SAP PRESS e-books

Print or e-book, Kindle or iPad, workplace or airplane: Choose where and how to read your SAP PRESS books! You can now get all our titles as e-books, too:

- By download and online access
- For all popular devices
- And, of course, DRM-free

Convinced? Then go to www.sap-press.com and get your e-book today.

Production Planning with SAP S/4HANA®

SAP PRESS is a joint initiative of SAP and Rheinwerk Publishing. The know-how offered by SAP specialists combined with the expertise of Rheinwerk Publishing offers the reader expert books in the field. SAP PRESS features first-hand information and expert advice, and provides useful skills for professional decision-making.

SAP PRESS offers a variety of books on technical and business-related topics for the SAP user. For further information, please visit our website: *www.sap-press.com*.

Mahesh Babu MG
PP-DS with SAP S/4HANA
2020, 476 pages, hardcover and e-book
www.sap-press.com/4951

Caetano Almeida
Material Requirements Planning with SAP S/4HANA
2020, 541 pages, hardcover and e-book
www.sap-press.com/4966

Jawad Akhtar, Martin Murray
Materials Management with SAP S/4HANA (2nd Edition)
2020, 939 pages, hardcover and e-book
www.sap-press.com/5132

Justin Ashlock
Sourcing and Procurement with SAP S/4HANA:
Business Processes and Configuration (2nd Edition)
2020, 716 pages, hardcover and e-book
www.sap-press.com/5003

Jawad Akhtar
Quality Management with SAP S/4HANA
2020, 950 pages, hardcover and e-book
www.sap-press.com/4924

Jawad Akhtar

Production Planning with SAP S/4HANA®

Rheinwerk
Publishing

Editor Rachel Gibson
Acquisitions Editor Emily Nicholls
Copyeditor Melinda Rankin
Cover Design Graham Geary
Photo Credit Shutterstock.com: 1450091936/© H_Ko
Layout Design Vera Brauner
Production Kelly O'Callaghan
Typesetting SatzPro, Krefeld (Germany)
Printed and bound in Canada

ISBN 978-1-4932-2167-7
© 2021 by Rheinwerk Publishing, Inc., Boston (MA)
2nd edition 2021

Library of Congress Cataloging-in-Publication Control Number: 2021029410

Contents at a Glance

Dear Reader,

When it comes to jobs, "editor" and "production planner" seem about as different as you can get. But in my experience, they both require a sharp eye, a careful attention to detail, and a healthy amount of skepticism that everything will run (or read!) smoothly with no outside interference. All the moving pieces must be accounted for, whether that's monitoring the progression of each chapter, section, and subsection through editing or scheduling machine downtime for maximum productivity.

As such, a production planner's job is easiest when everything is running smoothly—no oversights, last-minute repairs, or sudden inventory shortages. Similarly, an editor's job is easiest when the completed manuscript proves to be both well organized and well written. Author Jawad Akhtar has handed me just that. Even while updating over 1,000 pages of detailed content, his prompt communication, impeccable organization, and early delivery prove he can write a book like a well-oiled machine.

What did you think about this second edition of *Production Planning with SAP S/4HANA*? Your comments and suggestions are the most useful tools to help us make our books the best they can be. Please feel free to contact me and share any praise or criticism you may have.

Thank you for purchasing a book from SAP PRESS!

Rachel Gibson
Editor, SAP PRESS

rachelg@rheinwerk-publishing.com
www.sap-press.com
Rheinwerk Publishing · Boston, MA

Contents

4   Process Manufacturing Configuration

Part III Production Planning Workflows

6   Production Planning for Discrete Manufacturing   195

7   Production Planning for Process Manufacturing

8   Production Planning for Repetitive Manufacturing

Part IV Production Planning Tools

9   Kanban

10   Batch Management

11 Sales and Operations Planning 519

12   Demand Management   591

13 Foundations of Material Requirements Planning 643

14   Running Material Requirements Planning   707

15   Demand-Driven Replenishment   741

16   Long-Term Planning   807

17   Predictive Material and Resource Planning

18   Capacity Requirements Planning

19 Production Planning and Detailed Scheduling   893

Part V Monitoring and Evaluating Production Planning

23 Standard Planning Analysis

24 SAP Fiori Apps for Production Planning

Contents

Acknowledgments

Like my previous seven books, this book is dedicated to the loving memory of my parents, who have left for their eternal abodes. If you are blessed with one or both living parents, please take great care of them and spend as much time with them as possible, for they are the true source of all our professional and personal successes in life.

I wish to express my enormous admiration for my acquisitions editor at Rheinwerk Publishing, Emily Nicholls. Emily has trusted me to create and present the very best book we possibly could in this second edition of *Production Planning with SAP S/4HANA*.

At Rheinwerk Publishing, I have always been greatly impressed by its managing director, Florian Zimniak, who treats his authors as the greatest asset, which ensures that they keep coming back for many more projects.

Finally, to my editor, Rachel Gibson: It's a sheer pleasure to collaborate with her on our first book project together! My appreciation also goes out to the unsung and unseen publishing team, such as the copyeditor, the production team, the design team, and so on, who tirelessly work behind the scenes to bring out the very best in each book.

Last, but not least: To my readers—I am truly humbled and honored by all the appreciation I've received from all of you over the years. I hope that, like my previous seven books and several E-Bites, this book also meets your expectations and becomes a stepping-stone in your SAP S/4HANA career.

Preface

Logistics and supply chain management today are far more volatile, uncertain, complex, and ambiguous than before due to globalized sourcing, which causes longer lead times. Manufacturing complexities, including outsourced and subcontracted manufacturing, incessant and endless introduction of new products and features, and customers' lower tolerance of time to wait for the required products are causing companies to constantly try to stay a step ahead or risk being overtaken by their competition. But whatever happens in the real world in general and in a company in particular should also be correspondingly mapped in SAP S/4HANA so that the business processes of a company can run smoothly. The second edition of this book, *Production Planning with SAP S/4HANA*, covers not only the standard manufacturing processes but also some of the newer and more innovative production planning and control tools, as well as reporting features and functionalities, introduced in SAP S/4HANA.

In this book, a four-step approach is adopted to ensure that a logical, step-by-step, sequential set of activities are performed in the SAP S/4HANA system that correspond to meeting the actual business needs of a company:

1. *Configuration* is a backend SAP system activity and must occur only once during an SAP implementation project.
2. *Master data* is a frontend input activity that also often happens only once or only occasionally. Master data remains largely unchanged for a much longer period of time and is used in routine business transactions.
3. *Transactions*, or business processes, such as creating a production order, goods issue (GI), or goods receipt (GR), are also input activities and take place as frequently as needed.
4. Finally, *reporting and analysis*—for example, to determine the number of open production orders or production wastages—are *outputs* of all these previous input activities.

As an SAP consultant, you must always stay focused on the *output* (reporting) during the SAP implementation project. Doing so means you'll need to ensure the necessary data *inputs* are in place in the system to be able to produce the necessary outputs. (Remember, when data is incorrect or missing, data outputs will also be incorrect or incomplete!)

Goals of This Book

The first goal of this book is to provide a step-by-step approach to configure and implement three different production types in production planning (PP): discrete manufacturing, process manufacturing, and repetitive manufacturing (REM).

The book lays the initial foundation in the form of configuration and then explains how the configuration impacts actual business processes. The *from configuration to business process* approach is maintained throughout the book.

The next goal is to provide comprehensive coverage of the PP workflow tools available. There are also significant "hidden" or lesser-used functionalities in PP that you can integrate, even when (and long after) the SAP system implementation is complete. These tools are covered to bring greater optimization to the business processes and greater return on investment in the SAP system.

The book offers several real-life examples and other modeling hints and tips to help decide which option best meets the business needs of the company. Screenshots using SAP S/4HANA 2020 are used extensively and are duly supported by in-depth coverage of concepts and terminologies. The menu paths or transaction codes to perform each step are provided. Where specific or unique data is used, all necessary prerequisites and hints are given to set up the data or meet the prerequisites before attempting to run a business process. This book can only cover so much of any topic, but we highly encourage exploring and trying out a large number of options, icons, menu paths, and the like to continue the process of self-learning and eventually become an expert in PP.

In this book, we also cover several cross-component functionalities to leverage their strengths, not only in PP but also in other logistics components that are implemented in a company. For example, you can use the classification system, Early Warning System (EWS), predictive material and resource planning (pMRP), flexible planning standard analysis, information systems, reporting, and SAP Fiori apps in many other logistics components.

Target Audience

This book is intended for all readers who use PP in the SAP system, such as the team leader, project team members in an SAP system implementation, integration managers, production planners, or production controllers working in operational positions in the company. Because this book covers three different production types—discrete manufacturing, process manufacturing, and REM—it tends to benefit those readers who are either transitioning or intending to transition from companies using different production types. In addition, if a company is embarking on production and capacity expansion, then this book can help by facilitating the creation of the new enterprise structure needed in the SAP system to support the expansion. Finally, this book can be an invaluable reference for SAP system consultants and even business process owners who are considering the transition to a consulting career and need a comprehensive understanding of the required concepts and fundamentals.

Structure and Content

This book takes a deep-dive approach to deliver in-depth and comprehensive coverage of discrete manufacturing, process manufacturing, and REM in SAP. It begins by covering the enterprise structure you need to set up in PP, which also reflects the interdependencies of the enterprise structures of other areas. The configuration basics for each production type are covered next. Similarities and differences in various production types are highlighted to comprehensively differentiate one from the other. The configuration of each production type is then put to actual use to show the impact of the configuration on the business processes. A business process must be completely understood before modeling and configuring it in the SAP system.

The book then transitions to cover the PP workflow tools available. It covers how to optimize the production processes by using several latent features that are often not as frequently used to bring about business processes improvements. This book moves toward its conclusion by covering reporting capabilities, including those presented by SAP Fiori applications.

In summary, the following structure is used:

In Part I, which starts with **Chapter 1**, we first present a comparison of the functionality available in SAP ERP with that in SAP S/4HANA. Next, we'll discuss the various manufacturing types and their unique characteristics. We'll also explain how to decide which manufacturing type is suitable for a particular manufacturing process. In addition, we'll provide an overview of the five applications of SAP Integrated Business Planning for Supply Chain (SAP IBP), which is the next-generation, SAP HANA-powered, cloud-based materials planning tool.

In **Chapter 2**, we discuss the enterprise structure that is needed in PP, which also depends on the enterprise structures of other areas, such as financials (FI), materials management (MM), or sales and distribution (SD). The enterprise structure forms the backbone of the SAP system, to which all the important business processes of the company are mapped. Eventually, reporting is often based on important elements from the enterprise structure.

In Part II, we move forward to cover the configuration basics you need to set up for each production type. The primary focus of the three chapters in this part is on the configuration only; the actual and practical use of configuration is covered with the business processes in later chapters. **Chapter 3** covers the discrete manufacturing configuration, **Chapter 4** attends to the process manufacturing configuration, and **Chapter 5** covers the configuration details for REM.

In Part III, the book transitions to the PP workflow for each production type and makes logical connections to the business processes of each production type for which the configuration was undertaken in the relevant chapters earlier. **Chapter 6** provides an in-depth coverage of the PP business processes in discrete manufacturing. **Chapter 7** highlights the similarities and differences between discrete and process manufacturing, but it remains primarily focused on the process industry-specific functionality known as *process management*. Process management then matures into a user-friendly functionality known as Execution Steps (XSteps). XSteps can also be used in discrete manufacturing. In the same chapter, we also cover how to use the process manufacturing cockpit. The focus of **Chapter 8** is on the important business processes of REM, in which, once again, we make consistent and logical links to the configuration chapter.

[»]

Note

As is always standard in testing, checking, and validating the configuration, the agreed-upon objects are first configured during SAP implementation projects. These configured objects are then assigned to the master data. The master data is then used in business processes or transactions. Finally, the configured objects are often used as selection criteria in various SAP standard reports. In other words, the relationships among these elements follows this pattern: configuration → master data → transactions → reports.

This book follows the same approach to show the logical, predecessor-successor relationships of the preceding four elements.

Next, in Part IV, we discuss the PP workflow tools. We start with the replenishment process, kanban, in **Chapter 9**, followed by batch management in **Chapter 10**, which is used extensively in process manufacturing. **Chapter 11** focuses on sales and operations planning (S&OP), in which we cover the product group, flexible planning, and standard analysis in flexible planning. Forecasting as an invaluable planning tool is also covered in this chapter. **Chapter 12** covers demand management, including several planning strategies and production methods. The foundations of material requirements planning (MRP) are covered in **Chapter 13**, in which we discuss the planning calendar and MRP areas. In **Chapter 14**, we discuss the MRP tools, such as MRP Live. **Chapter 15** covers demand-driven replenishment, while **Chapter 16** covers long-term planning (LTP) to simulate what-if planning scenarios. **Chapter 17** carries forward the concepts of LTP and introduces the newer simulation tool, pMRP. **Chapter 18** details how to manage capacity requirements planning (CRP) in SAP S/4HANA systems, including evaluation and leveling. **Chapter 19** covers the configuration, master data, business processes, and reporting in embedded production planning and detailed scheduling (PP-DS) in SAP S/4HANA. **Chapter 20** is on SAP Manufacturing for production engineering and operations, which is finding greater use in discrete manufacturing.

Finally, in Part V, monitoring and evaluation in PP is discussed. **Chapter 21** shows how to quickly set up user-defined alerts in the SAP system with EWS to closely monitor important deviations to your business processes and make quick decisions and actions. EWS can also be used in other logistics functions if needed. In **Chapter 22**, you'll learn about many features, functionalities, menu paths, navigation tools, and options available to run a large number of standard reports in SAP. The concepts developed here will enable expanding your knowledge horizon to explore standard reports available in other logistics areas. In **Chapter 23**, several standard analyses for PP are discussed. Finally, **Chapter 24** covers a large number of SAP Fiori apps for PP.

This edition of the book is certainly a significant expansion of the areas and functionalities that PP offers, but note that the following are not covered:

- Variant configuration
- Distribution resource planning

Throughout the book, we've also provided several elements that will help you access useful information (see the following boxes).

[+]

Tips and Tricks

Boxes with this symbol provide recommendations for how to simplify your work.

[«]

Notes

Boxes with this symbol contain additional information or important contents to keep in mind.

[Ex]

Examples

Boxes with this symbol provide practical scenarios and explain, in detail, how particular functions can be applied.

[!]

Warnings

Boxes with this symbol contain details worth considering. Moreover, they warn you about common errors or problems that might occur.

PART I

Core Production Planning Concepts

Chapter 1

Introduction to Production Planning with SAP S/4HANA

While it's true that today's logistics and supply chain management is far more volatile, uncertain, complex, and ambiguous due to globalized supply chains and shorter product lifecycles, production planning in SAP S/4HANA offers several planning tools to help reduce volatility, uncertainty, complexity, and ambiguity.

A company that is in the business of manufacturing a product and selling it to customers goes through the rigor of production planning and then production execution. Production planning with SAP S/4HANA (referred to as PP throughout this book) plays a critical role in the logistics and supply chain functions of a company to accomplish just this. PP enables a company to benefit from historical data when preparing a forecast that can then be used in sales, operations, materials, capacity, and production planning.

From an initial sales plan or sales orders from customers to the highly integrated and complex chain of interdependent activities in logistics in the SAP system, PP reflects its strength, both in planning and execution. It seamlessly integrates with the sales, procurement, quality, maintenance, projects, human capital, finance, and controlling functions of a company.

This chapter provides an overview of the three manufacturing types: discrete, process, and repetitive. This will then be followed by an overview of some of the important production planning tools available in SAP S/4HANA. The importance of production planning in the product costing business process will also be highlighted. We'll also provide a table comparing the features and functionalities available in SAP Enterprise Resource Planning (SAP ERP), the predecessor of SAP S/4HANA, with those in SAP S/4HANA. Finally, we'll also provide a table that compares the different production types and give a brief overview of another planning tool offered by SAP: SAP Integrated Business Planning for Supply Chain (SAP IBP).

1.1   Production Planning and Control

Production planning is the core of any manufacturing process. SAP helps with setting up and streamlining specific planning and production processes in order to maximize efficiency in the workplace when working with different types of manufacturing. In the following sections, we'll introduce PP, cover the features and characteristics of various production types, and discuss important business processes.

1.1.1   Production Planning Overview

The SAP S/4HANA system is made up of several different functionalities in addition to PP, and they all work together to cover end-to-end business processes, such as procure-to-pay, plan-to-produce, order-to-cash, maintenance management, and hire-to-retire. They do by ensuring seamless flows of material and information through the integration processes.

In general, the entire process of production planning and control starts when the company forecasts the demand of a product and prepares a sales plan. The sales plan is synchronized with a production plan to take the project realities into account, such as capacity or warehouse constraints. Various simulated models are considered, and a finalized production plan becomes the basis of material requirements planning (MRP). MRP helps production and procurement planners know when to procure and produce what materials for their eventual availability and dispatch to the customer. The production execution accounts for and records each production detail, including yield, rework, scrap, coproducts, or by-products generated during the production processes. Quality checks in the production processes ensure minimal customer returns or other in-process or line rejections. The produced product is sold to a customer, and the production plan continues to be a monitoring barometer against the sales plan.

Of course, this information is great for providing a bird's-eye view of the production planning process. We'll help you understand how the individual objects you have to work with in the SAP system help streamline and manage your business processes in the sections ahead.

PP includes the following production types and production planning tools:

- **Master data**
  Master data is the data that remains in the SAP system for a long time and doesn't change frequently. This includes the material master, work centers, resources, production lines, routings, master recipe, rate routing, bill of materials (BOM), and production version.

- **Sales and operations planning (S&OP)**
  Both standard S&OP and flexible planning tools are available to forecast sales and production plans to meet customers' requirements for products.

- **Production planning**
  This includes material forecasting, demand management, long-term planning (LTP), predictive material and resource planning (pMRP), and master production scheduling (MPS).

- **Material requirements planning (MRP)**
  This attends to standard and unique customers' requirements via various planning and production methods.

- **Demand-driven replenishment (DDR)**
  This reduces the bullwhip effect so commonly found in the supply chain via timely adjustments to the supply plan due to a change in demand.

- **Production planning and detailed scheduling (PP-DS)**
  This introduces advanced capacity planning and heuristics for materials planning.

- **Discrete manufacturing, or shop floor control (SFC)**
  Production orders processing, goods issues (GIs) and goods receipts (GRs), and confirmations are used for complex manufacturing processes in which there may be a need for intermediate or interim storage.

- **Process manufacturing, or production planning for process industries (PP-PI)**
  Process orders processing, process management, material quantity calculation, GI/GR, and confirmations are used for production processes of liquid-based or flow-based materials.

- **Repetitive manufacturing (REM)**
  REM adopts the lean manufacturing principle in which the production process generally is not only simple but also consistent over a considerable period of time.

- **Capacity requirements planning (CRP)**
  This consists of capacity evaluation and capacity leveling. *Capacity evaluation* reflects the load and overload at work centers/resources, whereas *capacity leveling* helps a planner optimize the production processes.

- **Product cost controlling (CO-PC)**
  This completely integrates with PP and is responsible for ensuring all production-related costs are accounted for, including overheads, variances, and work in process (WIP).

- **Kanban**
  This system replenishes stocks based on a pull system by using kanban cards. Kanban works well for both in-house-produced materials and outside-procured materials, as well as interplant stock transfers.

- **Distribution resource planning (DRP)**
  This enables planning the demand of products at distribution centers.

- **Embedded analytics**
  A large number of embedded analytics and standard and flexible analysis reporting options are available in PP.

1.1.2   Characteristics of Production Types

A *production type* characterizes the frequency, complexity, or stability with which a product is produced in the production process. When implementing an SAP system, one of the first decisions a company makes is which production type to implement to reflect the complexity (or simplicity) of the production process. For example, if the production process is relatively simple with a linear production line involving one operation and one work center, then it makes sense to implement the REM production type to enable the company to benefit from lean manufacturing. Similarly, the process manufacturing production type is more suited to scenarios in which the product is generally in liquid form and flows or where the manufacturing process is generally continuous. The discrete manufacturing production type is used when the production process is order-based, when it involves special procurement types, or when products are stored in interim storage locations between the production processes.

We discuss each of the three main production types in the following sections. Although this book will primarily cover discrete, process, and repetitive production types, these sections also briefly cover engineer-to-order (ETO) to provide a comprehensive look at production types. Kanban is discussed briefly in these sections, but there is also a chapter dedicated to it in this book (Chapter 9).

Discrete Manufacturing

The *discrete manufacturing* production type, which is also known as *shop floor control*, describes the production of a product on the basis of production orders. Discrete manufacturing is implemented when products change frequently, the demand pattern is irregular, and the production is workshop0oriented in character. A range of master data is required for discrete manufacturing; the most important pieces are the material, BOM, work center, routing, and production version.

> **Example**
>
> In steel rerolling mills, the entire production process passes through five different production steps. However, customers can place orders based on a different level of the processed good. Hence, the company has to produce and also store a semifinished good at each production step to meet its customer's demand. Automotive, consumer goods, and building products are some of the other industries in which discrete manufacturing is implemented.

The production process in discrete manufacturing starts when a production order is created and processed. A production order can be created either manually or by converting a planned order that the system generated after an MRP run. A production order is a request to the production department to produce the product at a specific time and in a specific quantity. It specifies the work centers and material components that are required for production. The creation of a production order automatically creates reservations for the required material components. Purchase requisitions are created for externally procured material components and services, and capacity requirements are created for the work centers at which each operation of the order will be executed. The discrete manufacturing process is shown in Figure 1.1.

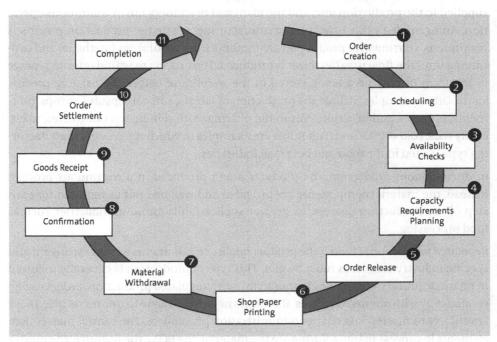

Figure 1.1 Discrete Manufacturing Process Flow

Production orders are released on the release date so long as the required materials and capacity are available. The production order-related documents (known as *shop floor papers*) are printed to prepare for production execution. The capacity situation is evaluated, and any required capacity leveling is carried out in any phase of production order processing, although this is usually ensured before the actual production starts.

The components required to produce the products are issued with reference to the production order, the product is produced on the basis of the production order, and the finished quantity is confirmed with reference to the production order. The product is put into a storage location, and the GR is posted. Finally, the settlement of the production order is ensured.

Note

Chapter 3 covers discrete manufacturing configuration, and Chapter 6 details the business processes of discrete manufacturing.

Process Manufacturing

Process manufacturing is the batch-oriented and recipe-oriented production of main products or coproducts in the process industry. Manufacturing can be in the form of continuous production, discontinuous production, or regulated production. In *continuous production*, the product is continuously produced, raw material is continuously supplied to the production line, and the plant and machinery are in continuous operation. An example of this is fertilizer manufacturing, where the production process is continuous, starting with production of ammonia from natural gas (methane) and continuing until the final urea/fertilizer is produced. The process may find interim storage in the form of bulk urea being stored in the warehouse before the bagging process starts. Other examples include the production of tablets, soft gel capsules, syrups, ointments, capsules, and injection vials in the pharmaceutical industry. Chocolates, cakes, candy bars, cold drinks, and fruit juices are examples in which the process manufacturing type is used in the food and beverage industries.

In *discontinuous production*, the products aren't produced in a continuous process. Instead, the material components are provided and weighed out as required for each step of the production process. Its greater application is found in industries such as food processing.

Regulated production is used if the product quality requirements are very stringent and specific industry standards must be met. This type of production is generally followed in pharmaceutical or cosmetics manufacturing. In regulated production, orders can be created only with approved recipes. If changes need to be made to master recipes, these are subject to master data change administration procedures. The central master data elements in process manufacturing are the material, the BOM, the resource, the master recipe, and the production version.

The business process in process manufacturing starts when a *process order* is created and processed in accordance with a master recipe. A process order is a request to the production department to produce a product at a specific time and in a specific quantity, and it specifies the resource and material components required for production.

A process order can be created either manually or when a planned order that was created in the PP process is converted. The creation of a process order automatically creates reservations for the required material components. The system automatically creates purchase requisitions for externally procured material components and services, and capacity requirements are created for the resources at which the order will be executed. Process orders are released on the release date, provided the required materials and capacity are available. At the time of release, you can run an automatic batch-determination process for components that are subject to a batch management requirement. The relevant documents in the process order can be printed to prepare for the execution of the process order. The process manufacturing flow is shown in Figure 1.2.

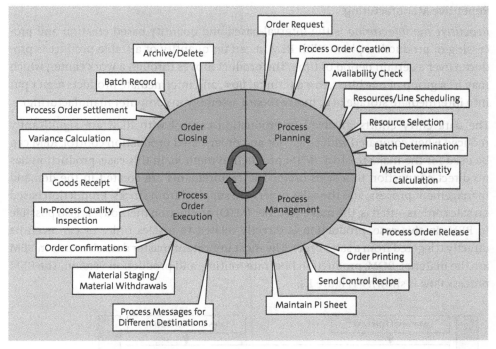

Figure 1.2 Process Manufacturing Process Flow

The capacity situation is evaluated, and any required capacity leveling can be carried out in any phase of the process order processing, although this is usually ensured before the actual production commences.

Note

Chapter 18 covers how to use capacity requirement planning for evaluation and leveling.

The actual production can now begin, with or without the use of process management. Process management is implemented to execute a process order, which serves as the interface between the SAP system and process control. The flexible structure of this interface makes it possible to connect automated, semiautomated, and manually controlled plants and equipment to the production process. Process management extensively uses the classification system, which works throughout the SAP S/4HANA functional areas.

Note

Chapter 4 and Chapter 7 cover the configuration and business processes of process manufacturing, respectively.

Repetitive Manufacturing

Repetitive manufacturing is the interval-based and quantity-based creation and processing of production plans. With REM, a certain quantity of a stable product is produced over a certain period of time. The product moves through a work center, which may be a group of machines, in a continual flow, and intermediate products aren't put into intermediate storage (e.g., motherboard assembly in computer manufacturing).

The data entry efforts involved in production control with REM are significantly reduced when compared with single-lot and order-based production control. REM can be used for the make-to-stock (MTS) production method. In this case, production has no direct connection to a sales order. The requirements are created in the demand management process, and the sales orders are supplied from stocks. Production based on sales orders—that is, the make-to-order (MTO) production method—is also possible in REM. In this case, production is directly related to a sales order or can even be directly triggered from a sales order. The most important master data elements in REM are the material, BOM, production line, rate routing, and production version. The REM process flow is shown in Figure 1.3.

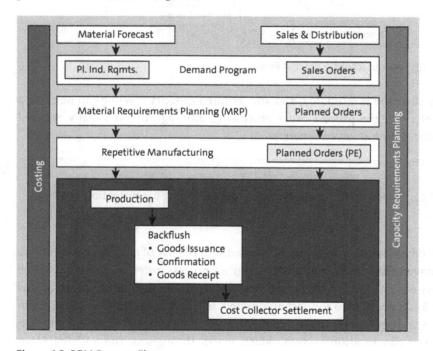

Figure 1.3 REM Process Flow

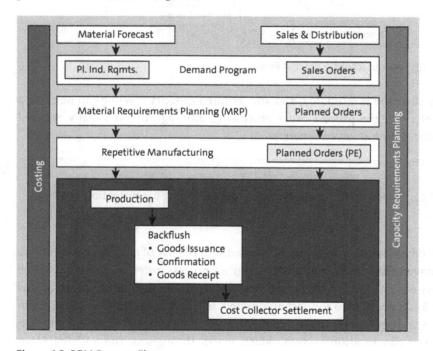
Note

Chapter 5 covers the configuration details of REM, and Chapter 8 details the business processes.

Engineer-to-Order

The *engineer-to-order* production type attends to the complexities and challenges involved when a sales order-based MTO production method is unable to fulfill the requirements. In the MTO production method, the system is unable to make a distinction between the predecessor-successor relationships in the production process; for example, a material's production can't be initiated (successor) until the production of the previous product (predecessor) is ensured. In ETO, the system uses the work breakdown structure (WBS) and networks for scheduling and coordinating the production processes and also managing cost accounting. All produced goods are specific to the project, and the system maintains project-based inventory.

Kanban

With *kanban*, a material is produced or procured only when it's actually required. A specific quantity of the components required to produce a material are stored on-site and in containers. When a container is empty, this component is replenished according to a predefined replenishment strategy (in-house production, external procurement, or stock transfer). In the interval between the request for replenishment and the delivery of the refilled container, the other available containers simply do the work of the empty one.

The replenishment process is largely automatic in the kanban procedure, thereby greatly reducing the amount of manual posting work required. The material isn't pushed through the production process as specified by an overall plan; rather, it's requested by one production level (consumer) from the previous production level (source) as and when needed. It adopts the "pull" strategy in the production process.

In kanban processing, *production supply areas* (PSAs) divide the plant. The components required for production are stored in these PSAs, and various work centers take what they need from them. A kanban control cycle is defined to specify how a material should be obtained within a PSA. The control cycle defines a replenishment strategy for the material that specifies, for example, whether the required material is to be produced in-house or procured externally. The control cycle also specifies the number of containers in circulation between the consumer and source, as well as the quantity per container.

Replenishment strategies specify how a material component should be replenished and which of the following replenishment elements should be created for this purpose:

- In-house production
- Manual kanban
- Replenishment with run schedule quantity
- Replenishment with production order
- Replenishment by purchase order

- Replenishment with schedule agreement
- Replenishment with reservation
- Replenishment with direct transfer posting
- Replenishment with summarized just-in-time (JIT) call
- Stock transfer
- Replenishment by transport requirements of a warehouse management-administered storage location

The replenishment process with kanban entails that a material is produced at a machine. The components required to produce it are available on-site in containers and are ready for withdrawal. If one of these containers is empty, the source that is responsible for its replenishment has to be informed. If kanban processing without an SAP system support is being used, the consumer sends a card to the work center (source). The card contains the information about which material is required, in what quantity, and where it should be delivered to.

[»]

Note

The replenishment process gets its name from the Japanese word for these cards (*kanban*).

The source can now produce or procure the material and then refill the container. If kanban processing with SAP support is in place, the containers are managed in the system and have a specific status. After the last component is withdrawn from a container, the status of that container is simply changed from **Full** to **Empty**. This status change is the kanban signal, and it can be set by passing a barcode reader over the card attached to the container. It's also possible to have the system display the containers in a production area in the form of a kanban table and to make the status change there. The kanban signal now triggers the replenishment process and creates, for example, a run schedule quantity in accordance with the replenishment strategy. The source then processes the run schedule quantity, and the finished material is sent to the container. The status of the container is set to **Full** again (through the barcode or kanban table), and the GR for the material is posted with reference to the procurement element.

[»]

Note

Kanban is discussed in Chapter 9.

1.1.3   Processes in Production Planning and Control

The following sections discuss the main processes in PP in SAP S/4HANA.

Sales and Operations Planning

The S&OP process is used to determine the quantities for production. Sales planning, which is also known as demand planning, covers future requirements without considering stocks and available capacities. The historical sales figures serve as a basis for sales planning. Operations planning use the results of the sales planning process to plan the production quantities and takes initial stocks and capacities into account.

> **Note**
> Chapter 11 covers S&OP.

Demand management aligns sales planning with the customer requirements in accordance with the planning strategy and thus calculates the independent requirements for production. The planning methods that demand management looks for are MTS, MTO, and planning with final assembly.

> **Note**
> Chapter 12 covers demand management.

Material Requirements Planning

MRP is one of the most important functions of PP. The system performs net quantity calculations for component requirements while taking scrap and lot sizes into account. MRP calculates requirement coverage elements for all MRP levels, such as plant, material, product group, and MRP areas, and it takes into account the lead times, lot sizes, and scrap quantities. MRP also enables capacity planning.

> **Note**
> Chapter 13 and Chapter 14 cover MRP.

Long-term planning (LTP) is a simulation tool for MRP that examines how a change in planned independent requirements (PIRs) will affect capacity utilization, stocks, and external procurement. LTP is also suitable for short-term simulations. Another simulation tool available in SAP S/4HANA is pMRP, which offers an intuitive interface to simulate various scenarios to balance materials and capacities planning. The consensus or finalized simulated plan from pMRP can be transferred to operative planning, which forms the basis of an MRP run.

> **Note**
> Chapter 16 covers LTP, while Chapter 17 covers pMRP.

Capacity Requirements Planning

For detailed production planning while taking available capacities into account, CRP schedules the worklist in detail, which usually consists of the processes for created or released production orders. CRP delivers a production sequence that is feasible from the capacity viewpoint. CRP consists of capacity evaluation and capacity leveling.

[»]

> **Note**
>
> Chapter 18 covers CRP.

Demand-Driven Materials Requirements Planning

Demand-driven replenishment (DDR) functionality available in SAP S/4HANA is based on the demand-driven material requirements planning (DDMRP) concept promoted by the Demand Driven Institute. DDR effectively *positions* buffers at strategic inventory locations in the logistics and supply chain, *protects* the flow of materials and relevant information by evaluating buffer profiles, and then dynamically adjusts these buffers. In short, an efficient *pull* system is put in place to reduce variabilities between demand and supply through demand-driven planning.

[»]

> **Note**
>
> Chapter 15 covers DDR.

Production Planning and Detailed Scheduling

Production planning and detailed scheduling in SAP S/4HANA enables extensive production, procurement, and sales planning of materials by taking capacity and scheduling considerations and constraints into account.

[»]

> **Note**
>
> Chapter 19 covers PP-DS.

Production Engineering and Operations

SAP Manufacturing for production engineering and operations bridges the gap between engineering and manufacturing by ensuring that all engineering changes made in a product's design are completely and correctly reflected in the operations or the manufacturing process. Production engineering and operations also undertakes a comprehensive change impact analysis to identify all the objects that are affected by a change and how to introduce the change.

[«]

1

> **Note**
> Chapter 20 covers production engineering and operations.

Production Control

The central controlling and recording element—the production process—is the production order in discrete manufacturing, the process order in process manufacturing, and the run schedule quantity in REM. While the previous processes dealt with production planning, production execution is concerned with how the actual production as specified in the production order is recorded and controlled, from material withdrawal to order confirmation to storage and invoicing.

1.1.4   Product Cost Controlling

The product cost controlling (CO-PC) functionality is a subset of controlling (CO) and comprehensively integrates with PP. In fact, PP is unable to function completely until CO-PC is in place. CO-PC helps to ensure that the total cost of goods manufactured (COGM) and total cost of goods sold (COGS) are completely accounted for. To calculate COGM, you need firsthand information about the cost of all raw materials and components used. The activity rates for each work center (resource) also should be known. The material and activities costs are also known as *direct costs* and are individually assigned to the order without any allocation. *Overhead costs* are determined by overhead charges. Examples of overhead costs are the electricity consumed in the production process and the salaries of employees involved in the production of goods.

There is also a method of assigning a *costing sheet* to an order type, which, for example, may contain details such as that 2% of the raw material costs will equal the electricity cost of producing a material. Before the actual business processes in PP, such as order creation, begin, the product costing team runs a *material cost estimate* in the SAP system. When running the material's standard cost estimate, the system refers to the complete master data information of PP, such as BOM, routing, work center, and production version. It draws information from CO, such as activity types and activity rates. The material cost estimate is first saved and then released. Then, on creating an order, the system performs planned cost calculations within the order. On performing production execution activities, such as GI, confirmation, GR, and recording of coproducts or by-products, the system continuously updates the actual cost and presents a comparison of planned costs with actual costs.

The WIP, overhead, variances, and finally settlement are some of the functions managed by the product costing team. When an individual order is settled, the system updates the material price based on the price control. If the price control in the material master (finished or semifinished good) is a standard price, the system reflects all differences and variances to the price difference account. If the price control in the material master is a moving average, the system updates the material price. Order-based settlement is a mandatory requirement in discrete and process manufacturing.

The process differs slightly in REM, in which either the material's standard cost estimate is used or a product cost collector (PCC) is created with infinite validity. A PCC is preliminary costing, and all the product costs are summed up in the PCC for a material before the actual settlement takes place. In REM, the settlement process isn't order-based but period-based.

1.2   Comparison Table of Production Types

Table 1.1 provides a selective comparison of the three types of production highlighted in this book: discrete, process, and REM. Here you can find the typical properties of each production type. In a few cases, there might be exceptions that are very rare or special and aren't worth mentioning here.

Characteristics	Discrete Manufacturing (SFC)	Process Manufacturing (PP-PI)	Repetitive Manufacturing (REM)
General Characteristic			
Industry types	Automobiles, pumps, engines, computers, toys, and electronics, such as televisions and computers	Chemicals, paints, fertilizers, processed foods, pharmaceuticals, beverages, and so on	Consumer goods, mechanical and electronic parts, and so on
Product stability and complexity	Complex production process with intermediate storages	Complex production process and generally without or bulk intermediate storage (mostly continuous flow and liquid-based production)	High-volume (mass production), highly stable, and without any production complexities
Production flow	Order-based and complex	Order-based and mostly used in producing materials that flow (or can't disassemble)	Lean (simple) manufacturing without order types and only through planned orders
Changeover	Frequent	Frequent	Infrequent
MTS and MTO	Supported	Supported	Supported

Table 1.1 Comparison of Discrete, Process, and Repetitive Manufacturing

Characteristics	Discrete Manufacturing (SFC)	Process Manufacturing (PP-PI)	Repetitive Manufacturing (REM)
Batch management	Yes	Yes (extensive utilization)	Yes
Active ingredient management	Not available	Available	Not available
Material quantity calculation	Not possible	Possible	Not possible
Components staging	With reference to production order	With reference to process order	Components staged periodically and anonymously (order reference is a typical reference in REM)
Planning strategies: MTO and MTS	Supported	Supported	Supported
Completion confirmation (backflush)	For individual operations or orders	For individual phases or orders	Period-based confirmation with backflush
Order-related production	Yes (production order)	Yes (process order)	Period-based with planned orders
Production-based	Lot size-based production	Lot sized-based production	Period- and quantity-based production
Cost object controlling	Order-based costing	Order-based costing	Period-based costing (using PCC)
Settlement	Settlement at order level	Settlement at order level	Settlement at the material level; production version-specific CO-PC is also possible for better evaluation

Table 1.1 Comparison of Discrete, Process, and Repetitive Manufacturing (Cont.)

Characteristics	Discrete Manufacturing (SFC)	Process Manufacturing (PP-PI)	Repetitive Manufacturing (REM)
Process management	Process integration (process control), control instruction (control recipe), operational method sheet (process instruction sheet [PI sheet])	Control recipe (sent as process instructions)	Operational methods sheet (OMS)
Master Data			
Material master	Yes	Yes	Yes (**REM** checkbox and REM profile maintenance in material master)
Work scheduling view activated	Yes	Yes	No (maintaining REM details in **MRP 4** view of material master is necessary/sufficient)
BOM	BOM (Transaction CS01)	List of materials (Transaction CS01)	BOM (Transaction CS01)
Work center	Work center (Transaction CR01)	Resource (Transaction CRC1)	Production line (Transaction CR01)
Work center hierarchy	Work center hierarchy	Resource network	Possibility for work center hierarchy in REM planning to get a synchronous overview of several production lines (Transaction MF50); possibility for line hierarchies to monitor and plan the load on several capacities along a production line
Routing	Routing (Transaction CA01)	Master recipe (Transaction C201)	Rate routing (Transaction CS21); complete support from REM for standard routing (Transaction CA01)

Table 1.1 Comparison of Discrete, Process, and Repetitive Manufacturing (Cont.)

1

Characteristics	Discrete Manufacturing (SFC)	Process Manufacturing (PP-PI)	Repetitive Manufacturing (REM)
Production version	Mandatory (Transaction C223)	Mandatory (Transaction C223)	Mandatory (Transaction C223)
Transactional Data			
Manufacturing order	Production order (Transaction CO01)	Process order (Transaction COR1)	Run schedule quantity (Transaction MF50)
Collective availability check	Transaction COMAC Transaction COHV (on the **Mass Processing** tab, select **Material Availability Check** from the dropdown)	Transaction COHVPI (on the **Mass Processing** tab, select **Material Availability Check** from the dropdown)	Planned orders (Transaction MDVP)
Process management	Execution Steps (XSteps)	Control instructions and XSteps	OMS (Transaction LDE1)
Confirmation	At operation level (Transaction CO11N)	At phase level (Transaction COR6N)	Confirmation with or without reporting point backflush (Transaction MFBF)
Printing	Shop floor papers (Transaction CO04)	Shop floor papers (Transaction COPI)	Production list (Transaction MF51)
Order confirmation	For production order (Transaction CO15)	For process order (Transaction CORK)	For material or for planned orders of material (Transaction MFBF)
Mass processing	Transaction COHV	Transaction COHVPI or CORM	Transactions COHV and COHVPI; availability of several mass processing functions with the deselection of **Production** or **Process Order**, respectively, and the selection of **Planned Order**
Status management	Yes	Yes	No

Table 1.1 Comparison of Discrete, Process, and Repetitive Manufacturing (Cont.)

Characteristics	Discrete Manufacturing (SFC)	Process Manufacturing (PP-PI)	Repetitive Manufacturing (REM)
Confirmation of activities	Yes	Yes	Yes
Separation of final confirmation and GR possible	Yes	Yes	No
In-process (during production) inspection	Possible at operation level only (inspection type 03)	Possible at operational and phase level (inspection type 03)	Possible (inspection type 13)

Table 1.1 Comparison of Discrete, Process, and Repetitive Manufacturing (Cont.)

1.3   Production Planning Features in SAP ERP and SAP S/4HANA: A Comparison

Table 1.2 provides a selective comparison of the features and functionalities available in SAP ERP versus SAP S/4HANA. It also highlights some of the simplifications available in SAP S/4HANA.

Feature	In SAP ERP	In SAP S/4HANA
PP-DS	A component of SAP Advanced Planning and Optimization that interfaces with SAP ERP via middleware.	Embedded (with additional license cost).
Production engineering and operations	Not available.	Embedded (with additional license cost).
pMRP	Not available.	Both pMRP and its predecessor from SAP ERP, LTP, are simulative tools and both are available in SAP S/4HANA.
MRP Live	Not available.	Available. MRP Live offers far greater options to select relevant parameters such as multiple plants, materials, and MRP controllers. It also handles master production scheduling (MPS) materials in addition to MRP materials in a single transaction.

Table 1.2 Production Planning in SAP ERP and SAP S/4HANA: Features Comparison

Feature	In SAP ERP	In SAP S/4HANA
Externally procured material	Options to create planned orders and purchase requisitions were available.	Only purchase requisitions are created during the MRP run via the MRP Live transaction for material marked for external procurement.
Delivery schedule lines for externally procured materials	Option to choose creation of delivery schedule lines for externally procured materials.	Delivery schedule lines are automatically created during the MRP run via the MRP Live transaction.
Production version	<ul><li>Optional for discrete manufacturing; mandatory for process and repetitive manufacturing.</li><li>Selection method based on validity date, lot size, and explosion date were available.</li><li>No mass creation functionality for production version exists.</li></ul>	<ul><li>Mandatory for all production types (discrete, process, repetitive).</li><li>Selection method is not available, and production version with latest 'valid from' date is considered.</li><li>For mass creation of production versions, two reports are available (via Transaction SM38): CS_BOM_PRODVER_MIGRATION CS_BOM_PRODVER_MIGRATIONO2</li></ul>
Process management	ABAP list-based process instructions and browser-based PI sheets.	Browser-based PI sheets and XSteps available.
Quota arrangement	Option to choose quota arrangement usage available.	Quota arrangement is always considered by the MRP Live transaction during the MRP run.
Repetitive manufacturing (REM)	Action control, fair share rule, push distribution, and deployment horizon are available to choose from.	All are now considered by default and hence not available in SAP S/4HANA.
Planning file entry	Net change planning in the planning horizon (NETPL) is available.	NETPL is unavailable as MRP Live always determines the shortages and requirements of all materials in the scope of planning.
Bill of materials (BOM) header quantity range	This available functionality enables a user to define a quantity range for which the BOM is applicable.	Not available.
MRP area for storage location	Available.	Unavailable.

Table 1.2 Production Planning in SAP ERP and SAP S/4HANA: Features Comparison (Cont.)

Feature	In SAP ERP	In SAP S/4HANA
Consumption mode in MRP	The following consumption modes are available: • Backward consumption only • Backward/forward consumption • Forward consumption only • Forward/backward consumption	In addition to the four consumption modes available from SAP ERP, a fifth consumption mode, period-based consumption, is available. In this new consumption method, sales orders, dependent requirements, or material reservations consume planned independent requirements (PIRs) that lie within the consumption period of the PIRs.
Monitor internal and external requirements	Functionalities not available. A user can only check the material situation in Transaction MD04 and then run MRP to attend to the requirements.	The Monitor Material Coverage, Monitor Internal Requirements, and Monitor External Requirements SAP Fiori apps provide far greater visibility into the internal and external requirement situations.
Analyze PIR quality	Not available.	A planner can analyze how accurately the forecasted quantities in the PIRs for materials match the quantities that were actually delivered to customers. The data can be analyzed for monthly periods in the past.
Excess component consumption, material scrap, and component scrap	Not available.	These apps provide a comparison of the expected scrap percentage defined in the master data and the actual excess consumption or scrap recorded in the production process.

Table 1.2 Production Planning in SAP ERP and SAP S/4HANA: Features Comparison (Cont.)

The next section covers core applications of SAP IBP.

1.4   SAP Integrated Business Planning for Supply Chain

SAP IBP is an SAP HANA-based cloud solution to manage the strategic, tactical, and operational objectives of a company—all in an integrated environment. Some of the key highlights of SAP IBP are real-time simulations of business scenarios to bring demand, supply, and financial models together; a collaborative approach to reaching consensus on important business decisions; and a user-friendly interface—all while using the enormous data processing prowess of SAP HANA. To ensure a quick and steep learning and adoption curve, all SAP IBP components use a familiar Microsoft Excel interface.

The six main components of SAP IBP are as follows:

- **SAP IBP for sales and operations**
  SAP IBP for sales and operations is often the first component that companies implement because they almost always start with long-term and mid-term sales planning that then needs to be synchronized with operations (production, procurement, logistics) planning. The ability to use different forecasting models coupled with the ability to simulate various demand, supply, and financial models provides a holistic view of the entire supply chain network, which includes customers, suppliers, manufacturing units, and distribution units.

- **SAP IBP for demand**
  The ability to predict demand of products is perhaps one of the most critical success factors in the entire planning process because it impacts the full upstream planning of procurement, production, and inventory. Even the best forecasting tools can only predict the demand to a certain degree of accuracy; the key to better demand planning lies in a collaborative and consensus-based approach to predicting demand and working backward to ensure timely supplies. However, with this SAP IBP component, the possibility to adopt a demand-driven approach to material planning becomes a reality in the short to medium term when verifiable demand signals, such as confirmed sales orders, help supply chain planners quickly adapt supplies. This business process is known as *demand sensing*.

- **SAP IBP for response and supply**
  Like SAP IBP for demand, this SAP IBP component also takes advantage of DDMRP to account for the demand variability or supply disruptions that can't be planned for in advance. Starting with rough-cut capacity planning, the SAP IBP for response and supply component simulates and evaluates different planning scenarios to strike a balance among demand, supply, and capacity constraints while taking into account the procurement, production, inventory, and warehousing costs. The output from this SAP IBP component forms the basis for input into the SAP IBP for sales and operations component. The response planning takes into account the demand variability and how best to allocate constrained supplies to meet the highest service level and fill rate while keeping all costs to a minimum.

- **SAP IBP for inventory**
  SAP IBP for inventory enables complete modeling of the inventory network—that is, from raw material supplier to the end customer and all the logical supply chain links involved among them. This SAP IBP component uses an advanced algorithm to balance inventory investment with service levels at each supply chain link to come up with optimum inventory and service levels for each product and physical location combination. For example, in a multisourcing environment, where one product can be sourced or distributed from multiple sources, this SAP IBP component strikes the

right balance by considering transportation costs, replenishment lead time, targeted service level, and fill rate to suggest where and how much of a product's inventory should be available at a specific location.

- **SAP Supply Chain Control Tower**
  This SAP IBP component is a dashboard and analytics tool to provide real-time, end-to-end visibility of the entire supply chain of the company. Apart from the ability to set up user-defined alerts when there's a potential disruption to the supply chain, this SAP IBP component also can drill down to the lowest level to evaluate the root cause leading to supply chain issues or disruptions. The process management functionality enables all stakeholders to gain complete visibility into the status of various business processes, such as if a sales forecast is approved, a demand plan is created, or a financial review of the annual sales plan hasn't started yet. This SAP IBP component can also integrate with different SAP logistics and supply chain components such as SAP ERP, SAP S/4HANA, SAP Extended Warehouse Management (SAP EWM), and SAP Transportation Management (SAP TM), as well as non-SAP systems.

- **SAP IBP for demand-driven replenishment**
  SAP IBP for DDMRP works in two big blocks. The first block covers the first two DDMRP components (strategic inventory positioning; buffer profiles and levels), whereas the second block tackles the remaining three DDMRP components (dynamic adjustment, demand-driven planning, and visible and collaborative execution).

Because SAP IBP is a cloud-based solution, it can integrate with on-premise SAP ERP systems, including SAP ERP, SAP Advanced Planning and Optimization, and SAP S/4HANA, all via SAP Business Technology Platform.

1.5   Summary

This chapter provided an overview of the various manufacturing types available in SAP S/4HANA, and the corresponding comparison table will make it easier for a PP consultant or even a production planner to choose which manufacturing type best suits their business needs. The overview of various production planning tools available in SAP S/4HANA should convince a production planner to use as many of them as is possible or practical to bring some degree of stability and sanity to today's complex logistics and supply chain management.

Chapter 2 will discuss the internal organizational structure of SAP from a PP perspective.

Chapter 2

Organizational Structure in SAP

Production planning with SAP S/4HANA is a direct and in-depth reflection and mapping of the business processes that a company either currently follows as a part of industrial operations or will transition to when the implementation of the SAP system is complete. This chapter is a discussion of the organizational structure of all the core units.

This chapter provides an overall understanding of how business functions and the SAP system interact and work together. After covering the basics, this chapter will slowly move into some specific details on how production planning (PP) works in the SAP system.

From a PP perspective, the important organizational units are company code, plant, and storage location. The following sections will review the structure as it applies to PP and will discuss the importance of the organizational units and explain how they work together to accomplish the organizational, legal, and reporting requirements of the company. We'll also explain the SAP calendar, which is an essential part of maintaining your entire system schedule.

2.1 Breaking Down the Structure into Units

During an SAP system implementation, one of the first and most intensive activities undertaken is the finalization of the organizational structure. This involves having intermodular and intramodular discussions and deliberations to ensure that SAP can cover the legal aspect of the company's organizational structure, as well as attend to specific reporting needs. In other words, the business process owners, business analysts, and SAP system consultants review the existing organizational structure of the company and then simultaneously begin mapping it in the SAP system.

A practical approach to adopt while finalizing the organizational structure in the SAP system is to ensure that the organizational structure isn't so generic that it loses its significance and prevents the business process owner from extracting the required information from the system, nor is it so minute or detailed that it becomes cumbersome to collate and consolidate the information. Also, it's best to keep a forward-thinking view of the organizational structure. If there's a need for certain organizational elements in the SAP system in the future, for example, it's better to have them available in the system than to add them at a later point.

The organizational structure in the SAP system is equally applicable to all manufacturing types—discrete, process, or repetitive. Take a look at Figure 2.1, which shows the client as the highest level of the organizational structure in the SAP system. The profitability analysis of the company is performed at the *controlling area* level, and the cost center and profit center accountings are performed at that level as well.

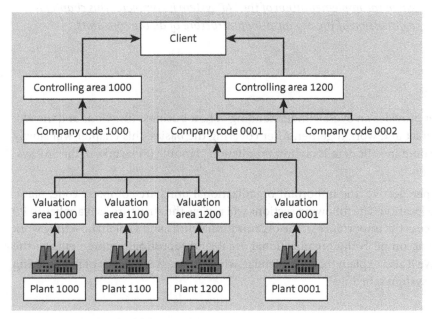

Figure 2.1 Organizational Structure in SAP

A company can consist of several legal entities, each including separate, individual financial statements that must be prepared at the end of the financial year. This is reflected as a separate *company code* for each legal entity.

The *valuation area* represents the level at which the company values its material stock consistently. It's part of the logistics area of the SAP system. A one-to-one relationship exists between the valuation area and the plant. For example, a material at one plant may have a different standard price than at another plant.

The diagram shown in Figure 2.2 represents the *organizational unit* of PP, wherein the company code attains the highest level. Within each company code, there can be one or multiple *plants*. Within each plant, there can be one or multiple physical and virtual *storage locations*.

The next sections will explain each unit in greater detail.

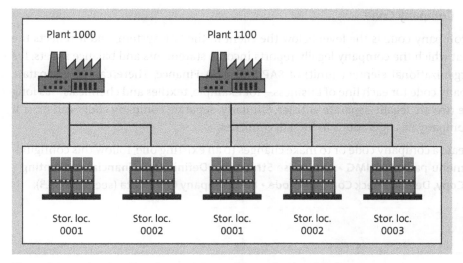

Figure 2.2 Production Planning and Control Organizational Unit

2.1.1   Client

A *client* represents the highest element of the SAP system's organizational structure. Often, the client represents a company or a group of companies, within which there are several independent company units. An SAP system can contain several clients in logical units. The additional organizational elements and the master and transaction data are created and managed within a client.

From the SAP system's landscape perspective, normally there are three clients (systems): development (DEV), quality assurance (QAS), and production (PRD). The actual configuration of the SAP system takes place in the DEV system, which is then transported to the QAS system for testing and training. The final configuration eventually moves to PRD, which is the final and live system in which the business process owners of the company make real-time live entries.

> **Note**
>
> In an SAP system, the word *client* has a specific meaning, and a clear understanding of what this word means in this context is important. In general speech, a client is a customer to whom the company provides services. In an SAP system, however, it refers to a corporate group, which is the highest organizational element. Clients in an SAP system are also used to differentiate among real-time data, test data, and development data.

2.1.2   Company Code

The company code is the level below the client in the SAP system, and it reflects the level at which the company legally reports income statements and balance sheets. It's an organizational element (unit) of SAP S/4HANA Finance. There can be a separate company code for each line of business—for example, textiles and chemicals—as long as the two are legally separate entities. Similarly, separate company codes can exist if the company has operations in foreign countries.

To create a company code or to make changes to an existing one, follow this configuration menu path: **SAP IMG · Enterprise Structure · Definition · Financial Accounting · Edit, Copy, Delete, Check Company Code · Edit Company Code Data** (see Figure 2.3).

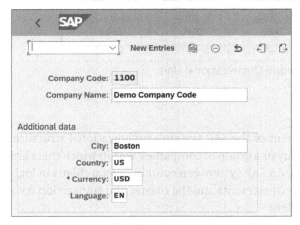

Figure 2.3 Company Code

[+]

Tips and Tricks

The configuration menu paths in this book each begin with **SAP Menu · Tools · Customizing · IMG · SPRO** followed by clicking on **Display Reference IMG** or pressing F5. For the sake of brevity, each menu path won't include that repetitive section of the path but rather will only begin the configuration menu path with **SAP IMG**.

Wherever possible or available, the relevant configuration transaction code is also shared to facilitate the configuration efforts.

[+]

Tips and Tricks

In general, when creating a company code, it's *always* recommended to copy from an existing company code. In a standard system, company code 0001 is provided by SAP for this purpose. When copying company codes, the system also copies parameters specific to company codes. If necessary, these parameters can be changed within the relevant application, which is less time-consuming than creating a new company code and also reduces the chance of error when maintaining the settings for a new company code.

Note

During the SAP implementation project, the financials (FI) team decides on company codes with the client and works on their creation in the SAP system.

2.1.3   Plant

A *plant* is an organizational unit within logistics. You can classify a plant from the point of view of production, procurement, maintenance, warehouse, or planning. For example, the plant can be a manufacturing site, a head office, or a distribution center within a company. It organizes the tasks for the production logistics, and it can be a physical production site or the logical grouping of several sites in which materials are produced or goods and services are provided. Different production locations are mapped with the plant in the SAP system. At the plant level, the following tasks can be performed:

- Managing inventory
- Evaluating and performing physical inventory of stocks
- Managing demand
- Planning production
- Executing and controlling production
- Performing material requirements planning (MRP)

In the organizational structure of the SAP system, only one company code can be assigned to a plant. However, multiple plants can be assigned to the same company code.

To create a new plant or to make changes to the existing plant, follow menu path **SAP IMG • Enterprise Structure • Definition • Logistics—General • Define, Copy, Delete, Check Plant**, or use Transaction OX10.

Note

During the SAP implementation project, the materials management (MM) team decides on and works on the creation of plants in the SAP system.

Figure 2.4 shows the change transaction screen of plant 1105, with the provision to enter the complete address and other details. It's important to use the **Factory Calendar** field to assign a factory calendar to a plant so that the system can plan out all the working and nonworking days of the plant.

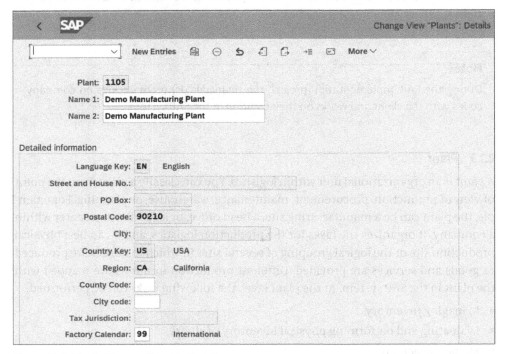

Figure 2.4 Plant: Change Transaction Screen

[»]

> **Note**
>
> Creating a factory calendar is covered in Section 2.2.

After the creation of the plant, the next step is to assign the plant to the company code. A plant can only be assigned to one company code, and multiple plants can be assigned to the same company code. It's mandatory to assign a plant to a company code.

To make a plant company code assignment, follow configuration menu path **SAP IMG · Enterprise Structure · Assignment · Logistics—General · Assign Plant to Company Code**, or use Transaction OX18 (see Figure 2.5). Choose the **New Entries** icon to create a new plant company code assignment.

[»]

> **Note**
>
> The MM team creates the plant company code assignment in the system.

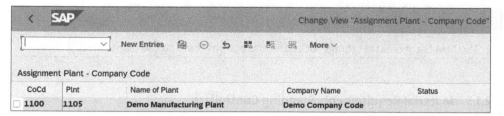

Figure 2.5 Assignment of Plant to Company Code

2.1.4   Storage Location

A *storage location* is the physical or virtual storage site for the materials. Examples of physical storage locations include a raw materials store, components store, returned goods store, finished goods store, and so on, whereas the virtual storage location can be self-defined and may be a scrap yard or a production shop floor in which semifinished goods are temporarily stored.

Even storage tanks or silos for storing bulk chemicals, oils, or grains can be treated as storage locations in the system. However, the limitation is that a storage location in the SAP system doesn't have the provision to define the maximum storage capacity of an individual tank or silo. This provision is available in the embedded SAP Extended Warehouse Management (SAP EWM) app in SAP S/4HANA.

Many storage locations can be created as needed within a plant, but one storage location can be assigned to one plant only.

To create a new storage location or to make changes to the existing storage location, follow configuration menu path **SAP IMG · Enterprise Structure · Definition · Materials Management · Maintain Storage Location**, or use Transaction OX09. Figure 2.6 shows the plant 1105 and several storage locations with this plant. Here, add both the storage location code and the **Addresses of Storage Locations**.

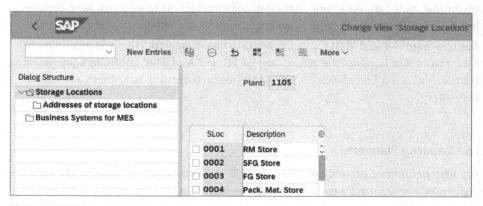

Figure 2.6 Storage Locations

[»]
> **Note**
>
> The MM team creates storage locations and assigns them to the plants.

2.1.5   Material Requirements Planning Controllers

An *MRP controller* can be an individual role or group of roles performing the same task. For example, if three people in a company manage the packaging materials procurement, then it makes sense to define one MRP controller for this. The MRP controller is primarily responsible for attending to the requirements of materials. When defining the MRP controller, the focus must remain on making sure it's defined based on responsibility, role, or area of work, instead of on an individual. For example, there may be one MRP controller who is responsible for raw materials only, while another one may be responsible for packaging materials. There may also be an MRP controller who is only responsible for managing consumables.

The MRP controller is assigned in the **MRP 1** view of the material master. When selecting the relevant MRP type in the material master by indicating that planning will be done on the material, the system prompts the user to enter the MRP controller. Again, the MRP controller should be based on the position or responsibility rather than on the person. Later, when using several standard reports and embedded analytics, MRP controller will be used as one of the selection criteria, among others.

To configure the MRP controller in SAP, follow configuration menu path **SAP IMG • Production • Material Requirements Planning • Master Data • Define MRP Controllers**.

[»]
> **Note**
>
> MRP controllers are used extensively by both production and procurement departments and the corresponding PP and MM areas. MRP controllers for procurement may be for raw materials, packaging materials, consumables, or spare parts. MRP controllers for production may be for finished goods, semifinished goods, or assemblies.
>
> The two teams (PP and MM) must coordinate in finalizing production and procurement MRP controllers because the bifurcation of PP and MM MRP controllers (including transaction codes) isn't obvious. It's best to agree on them and make them available in the system.

2.1.6   Capacity Planners

A *capacity planner* or *capacity planner group* is responsible for evaluating the current work center's or resource's capacity and, if needed, also for performing capacity leveling. When creating a new work center, it's also important to assign the person responsible in a specific field. The capacity planner can handle the role of person responsible for the work center as well. For example, it may make sense to combine all of the packing units of similar products into one capacity planner if the same person is responsible for it. If a company produces 10 different sizes of tomato ketchup—from a packet to a gallon size—and the same capacity planner is responsible for ensuring that various machines' capacities for each packing size are available, then simply agree to have one capacity planner in the SAP system, together with its code.

The capacity planners are assigned in the capacity header data of the work center (resource). Then, in all the capacity evaluation and leveling reports, the capacity planner is available as a selection criterion for the planner to choose from and that enables the system to display only relevant information.

To create a capacity planner, follow configuration menu path **SAP IMG · Production · Capacity Planning · Master Data · Capacity Data · Set up Capacity Planner.**

2.1.7 Production Schedulers

A production scheduler is responsible for ensuring that production execution and operation takes place per the production plan. The production scheduler immediately attends to or takes remedial action where necessary. To define a production scheduler, follow configuration menu path **SAP IMG · Production · Shop Floor Control · Define Production Scheduler**, or use Transaction OPJ9 (see Figure 2.7). Production schedulers are assigned in the **Work Scheduling** view of the material master.

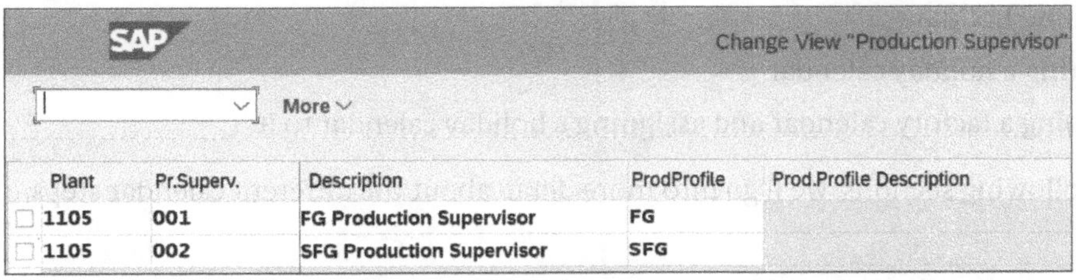

Plant	Pr.Superv.	Description	ProdProfile	Prod.Profile Description
1105	001	FG Production Supervisor	FG	
1105	002	SFG Production Supervisor	SFG	

Figure 2.7 Production Scheduler with Production Profile Assignment

The next section discusses the SAP calendar, which is alternatively referred to as a factory calendar in the SAP system.

2.2 SAP Calendar

For all of the planning and scheduling to effectively take place, it's imperative that a calendar exists in the system. This calendar is then assigned to the plant. First, all of the national holidays have to be defined, followed by combining all of the individual holidays in the holiday calendar. This holiday calendar then is assigned to the factory calendar.

To create a new calendar, follow configuration menu path **SAP IMG · SAP NetWeaver ·**
General Settings · Maintain Calendar, or use Transaction SCAL (see Figure 2.8). Here the
options to maintain the requisite details, such as **Public holidays, Holiday calendar,** and
Factory calendar, are available.

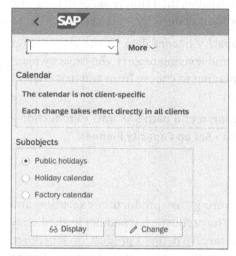

Figure 2.8 SAP Calendar

The SAP calendar creation function includes three individual steps:

1. Defining holidays
2. Creating a holiday calendar
3. Defining a factory calendar and assigning a holiday calendar to it

In the following sections, we'll go into more detail about the different calendar steps.

2.2.1   Public Holidays

Select the **Public holidays** radio button shown previously in Figure 2.8, and then choose
the **Change** icon. Select the **New Holiday** icon and then select whether it's a fixed date
or a floating public holiday. A floating public holiday depends on factors such as moon
sighting to decide the holiday. In Figure 2.9, selecting **Floating Public Holiday** leads to
the **Floating Public Holidays** dialog box, in which you can choose the holiday to be any
specific date or day, or even tied to a particular religious denomination, such as Bud-
dhist, Christian, Islamic, or Jewish.

Create/Change Public Holidays: Details
Holiday: New Year:
Public holiday is already being used
Type of Public Holiday
with fixed date
with a fixed day from date
Distance to Easter
Easter Sunday
Floating Public Holiday

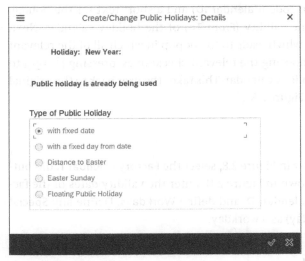

Figure 2.9 Public Holidays

2.2.2 Holiday Calendar

After defining and saving a public holiday, the system again returns to the screen shown previously in Figure 2.8. Selecting the **Holiday Calendar** radio button offers of a list of all of the holidays defined so far. Choose **New Entry**, which leads to the screen shown in Figure 2.10.

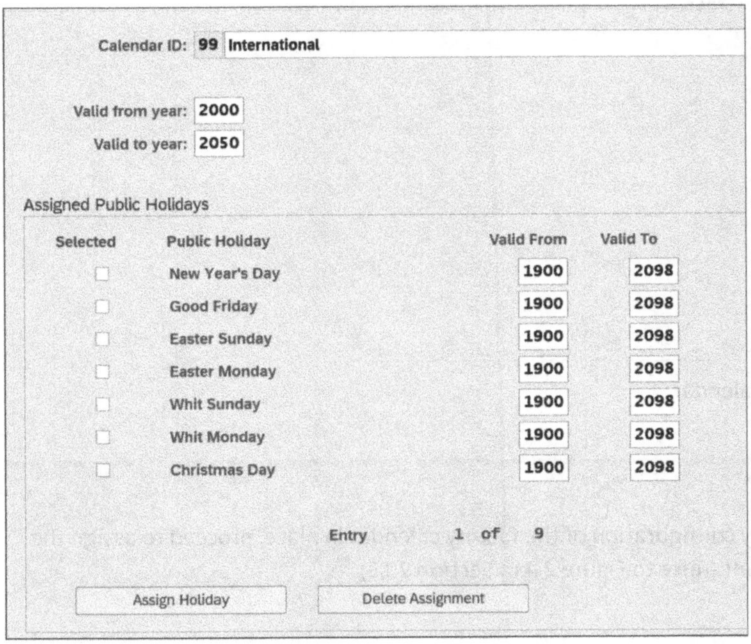

Calendar ID: 99 International
Valid from year: 2000
Valid to year: 2050
Assigned Public Holidays
Selected
Public Holiday
Valid From
Valid To
New Year's Day 1900 2098
Good Friday 1900 2098
Easter Sunday 1900 2098
Easter Monday 1900 2098
Whit Sunday 1900 2098
Whit Monday 1900 2098
Christmas Day 1900 2098
Entry 1 of 9
Assign Holiday
Delete Assignment

Figure 2.10 Public Holiday Calendar

After providing the identification code (**Calendar ID**) and a short text for the holiday calendar in this screen, define the validity (**From/To**) of the holiday calendar. Next, select the **Assign Holiday** button, which leads to the popup in which all of the relevant public holidays are selected by choosing the relevant checkboxes, pressing [Enter] to confirm, and finally saving the holiday calendar. This takes the user back to the original **Calendar** screen shown earlier in Figure 2.8.

2.2.3   Factory Calendar

Finally, in the screen shown earlier in Figure 2.8, select the **Factory calendar** radio button, which leads to the screen shown in Figure 2.11. Enter the validity dates of the factory calendar, assign a **Holiday Calendar ID**, and define **Workdays**. Define any **Special Rules** to denote any holiday (off day) as a workday.

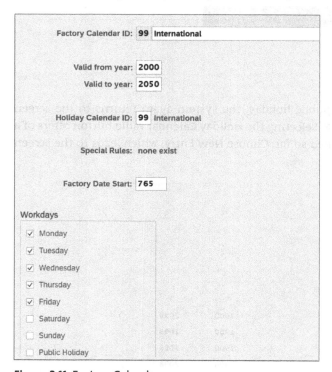

Figure 2.11 Factory Calendar

[»]

Note

With the necessary configuration of the factory calendar in place, proceed to assign the calendar in the plant (refer to Figure 2.4 in Section 2.1.3).

2.3   Summary

This chapter explained the importance of mapping most, if not all, of the important actual business processes of a company in the SAP system during its implementation. We also highlighted the importance of the enterprise structure of not just PP but of the entire organization, along with interdependencies. The reference table acts as an invaluable guide to understanding the importance of several PP-specific configuration elements, such as MRP controllers, production schedulers, and capacity planners.

The next chapter covers the configuration details of PP for discrete manufacturing.

PART II
Production Planning Configuration

Chapter 3
Discrete Manufacturing Configuration

Implementing discrete manufacturing, also known as shop floor control, involves a series of logical and sequential configuration steps to ensure complete mapping of configuration with the business processes of the company.

During an SAP S/4HANA implementation project, when it's established that discrete manufacturing will most closely serve the business needs of the company, the next logical step is to have intensive discussions and several workshops to agree on the configuration objects of discrete manufacturing. Configuration of the discrete manufacturing production type forms the basis on which the business processes of the company will run. For example, how should the system behave when it comes across a material or capacity shortage during production order creation or release? How should it behave when the actual production exceeds the defined underdelivery or overdelivery of the material? What should the system do if it's unable to schedule production within the defined basic dates? For each of these (and many more) questions, controls on the degree of freedom or flexibility (or strictness) can be set that will enable the system to allow or disallow certain options when performing relevant business functions. For example, the system can be configured to allow creating a production order despite a component shortage, but to stop a user from releasing it until the requisite components for production are available in stock.

In this chapter, we begin by covering the configuration basics needed to set up the master data used in discrete manufacturing. Then we follow a step-by-step process to create a new production order type, PP10, including assigning it a new number range. The subsequent configuration steps covered for this order type and in this chapter are sufficient to enable a business user to run end-to-end business processes in SAP. Chapter 6 will cover the business processes side of the configuration undertaken in this chapter.

If, as an SAP consultant or as a business process owner, this is your first time configuring and implementing production planning (PP), we suggest following the step-by-step approach in this chapter. Because PP integrates with several other functional areas, such as materials management (MM), quality management (QM), and, most importantly, product cost controlling (CO-PC), we suggest maintaining close coordination throughout by consulting the resources of these functionalities.

[»]
> **Note**
>
> The business processes of discrete manufacturing and process manufacturing are also similar in a lot of ways. Any differences are specifically covered in the relevant chapters (process manufacturing is covered in Chapter 4).

[»]
> **Note**
>
> Refer to Chapter 1 for a features comparison among discrete manufacturing, process manufacturing, and repetitive manufacturing (REM), as well as to learn how to decide which manufacturing type is most relevant for a given industry.

3.1   Material Master

The configuration of the material master is primarily managed within MM. During an SAP system implementation, the MM team coordinates with the client to discuss and agree on a large number of MM-specific configuration objects, which also include material types. A *material type* is a unique identification to distinguish materials used in various business processes. Some examples of material types are raw materials, semifinished goods, trading materials, packing materials, nonvaluated materials, spare parts, and consumables. However, the importance and involvement of PP can't be overemphasized here because the material requirements planning (MRP) and work scheduling views of the material master are very important to PP, from both a planning and an execution perspective. The PP information is maintained in the MRP views of the material master to enable the system to perform reliable material planning. The work scheduling view controls how production execution should take place.

Apart from the option for quantity and value updates, it's also possible to control the views that the system makes available to the end user during material master creation. For example, the purchasing view isn't normally available for finished goods because the company doesn't purchase finished goods. Similarly, for raw materials, the sales views aren't available because the company normally doesn't sell its raw materials.

To set up the material type attributes, follow configuration menu path **SAP IMG · Logistics—General · Material Master · Basic Settings · Material Types · Define Attributes of Material Types**.

Figure 3.1 shows the configuration view of **Material Type FERT (Finished Product)**. On the lower-right side of the screen, the option to control the views that the system makes available during material master creation is selected. At the bottom of the screen (not shown) is the **Price Control** field, which enables selecting whether the material will have a moving average price or standard price.

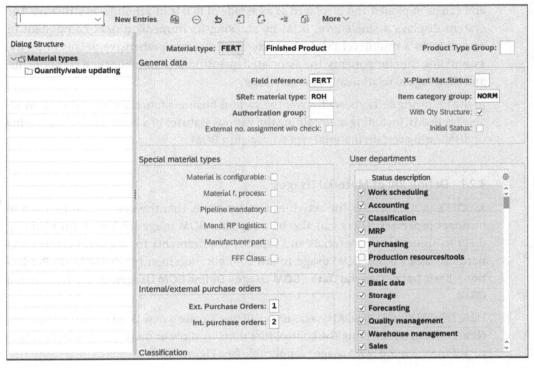

Figure 3.1 Material Types

3.2   Bill of Materials

Similar to the material master, a material's bill of materials (BOM) is used extensively in various areas of the supply chain, including planning, production, sales, and costing. A BOM is a formally structured list of components that is needed to produce a material. These components may be raw materials or packing materials procured directly from vendors or subassemblies produced in-house.

The BOM has a large number of functions. A user can have a BOM that is specific to engineering/design only, whereas another BOM of the same material can be used for costing purposes. There can be a production BOM and also a sales BOM. In a sales BOM, the system "explodes" the components and makes them an integral part of sales processing. For example, when a company sells a new car, it also includes accessories, such as a spare tire, a tire-changing toolkit, and an owner's manual, among other things. These accessories are, in fact, components in a sales BOM.

A material BOM is a central component in MRP. When the system runs the MRP on a material, it looks for its BOM to plan not just at the finished goods level but also at the components level and raw materials level. The material BOM is always a single level and can be exploded and displayed as a cascade of BOMs in a multilevel structure. The system displays a single-level BOM by showing its immediate next component or assembly. In a multilevel BOM, the system reflects comprehensive details of all the assemblies, the components, the associated quantities of assemblies and components, and their logical relationships to each other.

In the following sections, we'll cover the various business functions and controls available for BOMs, including maintaining the various statuses of a BOM, as well as allowing or disallowing certain material types' usage in a BOM.

3.2.1   Define Bill of Material Usages

A BOM's usage controls the activities and functions that the system can perform in business processes. There can also be a separate BOM usage for long-term planning (LTP) to simulate the materials and capacity requirements for a given business scenario. To create a new BOM usage, follow configuration menu path **SAP IMG · Production · Basic Data · General Data · BOM Usage · Define BOM Usages**, or use Transaction OS20.

Here several standard BOM usages are available. Create a new BOM usage by choosing **New Entries** and selecting the control functions to allow or disallow the business processes in which the BOM usage is applicable (see Figure 3.2).

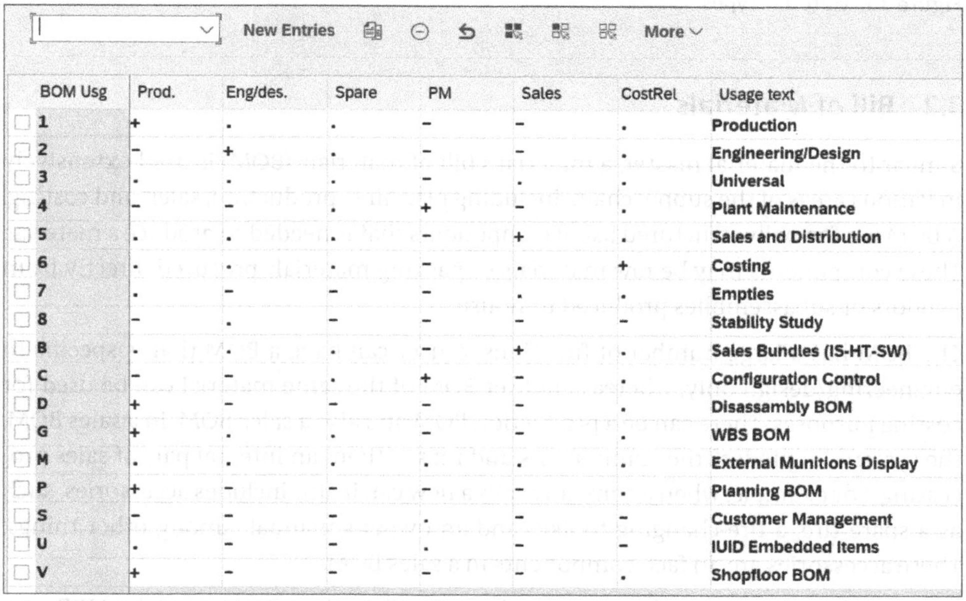

BOM Usg	Prod.	Eng/des.	Spare	PM	Sales	CostRel	Usage text
1	+	.	.	-	-	.	Production
2	-	+	.	-	-	.	Engineering/Design
3	.	.	.	-	.	.	Universal
4	-	-	.	+	-	.	Plant Maintenance
5	.	.	.	-	+	.	Sales and Distribution
6	.	.	.	-	.	+	Costing
7	.	-	-	-	.	.	Empties
8	-	.	-	-	-	-	Stability Study
B	.	.	.	-	+	.	Sales Bundles (IS-HT-SW)
C	-	-	.	+	-	.	Configuration Control
D	+	-	-	-	-	.	Disassambly BOM
G	+	.	.	-	-	.	WBS BOM
M	.	.	.	.	.	.	External Munitions Display
P	+	-	-	-	-	.	Planning BOM
S	-	-	-	.	-	-	Customer Management
U	.	-	-	.	-	-	IUID Embedded Items
V	+	-	-	-	-	.	Shopfloor BOM

Figure 3.2 BOM Usages

3.2.2 Allowed Material Types in the Bill of Materials Header

It's possible to control the material types that the system allows for creation of a material BOM. For example, normally creating a material BOM for spare parts or consumable material types isn't required. This control on material types for BOM creation also helps prevent the creation of unnecessary or unwanted material BOMs. During the SAP project, if several company-specific material types are configured by the MM consultant, then they must be specifically identified and perform the necessary configuration for all of the material types that will have any BOM usage.

To specify the material types for a material BOM creation, follow configuration menu path **SAP IMG · Production · Basic Data · Bill of Material · General Data · Define Material Types Allowed for BOM Header**, or use Transaction OS24.

Figure 3.3 shows that the BOM usage for the material type at the header level can be specified. The * symbol denotes that a BOM can have all usage types and can also be used in all material types at the header level.

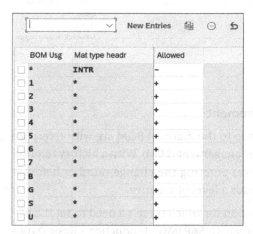

BOM Usg	Mat type headr	Allowed
*	INTR	–
1	*	+
2	*	+
3	*	+
4	*	+
5	*	+
6	*	+
7	*	+
B	*	+
G	*	+
S	*	+
U	*	+

Figure 3.3 Allowed Material Types in BOM Header

> **Note**
>
> In addition to maintaining the control function of the material type at the BOM header level, it's possible to do the same for a material at the BOM item level. To do so, follow configuration menu path **SAP IMG · Production · Basic Data · Bill of Material · Item Data · Define Material Types Allowed for BOM Items**, or use Transaction OS14.

3.2.3 Bill of Material Status

Different applications of a material BOM based on its status can be controlled. For example, during new product development, a material has a BOM status of **Engineering/Design**. When the engineering/design departments approve it, the next status can be **Costing** to enable the product costing team to calculate the cost of the material. Finally, when the costing department also approves the material BOM, it can attain the status of **Production**. This status enables the production team to begin producing the material. When the BOM has a **Production** status, it becomes available during the production order creation, whereas when its status is either **Engineering/Design** or **Costing**, it isn't available in production order creation. All these statuses in which all functions are possible can also be set.

To create or set the BOM status, follow configuration menu path **SAP IMG · Production · Basic Data · General Data · Define BOM Status**, or use Transaction OS23. Figure 3.4 shows the option to control whether the BOM status should allow business functions, such as being available during MRP explosion, for costing, or for work scheduling (production).

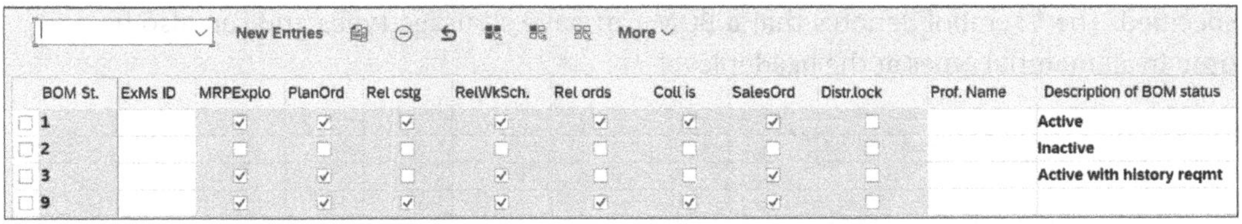

BOM St.	ExMs ID	MRPExplo	PlanOrd	Rel cstg	RelWkSch.	Rel ords	Coll is	SalesOrd	Distr.lock	Prof. Name	Description of BOM status
1		✓	✓	✓	✓	✓	✓	✓	☐		Active
2		☐	☐	☐	☐	☐	☐	☐	☐		Inactive
3		✓	✓	☐	✓	☐	☐	✓	☐		Active with history reqmt
9		✓	✓	✓	✓	✓	✓	✓	☐		

Figure 3.4 BOM Statuses

3.2.4   Bill of Material with History Requirement

It's possible to control whether changes made to the material BOM are with reference to a change number or engineering change management (ECM). With a history requirement or change number, the system requires entering the change number before it allows making the desired changes, which adds a level of security.

To select the BOM usage and status combination for which there's a need to set the history requirements, follow configuration menu path **SAP IMG · Production · Basic Data · General Data · Configure History Requirement for BOMs**, or use Transaction OS25. On the screen that appears, mark the required BOMs with a history requirement by selecting their checkboxes.

3.2.5   Item Category in Bill of Material

The item category provides further divisions to the different BOM classes. While some item categories are relevant for production or for planning, others are merely to provide information.

The following are some of the most important predefined item categories:

- **L: Stock item**
  Stock items contain components that are stored in a warehouse and included as a part of inventory management (IM).

- **N: Nonstock item**
  A nonstock item is a material that isn't available in stock but is procured directly for the given production order. A nonstock item has direct relation to the procurement process. There is also no need to have a material master (item code) for nonstock material. If a nonstock material is used, then it also requires filling in the procurement details, such as cost element, purchasing group, material group, and price.

- **R: Variable-size item**
  In this item category, a formula is used to define the sizes of the variables to enable the system to perform calculations and suggest the component's quantity.

- **T: Text item**
  The text item has a descriptive character.

- **M: Intra material**
  This item category is commonly used in master recipes (process industry). Materials that are temporarily used in process engineering are recorded as components with this item category.

The material input parameter (**MatInpt**) indicates whether a material reference to the item exists. This isn't the case with document items or nonstock items. The IM parameter (**InvMg**) allows for setting that up for only using those materials whose quantities are managed in IM.

To maintain a new item category or make changes to the existing ones, follow configuration menu path **SAP IMG • Production • Basic Data • Item Data • Define Material Types Allowed for BOM Header**, or use Transaction OS24. Select or deselect the checkboxes to meet your business needs.

3.2.6 Variable-Size Item Formulas

In the fabrication industry, components issued to produce an assembly are often based on a formula. For example, to produce the fuel tank of a motorcycle, the warehouse issues the steel sheet based on the formula, which calculates the requirement. When assigning a variable-size item in the BOM of the material with item category R, the system enables the option to enter the variable-size details in the relevant area of the BOM's item details area.

> **Note**
>
> Before creating a formula for a variable-size item, a unique unit of measure to denote the formula can be defined via Transaction CUNI.

To create a variable-size item formula, follow the SAP system configuration menu path **SAP IMG • Production • Basic Data • Item Data • Define Variable-Size Item Formula**, or use Transaction OS15. Figure 3.5 shows the list of available formulas that can be used, or a new one can be created.

Formula	Formula	DimRes	Formula text
☐ F1	ROMS1 * ROMS2	SURFAC	Area of a rectangle
☐ F2	ROMS1 * ROMS1 * PI	SURFAC	Area of a circle
☐ U1	ROMS1 + ROMS2 + ROMS3	LENGTH	Perimeter of a triangle
☐ U2	2 * ROMS1 + 2 * ROMS2	LENGTH	Perimeter of a rectangle
☐ V1	ROMS1 * ROMS2 * ROMS3	VOLUME	Volume of a rectangular parallelepiped

Figure 3.5 Variable-Size Item Formulas

3.2.7   Bill of Material Explosion Types

It's possible to control how the system takes a specific component's explosion into account in the **Basic Data** view of the BOM creation screen. This control allows you to set whether direct production, a phantom assembly, or even LTP is deactivated. For example, if there's a business need for the system to plan a particular component in LTP, you can set its explosion type status in the **Basic Data** view of the material's component. If the desired configuration settings aren't found, then they can be configured using the configuration menu path **SAP IMG · Production · Basic Data · Item Data · Define Explosion Types**.

3.2.8   Bill of Material Selection (Order of Priority)

It's possible to control how the system makes an automatic selection of a BOM to incorporate it in, say, a planned order during an MRP run. For example, during the MRP run, if the system is unable to find a material's BOM for production (BOM usage 1), then the next BOM selection priority that is set as universal (BOM usage 3) can be selected.

To configure the BOM selection and its order of selection priority, follow the configuration menu path **SAP IMG · Production · Basic Data · Bill of Material · Alternative Determination · Define Order of Priority for BOM Usages**, or use Transaction OS31. Here, define the selection ID to combine all BOMs with one unique ID. Then define the selection priority of each BOM, and finally assign the BOM usage, such as production or universal.

3.3   Work Center

A *work center* is a machine or a group of machines, a person or a group of persons, or a group of persons and machines that adds value to the manufacturing process. During an SAP implementation project, the production team and the product costing team discuss and mutually agree on the number of work centers that needs to be available.

The decision is primarily focused on ensuring that the production department is able to schedule and plan work centers and machine capacities, whereas the product costing team ensures that the reporting for both activities and cost centers is available. For example, if the packaging process incurs significant costs that the product costing team needs to monitor, then it makes sense to create a packaging work center and assign a separate cost center and associated activities to it. If these costs don't require separate monitoring, then the production line cost center is sufficient.

In the following sections, we explain how to make field selections in the work center so that during creation of the work center, the system either makes a field entry mandatory or optional. We also discuss how to use a standard value key (SVK) to define which activities are important for an operation from a business perspective. Defining formulas for the work center that can be used in capacity requirements planning (CRP), scheduling, and costing is also discussed. Location groups to account for the time it takes to move a product from one work center to another and the corresponding system to consider this during scheduling is also discussed. Finally, we discuss using a control key for operations as a control function to decide if, for example, scheduling or printing for an operation is allowed.

3.3.1 Work Center Category

A *work center category* is a control function that ensures which master data applications and business processes of discrete manufacturing the work center can be used in. For example, work center category 0007 is available for rate routing in REM, and in this category the available application option for REM can be found. In the same way, work center category 0008 is available and used for process manufacturing, and in this category, the master recipe application can be found.

To create a work center category, follow configuration menu path **SAP IMG · Production · Basic Data · Work Center · General Data · Define Work Center Category**, or use Transaction OP40. Select the work center category **0001** used in discrete manufacturing, and double-click the **Application** folder. The available applications in the resulting screen are shown in Figure 3.6 for **Cat.** (category) **0001**.

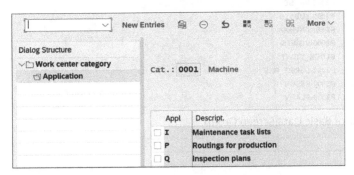

Figure 3.6 Application of Work Center Category

3.3.2   Field Selection in the Work Center

It's possible to control the fields in the SAP system for which entry is mandatory, optional, an input option, or hidden from display. For example, during the work center creation, if a user must enter information in a specific field, then selecting the **Req.** radio button will ensure a mandatory entry. When a user enters information in one field, the system can also control prompting the user or preventing the user from performing any dependent function. This option works when one modifiable field relates to the influencing fields. For this example, on selecting the work center category as **0001** as an influencing field, the system makes the **Backflush** field indicator (a modifiable field) a mandatory entry. So whenever a user creates a work center with category 0001, selecting the **Backflush** field is also mandatory.

> **Note**
>
> The field selection option isn't just restricted to work centers; it can also be used in BOMs, routings, and confirmations.

To define field selection in a work center, follow configuration menu path **SAP IMG • Production • Basic Data • Work Center • General Data • Define Field Selection**, or use Transaction OPFA. Figure 3.7 shows that the **Basic data** screen group has several modifiable fields, such as **Backflush** or **Person Responsible**.

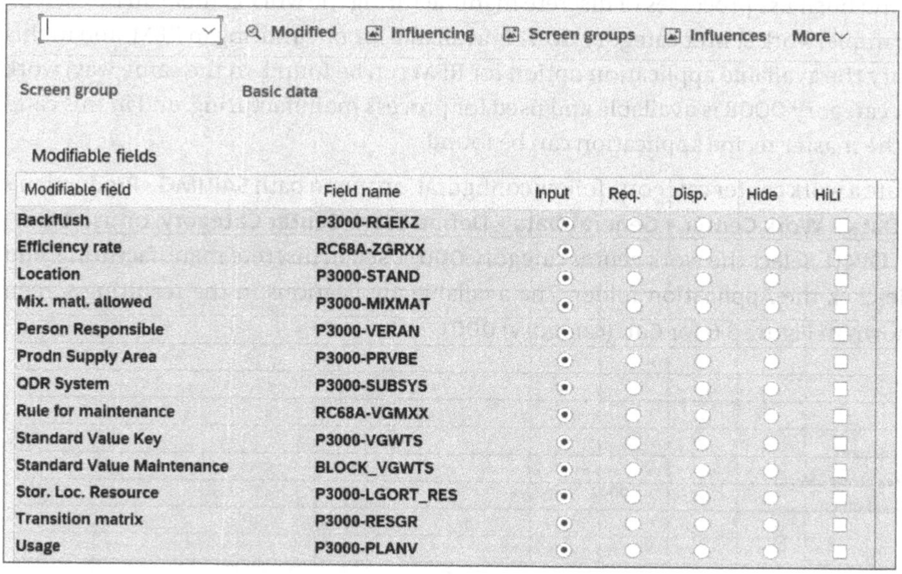

Modifiable field	Field name	Input	Req.	Disp.	Hide	HiLi
Backflush	P3000-RGEKZ	●	○	○	○	☐
Efficiency rate	RC68A-ZGRXX	●	○	○	○	☐
Location	P3000-STAND	●	○	○	○	☐
Mix. matl. allowed	P3000-MIXMAT	●	○	○	○	☐
Person Responsible	P3000-VERAN	●	○	○	○	☐
Prodn Supply Area	P3000-PRVBE	●	○	○	○	☐
QDR System	P3000-SUBSYS	●	○	○	○	☐
Rule for maintenance	RC68A-VGMXX	●	○	○	○	☐
Standard Value Key	P3000-VGWTS	●	○	○	○	☐
Standard Value Maintenance	BLOCK_VGWTS	●	○	○	○	☐
Stor. Loc. Resource	P3000-LGORT_RES	●	○	○	○	☐
Transition matrix	P3000-RESGR	●	○	○	○	☐
Usage	P3000-PLANV	●	○	○	○	☐

Figure 3.7 Modifiable Fields of Basic Data Screen Group

Five options are available in the modifiable fields:

- **Input**
  The entry in this field is optional.

- **Req. (required)**
  The entry in this field is mandatory.

- **Disp. (display)**
  There's no entry in this field because it's available for display only.

- **Hide**
  The system hides this field, and it isn't displayed.

- **HiLi (highlight)**
  Any specific field can be highlighted for the user's attention. For example, when marking a field entry as **Req.**, the HiLi checkbox can also be selected to enable the user to quickly see the fields requiring entries.

Double-click the **Backflush** field, or click the **Modified** button. In the screen that appears, as shown in Figure 3.8, click on the **New values** button. In the popup that appears, enter the work center category as "0007", and choose **Continue**. Select the **Req.** radio button to ensure that whenever a user creates a work center of category 0007, selecting the **Backflush** indicator is mandatory.

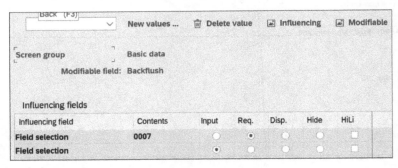

Figure 3.8 Modifiable Field with Influences

Repeat the same with work center category **0014**, but this time select the **Hide** radio button. The system won't show the **Backflush** field when the user creates a work center with work center category 0014.

3.3.3 Formulas for the Work Center

The system uses previously defined parameters to define formulas that can then be used in CRP or scheduling. The following parameters can be used:

- SAP_08 Base quantity
- SAP_09 Operation quantity
- SAP_11 Number of operation splits

A formula definition also holds the control for the following applications:

- CRP
- Scheduling
- Costing

To define the formula parameter, if it's different from the ones already available, use the configuration menu path **SAP IMG** · **Production** · **Basic Data** · **Work Center** · **Costing** · **Work Center Formulas** · **Define Formula Parameters for Work Centers**, or use Transaction OP51.

To define the formula that can be used in the work center for costing, CRP, and scheduling, follow the configuration menu path **SAP IMG** · **Production** · **Basic Data** · **Work Center** · **Costing** · **Work Center Formulas** · **Define Formula for Work Centers**, or use Transaction OP54.

In Figure 3.9, notice the formulas for calculating the production processing duration.

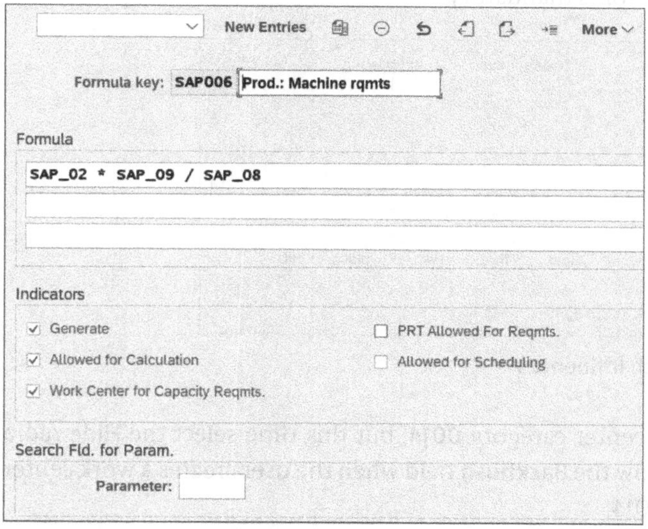

Figure 3.9 Formula Definition in Work Center

The system calculates the capacity requirement as follows:

Capacity requirement = Standard value × Order quantity ÷ Base quantity

The processing duration can be reduced if the operation is processed simultaneously at several work centers per the following formula:

Duration = Standard value × Order quantity ÷ Base quantity ÷ Number of splits

In Chapter 6, these formulas will be assigned in the **Scheduling**, **Capacities**, and **Costing** tabs of a work center.

Figure 3.10 shows the **Formula Key** ZPOWER and the associated **Formula** that also uses the parameter ZPOWER in formula calculation. This ZPOWER formula key is then assigned to a standard value key (SVK).

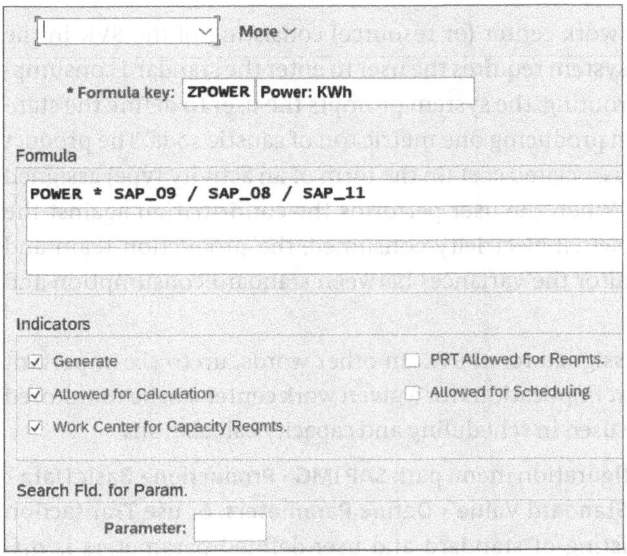

Figure 3.10 Self-Defined ZPOWER Parameter Used in Formula Key

3.3.4 Standard Value Key

During the course of an SAP implementation project, one of the main areas where the production and the product costing teams collaborate is in defining the SVK, which consists of individual parameters that are then grouped together as one SVK. The SVK is assigned in the **Basic Data** view of the work center and also entered in the formula that the system will use for each of the parameters. The following sequence of steps is used to define an SVK:

1. Define the parameters.
2. Assign the parameters to the SVK.
3. Create a formula for the work center.
4. Assign a formula against each parameter.

Let's explain this with an example. Suppose that in addition to monitoring and recording standard durations, such as setup, machine, or labor, your product costing department also wants to record the electricity and steam consumed in producing a product. The reason to record these two unique parameter values is that a significantly high cost is associated with these values. For example, in the caustic soda industry, electricity consumption (power) is excessive and is closely monitored, so it's a critical cost component that the company wants to monitor and control. Similarly, in the steel rerolling industry, electricity and natural gas form significant costs of the finished product and therefore must be recorded and monitored. When determining the parameters to use and monitor for SVK, check and confirm with the company to see if these parameters are quantifiable and measurable for recording in the SAP system.

When the user uses a specific work center (or resource) consisting of the SVK in the routing (or master recipe), the system requires the user to enter the standard consumptions. For this example, in the routing, the system prompts the user to define the standard electricity consumption in producing one metric ton of caustic soda. The product costing team will also have an associated cost (in the form of an activity type) assigned to this parameter (electricity). When the user performs the confirmation against the process order and enters the actual electricity consumed, the production team and product costing team can monitor the variances between standard consumption and actual consumption.

Up to six parameters can be assigned to an SVK. In other words, up to six important parameters that have direct cost implications for a given work center can be monitored and recorded. SVKs can also be used in scheduling and capacity calculations.

To define a parameter, use configuration menu path **SAP IMG · Production · Basic Data · Work Center · General Data · Standard Value · Define Parameters**, or use Transaction OP7B. The initial screen consisting of standard and user-defined parameters is displayed. Double-click **SAP_02**, and the screen shown in Figure 3.11 appears. The standard parameter with **TIME** as a **Dimension** and **Standard Value Unit** in **MIN** (minutes) is displayed. If a self-defined parameter is created, such as power, steam, or electricity, then give the dimension and the unit of measure in which to record the consumption value.

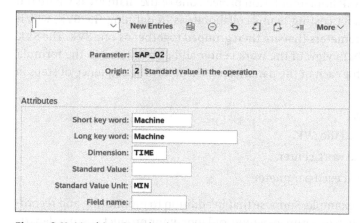

Figure 3.11 Machine Standard Parameter with Unit of Measure

Next, to create the SVK, follow configuration menu path **SAP IMG · Production · Basic Data · Work Center · General Data · Standard Value · Define Standard Value Key**, or use

Transaction OP19 (or Transaction OPCM). Figure 3.12 shows the **Std Val. Key** SAP1, which consists of the standard parameters **SAP_01**, **SAP_02**, and **SAP_03**. If any self-defined parameters need to be part of the SVK, then maintain them here. As noted previously, up to six parameters can be maintained in an SVK. Make sure to select the **Generate** checkbox when defining SVK because then the system automatically performs the calculations defined in the formulas. Otherwise, it does the calculation for scheduling and capacity planning during production order creation, which often leads to system performance issues.

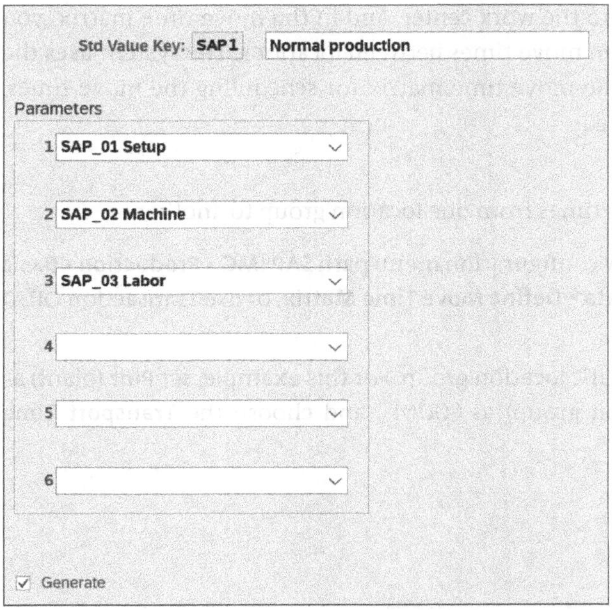

Figure 3.12 Standard Value Key Formula

Figure 3.13 shows an example of a self-defined SVK, ZCL1, containing two parameters (machine hours and rework hours) that a cladding manufacturing company wants to record, monitor, and make part of its product costing.

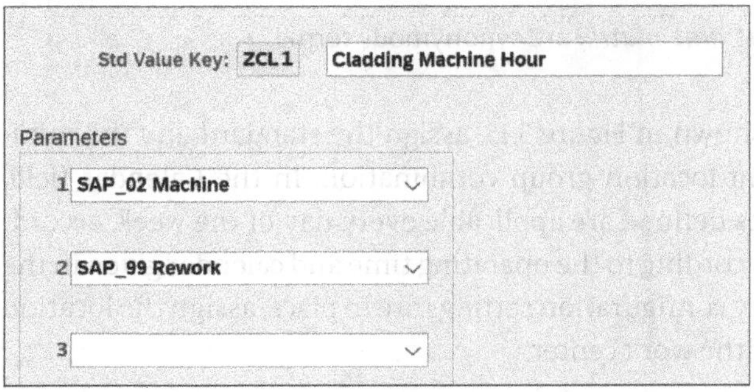

Figure 3.13 Self-Defined SVK Containing Self-Defined Parameters

3.3.5 Location Groups

A *location group* consists of a physical location where each work center is located. Several work centers can be combined into one location group if they are in close proximity to one another. Use the move time matrix to provide standardized values to different transitions times (also known as *interoperation times*), such as queue time, wait time, and move time. If there's no business need to use the move time matrix, then maintain this transition's time information either in the work center or in the routing.

The location group is assigned to the work center, and in the move time matrix, you define the normal and minimum move times between locations. The system uses the working times maintained in the move time matrix for scheduling the move times. Basically, two steps are performed:

1. Maintain the location groups.

2. Maintain the matrix of move times from one location group to another.

To set up location groups, follow configuration menu path **SAP IMG · Production · Basic Data · Work Center · General Data · Define Move Time Matrix**, or use Transaction OP30 (or Transaction OPJR).

Figure 3.14 shows the plant-specific location group. For this example, set **Plnt** (plant) as "1000", set **Loc. Group** (location group) as "0001", and choose the **Transport Time Matrix** folder.

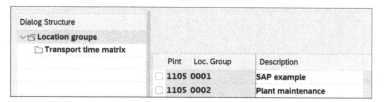

Figure 3.14 Location Groups/Transport Time Matrix

Note

Move time matrix and *transport time matrix* are synonymous terms.

In the screen that appears, as shown in Figure 3.15, assign the standard and the minimum move times for the plant-location group combination. In the **Calendar** field, choose whether the move times defined are applicable every day of the week, according to the factory calendar, or according to the operating time and calendar given in the work center. When the necessary configuration settings are in place, assign the location group in the **Scheduling** area of the work center.

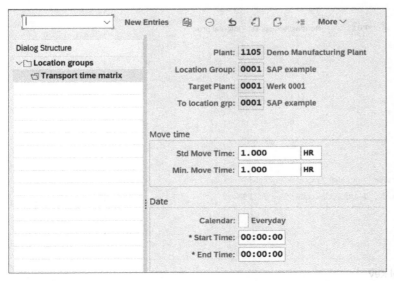

Figure 3.15 Transport Time Matrix

3.3.6 Control Key for Operations

A *control key* acts as a central function to control which actions a user or system can or can't perform on a specific work center. Select the relevant checkboxes and make the relevant settings in the control key, as shown in Figure 3.16. Then, assign this control key in the **Default Values** area of the work center (or resource). On assigning the work center to the material's routing, the control key becomes an integral part of the operation and acts as a control function.

In a control key, it's possible to define, among other things, whether some or all of the following functions are possible:

- Scheduling
- CRP
- Inspection characteristics required for in-process (during production) inspection
- Automatic goods receipt (GR)
- Scheduling for external operations

The confirmation type required for a work center can also be controlled. For example, it's possible to control whether confirmation is required or optional for a given operation during the order confirmation process. Further, whether an operation is a milestone confirmation can also be controlled. In a milestone confirmation, all of the preceding operations are automatically confirmed as soon as the operation is confirmed as having a milestone confirmation.

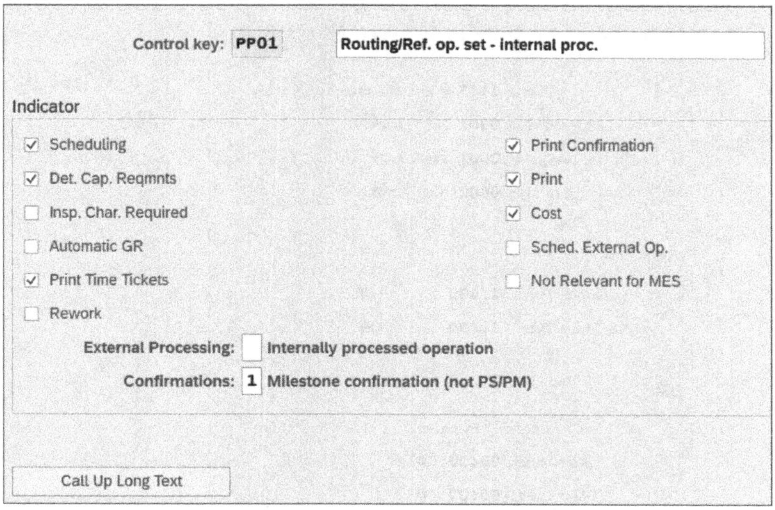

Figure 3.16 Control Key

[»]

Note

Chapter 6 will cover how to assign this control key in the **Default Values** area of the work center.

3.4   Routing

A *routing* is a set of operations that the material will undergo during the entire production process at relevant work centers. For example, a raw material is transformed into a finished product due to undergoing various operations (defined in the routing) performed at the relevant work centers.

Most of the important parameters for routing selection are made in the order type-dependent parameters (Section 3.6), in which you incorporate controls such as routing selection as a mandatory or an optional requirement. The order type-dependent parameters also control whether routing selection is an automatic or manual process.

To set up the routing parameters, follow the configuration menu path **SAP IMG · Production · Basic Data · Routing · Routing Selection · Select Automatically**, or use Transaction OPEB. In Figure 3.17, the selection **ID** specifies the selection sequence according to which the system will select the planned type, usage, and status of the routing. The following list explains the first few columns:

- ID

  Combines all of the different priorities listed in the next column, **SP**.

- **SP**
  Lists the sequence in which the system will look for relevant routing during production order creation. In other words, it's the priority setting for routing selection.

- **Task List Type**
  Refers to the task list type that the system will consider, such as **N** for routing, **R** for rate routing, and **S** for reference operation set.

- **Plan Usage**
  Controls whether the routing is only used for production or is available for inspection plan usage too. The value **3** denotes that this routing will be available for all types of usages.

- **Description**
  The description that appears after you select relevant usage from the **Plan Usage** field.

- **Status**
  Denotes the status that the system should look for in a routing or in a reference operation set and, if found, incorporate in the production order.

- **Description of the Status**
  The description that appears after you select the relevant usage from the **Description of the Status** field.

ID	SP	Task List Type	Plan Usage	Description	Status	Description of the Status
01	1	N	1	Production	4	Released (General)
01	2	N	1	Production	2	Released for Order
01	3	2	1	Production	4	Released (General)
01	4	2	1	Production	2	Released for Order
01	5	V	1	Production	4	Released (General)
01	6	V	1	Production	2	Released for Order
01	7	P	1	Production	4	Released (General)
01	8	P	1	Production	2	Released for Order
02	1	R	1	Production	4	Released (General)
02	2	R	1	Production	2	Released for Order
03	1	3	1	Production	4	Released (General)
03	2	3	1	Production	2	Released for Order
04	1	2	1	Production	4	Released (General)
04	2	2	1	Production	2	Released for Order
Q1	1	Q	1	Production	4	Released (General)

Figure 3.17 Automatic Routing Selection

[«]

Note

The selection IDs can be used during scheduling of orders (planned orders or production orders). Use Transaction OPU3, OPU4, or OPU5 to assign the relevant selection IDs to the order. See Section 3.6.1 for how to incorporate selection IDs into production orders (Transaction OPU3).

3.5 Production Order Configuration

During an SAP implementation, the PP consultant conducts workshops and finalizes several configuration objects, including order types and their number ranges. An *order type* is a unique identification and control function that enables the business process owner to quickly perform several functions, such as creating an order, automatically releasing an order, or scheduling an order.

The decision to create and make available different order types depends on how the company wants to see data, information, and depth of planning and controls required. For example, a company might want to sort all orders by separating all of the rework production orders from the normal production orders. This logical segregation of two different order types enables the planner to not only quickly segregate the available data in the system in the form of reports but also put in place the necessary system authorizations. Normally, companies also prefer to have production order types in direct relation to work centers. For example, in the cold-rolled steel sheets industry, if there are five different work centers, such as cold-roll sheets uncoiling, pickling, annealing, recoiling, and packing, then it makes sense to have five different production order types to enable every work center to have clear visibility into the activities and controls involved. Similarly, in the automotive assembly, the main work centers may be press shop, paint shop, and final assembly. In the textile industry, the work centers might be spinning, weaving, bleaching and dyeing, stitching, and finishing. In a pharmaceutical company, there may only be a need to create two order types—the first for bulk medicines, such as pill, capsule, or tablet manufacturing, and the second for packing bulk medicines.

However, we suggest not overdoing it in this exercise: creating too many production order types can be confusing and also demands greater data entry and maintenance work. Instead, use operations and other work center criteria to meet your reporting needs. In the following sections, we'll discuss how to create a new production order type in discrete manufacturing and assign it a new number range.

3.5.1 Maintain Order Types

An order type controls the following functions directly or through additional profiles:

- Internal and external number assignment
- Classification system
- Commitments management
- Status management for the different production statuses
- Settlement
- Scheduling

When defining an order type, the system automatically assigns the relevant order category. An order category distinguishes among various order types, not just in the production processes but also in plant maintenance (PM), quality management, or controlling (CO) orders. Whenever you create a new order type for a particular application, the system automatically assigns the correct order category.

Figure 3.18 shows the list of order categories available in the SAP system when you hover over **Order category** and press F4 . A **PP Production Order** uses **Order category 10**, whereas the **Order category** for a **Process Order** is **40**.

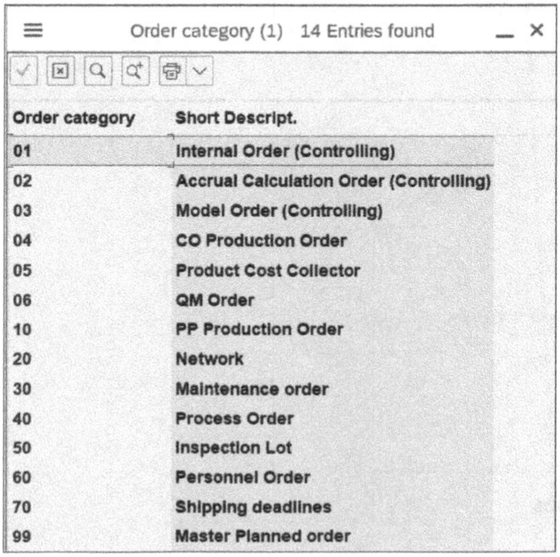

Order category	Short Descript.
01	Internal Order (Controlling)
02	Accrual Calculation Order (Controlling)
03	Model Order (Controlling)
04	CO Production Order
05	Product Cost Collector
06	QM Order
10	PP Production Order
20	Network
30	Maintenance order
40	Process Order
50	Inspection Lot
60	Personnel Order
70	Shipping deadlines
99	Master Planned order

Figure 3.18 Order Categories

To create a new order type, follow the configuration menu path **SAP IMG • Production • Shop Floor Control • Master Data • Order • Define Order Types**, or use Transaction OPJH.

In Figure 3.19, notice that the system automatically assigns **Order category 10** to the production order. Create **Order Type** "PP10", and give a short description. For the **Settlement Profile**, coordinate with the product costing team to assign the appropriate settlement profile to the production order.

Tips and Tricks

To save the effort of defining all the parameters in any configuration object and also to lessen the chance of errors, we suggest copying from one of the standard objects available and then making the desired changes to the newly created object. The copy function is available in all configuration objects. Look for the **Copy As** button, as shown in the menu bar in Figure 3.19.

For this example, copy the standard and previously available production order **PP01** to create the new production order type **PP10**.

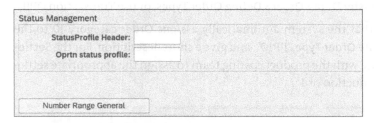

Figure 3.19 Maintain Production Order Types

Scroll down in the screen shown in Figure 3.19 and click the **Number Range General** button shown in Figure 3.20 to define the new number range for the newly created **PP10** production order type.

Figure 3.20 Number Range Creation

[»]

Note

Transaction CO82 can also be used to create a new number range group and define the interval for the production order. On the initial screen, click **Change Groups**, and then perform all of the steps listed in Section 3.5.2.

3.5.2   Number Ranges

On the initial screen that appears, choose **Group • Insert**. In the screen that appears, as shown in Figure 3.21, enter the new number range group. All production orders assigned to this number range group will use this number range. For this example, enter "Turbine" in **Group**, and define the new number range interval as "80000001" to "84999999". To facilitate the number range creation process, the system displays the existing number ranges available (if any) in the lower half of the screen. The newly defined number range can't overlap with the existing number ranges. Click the **Insert** button, and the system enables defining a new number range interval. In this example, the newly defined number range is assigned the tag **25**, as shown on the left-hand side of Figure 3.21. This number range tag will be used to assign the number range to the newly created production order type PP10.

Next, perform the following steps:

1. Select the **Turbine Manufacturing** checkbox, which represents the new number range group.

2. At the bottom of the same screen, look for **Not Assigned**, including the new created order type **PP10**. Click order type **PP10**, and then click **Select**.

3. Click the **Element/Group** icon.

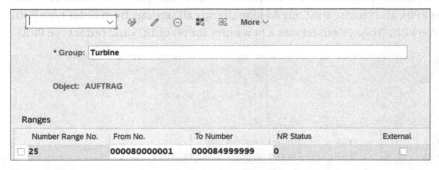

Figure 3.21 Insert Group Screen to Enter New Number Range Interval

If these steps were successfully followed in order, the final screen will look like Figure 3.22. Here the system assigns the newly created number range group **25** to the newly created order type **PP10**.

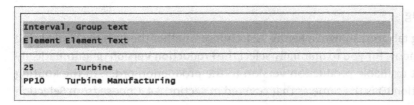

Figure 3.22 Number Range Group Assigned to Order Type PP10

In Chapter 6, you'll see that the production order for order type PP10 has the number range assigned in this step.

3.6   Order Type-Dependent Plant Parameters

After defining the new order type, the next step is to define order type-dependent plant parameters. In this step, several settings are made to enable the system to control different functions during production order creation. For example, it's possible to control whether the system should automatically select the production version or provide the user with the option to select it manually in a popup that appears during production order creation. Similarly, a batch search strategy can be assigned for batch-managed materials. Further, controlling which information the system should update to make it a part of the order information system and logistics information system (LIS) is possible. Finally, coordinate with the product costing team to enable them to make relevant settings from a cost center accounting (within SAP S/4HANA Finance) perspective.

To set up order type-dependent plant parameters, follow the configuration menu path **SAP IMG · Production · Shop Floor Control · Master Data · Order · Define Order Type-Dependent Plant Parameters**, or use Transaction OPL8. In Figure 3.23, notice the plant and order type combinations already available. For this example, select **Plant 0001** and **Order Type PP01**, and choose the **Copy As** icon to copy all settings from order type PP01 to order type PP10. The system creates a new entry for plant 1105 and order type PP10.

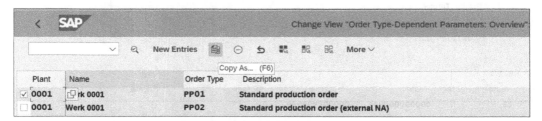

Figure 3.23 Available Order Type-Dependent Parameters

We'll now walk through the different tabs that are available for order type-dependent parameters.

3.6.1   Planning

In the **Planning** tab area, shown in Figure 3.24, choose whether the system should bring up a popup window for you to manually select the **Production Version** or automatically assign the first available production version to the production order. In the **Routing** area, the **Selection ID** is the same as that covered in Section 3.4. Choose from **Selection**

ID for automatic or manual routing selection (or reference operation set) during production order creation. Also, choose whether it's mandatory or optional for the system to have a routing (or reference operation set) available during production order creation. Select the **Check Op. Details** checkbox to enable the system to check and automatically copy the work center details in the routing. The routing header text can also be copied into the production order.

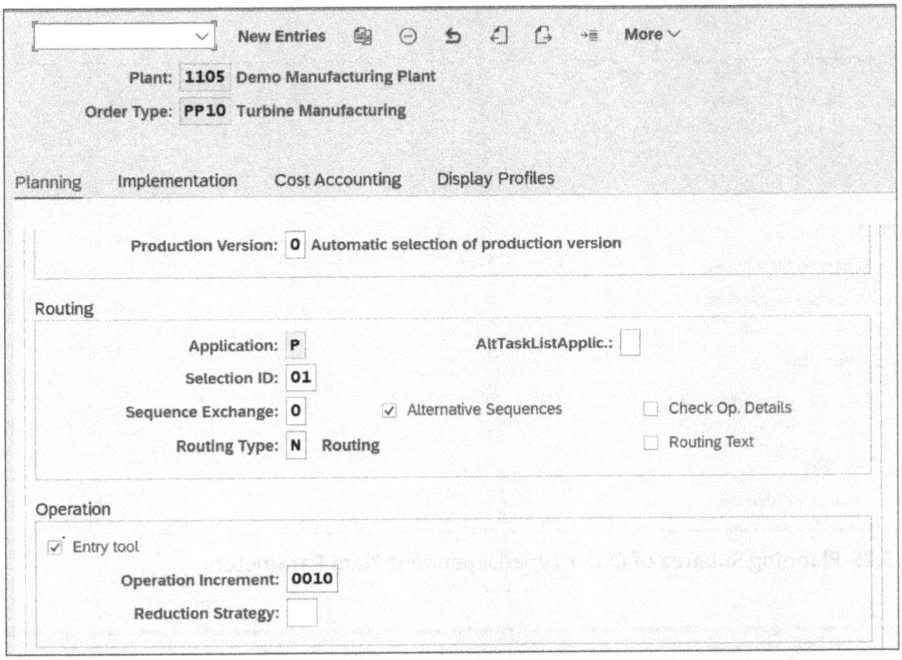

Figure 3.24 Planning Tab of Order Type-Dependent Plant Parameters

In the **Bill of Material** area, choose to either use the standard BOM application or enter a custom-defined BOM application, if it's previously created. Scroll down on the same screen to see the area shown in Figure 3.25.

In the **Batch Determination** area, enter the previously created batch-search strategy (primarily used in the process industry, but also in discrete manufacturing for batch-managed materials). We suggest coordinating with the MM team to define the batch search strategy and then assign it in the **Search Procedure** field. **Substitute MRP Ctrller** or **Substitute Scheduler** can be assigned if the system is unable to find it in the material master or when creating a production order without reference to a material. An MRP controller is assigned in the **MRP 1** view of the material master and the production scheduler (supervisor) in the **Work Scheduling** view of the material master.

When creating a production order, choose when the system should create reservations for in-house or stock-based materials and purchase requisitions for externally procured materials. Finally, on this screen, enter **Inspection Type** "03" to enable the system to perform in-process (during production) inspection of the material. This is an integration point between PP and QM (see Figure 3.25).

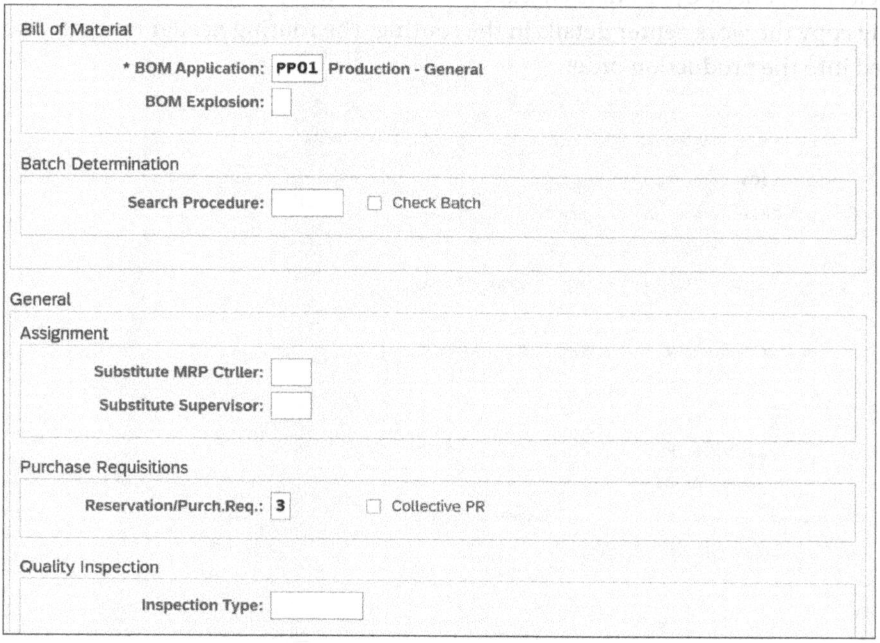

Figure 3.25 Planning Subarea of Order Type-Dependent Plant Parameters

[»]

> **Note**
>
> Chapter 10 covers batch management.

3.6.2   Implementation

In the **Implementation** tab (shown in Figure 3.26), make sure to select all of the relevant checkboxes, especially for the **Shop Floor Information System** and **Documentation of Goods Movement** areas. Selecting these checkboxes will enable the system to automatically update the LIS with the option to view documented goods movements (goods issue [GI] or goods receipt [GR]) for the production orders. The documented goods movements in the production order information system (Transaction COOIS) also show up in the complete GI/GR details.

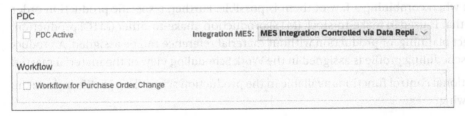

Planning   Implementation   Cost Accounting   Display Profiles

Status Change Documents

☐ For Order Header

☐ For Operation

☐ For Material

☐ For Production Resource/Tool

Shop Floor Information System

☑ Update   I01

Release Versions

☐ Header   ☐ Item   ☐ Operation

Documentation of Goods Movements

☑ GR for Purchase Order

☑ GR for Production Order

☑ Planned Goods Issue

☑ Unplanned Goods Issue

Figure 3.26 Implementation Tab of the Order Type-Dependent Plant Parameters

Scrolling down the screen, make any specific settings for work in process (WIP) batches (see Figure 3.27), which we'll cover in detail in Chapter 10.

PDC

☐ PDC Active   Integration MES: **MES Integration Controlled via Data Repli.** ⌄

Workflow

☐ Workflow for Purchase Order Change

Figure 3.27 WIP Batch Settings

3.6.3   Cost Accounting

Figure 3.28 shows the **Cost Accounting** tab. We suggest coordinating with the CO resource (who handles cost object controlling) to ensure that the necessary configuration settings are in place.

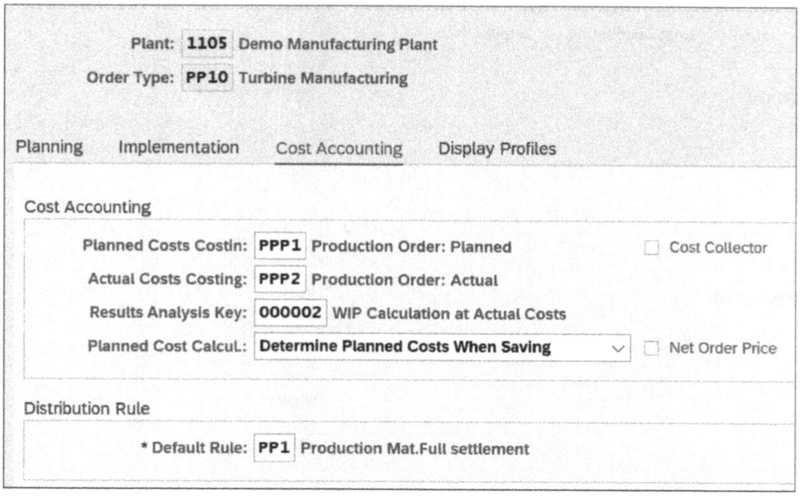

| Plant: | **1105** | Demo Manufacturing Plant |
| Order Type: | **PP10** | Turbine Manufacturing |

Planning   Implementation   Cost Accounting   Display Profiles

Cost Accounting

Planned Costs Costin:	**PPP1**	Production Order: Planned	☐ Cost Collector
Actual Costs Costing:	**PPP2**	Production Order: Actual	
Results Analysis Key:	**000002**	WIP Calculation at Actual Costs	
Planned Cost Calcul.:	**Determine Planned Costs When Saving** ⌄		☐ Net Order Price

Distribution Rule

| * Default Rule: | **PP1** | Production Mat.Full settlement |

Figure 3.28 Cost Accounting Tab of Order Type-Dependent Plant Parameters

3.7   Production Scheduling Profile

A *production scheduling profile* is used to define the tasks of the production order that the system automatically executes during creation or release of a production order. For example, the system can automatically release the production order as soon as it's created, or the system can automatically send the shop floor papers for printing after an order is released. This saves the user the time and effort of performing individual functions when combining a few of them is possible. Further, a specific production order type that is used in make-to-stock (MTS) production, make-to-order (MTO) production, project planning, or production without material reference can be assigned. A production scheduling profile is assigned in the **Work Scheduling** view of the material master.

Additional control functions available in the production scheduling profile include the following:

- Automatic actions on creating a production order
- Automatic actions on releasing a production order
- Material availability
- Capacity availability
- Automatic GR (along with the control key; Section 3.3.3)
- Confirmation controls
- Batch management settings

To create a new production scheduling profile, follow the configuration menu path **SAP IMG** • **Production** • **Shop Floor Control** • **Master Data** • **Define Production Scheduling**

Profile, or use Transaction OPKP. In the **Automatic Actions** area shown in Figure 3.29, it's possible to control whether the system should automatically release a production order on its creation. This is applicable in those business scenarios in which a formal or separate approval on the release of the production order isn't required and thus immediate creation and release serve your purposes. Similarly, on release of the production order, controls can be put in place for whether the system is to automatically execute the printing function, schedule the order, or even create control instructions (see the information on process management in Chapter 4, Section 4.4, and on Execution Steps [XSteps] in Chapter 7, Section 7.7).

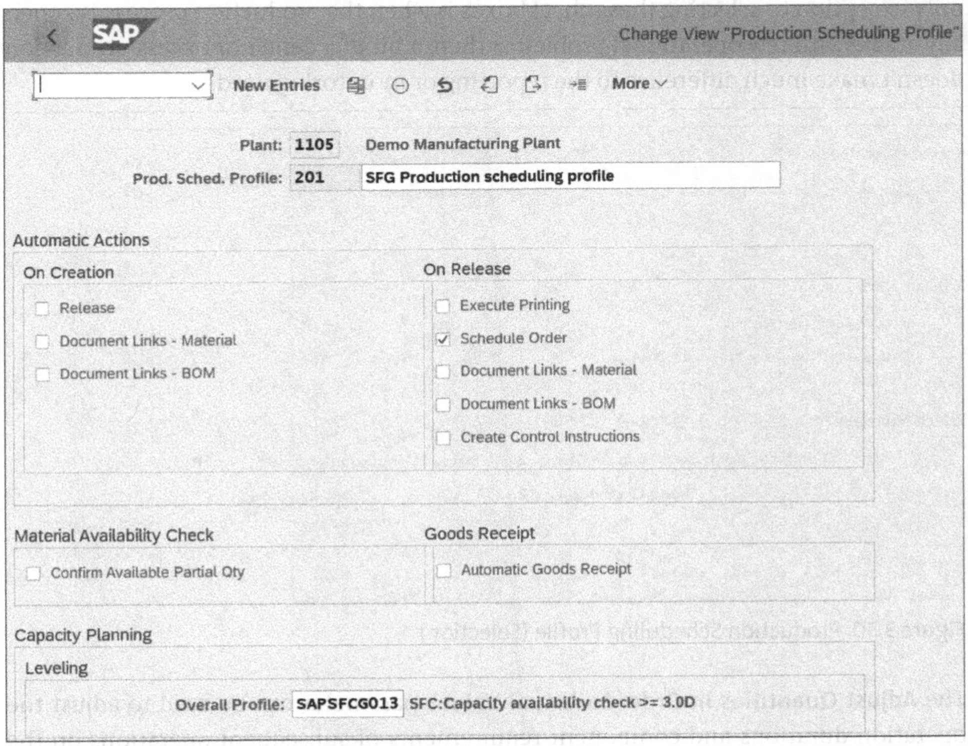

Figure 3.29 Production Scheduling Profile (Selection)

> **Note**
> Process integration is a relatively new offering for discrete manufacturing, including creation of control recipes. Refer to Chapter 4 and Chapter 7 for in-depth coverage of process management; the underlying workings and concepts are the same for discrete manufacturing.

For capacity planning, an overall profile is assigned, and then in the production order screen, the user can navigate to the capacity planning screen, in which the system uses the profile assigned here. Further controls can be put in place for whether the system should confirm the capacity availability, as well as to perform finite scheduling during production order creation.

Scroll down the screen to see the options shown in Figure 3.30. Here we recommend not setting the **Confirmation** area checkboxes. This ensures that the system automatically updates the production deficit or surplus (excess) in the production order as soon as the necessary business processes, such as confirmation and GR, are performed. The only exception to selecting these checkboxes is when the production process is generally stable with few operational problems; then, a bit of a deficit or excess production doesn't make much difference to the reporting or monitoring needs.

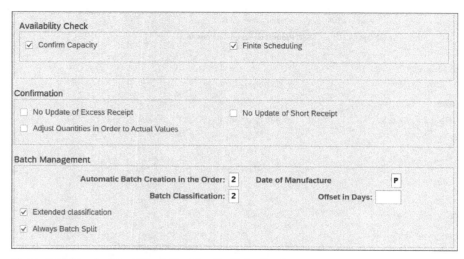

Figure 3.30 Production Scheduling Profile (Selection)

The **Adjust Quantities in Order to Actual Values** parameter can be used to adjust the operation durations and component requirements of subsequent operations on the basis of a scrap-adjusted quantity calculation. The system reschedules the relevant operations.

It's also possible to control how the system handles the batch-managed materials and if it should automatically create the batch during production order creation, during its release, or not at all. If the company plans to integrate warehouse management (WM) or embedded SAP Extended Warehouse Management (SAP EWM) into the production process, then we suggest coordinating with the relevant WM/SAP EWM resource to make the necessary settings on this screen (see Figure 3.31).

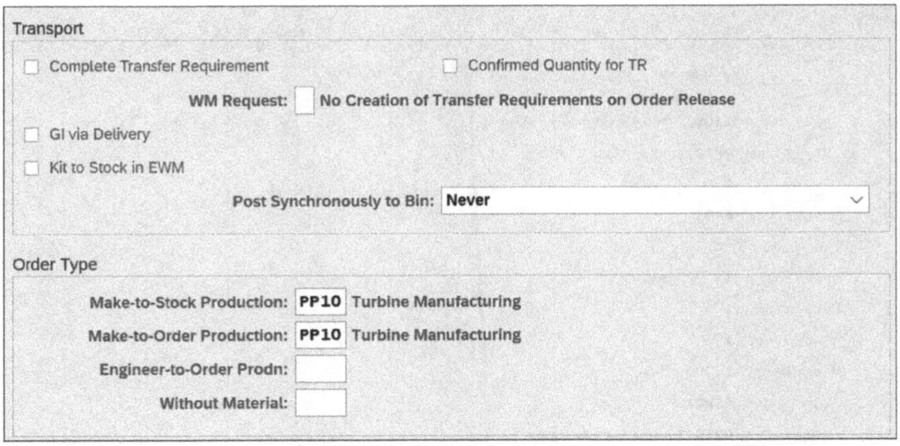

Figure 3.31 Order Types Assignment in Production Scheduling Profile

3.8   Default Values for the Generation of Operations

During the production order creation, if the system is unable to find routing or a reference operation set, it no longer allows the user to create the production order. Further, to create a production order without reference to a material, the system still needs a routing or reference operation set.

When creating a production order for a material, the system looks for its master data, such as a BOM and routing. Routing consists of operations involved in the production of a material. If the master data is maintained, especially routing data, then the system can refer to the default values to generate operations.

To manage these business scenarios, set default values for the generation of operations with a plant and order type combination. To do so, follow the configuration menu path **SAP IMG • Production • Shop Floor Control • Operations • Task List Selection • Define Default Values**, or use Transaction OPJG.

For **Plant 1105** and **Order Type PP10**, we suggest making entries in all of the fields, as shown in Figure 3.32.

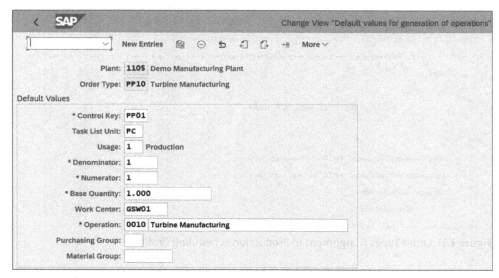

Figure 3.32 Default Values for Generation of Operations

3.9   Availability Check

An *availability check* enables the system to check and validate whether one or all of the required resources, whether materials, capacities, or production resources/tools (PRT), are available in the production process. A production planner and scheduler want a comprehensive overview of material and capacity availability or shortages to take necessary action, if required. In case of missing component availability, the system maintains an entry in the missing parts information system. Moreover, controls can be put in place for whether the system should allow creation or release of the production order if it finds a shortage of a material or capacity needed to produce the goods.

Several options are available to perform material or capacity availability checks. You can manually check these within the production order creation screen, or you can even use a separate transaction to perform the material availability check. Alternatively, you can make the settings in the availability check for the system to perform these functions automatically.

There are three different types of availability checks in the SAP system:

- **Material availability check**
  Checks the availability of the components for the production order either against actual stocks (and optionally receipts) or against the planning.

- **Capacity availability check**
  Checks whether sufficient free capacity is available for the order's operations.

- **PRT check**
  Checks a status in the master data to determine whether the required PRT is free.

> **Note**
> See Chapter 18 for more information on CRP.

The system makes availability checks on two levels:

- During production order creation
- During production order release

The following sequence of steps is involved in the availability checks:

1. Define the checking group.
2. Define the checking rule.
3. Define the scope of the check.
4. Define the checking control.

We cover each of these steps in the following sections.

3.9.1 Define the Checking Group

To set the availability checking control, follow the configuration menu path **SAP IMG • Production • Shop Floor Control • Operations • Availability Check • Define Checking Group**, or use Transaction OVZ2. In Figure 3.33, the availability **(Av) 01** for **Daily requirements** has options to enter **TotalSales** and **TotalDlvReqs** on a daily, weekly, or monthly basis. If the **No PAC** checkbox is selected, then the system switches off the available-to-promise (ATP) check.

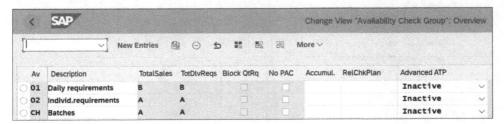

Figure 3.33 Availability Checking Control

3.9.2 Define the Checking Rule

A checking rule can be defined to cater to various functional areas such as sales and distribution (SD), MRP, production order processing, or IM. This enables configuring and integrating different checking rules for different applications to meet the business needs. To define the checking rule, follow the configuration menu path **SAP IMG • Production • Shop Floor Control • Operations • Availability Check • Define Checking Rule**.

3.9.3   Define the Scope of the Check

From the combination of the previously defined availability checking control as **01** (**Daily requirements**) and **Checking Rule** as **PP**, we proceed to define the scope of the check. This step primarily defines which inward and outward movements and stock types the system should consider during the availability check—for example, if the system should consider purchase orders whose GRs on the delivery dates will ensure material availability. Similarly, you can set the relevant settings for the system to include (or exclude) firmed planned orders in its quantity and material availability calculation.

In the standard settings, the system only considers available unrestricted stock for the availability check; however, there may be business needs in which quality stock may also be considered as available stock during an availability check. For example, in ice cream manufacturing, the stock is kept in quality inspection even during transportation from one plant to another, until it reaches its destination. If such quality stock should be included in the material availability check, then set the relevant indicator.

To define the scope of the check, follow the configuration menu path **SAP IMG · Production · Shop Floor Control · Operations · Availability Check · Define Scope of Check**, or use Transaction OPJJ.

In the screen shown in Figure 3.34, choose the stock types and inward/outward movements that best meet the business scenarios. Scroll down and notice that in the **Receipts in Past** field (not shown), you can control whether the system should consider all of the past and future receipts or future receipts only.

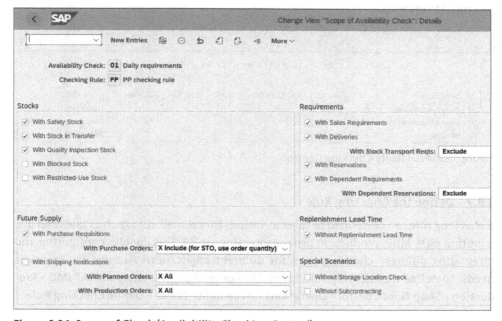

Figure 3.34 Scope of Check (Availability Checking Control)

3

Now proceed to assign the checking group in the **MRP 3** view of the material masters for all the components in the **Availability Check** field. For this example, use availability checking group **01** and assign it in the **MRP 3** view of the material masters for all the *components* used in producing the semifinished product (**Turbine Manufacturing**).

3.9.4 Define the Checking Control

As mentioned previously, you maintain comprehensive availability checks of material, PRT, and capacity during production order creation and release. Because creation and release of production orders are two important business functions, define the level of controls for each business function. For example, if there's a long lead time between production order creation and release, skip some of the availability checks, such as for capacity or PRT, until the order is ready to be released. Similarly, instead of a stringent control meaning that the system doesn't allow the release of a production order until the material is available to produce it, select the option in which the user decides when to release the production order, which meets business needs more closely so that at least partial production can commence.

To set up a checking control for production order creation and release, follow the configuration menu path **SAP IMG • Production • Shop Floor Control • Operations • Availability Check • Define Checking Control**, or use Transaction OPJK. On the initial screen, there are several order type and plant combination entries. For this example, copy the standard settings of plant 0001 and order type PP01 and both business functions (**1**: creation, **2**: release) to the newly created order type PP10 and for plant 1000. The screen shown in Figure 3.35 appears after completing the copy function.

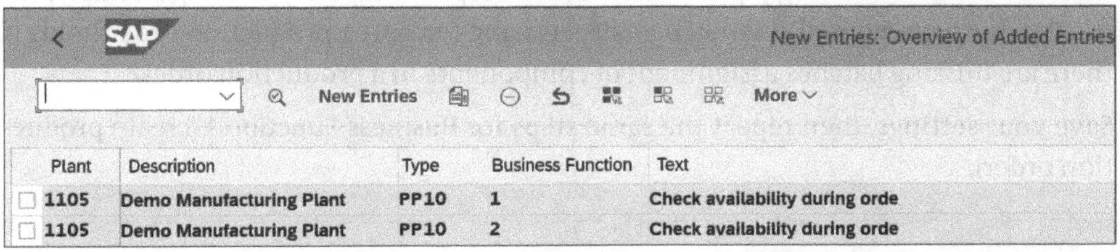

	Plant	Description	Type	Business Function	Text
☐	1105	Demo Manufacturing Plant	PP10	1	Check availability during orde
☐	1105	Demo Manufacturing Plant	PP10	2	Check availability during orde

Figure 3.35 Checking Controls in Creation and Release of Production Order

Double-click **Plant 1105**, **Type PP10**, and **Business Function 2** (release). In the screens shown in Figure 3.36 and Figure 3.37, notice that there are four distinct areas: **Material Availability**, **PRT Availability**, **Capacity Availability**, and **Batch Assignment**. In the **Checking Rule** field, assign the rule **PP** that was discussed previously. For **PRT Availability**, select the **No Check** checkbox, and the system won't check for PRT availability during production order release. There can be different settings when creating a production order (**Business Function 1**) as compared to when a production order is released.

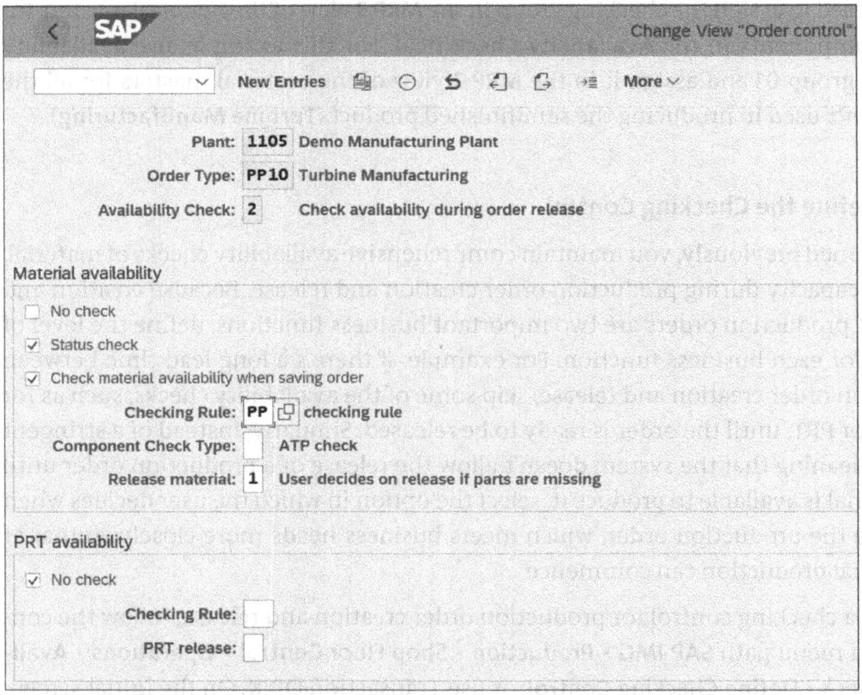

Figure 3.36 Availability Checks during Production Order Creation

For **Capacity Availability** in Figure 3.37, assign an overall profile, and also select option **1** for the **Release Order** field. This option enables the user to decide on a runtime basis whether to allow creating a production order despite a capacity shortage. Finally, for the **Batch Assignment**, the same logic of releasing (or not) a production order holds if there are missing batches assignment of components in a production order.

Save your settings, then repeat the same steps for **Business Function 1** (create production order).

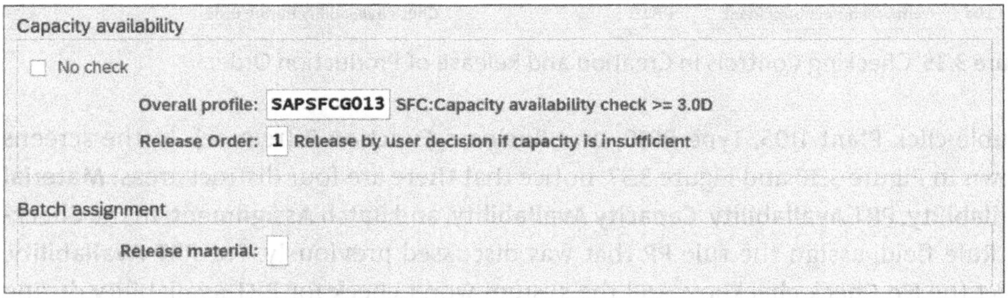

Figure 3.37 Availability Check for Capacity

3.10 Scheduling

During the planning of planned orders that are created during MRP, the system needs to incorporate dates of production for the individual operations in the production order. Apart from specific production times (setup and machine), there may also be a need to add transition times, such as wait time, queue time, and move time, as well as safety times, such as opening period, float before production, or float after production.

Before we cover the scheduling in detail, it's important to note how the system takes the various dates into account during scheduling:

- There are two scheduling types in SAP: basic dates scheduling and lead-time scheduling.

- For planned orders, the planner can have only basic date scheduling (only basic dates). For production orders, the planner can have both (basic and production dates).

- Whenever the system carries out lead-time scheduling, it automatically carries out basic date scheduling beforehand.

In finite scheduling and reduction of lead time scheduling, the first step the system takes is to define the start and end dates of the production order without taking capacity constraints into account. The objective is to evaluate whether the dates are synchronized for timely and complete production. Primarily, there are two types of scheduling:

- **Backward scheduling**
  Determines the start date of the production order based on the latest finish date that you define in the production order.

- **Forward scheduling**
  Determines the end date of the production order based on the earliest start date that you define in the production order.

In finite scheduling, the system carries out individual planning (scheduling) for the production order and doesn't take interdependencies of various orders into account. If the system can't manage the production within the stipulated dates, then the lead time can be reduced with overlapping, splitting, or reducing the transition times. If the system should consider reduction during the planned orders creation stage (during an MRP run), then use Transaction OPU5 to configure it. Here are some of the steps to take to reduce the lead time and to optimize the production process:

1. If a float before production is defined as three days, then reduce or eliminate this time to enable the system to bring back the production schedule to meet the target finish date. This also applies to the opening period and float after production. Use Transaction OPU3 to achieve this.

2. Similarly, the splitting function divides a large production lot into several smaller lots, provided there are several individual capacities to manage it in parallel.

3. With overlapping, the system passes the processed parts of the total lot directly on to the next machine.

4. Reduce other times, such as queue time and wait time, where possible.

5. Add another workday or shift to the factory calendar to increase the number of available production hours.

In the following sections, we explain the different scheduling types available for production orders and how the system adjusts the scheduled dates if these aren't within the time frame of the basic dates. We also discuss how the scheduling margin key enables various buffers in production to account for any unforeseen or unexpected delays.

3.10.1 Scheduling Types for Production Orders

As previously covered, there are two primary types of scheduling: backward scheduling and forward scheduling. The other available options are backward or forward scheduling with time and current date. In **Current Date**, the system performs forward scheduling and uses the current date (today's date) as the basic start date in the planning.

With the **Only Capacity Requirements** scheduling type, the system calculates the capacity requirements only. The individual operations aren't scheduled, and the basic dates are copied as operation dates.

To set up the scheduling type, follow the configuration menu path **SAP IMG • Production • Shop Floor Control • Operations • Scheduling • Specify Scheduling Type**, or use Transaction OPJN.

3.10.2 Scheduling Parameters for Production Orders

A scheduling type can be assigned in the scheduling parameters of the production order. Make other settings in the scheduling parameters for the production order; it's possible to control it even up to the production scheduler level.

To set the scheduling parameters for the production order, follow the configuration menu path **SAP IMG • Production • Shop Floor Control • Operations • Scheduling • Define Scheduling Parameters for Production Orders**, or use Transaction OPU3. The screens in Figure 3.38 and Figure 3.39 show **Plant 1105** and **Order type PP10** with no specific production scheduler. Select the **Generate Capacity Reqs.** checkbox to enable the system to generate capacity requirements during scheduling.

The **Adjust Dates** field describes whether the system determines the basic start and finish dates during scheduling. In backward scheduling, this applies to the basic start dates. Further, this only applies if lead-time scheduling creates production dates so that the time frame given by the basic dates isn't sufficient to include the production dates from lead time scheduling anymore. In this case, one of the two basic dates is adjusted automatically.

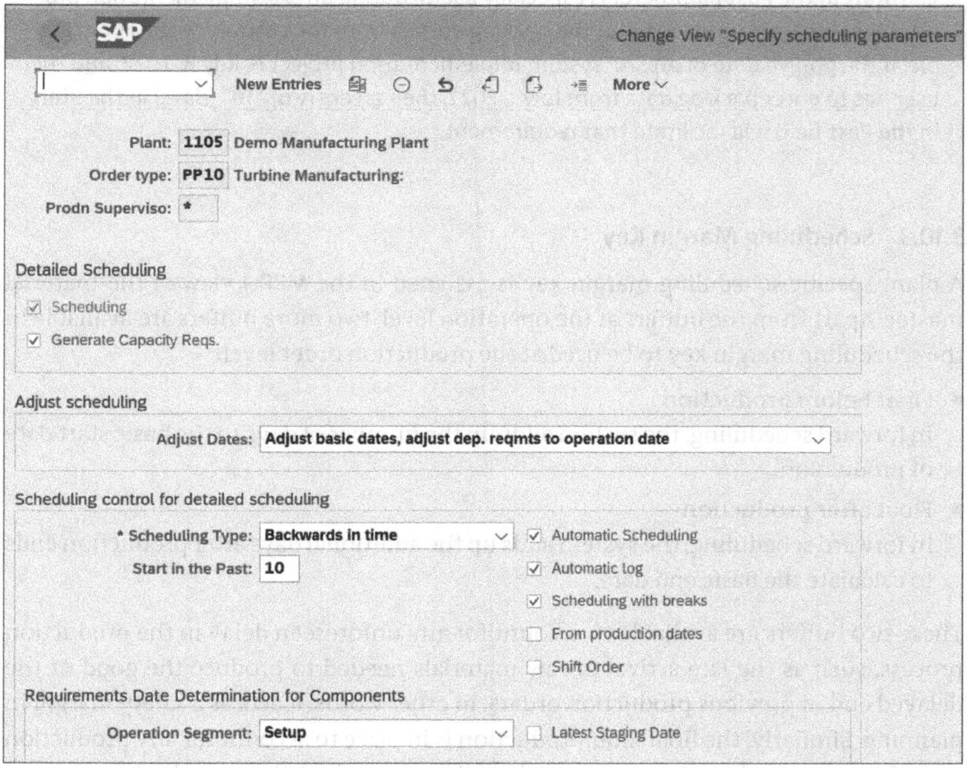

Figure 3.38 Scheduling Parameters for Production Order: Part 1

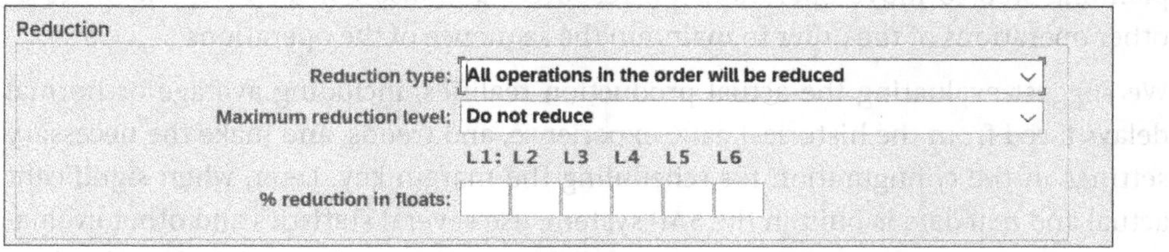

Figure 3.39 Scheduling Parameters for Production Order: Part 2

The **Start in the Past** parameter specifies how many days in the past the basic start date may be before the scheduling type is overridden and the today scheduling (forward scheduling from today) is used. Here, first set the **Scheduling Type** that the system will consider in production order scheduling.

[+]

Tips and Tricks

The **Start in the Past** parameter is especially useful during an SAP implementation project when the user needs to enter the backlog entries from the cutover dates. For example, if the go-live date of an SAP system implementation project is July 8, 2022, and the user has to enter backlog data from July 1, 2022, then an entry of "10" (days) in the **Start in the Past** field will facilitate that requirement.

3.10.3   Scheduling Margin Key

A plant-specific scheduling margin key is assigned in the **MRP 1** view of the material master. Apart from the buffers at the operation level, two more buffers are available in the scheduling margin key to be used at the production order level:

- **Float before production**
  In forward scheduling, the system adds up the number of days to the basic start date of production.

- **Float after production**
  In forward scheduling, the system adds up the additional days after production ends to calculate the basic end date.

These two buffers are available to account for any unforeseen delay in the production process, such as the late arrival of raw materials needed to produce the good or the delayed end of previous production orders. In other words, it acts as a safety margin in planning. Similarly, the float after production is in place to account for any production or unforeseen machine breakdown delays that may affect the overall planning and scheduling. Further, these floats provide a certain degree of freedom from the capacity-planning step to move operations on resources and also consider dependencies of other operations of the order to maintain the sequence of the operations.

We suggest evaluating the actual production realities, including average or normal delays faced from the historical data, experience, and trends, and make the necessary settings in the configuration for scheduling the margin key. Later, when significant actual and real data is built in the SAP system, use several statistics and other evaluation reports and information systems available in PP to revisit and update the data, which forms the basis for planning.

Finally, apart from floats before and after production, the scheduling margin key also contains the opening period and the release period. The *opening period* is a time interval at the beginning of the planned order and is used for the (collective) conversion of planned orders into production orders. The opening date is the beginning of the opening period and is prior to the basic start date of the planned order. The *release date* is the beginning of the release period and is prior to the start date of the production order. The released period may also be considered as the time it takes from creating a production order to its release, due to internal company processes and controls in place.

To set up the scheduling margin key, follow the configuration menu path **SAP IMG · Production · Shop Floor Control · Operations · Scheduling · Define Scheduling Margin Key**.

For scheduling margin **Key 001** for **Plnt 1105**, the **Opening Period** is **10** days, the **Float After Production** is **1** day, the **Float Before Production** is **2** days, and the **Release Period** is **3** days (Figure 3.40).

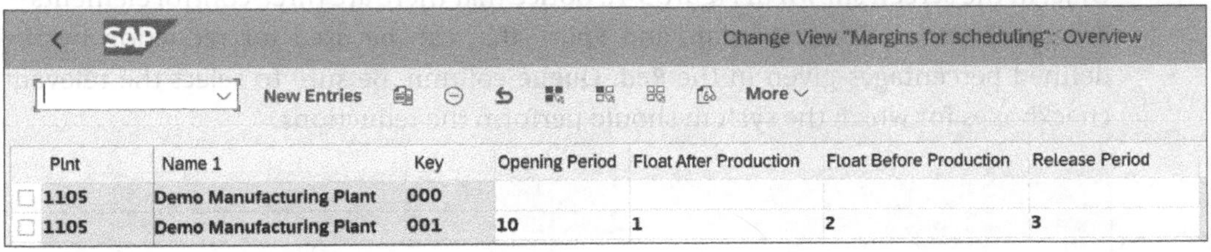

Plnt	Name 1	Key	Opening Period	Float After Production	Float Before Production	Release Period
☐ 1105	Demo Manufacturing Plant	000				
☐ 1105	Demo Manufacturing Plant	001	10	1	2	3

Figure 3.40 Scheduling Margin Key

3.11 Reduction Strategy

It's only logical and practical to maintain buffers during the production processes to account for any unforeseen or other business contingencies. However, when needed, reducing or eliminating several of these buffers can be helpful, especially when the system is unable to schedule a feasible and practical production plan.

To cancel buffers, use a reduction strategy, which consists of reduction types and reduction levels. In a reduction type, define whether the reduction is applicable to all operations of the production order or only to the critical part. In a reduction level, define the levels (up to six) to which the floats can be reduced. Define the percentage reduction at each level. For this example, set the **Reduction Level** to level **2**, and then define the percentage reduction in floats as 50% and 100%, respectively. Although different reduction levels can be set up, the system always tries to make it without a reduction in the first place. If unable to do so, and if the system is able to meet the scheduling needs during the first reduction in floats by 50%, no further reduction will take place; otherwise, it will move to the next reduction level.

> **[!]**
>
> **Warning**
>
> We suggest avoiding using all six reduction levels for system performance reasons. The system first schedules the planned order with standard scheduling, but with each reduction level, the required system's resources to achieve the reduction increase greatly.

The reduction levels only reflect the reduction of the operations by shortening the queue, wait, and move times, as well as through splitting and overlapping.

If the reduction strategy isn't maintained in the routing, then the system uses order type-dependent parameters at the plant level to perform reduction. A *reduction strategy* refers to the percentages by which the system reduces the interoperation times, such as transport time, and performs further reduction with overlapping and splitting.

To set the reduction strategies, follow the configuration menu path **SAP IMG • Production • Shop Floor Control • Operations • Define Reduction Strategies**, or use Transaction OPJS. In the screen shown in Figure 3.41, notice that there are three control elements— **Transport** (move time), **Overlap**, and **Split**—that can be used for reduction by the defined percentages given in the **Red. Queue** column. Be sure to select the relevant checkboxes for which the system should perform the reductions.

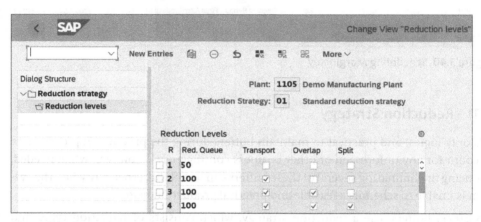

Figure 3.41 Reduction Levels

3.12   Confirmation

So far, all of the configuration work undertaken is merely at the various planning stages. From the initial material forecast to running MRP to generation of planned orders, conversions to production orders are all planning activities with no financial implications. For example, the production order creation signals to the production department to start production of the material. The production order quantity denotes the target or the planned quantity for production. The release of a production order enables the system to activate certain business functions, such as printing shop floor papers, allowing issuance of components, or enabling confirmation of operations. When the production department has actually produced some or all of the target/ planned quantity, it proceeds to confirm this produced quantity in the SAP system.

It's imperative that the user performs the confirmation as soon as the actual production data is available and ready for entry in the system. The data entry confirmation can also be an automatic process initiated via a barcode using a conveyor belt. Alternatively, the business normally agrees on the frequency at which it will perform confirmation—for example, once at the end of every eight-hour shift or once in 24 hours. The confirmation process also enables several other business processes, such as automatic GI (backflush), automatic GR, capacity reduction of the relevant work center, and updating costs.

The following sections will discuss the various options and controls available for confirmation of an order.

3.12.1 Process Overview

When performing the confirmation step against a production order, whether it's for an entire order or a milestone confirmation, the system makes actual data updates of the following objects:

- Yield
- Scrap
- Rework

Depending on the settings already made, when confirming an order, the system updates the following data in the production order:

- Quantities (yield, scrap, rework), activities, dates, and order status
- Backflush of the components
- Automatic GR
- Capacity reduction of the relevant work centers
- Costs based on actual data entered during confirmation
- Excess/shortage quantities for MRP-relevant materials

On the configuration side of confirmation, several checks and controls can be incorporated during the confirmation, including but not limited to the following:

- Time when the system should backflush components
- Check operations sequence
- Check underdelivery and overdelivery quantity tolerances
- Check if QM in-process results (during production) are entered for an operation
- GR control for coproducts
- Actual cost of error handling during confirmation
- Quantity (goods movements) of error handling during confirmation

It's also possible to control the screen layout of the confirmation to suit any unique business needs. Controls even can be placed on the fields for which data entry is required, optional, or hidden. See Section 3.12.3 for how to manage this.

Now let's discuss the specifics of confirmation.

3.12.2   Parameters for Order Confirmation

To set up parameters for order confirmation, follow the configuration menu path **SAP IMG · Production · Shop Floor Control · Operations · Confirmation · Define Confirmation Parameters**.

For **Plant 1105** and **Order Type PP10** (Figure 3.42), the **Process Control** field controls when the system should perform some or all of the following steps:

- Goods movements, such as backflush
- Automatic GR
- Actual costs calculation

If the **Process Control** field is left blank, then the system performs all activities online and immediately. Refer to Section 3.12.4 for how to control the settings as online, immediate, or in the background.

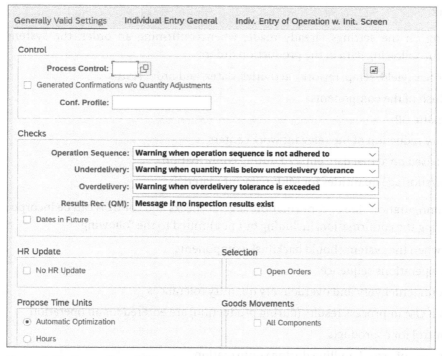

Figure 3.42 Generally Valid Settings Tab of Confirmation Parameters

The **Checks** area controls whether the system should ensure that the user adheres to the **Operation Sequence**, with varying degrees of controls, from no check to warning to error. Similarly, if the minimum and maximum tolerance limits in the **Underdelivery** and **Overdelivery** fields are maintained in the **Work Scheduling** view of the material master, the system copies this information during production order creation. When performing confirmation of the order and entering the yield, the system checks to see if it's within the tolerance limits and acts according to the level of control set. If there is an error message, the system won't allow proceeding further or saving the confirmation until the error is corrected. The system considers the sum of yield and rework quantities for underdelivery/overdelivery calculation.

Note

During the SAP implementation project, discuss and agree with the client on the level of control required and then make the necessary settings. In general, the control should neither be too loose nor too stringent to meet the day-to-day working needs of business process owners. The level of control also depends on the stability of production processes and business maturity to reflect that optimum production should be within the defined tolerance limits. If there are large variations and deviations in yield, then a less stringent control will suffice.

Tips and Tricks

If the underdelivery or overdelivery control is set as an error setting, the system won't allow the production supervisor to exceed the defined tolerance limits. To attend to this, make changes in the **Goods Receipt** tab of the production order and perform the confirmation process again. This enables the user to deviate from a one-time or limited deviation to the standard tolerance limits.

In the **Results Rec. (QM)** field and for in-process (during production) inspection, the system creates a quality inspection lot for one or more operations. This is an integration point between PP and QM processes. It's possible to control whether the system should check to see if the inspection results of an operation for the inspection lot are already entered before it allows performing the confirmation of the next operation.

In the **Goods Movements** area of the screen, set the necessary controls for whether the system should perform goods movement for all of the components by selecting the checkbox.

Click the **Individual Entry General** tab, and the screen shown in Figure 3.43 appears. Here, select the **Confirmation Type** that the system makes available during the confirmation process. It can be a **Partial confirmation**, **Final confirmation**, or **Automatic final confirmation**.

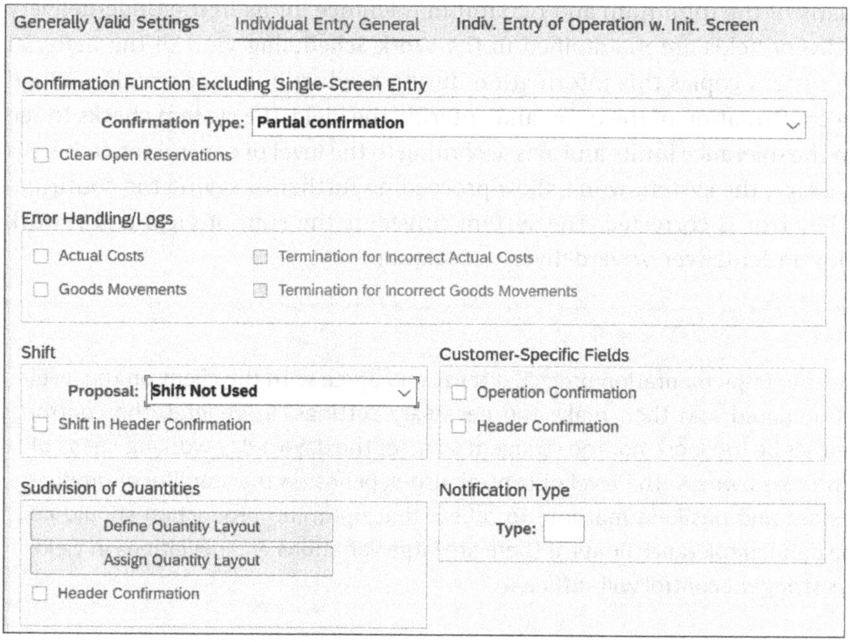

Figure 3.43 Individual Entry General Tab of Confirmation Parameters

The settings depend on how frequently the business performs the confirmation process. If there are large and frequent numbers of confirmations against a production order, then it makes sense to set **Partial Confirmation** as the default. When performing the final confirmation against the production order, manually set the **Confirmation Type** as **Final Confirmation**. For **Automatic Final Confirmation**, the system checks whether the confirmed quantity is equal to or less than the production order quantity. If it's less, then it automatically sets the status as **Partial Confirmation**, whereas if the confirmation quantity is equal to or exceeds the production order quantity, then it automatically sets the status as **Final Confirmation**.

For **Actual Costs** and **Goods Movements** in the **Error Handling/Logs** area, set whether the system should terminate the confirmation processing until the error is corrected.

Click the **Indiv. Entry of Operation w. Init. Screen** tab, and the screen shown in Figure 3.44 appears. The system offers a large number of checkboxes to facilitate data entry work. For example, if the **Propose** checkbox in the **Quantities** area is selected, the system proposes the quantity that a production supervisor needs to confirm for an operation or an order. Select the **Display** checkboxes to display any information for reference purposes.

We suggest selecting the **Actual Data** radio button in the **Screen Control Time Ticket** area so that the system automatically proposes the data (quantity and activities) that need to be confirmed. Otherwise, on the actual confirmation screen, manually click the **Actual Data** icon to view the data that needs to be confirmed.

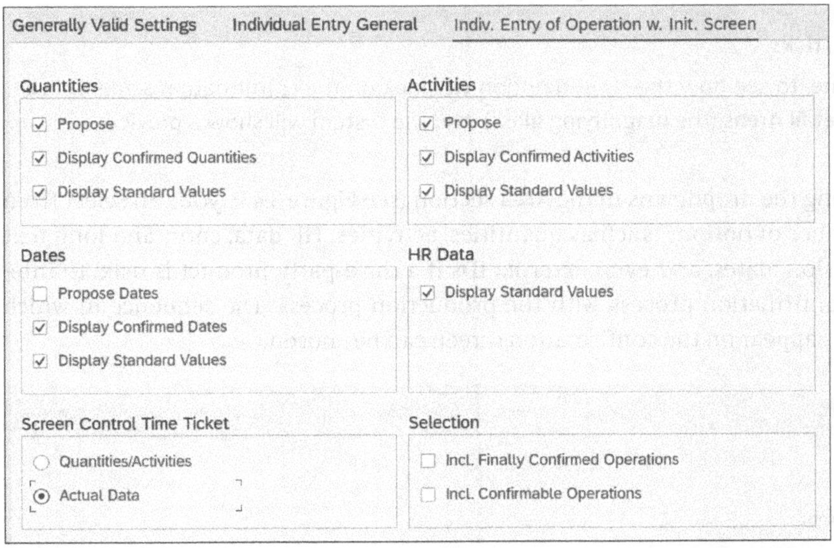

Generally Valid Settings	Individual Entry General	Indiv. Entry of Operation w. Init. Screen

Quantities
- ☑ Propose
- ☑ Display Confirmed Quantities
- ☑ Display Standard Values

Activities
- ☑ Propose
- ☑ Display Confirmed Activities
- ☑ Display Standard Values

Dates
- ☐ Propose Dates
- ☑ Display Confirmed Dates
- ☑ Display Standard Values

HR Data
- ☑ Display Standard Values

Screen Control Time Ticket
- ○ Quantities/Activities
- ◉ Actual Data

Selection
- ☐ Incl. Finally Confirmed Operations
- ☐ Incl. Confirmable Operations

Figure 3.44 Indiv. Entry of Operation w. Init. Screen Tab of Confirmation Parameters

3.12.3 Single Entry Screen for Confirmation

It's also possible to control how the system displays the information on the confirmation screen (Transaction CO11N for discrete manufacturing or Transaction COR6N for process industries). In this step, set up a profile and assign that profile to an individual user in the CORUPROF user parameter.

A profile for a single-entry screen controls the user-defined layout for confirmation. In the layout, define the fields and the sequence in which they appear on the confirmation screen. For example, if the production supervisor likes to have a provision to enter long text in the confirmation screen to enable the process operator to write extensive shift details, select the relevant option. Similarly, a control can be set for whether the system should list the activities to be confirmed as individual fields or in a tabular form.

To define a single-entry screen for confirmation, follow the configuration menu path **SAP IMG · Production · Shop Floor Control · Operations · Confirmation · Single Screen Entry · Define Single Screen Entry**, or use Transaction OPKO. In Figure 3.45, define the header area so that during the actual confirmation, the system brings up the relevant fields to enter the details. For example, choose whether the system should only allow entering the confirmation number at the header level or should allow entering the production order number together with its operation.

[+] **Tips and Tricks**

At any time, to see how the chosen option will look on the confirmation screen, click **Display Detail Areas** (the magnifying glass), and the system will show a preview.

When clicking the dropdowns in the **Area** section (see Figure 3.45), you can select from a large number of options, such as quantities, activities, HR data, short and long text entry provision, dates, and even external IDs if a third-party product is used to integrate the confirmation process with the production process. The sequence in which these details appear on the confirmation screen can be chosen.

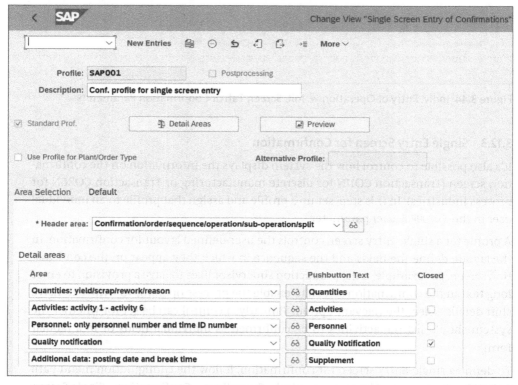

Figure 3.45 Single-Entry Screen of Confirmation

In the **Pushbutton Text** fields, define the text of the pushbuttons to suit your business needs. The **Closed** checkbox enables having a minimized (closed) view of the information on the confirmation screen, which can be opened when the production supervisor is ready for data entry.

[+]

Tips and Tricks

To check that settings are correct, with no duplication or other layout error, use the **Detail Areas** button for a consistency check. Also, use the **Preview** button to simulate the confirmation screen.

[«]

Note

Activate the CONFPP07 enhancement if there's a need for more than one reason for variances. As a practical workaround (without activating the enhancement), in the screen shown in Figure 3.45 under **Detail Areas**, incorporate **Additional data: Reason** as many times as needed from the dropdown list.

3.12.4 Time of Confirmation

If there is a large number of confirmations that the production supervisor needs to perform on a daily basis, then it's practical to perform confirmations in the background, such as quantity update or backflush, when there is less of a workload on the system. However, if an immediate update of all quantity and activities data posted is required, then set the necessary settings. These are the same settings used for the **Process Control** field at the beginning of Section 3.12.2. To set up the time of confirmation, follow the configuration menu path **SAP IMG · Production · Shop Floor Control · Operations · Confirmation · Single Screen Entry · Define Time for Confirmation Processes**, or use Transaction OPKC. In Figure 3.46, choose when the system should update the following:

- **Auto GR** (automatic GR)
- **Backflush**
- **Actual Costs**

Figure 3.46 Process Control for Confirmation

The available update options are listed here:

- **Immediately Online**
- **Later in Background Job**
- **Immediately in Update Program**

We'll cover how to set up background jobs in Section 3.16.

3.13   Reason for Variances

During confirmation against the production order, when the yield, scrap, and rework is recorded, a reason for variance between the planned and actual production can be assigned. For example, assume that due to machine malfunction or defective components, the actual production was less than planned. In that case, assign the specific reason for this deviation or variance. Similarly, when entering the scrap quantity, give the reason for variance. Later, when executing the production order information system (Transaction COOIS) or even using embedded SAP Fiori analytics, filter out the information based on the reason for variance. This helps clarify the reasons behind the problems and helps the production supervisor take corrective or preventive actions.

As a PP consultant during an SAP implementation project, maintain a complete list of plant-related reasons for variances and configure them accordingly in the system. Perform multiple partial confirmations and enter different reasons for variance for each deviation.

> **Note**
>
> If there's a business need to enter multiple reasons for variances, engage an ABAP resource and activate the CONFPP07 enhancement.

A user status can also be assigned to a reason for variance to add further control in the confirmation.

> **Note**
>
> To set up a new status profile, use Transaction BS02.

To configure a new reason for the variance for a given plant, follow the configuration menu path **SAP IMG • Production • Shop Floor Control • Operations • Confirmation • Define Reasons for Variances**, or use Transaction OPK5. Figure 3.47 lists the reason for variance for **Plant 1105**. On selecting a specific reason for variance and clicking the **User Status** folder, the system prompts you to enter the status profile and then the user status.

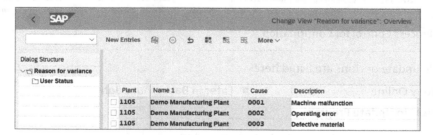

Figure 3.47 Reasons for Variance

3.14 Trigger Points

Trigger points are automatic functions that the system can perform when it's able to meet a user-defined condition. For example, when a user releases an operation, the system can automatically release all preceding operations via a trigger point. Minimal configuration steps are involved in trigger points: Simply define the trigger point usage and then define a group for the trigger points.

The **Trigger Point Usage** field provides a unique identification to list trigger points that will have a common usage. This enables a production supervisor to quickly select the relevant trigger point based on its usage. To define the (standard) trigger points usage, follow menu path **SAP IMG • Production • Shop Floor Control • Master Data • Trigger Point • Define (Standard) Trigger Point Usage**. On the initial screen, enter an alphanumeric key, and give a short description of the trigger point usage.

All of the trigger points can be grouped together and can then be assigned to an operation. Doing so saves the time and effort involved in individually creating and assigning trigger points.

To define a group for standard trigger points, follow menu path **SAP IMG • Production • Shop Floor Control • Master Data • Trigger Point • Define Group for Standard Trigger Points**. On the initial screen, enter an alphanumeric key and give a short description of the trigger points group.

3.15 Define Print Control

During the production process, there's often a business need to print several shop floor papers—for example, production order, pick list, or GI slip. The SAP system offers standard layouts for each shop floor paper. During an SAP system project implementation, engage an ABAP resource to develop new scripts or modify the scripts of the shop floor papers to fulfill a client's requirements. It's recommended to discuss and evaluate all of the shop floor papers needed as printouts with the client. For example, eliminate the layout development of a confirmation and its printout requirement if there's an SAP system terminal from which to make live data entries, or use an upload program to automatically enter confirmation. Further, if Adobe Document Services is installed, then it's also possible to create PDF printouts of the shop floor papers.

To make the necessary settings to print shop floor papers, follow the configuration menu path **SAP IMG • Production • Shop Floor Control • Operations • Define Print Controls**, or use Transaction OPK8. The resulting screen, shown in Figure 3.48, lists the shop floor papers that you can individually work on and for which you can make the desired settings.

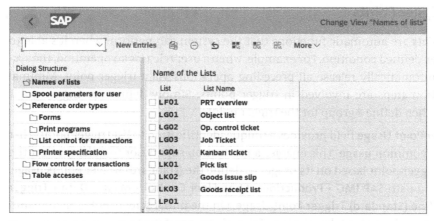

Figure 3.48 Printing Shop Floor Papers

Note

Chapter 6 shows how we used list **LG01** (**Object list**), shown on the right-hand side of Figure 3.48, to get printouts with the SAP system standard layout.

3.16   Background Jobs

To optimize the SAP system's resources, which will help to improve performance and minimize undue burdens, there are several processes that can be set up as background jobs. A *background job* enables defining the frequency with which the system automatically performs the desired function without manual intervention. For example, if MRP is run on a weekly basis and planners are generally satisfied with the results, then set up a background job to automatically convert planned orders into production orders.

To set up a background job, follow the configuration menu path **SAP IMG · Production · Shop Floor Control · Operations · Schedule Background Jobs**, or use Transaction SM36.

We suggest clicking the **Job Wizard** icon and using the wizard because it provides a step-by-step approach for setting up a background job. Table 3.1 lists the program names of selected background jobs that can be set up, and the system asks for this information. Before setting up the background job, also set up the variant of the background job so that the system processes only the relevant data.

Function	Program Name
Convert planned orders into production orders	PPBICO40
Print production orders	PPPRBTCH

Table 3.1 Background Jobs

Function	Program Name
Print shop floor papers	PPPRBSEL
Mass processing	COWORKDISPATCHNEW
Confirmation: Componentized processes (GR, GI, HR, actual)	CORUPROC
Confirmation: Fast entry records	CORUPROC1

Table 3.1 Background Jobs (Cont.)

Tips and Tricks

On the initial screen of Transaction SE38, enter the program name listed in Table 3.1 and choose **Execute**. The system navigates to the screen to set screen parameters and save them by pressing ⌈Ctrl⌋+⌈S⌋ or by choosing **Goto • Variants • Save as Variant**.

Read additional documentation on the background program by clicking the **Information** icon, where available.

3.17   Summary

The logical and sequential configuration steps that we undertook in this chapter will enable a production planner and production supervisor to perform the same set of steps and activities in configuration steps in process manufacturing. If all of the steps covered in the chapter are followed in a sequential and logical order, then all of the major business processes and scenarios of production with production orders (shop floor control) are covered. See Chapter 6 for more details that will align with the business processes.

The next chapter covers process manufacturing configuration.

Chapter 4
Process Manufacturing Configuration

Configuration basics in process manufacturing are generally the same as in discrete manufacturing. However, the process management functionality demands in-depth coverage because it's unique to process manufacturing only.

The configuration basics of process manufacturing are similar to those in discrete manufacturing. For example, the steps to define order types, assign number ranges, and define the screen layout for confirmation are the same in both production types. We recommend reading Chapter 3 and Chapter 6 for an in-depth understanding of the configuration settings and business processes, respectively.

The focus of this chapter is primarily on the configuration that is unique only to process manufacturing—for example, the master recipe profile that is only used in process manufacturing. At the same time, this chapter gives extensive coverage to the configuration area of process management.

We'll start by covering the standard settings and tools that can be used to optimize most of the configuration work related to process management. We then cover process messages and process message categories, followed by control recipes and PI sheets. Next, we'll discuss the process instructions, types, and categories, as well as how the system can facilitate several configuration steps using wizards. Using the scope of generation functionality further reduces the data maintenance efforts involved in process management. We'll also cover background jobs for sending control recipes and how to send process messages back to the SAP S/4HANA system as scheduled (background) jobs.

The concepts and the basics covered in this chapter learn will enable the implementation of a newer and more user-friendly functionality of process management known as Execution Steps (XSteps). It's also possible transition from process management to XSteps and still use all the configuration steps that are discussed in this chapter.

We'll also show how the entire configuration undertaken so far facilitates the quick definition, simulation, and activation of process manufacturing cockpits. We present a simple example of how to use a self-defined process instruction type and incorporate its details in the PI sheet. When the system sends process messages back to its predefined destination, it also sends the details of the self-defined process instruction characteristic.

Note

Refer to Chapter 1 for features comparison among discrete manufacturing, process manufacturing, and repetitive manufacturing (REM), as well as how to decide which manufacturing type is most relevant for a given industry.

Let's get started.

4.1   Master Data in Process Industries

The master data in process manufacturing is similar to the master data of discrete manufacturing. For detailed configuration settings and business processes, refer to Chapter 3 and Chapter 6, respectively.

The following master data are specific to process industries and will be the main topics covered in this section:

- Resource
- Materials list (bill of materials [BOM])
- Master recipe
- Production version

The *resource* in process manufacturing is similar to the work center in discrete manufacturing, and the creation of the *materials list* in process manufacturing is similar to the BOM in discrete manufacturing, so we won't cover these master data items here (see Chapter 3 and Chapter 6). For process industries, it's mandatory to have a master recipe and production version in the system. While the configuration of the master recipe has some uniqueness and is covered in this chapter, the creation of the production version is once again the same for discrete manufacturing and therefore isn't covered here.

4.1.1   Master Recipe Profile

Although most of the details in the master recipe profile are the same as in routing, the one exception is the option available for process management. Depending on the master recipe profile used during master recipe creation, the system offers the following options for process management:

- **Process Instructions**
- **XSTEPS**
- **XSTEPS OPTIONAL**

If the **XSTEPS OPTIONAL** option is chosen during the master recipe creation, the system provides the option to either select **Process Instructions** or **XSTEPS**. Both of them cannot be used at the same time. In addition, if process instructions were previously used in the master recipe and now the company wants to transition to XSteps, the system issues a warning message that it won't be possible to revert back to process instructions after saving the master recipe with XSteps activated.

To set up the master recipe profile, follow menu path **SAP IMG · Production Planning for Process Industries · Master Data · Master Recipe · Define Profile with Default Values**, or use Transaction OPN1. Choose **Profile/Recipe** on the initial screen, which brings up the overview of the master recipe profile with three entries.

Select **Profile PI01_XS**, and choose the **Details** icon, which leads to Figure 4.1. Here, the available fields can be updated, which then apply when a master recipe is created. Assigning a profile is a mandatory requirement when creating a master recipe. Notice the **Process Instruction Maintenance** dropdown in the **Process Management** area and the available options, including **XSTEPS OPTIONAL**.

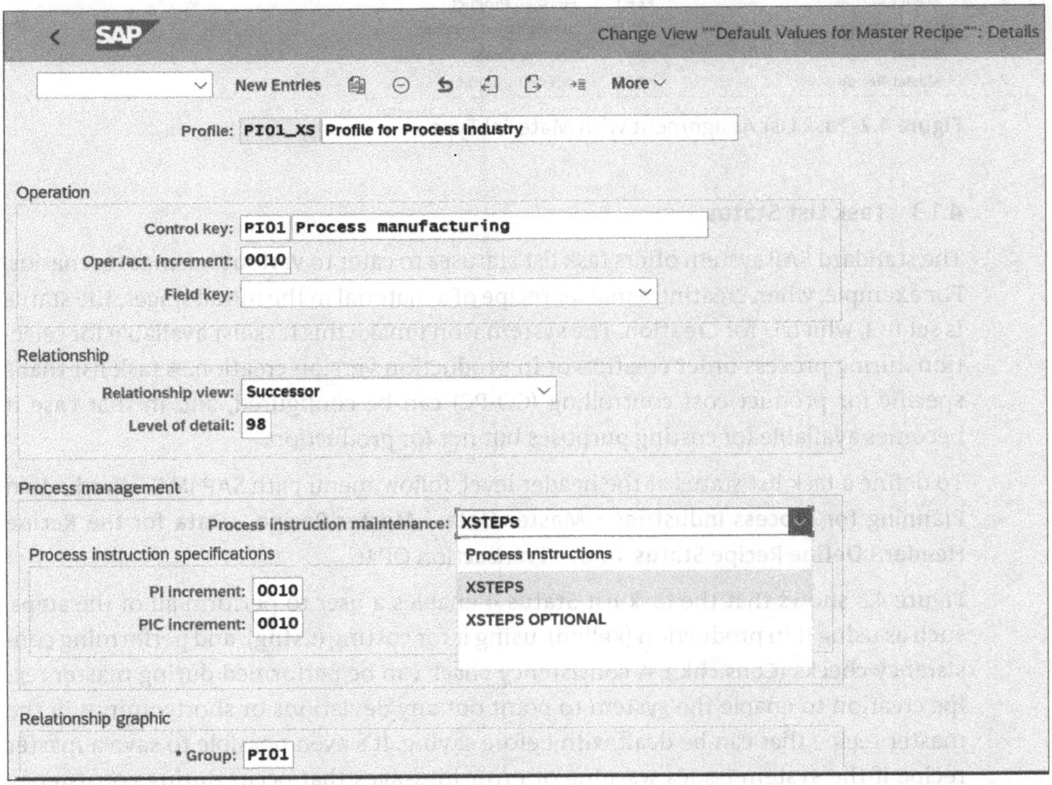

Figure 4.1 Master Recipe Profile

4.1.2   Task List Assignment to Material Types

Task list type 2 is used for a master recipe. When a process order is created, the system looks for the relevant master recipe and for task list type 2 to assign it to the process order. A *task list* consists of operations, phases, activities, control keys, and the relationship to the BOM. If a company has material types other than those available in a standard SAP system, then maintain the task list relationship for each material type.

To define the task list assignment to the material type, follow menu path **SAP IMG • Production Planning for Process Industries • Master Data • Master Recipe • Assign Material Types**. On the screen shown in Figure 4.2, choose **New Entries** to define the task list type (**TLType**) as **2** and the company-specific material types used in process manufacturing.

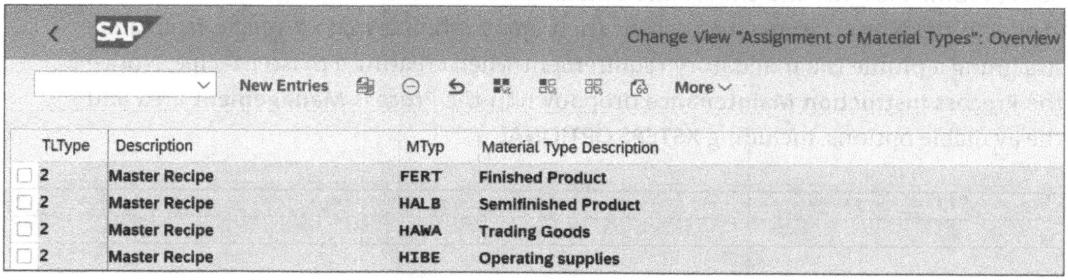

TLType	Description	MTyp	Material Type Description
2	Master Recipe	FERT	Finished Product
2	Master Recipe	HALB	Semifinished Product
2	Master Recipe	HAWA	Trading Goods
2	Master Recipe	HIBE	Operating supplies

Figure 4.2 Task List Assignment with Material Type

4.1.3   Task List Status

The standard SAP system offers task list statuses to cater to various business scenarios. For example, when creating a master recipe of a material in the initial stages, the status is set to 1, which is for **Creation**. The system won't make this task list available for selection during process order creation or in production version creation. A task list that's specific for product cost controlling (CO-PC) can be configured, and in that case it becomes available for costing purposes but not for production.

To define a task list status at the header level, follow menu path **SAP IMG • Production Planning for Process Industries • Master Data • Master Recipe • Data for the Recipe Header • Define Recipe Status**, or use Transaction OP46.

Figure 4.3 shows that the task list **Status 4** enables a user to perform all of the steps, such as using it in production (**RelInd**), using it for costing (**Cstng**), and performing consistency checks (**Cons.chk.**). A consistency check can be performed during master recipe creation to enable the system to point out any deviations or shortcomings in the master recipe that can be dealt with before saving. It's even possible to save a master recipe if the system issues warning or error messages that occur during consistency checks and then correct the errors later on.

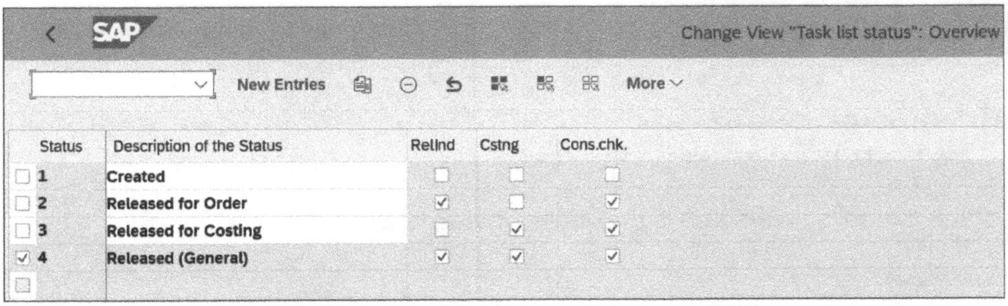

Figure 4.3 Task List Status

4.2   Order Type-Dependent Parameters

For better control of various order types configured in the SAP system, different order types are created within a plant. For example, there may be one order type for finished goods, another for semifinished goods, and a third one to capture rework details from normal production. Each order type can have a separate number range and its own order type settings. Further, authorizations to users can be controlled based on the order type and plant combination. In order type-dependent parameters, make settings that are applicable each time a user creates a process order for that specific order type and plant combination.

To set up order type-dependent parameters, follow menu path **SAP IMG • Production Planning for Process Industries • Process Order • Master Data • Order • Define Order Type-Dependent Parameters**, or use Transaction COR4. On the initial screen, select **Plant 1105** and **Order Type PI01**, which leads to the **Master Data** tab. We'll discuss each of the tabs for configuring parameters in the following sections.

4.2.1   Master Data

Figure 4.4 shows the **Master Data** tab of order type-dependent parameters. Here, select **Automatic Selection of Production Version** from the **Production Version** dropdown, and the system assigns the first available and valid production version during planning and production execution steps. Alternatively, use the **Manual Selection of Production Version** option, and the system opens a popup during process order creation to enable the user to select a production version manually.

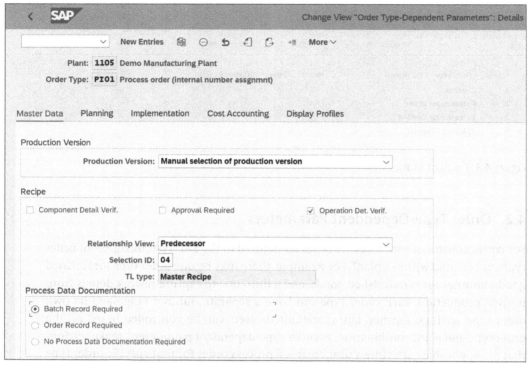

Figure 4.4 Order Type-Dependent Parameters: Master Data Tab

If the **Approval Required** checkbox is selected, then the process order must first be approved before it can be released. When a user creates a process order, the system requires the order to be approved before allowing the user to release it. Similarly, if the automatic process order release during creation (in the production scheduling profile) is set up, the system overrules the automatic release settings if the approval process is set up (Section 4.3).

> **[»]**
>
> **Note**
>
> To grant approval to a process order during its creation, follow menu path **Process Order • Functions • Approval • Individual Approval**.

4.2.2   Planning

In the **Planning** tab, select the **Scrap** checkbox if a business process has a need for it (Figure 4.5). Normally, in process industries, the scrap option or its recording finds less use.

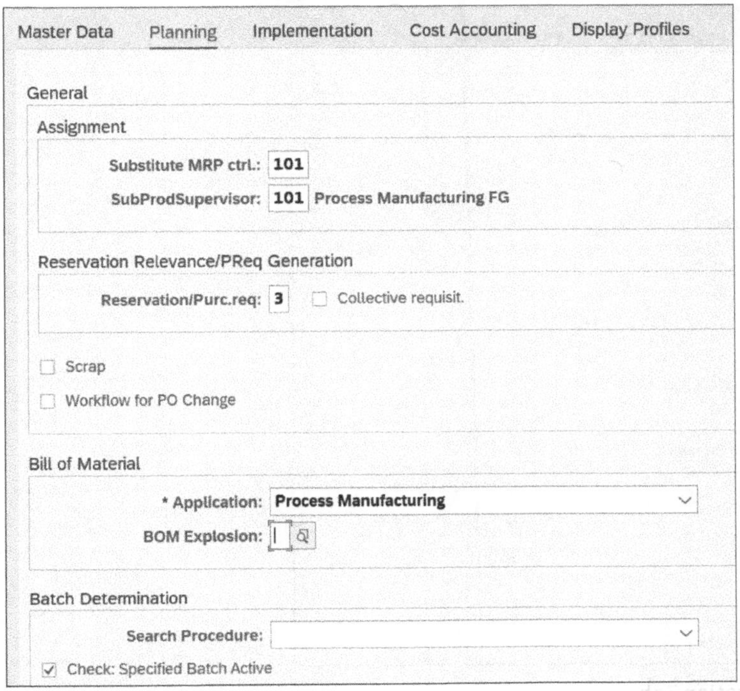

| Master Data | Planning | Implementation | Cost Accounting | Display Profiles |

General

Assignment

Substitute MRP ctrl.: `101`

SubProdSupervisor: `101` Process Manufacturing FG

Reservation Relevance/PReq Generation

Reservation/Purc.req: `3` ☐ Collective requisit.

☐ Scrap

☐ Workflow for PO Change

Bill of Material

* Application: `Process Manufacturing` ∨

BOM Explosion: `|` 🔍

Batch Determination

Search Procedure: ∨

☑ Check: Specified Batch Active

Figure 4.5 Planning Tab

For example, in the fertilizer industry, any visible or overflow material (spilled-over material) is automatically sent back in the production process chain, so there is no scrap recording during production. However, in the steel rerolling industry, it's common to have production scrap, so the **Scrap** option needs to be activated in such business scenarios. For a PP-QM integration scenario, assign the relevant inspection type for in-process inspection in the **Planning** tab and make settings for batch determination. Chapter 10 covers batch management.

4.2.3 Implementation

In the **Implementation** tab, make sure to select all the relevant checkboxes, especially for the **Shop Floor Information System** and **Documentation of Goods Movement** areas (Figure 4.6). Selecting these checkboxes will enable the system to update the logistics information system (LIS) and the user will be able to see the documented goods movements (goods issue [GI] or goods receipt [GR]) for the process orders. The documented goods movements in the process order information system (Transaction COOISPI) also will show all the relevant details.

Figure 4.6 Implementation Tab

4.2.4   Cost Accounting

In the **Cost Accounting** tab, we suggest coordinating with a controlling resource (responsible for cost object controlling) to ensure that the necessary configuration settings are in place.

4.3   Production Scheduling Profile

The production scheduling profile in process manufacturing is similar to that in discrete manufacturing. However, in process manufacturing, it provides an option to automatically generate the control recipe when a process order is released. A control recipe enables the process operator to record important plant parameters. We cover the details of control recipes in Section 4.4.1.

To set up the production scheduling profile, follow menu path **SAP IMG · Production Planning for Process Industries · Process Order · Master Data · Define Production Scheduling Profile**, or use Transaction CORY (see Figure 4.7).

On the initial screen, select **Plant 1105** and **PS Profile** (production scheduling profile) **PI01**. In this example, the **Generate Cntrl Recipe** checkbox in the **On Release** area (within the **Automatic Actions** area) isn't selected. In Chapter 7, we'll show how to manually generate a control recipe when a process order is released.

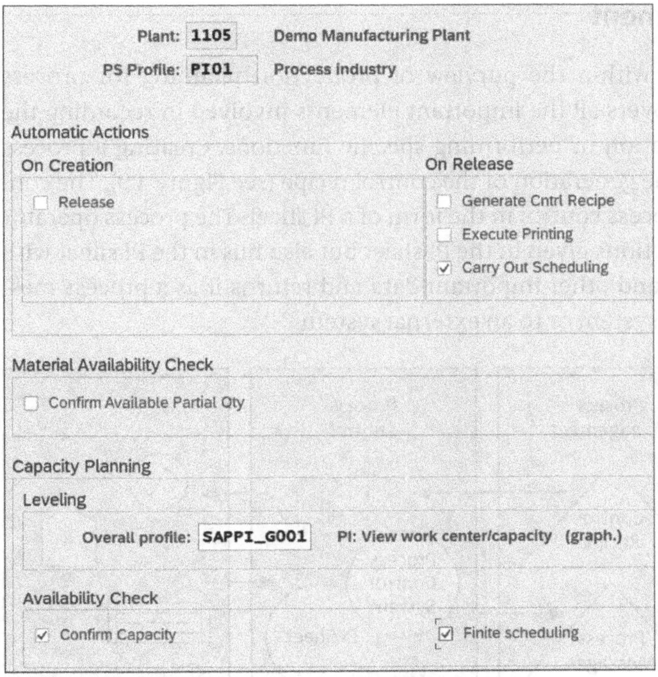

Figure 4.7 Production Scheduling Profile

Using Transaction MM02 to change the material master, assign the production scheduling profile in the **Work scheduling** tab (see Figure 4.8). Whenever a process order of this material and plant combination is created, the system automatically triggers the settings made in the production scheduling profile.

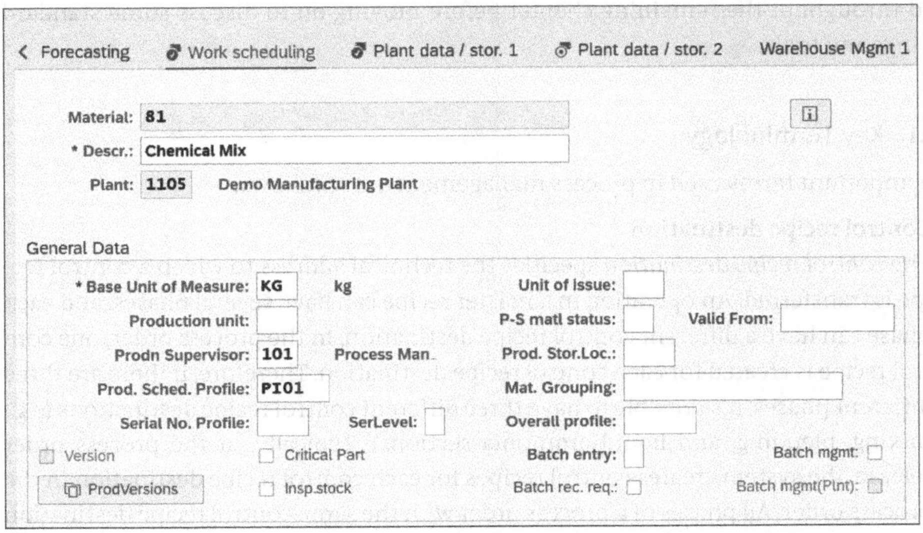

Figure 4.8 Production Scheduling Profile in Material Master

4.4   Process Management

Process management falls within the purview of production planning for process industries (PP-PI), which covers all the important elements involved in recording the process parameter information or performing specific functions. Creating a process order forms the basis for the generation of the control recipe (see Figure 4.9). The control recipe is sent to the process control in the form of a PI sheet. The process operator not only follows the instructions given in the PI sheet but also fills in the PI sheet with relevant plant parameters and other important data and returns it as a process message back to either the SAP system or to an external system.

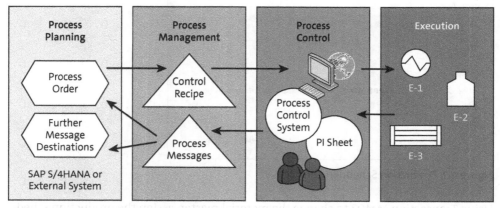

Figure 4.9 Process Management Overview

Although this section applies more to the business process side of process management, it's important to have a basic understanding of the concepts and terminologies used throughout the remaining chapter before moving on to discuss some standard settings and tools.

4.4.1   Key Terminology

The important terms used in process management are as follows:

- **Control recipe destination**

    The *control recipe destination* specifies the technical address to which a control recipe is transferred. An operation in a master recipe can have several phases, and each phase can have a different control recipe destination. In the process order, one control recipe is created for each control recipe destination. Therefore, if there are three different phases, it's possible to have three different control recipe destinations (e.g., mixing, blending, and liquid ammonia sections). Typically, at the process order release, the system creates control recipes for each control recipe destination in the process order. All phases of a process order with the same control recipe destination are combined into the same control recipe. A control recipe destination defines whether the process instruction of a phase is transferred to an external system (process control system [PCS]) or is converted to a PI sheet for a line operator. It also specifies which system or line operator executes the process instructions of a phase.

- **Process instruction characteristic**
  A released characteristic within a characteristic group is available for use in process instruction. Process instruction characteristics are allocated to process instructions either directly in the master recipe or by process instruction category. Process instruction, together with the corresponding characteristic value, determines the information transferred or requested—that is, the status of the control recipe. It also determines how the requested data is processed (e.g., the message category to be used to report the data).

- **Process instruction category**
  The process instruction category specifies the type of process instruction (i.e., process parameter or process data request). It also specifies the characteristics of this process instruction—that is, information to be sent via this instruction.

- **Process message characteristic**
  A released characteristic within the characteristic group is available for use in process messages. Process message characteristics are allocated to process message categories. Process message characteristics, together with the corresponding characteristic values, determine the content of the process message. The process message can be sent to an external system, SAP Office mail recipients, or custom-defined ABAP tables.

- **Process message category**
  The process message category specifies the characteristics to be allocated to a process message—that is, the information to be sent. It also specifies the message destinations for the process message. Every process message sent via process management must be assigned to a process message category.

- **PI sheet**
  A PI sheet is used as an input and output form for plant parameters and is customizable according to individual production processes. This customized PI sheet is part of either the configuration activity or master data management. Due to its intuitive features, a PI sheet can be used for many functions, such as calling up a transaction while remaining in a PI sheet, displaying documents, recording shift highlights, posting GI/GR, undertaking confirmation of a phase, calculating results, and jumping to record results for quality inspections.

To create a custom process message or a custom process instruction, a user can leverage knowledge of and experience in creating characteristics in the classification system. The only difference between classification and process message/instruction creation is that the former doesn't offer the option to incorporate details specific to process management. In the example in the following section, we'll show how to use process instruction to fetch a field, **Process Order Start Date**, from the process order automatically and integrate it into the PI sheet.

Now let's discuss the important one-time settings to make in the SAP system to activate process management. This entails sequence steps, in which the standard settings delivered by the SAP system are copied to specific plants.

4.4.2   Standard Settings and Tools

The system offers a large number of standard process messages, process message categories, process instructions, and process instruction categories. These are all available in the SAP system's plant 0001. All of these standard settings from plant 0001 can be copied, except process instruction categories, which need to be copied manually. An easier way to do this is to copy the SAP system reference plant 0001 to the desired plants.

A few important steps need to be performed in the right sequence to ensure that minimal work and effort are involved in integrating process management in the business processes. Use menu path **SAP IMG • Production Planning for Process Industries • Process Management • Standard Settings**, as shown in Figure 4.10.

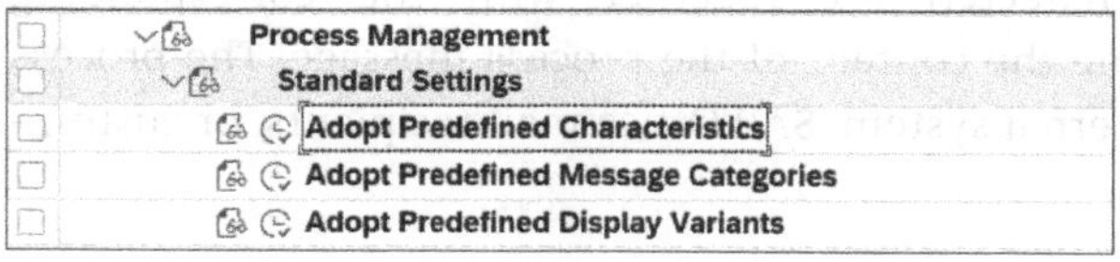

Figure 4.10 Standard Settings in Process Management

Next, follow these steps:

1. Use Transaction O23C to transport predefined characteristics from the SAP system reference client, which is 0001, to the SAP system client. The **Copy Object Lists** screen appears when the first step is successfully performed.

2. Access Transaction O22C to transport preconfigured process message categories from the SAP system reference plant 0001 to the desired plants. The screen shown in Figure 4.11 appears after entering the target plant.

3. Enter the target plant (in this example, "1105"). Use the **Copy** icon to copy it to the target plant. The system issues a warning message: **The SAP standard settings are copied to your target plant. Objects with identical names are overwritten.**

4. When the **Do You Want to Copy?** message appears, click **Yes**.

5. Access Transaction CO60_VM to transport the PI sheet's display variants from the SAP reference plant to the login client. Make sure to select all available display variants, and choose **Save** before exiting the screen.

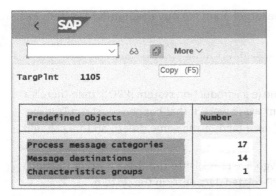

Figure 4.11 Predefined Objects of Process Messages

The SAP system also offers standard characteristics groups in process management, both for process instructions and for process messages. The system groups the process instruction characteristics in group PPPI_01; it groups the process message characteristics in group PPPI_02. When creating a self-defined process instruction or process message characteristic, ensure that you assign it to the relevant characteristics group to enable it to work correctly.

> [+]
>
> **Tips and Tricks**
>
> To ensure that you see the characteristics groups (PPPI_01 or PPPI_02) in the dropdown, click **Customize Local Layout** (or press (Alt)+(F12)) on the main screen, select **Options • Interaction Design • Visualization and Interaction**, and then choose **Show Keys within the Dropdown Lists**.

When implementing process management, ensure that you release the process instruction and process message groups to the requisite plants. To release a process messages group, use menu path **SAP IMG • Production Planning for Process Industries • Process Management • Process Messages • Define Characteristics Groups for Process Messages • Release for Process Messages**, or use Transaction OO8C.

To release a process instructions group, use menu path **SAP IMG • Production Planning for Process Industries • Process Management • Process Instructions • Define Characteristics Groups for Process Instructions • Release for Process Instructions**, or use Transaction OO9C.

If the process messages or process instruction groups aren't defined, available, or released for the desired plant, simply copy them with reference to another plant, where these are available and released.

To copy all settings from reference plant 0001 to the desired plant, use menu path **SAP IMG • Production Planning for Process Industries • Process Management • Tools • Copy Settings between Plants**, or use Transaction O2OC. In the ensuing screen, enter the reference plant, which is "0001", and the target plant to copy the standard system's settings ("1105" in this example).

[+]

> **Tips and Tricks**
>
> If using a new SAP client for the first time (e.g., production system [PRD]), then there's a possibility that the process management won't work. If that happens, just run Transaction O23C and then Transaction O22C once (and in the same order), and this should solve the problem.
>
> Alternatively, make it a part of the SAP go-live checklist to run these two transactions in the PRD system before starting any PP-related data entry in the system.

4.5   Process Messages

Process messages enable the process operator to send the requested data back to the SAP system, which then performs the necessary functions. For example, say a production supervisor wants the process operator to inform (through process messages) about the consumption (GI) of all of the materials used in the production process (against a process order). The process operator fills in the PI sheet, which contains the provision to record actual material consumption details, and marks the status of the PI sheet as **Complete**. The process operator then sends the process message containing the consumption details to the process message destination in the SAP system, after which the system will perform the actual GI posting against the process order in the system.

The system offers a large number of standard process messages and process message categories, but it's still possible to define your own process messages to attend to specific business needs. For example, there might be some specific information that the system should send back to the SAP system based on the process operator's input in the PI sheet.

In the following sections, we'll go through the details of how to create or define and set up a process message. The first step is to create a process message characteristic.

4.5.1   Create a Process Message Characteristic

The first step is to follow menu path **SAP IMG • Production Planning for Process Industries • Process Management • Process Messages • Define Characteristics for Process Messages • Create Characteristics for Process Messages**, or use Transaction O25C.

For this example, create process message characteristic **ZPI_Creation_Date**, and define the characteristics group (**Chars Group** field) as **Process Message Characteristic** in the **Basic Data** tab. Define the **Data Type** as **Date**. In Chapter 7, we'll show how to use this self-defined process message to send details back to the SAP system.

4.5.2   Process Message Destination

To create a new process message destination, use menu path **Production Planning for Process Industries • Process Management • Process Messages • Process Messages Destinations • Define and Set up Process Messages Destinations**, or use Transaction OO3C.

For this example, create a new **Destination PP20** process message for **Plant 1105**, and then choose **Target Fields/Message Destinations** on the left-hand side of the screen. The **Change View** screen shown in Figure 4.12 appears. Here the system allows you to enter the process message characteristic, "ZPI_CREATION_DATE", which was created in the previous step.

It's possible to set a self-defined process message destination so that the system can send the process messages to the defined destination. When the system receives information from process messages, it processes them in the SAP system using function modules. For external systems, the process messages with information are sent back to the SAP system using remote function call (RFC) connections. Select the **Individual** checkbox (not shown) if the system should process each process message individually. This option is generally used in complex process messages involving function module destinations.

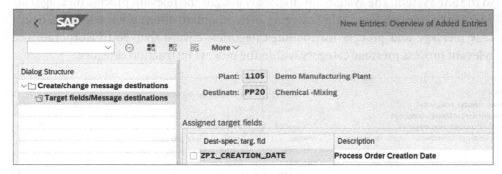

Figure 4.12 Target Field in Process Message Destination

Note

We suggest engaging an SAP NetWeaver resource to manage the configuration of RFC destinations.

4.5.3   Process Message Categories

In process management, the system first sends the control recipe to the control recipe destination as a manual or automatic (background) job. The plant operator receives the control recipe in the form of a PI sheet and fills in the requisite data. When the data entry is complete, the process operator sets the status of the PI sheet as **Complete**. This enables the system to communicate the data back into the SAP system in the form of *process messages*, instructions to proceed with performing the necessary functions, such as data entry or data updates.

The system embeds the process message category within the process instruction category. For example, the system embeds the PI_PROD process message category within the APROD_1 process instruction category. The APROD_1 process instruction category enables a process operator to record the production and also perform GR against the process order through the PI_PROD process message category. When a user creates a process order, generates a control recipe, sends it to the control recipe destination, maintains the PI sheet, and sets the status to **Complete**, the system processes the process messages by sending the completed data, such as quantity produced or GI, to the SAP system, which then process the data using function modules or Business Application Programming Interfaces (BAPIs).

There are several process message categories that cater to different business scenarios, such as the material consumption message, messages about the control recipe status, confirmation of a phase, or even new batch creation messages (provided that batch management is already active for the material).

Figure 4.13 shows the list of selected and standard process message categories available in the SAP system. The system automatically assigns the relevant process message category in the process instruction category in the standard offering. For self-defined process message and process instruction categories, ensure that you incorporate the relevant process message category within the process instruction category.

Dialog Structure	Plant: **1105** Demo Manufacturing Plant		
✓ **Process message categories**	Process message categories		
☐ Characteristics/Message categories			
✓ ☐ Destinations/Message categories	ProcMessage Cat	Description	SndA
☐ Characteristics/destination-specific target fields	○ DPREAD	Message for read data point	☐
	○ EHS_CE01	Secondary data - frontend appl. call	☐
	○ EHS_CS01	Secondary data - server call	☐
	○ EHS_DATA	Secondary data - data server result	☐
	○ EHS_ERR	Secondary data - error message	☐
	○ EHS_REQ	Secondary data - request to data server	☐
	○ EHS_RES	Secondary data - ext. system result	☐
	○ NREAD	Message with one numeric value	☐
	○ PI_BT_CL	Batch Characteristic Value Assignment	☐
	○ PI_BT_CR	Batch Creation	☐
	○ PI_COMM	Comment Message	☑
	● PI_CONS	Material Consumption Message	☑
	○ PI_CRST	Message on Control Recipe Status	☑
	○ PI_CRST2	Control recipe status via order	☐
	○ PI_HUCNS	GI posting for HUs	☑

Figure 4.13 Overview of Process Message Categories

The screen shown in Figure 4.14 appears when the **PI_CONS** process message category is selected and you double-click **Destinations/Message Categories.** On the right-hand side of the figure, the system assigns the destination (**Dest**) PI04 to which it will send the process messages. Further mapping the source and target characteristics to be sent to specific destinations is possible.

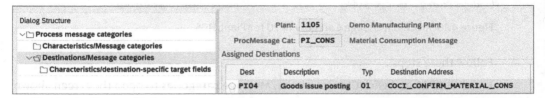

Figure 4.14 Process Message Categories

To view the list of standard process message destinations available in the SAP system, place the cursor on the **Dest** field and press F4.

The screen shown in Figure 4.15 appears when **PI_CONS** is selected in the **ProcMessage Cat** field and PI04 **Goods issue posting** is selected in the **Destination** field.

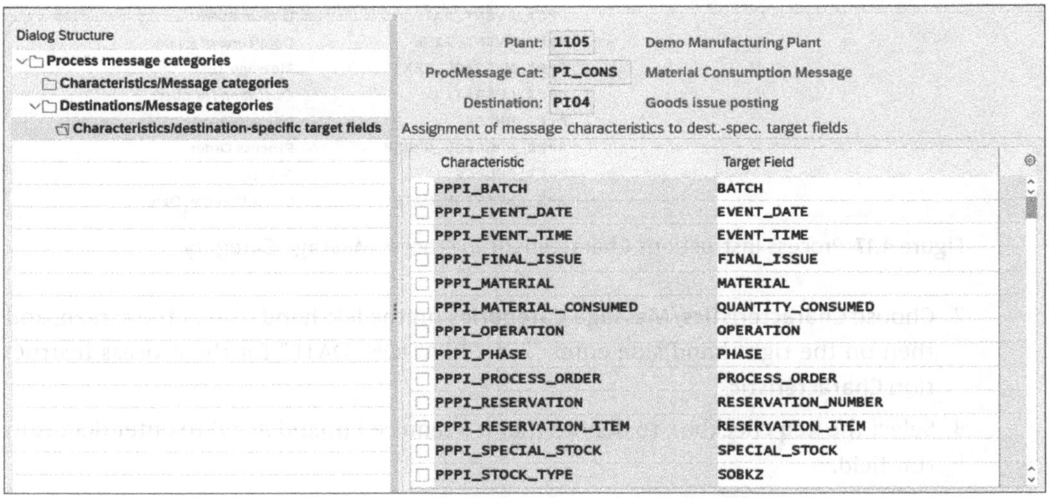

	Plant: 1105	Demo Manufacturing Plant
	ProcMessage Cat: PI_CONS	Material Consumption Message
	Destination: PI04	Goods issue posting

Assignment of message characteristics to dest.-spec. target fields

Characteristic	Target Field
PPPI_BATCH	BATCH
PPPI_EVENT_DATE	EVENT_DATE
PPPI_EVENT_TIME	EVENT_TIME
PPPI_FINAL_ISSUE	FINAL_ISSUE
PPPI_MATERIAL	MATERIAL
PPPI_MATERIAL_CONSUMED	QUANTITY_CONSUMED
PPPI_OPERATION	OPERATION
PPPI_PHASE	PHASE
PPPI_PROCESS_ORDER	PROCESS_ORDER
PPPI_RESERVATION	RESERVATION_NUMBER
PPPI_RESERVATION_ITEM	RESERVATION_ITEM
PPPI_SPECIAL_STOCK	SPECIAL_STOCK
PPPI_STOCK_TYPE	SOBKZ

Figure 4.15 Process Message Category PP_CONS and Destination PP04

On the right-hand side of the screen, the system maps each process instruction characteristic (source characteristic) with the process message characteristics (target characteristic/field). The **Characteristic** column lists all of the process instruction characteristics, whereas the **Target Field** column enables mapping of each process instruction characteristic to its respective process message characteristic.

Now let's walk through the entire set of activities involved in process messages with an example. The example in Figure 4.16 defines the **PP20** process message category.

Figure 4.16 Process Message Category PP20 for Plant 1105

Follow these steps:

1. Select **PP20** and click **Characteristics/Message categories** to open the screen shown in Figure 4.17. Now you see **PP20** in the **ProcMessage Cat** field and **1105** in the **Plant** field.

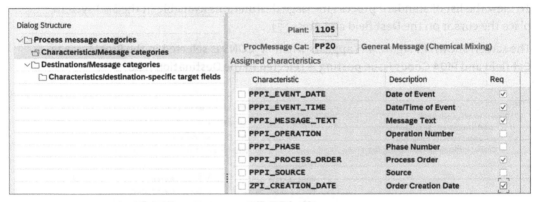

Figure 4.17 Process Instructions Characteristic in Process Message Category

2. Choose **Characteristics/Message Categories** on the left-hand side of the screen, and then on the right-hand side enter "ZPI_CREATION_DATE" for the process instruction **Characteristic**.

3. Select the **Req** checkbox to denote that it's required (mandatory) to enter details in this field.

4. Double-click **Destinations/Message Categories** on the left-hand side, and the screen shown in Figure 4.18 appears. Incorporate the **Destination PP20 (Chemical Mixing)** process message.

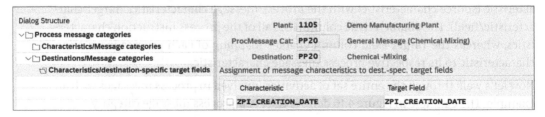

Figure 4.18 Process Message Destination in Process Message Category

5. Select **Process Message Destination PP20**, and choose **Characteristics/Destination-Specific Target Fields** on the left-hand side. On the right-hand side of this screen, perform one-to-one mapping of the process instruction characteristic with the process message characteristic for the **Destination PP20** process message. For this example, map the **ZPI_CREATION_DATE** process instruction characteristic with the **ZPI_CREATION_DATE** process message characteristic.

4.6   Process Instruction Category

A *process instruction category* consists of different process instruction types. In the master recipe, you have to assign the process instruction category, which then automatically incorporates the different process instruction types assigned to the process instruction category.

In the following section, we deliberately took a longer route to explain the various process instruction types in order to cover the concepts and the fundamentals involved in each type. Toward the end of this section, we also show how to use a wizard to create any of the seven different process instruction categories for various business scenarios.

4.6.1   Process Instruction Types

When a process instruction category is defined, it's mandatory to assign a process instruction type to enable the system to process the data accordingly. Eight different process instruction types are available:

- Process parameters
- Process data requests
- Process message subscriptions
- Calculations
- Inspection results requests
- Dynamic function calls
- Sequence definitions
- Universal

Table 4.1 summarizes the different process instruction types, which are also explained in detail later. Universal isn't included here because it applies to all types.

We discuss each of these in the following sections.

Process Instruction Type	Process Instruction Type Description	Usage in PI Sheets (Types 1 and 4)	Usage in External PCS (Types 2 and 3)	Sending Process Parameter Details	Process Message Requests to Process Message Destinations
1	Process parameters	✓	✓	✓	
2	Process data requests	✓	✓		✓
3	Process message subscriptions		✓		✓
4	Process data calculation formulas	✓			✓
5	Inspection results requests	✓			✓
6	Dynamic function calls	✓			✓
7	Sequence definitions	✓		✓	✓

Table 4.1 Process Instruction Categories

Process Instruction Type 1: Process Parameters

Process instruction type 1 is the simplest of all because it only requires the user to enter parameter values. In the PI sheet, there is a label for the process parameter, which is where the user enters the parameter value. Figure 4.19 shows the screen for the process instruction category **AMAT_1** for process instruction type 1. If this process instruction type is used in the process order (or in the master recipe), the system automatically fills in most of the details, such as material number, short text, issuance quantity for the operation, and phase. In column **A** (for automatic), the system automatically fills in all of the requisite fields.

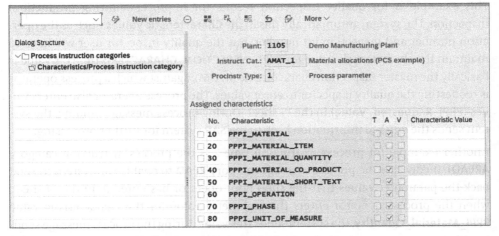

Figure 4.19 Process Instruction Type 1: Material Assignment

Process Instruction Type 2: Process Data Requests

Process instruction type 2 requires the user on the shop floor to enter the required data and send it back to the SAP system through process messages so that the system is able to perform the necessary data entry or updates. Either the system requires the user to enter the process parameter value manually, or the system can fill in the value automatically, depending on how you've set up the process instruction characteristics. We'll cover both types of process parameter value entry (manual input and automatic).

Figure 4.20 shows the screen for the process instruction category **AQMSMR_1** and process instruction type **2**. It contains the process message category **PI_QMSMR** to enable the system to send back the parameter values that the shop floor operator has entered.

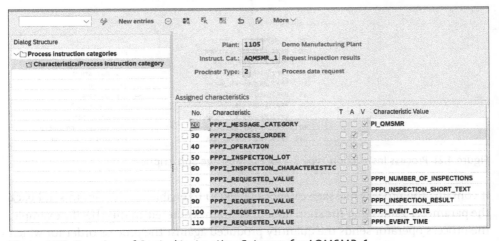

Figure 4.20 Overview of Control Instruction Category for AQMSMR_1

This example is for quality inspection results for in-process (during production) inspection. The system automatically fills in the **Characteristic Values**, such as the operation number and inspection lot number, but the quality inspector user will have to maintain the characteristic value for **PPPI_INSPECTION_CHARACTERISTIC**. This value is basically the master inspection characteristic (in QM), against which a process operator is requesting the quality inspector to enter values. The process operator also enters values (**PPPI_Requested_Value**) in the PI sheet. During process message sending, the system sends the entered information back to the SAP system for further processing.

Another example for process instruction type 2 is the process instruction category **AREAD1**. It contains the process message category **READ** to enable the system to send back the parameter values that the shop floor operator has entered. In the PI sheet, when the process operator enters the parameter value for the characteristic value **PPPI_Material_Quantity**, the system sends this value during the process message sending. The system automatically fills in the characteristic values for the **PPPI_Event_Date** and **PPPI_Event_Time**, with the date and time the user enters the requested process parameter values.

Later, we'll also show how the system automatically fills in the characteristic value for a self-defined process instruction characteristic.

Process Instruction Type 3: Process Message Subscriptions

Figure 4.21 shows the screen for the process instruction category **APROD_1** and process instruction type **3**.

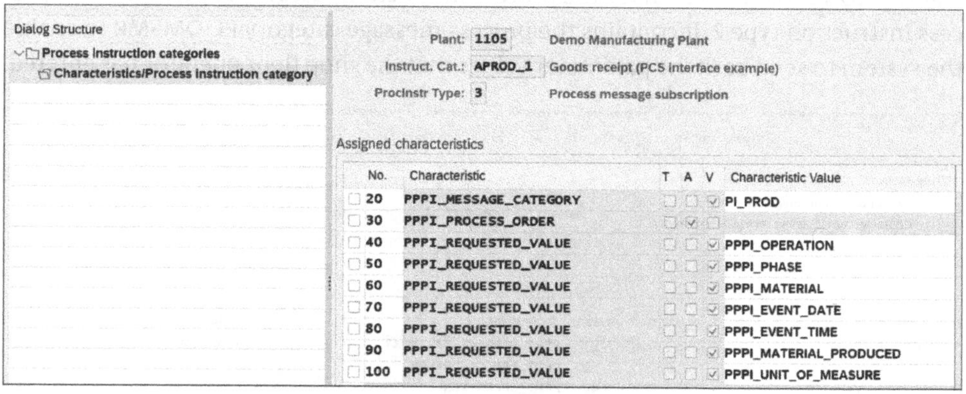

Figure 4.21 Process Instruction Type 3: Process Message Subscription

It contains the process message category **PI_PROD** to enable the system to send back the parameter values that the shop floor operator has entered. In this specific example, the process operator sends the quantity produced against the process order for which the operator wants to record GR against the process order. The process operator records the goods produced information in the PI sheet and sets the status of the PI sheet as **Complete**. Upon processing the process message—that is, sending it back to the SAP system—the system updates the goods produced information in the process order and also creates the material and accounting documents.

Process Instruction Type 4: Calculations

In this process instruction type, the system can perform calculations in the PI sheet based on the calculation formula defined. The system uses the process message category to send back the calculated value to the predefined destination. The standard process message category is NREAD.

Table 4.2 provides the details of some of the important process instruction characteristics that can be used for calculation. You can also refer to Figure 4.22 for more information.

Characteristic	Characteristic Value	Details
PPPI_INPUT_REQUEST	KS PRODUCTION	Define any characteristic value, and the system displays it accordingly in the PI sheet.
PPPI_VARIABLE	B	This is the variable that is defined for the calculated value.
PPPI_EVENT	PARAMETER_CHANGED	If this characteristic and its value are used, the system automatically does the calculation. If not, the user will have to manually choose the **Calculator** icon to trigger calculation.
PPPI_CALCULATED_VALUE	NH3_02	This characteristic value was already created using Transaction CT04 and is assigned here. It governs and controls several parameters, such as whether the field input is mandatory, whether a negative data entry is possible, or whether a user can select a value from the dropdown option in the PI sheet.
PPPI_CALCULATION_FORMULA	A*20	This is the calculation formula. The variable A needs to be previously defined in the PI sheet. Up to eight lines of characteristic can be used to define a long or complex formula.
PPPI_UNIT_OF_MEASURE	KG	This is the unit of measure of the calculated value.

Table 4.2 Process Instruction Characteristics for Calculation

In Figure 4.22, maintain a field description for **Characteristic PPPI_INPUT_REQUEST**, and the system will display it in the PI sheet. Then define the formula that the system will use in the calculation in the value field for **Characteristic PPPI_CALCULATION_FORMULA**. If the formula is too long to fit on one line, the formula can be entered in up to eight characteristics: just add a new line, enter the "PPPI_CALCULATION_FORMULA" characteristic, and continue entering formula details in the value field until the formula is complete.

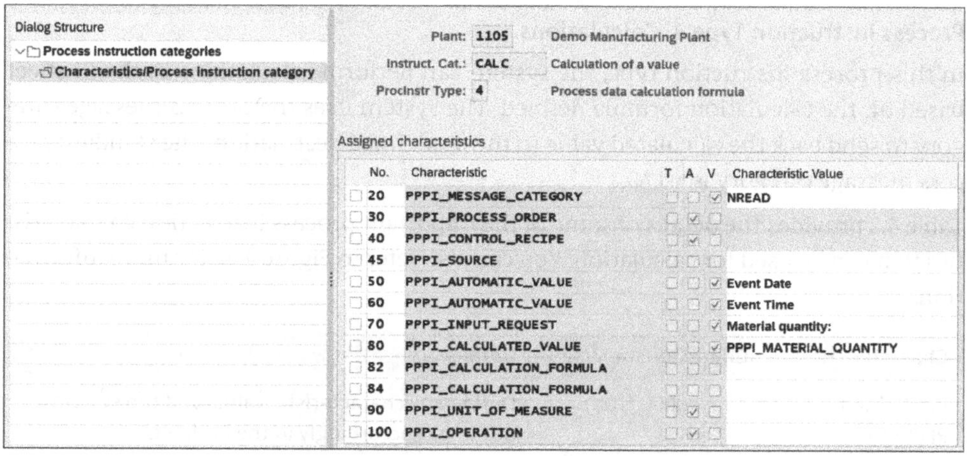

Figure 4.22 Process Instruction Type 4: Calculation

Process Instruction Type 5: Inspection Results Requests

In this process instruction type, navigate to the screen or transaction within the PI sheet in which a quality inspector can record inspection results of an operation or a phase. In other words, this provides the option to record the quality results. The standard process instruction category available for operations is QMJUM; for phase, it's QMJUM_PH. Depending on the process instruction category selected, either define the operation (see Table 4.3) or the phase (see Table 4.4) or both.

Characteristic	Characteristic Value	Details
PPPI_OPERATION	–	The operation for which you want to record quality inspection results

Table 4.3 Process Instruction Type 5 for Operation

Characteristic	Characteristic Value	Details
PPPI_PHASE	–	The phase for which you want to record quality inspection results

Table 4.4 Process Instruction Type 5 for Phase

Process Instruction Type 6: Dynamic Function Calls

Process instruction type 6 uses the dynamic function call, wherein a user can call any SAP system transaction in the PI sheet to facilitate a business process. For example, before initiating the process of GI against a process order within the PI sheet, the process operator wants to quickly check the stock overview of the materials. Similarly, while remaining in the PI sheet, a user also wants to perform the phase confirmation of the process order. In the first example, the relevant transaction is MMBE for a stock overview. In the second example, the user can call or navigate to the phase confirmation Transaction COR6N.

Table 4.5 provides an overview of each process instruction characteristic and its function.

Characteristic	Characteristic Value	Details
PPPI_FUNCTION_NAME	COPF_CALL_TRANSACTION	The system uses this function module to call up a transaction.
PPPI_BUTTON_TEXT	Display Process Order	The system displays the text **Display Process Order** (or any other text) on the pushbutton in the PI sheet.
PPPI_FUNCTION_DURING_DISPLAY	Allowed	This control function determines whether the system should show or forbid display of the desired information.
PPPI_EXPORT_PARAMETER	NEW_SESSION	–
PPPI_INSTRUC-TION	–	–
PPPI_EXPORT_PARAMETER	TCODE	–
PPPI_TRANSAC-TION_CODE	COR3	This is the transaction code that you want to use to display a process order.

Table 4.5 Process Instruction of Type 6

In Figure 4.23, the process instruction category **C_DURAT** enables calculating the duration.

For each export parameter (**PPPI_EXPORT_PARAMETER**), such as **I_START_DATE** or **I_START_TIME**, enter the values in **PPPI_STRING_VARIABLE**, and the system automatically calculates the duration. This duration can be used for calculating machine hours or production duration. The system uses function module COPF_DETERMINE_DURATION.

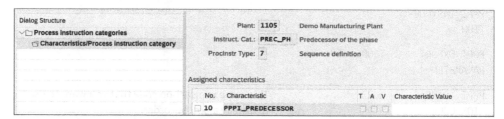

Figure 4.23 Process Instruction Type 6: Calculation of Duration

Process Instruction Type 7: Sequence Definitions

When process instruction type 7 is incorporated in the process instruction of a master recipe, the system prompts the user to enter the phases' relationships with each other. This enables the system to provide the business process owner with the necessary control so that unless a predecessor phase is complete, the successor phase can't start, or its data entry in the PI sheet can't be made. When a process operator sends a process message of a predecessor phase, only then will the system enable entering the details of operation of the next (successor) phase. In this process instruction type, assign the following process instruction character, along with its value (see Figure 4.24).

Figure 4.24 Process Instruction Type 7: Sequence Definition

Process Instruction Type 0: Universal

We've discussed how each process instruction type differs—but you also can use process instruction type 0 to attend to specific business processes that the standard process instruction types don't cover. In addition, if a company is planning to implement the process manufacturing cockpit, all of the process instruction categories will need to be defined as type 0 to enable the system to use them. See Section 4.9 for more on configuring the process manufacturing cockpit in the SAP system.

4.6.2 Using a Wizard or Process Instruction Assistant

With the exception of process instruction type 0, using a wizard helps with defining the category of each process instruction type. For example, if a user wants to create a new process instruction type 4 (calculation) for a new process instruction category, use the **PI Assistant** button to open this step-by-step instruction tool, which eliminates the need to know the complexities involved, such as a characteristic's PPPI_INPUT_VALUE.

Table 4.6 lists the standard process instruction categories available in the SAP system to enable business users to perform routine process management functions.

PI Category	PI Category Description	PI Category Type
AACT_1	Activity for phase (PCS example)	1
ACONS_1	Matl Consumption (PCS Interface Example)	3
ACRST_I	Change ctrl recipe status (PCS example)	3
AMAT_1	Material allocations (PCS example)	1
AOPST_I	Change operation status (PCS example)	3
AORD_1	Order data (PCS example)	1
APHACT_1	Confirmation of activity (PCS example)	3
APHAR_1	Parameter for phase (PCS example)	1
APHASE_1	Phases (PCS example)	1
APHSQ_1	Predecessor/successor of a phase	1
APHST_1	Change phase status, minimum scope (PCS)	3
APHST_2	Change phase status incl. resource (PCS)	3
APHST_I	Change phase status, all charact. (PCS)	3
APROD_1	Goods receipt (PCS interface example)	3
AQMSMR_1	Request inspection results	2
AREAD1	Request a measured value	2
AREAD2	Request two measured values	2
ASRACT_1	Confirm. of activity for sec.res. (PCS)	3
ASRST_I	Status of secondary resource (PCS)	3
BATCH_CL	Value assignment to batch characteristic	2
BATCH_CR	Batch creation	2

Table 4.6 Available Process Instruction Categories

PI Category	PI Category Description	PI Category Type
CALC	Calculation of a value	4
CONF_PH	Confirmation - create for phase	6
CONS_1	Material consumption, minimum scope	2
CONS_2	Material consumption, batch in message	2
CONS_3	Mat.consumption, storage locat. in mess.	2
CONS_4	Mat. consumption, reservation in message	2
CONS_5	Mat.consumpt., final issue ind. in mess.	2
CONS_BDR	Mat.consumption, batch determinat., split	2
CONS_BDS	Mat. consumption, batch determination	2
CONS_C	Mat. consumption, target/actual value	2
CONS_I	Material consumption, all message char.	2
CRST_I	Change control recipe status	2
C_DURAT	Calculation of a time interval	6
C_END_T	Calculation of an end date	6
C_STRT_T	Calculation of a start date	6
DOC_SHOW	Display a document	6
DOC_SHW2	Show document via URL	0
INSTR	Control instruction with note	1
MAT_CALC	Call material quantity calculation	6
MFLOW_BW	Material flow, backward flushing	2
MFLOW_FW	Material flow, forward flushing	2
MI_HUCMP	Identification	6
MI_HUCNS	Separate GI posting for HU	6
MI_HUSQU	Sequence check for HUs	6
MI_HUSTC	Check completeness of picking	6
MI_HUSTG	Picking for HUs	6
MI_MATBA	Mat.ident. on material/batch level	6

Table 4.6 Available Process Instruction Categories (Cont.)

PI Category	PI Category Description	PI Category Type
PHST_1	Change phase status, minimum scope	2
PHST_I	Change phase status, all charact.	2
PH_ACT	Activity confirmation for phase	2
PH_CON	Time ticket confirmation for phase	2
PMC_LAY1	Ex.: Layout definition with 2 frames	0
PMC_LAY2	Ex.: Layout definition with 3 frames	0
PMC_LAY3	Ex.: Layout definition with default style	0
PMC_LAY4	Ex.: definition of a header area	0
PMC_LAY5	Ex.: layout definition w/ simple style	0
PM_MDOC	Message for meas. point, plant maint.	2
PREC_PH	Predecessor of the phase	7
PROD_1	Goods receipt, minimum scope	2
PROD_2	Goods receipt, batch in message	2
PROD_3	Goods receipt, storage location in mess.	2
PROD_4	Goods receipt, order item in message	2
PROD_5	Goods receipt, final deliv. ind. in mess	2
PROD_I	Goods receipt, all message characterist.	2
QMJMP	Jump to QM results recording for operatn	5
QMJMP_NS	Jump to QM for new sample drawing	6
QMJMP_PH	Jump to QM results recording for phase	5
QMJMP_SD	Jump to sample-drawing processing	6
QMRES	Record a value relevant to QM	2
QMRES_PH	Record inspection result for phase	2
READ1	Request a measured value	2
READ2	Request two measured values	2
READ2_S	Tabular request with signature	2
READR	Data request with display of oth. values	2

Table 4.6 Available Process Instruction Categories (Cont.)

PI Category	PI Category Description	PI Category Type
RECON	Material Reconciliation	6
SIGN	Request a signature	2
SR_ACT	Activity confirmat. for sec.resource	2
SR_CON	Time ticket confirmation for sec.res.	2
SR_END	End of secondary resource	2
SR_START	Start of secondary resource	2
TA_CALL	Call any transaction	6
TMS_CNS1	Matl Consumption: Batch Mgmt Reqmt/Phase	2
TMS_CNS2	Matl Cons.: No Batch Mgmt Reqmt/Phase	2
TMS_CNS3	Matl Cons.: Batch Mgmt Reqmt/Operation	2
TMS_CNS4	Matl Cons.:No Batch Mgmt Reqmt/Operation	2
TMS_PP	Represents RMS Process Parameter	2
TMS_PPT	Represents RMS Process Parameter (Text)	2
TMS_PROD	Goods Receipt, Minimum Scope	2
TMS_PR_F	Label Printing: Finished Product	6
TMS_PR_I	Label Printing: Stream	6

Table 4.6 Available Process Instruction Categories (Cont.)

4.6.3   Creating a Self-Defined Process Instruction Category

Now that we've covered the basics of the process instruction category, let's create a self-defined process instruction category of type 0 as an example. In Chapter 7, we'll show how to use this self-defined process instruction category, PP20.

To create a new process instruction category, use menu path **SAP IMG · Production Planning for Process Industries · Process Management · Process Instructions · Define Process Instruction Categories (General)**, or use Transaction O12C.

On the initial screen that appears, enter "1105" in the **Plant** field, and choose the **Continue** icon to open the screen shown in Figure 4.25.

The screen that appears shows the list of available process instruction categories for **Plant 1105**. Notice the **ProcInstr.type** field; if the cursor is placed on this field and F4 is pressed, the system shows a dropdown list of process instruction types. These are the same process instructions that we covered in Section 4.6.1. Choose **New Entries**, and Figure 4.25 appears.

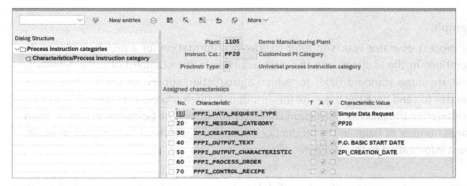

Figure 4.25 Overview Screen of Process Instruction Category PP20

In the initial screen that appears, define the process instruction category **PP20** as type **0** (universal) and give a short **Description**. Next, select the **Process Instruction Category** and double-click the **Characteristics/Process Instruction Category** field on the left-hand side of the screen to enter specific process instruction characteristics. For this example, enter the characteristics as shown in Table 4.7.

Characteristic	Characteristic Value
PPPI_DATA_REQUEST_TYPE	Simple Data Request
PPPI_MESSAGE_CATEGORY	PP20
ZPI_CREATION_DATE	
PPPI_OUTPUT_TEXT	P.O. Basic Start Date
PPPI_OUTPUT_CHARACTERISTIC	ZPI_CREATION_DATE
PPPI_PROCESS_ORDER	
PPPI_CONTROL_RECIPE	

Table 4.7 Self-Defined Process Instruction Category PP20

Table 4.7 consolidates the configuration made so far. It incorporates the process message category PP20 as well as the self-defined process instruction characteristic ZPI_ CREATION_DATE. See Section 4.6.4 to create a self-defined process instruction characteristic. Also note that the system automatically fills in the characteristic values that are blank in the preceding table.

4.6.4 Creating a Self-Defined Process Instruction Characteristic

Although the SAP system offers a large number of standard process instruction (and process message) characteristics, unique business processes or business needs often require custom-defined or self-defined characteristics.

For our example, create a simple self-defined process instruction characteristic that automatically fetches the process order basic start date when the user creates the process order. Use this characteristic to display this information (process order end date) in the PI sheet. Although this example uses automatic value assignment—that is, the system automatically fills in the date field—it can also be used to request that the process operator send the requisite information in the form of a process message. Process instruction characteristics can also be used to define the RFC destination to which a production supervisor wants process operator to send process instructions for an external control system.

To create a new process instruction characteristic, follow menu path **SAP IMG · Production Planning for Process Industries · Process Management · Process Instructions · Define Characteristics for Process Instructions · Create Characteristics for Process Instructions**, or use Transaction O25C.

Figure 4.26 displays the initial screen to create the process instruction characteristic. Notice the similarities in creating a standard characteristic (Transaction CT04) when compared with creating a process instruction characteristic.

For this example, create **ZPI_CREATION_DATE** and click the **Basic Data** tab. In this tab, it's important to ensure that the **Char.** (characteristics) **Group** is defined as a process instruction characteristic (**PPPI_02**). This is the same characteristic group that we covered in Section 4.4.2.

Define the **Data Type** as **DATE Date Format** and click the **Proc. mgmt** icon. The system displays a popup that allows incorporating additional process instructions and process message details. If the cursor is placed on the **Table** field and F4 pressed, or you click the dropdown option, the dialog box shown in Figure 4.27 appears. This screen provides the option to select any of the five tables available: **Process Order (Header)**, **Operation**, **Phase**, **Resource**, and **Material (Header)**. Depending on the table selected, the system displays the fields associated with it.

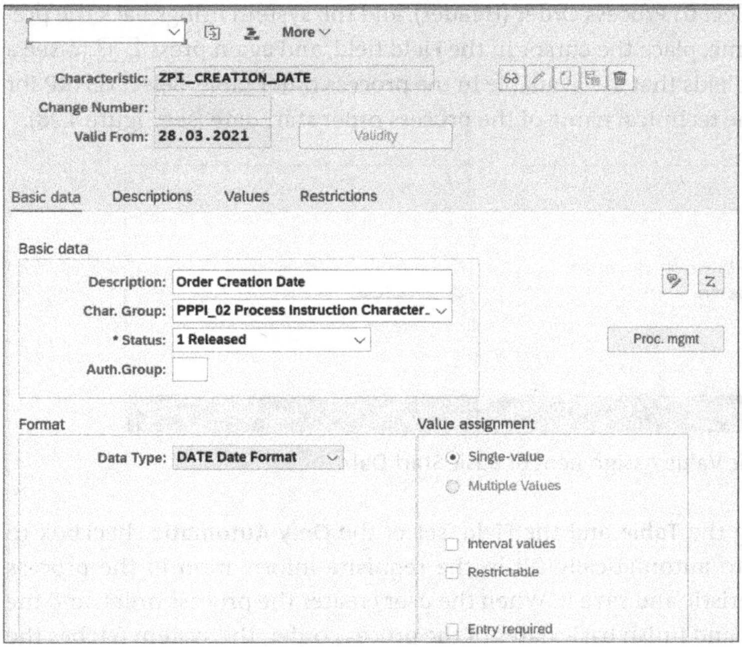

Figure 4.26 Creating Process Instruction

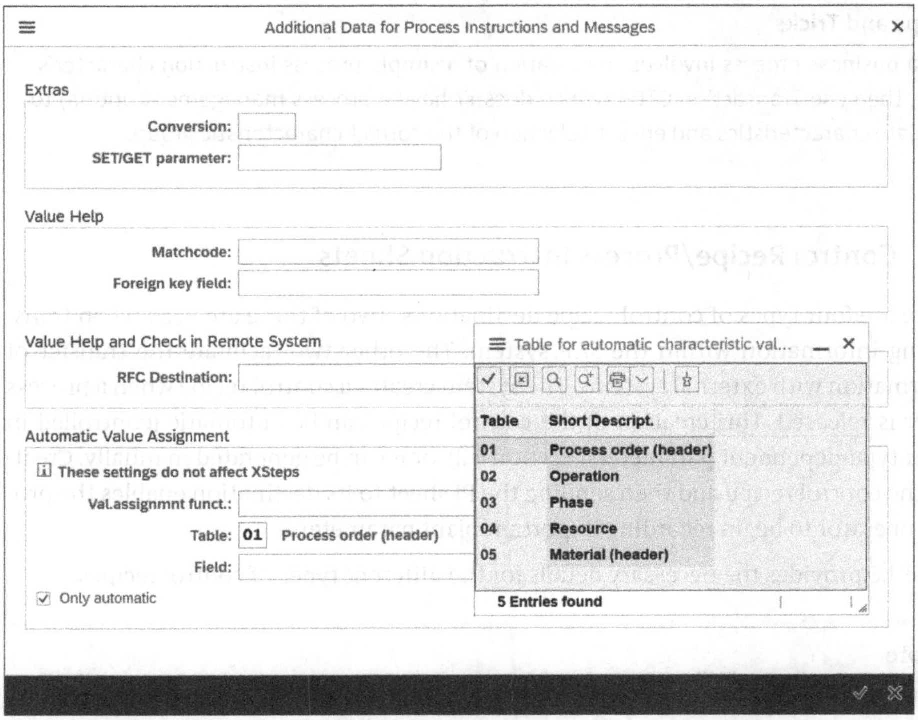

Figure 4.27 Automatic Value Assignment for Process Order Tables

For this example, select **01 Process Order (Header)**, and the system brings back the previous screen. This time, place the cursor in the **Field** field, and again press F4 to see a limited selection of fields that are available in the process order table. Select **GSTRP** for the **Field**, which is the technical name of the process order start date (see Figure 4.28).

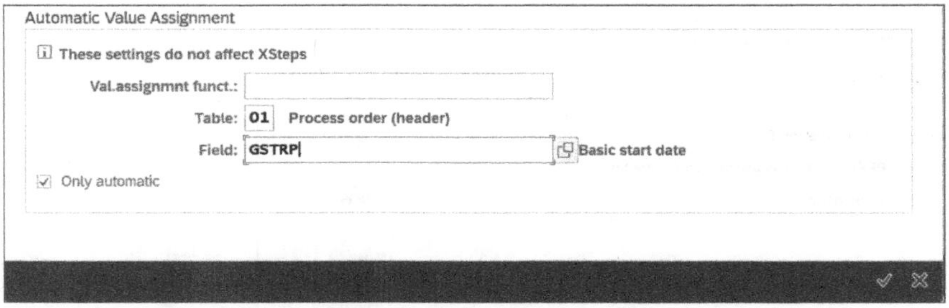

Figure 4.28 Automatic Value Assignment of Basic Start Date

Apart from entering the **Table** and the **Field**, select the **Only Automatic** checkbox to enable the system to automatically fill in the requisite information in the process instruction characteristic and save it. When the user creates the process order, and the system assigns start and finish basic dates of the process order, the system fetches the basic start date of the process order and makes it an integral part of the PI sheet.

[+]   **Tips and Tricks**
If a business process involves the creation of a simple process instruction characteristic, then use Transaction CT04 (which doesn't have a process management option) to create characteristics and ensure selection of the correct characteristic group.

4.7   Control Recipe/Process Instruction Sheets

There are four types of control recipe destinations. Two of these are used when transferring information within the SAP system. The other two facilitate the transfer of information with external systems. The system creates a control recipe when a process order is released. This creation of the control recipe can be automatic (controlled in order type-dependent parameters; Section 4.2), or it can be generated manually. Creating the control recipe and then sending the PI sheet to its destination enables the process operator to begin recording important plant parameters.

Table 4.8 provides the necessary details for the different types of control recipes.

[»]   **Note**
Although still available in SAP S/4HANA 2020, ABAP list-based PI sheets are already obsolete and may not be available in future releases of SAP S/4HANA.

Control Recipe Destination Type	Destination Location	Output Type
1	SAP system	ABAP list-based PI sheet
2	External control system	External control system
3	External control system	External system
4	SAP system	Browser-based PI sheet

Table 4.8 Control Recipe Destination Types

If the control recipe destination is of either type 1 or 4, then the system sends the recipes to different destinations within the SAP system. The system creates a control recipe, either user-driven (manually) or automatically, and consolidates the process instructions for a given order and destination in the form of the PI sheet. The PI sheet contains user-defined details—for example, process notes, process steps, input fields, calculations, options to sign the phases of the PI sheet, details to enter GI (consumption), and navigation to the confirmation screen or to record in-process quality results. When the process operator sets the status of the PI sheet to **Complete**, the system sends the data back to the SAP system in the form of process messages. The system then uploads the information from the process messages into the SAP system tables using function modules and BAPIs. If the control recipe destination is of either type 2 or 3, then the system consolidates the process instructions in the control recipe of the process order and sends them to an external PCS.

An internal SAP system destination can be any logical or virtual destination where the process operator receives the PI sheet and fills in the data. For example, internal destinations could include mixing unit, packing unit, blending, ammonia section, urea section, or quality section. For external destinations—that is, external PCSs—these are the RFC destinations of the external system.

It's also possible to integrate a digital signature using an SAP system login and password. The following options are available for use with digital signatures:

- Activating or deactivating the PI sheet
- Locking or unlocking PI sheet
- Changing the status of the PI sheet to **Complete**
- Entering each parameter value in the PI sheet

Digital signature options are also available in case a parameter value deviates from predefined limits, as well as for completion of each phase in the PI sheet. If there's a business need to automatically generate process instructions to minimize maintaining them in the master recipe, then this can be achieved when creating the control recipe destination. See Section 4.7.2 for information on the scope of generation. In the following sections, we'll explain how to set up a control recipe destination and how to make the necessary settings for the scope of generation for process instructions.

4.7.1   Create a Control Recipe Destination

To create a new control recipe destination, follow menu path **SAP IMG · Production Planning for Process Industries · Process Management · Control Recipe/PI Sheets · Control Recipe Destinations · Define and Set Up Control Recipe Destinations**, or use Transaction O25C.

In the screen shown in Figure 4.29, create a new control recipe destination **PP** of **Type 4** (browser-based PI sheet). Give a short description and set the **Destination address** as **Chemical Mixing**. Select the **SortMat** checkbox to enable the system to display materials in the same order in which they appear in the master recipe or in the process order. If the cursor is placed on the **Type** field and ⌊F4⌋ pressed, or the dropdown option is used, then the system will display the four different types of control recipe destinations available to choose from (this is the same as in Table 4.8).

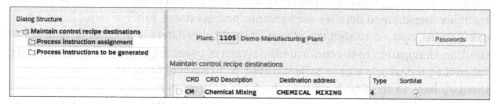

Figure 4.29 Control Recipe Destination: Overview

Figure 4.30 shows the details screen to create the control recipe destination. The options to incorporate digital signatures in some or all of the processes are shown.

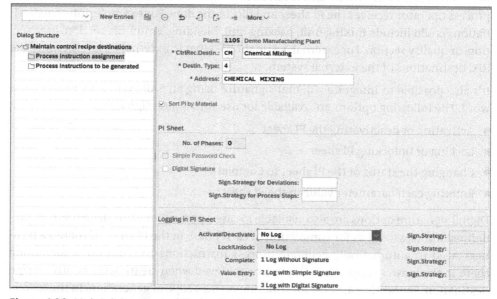

Figure 4.30 Maintaining Control Recipe Destination

4.7.2   Scope of Generation

In some situations, the process operator enters the same data. It's possible to automate the entry of this data so that it's the same every time with the use of scope of generation. This is helpful in the following situations:

- To confirm the quantity produced or activities consumed at the end of each phase
- To enter shift details at the end of every phase or operation
- To ensure that each master recipe created for a specific destination should have standard instructions and notes, which then become visible in the PI sheet

Figure 4.31 shows the **New Entries: Overview of Added Entries** screen that appears during the creation of control recipe destination **10** for **Plant 1105** and when choosing **Process Instructions to Be Generated** on the left-hand side.

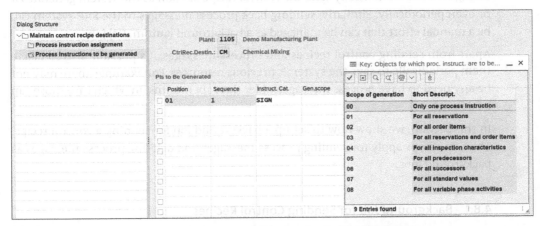

Figure 4.31 Process Instructions to Be Generated during Control Recipe Creation

Place the cursor on the **Position** field and press ⌕F4⌕, and the dialog box appears. Here, define the position in the control recipe to place the process instruction category. It can be at the start or end of a control recipe, an operation, or a phase.

When a position is maintained, the next step is to assign a process instruction category, place the cursor on the **Gen.scope** field, and press ⌕F4⌕. This opens the screen shown in Figure 4.31, wherein the scope of generation is available to enable the system to generate process instructions based on the given details. For example, select the **01** option for the GI process instruction category. When the system creates a process order and incorporates the materials list based on the BOM, it also simultaneously creates a reservation with item numbers. To record consumption (GI) against the process order using the PI sheet, select the relevant process instruction category (**CH_CONS** or **CH_CONS2**) and define the scope of generation as **01** (**For All Reservations**).

For this example, assign the instruction category **SIGN** that the system will generate once and at the end of the PI sheet (refer to Figure 4.31).

Tips and Tricks

When creating the process instruction category **SIGN**, make sure to assign a characteristic value (e.g., **PI Completion Signoff**) to the process instruction characteristic **PPPI_INPUT_VALUE**.

4.8 Background Jobs

Background jobs help to automate processes that otherwise require manual intervention. For example, when a user creates a process order and generates its control recipe, it will have to be manually sent it to the control recipe destination. The system can be configured to automatically send the control recipe as soon as the system generates it or even periodically. Similarly, sending back process messages to the SAP system can be a manual effort that can be managed as a background (automatic) job.

Apart from sending control recipes and process messages, it's possible also to delete them periodically to save the system's precious resources. For example, there may not be any need to have process messages older than six months, in which case those can be deleted.

In this section, we show how to set up a background job for sending a control recipe. The same steps apply for sending process messages and deleting process messages as background jobs.

4.8.1 Background Job for Sending Control Recipes

To set up the background job for sending a control recipe as soon as the system creates it, follow menu path **SAP IMG • Production Planning for Process Industries • Process Management • Control Recipe/PI Sheet • Define Background Job for Sending**, or use Transaction SM36. Figure 4.32 shows the initial **Define Background Job** screen to define the background job. Enter "ZPP_PI_SEND" in the **Job Name** field and press ⌈Enter⌋.

Figure 4.32 Defining Background Job to Send Control Recipe

On the next screen, enter "SAP_NEW_CONTROL_RECIPES" in the **Event** field, which causes the system to send the control recipe as soon as the system creates it. If the **Start**

Condition button is clicked, the schedule for sending control recipes to various destinations can be defined. Also assign the program name **RCOCB006** to set up the background job.

> **Tips and Tricks** [+]
>
> Use the **Job Wizard** button to enable the system to provide guidance in a step-by-step process to set up a background job, not just for sending a control recipe to a destination but for any background job. It's important to know the program name for which to define the background job.

4.8.2 Background Job for Sending Process Messages

In Transaction SM36, use program RCOCB004 to send newly created process messages as a background job. The system also processes the process messages that have statuses of **To Be Submitted** and **To Be Submitted with Warning**. This program is for sending process messages within the plant. If process messages need to be sent across different plants, then use program RCOCB002. The corresponding event is SAP_NEW_PROCESS_MES-SAGES.

> **Tips and Tricks** [+]
>
> Whenever a background job is defined using Transaction SM36, there's also a requirement to assign a variant to it. Use Transaction SE38 to create a new variant for any background job (and its associated program). On the initial screen, enter the program name, click the **Variants** radio button, and then click the **Change** button. On the next screen, give the variant name, and click **Create**.

4.8.3 Background Job for Deleting Process Messages

The background program also enables deleting process messages as a background job. Use Transaction SM36 to set up the background job.

4.9 Process Manufacturing Cockpit

The process manufacturing cockpit finds diverse application in areas where the activities performed, actions taken, or results recorded aren't referencing any specific process order. In the cockpit, use of function calls—for example, to call up a transaction or to display a document—is possible. A cockpit can also be created for a predefined set of activities that a process operator performs on a specific resource or work center. The cockpit also facilitates input or output data entry, as well as calculations. The system creates a PI sheet with reference to a process order, and the system reflects any changes or updates made to it. In a cockpit, there's no need to give reference to a process order. Here are some examples in which creating process manufacturing cockpits meets business needs:

- There's a need to record values of five specific process parameters of the plant and report these back to the main control room. The reporting for the parameters doesn't reference a specific process order but is used to ensure that there is regular recording and consistent transmission of this information.

- The production process generates an ancillary product (a by-product of low value), but the production supervisor doesn't want to record it with reference to any specific process order nor to book the cost of the by-product generation to a process order. There's also a need to record its quantity every three days, along with other details, such as the date of recording, the person who recorded this information, and a signature.

- A company has installed a new production line for which it wants to ensure that the latest technical drawings and manuals are available for process operators to refer to. These drawings are for each work center or work station. In the process manufacturing cockpit, the process operator only has to click the relevant drawing's icon, and all details become visible.

Process manufacturing cockpits can be created for as many business applications or activities as needed. Because the cockpit uses a process instruction category, it's also possible to incorporate a process message category into it. When entries are made in the cockpit, the system generates process messages that can be sent to predefined destinations.

To define a process manufacturing cockpit, follow menu path **SAP IMG · Production Planning for Process Industries · Process Management · Define Process Manufacturing Cockpits** (see Figure 4.33).

Here, define **Cockpit PP10** for **Plant 1105**. Notice that a newly created cockpit can be checked for correctness by choosing the **Check** icon, and it can also be simulated by choosing the **Simulate** icon located at the bottom of the screen. Finally, ensure that you activate a process manufacturing cockpit so that it becomes available or changes made to the cockpit become effective. To activate the cockpit, choose the **Activate** icon.

For this example, select **Cockpit PP10**, and double-click **Assign Process Instructions to Cockpits**. This brings up the screen in Figure 4.34, where two different process instruction categories are maintained. The system only allows process instruction categories of type 0 (universal). The **Line No.** column defines the sequence in which the process instruction categories will appear in the process manufacturing cockpit. Create a new process instruction category with reference to the existing ones and assign it as type 0.

The **Ref** (reference) checkbox ensures that the system automatically reflects any changes made in the specific process instruction category.

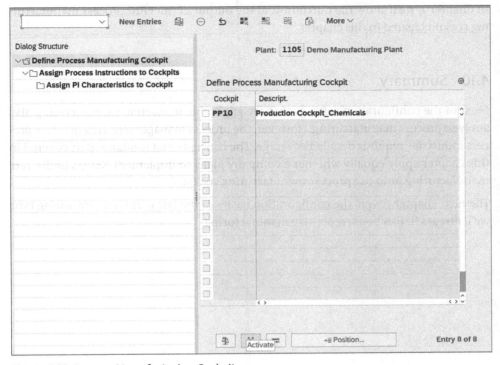

Figure 4.33 Process Manufacturing Cockpit

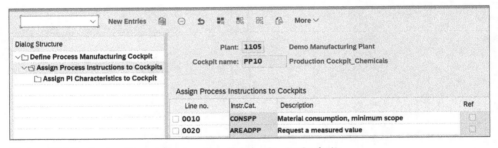

Figure 4.34 Assigning Process Instruction Categories to Cockpits

Tips and Tricks

A quick and easy way to use the desired process instruction category in the process manufacturing cockpit is to copy the original process instruction category as a reference and define it as type 0 (universal) during the copy function. In this example, the process instruction category **CONS_PI** is used as a reference to create a new process instruction category, **CONSPP**, which is defined as type 0 (universal).

In Chapter 7, we'll show the outcome and the output of the PP10 process manufacturing cockpit created in this chapter.

4.10   Summary

Most of the configuration settings that are applicable in discrete manufacturing also apply to process manufacturing. However, the process management area in PP for process industries requires detailed coverage. The concepts and fundamentals covered in this chapter apply equally whether a company plans to implement XSteps in discrete manufacturing or to use process manufacturing cockpits.

The next chapter covers the configuration basics of the last main manufacturing type we'll discuss in this book: repetitive manufacturing.

Chapter 5
Repetitive Manufacturing Configuration

Configuration steps in repetitive manufacturing include creating a repetitive manufacturing profile, setting scheduling parameters for a run schedule quantity (planned orders), and selecting backflush settings for use online or in the background.

The configuration steps in repetitive manufacturing (REM) are relatively straightforward, without many complexities when compared to discrete manufacturing or process manufacturing types. In fact, the very purpose of REM is to enable lean manufacturing in actual business scenarios with correspondingly fewer entries in the SAP S/4HANA system. REM may not be able to manage complex manufacturing processes, but it can be used to bring about significant process optimization with a decreased data entry workload and improved system performance.

This chapter begins by explaining how to set up the REM profile using the REM assistant. The assistant guides the user with a step-by-step approach to ensure that the correct settings are made during the REM profile creation stage. The assistant also provides the detailed function of each configuration step and gives recommendations where necessary. The desired production method, such as make-to-stock (MTS) or make-to-order (MTO), can be chosen. We deliberately took the long route to REM profile creation by using the assistant because we wanted to focus on explaining every available option in detail and with business examples.

At the end of REM profile creation by using the assistant, the "normal" or the prevalent method of creating an REM profile with a single screen (and multiple tabs) is explained. The options that aren't available in the REM profile assistant are also explained. If a REM profile is being configured for the first time, then it's recommended to use the REM profile assistant. But if you're familiar already with REM profile creation and the functionalities it offers, then proceed directly to using the single-screen REM profile creation option.

The chapter also covers scheduling REM planned orders and running the schedule quantity and then discusses the layout and display settings available on various screens in REM processing. The effects of the REM configuration will be become clear in Chapter 8, which covers the production planning for REM in detail. Finally, this chapter also covers the settings available to optimize day-to-day business transactions, such as backflushing.

> **Note**
>
> Refer to Chapter 1 for feature comparison among discrete manufacturing, process manufacturing, and REM, as well as to see how to decide which manufacturing type is most relevant for a given industry.

Let's get started.

5.1   Repetitive Manufacturing Profile

The REM profile offers several controls for important business functions that form the basis of regular or periodic data recording in the system. This includes options to post activities online or at a later date, automatic goods movements of all or some of the materials, and stock and/or automatic batch determination, among others. To create a REM profile using the REM profile assistant, follow SAP configuration menu path **SAP IMG · Logistics · Production · Repetitive Manufacturing · Control · Create Repetitive Manufacturing Profile Using Assistant**, or use Transaction OSPT.

The following sections will explain the steps involved in setting up a REM profile.

5.1.1   Repetitive Manufacturing Production Type

While creating a REM profile, decide whether to use the profile for the MTO or MTS production method. Alternately, separate REM profiles can be catered to meet MTO or MTS business scenarios.

> **Note**
>
> Chapter 12 covers MTO and MTS production methods.

Depending on the option selected, the system correspondingly displays the relevant screens and options to choose from. If MTO production is chosen, then a profile suited to REM that references the sales order is created. If MTS production is chosen, a profile suited to REM that doesn't reference the sales order is created.

It's also possible to use a REM profile template to copy previously created and available REM profiles to create a new REM profile. This step copies all the settings of the REM template profile into the new REM profile, and then the desired changes can be made where needed.

[+]

> **Tips and Tricks**
>
> Choose the **Meaning** icon available on each screen of REM profile creation to get information on the underlying concept for that functionality or area.
>
> Choose the **Recommendation** icon available on each screen of REM profile creation to see system advice on recommended settings.

For this example, create a REM profile for an MTS production method. Figure 5.1 shows the initial screen to create a REM profile using the assistant. For this example, select the **Make-to-Stock—REM** radio button, and then choose **Next**.

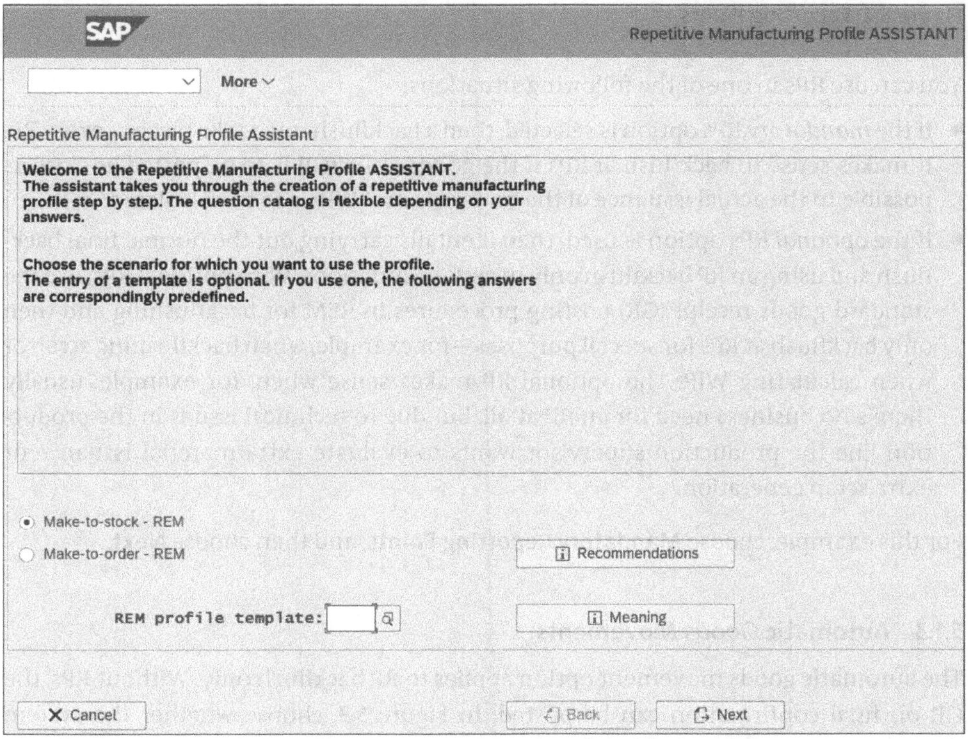

SAP   Repetitive Manufacturing Profile ASSISTANT

[_____ ∨]   More ∨

Repetitive Manufacturing Profile Assistant

Welcome to the Repetitive Manufacturing Profile ASSISTANT.
The assistant takes you through the creation of a repetitive manufacturing
profile step by step. The question catalog is flexible depending on your
answers.

Choose the scenario for which you want to use the profile.
The entry of a template is optional. If you use one, the following answers
are correspondingly predefined.

(•) Make-to-stock - REM
(○) Make-to-order - REM   [i] Recommendations

        REM profile template: [____] 🔍   [i] Meaning

[✕ Cancel]   [⟨ Back]   [⟲ Next]

Figure 5.1 Initial Screen of Repetitive Manufacturing Profile Assistant

5.1.2   Reporting Points

A *reporting point* (RP) enables the system to record consumption or other details, such as identifying the work in process (WIP) and better stock visibility in inventory management (IM), which are specific to actual information in time and equally helpful in reporting. As shown in Figure 5.2, select whether the system should include no RPs or make the RPs mandatory or optional. An RP serves the same purpose as a milestone does in routing for discrete manufacturing. If the **Mandatory Reporting Points** option is selected, then an RP has to be defined at the time of assembly or component backflush.

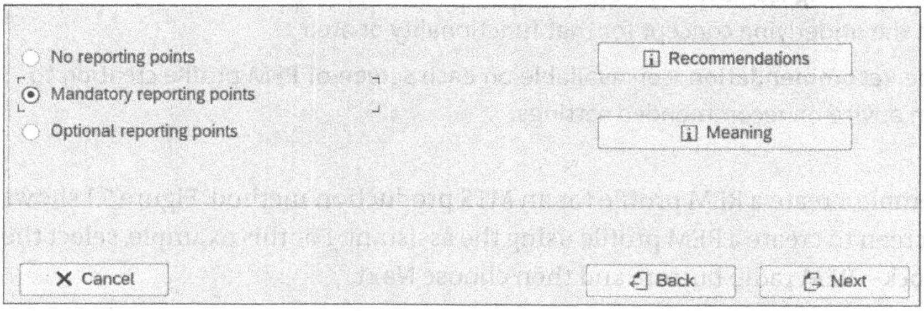

Figure 5.2 Reporting Points

You can use RPs in one of the following situations:

- If the *mandatory* RPs option is selected, then a backflush must take place at every RP. It makes sense to backflush at RPs if the goods issue (GI) is to be posted as close as possible to the actual issuance of the materials or if WIP is to be calculated.
- If the *optional* RPs option is used, then it entails carrying out the normal final backflush and using an RP backflush only in certain situations. With optional RPs, use the standard goods receipt (GR) posting procedures in REM for backflushing and then only backflush at RPs for special purposes—for example, when backflushing scrap or when calculating WIP. The optional RP makes sense when, for example, usually there's no business need for an RP at all, but due to technical issues in the production line the production supervisor wants to evaluate extra material issuance or extra scrap generation.

For this example, choose **Mandatory Reporting Points**, and then choose **Next**.

5.1.3   Automatic Goods Movements

The automatic goods movement option applies to RP backflush only. Without RPs, the GR on final confirmation can be posted. In Figure 5.3, choose whether the system should perform automatic GR at the time of assembly backflush. When assembly backflush is recorded and the yield is confirmed, the system automatically performs the GR at the last RP.

When using optional RPs, choose the **Automatic GR** setting because usually the components are backflushed along with the GR posting.

When using mandatory RPs, the production supervisor can only backflush at RPs. The normal GR posting isn't available here. Therefore, for mandatory RPs, the recommendation is to define the last workplace on the production line as an RP with the **Automatic GR** setting. If the **Automatic GR** option is set, the production supervisor has to post activities and GIs manually for operations that lie after the last RP. This is normally an exception to the preceding rule/recommendation.

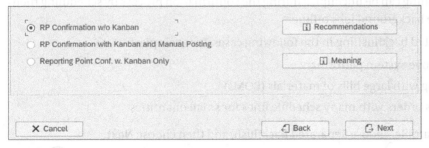

Figure 5.3 Automatic GR

For this example, choose **Automatic GR**, and then choose **Next**.

> **Note**
>
> While configuring the REM profile using the assistant, the system displays either the screen shown in Figure 5.3 or the screen shown ahead in Figure 5.4. This is dependent on the option that was previously selected while creating a REM profile.

5.1.4   Reporting Points Confirmation and Kanban

Depending on the system release, select whether to use RPs with or without kanban, as shown in Figure 5.4. RP with kanban enables monitoring of the production process at the intermediate level by using kanban for processing products in individual operations. The RPs record the confirmation that an operation has been completed. For this example, choose **RP Confirmation w/o Kanban**, and then choose **Next**.

Figure 5.4 RP Confirmation for Kanban

5.1.5   Activity Posting

On the next screen, choose whether or not the system will also post the activities to a product cost collector at the time of assembly backflush by choosing the **Post Activities** or **No Activity Posting** radio button (see Figure 5.5). Activities may be machine hours, labor hours, or processing time, and they are defined in rate routing. If a company follows a lean manufacturing approach, in which even the data entry effort is minimal, activity posting involves additional use of the system's resources, such as material calculation and price updates. Activity posting should only be considered if it's significant when compared with cost. We suggest engaging a product cost controlling (CO-PC) resource to help with the decision-making process about activity posting.

If the system is instructed to post production activities, it calculates these activities either on the basis of details from the standard cost estimate or from preliminary costing in the cost collector for material. The system also posts the activities during the confirmation process. For this example, choose **Post Activities**, and then choose **Next**.

Figure 5.5 Activities Backflush

5.1.6   Separated Backflush

In this step, choose whether the system should perform separated backflushes or not by selecting the **Separated Backflush** or **No Separated Backflush** radio button. This option is primarily used to improve a system's performance, especially if it becomes slow due to a large number of confirmations. With separated backflush, certain aspects of backflushing can be uncoupled during the confirmation process by scheduling them as separate background jobs offline.

Use separated backflushing in the following cases, for example:

- To improve system performance
- If dealing with large bills of materials (BOMs)
- For sales orders with many schedule lines for small quantities

For this example, choose **Separated Backflush**, and then choose **Next**.

If the **No Separated Backflush** option is selected, then Figure 5.6 will appear, with an option to choose whether the system should simultaneously post GR and GI in the same assembly confirmation transaction or separately. In REM, the final confirmation also encompasses GR. Choose whether to also post GI during the confirmation process. If the **Post GR Only** option is selected, then the GIs for the components can be posted collectively—for example, using the GI transaction in REM.

For this example, choose **Post GR and GI** in the assembly confirmation.

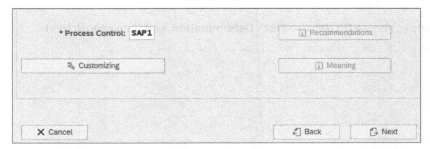

Figure 5.6 Automatic GR and GI

5.1.7 Process Control

In Figure 5.7, choose when GI and calculation of costs are performed and whether GI and calculation of costs are aggregated during confirmation. While the option to let the system perform several steps/functions together is available, use the **Process Control** option to customize the process according to the business needs. Click the **Customizing** button on this screen to make the necessary changes. (We'll cover the customization of process controls later in Section 5.5.)

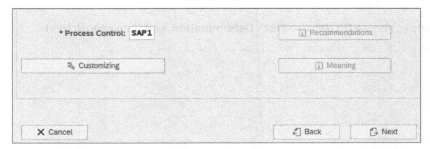

Figure 5.7 Process Control in Backflushing

It's important to note that this option is only available if **Separated Backflush** is chosen in the previous step. In that case, defining the process control for this separated backflush is required, and there are four options available to maintain.

For this example, enter "SAP1" for the **Process Control**, and choose **Next**.

5.1.8 Firming Planned Orders

It makes sense to firm the planned orders when these are created in the REM planning table because a firmed planned order won't change during the material requirements planning (MRP) run. Options to not firm the planned order at the time of its creation and to firm planned orders in the planning time fence only are also available.

For this example, choose **Firm Planned Orders in Plng Time Fence**, and then choose **Next** (Figure 5.8).

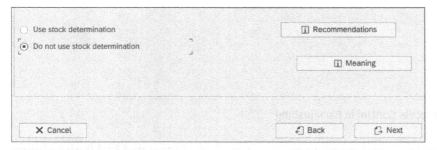

Figure 5.8 Firming Planned Orders in REM

5.1.9   Automatic Stock Determination

It's possible to take advantage of the system performing the automatic stock determination at the time of component or assembly backflush by selecting the **Use Stock Determination** radio button (see Figure 5.9). The prerequisite is that the automatic stock determination procedure is already set up in the system. Stock determination enables the system to suggest available stock for consumption based on the defined criteria.

For this example, choose **Do Not Use Stock Determination**, and then choose **Next**.

Figure 5.9 Stock Determination

5.1.10   Batch Determination Procedure

Similar to the previous automatic stock determination procedure, choose whether or not the system should perform the batch determination procedure in REM by selecting **Separate Batch Search Procedure** or **No Separate Batch Search Proc**. The material in this case must be batch-managed to use this functionality. Batch determination enables the system to suggest available batches for consumption based on the defined criteria. For this example, choose **No Separate Batch Search Proc.**, and then choose **Next**.

> **Note**
> Batch determination is covered in Chapter 10.

5.1.11 Reduction in Planned Order Quantities

In the screen shown in Figure 5.10, choose whether the system should reduce the production quantities in the planned order or in the run schedule quantity (RSQ) while performing assembly confirmation of a material. Also choose whether the system should reduce the planned order quantity only if it pertains to a specific production version. As each production version reflects a production line, this option enables reduction of planned order quantities as soon as the goods on the production line (in direct relation to the production version) are produced.

For this example, choose **All**, which causes the system to reduce planned order quantities in all cases. Choose **Next**.

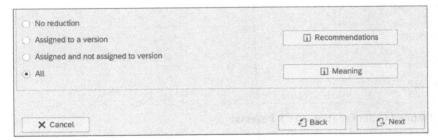

Figure 5.10 Reduction in Planned Order Quantities

5.1.12 Reduction Period

In Figure 5.11, choose the period in days during which the system should reduce the planned order quantities. The system considers the reduction period from today and expands to consider the defined dates in the future. For example, if a company is consistently faced with overproduction and wants to avoid additional production for the defined days in the future, then maintain the reduction period here. In addition, note that the system reduces the planned order quantities dates of the past in any case and accords them higher priority than the current date or future dates.

For this example, enter "3" in the **Reduction Period** field, and then choose **Next**.

Reduction period: **3**

Recommendations

Meaning

X Cancel   Back   Next

Figure 5.11 Reduction Period for Planned Orders

5.1.13   Create New Planned Orders on Goods Receipts Reversals

In Figure 5.12, choose whether the system should automatically create planned orders for reversed quantities. If this option is not chosen, then the system automatically creates planned orders during the MRP run if necessary. For this example, choose **No Planned Order Creation**, and then choose **Next**.

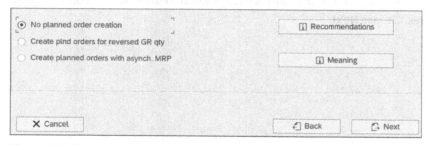

Figure 5.12 Planned Order Creation on GR Reversals

5.1.14   Online Error Correction

In this step, choose how the system processes errors encountered during transaction postings, such as a failed component backflush due to a mismatch in IM. Other types of errors may include an insufficient quantity of a component's stock in a component backflush, a missing storage location for GI or GR, and so on. If the **No Online Correction** or **Optional Online Correction** option is selected, then use a separate transaction to address errors separately, provided that reprocessing records are created (see the next step). It's also possible to choose **Online Correction Mandatory**. For this example, choose **Optional Online Correction**, and then choose **Next**.

5.1.15   Reprocessing Errors Log Maintenance

During automatic goods movement processing, such as backflushing, sometimes the processing isn't successful due to insufficient stock, an incorrect storage location, or missing or nonupdated rates for activity types. All such unsuccessful records end up in error log maintenance for reprocessing and to note that they haven't been resolved yet.

In Figure 5.13, choose how the system should manage all reprocessing records of all items that caused the errors. The available options are that the system won't maintain any reprocessing record, the system will maintain collective reprocessing records, or the system will maintain individual and collective reprocessing records of errors. For this example, choose **Indiv. and Cumul. Reprocessing Records**, and then choose **Next**.

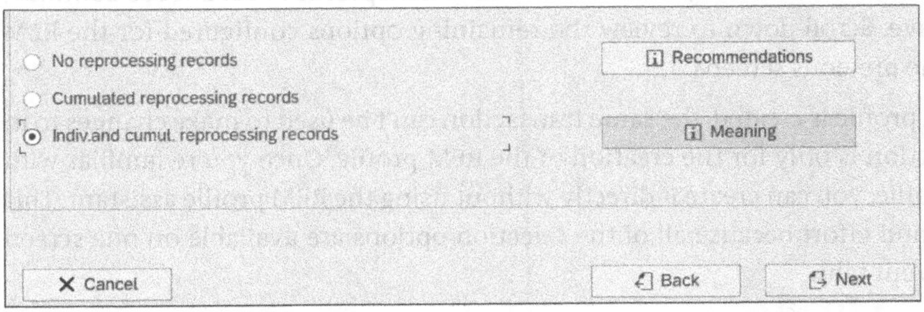

Figure 5.13 Reprocessing Incorrect Records

5.1.16 Movement Types for Stock Postings

In Figure 5.14, the system provides standard movement types that the system uses to perform various IM transactions. For example, for GI against a REM planned order, the movement type is 261, and its reversal is reflected in movement type 262.

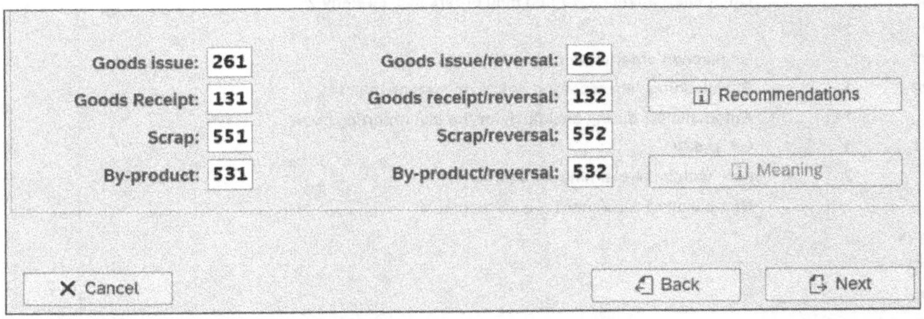

Figure 5.14 Movement Types for MTS Production

If there's any customized movement type to record an inventory transaction, then enter it on this screen. The prerequisite for using a customized movement type is that it's already maintained in the system previously and then is assigned on this screen. Choose **Next**.

5.1.17   Naming the Repetitive Manufacturing Profile

Finally, the last screen of the REM profile creation process using the assistant appears. On this screen, enter "PP10" for the **REM Profile**, and give it a short description. It's possible to go back and make changes to any of the settings so far.

5.1.18   Summary of Repetitive Manufacturing Profile Settings

Figure 5.15 shows the overview/summary screen of REM profile PP10. Choose **Continue**, and then save. Scroll down to review the remaining options configured for the REM profile in the previous screens.

After a REM profile is created, the same transaction can't be used to make changes to it; that transaction is only for the creation of the REM profile. Once you're familiar with the REM profile, you can create it directly without using the REM profile assistant. This saves time and effort because all of the selection options are available on one screen and in different tabs.

Parameter	New Value	Description of New Value
REM Profile	PP10	
Activities	2	Post activities
Costing	1	Using preliminary cost estimate for product cost collector
Backlogs	3	As 2, plus create individual postprocessing records
Error correct.	0	No online correction
Reduc.prod.qts	3	Other alternatively assigned plnd orders incl. strategy 2
Reduct.period	3	
Planned Orders		No planned order creation
Reporting point	1	Backflushing with reporting points (milestone logic)
Automatic GR	1	Automatic GR during backflush for the last reporting point
Post GR and GI	1	GR and GI
Firming logic	2	Firm within the planning time fence
Total reqmts		No totaling of dependent requirements
W/o Phant. Assys		
Process Control		
Stk Determ.Rule		
Search proced.		
Goods Issue	261	
GI/reversal	262	
Goods Receipt	131	
GR/reversal	132	
Scrap	551	
Scrap/reverse	552	

Repetitive Manufacturing Profile ASSISTANT

Figure 5.15 Overview of REM Profile after All Settings Are Made

To make changes or to update any field in the already created REM profile, follow SAP configuration menu path **SAP IMG** · **Production** · **Repetitive Manufacturing** · **Control** ·

Define Repetitive Manufacturing Profiles, or use Transaction OSP2. Here, make the desired changes to REM profile PP10. For this example, scroll down and choose **Backflush Using Standard Cost Estimate for Material** (not shown), and then save the REM profile (see Figure 5.16).

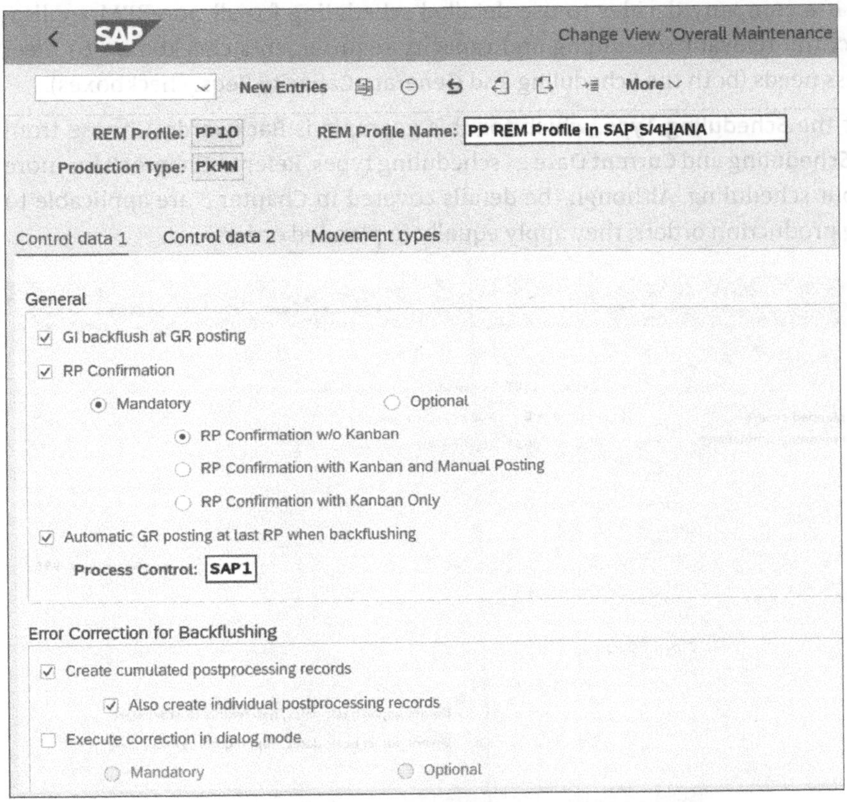

Figure 5.16 Overall Maintenance of REM Profile

5.2 Scheduling Planned Orders

The next basic configuration topic we'll discuss is scheduling planned orders. As in the discrete manufacturing or process manufacturing types, a production planner can take advantage of the available scheduling options. The scheduling parameters for planned orders in REM are set by following the configuration menu path **SAP IMG · Production · Repetitive Manufacturing · Planning · Define Scheduling Parameters for Planned Orders**. The initial screen appears for maintaining the scheduling parameters for a planned order. Because the order type for the REM planned order is PE, enter "1105" for **Plant** and "PE" for **Order Type**, and double-click the **Plant** field (**1105**). It's important to note here that the PE order type is identical to the RSQ.

After this selection, choose the **Detail** icon. This brings up the detailed screen to set scheduling parameters for the REM planned order for order type PE and plant 1105 (see Figure 5.17).

Because REM uses rate-based scheduling, select the **Takt Time/Rate-Based Scheduling** checkbox. If a company decides to use detailed scheduling for all non-REM applications, select the relevant scheduling and capacity requirements checkboxes to meet the business needs (both the **Scheduling** and **Generate Capacity Reqs.** checkboxes).

Also select the **Scheduling Type**, which for this example is **Backwards**. Choose from **Backward Scheduling** and **Current Date** as scheduling types. Refer to Chapter 3 for more details about scheduling. Although the details covered in Chapter 3 are applicable to scheduling production orders, they apply equally to planned orders.

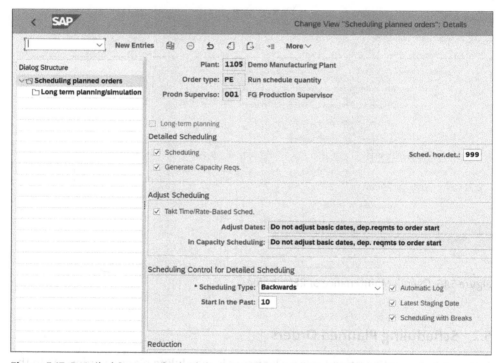

Figure 5.17 Detailed Screen of Scheduling Parameters for Planned Orders

5.3   Display

Different options to control how different settings will appear in the SAP system can be made. The following sections cover two display options.

5.3.1 Entry Parameters for a Planning Table

It's possible to choose how the display entry parameters of the REM planning table should look or how to present the requisite information. The settings you make in this section will eventually be available on the initial parameters selection screen of the REM planning table (Transaction MF50). To maintain or change the entry parameters of the planning table, follow configuration menu path **SAP IMG • Production • Repetitive Manufacturing • Planning Table • Maintain Entry Parameters** (see Figure 5.18).

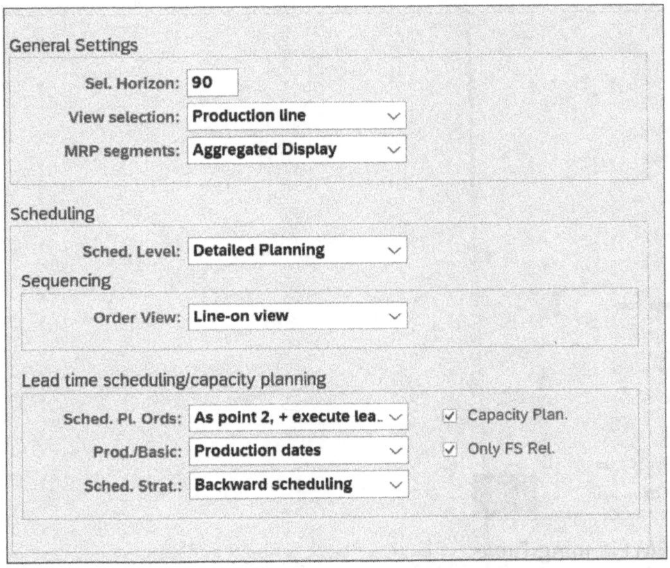

Figure 5.18 Entry Parameters of REM Planning Table

The impact of the preceding configuration on the parameters selection screen of the planning table will be visible (Transaction MF50) in Chapter 8.

5.3.2 Maintain Rows Selection

Information display within the planning table can be controlled, including receipts, requirements, and stock situations. To configure rows selection in the planning table, follow the configuration menu path **SAP IMG • Production • Repetitive Manufacturing • Planning Table • Maintain Rows Selection**. For this example, select all the checkboxes (see Figure 5.19); in a real-world situation, select only the checkboxes relevant to your business needs to keep things lean when dealing with your company's unique situation.

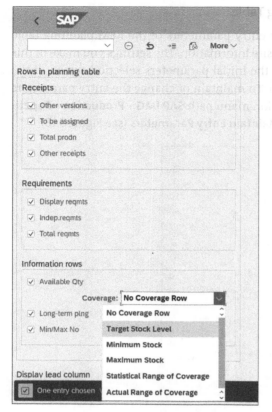

Figure 5.19 Visible Rows in REM Planning Table

5.4   Material Staging

A *pull list* is basically a movement of stock (stock transfer) from storage location to storage location that uses inventory movement type 311. It's also known as *material staging*. The previously configured stock determination and batch search procedures can be assigned on this screen. For the necessary settings, follow the configuration menu path **SAP IMG • Production • Repetitive Manufacturing • Material Staging • Define Control Data for Pull List** (see Figure 5.20).

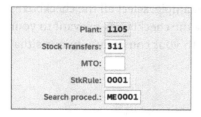

Figure 5.20 Pull List Control

5.5   Global Settings for Confirmation and the Logistics Information System

Some settings are maintained at the global level. This includes the period the system is to take into account when automatically updating statistics (the logistics information system [LIS]) of the planning figures. It also includes an option allowing a production planner to require the system to display the planned order number of the RSQ number during backflushing.

To configure the necessary settings, follow the configuration menu path **SAP IMG • Production • Repetitive Manufacturing • Backflushing • Maintain Global Settings for Confirmation and LIS**. In the **Start: Current Date+** and **Finish: Current Date+** fields (see Figure 5.21), choose to start from the current date (the earliest) and give any number of days for the future date.

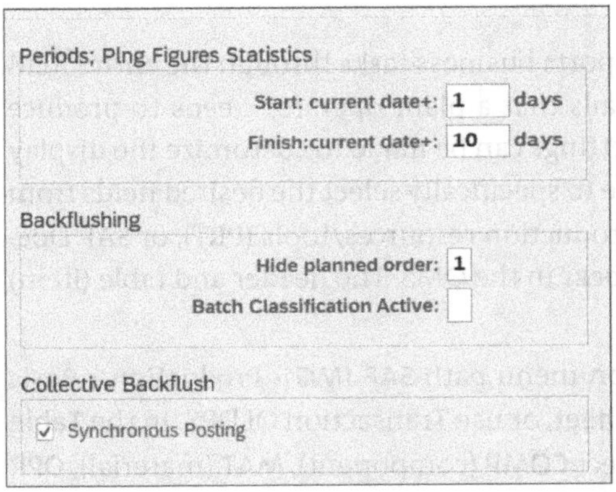

Figure 5.21 Field Selection Table in REM

When the process control for confirmation is maintained, it can control when the system should update the transactions, such as during backflush or activity costs calculation. The system can update the information immediately and online by using an update program or later in a background program. It's therefore important to ensure selecting the process control while creating the REM profile.

On the screen shown in Figure 5.22, place the cursor in the **Backflush** field and press ⏎F4; the dropdown on the right side of the screen then appears. From the dropdown, choose one of the three backflushing options available. To set the relevant parameters, use configuration menu path **SAP IMG • Production • Repetitive Manufacturing • Backflushing • Separate Backflushing Processes • Define Confirmation Processes**.

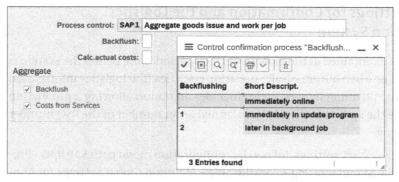

Figure 5.22 Process Control Confirmation Parameters

5.6   Operational Methods Sheet

The operational methods sheet (OMS) supports business tasks through the entire REM cycle. An OMS shows the production details that a plant operator needs to produce goods. Several layout and configuration settings can be made to customize the display layout of an OMS. For example, it's possible to specifically select the desired fields from the work center, operation, component, production resources/tools (PRT), or SAP Document Management service that must appear in the OMS. The header and table (item) details can be separately customized.

To create an OMS, follow the configuration menu path **SAP IMG · Production · Basic Data · Line Design · Operational Method Sheet**, or use Transaction OLDPS. In the **Table Assignments** area shown in Figure 5.23, select **COMP** (component), **MAT** (material), **OPR** (operation) or **PRT**, for example, from the **Table ID** column. Next, use the **Assign Fields** folder available on the left-hand side of the screen to choose the field to appear in the OMS.

Dialog Structure
- ∨ ☐ Header data template
  - ∨ ☐ Table assignments
    - ☐ Assign fields

Template: **SAPS4REM**

Table Assignments

Table ID	Table ID	No. of Word table	Automatic Adjustment	First data line
☐ COMP	COM	4	✓	2
☐ MAT	MAT	1	✓	2
☐ OPR	OPR	3	✓	2
☐ PRT	PRT	5	✓	2
☐ TST	TSK	2	✓	2

Figure 5.23 Operational Methods Sheet

In Chapter 8, we'll show how the settings made here enable displaying (and printing) the OMS in REM. Integration with Microsoft Word must be in place as well. The prerequisite is to have at least Word for Windows 95 installed and macros enabled. The template file is placed within the SAP system, which the system refers to while creating the OMS.

5.7 Summary

The REM profile is the main configuration activity, and it controls the various functions that can be performed in REM. The configured REM profile is assigned in the material master. The scheduling parameters of RSQs can be configured, and you can alter the display layout of the planning table. Controls can be maintained for when the system performs automated functions, such as backflushing, either online or in the background.

The next chapter will cover the business processes associated with discrete manufacturing in the SAP S/4HANA system. The chapter will build upon the configuration concepts and understandings that were developed in Chapter 3.

PART III
Production Planning Workflows

Chapter 6
Production Planning for Discrete Manufacturing

This chapter covers the important business processes and functions that are used in discrete manufacturing. We'll discuss vital and logical links to explain how the configurations that were made in Chapter 3 match with the business processes when dealing with products or materials that are subject to high changeability.

Discrete manufacturing, which is also interchangeably referred to as *shop floor control* (SFC) in the SAP system, is characterized by frequent changes to products on the production lines. The demand for the product is generally irregular, and often the entire production process is complex, including the routing (the sequence of work steps). The assemblies are often placed in interim storage, and the components are staged with reference to a production order.

Discrete manufacturing finds extensive implementation in the high-tech, steel sheets recoiling, pumps, textile, steel rerolling, and automobile industries. Production planning (PP) for discrete manufacturing helps with production order creation, material/capacity availability checks, variance calculation, and much more. It also helps manage and smooth out some of the related business processes that are involved with this type of manufacturing, including scheduling, costing, and goods issue/goods receipt (GI/GR). To help manage the business processes seamlessly, PP for discrete manufacturing works with most other functionalities in SAP S/4HANA.

> **Note**
>
> The master data and processes in discrete manufacturing and process manufacturing have significant similarities. While the specific master data details of process manufacturing are covered in Chapter 7, this chapter covers the general master data and process specifics in detail.

This chapter begins with an overview of discrete manufacturing and explains how it fits in the planning and production perspectives. Important discrete manufacturing master data is covered next, with extensive focus on creating a material, bill of materials (BOM), work center, routing, and finally production version. The concepts and the fundamentals covered in this chapter apply equally to process manufacturing and repetitive manufacturing (REM). After covering the master data creation, the same master data is used to cover end-to-end business processes of discrete manufacturing—from production order creation to completion and settlement.

Finally, some additional functions available in discrete manufacturing are also covered to optimize the business processes. Let's get started with an overview of discrete manufacturing.

6.1   Process Overview

Figure 6.1 illustrates the end-to-end process flow in discrete manufacturing. The process begins when requirements from manually created planned orders, material requirements planning (MRP), or sales and distribution (SD) flow in, based on which the production process must initiate.

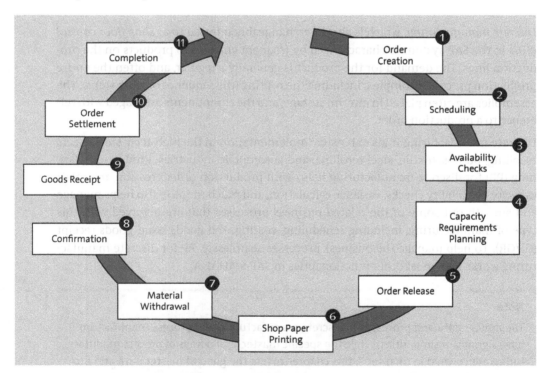

Figure 6.1 Process Flow in Discrete Manufacturing

To initiate the production process, you need a production order ❶. The system schedules the order ❷, and it checks for material and production resources/tools (PRT) requirements and their availability ❸ to see if it's able to produce the required quantities or not. It also checks for the capacity ❹ needed to produce the material. If the system is unable to find the requisite capacity, it reflects an overload.

The next step is to release the production order ❺ to enable the system to perform additional functions. Several functions can't be performed until the order is released, including printing shop floor papers ❻. The production execution step is the actual and physical production of material, and the first step toward production is material withdrawal from the warehouse ❼.

The plant operator then enters the operation or order confirmation to record the actual processing of material or production, including scrap produced or rework required ❽. The production department delivers the produced material to the warehouse, which performs the GR against the production order ❾. The last two steps reflect SAP S/4HANA Finance's controlling (CO) functionality's integration with PP, in which order settlement ❿ takes place and the production order is closed ⓫.

6.2   Master Data

Before running processes and transactions in the SAP system, it's imperative to set up complete and comprehensive master data. In discrete manufacturing (and in other manufacturing types), if the master data is set up in the right sequence, then it's much easier to connect with other types of master data because the predecessor-successor relationship is already taken care of.

The following steps outline the procedure that needs to be followed to set up master data correctly, which is discussed in more detail in the following sections:

1. Create the *material master* of the product (a finished good or an assembly) that needs to be produced. Also, create the material master for the raw material that will eventually become part of the production process.

2. Create the *BOM* of the product that needs to be produced and assign components, together with the quantities needed to produce the product. If applicable, also define a scrap percentage at the operation or component levels. Similarly, if required, also maintain details of coproducts or by-products in the BOM.

3. Create the *work center*.

4. Create a *routing* for the material and assign the previously created work center.

5. Create the *production version* for the material, and assign the material's BOM and routing to it.

Due to the highly diverse nature of the material master creation process, we cover it briefly in this chapter, while offering much greater coverage of the PP-specific master data (specifically the BOM, work center, routing, and production version).

> **Note**
> Refer to Chapter 3 for a more in-depth understanding of the configuration specifics for discrete manufacturing.

6.2.1   Material Master

A *material master* is whatever the company wants to maintain as an inventory item. Examples are far ranging and include the following: a finished product that the company first produces in-house and then sells, a raw material it procures and consumes in the production process, consumables (e.g., greases, lubricants, or gloves), trading goods that it buys and then sells, or spare parts for maintenance on machines.

Creating and maintaining information on a material master is the collective and combined responsibility of a company's various departments and divisions. A material master is a central element; therefore, everyone contributes their share of maintaining different information. In the SAP system, maintaining logically structured information absolutely helps the relevant departments efficiently perform day-to-day business functions.

[Ex]

Example

A company produces a finished good (a product). For this product, the company needs to maintain information for producing the product, selling it, maintaining planning and design data, quality control and life span, costing, and more.

More than likely, one person or department won't know all of the information related to many business functions. For example, the sales personnel may not know the quality tests a product goes through. Similarly, the production department won't necessarily care about the selling price of the product because it's primarily concerned with or focused on producing it. However, the salesperson needs instant access to selling price and the applicable taxes or discounts on creation of a sales order. Similarly, the production supervisor wants better control over the underdelivery and overdelivery tolerances allowed for a material, whereas the warehouse in charge needs instant information about storing the product.

To add greater visibility to the entire material master creation process, the SAP system provides *views* in which the relevant departments of the company (depending on which SAP functionality they're working with) can fill in their share of information. The **Basic Data** view contains basic information that is applicable to the entire material master, such as base unit of measure, gross and net weights, volume, product hierarchy, and design/drawing information. We cover the details of these views later in this section.

When creating a material master, it's also important to define the *material type*—that is, whether it's a raw material, a semifinished product, a trading good, a spare part, or a consumable item. The material type controls the views that it makes available for the user to maintain information for later use. The views contain either organization-independent or organization-dependent details. The organization-independent information includes, for example, the material description or its weight and volume. The organization-dependent information—that is, information specific to a plant or storage location—may include the planning or the forecasting data that is unique to a plant only. For a different plant (organization-dependent), the planning or forecasting data may be different.

Table 6.1 provides an overview of plant-independent and plant-dependent views of the material master. A checkmark in a column denotes the data that needs to be maintained for a given function.

Material View	Organization-Independent	Plant	Storage Location	Storage Number	Sales and Distribution
Basic Data 1 and 2	✓				
Classification	✓				
Sales: Sales Org.	✓				✓
Sales: General/Plant	✓	✓			
Foreign Trade/Export Data		✓			✓
Sales Text		✓			✓
Purchasing		✓			
Foreign Trade/Import Data		✓			
Purchase Order Text	✓				
MRP 1–4		✓			
Advanced Planning		✓			
Forecast		✓	✓		
Work Scheduling		✓			
Plant Data/Storage 1 and 2	✓	✓	✓		
Warehouse Management 1 and 2		✓		✓	
Quality Management		✓			
Accounting 1 and 2		✓			
Costing 1 and 2		✓			

Table 6.1 Material Master Views

The following is a broad explanation of the data in some of the views of the material master:

- **Basic data**

  These views consist of information such as base unit of measure, which is the smallest unit of measure in which a company maintains the product's inventory. It consists of gross weight, net weight, volume, product hierarchy, size/dimension, and design/drawing details by using the SAP Document Management service.

- **Classification**

  This view enables classifying specific materials with identical or similar characteristics into groups and categorizing those groups based on specific characteristics. Due to its diverse and practical nature, it's available in several areas of the SAP system. You can classify materials, as well as customers and equipment. When there isn't any other option to do so, classification can be used to maintain material-specific information.

- **Sales**

  These views contain details such as the delivering plant, selling unit of measure, taxes, conditions (e.g., gross price and taxes), sales order text, transportation group, loading group, and item category. These views are maintained for materials that a company wants to sell.

- **Purchasing**

  This view contains the purchase unit of measure, purchase group, material group that groups together materials with similar attributes, purchasing value key that incorporates underdelivery and overdelivery tolerances, GR processing time, and batch management. For externally procured materials, maintaining this view is mandatory.

- **MRP**

  These views enable a materials planner to define how to procure a material and how to plan and control this material within the production process. The definition of the procurement type specifies whether a company procures the material externally or produces it in-house, or if both scenarios are possible. It enables specifying whether the material follows reorder point planning or is demand-driven. Using a strategy group, controls can be maintained for whether a material uses make-to-stock (MTS), make-to-order (MTO), or assemble-to-order (ATO) production. Material planning for a procured or produced material requires maintaining some or all of the MRP views.

[»]

Note

Chapter 13 and Chapter 14 cover MRP.

- **Advanced planning**

  Production planning and detailed scheduling (PP-DS) with SAP S/4HANA introduces the advanced capacity planning and heuristics for materials planning that were previously available in SAP Advanced Planning and Optimization (SAP APO). PP-DS transactions are executed directly in SAP S/4HANA, thereby eliminating the need for a separate installation to run PP-DS transactions. The material master and the work center creation are also synchronous, which means that a material or a work center that has just been created can be immediately available for planning in PP-DS.

- **Forecast**

  This view enables a materials planner to define the forecasting parameters and models, such as constant, seasonal, moving average, or trend. If the forecasting data properties are already known, then make a selection from one of the available forecasting models. If model to select isn't known, the system provides an option for automatic model selection. It requires defining the number of historical and forecast periods, based on which the system runs forecasting.

> **Note**
>
> Chapter 11, Section 11.4 covers forecasting.

- **Work scheduling**

  This view contains details for underdelivery and overdelivery tolerances for in-house production, the production scheduler, the production scheduling profile that controls several business functions, the production unit of measure, and the production time in days. For material produced in-house, maintaining this view is mandatory. It's possible to have a different unit of measure, which in this case is the production unit of measure and may be different from the base unit of measure.

- **Plant data**

  This view contains information such as storage bin, temperature conditions, and shelf life data for batch-managed materials, including maximum storage period, minimum remaining shelf life, and total shelf life.

- **Quality management**

  This view provides the option to select different inspection types that a material may go through—for example, finished goods inspection, raw material inspection, and in-process (during production) inspection. The quality management (QM) procurement key denotes whether raw material must be quality-managed and the relevant certificate type.

- **Accounting**

  These views contain the price control indicator—that is, whether the material will be valued at a standard price or moving average price—and the valuation class.

■ **Costing**
These views contain details such as overhead group, origin group, and variance key.

> **Note**
>
> The creation of material types and also the material master is largely driven by materials management (MM) processes, with other functional areas supporting and facilitating it.

Now let's create a new material and maintain some of the important views. To create a new material master, follow menu path **Logistics · Production · Material Master · Create (General) · Immediately,** or use Transaction MM01 (see Figure 6.2). On the initial screen that appears, select **M Mechanical Engineering** as the **Industry sector** and **FERT Finished Product** from the dropdown (not shown) as the **Material Type.**

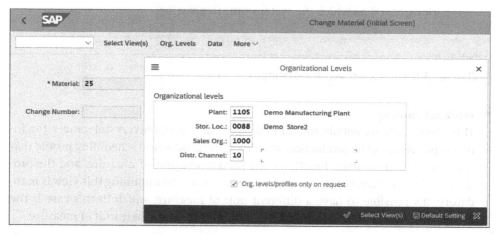

Figure 6.2 Initial Screen for Material Master Creation

Next, click the **Select View(s)** in Figure 6.2, and the screen shown in Figure 6.3 appears, showing the list of views that were briefly covered earlier. There's no need to select and maintain all the views, only those that will eventually be used in a company's business processes. For example, if material planning is not required, then there's no need to maintain **MRP** views of the material.

Select the **Basic Data** views, and the screen shown in Figure 6.4 appears, showing the **Basic Data** 1 tab of the material master. Here, the system automatically assigns it an internal material number, **25.** In this view, maintain information such as **Base Unit of Measure, Gross Weight,** and **Net Weight.** The right-hand side of the screen shows the various views that can be maintained for this material.

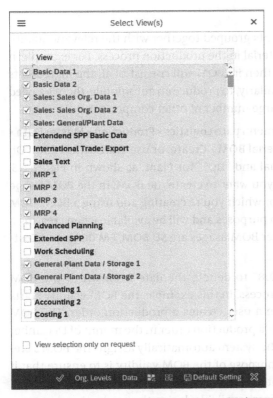

Figure 6.3 Selecting View Options in Material Master Creation

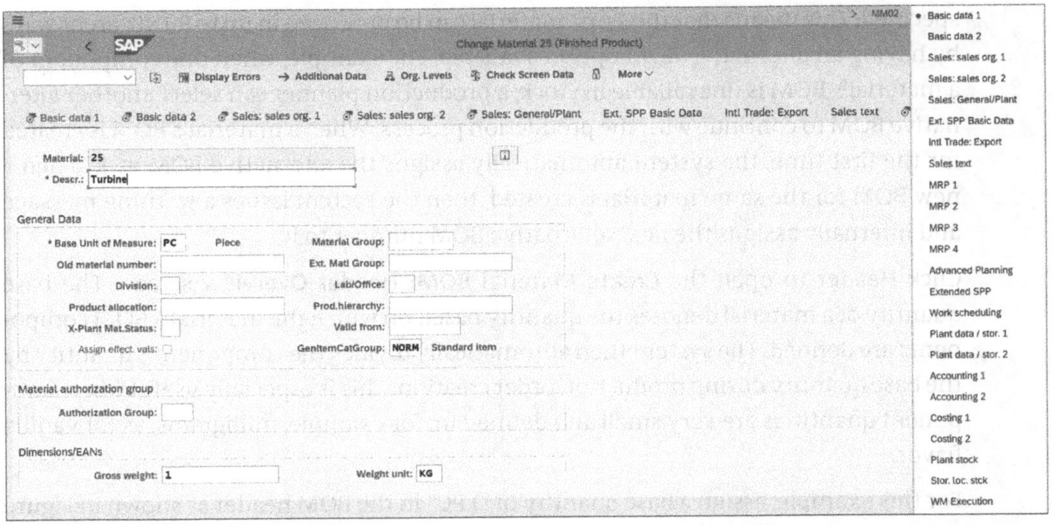

Figure 6.4 Basic Data View of Material Master

6.2.2   Bill of Materials

A material's BOM consists of components grouped together with the relevant quantities that are needed to produce the material in the production process. For example, if vanilla ice cream is the main product, then its BOM will consist of all the ingredients (components) needed to produce it. Similarly, to produce an automobile, there's a need for an engine, a chassis, a body, and a large number of other components.

To create the BOM of a material, follow menu path **Logistics • Production • Master Data • Bills of Material • Bill of Material • Material BOM • Create**, or use Transaction CS01. On the initial screen, enter "25" for **Material** and "1105" for **Plant**, as shown in Figure 6.5. This is the material number for which you want to create the BOM. In the **BOM Usage** field, enter "1" to specify the purpose for which you're creating and using a BOM. **BOM Usage 1** denotes that it's for production purposes and will be available when creating a production order for this material. Other BOM usages are **SD BOM**, **PM BOM**, and **Costing BOM**.

Enter the **Valid From** field as "11.01.2018" to denote the date from which the BOM becomes available in the production process. In this example, the BOM validity starts from January 11, 2021 (11.01.2021), when a user creates a production order. The BOM won't be available when the user creates a production order in the month of December 2020, for example. If no date is given, the system automatically assigns the BOM's creation date as the **Valid From** date. The purpose of the BOM validity is to ensure that if the company has a new BOM starting at a later date, then the validity of the new BOM can be set accordingly, which then becomes available during the production process.

In the **Alternative BOM** field, up to 99 different alternative BOMs for a material can be specified. This means that the same material can be produced in up to 99 different ways by having an alternative BOM option available. For example, when one component of a material's BOM is unavailable in stock, a production planner can select another alternative BOM to continue with the production process. When a material's BOM is created for the first time, the system automatically assigns the alternative BOM as 1. When a new BOM for the same material is created, then the system issues a warning message and internally assigns the next alternative BOM number to it.

Click **Header** to open the **Create Material BOM: Header Overview** screen. The base quantity of a material denotes the quantity based on which the material's BOM components are defined. The system then automatically divides the component's quantity by the base quantity during production order creation. This is especially useful when component quantities are very small and defined in, for example, milligrams, as for vanilla flavor.

For this example, assign a base quantity of "1 PC" in the BOM header as shown in Figure 6.5. The components and their quantities that you define in the BOM now denote the requirements to produce one piece of material 25.

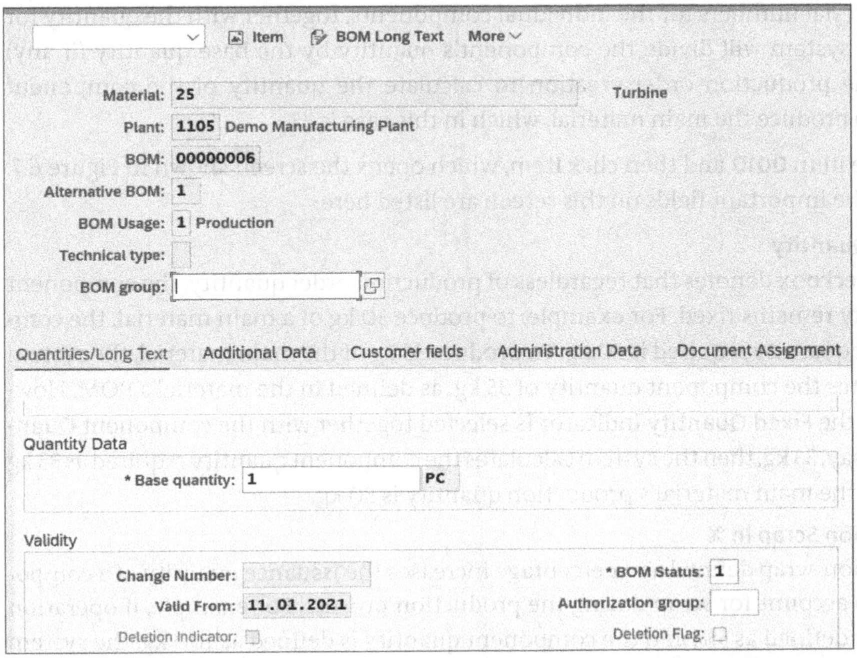
Item
BOM Long Text
More
Material: 25
Turbine
Plant: 1105 Demo Manufacturing Plant
BOM: 00000006
Alternative BOM: 1
BOM Usage: 1 Production
Technical type:
BOM group:
Quantities/Long Text
Additional Data
Customer fields
Administration Data
Document Assignment
Quantity Data
* Base quantity: 1
PC
Validity
Change Number:
* BOM Status: 1
Valid From: 11.01.2021
Authorization group:
Deletion Indicator:
Deletion Flag:

Figure 6.5 BOM Header

The **BOM Status** field controls whether the BOM is active and is available for usage. The value 1 denotes that it's active. If there's a business need to deactivate a BOM, then simply changing the status of the BOM to **Inactive** at any time will serve the purpose.

Click the **Item** button to go to the screen shown in Figure 6.6, which shows the item overview of the BOM.

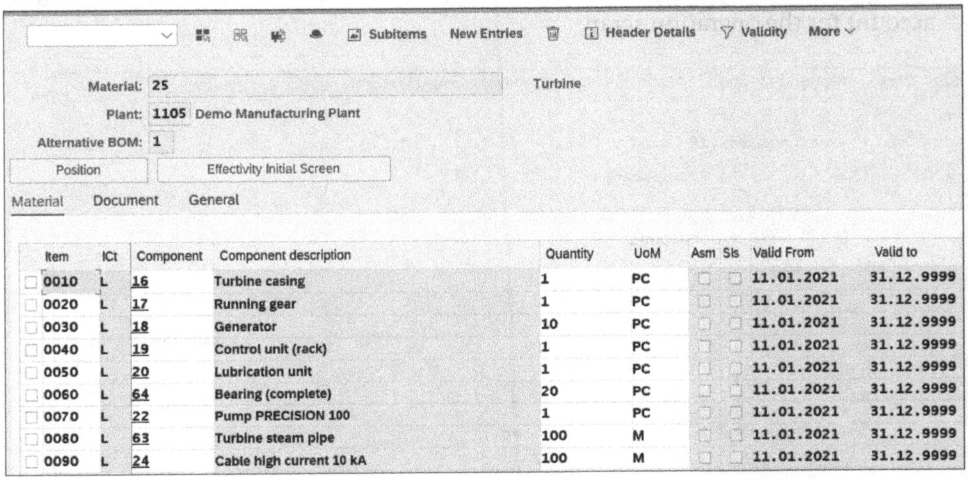
Subitems
New Entries
Header Details
Validity
More
Material: 25
Turbine
Plant: 1105 Demo Manufacturing Plant
Alternative BOM: 1
Position
Effectivity Initial Screen
Material
Document
General
Item ICt Component Component description Quantity UoM Asm Sls Valid From Valid to
0010 L 16 Turbine casing 1 PC 11.01.2021 31.12.9999
0020 L 17 Running gear 1 PC 11.01.2021 31.12.9999
0030 L 18 Generator 10 PC 11.01.2021 31.12.9999
0040 L 19 Control unit (rack) 1 PC 11.01.2021 31.12.9999
0050 L 20 Lubrication unit 1 PC 11.01.2021 31.12.9999
0060 L 64 Bearing (complete) 20 PC 11.01.2021 31.12.9999
0070 L 22 Pump PRECISION 100 1 PC 11.01.2021 31.12.9999
0080 L 63 Turbine steam pipe 100 M 11.01.2021 31.12.9999
0090 L 24 Cable high current 10 kA 100 M 11.01.2021 31.12.9999

Figure 6.6 BOM Item Overview

Enter material numbers for the individual components, together with the quantity for each. The system will divide the component's quantity by the base quantity (if any) during the production order creation to calculate the quantity of the component needed to produce the main material, which in this case is 25.

Select line item **0010** and then click **Item**, which opens the screen shown in Figure 6.7. Some of the important fields on this screen are listed here:

- **Fixed Quantity**

  This checkbox denotes that regardless of production order quantity, the component quantity remains fixed. For example, to produce 50 kg of a main material, the component quantity required is 50 kg. To produce 35 kg of the main material, the system calculates the component quantity of 35 kg, as defined in the material's BOM. However, if the **Fixed Quantity** indicator is selected together with the component **Quantity** of, say, 35 kg, then the system calculates the component quantity required as 35 kg even if the main material's production quantity is 50 kg.

- **Operation Scrap in %**

  Operation scrap defined as a percentage increases the issuance quantity of a component to account for scrap during the production process. For example, if operation scrap is defined as 5%, and the component quantity is defined as 100 kg, the system automatically calculates the required component quantity as 105 kg to account for the operation (during production) scrap. It's mandatory to select **Net ID** (not shown) when defining operation scrap.

- **Component Scrap (%)**

  Component scrap is defined as a percentage increase of the issuance quantity of a component to account for scrap during the production process. For example, if component scrap is defined as 10%, and the component **Quantity** is defined as 100 kg, the system automatically calculates the required component quantity as 110 kg to account for the operation scrap.

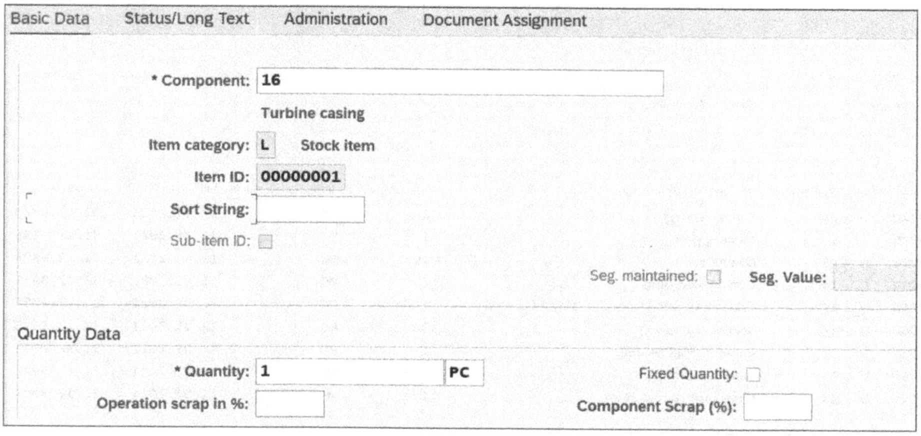

Figure 6.7 Detailed View of BOM Item

If both scrap types that are selected are defined (operation scrap as well as component scrap), the system considers both scrap types during the component quantity calculation. During the MRP run, the system takes all of these scrap definitions into account to suggest planning proposals.

Scroll down the screen (see Figure 6.8). If the normal production of a product also generates a coproduct, then select the **Co-product** checkbox.

If the production process in a business scenario entails that the main material can also be one of its BOM components, then this is only possible if the **Recurs.** (recursive) **Allowed** checkbox is selected.

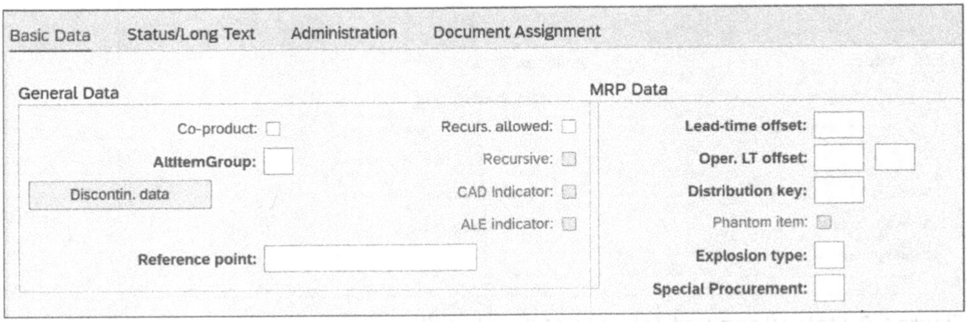

Figure 6.8 Additional Details in BOM Item

In the **MRP Data** area of the screen, the **Lead-Time Offset** field helps with planning a component's availability. For example, to produce material as soon as the first shift starts in the morning, a production supervisor approaches the warehouse supervisor to issue the requisite components one day earlier. To handle this scenario, enter "–1" so that the component's required availability date is one day earlier than the planned start date of the production. The negative number of the workday reflects that the production supervisor needs components earlier than the start date of production, and a positive number of days is used to show that there's no need to have the components until the defined number of days after the start of production. The system ignores this option if the production process follows lead-time scheduling (and not just basic date scheduling). To enable this behavior for lead-time scheduling, assign the components to the corresponding operations in the routing. Note that such a positive or negative lead time is always independent from lot size.

The **Special Procurement** field enables a materials planner to define a component-specific special procurement, like a phantom assembly or a procurement from another plant. Maintaining a special procurement type at the component level gives it a higher precedence than at the material level. During an MRP run, the system explodes the material BOM and evaluates parameters maintained at the component level for planning purposes before it looks for the information at the material level.

Click the **Status/Lng Text** tab shown in Figure 6.7 to see the fields in Figure 6.9.

Enter the **Prod. Stor. Location**. During the backflush process in SFC, the system looks for information in this field because it acts as an issue storage location. If the customer or vendor supplies the material instead of the company using its own material in production, then select the relevant option from the **Mat. Provision Ind.** dropdown field. Finally, it's also possible to control whether the component is considered during product cost calculation or if the system excludes it by selecting the relevant option in the **CostingRelevncy** field.

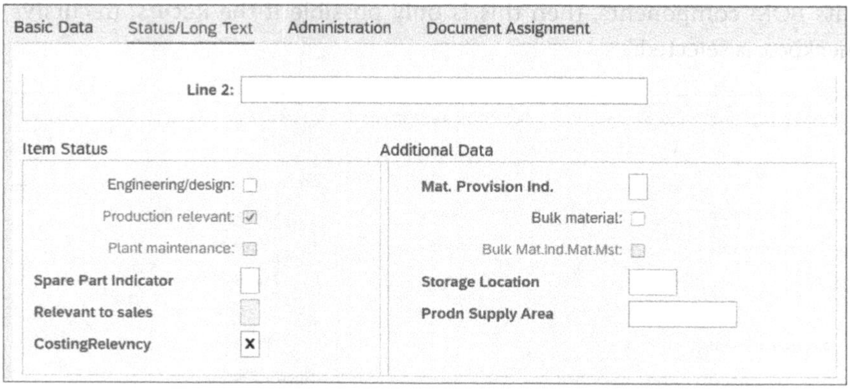

Figure 6.9 Status/Long Text Tab of BOM Item Details

[+] **Tips and Tricks**

Mass changes to BOMs can be made to attend to any new business requirements. For example, a materials planner might want to replace an old and obsolete component number in all of the material BOMs in which it's currently in use or to change the component's quantity in all of the material BOMs in which it's in use. For such business scenarios, use Transaction CS20 to make mass changes to the BOM. On the upper half of the screen, define the selection criteria; in the lower half of the screen, define the changes that need to be made. When making the desired changes, be sure to select one of the several radio buttons available.

6.2.3   Work Center

A *work center* can be a production facility, a processing unit, a machine or group of machines, or even a laborer or group of laborers directly involved in the production process. It's also possible to group together machines and laborers in a single work center. To create a work center, follow menu path **Logistics · Production · Master Data · Work Centers · Work Center · Create**, or use Transaction CR01.

> **Note**
>
> For process industries, create a resource by following menu path **Logistics • Production – Process • Master Data • Resources • Resource • Resource • Create**, or use Transaction CRC1.

On the initial screen, enter **Plant** "1105" for the relevant new work center. It's mandatory to assign a plant while creating a work center. Enter the **Work Center** as "TURBO1". This is an alphanumeric identification to denote a work center. Enter "0001" in the **Work Center Category** field; this is a control function used to ensure that only the relevant screens are eventually available during work center creation. Work center category 0001 denotes a machine, whereas 0007 denotes a production line.

Other important functions on the screen are **Copy from Plant** and **Copy from Work Center.** Select the checkboxes of the reference work center views that need to be copied to the new work center. These functions help in reducing data entry efforts during the new work center creation by automatically making available all of the necessary information from the reference work center to the new work center, which you can change as needed.

In the following sections, we'll cover the various tabs available in a work center and the data to be maintained, as well as the data's impact on business processes.

Basic Data

Click the **Basic Data** tab of the work center, and enter a short description of the work center. In the **Usage** field, enter "009" (see Figure 6.10). A *usage* is a control function that controls whether this work center eventually becomes available for various other tasks, such as the creation of a routing or the production version. Usage 009 denotes using this work center in all task list types.

Two important fields on this screen are as follows (not shown):

- **Shift Note Type**
  A *shift note* is an option to record the important shift-related details of a work center. These can be general details of the shift, as well as any specific problems encountered at this specific work center during the production process.

- **Shift Report Type**
  A *shift report* compiles and consolidates all of the information from a single shift note or multiple shift notes and is available either in PDF format or other formats, as well as in the layout defined for a company. The user can also digitally sign a shift report before a printout is possible and send a shift report by email.

Recall from Chapter 3 that we discussed the configuration of the **Standard Value Key** field, in which you entered "SAP1". The standard value key (SVK) consists of three activities to note and record during the production process when the TURBO1 work center was used. An SVK denotes activities performed on the work center, as well as the option to record them or otherwise. Some of the activities are production time, setup time, processing time, or labor time. If you enter "SAP1", the system automatically brings up three activities (**Setup**, **Machine**, and **Labor**) for which the actual details in the confirmation process are recorded (see Figure 6.10).

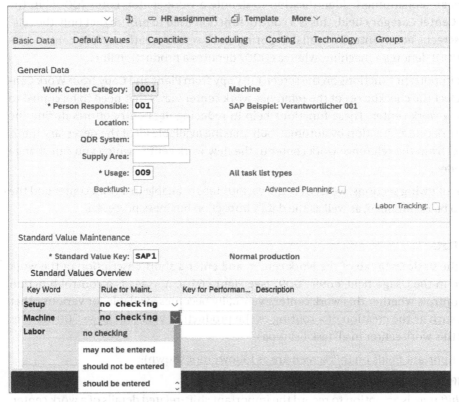

Figure 6.10 Basic Data View of Work Center

Enter "Machine" under **Key Word**, and select **3 Must Be Entered** under **Rule for Maint**. If this activity is marked as **Must Be Entered**, then during the creation of a routing, the production supervisor is required to enter the actual duration of the activity; otherwise, the system won't allow you to save the routing. Other maintenance options are **May Not Be Entered**, **Should Not Be Entered**, and **Should Be Entered**, which offers various degrees of control, from an information message to a warning message, if the requisite information (duration, in this case) isn't recorded during confirmation.

In addition, select the **Backflush** checkbox on this screen so that the system automatically issues components at the work center (in this example, TURBO1) during the confirmation process.

> **Note**
>
> In Chapter 3, we made the field settings that require the selection of the **Backflush** field.

Default Values

Click the **Default Values** tab to see the options shown in Figure 6.11.

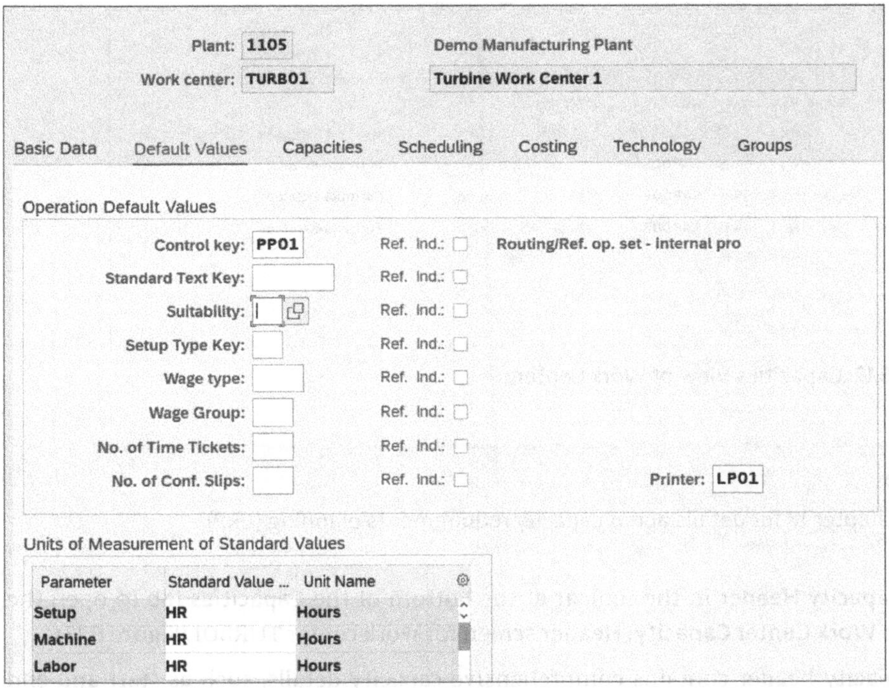

Plant:	1105		Demo Manufacturing Plant
Work center:	TURBO1		Turbine Work Center 1

Basic Data   Default Values   Capacities   Scheduling   Costing   Technology   Groups

Operation Default Values

		Ref. Ind.: ☐	Routing/Ref. op. set - internal pro
Control key:	PP01		
Standard Text Key:		Ref. Ind.: ☐	
Suitability:	| ⌗	Ref. Ind.: ☐	
Setup Type Key:		Ref. Ind.: ☐	
Wage type:		Ref. Ind.: ☐	
Wage Group:		Ref. Ind.: ☐	
No. of Time Tickets:		Ref. Ind.: ☐	
No. of Conf. Slips:		Ref. Ind.: ☐	Printer: LP01

Units of Measurement of Standard Values

Parameter	Standard Value ...	Unit Name	⚙
Setup	HR	Hours	
Machine	HR	Hours	
Labor	HR	Hours	

Figure 6.11 Default Values View of Work Center

Assign the **Control key** "PP01" to the work center. A *control key* is a control function that determines whether a production supervisor can perform an activity or a task associated with the work center or not. A control key controls several functions, such as scheduling, cost, automatic GR, print confirmation, and print. If any of the checkboxes of the control key aren't selected, then that step or function on this work center (TURBO1) can be performed. For example, if the **Scheduling** checkbox isn't selected in the control key, then the system won't perform scheduling on this work center.

[»]

Note

Chapter 3, Section 3.3.6, covers how to configure a control key.

Capacities

Click the **Capacities** tab to see the options shown in Figure 6.12. Enter "SAP005" in **Setup Formula**, which denotes the setup formula that the system will use during capacity calculation. For the **Processing Formula**, enter "SAP006", and for the **Teardown Formula**, enter "SAP007". These formula entries are for **Capacity category 001**, which is for **Machine**.

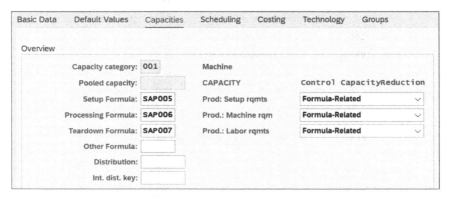

Figure 6.12 Capacities View of Work Center

[»]

Note

See Chapter 18 for details about capacity requirements planning (CRP).

Click **Capacity Header** in the toolbar at the bottom of the **Capacities** tab to open the **Change Work Center Capacity: Header** screen for work center TURBO1 (Figure 6.13).

The capacity header contains comprehensive capacity details, such as start and end time of shift, breaks, overload percentage allowed for capacity, shifts and intervals, and factory calendar.

[»]

Note

Refer to Chapter 2 for information about setting up the factory calendar and capacity planner group.

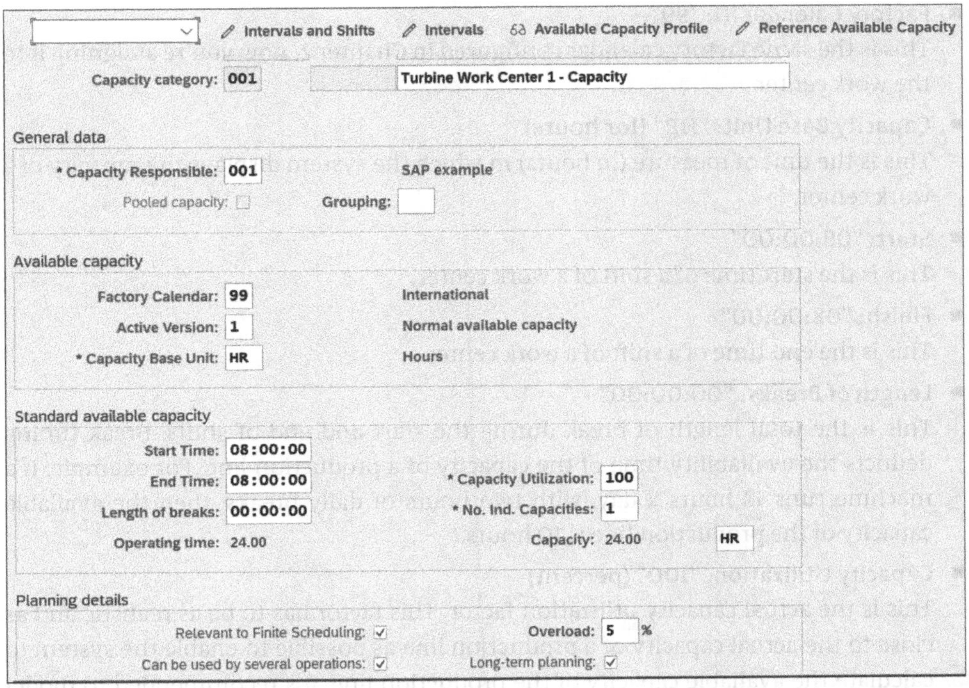

Figure 6.13 Capacity Header

For this example, maintain the following in each field:

- **Short Text for Capacity (not shown): "Turbine 01"**
  This short text describes the capacity category—for example, a specific production line or machine.

- **Capacity Responsible: "001"**
  It's important to assign a capacity planner group to a work center so that during evaluation of capacities, the capacity planner group can be one of the evaluation criteria. The capacity planner group shouldn't be the name of the person but instead the name of the area or domain of responsibilities.

- **Grouping: "51"**
  If, apart from the normal shift timings during the entire calendar year (factory calendar), a company has any specific slow or busy seasons in which either an increase or decrease in the number of shifts or intervals takes place, then a production planner can logically group these using the grouping function. For example, in several countries, Fridays have longer breaks; in other countries, Saturday is a half working day. Such business scenarios can be addressed using grouping, which doesn't fall under normal start, finish, and break timings.

6

- **Factory Calendar ID: "99"**
  This is the same factory calendar configured in Chapter 2; now you're assigning it to the work center.

- **Capacity Base Unit: "HR" (for hours)**
  This is the unit of measure (in hours) in which the system displays the capacity of a work center.

- **Start: "08:00:00"**
  This is the start time of a shift of a work center.

- **Finish: "08:00:00"**
  This is the end time of a shift of a work center.

- **Length of Breaks: "00:00:00"**
  This is the total length of break during the start and end of shifts. Break timing deducts the availability time of the capacity of a production line. For example, if a machine runs 12 hours a day, with two hours of daily breaks, then the available capacity of the production line is 10 hours.

- **Capacity Utilization: "100" (percent)**
  This is the actual capacity utilization factor. This factor has to be as realistic and as close to the actual capacity of a production line as possible to enable the system to calculate the available capacity of the production line. It's recommended to model for statistically unforeseen downtimes. When the SAP system has built up a significant amount of data, use one of many available statistics reports on capacities to update the information in this field. For example, say that a capacity planner has maintained a value of 100% in this field, but the statistics reports reveal that capacity is never utilized by more than 90%. In this case, updating the information to 90% here ensures realistic and practical capacity planning, and there's a greater confidence in the system-generated results. (Refer to Chapter 19 on reporting.)

- **No. Ind. Capacities: "1"**
  This is the number of individual capacities associated with a production line. For example, four individual ice cream mixers are created as one production line. Thus, the individual capacities are four in number and directly multiplied by the timings for the capacity of the production line. For example, if the available capacity of a production line is 10 hours in a day, and there are four individual capacities, then the total available capacity of the production line is 40 hours. If splitting is going to be used in a routing and you will also define the number of splits, then it's important to also define the number of capacities because the system checks for this information during scheduling.

- **Relevant to Finite Scheduling**
  This checkbox causes the work center to consider capacity overload during capacity evaluation.

- **Overload: "5%"**
  A capacity overload in percentage directly increases the capacity availability of the production line by the defined percentage. If, for example, the total capacity of a production line is 40 hours with 10% overload, then the available capacity is 44 hours. A 10% overload of 40 hours is four hours, and it adds up to 40 hours to show the total available capacity at 44 hours.

- **Long-Term Planning (checkbox)**
  This checkbox enables the system to consider the production line availability during long-term planning (LTP). LTP typically is a simulative planning of material and production lines over a longer period.

> **Note**
> See Chapter 16 for detailed information on LTP.

Click the **Intervals** button, and then in the screen shown in Figure 6.14, you can assign specific intervals or shifts that are applicable for the defined duration. For this example, define that from **01.01.2022** until **01.10.2022**, there will be a shift **Sequence** consisting of a seven-day cycle (**Length of Cycle**).

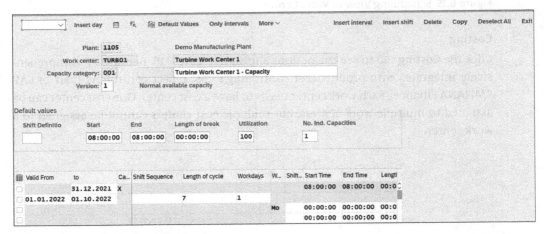

Figure 6.14 Interval in Capacity Header

Scheduling

Click the **Back** icon, then click the **Scheduling** tab to see the options shown in Figure 6.15. Enter the standard formulas available for discrete manufacturing, as covered in detail in Chapter 3.

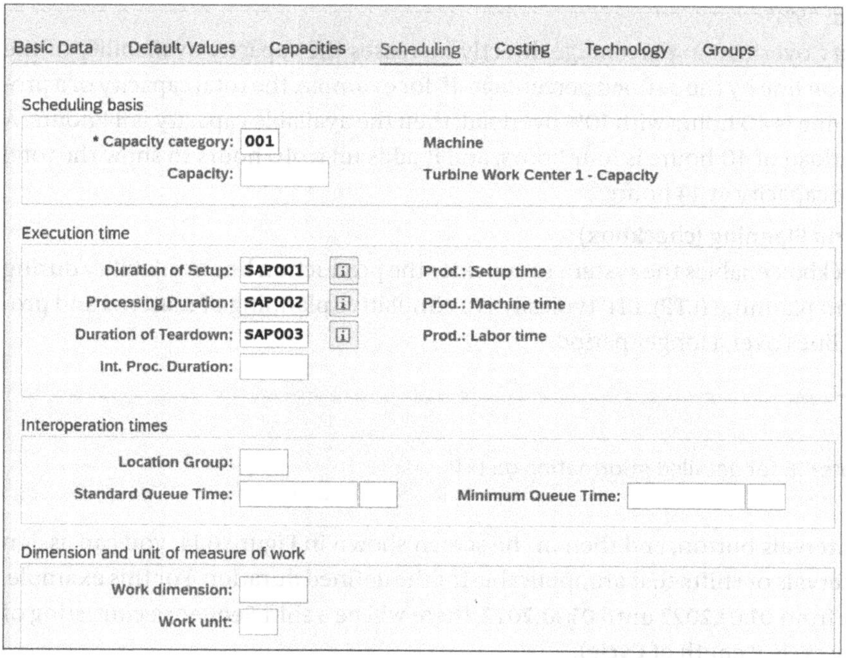

Figure 6.15 Scheduling View of Work Center

Costing

Click the **Costing** tab to see the options shown in Figure 6.16. Because PP comprehensively integrates with product cost controlling's cost object controlling (part of SAP S/4HANA Finance), each work center needs to have a cost center. One cost center can be assigned to multiple work centers, but multiple cost centers cannot be assigned to a work center.

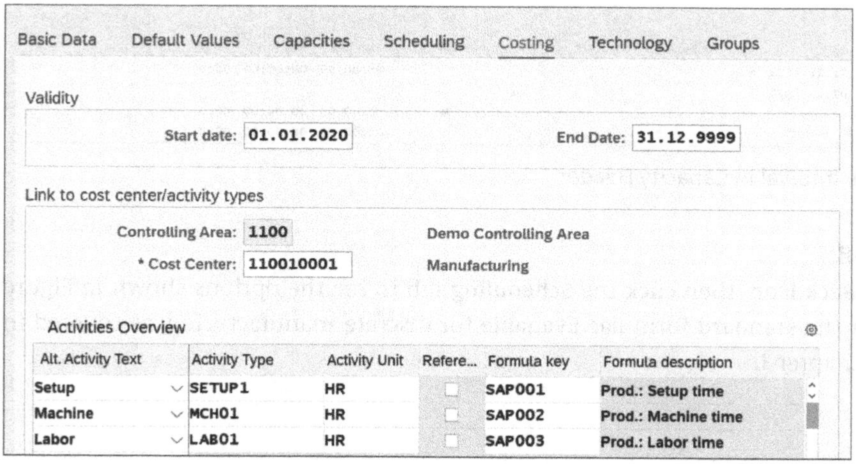

Figure 6.16 Costing View of Work Center

6

> **Note**
> Coordinate with the CO person to ensure that each cost center and associated activity type for the given controlling area has price planning. In the same step, ensure that activity types and cost centers are already in place so as to assign them in the work center. This is an integration point between PP and CO.

Enter the following details:

- **Start Date: "01.01.2020"**
  This is the start date of the availability of the cost center for the work center.

- **End Date: "31.12.9999"**
  This is the end date of the availability of the cost center for the production line.

- **Cost Center: "110010001"**
  Every work center requires direct assignment of a cost center so that when work is performed using the work center, the system is able to accumulate all of the costs on the designated cost center.

- **Activity Type (Alt: Activity Text Setup): "SETUP1"**
  The activity type denotes the predefined rate at which the system calculates the costs incurred to perform machine setup.

Repeat the same process of entering activity types and formulas for the other remaining two activities, **Machine** and **Labor**, and then save the work center.

6.2.4   Routing

The routing of a material can contain a series of operations. The operation details are defined for each operation based on the production quantity, production time, and associated unit of measure. You assign work centers to the routing, which should also contain an SVK, in which the standard values for setup time, production time, and teardown time are defined. The routing is the sequence of logical production processes through which a product will, for example, transform from a raw material into a finished product.

To create the routing of a material, follow menu path **Logistics • Production • Master Data • Routings • Routings • Standard Routings • Create**, or use Transaction CA01.

Figure 6.17 shows the initial screen to create a routing. Enter the **Material** as "25" and **Plant** as "1105". In the **Key Date** field, enter "14.03.2021" to denote the date when the routing becomes available in the production process. Because the routing validity starts on March 14, 2021 (14.03.2021), when a production planner creates a production order—for example, for the month of January 2021—this routing won't be available.

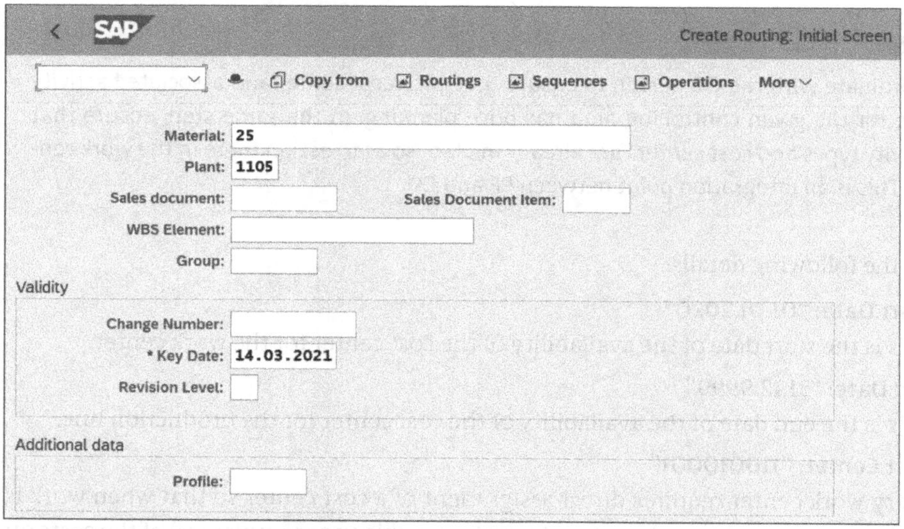

Figure 6.17 Initial Screen for Routing

If no date is given during routing creation, then the system automatically assigns the routing's creation date as the valid from date.

The following sections will discuss the various elements and options available in the routing.

Header Details

Click **Routings**. In the header details of the routing, shown in Figure 6.18, enter the following:

- **Usage: "1" (for Production)**
  This makes the routing available during subsequent production activities, in which the system uses the routing during production order creation.

- **Status: "4" (for Released)**
  This makes the routing available during subsequent production activities, in which the system uses the routing during creation of the production order. If the status of the routing is set to **Being Created** (1), it won't be available when you create a production order for the material.

- **Planning Work Center: "TURBO1"**
  This is the work center that was previously created and is now used in the planning and production of the material.

Note

Normally, a production planner should have several work centers already created before creating a routing. The **Planning work center** field should either be left open/

blank or made to include the "bottleneck" work center that the production planner wants to evaluate during the planning process.

The **From Lot Size** field denotes that the smallest quantity of the production order must be at least 1 PC for the system to consider using this routing. The **To Lot Size** field denotes the maximum quantity of the production/order.

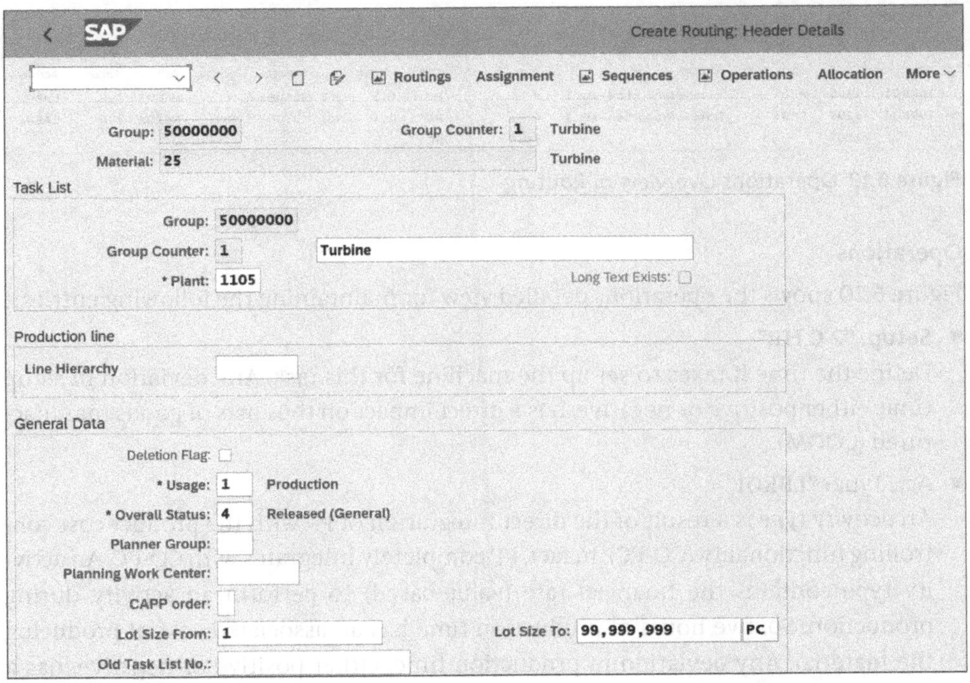

Figure 6.18 Header Details in Routing

The **Parameters for Dynamic Modification/Inspection Points** area of the screen is the integration point between PP and QM in SAP. The parameters entered here determine whether the system carries out an inspection for the inspection type, for the individual inspection lot, or for the master inspection characteristics.

Note

Because QM also integrates with discrete manufacturing, we recommend engaging a QM resource for this activity.

Click the **Operation** button to access the screen in Figure 6.19, where you can maintain the **Work Center** as "TURBO1". This denotes assigning a previously created work center to an operation, which is used in the production of material and for which the routing is being created. An operation defines, for example, a single-level detail of a production step. The second work center, TURBO2, denotes the second step in the production process. Double-click **Operation 0010**, which opens the screen in Figure 6.20.

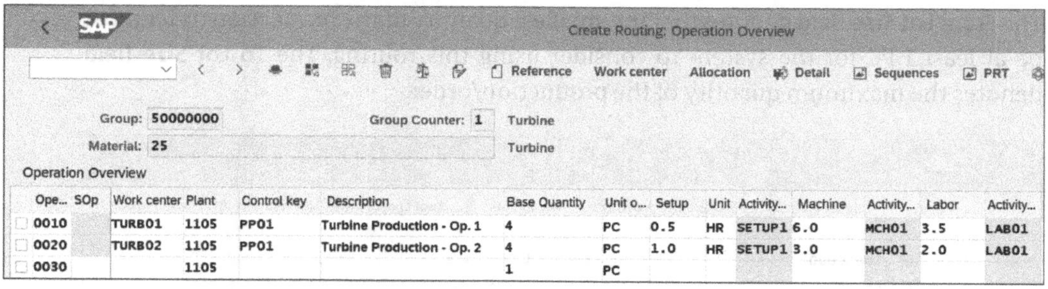

Ope...	SOp	Work center	Plant	Control key	Description	Base Quantity	Unit o...	Setup	Unit	Activity...	Machine	Activity...	Labor	Activity...
0010		TURBO1	1105	PP01	Turbine Production - Op. 1	4		PC	0.5	HR	SETUP1 6.0	MCH01	3.5	LAB01
0020		TURBO2	1105	PP01	Turbine Production - Op. 2	4		PC	1.0	HR	SETUP1 3.0	MCH01	2.0	LAB01
0030			1105			1		PC						

Figure 6.19 Operations Overview of Routing

Operations

Figure 6.20 shows the operations detailed view for maintaining the following entries:

- **Setup: "2.0 HR"**
  Define the time it takes to set up the machine for this task. Any deviation in setup time, either positive or negative, has a direct impact on the costs of goods manufactured (COGM).

- **Act. Type: "LBRO1"**
  An *activity type* is a result of the direct integration of PP with the product cost controlling functionality (CO-PC). In fact, PP completely integrates with CO-PC. An activity type contains the financial rate (value-based) to perform an activity during production. So, five hours of production time has an associated cost of producing the material. Any deviation in production time, either positive or negative, has a direct implication on the COGM.

- **Machine: "1.0 HR"**
  Recall that you defined in the work center that recording duration information in the routing is mandatory (in the rule for maintenance when the **Must Be Entered** option was selected), so it's mandatory to define the time it will take in this work center's operation of the manufacturing process.

- **Labor: "1.0 HR"**
  Define the time it takes to dismantle or tear down the setup of the machine or the production line. Any deviation in teardown time, either positive or negative, has a direct implication for COGM.

Enter the **Act. Type** for each of the three activities: **Setup**, **Machine**, and **Labor**. These durations are for the **Base Quantity** of **4 PC** of material **25** produced.

Notice that the system automatically incorporates the **Control Key** that was defined in the work center, **TURBO1**, in the previous step.

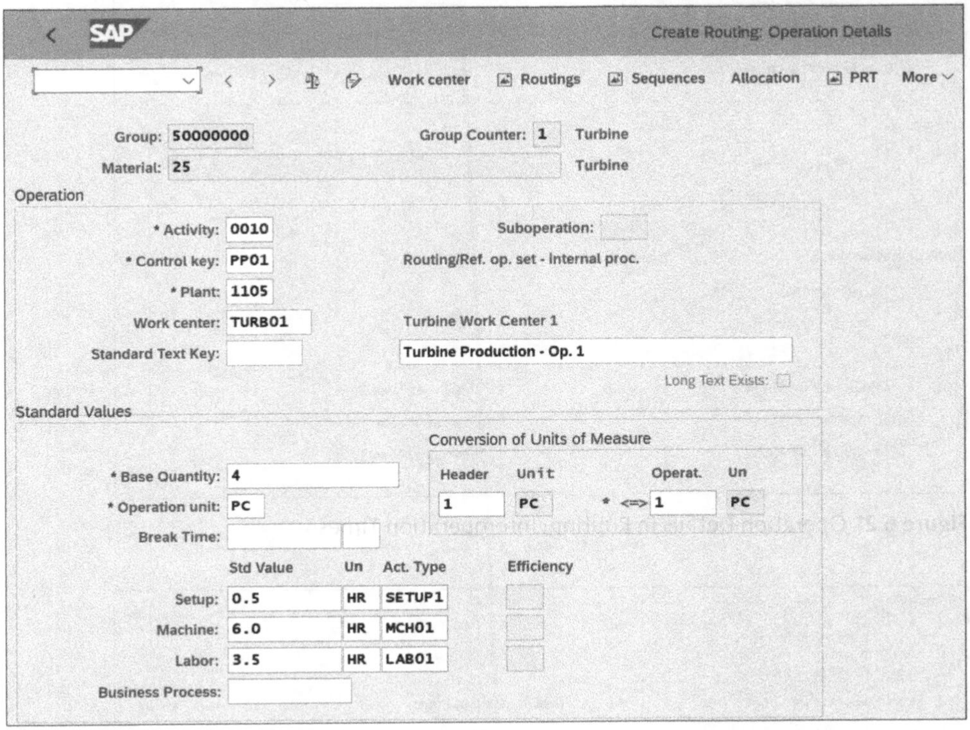

Figure 6.20 Operation Details in Routing

Scroll down to see the screen area shown in Figure 6.21. Here, assign the reduction strategy that was configured for plant 1105 in Chapter 3. Selecting the **Teardown/Wait Parallel** (simulation) checkbox here enables a planner to see simulated details during scheduling. Normal and minimum interoperation times can be defined. The interoperation times consist of wait time, queue time, and move (transport) time. During reduction—that is, during scheduling conflicts in basic dates—the system switches to minimum interoperation times, as well as further reduction based on the reduction strategy and reduction levels defined.

Scroll down the same screen to see the screen areas shown in Figure 6.22. With **Splitting**, a production planner can divide a large production lot into several smaller lots provided there are several individual capacities to manage it. The system checks the number of splits with individual capacities defined in the work center.

With **Overlapping**, the system passes the processed parts of the total lot directly on to the next machine. Define the minimum overlap time and the minimum send-ahead quantity to the next operation if there's a business need for it.

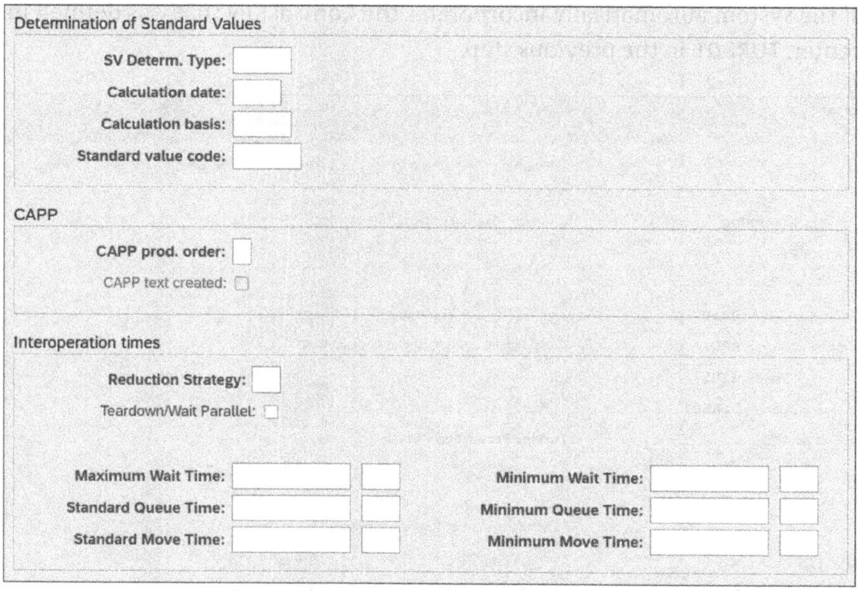

Figure 6.21 Operation Details in Routing: Interoperation Times

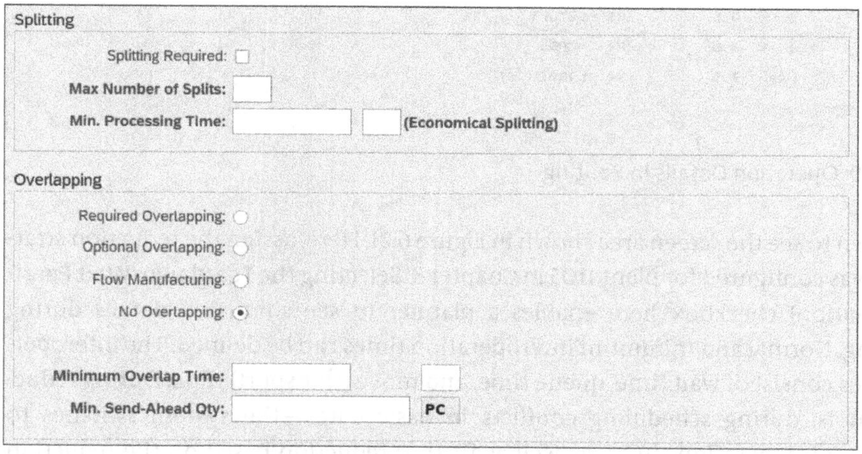

Figure 6.22 Item Details in Routing: Splitting and Overlapping

The information in the **General Data** tab (see Figure 6.23) relates to the percentage scrap (planned) for the operation and integrating with the HR system. For example, the person doing the confirmation on the shop floor can be integrated with the HR system.

Scroll down further on the same screen to see the screen area shown in Figure 6.24. Here, the **Subcontracting** checkbox reflects the details that can be maintained in case the material processing involves subcontracting. A subcontracting process entails engaging the services of a vendor to perform some of the steps in the production process, for which either there isn't an in-house expert or the company finds it more cost-effective to outsource those steps.

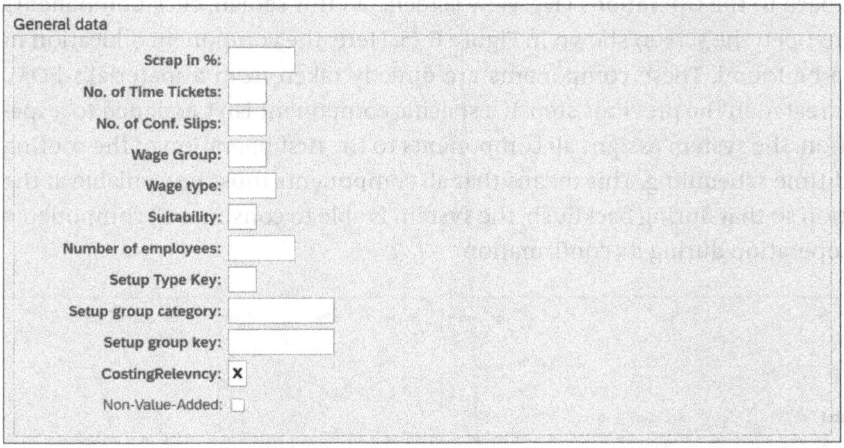

General data

Scrap in %:	
No. of Time Tickets:	
No. of Conf. Slips:	
Wage Group:	
Wage type:	
Suitability:	
Number of employees:	
Setup Type Key:	
Setup group category:	
Setup group key:	
CostingRelevncy:	X
Non-Value-Added:	☐

Figure 6.23 Item Details in Routing: General Data

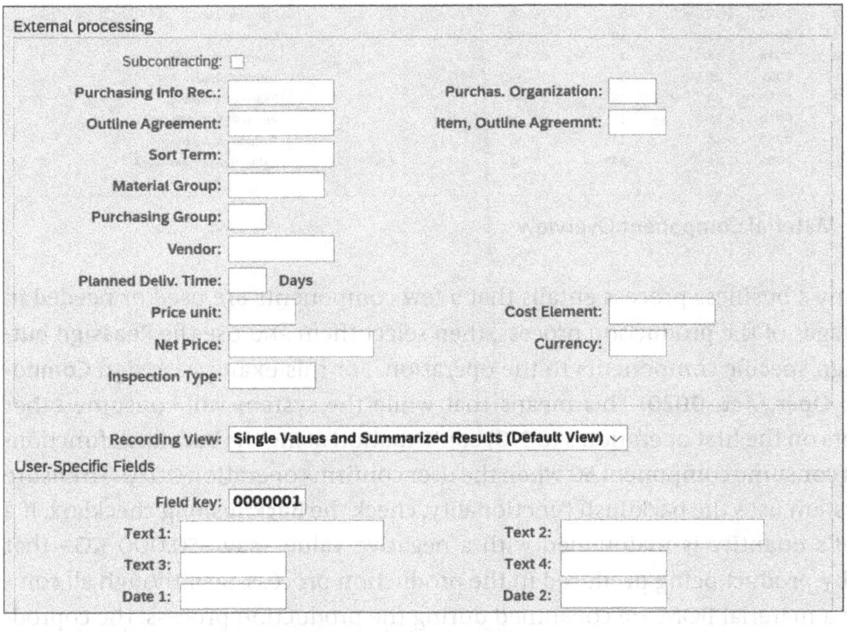

External processing

Subcontracting: ☐			
Purchasing Info Rec.:		Purchas. Organization:	
Outline Agreement:		Item, Outline Agreemnt:	
Sort Term:			
Material Group:			
Purchasing Group:			
Vendor:			
Planned Deliv. Time:	Days		
Price unit:		Cost Element:	
Net Price:		Currency:	
Inspection Type:			

Recording View: Single Values and Summarized Results (Default View) ⌄

User-Specific Fields

Field key: **0000001**

Text 1:		Text 2:	
Text 3:		Text 4:	
Date 1:		Date 2:	

Figure 6.24 Item Details in Routing: Subcontracting

Select the **Subcontracting** checkbox and maintain the procurement details in the remaining fields. When a production planner creates a production order for the material, the system will simultaneously create a purchase requisition for the subcontracting operations. The **User-Specific Fields** section can be used to maintain additional details related to routing that can't be maintained elsewhere.

Components Assignment

Next, press F6, or follow menu path **Goto • Operations Overview**, and the system brings you back to the **Operations Overview** screen. On this screen, click **Components Allocation** to open the screen shown in Figure 6.25. Here, the component allocation in routing can be found. These components are directly taken from a material's BOM, which you created in the previous step. If a specific component isn't assigned to a specific operation, the system assigns all components to the first operation of the routing during lead-time scheduling. This means that all components must be available at the first operation so that during backflush, the system is able to consume all components in the first operation during its confirmation.

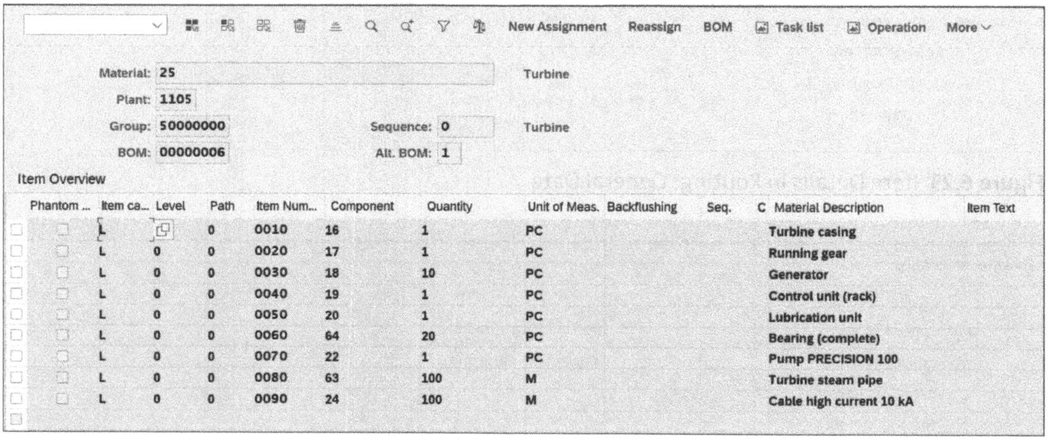
New Assignment
Reassign
BOM
Task list
Operation
More
Material: 25
Turbine
Plant: 1105
Group: 50000000
Sequence: 0
Turbine
BOM: 00000006
Alt. BOM: 1
Item Overview
Phantom ... Item ca... Level Path Item Num... Component Quantity Unit of Meas. Backflushing Seq. C Material Description Item Text
L 0 0010 16 1 PC Turbine casing
L 0 0 0020 17 1 PC Running gear
L 0 0 0030 18 10 PC Generator
L 0 0 0040 19 1 PC Control unit (rack)
L 0 0 0050 20 1 PC Lubrication unit
L 0 0 0060 64 20 PC Bearing (complete)
L 0 0 0070 22 1 PC Pump PRECISION 100
L 0 0 0080 63 100 M Turbine steam pipe
L 0 0 0090 24 100 M Cable high current 10 kA

Figure 6.25 Material Component Overview

If a company's business process entails that a few components are used or needed in the later stages of the production process, then select them and use the **Reassign** button to assign specific components to the operation. For this example, assign **Component 50** to **Oper./Act. 0020**. This means that while the system will consume other components on the first operation's (0010) confirmation using the backflush functionality, it will consume component 50 when the user confirms operation 0020. To ensure that the system uses the backflush functionality, check the **Backflushing** checkbox. If a component's quantity is maintained with a negative value—say, -50.000 KG—that denotes a by-product being produced in the production process. So although all components in a material BOM are consumed during the production process, the coproducts or by-products are generated or produced.

Material Assignment

Go back to the routing header screen, click **MatlAssignment**, and the popup shown in Figure 6.26 appears. **Material 25 in Plnt 1105** is assigned an internal group as 50000000 with the group counter (**GrC**) set to 1. Later, we'll use this group (50000000) and the group counter (1) to create the next PP master data element, which is the production version. It's important to add that every combination of a group and the group counter reflect certain planned working processes.

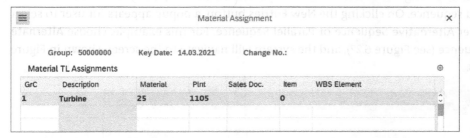

Figure 6.26 Material Assignment

Several materials together with their respective plants can be assigned to this routing group. All such materials belonging to this routing group will have the same group but will have ascending group counter numbers.

> **Tips and Tricks**
>
> If there are several materials undergoing the same production process, there's no longer a need to create separate routings for each. Just create one routing and assign relevant materials (with plants) to it. This saves time and effort in creating an important master data element (routing) and also eliminates or reduces redundant data entry efforts.

Sequences

Whenever we refer to routing, we imply that it will be a sequence of operations in a logical order. For example, when we define operations 10, 20, and 30 for a routing, we indicate that operation 10 will be the first step of the production process, then operation 20, and finally operation 30. It also means that we confirm the operations in the same sequence. However, you can also maintain parallel and alternate sequences in routing. *Parallel sequences* enable you to split up the production process if you can carry out specific production steps of an order simultaneously. *Alternative sequences* represent alternatives that enable you to produce a product in the production process in different ways.

The sequence overview can be called by clicking the **Sequences** icon in the initial routing screen. The sequence overview displays all parallel and alternative sequences contained in the routing:

- The system numbers the sequences and also contains a sequence category. The standard sequence contains sequence category 0.

- The parallel sequences contain sequence category 1.
- The alternative sequences contain sequence category 2.

When a routing is first created and an operation is defined, the system contains a standard sequence. On clicking the **New Entries** button, a popup appears for user to select either **Alternative Sequence** or **Parallel Sequence**. For this example, choose **Alternate Sequence** (see Figure 6.27), and the system will navigate to the screen shown in Figure 6.28.

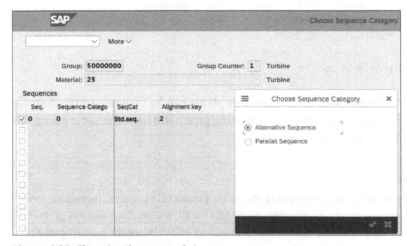

Figure 6.27 Choosing Sequence Category

In Figure 6.28, **Sequence 1** refers to the first sequence with reference to the original operation's sequence, which is **0**. The **Branch Operation** field stipulates the operation during which the system should proceed with the parallel sequence. The **Return Operation** field denotes the operation number that the system must return to or branch back to after the parallel operation. It's mandatory to define the return operation.

Figure 6.28 Sequence Details

Figure 6.28 shows a sequence overview for material 25. It stipulates that the system will branch off to an alternate sequence on operation **0010** and will return to a standard sequence in operation **0020**. For the alternative sequence, you can define the minimum and maximum lot sizes (**Lot Size From** and **Lot Size To**) that are applicable for the alternative sequence.

Production Resources and Tools

Production resources and tools (PRTs) are movable operating resources that you can assign to internal and external operations in the routing. Examples of PRTs include tools, materials, documents or drawings, and test equipment. PRTs play an important role in facilitating the production process. For example, to move heavy metal containers from one production line to the next, you need a pair of large metal hooks, which is a PRT.

You can assign a PRT to an operation of a routing by clicking the **PRT** icon. On the screen shown in Figure 6.29, assign a **Material** PRT "26", and assign a **Quantity** of "1.000". You can use this screen to create more PRTs, such as documents and equipment, by using the corresponding **Document** and **Equipment** buttons.

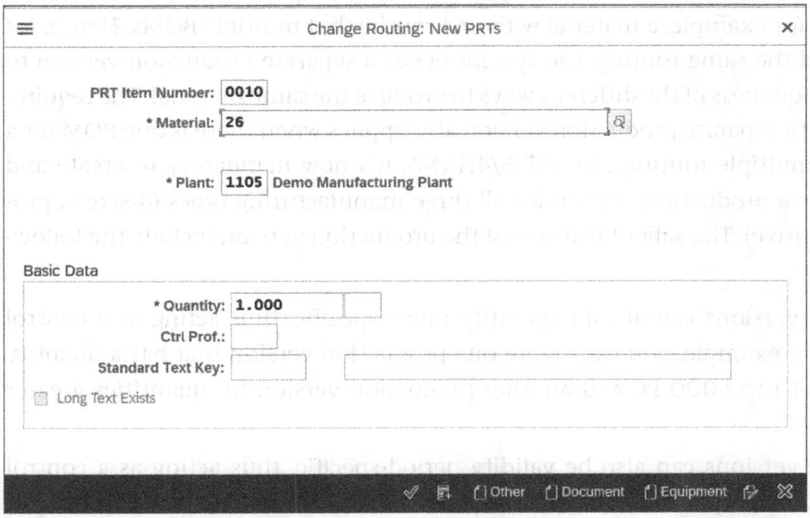

Figure 6.29 PRT Assignment

Delete Task List

One of the advantages of PP master data is that the master data can be deleted from the system, which avoids having to archive it. Problematic master data—for example, a wrongly created a work center or an incorrect routing—can be deleted. Any PP master data that isn't in use can also be deleted.

To delete a routing or, in fact, any task lists (e.g., rate routing, master recipe, or inspection plan), use Transaction CA98. On the initial screen, enter the selection parameters and choose the relevant deletion options.

Engineering Workbench

The Engineering Workbench can be used to create or make changes to PP master data, such as BOMs or routings. The Engineering Workbench is an interactive and intuitive tool to enable making collective changes to, for example, BOM headers of several materials at once.

Use Transaction CEWB to access the Engineering Workbench. In the initial popup, select the work area to work on. The work area can be the BOM header, BOM item, routing header, or routing item. On the parameter selection screen, enter the parameters, and then choose **Load BOMs and Task Lists**. In the ensuing worklist, make the desired changes to PP master data or create a new worklist.

6.2.5   Production Version

Production versions denote different ways in which a company produces a material. This includes, for example, a material with one routing but multiple BOMs. Hence, for each BOM and the same routing, the system needs a separate production version to denote the uniqueness of the different ways to produce the same material. The requirement to create a separate production version also applies when there is one BOM for a material but multiple routings. In SAP S/4HANA, it's now mandatory to create and make available a production version for all three manufacturing types (discrete, process, and repetitive). The salient features of the production version include the following:

- Production versions can also be quantity range-specific, thus acting as a control function. For example, you can create one production version that has a quantity limitation of 1 to 1,000 PC and another production version for quantities greater than 1,000 PC.

- Production versions can also be validity period-specific, thus acting as a control function. For example, there may be one production version that is valid from April 1, 2019, until March 31, 2020. From April 1, 2020, on, there may be a new production version. When the system has to assign a production version to the production order, it searches for specific validity dates. When the system finds the relevant production version, it automatically assigns it.

- If the system is able to find multiple production versions fulfilling the search and application criteria, it assigns the first available production version to the production order.

To facilitate production version creation in SAP S/4HANA, a new report, report CS_ BOM_PRODVER_MIGRATION, is available. To execute the report/worklist, use Transaction SE38, enter "CS_BOM_PRODVER_MIGRATION" on the screen that appears, and click **Execute** or press F8. On the screen that appears, choose materials and the associated plants; alternately, simply entering a plant will bring up all the materials for which BOMs exist and the qualities for production version creation. To simulate production version creation, choose the **Run in Simulation Mode** radio button and click **Execute**. To create production versions in actual mode, choose the **Run in Actual Mode** radio button.

A production planner can choose to approve individual, selective, or all production versions creation and then click **Approve**. A message appears to confirm creation of the production version.

To create a new production version, follow SAP menu path **Logistics • Production • Master Data • Production Versions**, or use Transaction C223.

In Figure 6.30, and in the **Selection Conditions** area, enter the **Plant** as "1105", enter the **Material** as "25", and then press Enter. If the system is unable to find any production version for the material, then the lower half of the screen is blank. If it does find versions, then the system displays the relevant production versions.

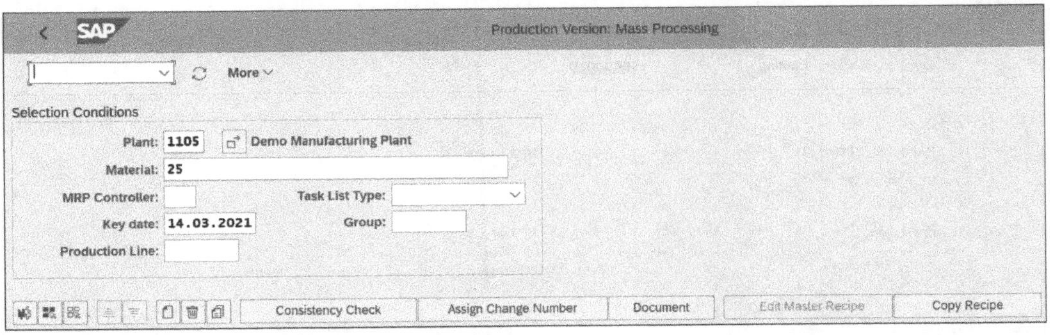

Figure 6.30 Production Version Initial Screen

From the menu bar available at the center of the production version creation screen, you have just about all of the options normally needed while creating production version master data. This includes copying, deleting, copying from a template, and so on. Choose **Create Production Version** to open the screen shown in Figure 6.31. Enter the basic details, such as **Plant** "1105", **Production Version** "0001", **Production Version Text**, **Valid from** "14.03.2021", and **Valid to** "31.12.9999".

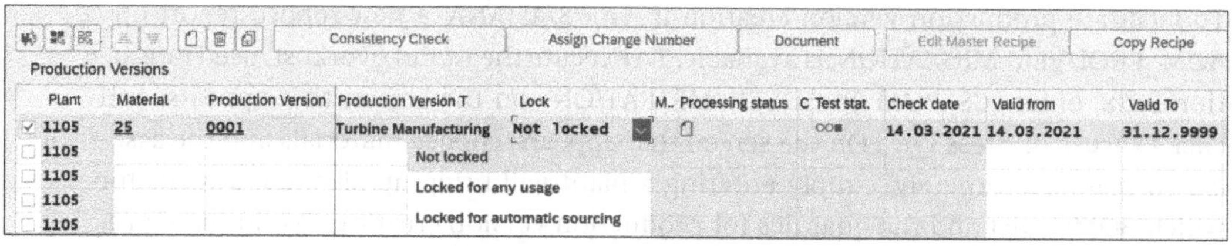

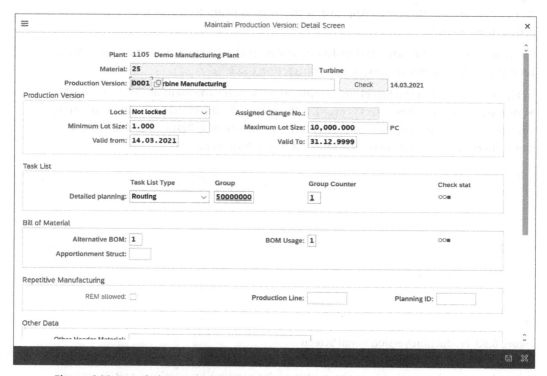

Figure 6.31 Overview Screen of Production Version

Select the first line item, and double-click it, or click the **Detail** icon, which brings up the screen shown in Figure 6.32.

Figure 6.32 Detailed Screen of Production Version

Enter the details as listed in Table 6.2.

Field	Value	Additional Details/Remarks
Material	25	—
Production Version	0001	—

Table 6.2 Parameters Entry in Production Version

Field	Value	Additional Details/Remarks
Valid From	14.03.2021	This field is the start of the validity date of the production version.
Valid To	31.12.9999	This field is the end of the validity date of the production version.
Detailed Planning	**Routing** (N)	Task list type **N** denotes that it's a routing. Each task list type represents a different function. Type list type **R** represents a rate routing, whereas task list type **Q** represents a quality inspection task list. Enter the routing that was created in the previous step. For this example, enter routing **Group** "50000000" and a **Group Counter** of "1".
Alternative BOM	1	This is the BOM that was crated in the previous step.
BOM Usage	1	This field is the BOM usage, where 1 refers to the usage production.

Table 6.2 Parameters Entry in Production Version (Cont.)

The **Lock** field provides the flexibility to lock or unlock the production version anytime to allow or restrict accesses to the production version during production order creation. A locked production version won't be available for selection during production order creation.

Finally, click the **Check** button located at the top right-hand side of the screen to evaluate whether the details incorporated in the production version, such as BOM and routing, are correct and valid. It's important to note here that data in the production version that doesn't make sense can be added, such as selecting an incorrect work center as a production line.

The system confirms that it's able to find a relevant task list (routing), as well as a BOM, which meets the other criteria of the production version. This includes having validity dates of the routing and BOM, which falls within the validity specified in the production version, as well as the lot sizes mentioned in the production version (see Figure 6.33). Click the **Cancel** icon.

The green traffic lights for the task list and the BOM denote that the consistency check was successful, and this production version will be available to users during production order creation. If a warning or error is observed during consistency check, the system denotes it with a yellow or a red sign, respectively. In the production version, it's possible to check if previously created and unchecked production versions are still valid or not.

Click **Close Detailed Screen and Adopt Changes**, then save the production version.

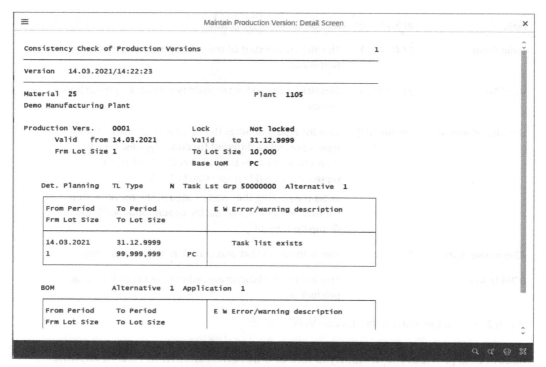

Figure 6.33 Results of Production Version Consistency Check

6.3   Production Order Management

The *production order* is the formal element that informs the production department how to proceed with producing a product. It contains details of production quantities, the components required to produce the material, the operations (consisting of work centers) that are involved in production, and the scheduling details of production, among many other details. Due to the highly integrated nature of production with CO-PC, all planned costs are in place when a production planner first creates the production order.

The master data of a material that was covered in the previous sections forms the core and the central information for the production order. In other words, when a production order is created for a material, the system looks for its BOM, routing, and production version (if applicable). The system copies all of the information from the master data so that minimal efforts are involved in production order creation. Regardless of whether a production order is created by converting planned orders from MRP or manually, the system fetches the master data in the production order. It's also possible to individually or collectively convert planned orders of MRP into production orders. Further, a production order can also be created without reference to any planned order.

The production order is also the central component used to record and update all of the activities or functions that the users perform. For example, a production planner can manually or automatically enable the system to check and perform the following functions or activities in the production order (depending on the configuration settings): checking material or capacity availability, generating the control instruction, calculating planned costs, and more.

Later, when performing functions with reference to the production order, such as GI, confirmation, or yield/scrap updates, the system keeps updating the information.

The production order consists of the following elements, which we'll discuss in the following sections:

- **Header data**
  Contains organizational information such as the order number and costs, quantities, and dates for the order as a whole.

- **Operations data**
  Contains detailed operation dates, default values, and the confirmed quantities and dates.

- **Components data**
  Contains detailed information about components, such as the requirements quantity and reservation number.

- **Reread master data**
  Enables rereading the master data to ensure the production order has the most up-to-date information.

- **Statuses**
  Controls and displays various system or user-defined statuses of a production order.

- **Trigger points**
  Contains detailed information about trigger points—that is, actions or statuses that trigger other actions.

To create a production order, follow menu path **Logistics · Production · Shop Floor Control · Order · Create · With Material**, or use Transaction CO01.

On the initial production order screen, enter **Material** "25", production **Plant** "1105", and order **Type** "PP10", as configured in Chapter 3. Choose **Continue**.

6.3.1 Header Data

Figure 6.34 shows the header data screen of the production order. It consists of information that is applicable to the entire order, such as production order number, the material number, the plant, and the order type. The **General** tab includes the planned production quantity, the scrap quantity, the scheduling details, and the reduction details. If a planned order was converted into a production order, the system automatically copies the details from the planned order, such as quantity, scrap percentage (and its equivalent quantity), BOM, routing (if available), scheduling, and capacity details.

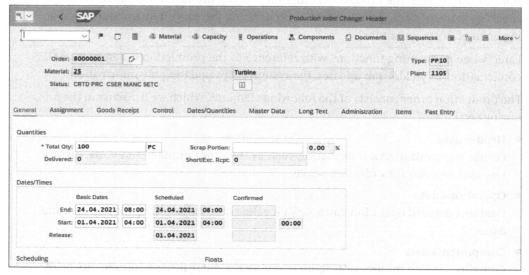

Figure 6.34 Production Order Header

When subsequent business functions, such as confirmation, are performed, the system automatically updates the relevant fields, at both the production order level and the operation level.

Note the large number of system statuses, which the system keeps on updating as a production planner continues to perform business functions. These business functions can include activities such as releasing or printing the production order, providing confirmation, and closing or locking the production order.

Further, if **User Status** is set up at the production order level, then it also becomes visible just below the **System Status** in the production order header.

The following is some of the information available in various tabs of the production order header:

- **Assignment**
  This view contains the responsible MRP controller, the production scheduler, the sales order number and its item number (for MTO production), and the work breakdown structure (WBS) element (for engineer-to-order [ETO]).

- **Goods Receipt**
  This view contains control parameters for goods movements, deviation tolerances, GR processing time, and production location.

- **Control**

  This view contains the parameters for the calculation, the production scheduling profile, and the control parameters for scheduling: creating capacity requirements, scheduling allowing for breaks, and automatic rescheduling in the event of scheduling-relevant changes.

- **Dates/Qties**

  This view contains the overview of planned and actual times and quantities.

For this example, in the **Total Qty** field shown in Figure 6.34, enter "100". The system automatically calculates the **Scrap Portion** field if it was maintained in the **Assembly Scrap** field of the **MRP 1** view of the material master. Because we configured the system to perform backward scheduling, it asks for the end basic date. Enter "24.04.2021", and the system automatically calculates the **Start Basic Date**. Notice that it takes the floats into account, as **Sched. Margin Key 001** (not shown) is in place and enables the system to calculate schedule dates. It also performs reduction up to level 2.

Let's now evaluate the information maintained in the operations view of a production order. Click the **Operation Overview** icon.

6.3.2   Operation Overview

The **Operation Overview** screen details the sequence in which a product will undergo a production process. It uses information from the routing and the operations that are scheduled for the order. The system denotes each operation with an operation number, together with the associated work center and the control key that you defined in the work center. The control key determines the functions that the user can perform for an operation, such as printing and whether confirmation is required or not allowed. It also controls scheduling and CRP. Other details that are available in this screen are trigger points, the PRTs, and an assignment flag for material components.

Figure 6.35 shows the **Operation Overview** screen of a production order. Double-click **0010** in the **Op.** column and the system will navigate to the operation detail screen.

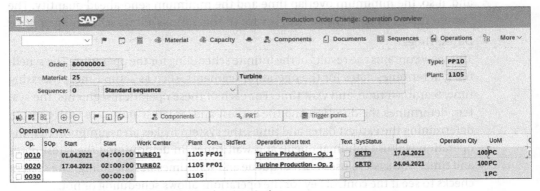

Figure 6.35 Operation Overview in Production Order

The detail operation screen shown in Figure 6.36 has several tabs, of which some of the important ones are described here:

- **General**
  This view contains general information on the operation, such as the percentage scrap, number of shop floor papers to print, and setup type key. It also contains the cost calculation relevance indicator, which specifies whether the operation is included in the cost calculation.

- **Default Values**
  This view contains the default and standard values copied from the routing and directly relates to the operation quantity—that is, the planned values for performing the operation and the corresponding units of measure.

- **Ext. Processing**
  This view contains information on externally processed operations such as subcontracting, which involves operations processed at the supplier's end. The material-supplier relationship known as the *purchasing info record* is entered in this view. The system checks to see if the control key for the operations allows external processing or not. If it doesn't, then details related to external processing can't be maintained.

- **Transition Times**
  This view contains scheduling data that affects the operation segments outside the execution time. This data includes the reduction strategy and level and the pertinent transition times: wait time, queue time, and move time. The system checks to see if the control key for the operation allows scheduling or not.

- **Splitting**
  In this view, maintain splitting data that controls whether, how, and when an operation may or must be split during the scheduling. The system checks to see if the control key for the operations allows scheduling or not.

- **Overlap**
  In this tab, maintain data on operations that the system can consider in overlapping during production order scheduling. The system verifies if overlapping is required and, if so, the minimum overlap time and the minimum send-ahead quantity. The system checks to see if the control key for the operations allows scheduling or not.

- **Dates/Times**
  This view contains the results of the infinite scheduling for the operation. The scheduling determines dates for the operation segments, such as setup time, processing time, teardown time, and wait time. For each of these operation segments, the system determines the duration and the earliest and/or latest start date with time. In determining the earliest dates and times, the system makes an assumption that the operation will use minimal queue and wait times. In determining the latest dates and times, the system uses normal queue and wait times in scheduling. The system checks to see if the control key for the operations allows scheduling or not.

- **Qties/Activities**
  In this view, the system displays the confirmed quantities and activities for the operation.

- **Dates Confirmed**
  This view contains the actual processing dates for the operation.

- **Capacity Requirement Assignment**
  In this view, the total requirement of the operation can be split into subrequirements.

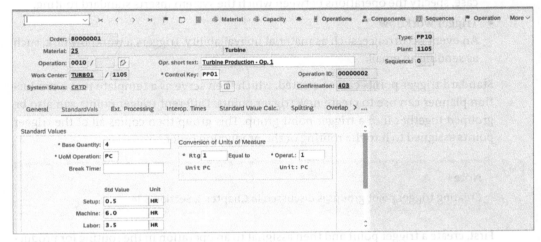

Figure 6.36 Detailed View of Operation

6.3.3 Standard Trigger Points

As an SAP system consultant or a business process owner, it's always a good approach to look for ways to optimize existing business processes and functions, especially when the processes have matured and the company can transition from manual intervention to automation.

Using a *trigger point* enables the system to perform predefined functions when an event occurs in a production order. Trigger points automatically trigger functions—for example, releasing all subsequent operations when the first operation is released. Trigger points can be assigned in the routing or to individual production orders.

The following functions can be performed with trigger points:

- **Release of directly following operations**
  An event occurrence triggers the automatic release of the subsequent operations.

- **Release up to release point**
  An event occurrence triggers the release of all subsequent operations, up to and including the next operation, which is given the **Release Stop** indicator.

- **Release of previous operations**
  An event occurrence triggers the release of all previous operations.

- **Create order with template**
  An event occurrence (e.g., a material is faulty) means that the system creates a new production order to postprocess the material. The system creates an order using standard routing without reference to a material.

- **Include standard routing**
  An event can incorporate a standard routing in an existing production order. In this case, specify the operations between which the system inserts standard routing.

- **Trigger workflow**
  An event occurrence, such as material unavailability, triggers a workflow task, such as sending an email.

Standard trigger points can be created, which then serve as a template that a production planner can use to create new trigger points. Different trigger points can also be grouped together into a trigger point group. This group then copies all of the trigger points assigned to it to the routing or the production order.

[»]

> **Note**
> Creating trigger point groups is discussed in Chapter 3, Section 3.14.

First, create a trigger point and then assign it to an operation in the routing (or production order). Give a short text for the trigger point, and then assign this trigger point to the **TrigPointUsage** "FERT" and **TriggerPtGroup** "FERT".

Next, select the **TrigPointFuncts** checkbox in the **Usage** area, then select one of the trigger point functions, such as **Release Succeeding Operations** when the **Syst.Sts** (system status) is **CRTD** (created). Click the **Parameters** icon, and the **Parameters for Function** popup appears. Here, specify an event so that when the system status of the operation of an order is **CRTD** (created), this triggers an automatic release of succeeding operations. The **Status Change** field enables a production planner to define if a particular event sets or resets the status.

Depending on which trigger point function a production planner chooses to implement, the system then brings up the corresponding parameter's entry options. For example, if the **Create Order with Reference** function is selected, the system asks the user to enter the status (e.g., **Partially Confirmed** or **Scheduled**), which it will check to activate the trigger function. It then asks user to define parameters, such as routing group number, group counter, and production order type.

6.3.4 Components Overview

At any time in the production order creation screen, navigate to **Components Overview**. The system reads the BOM data to bring up the components that will be used in the production process. Assign each component of the BOM to an operation in the production order. If this isn't done, then the system automatically assigns all components to the first operation. This assignment can also be changed by using the **Reassign** option. For nonstock components, the system creates a purchase requisition when the production order is created and saved. This is an integration point between PP and MM. During the entire procurement process, the system maintains the link with the production order.

Figure 6.37 shows the components overview screen of the production order. The details covered here are the same as previously covered in the BOM master data creation.

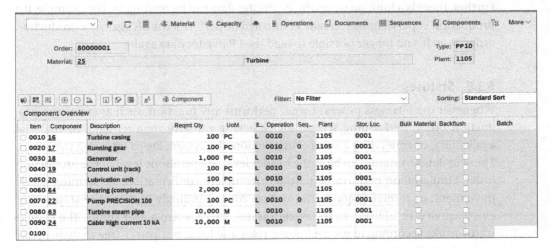

Figure 6.37 Components Overview

Figure 6.38 is the detailed view of the first component, **16**, of the material BOM.

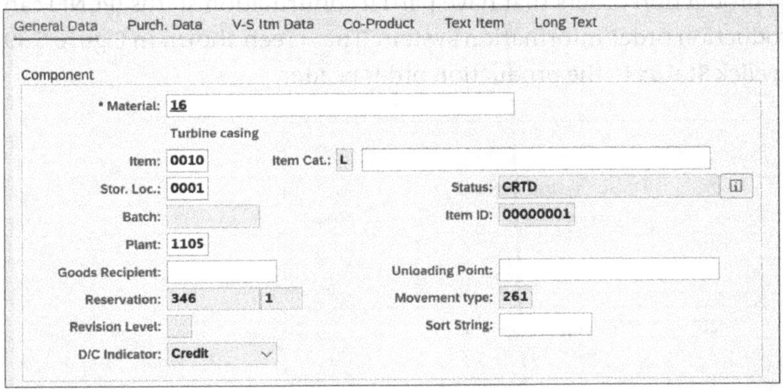

Figure 6.38 Detailed View of Component in Production Order

6.3.5   Reread Master Data

When a production order is created, the system reads the relevant PP master data and makes it an integral part of the production order. In the SAP system, first the master data is created and then this master data is used in day-to-day business transactions, such as production order creation. The system doesn't automatically read any changes made to the master data later on. For example, a production order of a material was already created, and that reads the PP master data, including its BOM. Now, if changes in a material's BOM are made, the system doesn't automatically reflect these changes in the newly created production order. If there's a business need to reread the master data, this can be achieved by choosing **More • Functions • Read PP Master Data** in the production order screen. If any interactive or manual changes were made in the production order, reading PP master data again will overwrite all changes made.

Further, there is a limit on when the PP master data can be read again. For example, if a production supervisor has already confirmed or performed a GR against a production order, then it's no longer possible to read the PP master data again.

6.3.6   Statuses

Whenever the business process owner performs any function, such as creating a production order, performing scheduling, checking capacity requirements or material availability, or generating a control instruction, the system keeps updating the status. These updates in status can be at the header level or operations level of the production order. Similarly, on performing partial or complete confirmation, performing goods movement, or receiving goods, the system correspondingly updates the status after every activity. In addition to the system status, there is also a user status. The system status works according to preconfigured rules and logic, but you're free to define your own rules in the user status.

When using the production order information system (Transaction COOIS), a production supervisor can choose status or user status as one of the selection parameters. For example, all of the production orders that have partial confirmation status (**PCNF**) can be listed in the production order information system. The screen shown in Figure 6.39 appears when you click **Status** in the production order header.

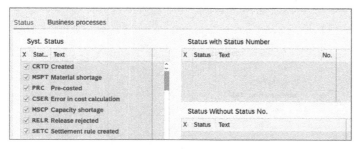

Figure 6.39 Status View of Production Order

6.3.7 Scheduling

Building on the information covered in the work center discussion (Section 6.2.3) and in the routing discussion (Section 6.2.4), this section provides more in-depth information on the factors that the system considers when scheduling production orders. For example, the system takes the following into account from the work center: factory calendar, shift timings, maximum capacity utilization (in percentage), overload percentage, and number of individual capacities. From the routing, it considers information such as setup, processing, transition times, splitting, and overlapping.

When the system performs scheduling for the production order, it takes the following factors into consideration (we'll discuss these in more detail in the following sections):

- Dates in the production order
- Finite scheduling
- Transition times
- Splitting
- Overlapping
- Float before production and safety time
- Reduction

When the basic dates are entered into a production order, the system performs comprehensive scheduling and also takes the dates and times into account. The dates may be the opening period and float before production (defined in **Scheduling Margin Key**), and the times may be transition times, such as wait, move, or queue times.

Dates of the Production Order

Depending on how the scheduling type for the production order has been configured, the system takes the basic dates into account. Refer to the production order creation screen shown previously (Figure 6.34): the backward scheduling type was defined, and the system prompted the user to enter the end date (**Basic**) (e.g., "24.04.2021") and calculated the scheduled start date as 01.04.2021 at 04:00. The system arrives at this schedule based on the following factors (and in the same sequence by performing forward scheduling):

- Float before production
- Operations times
- Safety time (float after production)
- GR processing time

In MRP, if backward scheduling is used, then the system starts with the planned availability date. Therefore, the first object that the system considers is the GR processing time to get the basic order finish date. Then, based on the in-house production time, the system calculates the basic order start date. Afterward, starting from the basic order finish date, the float after production is considered to get the production finish date. From there (due to backward scheduling), the operations are considered for calculating the production start date. Finally, the float before production is applied, and, if necessary and allowed by configuration Transaction OPU5, the initial basic start data is adjusted. The durations of the operations are made up of waiting, setup, edit, teardown, and transport. In the production order, the system displays the operation dates and timings on the **Dates/Times** tab. Figure 6.40 shows the operation details screen of **Operation 0010**. Starting from the queue time, it takes the setup, processing, teardown, wait, and finally move times into account for the operation.

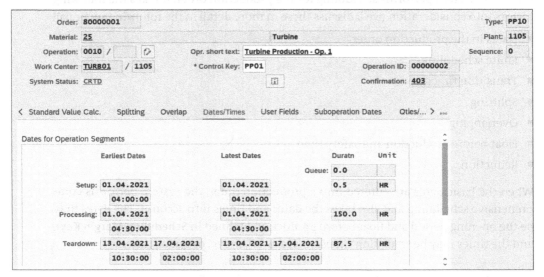

Figure 6.40 Date and Time Details in Operation View

Finite Scheduling

The objective of finite scheduling is to create an organization type in capacity planning that takes into account current capacity loads. *Finite scheduling* calculates the start and finish dates for operations in an order. Infinite scheduling doesn't give the capacity requirement due consideration, and it also doesn't take into account the interdependencies of production orders.

The system uses backward and forward scheduling. In backward scheduling, the system determines the start date of the production order based on the latest finish date. In forward scheduling, the system determines the finish date of the production order based on the earliest start date. Apart from scheduling, material availability is another very important factor that needs to be taken into account. If it isn't possible to manage production within the given dates, then a production planner can minimize the lead time by overlapping, splitting, and reducing the transition times, float before production, and safety time. During finite scheduling (capacity planning), you can also use the float times as degrees of freedom to move operations for a feasible plan for the resource-critical operations; that is, the production dates can be variable within the limits of the basic order dates.

Splitting

Splitting can be used to split an operation into several suboperations that can be processed in parallel with each other. This reduces the overall lead time of the operation. A prerequisite for splitting is that the work center capacity must contain multiple individual capacities; otherwise, parallel processing isn't possible. The system looks for this split information in the capacity header of the work center.

Figure 6.41 shows the **Splitting** tab in the operations view. The system only performs the splitting during scheduling if the **Required Splitting** indicator is checked; otherwise, it considers splitting during reduction. If the number of splits and the minimum processing time aren't specified, the system distributes the processing time equally among the number of available capacities.

The **Maximum Number of Splits** field specifies the maximum number of splits that may take place for the operation. For an economical and practical perspective, **Minimum Processing Time** must also be set.

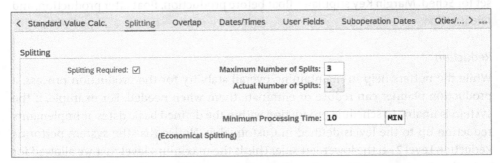

Figure 6.41 Splitting in Operation View of Production Order

Overlapping

Maintain the **Overlapping** parameters, the **Minimum Send-Ahead Qty**, and the **Minimum Overlap Time** in the operation data of the routing. These parameters relate to the overlapping with the follow-up operation.

During scheduling, if the minimum overlapping time isn't reached, no overlapping takes place. This is the case, for example, when the remaining processing time after the processing of the minimum send-ahead quantity is too small. The minimum overlapping relates to the processing time. Transition times, such as wait time or move time, don't contribute to the minimum overlapping time.

Depending on the settings made in the routing or production order for overlapping, when the system schedules the order, it performs overlapping during reduction (**Optional Overlapping**), always (**Required Overlapping**), or never (**No Overlapping**).

Figure 6.42 shows the **Overlap** tab in the production order.

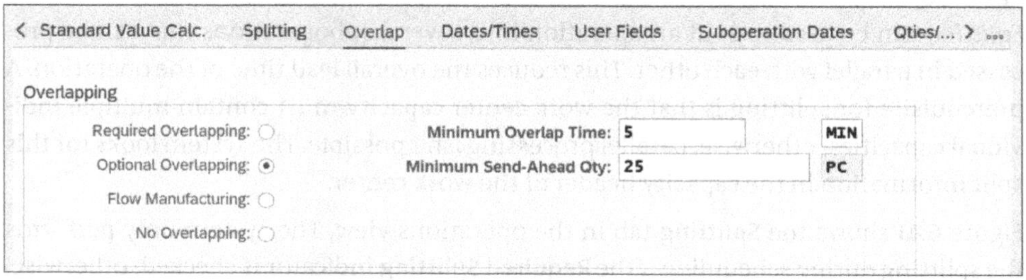

‹ Standard Value Calc.   Splitting   Overlap   Dates/Times   User Fields   Suboperation Dates   Qties/... › ...

Figure 6.42 Overlapping in Operation View of Production Order

Float before Production

In Chapter 3, Section 3.10.3, we covered the scheduling margin key, which provides additional buffers to the production process from unforeseen delays. Refer to Figure 6.34 again and examine the **Floats** area on the lower-right side of the screen. The float set for **Sched. Margin Key** stipulates float before production, float after production, and release time.

Reduction

While the buffers help in maintaining overall stability for the production process, a production planner can reduce or eliminate them when needed. For example, if the system is unable to schedule production within the defined basic dates, it implements reduction up to the levels defined in Customizing. Notice that the system performs **Reduction Level 2** on the lower-left side. This is the maximum level that we allowed for reduction in Chapter 3. The system first tries to resolve the scheduling issue without reduction, then with reduction level 1, and, only if necessary, finally with reduction level 2. Before making a reduction, the system considers whether the production dates (after scheduling) are within the basic dates; if so, it makes no reduction. If not, the system continues the reduction process until it either meets the basic production dates or reaches the last reduction level, whichever comes first.

For example, the system is configured to reduce up to two levels; however, if the system is able to meet the basic production date after first-level reduction, it secures the production dates. In this case, it doesn't proceed to the next reduction level. For such cases, there is also the option to let the system adjust the basic dates to the new lead-time scheduling situation in Customizing Transactions OPU5 and OPU3 (this is recommended). Otherwise, there might be production dates outside the basic dates, and the corresponding exception message occurs.

6.3.8   Availability Checks

Depending on how the *availability checks* are configured, this step can be performed either automatically during production order creation or its release, or interactively (manually) within the production order creation screen. Further, the material availability check for an individual production order or for a large number of production orders collectively can also be performed.

Three different types of availability checks are available for a production order:

- **Material availability check**
  Checks the availability of the components for the production order, either against actual stocks (and optionally receipts) or against the planning.

- **Capacity availability check**
  Checks whether sufficient free capacity is available for the order's operations.

- **PRT check**
  By checking a status in the master data, checks whether the required PRT is free.

For automatic availability checks, make the relevant configuration settings to enable the system to check for one or all of the availability checks during an order creation or order release (refer to Chapter 3, Section 3.9 for these). For example, if there is a significant lead time between order creation and its release, a production planner can choose not to perform a capacity check on order creation but instead during order release.

Further, it's also possible to set how the system should proceed if it finds missing capacity, missing PRTs, or a material shortage (due to missing parts) during the availability check. The following options are available for material, capacity, and PRT checks during order creation or release:

- Disallow order creation or release when there is a shortage.
- Allow order creation or release when there is a shortage.
- Allow the user to decide (interactively) to allow creation or release of an order when there is a shortage.

In the following sections, we'll discuss material and capacity availability checks.

Material Availability Check

Despite all of the planning, checks, and balances in place, and even when keeping the minimum stock levels, it's imperative for a production planner to consistently check material availability to ensure there is no disruption in the entire production process. The immediate and visible purpose of the material availability check is to ensure that the requisite components are available for the production order. If not, the system creates an entry in the missing parts list, which the production and the procurement planners can work on together to procure the components. So for in-house-produced parts, the production planner can coordinate internally to ensure the requisite component's availability. For externally procured material, the procurement planner can take advantage of the missing parts list to coordinate and attend to procurement priorities.

With every availability check that is performed, the system correspondingly updates its status. In the material availability check, for example, the system assigns a **NMVP** status if it makes no material availability check. A production order whose component requirements are checked and confirmed attains the **MABS** (material confirmed) status. If the system can't confirm the availability of one or several components, the order receives the **FMAT** (missing material) status, and the system creates a missing parts list. In the production order, click the **Component availability** button. If all components are available, then the system issues an information message to confirm material availability; otherwise, the popup shown in Figure 6.43 appears. Click the **Missing Parts Overvi** (overview) button.

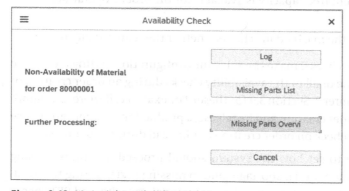

≡	Availability Check	✕
	Log	
Non-Availability of Material		
for order 80000001	Missing Parts List	
Further Processing:	Missing Parts Overvi	
	Cancel	

Figure 6.43 Material Availability Check

Figure 6.44 shows the missing parts overview, missing parts list, and other detailed information on the production order, such as the requirements quantity and the component's availability situation.

No. of Components Checked:			9						
Missing Parts:			8						
Overall commitment date could not be determined									

	Material	Material description	Plant	Stor. Loc.	Reqmt Qty	Reqmts date	Cnf/allcQt	CmmttdDate	Miss. Part	F
☐	16	Turbine casing	1105	0001	100	01.04.2021	0		X	
☐	17	Running gear			100	01.04.2021	0		X	
☐	18	Generator			1,000	01.04.2021	17		X	
☐	19	Control unit (rack)			100	01.04.2021	0		X	
☐	20	Lubrication unit			100	01.04.2021	0		X	
☐	24	Cable high current 10 kA			10,000	01.04.2021	0		X	
☐	63	Turbine steam pipe			10,000	01.04.2021	2,015		X	
☐	64	Bearing (complete)			2,000	01.04.2021	350		X	

Figure 6.44 List of Missing Components

This example shows how to interactively check for material availability within the production order change screen (Transaction CO02), but the system also offers a method called the *missing parts information system*. It's recommended to first perform a mass availability check on production orders, and then, if this activity finds missing parts, use the missing parts information system to further work on producing or procuring the components.

To access the missing parts information system, follow menu path **Logistics • Production • Shop Floor Control • Information System • Missing Parts Info System**, or use Transaction CO24. Figure 6.45 shows the initial screen on which you assign the **Plant** as "1105". In the **Selection from Orders** area, enter the **Material** as "25" for the system to check for missing components.

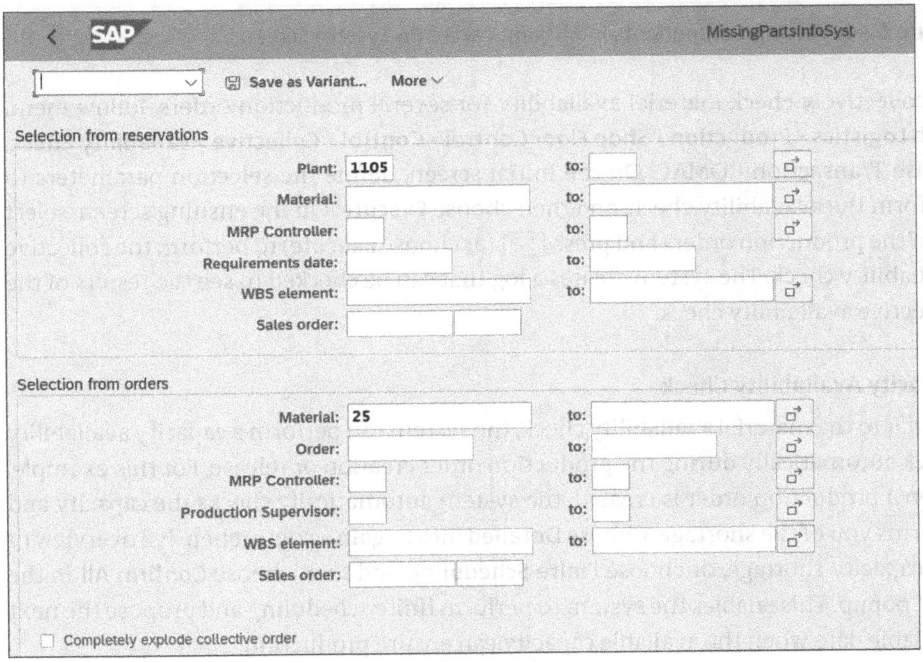

Figure 6.45 Initial Screen of Missing Parts Information System

Press F8 or choose **Execute**, and the screen shown in Figure 6.46 appears, listing the missing components against production order 80000001.

Tips and Tricks

If the missing parts information system is run for the first time in a newly created SAP system client, the system may produce an error stating that it requires running a specific program first. Use Transaction SE38 and program PPCOXPR1, and choose **Execute** (or press F8). This activity needs to be performed only once for a given SAP system client.

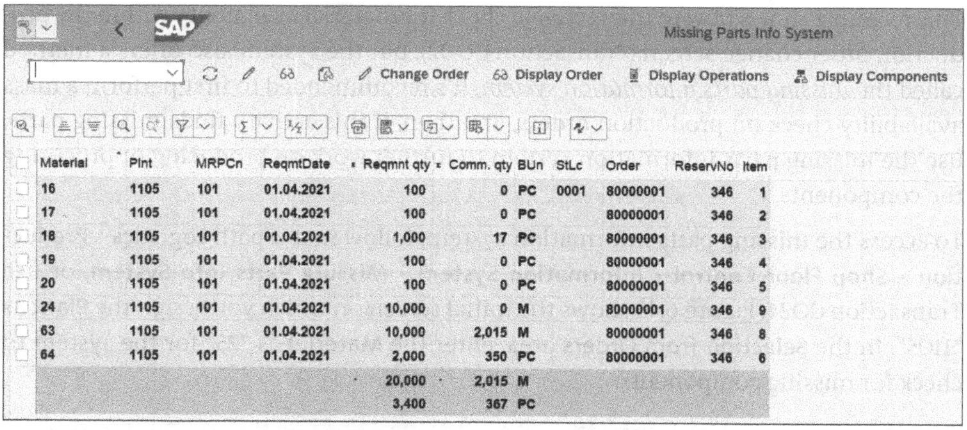

Material	Plnt	MRPCn	ReqmtDate	Reqmnt qty	Comm. qty	BUn	StLc	Order	ReservNo	Item
16	1105	101	01.04.2021	100	0	PC	0001	80000001	346	1
17	1105	101	01.04.2021	100	0	PC		80000001	346	2
18	1105	101	01.04.2021	1,000	17	PC		80000001	346	3
19	1105	101	01.04.2021	100	0	PC		80000001	346	4
20	1105	101	01.04.2021	100	0	PC		80000001	346	5
24	1105	101	01.04.2021	10,000	0	M		80000001	346	9
63	1105	101	01.04.2021	10,000	2,015	M		80000001	346	8
64	1105	101	01.04.2021	2,000	350	PC		80000001	346	6
				20,000	2,015	M				
				3,400	367	PC				

Figure 6.46 Missing Components in Missing Parts Info System Screen

To collectively check material availability for several production orders, follow menu path **Logistics • Production • Shop Floor Control • Control • Collective Availability Check**, or use Transaction COMAC. On the initial screen, define the selection parameters to perform the availability check, and then choose **Execute**. On the ensuing screen, select all of the production orders and press F8 (or choose **Execute**) to perform the collective availability check. The system creates a log that can be checked to see the results of the collective availability check.

Capacity Availability Check

Similar to the material availability check, the system can perform a capacity availability check automatically during the production order creation or release. For this example, when a production order is created, the system automatically checks the capacity and informs you of the shortage. Choose **Detailed Info** to gain a comprehensive overview of the capacity shortage, or choose **Finite Scheduling** and then choose **Confirm All** in the next popup. This enables the system to perform finite scheduling and propose the next available date when the available capacity can ensure production.

Further, when you're on the production order creation or change screen, choose the **Capacity Availability Check** (see Figure 6.47). A screen offers the option to release a production order despite capacity shortage or to cancel an order release. (This is the same setting previously configured in Chapter 3.)

Alternately, use the following menu path within the production order: **More • Goto • Capacity Planning Table** (see Figure 6.48).

[»]

Note

Chapter 18 describes CRP in detail.

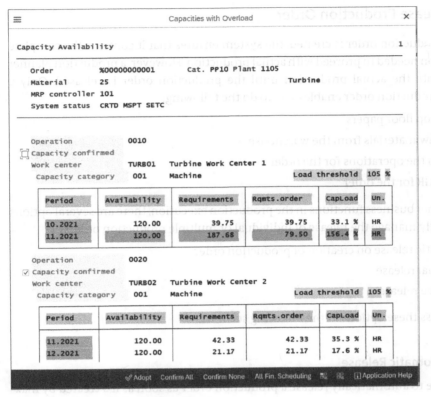

Figure 6.47 Capacity Availability Check

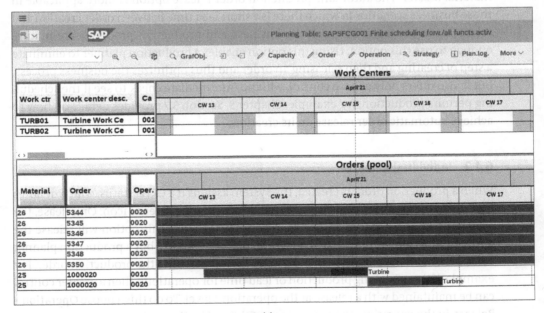

Figure 6.48 Capacity Requirements Planning Table

6.4   Release Production Order

When a production order is created, the system ensures that it contains the complete information needed to proceed with actual production. However, a production planner can't initiate the actual production until the production order is released. Only a released production order enables you to do the following:

- Print shop floor papers
- Withdraw materials from the warehouse
- Confirm the operations for the order
- Record GR for the order

As with other business functions in the production execution, there are several options to efficiently manage the release of individual or multiple production orders:

- Automatic release on creation of production order
- Individual release
- Collective release

We'll discuss these options in the following sections.

6.4.1   Automatic Release

It's possible to automatically release a production order as soon as it's created by making the relevant settings in the production scheduling profile and assigning it to the material master. The automatic production order release option is more applicable in those business scenarios in which there is a short lead time between order creation and release or in scenarios in which the business and production processes are mature enough to use this option. Using this option enables a production planner to eliminate a step of creating and then releasing an order and thus optimizes the business process, but it also offers only a loose control, with no intermediate check to see if the scheduling permits production, for example. Chapter 3, Section 3.7 provides details on how to achieve automatic order release on its creation.

6.4.2   Individual Release

When a production order is created, the system assigns it a **CRTD** status, which denotes that it's in the creation stage. It's released by clicking the **Release** icon. On release, the system updates the status of the order from **CRTD** to **REL**. This option will release the entire production order and thus release all of its operations, but a production planner can also control the release of an individual operation within the production order. For example, if there is a long production or lead time for operations, then a greater control can be maintained with a release at the operation's level. To do this, choose **Operation • Release** in the operation overview screen of the production order.

Figure 6.49 shows the popup to let the user decide if the production order can still be released despite a material, capacity, or PRT shortage.

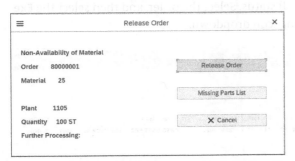

Figure 6.49 Option to Release Production Order or Not

To avoid having to release individual operations, use a trigger point, which we covered earlier in Section 6.3.3.

6.4.3   Collective Release

To release several production orders simultaneously, use the collective release option. To do so, follow menu path **Logistics • Production • Shop Floor Control • Control • Collective Release**, or use Transaction CO05N.

Figure 6.50 shows the parameter selection screen to define the parameters, such as material number, plant, order type, MRP controller, or production supervisor, which will enable the system to bring up relevant orders for release.

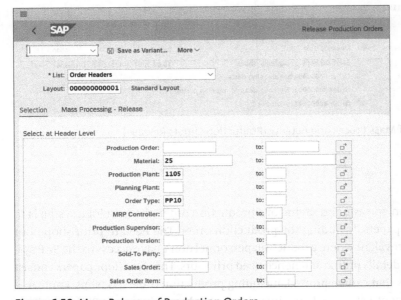

Figure 6.50 Mass Release of Production Orders

For this example, define **Material** as "25" and production **Plant** as "1105", and choose **Execute** or press ⌐F8⌐. The screen shown in Figure 6.51 appears, consisting of a production order that has the **CRTD** (created) status. Select the order, and then select the **Execute** option from the **Mass Processing** icon dropdown.

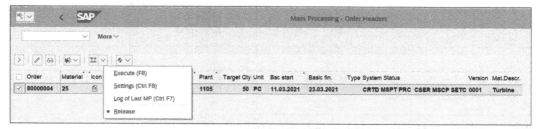

Figure 6.51 Mass Processing of Production Orders: Detailed Screen

The mass processing log appears and shows that the collective release of production orders was successful (Figure 6.52). During the production order's release, the system also carried out the material availability check; on finding no missing part (material shortage) or other issue, it successfully executed the release function.

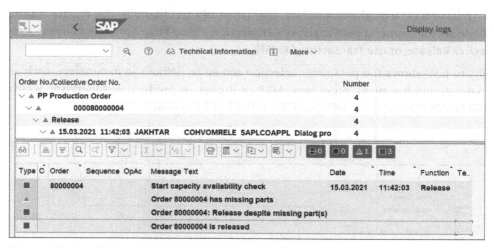

Figure 6.52 Log of Mass Processing Activity (Production Orders Release)

6.5   Printing

Upon the creation, release, and saving of a production order, the next logical step is to print shop floor papers, including the production order. The need to print shop floor papers is more prevalent where production personnel don't have access to the SAP system to check the details online and hence need printouts. The shop floor papers consist of several objects that can be printed, including production orders, GI slips, confirmation slips, document lists, pick lists, time tickets, kanban tickets, and PRT overviews.

Depending on the company's business needs, a production planner can print some or all of them and hand them over to concerned production personnel for their information. If required, shop floor papers can be saved as PDFs using the Adobe Document Services.

The layout, printer settings, and other configuration settings were covered in Chapter 3. For this example, use the standard form (layout) for production orders that the SAP system provides for various shop floor papers.

It's also important to note that a production order (or other shop floor paper) can only be printed once after it's released. Use the manual option to print the shop floor papers, or control the printing from the production schedule profile, in which a checkbox can be selected that causes the system to automatically perform the printing function on release. A production planner can individually print the shop floor papers of a production order by using the change production order transaction (Transaction CO02) and selecting **More • Order • Settings • List Control**.

To print shop floor papers, follow menu path **Logistics • Production • Shop Floor Control • Control • Print**, or use Transaction CO04N. On the resulting screen, shown in Figure 6.53, enter these parameters: **Production Plant** "1105", **Order Type** "PP10", and **Production Order** "80000002". In the **Mass Processing—Printing of Shop Floor Papers** tab, select the **Display Applicat. Toolbar** checkbox and click **Execute**. When using Transaction CO04, maintain these same parameters and choose the **Original Printout** radio button.

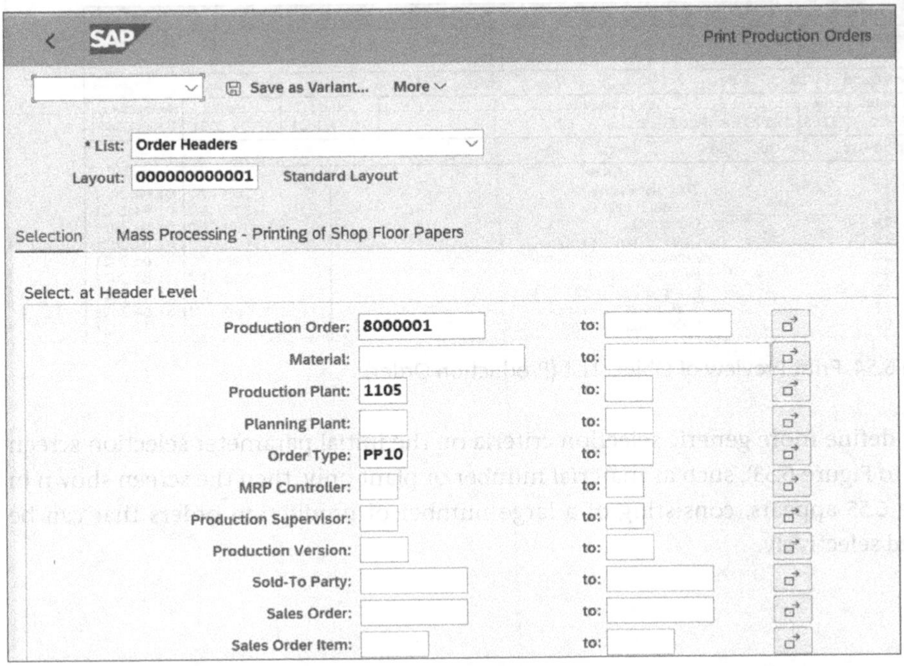

Figure 6.53 Initial Screen to Print Shop Floor Papers

Note

An original shop floor paper can only be printed once. For any subsequent print requirement of the same shop floor paper, select **Reprint**.

Choose **Execute** or press F8, and the screen shown in Figure 6.54 appears, showing the **Object List** (production order) print preview. It contains just about all of the information needed on a production order, such as order start and end dates, the operations involved in production, and the components required at each operation.

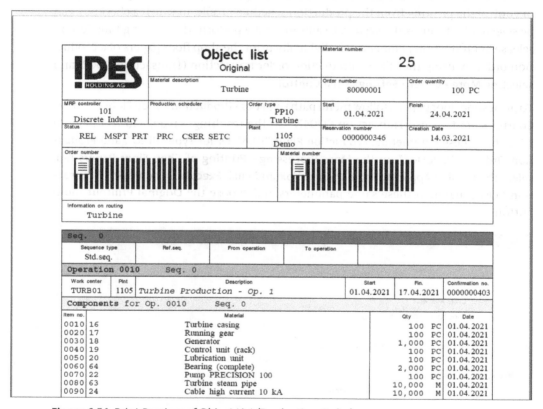

Figure 6.54 Print Preview of Object List (Production Order)

If you define more generic selection criteria on the initial parameter selection screen (refer to Figure 6.53), such as material number or plant only, then the screen shown in Figure 6.55 appears, consisting of a large number of production orders that can be printed selectively.

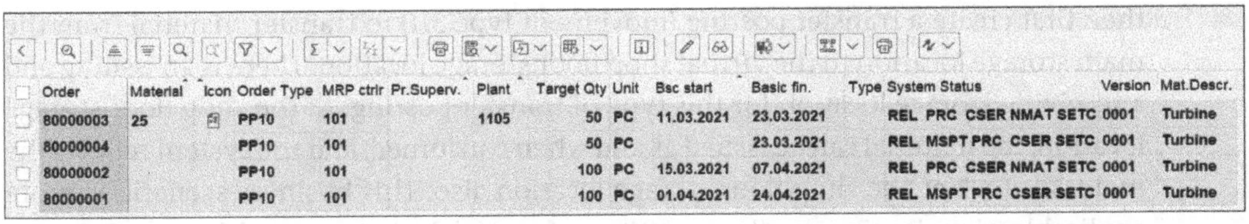

Order	Material	Icon	Order Type	MRP ctrlr	Pr.Superv.	Plant	Target Qty	Unit	Bsc start	Basic fin.	Type System Status	Version	Mat.Descr.
80000003	25	🖼	PP10	101		1105	50	PC	11.03.2021	23.03.2021	REL PRC CSER NMAT SETC	0001	Turbine
80000004			PP10	101			50	PC		23.03.2021	REL MSPT PRC CSER SETC	0001	Turbine
80000002			PP10	101			100	PC	15.03.2021	07.04.2021	REL PRC CSER NMAT SETC	0001	Turbine
80000001			PP10	101			100	PC	01.04.2021	24.04.2021	REL MSPT PRC CSER SETC	0001	Turbine

Figure 6.55 Item Overview of Shop Floor Papers for Printing

6.6 Material Withdrawal

After the system creates a production order (even before the production order is released), it automatically creates a material reservation. This reserve will be pulled in the next actual production process. The next business function is to withdraw material from the warehouse. During the SAP system implementation, the production team and the product costing team decide which components will form BOMs and which will be charged off to the production cost center. For example, low-value items, such as greases, scrubbers, cleaning solutions, and lubricants, are used in the production process but aren't the components used in manufacturing a product. Similarly, bulk material isn't part of the BOM. There are three ways in to perform material withdrawal against the production order, which we'll discuss in detail in the following sections:

- GI against production order
- Picking list
- Backflush

On GI posting, the system enables several activities in the background:

- Reduces the stock quantity of the material by the withdrawn quantity at both the plant level and storage location level
- Updates the consumption statistics, as these consumption figures eventually facilitate forecasting
- Reduces the reservation with the quantity withdrawn
- Debits the production order with the actual costs
- Creates a material document showing the GI and an accounting document, consisting of all postings in SAP S/4HANA Finance (material stock and consumption accounts)

6.6.1 Goods Issuance against the Production Order

The system uses movement type 261 for GI against the production order. This means that the material is directly withdrawn from the warehouse against the production order or is first transferred from the main warehouse to the virtual production floor storage location and then posts GI to match consumption. If the second option is used, then first create a transfer posting (movement type 311) to transfer material from the main storage location to the virtual shop floor storage location. There is an issuing and a receiving storage location for this type of transfer posting. At the shop floor storage location, the material can be issued as and when consumed, and the system reflects the material stock at the shop floor storage location also. This business scenario is more applicable when issuing smaller quantities of materials that are used frequently.

To perform GI against the production order, follow SAP menu path **Logistics · Materials Management · Inventory Management · Goods Movement · Goods Movement**, or use Transaction MIGO. Figure 6.56 shows the initial screen in which you select **Goods Issue** from the first dropdown list and then select **Order** from the next dropdown list. Next, enter the production order number as "80000001". It's also important to note that the system should use movement type 261, which we discussed earlier. This is shown on the far-right side of the screen in the **GI for Order** field.

On pressing [Enter], the system brings up the list of components directly from the production order (see Figure 6.56). This screen shows the same components that the system reads from the production order's components overview screen and suggests these components for GI. Changes can be made to the quantities if desired, and you can also enter the storage location (**SLoc**) from which to issue the components. Finally, select the **OK** checkbox for each component that needs to be issued. Save the entries, and the system creates a material document number (and a corresponding accounting document).

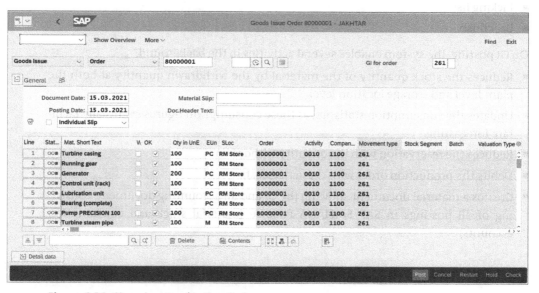

Figure 6.56 GI against Production Order

Figure 6.57 shows the display production order screen (Transaction CO03), in which you navigate to the **Components Details** screen. It shows **Reservation 346** and item **3** for the production order, along with the **Requirement Qty** of **1,000** and the **Withdrawal Qty** of **200** (after the GI step).

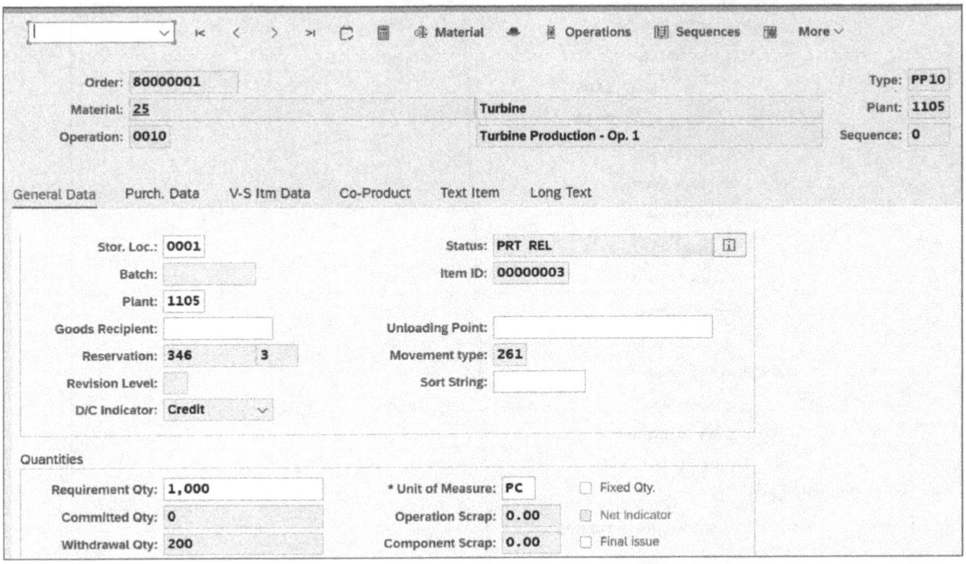

Figure 6.57 Material Withdrawal in Component View of Production Order

6.6.2 Picking List

Picking is another process of material withdrawal from the warehouse. A *picking list* is an intuitive and interactive option that the warehouse supervisor can use to issue materials against production orders. To issue components by using a picking list, follow menu path **Logistics • Production • Shop Floor Control • Goods Movements • Material Staging • Pick**, or use Transaction CO27.

Figure 6.58 shows the initial screen that offers a large number of options to enter parameters, based on which the ensuing picking list will appear. For this example, define these parameters: **Material** "25", **Plant** "1105", **Work center** "TURBO1", and **Plant** (for work center) "1105".

Choose **Execute** or press F8 to open the screen shown in Figure 6.59. This screen consists of several production orders against which a warehouse supervisor can initiate the picking process. Select the first four components that pertain to **Order 80000001** by setting the checkboxes (the first column on the left-hand side of the screen) against each component, and click the **Picking** button in the toolbar.

257

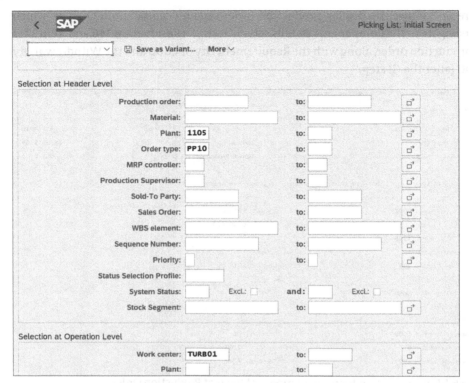

Figure 6.58 Initial Screen of Picking List

Order	Material	Item	Reqmts date	Reqmt Qty	Qty wthdrn	BUn	Material description	Batch	Seq.	Opr.	RItem	Plant	SLoc	Type	Status
80000001	18	0030	01.04.2021	1,000	200	PC	Generator		0	0010	3	1105			PRT REL
	64	0060	01.04.2021	2,000	200	PC	Bearing (complete)		0	0010	6	1105			PRT REL
	63	0080	01.04.2021	10,000	100	M	Turbine steam pipe		0	0010	8	1105			PRT REL
	24	0090	01.04.2021	10,000	100	M	Cable high current 10 kA		0	0010	9	1105			PRT REL
80000004	16	0010	11.03.2021	50	0	PC	Turbine casing		0	0010	1	1105			REL
	17	0020	11.03.2021	50	0	PC	Running gear		0	0010	2	1105			REL
	18	0030	11.03.2021	500	0	PC	Generator		0	0010	3	1105			REL
	19	0040	11.03.2021	50	0	PC	Control unit (rack)		0	0010	4	1105			REL
	20	0050	11.03.2021	50	0	PC	Lubrication unit		0	0010	5	1105			REL
	64	0060	11.03.2021	1,000	0	PC	Bearing (complete)		0	0010	6	1105			REL
	22	0070	11.03.2021	50	0	PC	Pump PRECISION 100		0	0010	7	1105			REL
	63	0080	11.03.2021	5,000	0	M	Turbine steam pipe		0	0010	8	1105			REL
	24	0090	11.03.2021	5,000	0	M	Cable high current 10 kA		0	0010	9	1105			REL

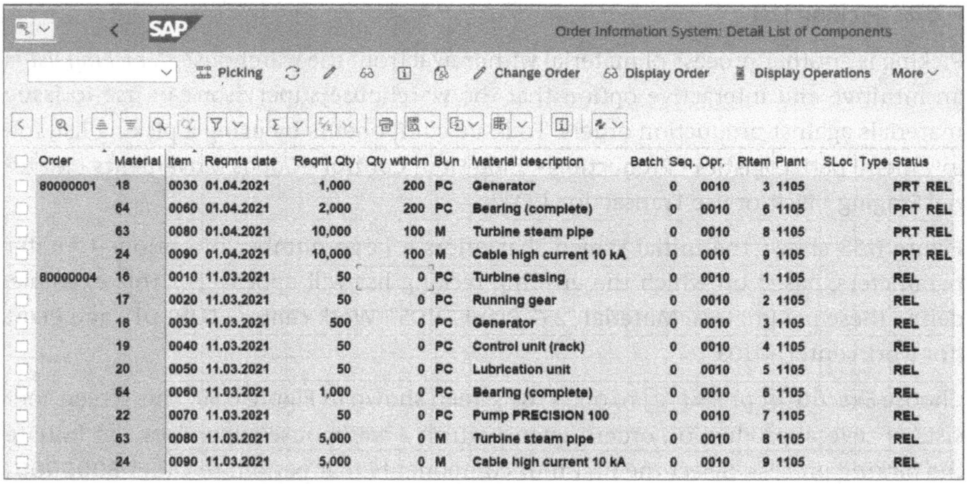

Figure 6.59 Goods Movements Overview in Picking List

Any last-minute changes to the issuance quantities can be made. If there are missing issuance storage locations, then maintain them on this screen. Notice that the **Movement Type** is **261**, which is for GI against the order. In this step, the system also performs the stock determination to ensure that the components required for issuance are available in stock. If any specific stock determination rules are configured and assigned in the **Stock Determ. Group** field in the **Plant Data/Storage 2** tab of the material master, then the system accordingly suggests the components during the picking function.

Choose **Save**, and the system performs the GI in the background. Then choose **Refresh**. The issued components—for which no further issuance is possible—won't be available in the picking list.

6.6.3 Backflush

In the backflush process, the system simultaneously posts the GI when an operation to which the components are assigned is confirmed. In this way, the system optimizes the confirmation process by performing a two-in-one function. For production orders, there are three ways to activate the backflush functionality in the production process:

- In the material master
- In the work center
- In the material component assignment

We'll discuss these in further detail in the following sections.

Activate Backflushing in the Material Master

Figure 6.60 shows the **MRP 2** view of the material master (component) with the **Backflush** field. Place the cursor on the field and press F4 ; the system brings up the two available options shown on the right-hand side of the screen. The first option is that the system always backflushes (1) this component during the confirmation process. The second option is that it will look for the work center to see if the backflush checkbox (2) is selected to enable it to execute the backflush function.

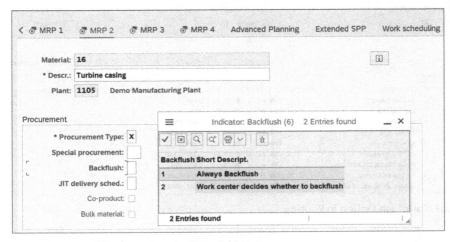

Figure 6.60 Backflush Options in Material Master

Activate Backflushing in the Work Center

Figure 6.61 shows the **Basic Data** tab of **Work Center TURB01** for **Plant 1105** (Transaction CRO2), where you can select the **Backflush** checkbox.

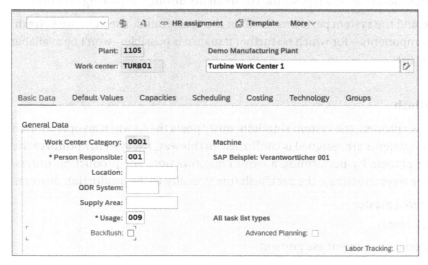

Figure 6.61 Backflush Option in Work Center

Activate Backflushing in the Material Component Assignment

Figure 6.62 shows the **Production Order Change: Component Overview** screen of the routing (Transaction CAO2), in which **Component 10000069** includes the **Backflush** option.

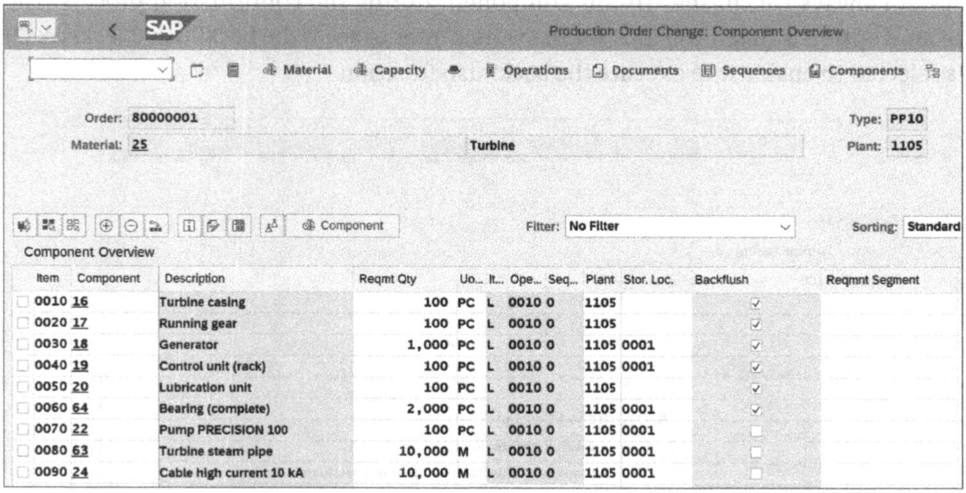

Item	Component	Description	Reqmt Qty	Uo...	It...	Ope...	Seq...	Plant	Stor. Loc.	Backflush	Reqmnt Segment
0010	16	Turbine casing	100	PC	L	0010	0	1105		✓	
0020	17	Running gear	100	PC	L	0010	0	1105		✓	
0030	18	Generator	1,000	PC	L	0010	0	1105	0001	✓	
0040	19	Control unit (rack)	100	PC	L	0010	0	1105	0001	✓	
0050	20	Lubrication unit	100	PC	L	0010	0	1105		✓	
0060	64	Bearing (complete)	2,000	PC	L	0010	0	1105	0001	✓	
0070	22	Pump PRECISION 100	100	PC	L	0010	0	1105	0001		
0080	63	Turbine steam pipe	10,000	M	L	0010	0	1105	0001		
0090	24	Cable high current 10 kA	10,000	M	L	0010	0	1105	0001		

Figure 6.62 Backflush Option in Routing

[+]

Tips and Tricks

If the **Backflush** indicator is in any of the master data elements (material master, BOM, or routing), it can be still selected in the **Production Order Change: Component Overview** screen of the production order (see Figure 6.63). However, this is applicable to the specific production order only and will in no way update the master data.

With the three backflush options just discussed, it's important to understand the sequence in which the system makes the decision of whether to backflush. Figure 6.63 shows the backflush decision-making process.

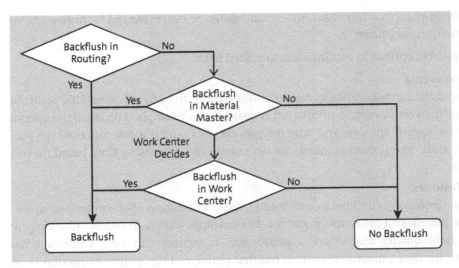

Figure 6.63 Decision-Making Process for Backflushing

6.7 Confirmation

To bring comprehensive visibility to the entire production process, the confirmation process provides the production scheduler and the MRP controller with important information: the quantities produced and confirmed for each operation or order. The types of confirmation that you can perform are listed here:

- Quantities/subsets
- Activities (setup time, processing time, etc.)
- Dates (start and end dates for setup, processing, etc.)
- Personnel data (personnel number, number of employees)
- Work centers used

As previously mentioned, a confirmation process automatically triggers some or all of the following business functions, depending on how the system is configured or the master data is set up:

- Updates the actual costs
- Reduces the capacities of the work centers involved
- Performs GI for backflush components
- Performs GR for the automatic GR material

The system calculates the remaining order quantity from the four quantity fields in the production order based on the following formula:

Remaining quantity = Total quantity – scrap – delivered + expected yield variation (due to underdelivery/overdelivery)

The available options in confirmation are listed here:

- **Time events**
  If a production supervisor wants the confirmations to be based on specific points in time, then *time events* confirmation is possible. For example, a production supervisor can specify the date and time the process starts and the date and time the process ends. The system automatically calculates the processing time based on this data.

- **Milestones**
  If an operation is defined as a *milestone*, the confirmation of the milestone operation includes all previous operations. For example, during in-process (during production) quality inspection, a production supervisor can only confirm scrap quantity after a quality inspection has first performed the quality inspection at an operation.

- **Progress confirmations**
  Like the milestone confirmation, the *progress confirmation* of an operation automatically includes all previous operations. However, in contrast to the milestone confirmation, there's no need to specifically mark an operation as a progress confirmation. A special characteristic of the progress confirmation is that each confirmation always considers the entire quantity that has been produced until the confirmation is triggered. A progress confirmation is useful if several partial confirmations are required and if it's easier to determine the total quantity rather than only the newly added quantity.

  It is also possible to confirm an entire production order. However, using this option will not bring up the option to confirm the details of the actual activities in this case. The system uses the standard activity details given in the production order.

Next, let's discuss the various options available to perform confirmation for a production order.

6.7.1 Confirmation at the Operations Level

A production supervisor may opt to confirm an operation either with a time ticket or a time event. For a confirmation with a time ticket, the system confirms the quantities, activities, dates, and personnel data of an operation. The activities that can be confirmed depend on the SVK, whereas the quantities that can be confirmed are yield, scrap, and rework. For dates, a production supervisor can specify the start and end of the execution, including time and calendar date.

To bring greater visibility to the production process, it's possible to periodically confirm the produced quantity at a work center. The frequency with which confirmation of an operation or an order is undertaken depends entirely on business needs. For example, in 24 hours, a production supervisor can confirm the quantities produced at the end of an eight-hour shift. This means there will be two partial confirmations and one final confirmation. On performing the final confirmation, the system no longer expects any further confirmation against the operation or the order. The partial confirmation option is especially useful and practical for operations with long lead times. On partially confirming an operation, the system assigns the production order a status of **PCNF**, whereas for final confirmation it assigns the **CONF** status.

To proceed with confirmation of a time ticket, follow menu path **Logistics • Production • Shop Floor Control • Confirmation • Enter • For Operation • Time Ticket**, or use Transaction CO11N.

Figure 6.64 shows the initial screen to confirm the time ticket. Enter the **Order** number as "80000001", enter **Operation** as "0010", and press ⌈Enter⌋. The system automatically brings up the data that can be confirmed. In this screen, enter the actual quantities, activities, and duration details to enable the system to perform automatic functions as discussed earlier (e.g., updating costs, releasing capacities, etc.).

> **Tips and Tricks**
> If the system doesn't automatically bring up the data that needs to be confirmed, click the **Actual Data** button.

Notice the **Confirm.type** field, which in this case has the value **Partial Confirmation**. In **Confirm.type** field, select the relevant option from the dropdown list. In the **Automatic Final Confirmation** option, the system checks whether the confirmed quantity is equal to, higher than, or less than the production order quantity. If it's less, then it automatically sets the status as **Partial Confirmation**; if the confirmation quantity is equal to or exceeds the production order quantity, then it automatically sets the status as **Final Confirmation**.

Further down this screen, a production supervisor can also assign a **Reason for Var.** (variance) in case there's a deviation between planned and actual production quantities.

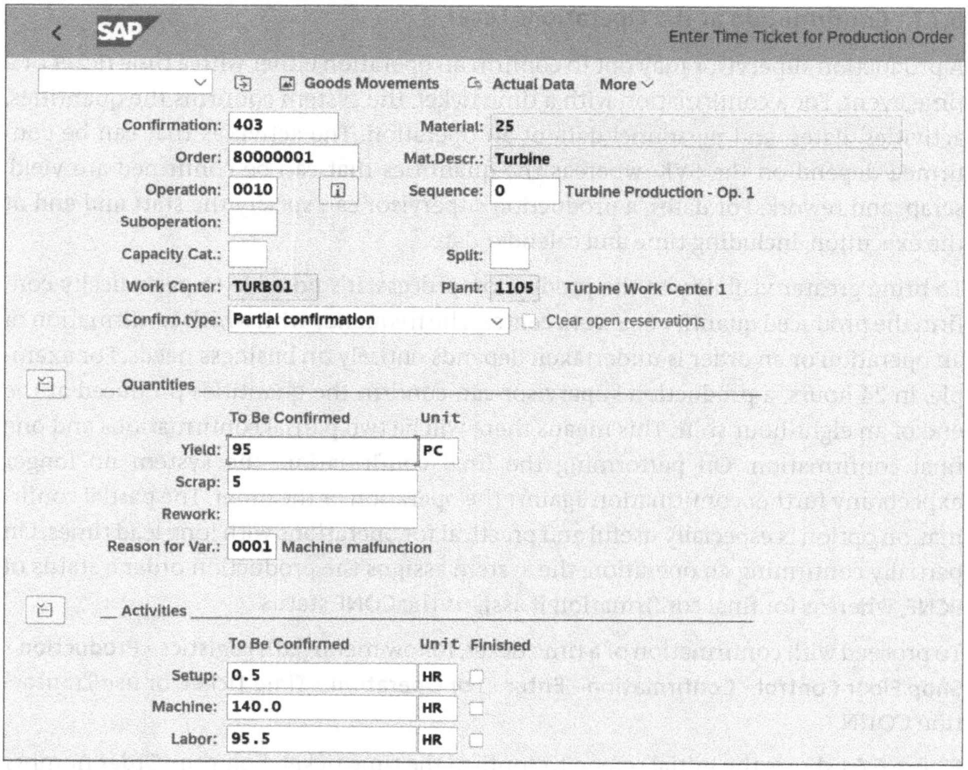

Figure 6.64 Operation Confirmation of Production Order

[+]
Tips and Tricks

Multiple reasons for variances can be added by using enhancement CONFPP07.

Figure 6.65 shows the lower half of the time ticket for the production order. Here, **Posting Date** is a mandatory field, and by default it uses the date of confirmation as the posting date. Other details, such as **Personnel No.**, are integration points between PP and the HR system. The **Notification Type** field is an integration point between PP and QM in which the system can automatically create a quality notification of notification type **F3** as soon as some scrap is recorded, as in this example.

It's also possible to enter long text to provide greater details regarding any problem encountered in the production process or any other findings worth recording during the production process.

Click **More · Goods Movements**, and the system navigates to the screen shown in Figure 6.66. This screen shows the components that the system will backflush on saving the confirmation. Notice that only three components are available for backflush on this screen.

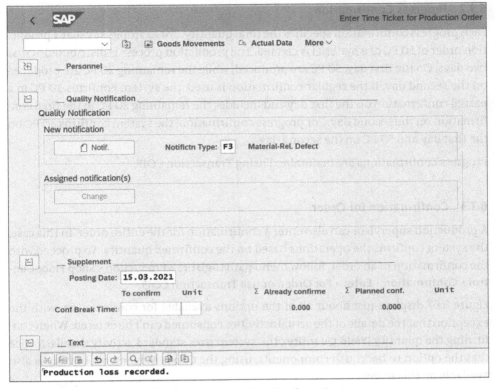

Figure 6.65 Additional Input Options in Operation Confirmation

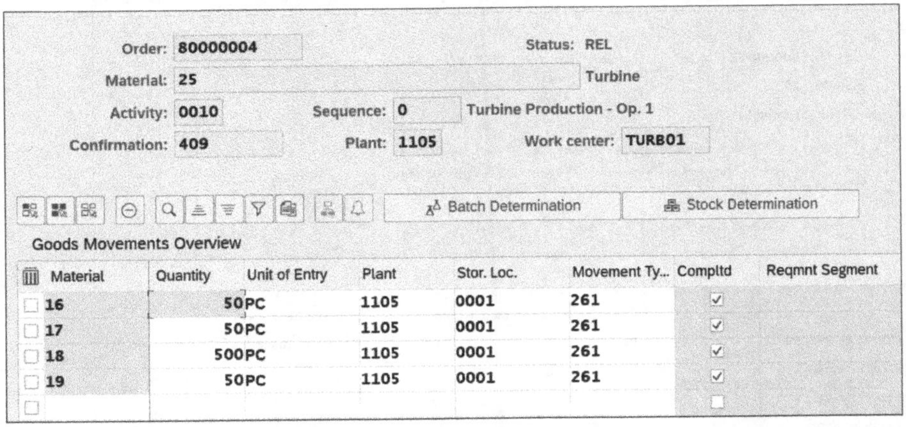

Figure 6.66 Goods Movements (Backflush) in Confirmation

Save the confirmation, and a message indicates the successful save of the confirmation (time ticket) and also that the system was able to successfully perform goods movement (which in this case is components backflush) for the four components. (In Section 6.9.1, we cover what to do if the goods movement fails.)

6.7.2   Progress Confirmation

Each progress confirmation specifies the total quantity. For example, say that a production order of 50 PC of a material is created. The production process is distributed across two days. On the first day, 30 PC are produced, while the remaining 20 PC are produced on the second day. If the regular confirmation is used, the system confirms 30 PC in a partial confirmation on the first day and includes the remaining 20 PC in the final confirmation on the second day. For progress confirmation, the system confirms 30 PC on the first day and 50 PC on the second day.

Progress confirmations are maintained using Transaction CO1F.

6.7.3   Confirmation for Order

A production supervisor can also enter a confirmation for the entire order. In this case, the system confirms the operations based on the confirmed quantity. To proceed with the confirmation of an order, follow menu path **Logistics • Production • Shop Floor Control • Confirmation • Enter • For Order**, or use Transaction CO15.

Figure 6.67 displays just about all of the options available for confirmation, with the exception that the details of the actual activities consumed can't be entered. When confirming the quantity (**Yield Quantity**), the system uses standard activity details. Notice that the option to backflush components, using the **Goods Movements** button, is also available on this screen.

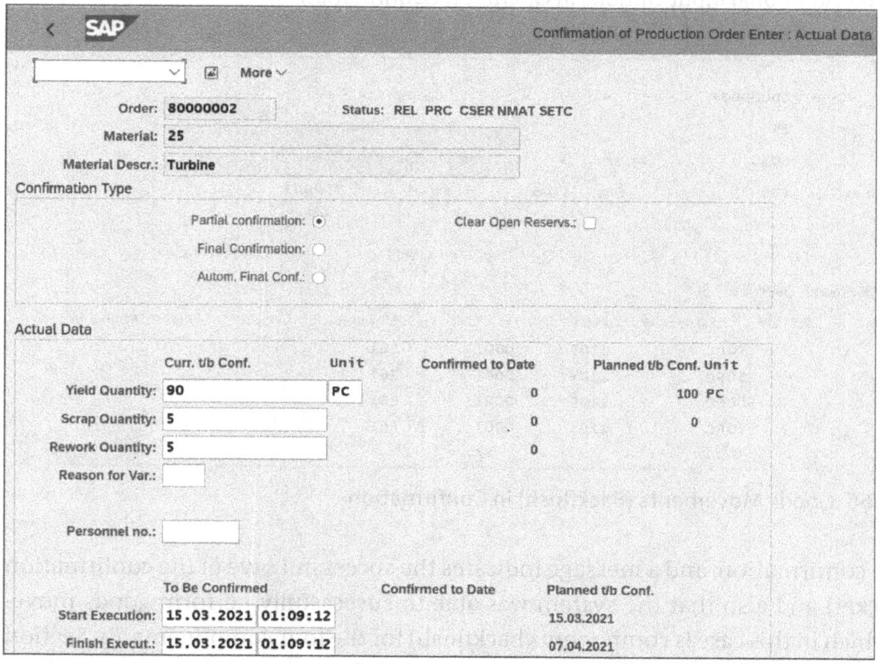

Figure 6.67 Production Order Confirmation

6.7.4   Confirmation Cancellation

If incorrect confirmation details are entered, such as for quantity or activities, then the confirmation can be cancelled using Transaction CO13. On the initial screen, enter the order number together with the operation number. On the next screen, choose **Save** to save the confirmation cancellation. There's no provision to make changes to a confirmation. A production supervisor will have to first cancel the confirmation and then do the confirmation again.

6.7.5   Display Confirmation

To display the entered confirmation, use Transaction CO14.

6.8   Goods Receipt

As soon as the last step or the operation in the production process is complete, the produced material is ready to be placed in stock for future sales or for consumption in the next assembly. This step increases the physical inventory of the material. When putting the material in stock, it can be posted in one of the following stock types:

- Unrestricted (freely usable) stock
- Quality inspection stock
- Blocked stock

If a company uses QM with PP in the production process, then the stock will go into quality inspection. The QM user performs the results recording and usage decision and also performs the stock posting of quality stock into unrestricted (or blocked) stock.

When a warehouse supervisor posts GR against the production order, the system carries out many activities in the background:

- The system increases the relevant stock type and also updates the information in the **Delivered Quantity** field of the production order.
- If the material is posted to consumption, then the system updates the consumption statistics, which facilitates the forecasting process.
- The system credits the production order, and the stock value increases.
- If material is posted to consumption, the system debits the recipient.
- The system updates the general ledger accounts in SAP S/4HANA Finance, such as the material stock account and the factory activity account.
- The system creates a material document showing the GR, as well as an accounting document, consisting of all postings in SAP S/4HANA Finance.

Either a manual or automatic process to perform the GR can be used, which we'll discuss in the following sections.

6.8.1   Goods Receipt: Manual Process

To perform GR against the production order, follow menu path **Logistics · Materials Management · Inventory Management · Goods Movement · Goods Movement**, or use Transaction MIGO. Figure 6.68 shows the initial screen to first select the **Goods Receipt** dropdown option, and then from the next dropdown, select **Order**. Enter the production order number as "80000001".

It's important to note that the system uses movement type **101**, as shown on the far-right side of the screen in the **GR Goods Receipt** field. On pressing [Enter], the system brings up the details of the material to perform GR against the production order (see Figure 6.68).

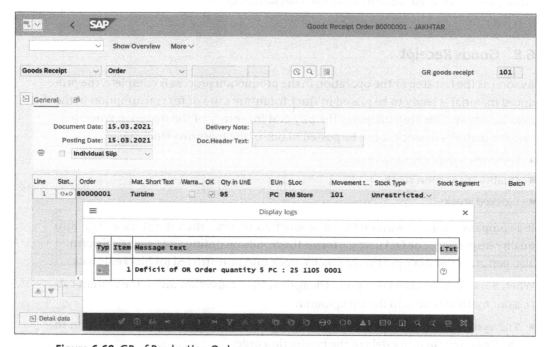

Figure 6.68 GR of Production Order

Make any changes to the quantity to reflect the actual GR quantity and enter the storage location (**SLoc**) of the receiving storage location. Finally, select the **OK** checkbox. Save the entries, and the system creates a material document number (and a corresponding accounting document). Notice the popup message that denotes a deficit of 5 PC between the quantity noted in a production order versus the goods being received in the warehouse. The deficit happened due to the scrap being recorded earlier in the production process.

For this example, we performed the GR of 95 PC of material 25 against the production order.

[«]

> **Note**
>
> The GR of a coproduct can also be performed in the same way.

Go back to the display production order screen (Transaction CO03). The system has updated the **Delivered** field to reflect the GR against the production order (see Figure 6.69).

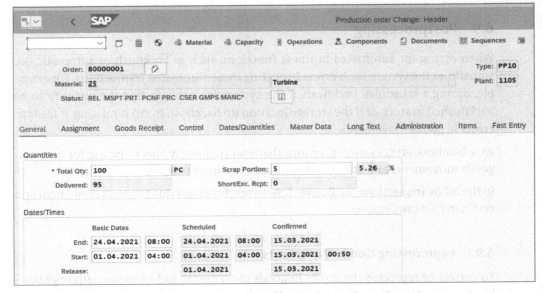

Figure 6.69 Shortage/Excess Production Updates in Production Order

The system updates two fields, **Delivered** and **Short/Exc. Rcpt**. A negative quantity in the latter field reflects a shortage in production and its eventual GR.

Depending on how the confirmation parameters of the production order are set up, the system either issues a warning or an error message if it finds confirmation that the GR quantity deviates from the predefined tolerance limits. Upper and lower tolerance limits can be maintained in the **Work Scheduling** view of the material master. If these tolerance limits aren't maintained, then the system infers this to be 0% tolerance and doesn't allow any underdelivery or overdelivery.

6.8.2 Goods Receipt: Automatic Process

To optimize the business process and eliminate manual data entry efforts, automatic GR against the production order can be performed when the last operation is confirmed. To activate automatic GR, make settings at two different configuration objects: the control key and production scheduling profile.

In each of these configuration objects, select the **Automatic Goods Receipt** checkbox. Then, assign the control key in the **Default Values** tab of the work center and assign the **Production Scheduling Profile** in the **Work Scheduling** view of the material master.

[»]

> **Note**
>
> We covered the automatic GR settings in Chapter 3.

6.9   Postprocessing

When opting for automated business functions, such as backflush or automatic GR, sometimes the system faces errors in posting these automated transactions. For example, during a scheduled backflush, if the system is unable to find the quantity to be backflushed in stock or if the storage location (to backflush from) is missing, it leads to errors in goods movements.

As a business process owner, ensure that you frequently check the log for errors in goods movements and attend to the issues in a timely fashion.

In the following sections, we'll cover how to resolve errors due to goods movement and errors in cost calculations.

6.9.1   Reprocessing Goods Movements

To correct or reprocess the errors in goods movements, follow menu path **Logistics • Production • Shop Floor Control • Confirmation • Reprocessing • Goods Movement**, or use Transaction COGI.

On the initial parameter selection screen, enter several relevant parameters so that the system only brings up the relevant records for processing. For this example, enter **Plant** "1105" and **Material** "25", and choose **Execute**.

Figure 6.70 consists of a list of four records that need to be reprocessed. Select a record and click **Display Errors** to see the nature of the error, as shown in Figure 6.71.

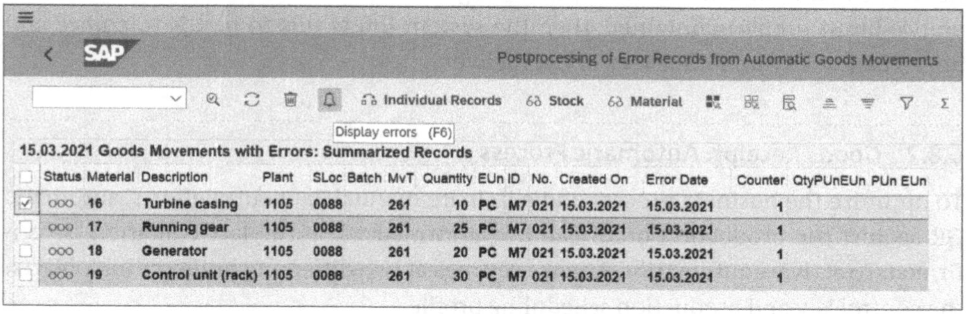

Figure 6.70 Postprocessing Records of Automatic Goods Movements

Figure 6.71 shows that the system found a deficit quantity in storage location 0088, which leads the system to terminate automatic goods movement processing. Select all four records and click the **Change Details** button.

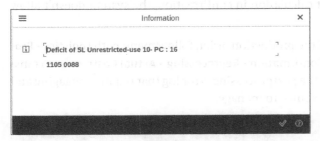

Figure 6.71 Error Details in Automatic Goods Movements

On the screen shown in Figure 6.72, change **SLoc** (storage location) from "0088" to "0001" for each of the four records, and then click the **Back** icon.

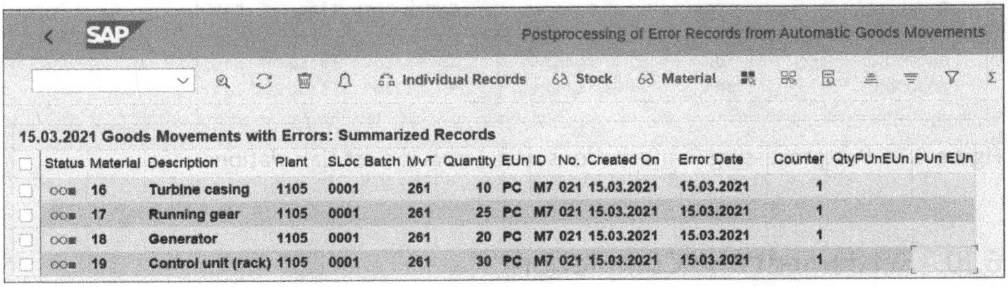

Status	Material	Description	Plant	SLoc	Batch	MvT	Quantity	EUn	ID	No.	Created On	Error Date	Counter	QtyPUnEUn	PUn	EUn
○○■	16	Turbine casing	1105	0001		261	10	PC	M7	021	15.03.2021	15.03.2021	1			
○○■	17	Running gear	1105	0001		261	25	PC	M7	021	15.03.2021	15.03.2021	1			
○○■	18	Generator	1105	0001		261	20	PC	M7	021	15.03.2021	15.03.2021	1			
○○■	19	Control unit (rack)	1105	0001		261	30	PC	M7	021	15.03.2021	15.03.2021	1			

15.03.2021 Goods Movements with Errors: Summarized Records

Postprocessing of Error Records from Automatic Goods Movements

Figure 6.72 Goods Movements with Errors

Figure 6.73 shows the successful reprocessing status of all four records, indicated by a green traffic light. Save the records, and the system reprocesses them and posts the GI.

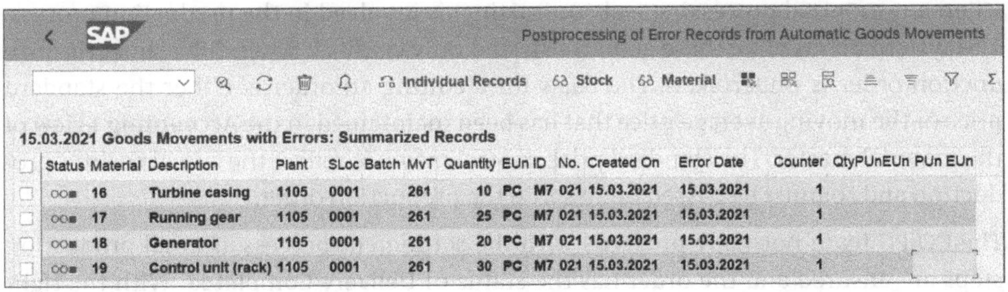

Status	Material	Description	Plant	SLoc	Batch	MvT	Quantity	EUn	ID	No.	Created On	Error Date	Counter	QtyPUnEUn	PUn	EUn
○○■	16	Turbine casing	1105	0001		261	10	PC	M7	021	15.03.2021	15.03.2021	1			
○○■	17	Running gear	1105	0001		261	25	PC	M7	021	15.03.2021	15.03.2021	1			
○○■	18	Generator	1105	0001		261	20	PC	M7	021	15.03.2021	15.03.2021	1			
○○■	19	Control unit (rack)	1105	0001		261	30	PC	M7	021	15.03.2021	15.03.2021	1			

15.03.2021 Goods Movements with Errors: Summarized Records

Postprocessing of Error Records from Automatic Goods Movements

Figure 6.73 Log for Automatic Goods Movements before Posting

6.9.2 Cost Calculation

Similar to automatic goods movement errors, cost calculation errors arise during the confirmation process when the system updates the costs based on entered data, such as activities. Depending on how the system is configured, errors occurring during the confirmation process and cost calculation can appear as warnings or errors. For warnings, the system allows saving the confirmation so that the errors can be processed later on. For errors during cost calculation in confirmation, the system doesn't allow saving the confirmation.

To reprocess the actual costs of the production order, follow menu path **Logistics • Production • Shop Floor Control • Confirmation • Reprocessing • Actual Costs**, or use Transaction COFC. Figure 6.74 shows the postprocessing error log that requires engaging and coordinating with the CO-PC resource to manage.

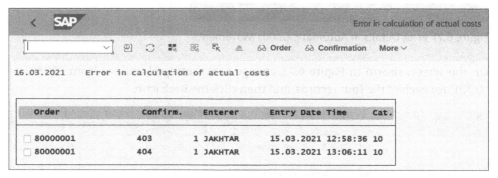

Figure 6.74 Postprocessing Confirmations with Errors in Cost Calculations

6.10   Settlement and Completion

When a production order is created, the system calculates the planned cost of the order. Thereafter, every business function that is performed will directly reflect as costs, which continue to accrue. This occurs, for example, when components are withdrawn against a production order, when an operation's activities are confirmed, or when any external processing (subcontracting) is involved in the production process. The system debits all of these actual costs and only credits it when GR against the production order is undertaken. The basis for crediting an order is either the standard price or the moving average price that has been maintained in the **Accounting 1** view of the material master. The standard price control may not reflect the actual costs of production and so must be passed on to settle the production order.

The CO-PC team normally proceeds with the settlement process after all production steps are ensured and the order has the status of **Delivery Completed**. With the right settings in place, the system assigns a settlement rule to the production order as soon as the order is created. A *settlement rule* defines the recipient to which the system will settle the order and distributes the percentages of costs to various settlement receivers. Some of the settlement receivers can be a material, a cost center, a project, or a sales order. Normally, the CO-PC team assigns the settlement receiver of the production order to the material account—so the settlement receiver is the material, and the settlement share is 100%. To display the settlement rule of a production order, choose **More • Header • Settlement Rule**.

When GR against the production order is performed, the system credits the production order and debits the material stock account. If the price control in the material master is standard price, then the system valuates the material at the standard price. Because the actual production costs often vary, the system posts the difference to the price difference account during the settlement process.

For the moving average price control in the material master, the system automatically valuates the material at the moving average that it determines. For the moving average calculation, it takes the total value of the material stock account and divides it by the total quantity of material available in all of the storage locations.

The *overheads* can be separately evaluated, which must be part of CO-PC. Overheads can be management or employee salaries, administration, and even utilities, such as electricity.

The *variances* can also be separately evaluated between planned and actual costs that occur due to the actual components and activities consumed that are different from (either larger than or smaller than) the plan according to the BOM and routing.

Similarly, as soon as the GI for the production order takes place, the system reflects this as work in process (WIP), and it remains so until the GR is posted and the stocks are updated. A production supervisor or even a cost controller can individually or collectively view the WIP details of production orders.

The completion of an order is logically divided into two distinct areas to distinguish logistical and accounting-based completion. When an order is technically completed and assigned the status **TECO**, the system updates the MRP-relevant details and deletes all reservations of components and capacity requirements. A production supervisor or even the cost controller can technically complete an order at any time by choosing **More • Functions • Restrict Processing • Complete Technically** in the order screen. After that, it isn't possible to make changes in the production order. Further, with a technically completed order, it also isn't possible to post costs to the order or perform any further confirmation.

While on the production order screen, a production planner can set the completion status by choosing **More • Functions • Restrict Processing • Close**. The system denotes the completion by the status **CLSD**. Both the completion and the technical completion steps can be achieved in mass processing steps. We explain the mass processing function in Section 6.11.4.

6.11   Additional Functions and Information Systems

In this section, we cover several of the functions that can be used to optimize business processes. We suggest checking out the features and functionalities available in each area, such as master data, transactional data, or reports. This can be achieved by navigating through each menu path and checking out the available options in the relevant folders (e.g., for the routing or work center).

6.11.1   From Planned Order: Individual Conversion

Although this entire chapter is primarily focused on covering the master data and the transactional data in the production processes, a production planner can also effectively use the planning data, which the system generates when the MRP is run. The output of MRP is the generation of planned orders, which can be converted into production orders for in-house production and purchase requisitions for external procurement. For in-house produced materials, it's important that the system is able to find the PP master data, such as BOM, routing, and production version.

There are two options to convert planned orders into production orders: interactive conversion in Transaction MD04 or individual conversion using Transaction CO40. With production order creation, all of the remaining functions are the same as covered in this chapter, such as its release, cost calculation, control instruction generation, and scheduling.

Note

See Chapter 13 and Chapter 14 on MRP.

6.11.2   From Planned Orders: Collective Conversion

Several planned orders can be converted into production orders collectively using Transaction CO41. On the initial screen, enter the selection parameters that the system will consider in bringing up the relevant planned orders. Assign an **Order Type** on the initial screen so that the collective conversion of planned orders to production orders is all of the same order type.

Note

Report PPBICO40 can also be used for the automatic conversion of planned orders into production orders in a batch job.

6.11.3   Production Order Creation without a Material

A production order without reference to a material can also be created; for example, there may be a business need to create a capacity placeholder for postprocessing or for maintenance works without using the maintenance orders. This option can also be used to record extra production costs incurred during rework and can reference the main (parent) production order for settlement.

Use Transaction CO07 to create production orders without a material. On the initial screen, enter the short text and assign a routing. If no routing is available, the system generates the operation from the default value that was defined in configuration.

6.11.4   Mass Processing

To process a large volume of transaction data or to simply optimize routine business processes, a production supervisor can use the mass processing functionality for the following functions:

- Performing confirmation
- Creating capacity requirements
- Picking
- Costing
- Checking material availability
- Generating control instructions
- Printing shop floor papers

For this example, perform the technically complete function using mass processing by following SAP menu pat, **Logistics • Production • Shop Floor Control • Control • Mass Reprocessing**, or by using Transaction COHV.

Figure 6.75 shows the initial parameters entry screen, in which the system offers a large number of parameters to select from. Enter **Production Plant** "1105", enter **Order Type** "PP10", and choose the **Mass Processing** tab.

On the next screen, select **Technically Complete** from the **Function** dropdown, and choose **Execute** (see Figure 6.76).

The system opens the worklist, where you can select **Production Order 80000002** and choose **Execute**. The system then displays the mass processing log (see Figure 6.77).

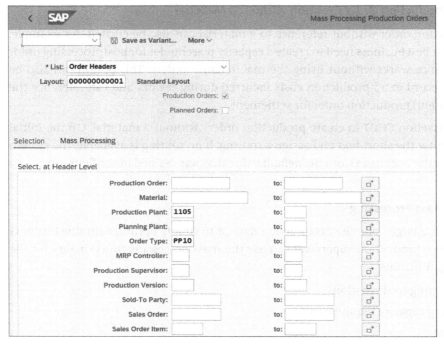

Figure 6.75 Initial Screen of Mass Processing Function

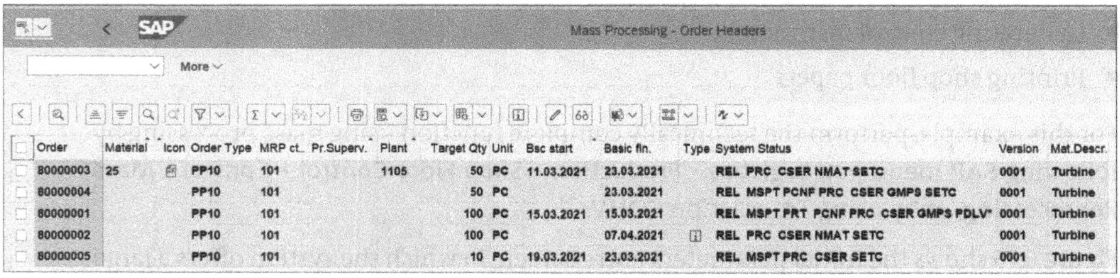

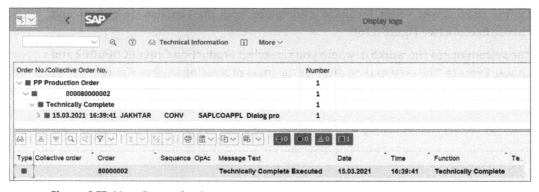

Figure 6.76 Confirmation through Mass Processing Function

Figure 6.77 Mass Processing Log

6.11.5 Information Systems

Due to the highly integrated nature of the SAP system, any activity or business function performed with reference to the production order automatically updates the relevant information.

Figure 6.78 shows the screen that appears after choosing **More • Production Order - Documented Goods Movements** within the production order display option (Transaction CO03), in which all of the GIs and receipts performed in MM are automatically updated.

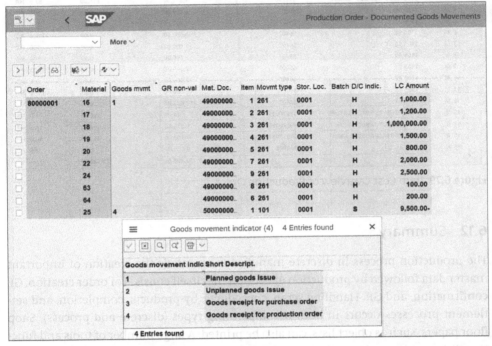

Figure 6.78 Documented Goods Movement in Production Order

Figure 6.79 shows the itemized costs of the production order, providing a detailed cost breakdown. It also keeps on updating the planned costs with actual costs to provide a quick evaluation. This is an integration point between PP and the CO-PC team.

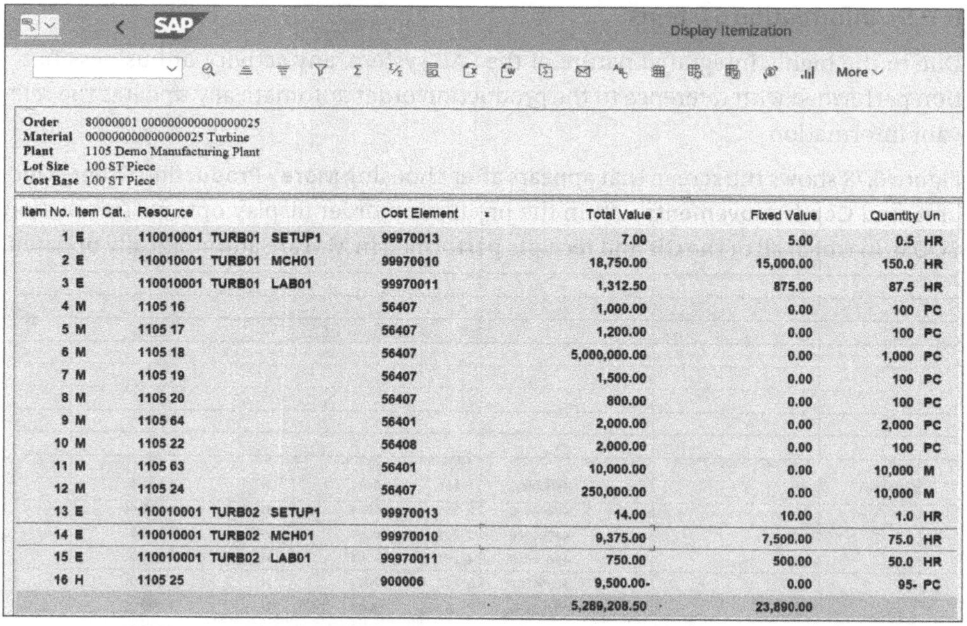

Order 80000001 000000000000000025
Material 000000000000000025 Turbine
Plant 1105 Demo Manufacturing Plant
Lot Size 100 ST Piece
Cost Base 100 ST Piece

Item No.	Item Cat.	Resource	Cost Element	Total Value	Fixed Value	Quantity	Un
1	E	110010001 TURB01 SETUP1	99970013	7.00	5.00	0.5	HR
2	E	110010001 TURB01 MCH01	99970010	18,750.00	15,000.00	150.0	HR
3	E	110010001 TURB01 LAB01	99970011	1,312.50	875.00	87.5	HR
4	M	1105 16	56407	1,000.00	0.00	100	PC
5	M	1105 17	56407	1,200.00	0.00	100	PC
6	M	1105 18	56407	5,000,000.00	0.00	1,000	PC
7	M	1105 19	56407	1,500.00	0.00	100	PC
8	M	1105 20	56407	800.00	0.00	100	PC
9	M	1105 64	56401	2,000.00	0.00	2,000	PC
10	M	1105 22	56408	2,000.00	0.00	100	PC
11	M	1105 63	56401	10,000.00	0.00	10,000	M
12	M	1105 24	56407	250,000.00	0.00	10,000	M
13	E	110010001 TURB02 SETUP1	99970013	14.00	10.00	1.0	HR
14	E	110010001 TURB02 MCH01	99970010	9,375.00	7,500.00	75.0	HR
15	E	110010001 TURB02 LAB01	99970011	750.00	500.00	50.0	HR
16	H	1105 25	900006	9,500.00-	0.00	95-	PC
				5,289,208.50	23,890.00		

Figure 6.79 Item Cost Overview of Production Order

6.12 Summary

The production process in discrete manufacturing entails the creation of important master data followed by production execution that itself consists of order creation, GI, confirmation, and GR. Handling scrap, coproducts, by-products, completion, and settlement processes occurs in both manufacturing types (discrete and process). Shop floor papers, such as object lists, can also be printed. A large number of tools and functionalities can be used to optimize the business processes, such as backflush, automatic GR, mass processing, and postprocessing. WIP batches can also be implemented to have better control over the entire production process.

The next chapter discusses the business processes in production planning for process industries (PP-PI).

Chapter 7
Production Planning for Process Manufacturing

Building on the important configuration of process manufacturing undertaken in Chapter 4, this chapter covers important business processes and functions, as well as the vital and logical links of configuration with those business processes. Greater focus is placed on process management in the master recipe, which is unique to process industries only but can also be implemented in discrete manufacturing if there's any business need for it.

Production planning for process industries (PP-PI) is characterized by product complexity. For many industries, it's necessary to integrate batch management and quality management (QM) with process manufacturing in PP-PI. Some of the industries in which process manufacturing finds extensive implementation include chemicals, edible oil refining, pharmaceuticals, fertilizers, beverages, food, and food processing. Any manufacturing industry that deals with liquids, where the product flows in a liquid or semisolid form, or where the processed material can't be brought back to its original state or disassembled, characterizes process manufacturing.

The chapter begins with an overview of process manufacturing and how it fits into the planning and production perspectives. The process manufacturing process flow provides a comprehensive and step-by-step explanation of each stage involved. Important process manufacturing master data is covered next, with extensive focus on the master recipe, in which the system facilitates not only material quantity calculation but also process management. We cover some of the standard features available in process management, such as input and calculated values, integration with the Document Management service, and digital signatures. We then cover the end-to-end business processes involved, from the creation of the process order to how process management integrates with it.

Next, we cover the highly versatile and intuitive functionality of Execution Steps (XSteps) when a company either wants to implement it or simply transition from process instructions to XSteps. More features and functionalities of XSteps are shown, as well at their correlations to the configurations made in Chapter 4.

We then cover process message evaluations and the process manufacturing cockpit (configured in Chapter 4) to see how they help to facilitate the business processes.

Because PP-PI processes, such as goods issue (GI), confirmation, and goods receipt (GR), are all similar to those in discrete manufacturing, we suggest revisiting the relevant sections of Chapter 3 and Chapter 6.

7.1   Process Manufacturing Overview

Figure 7.1 shows an overview of the end-to-end process involved in process manufacturing. The business processes involved can be divided broadly into the following areas:

- Process planning
- Process order execution
- Process management
- Order closure

Production planning in PP-PI begins when a materials planner converts the output of material requirements planning (MRP), which in this case is a planned order, into a process order. This is then followed by a material availability check to ensure that the required quantities of components needed to produce the material are available. If the material quantity calculation functionality is enabled in the master recipe of the material, the system calculates the components' quantities. If not, it reads the information from the material's bill of materials (BOM). At this stage, the system can perform batch determination of the components that are going to be used in the production process.

The next step is to proceed with releasing the process order, as well as printing the process order. With a released process order, a control recipe can be generated. A generated control recipe takes the form of a PI sheet. Several of these process order management activities can run automatically or in the background to minimize managing them manually. For example, a planner determines that on creating a process order, the system can automatically release it too. If not, the process order will have to be released manually. Alternatively, use a separate transaction to release a large number of process orders (mass processing), which again can be carried out as a manual task.

The materials management (MM) functionality plays an important role when raw materials and components need to be issued against a process order. QM processes, if integrated with production planning (PP), enable extensive in-process (during production) quality inspection checks. During this time, the planner also maintains the PI sheet and assigns it a **Complete** status. Then confirmation of the process order, either at the individual phase level or at the entire process order level, is undertaken. When goods are produced, it's again time to engage MM to ensure GR against the process order. Finally, sending the process messages back to the SAP system is the last step of process management.

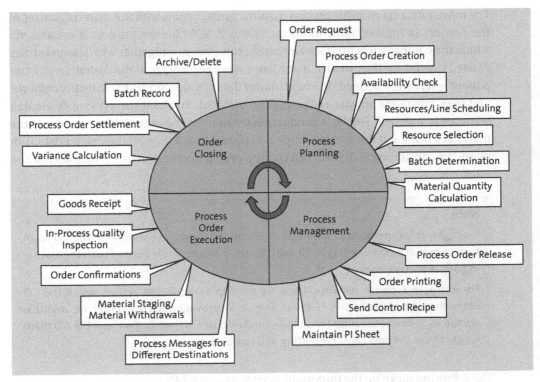

Figure 7.1 Production Planning and Execution in Process Industries

The cost object controlling activities, such as work in process (WIP) determination, variance calculation, and settlement, are order-specific in nature and are usually processed in the background. PP completely integrates with cost object controlling in the SAP system, so it's imperative that extensive coordination is ensured for comprehensive business processes mapping.

To optimize and bring greater visibility to the business processes, several additional processes and functionalities, such as digital signature, engineering change management (ECM), SAP Document Management service, coproducts and by-products, shift notes, and shift reports can be implemented and integrated. It's also possible to integrate QM during production (in-process quality inspection) or at the time of GR.

7.2   Master Data in Process Manufacturing

Process manufacturing has its own unique and often overlapping master data with other production types, such as discrete manufacturing or repetitive manufacturing (REM). If the master data is set up in the right sequence, it's much easier and more logical to interconnect the master data because the predecessor-successor relationship is already taken care of.

The master data creation for process manufacturing begins with the material master of the product (a finished good or an assembly). A BOM for the product is created, via which the company will produce and assign components, together with the quantities needed to produce the product. If needed, a scrap percentage at the operation or component level can be defined. The next master data creation step is to create the resource and then create the master recipe for the material, in which the previously created resource is assigned. Finally, a production version for the material is created and the material's BOM and the master recipe is assigned to it. When all the master data is in place, the controlling (CO) team can create a product cost estimate of the material and release it.

Note

It's highly recommended to maintain close coordination and liaison with the CO team to ensure that when working in PP, both teams are completely aligned with their working and reporting needs.

For example, for each resource, there's a need to assign a cost center, which the CO team should provide to the PP team. They may provide one cost center for multiple resources or one cost center for an individual resource, depending on how the CO team wants to see the cost center reporting and evaluation.

The following make up the important master data in PP-PI:

- Material master
- BOM
- Resource
- Production version
- Master recipe

We'll discuss each in detail in the following sections.

7.2.1   Material Master

The material master is the central master record in logistics and the supply chain. The system defines a *material* as a substance or commodity that a company buys or sells on a commercial basis. A material can also be either consumed or produced. A few examples of materials are raw materials, packing materials, consumables, semifinished goods, and finished goods. The material isn't just restricted to production-based processes but is used in all those processes in which the company wants to maintain inventory (stock items). Therefore, a company may also have materials that are used in plant maintenance (PM) processes or even have nonvaluated materials.

For PP-PI, there is extensive use of *batch management*. A *batch* is a uniquely identifiable partial quantity of a material. The batches of a material are managed in separate stocks. In a production process, a batch is a quantity of a specific material produced during a standardized production run. This quantity therefore represents a nonreproducible unit with unique specifications. The key properties of a batch are homogeneity and nonreproducibility.

A batch can be traced across the entire supply chain—that is, from the receipt of the raw material to processing in production and the creation of the final product, all of the way to sales and delivery to the customer. Complete batch traceability, batch determination, and batch derivation functionalities are available. The batch information cockpit (Transaction BMBC) can be used for complete top-down or bottom-up evaluation of material batches.

The system creates batches for a material, and the data of the material master is valid for all batches assigned to it. In contrast to the material master, a batch master record contains data that uniquely identifies the corresponding batch and characterizes the unit as one that can't be reproduced. The characteristic batch specifications are assigned using characteristics from the classification system in the material master and are inherited by the corresponding batch master records.

> **Note**
> Chapter 10 covers batch management.

7.2.2 Bill of Materials

The BOM in PP-PI is the same as in discrete manufacturing. Refer to Chapter 3 and Chapter 6 for a detailed understanding of the configuration and business processes involved in BOMs.

The material quantity calculation is unique only to PP-PI and uses components of the material defined in its BOM. When calculating the components' quantities that the system should use in reference to each other, it refers to the information in the BOM. See Section 7.2.5 concerning the master recipe for a detailed understanding of material quantity calculation.

To create a BOM, you use Transaction CS01.

7.2.3 Resource

The resource in process manufacturing is the same as the work center in discrete manufacturing. Refer to Chapter 3 and Chapter 6 for a detailed understanding of the configuration and business processes involved in work centers (resources in PP-PI). To create a resource, use Transaction CRC1.

The system offers and makes available standard configuration for PP-PI that can be used if a company's business processes aren't too complex. For example, set the **Usage** as "OO8" (for master recipe + process order) and **Standard Value Key** as "SAP4" (process manufacturing), in which only **Duration** is listed as an activity. The available control key available for use is PIO1 (Master Recipe/Process Order).

7.2.4   Production Version

A production version determines which alternative BOM the system should use in combination with the master recipe for process manufacturing. In PP-PI, it's mandatory to define a production version. The system uses the production version during the creation of a master recipe to identify the BOM for the material and pull the BOM details from the master recipe.

When creating the master recipe for a material and plant combination, it's mandatory to also enter the production version for the material on the initial screen. The production version should be created prior to the creation of the master recipe and then be used for creation of the master recipe.

To create a new production version, use Transaction C223. A production version can also be created in the **MRP 4** view of the material master or even in the **Work Scheduling** view. Refer to Chapter 6, Section 6.2.5 for a detailed understanding of the business process of a production version and how to create one in the SAP system.

> **[»]**
>
> **Note**
>
> Creating a production version directly from Transaction MM02 should be an exception because there may still be some incomplete data at this stage. Use Transaction C223 to achieve this objective instead.

7.2.5   Master Recipe Creation

Before creating a master recipe, a user can create a production version and include BOM details only (without the master recipe details because these aren't available at that time). Next, create the master recipe and give reference to the production version because it's a mandatory requirement to enter a production version during master recipe creation. Then, go back to the production version and incorporate the master recipe details, including the group number and group counter that the system generated when the master recipe is saved. The system suggests the master recipe group number and the group counter when the production version is again called up. With this approach, creating a master recipe makes a materials list (BOM) available in the master recipe, which can then also be used in the material quantity calculation.

A second approach that can be used in creating the master recipe is to first create a master recipe group without reference to a material and plant combination. When the system generates the recipe group number, create a production version of the material and enter the BOM and master recipe details. Finally, when the header material number is assigned in the change master recipe option for the master recipe group, the system prompts the user to enter a production version to enable it to explode the BOM.

To create a master recipe for which the production version already exists, follow SAP menu path **Logistics · Production—Process · Master Data · Master Recipes · Recipe and Material List · Create**, or use Transaction C201. On the initial screen of the master recipe, enter the **Material**, **Plant**, and **Profile** (see Figure 7.2), and the header screen appears. Recall from Chapter 4 that the master recipe's profile is a control function to allow or disallow certain functions, such as XSteps being optional or mandatory. The **Key date** controls when the master recipe will be available for production process. Either enter the key date manually or, if no entry is maintained, the system will use the date of master recipe creation as the key date.

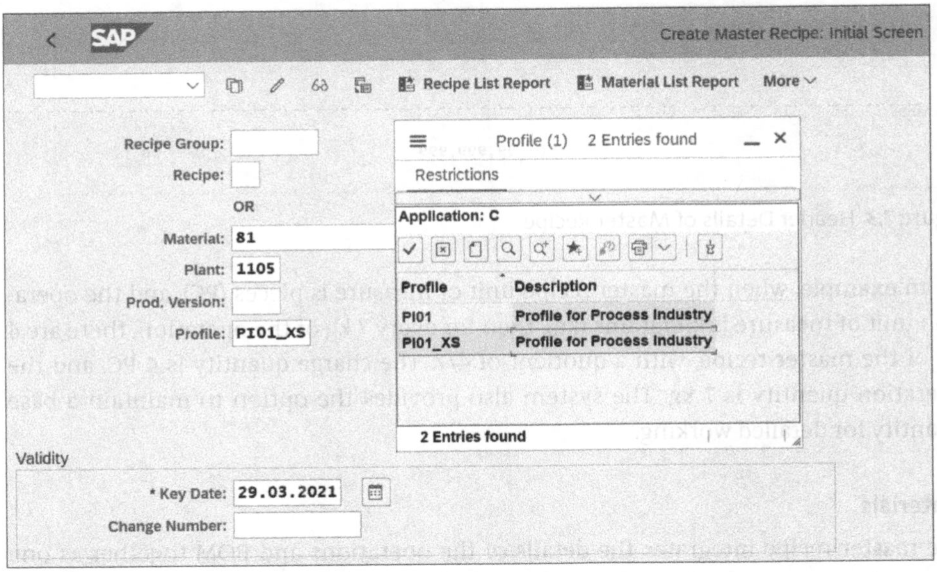

Figure 7.2 Initial Screen of Master Recipe Creation

We'll discuss the different elements of this screen in the following sections.

Recipe Header

Figure 7.3 shows the header details screen of the master recipe. The **Charge Quantity Range** area is valid for the lot size quantities in the master recipe. It contains the default values for the operation, phase, and secondary resources. A proportional relationship exists between the default values for operation quantities and their unit of measure versus the recipe quantities and their unit of measure. Compared with master recipes, maintain this relationship directly in the operation details in routing and rate routings.

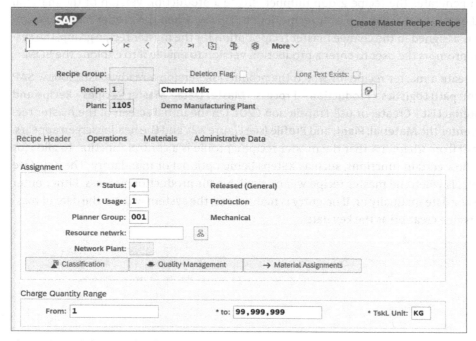

Figure 7.3 Header Details of Master Recipe

As an example, when the master recipe unit of measure is pieces (PC), and the operation unit of measure is kilograms (kg), then for every 7 kg of the operation, there are 4 PC of the master recipe, with a quotient of 4/7. The charge quantity is 4 PC, and the operation quantity is 7 kg. The system also provides the option to maintain a base quantity for detailed working.

Materials

The master recipe integrates the details of the operations and BOM together as one master data element by using the production version. The system explodes the BOM in the master recipe to bring up the details of the material BOM. The material BOM details in the task list (master recipe) help enable a feature unique to process manufacturing known as *material quantity calculation*.

[»] **Note**

It's crucial to adopt one of the two approaches mentioned previously for the creation of a production version in relation to the master recipe to ensure the master recipe contains the materials (BOM).

Material Quantity Calculation

In a process order, the system calculates the components' quantities directly from the BOM and takes the material quantity calculation into account.

With the material quantity calculation, the following options are available:

- Change the header product quantity with reference to components' quantities or even with respect to the active ingredient proportions.
- Calculate the planned scrap at the phase level; the system includes it in the planned production cost.
- Change components' quantities with reference to each other, the header product, or the active ingredient proportions (batch characteristics and their values).
- Change operation or phase quantities when these aren't in proportion to the product quantity.

For material quantity calculation to work effectively, make sure to create the master recipe with reference to the BOM consisting of components and quantities.

Because the planned scrap of the component is entered either in the material master or in the BOM, the system automatically increases the component quantity during planned order or process order creation. Use the planned scrap of a component as a variable to calculate the other component's quantity using the material quantity calculation formula.

When a process order is created, the system automatically calculates the quantities based on the formulas. For a formula that is processed at the batch level and also uses active ingredient proportions (batch characteristics values), the material quantity calculation needs to be triggered manually in the process order and after batch determination.

Note

Note that the system only considers batch characteristics with numeric values.

When the system explodes the BOM in the master recipe, go to the **Material Quantity Calculation** screen shown in Figure 7.4 by choosing **Goto • Material Quantity Calculation** or by clicking **Material Quantity Calc.** (calculation) in the **Materials** tab of the master recipe.

In general, the following steps are involved in entering the formula for the material quantity calculation:

1. On the screen shown in Figure 7.4, place the cursor on the field for which you want to change the quantity using a formula, and click the **Select Formula** button in the menu bar.

2. In the **Formula Definition** box, enter the formula or equation, which derives the output field value.

3. While creating a formula, double-click the variables to be included in the formula, or place the cursor on the variable and click the **Insert in Formula** button on the menu bar.

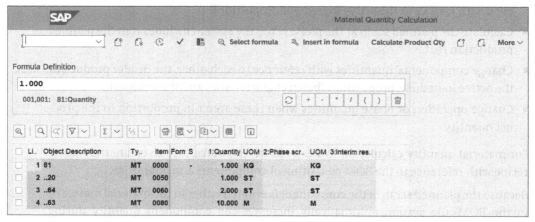

Figure 7.4 Material Quantity Calculation in Master Recipe

It's possible to use formula operators such as **+**, **−**, *****, **/**, **DIV**, and **MOD**, as well as exponential, rounding (**ROUND**), absolute values (**ABS**), truncation (**TRUNC**), **EXP**, **LOG**, **SIN**, **COS**, **TAN**, square root (**SQRT**), **IF THEN ELSE** conditions, and **IF THEN NOT** conditions.

Operations and Phases

Master recipes use a *phase*, which works in the same manner as operations do in routing for discrete manufacturing. It's easier to maintain detailed levels working at the phase level in the master recipe because a production supervisor can manage and incorporate more production details, including process management.

In the master recipe, assign activities such as production duration or labor hours at the phase level and not at the operation level. Hence, the confirmation of a process order is recorded for a phase and not an operation. A resource (work center) is assigned at the operation level. The phases below the operation then adopt the resource that was assigned at the operation level. The system assigns the standard values and activities (controlled by a control key in the resource) as active at the phase level and not at the operation level. The sum total of standard values at a phase is in fact the total time required to process the operation. The system assigns the components of the BOM (materials list) to phases and not to operations. However, integration of in-process quality inspections of QM can take place either at the operation level or phase level.

To create a phase below an operation, select the **Phase** checkbox in the **Operations** tab, which then automatically copies the resource from the operation. At the same time, when defining a phase, it's also necessary to assign the *superior* operation so that the system knows which specific phase relates to which operation.

Relationships among various phases, such as start-finish, finish-start, finish-finish, or start-start, can be maintained. The phases can work either in parallel or in overlapping sequences. In the **Operations** tab of the master recipe, access the phase relationship screen for phases by selecting the phases and choosing **Goto · Relationships**.

Individual control recipe destinations are assigned at the phase level and assign the process instructions in the respective phases of the master recipe. If the scope of generation is defined in the configuration of the process instructions, it reduces the data maintenance efforts at the master recipe level. Alternatively, maintain the desired process instruction details either in the master recipe or in the process order. For process instructions that have characteristic values based on a material, assign them at the master recipe level. To assign process instructions to the phases in the **Operations** tab of the master recipe, use the menu path **Goto · Process Management · Process Instructions**.

Figure 7.5 shows the **Operations** tab of the master recipe, in which the **Operation** is **0010**. Enter the **Resource** "MIX1" at the operation level, and the system automatically copies it in all of the phases below it. The phase is **0020** and is denoted by the **Phase Indicator** checkbox. When you define an operation as a phase, you also have to define the **Sup. Operation**, which, for this example, is **0010** (the operation).

The control recipe **Destination** is **CM**. This is the same control recipe destination that was configured in Chapter 4.

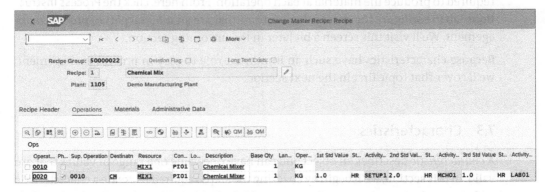

Figure 7.5 Operations Overview in Master Recipe

Notice that the system automatically copies the **Control key, PIO1**, from the **Resource MIX1**. Select the phase **0020** and double-click the line item **0020** (the operation, which is basically a phase), and the system brings up the screen shown in Figure 7.6.

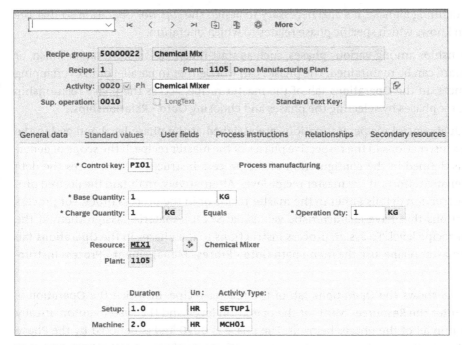

Figure 7.6 Standard Values in Master Recipe

This shows the **Standard Values** tab of the master recipe, where you can maintain the duration of the activities, such as the **Setup, Machine**, or **Labor** (not shown) hours required to produce the material at each operation. From here, click the **Process Instructions** tab to configure the process instructions that are an integral part of process management. We'll visit this screen a bit later in the upcoming section.

Because characteristics have such an important role to play in process management, we'll cover that topic first in the next section.

7.3   Characteristics

A *characteristic* describes an object and can have one value or a range of values that are valid. In this section, we'll begin by covering the steps required to create a characteristic and the available options. We'll also cover the associated configuration settings that can help users effectively create characteristics and put relevant controls in place.

Use Transaction CT04 to create a characteristic, via the menu path **SAP Menu · Cross-Application Components · Classification System · Master Data · Characteristics**.

In Figure 7.7, information related to the characteristic is defined, such as description, data type, number of characteristics, decimal places (if any), and unit of measure. Table 7.1 describes some of the important fields seen in the various tabs shown in Figure 7.7.

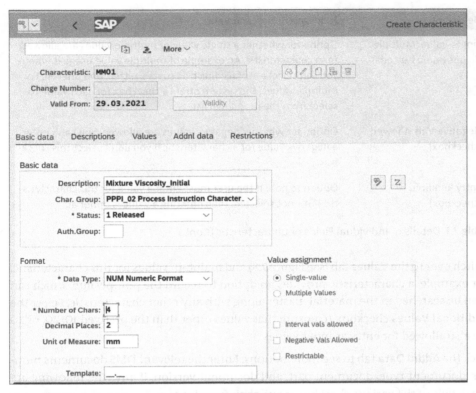

Figure 7.7 Basic Data Screen for Transaction CT04

Field Name	Field Description and Value
Description	Description of the characteristic; for example, thickness.
Char. Group	Groups together similar characteristics in one group.
Status	Status of the characteristic, for example, **Released**, to indicate it's ready for use.
Data Type	Indicates the type of data this characteristic has; for example, date, time format, or numeric format.
Number of Chars	Indicates the number of characters a value of this characteristic can contain.
Decimal Places	Indicates the number of decimal places if the format is numeric.
Unit of Measure	Unit of measure of the characteristic (quantitative/numeric), if any.

Table 7.1 Details of Individual Fields of Characteristic

Field Name	Field Description and Value
Single-value/Multiple Values (radio buttons)	Option for whether a single value or multiple values are allowed for a characteristic. An example of multiple value usage is when you can select a surface finish as coarse, pitted, and uneven. For multiple values, the system offers a checkbox for each value to select from the dropdown list.
Negative Vals Allowed (checkbox)	Option for whether negative values are allowed. You can't enter a negative value for a characteristic if you don't select this checkbox.
Entry Required (checkbox)	Option to note if the user must enter a value for this characteristic. If it's not selected, then entering a value is optional.

Table 7.1 Details of Individual Fields of Characteristic (Cont.)

Switch over to the **Values** tab (see Figure 7.8) and maintain values for this characteristic. For example, a characteristic provides an option to record the pump value, which can then be searched in the material master along with any other characteristic. Select the **Additional Values** checkbox to ensure that values other than the prefixed 10, 20, or 30 are also allowed for entry as input values.

Click the **Addnl Data** tab to see more options. Enter the relevant DMS documents number, document type, document part, and document version, if any. The following are the details of the various checkboxes and their functions:

- **Not Ready for Input**
  No value can be maintained for this characteristic. In other words, a preassigned default or calculated value automatically fills the characteristic field, and the user has no option to make an entry.

- **No Display**
  The system won't display a characteristic.

- **Display Allowed Values**
  If several values are already available from the **Values** tab of the characteristic, the system displays those values to facilitate the user during data entry.

- **Unformatted Entry**
  If this checkbox is selected, the system makes the provision to set the characteristic's field length to a maximum of 30 so the user can make multiple entries, separated by colons. If not selected, then the system displays the exact length of the characteristic for data entry.

- **Proposed Template**
  If selected, the system proposes or displays a template to help the user during data entry. Click back to the **Basic Data** tab to view the template details.

Finally, on the **Restrictions** tab, the use of a characteristic can be restricted to specific class types; otherwise, it will be available for use in all class types. For example, entering class type "001" will restrict this characteristic to the material class type only. Save the entries.

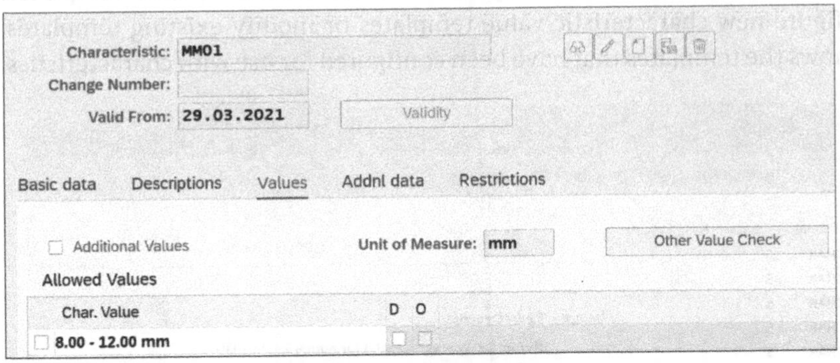

Figure 7.8 Allowed Values for Characteristic

> **Note**
> If a characteristic with a date format is created and then used in any class, the system will *not* provide the standard option of bringing up a calendar from which to choose a date. The user has to enter the date manually. If a user wants to have the calendar option in the dropdown of the date characteristic, then engage the assistance of an ABAP consultant.

> **Tips and Tricks**
> The standard system offers the provision to use a separate batch input program to upload large numbers of characteristics.

SAP includes a number of templates that can be used for the entry of information into the characteristic values. If a new template is required for a specific characteristic value, this can be configured.

Many characters are configured for use in the templates. These can be found using a configuration navigation path, **SAP IMG • Cross-Application Components • Classification System • Characteristics • Define Template Characters**.

Figure 7.9 shows the characters that are defined for use in the templates. The **Usage** field determines how the character is used via the following options:

- **1:** Numeric character that is valid for numeric and character formats.
- **2:** Alphanumeric character that is valid for character formats.
- **3:** Character that is valid for the character format.

- **4**: Preliminary sign that is valid for the character format.
- **5**: Separator that is valid for the character format.

By accessing the transaction using the configuration navigation path **SAP IMG • Cross-Application Components • Classification System • Characteristics • Define Templates**, you can configure new characteristic value templates or modify existing templates. Figure 7.10 shows the templates that have been configured for use with characteristics.

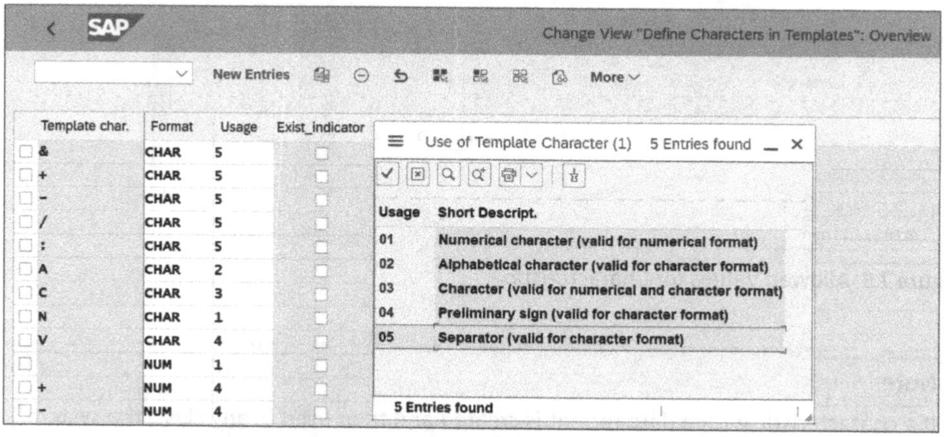

Template char.	Format	Usage	Exist_indicator
&	CHAR	5	
+	CHAR	5	
-	CHAR	5	
/	CHAR	5	
:	CHAR	5	
A	CHAR	2	
C	CHAR	3	
N	CHAR	1	
V	CHAR	4	
	NUM	1	
+	NUM	4	
-	NUM	4	

Usage	Short Descript.
01	Numerical character (valid for numerical format)
02	Alphabetical character (valid for character format)
03	Character (valid for numerical and character format)
04	Preliminary sign (valid for character format)
05	Separator (valid for character format)

Figure 7.9 Define Characters for Characteristic Templates

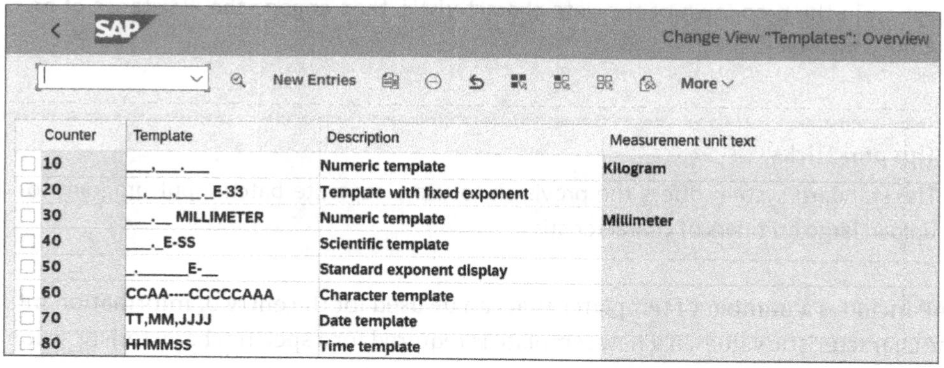

Counter	Template	Description	Measurement unit text
10	___,___.___	Numeric template	Kilogram
20	_,___,___.__E-33	Template with fixed exponent	
30	___.__ MILLIMETER	Numeric template	Millimeter
40	___._E-SS	Scientific template	
50	_.______E-__	Standard exponent display	
60	CCAA----CCCCCAAA	Character template	
70	TT,MM,JJJJ	Date template	
80	HHMMSS	Time template	

Figure 7.10 Creation and Modification of New Characteristic Value Templates

7.4 Process Management

Because a large number of features and functionalities of process instructions exist within an operation's phase of the master recipe, it warrants a separate section in this chapter. This section deals with process instructions (which is a part of process management) that need to be defined in the **Process Instructions** tab shown previously in Figure 7.6.

In a manufacturing organization, a permanent requirement is to monitor system performance and plant parameters. For example, when the production of a certain item is scheduled, the plant operator needs to have a series of clear and comprehensive instructions to follow. Similarly, the plant operator is required to record and report back data, such as steam temperature twice a shift or an abnormal vibration in the suction pump, so that it will be available for future reference or corrective action.

Therefore, a functionality is needed in the SAP system that can transfer and communicate all such information in a timely manner from the plant operator back to the process control system (PCS). This has been made possible by the process management functionality.

Note

Transmitting information between an SAP system and a PCS is made possible by defining the type of the control recipe destination. We focus on the transfer to PI sheets to show that implementing process management can still yield significant added value without integrating SAP with a PCS.

Process management completely integrates with core functional areas such as MM, QM, and DMS. It offers functionality such as GIs and GRs, process order confirmations, and results recording of quality inspection data. All of this information helps in analysis and report generation functions, not to mention benefiting the business process owners who are directly using the information.

The following summarizes the functions supported by process management in PP-PI:

- Receiving control recipes from released process orders
- Sending control recipes to process operators or PCSs
- Preparing process instructions as texts so that the process operators can display them on their computer screens
- Receiving, checking, and sending process messages with actual process data
- Monitoring process messages and control recipes
- Manually creating process messages

In the following sections, we'll cover some of the elements of process management and how to intuitively create a PI sheet.

7.4.1 Elements in Process Management

Figure 7.11 illustrates the various elements involved in process management for data flow. Starting from the top left, creating a process order forms the basis for the generation of the control recipe.

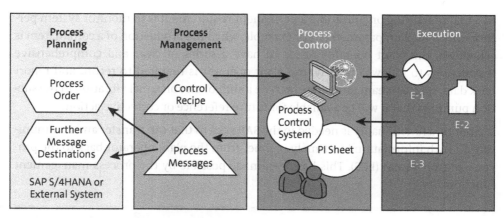

Figure 7.11 Overview of Process Management

The system sends the control recipe in the form of a PI sheet to the predefined control recipe destinations. The process operator follows the instructions given in the PI sheet and also fills the PI sheet with relevant plant parameters and other important data, and then returns it as a process message either to the SAP system or to an external system.

7.4.2   Integrating Process Management

In an automated environment, object linking and embedding (OLE) for process control (OPC) and SAP OPC Data Access enable the system to read and write data points and events using the OPC server for the SAP system. This function is also available in production orders (discrete manufacturing).

> **Note**
>
> OPC is a standard that uses component object model/distributed component object model (COM/DCOM) technology to define interfaces independent of the manufacturer for use in an industry. SAP designed the OPC standard especially for the process control level. OPC servers allow access to various data sources, such as PCSs, programmable logic controllers, and temperature sensors, and thus provide process data that can be requested by OPC clients.

With SAP Manufacturing Integration and Intelligence, the SAP system offers an adaptive manufacturing solution for production. SAP Manufacturing Integration and Intelligence provides manufacturing companies increased flexibility through improved linking of the SAP system to the production process level and by making real-time information available. SAP Manufacturing Integration and Intelligence can be used in both the process order and production order environment. It provides standardized, preconfigured connectors to enable real-time data integration in manufacturing execution systems (MESs) and supervisory control and data acquisition (SCADA) systems.

A process operator can run real-time analyses and display the results in browser- and role-based dashboards. These analyses provide important information for checking and supporting decision-making, such as warnings, job lists, analyses, reports, and real-time messages about production variance.

7.4.3 Process Instructions

An operation in the master recipe may have several phases, and each phase requires a control recipe destination. After a control recipe destination is defined for an operation, it automatically applies to all phases of that operation. Within each phase, process management-related information is incorporated, including process message categories, process instruction characteristics, and control recipe destinations.

Process instructions are assigned to the phases in the **Operations** tab of the master recipe. To do this, select the specific phase, and use the following path in the **Operations** tab: **Master Recipe—Goto • Process Management • Process Instructions**.

In the resulting screen, shown in Figure 7.12, there are two process instruction categories, **AREAD1** and **PP20**. **AREAD1** relates to the request to the shop floor to get the measured value of the process parameter. The second process instruction category, **PP20**, is the same one that was configured in Chapter 4. The **Control Recipe Destination CM (Chemical Mixing)** is also one that was configured in Chapter 4.

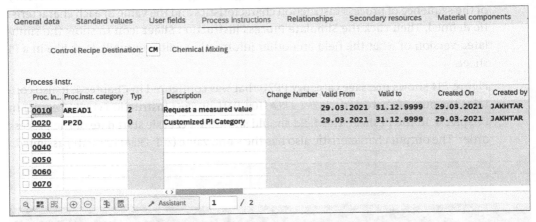

Figure 7.12 Process Instructions for Control Recipe Destination PP

> **Note**
>
> Implement SAP Note 2508866 in SAP S/4HANA if an error is faced during the selection of process instruction categories via F4 help.

Double-click **Proc. Instr.** (process instruction) **0010** (with **Proc.instr. category AREAD1**) to go to the screen shown in Figure 7.13.

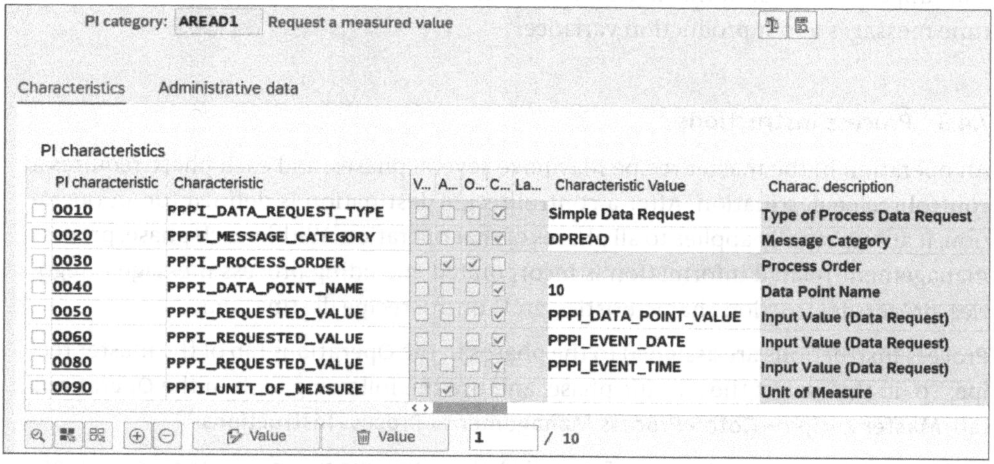

PI characteristic	Characteristic	V...	A...	O...	C...	La...	Characteristic Value	Charac. description
0010	PPPI_DATA_REQUEST_TYPE				☑		Simple Data Request	Type of Process Data Request
0020	PPPI_MESSAGE_CATEGORY				☑		DPREAD	Message Category
0030	PPPI_PROCESS_ORDER		☑	☑				Process Order
0040	PPPI_DATA_POINT_NAME				☑		10	Data Point Name
0050	PPPI_REQUESTED_VALUE				☑		PPPI_DATA_POINT_VALUE	Input Value (Data Request)
0060	PPPI_REQUESTED_VALUE				☑		PPPI_EVENT_DATE	Input Value (Data Request)
0080	PPPI_REQUESTED_VALUE				☑		PPPI_EVENT_TIME	Input Value (Data Request)
0090	PPPI_UNIT_OF_MEASURE		☑					Unit of Measure

PI category: **AREAD1**   Request a measured value

Characteristics   Administrative data

PI characteristics

Value   **Value**   1   / 10

Figure 7.13 Process Instruction Characteristics for PI Category AREAD1

A major benefit that process management offers is that its results can be checked for consistency and simulated to ensure completeness and correctness. Click the **Check Process Instruction** icon located at the top-right of Figure 7.13 to check the consistency of the sequence of process instruction characteristics and the value of each characteristic defined. Then click the **Simulate Process Instruction Sheet** icon to show the simulated version of what the field and other information will eventually look like in a PI sheet.

Figure 7.14 shows message category PP2O that was configured in Chapter 4. It also contains the output characteristic ZPI_CREATION_DATE process instruction created earlier in Chapter 4. In the PI sheet, this field should show the PO basic start date of the process order. The output characteristic also has the same value (ZPI_CREATION_DATE) assigned.

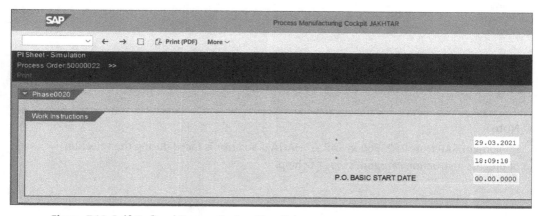

Figure 7.14 Self-Defined Process Instruction Category

7.4.4 Process Instruction Sheet

Figure 7.15 and Figure 7.16 show a general example of different sections of a PI sheet, displaying input fields, calculations, tables, values to choose from a dropdown, and operator's notes as some of the options available.

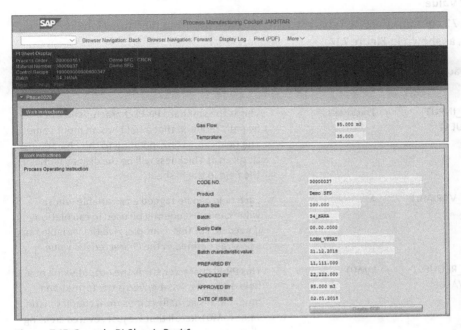

Figure 7.15 Sample PI Sheet: Part 1

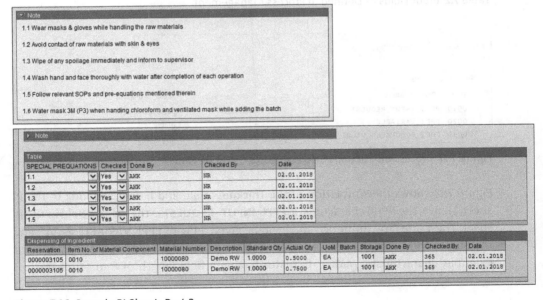

Figure 7.16 Sample PI Sheet: Part 2

The following sections explain some of the options available in the PI sheet and the data or other information that needs to be maintained for using a specific function/option.

Input Value

Table 7.2 contains the PP-PI characteristics needed for input field functionality in the PI sheet, as shown in Figure 7.17.

Characteristic	Characteristic Value	Description
PPPI_INPUT_REQUEST	Thickness	This is the standard **PP-PI** characteristic whenever it's required that a field has an input value. The field value corresponding to this characteristic given as **Thickness** will be the display name of the field in the PI sheet.
PPPI_VARIABLE	A	Each field can be tagged as a variable whose value can subsequently be used in calculations, if needed. For this example, give the variable tag as "A", as defined in the characteristic value.
PPPI_REQUEST-ED_VALUE	MM01	This **PP-PI** characteristic is the output value of a field. However, what governs the format and other details actually comes from characteristic value **MM01**. Recall that we just covered creating characteristic MM01 in Section 7.3.

Table 7.2 Input Fields as Defined in Process Management

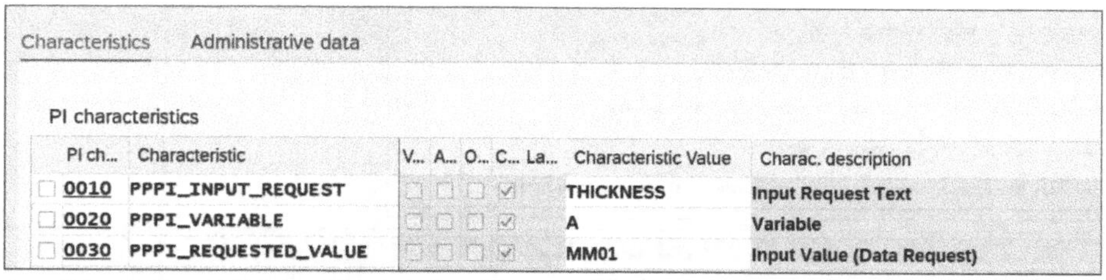

Pi ch...	Characteristic	V...	A...	O...	C...	La...	Characteristic Value	Charac. description
0010	PPPI_INPUT_REQUEST				☑		THICKNESS	Input Request Text
0020	PPPI_VARIABLE				☑		A	Variable
0030	PPPI_REQUESTED_VALUE				☑		MM01	Input Value (Data Request)

Figure 7.17 Process Instructions Characteristics for Input Value

Figure 7.18 shows the simulation of the **Thickness** field and how it will look in the PI sheet. Hence, the PP-PI characteristic **PPPI_INPUT_REQUEST** is the display field in the PI sheet. The value (any numeric value) will be given a tag of **PPPI_VARIABLE** as "A", and the output format of the numeric value will be governed by characteristic **MM01**. For example, characteristic **MM01** stipulates having a field length of four (4) characters with two decimal places and no negative values. In such a case, values such as 5.35 or 5.88 are acceptable, but –5.28 isn't acceptable in the PI sheet. The decimal is also counted as a character.

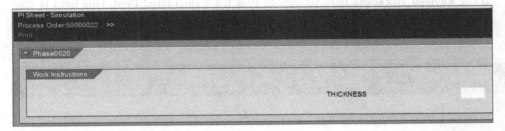

Figure 7.18 Input Value in PI Sheet

> **Tips and Tricks**
>
> If a PP-PI characteristic isn't going to be used in any subsequent calculation and if it's being used only for data entry purposes, then eliminate the entire **PPPI_VARIABLE** row and its value **A**.

Calculated Value

A PI sheet can be extensively used for all kinds of calculations, as long as all of the relevant parameters required for calculation are available in the same PI sheet.

Table 7.3 contains the PP-PI characteristics needed for the calculation field functionality in the PI sheet. If the calculation formula is too long for a single line, it can be continued on the next line (up to eight lines can be used for the calculation formula). In addition, while using variables in a calculation formula, they must previously be defined in the same PI sheet.

Characteristic	Characteristic Value
PPPI_INPUT_REQUEST	Revised thickness
PPPI_VARIABLE	B
PPPI_CALCULATED_VALUE	MM01
PPPI_CALCULATION_FORMULA	A*1.05
PPPI_EVENT	Parmeter_changed

Table 7.3 Calculation Fields in Process Management

The simulated version of the calculated field will appear as shown in Figure 7.19. The system automatically calculates the **Revised Thickness** field by using the formula that you defined in the master recipe for this field. Notice a small calculator icon right next to the **Revised Thickness** field to denote that it's a calculated field. This field is also noneditable. If you make changes to the parameter value **Thickness**, the system automatically updates the calculated values.

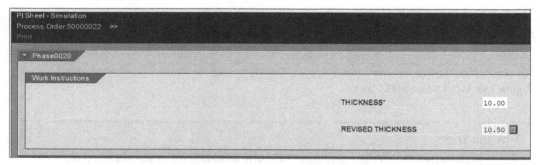

Figure 7.19 Calculation Field in PI Sheet

Repeat Data Request

Table 7.4 contains the PP-PI characteristics needed for the repeat data input request functionality in the PI sheet.

Characteristic	Characteristic Value
PPPI_DATA_REQUEST_TYPE	Repeated Data Request
PPPI_MESSAGE_CATEGORY	DPREAD
PPPI_PROCESS_ORDER	
PPPI_DATA_POINT_NAME	10
PPPI_REQUESTED_VALUE	PPPI_DATA_POINT_VALUE
PPPI_REQUESTED_VALUE	PPPI_EVENT_DATE
PPPI_REQUESTED_VALUE	PPPI_EVENT_TIME
PPPI_UNIT_OF_MEASURE	KG

Table 7.4 Input Groups as Defined in Process Management

They will result in a display as shown in Figure 7.20.

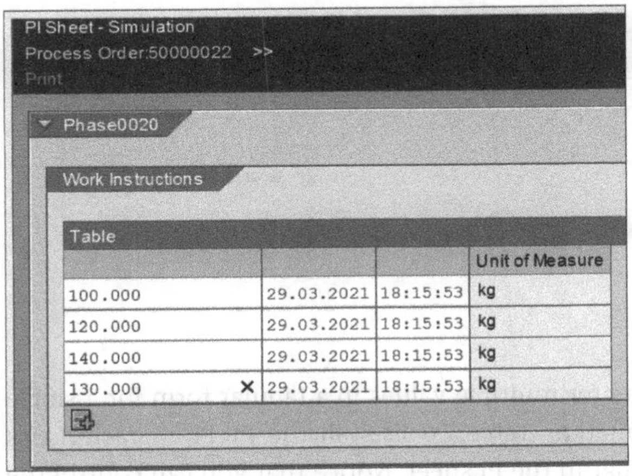

Figure 7.20 PP-PI Characteristics for Input Group Field Functionality in PI Sheet

Call Function

As explained in Table 7.5, a PI sheet can be used to call up a transaction while remaining within the PI sheet's screen. The process instruction characteristics together with their values call up the **Display Process Order** transaction while remaining in the PI sheet. **PPPI_Button_Text** enables a user to define a meaningful description of the icon while remaining in the PI sheet. Set the icon text as **Display Process Order** and set **PPPI_Transaction_Code** as **COR3** for this example, but note that these fields are flexible and can be set to whatever is needed.

Characteristic	Characteristic Value
PPPI_FUNCTION_NAME	COPF_CALL_TRANSACTION
PPPI_BUTTON_TEXT	Display Process Order
PPPI_FUNCTION_DURING_DISPLAY	Allowed
PPPI_EXPORT_PARAMETER	New_Session
PPPI_INSTRUCTION	
PPPI_EXPORT_PARAMETER	TCODE
PPPI_TRANSACTION_CODE	COR3

Table 7.5 PP-PI Characteristics and Their Values for Call Functions as Defined in Process Management

The simulated version of the characteristics is shown in Figure 7.21. When the **DISPLAY PROCESS ORDER** button shown here is clicked, it brings up Transaction COR3 (Display Process Order).

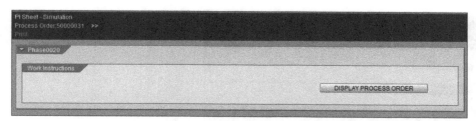

Figure 7.21 Call Function in PI Sheet

Table Entry

Often there is a business need to enter multiple values in a tabular form for a single value or multiple values of parameters. Table 7.6 lists all the PP-PI characteristics needed to use the table-entry format in the PI sheet. Notice that you can control the table size (minimum four values, maximum six values in this example).

Characteristic	Characteristic Value
PPPI_DATA_REQUEST_TYPE	Repeated Data Request
PPPI_MINIMUM_TABLE_SIZE	4
PPPI_MAXIMUM_TABLE_SIZE	6
PPPI_INPUT_REQUEST	Shift-wise Flow Reading
PPPI_VARIABLE	ABC
PPPI_REQUESTED_VALUE	MM03

Table 7.6 Activating Format with Multiple Values

Figure 7.22 illustrates the simulated version table entry format and shows the option to enter six values. The option to maintain decimal places for each value is controlled via characteristic MM03.

Figure 7.22 Table in PI Sheet

Long Text Input

In general, at the end of every shift, a company requires the process operator to prepare shift highlights and/or other important details. To do this, you can use the long text functionality in the PI sheet. Table 7.7 lists the PP-PI characteristics needed for the long text functionality in a PI sheet.

Characteristic	Characteristic Value
PPPI_INPUT_REQUEST	Shift Highlights
PPPI_REQUESTED_VALUE	PPPI_MESSAGE_TEXT

Table 7.7 Required PP-PI Fields for Activating Text Box in PI Sheet

Figure 7.23 shows the text box that becomes available in the PI sheet, in which the process operator has entered shift details.

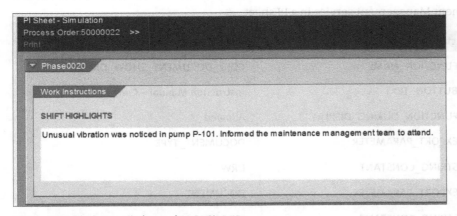

Figure 7.23 Shift Details (Notes) in PI Sheet

Instructions and Notes

In general, businesses want to make sure that the line operator has easy and instant accessibility to various instructions and other notes during the course of the shift. The functionality of instructions and notes is useful in such scenarios.

Table 7.8 provides a list of the PP-PI characteristics needed to maintain instructions and notes in a PI sheet. To enter the desired text that you want to display on the PI sheet, select the characteristic **PPPI_INSTRUCTION** (or **PPPI_NOTE**), and click the **Value** icon at the bottom of the screen. You can enter the text that you want to see being displayed in the PI sheet, as well as use some of the formatting options, such as bold, italic, large fonts, or text alignment center/right.

Characteristic	Characteristic Value
PPPI_INSTRUCTION	–
PPPI_NOTE	–

Table 7.8 PP-PI Fields for Activating Instructions and Notes in PI Sheet

Document Management Service in the Process Instruction Sheet

Sometimes the line operator is required to refer to a specific user manual or machine instruction manuals to perform a task or to rectify a production problem during operation. For this purpose, process management completely integrates with SAP Document Management service, which is a central repository used to store important documents and other references for use.

Table 7.9 contains the PP-PI characteristics that you need to maintain to activate SAP Document Management service in a PI sheet.

Characteristic	Characteristic Value
PPPI_FUNCTION_NAME	COPF_DOCUMENT_SHOW_DIRECT
PPPI_BUTTON_TEXT	Instruction Manual – Complete
PPPI_FUNCTION_DURING_DISPLAY	Allowed
PPPI_EXPORT_PARAMETER	DOCUMENT_TYPE
PPPI_STRING_CONSTANT	DRW
PPPI_EXPORT_PARAMETER	DOCUMENT
PPPI_STRING_CONSTANT	10000000001
PPPI_EXPORT_PARAMETER	DOCUMENT_PART
PPPI_STRING_CONSTANT	000
PPPI_EXPORT_PARAMETER	DOCUMENT_VERSION
PPPI_STRING_CONSTANT	00

Table 7.9 PP-PI Characteristics for Activating SAP Document Management Service

Digital Signature on Completion of the Process Instruction Sheet

A digital signature in the SAP system is a process of authenticating information and requires the user to enter his name along with a password before the system can accept an entry or perform a function. For example, when a function is executed, the user is required to digitally sign the PI sheet in the popup box that appears.

7.5 Process Order Execution

When compared with production order execution in discrete manufacturing, process order execution has differences as well as similarities:

- Batch allocation, either automatically or manually, can occur within the process order.
- The system automatically executes the formulas of the material quantity calculation that is defined in the master recipe using batch allocations.
- When a process order is released, the system can create the control recipe automatically, or the user can click the relevant icon within the process order creation screen to do it manually.
- A user can also create a test control recipe in a process order to check or validate settings.
- The system creates a control recipe for each control recipe destination of the process order. If there are three control recipe destinations in the process order, then the system creates three control recipes for the process order.
- Integration points, such as in-process inspection, finished goods inspection, capacity requirements planning (CRP), material requirements planning (MRP), sales and operations planning (S&OP), and long-term planning (LTP), also remain the same.

Figure 7.24 illustrates the important elements in a process order.

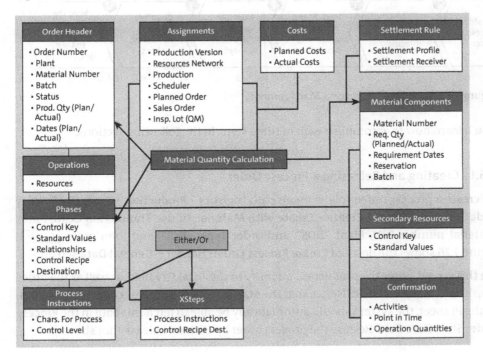

Figure 7.24 Elements of Process Order

7.6 Process Management in Action

The main steps involved in process management are listed here, with numbers corresponding to each step, as shown in Figure 7.25:

❶ The first step is the process order creation. The process order reads the material master data, including the master recipe and materials list (BOM). It also takes the material quantity calculation into account. The master recipe contains all the information related to process management and is used for the generation of a control recipe.

❷ When the process order is released and the control recipe is generated, the system creates a PI sheet.

❸ The next step is to send the generated control recipe to the predefined destination in the master recipe (in this example, it's **PP—Chemical Mixing**).

❹ The PI sheet is now available at the destination, and the PI sheet can be maintained.

❺ The status of the PI sheet can be updated as **Complete**. Once completed, no further changes to the PI sheet are possible. If necessary, an incomplete PI sheet can also be saved.

❻ The last step is to send the process messages to their required locations so that the system can perform the necessary predefined actions.

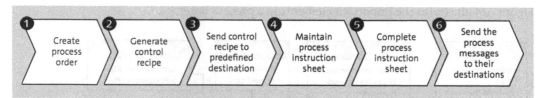

Figure 7.25 Main Steps in Process Management

You'll learn how to accomplish each of these steps in the following sections.

7.6.1 Creating and Releasing a Process Order

To create a process order, follow menu path **Logistics · Production – Process · Process Order · Process Order · Create · Create with Material**, or use Transaction COR1. Enter **Material** number "81", **Plant** "1105", and order **Type** "PI01", and then press ⌊Enter⌋. Figure 7.26 shows the detailed **Create Process Order: Header—General Data** screen.

On this screen, enter the production quantity in the **Total Qty** field, as well as the order finish date in the **End** field. Notice that the **Start** date of the process order is **01.04.2021**. In the PI sheet, the system should automatically be able to fetch this date in the **Process Order Start Date** field. Release the process order by clicking **Release** (not shown).

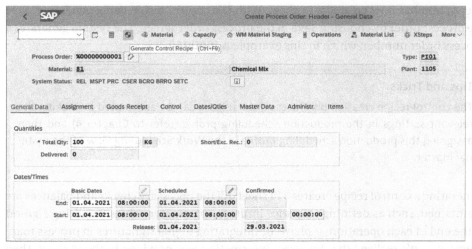

Figure 7.26 Header Screen for Process Order Creation

7.6.2 Generating a Control Recipe

After releasing the process order, choose the **Generate Control Recipe** button at the top of the **Change Process Order** (refer to Figure 7.26) to generate a control recipe. An information message appears at the bottom of the screen to inform you that the system created a control recipe (see Figure 7.27) and also generated a log.

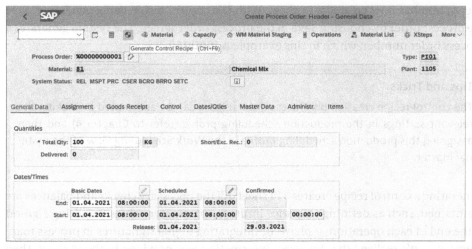

Figure 7.27 Control Recipes Created

The system has now created a PI sheet. With the control recipe being generated, save the process order by choosing **Save** in the process order screen. The system generates a process order number, which in this example is **1000040**.

[+]

> **Tips and Tricks**
>
> The control recipe creation on process order release can be automated by making the relevant settings in the production scheduling profile (refer to Chapter 4) and then assigning this production scheduling profile in the **Work Scheduling** view of the material master.

Generating a control recipe creates a PI sheet. All the necessary checks and balances are maintained, such as defining tolerance limits for parameter values, requiring sign-off at the end of each operation or phase, or integrating digital signatures in process management. If it's realized that incorrect information was provided in the PI sheet, then create a new PI sheet (by generating a new control recipe) to attend to this scenario. This situation arises after a user has already performed all the necessary steps in process management.

To generate a new PI sheet, follow these steps:

1. Use Transaction CO67. On the **Worklist for PI Sheets** screen containing the PI sheet with the **Complete** status, select the PI sheet. Then choose **PI Sheet · Delete**.

   The system issues a message stating that the selected entry (PI sheet) was deleted.

2. Use Transaction CO57 to create a process message manually. In this option, enter the **Plant**, and use **Process Message Category PI_CRST**. Enter the process order number of the deleted control recipe, enter the number of the deleted control recipe (from the previous step), and set the **Control Recipe Status** as **00007 (Discarded)**.

3. Save the process message, and the system states that a new process message has been created, including the process message number.

4. Use Transaction CO54XT, and on the initial parameter selection screen, enter the process order number and the process message category as "PI_CRST". Press [F8], or click the **Message List** icon.

5. Select the process message number created in the previous step and click the **Send** icon to send the process message. The system issues an information message to inform you that the process message has been processed.

6. Use Transaction CO53XT. On the initial screen, enter the **Plant**, the process order number, and the destination address (in this example, it's "Chemical Mixing"). Press [F8], or click the **Display** icon.

7. In the **Control Recipe Monitor** screen, select the relevant control recipe number, and click the **Delete** icon. The system issues an information message that the control rec-

ipe has been deleted and, at the same time, assigns the status of the control recipe as **Discarded**.

8. Use Transaction COR2 for the change in process order, and click the **Generate Control Recipe** icon to create a new PI sheet for the same process order.

7.6.3   Downloading and Sending a Control Recipe

A control recipe can be manually downloaded to a destination in a nonautomated environment (as a background job). To do so, follow menu path **Logistics • Production – Process • Process Management • Control Recipe • Control Recipe Monitor**, or use Transaction CO53XT. Figure 7.28 shows the initial screen with selection parameters for the control recipe. For this example, use the same **Manufacturing Order** number **1000040**, and assign the **Destination Address** as **Chemical Mixing** (PP), which was configured in Chapter 4. Click the **Created, Sent** button to view the generated control recipe.

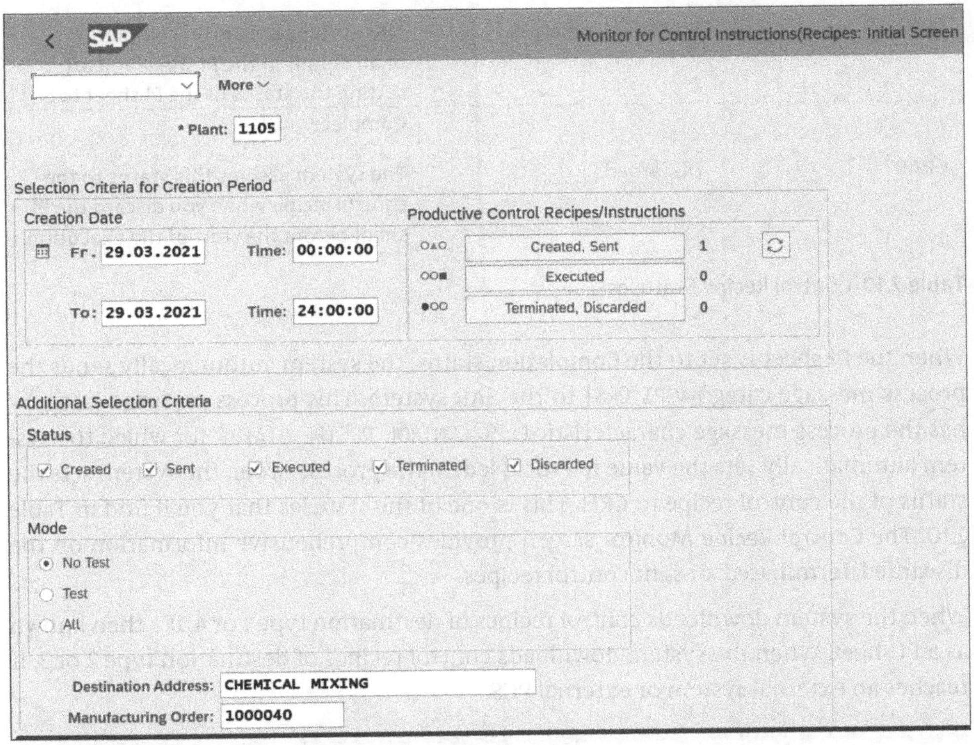

Figure 7.28 Initial Screen of Control Recipe Monitor

In the screen shown in Figure 7.29, select the line item, and click the **Send** button to send the control recipe to destination PP. The status will be updated from **Created** to **Sent**.

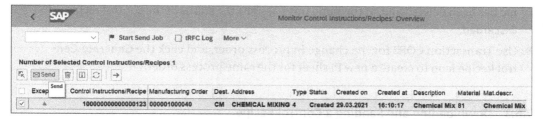

Figure 7.29 Control Recipe Monitor

The control recipe has the statuses detailed in Table 7.10.

Control Recipe Status	Control Recipe Description	Details
CRCR	Created	This status appears in the process order when the system generates a control recipe.
CRFI	Processed/finished	This status appears on completion of all details in the PI sheet and after setting the status of the PI sheet to **Complete**.
CRAB	Discarded	The system assigns this status to the control recipe when you discard the PI sheet before the start of the execution.

Table 7.10 Control Recipe Statuses

When the PI sheet is set to the **Completion** status, the system automatically sends the process message category PI_CRST to the SAP system. This process message category has the process message characteristic PPPI_CONTROL_RECIPE_STATUS, for which the system automatically sets the value to **Processed**. In the process order, the system sets the status of the control recipe to **CRFI**. This is one of the statuses that you'll find in Table 7.10. The **Control Recipe Monitor** screen provides comprehensive information on the discarded, terminated, or sent control recipes.

When the system downloads control recipes of destination type 1 or 4, it's then known as a PI sheet. When the system downloads control recipes of destination type 2 or 3, it reaches an external system or external PCS.

[»]

Note

A background job can be scheduled for downloading and sending control recipes with the program RCOCB006 (batch job name: SAP_NEW_CONTROL_RECIPE).

Refer to the detailed settings of the background job covered in Chapter 4, Section 4.8.

7.6.4   Maintaining Process Instruction Sheets

To maintain the PI sheet, follow menu path **Logistics • Production—Process • Process Management • Process Instruction Sheet • Worklist—Maintain**, or use Transaction CO55. You can click **All Selections** so that the system can offer you more selection options on the initial screen than are visible when you first execute Transaction CO55. For example, apart from new and in-process PI sheets, you can also select PI sheets that you discarded and terminated (see Figure 7.30). This transaction can also be used to display completed PI sheets by selecting the relevant checkbox.

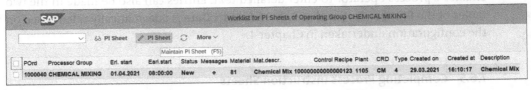

	SAP					Worklist for PI Sheets/Work Instructions

```
[            ⌄]   🖫 Save as Variant...   🗇   🗗   More ⌄

                              * Plant:  1105                              ⬚⟋
                    * Processor Group:  CHEMICAL MIXING                   ⬚⟋
               Max. number of PI sheets:        500

  Status
        ☑ New                              Planned for the next:  [   ]  Hours

                    In Process:  ☐

  Process Order
                         Resource:  [            ]          to:  [        ]      ⬚⟋

  Material
                  Material Number:  81                       to:  [        ]      ⬚⟋
```

Figure 7.30 Initial Screen for PI Sheets

Enter **Plant** "1105" and **Processor Group** (which is the description of the control recipe destination) as "CHEMICAL MIXING", and then choose **Execute** or press F8. The corresponding PI sheet's worklist is now available for maintenance (see Figure 7.31).

	SAP					Worklist for PI Sheets of Operating Group CHEMICAL MIXING								
[⌄]	👓 PI Sheet	✏ PI Sheet	⟳	More ⌄										
			Maintain PI Sheet (F5)											
	POrd	Processor Group	Erl. start	Earl.start	Status	Messages	Material	Mat.descr.	Control Recipe	Plant	CRD	Type	Created on	Created at	Description
☐	1000040	CHEMICAL MIXING	01.04.2021	08:00:00	New	♦	81	Chemical Mix	100000000000000123	1105	CM	4	29.03.2021	16:10:17	Chemical Mix

Figure 7.31 Worklist of PI Sheets for Operating Group Production Floor

This is the process instruction worklist, which meets the selection criteria. For this example, there is only one PI sheet in the worklist. Select the relevant PI sheet and choose **Maintain PI Sheet** (see Figure 7.31) to start data input (data maintenance).

Figure 7.32 shows the PI sheet with all of the input fields available for maintenance.

The PI sheet may contain several fields and other important functions already filled in, such as default views or calculation fields.

Enter the value for the **Thickness** parameter. A red asterisk next to the parameter denotes that it's a mandatory field that needs to be maintained.

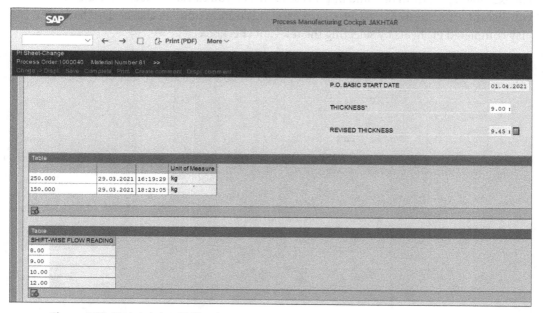

Figure 7.32 Maintaining PI Sheet

[+]   Tips and Tricks

It's possible to control whether an entry in the field is optional or mandatory by selecting the relevant checkbox in the characteristic (Transaction CT04).

The **SHIFT HIGHLIGHTS** text box (not shown, but located further down the same screen) enables a process operator to enter detailed text. Entries can also be made in the two tables of the PI sheet. Notice that **P.O. Basic Start Date** is automatically filled based on the configuration undertaken in Chapter 4.

7.6.5   Completing Process Instruction Sheets

When all entries are made in the PI sheet, it can either be saved or marked as **Complete** by using the light-blue colored buttons at the top of the PI sheet (refer to Figure 7.32). The **Save** function in a PI sheet can be used as many times as needed to save partial and incomplete information. The **Complete** function is used when all details in the PI sheet have been incorporated. Note that after using the **Complete** function, it's no longer possible to make changes to the PI sheet.

[«]

> **Note**
>
> If relevant settings are made in the configuration (Chapter 4) of the control recipe destination, then the system shows a popup message to digitally sign the PI sheet on completion.

7

7.6.6   Sending Process Messages

The PI sheet automatically creates a process message with all the information that the system needs to send to specific destinations. This information may be a GI against a process order, a GR against a process order, or a confirmation of a process order. Sending the process message executes the function module with the gathered information.

Process messages in a productive system are typically sent via a background job of program RCOCB002 (cross-plant) or program RCOCB004 (plant-specific).

[!]

> **Warning**
>
> Be sure to monitor process messages: sometimes a process message sending fails if, for example, data is missing from the PI sheet. It's possible to monitor and delete process messages with Transaction CO54XT and manually create them with Transaction CO57.

It's also possible to create, test, check, and monitor process messages, although the system doesn't process these process test messages at the destination as it does for normal process messages. Test process messages are created to check whether the system is able to transfer all the relevant information from various systems and destinations.

To send a process message, follow menu path **Logistics • Production – Process • Process Management • Message • Message Monitor**, or use Transaction CO54XT. Enter the **Plant** and the **Creation Date** range for the process message (see Figure 7.33), and then click the **To Be Sent** button to send the messages.

In the process messages worklist shown in Figure 7.34, there are two process messages categories, **Sign** and **PI_COMM**, that the system needs to send. Notice that the sender of these process messages is **Chemical Mixing** (configured in Chapter 4). Select the first process message, **SIGN**, and click **Change** (the pen icon).

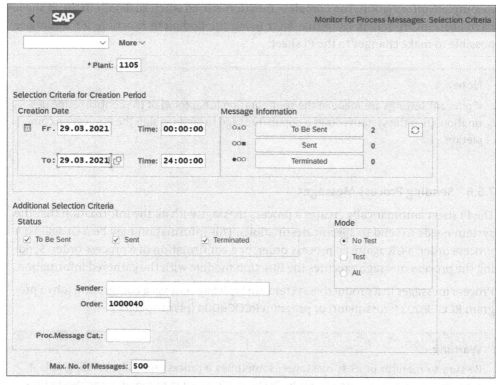

Figure 7.33 Process Messages Monitor

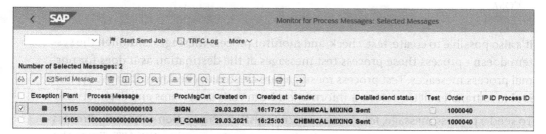

Figure 7.34 Process Messages from Production Floor Sender

In Figure 7.35, the system automatically incorporates **Char. Value**, which is the date (**29.03.2021**) for the ZPI_CREATION_DATE characteristic.

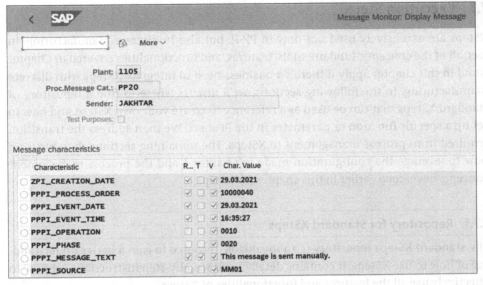

Figure 7.35 Process Message with Message Category PP

Some of the other salient features of process messages are as follows:

- For process message categories that have errors or are terminated during processing, these can be resubmitted for processing using the **Process Messages Monitor** screen.

- Process messages can be created manually using Transaction CO57. Then these manually created process messages are visible in the **Process Messages Monitor** screen, where they can be processed further.

- The system uses Business Application Programming Interfaces (BAPIs) or function modules to update the process messages. The system processes the received process messages using these function modules.

- The system uses a remote function call (RFC) connection to communicate with an external PCS using process messages. It's important to define the RFC destination for every external system, so it's recommended to engage an SAP NetWeaver (basis) consultant for this task.

- The system issues alerts for critical situations or milestones in the production run. The alerts can be from either the external control system or the internal shop floor operator.

- A special destination type is used in the process message, SAP Office user, to inform specific SAP system users about the status of process messages (and also control recipes).

7.7 Execution Steps

XSteps are extensively used not only in PP-PI but also in discrete manufacturing. In fact, all of the concepts, fundamentals, features, and functionalities covered in Chapter 4 and in this chapter apply if there's a business need to integrate XSteps with discrete manufacturing. In the following sections, we'll discuss where to find a repository of standard XSteps that can be used as a reference to create your own XSteps and how to set up a specific function or parameter in the PI sheet. We then address the transition required from process management to XSteps. The remaining sections then focus on how to leverage the configuration made in Chapter 4 and the process management concepts developed earlier in this chapter for XSteps.

7.7.1 Repository for Standard XSteps

The standard XSteps repository is an invaluable resource to gain a better understanding of how to use XSteps. It contains detailed and step-by-step instructions for how to effectively use all the features and functionalities of XSteps.

To access the repository of standard XSteps, follow menu path **Logistics • Production—Process • Master Data • Standard XStep Repository**, or use Transaction CMXSV. For this example, enter **Plant** "1105", and choose **Execute**. The screen shown in Figure 7.36 appears, containing comprehensive details on XSteps.

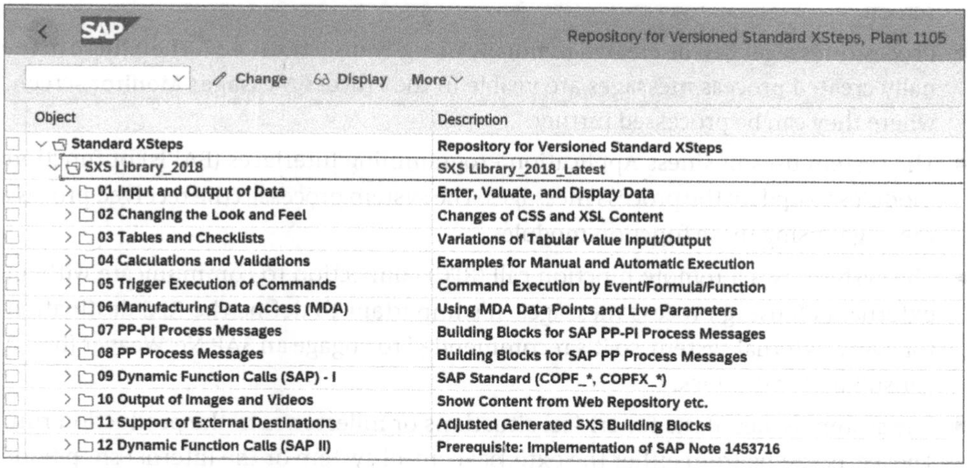

Figure 7.36 XSteps Repository

SAP provides a standard XSteps library that can be downloaded from the SAP Store (*https://store.sap.com*) in an XML format and imported into the SAP system. The XSteps provided in this library can be used as a starting point or even as a model for the creation of your own XSteps. They are included on the SCN SAP Core Manufacturing Sample Application and Best Practices, which is provided by SAP and can be downloaded for free from the SAP Store. Download a file called *Basic_Standard_XStep_Templates.zip*. This file contains detailed technical documentation about the implementation of XSteps and a folder called *XML_files_V_1_0* (the name may change if a new version is delivered) that contains XML files with the standard XSteps.

After downloading and extracting the content of the file, it can be imported into the system.

> **Note**
> Refer to SAP Note 2625835 for a detailed understanding of and step-by-step instructions to implement the technical and the functional areas of XSteps.

7.7.2 Importing the Standard XSteps Library

To import the XML file containing the standard XSteps library, use Transaction CMXSV. After executing Transaction CMXSV, define the plant by populating the **Plant** field in the initial screen that the system displays. Click the **Execute** icon or press the [F8] key to access the XSteps repository.

With the repository open, right-click the **Standard XSteps** folder and then choose **Create • Folder** to create a new folder to store the standard XSteps.

The newly created folder appears in the next screen with the description **<Folder>**. After double-clicking this folder, change the description in the popup screen that appears. The next step is to import the downloaded XML file containing the standard XSteps library to the newly created folder. To complete this step, right-click the folder just created, and select the **Import Standard XStep** option.

In the popup screen that appears, select the file named **SXS Library BASICS V1_0.XML** under the previously mentioned folder, **XML_files_V_1_0**, and then click the **Open** button.

7.7.3 Switching from Process Instructions to Execution Steps

Whenever transitioning from process instructions to XSteps in the master recipe, the system issues the warning message that all previously created process instructions become invalid when the changes made in the master recipe are saved. In addition, the profile in the master recipe (see Chapter 4, Section 4.1.1) should allow for the creation of XSteps. A warning message appears when the **XSteps** icon (in the master recipe) is clicked (this icon is located right next to **More** dropdown in Figure 7.37). Choose **Yes** to proceed further (see Figure 7.37).

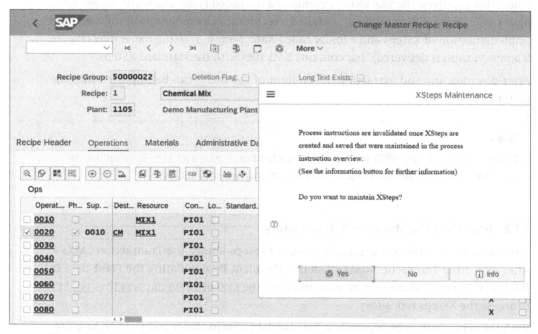

Figure 7.37 Switching from Process Instructions to XSteps

7.7.4   General Information

On the XSteps creation screen in the master recipe, click **XStep Tree**, and the system creates an **XSteps** icon on the left-hand side of the screen. Select the **XStep Tree** icon again, right-click, and select **Properties** from the dropdown.

[+]   Tips and Tricks

Relevant fields in XSteps, such as process instruction or calculation, can also be selected, followed by pressing [Enter]; the system then will bring up the **Properties** option, wherein the desired changes can be made.

In the **Node Attributes** screen that appears as shown in Figure 7.38, enter a short description, which then becomes visible throughout the XSteps tree. Click the **Parameters** tab to bring up the next screen, which is described in the next section.

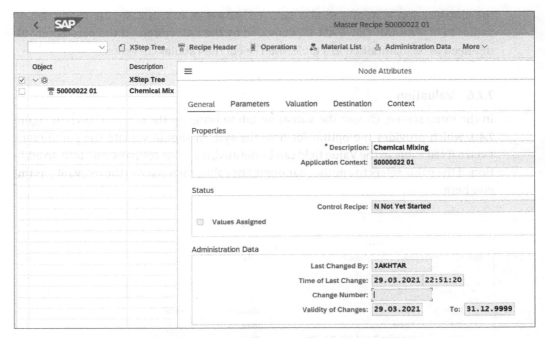

Figure 7.38 Node Attributes in XSteps

7.7.5 Parameters

Figure 7.39 shows the screen in which to define all the parameters that will be used in the XSteps for data entry or calculation. If the parameters aren't defined on this screen, it won't be possible to select them when needed; for example, it won't be possible to create an input value in the process instructions. If it's only a numeric value that won't be subsequently used in calculation, then there's no need to define the parameter.

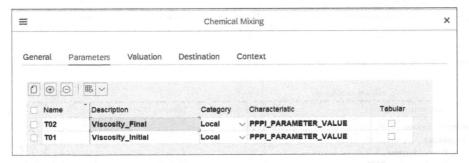

Figure 7.39 Parameters in XSteps

For this example, define two parameters, **T01** and **T02**, and give a short description for each. It's important to enter the **Characteristic** ("PPPI_PARAMETER_VALUE", in this example). The characteristics that were previously created using Transaction CT04 (in the classification system) can also be used. However, in this case, use characteristic value "PPPI_PARAMETER_VALUE", delivered by the SAP system. If the parameter values need to be maintained in a table, then select the **Tabular** checkbox.

7.7.6   Valuation

In the same screen, choose the **Valuation** tab to bring up the screen shown in Figure 7.40, which provides the option for how the system should valuate the parameters. Even a fixed value in the **Value** field can be defined, if a value remains constant. In addition, if the value refers to another parameter or value, then refer to the relevant parameter here.

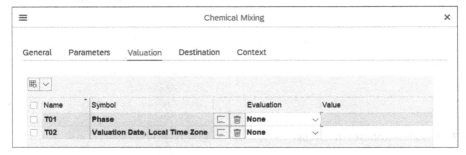

Figure 7.40 Valuation in XSteps

7.7.7   Control Recipe Destination

Click the **Destination** tab, and on the screen shown in Figure 7.41, assign the control recipe destination defined in Chapter 4. For this example, double-click the control recipe destination, **Chemical Mixing** (CM), which was defined in Chapter 4 and is now assigned here.

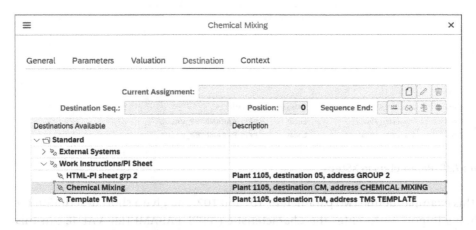

Figure 7.41 Destination in XSteps

Choose the **Close** icon (not shown).

After successfully maintaining the details in the previous four figures, the screen appears as shown in Figure 7.42. The next step can be performed, which is the creation of process instructions in the XStep tree. To do so, place the cursor on the **Chemical Mixing** field (in the XStep tree), and right-click to bring up the available options. From the available options, choose **Create · Process Instruction**.

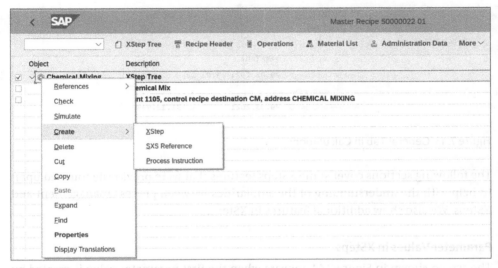

Figure 7.42 Process Instruction Creation in XSteps

7.7.8 Process Instructions

A new process instruction can be created by right-clicking **New Process Instruction**, choosing **Create · Control Data**, and then choosing the appropriate option. Here, input the input parameters, output parameters, and function modules can be freely defined, or even the control data; for example, calculations, process messages, commands, or function calls can be managed.

The screen shown in Figure 7.43 appears when a process instruction is selected and the properties are brought up (by either pressing Enter or right-clicking to select the **Properties** option). For this example, enter a description to identify the process instruction.

> **Note**
> Now that we've explained how to access the **Properties** option of any element in XSteps, we'll only cover the details of the element, such as input value, output value, or calculation, without repeatedly referring to the **Properties** option.

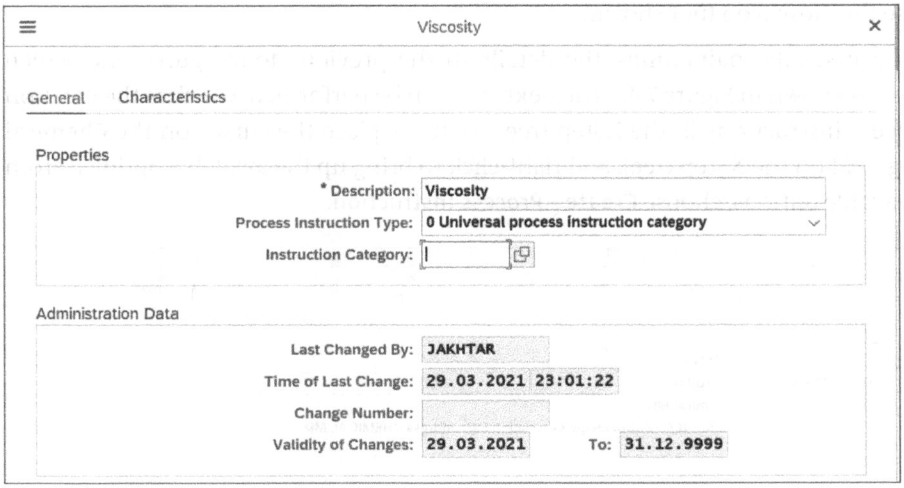

Figure 7.43 General Tab in Calculations

The following sections cover some XSteps features that were previously touched upon to help with the understanding of the similarities between process management and XSteps. We also show additional features in XSteps.

Parameter Values in XSteps

The screen shown in Figure 7.44 appears when the first parameter value is created by choosing **Create • Entry • Parameter Value**. In **Description**, enter "Viscosity_Initial", and from the **Parameters** area, select **T01 Viscosity_Initial** from the **Name** dropdown list. Notice that this is one of the same parameters defined when the XStep tree was first created. The remaining three tabs provide in-depth options to validate the values entered for a parameter. A user can choose to always accept a value, accept it with a digital signature, or never accept an out-of-range value. It's also possible to create your own text that the system will display in case of a failed check.

Repeat the same process to create the second parameter value, with a description of "Viscosity_Final", and select the parameter's name from the **Name** dropdown list.

[+]   Tips and Tricks

As an alternative, choose **Create • Entry • Numeric Value** to achieve the same results as just described, but ensure you select the **Parameters** option from the dropdown list in the **Default Value** tab.

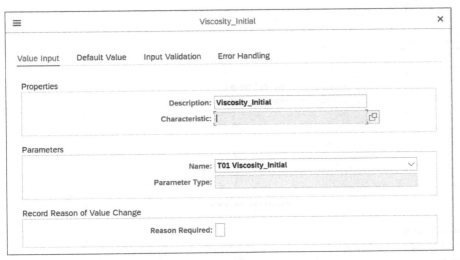

Figure 7.44 Characteristic Details and Validation in XSteps

Calculation in Execution Steps

Now that two parameter values are created in the XStep tree, let's use them in calculations. Any kind of calculation can be performed, as long as the parameters are already defined in the XStep tree. For this example, use the simple calculation of subtracting the value of one parameter from the other to display the result as a calculated field.

To perform calculation, choose **Create · Control Data · Calculation**. The screen shown in Figure 7.45 appears. Enter a short description: "Difference". In the lower half of the screen, enter "T02 - T01" in the **Calculation Formulas** box.

An important aspect to note is the **Event** field, in which "PARAMETER_CHANGED" is entered. An *event* is a control function that triggers the necessary action when the user or the system fulfills a certain and predefined event. For this example, stipulate that whenever there is a change (an event) in the **Viscosity Difference** field, the system should automatically calculate and update the value in the field. If an event isn't defined, then the user will have to manually click the **Calculator** icon to update the calculation in the **Viscosity Difference** field, based on any changes made to the parameter values.

Other examples of events include the system unlocking the table fields when the user maintains the PI sheet, locking the tables when all entries in the table are made, or activating or deactivating the PI sheet.

Tips and Tricks

To view all the available options in events, place the cursor on the **Event** field and press F4, or click the dropdown option.

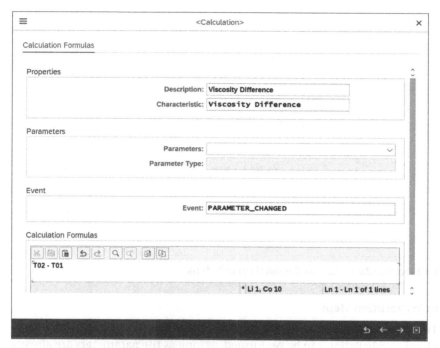

Figure 7.45 Calculation Formula in XSteps

To simulate the fields, place the cursor on either the XStep tree or on the process instruction and then either press ⟨F8⟩ or right-click and choose **Simulate**.

Figure 7.46 shows how the screen looks when not only the two parameters are entered but also the calculation. Notice that the calculated field **Viscosity Difference** has a small **Calculator** icon next to the field to denote that this is a calculated value.

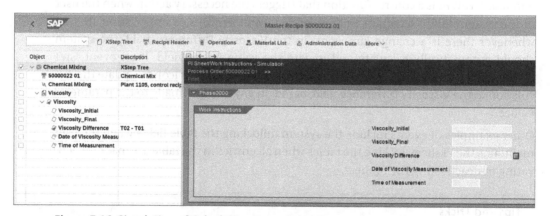

Figure 7.46 Simulation of Calculation Formula in XSteps

Many input, output, and control options are available in the XStep tree, so we briefly discuss the most relevant ones in the following sections.

Note

We encourage exploring the large number of options available in XSteps, including the option to incorporate website addresses and images/figures (e.g., hazard or gloves signs), the option to enter long text or a short note, and so on. It's possible to immediately simulate the results to see if the settings are correct. If they aren't correct, the system provides the guidance to correct them or points out the shortcoming or deviation.

Output Characteristics and Values in Execution Steps

If there is a business need to display a fixed value in an XStep or subsequently in the PI sheet, then use the **Output Characteristic** option. For example, enter the description "Value Output (Fixed)" and use the PPPI_Parameter_Value characteristic with a fixed value of 40. On the left-hand side of the same figure, again use the **Output Characteristic** option, but this time, select **Note** as the **Characteristic**, and in the **Long Text** field, enter the text shown. This is fixed text that will display when the PI sheet is processed.

Control Instruction

The description of how each control instruction in the PI sheet appears can also be changed. This option helps combine the relevant process instructions in one visual tab so that it's easier for the line operator to either enter the details of the process parameters or simply use the available functions. To ensure that the system displays control instructions as a tab, first enter the desired description of the control instruction, and then select the **Control Instruction** characteristic from the dropdown menu.

Tables in Execution Steps

To generate a table in the PI sheet using XSteps, first create a process instruction and then choose **Create · Control Data · Table**. Figure 7.47 provides the option to enter the minimum and maximum number of lines (rows) that must appear in the table.

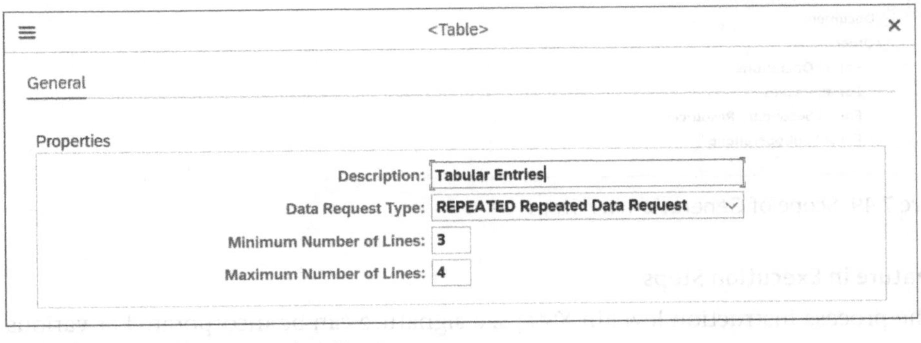

Figure 7.47 Tables Settings in XSteps

When a table is created, maintain the input value of the parameters by choosing **Create · Entry · Numeric Value (or Parameter Value)**. Figure 7.48 shows an example of a table created in XSteps with calculation and signature options.

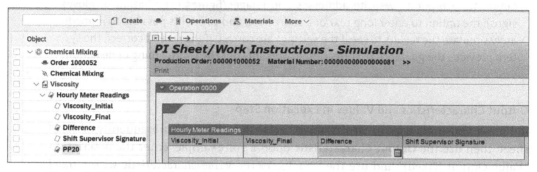

Figure 7.48 Tables in XSteps

Scope of Generation in Execution Steps

Whenever an XStep is created, the system provides the option to define the scope of generation, just as it does for process instructions. In this step, define the scope of generation for materials, resources/work centers, documents, or orders. The generation options in XSteps are far greater when compared to process instructions. Figure 7.49 lists the available options for scope of generation.

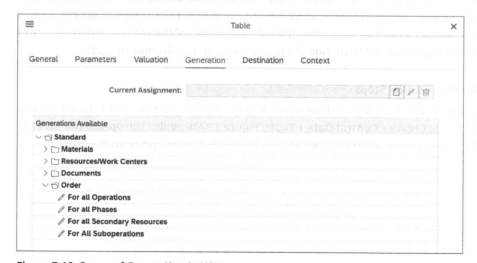

Figure 7.49 Scope of Generation in XSteps

Signature in Execution Steps

At the process instruction level in XSteps, a signature can be incorporated at various steps of data entry (or other input) to validate the information entered (see Figure 7.48

again). Even entering details of a digital signature is possible; the digital signature functionality is already configured in the system and can be chosen via **Create · Control Data · Signature**.

Process Messages in Execution Steps

At the same level on which a signature is entered in the process instruction, the option to select the associated process message is also available. To do so, choose **Create · Control Data · Process Message**. Use the same process message example here that was created in Chapter 4. Enter **Process Message Category** "PP20", and the relevant message characteristic automatically appears.

Execution Steps Overview

Place the cursor on any level and press ⌨F8 to simulate the PI sheet, and it will appear on the right-hand side of the figure.

> **Tips and Tricks**
> Use the drag-and-drop option on any element in XSteps to move it to desired location. For example, if **Table Entries** should appear earlier in the XStep tree, simply select it and drag it to the desired new location.

7.8 Process Messages Evaluation

The system offers process messages evaluation as a report that can be used to access information on process messages. The process messages evaluation integrates with Microsoft Excel and offers the option to save the evaluated information either as a pivot table or simply as an Excel worksheet.

All the standard or self-defined process message characteristics can be used in the evaluation. It's possible to self-define the layout for evaluation—that is, to decide how the system should display the information during evaluation. But it's important to first create an evaluation version before using it to evaluate process messages.

For process messages evaluation, use menu path **Logistics · Production—Process · Process Management · Evaluation · Process Messages**, or use Transaction CO52.

On the initial screen, first enter the **Plant** as "1105" and the **Evaluation version** as "SAPS4", and then choose the **Create** icon. But first, create an evaluation version before using it in process messages evaluation. A new evaluation version can also be created with reference to an existing version. To create an evaluation version, simply enter the **Plant**, and click the **SAP XXL** icon. The system brings up the screen shown in Figure 7.50, wherein a user can select the relevant checkboxes and save. The system asks the user to enter the **Evaluation Version** and its **Description**.

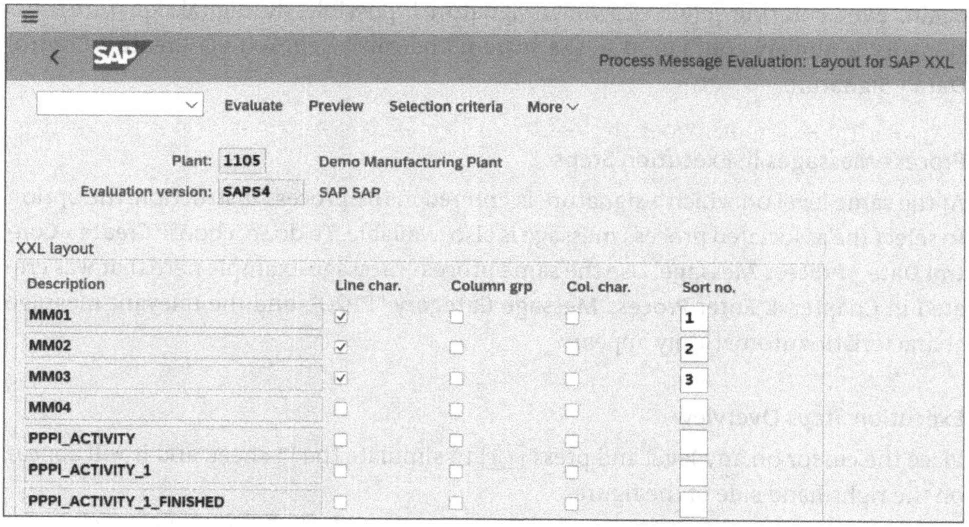

Figure 7.50 Selection Screen of Process Messages Evaluation

For this example, shown in Figure 7.50, use the previously created **Evaluation Version SAPS4**, and select the checkboxes in the line (**Line Char.**) and column characteristics (**Col. Char.**) columns for the characteristics (process messages) that need to be evaluated. For the **Line Char.** option, select the requisite checkboxes so that the data appears in horizontal lines (in rows). For the **Col. Char.** option, select the requisite checkboxes so that the data appears in columns. For this example, the control recipe status appears in a column, whereas the control recipe destination appears in a row.

If the **Evaluate** option is selected, the system downloads the information either in an Excel spreadsheet or in a pivot table format. Alternatively, the **Preview** option can be used. The first column and the related rows will show the control message ID. In the second column, the first row pertains to the control recipe status, whereas the second row reflects the control recipe number.

7.9   Process Manufacturing Cockpit

Building on the configuration made in Chapter 4 for the process manufacturing cockpit, PP10, we now show how it appears when a user wants to use it for data entry and reporting purposes. To access the process manufacturing cockpit, use the menu path **Logistics • Production—Process • Process Management • Manufacturing Cockpit • Start**, or use Transaction COPOC.

On the initial screen, enter the **Plant** as "1105" and the cockpit **Name** as "PP10". Choose **Execute**.

Figure 7.51 shows the manufacturing cockpit PP10, in which the required details are maintained. All details are optional, except for the **Material Quantity Consumed** field, which is mandatory, as denoted by the red asterisk. When exiting the process manufacturing cockpit, the process messages automatically become available in the message monitor (Transaction CO54XT). From there, these can be sent to the predefined destinations.

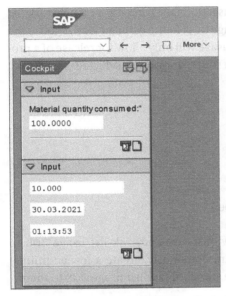

Figure 7.51 Process Manufacturing Cockpit: PP10

7.10 Resources Network

A *resource network* is a group of individual resources used in the production process. The ability for a user to pick and choose from the available or even required resources during process order creation ensures smoother production. Using a resource network also eliminates the need to create a production version for every variant of the production.

We'll show a real-time example in which several resources are available and can be used for similar production processes, but the business process entails a user deciding which resource to use just before production begins. For this purpose, a planning resource is defined that is only used for planning and represents several resources that can be used in the same way. There's a case of three equivalent resources (mixes), and the business requirement is that the user wants to dynamically (and in real-time) select the actual resource while creating a process order level (before release).

To map this business requirement in SAP S/4HANA, the resource network functionality is used. It begins with creating a specific task list usage type and selecting the relevant checkbox. This is then followed by creating relevant master data, including creating the resource network, followed by creating a resource hierarchy, and then assigning them to a master recipe. When a process order is created and is ready to be released, the system will prevent the user from doing so until one resource from a resource network is selected first.

Let's go through this step by step.

Access the screen shown in Figure 7.52 via Transaction OP45 and create a new task list usage, Z08, by copying the standard task list usage 008. In the detailed view, choose the **Until Rel.** checkbox to denote that this task list usage will only allow for release of a process order *after* one of the resources from the resource network is selected.

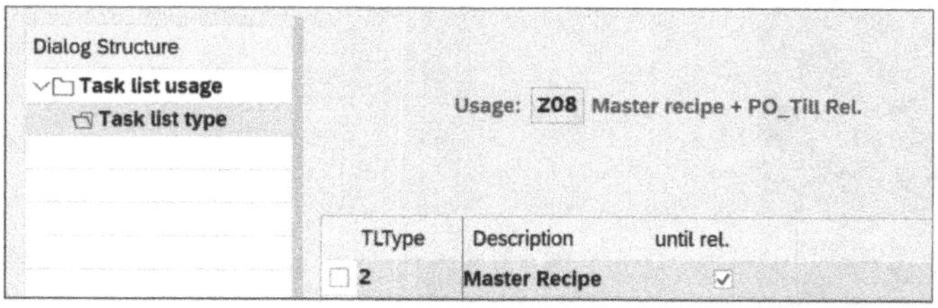

Figure 7.52 Configuration Settings for Task List Type 2

Then, using Transaction CRC1, assign the previously created task list usage Z08 to **Resource Mix_Plan**, as shown in Figure 7.53. Simultaneously, create a few additional resources (Mix1, Mix2, and Mix3) and assign the standard task list usage 008 to them.

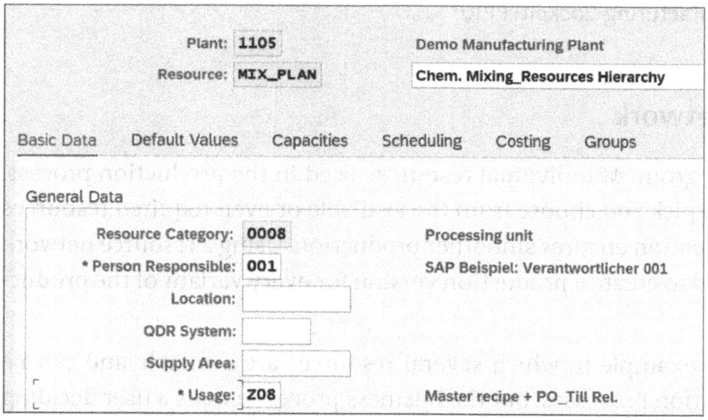

Figure 7.53 Assigning Task List Usage in Planning Resource

Access Figure 7.54 via Transaction CR24 to create **Resource Network MIX_RN**. Here, assign all the previously created resources, including the planning resource **MIX_PLAN** by first choosing **New Assignment** and then entering individual resources in the popup that appears. Be sure to also select the **Assignment Indicator** checkbox for each of the resources being added to the resource network. To create a relationship among these assigned resources in a resource network, choose **Graphic** in Figure 7.54, which brings up Figure 7.55.

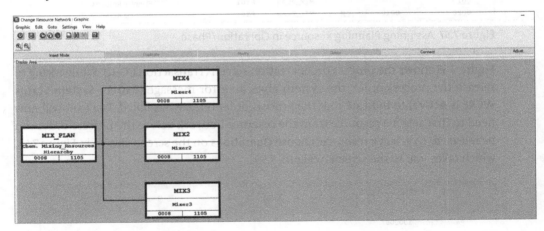

Figure 7.54 Resource Network and Assignment of Resources

The three resources in the resource network **MIX_PLAN** shown in Figure 7.55 appears connected to the planning resource **MIX_PLAN**. To connect a resource, first select the relevant resource, then choose **Connect**, shown on the right-hand side of Figure 7.55. Choosing a resource will also enable currently disabled options, such as **Duplicate**, **Modify**, and even **Delete** to delete a resource from a resource network.

Figure 7.55 Creating Resource Network

Access the screen shown in Figure 7.56 via Transaction C201 or C202 (create or change a master recipe), and then in the **Recipe Header** tab, enter "MIX_RN" for **Resource Netwrk** to assign it. Next, choose the **Operations** tab shown in Figure 7.56, which opens the screen shown in Figure 7.57.

On the screen shown in Figure 7.57, assign only the planning resource MIX_PLAN at the operation and phase levels, and maintain any additional details if required.

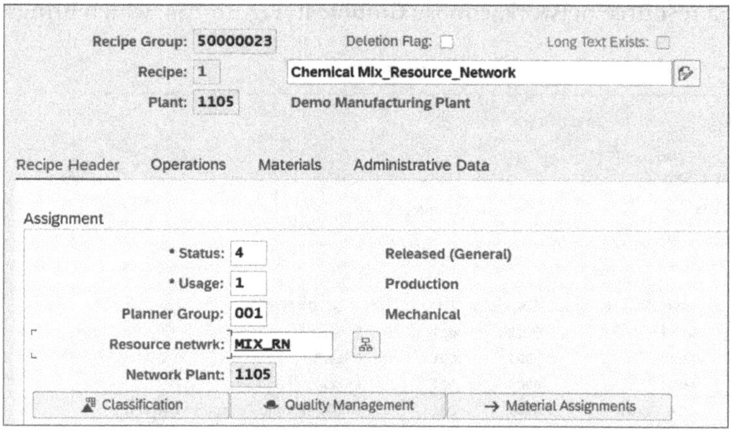

Figure 7.56 Assigning Resource Network in Master Recipe

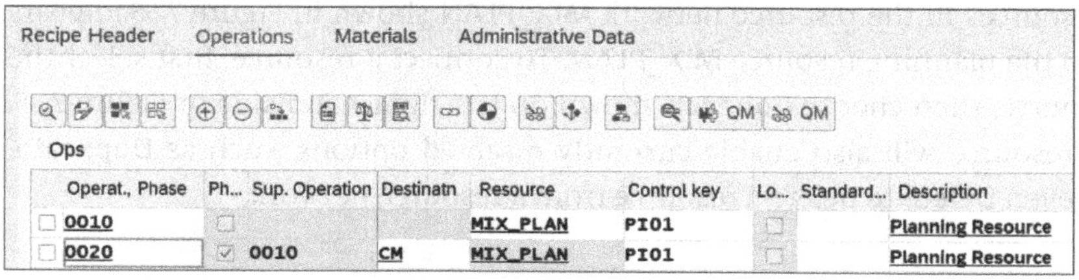

Figure 7.57 Assigning Planning Resource in Operation/Phase

Figure 7.58 shows the process order creation screen (Transaction COR1). While trying to release the process order, the system gives an error message (**BS013—System Status WCRE Is Active**) to indicate that the process order release has failed. The user will now need to first select a resource from the resource network before the process order can be released. To select a resource, choose **Operations** on the screen shown in Figure 7.58, which takes you to the screen in Figure 7.59.

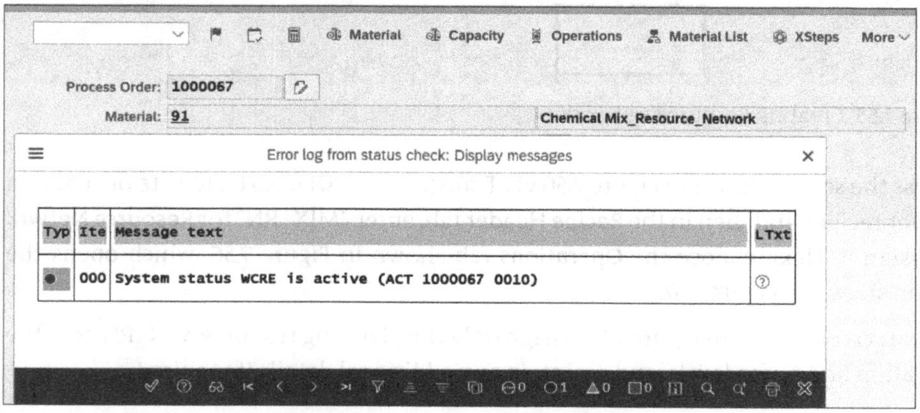

Figure 7.58 Error Messages when Releasing Process Order

Figure 7.59 shows the operations view of a process order and consists of the same planning resource, MIX_PLAN. To choose an actual resource from the resource network, first select **Operation 0010** and then choose **Execute Resource Selection**, shown in Figure 7.59; the screen shown in Figure 7.60 appears.

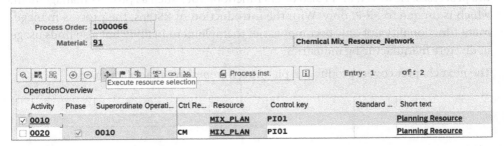

Figure 7.59 Resource Selection

Figure 7.60 is the popup to enable the user to select one of the resources from the resource network. Place the cursor on the relevant resource and click **Choose**. The planning resource MIX_PLAN shown in Figure 7.59 will be replaced with the chosen resource. To choose a different resource from the resource network, choose **Execute Resource Selection** again.

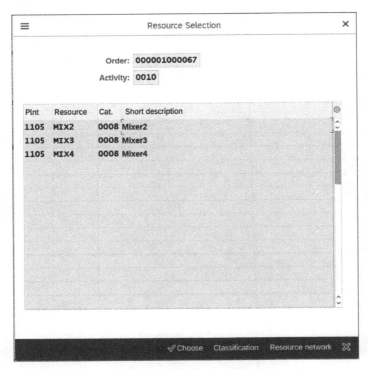

Figure 7.60 Choosing Resource from Resource Network

7.11   Summary

In general, the production processes in process industries are no different from those in discrete manufacturing, except that PP-PI offers options to record greater details of the processes. However, PP-PI also offers functionalities such as process management, which is unique to PP-PI only. With the introduction of XSteps, the process management functionality not only becomes easier to implement in PP-PI but also finds usage in discrete manufacturing industries.

The next chapter covers production planning in repetitive manufacturing.

Chapter 8
Production Planning for Repetitive Manufacturing

This chapter covers the important business processes and functions in repetitive manufacturing, along with the vital and logical links to required configuration.

Repetitive manufacturing (REM) is mainly used for production scenarios with high repetition rates, high product stability, and low product complexity. REM is characterized by quantity-based and period-based production (uninterrupted production over a longer period of time). The REM type is often mixed up with takt-based flow manufacturing, which is usually used whenever the production process is based on takt time (e.g., in the automobile industry). Both production types (REM and takt-based flow manufacturing) have different business backgrounds and properties, and they use different SAP technology, different master data, and even different planning tools.

> **Note**
>
> Refer to Chapter 1 for comparisons of discrete manufacturing, process manufacturing, and REM, as well as how to decide which manufacturing type is most relevant for a given industry.

This chapter will discuss what REM is and how it fits into the planning and production perspectives. A walk through the REM process flow will provide a comprehensive, step-by-step understanding of each process involved. We'll discuss the important REM master data and walk through how to run the end-to-end material requirements planning (MRP) process and how to use planning to optimize the production and procurement processes. We'll also discuss performing the material availability check for missing components, as well as the capacity available check and overload, if any.

Then, the actual and daily business processes in REM are covered: planning tables and material staging, based on the current material situation; the creation of a production list; REM confirmation at the assembly, components, and activity levels; and capacity requirements planning (CRP). Next, the chapter moves toward handling scrap at various levels, cancellations, and reversals. A short discussion on cost object controlling is next, followed by discussing heijunka and its role in REM. Finally, the chapter concludes with a few important evaluation reports available in REM.

This chapter links the discussion to the configuration that was made in Chapter 5 as often as possible. If deemed necessary, pointers to necessary configurations are given in this chapter.

8.1   Overview

Companies that work with high-volume and mass-produced materials (e.g., pens, pencils, keyboards, or batteries) find that REM best reflects their production processes, rather than discrete manufacturing or process manufacturing. If the actual business process is quite simple and straightforward, consider implementing the lean REM production type, so long as it's able to fulfill the business needs from a functional perspective.

The SAP S/4HANA system supports and offers make-to-order (MTO) REM, which enables handling of configurable materials. REM supports handling unit management, in which goods and packaging are mapped as a logistic unit. Serial number assignment for unique identification is also possible in REM. Make-to-stock (MTS) REM is equally possible.

The following sections will cover how REM plays a central role in production planning and production execution and will discuss the REM process flow.

8.1.1   Roles of Repetitive Manufacturing in Planning and Production

Figure 8.1 provides an overview of the role of REM in the planning and production areas of the SAP system. The planning process starts with requirements coming from sales and distribution (SD) or from the material forecast and then becomes a part of demand management. The system runs the MRP based on the figures given in the demand program, and the outcome of the MRP run (planning run) is the creation of procurement proposals. These procurement proposals can be planned orders (order proposals), purchase requisitions for external procurement, or delivery schedules for scheduling agreements with vendors. In REM, the planned orders can't be converted because these are sufficient to trigger the production process. In fact, the REM planned orders obtain the new order type of the *run schedule quantity* (RSQ) when the system assigns a production version to them.

After actual production execution, the relevant information is recorded in the system, such as components consumption, activities consumption, and production yield. Because REM is a period-based manufacturing type, the product costing team finally proceeds to the settlement process, in which variances and overheads are also settled during the cost collector settlement.

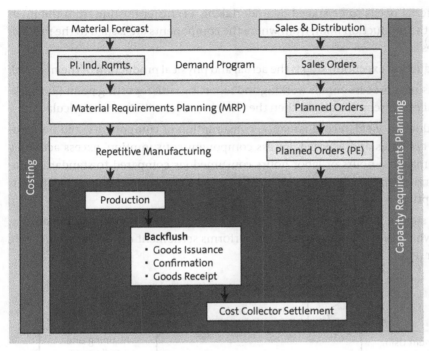

Figure 8.1 REM in Production Planning

8.1.2 Repetitive Manufacturing Process Flow

Figure 8.2 illustrates the end-to-end process flow in REM.

The process flow sequence is as follows:

❶ The process begins when requirements from MRP (through planned independent requirements [PIRs]) or SD flow in, based on which the production must initiate.

The system covers the infinite requirements with planned orders during the MRP run.

❷ The system performs the line loading and checks the capacity requirements to see if it's able to produce the required quantities. If not, it's overloaded.

❸ The system checks for the availability of the components needed to produce the material.

❹ The operational methods sheet (OMS) that contains detailed instructions for producing the material can be printed.

❺ It's also possible to print the production list, which contains quantities to produce and important dates. A production list specific to a material or to a production line can also be printed. Following the lean manufacturing principle, these are the only two shop floor papers.

⑥ The material needs to be staged by undertaking a transfer posting from the main store to the production floor, from where the components are issued to the production lines.

⑦ The production execution step is the actual and physical production of the material.

⑧ If the business process entails working and reporting with reporting point (RP) backflush (milestone confirmation), then the work in process (WIP) can be calculated.

⑨ The production yield, record issuance, consumption of components, and postproduction activities are recorded. Excess component consumption, excess activities such as machine hours or labor hours consumed (as compared to standard durations), and scrap can also be recorded. It's also possible to record any deviation in consumption.

⑩ The last step reflects the integration of controlling (CO) with production planning (PP), in which the product costing team performs settlement using the product cost collector (PCC).

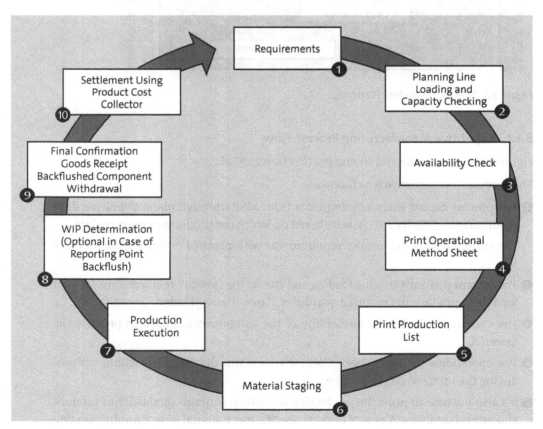

Figure 8.2 Process Flow in REM

[«]

> **Note**
> Quality management (QM) processes can also be integrated into the REM production process to ensure that all product produced in-house will go through quality checks before being dispatched to customers.

8.2   Master Data

Before running processes and jobs in the SAP system, it's imperative to set up complete and comprehensive master data. REM has its own unique master data that often overlaps with other production types, such as discrete manufacturing or process manufacturing. If master data is set up in the right sequence, it's much easier and more logical to interconnect because the predecessor-successor relationship is already taken care of.

Table 8.1 provides an overview of the master data that is needed in REM. It begins with the material master of the product (a finished good or an assembly), specifically marked as the REM type in the **MRP 4** view of the material master by selecting the relevant checkbox and also assigned the REM profile, which was previously configured (in Chapter 5).

Material	Production Version
■ Activating **REM** indicator ■ Assigning REM profile ■ Assigning production supervisor in the **Work Scheduling**	■ Activating **REM** indicator ■ Rate-based planning ■ Bill of material (BOM) assignment ■ Production line ■ Receipt storage location
Bill of materials (BOM)	**Cost object controlling**
■ Material BOM	■ PCC or even product cost estimate
Work center (production line)	**Rate routing**
■ Production line as work center	■ Assign work center (production line)—usually one operation ■ Production rate (quantity per time)

Table 8.1 Master Data of REM

A BOM of the product that needs to be produced is created, and the components together with the quantities needed to produce that product are assigned. If needed, a scrap percentage at the operation or component level can also be defined.

8

Then a work center or production line is created, followed by creating a rate routing for the material, in which the previously created work center is assigned.

Finally, a production version for the material is created and assigned the material's BOM and rate routing. The **REM** checkbox is selected to denote that the material produced will follow the REM process.

When all of the logistics master data is in place, the CO team can create PCCs of the material. This can be specific to the production version or can be independent of the production version.

[»]

> **Note**
>
> It's highly recommended to maintain close coordination and liaison with the CO team to ensure that when working in PP, both teams are completely aligned in terms of their working and reporting needs.
>
> For example, each work center (production line) requires assigning a cost center, which the CO team should provide. It may provide one cost center for multiple work centers or one cost center for an individual work center, depending on how the team wants to see the cost center reporting and evaluation.
>
> One possible approach to having several cost centers within one production line is accomplished by incorporating additional cost-relevant operations (in the rate routing) and still keeping the principle of just one work center for production (and PP).

Let's now discuss how to set up each of the REM-specific master data areas.

8.2.1   Material Master

The first step in creating REM-specific master data begins with creating the necessary settings in the material master of the product (an assembly or a finished good). To change the material master, follow menu path **Logistics · Materials Management · Material Master · Material · Change · Immediately**, or use Transaction MM02. On the resulting screen, enter **Material** number "72", and press [Enter] to bring up the organizational level, wherein **Plant** "1105" and **Stor. Loc.** "0001" are entered. Choose **Continue** to bring up **Select Views**, in which you select **MRP 4** and press [Enter] again.

On the screen shown in Figure 8.3, maintain the details related to REM production processes in the **MRP 4** view of the material master. Next, select the **Repet. Manufacturing** checkbox, which denotes that the material will undergo the REM production process. Select **PP10** in the **REM Profile** field.

[»]

> **Note**
>
> This is the same REM profile that was configured in Chapter 5.

A *REM profile* is a four-digit code that determines the following:

- The movement type that the system uses to post goods receipts (GRs) and goods issues (GIs)
- How the system reduces planned orders and RSQs in the confirmation process
- How the system makes the correction in the assembly's components (according to BOM), which enables you to define whether GI posting isn't possible in the system due to forgotten GR postings or whether the system should process the same later on in a separate backflush processing transaction
- How the system deals with production activities during confirmation, such as setup or machine hours

Save the settings in the material master, while also ensuring that you assign a production supervisor in the **Work Scheduling** view of the material master.

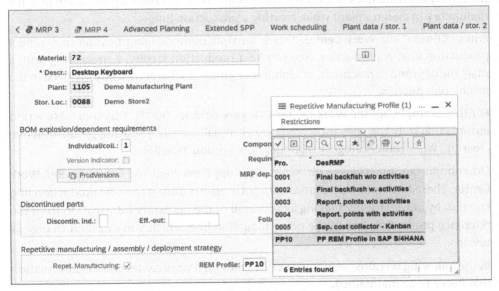

Figure 8.3 REM Indicator in MRP 4 View of Material Master

8.2.2   Bill of Materials

The process used to create a material BOM for REM is no different from the process in discrete manufacturing. Refer to Chapter 6, Section 6.2.2, in which the details of material BOM creation are covered.

8.2.3   Work Center (Production Line)

The alternative term for a work center is a *production line* in the SAP system. *Work center* is specific to discrete manufacturing, whereas *production line* is specific to REM.

Production lines are usually created as simple work centers in the system (and because the SAP system refers to these as *work centers*, we'll use both terms throughout this chapter to maintain a logical connection between the SAP terms and real-world business scenarios). In the work center, the availability of the production line is defined. In REM, following the lean manufacturing principle, all workstations in the production line aren't modeled as individual work centers. Rather, the entire production line (with all of its work centers) is modeled as one work center. The production line created as the work center is entered in the **Production Line** field in the production version. This same work center is specified in the single operation of the rate routing. Production lines that need to include or model more than one work center can be represented in a line hierarchy.

To create a work center (production line), follow menu path **Logistics · Production · Master Data · Work Centers · Work Center · Create**, or use Transaction CR01. On the initial screen to create the work center, enter **Plant** "1105" to create a production line. It's mandatory to assign a plant while creating a production line.

Enter "KBASSY" for **Work Center**. This is an alphanumeric identification to denote a production line. A production line can be a production facility, a processing unit, a machine or group of machines, or a laborer or group of laborers directly involved in the production process.

For this example, set the **Work Center Category** field as "0007". This control function ensures that only the relevant screens are eventually available during production line creation. Work center category 0007 denotes a production line.

Other important functions in this screen are **Copy from Plant** and **Copy from Ref. Work Center**. These functions help reduce data entry efforts during the new production line creation by automatically making available all of the necessary information from the reference production line in the new production line, which you can then change as needed.

In the following sections, we'll cover the five tabs for a work center and the information that needs to be maintained.

Basic Data

Figure 8.4 shows the **Basic Data** tab of a production line. Here, enter a short description of the production line in the text box at the top-right of this screen. In the **Usage** field, enter "009". A *usage* is a control function that controls whether this production line eventually becomes available for various other tasks, such as during the creation of rate routing or the production version. A usage of 009 denotes that this production line can subsequently be used in all task list types.

In the **Standard Value Key** field, enter "SAP3". A standard value key (SVK) denotes activities performed on a specific production line, as well as the option to record them.

Some of the activities include production time, setup time, processing time, and labor time. For REM, the SAP system already provides the SAP3 SVK, which can be used.

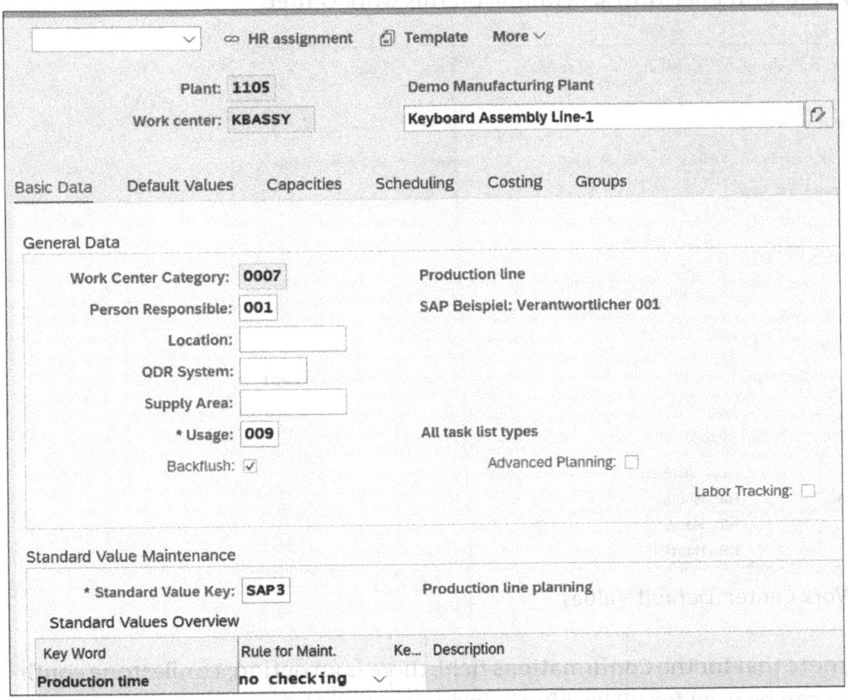

Figure 8.4 Work Center: Basic Data

Enter the production time as a rule for maintenance. If the **Production Time** is assigned as **Must Be Entered** from the dropdown list, then it's required to enter the actual duration of the activity during the confirmation of the REM planned order. Otherwise, the system won't allow the production supervisor to save the confirmation. Other maintenance options are **May Not Be Entered**, **May Be Entered**, or **Should Be Entered**, offering various degrees of control, from an information message to a warning message, if the requisite information (duration, in this case) isn't recorded during confirmation.

Default Values Tab

Click the **Default Values** tab to see the screen shown in Figure 8.5, wherein the PP01 control key is assigned to the work center. A *control key* is a control function that manages whether a production supervisor can perform an activity or a task associated with the work center. Place the cursor on the **Control Key** field and press F4.

With the cursor on the **Control Key** field, if the **Detailed Information** button is chosen, the system shows the details in the lower half of the same screen. Note that in REM, only the following checkboxes are included: **Scheduling**, **Det. Cap. Reqmnts.**, **Cost**, **Insp.char. required**, and **Confirmations**. No other checkboxes work for REM. If the checkbox isn't selected, then that step or function can't be performed on this work center (KBASSY). For example, if the **Scheduling** checkbox isn't selected in the control key, then the system won't perform scheduling on this work center.

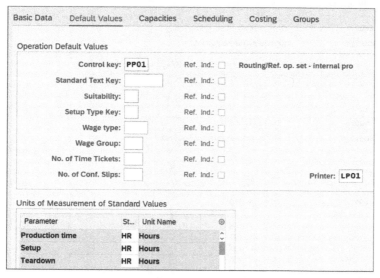

Figure 8.5 Work Center: Default Values

In addition, note that for the **Confirmations** field, there is an option, 1 (milestone confirmation), that can be used for RP backflush during confirmation.

> **Note**
>
> A control key is set up by using Transaction OPJ8.

Capacities Tab

Click the **Capacities** tab in the work center (production line) creation screen to see the options screen shown in Figure 8.6. On the **Capacities** tab, enter "SAPRO1" in the **Setup Formula** field; this denotes the setup formula that the system will use during capacity calculation. For **Processing Formula**, enter "SAPRO2". This is for **Capacity category 001** for **Machine** (shown at the top of the screen).

> **Note**
>
> See Chapter 18 for information on capacity requirements planning (CRP).

Click the **Capacity Header** button at the bottom of the **Capacities** tab. This brings up the header screen of the capacity for work center KBASSY, as shown in Figure 8.7. The capacity header contains comprehensive details about the capacity: start and end time of the shift, length of breaks, overload percentage allowed for capacity, shifts and intervals, and factory calendar.

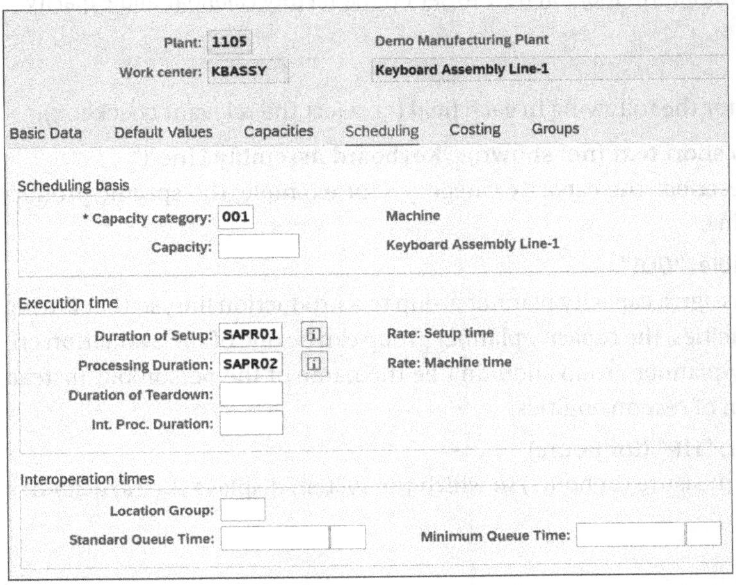

Figure 8.6 Work Center: Capacities

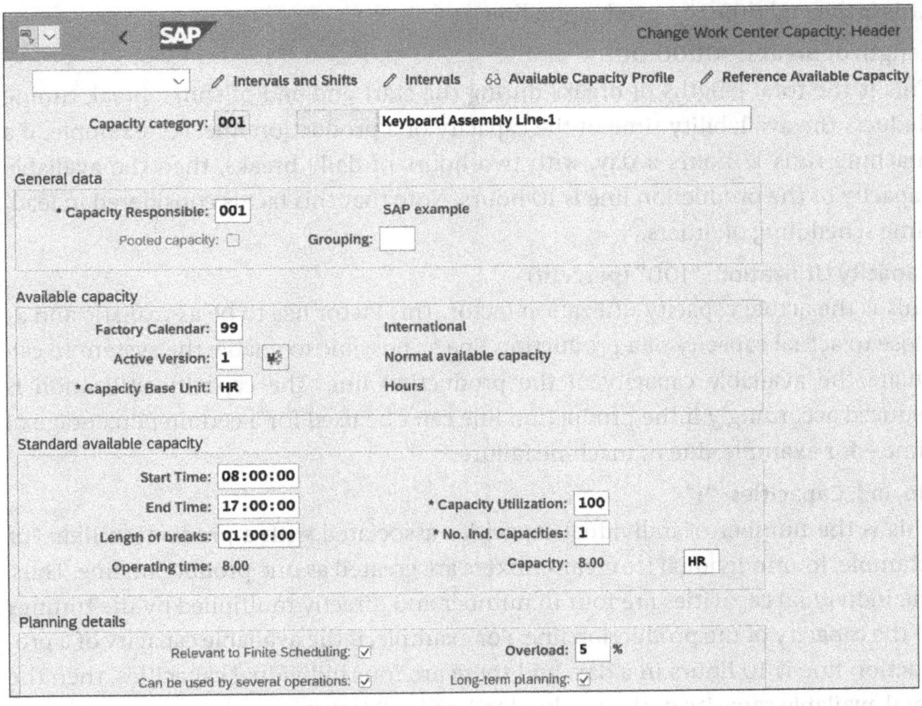

Figure 8.7 Work Center: Capacity Header

[»]

Note

Refer to Chapter 2 for information on how to set up the factory calendar and capacity planner group.

For this example, enter the following in each field (or select the relevant checkbox):

- **Capacity Category short text (not shown): "Keyboard Assembly Line-1"**
  This short text describes the capacity category—for example, the specific production line or machine.

- **Capacity Responsible: "001"**
  It's important to assign a capacity planner group to a production line, so that during evaluation of capacities, the capacity planner group can be one of the evaluation criteria. The capacity planner group shouldn't be the name of the person but instead the area or domain of responsibilities.

- **Capacity Base Unit: "HR" (for hours)**
  This is the unit of measure (in hours) in which the system displays the capacity of a production line.

- **Start: "08:00:00"**
  This is the start time of a production line.

- **Finish: "17:00:00"**
  This is the end time of a production line.

- **Length of Breaks: "01:00:00"**
  This is the total lengths of breaks during the start and end of shifts. Break timing deducts the availability time of the capacity of a production line. For example, if a machine runs 12 hours a day, with two hours of daily breaks, then the available capacity of the production line is 10 hours. Note that this fact is considered in lead-time scheduling of orders.

- **Capacity Utilization: "100" (percent)**
  This is the actual capacity utilization factor. This factor has to be as realistic and as close to actual capacity of a production line as possible to enable the system to calculate the available capacity of the production line. The capacity utilization is reduced accordingly if the production line can't be used for a certain percentage of time—for example, due to machine failure.

- **No. Ind. Capacities: "1"**
  This is the number of individual capacities associated with a production line. For example, four individual ice cream mixers are created as one production line. Thus, the individual capacities are four in number and directly multiplied by the timings of the capacity of the production line. For example, if the available capacity of a production line is 10 hours in a day, and there are four individual capacities, then the total available capacity of the production line is 40 hours.

- **Relevant to Finite Scheduling**
  This checkbox requires the system to consider capacity overload during capacity evaluation.

- **Overload %**
  A capacity overload in percentage directly increases the capacity availability of the production line by the defined percentage. If, for example, the total capacity of a production line is 40 hours with 10% overload, then the available capacity is 44 hours. A 10% overload for 40 hours is 4 hours, which adds to the 40 hours to show the total available capacity at 44 hours. Because you're considering an overload, maintain "5" here to denote that a 5% capacity overload is allowed.

- **Long-Term Planning**
  This checkbox enables the system to consider the production line availability during long-term planning (LTP). LTP refers to a simulative planning of material and production lines over a longer period.

> **Note**
> See Chapter 16 for more information about LTP.

Scheduling
Click the **Back** icon, then click the **Scheduling** tab (see Figure 8.8). Enter the standard formulas available for REM (these are covered in detail in Chapter 6).

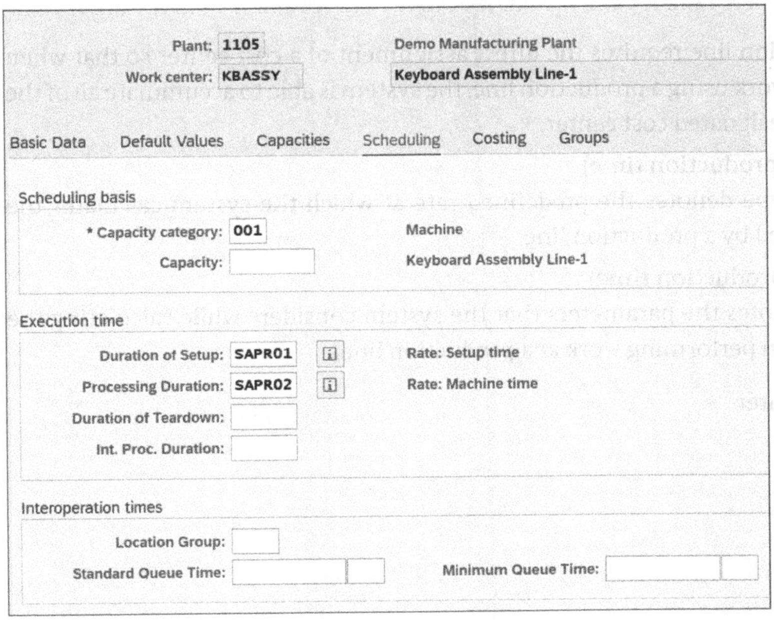

Figure 8.8 Work Center: Scheduling

[»]

> **Note**
>
> See Chapter 18 to learn more about CRP.

Costing

Because PP comprehensively integrates with the cost object controlling functionality in product cost controlling (CO-PC), each work center needs to have a cost center. It's possible to assign a single cost center to multiple work centers in the **Costing** tab, but multiple cost centers can't be assigned to a single work center.

[»]

> **Note**
>
> It's highly recommended to coordinate with the CO person to ensure that each cost center and associated activity type for the given controlling area has price planning.
>
> In the same step, ensure that activity types and cost centers are also in place, so these can then be assigned in the rate routing.

In the screen shown in Figure 8.9, enter the following details:

- **Start Date**
  This is the start date of the availability of the cost center for the production line.

- **End Date**
  This is the end date of the availability of the cost center for the production line.

- **Cost Center**
  Every production line requires the direct assignment of a cost center so that when you perform work using a production line, the system is able to accumulate all of the costs on the designated cost center.

- **Activity Type (production time)**
  The activity type denotes the predefined rate at which the system calculates the work performed by a production line.

- **Formula Key (production time)**
  A formula denotes the parameters that the system considers while calculating the cost incurred in performing work at a production line.

Save the work center.

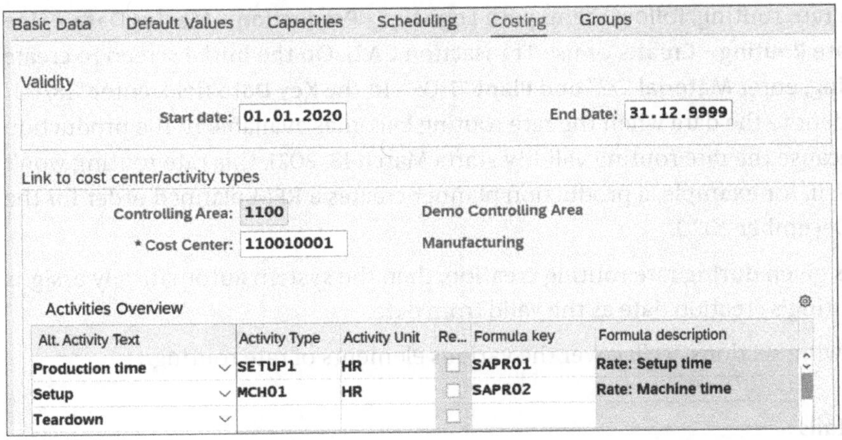

Figure 8.9 Work Center: Costing

8.2.4 Rate Routing

Rate routings are designed for the maintenance of production rate-based task lists and are used in REM, among other business scenarios. In a standard routing, the base quantity (e.g., pieces) generally remains constant, and the time-related data, such as the processing time, is maintained using standard values. Rate routing works exactly the opposite. The production quantities are maintained on the basis of individual items, and the reference time is constant. Thus, a rate routing describes the quantity of an item that must be produced within a given period of time.

A rate routing can contain a series of operations. The production rate is defined for each operation based on the production quantity, production time, and associated unit of measure. The production rate is determined as the quotient of the production quantity and production time. This enables a production planner to determine the production quantity in terms of tons per shift, for example. Usually, only one operation is production-relevant, and the others may be controlling- or print-relevant. Using line hierarchies, several production-relevant operations can support capacity leveling on different work centers along the production line.

All other aspects of the functionality and maintenance of standard routings and rate routings are identical. Work centers are assigned to the rate routing, which should also contain the SVK in which the standard values for production time, setup time, and teardown time are predefined.

A *reference routing* is used as a reference or template in routings. A reference rate routing contains a sequence of operations. As with a rate routing, the production rate for an operation is defined on the basis of the production quantity and reference time. The functionality and maintenance of reference routings are similar to those of reference operation sets.

To create a rate routing, follow menu path **Logistics** • **Production** • **Master Data** • **Line Design** • **Rate Routing** • **Create**, or use Transaction CA21. On the initial screen to create a rate routing, enter **Material** "72" and **Plant** "1105". In the **Key Date** field, enter "18/03/2021" and denote the date when the rate routing becomes available in the production process. Because the rate routing validity starts March 18, 2021, this rate routing won't be available if, for example, a production planner creates a REM planned order for the month of December 2020.

If no date is given during rate routing creation, then the system automatically assigns the rate routing's creation date as the valid from date.

In the following sections, we'll cover the various elements of rate routing.

Header Details

Click the **Header** icon. In the header details of the rate routing, enter the following:

- **Usage: "1" (for production)**
  This makes the rate routing available during subsequent production activities, in which the system will use the rate routing during the creation of the REM planned order.

- **Status: "4" (released)**
  This makes the rate routing available during subsequent production activities, in which the system will use the rate routing during the creation of the REM planned order. If the status of the rate routing is set to **Being Created (Status 1)**, it won't be available when a REM planned order for the material is created.

- **Planning Work Center: "KBASSY"**
  This is the production line that was previously created and is now used in the planning and production of the material.

- **From Lot Size: "1" PC**
  This denotes that the smallest quantity of the REM planned order must be at least 1 PC for the system to consider using this rate routing. In other words, this rate routing is applicable when you create the REM planned order of a quantity greater than or equal to 1 PC.

- **To: "999,999" PC**
  This denotes that the maximum quantity of the REM planned order is 999,999 PC for the system to consider using this rate routing. In other words, this rate routing is applicable when a REM planned order with a quantity greater than or equal to 1 PC but less than or equal to 999,999 PC is created.

[»]

Note
Because QM also integrates with REM, engage the QM resource for this activity.

Click the **Operations** button. The resulting screen is shown in Figure 8.10, in which **KBASSY** is the work center (**Work Ctr** column). This denotes assigning a previously created work center (production line) to an operation, which is used in the production of a material and for which you're creating the rate routing. An operation defines a single level of detail for a production step.

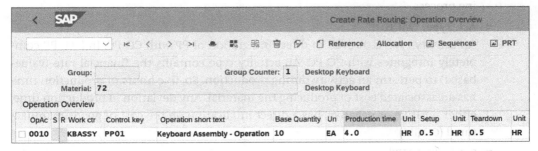

Figure 8.10 Routing: Operation Overview

Operations

Select and double-click the first line item, **Operat 0010**, and the screen shown in Figure 8.11 appears.

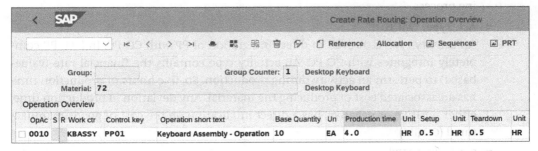

Figure 8.11 Routing: Operation Details

Here you see the operation's detailed view, in which you can enter the following:

- **Production Time: "4.0 HR" (hour)**
  It was defined in the production line that recording duration information in rate routing is mandatory (by using the maintenance control **Must Be Entered**); hence, you must define the time it will take for the production line step of the manufacturing process.

- **Act. Type: "MCH01"**
  An activity type is a result of direct integration of PP with CO-PC. In fact, PP completely integrates with CO-PC. An activity type contains the financial rate (value-based) to perform an activity during production. So, five hours of production time has an associated cost of producing the material. Any deviation in production time, either positive or negative, has a direct implication on the cost of goods manufactured (COGM).

- **Setup: "0.5 HR"**
  This is the time it takes to set up the machine or the production line for this task. Any deviation in setup time, either positive or negative, has a direct implication on COGM.

- **Teardown: "0.5 HR"**
  This is the time it takes to dismantle or tear down the setup of the machine or the production line. Any deviation in teardown time, either positive or negative, has a direct implication on COGM.

Components Allocation

Next, press F6 or choose **Goto • Operations Overview**, and the system brings up the **Operations Overview** screen. On this screen, click the **Components Allocation** icon.

Figure 8.12 shows the component allocation in rate routing. These components are directly taken from a material's BOM, which was created in the previous step.

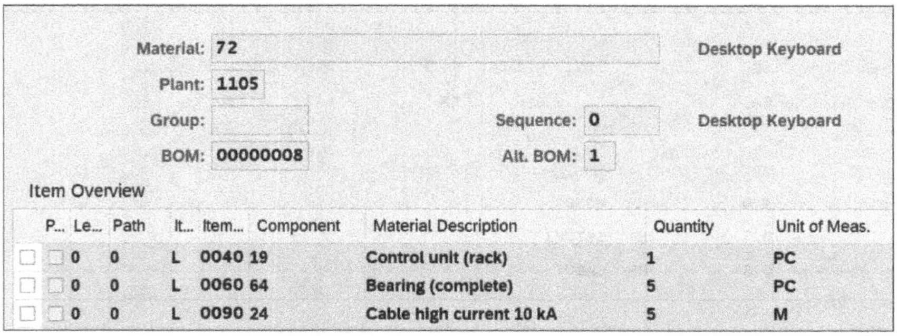

Material:	**72**				Desktop Keyboard
Plant:	**1105**				
Group:			Sequence:	**0**	Desktop Keyboard
BOM:	**00000008**		Alt. BOM:	**1**	

Item Overview

P...	Le...	Path	It...	Item...	Component	Material Description	Quantity	Unit of Meas.
	0	0	L	0040	19	Control unit (rack)	1	PC
	0	0	L	0060	64	Bearing (complete)	5	PC
	0	0	L	0090	24	Cable high current 10 kA	5	M

Figure 8.12 Material Component Overview in Routing

If a specific component isn't assigned to a specific operation, the system assigns all components to the first operation of the rate routing. This means that all components must be available at the first operation so that during backflush, the system is able to consume all components in the first operation.

If a business process entails that a few components are used or needed in the later stages of the production process, then select them and use the **Reassign** button to assign specific components to the operation.

Because there is only one operation in REM, the preceding scenario of material assignment is broadly more applicable in discrete manufacturing than in REM.

Material Assignment

Going back to the rate routing header screen, click the **Assignment** button. A production planner can assign several materials, together with their respective plants, to this rate routing group (**50000003**). All such materials belonging to this rate routing group will have the same group but with an ascending group counter number.

In other words, several materials undergoing the same production process need separate routings for each. Just create one rate routing and assign relevant materials (with plants) to it. This saves time and effort in creating an important part of the master data (rate routing) and also eliminates or reduces redundant data entry efforts.

Save the rate routing.

8.2.5 Production Version

Production versions denote different ways in which a company produces a material—for example, a material with one rate routing but multiple BOMs. Therefore, for each BOM and the same rate routing, the system needs a separate production version to denote uniqueness during the REM planned order creation. The requirement to create a separate production version also applies when there is one BOM for a material but multiple routings. In the REM process, it's mandatory to create a production version and make it available.

The production version can also be specific to the quantity range, thus acting as a control function. For example, one production version can be created that has a quantity limitation of 1 to 1,000 PC and another production version for a quantity greater than 1,000 PC.

The production version can also be specific to the validity period, thus acting as a control function. For example, a production version can be valid from April 1, 2018, to March 31, 2021. From April 1, 2021, on, a new production version is effective. When the system has to assign the production version to the REM planned order, it searches for specific validity dates and automatically assigns the relevant production version when it's found.

If the system is able to find multiple production versions fulfilling the search and application criteria, it assigns the first available production version to the REM planned order. The first available production version refers to the list that can be called from the material master (in the **MRP 4** or **Work Scheduling** views). To create a new production version, follow SAP menu path **SAP Menu · Logistics · Production · Master Data · Production Versions**, or use Transaction C223.

In the **Selection Conditions** area of the screen shown in Figure 8.13, enter **Plant** "1105" and **Material** "72", and then press ⌷Enter⌷. If the system is unable to find a production version for the material, then the lower half of the screen appears blank. If the system is successful, then it displays the relevant production versions.

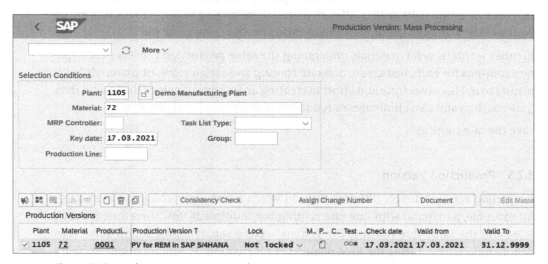

Figure 8.13 Production Version: Initial Screen

A menu bar is available at the bottom of the production version creation screen that has just about all of the options normally needed while creating production version master data, including copying, deleting, copying from a template, and so on.

Click the **Create Production Version** icon, and an almost empty screen appears for maintaining details, as shown in Figure 8.14.

Figure 8.14 Production Version of Material 72

Enter the details as noted in Table 8.2.

Field	Value	Additional Details/Remarks
Material	72	–
Production Version	0001	–
Minimum Lot Size	1.0	This field sets the minimum REM planned order quantity for which the system offers this production version for selection. Leaving this field blank entails that there is no minimum quantity limit.
Maximum Lot Size	99,999,999.000	This field sets the maximum planned order quantity for which the production version is applicable.
Valid from	17.03.2021	This field denotes that when the REM planned order creation starting on or after 17/03/2021, the system offers this production version for selection. If the start date of the REM planned order is before 17/03/2021, the system won't make this production version available for selection. If this field is left blank, the system automatically incorporates the current date as the validity start date of the production version.

Table 8.2 Parameters Entry in Production Version

Field	Value	Additional Details/Remarks
Valid to	31.12.9999	This field sets the end validity date of the production version.
Detailed Planning	Rate Routing	Task list type **R** denotes that it's a rate routing. Each task list type represents a different function; for example, task list type **Q** represents quality inspection.
		For this example, enter rate routing **Group** "50000003" and **Group Counter** "1".
Alternative BOM	1	This is the BOM that you created in the previous step.
BOM Usage	1	In this field, 1 refers to the usage production.
REM Allowed	Select checkbox	This checkbox selection is mandatory to denote that the production version is applicable and becomes available during the REM process.
Production Line	KBASSY	Because REM is generally a simpler production process, only one production line (work center) is involved.
Receiv. Location (not shown)	0001	Entering a value makes it a default setting, and the system automatically proposes it during GR or confirmation of the REM planned order.

Table 8.2 Parameters Entry in Production Version (Cont.)

The **Lock** field in the **Production Version** area of the screen provides the flexibility to lock or unlock the production version anytime to allow or restrict access to the production version during the REM planned order creation. A locked production version won't be available for selection during the REM planned order creation.

Finally, click the **Check** button (consistency check) to evaluate if the details incorporated in the production version are correct and valid.

The system confirms that it's able to find a relevant task list (rate routing) as well as the BOM, which meets the other criteria of the production version. This includes having validity dates for the rate routing and the BOM, which falls within the validity specified in the production version, as well as the lot sizes mentioned in the production version. Click the **Cancel** icon.

The green traffic light against the task list and the BOM indicates that the consistency check was successful, and this production version will be available to the user during REM planned order creation. If a warning or error is observed during the consistency check, the system indicates that with a yellow or a red traffic light, respectively.

> **Note** [«]
>
> The consistency check isn't a prerequisite to using a correct production version. But using this option can give you confidence that eventually a valid production version will be available to work with.

Click on **Close Detailed Screen and Adopt Changes**, then save the production version.

> **Note** [«]
>
> If detailed scheduling and capacity planning functionalities are required in the REM business processes of a company, then it's recommended to use a routing (instead of a rate routing) and assign it to the production version. Details of how to create a routing were covered in Chapter 6.
>
> We'll still cover detailed scheduling and capacity planning in REM while using a rate routing in this chapter. The formulas used in rate routing (such as SAPRO2 in this example) should allow scheduling and capacity calculation and this can be achieved by selection the relevant checkboxes in the formula being used in the rate routing (Transaction OP55).

8.3   Material Requirements Planning in Repetitive Manufacturing

Extensive coverage on MRP is provided in Chapter 13 and Chapter 14. In this section, however, we will show how to use MRP for preplanning of REM-based manufacturing types. The preplanning process entails that a production planner has already planned to produce predetermined quantities of a product and use MRP for comprehensive planning, including the components (BOM) of the product. It's important to note that there are no REM-specific details for MRP; REM uses standard MRP. For example, preplanning isn't a prerequisite for REM. REM based planning can also be used on sales orders only (MTO). For this example, we use strategy 40 (MTS production method), which is a typical case in REM. Any planning strategy in conjunction with REM (MTO and MTS) can be used. We'll focus on a typical real-world example in the keyboard manufacturing industry.

For normal and standard planning, the planning process starts with either a sales order forming the basis of planning or quantities calculated from forecasting. Any or all of these quantities are forwarded to demand management, which ends up forming the PIRs. The MRP considers PIRs and generates procurement proposals, including planned orders. A production planner evaluates the planning results and converts them into procurement elements for external procurement; these don't need to be converted any further or for REM types. The steps are as follows:

1. **Maintain planned independent requirements**

   Use Transaction MD61 to enter the PIRs into the screen shown in Figure 8.15. Enter **Material** "72", **Plant** "1105", and **Version** "00", and then define the planning horizon from "19/03/2021" to "01/01/2022". Press ⌈Enter⌋. Next, enter planning quantities as maintained in Figure 8.15, and save the PIR. The next step is to run the MRP.

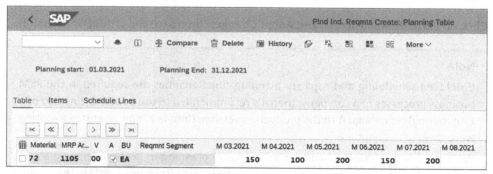

Figure 8.15 Planned Independent Requirements

2. **Run material requirements planning**

   In this step, the materials planner runs MRP Live by using Transaction MD01N. Figure 8.16 shows the initial screen to run MRP. Set the parameters as shown, and click **Execute** (not shown) to begin the process of running MRP. As soon as the system completes the planning process (MRP run), it displays the planning results.

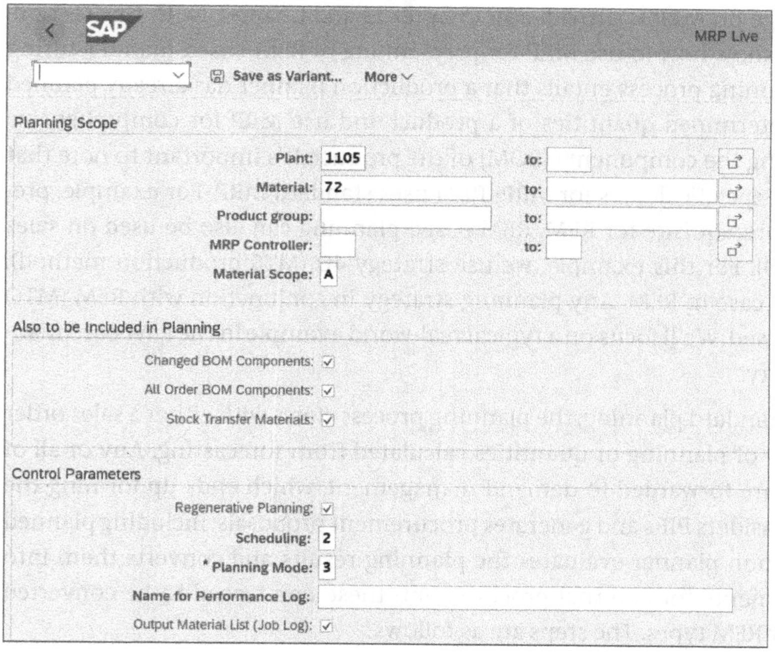

Figure 8.16 Initial Screen of MRP Live

3. Display planning results

Figure 8.17 shows the planning results for both material 72 and its associated components. The next step is to evaluate the planning results of material 72 by either double-clicking the material directly or first saving the planning results and then using Transaction MD04 for the material and plant combination to see the stock/requirements list. For this example, use the first option: double-click the planning results of material 72 (the last material in the list).

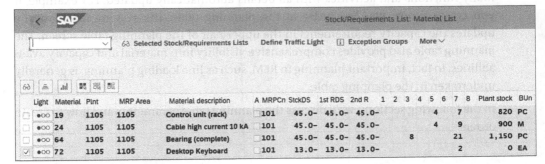

Light	Material	Plnt	MRP Area	Material description	A	MRPCn	StckDS	1st RDS	2nd R	1	2	3	4	5	6	7	8	Plant stock	BUn
●○○	19	1105	1105	Control unit (rack)	101		45.0-	45.0-	45.0-				4			7		820	PC
●○○	24	1105	1105	Cable high current 10 kA	101		45.0-	45.0-	45.0-				4			9		900	M
●○○	64	1105	1105	Bearing (complete)	101		45.0-	45.0-	45.0-			8				21		1,150	PC
●○○	72	1105	1105	Desktop Keyboard	101		13.0-	13.0-	13.0-							2		0	EA

Figure 8.17 Planning Results of MRP Run

The system also creates multiple planned orders to cater to the PIRs (see Figure 8.18).

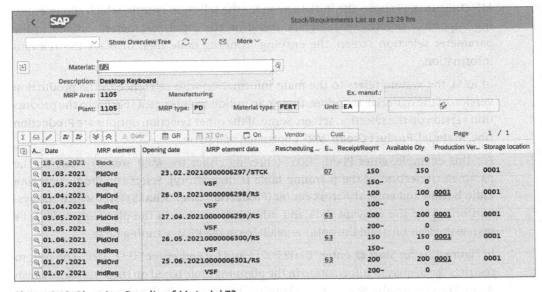

A...	Date	MRP element	Opening date	MRP element data	Rescheduling ...	E...	Receipt/Reqmt	Available Qty	Production Ver...	Storage location
🔍	18.03.2021	Stock						0		
🔍	01.03.2021	PldOrd	23.02.20210000006297/STCK			07	150	150		0001
🔍	01.03.2021	IndReq		VSF			150-	0		
🔍	01.04.2021	PldOrd	26.03.20210000006298/RS				100	100	0001	0001
🔍	01.04.2021	IndReq		VSF			100-	0		
🔍	03.05.2021	PldOrd	27.04.20210000006299/RS			63	200	200	0001	0001
🔍	03.05.2021	IndReq		VSF			200-	0		
🔍	01.06.2021	PldOrd	26.05.20210000006300/RS			63	150	150	0001	0001
🔍	01.06.2021	IndReq		VSF			150-	0		
🔍	01.07.2021	PldOrd	25.06.20210000006301/RS			63	200	200	0001	0001
🔍	01.07.2021	IndReq		VSF			200-	0		

Figure 8.18 Planning Results of Material 72

> **Note**
>
> In principle, manual changes to the REM planned orders should only be made in Transaction MD04.

Save the MRP results, and all of these planning details will become available in the REM planning table.

8.4   Planning Table

The planning table in REM is highly interactive and enables the planner to perform many functions and activities with all details automatically updated. For example, if you create a new planned order in the planning table, the system automatically updates the capacity requirements in the upper half of the planning table screen. The planning table also provides comprehensive visibility into material and capacity availabilities. In fact, important planning in REM, such as line loading planning, is generally undertaken in the planning table.

In the following sections, we'll discuss the planning table parameters and how to create orders.

8.4.1   Parameters Selection

To access the planning table in REM, follow menu path **Logistics • Production • Repetitive Manufacturing • Planning • Planning Table • Change Mode**, or use Transaction MF50. Figure 8.19 shows the initial screen for the selection criteria, which allows entering important selection parameters. Based on the input parameters defined in the parameter selection screen, the ensuing planning table then displays the relevant information.

In REM, the system refers to the main information with reference to the production version of the material; therefore, there's an option to enter data specific to the production version on the selection screen. Some of the other selection options are **Production Line**, **Material**, **Product Group**, **MRP Controller**, and so on.

For this example, enter **Plant** "1105" (entering either the **MRP area** or **Plant** on the parameter selection of the planning table is mandatory). Select the **Production Line** radio button and enter the work center (**Production Line**) "KBASSY", for which the system brings up the relevant data and other information in the planning table. Let's review the four tabs and the options available in the REM planning table.

In Figure 8.20, for **Start ❶**, enter "01.02.2021"; and for **End**, enter "31.12.2021". The system restricts the display of information in the planning table based on these start and finish dates. The system also won't show planning information in the planning horizon that lies outside the planning horizon. Assign the **Period** field as **Week**, and the system shows planning details in a weekly basket. A production planner can also choose to display planning information in the planning table, either in days or weeks.

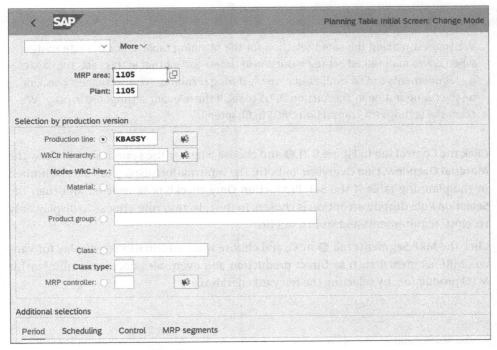

Figure 8.19 Initial Screen of Planning Table

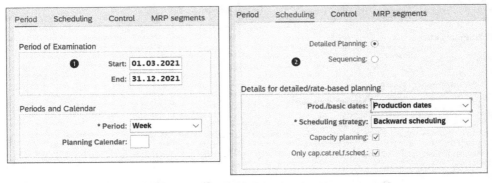

Figure 8.20 Period of Examination and Scheduling in REM Table

Click the **Scheduling** tab ❷. The scheduling options available in this screen enable the selection options, to make them available in the planning table. Choose whether the system will perform rate-based planning and select whether it should consider basic dates or production dates during planning. The system can also bring up capacity planning and leveling options by selecting the relevant checkbox.

Note

We suggest making the same selection for the planning table as for the rate routing when it was maintained in the production version—except that in this case, the capacity requirements can be evaluated properly during planning. We also suggest checking on the configuration in Transaction OPU5 to see if the relevant settings are in place. We cover the settings for Transaction OPU5 in Chapter 3.

Click the **Control** tab in Figure 8.21 ❸ and choose whether the system should show the **Material Overview, Line Overview**, or both. The information display can also be limited in the planning table if the **Sel. Production Only** checkbox is selected and then the **Selection Rule** dropdown option is chosen. In the selection rule, choose to display only receipts, requirements and stocks, or PIRs.

Click the **MRP Segments** tab ❹ next, and choose what information to display for various MRP elements, such as **Direct production** and even sales document number for MTO production, by selecting the relevant checkboxes.

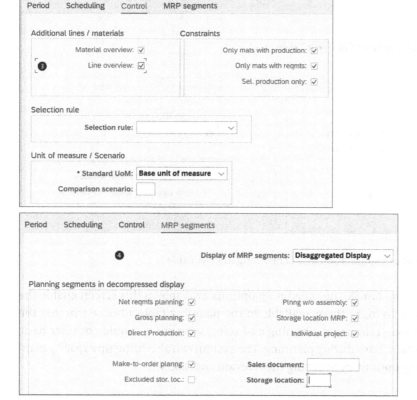

Figure 8.21 Control and MRP Segments in REM Table

All of the parameter selection options are the same as configured in Chapter 5, Section 5.3, but there's flexibility to change parameters, as we've done with **Scheduling Strategy** in the **Scheduling** tab of the **Planning Table Initial Screen: Change Mode**. In the configuration for the scheduling strategy, we defined the scheduling strategy as **Forward Scheduling**, whereas in the **Scheduling** tab, we changed this to **Backward Scheduling**.

Click the **Execute** button located at the bottom right-hand corner of the **Planning Table: Initial Screen** shown earlier in Figure 8.19, and the screen shown in Figure 8.22 appears. The upper half of the screen displays the complete capacity data, including the required and available capacities of the KBASSY production line that was maintained in the production version previously.

Total Capacity Data	Un	Due	W 11 (15.03)	W 12 (22.03)	W 13 (29.03)	W 14 (05.04)	W 15 (12.04)	W 16 (19.04)	W 17 (26.04)	W 18 (03.05)	W 19 (10.05)	W 20 (17.05)
KBASSY /001 Keyboard Ass. %		35.625	100	141.25	275	200	291.25	200	200	176.25	200	101.25
Requireme- Keyboard Asse.H		29	8	57	88	64	117	80	80	71	80	41
Available- Keyboard Assem.H			8	40	32	32	40	40	40	40	40	40

Material Data	Un	Due	W 11 (15.03)	W 12 (22.03)	W 13 (29.03)	W 14 (05.04)	W 15 (12.04)	W 16 (19.04)	W 17 (26.04)	W 18 (03.05)	W 19 (10.05)	W 20 (17.05)
Desktop Keyboard 72	•••											
Available Quantity	EA				100	100	300	300	300	300	300	300
Preplanning	EA	150			100						200	
Σ Total Requirements	EA	150			100						200	
Minimum Stock Level	EA		28	28	28	36	36	36	36	43	43	43
0001 KBASSY	EA	100			200	100		200			150	
Not Assigned	EA	140										
Σ Total Production	EA	240			200	100		200			150	

Figure 8.22 Planning Table

The lower half of the screen displays material-specific information. In the **Preplanning** field, the system displays the same PIRs that were created in an earlier section (refer to Section 8.3).

The planning table also displays the settings made in Chapter 5, Section 5.3, including the display of available quantity, total production, total requirements, and the actual coverage as target stock.

> **[+] Tips and Tricks**
>
> If a production planner is unable to see editable fields such as **KBASSY** or **Not Assigned**, as shown in the planning table in Figure 8.22, double-click the **Not Assigned** field under **Material Data**, and these fields will appear.

8.4.2   Creating a Repetitive Manufacturing Planned Order

As a planner, changes to the existing planning elements, such as planned orders, and the creation of new planned orders to account for production constraints or other practical realities, such as an unplanned plant or machine shutdown, have to happen. Because the REM planning table is interactive, all these important planning functions and much more within the REM planning table is possible. On exiting the REM planning table, save the interactive planning to enable the system to update the information accordingly.

For this example, create a new planned order by placing the cursor in the **KBASSY** field and entering a quantity of "350" for any week (column **W 41(15.03)**). Then double-click the field in which the quantity 350 was entered to open the screen shown in Figure 8.23.

Figure 8.23 Planned Order Creation in Planning Table

Here, the system has given a temporary planned order number (**Plnd order: 9999999006**) and enables making changes to the production version, production line, or production start or finish dates. The **Fxd** checkbox can be chosen, which will ensure that no changes are made to the planned order during the MRP run. Click the **Adopt** button, and the details are copied to the planning table.

Double-click the **Quantity** field, and this time the system assigns a permanent planned order number to which a large number of requisite changes can be made, if desired. To make changes to the planned order, click the **Change** icon (not shown), and the screen shown in Figure 8.24 appears. This screen shows that the REM planned order is referred to as **Run Schedule Quantity**, which is due to the fact that it has created the new quantity directly on the production line. The **Order Quantity** can be changed and the **Scrap Quantity** can be added to account for any production losses (see Figure 8.25). The system automatically copies all other details, such as storage location data and the production version number, from the REM master data. Scroll down and the system also automatically selects the **Repetitive Mfg** checkbox from **Version 0001** (not shown).

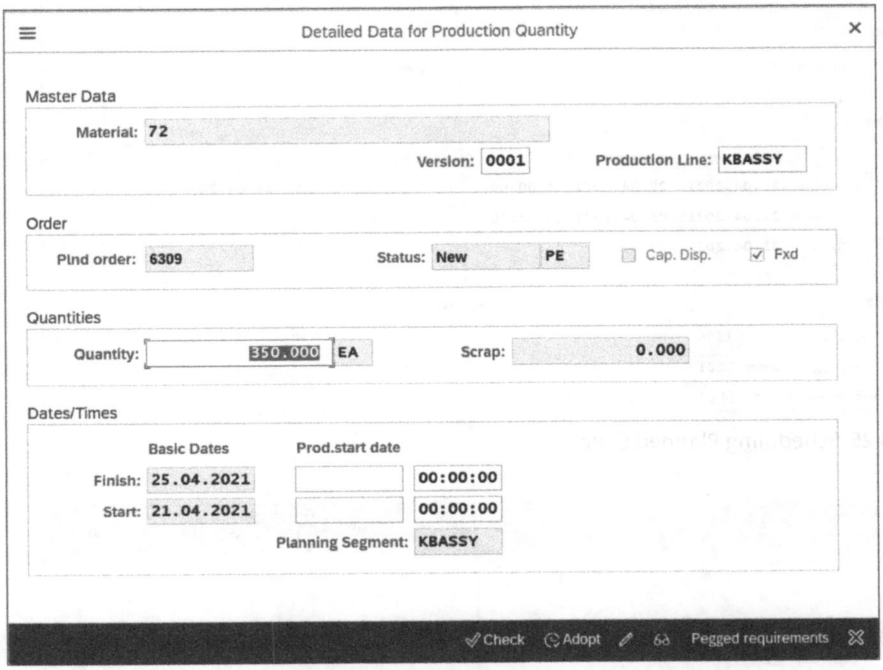

Figure 8.24 Header Screen of Planned Order (Run Schedule Quantity)

The **Planned Order** checkbox in the **Firming** area (see Figure 8.25) indicates that during the MRP run, the system won't make automatic changes to this REM planned order. The system automatically firms all manually created REM planned orders, according to the settings made in the REM profile in Chapter 5.

Click **Schedule Planned Order** at the top of the screen, and the system shows the **Detailed Scheduling** tab. When detailed scheduling for the material is performed, you can choose **More • Goto • Capacity Leveling** in the planned order, and the screen shown in Figure 8.26 appears, showing the capacity requirement.

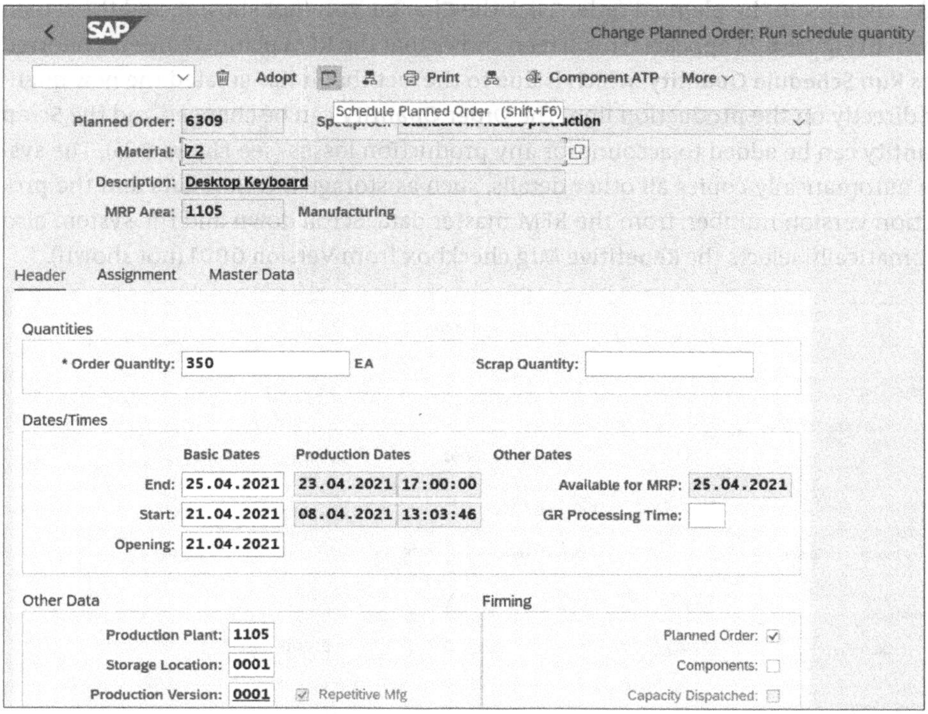

Figure 8.25 Scheduling Planned Order

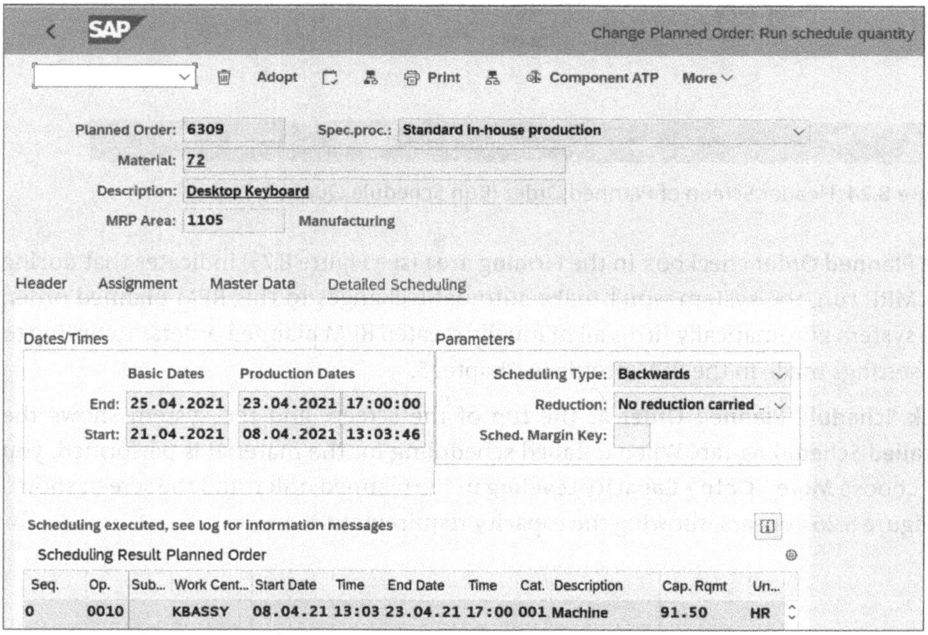

Figure 8.26 Capacity Planning

Clicking **Component ATP** (available to promise) in Figure 8.26 will bring up the **Availability Check** screen shown in Figure 8.27, indicating that for the three components checked, the system found that all components are available.

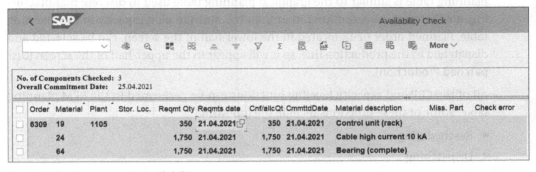

Figure 8.27 Components Availability

> **Tips and Tricks**
>
> In the **Change Planned Order** screen, a large number of activities and functions can be performed—for example, components availability check, capacity check, or re-exploding the BOM for the material.
>
> As an MRP planner, decide whether to use Transaction MD04 or Transaction MF50 for daily work. In Transaction MF50, work can be managed on a periodic basis, whereas in Transaction MD04, all work is order-based.

8.4.3 Capacity Planning

Go back to the REM planning table and set up graphics for capacity planning by navigating to **More • Capacity Requirements Planning • Graphical Planning Table**. Within the REM planning table shown in Figure 8.28, evaluate the capacity situation (located in the upper half of the screen).

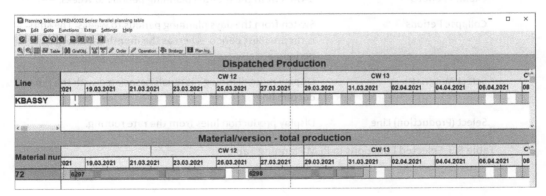

Figure 8.28 Capacity Planning

In general, at this stage, the capacity situation at the work center is agreed upon and already known, except in cases of urgent or immediate business need, such as sequence planning (within shifts or in days). The capacity planning function in the REM planning table is similar to the graphical planning table used in discrete manufacturing. It's therefore an exception rather than the norm to plan capacity in the planning table. Planned order 6297, located in the lower-half of the screen, can be selected and dispatched to the production line, so it will appear in the upper-half of the screen (**Dispatched Production**).

All of the CRP and capacity leveling functions can be performed in the REM planning table. Some of these functions include the following:

- Rescheduling
- Dispatching
- Performing deallocation
- Making changes to the REM planned order
- Making changes to the rate routing operations

[»]

> **Note**
>
> See Chapter 18 for more about CRP.

8.4.4   Changes and Evaluations

Any changes or evaluations in the planning table can be made, and the system updates all information on a real-time basis. Some of these functions are listed in Table 8.3.

Function	Function Detail
Create New Planned Order	Place the cursor on the **Not Assigned** field in the planning table, then click this icon to create a new planned order.
Expand Periods	Switch from the months planning periods to weeks.
Collapse Periods	Switch from the days planning periods to weeks. The shift is the smallest period, whereas the month is the largest period.
Select Material	Display more planning materials associated with the production line.
Select (Production) Line	Display production lines from the rate routing.

Table 8.3 Selected Functions in REM Planning Table

Function	Function Detail
Hide Material	Hide the already-displayed materials.
Hide (Production) Line	Hide the already-displayed production lines.
Graphical Planning Table	Display a graphical version of capacity planning.

Table 8.3 Selected Functions in REM Planning Table (Cont.)

8.4.5 Range of Coverage

If the necessary configuration for the range of coverage profile is already undertaken and this coverage profile is assigned to the material master in the **MRP 2** view of the material master, then the option to evaluate the coverage becomes available in the planning table. This has to be first activated in the **View** menu. The range of coverage profile contains the parameters for calculating the dynamic safety stock. This is a statistical calculation on the basis of average daily requirements. The range of coverage profile includes, for example, maximum stock level, minimum stock level, target stock, statistical, and actual range of coverage.

If the configuration was undertaken to display **Minimum Target Stock** in the **Coverage** field (refer to Chapter 5, Section 5.3.2, showing the **Coverage** field and the **Target Stock Level** value), then the system displays **Minimum Target Stock** as a default setting in the REM planning table. To change this display in the REM planning table, choose **More · View · Range of Coverage Profile** (see Figure 8.29). The maximum stock level can also be displayed in the planning table.

Material Data	Un	W 12 (22.03)	W 13 (29.03)	W 14 (05.04)	W 15 (12.04)	W 16 (19.04)	W 17 (26.04)	W 18 (03.05)	W 19 (10.05)	W 20 (17.05)	W 21 (24.05)
Desktop Keyboard 72	●●●										
Available Quantity	EA					350	350	350	350	350	350
Preplanning	EA		100					200			
Σ Total Requirements	EA		100					200			
Actual Range of Cov.	●●●					26	25	42	37	32	28
0001 KBASSY	EA	150	100			350	200				
Not Assigned	EA										
Σ Total Production	EA	150	100			350	200				

Figure 8.29 Actual Range of Coverage in REM Planning Table

> **Note**
>
> We encourage exploring the features and functionalities in the planning table for REM. For example, clicking the **Situation** icon in the REM planning table will bring up the screen shown in Figure 8.30.

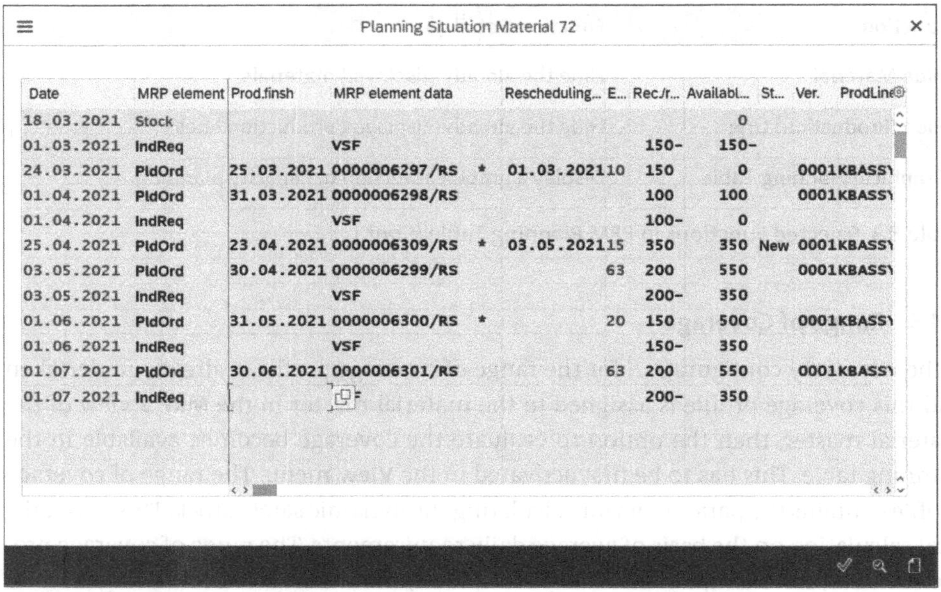

Date	MRP element	Prod.finsh	MRP element data		Rescheduling...	E...	Rec./r...	Availabl...	St...	Ver.	ProdLine⊛
18.03.2021	Stock							0			
01.03.2021	IndReq		VSF				150–	150–			
24.03.2021	PldOrd	25.03.2021	0000006297/RS	*	01.03.2021	10	150	0			0001KBASS\
01.04.2021	PldOrd	31.03.2021	0000006298/RS				100	100			0001KBASS\
01.04.2021	IndReq		VSF				100–	0			
25.04.2021	PldOrd	23.04.2021	0000006309/RS	*	03.05.2021	15	350	350	New		0001KBASS\
03.05.2021	PldOrd	30.04.2021	0000006299/RS			63	200	550			0001KBASS\
03.05.2021	IndReq		VSF				200–	350			
01.06.2021	PldOrd	31.05.2021	0000006300/RS	*		20	150	500			0001KBASS\
01.06.2021	IndReq		VSF				150–	350			
01.07.2021	PldOrd	30.06.2021	0000006301/RS			63	200	550			0001KBASS\
01.07.2021	IndReq		VSF				200–	350			

Figure 8.30 Planning Situation

8.5   Material Staging

Material staging refers to the step in which the components from the replenishment storage location are transferred to the issuing storage location. These components are consumed during the actual production process. This step involves the stock transfer transaction with standard movement type 311, and it transfers stock from the replenishment storage location to the issuing storage location. The system issues or backflushes the components of the material from an issuing storage location.

[+] **Tips and Tricks**

The alternative term used for material staging is *pull list*. A pull list provides details on which material's components are faced with shortages. At the same time, it also triggers stock transfers. Storage location MRP or kanban can also be used as the pull list.

The current or existing material situation of the planned orders can be viewed before proceeding to stage the materials. Evaluating the current material situation gives a materials planner a better idea, and it helps in deciding which components should be staged first. Material staging in REM is typically carried out with reference to a certain time horizon or a certain time interval—for example, a shift or until the end of the week. Except for MTO, materials aren't staged with reference to any specific planned order. Similarly, the GR of the material produced is period-based, with or without reference to planned orders.

In the following sections, we'll explain how to view the current situation, trigger replenishment, evaluate the material documents that the system created for material staging, and perform collective availability checks.

8.5.1 Current Situation

To view the current situation in the pull list, follow menu path **Logistics · Production · Repetitive Manufacturing · Material Staging · Pull List—Current Situation**, or use Transaction MF63.

In the initial parameter selection screen, choose from a large number of selection options and also define the end date for requirements in the **Selection Horizon for Rqmts** field. This is the date until which the system will consider requirements of materials. There are also selection options if a company uses the kanban production process or has integrated with either warehouse management in SAP S/4HANA or embedded SAP Extended Warehouse Management (SAP EWM) in SAP S/4HANA.

For this example, define the **Plant** as "1105" (this is a mandatory entry requirement), and set the **Selection Horizon for Rqmts** as "18/03/2021", the end date until which the system will consider all materials requirements. If the materials requirements lie outside the horizon, they won't show up in the current list of material staging.

Further limit the selection to **Production Line** (work center) "KBASSY", and choose **Execute** or press F8. This brings up the screen shown in Figure 8.31.

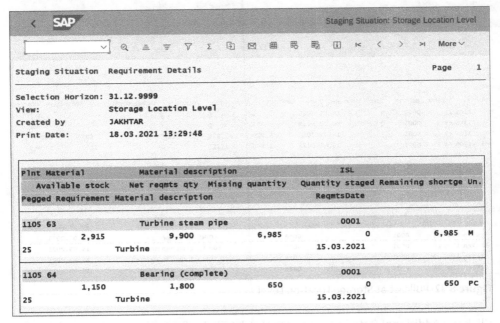

Figure 8.31 Staging Situation: Storage Location Level

The system shows the current stock and requirements situation of the planned orders in detail. It also shows the available stock, as well as the shortage quantities for the period under evaluation. The system shows the shortage quantity of each individual material.

8.5.2   Trigger Replenishment

To trigger replenishment from one storage location (replenishment storage location) to another (issuing storage location within a plant), follow menu path **Logistics • Production • Repetitive Manufacturing • Material Staging • Pull List—Trigger Replenishment,** or use Transaction MF60.

Enter the initial parameters in the selection screen, which brings up the screen shown in Figure 8.32. Note that the subsequent screen appearance will greatly depend on the parameters that were defined on the initial parameter selection screen.

In the upper half of Figure 8.32, the system shows a summarized view of four materials (25, 45, 63, and 64); the system needs varying quantities against various planned orders. This shows the same quantity shortage seen previously in Section 8.5.1.

Click the **Replenishment Proposals** button shown in Figure 8.32, and the details in the lower half of the screen appear, including details of various requirements for the three materials.

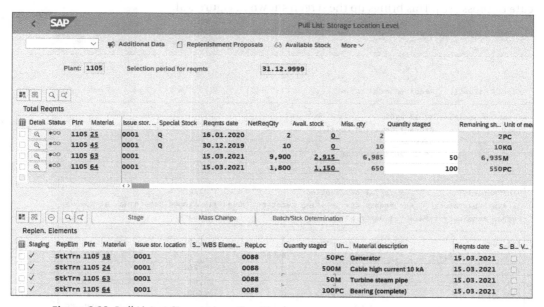

Figure 8.32 Pull List at Storage Location Level

Click the **Additional Data** button to see the detailed information on the requirements for each of the materials. For the third material, enter the **Quantity Staged** as "50", and in the lower half of the same screen, enter the **RepLoc** (replenishment storage location) as "0088".

The system is able to detect the replenishment storage location automatically if was activated in the global settings of the transaction. Select the line item and click the **Stage** button.

If the staging is successful, the system displays the relevant message on the left-hand side of the screen (see the **Staging** column and the green checkmark) and also turns the status traffic light green. Because this is a transfer posting between two storage locations, the system creates a material document. A material document records the details of inventory movements. Use Transaction MIGO to view the material document created after material staging.

8.5.3 Collective Availability Check

As a production planner, it's important to frequently and consistently monitor the availability of the components that are needed to produce the material. While an availability check of an individual planned order can always be performed in REM, it's more efficient to do a collective availability check on several materials simultaneously to gain a better understanding of the material availability situation and then plan or take action accordingly.

In the collective availability check option, use a large number of selection parameters to choose the information that the system should display.

To perform a collective availability check, use menu path **Production • Repetitive Manufacturing • Planning • Collective Availability Check**, or use Transaction MDVP. On the initial screen, enter the desired parameters, and choose **Execute** or press [F8]. If the system finds a materials shortage, it identifies the shortage with a red traffic light. Click the **Missing Parts** icon for an in-depth analysis and evaluation; it contains details of the requirements versus available quantities, as well as the dates when the required and shortage material should be in store to timely initiate the production process. The availability check function in SAP checks the availability but isn't able to trigger replenishment.

8.6 Production List

A *production list* is a list of REM planned orders that can be printed for information and record-keeping purposes. A production list can also be created and printed for a specific production line or work center hierarchy. This is helpful for production supervisors and line operators (shop floor) who don't have access to the SAP system, to allow for information access and for necessary planning and action, where needed. On the selection screen, choose how the ensuing production list should appear as an output.

To create a production list, follow menu path **Logistics · Production · Repetitive Manu-facturing · Planning · Production List**, or use Transaction MF51.

In the initial selection parameters screen, choose to print the production list based on the defined period and whether the system should consider only firmed planned orders, scheduled planned orders, or dispatched planned orders.

For this example, define the period of examination as **18/03/2021** to **01/09/2021**, and enter the **Production Line** as "KBASSY". Choose **Execute** or press F8 to open the screen shown in Figure 8.33. This screen shows the production list of REM planned orders. In the period under evaluation, there are a few REM planned orders in the production list. These are RSQs, which means that can proceed with production because they are already assigned to the production line KBASSY.

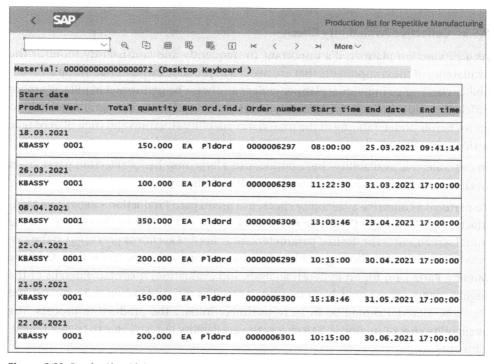

Figure 8.33 Production List

[+]   **Operational Methods Sheet**
The OMS is primarily used for production personnel to have a clear understanding of and step-by-step directions for producing a material. The layout can be configured to set the information that needs to appear in an OMS. It integrates with Microsoft Word, and any last-minute changes can be made before printing it. Further, there is an option to print the sheet at the header level or at the operation level.

To print an OMS, follow menu path **Logistics • Production • Master Data • Line Design • Rate Routing • Print Operational Method Sheets**, or use Transaction LDE1. On the initial parameter selection screen, enter **Material** "72" and **Plant** "1105". It's also important to select a template for either the cover sheet or individual operation, or both. For this example, select the template for the individual operation, and choose **Execute** or press ⌨F8. Word opens, and when the system asks you to choose to enable or disable the macros. In this example, choose **Enable Macros**.

8.7 Confirmation

Assume that a company manufactures products on a long production line with a long lead time. With long lead times, the GIs for the components may be posted much later in the system than when they are actually physically withdrawn. All components used along the production line are usually backflushed during final confirmation. However, the GIs for the first components at work centers are posted on time and not by back-flushing with a final confirmation at the end of the production line.

An REM confirmation indicates that the actual production happened and the production supervisor is now entering the details of the goods produced in the system. It's important to note that during the assembly backflush, the system automatically posts the component consumptions (GI).

Depending on how the REM profile is set up and assigned to a material, the system accordingly performs the necessary functions. In this case, it makes sense to use RP confirmation to post the withdrawal of components (and production activities) at an earlier stage after operations are already completed.

In the following sections, we cover how to perform confirmation for REM assembly, REM components, and REM activities. We'll give also an overview of when and how backflushing should be used in REM situations, as well as the different types of back-flushing that are available in REM.

8.7.1 Overview

When the GR is posted for the finished parts during confirmation, a number of different actions are performed by default (these are controlled to a large extent using the REM profile):

- Posting GI for the components used by using the backflush option
- Reducing RSQs/planned orders and the associated capacity requirements on the production lines
- Posting production costs incurred (material costs, production activities, overhead costs) to a PCC

- Creating a data entry document (material and/or financial document)
- Updating statistics in the logistics information system (LIS)

Other optional actions (see the **Details** icon in the confirmation transaction) include the following:

- Taking account of the setup costs for material quantities that are independent of their lot sizes
- Posting component/assembly scrap
- Performing collective entry for different materials in a line
- Archiving confirmation documents
- Performing GI confirmation only or activity confirmation only (more/less activity)
- Using RP confirmations
- Decoupling confirmation processes
- Performing aggregation
- Using postprocessing and reversal options

In addition, production based on sales orders enables confirmation with reference to sales orders.

> **Note**
>
> We configured REM profile PP10 in Chapter 5, Section 5.1; revisit that chapter to see the settings that were made.

Although the system-recorded components' consumption is based on a BOM calculation, it's possible to make changes to consumption quantities during the REM assembly backflush. Separately, a production supervisor can also use this component's backflush option to record excess component consumption, either against a specific REM planned order or for general consumption during the production process.

The confirmation can be any of the following types:

- **Assembly confirmation**
  The production of goods is complete, and the production supervisor wants to record the yield of the produced material. At the same time, there's also a need to record the consumption of the components against the produced goods based on the standard BOM. The user can also record the assembly scrap on the same screen with a different posting.

- **Component confirmation**
  Extra consumption of the components against the produced goods based on the standard BOM can be recorded. Component scrap can also be recorded on the same screen. Further, components can be issued out if backflush isn't applicable (this scenario isn't used often).

- **Activity confirmation**
  Excess consumption of the activities, such as machine hours, labor hours, or setup hours, against the produced goods based on the rate routing can be recorded. Further, activity scrap can also be recorded on the same screen.

As with assembly backflush, several options are available on the component backflush screen:

- Record corresponding information during REM confirmation and backflush. This flexibility is available because the REM production type caters to all MTS or MTO productions.
- Record components' scrap, either with reference to the assembly material or as standalone. The movement type for scrap is 551.
- Reverse the material document for an already posted consumption or scrap.
- Perform a reversal function, without reference to any material document.

8.7.2 Assembly Confirmation

To access the REM confirmation for an assembly backflush, follow menu path **Logistics • Production • Repetitive Manufacturing • Data Entry • Repetitive Manufacturing Confirmation**, or use Transaction MFBF. In the initial screen of REM confirmation, select the **Assembly Backflush** radio button (see Figure 8.34). Use this screen to confirm the production yield and to record components' consumption and activities (if configured in the REM profile).

Also, record assembly scrap, if any, by choosing the **Scrap** button. We cover how to record assembly scrap later in this chapter in Section 8.8.3.

Click the **Details** button. The system brings up the REM profile (in this example, PP10), in which the following can still be changed:

- Post activity backflush
- Stock posting to unrestricted, quality, or blocked stock
- Backflushing options—for example, from online to background
- Post ordering costs

Maintain the posting date as the document date on which to post the REM assembly backflush. Further, use this screen for document-specific or document-neutral reversals of the entered values. We cover document-specific reversal in Section 8.8.

It's also important to note that there's flexibility to record the yield of the assembly without reference to the REM planned order because then the system is able to account for period-based confirmation. However, doing so won't reduce the quantity specific to the planned order for the MTS scenario (if such settings are made in the REM profile). For MTO, the system reduces the planned order quantity.

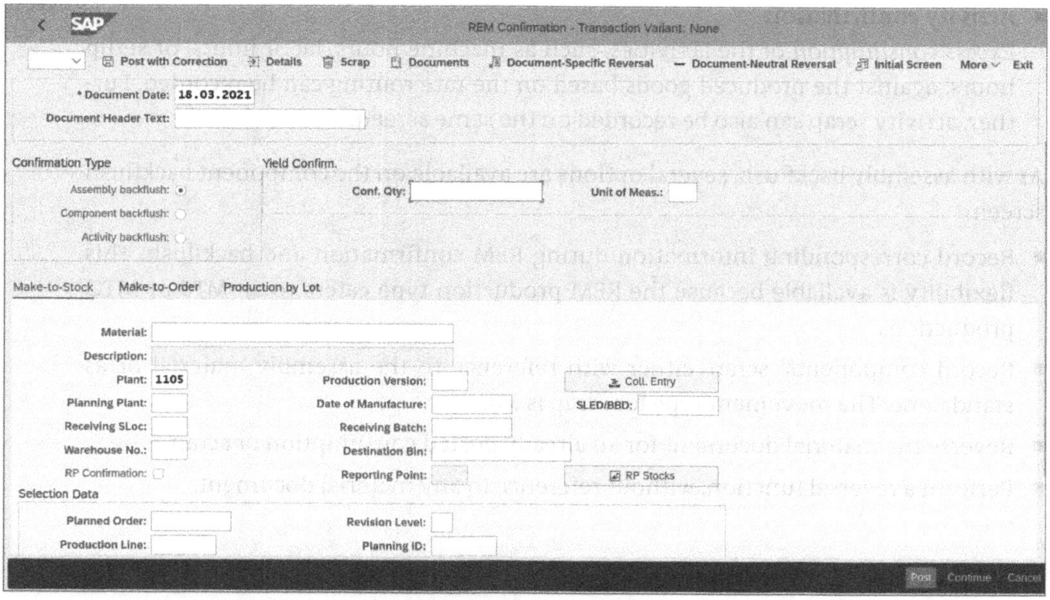

Figure 8.34 Assembly Backflush in REM Confirmation

The three tabs **Make-to-Stock, Make-to-Order,** and **Production by Lot** cater to various production scenarios.

8.7.3   Component Confirmation

As soon as the **Component Backflush** radio button shown previously in Figure 8.34 is selected, the system offers the following two options:

- **No BOM explosion (Manual Component Entry)**
  In this option, enter the assembly in the **Material** field so that the system is able to find the link with the PCC. If **No BOM Explosion** is selected, the **Process Component List** is empty.

- **Propose Components Acc.to BOM**
  This option enables entering a quantity of the assembly material, and the system explodes the assembly BOM and proposes the component quantities for backflush or excess consumption. When selecting this option, provide the reference quantity of the assembly material.

A production supervisor can also select if excess component consumption for a specific RP or after the last RP took place by selecting the relevant radio button. This radio button only appears if a valid RP is entered.

8.7.4 Activities Confirmation

When selecting the **Activity Backflush** radio button in the REM confirmation screen (Transaction MFBF), shown earlier in Figure 8.34, the system displays the following two options:

- **No Planned Activities from Rate Routing**
  In this option, enter the material number together with the activity types, as well as the corresponding duration of each activity. The system doesn't make any suggestions.

- **Fetch Planned Activities from Rate Routing**
  With this option, enter the quantity of the assembly material and the system refers to the rate routing of the assembly material and proposes the details. When selecting this option, give the reference quantity of the assembly material.

8.7.5 Actual Assembly Confirmation

In the screen shown in Figure 8.35, perform the actual assembly backflush posting for **Material 72**, **Plant 1105**, and **Production Version 0001**. The yield confirmation for the material in this REM assembly backflush is **10 EA**. Because the configured and assigned REM profile PP10 stipulates that there should be mandatory RP backflushing, select the **RP Confirmation** checkbox, and also assign **Reporting Point 0020**.

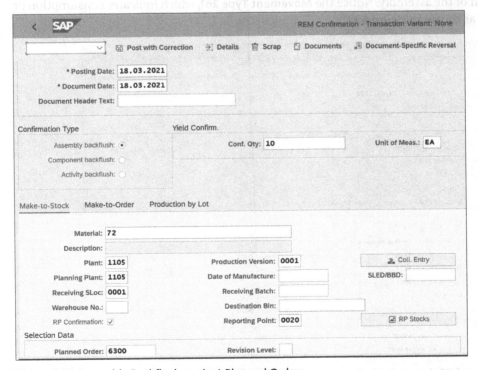

Figure 8.35 Assembly Backflush against Planned Order

RP backflush in REM occurs when the system is able to automatically backflush several operations in the processing sequence. Using the RP backflush procedure, a production supervisor can backflush components synchronized with actual consumption as much as possible. From the controlling perspective, RP backflush displays WIP for assemblies that haven't completely been backflushed. The REM profile controls whether to use the RP backflush for a material; further, the control key is used to determine whether an operation is an RP operation (milestone). If so, then all previous operations that haven't been confirmed yet or all previous operations that aren't mandatory RPs are automatically backflushed together. If several operations are marked as RPs, the system should backflush components according to the processing sequence of the RP operations.

Save the entries at this stage, and the system performs the following three functions:

- Performs GR (yield confirmation) of 10 PC for material 72
- Performs backflush (GI) of components according to the BOM of 72
- Records and updates activities according to the rate routing of material 72

Click the **Post with Correction** button in the menu bar to open the screen shown in Figure 8.36, which shows that the system is performing two functions simultaneously. First, it's confirming the yield of **10 EA** for the assembly **Material 72**; then, in the second step, it's recording the consumption of all the components that are used in the production of the assembly. Notice the **Movement Type 261**, which indicates consumption or GI, as shown in Figure 8.37.

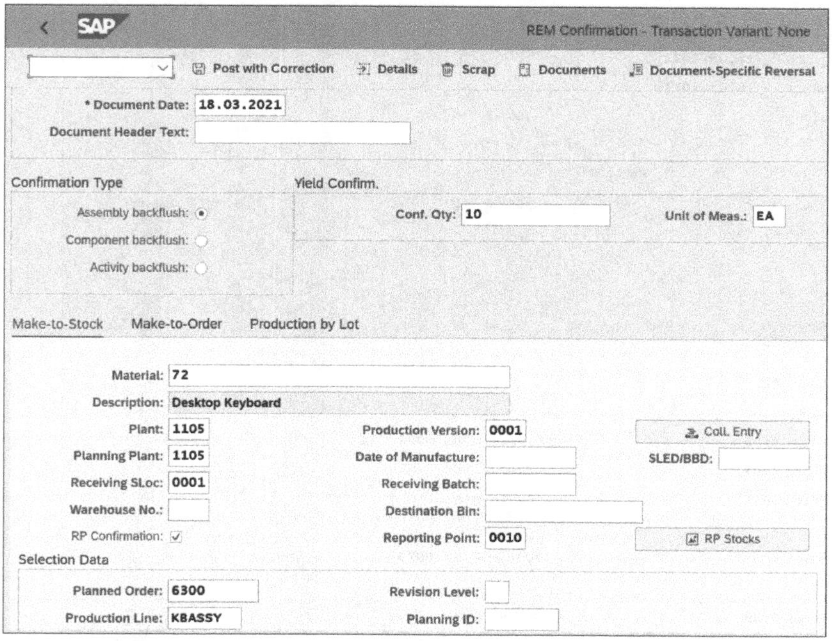

Figure 8.36 Components Overview of Assembly Backflush

The quantity of any component can be changed, if needed, and addition or deletion of components is possible as necessary. For example, to overwrite (change) the quantity of component 10, overwrite the quantity given in the **Quantity** column (see Figure 8.37).

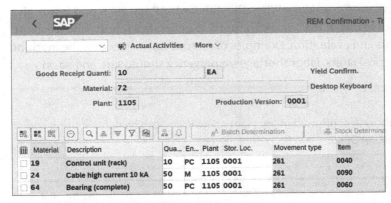

Figure 8.37 Posting Excess Consumption

Similarly, to delete a component from this figure, first select the component, and then click on the **Delete** icon. In the ensuing screen of **Processing Activities** (see Figure 8.38), make changes to the activities such as machine hours or labor hours.

Figure 8.38 Processing Activities

It takes the standard duration details from the rate routing of material 72. Make any changes to the durations to reflect actual durations (whether on the higher or lower side), and the system correspondingly and automatically updates the cost details when you save the confirmation.

In the **Reason** field, define the reason for the excess consumption of activities. This is also known as the *reason for variance*. When the standard SAP system report is run, give reasons for variance as one of the selection criteria to generate a report, which eventually helps in analysis and evaluation. Examples of reasons for variance can be machine malfunctions, electrical faults, labor shortages, emergency shutdowns, and so on.

[»]
> **Note**
>
> Reasons for variances in confirmation are plant-specific and can be defined using configuration Transaction OPK5.

[+]
> **Tips and Tricks**
>
> When defining reasons for variance, we recommend taking past experiences into account for the major or possible reasons that resulted in delayed production, excess consumption, and so on. Also consider which reasons are important for analysis and reporting purposes and thus should be available as a selection option when running standard or custom-developed reports.

When saving the REM assembly backflush, the system issues the following message at the bottom of the screen confirming the goods movements (GI and GR) and activities posting: **GR and GI with document XXX and activities posted**. This means that the system successfully posted GR (production yield), GI (components consumption), and recording of the actual production activities durations. It's important to add that the business process depends on whether the planned activities, per the rate routing, have been adjusted manually during the confirmation according to the real production efforts or not.

8.7.6   Separated Backflush

If a large number of backflush processes need to be managed—that is, a high volume of data entry for GI and for activity postings—then use the separated backflush functionality. In separated backflush, the system posts GI and activities during a slower time of the day (or it can even be scheduled at night). The separated backflush option is controlled in the REM profile creation (configuration).

To perform separated backflushing, follow SAP menu path **Logistics • Production • Repetitive Manufacturing • Data Entry • Separated Backflush**, or use Transaction MF70.

Enter the appropriate parameters on the initial screen, and select the appropriate checkboxes, such as **Post Goods Issue** and/or **Post Production Activities**.

8.7.7 Postprocessing of Components

If it was defined that the system should not perform online error correction during REM confirmation, then these errors can be corrected later on. The nature of the error can be that there were insufficient component quantities for backflush (GI) during confirmation—for instance, due to incorrect or delayed postings in materials management (MM). Alternatively, there can be errors when the system is unable to find the storage location to backflush (GI) components from.

It's important to ensure that these errors are attended to in a timely manner because they continue to accumulate in the incorrect goods movement log. To postprocess components (or other errors), follow the SAP menu path **Logistics • Production • Repetitive Manufacturing • Data Entry • Postprocess • Postprocessing Individual Components,** or use Transaction COGI.

> **Note**
>
> To use Transaction COGI, select the **Also Create Individual Postprocessing Records** option in the REM profile.

Enter the appropriate parameters on the initial screen, and choose **Execute** or press F8. The ensuing screen lists all the confirmations in which the system found errors and wasn't able to process them successfully. The details of the errors can be displayed to help a production supervisor understand why they occurred—for example, because of a missing storage location.

> **Note**
>
> The standard tool for REM postprocessing is Transaction MF47.

8.7.8 Collective Confirmation

The SAP system provides an option to collectively enter a large volume of data at once that you don't need to enter and post individually. However, this option is limited to recording assembly backflush and assembly scrap. As already covered, with assembly backflush, the system records production yield and consumes components according to the BOM. For assembly scrap, it consumes additional components of the assembly with reference to the assembly's BOM.

To use the collective confirmation functionality, follow menu path **Logistics • Production • Repetitive Manufacturing • Data Entry • Collective Entry**, or use Transaction MF42N (see Figure 8.39).

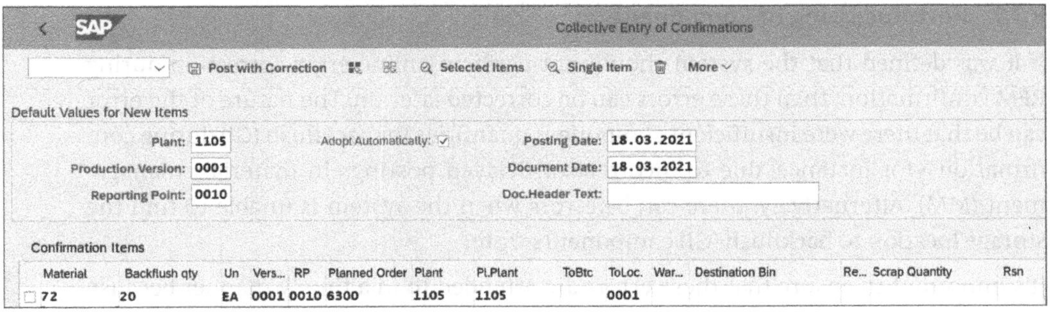

Figure 8.39 Collective Confirmations

For this example, enter the details shown, including assembly **Material** "72", **Backflush qty** of "20" **PC**. Also, while not shown here, in the second line, enter the **Material** "72" and the **Scrap** quantity of "1" **PC**. The system creates two material documents, the first for the assembly backflush and the second one for assembly scrap (excess components consumption, without any yield).

8.8   Reversals and Scrap

In a normal business scenario, the process operator occasionally faces a situation in which there was a data entry error or the confirmation details posted in the system differ from the actual production figures. In such cases, reversal becomes inevitable. In REM, document-specific reversal or document-neutral reversal can be performed. A reversal is also possible while remaining in the REM confirmation screen (Transaction MFBF) and selecting the **Doc-Specific Cancellation** icon. When this option is selected, the system navigates to Transaction MF41. Alternatively, use a separate transaction code (Transaction MF41) to reverse a specific document (we use this option in this example).

In the following sections, we'll discuss how to perform reversal of the documents already posted in the system, such as during RP backflush. As already stated, there are two types of document reversals. In *document-specific reversal*, select a specific document that needs to be reversed. On the other hand, in *document-neutral reversal*, simply correct the total confirmed quantity—for example, for a day. In this case, just reverse the difference between the previously posted quantity with the correct quantity, which reduces the overall posting efforts. Later in this section, we also cover how to manage REM actual scrap for component, assembly, and activity.

8.8.1   Document-Specific Reversal

To proceed with a document-specific reversal of confirmation, follow menu path **Logistics · Production · Repetitive Manufacturing · Data Entry · Reverse**, or use Transaction

MF41. In the initial screen for parameters selection (see Figure 8.40), provide as much detail as possible or available to enable the system to bring up only the relevant documents for reversal.

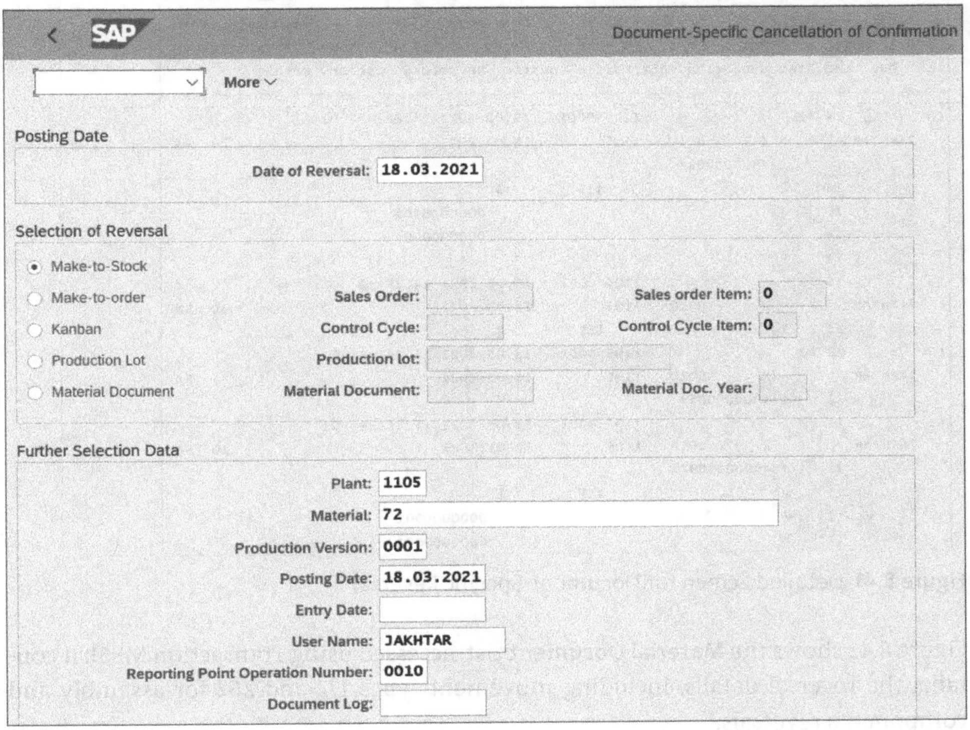

Figure 8.40 Document-Specific Cancellation of Confirmation

For this example, define the posting date or **Date of Reversal** as "18.03.2021", which means the system will post the reversal on that posting date.

To limit the selection further, enter **Plant** "1105", **Material** "72", and **Production Version** "0001", along with more parameters, as shown. Choose **Execute** or press F8 to open the screen shown in Figure 8.41, which shows a selective list of material documents and the corresponding RP documents. Place the cursor on the material document, which is **4900000095**, and click the **Reverse** button. Upon a successful reversal (of both material documents and activity posting), a message appears at the bottom of the screen: **Material movement with document and posting reversed**.

On reversal, the system reverses the production yield confirmation with movement type 132, whereas the component consumption is reversed with movement type 262. The document number of the reversal document posted is 4900000096. These are the standard reversal movement types for REM. The material document reversal and the associated reversal movement types also validate the settings that were made in Chapter 5, Section 5.1.16.

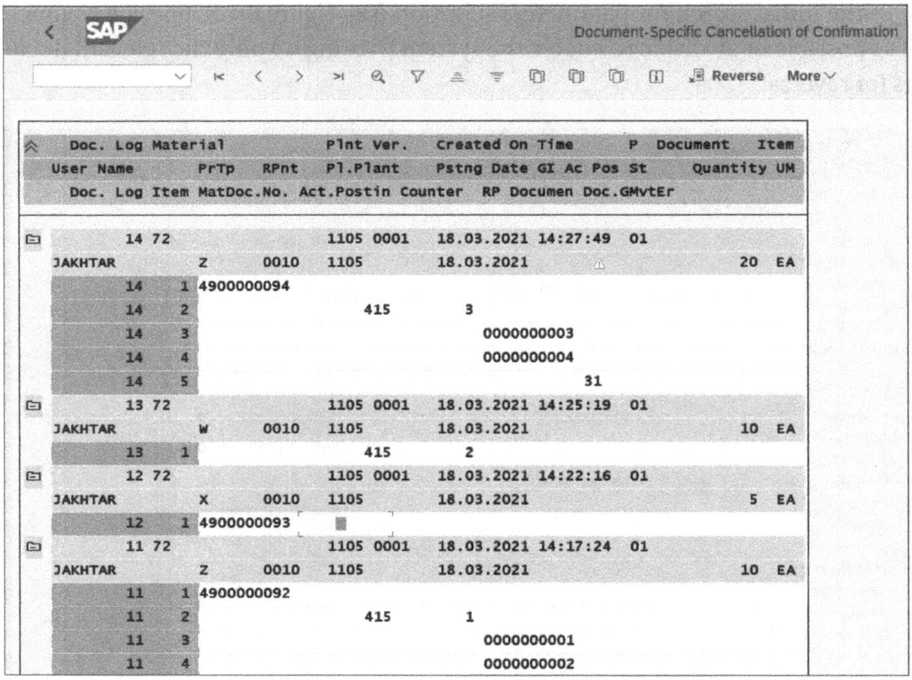

Figure 8.41 Detailed Screen for Document-Specific Reversal

Figure 8.42 shows the **Material Document List**, accessed using Transaction MB51. It contains the reversal details, including movement types 132 and 262 for assembly and components reversals.

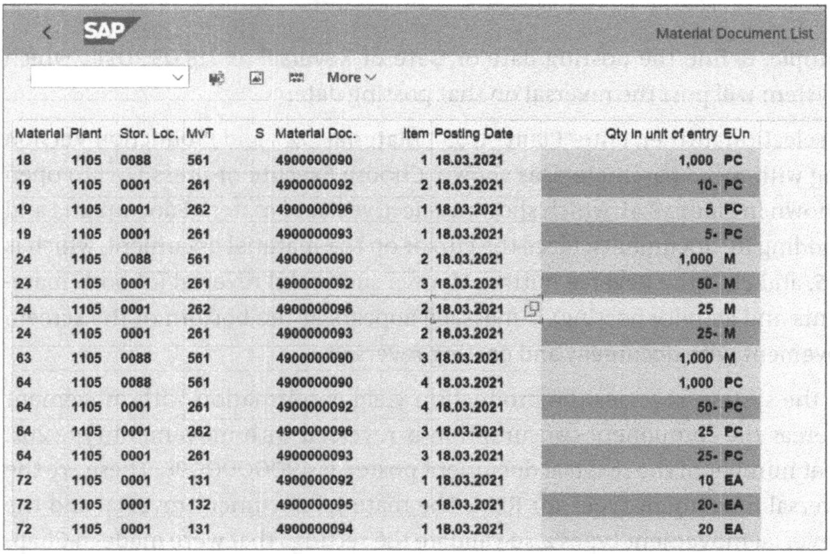

Material	Plant	Stor. Loc.	MvT	S	Material Doc.	Item	Posting Date	Qty in unit of entry	EUn
18	1105	0088	561		4900000090	1	18.03.2021	1,000	PC
19	1105	0001	261		4900000092	2	18.03.2021	10-	PC
19	1105	0001	262		4900000096	1	18.03.2021	5	PC
19	1105	0001	261		4900000093	1	18.03.2021	5-	PC
24	1105	0088	561		4900000090	2	18.03.2021	1,000	M
24	1105	0001	261		4900000092	3	18.03.2021	50-	M
24	1105	0001	262		4900000096	2	18.03.2021	25	M
24	1105	0001	261		4900000093	2	18.03.2021	25-	M
63	1105	0088	561		4900000090	3	18.03.2021	1,000	M
64	1105	0088	561		4900000090	4	18.03.2021	1,000	PC
64	1105	0001	261		4900000092	4	18.03.2021	50-	PC
64	1105	0001	262		4900000096	3	18.03.2021	25	PC
64	1105	0001	261		4900000093	3	18.03.2021	25-	PC
72	1105	0001	131		4900000092	1	18.03.2021	10	EA
72	1105	0001	132		4900000095	1	18.03.2021	20-	EA
72	1105	0001	131		4900000094	1	18.03.2021	20	EA

Figure 8.42 Material Document with Reversal Movement Types

8.8.2   Document-Neutral Reversal

To proceed with the document-neutral reversal of confirmed quantities, use Transaction MFBF (the REM backflush screen). Enter the **Plant** and **Material**, click the **Document-Neutral Reversal** button in the toolbar, and enter the quantity that you want to reverse. Finally, click the **Post** icon to post the reversal in the system (refer to Figure 8.36).

8.8.3   Repetitive Manufacturing Actual Assembly Scrap

At any time during the REM confirmation screen for assembly, component, or activity backflush (Transaction MFBF), switch the screen layout to record scrap for any of these three backflush types. To do so, click the **Scrap** icon available on the REM confirmation screen. For this example, show the assembly backflush for the material by using the reference quantity.

The system consumes the components per the BOM of the material (assembly) along with activities. It uses movement type 261 to consume the components without recording any assembly yield.

After clicking the **Scrap** icon, select the **Backflush RP scrap** radio button and enter the reference scrap quantity of "3", and the screen shown in Figure 8.43 appears. As usual, also maintain reference to **Material 72** and **Plant 1105**.

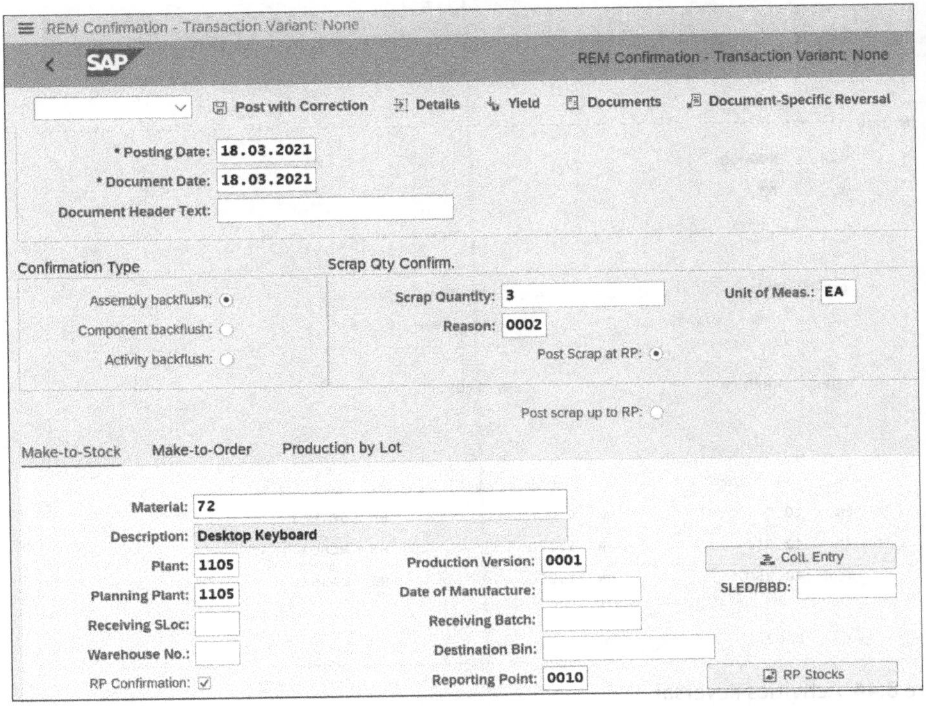

Figure 8.43 Scrap Posting for Assembly

8.8.4   Repetitive Manufacturing Actual Component Scrap

If there's a need to post scrap with reference to component scrap, select the appropriate radio button, and then the system will post the GI to scrapping while booking the cost of scrapped components to the PCC. The movement type for GI against scrapping is 551.

If there's a need to do actual components reversal with reference to the material (assembly), then give the reference quantity, which the system uses to calculate the components reversal. The component scrap is posted by clicking the **Save** icon, or by using the **Post with Correction** button in the toolbar to make any individual changes and then save those changes.

8.8.5   Repetitive Manufacturing Actual Activity Scrap

To record activity scrap with or without reference to a planned order but with reference to material, select the appropriate radio button. The system brings up the option to record activity scrap (reversal of record activities) with or without reference to a material's rate routing. If the activity scrap is posted with reference to the material, then enter the reference quantity, which the system uses to calculate the activity reversal. The activity scrap is posted by clicking on the **Save** icon, or by using the **Post with Correction** icon (see Figure 8.44) to make any individual changes and then save those changes.

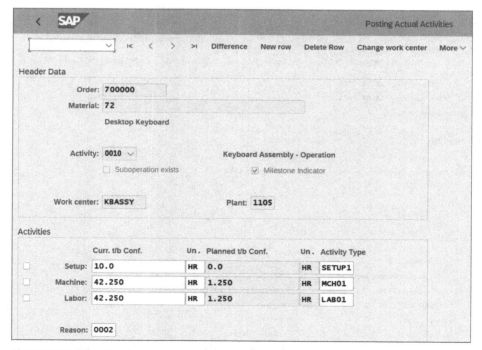

Figure 8.44 Activities Reversal

8.8.6 Reset Reporting Point Confirmation

A specific quantity posted against RP confirmation can also be reset. This is necessary when there's a need to cancel a milestone confirmation due to incorrect entry and you must also reset the stock posted up to that RP confirmation.

To reset the RP confirmation, follow menu path **Logistics • Production • Repetitive Manufacturing • Data Entry • Reset RP Confirmation**, or use Transaction MF4R. On the initial screen, the system provides the option to enter a document and the posting dates and make further selections, which are specific to the material or production line. Click the **RP Overview** icon to display RP information. When the desired parameters are selected, click the **Save** icon (on the initial screen), and the system resets the RP confirmation.

8.9 Costing Activities (Cost Object Controlling)

Before recording the actual yield confirmation, components backflush, or activities recording, all of which have financial implications, it's recommended to coordinate with the cost object controlling person to ensure that the necessary and preliminary work on the costing side is taken care of. Some of these activities include the following:

- Creating a PCC
- Creating a material cost estimate
- Releasing the material cost estimate
- Performing settlement

During confirmation in REM, the material costs for the components and the production activities (unless a material cost estimate with price update has been carried out in advance) are automatically posted to the PCC during backflushing. The option to post activities is enabled in the REM profile before the activities can be posted. The PCC is debited with the material costs, production activities, and overhead. A PCC such as an order (a cost controlling object) may have an infinite validity. In the REM profile, a cost controller defines whether the actual data entry of the activities is to be made with reference to the standard material cost estimate or according to preliminary costing for the PCC. While creating a PCC, decide whether there should be several production version-specific cost collectors or one production version-independent cost collector.

During confirmation, the PCC is credited with the valuation price (materials controlled with standard price) or with the moving average price of the assembly (materials controlled with the moving average price).

Overheads aren't determined with reference to an operation—that is, not for each goods movement or activity confirmation. Rather, they are determined periodically during period-end closing in CO using an overhead structure and are posted to the PCC.

Components different from the planned components may be used in production, or the overhead cost rates may change. This results in variances in the PCC, and a settlement must be carried out. The aim of the settlement is to credit the PCC in full. During settlement, the costs not yet credited to the PCC are transferred. For a material that is valuated using the standard price, the variant costs are posted to the price difference account.

Settlement in REM is always based on the period and on the costs in the PCC (product-related cost object controlling).

8.10   Heijunka

REM is also often used in production planning in the Japanese automobile industry and is known as *heijunka*. Heijunka is used effectively for production smoothing, and it also uses sales and operations planning (S&OP), demand management, MRP, CRP, and sequencing.

Heijunka allows for even distribution according to the Every Part Every Interval (EPEI) principle. EPEI suggests that you have every part on the schedule for every period; that is, a small amount of each part is produced every shift, every day, every week, or every month, depending on how the scheduling periods are defined. Heijunka then distributes orders evenly over a specific period and sequences them according to the principle of equal distribution. In Japanese, *heijunka* means *leveling*. Leveling can be done by volume or by product. If, for example, a family of products that uses the same production process has demand that varies between 500 and 800 units, then it might seem like a good idea to produce the exact amount that was ordered by the customer. Distributing the demand in equal, average quantities over a certain period of time provides a much more reliable supply to fulfill fluctuating order quantities.

Many value streams produce a mix of products, and, therefore, decisions have to be made in terms of product combinations and sequences. The economic order quantities play an important role and are driven by changeover times and the inventory required. Implementing heijunka results in a different situation: it reduces the time and cost of changeovers so that smaller and smaller batches aren't prohibitive and lost production time and quality costs aren't significant. The demand for products could be leveled for upstream processes, reducing lead times and total inventories along the entire value stream.

As mentioned earlier, in a REM environment, the option of using heijunka is already available. There is an option in takt-based scheduling to plan according to the heijunka principle of equal distribution. Heijunka—the scheduling of rates according to equal distribution—is just such a mixed model scheduling method. In fact, you'd look at the demand of the total week and then distribute the rates according to EPEI.

First, we must split the demand into lot sizes that allow equal distribution. The MRP run does that automatically by taking the total weekly demand and splitting it into individual planned orders according to the lot-sizing procedure maintained in the **MRP 1** view of the material master (lot sizing is covered in detail in Chapter 12). To show how this looks in the SAP system, create a model mix using Transaction LDD1 (to create) or Transaction LDD2 (to maintain). A prerequisite for line balancing is the existence of a line hierarchy with a maximum rate. Line hierarchies are created using Transaction LDB1 and represent the assembly line with all its work centers.

Note that the line hierarchy doesn't represent the flow of the product but rather the hierarchy of the work centers the product flows through (or doesn't flow through). The line hierarchy can consist of line segments and feeder work centers assigned to a level-by-level hierarchical structure. The line hierarchy can have a scheduling segment (usually the bottleneck work center) that is then used in the production version of the materials being assembled on the line. In the production version, you also assign the routing that is used to assemble the product, which consists of a sequence of operations that follows the assembly line.

8.11 Reporting

We'll be covering standard reporting extensively in Chapters 22, 23, and 24, including several reports available specifically for REM. In the following sections, we briefly cover two of them:

- Document log information
- RP statistics

8.11.1 Document Log Information

The SAP system maintains a comprehensive log of each and every material document posted or canceled, which is known as the *document principle*. As a planner, it's often important to have access to the material document information for evaluation purposes, as well as for identifying individual documents against which incorrect or incomplete entries were made and must now be reversed or canceled.

To access the document log information in REM, follow menu path **Logistics • Production • Repetitive Manufacturing • Evaluations • Display Data Entry Documents**, or use Transaction MF12. On the initial parameters selection screen, enter the parameters, such as **Plant**, **Material**, **Production Version**, or **Posting Date**, and choose **Execute** or press F8. Not only does the system bring up relevant documents for display, but it also provides the option to reverse any document if needed. We've already covered document-specific reversal in Section 8.8.1 (see Figure 8.45).

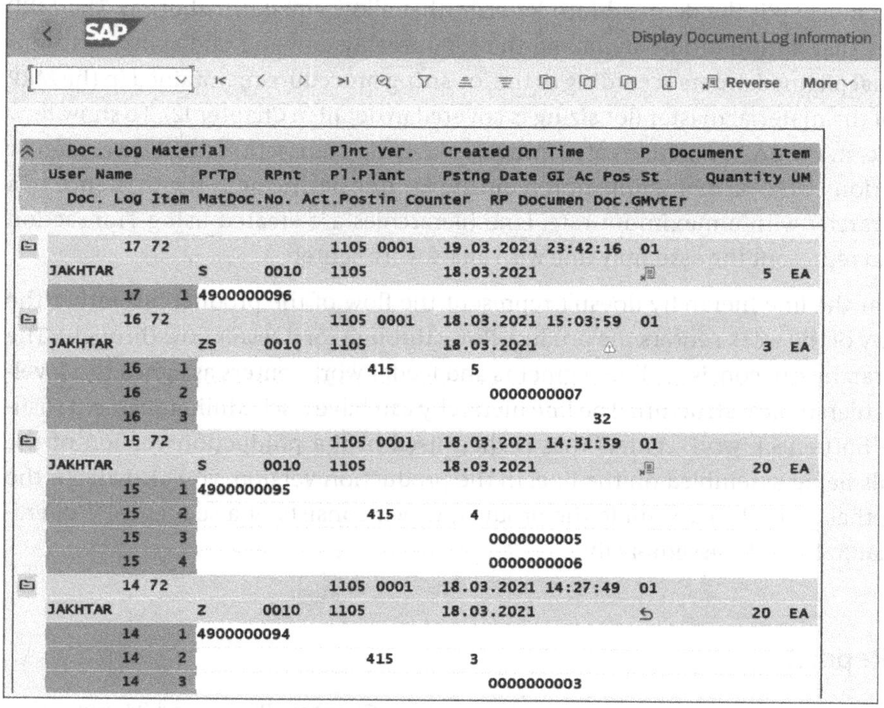

Figure 8.45 Document Log Information

8.11.2   Reporting Point Statistics

RP statistics is one of the several statistics reports available to facilitate evaluation. To access RP statistics, follow menu path **Logistics • Production • Repetitive Manufacturing • Evaluations • LIS Statistics • Reporting Point Statistics**, or use Transaction MCRM. On the initial parameter selection screen, enter the relevant parameters, such as **Material**, **Plant**, **Production Version**, or **RP**. A period of evaluation can also be provided so that the system only brings up relevant information. Choose **Execute** or press $\boxed{\text{F8}}$ and the screen shown in Figure 8.46 appears.

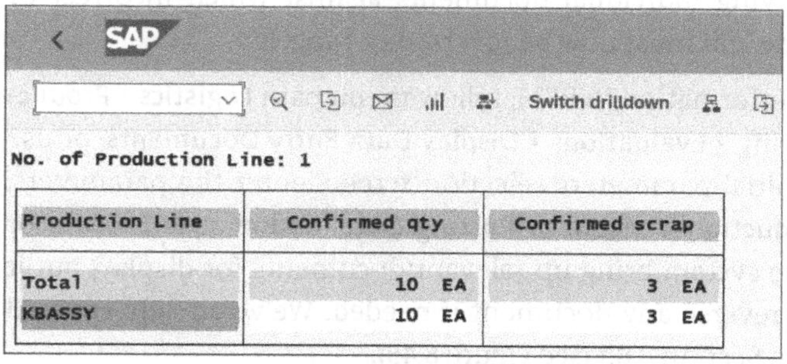

Figure 8.46 REM Reporting: RP Statistics

This statistics report provides details on the confirmed quantity at each RP, as well as the confirmed scrap recorded. Switch to different views—for example, date-wise evaluation, RP-wise evaluation, production version-wise evaluation, or production line-wise evaluation—by clicking the **Switch Drilldown** button and then selecting the desired radio button. These RP evaluations can be used as valuable reporting tools to evaluate the WIP.

8.12 Summary

For material produced in bulk quantity and with relatively fewer production steps and complexity when compared with production types such as discrete manufacturing or process manufacturing, companies can implement the REM production type. Line loading, material staging, backflush assembly, components, and activities can be planned and recorded as frequently as is deemed necessary and practical from the business perspective. All costs associated with REM production of a material continue to accumulate in the PCC, and the company can periodically settle these. Due to the highly integrated nature of PP with CO-PC, you must maintain extensive coordination to ensure that the inventory, financial, and business results are in line with the company's business processes.

The next chapter discusses kanban.

PART IV
Production Planning Tools

Chapter 9

Kanban

Kanban was invented at Toyota Motor Corporation in 1953 by Mr. Taiichi Ohno. At the time, the automotive industry as a whole was improving itself with the implementation of what Toyota called the »Toyota Production System«. This simple system was based on a physical, card-based signal for materials replenishment. In Japanese, kan means card and ban means signal.

In a kanban environment, when production workers take the last part from a bin, they flag a signal for other workers, who would make more of the required parts and ensure delivery to the assembly line. Since the system's start, many companies in several industries have used simple kanban techniques to drastically improve their manufacturing execution speed and reduce inventory, with minimal planning.

In kanban, material flow is organized using containers that are kept directly at the appropriate work centers in production. Each container holds whatever quantity of material the work center personnel need for a certain period of time. As soon as a demand source (the material-consuming work center) empties a container, the demand source initiates a replenishment request to a supply source (the source that ensures material replenishment). The supply source for the required material can be another production unit within the factory, from another factory of the same company, an external supplier, or even another warehouse. The demand source can use material from other "buffer" containers until a supply source fills and returns the empty containers.

In this chapter, we'll discuss the configuration settings required to setup kanban in SAP S/4HANA for not just in-production processes but also for procurement and interplant or interstore transfer. We'll also discuss the kanban storage location, as well as settings for a kanban board. Then, we'll discuss setting up kanban master data. This will then be followed by discussing end-to-end business processes of kanban in a step-by-step manner. The chapter will conclude with discussing kanban reporting and analysis.

In the following sections, we'll discuss an overview of kanban, as well as the push-pull principle that underpins kanban and the three possible replenishment strategies that can be used to control kanban. With the push-pull principle, the demand source asks the supply source to push the material for consumption, and then it can pull on its availability. The three replenishment strategies cover how PP component can be used for kanban replenishment and how MM covers procurement and stock transfer as kanban replenishment choices.

9.1 Kanban Overview

Figure 9.1 shows the standard kanban flow between demand source and supply source.

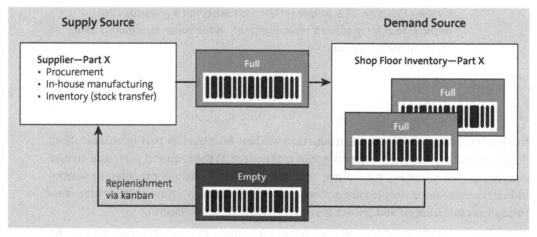

Figure 9.1 Kanban Process

Companies can integrate some of the business operations of electronic kanban to reduce inventory and simplify material movements and production planning. Electronic kanban uses the SAP S/4HANA system's kanban monitor, which completely maps with the actual and real-life kanban processes.

Note

In the initial days of introducing kanban to streamline replenishment in manufacturing processes, all business processes were manual or relied on the supply source visually and physically seeing the kanban cards at the demand source.

With the advent and extensive introduction and integration of technologies such as scanners and barcode readers for data capture and data transmission to business application systems such as SAP to trigger replenishment, manual kanban eventually transformed into *electronic* kanban. For the sake of simplicity, we'll be referring to electronic kanban simply as kanban going forward in this chapter.

Kanban aims to give personnel significant control over the production process and to reduce the manual tasks they must perform. This self-management process and the fact that production personnel create replenishment elements close to when they're actually consumed leads to inventory reduction while also shortening lead times. Kanban triggers replenishment only when there is a material requirement and not before, thus providing material to the production process only and exactly when required.

Materials ready for use remain near the work center in small material buffers so that planners don't have to plan for material staging. Instead, consumed materials are replenished immediately. Another advantage of kanban is that the transmission of replenishment data is well automated. Scanning the *barcode* on a kanban card is enough to transmit the data required to initiate replenishment and to post the goods receipt upon receiving material. The kanban signal for delivery of a material can be triggered by a demand source sending a *card* to a supply source. This card contains details about the required material, its quantity, and its delivery location. It's also common practice to refer to a material-carrying container as a kanban.

Following are some advantages of kanban:

- Replenishment elements integrate with the SAP S/4HANA system
- Improves monitoring of kanbans in circulation via a kanban board and access to additional evaluations
- Integrates with printing and transmission functions
- Can forecast from material requirements planning (MRP) or long-term planning (LTP)
- Integrates with cost accounting
- Integrates with capacity requirements planning (CRP)
- Integrates with engineering change management (ECM)

Note

Because kanban integrates with production planning (PP) and materials management (MM), we recommend maintaining close coordination between these SAP resources and the consultants for the company or project. Only then will a company be able to realize the true benefits of integrating kanban into business processes. In this chapter, in addition to discussing the kanban replenishment process in PP, we've also covered two kanban replenishment processes in MM (procurement and stock transfer).

Now, let's quickly discuss why some companies hesitate to implement kanban in production, procurement, or the stock transfer processes. The problem some organizations have with implementing kanban lies not in the production method but in meeting the *prerequisites* necessary for kanban. To use kanban effectively, a number of conditions must be met:

- The supply source must be able to deliver the material quickly and in small lots. Setup times should be short, and the availability of components and capacity to process them should be ensured.

- The parts controlled using kanban should be consumed relatively uniformly over the replenishment time. If a material is used in large quantities sometimes but in smaller quantities at other times, then a large number of containers is necessary to ensure material availability. There will then be relatively high levels of stock during periods when the material is used less.

- The material should not be produced in advance, as this would lead to unnecessary materials being procured and stored.

9.2   Push-Pull Principle

In traditional production and MRP, the system calculates the production quantities and dates at the product level based on customer requirements or planned independent requirements (PIR). The system determines the required quantities and materials staging dates in the bill of materials (BOM) explosion, which means that the system reads every component of the BOM to determine the components' quantities required on specific dates. The system calculates lot sizes by referring to the lot-sizing procedure. Lots are generally completed at each manufacturing level before becoming available at the next manufacturing level.

The component staging dates, determined by MRP, are used to schedule the production of parts or, for purchased parts, the order dates. At the time of scheduling, exactly when the material is needed for the next manufacturing level often is not known. The material is *pushed* through production on the basis of the times calculated (the *push principle*). This procedure can result in queue times before the start of production, which are generally addressed by increasing lead times or by using a float after production (as an order buffer). This often leads to the use of increased safety stocks to achieve constant service levels.

With kanban, instead of pushing materials through production by higher-level planning, materials are called out (or *pulled*) from the supply source by production at the manufacturing level only when needed (the *pull principle*). When a container is empty, the production personnel creates a kanban signal; that is, the demand source calls out the required material to the supply source using a card (a kanban).

Figure 9.2 demonstrates the push-pull principle of materials. The upper half illustrates push, and the lower half illustrates pull (kanban).

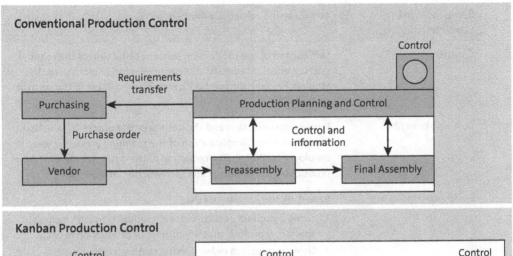

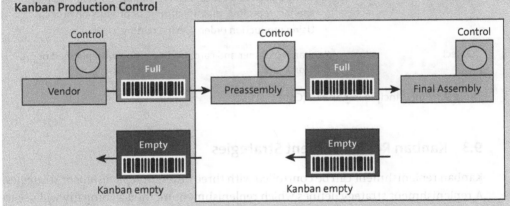

Figure 9.2 Push-Pull Principle

Table 9.1 summarizes kanban's key characteristics when integrated into production processes for discrete and repetitive manufacturing.

Replenishment Characteristics	Advantages Realized via Kanban
Principle	Pull production. Consumption controls replenishment (on direct request from demand source) only.
Procedure	Material flow using containers. When the demand source empties a container, the replenishment signal is triggered (internal production, external vendor, storage location). Requirements-based material request at the time of actual demand only.
Technique	Self-controlling control cycles and supply areas.

Table 9.1 Pull Principle in Kanban

Replenishment Characteristics	Advantages Realized via Kanban
Control	Self-control of the production process, reduction of the manual posting effort, automatic replenishment, no need to plan the staging. Replenishment data constantly available in the control cycle.
Business benefits	Process optimization and shortening of the process chain. Lean manufacturing. Simplification of the planning process, more employee responsibility, reduction of the administrative effort in production. Reduction of stocks, reduction of lead times.
Backflush controlling	By setting the kanban to **FULL**: 1. Using a product cost collector in conjunction with manual kanban, repetitive manufacturing, or production orders. 2. Using production order-specific costing.
Object	Kanban (container and card) in connection with planned or production order

Table 9.1 Pull Principle in Kanban (Cont.)

9.3   Kanban Replenishment Strategies

Kanban replenishment can be controlled with three different *replenishment strategies*. A replenishment strategy defines which replenishment method a company will use to produce or procure the container quantity—that is, the replenishment element (e.g., a production order, a purchase order, a reservation) that the system will create when the kanban is set to **EMPTY**. Let's take a look at all three replenishment strategies.

With *in-house production*, replenishment can be organized using planned orders (repetitive manufacturing), production orders (discrete manufacturing), manual kanban, or container control/MRP (a mix of kanban and MRP). With replenishment using container control/MRP, replenishment elements are created not in kanban but in MRP. Setting the container status to **FULL** or **EMPTY** then simply controls the material flow. The person responsible for production is mentioned in the supply source. This individual is responsible for the area of production that delivers materials to other production areas.

In *external procurement*, replenishment can be organized using purchase orders, delivery schedules, stock transport orders, stock transport scheduling agreements, source lists, or container control/MRP. The supply source can be a vendor or a supplying plant. If deliveries refer to a specific quantity or a value contract, then this information is maintained in the control cycle. With plant-to-plant relationships, a delivering plant is entered instead of a vendor.

With *stock transfer*, replenishment can be organized by using stock transfer reservations, direct transfer posting, or container control/MRP. With stock transfer, the supply source is a delivering storage location. A storage location must be assigned to every supply area. The system posts all the goods movements in inventory management from or to a supply area using this storage location. On material staging at a supply area, the system posts the corresponding goods receipt to the assigned storage location. On material withdrawal from a supply area, the system posts the corresponding goods issue from the assigned storage location. A supply area or groups of supply areas can be assigned to a single storage location, but multiple storage locations cannot be assigned to a single supply area. From the demand source view, the responsible person is in charge of organizing material replenishment at the supply area. The responsible person can be a group representative, a materials controller, a team leader, or an MRP controller.

For some bulk materials, it makes sense to procure or withdraw them against *cost centers* as these are low-cost, high-use consumable materials.

The system represents all kanban operations, such as material receipts or material consumption, by status changes. If a kanban is empty, the employee in production sets the status of the kanban to **EMPTY**. This kanban status also automatically triggers replenishment; that is, the supply source receives the signal from the demand source to refill the kanban. When the replenished kanban returns to the demand source, the employee at the demand source sets the kanban to the **FULL** status. These two statuses are generally sufficient to control the material flow in kanban production control and are usually the only two used. The progress of production in kanban is controlled by setting the kanban to the appropriate status. Other kanban statuses are also available, as we'll discuss in Section 9.6.1. The general kanban practice is to have two barcodes: one with the serial number and the empty code and one with the serial number and the full code. When the production person scans the appropriate barcode, the system performs the empty or full transaction.

Table 9.2 compares kanban with and without MRP to help a planner decide which option to choose.

Kanban without MRP	Kanban with MRP
MRP creates no receipt elements. Forecast is through long-term planning.	MRP creates receipt elements (not delivery relevant) as a forecast.
The system creates replenishment elements (delivery relevant) by kanban per container.	Replenishment elements (delivery relevant) are created by kanban per container (in container control, printing the cards triggers replenishment).

Table 9.2 Kanban with and without MRP

Kanban without MRP	Kanban with MRP
Components of kanban parts can only be procured using consumption-based planning or with kanban.	Components of kanban parts can be planned to appropriately reflect business needs.

Table 9.2 Kanban with and without MRP (Cont.)

Table 9.3 provides a comparison to help a planner decide between using MRP and kanban to replenish some materials.

MRP	Kanban
Long- and short-term planning tool	Demand-based/short-term replenishment tool
Driven by BOMs, dates, lead times, and floats	Signal-based replenishment
Central control (planners and MRP run)	Decentralized control: fill empty kanbans
Lot size determines quantity produced	Kanban quantity determines quantity produced or procured
Complex organization (planners and master schedulers)	Simple organization: supervisors and workers control production
Centralized inventory	Inventory generally available on the factory floor (in kanbans)
Push principle	Pull principle: usage drives more production

Table 9.3 MRP versus Kanban

Let's delve now into kanban configuration.

9.4 Configuring Kanban

This section covers the details to configure kanban, including both standard settings and, when standard settings are unable to cover an organization's business needs, user-defined settings.

In the following sections, we'll first configure both the number ranges for the control cycle and the kanban ID number that the system will use at the time of creation for new kanbans. Then we'll cover configuring the MRP controller, the person responsible for monitoring kanbans at the demand and supply sources. Because kanbans are generally physically stored on the production shop floor, we'll also cover how to set up a Kanban storage location. With these configuration settings in place, the configured objects will be assigned to a production supply area.

9.4.1 Number Range for the Control Cycle

A *control cycle* is the critical kanban master data that maintains information about how the system will create replenishment elements when a demand source sets a kanban to **EMPTY**. To define an internal number range for the control cycle, follow the configuration menu path **SAP IMG • Production • KANBAN • Define Number Range for Control Cycle**. On the screen that appears, choose **Change Intervals**. Select the **Ext** (external) checkbox if there's any unique business need to externally assign a number to control cycle.

9.4.2 Number Range for the Kanban ID Number

The system assigns a unique internal identification (ID) number to every kanban that it creates. To define the internal number range for the kanban ID number, follow menu path **SAP IMG • Production • KANBAN • Define Number Range for Kanban ID Number**. On the screen that appears, choose **Change Intervals**. Here, maintain only the internal number range for the kanban ID.

9.4.3 MRP Controllers

A MRP controller is a person responsible for the supply area. To define MRP controllers, use Transaction OMD0 or follow menu path **SAP IMG • Production • Material Requirements Planning • Master Data • Define MRP Controllers**. On the screen that appears, maintain plant-wide MRP controllers while maintaining details in the additional MRP controller screen.

9.4.4 Kanban Storage Location

To define kanban storage locations, use Transaction OX09, or follow menu path **SAP IMG • Enterprise Structure • Definition • Materials Management • Maintain storage location**. On the screen that appears, enter "1105" for **Plant**, and maintain the storage location along with the address details.

9.4.5 Kanban Board

A kanban board is an intuitive, graphical dashboard that allows business users not only to have comprehensive visibility of various kanban statuses but also to perform several important business functions, including the ability to change a kanban status. Changing a status in a kanban board also automatically triggers the replenishment process.

It's possible to control the fields or the information that a user will see (or not see) in the demand or supply source of the kanban board. To do so, follow menu path **SAP IMG • Production • KANBAN • Kanban Board • Define Kanban Display in the Kanban Board**.

Figure 9.3 shows the kanban board's **Demand Source View** options. Here, you define how often the system will automatically update or refresh the statuses of various kanbans in the kanban board (**Refresh**). Also, set the sort priority order for various elements that will be displayed in the demand source view.

In SAP S/4HANA, the Kanban Board app is also available to perform the necessary business functions, and we'll also cover this app in this chapter.

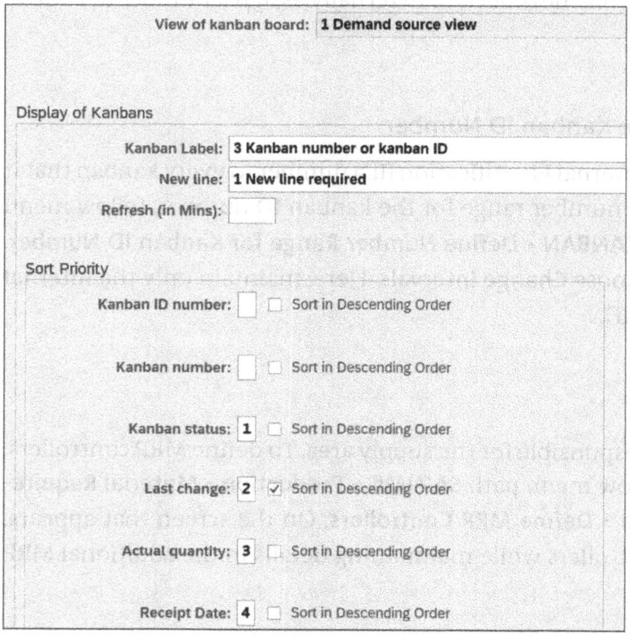

View of kanban board:	**1 Demand source view**

Display of Kanbans

Kanban Label:	**3 Kanban number or kanban ID**
New line:	**1 New line required**
Refresh (in Mins):	

Sort Priority

Kanban ID number:		☐ Sort in Descending Order
Kanban number:		☐ Sort in Descending Order
Kanban status:	1	☐ Sort in Descending Order
Last change:	2	☑ Sort in Descending Order
Actual quantity:	3	☐ Sort in Descending Order
Receipt Date:	4	☐ Sort in Descending Order

Figure 9.3 Settings for Kanban Board (Demand Source View)

9.4.6   Production Supply Area

In the kanban process, the material is staged directly in production in specific areas known as *supply areas* or *production supply areas*. A supply area can be used by one or more work centers and acts as a buffer zone for necessary materials—for example, on shelves or in marked-out areas on the floor. The primary purpose of maintaining a supply area is to organize material flow for kanban, but the supply area may not exist as an inventory management object. Therefore, it's mandatory to assign a storage location to the supply areas. Inventory management for posting goods receipts, for example, takes place at the storage location assigned to the supply area.

A responsible person (MRP controller) is also assigned for each supply area. This step ensures identification of a person responsible at the demand source for material processing and for monitoring stocks at the supply area. For in-house production, maintain a person responsible in the control cycle, which defines who is responsible at the supply source for replenishment and, if necessary, for delivery to the demand source.

The *unloading point* in the supply area is especially useful. With external procurement, it's often the case that the supplier delivers materials not directly to the supply area but to a certain unloading point, from which kanbans are transported to the supply area. The unloading point defines where the supplier has to deliver the material (e.g., gate 5).

One storage location can be assigned to several supply areas, but several storage locations cannot be assigned to one supply area.

To define a supply area, use Transaction **PK05** or follow menu path **Logistics • Production Planning • Production • KANBAN • Production Supply Areas • Maintain**. Although creating the production supply area is a configuration step, it isn't covered in the configuration menu; instead, this option is available in the main SAP menu.

Enter "1105" for **Plant** to indicate where to create a supply area, and then enter the appropriate details in fields such as **Stor. Location**, **Responsible**, and **Unloading Point**. For this example, we created a kanban supply area in plant 1105 and assigned storage location 0001 to it, as shown in Figure 9.4.

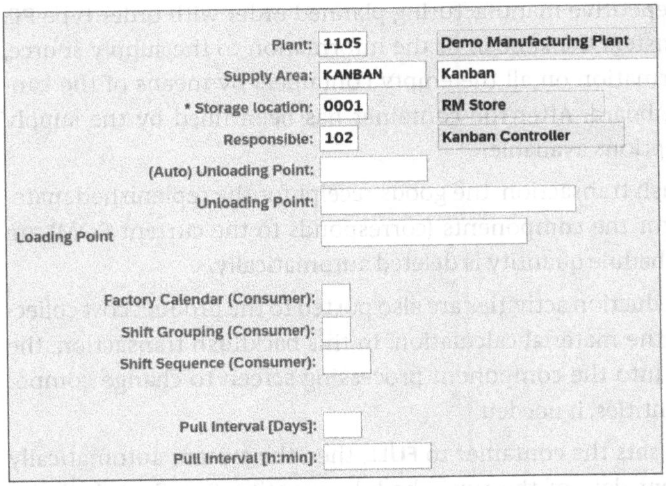

Plant: **1105**	Demo Manufacturing Plant
Supply Area: **KANBAN**	Kanban
* Storage location: **0001**	RM Store
Responsible: **102**	Kanban Controller
(Auto) Unloading Point:	
Unloading Point:	
Loading Point	
Factory Calendar (Consumer):	
Shift Grouping (Consumer):	
Shift Sequence (Consumer):	
Pull Interval [Days]:	
Pull Interval [h:min]:	

Figure 9.4 Production Supply Area

9.4.7 Configuring Kanban Strategies

The SAP S/4HANA system offers three main kanban strategies for replenishment: in-house production, external procurement, and stock transfer. The following subsections will discuss configuring each of these strategies in turn.

In-House Production

Depending on the manufacturing type (discrete manufacturing or repetitive manufacturing), the following are three options to define a kanban strategy for in-house production:

- **Processing with cards and product cost collector (manual kanban)**
  The system does not create a replenishment element when the demand source sets the kanban's status to **EMPTY**. Rather, the system transfers the kanban or the information to the supply source. The supply source receives the information either via the kanban (card) or via the kanban board. The supply source produces the kanban quantity. In this case, the backflush functionality is used or by setting the kanban's status to **FULL**. If the status is set to **FULL** or the backflush transaction is posted without component processing, then the system explodes the current BOM. If there's a business need to change components, then it's recommended to work with the backflush transaction, in which it's possible to branch into the component processing functions. In the backflush, the production activities are posted to the product cost collector according to the material calculation.

- **Processing with planned order (run schedule quantity) and product cost collector**
  When the demand source sets a kanban to **EMPTY**, the system creates a run schedule quantity (forward scheduling as basic scheduling, no lead time scheduling). The run schedule quantity is a repetitive manufacturing planned order with order type PE. The demand source transfers the kanban or the information to the supply source, which receives the information on all the empty containers by means of the kanbans or via the kanban board. After the container has been filled by the supply source, there are three options available:

  - In the kanban backflush transaction, the goods receipt for the replenished material and goods issue for the components (corresponds to the current BOM) are linked, and the run schedule quantity is deleted automatically.

  - Material costs and production activities are also posted to the product cost collector corresponding to the material calculation. In this backflush transaction, the user can also branch into the component processing screen to change component materials or quantities, if needed.

  - If the demand source sets the container to **FULL**, then the system automatically backflushes the current data of the run schedule quantity. Backflush includes goods receipt for the replenished material, goods issuance for the components, and deletion of run schedule quantity.

  For repetitive manufacturing integration with cost accounting, the collection of material costs, production activities, and overhead rates at a cost collector are settled periodically. Chapters 5 and 8 covered repetitive manufacturing.

- **Production order (discrete manufacturing)**
  When the demand source sets a kanban to **EMPTY**, the system creates a production order for the kanban quantity for the supply source. Depending on the configuration settings, the system can automatically release and print the production order. The empty kanban and the kanban information is transferred to the supply source. The supply source receives the kanban or the shop floor papers or uses the kanban board, and the order is produced. On order completion, the supply source backflushes the

quantity produced (with the backflush transaction in the production control menu). Using the control key in the routing, it's possible to set the backflush to automatically post the goods receipt (but not the reverse). For discrete manufacturing integration with cost accounting, the collection of material costs, production activities, and overhead rates in the production order is settled individually. Chapters 3 and 6 covered discrete manufacturing. In this chapter, we'll provide an example of setting a kanban to **EMPTY** and show how doing so leads to automatic production order creation.

To set up a replenishment strategy for in-house production, follow the configuration menu path **SAP IMG • Production • KANBAN • Replenishment Strategies • Define In-House Production Strategies**. Then, on the initial screen that appears, enter "1105" for **Plant** and then choose **In-House Prod. 0006 (Production Order)**; the screen shown in Figure 9.5 will appear.

Figure 9.5 shows the various settings available for discrete manufacturing-oriented kanban replenishment.

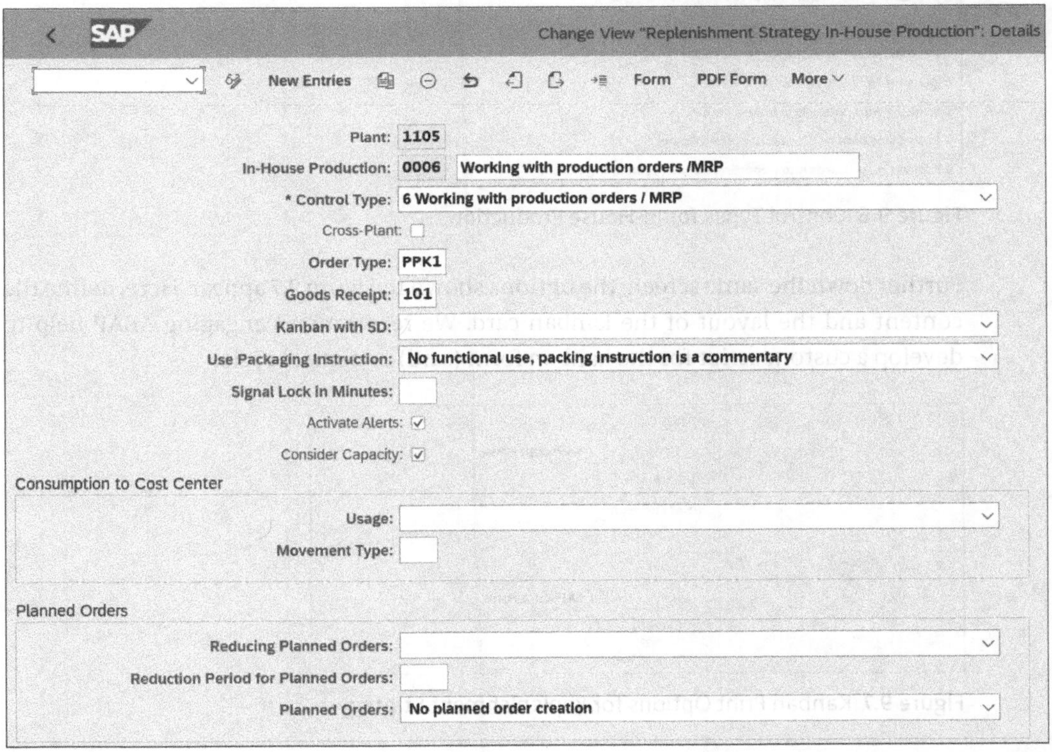

Figure 9.5 Replenishment Strategy: In-House Production

Choose a **Control Type** option from dropdown list (see Figure 9.6) and then manually assign the **Order Type PPK1** that the system creates at the time of creating a production order. Further control settings can be maintained that best reflect the business needs.

The **Signal Lock** functionality reduces the risk of incorrect input, particularly via the barcode scanner. For example, the signal will not take a status change into account within five minutes of a previous status change if a value of "5" is maintained in this field. The **Activate Alerts** indicator activates the alerts for a kanban in the alert monitor.

Tips and Tricks

The system-delivered standard kanban settings for in-house replenishment are generally sufficient to cater to all kind of business needs (see Figure 9.7). However, if there's a unique business need to maintain kanban replenishment strategy, we suggest copying from the standard strategy and then making the desired changes.

Figure 9.6 shows the various **Control Type** options available for in-house production.

3 Working with production orders
1 Working with kanbans and cost collector
2 Processing with Planned Orders and Cost Collector
3 Working with production orders
4 Replenishment using containers / MRP
5 Working with planned orders / MRP
6 Working with production orders / MRP
7 Processing with Cards and Reporting Points
8 Processing w. Cards and Reporting Points/Preplanning w. MRP

Figure 9.6 Control Types for In-House Production

Further down the same screen, the options shown in Figure 9.7 appear. Here, define the content and the layout of the kanban card. We recommend engaging ABAP help to develop a custom script for the kanban form (card) or control cycle.

Print Kanban
Form Type:
1 SAPscript Form
SAPScript Form:
Print Function:
Print Control Cycle
Form Type:
1 SAPscript Form
SAPScript Form:
Print Function:

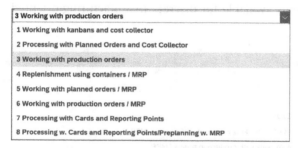

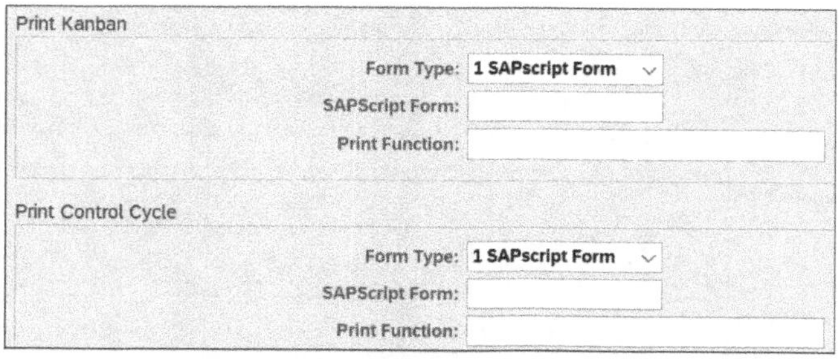

Figure 9.7 Kanban Print Options for Replenishment Strategy

External Procurement

Depending on the procurement type (purchase order, scheduling agreement, or stock transfer order), there are the following options to define a kanban strategy for external procurement:

- Purchase order
- Scheduling agreement schedule line
- Stock transfer order (plant to plant); cross-company code also possible
- Schedule line for stock transfer
- Scheduling agreement (plant to plant); cross-company code also possible
- Source list
- Quantity/value contract can be specified; contract release order for outline agreement

Let's take a look at some of the available control type options associated with external procurement:

- **Source list**
  When several control cycles have the same supply source available, then maintain this business scenario using the source list. For processing with an outline agreement (quantity/value contract), the outline agreement is specified in the source list. There is always exactly one supply source (no quota arrangement).

- **Purchase orders**
  The system creates a purchase order (possibly with reference to a quantity or a value contract) when a kanban's status is set to **EMPTY**. The delivery date for the purchase order is determined by forward scheduling using the planned delivery time from the purchasing info record and the goods receipt processing time from the material master. There is a 1:1 relationship between a purchase order and a kanban. The kanban indicator is set in the purchase order, and a vendor delivers goods to the location determined; the receiving storage location is taken from the control cycle, so maintenance in the material master isn't necessary.

  Either a vendor delivers goods to a central goods receipt location, or goods are delivered directly to the supply area. If the goods are delivered directly to the production line, the status change (by barcode or kanban board) triggers an immediate goods receipt posting using the target data. The goods receipt can also be posted manually using the goods receipt transaction (such as in cases in which there's a need to make any changes or if the warehouse supervisor wants to enter any additional data).

  When the goods receipt is posted, the system changes the status in the background. For this type of goods receipt posting, the system issues an information message indicating that the goods receipt will be carried out for the kanban. In the case of underdelivery (e.g., posting a lower actual quantity in the kanban signal transaction than the actual physical quantity), remaining quantities of the purchase order remain open. Therefore, for underdelivery, the goods receipt should be posted in inventory management and the final delivery indicator should be set.

- **Process with schedule lines**
  When a kanban's status is set to **EMPTY**, the system automatically creates a schedule

line. The schedule line is transferred to the vendor. On goods receipt, there is no 1:1 relationship between a kanban and the scheduling agreement schedule line. In the manual goods receipt, if the scheduled quantity is not equal to the goods receipt quantity, then the goods receipt quantity must be divided among empty kanbans. The kanban indicator must be set in the additional data for the scheduling agreement item to which the kanban process applies. Scheduling agreement items with the kanban's indicator cannot have entries for MRP in the source list. The scheduling agreement item for the kanban process must be assigned to the same storage location as the supply area for which the material is being procured.

- **Process with stock transfer orders/stock transport scheduling agreements (plant to plant)**
  When a kanban is set to **EMPTY**, the system creates a purchase order (which is basically a stock transport order) in the receiving location and a release order in the delivering plant. The release order is procured and then posted using the goods movement type 351. In the receiving location, posting takes place with movement type 101. However, instead of posting the goods receipt, the status can also be set to **FULL** (in which case the goods receipt takes place in the background).

  The system supports the process with stock transfer orders/stock transfer scheduling agreements between two plants from different company codes. The procedure for using the source list is similar to the procedure for standard purchase orders or for scheduling agreements. The only difference is that the system reads the source list to determine the source of supply. The vendor or the outline agreement (scheduling agreement or quantity/value contract) is maintained in the source list. Because the kanban process entails requiring material only when needed, which differs from the scheduling agreement in which a vendor delivers materials according to a predefined schedule, there's no option to maintain a kanban indicator in a scheduling agreement. Moreover, only one entry is allowed so that the scheduling agreement can be specifically identified in kanban procedures.

To set up a replenishment strategy for stock transfer, follow the configuration menu path **SAP IMG • Production • Kanban • Replenishment Strategies • Define External Procurement Strategies**. Refer to Section 9.6.2, in which we discuss kanban replenishment via procurement.

Stock Transfer

Choose one of the following options to define a kanban strategy for stock transfer:

- **Stock transfer with a reservation**
  Create a stock transfer reservation as a planned receipt at the production storage location and a material reservation as a planned issue at the issuing storage location. Posting the stock transfer for the reservation (from the issue storage location to the production storage location) or a manual transfer posting (movement type 311) sets

the status to **FULL**. The planned receipt is always on the posting day. Refer to Section 9.6.3, in which we discuss Kanban replenishment via stock transfer.

- **Direct transfer posting**
  Post the stock transfer from the issuing storage location to the receiving storage location. This option only changes the Kanban's status from **EMPTY** to **FULL**.

Withdrawal and Procurement to Cost Center

Bulk material that isn't backflushed via kanban can be procured. This bulk material isn't part of the assembly BOM and therefore can't be assigned to an assembly. For this reason, the costs for this bulk material must be posted to a cost center as material overhead costs. For example, if grease is used in the production process but there isn't usually a certain consumption of grease assigned to every assembly or it isn't made a part of a BOM, then grease is treated as a bulk material and its consumption is posted to a cost center.

Let's discuss the two options for this kanban process:

- **Withdrawal to cost center**
  In this option, on setting a kanban to **FULL**, the system initially posts the material to the storage location of the demand source (supply area). When a kanban is set to **EMPTY**, the system posts the quantity available to cost center. The advantage of this procedure is that the warehouse stock in production is available in the storage location and the bulk material also can be procured by means of in-house production.

- **Procurement to cost center**
  The material is consumed directly to a cost center. Here, the system posts the material to a cost center on setting a kanban to **FULL**. The material therefore is not available in the storage location. A bulk material can be procured via kanban using an external procurement and stock transfer.

To use these options, the following are the prerequisites:

- Set the **Bulk material** checkbox in the MRP 2 view of the material master. This setting will ensure that the system does not backflush this material.

- Configure a kanban replenishment strategy that plans the procurement or the withdrawal to a cost center. The system provides the necessary configuration settings option regardless of the kanban replenishment strategy to work with. The movement type for consumption to a cost center is 201 (goods issuance to cost center).

- When a control cycle is created for the material, enter this replenishment strategy for the bulk material and also maintain the cost center in the control cycle on the **Sequential Control** tab. However, when the control cycle refers to a scheduling agreement or contract in which procurement is charged off to a cost center, there's no need to maintain a cost center in the control cycle because the scheduling agreement or contract was already previously assigned to an account (a cost center). The **Cost Center** field isn't ready for input in this case.

9.4.8   Kanban Statuses

A kanban status not only denotes the current status of a kanban but also acts as a control function. It's possible to control both the sequence of various kanban statuses and whether flagging a specific kanban status is optional, mandatory, or forbidden. Further, the short text of various kanban statuses can be modified to closely reflect business needs.

To change the short text of a kanban status, follow menu path **SAP IMG · Production · KANBAN · Status · Maintain Short Text for Container Status**.

Figure 9.8 shows the editable language-dependent kanban status short text.

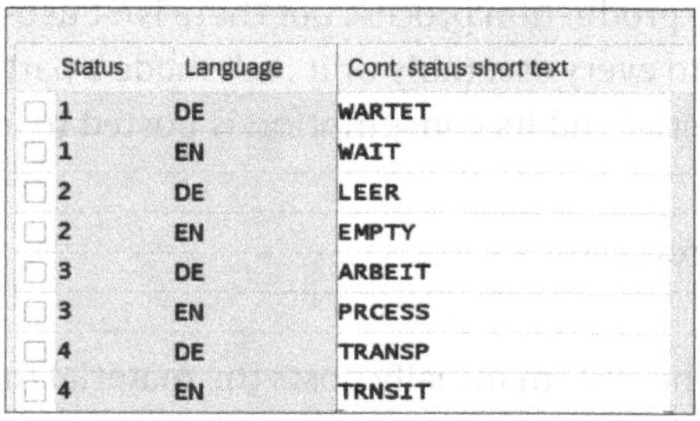

Status	Language	Cont. status short text
1	DE	WARTET
1	EN	WAIT
2	DE	LEER
2	EN	EMPTY
3	DE	ARBEIT
3	EN	PRCESS
4	DE	TRANSP
4	EN	TRNSIT

Figure 9.8 Statuses of Kanban Containers

A status can be marked as *forbidden* or *mandatory*; two statuses, **EMPTY** and **FULL**, are always mandatory. If any specifications aren't made, then the system sets a *planned status*. These statuses can be manually skipped, and the system skips *optional statuses*, but these can set manually. If a kanban's signal is triggered without the next status being specified, the system searches the next mandatory or planned status in the relevant status sequence. If a status sequence has not been defined, then the sequence **EMPTY** and **FULL** is mandatory, and all others are optional. The following statuses are available: 1, **WAIT**; 2, **EMPTY**; 3, **IN PROCESS**; 4, **IN TRANSIT**; 5, **FULL**; 6, **IN USE**; and 7, **ERROR**.

When a new kanban is included in the control cycle, the system assigns it the **WAIT** status, and it can then be set to **EMPTY**. If certain kanbans are not to be refilled immediately, then these can be assigned the **WAIT** status at the demand source in the kanban board for information purposes. If the independent supply source/separation of status change and replenishment have been defined in the control cycle, then the kanban's signal from the demand source doesn't trigger replenishment. Instead, the kanban is assigned the **WAIT** status until the supply source triggers replenishment. The **IN PROCESS** status indicates that the requested material is currently being produced by the supply source. **IN TRANSIT** indicates that the material is currently on its way to the demand source. **IN USE** indicates that the demand source is currently withdrawing material. **ERROR** is set by the system and indicates that the selected status can't be set successfully. The statuses **WAIT, IN PROCESS, IN TRANSIT**, and **IN USE** are only useful when working with the kanban board. These color-coded statuses can be seen clearly in the kanban board, and they indicate exactly how far production has progressed. They can be set manually, using barcode entry, or, more often, using the kanban board itself.

To set up or change the kanban status sequence, follow the configuration menu path **SAP IMG · Production · KANBAN · Status · Define Status Sequence**.

In Figure 9.9, the plus signs to the right of **Status 2** and **Status 5** indicate that **Status Sequence EXT** has mandatory (**Required**) **EMPTY** and **FULL** statuses; the remainder are all either **Optional** (.) or **Not allowed** (forbidden; -). Later, we'll assign the **INH** status sequence to the control cycle for in-house-produced kanban material.

It's possible to switch the goods receipt activity off or on during a status change. For example, say that a planned order has three operations, and three control cycles are created, one for each operation. A separate supply area is created for each individual control cycle. For the first two control cycles, choose manual kanban as the replenishment strategy and define a status sequence in which the goods receipt is not active. For the last control cycle, select the kanban with planned orders replenishment strategy. However, don't deactivate the status sequence for which the goods receipt is possible. On setting a kanban to **FULL**, the system posts the goods receipt for the last control cycle. All control cycles work with the same material number.

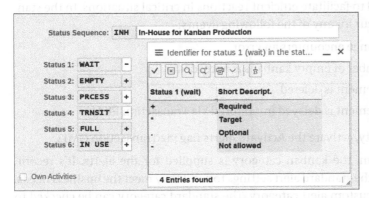

Figure 9.9 Status Sequence and Controls of Kanban Containers

A kanban can also be automatically printed when it attains the desired status, creating a kanban card that contains barcode information and can be pasted on the physical kanban container. To set actions (such as goods receipt or kanban printing) for a particular status or range of statuses, follow menu path **SAP IMG · Production · KANBAN · Status · Define Activities for Status Change**.

On the screen shown in Figure 9.10, choose from the range of kanban statuses for the **INH** status sequence and then select the desired action for the status, such as goods receipt or printing.

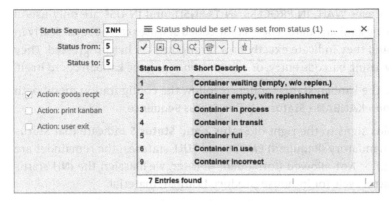

Figure 9.10 Container Statuses to Trigger Automatic Actions

For this example, select **5** (**Container full**) for both the **Status From** and **Status To** fields and select the **Action: Goods Recpt** checkbox. These choices ensure that as soon as the kanban status is set to **FULL**, the system will automatically post goods receipt for the replenishment element.

9.4.9   Kanban Alerts

Kanban alerts are used to facilitate efficient reactions in critical situations. In the standard system, alerts occur for any of the following events:

- A kanban status change encounters an error
- The maximum number of empty kanbans is exceeded
- A replenishment element is deleted
- A replenishment element is delayed (monitored via Transaction PKAL)

To use this functionality, activate the **Activate Alerts** flag via Transaction OM12.

In the standard system, the kanban category is supplied for the alerts. It's recommended to first check the standard alert settings to see if they meet the business needs. If they don't, create a custom alert category. The standard category can be checked to define a custom alert by using the BADI_Kanban_MODIFY_ALERTS BAdI. Seek help from an ABAP resource to implement this BAdI.

> **Tips and Tricks**
>
> To display the errors accumulated during the kanban processes, use the standard Transaction PK50 (Error Display). We'll cover this in more detail in Section 9.6.

9.5 Setting Up Kanban Master Data

Master data is the backbone of every successful replenishment process. This section will cover how to set up necessary and kanban-specific master data in the SAP system, such as production orders, purchase orders, scheduling agreements, and process or planned orders. For this example, material 101 (a semifinished material) in plant 1105 is used.

In the following sections, and as a part of kanban master data maintenance, we'll cover the specific settings needed. We'll also show how to maintain kanban-specific master data for manufacturing-specific business scenarios.

9.5.1 Kanban Control Cycle

The control cycle is the most important master data used for the kanban process and defines the relationship between the demand and the supply sources. The control cycle contains the following control data for kanban production:

- Kanban circulation (the number of kanbans and the kanban quantity)
- Replenishment strategy (external procurement, in-house production, or stock transfer)
- Printing kanbans
- The delivery address
- The basic data required for automatic kanban calculation (if necessary)
- The process control data

A few examples of the process control data include the indicator for a separate goods receipt, the status sequence key, and the indicator for the logic for triggering replenishment for one-card kanban.

Control cycles for classic kanban can be maintained. The system uses these control cycles for kanban with quantity signals or for one-card or event-driven kanban. In event-driven kanban, the system only creates a kanban when required; for example, a certain event based on actual material consumption triggers the kanban process.

The control cycle is created by using Transaction PK01 (there is no menu path available). On the initial screen that appears, enter "101" for **Material**, "1105" for **Plant**, and "KANBAN" for the **Supply Area**, for which the control cycle is defined. Choose the **Classic Kanban** radio button, press Enter, and the screen shown in Figure 9.11 appears.

On this screen, enter short text for **Storing Position** to denote the physical location to place the kanban container. For this example, enter "4" for **No. of Kanbans** and "2" for **Maximum Empty**; this indicates that there will be four kanbans at this supply area and that a maximum of two kanban containers can remain empty at any time. Maintain the printer settings that the system will use to print the kanbans' barcodes. Maintain the replenishment quantity in the **Kanban Quantity** field as "50" **EA.** The system will automatically create a production order of quantity 50 each time a kanban is set to **EMPTY** status.

The system allows prompts the user to choose the replenishment strategy for a kanban. In this example, choose in-house production as the replenishment strategy by selecting the **In-House Prod.** radio button (not shown). After selecting the replenishment strategy, choose **Replenishment Strategy 0006** from the dropdown (see Figure 9.11), and maintain the data in the **Person Respons.** (responsible) and **Prod.** (production) **Version** fields.

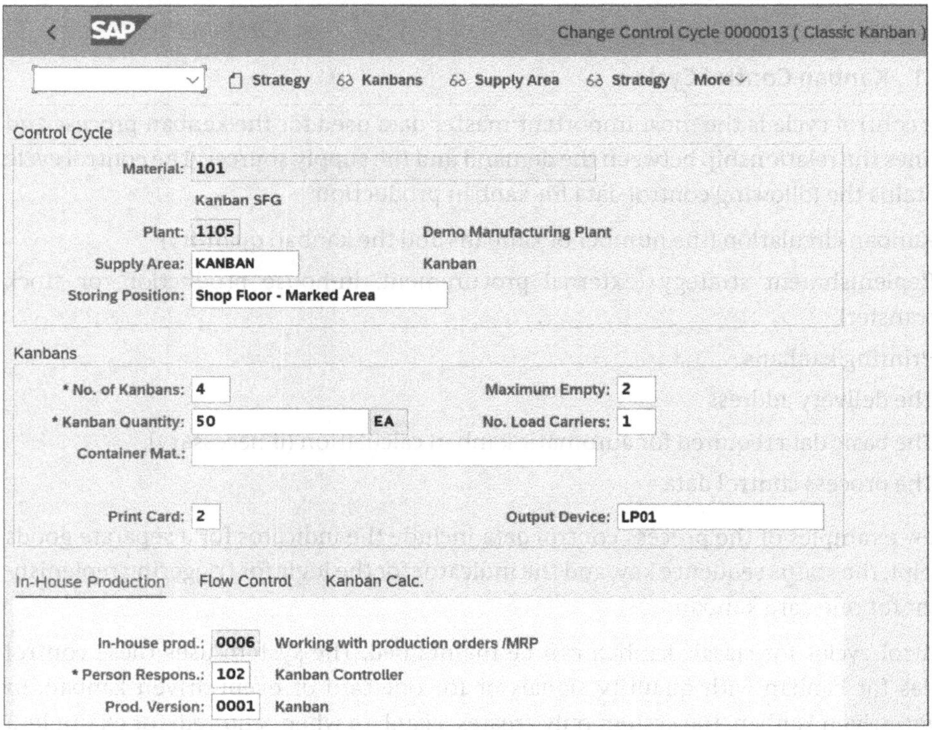

Figure 9.11 Replenishment Strategy (External Procurement) in Control Cycle

Next, choose the **Flow Control** tab (see Figure 9.12).

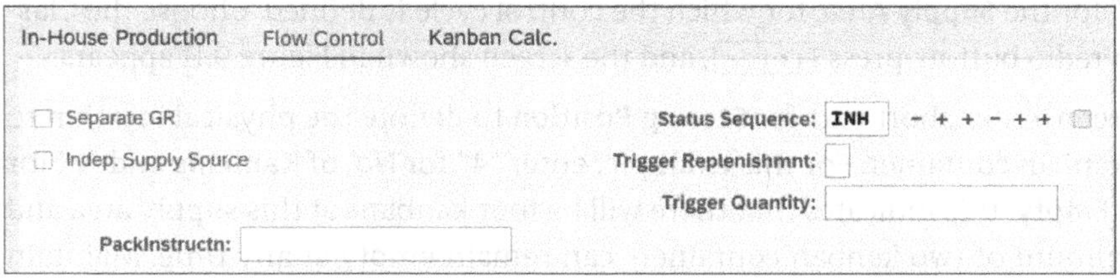

Figure 9.12 Flow Control in Control Cycle

On the screen shown in Figure 9.12, select **Separate GR** (goods receipt) if a company doesn't want to link a kanban **FULL** status with automatic goods receipt for a production or a purchase order. This setting may be useful in the following situations:

- The company posts goods receipts for externally procured materials in a central warehouse.
- The goods receipt posting is automatically linked to the backflush, as is always the case in repetitive manufacturing. Here, for example, a production supervisor can separate the backflush posted by the supply source from the status change initiated by the demand source.
- If planned orders (REM), manual kanban, and scheduling agreement schedule lines are used, then it's mandatory to post the goods receipt before the status can be set to **EMPTY** again.

With the **Independent Supply Source** indicator, it's not the demand source but the supply source that triggers replenishment. The demand source sets the kanban status to **EMPTY**, but the system doesn't create a replenishment element and sets the kanban status to **WAIT**. While remaining in the kanban board screen, the supply source triggers replenishment for these kanbans, thereby setting the status of such kanbans to **EMPTY**. The independent supply source thus determines the time of replenishment itself.

Next, assign the previously configured **INH** status sequence in this step to control how the system does or doesn't allow the user to set various statuses. For triggering replenishment when the kanban status is **IN USE** or **WAIT** or on reaching a trigger quantity, maintain the relevant details in the **Flow Control** tab (Figure 9.12). Next, choose the **Kanban Calc.** and the screen shown in Figure 9.13 appears.

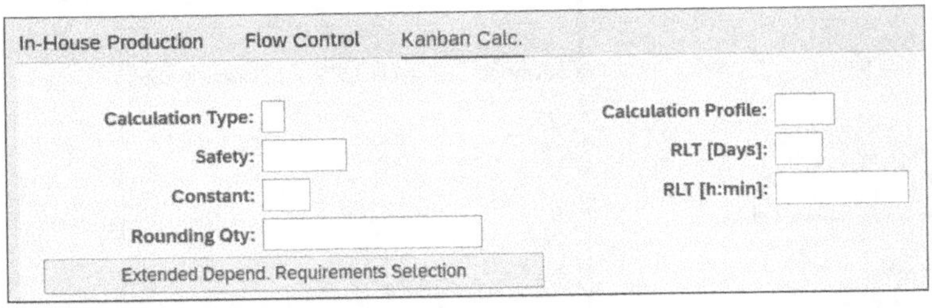

Figure 9.13 Kanban Calculation in Control Cycle

Figure 9.13 shows the kanban calculation details. The value 1 for **Calculation Type** enables the system to calculate the number of kanbans necessary to fulfill the production requirements. In the **Calculation Profile** field, maintain a number for the data to use for the automatic calculation of the kanban circulation. The system uses the calculation profile if the replenishment lead time is less than one day.

The system uses the following formula for automatic kanban calculation:

$$K = ((AC \times RT \times SF) \div Cont.) + C$$

The symbols are defined as follows:

- K = Number of kanbans
- AC = Average consumption per unit of time (from dependent requirements)
- RT = Replenishment time per kanban (from control cycle or material)
- Cont. = Quantity per kanban
- SF = Safety Factor
- C = Constant

Save the control cycle after the necessary input is made.

> **Tips and Tricks**
>
> The control cycle can also be maintained by using Transaction PKMC or following menu path **Logistics • Production Planning • Production • KANBAN • Control Cycle • Control Cycle Maintenance**.

9.5.2 Material Master/Production Version

Although this example primarily covers kanban replenishment via discrete manufacturing (production order), maintain the following settings if a company uses repetitive manufacturing (planned orders or run schedule quantity):

- Using Transaction MM02, choose the **MRP 2** tab of the material master and assign the **Proposed Supply Area** as "KANBAN", which is the same production supply area previously configured in Section 9.4.6 (see Figure 9.14).

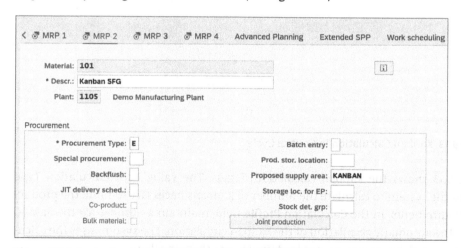

Figure 9.14 Assigning Proposed Supply Area in Material Master

- Using Transaction C223, maintain information for **Default Supply Area** in a production version.

9.5.3   Bill of Materials

If one or more components of a material BOM are replenished via kanban, then maintain the production supply area in the material BOM. To do so, use Transaction CS02 and navigate to the item details of the component. Then, choose the **Status/Lng Text** tab to maintain the production supply area (previously configured in Section 9.4.6) in the **Prodn Supply Area** field for each of the components that will undergo replenishment via kanban.

9.6   Replenishment with Kanban

In the following sections, we'll cover the impact of kanban configuration and kanban master data on the three kanban replenishment strategies: production, procurement, and stock transfer. We'll also cover several associated topics, such as how to print kanban, how to handle kanban errors, and how to manually post a kanban goods receipt. Regardless of the kanban strategy used, we suggest reading all the sections; there's a significant amount of information common to all three kanban replenishment strategies. For example, regardless of the kanban replenishment strategy used, a user will most likely face kanban errors that require processing or rectification. We'll also cover how to address scenarios in which errors are encountered in the following sections.

9.6.1   Kanban Replenishment via Production

With the necessary kanban configuration in place and the master data set up, we can move forward with the business processes involved in replenishing a kanban through a procurement process.

To begin using the kanban board (in the Demand Source view), use Transaction PK13N or follow menu path **Logistics · Production Planning · Production · KANBAN · Control · Demand Source View**.

Figure 9.15 shows the initial parameters screen; here, enter "1105" for **Plant**, choose **Production** for **Supply Area** and enter "KANBAN," and enter "101" for **Material**. Choose the **Tabular View** checkbox, press Enter, and the screen shown in Figure 9.16 appears.

> **Note**
>
> Although our example uses the Demand Source view of the kanban board, the Supply Source view can also be used by using Transaction PK12N or following menu path **Logistics · Production Planning · Production · KANBAN · Control · Supply Source View**.

As soon as the system creates the control cycle, the kanbans attain **WAIT** status, as shown in Figure 9.16.

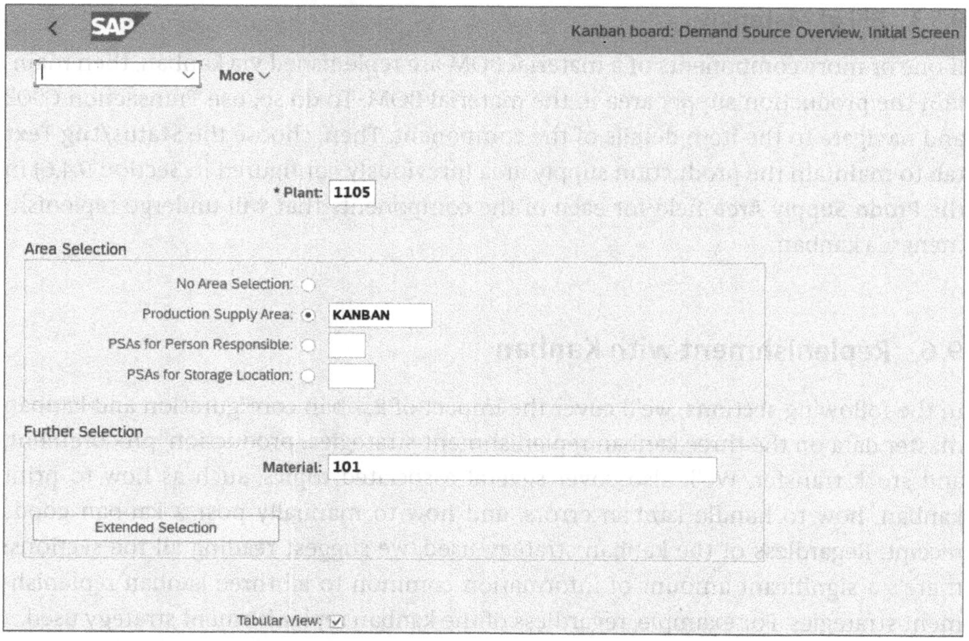

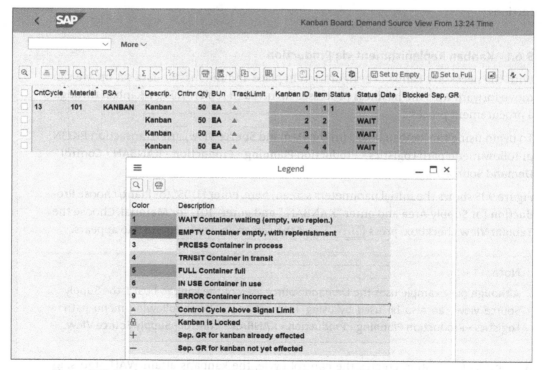

Figure 9.15 Kanban Board: Demand Source Overview, Initial Screen

Figure 9.16 Kanban Board in SAP GUI (Graphical User Interface)

If you choose the tabular view to display the kanban board, all information appears in a table. But if the tabular view isn't selected, then the left-hand side of the screen shows details such as supply area, material number, and kanban quantity, and the right-hand side shows the actual statuses of various kanbans through unique identification (using the internal number range defined in configuration) by means of various color codes.

Here, four kanbans (with **Kanban IDs** 1, 2, 3, and 4) with the **WAIT** status can be seen. To learn which kanban status each color code denotes, choose **Legend**, shown in the lower half of Figure 9.16.

Figure 9.17 shows the Kanban Board app, displaying the same information as that in Figure 9.16. A user has the option to use the SAP Fiori app or SAP GUI for accessing the kanban board, whichever is preferred. We'll use both interfaces.

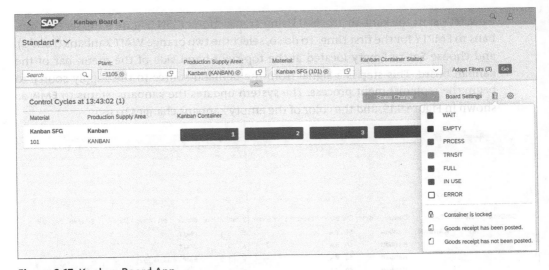

Figure 9.17 Kanban Board App

Before delving into replenishment via kanban, let's also take a quick look at the stock/requirements list for material 101 and plant 1105. The purpose of evaluating this list is to show how the system continuously updates the stock/requirements list based on various activities and actions performed during the kanban process.

To navigate to the stock/requirements list, use Transaction MD04 or follow menu path **Logistics • Production Planning • Production • Kanban • Evaluations • Stock/Requirements List**.

On the initial screen that appears, enter "101" for **Material** and "1105" for **Plant** and press ⌨Enter. The resulting screen is shown in Figure 9.18. The first thing to notice is that there isn't any stock at the plant and storage location level. Because the kanban process hasn't started yet, there aren't any replenishment elements, such as production orders or purchase orders.

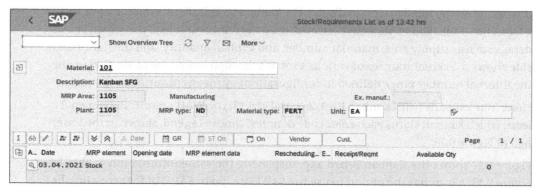

Figure 9.18 Stock/Requirements List without Any Replenishment Elements

Now, let's start the kanban process! Using Transaction PK13N (Figure 9.16), set two kanbans to **EMPTY** for the first time. To do so, select the two orange **WAIT** kanbans (1 and 2), and choose **Set to Empty** located at the top-right-hand side of the menu bar of the kanban board. This step is a signal from the demand source to the supply source to begin the replenishment process. The system updates the kanbans' status to **EMP**, as shown in Figure 9.19, and the color of the empty kanbans changes to red.

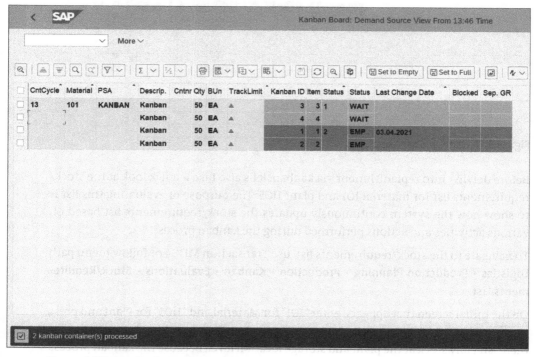

Figure 9.19 Two Kanbans with EMPTY Status

Tips and Tricks

To select multiple kanbans, click the first kanban and then hold Ctrl and select additional kanbans.

Setting the kanbans to **EMPTY** triggers creation of two production orders, as maintained in the control cycle.

Double-click **Kanban ID 1** in Figure 9.19 and the screen in Figure 9.20 appears. Figure 9.20 shows detailed information for **Kanban ID Number 1**, which links it to the production order **1000080**.

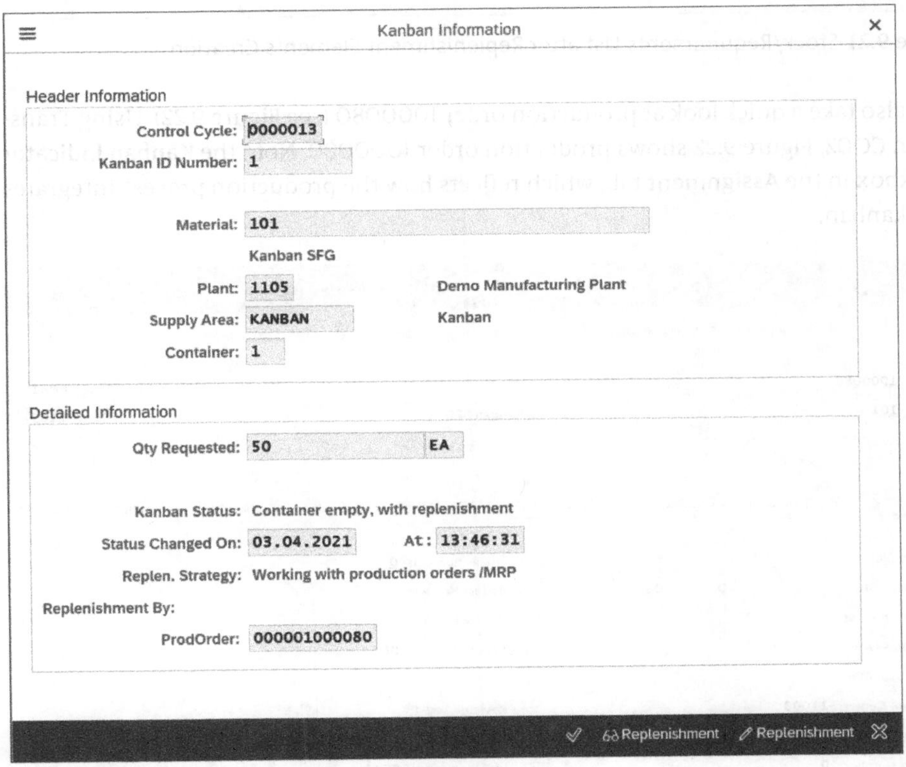

≡   Kanban Information   ×

Header Information

Control Cycle: 0000013
Kanban ID Number: 1

Material: 101
Kanban SFG

Plant: 1105   Demo Manufacturing Plant
Supply Area: KANBAN   Kanban
Container: 1

Detailed Information

Qty Requested: 50   EA

Kanban Status: Container empty, with replenishment
Status Changed On: 03.04.2021   At: 13:46:31
Replen. Strategy: Working with production orders /MRP
Replenishment By:
ProdOrder: 000001000080

✓   6ə Replenishment   ✎ Replenishment   ✕

Figure 9.20 Kanban Information: Detailed View

Using Transaction MD04 again, let's take a look at the newly created replenishment elements after two kanbans were set to **EMPTY** (see Figure 9.21). The system created two production orders (**1000080** and **1000081**, marked **PrdOrd** in the **MRP Element** column).

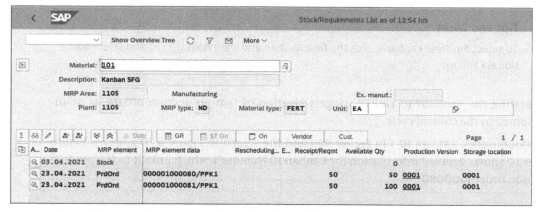

Figure 9.21 Stock/Requirements List after Replenishment Elements Creation

Let's also take a quick look at production order 1000080 (see Figure 9.22). Using Transaction CO02, Figure 9.22 shows production order 1000080. Note the **Kanban Indicator** checkbox in the **Assignment** tab, which reflects how the production process integrates with kanban.

Figure 9.22 Production Order with Kanban Indictor

Figure 9.23 shows the updated status of four kanbans in the Kanban Board app. The purple color of kanban ID **2** denotes that it's in process, which is the next target status based on the configuration. The colorless kanban ID **1** denotes that an error occurred when the user tried to set the next kanban status. We'll show how to handle kanban error processing shortly.

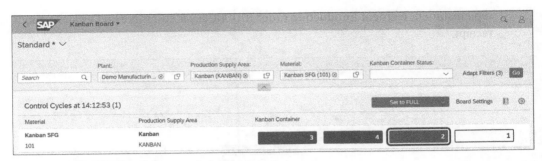

Figure 9.23 Kanban Board with Updated Kanban Statuses

Next, choose kanban ID **2** on the screen in Figure 9.23, and choose **Set to FULL** to denote that replenishment of kanban ID **2** has completed (goods are received). The kanban color changes to green to denote that it's full (see Figure 9.24). The system will display a message (not shown) that confirms the number of kanbans processed. At the same time, and on successful replenishment, the system changes the kanbans from **EMPTY** to **FULL** on the kanban board.

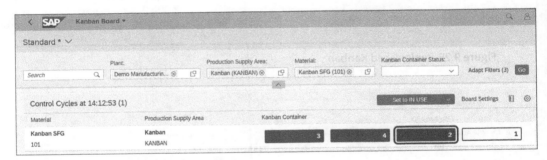

Figure 9.24 Setting Kanban to FULL Status

Figure 9.25 shows the status of kanban 1 as it appears after clicking it (if a user is using the SAP GUI version of the kanban board, then double-click the relevant kanban to view the details). Notice the material document number, **5000000060/2021**, against which the system posted the goods receipt when the status of the kanban was set to **FULL**.

There are three ways to set the kanban to full:

- Scan the barcode that denotes the **FULL** status.

- Use the kanban board's **Set to Full** button.

- Execute a normal goods receipt, which will automatically set the kanban to green (**FULL**).

Using Transaction MD04 for the stocks/requirement list, Figure 9.26 shows that the replenishment element (production order 10000081) is no longer in the system after the kanban was set to **FULL** via the automatic goods receipt. However, the second replenishment element (production order 10000080) is still there and awaits a goods receipt.

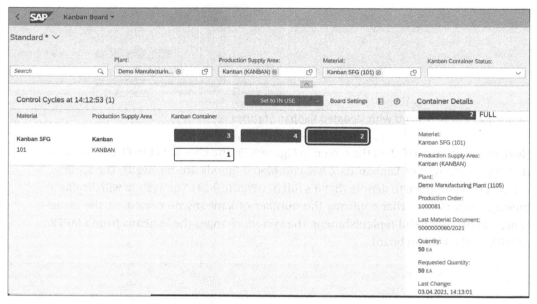

Figure 9.25 Replenished Kanban

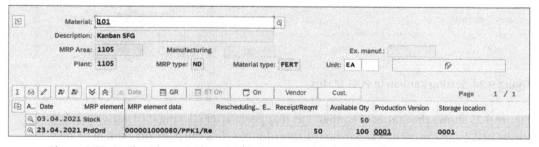

Figure 9.26 Replenishment Element (Production Order) Reduced

Let's now discuss the business processes of kanban replenishment via a procurement process.

9.6.2   Kanban Replenishment via Procurement

To set up a replenishment strategy for stock transfer, follow the configuration menu path **SAP IMG · Production · Kanban · Replenishment Strategies · Define External Procurement Strategies**. On the screen that appears, enter "1105" for the plant and "0001" (purchase order) for in the **External Procurement** field, as shown in Figure 9.27. Here you have nearly all of the same **Control Type** options that were available for in-house production. Because this replenishment strategy is for external procurement, the configuration settings here relate to kanban replenishment via the procurement process. Here, **Order Type** refers to the purchase order type that the system will create in kanban replenishment.

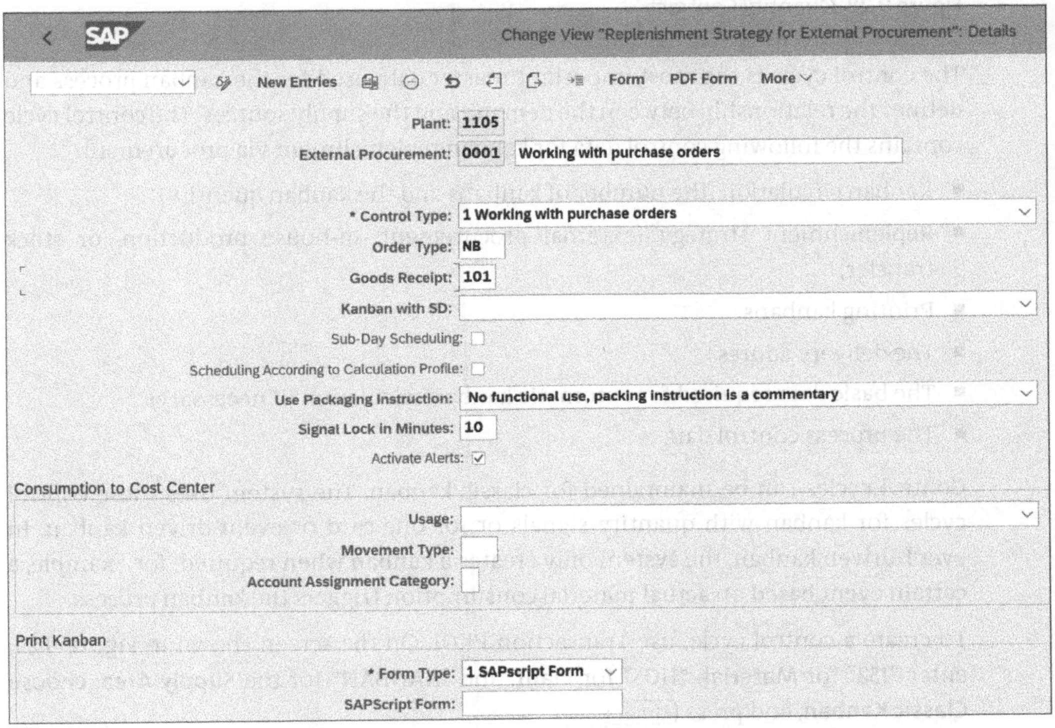

Figure 9.27 Control Types for Replenishment Strategy for External Procurement

The next step is to maintain the setting that will exclude the storage location from MRP. To do so, set up the MRP area for a specific storage location as discussed in Section 14.4 of Chapter 14.

The procurement department creates a quantity contract with the supplier for the materials that the production department needs to consume in kanban processes. To create a quantity contract, use Transaction ME31K or follow menu path **Logistics • Materials Management • Purchasing • Outline Agreement • Contract • Create**. Figure 9.28 shows the main details, including the **Supplier** (enter "100000"), **Material** (enter "152"), target quantity (**Targ. Qty**), and price (**Net Price**). When you save, the system will create quantity contract number 4600000001. We'll use this quantity contract number in the control cycle for kanban replenishment.

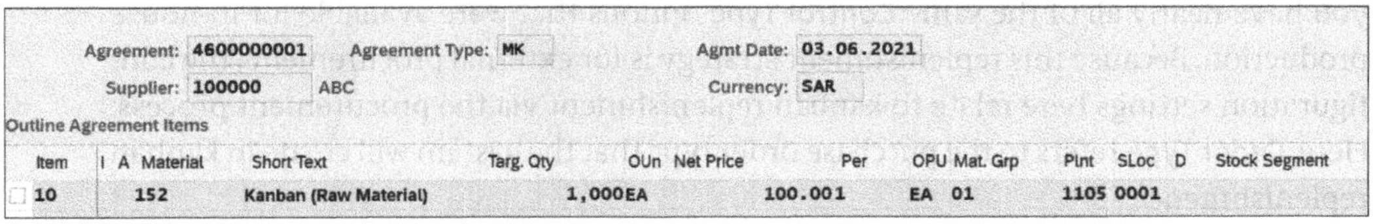

Agreement:	4600000001	Agreement Type:	MK			Agmt Date:	03.06.2021					
Supplier:	100000	ABC				Currency:	SAR					

Outline Agreement Items

Item	I	A	Material	Short Text	Targ. Qty	OUn	Net Price	Per	OPU	Mat. Grp	Plnt	SLoc	D	Stock Segment
☐ 10			152	Kanban (Raw Material)	1,000	EA	100.00	1	EA	01	1105	0001		

Figure 9.28 Quantity Contract

The control cycle is the most important master data used for the kanban process and defines the relationship between the demand and the supply sources. The control cycle contains the following control data for kanban replenishment via procurement:

- Kanban circulation (the number of kanbans and the kanban quantity)
- Replenishment strategy (external procurement, in-house production, or stock transfer)
- Printing kanbans
- The delivery address
- The basic data required for automatic kanban calculation (if necessary)
- The process control data

Control cycles can be maintained for classic kanban. The system uses these control cycles for kanban with quantity signals or for one-card or event-driven kanban. In event-driven kanban, the system only creates a kanban when required; for example, a certain event based on actual material consumption triggers the kanban process.

To create a control cycle, use Transaction PK01. On the screen shown in Figure 9.29, enter "152" for **Material**, "1105" for **Plant**, and "KANBAN" for the **Supply Area**, choose **Classic Kanban**, and press (Enter).

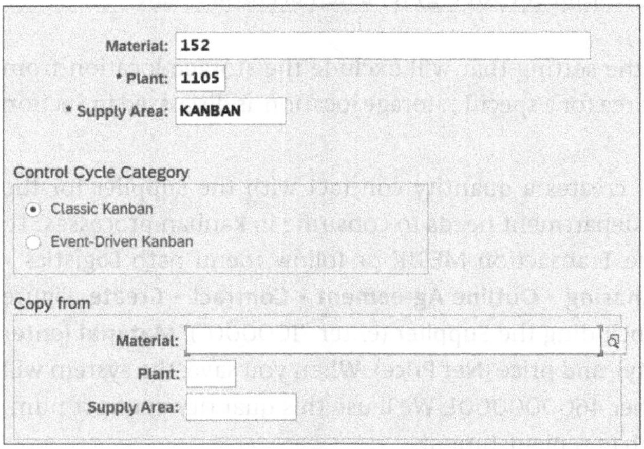

Material:	152
* Plant:	1105
* Supply Area:	KANBAN

Control Cycle Category

- ⦿ Classic Kanban
- ◯ Event-Driven Kanban

Copy from

Material:	
Plant:	
Supply Area:	

Figure 9.29 Control Cycle Creation

In Figure 9.30 , enter short text for **Storing Position** to denote the physical location to place the kanban container. For this example, enter "4" for the number of kanbans and "2" for **Maximum Empty**; this indicates that there will be four kanbans at this supply area and that a maximum of two kanban containers can remain empty at any time. Maintain the printer settings that the system will use to print the kanban's barcode.

Next, choose the replenishment strategy for a kanban. In this example, we chose external procurement as the replenishment strategy by selecting the **Ext. Proc.** radio button. After selecting the replenishment strategy, choose **Replenishment Strategy 0001**, as shown in Figure 9.30.

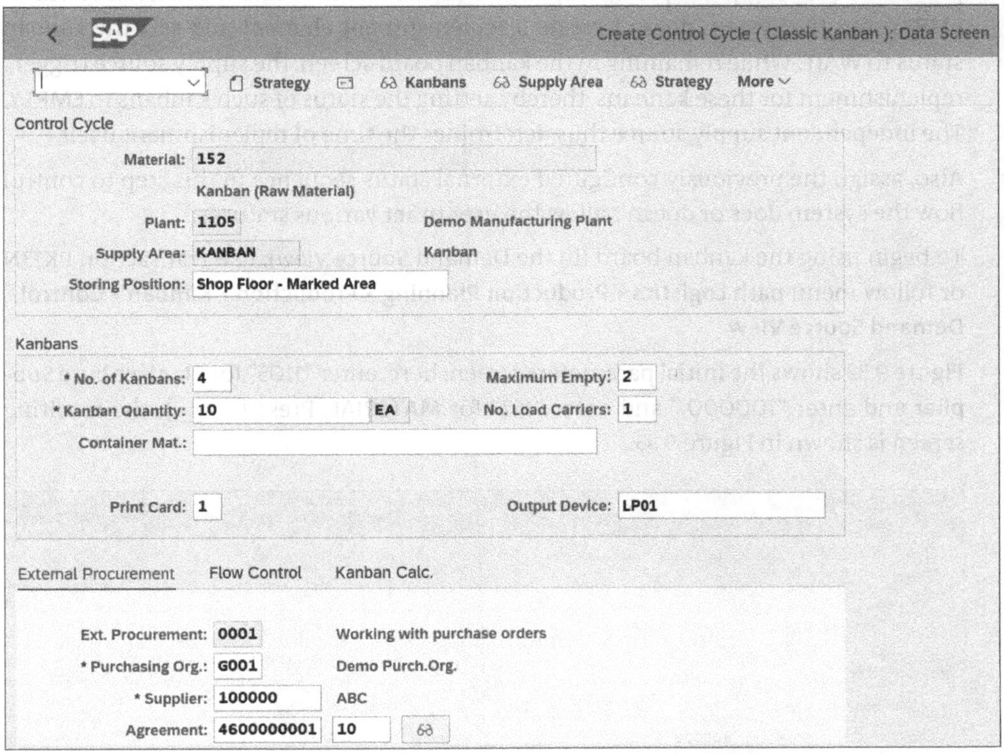

Figure 9.30 Replenishment Strategy (External Procurement) in Control Cycle

In Figure 9.30, enter specific details to replenish kanbans via external procurement. Enter "0001" for **Purchasing Organization**, "100000" for **Supplier**, and "4600000001" for **Agreement** (quantity contract), along with item number 10 from the quantity contract that was created in the previous step. Next, choose the **Flow Control** tab (see Figure 9.31).

In Figure 9.31, select **Separate GR** in case a company doesn't want to link a kanban **FULL** status with automatic goods receipt for a purchase or production order.

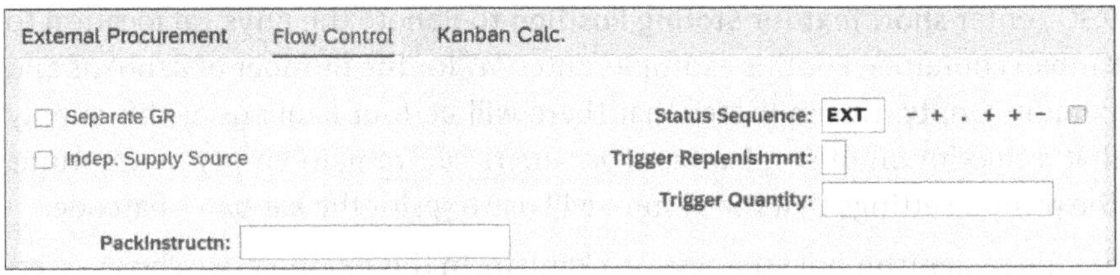

Figure 9.31 Assignment of Quantity Contract in Control Cycle

With the **Independent Supply Source** indicator, it's not the demand source but the supply source that triggers replenishment. The demand source sets the kanban status to **EMPTY**, but the system doesn't create a replenishment element and sets the kanban status to **WAIT**. While remaining in the kanban board screen, the supply source triggers replenishment for these kanbans, thereby setting the status of such kanbans to **EMPTY**. The independent supply source thus determines the time of replenishment itself.

Also, assign the previously configured external status sequence in this step to control how the system does or doesn't allow the user to set various statuses.

To begin using the kanban board (in the **Demand Source** view), use Transaction PK13N or follow menu path **Logistics • Production Planning • Production • Kanban • Control • Demand Source View**.

Figure 9.32 shows the initial parameters screen; here, enter "1105" for **Plant**, choose **Supplier** and enter "100000," and enter "152" for **MATERIAL**. Press ⌈Enter⌉; the resulting screen is shown in Figure 9.33.

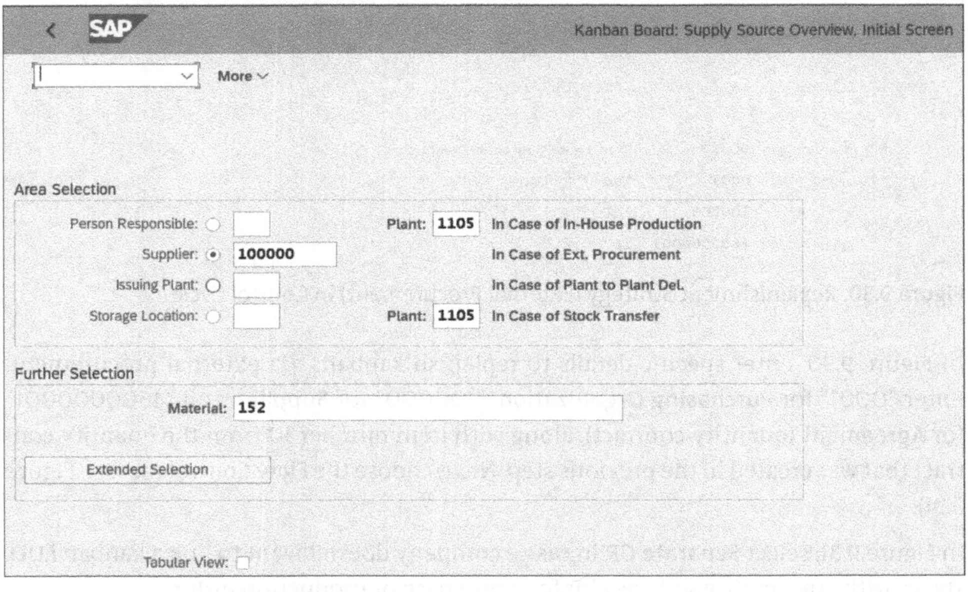

Figure 9.32 Kanban Board: Demand Source

[«]

Note

Although we used the **Demand Source** view of the kanban board here, a planner can also use the Supply Source view by using Transaction PK12N or following menu path **Logistics • Production Planning • Production • Kanban • Control • Supply Source View**.

As soon as the system creates the control cycle, the kanbans attain **WAIT** status, as shown in Figure 9.33. The left-hand side of the screen shows details such as supply area, material number, and kanban quantity, and the right-hand side shows the actual statuses of various kanbans through unique identification (using the internal number range defined in configuration) by means of various color codes. Here, there are four kanbans (001, 002, 003, and 004) with the **WAIT** status. To learn which kanban status each color code denotes, choose **Legend**, as shown in the lower half of Figure 9.33.

9

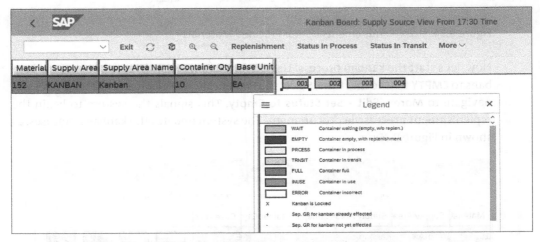

Figure 9.33 Kanban Board Legend, Identifying Kanban Status Colors

Before delving into replenishment via kanban, let's also take a quick look at the stock/requirements list for material 152 and plant 1105. The purpose of evaluating this list is to show how the system continuously updates the stock/requirements list based on various activities and actions that you perform during the kanban process.

To navigate to the stock/requirements list, use Transaction MD04 or follow menu path **Logistics • Production Planning • Production • Kanban • Evaluations • Stock/Requirements List**.

On the initial screen that appears, enter "152" for **Material** and "1105" for **Plant** and press [Enter]. The resulting screen is shown in Figure 9.34. The first thing to notice is that there isn't any stock at the plant and storage location level. Furthermore, the system also indicates that storage location 0001 isn't planned. This is the result of the storage location level setting previously established in the material master to exclude storage location 0001 from all forms of planning by creating an MRP area for storage location

0001 (MRP areas are discussed in detail in Chapter 14, Section 14.4). Because the kanban process hasn't started yet, there aren't any replenishment elements yet, such as purchase orders or production orders.

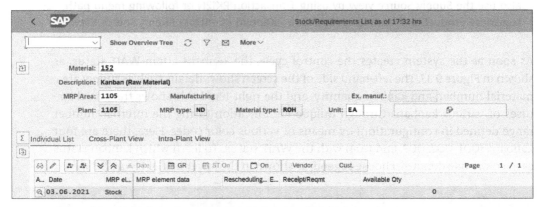

Figure 9.34 Stock/Requirements List for Procured Materials

Now, let's start the kanban process! Using Transaction PK13N (Figure 9.35), set the kanbans to **EMPTY** for the first time. Select the two purple **WAIT** kanbans (001 and 002) and navigate to **More • Edit • Set Status to Empty**. This signals the system to begin the replenishment process via procurement. The system updates the kanbans' statuses, as shown in Figure 9.35.

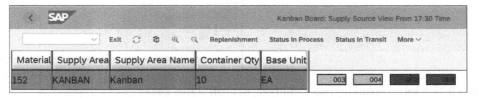

Figure 9.35 Available and Unused Kanbans

[+]   Tips and Tricks

To select multiple kanbans, click the first kanban and then hold `Ctrl` and select additional kanbans. To select several kanbans that are next to each other, click a kanban at one end of the board and drag the mouse cursor to the other end.

Figure 9.35 shows the status of kanbans 001 and 002 as **EMPTY**. The **EMPTY** status triggers the kanban replenishment process, as defined in the control cycle of the material-plant combination.

Setting the kanbans to **EMPTY** triggers generation of two purchase orders, which are basically contract release orders for the quantity contract maintained in the control cycle. A contract release order is a subset of the outline agreement (quantity or value contract) and is functionally the same as a purchase order. The difference between a contract release order and a purchase order is that the former links outline agreements, whereas the latter does not.

Using Transaction MD04, let's take a look at the newly created replenishment elements after two kanbans were set to **EMPTY** (see Figure 9.36). The system created two purchase orders (4500000011 and 4500000013, marked **POItem** in the **MRP EL...** column) as soon as the status of the two kanbans was set to **EMPTY**.

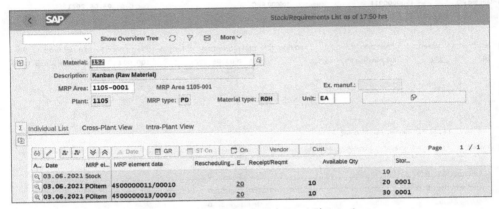

Figure 9.36 Stock/Requirements List with Replenishment Elements

Figure 9.37 shows information for kanban 11, which links it to purchase order 4500000011.

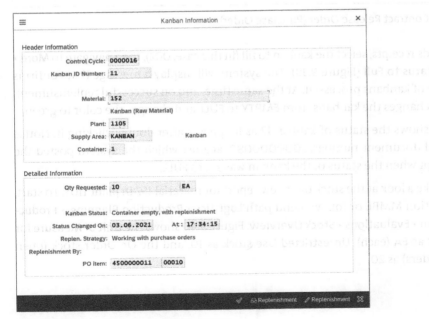

Figure 9.37 Detailed Kanban Information

Let's also take a quick look at purchase order 4500000011 (see Figure 9.38). Using Transaction ME23N, Figure 9.38 shows purchase order 450000011, which links to quantity contract 4600000001. Note the kanban indicator (**Kanban Indicat.**) in the **Delivery** tab, which reflects how procurement integrates with kanban.

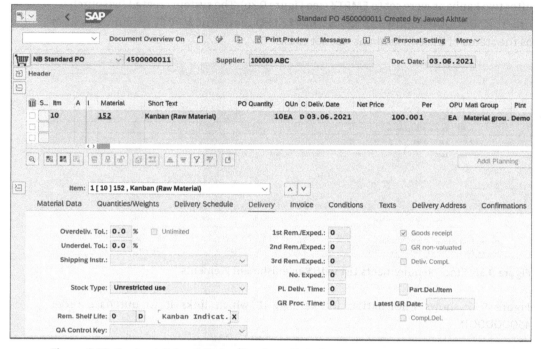

Figure 9.38 Contract Release Order (Purchase Order)

To post goods receipts, select the kanban to fill (in this case, 002), then navigate to **More · Edit · Set Status to Full** (Figure 9.39). The system will display a message that confirms the number of kanbans processed. At the same time, and on successful replenishment, the system changes the kanbans from **EMPTY** to **FULL** and changes the color to green.

Figure 9.39 shows the status of kanban 12 as it appears after double-clicking it. Notice the material document number, 5000000080, against which the system posted the goods receipt when the status of the kanban was set to **FULL**.

Let's now take a look at the stock overview report for material 152 in plant 1105. To start, use Transaction MMBE or follow menu path **Logistics · Production Planning · Production · Kanban · Evaluations · Stock Overview**. Figure 9.40 shows the **Unit of Measure** for material 152 as **EA** (each), **Unrestricted Use** stock as 10, and the **On Order** stock (open purchase orders) as 20.

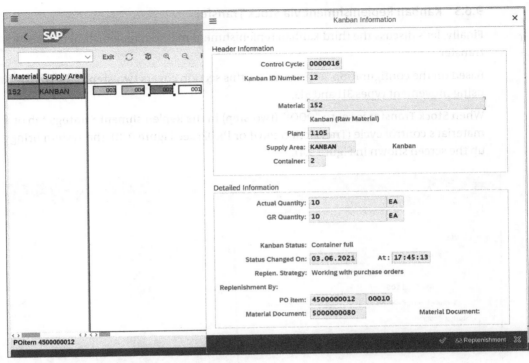

Figure 9.39 Empty Kanbans Awaiting Replenishment

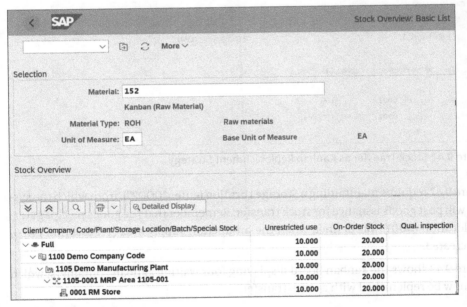

Figure 9.40 Stock Overview

9.6.3 Kanban Replenishment via Stock Transfer

Finally, let's discuss the third kanban replenishment method: replenishment via stock transfer.

Based on the configuration settings made, this section covers two-step stock transfers using movement types 311 and 313.

When **Stock Transfer** is set to "0001" (two-step) in the **Replenishment Strategy** tab of a material's control cycle (Transaction PKO1 or PKO2; see Figure 9.31), the system brings up the screen shown in Figure 9.41.

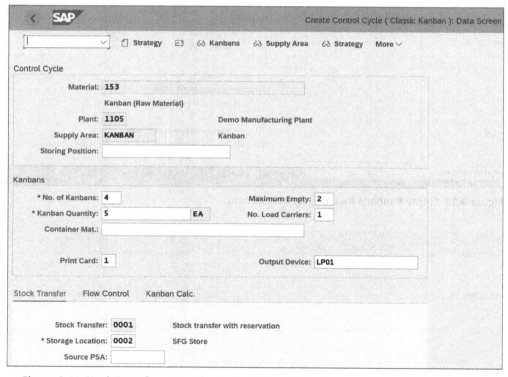

Figure 9.41 Stock Transfer as Kanban Replenishment Strategy

Figure 9.42 requires maintaining a **Storage Location** (enter "0002"), from which the system will post goods issuance for stock transfer. Remember that the goods receipt's storage location (**0001**) was defined when the production supply area (Transaction PKO5) was created.

Figure 9.42 shows the kanban board displaying four waiting kanban containers, which will now be replenished with a stock transfer.

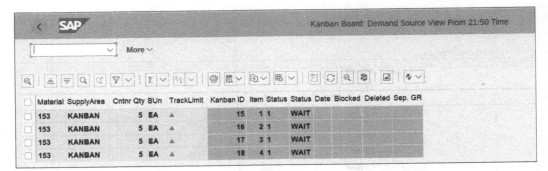

Figure 9.42 Kanban Board for Managing Stock Transfer Replenishment

In Figure 9.43, choose **KANBAN 15**, and then choose **More · Edit · Set Status to Empty** from the top menu items. After changing the kanban status to **EMPTY**, double-click **KANBAN 15** to open the screen shown on the right-hand side of Figure 9.43.

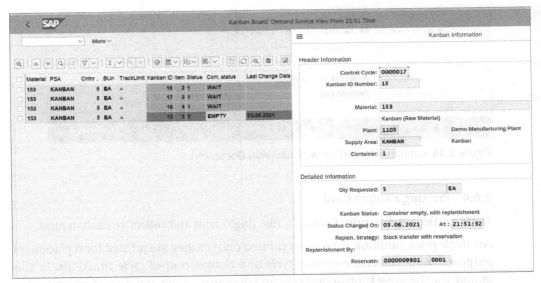

Figure 9.43 Kanban Information for Stock Transfer with Reservation

Figure 9.43 shows that the system will replenish kanban 15 in two steps. In the first step, and on marking the kanban as **EMPTY**, the system creates stock transfer reservation **9901**.

In the second step, set the status of kanban 15 to **FULL**, which not only updates the kanban's status and color to green, but also updates the stock transfer's goods movements' details (see Figure 9.44).

Figure 9.44 shows a goods receipt quantity (**GR Quantity**) of 5 while creating **Material Document 4900000140**, and the **Kanban Status** reads **Container Full**.

9   Kanban

Figure 9.44 Kanban Information with Material Document

9.6.4   Printing Kanban Card

There are two ways to print kanban cards: single print and collective kanban print.

For *single print*, cards are either only printed once or they are printed for replacement purposes using the *create control cycle* and *change control cycle* functions. In this option, use the same kanban card over and over again. Here, there are three options:

- The kanban card circulates between the supply source and the demand source with the container.
- The kanban card is passed from the demand source to the supply source without a container but returns to the demand source with one. The transport of the cards to the supply source has to be organized.
- The card remains at the demand source and is attached to the full kanban or is stored without a kanban at a predefined location. There is no information on the circulating kanbans, and the information on empty kanbans is kept at the demand source. Information is passed on to the supply source by means of the kanban board. When a kanban is delivered, the card has to be retrieved at the demand source.

442

With *collective kanban print*, kanban cards can be printed across the control cycle. In other words, collective kanban print allows collectively/mass printing several kanbans in one step. In the case of a print error, you can repeat the printing of certain kanbans (e.g., all kanbans that should have printed on a certain printer during a certain time period).

In a *renewed kanban print for each control cycle* run, the card is thrown away at the end of each cycle. The following options (using the **Kanban Print** field in the control cycle) are available:

- **1 Card Printed when Replenishment Is Triggered**
  With in-house production or stock transfer, the card is printed at the supply source. This means that the card doesn't have to be transported to the supply source. The card can be used as an extra written request for delivery (e.g., for in-house production with planned orders or manual kanbans). For production orders, printing is carried out using the print control for production orders; in all other cases, it's carried out using the kanban transaction.

- **2 Card Printed when Goods Receipt Is Posted**
  It makes sense to use this option for external procurement with central goods receipts. If a company uses a strategy in which the goods receipt is carried out automatically in the background as soon as the status is changed to **FULL**, then don't use this print control technique. The system prints the kanban on GR posting for a purchase order or a production order (or a stock transfer reservation) by using the GR function in inventory management (IM).

- **Blank**
  The kanban is printed instead of the GR papers and is attached to the kanban.

To print a kanban card, use Transaction PK17 or follow menu path **Logistics · Production · Kanban · Control Cycle · Print Kanban**. On the initial screen that appears, enter appropriate criteria to search for the kanbans that need to be printed and choose **Execute**. The system displays a list of kanbans that you can print. Choose the appropriate kanbans by selecting their checkboxes, then click **Print Selected Kanbans** and the system will print to the local network printer (see Figure 9.45).

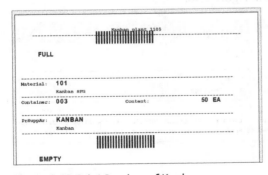

Figure 9.45 Print Preview of Kanban

9.6.5   Kanban Error Processing

Figure 9.46 shows the initial screen that displays and rectifies kanbans with processing errors. Enter parameters to ensure that the system only displays kanbans experiencing processing errors. For this example, enter "1105" for **Plant** and "KANBAN" for **Prodn Supply Area**. Choose **Execute** (not shown), and the screen shown in Figure 9.47 appears.

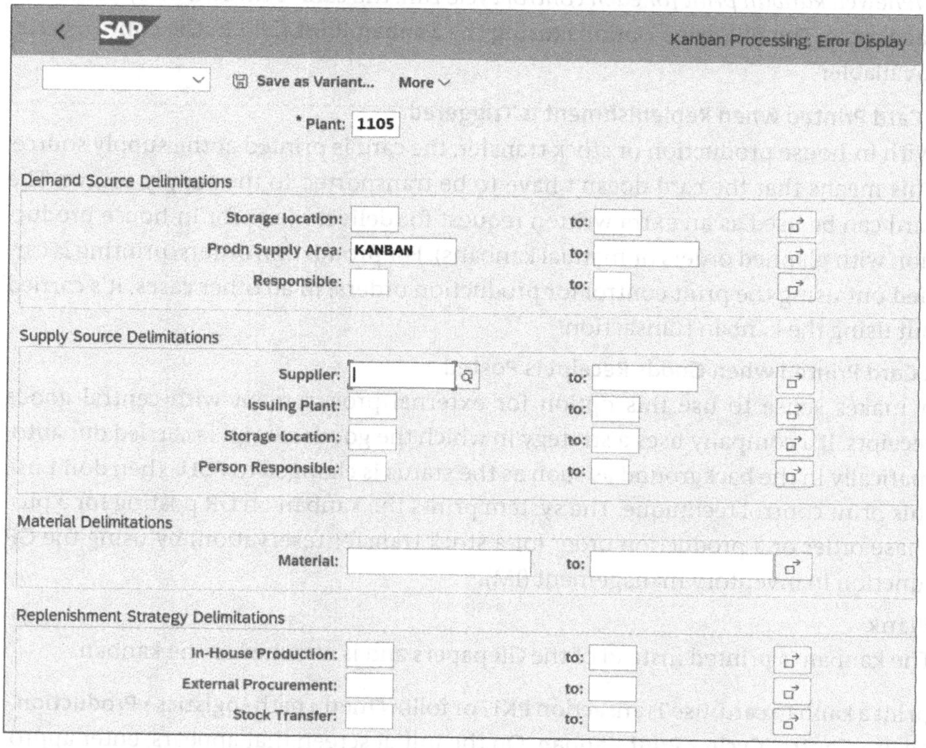

Figure 9.46 Initial Screen for Kanban Error Processing

Figure 9.47 shows that control cycle 13 has one kanban, 1, in need of error processing. Select the relevant checkbox for the kanban to correct, and then choose **Kanban Correction**. This will bring up the screen shown in Figure 9.48.

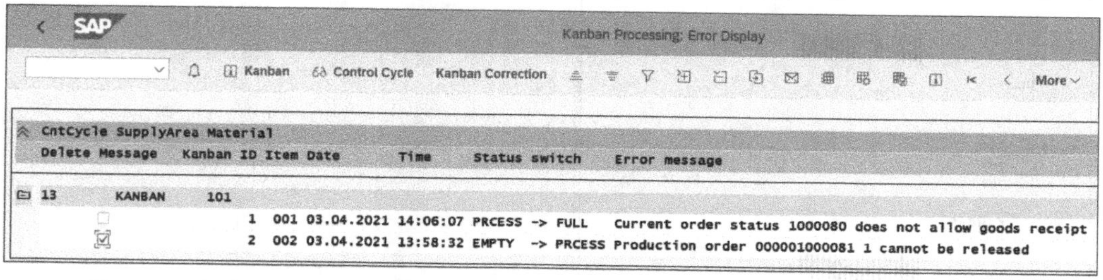

Figure 9.47 Kanban Error Processing

Figure 9.48 shows the details for kanban correction for control cycle 13. Here, the **Status** of kanban ID number 1 is **ERROR**. Double-click the ID of the kanban with an error, and the system will open the error correction options shown in the lower half of the screen.

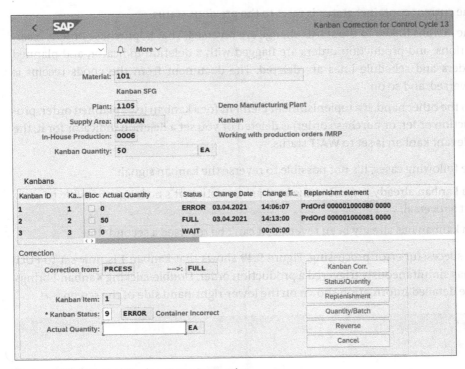

Figure 9.48 Detailed Kanban Error Processing

In the lower half of Figure 9.48, some of the error correction options are intended to correct the kanban's status or its quantity/batch, or even to reverse an already processed kanban. In this example, the production order wasn't released, the kanban status couldn't be set to **FULL**, and this led to the kanban error. Choose **Kanban Corr.**, and the system will prompt you to confirm the action. Choose **Yes**, and the system will update the status of the kanban to the correct setting. In this example, kanban 1 is correctly set to **FULL**, as this is the next status according to the status sequence.

As a rule, when a status change is incorrect, the kanban is always set to **ERROR**, and the kanban can't be used again until the kanban error correction is ensured. It's possible to define cases in which the system issues an error message that doesn't change the status of the kanban, but in all other cases the system sets the kanban status to **ERROR**.

For example, if there's an invalid cost collector for the backflush of a run schedule quantity, it's good business practice to set the **ERROR** status so that the user must complete the missing data. In other cases—for example, if the data is only temporarily locked by another user—an error message is sufficient. The user can repeat this action at any time, and the kanban retains its status.

Referring to Figure 9.48 again, in the case of a posting error, the user can *reverse* the last kanban signal (e.g., changing the status from **EMPTY** to **FULL**). To do so, click **Reversal**, and the system will perform the following actions:

- The current container status is reset to the previous status.
- The actions linked to the status change are reversed. That is, purchase orders, reservations, and production orders are flagged with a deletion indicator, and planned orders and schedule lines are deleted. The document from the goods receipt is reversed, and so on.
- On the other hand, if a replenishment element for a kanban (e.g., planned order, production order, or purchase order) is deleted or you set a deletion indicator for it, the relevant kanban is set to **WAIT** status.

In the following cases, it's not possible to reverse the kanban signal:

- If a kanban already processed the kanban correction, it's no longer possible to carry out a reversal.
- If a kanban has already been reversed, it can't be reversed a second time.

After successful error processing, Figure 9.49 shows that kanban 1 is now set to **FULL** and has simultaneously triggered a production order. Double-clicking **Kanban 1** brings up the detailed information shown on the lower-right-hand side of the screen.

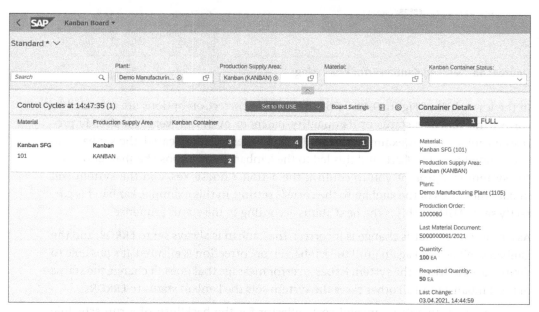

Figure 9.49 Updated Kanban ID 1 after Successful Error Processing

Figure 9.49 also shows that because the replenishment element is a production order, the system references the production order number 1000080. Also, setting the kanban status to **FULL** triggered the GR process, which resulted in the creation of material document 5000000061/2021.

9.6.6   Separated Post Goods Receipt

There's another kanban scenario in which goods receipts for production orders is undertaken as a separate step (via Transaction MIGO) instead of setting the kanban status to **FULL**. Separately posting goods receipts meets the business needs of those companies that have slightly longer lead times or that have some physical distance to cover to bring the kanban containers to the shop floor for use in production or assembly.

Choosing to separately post GRs still integrates with the kanban process; the system shows kanban containers with different identifications to denote cases in which GR has been undertaken or is awaited.

Once back at the kanban board (using Transaction PK13N), the screen will show the status of various kanban containers. In a separated GR, trying to change the kanban status to **Set to Full** does not adhere to the predefined status sequence of the control cycle and thus creates an error. The error message explains there's a need to first set the mandatory **In Process** status before updating the status to **Set to Full**.

A **FULL** status set for a kanban denotes it with green shading. However, a small dash sign to the right of kanban ID indicates that although the status of the kanban was marked as **Set to Full**, the system still needs to update its actual GR. Although the GR for the production order was performed separately in the previous step, this delay in the kanban status update is due to the configuration settings that determine the system will only update a kanban status after a predefined time interval (five minutes).

9.6.7   Kanban Signal: Two-Kanban Process

Instead of triggering the kanban signal by setting a kanban to **EMPTY**, it's also possible to withdraw quantities from kanbans in a control cycle using the *quantity signal*. The system reduces the actual quantity by the quantity specified in the quantity signal. At the same time, the system recognizes when the actual kanban quantity is zero and automatically sets the kanban to **EMPTY**. When the quantity is withdrawn from a container for the first time, the system sets the status to **IN USE**. If the withdrawal quantity exceeds the actual quantity of the kanban, the system reduces the actual quantity of the next kanban. This means the system first reduces kanbans with the **IN USE** status, and then reduces kanbans that have had the **FULL** status for the longest amount of time. When the quantity signal is used, the system updates only the actual quantity of the kanban and *does not* carry out stock postings. The system carries out the stock postings when backflushing the material. It's also possible to combine the kanban and the quantity signals.

The procedure is similar to the previous procedures. However, in this case the kanban is set to **EMPTY** when the remaining quantity in the kanban reaches or exceeds the trigger quantity. In this process, the parts are withdrawn with the quantity signal, but it's mandatory to maintain the trigger quantity and the logic in the control cycle. The withdrawal quantity can be posted either with the quantity signal or using a PDC system. The biggest disadvantage of using the quantity signal is the need to individually report quantities.

Kanban only manages the status of the kanbans and controls material flow and production using the kanban signals. In the case of underdelivery, remaining quantities of the production/purchase order remain.

Let's now examine the kanban signal through an example. First, create a control cycle (Transaction PK01) for a new material 103; define the total number of kanbans as two, each with a quantity of five. At any given time, only one kanban can remain empty. Also, specify that the kanban quantity should trigger replenishment and that the trigger quantity is three. When the kanban quantity signal indicates that a kanban quantity of three or less remains in a container, it will automatically trigger replenishment.

The kanban board in Figure 9.50 shows that the status of kanban 002 is **WAIT** and kanban 001 is **EMPTY**. Select kanban 001 and then click **To Full** so that system updates the kanban status as shown in Figure 9.51.

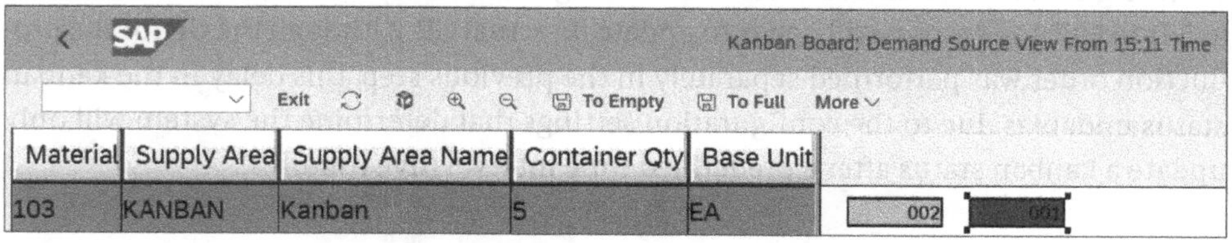

Figure 9.50 Two-Kanban Replenishment Using Quantity Signal

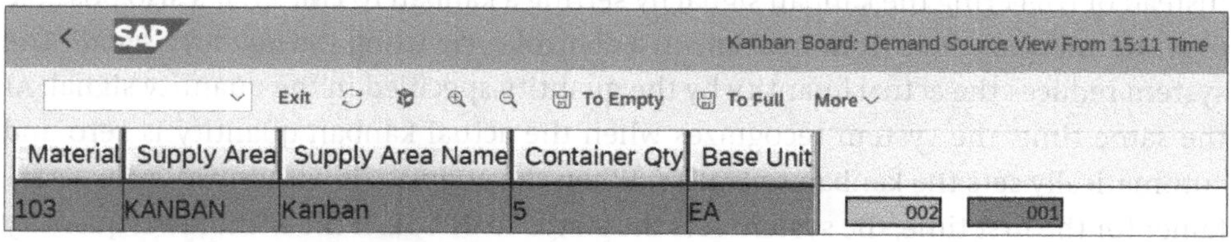

Figure 9.51 Kanbans with WAIT and FULL Statuses

Let's use the kanban quantity signal to denote withdrawal or consumption of material 103 from kanban 001. We'll also show how this automatically impacts the status of kanban 001.

To record quantity consumption of material using the quantity signal, use Transaction PK22 or follow menu path **Logistics · Production Planning · Production · KANBAN · Control · Kanban Signal · Quantity Signal**.

Figure 9.52 shows the screen for entering the **Kanban ID Number** (enter "001") and the **Withdrawal Quantity** (enter "4.000"). Save your entries. The system will update the information as shown at the bottom of the screen. You'll see that now the actual quantity that remains in kanban 001 is one, because four have been withdrawn.

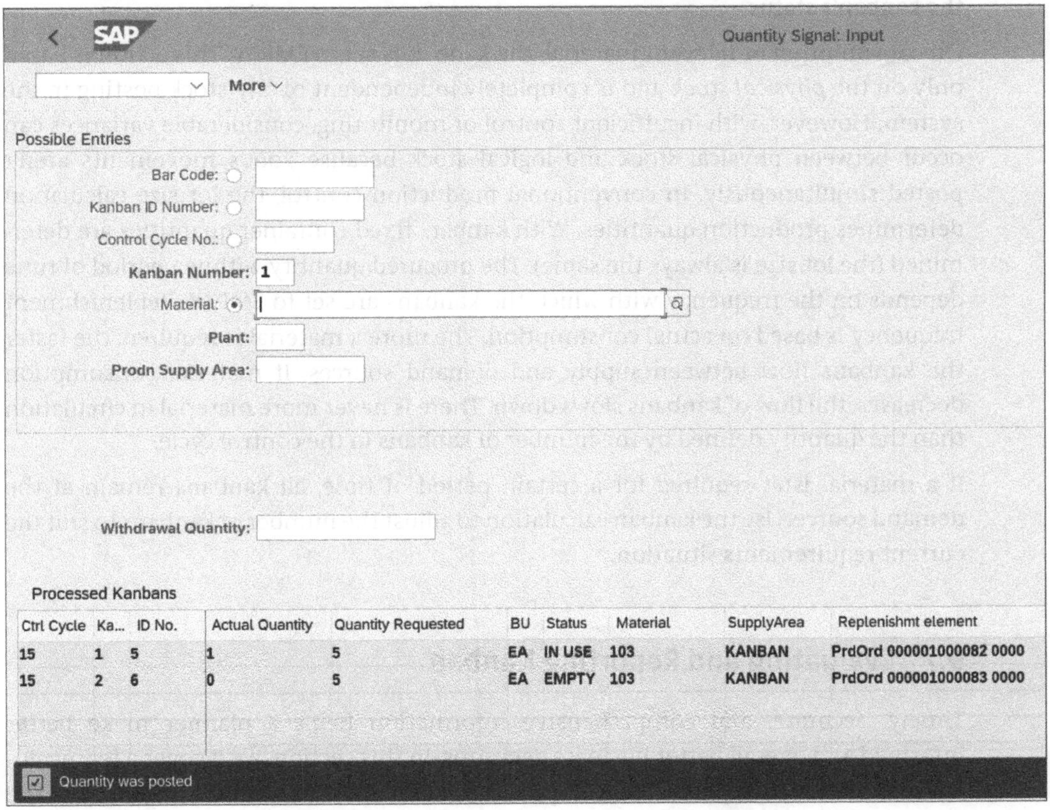
Quantity Signal: Input
More
Possible Entries
Bar Code:
Kanban ID Number:
Control Cycle No.:
Kanban Number: 1
Material:
Plant:
Prodn Supply Area:
Withdrawal Quantity:
Processed Kanbans
Ctrl Cycle Ka... ID No. Actual Quantity Quantity Requested BU Status Material SupplyArea Replenishmt element
15 1 5 1 5 EA IN USE 103 KANBAN PrdOrd 000001000082 0000
15 2 6 0 5 EA EMPTY 103 KANBAN PrdOrd 000001000083 0000
Quantity was posted

Figure 9.52 Kanban Quantity Signal

In this way, the system continuously rotates kanban statuses **EMPTY**, **WAIT**, and **FULL** for two kanbans using quantity signals.

Tips and Tricks

With kanban, it's possible for the system to automatically update statuses and quantities. However, due to human error, such updates often need adjustment. To make adjustments, use Transaction PK21 or follow menu path **Logistics • Production Planning • Production • Kanban • Control • Kanban Signal • Manual Entry**.

9.6.8   Logical Stock and Physical Stock

Setting a kanban to **EMPTY** doesn't lead to a goods issue posting. In general, the requested replenishment order is confirmed and kanban materials are backflushed simultaneously (goods issuance for components). The backflush has no influence on the kanban's status.

On consumption of relevant material, the kanban is set to **EMPTY**. This action is based only on the *physical stock* and is completely independent of any stock posting in the system. However, with insufficient control or monitoring, considerable variances can occur between physical stock and logical stock because goods movements aren't posted simultaneously. In conventional production control, the lot size calculation determines production quantities. With kanban, fixed container quantities are determined (the lot size is always the same). The procured quantity within a period of time depends on the frequency with which the kanbans are set to **EMPTY**. Replenishment frequency is based on actual consumption. The more a material is required, the faster the kanbans flow between supply and demand sources. If material consumption decreases, the flow of kanbans slows down. There is never more material in circulation than the quantity defined by the number of kanbans in the control cycle.

If a material isn't required for a certain period of time, all kanbans remain at the demand source. Use the kanban calculation to adjust the number of kanbans to suit the current requirements situation.

9.7   Evaluating and Reporting Kanban

Timely, accurate, and comprehensive information helps a planner make better informed and overall better business decisions. In this section, we'll cover a few evaluation and analysis reports that are specific to kanban. It's important to note that the kanban board only offers an overview of the kanbans at a certain point in time. The standard analyses in logistics information system (LIS) and in SAP Fiori apps provide tools for creating evaluations of kanban circulation for a specified interval.

9.7.1   Control Cycle and Kanban Evaluation

To access the control cycle and kanban evaluation, use Transaction PK18 or follow menu path **Logistics • Production Planning • Production • Kanban • Evaluations • Control Cycles/Kanbans**.

Figure 9.53 shows the initial screen of the control cycle and kanban evaluation. Enter the desired selection parameters so that the system only presents the information relevant for evaluation. Enter "1105" for **Plant** and "KANBAN" for **Prodn Supply Area**. Choose **Execute** (not shown), and the screen shown in Figure 9.54 appears.

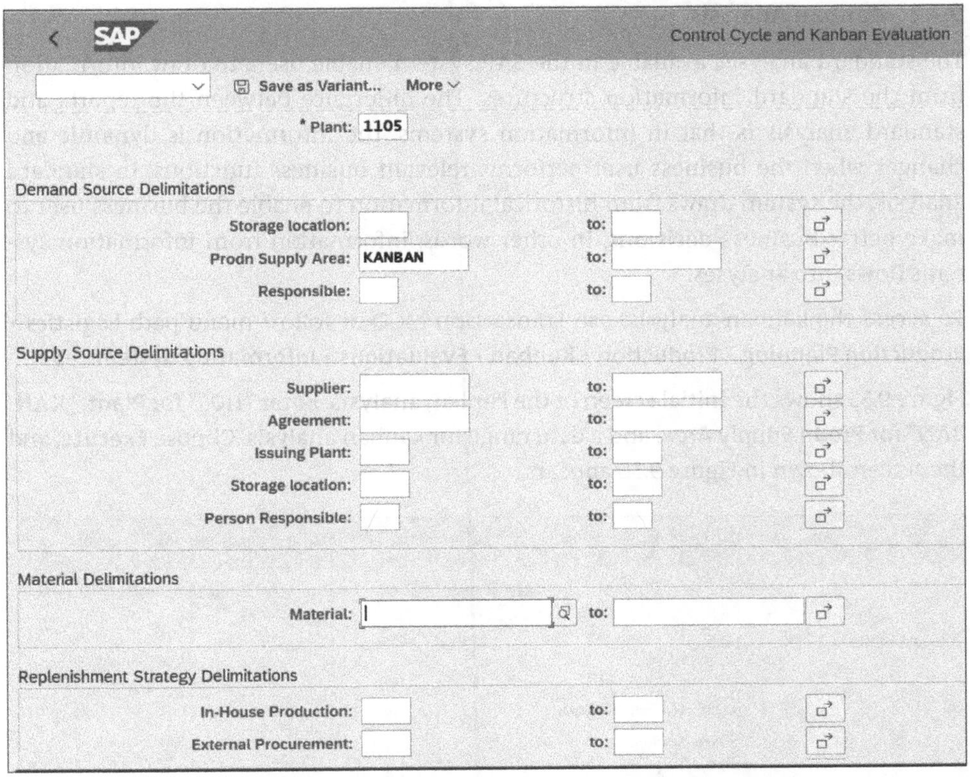

Figure 9.53 Initial Screen for Control Cycle and Kanban Evaluation

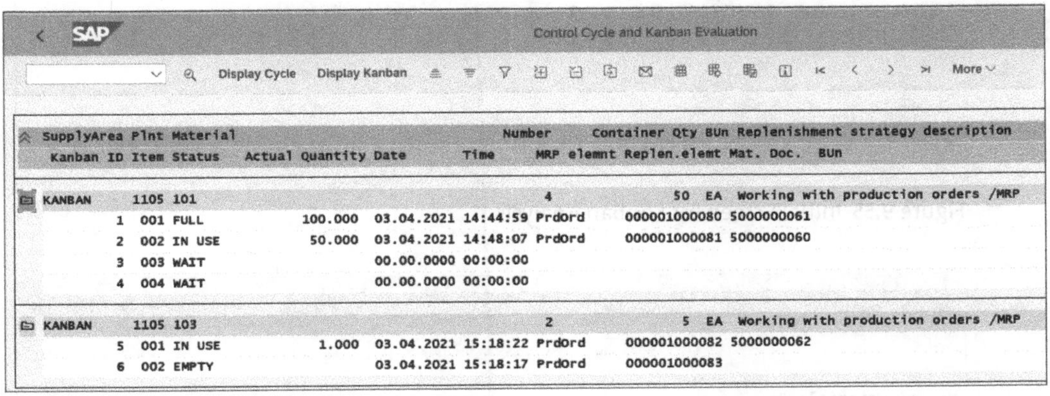

Figure 9.54 Control Cycle and Kanban Evaluation

Figure 9.54 shows the list of kanbans, their statuses, the replenishment elements (e.g., production order, purchase order, transfer posting), and material documents that were created as a result of any inventory posting.

9.7.2   Kanban Analysis

The standard analyses available in the SAP system enable users to draw information from the standard information structures. The difference between the reports and standard analysis is that in information systems, the information is dynamic and changes when the business user performs relevant business functions. In standard analysis, the system draws from historical information to enable the business user to make better business decisions. In other words, information from information systems flows into analyses.

To access the kanban analysis, use Transaction MCQ or follow menu path **Logistics • Production Planning • Production • Kanban • Evaluations • Information System**.

Figure 9.55 shows the initial screen of the kanban analysis. Enter "1105" for **Plant**, "KANBAN" **for Prodn Supply Area**, and a date range for kanban analysis. Choose **Execute**, and the screen shown in Figure 9.56 appears.

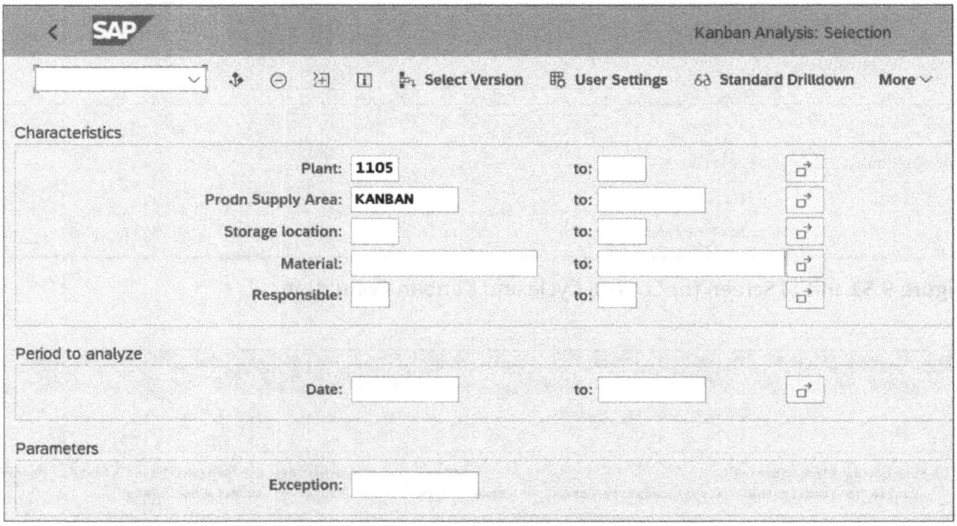

Figure 9.55 Initial Screen for Kanban Analysis

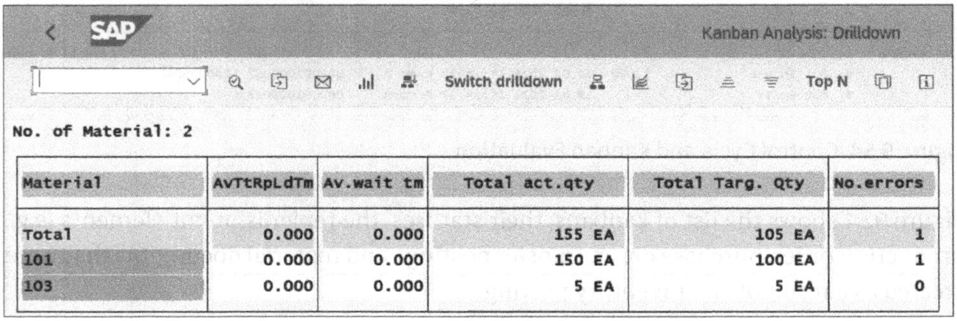

No. of Material: 2

Material	AvTtRpLdTm	Av.wait tm	Total act.qty	Total Targ. Qty	No.errors
Total	0.000	0.000	155 EA	105 EA	1
101	0.000	0.000	150 EA	100 EA	1
103	0.000	0.000	5 EA	5 EA	0

Figure 9.56 Kanban Analysis

Figure 9.56 shows some of the kanban key figures for plant 1105. As in all standard reports and analyses, a user can display or hide the available fields. Double-click a key figure, such as **Total Act. Qty**, and the screen shown in Figure 9.57 appears.

Figure 9.57 shows all of the important kanban key figures associated with plant 1105. From various lead times to quantities to additional information, the kanban analysis has them all covered.

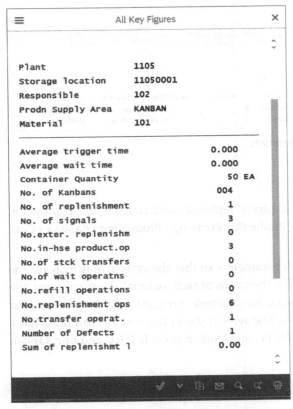

≡	All Key Figures	✕

Plant	1105
Storage location	11050001
Responsible	102
Prodn Supply Area	KANBAN
Material	101

Average trigger time	0.000
Average wait time	0.000
Container Quantity	50 EA
No. of Kanbans	004
No. of replenishment	1
No. of signals	3
No.exter. replenishm	0
No.in-hse product.op	3
No.of stck transfers	0
No.of wait operatns	0
No.refill operations	0
No.replenishment ops	6
No.transfer operat.	1
Number of Defects	1
Sum of replenishmt l	0.00

Figure 9.57 Key Figures for Kanban Replenishment

9.7.3   Delayed Replenishment Elements

It's important for a kanban planner to have visibility into kanbans facing delayed replenishment so that necessary alerts or actions can be implemented to prevent supply chain disruptions. The evaluation of delayed replenishment should provide not only the necessary visibility but also the option to issue timely alerts.

To evaluate or issue alerts for delayed replenishment elements, use Transaction PKAL or follow menu path **Logistics • Production Planning • Production • Kanban • Evaluations • Delayed Replenishment Elements**.

On the initial screen that appears, enter the plant, the delivery date (and the time), and other selection parameters in the relevant fields so that the system displays the desired information. If needed, select the **Trigger Alerts** checkbox to enable the system to issue alerts for all delayed kanbans.

Choose **Execute**, and the screen shown in Figure 9.58 appears. In this example, at least two kanbans are awaiting replenishment. The kanbans' statuses are set to **2** (container empty, with replenishment).

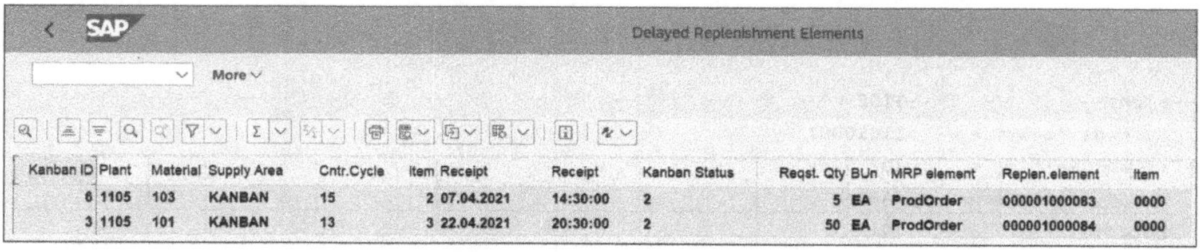

Kanban ID	Plant	Material	Supply Area	Cntr.Cycle	Item	Receipt	Receipt	Kanban Status	Reqst. Qty	BUn	MRP element	Replen.element	Item
6	1105	103	KANBAN	15	2	07.04.2021	14:30:00	2	5	EA	ProdOrder	000001000083	0000
3	1105	101	KANBAN	13	3	22.04.2021	20:30:00	2	50	EA	ProdOrder	000001000084	0000

Figure 9.58 Delayed Replenishment Elements

9.7.4 Kanban Plant Overview

To get a plant-wide overview of the kanbans' replenishment statuses, use Transaction PK11 or follow menu path **Logistics • Production Planning • Production • Kanban • Evaluations • Plant Overview.**

On the initial screen, enter selection parameters so that the system only displays the information needed. Figure 9.59 shows the status of each material, the supply area, the number of kanbans, and their statuses. For example, for material 101, there are four kanbans, each with a quantity of five. The system shows that one kanban (25%) has a **WAIT** status, one kanban (25%) is **EMPTY**, one kanban (25%) is **FULL**, and one kanban (25%) is **IN USE.**

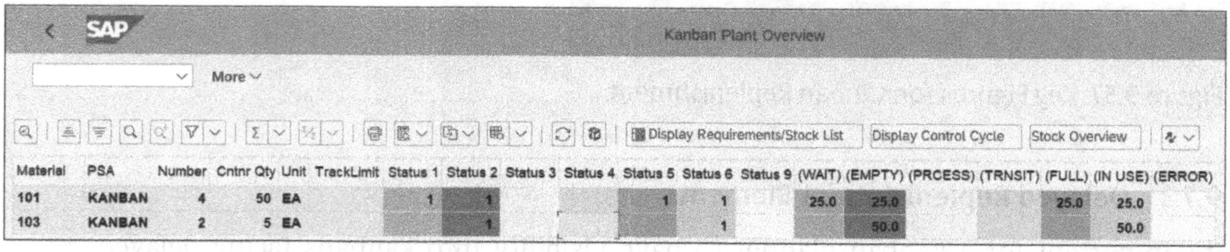

Material	PSA	Number	Cntnr Qty	Unit	TrackLimit	Status 1	Status 2	Status 3	Status 4	Status 5	Status 6	Status 9	(WAIT)	(EMPTY)	(PRCESS)	(TRNSIT)	(FULL)	(IN USE)	(ERROR)
101	KANBAN	4	50	EA		1	1			1	1		25.0	25.0			25.0	25.0	
103	KANBAN	2	5	EA			1				1			50.0				50.0	

Figure 9.59 Kanban Plant Overview

Figure 9.60 shows the Set Kanban Container Status app. This app can also be used to update the status of various kanbans. To do so, place the cursor in the **Enter Barcode** field; in the ensuing dropdown, choose from a list of all the available kanbans. After the relevant selection, the right-hand side of the screen will enable the user to make the desired changes or updates, such as changing from one status to another. Once the entries are successfully saved, they'll appear in the **Saved** tab, as shown in Figure 9.60.

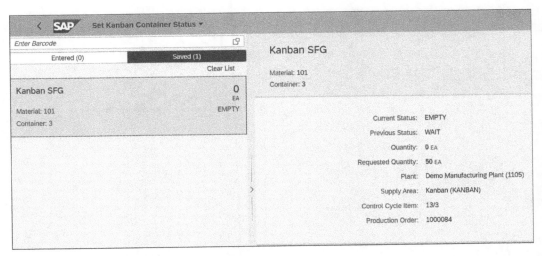

Figure 9.60 Set Kanban Container Status App

In addition, the Schedule Kanban Control Cycle Status Change app can be used to schedule regular updates to the statuses of various kanbans without manual entries.

9.8   Summary

Implementing kanban isn't restricted only to the production process; it can be implemented in procurement, stock transfer, and interplant transfer processes. In this chapter, we covered the kanban configuration that needs to be in place so that configured objects can be assigned to the master data. The entire production process using kanban was discussed, including the use of the Kanban Board app. We also discussed handling kanban errors, as well as kanban evaluation and reporting.

The next chapter is on batch management.

Chapter 10
Batch Management

*Batch management is an important part of a company's ability to pro-
cure, produce, store, and sell material. The batch defines a quantity of
material by characteristics unique to that batch. Those characteristics
determine how the material in that batch is used, sold, or moved.*

Certain material can be defined in SAP as being batch-managed. A batch is a quantity of
material that represents a homogeneous unit with unique specifications. The batch of
material may refer to a quantity of chemical that is produced in one process or a quantity of bottles of water that were filled on a certain filling line from a specific tank. There
are many ways in which a batch can be defined. In SAP, the batch is used to identify
units of material as they move through the system. The batch can have specific characteristics that enable it to be identified and used within the production planning (PP)
functionality. This chapter describes the processes involved in creating and changing a
batch and the process of batch determination. The first section gives an overview of the
batch and how it's used in industry.

We'll start out this chapter by covering the configuration settings needed to start using
the batch management functionality in the SAP system. After configuration, we cover
the requisite master data, followed by the business processes associated with batch
management, such as manually creating a batch master and how the system automatically creates the batch master during various business transactions. We'll then discuss
specialized but important batch management topics, such as automatic batch determination, batch derivation, and shelf-life expiration of batches. The chapter will conclude
with some important batch management reports, including the Batch Information
Cockpit (BIC).

10.1 Batch Management Overview

The definition of a batch differs among companies, industries, and countries. For
example, in the pharmaceutical industry, strict guidelines and regulations determine
what a batch is. These regulations on batches and batch control include the ANSI/ISA-
88 standard and the Food and Drug Administration (FDA) 21 CFR Part 11 specifications
in the United States.

Although there is no one exact definition of a batch, the following definition from ExxonMobil Aviation may help: "A batch is the specific quantity of a material produced in a single manufacturing process, i.e., under the same conditions, thus featuring identical properties. Each batch of material is given a batch number. Each batch of a material is tested with regard to relevant characteristics to ensure it meets the values or within the range for those characteristics."

A second definition of a batch is from Marathon Oil Company, and it significantly differs from other definitions: "A batch is a shipment of a single product that is handled through the pipeline without mixing with preceding or following shipments."

This third definition of a batch is from the Hawaiian Coffee Association:

> *A batch refers to a quantity of coffee coming to the roaster. Quantities of the same coffee arriving at different times would be viewed as separate batches. Changes from batch to batch—even of the same variety of bean—must be detected by the roaster if he is to produce coffees that are consistently the same.*

Whatever the definition, the fact is that the batch has to be identified by a batch record. This can be as simple as identifying bags of coffee beans as they arrive at the plant or as complex as identifying a batch by numerous qualifying characteristics to ensure quality and safety.

A batch of material can either be purchased from a vendor or produced internally. The need to manage materials by batch has been discussed; however, in SAP, the material must be identified as batch-relevant.

The identification of a batch record is especially important for the pharmaceutical industry due to the regulations set down by the FDA in the United States and other regulatory bodies across the world, such as the Drugs Controller General of India (DCGI), Bundesgesundheitsamt (BGA) in Germany, Health Canada, and the Medicines and Healthcare Products Regulatory Agency (MHRA) in the United Kingdom.

These regulatory bodies are primarily interested in public safety. Regulations such as FDA 21 CFR Part 11 in the United States are aimed at improving the efficiency of quality control and the quality assurance process. Each batch produced has to be quality tested, with the results stored electronically against the batch number.

The most critical use of the batch number in the pharmaceutical industry is for product recall. The batch number also can be used as the tracking device for companies in case of subsequent errors or contamination. Manufacturers publish product recalls every day, but for the pharmaceutical industry, product recalls can save lives.

A pharmaceutical company can voluntarily recall a product. If the company finds that a result from a test on a batch was incorrect, putting the batch out of tolerance, then the product made from that batch could be hazardous.

The errors could go all the way back to the vendor, if any of the material was purchased. If a vendor informs the company that a batch of purchased material was out of tolerance, then this batch must be traced through the production process to find all finished goods batches that may have used components or ingredients from the faulty batch.

In the United States, the FDA has the power to request that a company initiate a recall when it believes that a drug violates the Federal Food, Drug, and Cosmetic Act. A recall will be requested when the FDA concludes the following:

- A drug that has been distributed presents a risk of illness or injury or gross consumer deception.
- The manufacturer or distributor hasn't recalled the drug.
- FDA action is necessary to protect the public health.

In a recall, the manufacturer informs the retailer, wholesaler, or even consumer about how to identify the batch number on the product and which batch numbers are a part of the recall.

Let's begin with the configuration basics of batch management.

10.2 Batch Level and Batch Status Management

In the following sections, we'll follow a step-by-step approach for the configuration steps required to set up batch management in the SAP system.

10.2.1 Define the Batch Level

The batch can be defined at different levels, but by default it's defined at the plant level. At the beginning of an SAP implementation project, a materials management (MM) consultant helps the company decide the batch level at which it requires batch monitoring and reporting.

Use the following guidelines to determine that batch numbers are unique at the following three levels:

- **Plant and material combination level**
  In this level, the plant and material combination have unique batch numbers. Different material in the same plant can be assigned the same batch number, and the same material in different plants can also be assigned the same batch number. In this given context, the material is transferable from one plant to another, and although the batch number is the same, the specification of the destination batch will remain unchanged.
- **Material number level**
  As the batch numbers are created at the material level, the same batch numbers can be used for other material as well. After setting the batch level as the material in the system, a material can have the same batch number even though the materials are

in different plants with the same specifications. The same batch number can be reassigned for other materials with a different specification.

- **Client level**
  The batch level is set at the client level, which is the highest level. The same batch number can't be used for different material or different plants. The batch number assigned is rather unique and can be assigned only once; thus, every material will always have a new or different batch number.

The system's default setting is the plant level. As mentioned earlier, this can be customized to the batch level as needed. However, it's important to note that while switching to a higher level is always possible, lowering the batch level is only possible from the client level to the material level. This is because the batch data is organized so that it has to be converted whenever it's switched to another batch level.

To define the batch level, follow these steps:

1. Go to **SAP IMG · Logistics—General · Batch Management · Specify Batch Level and Activate Status Management**. Choose the batch level as just discussed (client, plant, or material level), and then save.

2. Choose **Batch Status Management** to activate batch management status in the client, select the **Active** checkbox, and then save.

3. Choose **Plants with Batch Status Management** and set the **Batch Status Management** checkbox in the resulting list for those plants where batch status management has to be active. Select the checkboxes and save.

4. Choose **Initial Status of a New Batch**, then specify which initial new batches are to be assigned for each *material type* and check the **Initial Status** box for each material type that will be batch-managed.

10.2.2 Batch Number Assignment

In this step, define the batch number range and assignments. To do so, follow menu path, **SAP IMG · Logistics—General · Batch Management · Batch Number Assignment · Activate Internal Batch Number Assignment**.

In the resulting screen, select the **Active** radio button to activate the internal batch number assignment. It's also possible to define whether internal batch number assignment is allowed for GRs that have an account assignment via **SAP IMG · Logistics—General · Batch Management · Batch Number Assignment · Internal Batch Number Assignment for Assigned Goods Receipt**.

In the next step, define the number ranges for internal batch number assignment by following menu path **SAP IMG · Logistics—General · Batch Management · Batch Number Assignment · Maintain Internal Batch Number Assignment Range**.

In the standard SAP system, you can set the number range object BATCH_CLT, and the number range 01 from 0000000001 to 9999999999 has been defined.

Similar to the internal batch number assignment, you can assign a number range for external number assignment. Follow menu path **SAP IMG · Logistics—General · Batch Management · Batch Number Assignment · Maintain Number Range for External Batch Number Assignment**.

Maintain the external number range by clicking the **Number Ranges** button and then the **Change Intervals** button. Here, use the already defined number range or create a new number range by clicking the **Inset Interval** button. Enter the number (**No.**), **From number**, and **To number**, and then click **Save**.

> **Note**
>
> SAP enhancement SAPLNOIZ can be used for internal batch number assignment. This enhancement comprises two function module exits to define number ranges or templates for batch numbers:
>
> - **EXI_SAPLV01Z_001**
>   This exit is used to replace the number range object and/or interval proposed with its own number range object by the system and/or interval. It's also used to stop the system from assigning an internal number based on the material or plant. This exit can be used to stop the dialog box from appearing.
> - **EXIT_SAPLV01Z_002**
>   This exit helps assign its own number or even change the number assigned by the system.

10.2.3 Creation of New Batches in the Production Process

This configuration step is how the system creates new batches for process/process orders. To define the new batch creation for process/process orders, follow menu path **SAP IMG · Logistics—General · Batch Management · Creation of New Batches · Define Batch Creation for Production Order/Process Order**, or use Transaction CORW.

Make specific settings in batch management for the existing production control profiles. Choose the production control profile for making the settings by selecting the required option (see Figure 10.1) for automatic batch creation:

- Automatic batch creation at order creation
- Automatic batch creation at order release
- No automatic batch creation in production/process order

Then select the batch classification option in the **Batch Classification** field. In addition, select the **Extended Classification** checkbox so that more batch-specific functionalities are available.

The production scheduling profile (**PS Profile**), which in this example is **101**, is then assigned in the **Work Scheduling** view of a material master.

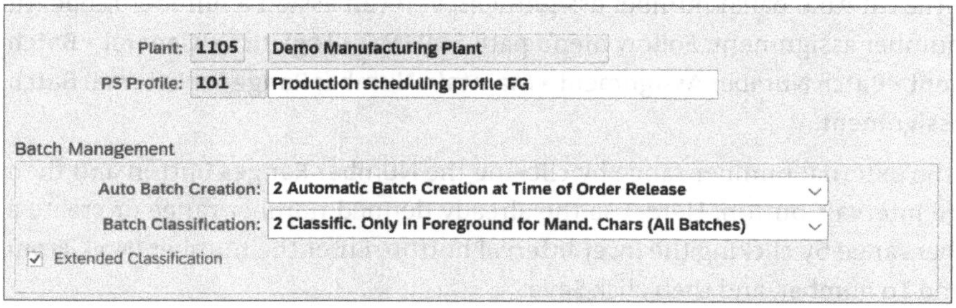

Plant:	**1105**	Demo Manufacturing Plant
PS Profile:	**101**	Production scheduling profile FG

Batch Management

Auto Batch Creation:	2 Automatic Batch Creation at Time of Order Release
Batch Classification:	2 Classific. Only in Foreground for Mand. Chars (All Batches)
☑ Extended Classification	

Figure 10.1 Batch Management in Production Process

10.2.4   Batch Creation for Goods Movement

The new batch creation settings for movement types can be defined. To do so, follow menu path **SAP IMG** · **Logistics—General** · **Batch Management** · **Creation of New Batches** · **Define Batch Creation for Goods Movements**.

For instance, when batch numbers aren't determined by the system automatically, the user may want to assign a batch number for goods receipt (GR) on a production or a process order (movement type 101) manually. To achieve this, choose the **Automatic/Manual without Check** option for movement 101, as shown in Figure 10.2.

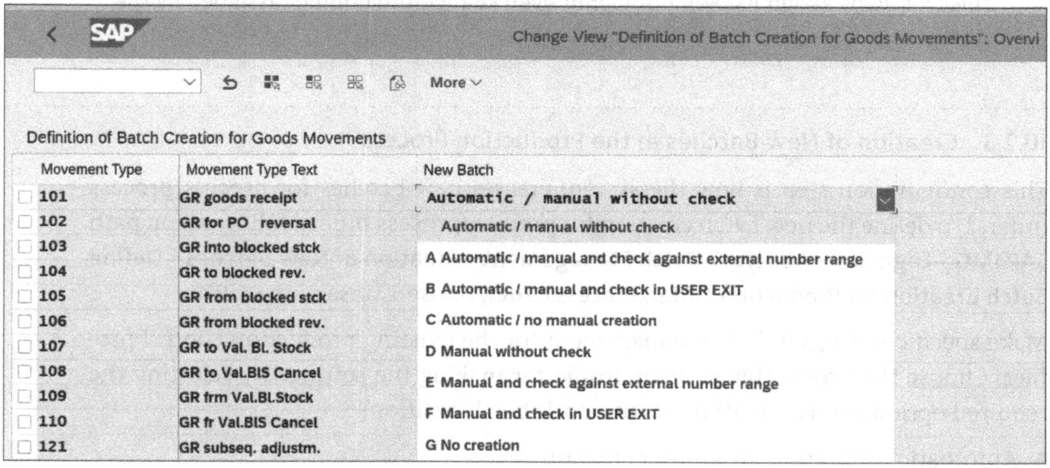

Change View "Definition of Batch Creation for Goods Movements": Overvi

Definition of Batch Creation for Goods Movements

Movement Type	Movement Type Text	New Batch
☐ 101	GR goods receipt	Automatic / manual without check
☐ 102	GR for PO reversal	Automatic / manual without check
☐ 103	GR into blocked stck	A Automatic / manual and check against external number range
☐ 104	GR to blocked rev.	B Automatic / manual and check in USER EXIT
☐ 105	GR from blocked stck	
☐ 106	GR from blocked rev.	C Automatic / no manual creation
☐ 107	GR to Val. Bl. Stock	D Manual without check
☐ 108	GR to Val.Bl5 Cancel	E Manual and check against external number range
☐ 109	GR frm Val.Bl.Stock	
☐ 110	GR fr Val.Bl5 Cancel	F Manual and check in USER EXIT
☐ 121	GR subseq. adjustm.	G No creation

Figure 10.2 Batch Management with Movement Type

For each material type, also define whether a new batch can be created via the batch master creation transaction (Transaction MSC1N). To do so, follow menu path **SAP IMG** · **Logistics—General** · **Batch Management** · **Creation of New Batches** · **Define Initial Creation of Data for Batch Master Transactions**. If a company wants to assign the batch numbers only automatically by the system and doesn't want the option to assign them manually, especially for finished products, then choose **Automatic/No Manual Creation** for material type FERT.

This ends the basic configuration settings needed for batch management. In the next section, we discuss how to set up master data in batch management.

10.3   Master Data in Batch Management

A first step when working with batch management is to identify the material that needs to be batch-managed and then update the material master record by setting the batch management requirement. Let's go over the different master data management processes and steps specific to batch management in the following sections.

10.3.1   Activate Batch Management in the Material Master

In the SAP system, batch master records always depend on material master records. Therefore, the first step is to define batch management requirements in the material master. Go to Transaction MM01 (Create Material Master), enter all of the required details, and select the **Batch Mgmt Rqt** (batch management requirement) checkbox to denote that the material has to be handled in batches (see Figure 10.3). The following views of the material master contain the checkbox for batch management:

- **Sales and Distribution**
- **General Plant Data**
- **Purchasing**
- **Work Scheduling**

All views are the same, and any changes/updates in one view appear in all views.

> **Tips and Tricks**
>
> The indicator for the material can be changed from batch-managed to non-batch-managed only if there has been no stock for the current period and the previous period. This is to allow for transactions posting of batch-managed materials in any previous period.
>
> In the SAP system, batches are posted *for* a material, so the batch master records are always dependent on material master records. If there is a mismatch of subjected material and batch requirement, all stocks need to be posted out from the previous fiscal year, the previous period, and the current period. To do this, reset the **Batch Mgmt Rqt** checkbox and repost the stock in batches into the system.
>
> Similarly, it's possible to cancel the batch requirement for any material that a company doesn't want to batch-manage anymore. If there's a need to reorganize the batch

master records, then it's mandatory to reset the **Batch Mgmt Rqt** checkbox to empty, post the required batch requirement, and then post the stock back into the SAP system using Transaction MIGO.

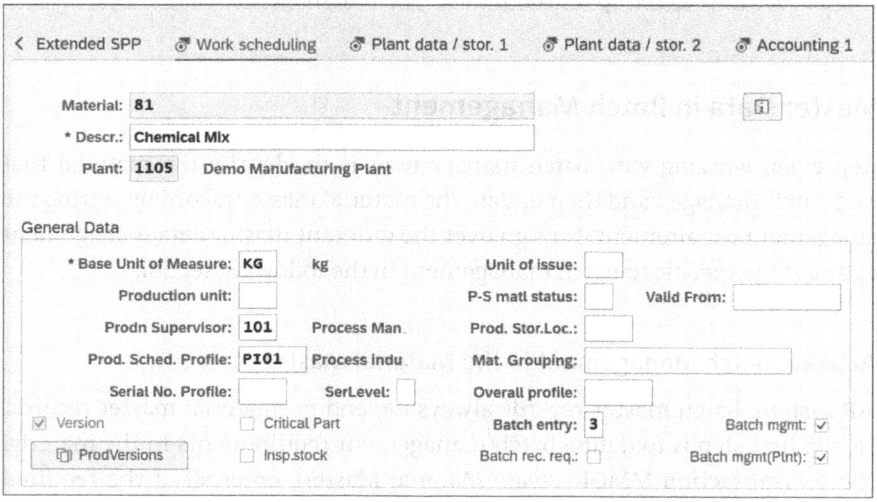

Figure 10.3 Activation of Batch Management in Material Master

10.3.2   Batch Classification

To differentiate batches of material depending on their individual properties, characteristics are used to define the properties. For example, the paint industry uses color, coverage, and viscosity as characteristics to classify different batches. The cold-roll coil industry uses finish, thickness, and quality to classify different batches.

These characteristics are created in the SAP system and assigned to the materials. The same classification concept as in materials classification is applied in defining batch classification.

Say that a company that deals with various types of paints wants to capture the characteristics of paint: shine, color, and viscosity. A class has to be created with the characteristics for coverage, color, and viscosity wavelength. This class has to be assigned to a material. Every time a new batch is created for the material, the characteristic values need to be entered. Let's briefly define characteristics and their assignment to a class specific to batch management.

Define Characteristics

First, create the various characteristics for the materials, such as thickness, viscosity, density, and so on. We've discussed the characteristics and classes in detail in Chapter 7, so we won't go into the same detail here.

To create characteristics, follow menu path **SAP Menu · Cross-Application Components · Classification System · Master Data · Characteristics**, or use Transaction CT04.

In the resulting screen, enter the **Characteristic** name, and click **Create**. Enter a description as shown in Figure 10.4. The **Status** field has **In Preparation**, **Locked**, and **Released** options. A **Released** status means that the characteristic can be used; a status of **In Preparation** or **Locked** means that it can't be used.

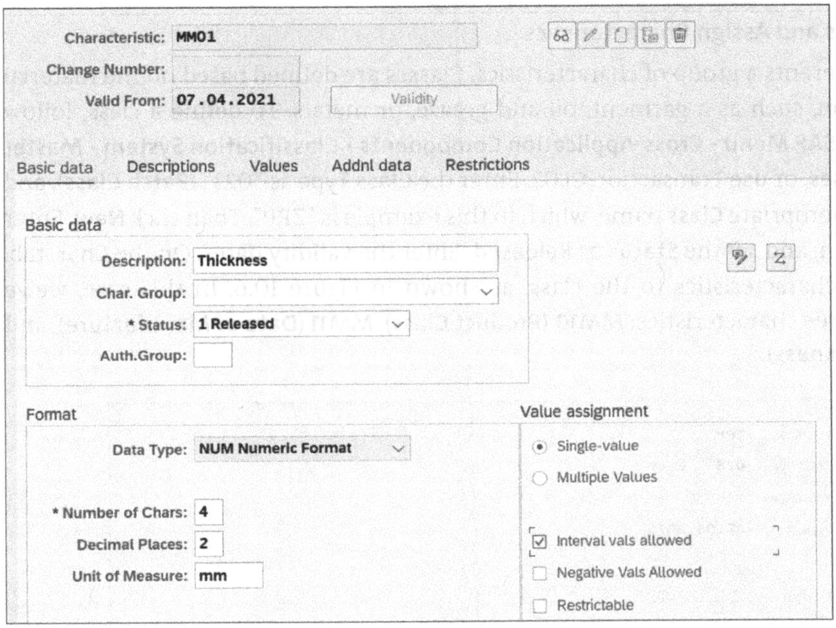

Figure 10.4 Characteristic

In the **Value Assignment** area, select either **Single-Value** or **Multiple Values**. The **Single-Value** radio button specifies that only one value can be assigned to this characteristic; the **Multiple Values** radio button is used when more than one value is possible.

Select the **Values** tab and enter the possible values for this characteristic, as shown in Figure 10.5.

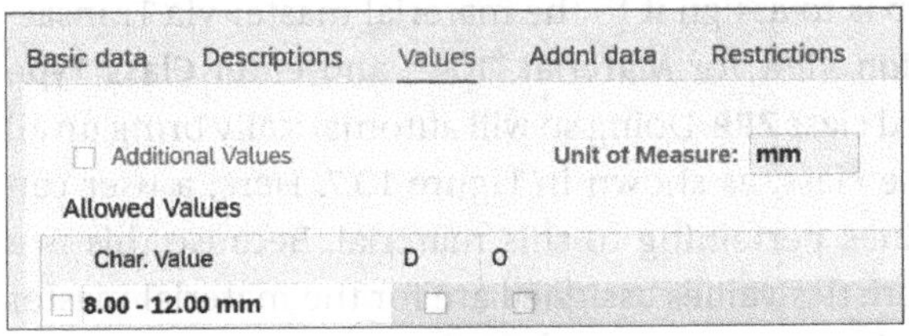

Figure 10.5 Characteristic Values

The **Additional Values** checkbox allows a user to enter characteristic values that aren't defined. After the values are defined, save the characteristic. In this example, we've set the **Thickness** characteristic, and the value of thickness can be within a range of 8.00 to 12.00 mm.

Now that a characteristic is created, the next step to assign existing characteristics to the class, which is explained in the following section.

Define Class and Assign Characteristics

A class represents a group of characteristics. Classes are defined based on the material classification, such as a garment, oil and grease, or metals. To define a class, follow menu path **SAP Menu • Cross-Application Components • Classification System • Master Data • Classes**, or use Transaction CL02. Enter the **Class Type** as "023" (**Batch Class**), and fill in the appropriate **Class** name, which in this example is "ZPP". Then click **New**. Enter a description, and set the **Status** as **Released**. Enter the validity dates. On the **Char.** tab, assign the characteristics to the class, as shown in Figure 10.6. In this case, we've assigned three characteristics: **MM10 (Product Class)**, **MM11 (Date of Manufacture)**, and **MM01 (Thickness)**.

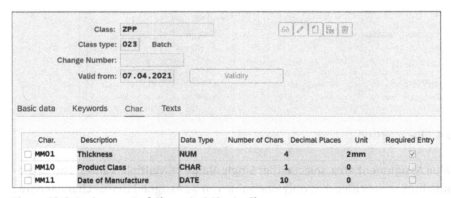

Figure 10.6 Assignment of Characteristics to Class

10.3.3   Assigning Classification in the Material Master

After a class is defined, the next step is to assign it to the material master via Transaction MM01. Choose the **Classification** view for **Material** "104", and enter **Class Type** "023" to assign the previously created class **ZPP**. Doing so will automatically bring up all three characteristics assigned to the class, as shown in Figure 10.7. Here, a user can maintain specific characteristic values pertaining to this material. Because this is a master data step, note that characteristics values assigned are for the material master only and *not* for batches of a material.

With requisite master data created for batch management, the next section discusses the business processes associated with batch management.

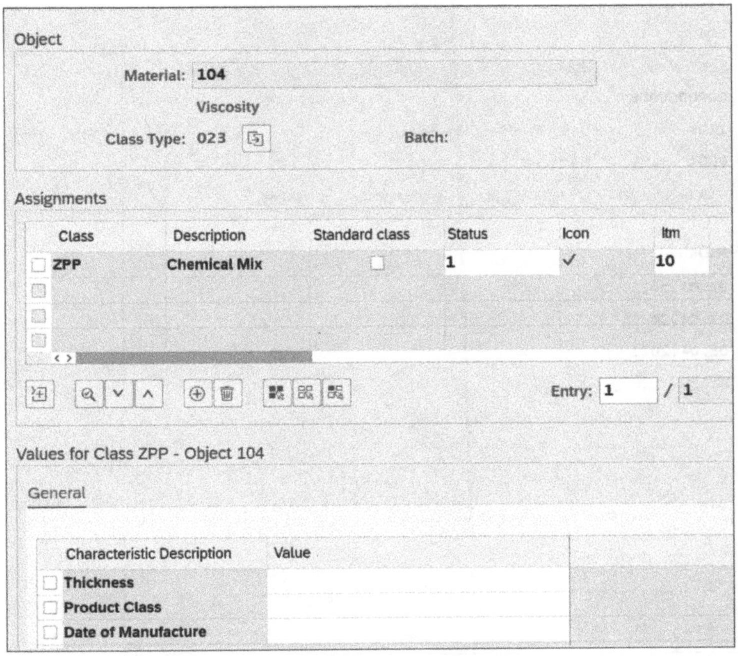

Figure 10.7 Classification View of Material Master

10.4   Business Processes of Batch Management

In the following sections, we'll cover the business processes of batch management in the SAP system. Some of these business processes include manually or automatically creating a batch, changing or deleting a batch, using the classification function in a batch, and attaching documents to a batch.

10.4.1   Create a Batch Master Manually

A batch master record for a material can be created manually or automatically in the background by the system when goods are received for the first time. A manually created batch of a material can then be assigned during stock posting, such as during GR of a material from the procurement or production processes.

To create batch master records manually, follow menu path **SAP Menu • Logistics • Central Functions • Batch Management • Batch Create**, or use Transaction MSC1N (see Figure 10.8).

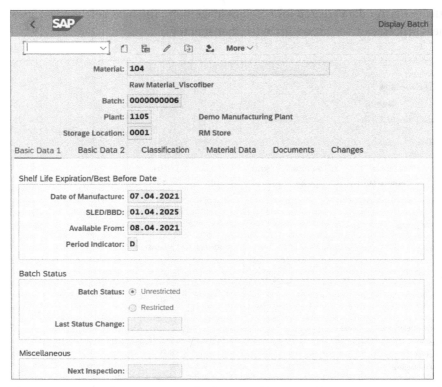

Figure 10.8 Manually Creating Batch of Material

Enter a material, plant, and storage location to create a batch master record. If an internal number range is defined, then the system will create the batch number automatically after ⌈Enter⌉ is pressed. The data in a material master applies in general for all the batches assigned to this master record. By contrast, a batch master record contains data that uniquely identifies the corresponding batch and characterizes the unit as one that can't be reproduced.

Various types of information are stored in the batch master record. Some can be updated manually, and some can be updated automatically. We'll discuss some of the relevant information in different tabs in the following sections.

Basic Data 1

Important fields and checkboxes in the **Basic Data 1** tab shown in Figure 10.8 are as follows:

- **Date of Manufacture**
  The date when the batch was produced can be entered into this field. In some industries, this field is also used as the date the material was tested or retested. If a material is found to be still in tolerance after the shelf-life date has expired, the material

can be retested, and the date of the retest is entered into this field, in addition to a new **Shelf-Life Exp. Date**. It's recommended to check with clients to determine whether they need to use this field.

- **SLED/BBD**

  The **SLED/BBD** (shelf-life expiration date) field is the date on which the shelf-life of this batch will expire. The shelf-life of a product can vary between plants. This date can be used in the sales process, as customers may have set a requirement on the acceptable number of days of shelf-life remaining. Some companies use this field to indicate the date on which a batch needs to be retested. If the company has implemented the quality management (QM) functionality, then the system uses this field to see if the material's batch expiration is about to be reached so that the system can create a quality inspection lot for retesting the material.

- **Available From**

  This field indicates when the batch will be available. For example, if a material needs to remain in the quality inspection process for a certain number of days after testing, then the quality department can enter a date to inform other departments of when the batch is expected to be available.

- **Batch Status**

  These radio buttons allow the batch to be classified as having restricted or unrestricted use. If the **Unrestricted** option is set, then the batch has no restriction placed on its use. If the **Batch Restr** option is set, the batch is treated like blocked stock in planning but can be selected by batch determination if the search includes restricted-use batches.

  The **Batch Status** can be set to restricted from unrestricted by changing the checkbox in the batch record. A material document will be posted that shows the movement of stock between the two statuses.

- **Next Inspection**

  This date field allows the quality department to enter the date of the next quality inspection of the batch, if applicable to this material. This field is helpful when a company must retest a material's batch after every predefined period. This material retesting process is known as *recurring inspection*.

- **Vendor Batch**

  If the material is purchased, then the batch number assigned by the vendor can be added to the batch record. It's important to any product recall procedure that the vendor batch number is noted. The **Vendor Batch** field (not shown) allows a 15-character string to be entered.

Basic Data 2

In this tab, maintain the **Texts** and **Freely Definable Date** fields. There are six date fields. This is optional and only necessary if a user wants to use these dates somewhere in the process. The other fields on the screen are six date fields: **Date 1**, **Date 2**, and so on. These fields don't have any standard functionality. The six **Date** fields can be used for whatever purpose is defined by the client. For example, these fields could contain the dates on which the material was inspected by the quality department.

Classification

In this tab, use the class that was assigned to a material during material master classification, and maintain the characteristics values here by clicking the **New** button (not shown). After clicking the **New** button, maintain the values of all the characteristics listed based on the material class, as shown in Figure 10.9.

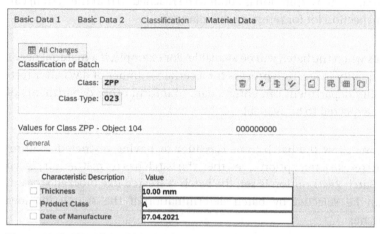

Figure 10.9 Classification Tab of Batch Master

Material Data

In this tab, use the information from the material master record. Clicking the **All Changes** icon will display the change history of the batch. This tab won't appear when a batch is created for the first time but will appear in change or display batch transaction (MSC2N and MSC3N respectively).

> **[+]** **Tips and Tricks**
>
> If there's also a business need to link documents to a batch, then a configuration step must be completed. Follow menu path **SAP IMG · Logistics—General · Batch Management · Batch Master · Activate Document Management for Batches**, or use Transaction ODOC.
>
> The configuration in Transaction ODOC is simply switching on the field to allow document management for batches. The options are **Active** and **Inactive**.

10.4.2   Changing a Batch

After the batch has been created, there may be occasion to amend the batch record, either to modify a characteristic or to add a new linked document. To change a batch record, follow menu path **SAP Menu • Logistics • Materials Management • Material Master • Batch • Change**, or use Transaction MSC2N.

The user can make changes to the batch record, but these changes are recorded and are available to review. The **Change Batch** screen has an extra tab in the change mode. This tab accesses a screen to view all changes made to the batch record. The **Changes** screen (refer to Figure 10.8) shows the changes made to the batch record. The information recorded includes the user who created and changed the record, as well as the fields that have been changed, including their values. This information is important to some companies because a strict audit record is needed to show compliance with federal or local regulations. In the pharmaceutical industry, companies manufacturing items that are to be consumed are under strict regulations from the FDA. Companies should at all times ensure that their record keeping is compliant with FDA regulations.

10.4.3   Deleting a Batch

There is no transaction used solely for deleting a batch, but a batch can be deleted through Transaction MSC2N.

Figure 10.8, shown earlier, shows the initial screen of the change batch transaction, which has a **Batch Deletion Flag** checkbox that can be set if the batch is to be deleted. However, setting the deletion flag doesn't immediately delete the batch. The checkbox allows the batch to be processed by an archiving program that will determine whether the batch can be deleted. If the batch can't be deleted, the deletion flag will remain until either the archiving program determines that the batch can be deleted or until the deletion flag is removed.

10.4.4   Automatic Creation of a Batch in Goods Movement

It's possible to define the automatic creation of batch numbers in the SAP system, whether for movement types or production and process orders. For instance, the system can be customized to automatically create unique batch numbers whenever goods are delivered against a process order. This means that every time goods with movement type 101 are received, the unique batch number for the material received is created by the system automatically.

Here we present an example of how the system automatically creates a batch master on GR with reference to a process order (movement type 101).

To receive goods with reference to a process order and via movement type 101, go to Transaction MIGO (see Figure 10.10). Enter the process order number "1000090" after selecting **Goods Receipt** followed by selecting **Order** from the two dropdowns located on the top-left side of the screen. In the item details, there's one more tab: **Batch**. Notice that the system has automatically created batch 16.

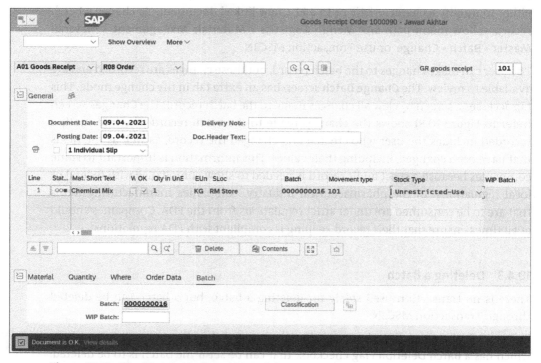

Figure 10.10 GR of Batch-Managed Material

Click the **Classification** button in the **Batch** tab in Figure 10.10 to enter the values of the characteristics, as shown in Figure 10.11.

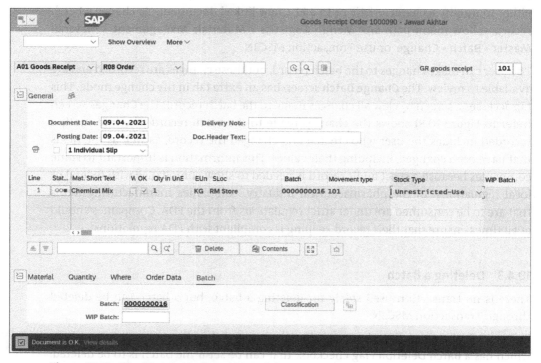

Figure 10.11 Classification View of Batch during GR

On the screen shown in Figure 10.11, maintain characteristic values such as **Product Class**, **Date of Manufacture**, and **Thickness**.

10.4.5 Stock Overview

The stock overview report can be used to view how the stock is kept under different batches. Use Transaction MMBE, enter the plant code and material number, and execute the report. The stock overview of a material and the respective batch numbers, such as batch number 16 that was just received in the previous step, can be seen. Figure 10.12 shows batch 16 of material 81 with quantity 1.0 KG.

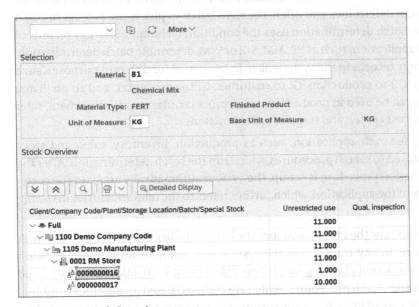

Figure 10.12 Stock Overview

When a batch-managed material needs to be issued out, and if there are multiple batches of the same material in stock, the system automatically lets the user choose the batch number from the material to be issued. If there's a business need to assign a batch number based on some strategy, the batch determination strategy should be configured. We cover the entire batch determination topic in the next section of this chapter.

Batch usage transactions can be used to track the batches and for analysis. Transaction MB56 will give the details of a batch where-used list. SAP also provides the BIC, a central tool for tracking batches, which is also discussed in this chapter.

10.5   Batch Determination

The batch determination process isn't unique to PP. The process is important in sales and distribution (SD), MM, and warehouse management as well. Batch determination uses strategy types, search strategies, and search procedures for a batch to be identified in the relevant area.

In a real-world scenario, a warehouse supervisor receives one material in a number of batches, and this will be kept in storage location stock or in warehouse storage bins. When the material needs to be issued out to production, a strategy needs to be in place for the system to choose different batches. Defining the strategy in the system by which the system determines and offers the right batch to pick is the process of batch determination. Batch determination uses the condition technique. Strategy records of the respective application, such as PP, MM, SD, or WM, determine batch determination. Different strategy records in the system have to be created for different purposes, such as goods issue (GI) to production, GI to customer, GI to cost center, and so on. Batch determination can be used in production order, process order, goods movement, sales order/delivery, cost center, and transfer order functions.

Configurations for each application, such as production, inventory, sales, and stock transfers, are stored in search procedures, which run the batch determination. After the batch determination procedure is set up, the system automatically accesses the corresponding entry of the application, which further refers to the relevant entries in configuration.

Figure 10.13 shows how the system searches the batch number using the batch determination procedure. In any transaction, the system will first determine the application area—PP and production planning for process industries (PP-PI), MM, WM, or SD—and then determine the search procedures, which are assigned based on different combinations ❶ ❷. In the case of PP or PP-PI, the system will determine the order type and plant from the transaction and then find a search procedure ❸ ❹. For MM, the system will find a search procedure based on movement type. For SD, the search procedure will be based on sales organization, distribution channel, division, and sales document type.

The search procedure helps the system determine the search type ❺. The search type helps to identify the condition types and condition tables ❻. The system will find the appropriate batch number based on the access sequence system.

In the following section, we start out with the necessary configuration steps required to set up automatic batch determination in the production process of PP-PI for process manufacturing (process order). However, the same logic and process steps we cover here can be used to set up automatic batch determination in other applications, such as PP (discrete manufacturing), MM, SD, and WM. These configuration steps are then followed by covering the necessary master data required for batch determination. Finally, we'll also show how the configuration and the master data setup eventually are reflected in the batch determination business process.

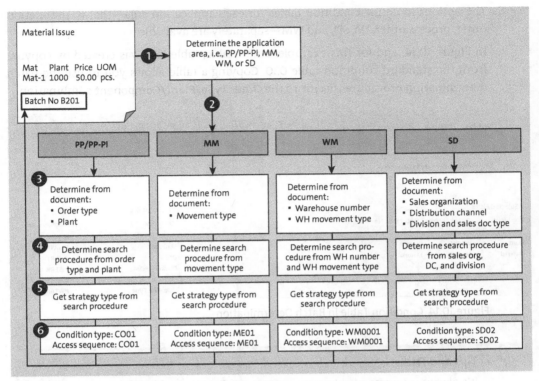

Figure 10.13 Batch Determination Flow in Logistics and Supply Chain

Next, let's perform the following configuration steps in their logical and sequential order.

10.5.1 Define Condition Tables

The batch determination condition table includes a number of fields for selection and to record and assign values to those fields.

There are five options for condition table creation, depending on which business process a company wants to use batch determination for:

- Production order (Transaction OPLB)
- Process order (Transaction OPLB)
- Inventory management (IM) (Transaction OMA1)
- SD (Transaction V/C7)
- WM (Transaction OMK4)

To define the condition table of a process order, follow menu path **SAP IMG · Logistic— General · Batch Management · Batch Determination and Check · Condition tables · Define Process Order Condition Tables**, or use Transaction OPLB.

The options to define condition tables for each application area—that is, production order, process order, IM, SD, and WM—separately are available.

In Figure 10.14, and for this example, a new table, table 550, was created by copying from the standard condition table 030. Copying a table allows you to use the batch determination procedure specific to the **Order Type/Plant/Component** combination.

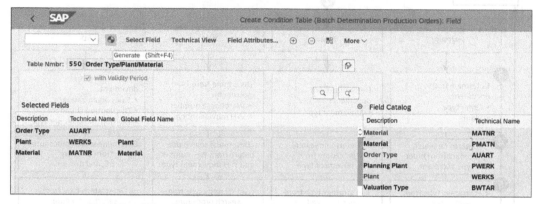

Figure 10.14 Condition Table in Batch Determination

[+] **Tips and Tricks**

It's always recommended to copy any new configuration object from an existing one and then make the desired changes to the newly configured object. Doing so not only saves time and effort but also reduces the chances of missing important configuration settings that will then be unable to give the desired results in transaction processing.

Figure 10.15 shows the newly created condition table 550, in which the three selected fields are **Order Type**, **Plant**, and **Material** (which is basically the component), as shown on the left-hand side of the figure.

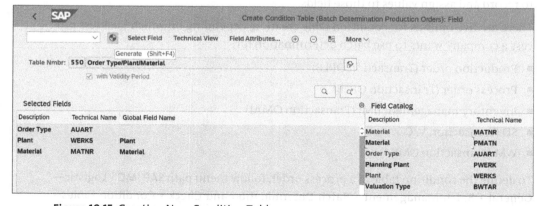

Figure 10.15 Creating New Condition Table

Choose additional fields from the catalog shown on the right-hand side of the same figure so that they too are available for selection during the batch determination procedure. For example, if the cursor is placed on **Valuation Type** from the field catalog and you click the **Select Field** button, then during the batch determination the system will only suggest batches of materials available with specific valuation types.

Choose **Generate**, and the system will create the condition table as shown in Figure 10.16. Here you can see the log generated on the successful creation of the new condition table 550.

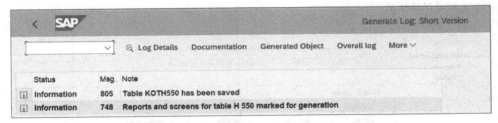

Figure 10.16 Log after Condition Table Creation

10.5.2   Define the Access Sequence

For each batch strategy type, there is a batch determination access sequence. This allows the batch strategy type to access the condition tables in the correct sequence. To define an access sequence for PP-PI, follow menu path **SAP IMG · Logistics—General · Batch Management · Batch Determination and Batch Check · Access Sequences · Define Process Order Access Sequences**.

Figure 10.17 shows the access sequence for a process order. Select the access sequence and choose **Edit**. Here, define the sequence of tables that the system should follow. For example, in Figure 10.17, the system will first search the **Order Type/Plant/Material** combination, then the **Order Type/Plant/Component** combination, and so on.

Dialog Structure	Access Sequence: **C001** OrdType/Plant/Material		
∨☐ **Access sequences**			
∨⬛ **Accesses**			
☐ **Fields**	Overview Accesses		
	No.	Table Number	Description
	☐ 5	550	Order Type/Plant/Material
	☐ 10	030	Order Type/Plant/Component

Figure 10.17 Access Sequence in Batch Determination

In the standard system for process orders, access sequences CO01 and CO02 are defined, just as in the standard SAP system for IM, and access sequences ME01 and ME02 are defined. And in the standard system for SD, access sequences SD01, SD02, and SD03 are defined. It's recommended to make a copy of the standard access sequences available and then make changes in the condition table sequences to meet any unique business requirements.

Here, select the standard access sequence **CO01** and make a copy of it by choosing **Copy As**. On the screen that appears, define the new access sequence as "ZPP" while confirming to copy all dependent entries from access sequence CO01 to ZPP.

Because this example uses the standard access sequence CO01, the previously created condition table 550 has been assigned (see Figure 10.18). The access sequence CO01 has three fields that the system will consider during batch determination: **Order Type**, **Plant**, and **Material**.

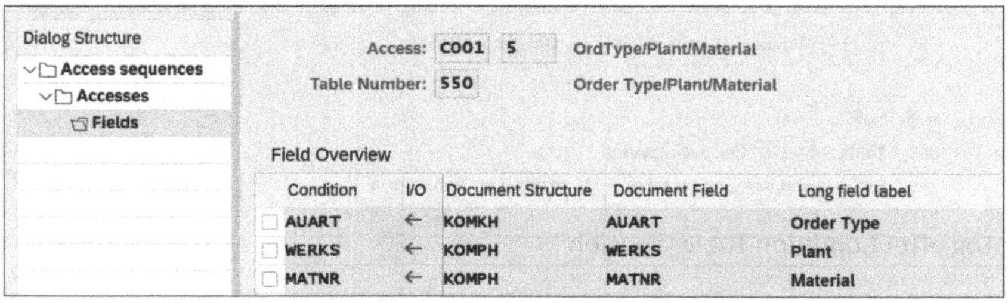

Figure 10.18 Newly Created Access Sequence CO01

10.5.3   Define Strategy Types

The *batch strategy type* is the specification that tells the system what type of criteria to use during the batch determination process. A batch strategy can be defined in the five areas already mentioned. Define the strategy types for each application area by following menu path **SAP IMG · Logistics—General · Batch Management · Batch Determination and Batch Check · Strategy Types · Define Process Order Strategy Types**. Choose the **New** button or copy the standard strategy type provided by SAP. It's recommended to copy the standard strategy type and make the required changes, then save the new strategy type. In this example, we created a new strategy CO03 and also assigned the previously configured access sequence CO01, as shown in Figure 10.19.

In Figure 10.19, we also assigned **Class Type 023** (**Batch**) and the previously created associated **Class ZPP**. This is the same class you created in the previous section for the batch determination processes, and you're now assigning it in the newly created strategy type CO03.

In the **Selection** area, there's an option to define the values of certain characteristics within a class. The values can be maintained by clicking the **Maint.** button. In addition, the following information is needed:

- **Selection Type**
  This field allows the user to determine how the batches are selected at the commencement of the batch selection. If the **Selection Type** field is left blank, then the system will display the batches that meet the selection criteria.

- **Sort Sequence**

   This field allows the user to choose a sort that will define how the batches are sorted if they're selected. **Sort Sequence** can be maintained on this screen if desired. Later in this section, we'll also cover how to create a sort sequence and assign it to a condition record.

- **Batch Split**

   This area contains the **No. of Splits** field that defines the number of batch splits that are allowed during the batch determination.

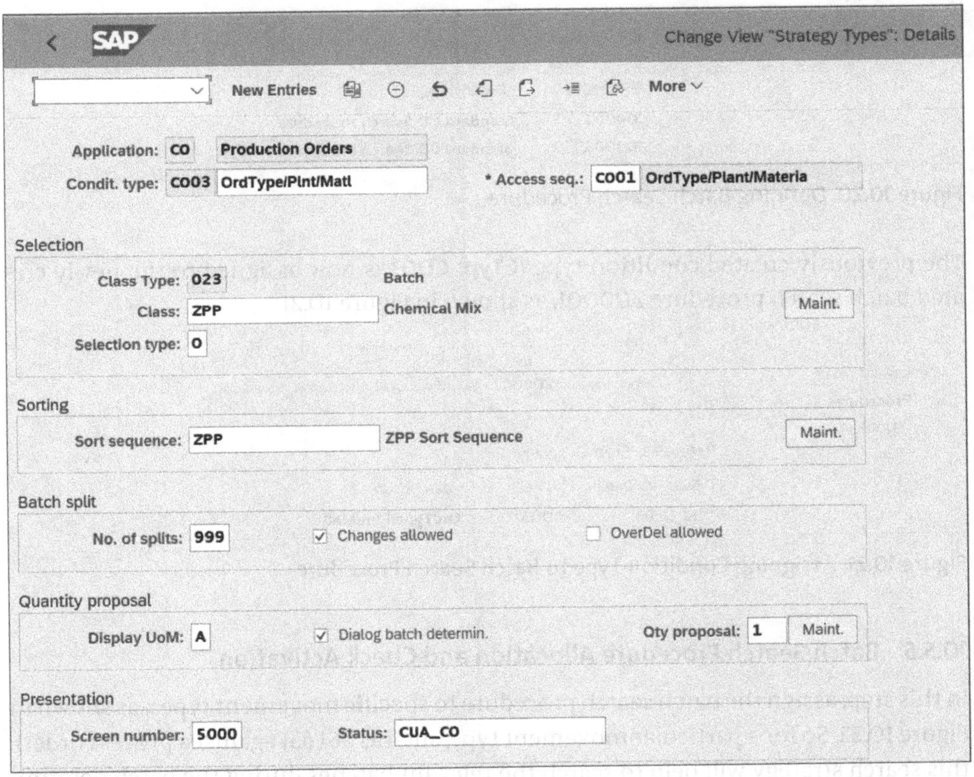

Figure 10.19 Strategy Type

10.5.4 Batch Search Procedure Definition

In this configuration activity, you'll define search procedures for batch determination in a process order. Follow menu path **SAP IMG · Logistics—General · Batch Management · Batch Determination and Batch Check · Batch Search Procedure Definition · Define Process Order Search Procedure**, or use Transaction OPLG (see Figure 10.20).

Choose **New Entries** to define the search procedure, or define it by copying the SAP-provided search procedure. As always, it's recommended to copy the standard procedure (so that any required settings aren't missed), make the required changes, and save the entries.

In Figure 10.20, we created a new batch search procedure ZC0001 by copying the standard procedure CO0001. After copying, select the newly created batch search procedure **ZC0001**, then click the **Control** folder located on the left-hand side of the screen.

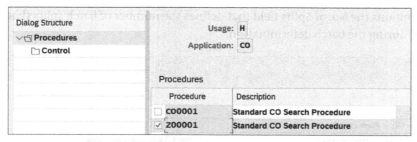

Figure 10.20 Defining Batch Search Procedure

The previously created condition type (**CTyp**) **CO03** is now assigned to the newly created batch search procedure Z00001, as shown in Figure 10.21.

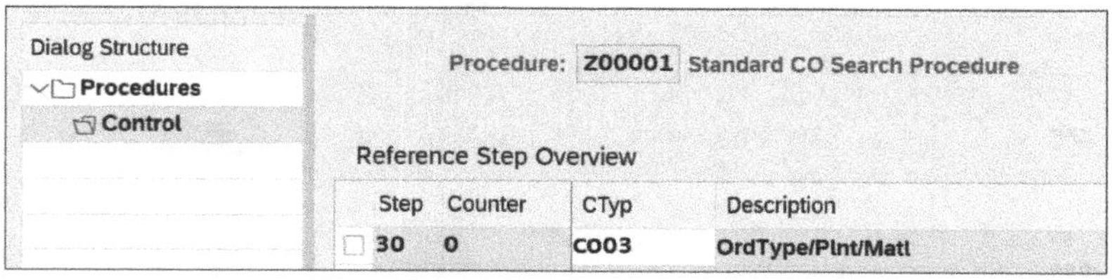

Figure 10.21 Assigning Condition Type to Batch Search Procedure

10.5.5   Batch Search Procedure Allocation and Check Activation

In this step, assign the batch search procedure to specific movement types, as shown in Figure 10.22. So for a particular movement type, such as 261 (GI against a process order), this search strategy will help to search the relevant batches during the batch determination process.

Follow menu path **SAP IMG • Logistics—General • Batch Management • Batch Determination and Batch Check • Batch Search Procedure Allocation and Check Activation • Assign Search Procedures to Production and Activate Check • Assign Search Procedure to Process Order and Activate Check,** or use Transaction CORC.

In Figure 10.22, the previously configured batch search procedure **Z00001** is assigned to **Plant 1105** and **Order Type PI01.** Be sure to select the **Check Batch** checkbox so that the system will trigger automatic batch determination when a process order of this plant-order type combination is created in the SAP system.

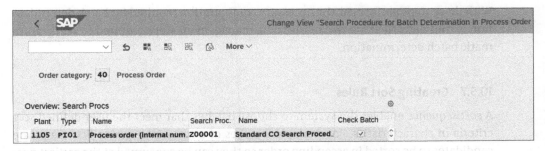

Figure 10.22 Assigning Batch Search Procedure to Movement Type 261

10.5.6 Batch Search Procedure for Process Orders

In this final configuration step, the previously configured batch search procedure ZC0001 is assigned to the plant-order type combination. Follow menu path **SAP IMG · Production Planning for Process Industries · Process Order · Master Data · Order · Define Order-Type-Dependent Parameters**, or use Transaction COR4.

Figure 10.23 shows that plant 1105 and order type PIO1 are assigned the batch search procedure Z00001. The **Check: Specified Batch Active** checkbox is also selected so that the system will use this assigned batch search procedure during process order creation.

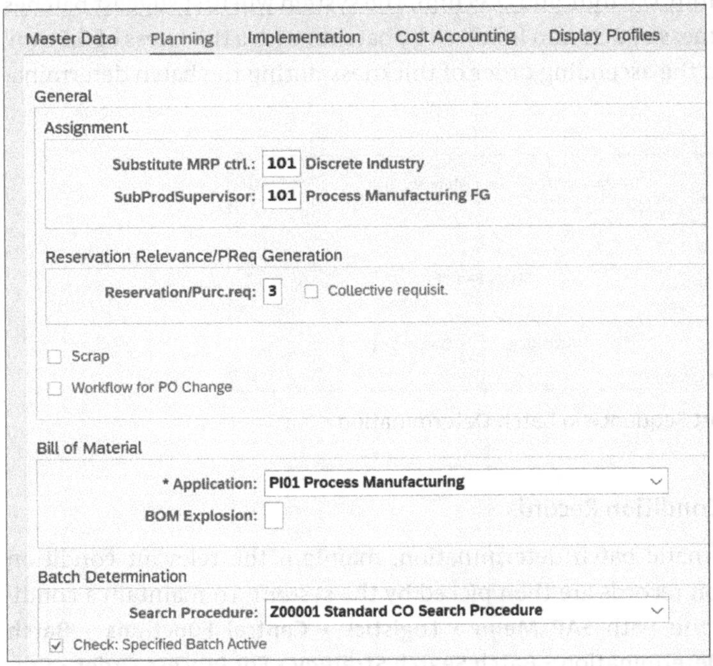

| Master Data | Planning | Implementation | Cost Accounting | Display Profiles |

General

Assignment

Substitute MRP ctrl.: **101** Discrete Industry
SubProdSupervisor: **101** Process Manufacturing FG

Reservation Relevance/PReq Generation

Reservation/Purc.req: **3** ☐ Collective requisit.

☐ Scrap
☐ Workflow for PO Change

Bill of Material

* Application: **PI01 Process Manufacturing**
BOM Explosion: ☐

Batch Determination

Search Procedure: **Z00001 Standard CO Search Procedure**
☑ Check: Specified Batch Active

Figure 10.23 Assigning Batch Search Procedure to Plant-Order Type Combination

With these steps performed, the necessary configuration required for batch determination is complete. Next are two master data management steps required to set up automatic batch determination.

10.5.7   Creating Sort Rules

A *sort sequence* enables the system to choose batches that meet the user-defined sort criteria of characteristics. For example, batches of a material *expiring first* are prime candidates to be sorted in ascending order so they can be consumed at the earliest possible date. This sort strategy is known as *first expiration, first out* (FEFO). Other sort strategies include first in, first out (FIFO) and last in, first out (LIFO). Any other type of sort sequence is also possible, which we'll soon show with an example.

Access the screen shown in Figure 10.24 by following menu path **Logistics · Central Functions · Batch Management · Batch Determination · Selection and Sort · Sort Rule · Create**, or by using Transaction CU70.

Create a new sort sequence ZPP, assign the previously created characteristic MM01, and select the **Ascending** checkbox. Doing so will lead to the system suggesting batches of material with values in ascending order during the batch determination process. For example, say there are four batches of a material with thicknesses (characteristic MM01) of 0.6 mm, 0.5 mm, 0.9 mm, and 0.35 mm. The system will first suggest batches of material with a thickness of 0.35 mm followed by batches with a thickness of 0.5 mm, and so on, to adhere to the ascending order of thickness during the batch determination procedure.

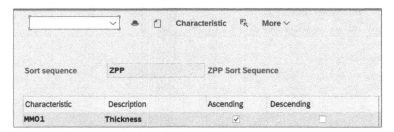

Figure 10.24 Creating Sort Sequence in Batch Determination

10.5.8   Maintaining Condition Records

As a last step in automatic batch determination, maintain the relevant condition records. These condition records are then picked by the system. To maintain a condition record, follow menu path **SAP Menu · Logistics · Central Functions · Batch Management · Batch Determination · Batch Search Strategy · For Process Order · Create**, or use Transaction COB1.

Select the strategy that you defined in the earlier configuration steps (in this case, **CO03**), and select the **Order Type (PI01)** and the **Plant (1105)** combination. Enter **Material** "104", as shown in Figure 10.25. Select the first line item, and then choose the **Sort** button to open the screen shown in Figure 10.26.

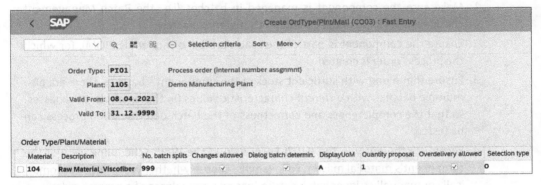

Figure 10.25 Batch Search Strategy

Figure 10.26 shows the complete details of the condition record. The previously created sort rule ZPP was assigned and marked characteristic MM01 (Thickness) in ascending order (**ASC** checkbox).

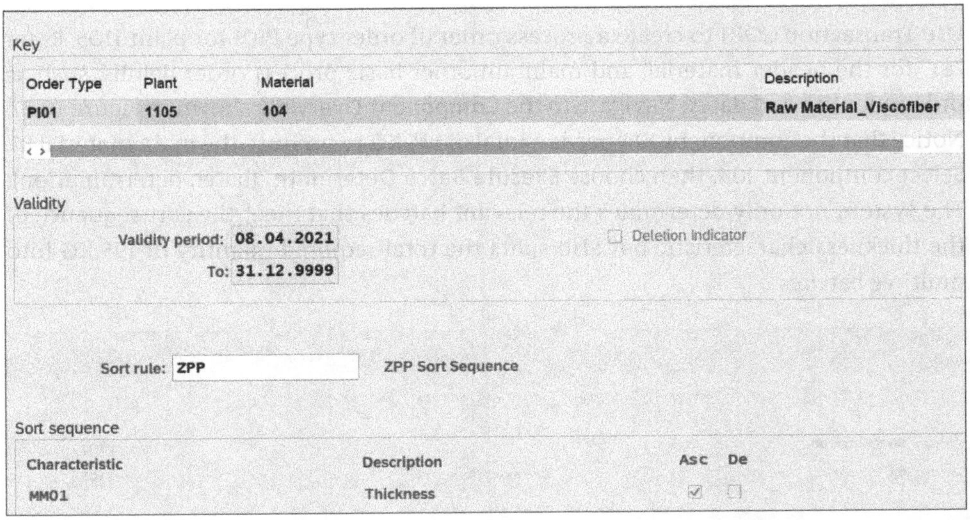

Key

Order Type	Plant	Material	Description
PI01	1105	104	Raw Material_Viscofiber

Validity

Validity period: 08.04.2021   ☐ Deletion Indicator
To: 31.12.9999

Sort rule: **ZPP**   ZPP Sort Sequence

Sort sequence

Characteristic	Description	Asc	De
MM01	Thickness	☑	☐

Figure 10.26 Assigning Sort Sequence in Batch Search Strategy

The configuration and master data setup required for the batch determination procedure is complete. Let's now run the business process that entails creating a process order of order type PI01 for plant 1105 for a finished good in which the component is material 104 undergoing the batch determination process.

[+]

Tips and Tricks

Before running the business process to test batch determination of a component, it's a good idea to use this checklist:

1. Make sure the component is managed in batches (i.e., the **Batch Management** checkbox is selected in the component's material master).

2. Ensure the component is part of the material's bill of materials (BOM), for which the process order is created.

3. Ensure that along with sufficient stock of the component's batches, there are also multiple batches with different characteristic values (in this example, thicknesses) so that the completeness and correctness of the batch determination process can be tested.

4. Reconfirm the entry in the **Batch Entry** field in the **Work Scheduling** view of the component's material master. For example, choose whether you want to automatically or manually trigger batch determination upon release of a process order.

5. If the same material is batch-managed in one plant but not in the other, then ensure that you select/deselect the **Batch Management (Plant)** checkbox.

10.5.9   Business Process

Use Transaction COR1 to create a process order of order type PIO1 for plant 1105. Enter "81" for the header material, and maintain other basic process order details, such as order quantity and dates. Navigate to the **Component Overview** shown in Figure 10.27. Notice that the component **104** needs a total of **195 KG** to produce the main material **81**. Select component **104**, then choose **Execute Batch Determntn.** (batch determination). The system not only determines the relevant batches that meet the sort sequence of the thickness characteristic but also splits the total required quantity of 195 KG into multiple batches.

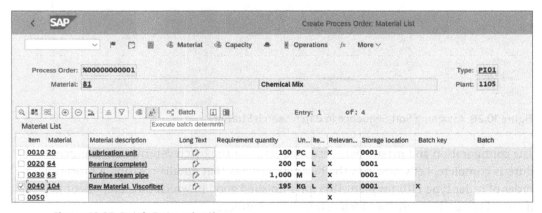

Figure 10.27 Batch Determination

Here, the system has automatically determined and then assigned four batches of material 104: 7, 8, 9, and 10. Let's evaluate this in more detail. The system first evaluates the thickness sort criteria to see which batch has the lowest thickness value and assign that batch's quantity to the process order. However, if the assigned batch's quantity isn't sufficient to cater to the complete requirement (in this case, 195 KG), the system proceeds to the next batch with the next highest thickness value and assigns the batch's quantity to the process order. The system continues in this way until multiple batches in the total required quantity are assigned to the process order.

Let's now also quickly check whether the batch determination for the process order is correctly configured.

Figure 10.28 and Figure 10.29 show that batch 7 has the lowest characteristic (thickness) value of 8.10 mm but is only available in a quantity of 100 KG, which was assigned to the process order. Next, the system found that batch 8 had the next highest thickness value of 8.50 mm in a quantity of 20 MT. This batch too was assigned to the process order while the system continued searching for more batches to meet a total required quantity of 195 KG. Next, it found that batch 9 with thickness value 9.20 mm had a quantity of 50 KG, which was therefore assigned to the process order. Finally, for the available quantity of 25 KG for the fourth batch (10) with the highest thickness value of 12.00 mm, the system accordingly assigned the same to the process order. These settings validate the ascending sort sequence of the thickness characteristic that was set up for batch determination.

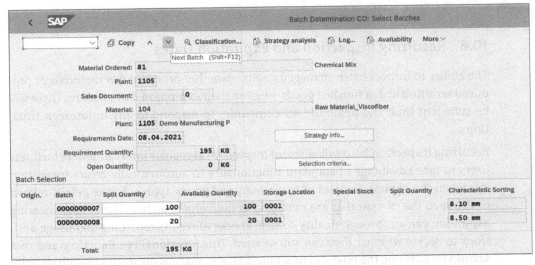

Figure 10.28 Batch Determination According to Sort Sequence: Part 1

Choose **Copy**, shown in Figure 10.28, and all four batches will be copied and assigned in the process order, as shown in Figure 10.30.

Figure 10.29 Batch Determination According to Sort Sequence: Part 2

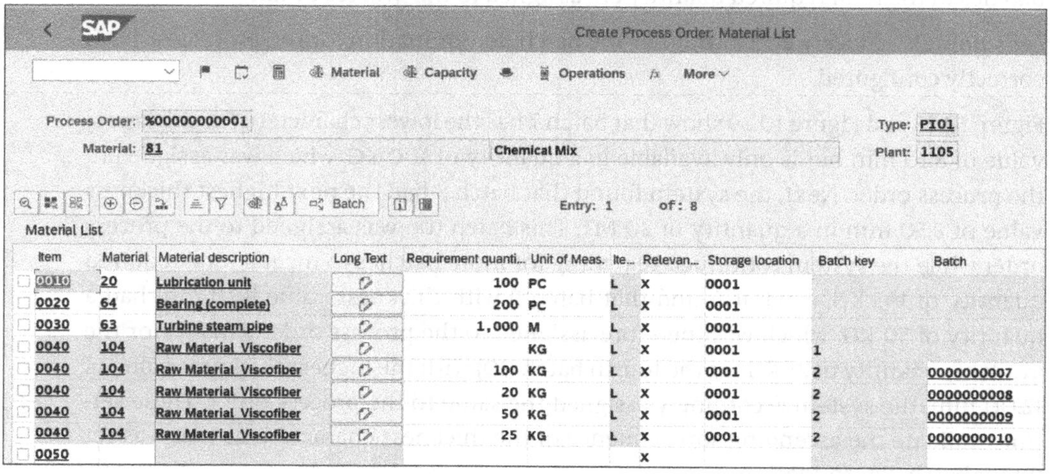

Figure 10.30 Multiple Batches Assigned

10.6   Recurring Inspection and Expiration Dates

The ability to inspect batch-managed goods—whether procured raw materials or produced semifinished or finished goods—before their expiration dates ensures there will
be sufficient time and flexibility for companies to respond to any unforeseen situations.

Recurring inspection (also called *repeat inspection*) at regular intervals allows business
users to take advantage of standard functionality to automatically create inspection
lots when the expiration dates of batch-managed goods approach. The details related
to the shelf life of materials are managed in individual batches. The batches nearing
expiration can go through quality control checks of results recording and usage decisions to decide whether they can still be used. This functionality offers time and cost
savings by enabling the business to act proactively and thus optimizes the full logistics
and supply chain operations of the company.

A significant challenge for any organization is to keep track of batch-managed materials with shelf life expiration dates. This is especially the case in process-based industries for slow-moving materials or materials with a short shelf life. Tracking this

information allows an organization to ensure that those materials are consumed first in the case of raw materials and sold first in the case of finished goods. This minimizes the material and financial costs associated with the need to destroy and scrap the goods or materials.

At the time of goods production, the system is able to calculate and suggest a *best before date* (BBD). Similarly, on procurement of goods, the system is able to calculate and suggest a *shelf life expiration date* (SLED). Therefore, it makes sense to ensure that recurring inspection takes place *before* the goods are about to expire.

> **Note**
>
> Although this example shows the integration between PP and QM in the SAP system, a company can still use several batch-specific functions even if QM isn't yet implemented.
>
> We recommend engaging a QM consultant to ensure an end-to-end integration among PP, MM, and QM functionalities for the batch-managed business processes covered in this section.

This section outlines the important master data needed to successfully set up recurring inspection. We'll show how to manually create an inspection lot that triggers the recurring inspection program and also touch on an automatic trigger option. For the QM part of the master data setup, we recommend engaging a QM consultant to cover the following QM-specific master data setup.

10.6.1   Quality Management Master Data Checklist

For recurring inspection to work correctly, you need to set up the following QM master data:

- Activation of recurring **Inspection Type 09** in the material master
- Inspection plan usage **9 (Material Check)**
- **Status** set to **4 (Released)**

In the following sections, we'll discuss how to activate the recurring inspection type, as well as the steps required to set up an inspection plan and set its status to released.

Activation of Recurring Inspection Type in the Material Master

Although the material may have been created previously, its QM view may still need to be activated. If the QM view is already activated, then activate the new inspection type for recurring inspection at the organizational level (plant). To activate the recurring inspection type, follow menu path **Logistics • Materials Management • Material Master • Material • Create (General) • Immediately**, or use Transaction MM01.

Enter material 106 and choose the **Select View(s)** button. Select the **Quality Management** view, and then choose **Organizational Levels**. Enter plant 1105, and choose **Continue**. This leads to the **Quality Management** view of the material master

Here, maintain an **Inspection Interval** of **10** days to denote that material inspection is due after every 10 days. In the case of recurring inspection, the system refers to the information maintained in this field to calculate the next inspection date. Choose **Insp. Setup**; in the ensuing popup, maintain **Inspection Type 09** for recurring inspection. Make sure to select the **Active** checkbox to activate this inspection type.

Back in the **Quality Management** view, this time choose the **Plant Data/Stor. 1** view, and the screen shown in Figure 10.31 appears.

Figure 10.31 shows the **Shelf Life Data** area, in which you maintain the shelf life data, including the minimum, maximum, and total shelf life of a material. While calculating or updating the SLED, the system looks for the date of manufacturing against the production/process order or date of GR against the purchase order and adds up the period, such as days or weeks from the total shelf life, to come up with the SLED/BBD. In this example, the system adds 20 days from the **Total Shelf Life** field to the date of manufacture to suggest a SLED/BBD. For SLED/BBD calculation, the system considers calendar days.

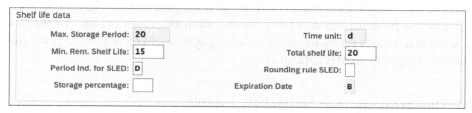

Figure 10.31 Shelf Life Data in Plant/Stor. 1 View of Material Maser

Tips and Tricks

The maximum storage period of a material should have the longest duration in terms of period. The total shelf life of a material must be greater than its minimum remaining shelf life. Further, it makes sense for an inspection interval (see Figure 10.32) to be less than the total shelf life.

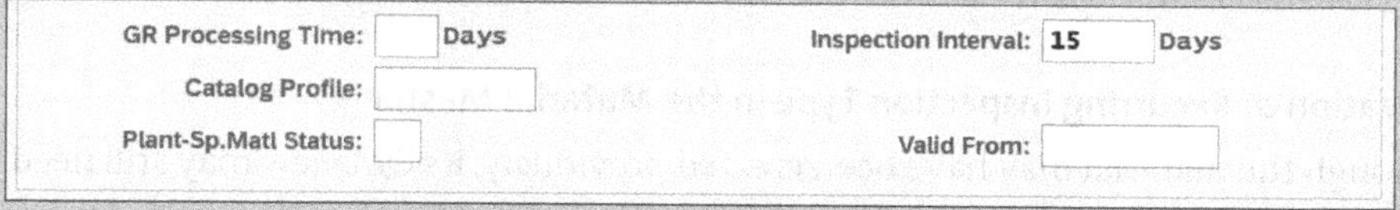

Figure 10.32 Inspection Interval in QM View of Material Master

Batch Master

Let's look at some of the details of the material's batch, which is about to expire. When materials are batch-managed, it's always the batch—not the individual material—that expires. To change the batch, follow menu path **Logistics • Materials Management • Material Master • Batch • Change**, or use Transaction MSC2N. Enter **Material** "106", **Plant** "1105", the storage location (**Stor. location**) where the batch is stored as "0001", and the material **Batch** number as **0000000012**. Press Enter, and the screen shown in Figure 10.33 appears.

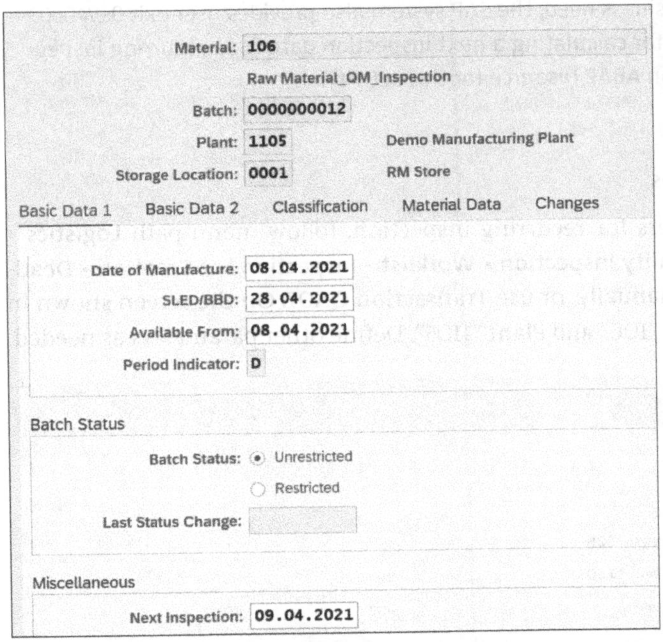

Material:	106
	Raw Material_QM_Inspection
Batch:	0000000012
Plant:	1105 Demo Manufacturing Plant
Storage Location:	0001 RM Store

Basic Data 1 | Basic Data 2 | Classification | Material Data | Changes

Date of Manufacture:	08.04.2021
SLED/BBD:	28.04.2021
Available From:	08.04.2021
Period Indicator:	D

Batch Status

Batch Status: ⊙ Unrestricted ○ Restricted

Last Status Change:

Miscellaneous

Next Inspection: 09.04.2021

Figure 10.33 Shelf Life Expiration Date and the Next Inspection Date

The **Next Inspection** field is of paramount importance for recurring inspection. Together with the inspection interval that we previously covered (in the QM view of the material master), the system calculates the next inspection date whenever a business user records the usage decision of an inspection. Here the next inspection date is April 9, 2021 (**09.04.2021**), and inspection should occur after every 15 days. On executing the recurring inspection program, which we'll cover next, the system adds another 15 days to this date. In reality, the system comes up with a date that is one day earlier than the date maintained in the **Next Inspection** field. This is to ensure that the quality inspector is able to inspect the material, record its results, and decide on its usage (the usage decision) at least a day before the product is set to expire.

The **Date of Manufacture** field in this case shows **08.04.2021** (April 8, 2021). For in-house production of finished or semifinished goods, this is the date when the user records GR against a process or process order. If this batch contains material (e.g., raw material) received against a procurement process, then at the time of recording its GR, the system prompts the warehouse person to enter the date of manufacturing mentioned with the accompanying vendor's quality certificate or supporting documents, such as a packing list. On executing the recurring inspection program, the system looks for the data maintained on shelf life expiration to come up with a new SLED/BBD.

[»]

> **Note**
>
> If you have any unique business need, the SAP system also provides user exit QEVA0003 to define a different logic for calculating a next inspection date for a recurring inspection. You need to engage an ABAP resource for this activity.

10.6.2   Business Processes

To set the initial parameters for recurring inspection, follow menu path **Logistics • Quality Management • Quality Inspection • Worklist • Inspection Lot Creation • Deadline Monitoring • Trigger Manually**, or use Transaction QA07. On the screen shown in Figure 10.34, enter **Material** "106" and **Plant** "1105". Define other parameters as needed.

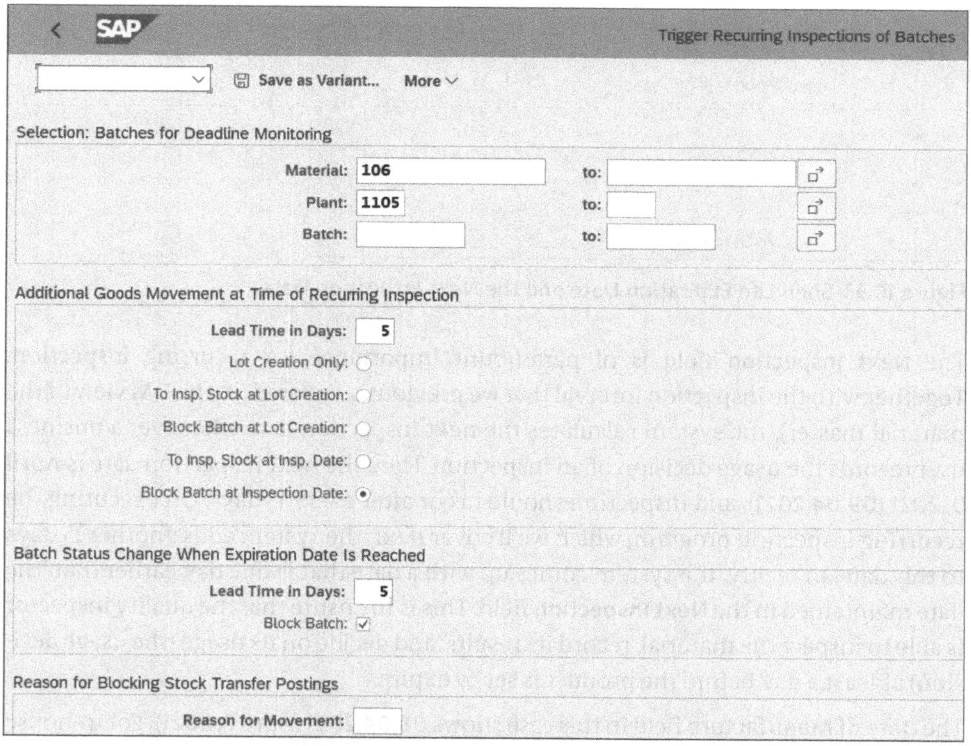

Figure 10.34 Deadline Monitoring (Recurring Inspection)

In this example, we define **Initial Run in Days** as "5" and that the material should transfer to quality inspection stock at the time of inspection lot creation (**To Insp.Stock at Insp. Date** checkbox) by the recurring inspection program. Therefore, all materials whose inspection dates fall in the next five days (from today's date or the date on which this transaction is run) are considered during the deadline monitoring program run. After such materials are identified, the system not only creates inspection lots for them but also moves the stock from unrestricted stock to quality inspection through the transfer posting process. Refer to Table 10.1 for information about the various fields and functions, which also eventually need be mapped with a company's business processes.

Field	Function/Description
Initial Run in Days	The number of days ahead in the next inspection date for the system to consider for recurring inspection purposes. If five days are maintained, and if today is December 15, 2021, then the system looks for all the material batches whose next inspection date is on or before December 20, 2021.
Lot Creation Only	The system only creates an inspection lot, but the batch is still in unrestricted use stock.
To insp. Stock at Lot Creation	The system creates an inspection lot and transfers the batch to quality inspection stock. The status of the batch changes to **Restricted**.
Block Batch at Lot Creation	An inspection lot is created, and the batch is blocked for any usage until the usage decision is made.
To Insp. Stock at Insp. Date	The system transfers the batch to inspection stock on the date when the user needs to perform quality inspection.
Block Batch at Inspection Date	The system transfers the batch to blocked stock on the date the user needs to perform inspection.

Table 10.1 Details of Fields and Functions in Recurring Inspection Manual Run

Choose **Execute** to see the detailed log shown in Figure 10.35. The system informs you that the batch's expiration date has been reached and the material's batch needs a recurring inspection, for which the system has automatically created inspection lot number 9000000001.

Tips and Tricks

To bring about organizational efficiency and optimization, a company can automate and schedule the recurring inspection process via scheduling jobs at regular intervals using Transaction QA06. The first step is to define a variant. The next step is to maintain the frequency with which the system runs the scheduled program for recurring inspections. It's best to schedule these programs during slow working hours (i.e., weekends or nights) to conserve the system's resources.

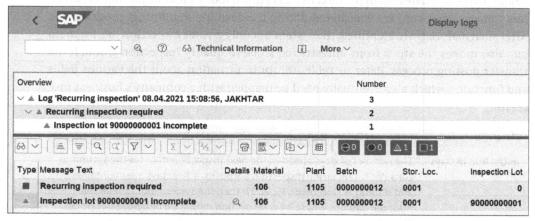

Figure 10.35 Log Display of Deadline Monitoring

Transaction MB5M, which is the shelf life list, can also be used to gain comprehensive visibility into materials whose shelf lives have ended or are about to end (see Figure 10.36).

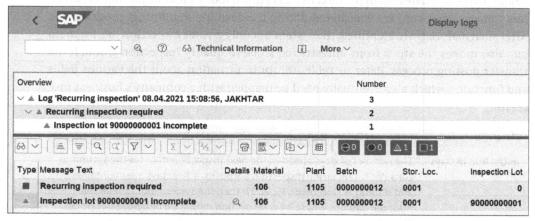

Figure 10.36 Shelf Life Expiry List

10.7   Batch Derivation

With batch derivation, a user can efficiently and automatically transfer a batch's characteristics values from the sender material's batches to the receiver material's batches, thereby saving time, data entry effort, and cost. Batch derivation enables a user to maintain one-to-one, one-to-many, and many-to-one relationships between the sender's and the receiver's materials for complete visibility of information and data.

Whenever a batch-managed material is processed in the production process, its characteristics change and the batch-managed material attains different physical and chemical attributes. These changed attributes are maintained as characteristic values of the batch-managed materials. With batch derivation, a user can control how the system manages the characteristic values flowing from a sender material to a receiver material.

In this section, we'll cover the basic configuration settings needed to activate batch derivation. Next, we'll move on to the master data you need to set up, including settings in the material master, classification, and batch derivation-specific settings. Finally, we'll cover the end-to-end business process in which we show how the settings made for master data are reflected in the batch derivation process. For this example, the sender material is 104 (a semifinished material that is consumed during the production process so as to produce finished good, 81), whereas the receiver material is 81 (a finished good).

Let's start with the configuration basics of batch derivation.

10.7.1   Configuration Basics

Activate batch derivation in the configuration settings by following menu path **SAP IMG • Logistics—General • Batch Management • Derivation of Batch Data • Activate Batch Derivation**, or by using Transaction DVSP. On the screen that appears, select the **Derivation Active** radio button, and save the settings.

In the following sections, we'll cover the end-to-end business process of setting up batch derivation master data, which entails setting up the details of the sender and receiver materials of a batch's data. We'll then use an example to show how the sender material's batch data automatically flows into a receiving material's batch data through the batch derivation process.

10.7.2   Classification in Material Master

In the material master of the sender material and receiver material, maintain the classification view, wherein class type 023 is incorporated, which is specific to batch-managed materials. To maintain the classification view or make changes to the already maintained classification view in the material master, follow menu path **Logistics •**

Materials Management · Material Master · Change · Immediately, or use Transaction MM02 (Figure 10.37).

In Figure 10.37, you can see ZPP of **Class Type 023 (Batch)**, and three characteristics, with descriptions given as **Product Class**, **Date of Manufacture**, and **Thickness**, respectively. On this screen, simply assign an already created class, which in this example is ZPP. After assigning an already created class, the system automatically assigns the characteristics associated with the class. There's no need to maintain any specific value to the characteristics (in the **Value** column) because you'll do that during the transactional data entry.

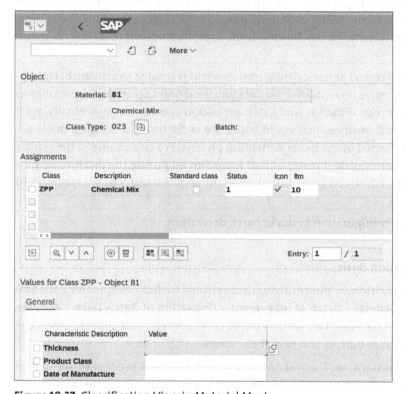

Figure 10.37 Classification View in Material Master

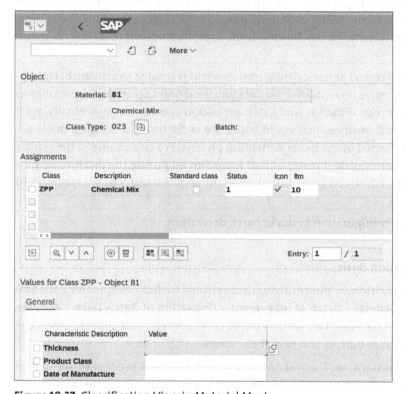

Note

The classification settings made for the sender material also apply to the receiver material, especially the common characteristics whose values the system should transfer during batch derivation. Although the preceding example shows classification details of receiver material 81, we've made similar classification settings for sender material 104. Refer to Chapter 7 for more on classification.

In the following sections, we'll cover the steps involved in setting up batch derivation, including maintaining details of sender and receiver materials' batch details and how a sender material's batch data flows into a receiver material's batch.

Classification: Class with Characteristics

It's important to understand how a class and characteristics are linked together. To view the structure of class ZPP and the characteristics associated with it, follow menu path **Cross-Application Components · Classification · Master Data · Classes**, or use Transaction CL02. On the initial screen, enter **Class** "ZPP" and **Class Type** "023" (**Batch**), then choose **Change**.

Figure 10.38 shows three characteristics—MM01, MM10, and MM11—whose descriptions appeared or were visible in Figure 10.37. We refer to several instances when the system interchangeably displays the characteristics or their descriptions. The data type of the first characteristic, MM10, is **CHAR** and consists of 10 characters; the data type of MM11 is **DATE**; and the data type of MM01 is **NUM**, with up to four characters. MM01 has a unit of measure of **mm** (millimeters) and two decimal places.

For this example of batch derivation, we'll all use the three characteristics to transfer their values from a sender material's batch to a receiver material's batch.

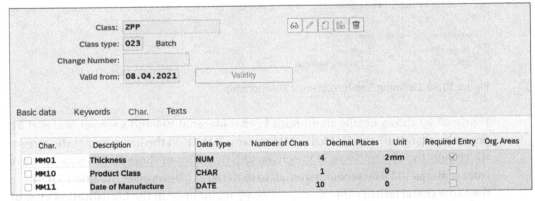

Figure 10.38 Characteristics Assignment in Class

Batch Derivation: Sender Material

For batch derivation settings for the sender material, including the characteristics, follow menu path **SAP Menu · Logistics · Central Functions · Batch Management · Batch Derivation · Sender Condition Records · Create**, or use Transaction DVS1. On the initial screen in which the standard **Strategy Type** option is available, the available key combinations offer the options to choose only the **Sender Material Number** radio button or the **Receiving material + Sending material** radio button. This key combination enables a user to maintain not just the sender material's information but also the receiver's material. Place the cursor on the **Strategy Type** field and press F4 to see the dropdown and to select condition type **BDS1**. After selecting **BDS1** and pressing ⎡Enter⎤, the system opens a popup screen to provide radio buttons to enable selecting a combination of both receiving and sending material information on the same screen, and only sender material number information. For this example, select the first radio button (**Receiving Material + Sending Material**) and choose **Continue**.

In Figure 10.39, enter "81" in the **Receiver Material** field and validity dates in the **Valid From** and **Valid To** fields. If validity dates aren't entered, then the system automatically sets the validity as from the date of creation of the condition record until **December 31, 9999**. If there's a business need to use a different validity than what the system proposes, use the **Validity** option (not shown).

Enter sender material "104" in the lower half of the screen. In this section of the screen, multiple sender materials can be entered for one receiver material. Select **Sender Material 104**, then choose **Details** from the top menu bar.

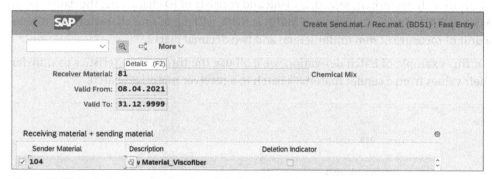

Figure 10.39 Defining Sender-Receiver Relationship

Figure 10.40 shows details about both **Sender Material 104** and **Receiver Material 81**. Enter the characteristics "MM01", "MM10", and "MM11" in the lower half of the screen, which tells the system to send the characteristic values of these three characteristics from material 104 (the sender material) to material 81 (the receiver material). These are the same characteristics that were previously maintained in the **Classification** view of material masters 81 and 104 (refer to Figure 10.37).

The next step is to define the event or instance when the system performs batch derivation for the receiver material. Automatic batch derivation is possible at the time when a production or process order is released, at GR of a production or process order, at GR of a purchase order, during a usage decision from a quality inspection process, or at transfer posting between two batches of different materials with common characteristics. It's also possible to perform manual batch derivation if there is any such business need. Choose **Condition Usage** or press ⎡F7⎤.

Select **Event 200** (see Figure 10.41) by clicking it once to highlight it; this will enable the system to perform batch derivation on the release of a production or a process order. Choose **Continue** and save the settings.

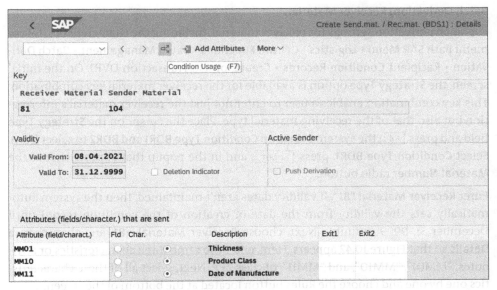

Figure 10.40 Attributes of Sender Material

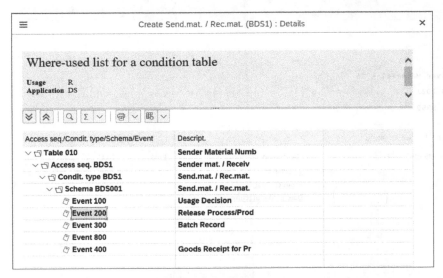

Figure 10.41 Choosing Event for Batch Derivation

So far, we've covered batch derivation for the sender material while also associating it with the receiver material. However, the setting for the receiver material is significantly more detailed than the setting for the sender material, especially in terms of how the system responds if batch derivation can't be performed on the receiver material or if one of the characteristic values derived from batch derivation is missing.

Batch Derivation: Receiver Material

For batch derivation settings for receiver material, including the characteristics, follow menu path **SAP Menu • Logistics • Central Functions • Batch Management • Batch Derivation • Recipient Condition Records • Create**, or use Transaction DVR1. On the initial screen, the **Strategy Type** option is available for the receiver material key combination. This key combination enables a user to enter not just the receiver material's information but also that of the receiving material type. Place the cursor on the **Strategy Type** field and press ⌁F4⌁; the system brings up **Condition Type BDR1** and **BDR2** to select from. Select **Condition Type BDR1**, press ⌁Enter⌁, and in the popup that appears choose the **Material Number** radio button.

Enter **Receiver Material** "81". If validity dates aren't maintained, then the system automatically sets the validity from the date of creation of the condition record until December 31, 9999 (infinity). Next, choose **Receiver Material—81**, and then choose **Details** so that Figure 10.42 appears. Here, enter the same three characteristics or attributes, "MM01", "MM10", and "MM11", of class ZPP. Next, select all of these characteristics one by one and choose the **Rules** button located at the bottom of the screen.

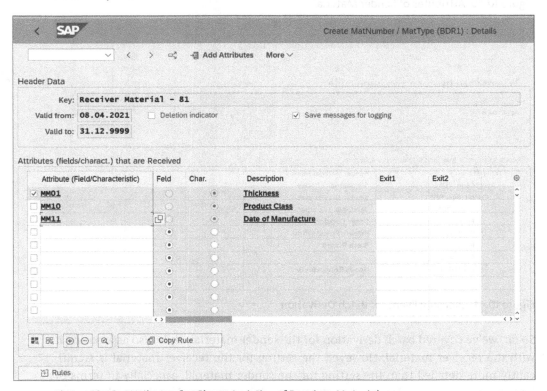

Figure 10.42 Attributes for Characteristics of Receiver Material

On the screen shown in Figure 10.43, define the rules for every individual characteristic that the system needs to follow if it can't perform batch derivation. In this example, we set the rules for the first characteristic **MM01**, in which we set the control level to **W Warning** in case the system finds the **Sender** field empty. An empty **Sender** field means that there is no characteristic value in the sender material's classification, so nothing transfers to the receiver material during batch derivation. These warning messages can also be turned into error messages if a user wants to ensure handling the batch derivation-related issues as soon as an error message appears. The second control setting for the same characteristic MM01 stipulates how the system reacts if it's able to find an already maintained value in the characteristic. If the system is to overwrite the value of this characteristic, it will do so with a warning message or bring up an error message that doesn't allow overwriting.

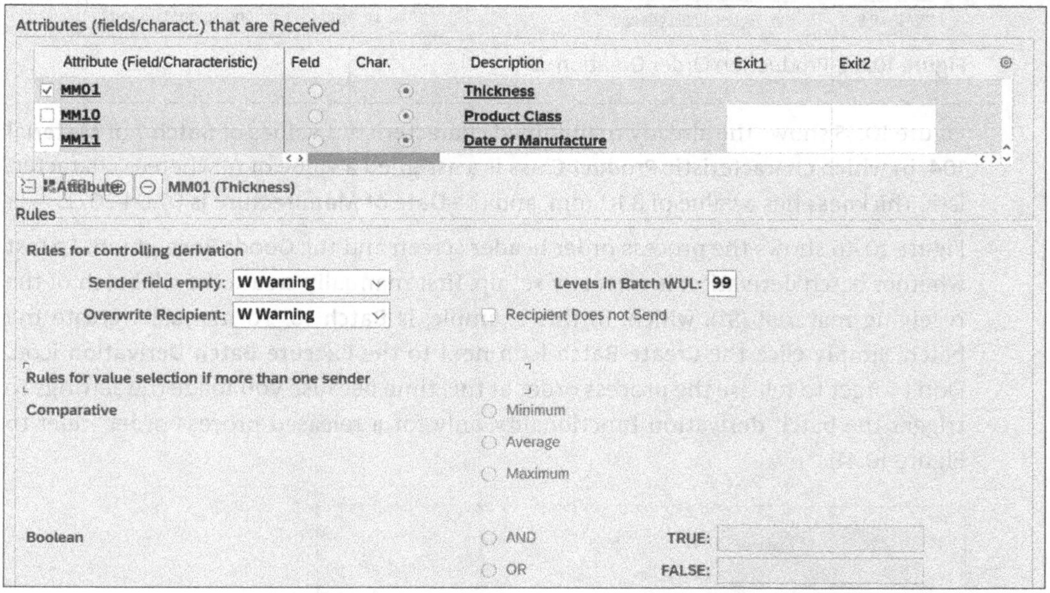

Figure 10.43 Rules for Characteristics of Receiver Material

Repeat the same rules setting for the remaining two characteristics, MM10, and MM11.

10.7.3 Business Processes

The business process of batch derivation begins with creating a process order for the receiver material 81 (the finished good) in which the system automatically assigns the sender material 104 as one of its components.

To create a process order, use Transaction COR1. Enter receiver **Material** "81", **Plant** "1105", and **Order Type** "PI01", then press ⏎Enter⏎. Maintain the order header details, such as the process order quantity and dates, and then navigate to the **Material List** shown in Figure 10.44. In the **Material List** view of the process order for the receiver **Material 81**, the system assigns a specific **Batch** number **7** of the sender material or **Component 104**. Double-click **Batch 7** so that Figure 10.45 appears.

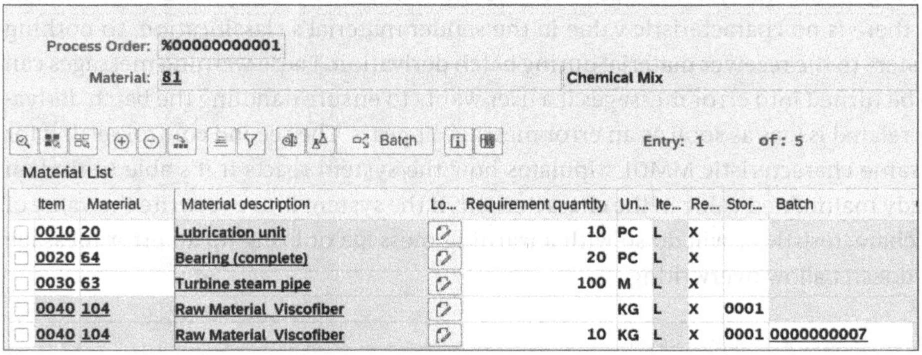

Process Order: %00000000001
Material: 81
Chemical Mix
Batch
Entry: 1
of: 5
Material List
Item Material Material description Lo... Requirement quantity Un... Ite... Re... Stor... Batch
0010 20 Lubrication unit 10 PC L X
0020 64 Bearing (complete) 20 PC L X
0030 63 Turbine steam pipe 100 M L X
0040 104 Raw Material_Viscofiber KG L X 0001
0040 104 Raw Material_Viscofiber 10 KG L X 0001 0000000007

Figure 10.44 Production Order Creation

Figure 10.45 shows the already maintained characteristics values of **Batch 7** of **Material 104**, in which characteristic **Product Class** is a assigned a value of A, whereas characteristic **Thickness** has a value of 8.10 mm, and the **Date of Manufacture** is 07.04.2021.

Figure 10.46 shows the process order header screen and the **Goods Receipt** tab. To test whether batch derivation is correctly set up, first manually create the GR batch of the receiving material (81), which, in this example, is **Batch 16**. To manually create the batch, simply click the **Create Batch** icon next to the **Execute Batch Derivation** icon. Don't forget to release the process order at this time because you made the settings to trigger the batch derivation functionality only for a released process order (refer to Figure 10.41).

Material: 104
Raw Material_Viscofiber
Batch: 0000000007
Plant: 1105
Demo Manufacturing Plant
Storage Location: 0001
RM Store
Basic Data 1
Basic Data 2
Classification
Material Data
Changes
Values for Class ZPP - Object 104
000000000
General
Characteristic Description
Value
Thickness
8.10 mm
Product Class
A
Date of Manufacture
07.04.2021

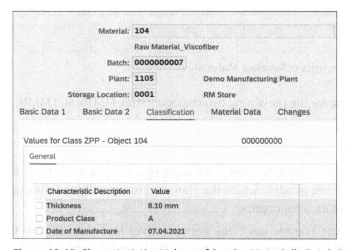

Figure 10.45 Characteristics Values of Sender Material's Batch 276

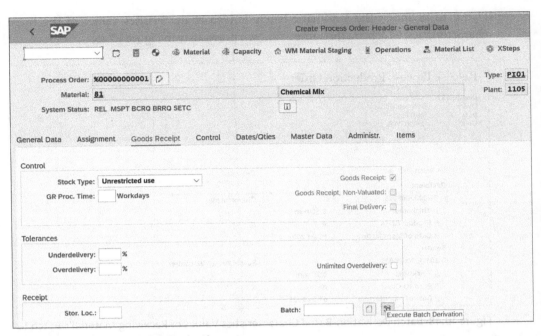

Figure 10.46 Executing Batch Derivation

Click the **Execute Batch Derivation** icon so that the screen shown in Figure 10.47 appears.

Figure 10.47 shows that the system has successfully performed batch derivation on receiver **Material 81** and its associated **Batch 16**. Choose **Details** so that the screen shown in Figure 10.48 appears.

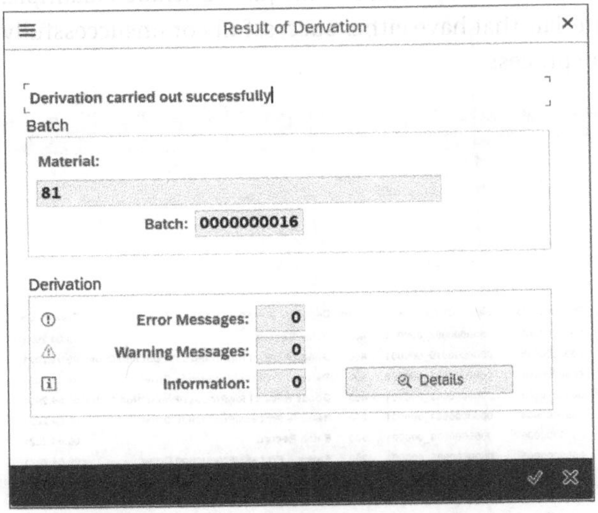

Figure 10.47 Results of Batch Derivation

Figure 10.48 shows the automatic batch-derived characteristics values of the three characteristics, which are the same as shown previously in Figure 10.45.

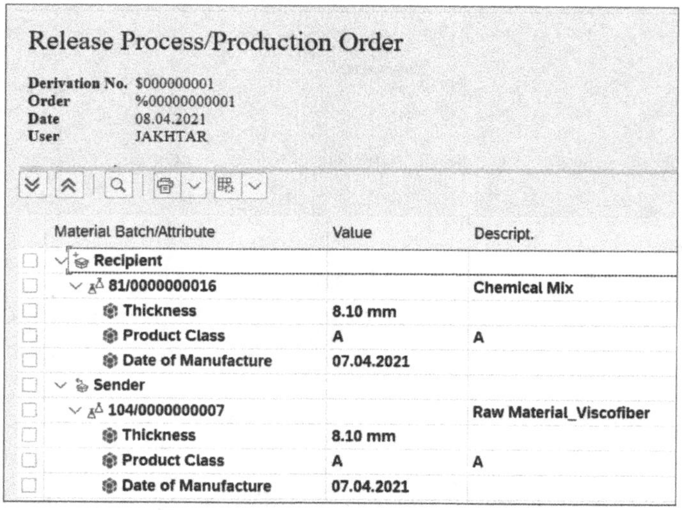

Figure 10.48 Batch Derivation-Based Characteristics Values of Receiving Material's Batch 16

10.7.4 Reporting

Transaction DVMO (Batch Derivation Monitoring Report) shows the status of batch derivations of different materials. The statuses with different traffic lights (red, yellow, and green) denote the current batch derivation status of various batches of sender and receiver materials.

While Figure 10.48 showed the batch derivation details of the just-concluded example, Figure 10.49 shows a range of materials that have either successfully or unsuccessfully gone through the batch derivation process.

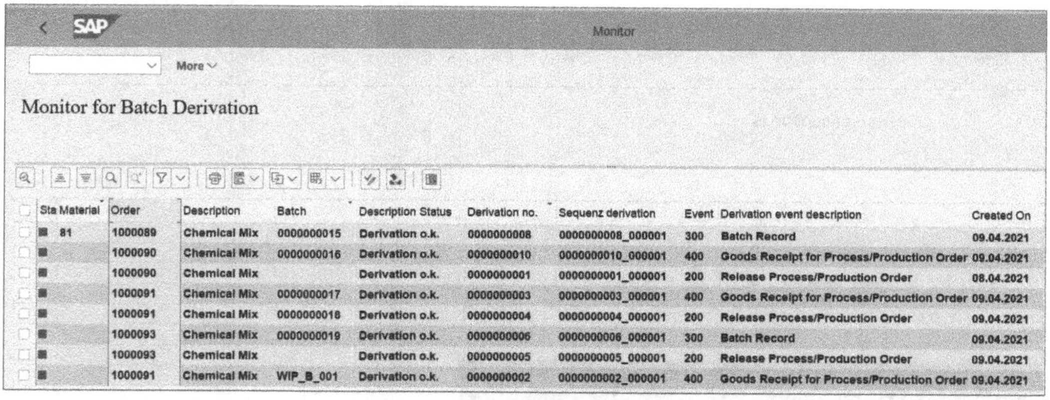

Sta Material	Order	Description	Batch	Description Status	Derivation no.	Sequenz derivation	Event	Derivation event description	Created On
81	1000089	Chemical Mix	0000000015	Derivation o.k.	0000000008	0000000008_000001	300	Batch Record	09.04.2021
	1000090	Chemical Mix	0000000016	Derivation o.k.	0000000010	0000000010_000001	400	Goods Receipt for Process/Production Order	09.04.2021
	1000090	Chemical Mix		Derivation o.k.	0000000001	0000000001_000001	200	Release Process/Production Order	08.04.2021
	1000091	Chemical Mix	0000000017	Derivation o.k.	0000000003	0000000003_000001	400	Goods Receipt for Process/Production Order	09.04.2021
	1000091	Chemical Mix	0000000018	Derivation o.k.	0000000004	0000000004_000001	200	Release Process/Production Order	09.04.2021
	1000093	Chemical Mix	0000000019	Derivation o.k.	0000000006	0000000006_000001	300	Batch Record	09.04.2021
	1000093	Chemical Mix		Derivation o.k.	0000000005	0000000005_000001	200	Release Process/Production Order	09.04.2021
	1000091	Chemical Mix	WIP_B_001	Derivation o.k.	0000000002	0000000002_000001	400	Goods Receipt for Process/Production Order	09.04.2021

Figure 10.49 Batch Derivation Monitor Cockpit

10.8 Batch Traceability of Work in Process Batches

Batch traceability is a key functionality used not only in the chemical and food industries but also in almost all industries, including in discrete manufacturing. SAP delivers the batch where-used list (Transaction MB56) in the SAP system. This where-used list enables business users to trace the batch from the finished product to the raw material (top down) or from the raw material to the finished product (bottom up). The work in process (WIP) batch is used to keep the batch traceability for a process order when several batches of raw material are consumed and several batches of a finished product are generated.

Transaction MB56 works well in most cases. However, there is a limitation on a process order with N:N batches. In a standard process order, there is no link between the raw material batch consumed and the finished product's batch received in the warehouse; therefore, the batch where-used list determines all the batches of raw material for each batch of the finished product.

Imagine, for example, that a problem was detected in a raw material batch after production. In this case, it isn't possible to identify exactly which batch of finished product was produced with this problematic batch of raw material. In previous releases, the only solution for this scenario was to create separate process orders for each raw material batch, but that required more data entry, inefficient business processes, and a significant amount of manual work.

In this example, we focus on the WIP batch functionality that is available in the system for production and process orders in SAP S/4HANA. More specifically, we explain how to enhance the batch where-used list to show a link between each raw material batch consumed and the respective finished product batch produced on a process order. Our example involves a simple process order with two operations and a few components.

In the following sections, we start with the necessary configuration needed to set up WIP batches, followed by the required master data setup. Then we transition to the business processes involved in WIP batches, and finally we conclude by using the BIC reporting tool to trace WIP batches.

10.8.1 Configuration Settings

The following are the configuration steps you need to perform before creating the confirmation profile.

Activating Work in Process Batch Business Functions

Two business functions are related to the WIP batch functionality that must be activated using Transaction SFW5: `LOG_PP_WIP_BATCH` and `LOG_PP_WIP_BATCH_02`. For the basic use of the WIP batch and for the scenario covered here, it's only necessary to activate the first business function. However, the second business function should be activated as well because it brings additional functionalities for the WIP batch, such as inventory valuation, use with documentary batches, and use on an order split.

To activate the business function using the Switch Framework (Transaction SFW5), select the business function and choose the **Activate Changes** button.

[!]

> **Warning**
>
> You can't deactivate these business functions after they're activated.

Activate Work in Process Batch

After the business function activation, it's also necessary to activate the WIP batch functionality in configuration. To complete this step, use Transaction OMCWB, choose the **Active** radio button, and then save.

[!]

> **Warning**
>
> Once activated, this configuration setting also can't be reversed. In other words, when a user allows the use of the WIP batch functionality in the SAP system, it isn't possible to get back to the original state in which WIP batches can't be used.

Activating the Original Batch

The next configuration step is to activate original batch reference material. To complete this step, execute Transaction OMT0. In the initial screen that appears (see Figure 10.50), select the **Original Batch Reference Material** checkbox and then save. Doing this enables the system to use this functionality in master data.

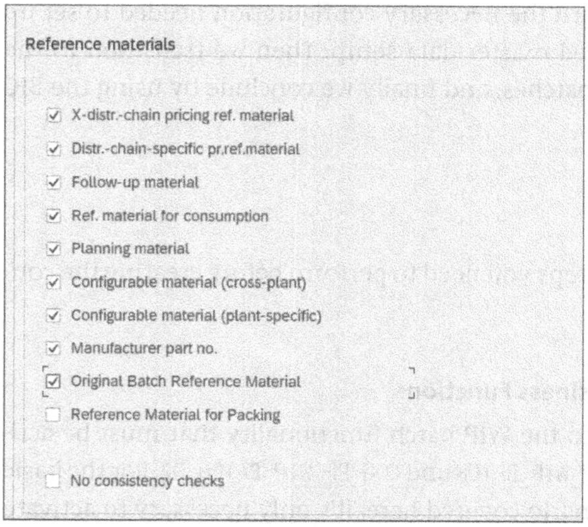

Reference materials

☑ X-distr.-chain pricing ref. material
☑ Distr.-chain-specific pr.ref.material
☑ Follow-up material
☑ Ref. material for consumption
☑ Planning material
☑ Configurable material (cross-plant)
☑ Configurable material (plant-specific)
☑ Manufacturer part no.
☑ Original Batch Reference Material
☐ Reference Material for Packing

☐ No consistency checks

Figure 10.50 Activating Original Batch Reference Material

Confirmation

Now that the WIP batch and original batch management functionalities are activated, the next configuration step is to create a new confirmation profile. Because the WIP batch information must be posted during the process order confirmation, the confirmation profile will include the WIP batch-specific subscreens.

For necessary configuration settings for the confirmation profile, use Transaction OPK1 and choose standard confirmation profile **SAP101**. On the next screen (see Figure 10.51), in the **Area Selection** tab, you need to add areas **8285 WIP Batch: Goods Receipts**, **8290 WIP Batch: Goods Issues**, and **8295 WIP Batch: WIP Batch Entry** to the standard **Profile SAP001**.

Use Transaction OPK0 if the WIP batch process is being implemented in discrete manufacturing (production order).

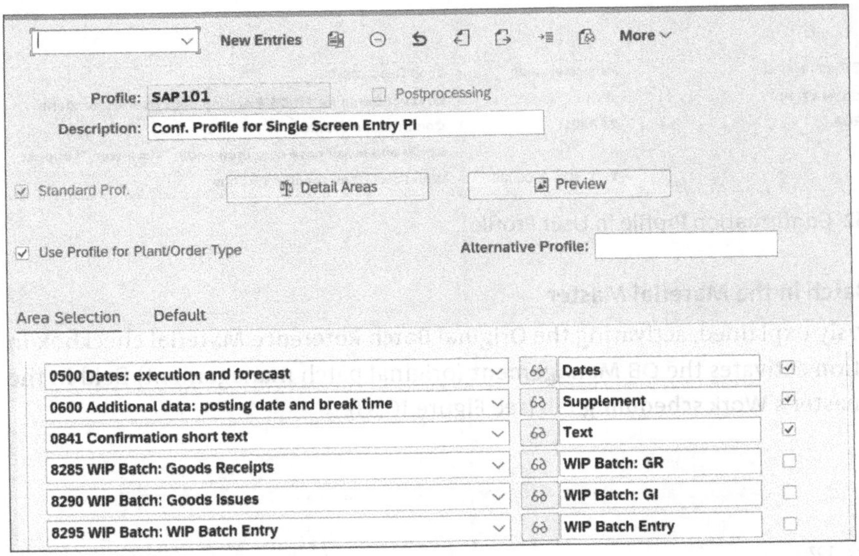

Figure 10.51 Confirmation Profile

Finally, use Transaction OMBB to switch on the option for a synchronous batch where-used list. In the screen that appears, select the **BaWU synchron.posting** checkbox for the relevant plant, which in this example is plant 1105.

10.8.2   Master Data Setup

Let's now delve into the requisite master data that you need to set up for WIP batches.

Confirmation Profile in the User Profile

To set the confirmation profile created in the previous step as the default while posting a confirmation using Transaction COR6N, choose the **Standard Prof.** (standard profile) checkbox on the initial screen of Transaction OPK1. However, because WIP batching is a very specific functionality that may not be used in all scenarios, here's an alternative. For each business user who posts a confirmation using WIP batch, it's possible to add this confirmation profile to the user parameters. User parameters are used to store user-specific settings. To add a new user parameter, use Transaction SU3, add the **Set/Get Parameter ID** as "CORUPROF", and enter the previously created confirmation profile ("SAP101") as the **Parameter value** (see Figure 10.52).

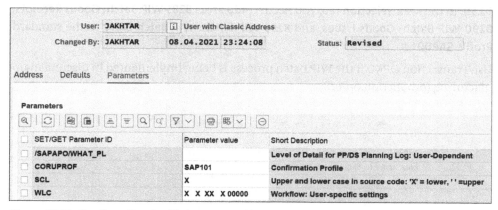

Figure 10.52 Confirmation Profile in User Profile

Original Batch in the Material Master

As previously explained, activating the **Original Batch Reference Material** checkbox in configuration activates the **OB Management** (original batch management) field in the material master's **Work scheduling** tab (see Figure 10.53).

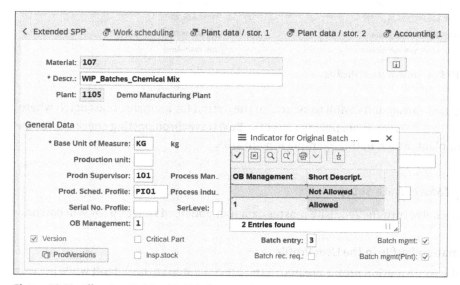

Figure 10.53 Allowing Original Batch Management in Material Master

The value of the **OB Management** field must be set to **1 (Allowed)** for the finished product, but it isn't necessary to set any value for the raw material. Also note that the **Batch Management** checkbox has been selected.

Let's now move to the business processes of WIP batches.

10.8.3   Business Processes

The business processes in WIP batches entail creating a process order, which is followed by confirmation, in which the WIP batches are created. The system automatically posts the GI and GR. We'll cover these processes in the following sections.

Process Order

Consider the example shown in Figure 10.54 of a regular process order that appears after executing Transaction COR2. This screen shows the **Material List**, in which one component, 104, is assigned batch number 7.

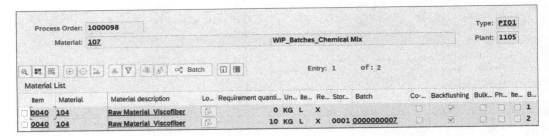

Figure 10.54 Process Order with Material List

To post the confirmation using WIP batches, you need to create a link between the raw material and the finished product. It isn't necessary to make any change in the process order header or components, and you can directly proceed to order confirmation.

Confirmation and Goods Issuance

When posting a confirmation using the WIP batch confirmation profile, you'll notice some of the following details:

- The button to display the **Goods Movements** overview isn't displayed.
- The GR goods movement is always proposed, even if automatic GR isn't set for the process order.
- The GI goods movements are always proposed, even if the **Backflush** checkbox isn't set for the components.
- All the goods movements are proposed without quantity.

Access the figure shown in Figure 10.55 using Transaction COR6N, then enter production **Order** "1000098" and its first **Phase**, which in this example is "0020". Scroll down the screen to evaluate the information provided here.

The same three areas—**WIP Batch: GR**, **WIP Batch: GI**, and **WIP Batch Entry**—that were set in the confirmation profile are displayed here. In the **WIP Batch: GI** area, the system may propose several components, of which we choose raw **Material 104** and its associated batch 7 for consumption (using **Mvmt Type 261**). Select this line item, then choose the **WIP Batch** button.

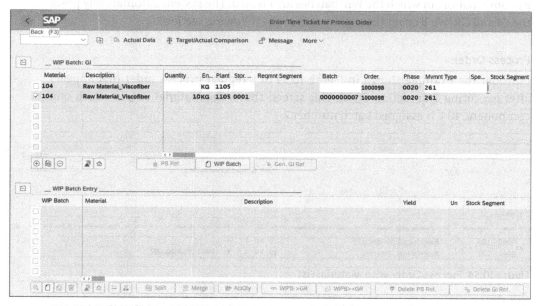

Figure 10.55 Confirmation with WIP Batches

In the popup screen that appears (see Figure 10.56), enter the name of the WIP batch in the **WIP Batch** field (e.g., "WIP_B_006"). With this process, a link between the raw material batch consumed and the WIP batch is being established. Click **Continue**.

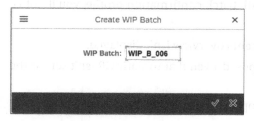

Figure 10.56 WIP Batch

The screen shown in Figure 10.57 prompts you to maintain characteristic values of WIP batch WIP_B_006. Figure 10.58 shows the newly created WIP batch WIP_B_006.

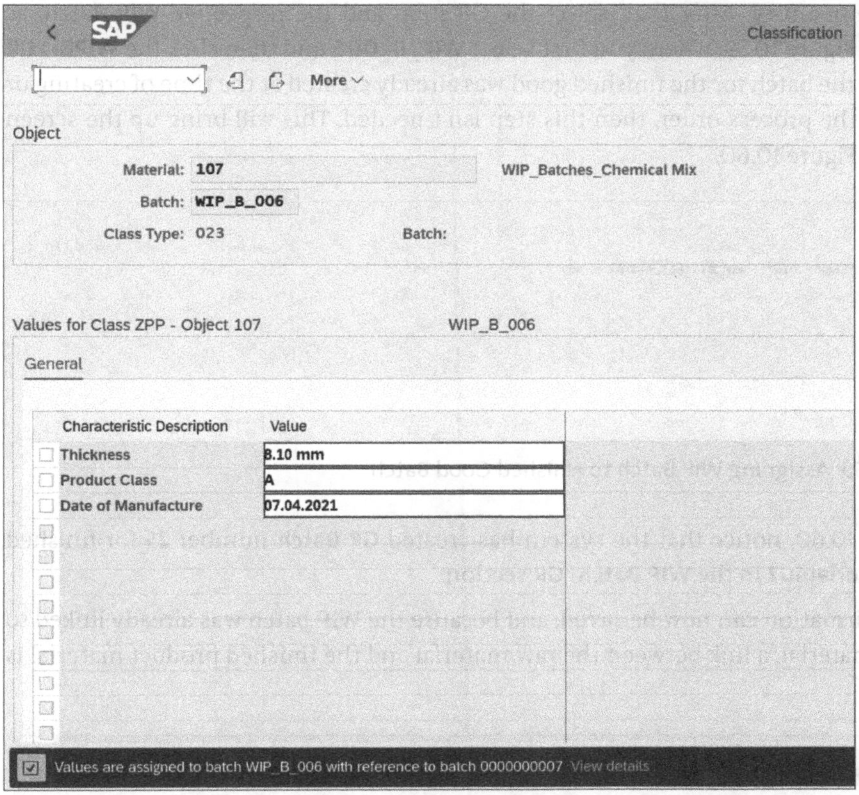

Figure 10.57 Maintaining Characteristic Values of WIP Batch

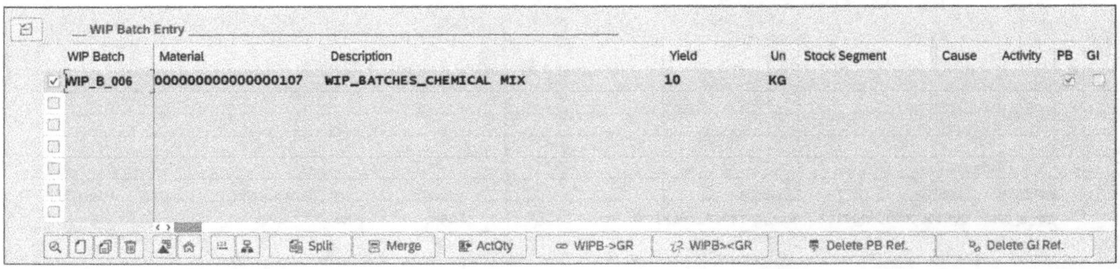

Figure 10.58 Yield Entry for WIP Batch

Next, maintain the standard confirmation details, such as the yield, scrap, rework, and associated activities (e.g., machine or labor hours) as is normally done in the confirmation process.

Work in Process Batch Goods Receipt

As explained previously in this section, the GR movement is proposed by default in the **WIP Batch: GR** section; however, it's proposed without a quantity, so you'll need to input the quantity. After that, select the GR item and the respective **WIP Batch**, as shown in Figure 10.59, where you first select **WIP_B_006** and then click the **WIPB->GR** button. If the batch for the finished good was already created at the time of creating or releasing the process order, then this step isn't needed. This will bring up the screen shown in Figure 10.60.

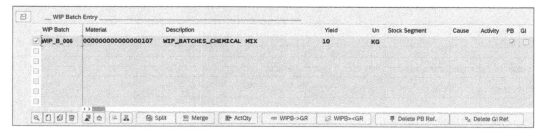

Figure 10.59 Assigning WIP Batch to Finished Good Batch

In Figure 10.60, notice that the system has created **GR Batch** number **25** for finished good **Material 107** in the **WIP Batch: GR** section.

This confirmation can now be saved, and because the WIP batch was already linked to the raw material, a link between the raw material and the finished product material is created.

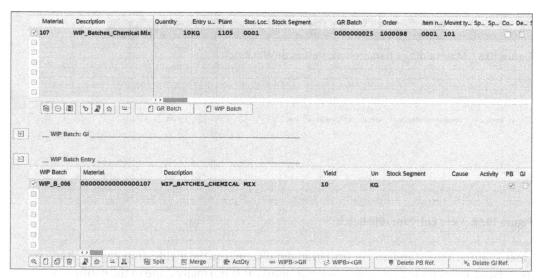

Figure 10.60 WIP Batch GR

This is how the system links up a raw material's batch to a WIP batch and then to a finished good's batch for the process order 1000098:

Raw material 104 (batch number 7): WIP batch (WIP_B_006): Finished good 107 (batch number 25).

We'll see the same link-up when we cover reporting in Section 10.8.4.

When posting GR of a finished goods batch, a few more screens or popups may appear to maintain additional details, such as date of manufacture or characteristic values of the finished good's batch that are created by the system at the time of GR.

> **Note**
>
> Now that you have a basic understanding of WIP batches and how they work is developed, we suggest exploring several additional features and functionalities available to handle all business processes.
>
> For example, in the earlier Figure 10.59, we showed how to link up the WIP batch with GR, but what if a user mistakenly created a wrong link? To undo or delink this linkage, use the **WIPB><GR** icon to correct the error.

10.8.4   Work in Process Batches Reporting

Access the **Batch Information Cockpit** screen (see Figure 10.61) using Transaction BMBC to see the report on WIP batches. Enter **Material** "107", its associated **Batch** "25", and **Plant** "1105", then choose **Selection** (at the top left in the menu bar).

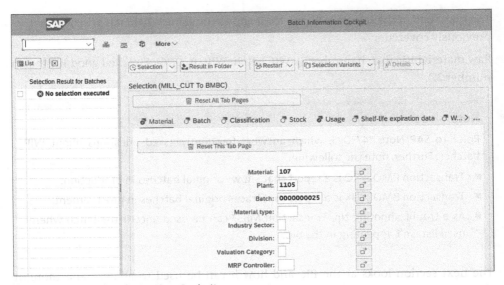

Figure 10.61 Batch Information Cockpit

Figure 10.62 shows **Batch (25)** for **Material 107**, which meets the selection criteria. Click this batch **25** on the left-hand side of the screen, then select **Usage** from the **Details** dropdown icon located on the top right-hand side of the screen.

For batch **25** for the finished good **107**, Figure 10.62 shows the **Top-Down Analysis** of the process order **1000098**, the raw material **104**, and its associated batch **07**. However, these screen details still don't show the associated WIP batch that was created during confirmation. To view the details of the WIP batch, click process order **1000098**, then choose **WIP Batch**.

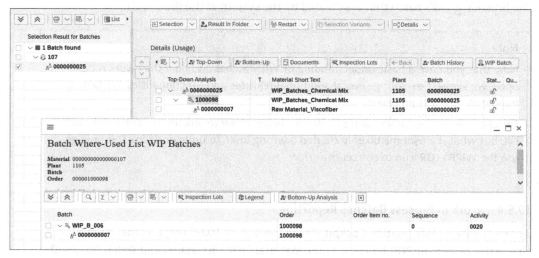

Figure 10.62 Batch Usage

The lower half of the screen in Figure 10.62 shows the same WIP batch's linkage that we previously covered:

Raw material 104 (batch number 7): WIP batch (WIP_B_006): Finished good 107 (batch number 25).

> **Note**
>
> Refer to SAP Note 1473025, which answers frequently asked questions about WIP batches. Further, note the following:
>
> - Transaction BMOBPRO is a report that shows original batches in production.
> - Transaction BMOBPUR is a report that traces original batches in procurement.
> - As a troubleshooting tip, Transaction MB57 can be used once if the batch where-used list isn't appearing in the BIC.

The next section looks at the BIC and how it can be used to analyze and monitor batches.

10.9   Batch Information Cockpit

In process industries, such as food and pharmaceuticals, traceability of the ingredients or components within a production or procurement process is of paramount importance. Batch traceability across logistics and supply chain processes is also a legal requirement in many industries and good manufacturing practice to maintain in case there is a batch recall. Companies often develop complex custom reports to view and analyze batch traceability when BIC can serve the same purpose. With BIC, you can do the following:

- Perform top-down and bottom-up traceability analysis. With top-down, a finished good traces all the raw, packaging, and semifinished materials that were used in making the finished product's batch. With bottom-up, it's possible to trace the ingredients or raw materials and trace all the finished goods that were made using these ingredients or raw materials' batches.

- Access the batch master to display and change information related to the batch directly from BIC while performing the traceability analysis of a batch.

- Display the stock information of the batch.

- Display the stock position of a material and its associated batches.

To access BIC, follow menu path **Logistics • Central Functions • Batch Management • Batch Information Cockpit**, or use Transaction BMBC. Figure 10.63 shows the initial screen to set parameters that the system then considers to bring up relevant batches of materials. Notice the various tabs available on the right-hand side, which can be used to enter specific information. The left-hand side of the screen provides search functionality.

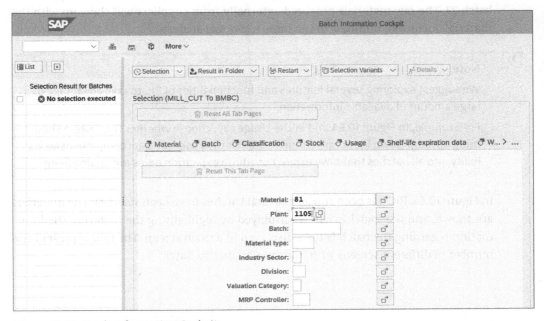

Figure 10.63 Batch Information Cockpit

For this example, enter **Material** "81", and **Plant** "1105". Choose **Selection**, then choose **Execute**. This brings up the screen shown in Figure 10.64. The left-hand side shows that the system is able to find the relevant material-plant-batch combination. The right-hand side appears when a user selects **Usage** from the **Details** dropdown.

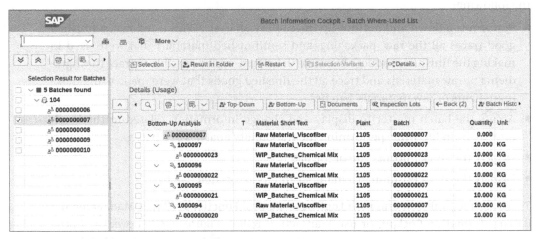

Figure 10.64 Bottom-Up Analysis

Figure 10.64 shows the bottom-up analysis for the batch 7 of material 81 in plant 1105. It shows that this batch was consumed in process order 1000097, which in turn produced batch 23. The raw materials procured externally from suppliers will show up with the material document numbers in the same top-down analysis.

> **Note**
>
> We suggest exploring several features and functionalities of BIC to take advantage of a large amount of available information.
>
> For example, in Figure 10.64 and in the **Usage** tab, choose whether the system should bring up a top-down list or bottom-up list. Similarly, a user can gain comprehensive visibility into all batches that have expired or whose expiration dates are approaching.

In Figure 10.65, BIC has been run and several batches have been selected. The materials are shown, and the matches can be displayed by highlighting the material. The information regarding the batch is then displayed in a main screen. The tabs represent the number of different screens with information on this batch.

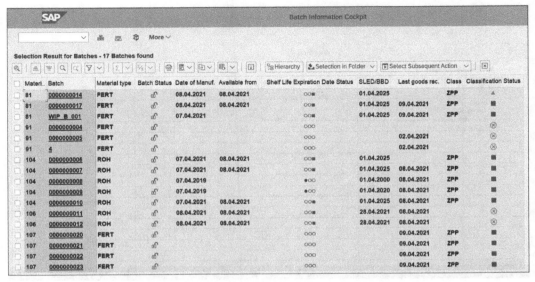

Figure 10.65 Central Area of Batch Information Cockpit

10.10 Electronic Batch Record

In highly regulated industries, such as pharmaceuticals, there's often a legal requirement to maintain a complete trail and record of all the batches used in the logistics and supply chain of manufacturing a product. Often it's not just the batches received from the procurement process or batches consumed in the production process that are important for record keeping; maintaining a complete record of various quality inspections that took place in the manufacturing process is important as well. The *electronic batch record* (EBR), or *batch record* for short, captures these inspection details too.

Access the screen shown in Figure 10.66 by following menu path **Logistics • Central Functions • Batch Management • Tools • Batch Record**, or using Transaction COEBR.

On the left-hand side, you can see a complete trail for material **81** and its associated **Batch 15**. As you drill down in the same node, the related process orders will appear, the two types of quality inspections (**04** for finished goods inspection, **03** for in-process inspection) if the PP-QM integration is in place, and the **Material List** (BOM) used in the production process.

On the upper-right side of the same screen, a user can only approve an EBR) for archiving with the **Approve** button if the statuses of various elements (e.g., process or process order, inspection lots, etc.) are set as required for electronic archiving. Here, the system also guides you to check all the prerequisites for EBR. After approval, an EBR can be archived by clicking the **Archive** button.

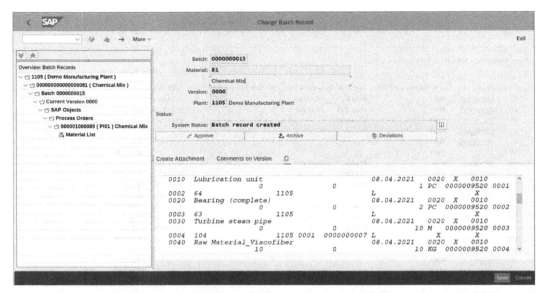

Figure 10.66 Electronic Batch Record

The lower-right side shows comprehensive details of the EBR in PDF format.

> **Note**
>
> We recommend engaging an SAP NetWeaver consultant to ensure that the necessary authorizations required for archiving electronic batches are granted. The SAP NetWeaver consultant will also set up a document repository required to store the EBRs being archived.

In some industries, such as consumer products or automotive suppliers, there are legal requirements to store where-used data of materials used for production and delivered to customers. Enabling recall actions becomes a mandatory and critical issue for these industries. Data can be recorded by managing all relevant materials in batches, but this method has a negative impact on data volume. When turning on batch management, entering a batch number becomes obligatory for all goods movements. Then all inventory postings must be executed on the batch level, and labor costs for IM will increase.

With the documentary batch record, it's important to ensure that a partial stock of a material is traceable without having to maintain a batch's data. This reduces the effort and complexities involved in maintaining batch data. The documentary batch record finds greater use in automotive and consumer goods industries but is unsuitable for use in dangerous goods.

Documentary batch processing can be achieved in the following ways:

- Documentary batches can be entered during goods movements.

- In a process order, entering documentary batches is only possible at backflush.

- In WM, entering documentary batches must be enabled during transport order confirmation.

10.11   Summary

Batch management is important to a large number of process-based industries. It has developed from just an identification of a group of items to a process that allows companies to perform product recalls, select and sell by batch characteristics, and identify expiring stock. As the drive for a competitive advantage continues, companies will further investigate how batch information can lower production time and hasten material to the customer.

Chapter 11 discusses sales and operations planning (S&OP).

10

Chapter 11
Sales and Operations Planning

Sales and operations planning strives to maintain a balance between demand planning and operations planning, which takes initial stocks, machine capacities, and constraints into account to finalize a realistic production plan. A planner can use standard sales and operations planning to come up with a feasible production plan or use flexible planning if there's a complex and diverse planning need.

Sales and operations planning (S&OP) is an iterative form of business process management, in which a planner uses several planning scenarios and versions until arriving at a production plan. A planner can then confidently use that plan in production, procurement, and capital investment processes.

With the complexities involved in global supply chain management processes, there has never been a greater appreciation for ensuring effective and efficient use of S&OP. S&OP is mainly about sales-driven forecasting and consolidating forecasts and uses only neutral key figures (numbers) for that. In contrast to this, production planning (PP), including material requirements planning (MRP) and capacity requirements planning (CRP), is all about production and takes into account requirements instead of key figures. Still, MRP in SAP S/4HANA doesn't consider capacities, but CRP does. For a value-based plan, a planner needs to transfer the sales or production figures to profitability analysis (CO-PA).

The biggest incentive for implementing S&OP in a company comes from the ability of a planner to evaluate various what-if models and to perform scenario planning in simulative modes, before passing on the finalized operations plan to demand management in the form of planned independent requirements (PIRs). Forecasting plays a major role in helping the planner arrive at a plausible operations plan.

[«]

> **Note**
>
> Long-term planning (LTP) and predictive material and resource planning (pMRP) are two additional tools available in SAP for planning and simulation. LTP offers several planning options, including simulating the components' requirements quantities, inventory controlling activities, and capacity requirements. LTP has its limitations, however. For example, LTP can't take into account a product's demand fluctuation or

the effect of changes in one key figure, such as sales quantity or production quantity, whereas both are possible in flexible planning. Refer to Chapter 16 and Chapter 17 for more information on LTP and pMRP respectively.

In this chapter, we'll start with an overview of what S&OP is and also introduce flexible planning, which a planner can use as an alternative. We'll give an explanation of all functions and tools that are a part of these planning types and a walkthrough of how to work with them and interpret their results. We also cover a lesser-known and -used application of flexible planning, known as *standard analysis reporting*. Standard analysis in flexible planning uses all the concepts and fundamentals that that are discussed in this chapter.

But first, let's start with an overview.

11.1   Standard Sales and Operations Planning

The following sections begin with an overview of S&OP and the similarities and differences between standard S&OP and flexible planning. It then moves on to cover forecasting and concludes with coverage of standard analysis in flexible panning.

11.1.1   Overview

In standard S&OP, a planner can plan individual materials or a group of materials (known as a *product group*). The product group consists of individual materials or other product groups and enables a planner to define the proportion factor (percentage) for each material in the overall product group. It also offers the option to aggregate and disaggregate at various planning levels. If the planning processes in a company are relatively simple and straightforward—that is, restricted to individual materials or a group of materials—then standard S&OP can fulfill the business needs.

Example

Consider the following business scenario: Before each financial year begins, the sales and production teams spend countless hours working on planning figures that are acceptable to both. The sales team uses forecasting tools to arrive at next year's sale figures (targets) based on historical data. The production team looks at things differently. They evaluate whether they are able to meet the demand of sales with the existing production capacities or not. The procurement planner needs a better understanding of how the production figures will impact the procurement process: Do the vendors even have the capabilities to meet the supply requirements of the company? The inventory controller (warehouse) is concerned about whether there is enough space in the warehouse to manage and store the produced quantities. The management of the company is interested in not only increasing the profitability of the product (and at the same time reducing costs) but also gaining a broader understanding of the capital tie-up involved and whether new investment (e.g., capacity enhancement or increasing the number of working shifts) is warranted. Further, knowing which products (or groups of products), regions, or markets can bring in greater revenue for the company also helps in the decision-making process.

This is where S&OP can help. In general, the entire planning exercise entails the creation of various planning versions in the system, adjusting sales or production figures until there is a mutual consensus. The finalized planning figures, which usually reflect a production plan, are sent forward to demand management, where they appear as planned PIRs with an active version. When the system runs the MRP, it considers the active PIRs to arrive at procurement proposals (in-house production and external procurement).

In the planning process, a planning table is needed in the SAP system that can take all of the important planning considerations into account and at the same time account for dependencies of one factor on another.

The flexible planning functionality, while very sophisticated, is also a slightly complex tool to manage. With better comprehension, the dividends that flexible planning offers are far higher and bring forth much more realistic planning figures, which the company can use to reap greater financial benefits. For example, with flexible planning, a planner can configure a planning layout (known as a *planning table*) of important key figures; include self-defined macros to manage complex calculations; perform forecasting (also possible in standard S&OP); take special events (e.g., trade shows or the Olympics) into account for increases in sales or take natural calamities (e.g., drought or flood) into account to factor in decreases in sales (or increases, if a company manufactures relevant products); and have a broader understanding of commitments (known as *pegged requirements*), such as capacities, materials, or production resources/tools (PRTs).

When deciding which S&OP options (standard S&OP or flexible planning) to use, it makes sense to evaluate the business requirements and at the same time strive to maintain simplicity and a straightforward approach to business processes. As mentioned already, standard S&OP offers a very limited set of functions, but being almost completely predefined, it enables a planner to immediately start taking advantage of the functionalities without any configuration. A general recommendation is to first try and cover your business process with standard S&OP, and then, if important functions are still missing, consider using the rather complex and sophisticated flexible planning tool instead. Flexible planning offers full functionality but requires configuration, many presettings, and definitions.

SAP offers several standard analysis reports in all logistics areas, consisting of characteristics and key figures for a period. A *characteristic value combination* (CVC) is the combination of characteristic values with which a planner wants to plan. Characteristics can be materials, plants, sales organizations, distribution channels, or purchase organizations. Key figures (values or quantities) can be quantity produced, quantity procured, operations quantity confirmed, production scrap (quantity), invoiced value, or purchasing value. The period can be an interval, such as six months.

For example, standard analyses bring forth information such as the purchase and invoiced values (key figures) of all the materials (characteristics) during the past six months (period). The standard analysis reports that SAP offers for each logistics functional area have predefined information structures with no option to add new key figures. However, it's also possible to create your own self-defined information structure in flexible planning by choosing the desired key figures from several available catalogs. A catalog consists of a large number of characteristics and key figures of a specific application area, such as PP or quality management (QM). Further, a planner can even define how frequently the system should update the values of key figures in flexible planning standard analysis. Hence, standard analysis in flexible planning isn't just applicable to the PP functionality; concepts and details covered in this chapter are equally applicable to other functionalities such as QM, plant maintenance (PM), materials management (MM), and sales and distribution (SD).

Note

See Chapter 23 for more on reporting, including standard analyses in PP.

The example of flexible planning from both perspectives (flexible planning and standard analysis in flexible planning) in this chapter remains primarily focused on SD and its integral correlation with PP processes.

Note

Regardless of whether a company implements standard S&OP or flexible planning, we encourage reading the entire chapter because several features and functionalities are applicable to both planning types and are eventually covered (not necessarily in the same section). For example, we cover the forecasting functionality within flexible planning, but it's also available and can be used in standard S&OP for a material or material group. We've also dedicated a separate section to forecasting. This is also true for events and rough-cut planning. An event tends to have an impact on planning figures. A rough-cut planning profile provides better visibility into capacity, material, or PRT situations. Similarly, we cover aggregation/disaggregation in standard S&OP but not in flexible planning, although the option is available in both planning types.

Figure 11.1 shows that S&OP can have key figures from one of the following three available options:

- **Sales information system (SIS)**
  SIS takes information from the sales history to propose a sales plan.

- **Profitability analysis**
  Information from CO-PA is used to help the planner makes a sales plan. The system derives this information from sales and profit planning.

- **Forecasting**
  Historical data is used to come up with a sales plan. Forecasting is covered in Section 11.4.

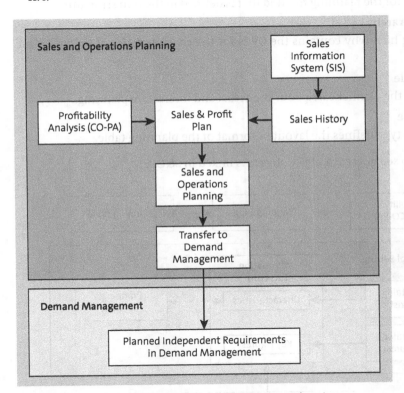

Figure 11.1 Process Overview of Sales and Operations Planning

The figures from S&OP are eventually transferred to demand management in the form of PIRs, which form the basis of MRP.

We list the objects used in S&OP (standard S&OP and flexible planning) and provide their logical relationships in Figure 11.2. The objects in S&OP form an integral part in the planning process, so it's important to have a comprehensive understanding of them:

- **Information structure (info structure)**
  This is the data structure that stores the important planning parameters. The planning data is stored in key figures for the CVCs. As previously explained, characteristics can be selection criteria based on which the system brings up relevant key figures. Key figures can be quantities or values—for example, the number of quality inspection lots, total purchase value of raw materials, operation quantities, or production quantities.

- **Planning method**
  The storage, aggregation, and disaggregation of data with regard to the planning level occur either as consistent planning or as level-by-level planning. In S&OP, the system looks for the planning method that is defined in the info structure.

- **Planning hierarchy**
  The planning hierarchy contains the CVCs for the characteristics of the info structure.

- **Planning table**
  This is where the planner carries out the actual and interactive planning.

- **Planning type**
  The planning type defines the layout or format of the planning table.

See Figure 11.2 to see how each of the objects is linked in S&OP.

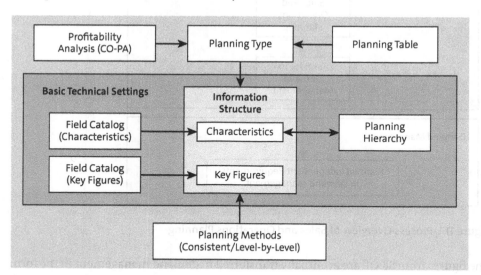

Figure 11.2 S&OP Objects

Figure 11.3 provides a graphical comparison between the planning methods available for standard S&OP and flexible planning.

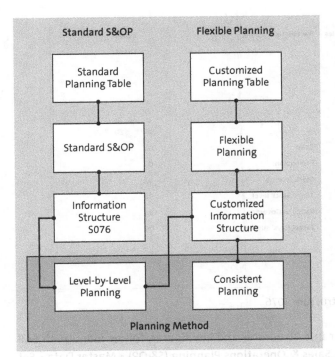

Figure 11.3 Standard S&OP, Flexible Planning, Level-by-Level Planning, and Consistent Planning

Now let's discuss the details of the objects used in standard S&OP and in flexible planning.

11.1.2   Information Structures

To create or change info structures, use menu path **SAP IMG • Logistics General • Logistics Information System (LIS) • Logistics Data Warehouse • Data Basis • Information Structures • Maintain Custom Information Structures**. Alternately, use Transaction MC21 to create info structures and Transaction MC22 to change them.

Figure 11.4 shows **Info Struct. S076**, which is used in standard S&OP.

The planning result is stored for each CVC among the six key figures listed in the figure. Values for other key figures, such as special production or sales order, for example, can't be stored in this (standard) info structure.

In standard S&OP, it isn't possible to change many settings, but we'll review them to provide a better comprehension of the parameters used in standard S&OP for info structures and key figures.

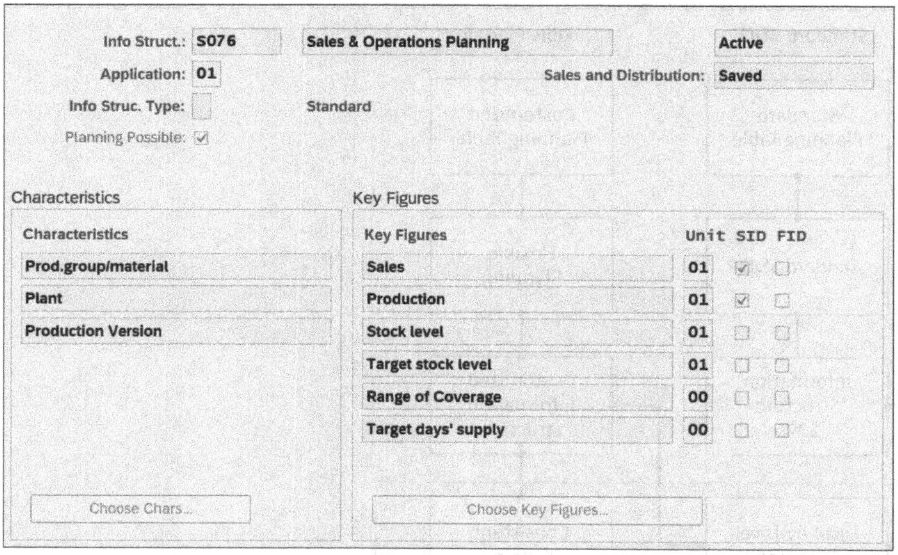

Info Struct.:	S076	Sales & Operations Planning		Active
Application:	01		Sales and Distribution:	Saved
Info Struc. Type:		Standard		
Planning Possible:	☑			

Characteristics

Characteristics
Prod.group/material
Plant
Production Version

Key Figures

Key Figures	Unit	SID	FID
Sales	01	☑	☐
Production	01	☑	☐
Stock level	01	☐	☐
Target stock level	01	☐	☐
Range of Coverage	00	☐	☐
Target days' supply	00	☐	☐

Choose Chars...   Choose Key Figures...

Figure 11.4 Standard SAP Info Structure S076

To view or set parameters for info structures and key figures, follow menu path **SAP IMG · Logistics · Production · Sales & Operations Planning (S&OP) · Master Data · Set Parameters for Info Structures and Key Figures**, or use Transaction MC7F.

On the screen shown in Figure 11.5, double-click the info structure (**Table**) **S076**, or select the same and choose **Details**, which opens the **Change View "Info structure planning parameters": Details** screen. This area stipulates that the planning method used in standard S&OP is level-by-level planning (denoted by I in the **Planning Method** field).

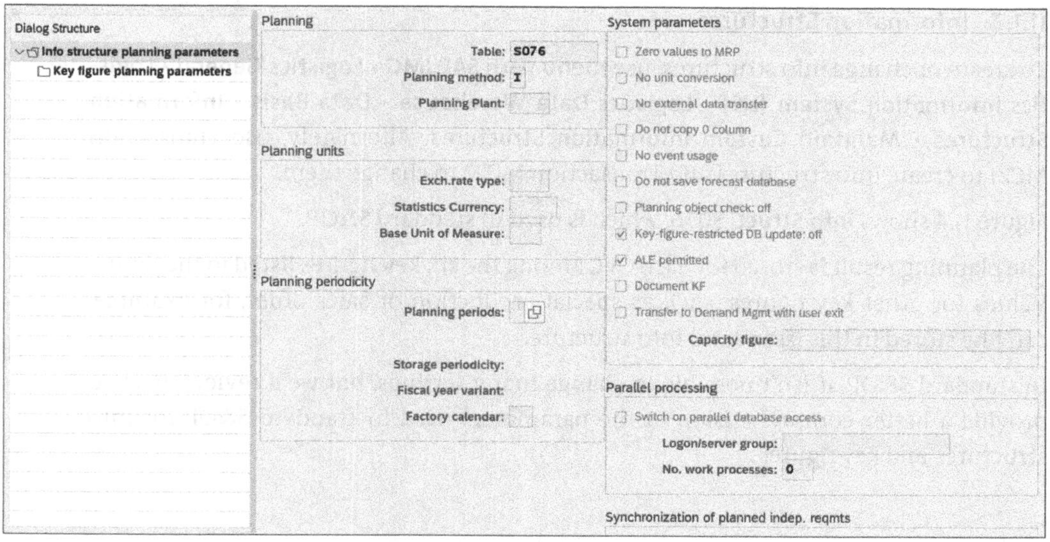

Dialog Structure
- ∨ 🗂 **Info structure planning parameters**
  - 🗀 **Key figure planning parameters**

Planning

Table:	S076
Planning method:	I
Planning Plant:	

Planning units

Exch.rate type:	
Statistics Currency:	
Base Unit of Measure:	

Planning periodicity

| Planning periods: | 🔲 |

Storage periodicity:
Fiscal year variant:
Factory calendar:

System parameters

☐ Zero values to MRP
☐ No unit conversion
☐ No external data transfer
☐ Do not copy 0 column
☐ No event usage
☐ Do not save forecast database
☐ Planning object check: off
☑ Key-figure-restricted DB update: off
☑ ALE permitted
☐ Document KF
☐ Transfer to Demand Mgmt with user exit

Capacity figure:

Parallel processing

☐ Switch on parallel database access

Logon/server group:
No. work processes: 0

Synchronization of planned indep. reqmts

Figure 11.5 Planning Parameters of Info Structure

Choose the **Key Figure Planning Parameters** folder on the left-hand side of the screen, and the screen shown in Figure 11.6 appears. The lower half lists the key figures available for standard info structure S076. Double-click the **ABSAT** field, and a popup appears (see Figure 11.7). Here, it's possible to control whether the key figure can be used for forecasting and to determine the type of aggregation (summation) of the entered data in the planning table.

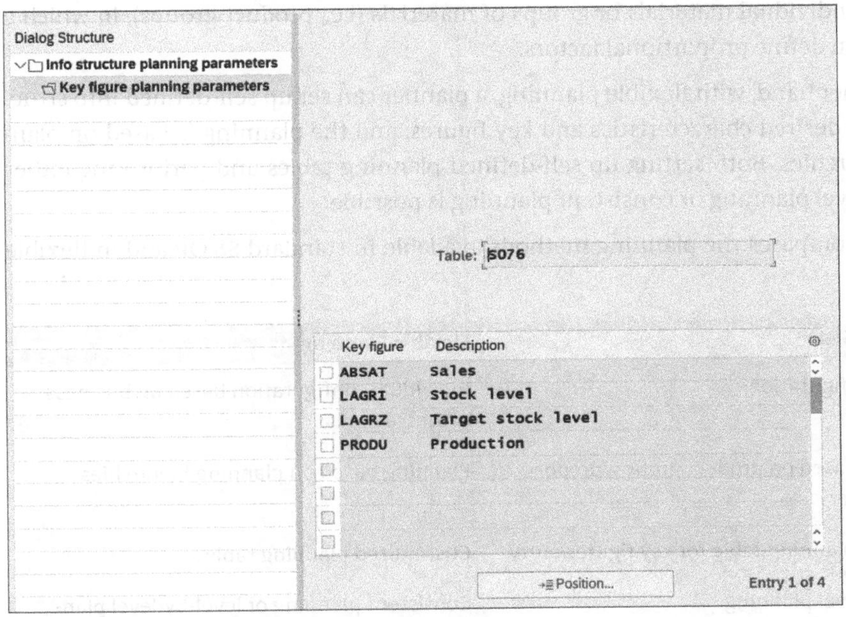

Figure 11.6 Key Figures Planning Parameters

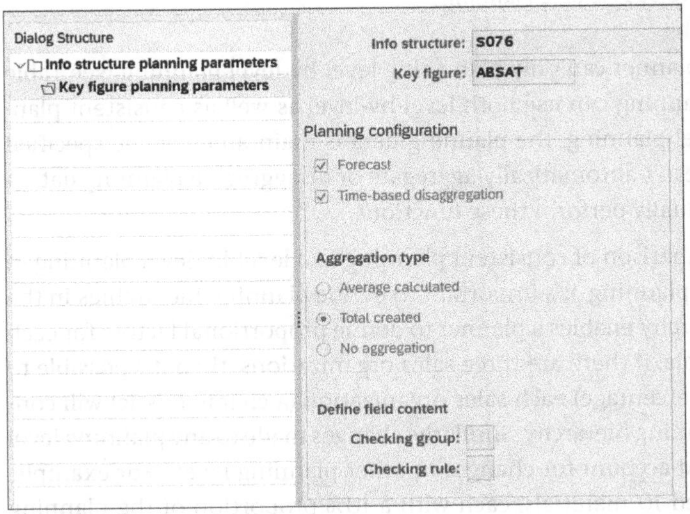

Figure 11.7 Details of Key Figure ABSAT

11.1.3   Planning Methods

Near the beginning of this chapter, we mentioned that in standard S&OP, the configuration and other settings are predefined, with limited options to customize parameters to meet the business requirements. For example, in standard S&OP, the configuration for info structure SO76 is preset with characteristics and key figures, as well as the planning table in which a planner maintains the planning figures. The planning is either based on individual materials or groups of materials (i.e., product groups), in which a planner can define proportional factors.

On the other hand, with flexible planning, a planner can set up self-defined info structures with desired characteristics and key figures, and the planning is based on planning hierarchies. Both setting up self-defined planning tables and performing either level-by-level planning or consistent planning is possible.

Table 11.1 compares the planning methods available in standard S&OP and in flexible planning.

Standard S&OP	Flexible Planning
Preset configuration	Individual configuration based on business processes
Planning based on product groups/proportional factors	Planning based on planning hierarchies
Standard planning table for key figures entry	Customized planning tables
Level-by-level planning	Consistent planning or level-by-level planning

Table 11.1 Standard S&OP versus Flexible Planning

With standard S&OP, a planner can only plan using level-by-level planning (see Table 11.2), whereas flexible planning can use both level-by-level as well as consistent planning. In the level-by-level planning, the planning data is maintained at the specified level only. Because it doesn't automatically aggregate or disaggregate planning data, a planner will have to manually perform these functions.

Table 11.2 provides a comparison of consistent planning and level-by-level planning in detail. To use consistent planning, it's important to define planning hierarchies in the system. A planning hierarchy enables a planner to define proportional factors for each characteristic. For example, if there are three sales organizations, then it's possible to define how much (as a percentage) each sales organization (a characteristic) will contribute in the overall planning hierarchy. Similarly, changes made to any planning level automatically update and account for changes in other planning levels. For example, initially a planner defined 10 materials, each with a 10% proportion of the planning results. Now, if a new material is added, the system automatically updates the proportional factor (100% ÷ 11 materials = 9.09% for each material). The system also automatically aggregates (adds up) and disaggregates (divides up) the planning data to present a consistent planning position in the planning table.

Consistent Planning	Level-by-Level Planning
Planning hierarchy	Product group
Storage at the lowest level; planning data at all levels	Storage at each level; planning data only at maintained level
Automatic aggregation and disaggregation	Aggregation and disaggregation as a planning step

Table 11.2 Consistent Planning and Level-by-Level Planning

11.1.4 Planning Types in Standard Sales and Operations Planning

The *planning type* defines the layout or the format of the planning table and thus represents the link between the planning table, where the actual planning is carried out, and the info structure, in which the planning data is stored. It's possible to create several planning types for one info structure. For example, two different planning types may contain planning data for two seasons (autumn and winter). The data is stored in the info structure, so the different planning types depend on each other because they use the same set of data. If level-by-level planning is used, then it's important to create a separate planning type for each planning level.

Standard S&OP has been configured with three planning types, which are used automatically in standard S&OP planning:

- **SOPKAPA**
  Planning type for the planning of individual product groups
- **SOPKAPAM**
  Planning type for the planning of individual materials
- **SOPDIS**
  Planning type for the dual-level planning of product group hierarchies

In the following sections, we'll go through the steps needed to create a product group that can be used in standard S&OP. We'll also show how to transfer the planning results of a product group to demand management as PIRs.

Create a Product Group

Figure 11.8 shows that in this example, we're using info structure S076 in standard S&OP to create a product group called Turbine_SOP for plant 1105. This product group has two materials, 25 and 108, with proportional factors of 60% and 40%, respectively. We explained aggregation and disaggregation earlier, but the proportional factor is specific to level-by-level planning only and either can be maintained manually or proposed automatically by the system.

To create the product group in the system, follow SAP menu path **Logistics • Production • SOP • Product Group • Create**, or use Transaction MC84. For **Product group Turbine_SOP** and **Plant 1105**, enter the materials, "25" and "108", and their proportional factors, "60" and "40" (percentages).

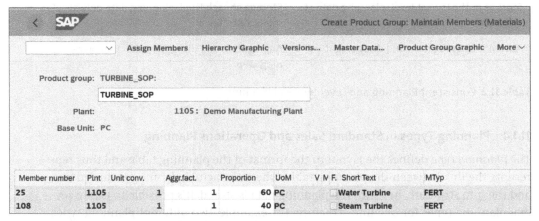

Figure 11.8 Creating Product Group Turbine_SOP

Choose the **Product Group Graphic** button to view the product group graphically (see Figure 11.9).

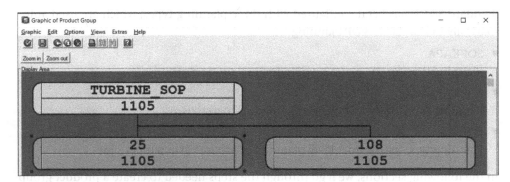

Figure 11.9 Graphical View of Product Group

In addition to the interactive entry, a planner can also calculate proportional factors on the basis of historical data via menu path **More • Edit • Calculate Proportional Factors**. Use this option to see how well the self-defined (manual) proportional factors compare with what the system proposes, which may help in preparing a realistic plan. Moreover, the proportional factors can be equally distributed via **More · Edit · Distribute Proportional Factors**. Save the product group.

Create a Plan for the Product Group

To plan the product group in standard S&OP, use menu path **Logistics · Production · SOP · Planning · For Product Group · Create**, or use Transaction MC81.

Figure 11.10 shows the initial screen of the rough-cut plan for the product. Enter **Product group** "Turbine_SOP" and **Plant** "1105", then press Enter to go to the **Define Version** dialog box. On this screen, enter planning **Version** "001" and a version description, and again press Enter to go to the **Create Rough-Cut Plan** screen.

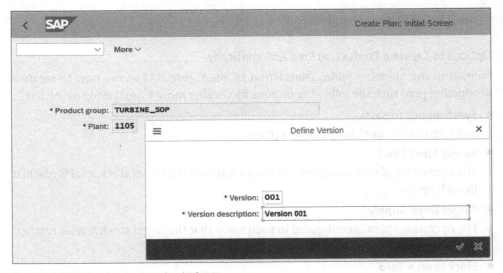

Figure 11.10 Planning in Standard S&OP

If the historical key figure data is already available in the system, then it can be imported to create a sales plan. Alternatively, manually enter the **Sales** quantities in the planning table, as we've done in this example, by entering sales data for the next nine months. On the screen shown in Figure 11.11, click the **More** dropdown menu to see several options to create a sales plan for the product group (or for an individual material, where applicable):

- **Transfer Plan from SIS**
- **Transfer CO-PA Plan**
- **Forecast**
- **Transfer Product Group Proportional from Production or from Sales**

To use any of these options, the system must have significant historical data to help in effective and reliable planning.

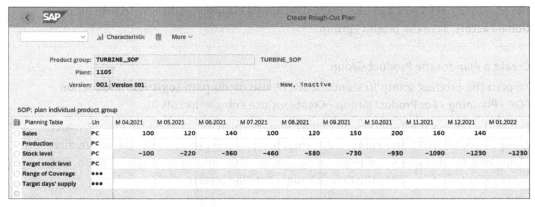

Figure 11.11 Sales Plan in Standard S&OP

Options to Create a Production Plan Automatically

Remain in the planning table (Transaction MC81). Figure 11.12 shows how to create a production plan with the following options by clicking **More** from the top menu bar:

- **Synchronous to Sales**
  Sales figures are used as operations plans.

- **Target Stock Level**
  The operations plan is configured in such a way that the target stock level is reached in each period.

- **Target Days' Supply**
  The operations plan is configured in such a way that the target stock level is reached in each period.

- **Stock Level = Zero**
  The operations plan is configured in such a way that the entire stock level is consumed.

Depending on the business requirement, choose if the production plan should be equal to the target stock level or if the target stock should eventually be zero at the end of the period. For this example, create the production plan as synchronous to the sales plan. This production plan has also taken the target stock levels into account at the end of each period.

It's important to note that these production figures have no direct implications on the production or procurement. The purpose of entering or incorporating these numbers (key figures, such as sales or production) is to come to a common understanding, wherein relevant stakeholders, be they from sales or production, can transfer the *finalized* key figures to demand management in the form of PIRs. For example, several planning versions are created in the system, from which input and feedback from sales and production are taken. The sales or the production figures are revised either in the same planning version or by creating a new version. The finalized version eventually transfers to demand management and reflects as PIRs with the **Active** checkbox selected.

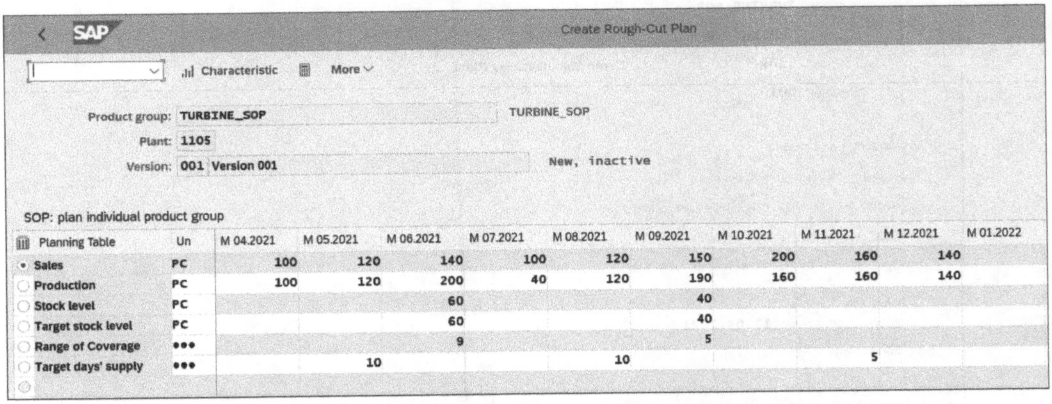

Planning Table	Un	M 04.2021	M 05.2021	M 06.2021	M 07.2021	M 08.2021	M 09.2021	M 10.2021	M 11.2021	M 12.2021	M 01.2022
Sales	PC	100	120	140	100	120	150	200	160	140	
Production	PC	100	120	200	40	120	190	160	160	140	
Stock level	PC			60			40				
Target stock level	PC			60			40				
Range of Coverage	•••			9			5				
Target days' supply	•••		10			10			5		

Figure 11.12 Options to Create Production Plan in Standard S&OP

The next step is to transfer the production plan to demand management, where the requirements of individual members (materials) of the product group are reflected as PIRs. When the transfer of the product group quantities to demand management takes place, the system disaggregates at the material level according to the proportional factor defined previously. In this example, a proportional factor of 60% and 40% is maintained for the two materials. The next section will show how the system disaggregates (divides up) the total planning quantities of the product group in a 60 to 40 ratio.

Transfer to Demand Management

A planner can directly transfer the planning figures from the planning table to demand management by selecting the relevant key figures (e.g., production) and using menu path **More • Extras • Transfer to Demand Management.** Alternatively, use menu path **Logistics • Production • SOP • Planning • For Product Group • Transfer PG to Demand Management**, or use Transaction MC75.

Figure 11.13 shows the initial screen to assign **Version** "001" of the product group and plant for transfer to demand management. The **Prod.Plan for Mat. or PG Members as Proportion of PG** radio button enables transferring the production plan to demand management.

Also, specify the requirement type and the version of PIR within which the system transfers the values. In this example, assign **Requirements Type** as "VSF" and **Version** as "00", and choose **Transfer Now**. A message log appears after the transfer is made.

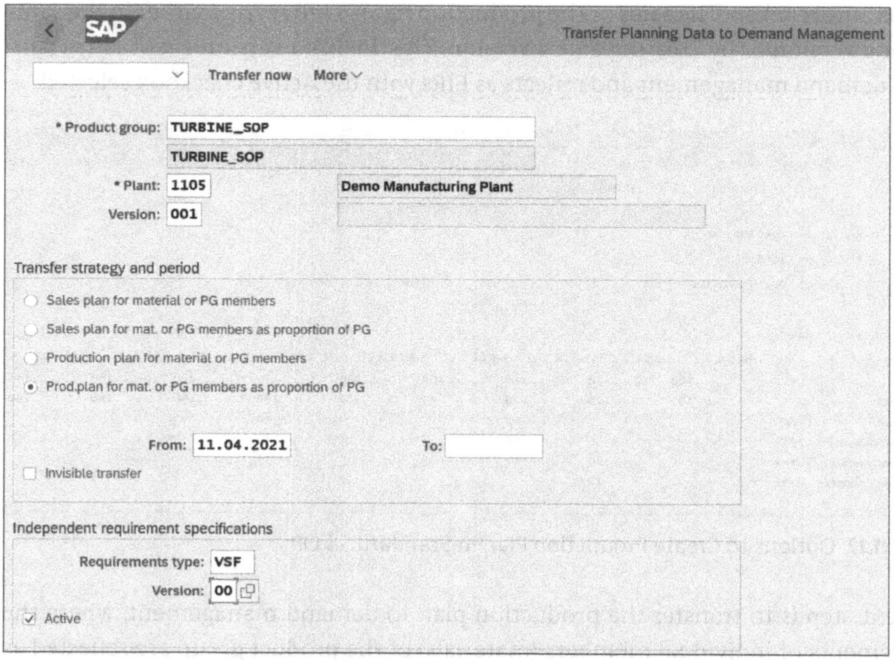

Figure 11.13 Transfer Product Group to Demand Management

Planned Independent Requirements in Demand Management

To check and confirm whether production figures of the product group were successfully transferred in demand management as PIRs, follow SAP menu path **Logistics • Production • Demand Management • Planned Independent Requirements • Display**, or use Transaction MD63.

On the initial screen, enter the selection parameters, such as **Product Group** "Turbine_SOP", **Plant** "1105", **Requirements Type** "VSF", and **Selected Version** "00", which were all previously defined in Figure 11.12. Press Enter, and you'll see the screen in Figure 11.14, which shows how the product group breaks down into individual members (materials), with the transferred quantity divided in a ratio of 60% to 40%.

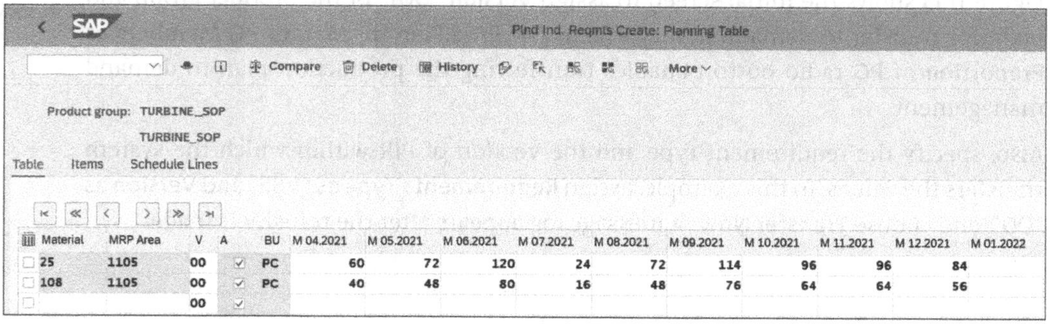

Figure 11.14 PIRs in Demand Management

11.1.5 Distribute Key Figures

During the course of planning the key figures, often the planner needs to make mass changes to several key figures at once. This can be tedious if done one by one or manually. Use the **Distribute** functionality to make mass changes to a key figure in the same row or column. The following are some of the changes that can be made:

- Perform mathematical calculations, such as addition, subtraction, multiplication, and so on, on all values (or a selection of values) of a key figure.
- Increase or decrease all the values (or a selection of values) of a key figure by a defined percentage.
- Distribute a value across the time series and replace the old values.

Figure 11.15 shows that the option to distribute key figures is available from the menu bar by clicking **Distribute** in the planning table. In the **Distribution Functions** dialog box that appears, enter a number in the **Val.** field, followed by selecting the right operand (**OP**). The list of available operands appears (shown on the right-hand side of Figure 11.15).

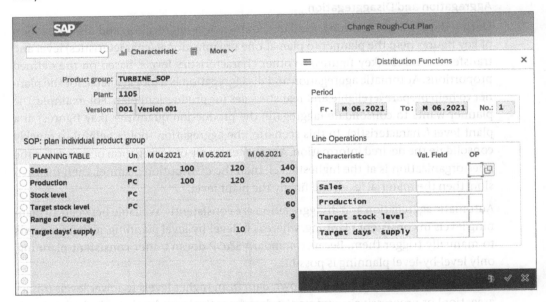

Figure 11.15 Distribution Functionality: Key Figures in S&OP

Figure 11.16 shows the graphical representation of the key figures, including sales, production, or stock level, to give the materials planner necessarily visibility of inward and outward movements of materials.

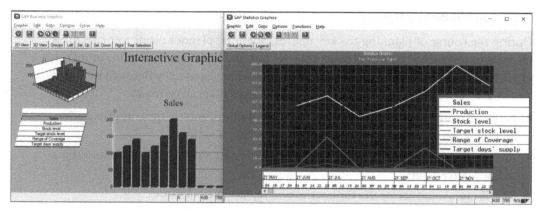

Figure 11.16 Graphical Representation of Key Figures in S&OP

The following sections cover aggregation and disaggregation, as well as tools and features available not only in standard S&OP but also in flexible planning.

Aggregation and Disaggregation

During the course of planning, available tools such as aggregation and disaggregation of key figures help the planner to plan at one organizational (characteristics) level and transfer the values (key figures) to other characteristics levels, based on the defined proportions. Automatic aggregation and disaggregation is a tool available for the planner to help prepare a reliable and realistic sales (or production) plan. For example, the planner wants to consolidate (aggregate) the production quantities (key figures) at a plant level (characteristic). In this scenario, the aggregation tool is helpful to quickly consolidate the desired information. Another example of aggregation occurs when the sales organization is at the highest level, then the distribution channel, then the division, then the material level, and finally the plant level.

Automatic aggregation and disaggregation are consistently available between all planning levels in consistent planning, whereas in level-by-level planning, a planner needs to manually trigger them. Because standard S&OP doesn't offer consistent planning, only level-by-level planning is possible.

The system enables a user to drill down data from higher levels to lower levels (disaggregation) or progressively sum up the data from the lower levels to the higher levels (aggregation of sum or average). The ultimate objective of planning, either in standard S&OP or in flexible planning, is to obtain a plan at the lowest level of the characteristic combination (e.g., at the product group or material level) and forward the plan to PP.

The planning hierarchy consists of CVCs and their disaggregation percentages. For example, if there's a CVC of sales organization, distribution channel, division, material, plant, statistics currency, and document currency, then a planner can view the historical sales data or a forecast plan for given key figures of the characteristics. The system disaggregates if the data is viewed from the lower levels of the hierarchy, and it aggregates the same if the data is viewed from the higher levels using the same set of disaggregation proportions.

Automatic Calculation of Proportional Factors

When the planning hierarchy is maintained, use Transaction MC9B (Using Planning Hierarchy) for consistent planning to allow the system to calculate the proportional factors based on the disaggregation proportions. These proportional factors become the base in consistent planning for the aggregation and disaggregation.

Time-Based Disaggregation

When rough-cut S&OP transfers the data in demand management, the system requires a *time-based disaggregation*. In S&OP, the planning is carried out in periods of weeks or months, whereas the PIR needs a current date for its planning activities. If the business process is simple, then the requirement of the period is scheduled for the first working day of the period without any further configuration. However, if there's a need for an in-depth and complex distribution of quantities, then a planner will need to define distribution strategies and period splits. The distribution strategy is assigned to the period split for weekly and monthly distribution. The period split, in turn, is assigned to the plant and the planning group.

Planning Hierarchy in Standard Sales and Operations Planning

The planning hierarchy in standard S&OP defines the proportion of one material with respect to others. For example, a material with a 40% proportional factor enables the system to divide all planning figures of this material to 40% of the total planning figures. A planning hierarchy master data is created in standard S&OP by maintaining product groups. The master data can also be generated automatically using Transaction MC8P for info structure S076. Alternatively, use program RMCPSOPP (by using Transaction SE38) to generate the master data for info structure S076. When a planner is in the product group as in standard S&OP or a planning hierarchy in flexible planning, it's important to define proportional factors. The system then uses these defined proportional factors either in level-by-level planning or in consistent planning.

Table 11.3 provides an overview of the usage of proportional factors in consistent planning and level-by-level planning.

Planning Mode	Calculation Method	Usage of Proportional Factors	Number of Levels
Level-by-level planning	–	Direct	Single
Consistent planning	Calculation based on the planning hierarchy	Multiplication of proportional factors of multiple levels	Multiple
Consistent planning	Calculation based on actual data	–	Multiple

Table 11.3 Usage of Proportional Factors in Disaggregation

To aggregate or disaggregate planning figures in standard S&OP, follow menu path **Logistics • Production • SOP • Disaggregation • Break Down PG Plan**, or use Transaction MC76. Having selected the product group, plant, and the version, the system will redirect the user to a screen in which changes to the proportional factor of each member of the product group can be made and in which they can select the relevant checkboxes to run the standard macros when the planning table screen for standard S&OP appears.

11.1.6   Working with Macros

Macros enable a planner to automate the linking of key figures in the planning table by using calculation rules. In standard S&OP, the system provides macros for the calculation of the projected stock level and for creating an operations plan on the basis of the sales plan. Macros can also be used in aggregation and disaggregation during level-by-level planning. It's not possible to define your own macros in standard S&OP.

In the planning table, first select the **Sales** line item, then choose **More • Macro**, which brings up the list of standard macros available to select from. For this example, choose **Aggregation: Sales**, which aggregates the individual sales figures for a material.

> **[»]**
>
> **Note**
> Self-defined macros in flexible planning are covered in greater detail in Section 11.2.6.

11.2   Flexible Planning

It's amply evident that standard S&OP offers limited options in terms of solutions to diverse and complex business scenarios and processes. If a company intends to carry out very lean and production-focused forecasting of sales figures, then it's recommended to check whether standard S&OP is able to fulfill the business needs.

For more complex planning scenarios, flexible planning can help. In flexible planning, a planner can plan and process planning data from any organizational unit, whether it's a sales organization, a distribution channel, or a production plant. Flexible planning begins with designing an *info structure*, which defines a structure with organizational units and business planning values—for example, forecast values in different periods, their relationships, and different views of planning values from different organizational units' perspectives, whether it's sales, production, or procurement. Gaining an in-depth understanding of how to define an info structure to fulfill business planning requirements is very important for successful implementation of flexible planning.

It's also possible to use info structures for product allocation. For example, in the automobile industry, it's common to assign sales quotas to different regions and to automotive dealers to ensure that a company's automobile is in every region it serves. In an info structure for production allocation, maintain a dealer-wise sales quota. During sales order creation for a specific dealer, the system then checks the information maintained in the info structure for product allocation to see if the dealer is still eligible to place orders. Similar to standard S&OP, in which everything is preconfigured, in flexible planning, a table is designed using the basic steps of configuring a self-defined info structure, setting the parameters for the info structure and key figures, and configuring the planning type.

This section will not only show how to successfully set up flexible planning but also specifically cover the update fields (key figures) involved in flexible planning. These update fields enable a planner to better use the flexible planning functionality when features such as macros, aggregation or disaggregation, events, and rough-cut planning aren't involved. The update fields apply to standard analysis in flexible planning.

S&OP can create a planning hierarchy and maintenance of disaggregation percentages for the CVCs in a hierarchy. As mentioned previously, a planning hierarchy is available in flexible planning only.

The section also covers self-defined macros, aggregation/disaggregation, events, and rough-cut planning profiles because all of these features hold significant value to the planner.

11.2.1   Creating a Self-Defined Info Structure

Because we've already covered the salient features of the info structure for flexible planning in Section 11.1.2, we'll now create the self-defined info structure in flexible planning.

To create and change these structures, follow menu path **SAP IMG · General Logistics · LIS · Logistics Data Warehouse · Data Basis · Information Structures · Maintain Custom Information Structures**. Alternately, use Transaction MC21 to create info structures and Transaction MC22 to change them.

Figure 11.17 shows the initial screen to create an info structure. For this example, define the **Info Structure** as "S655" and enter the description as "SOP: Info_Structure_Turbine". It's important to select the application because the resulting catalog (consisting of characteristics and key figures) will then appear accordingly. For this example, set **Application** as "01" for SD. It's also important to choose the **Planning Possible** checkbox to enable the user to perform planning functions in flexible planning.

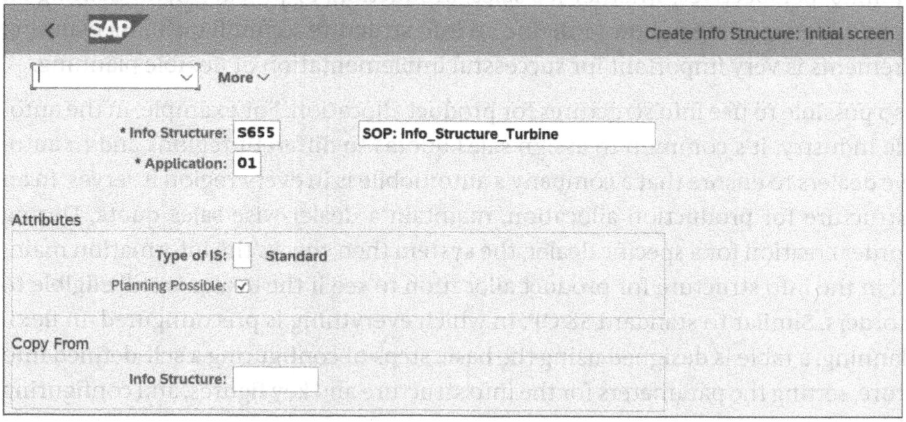

Figure 11.17 Self-Defined Info Structure Creation in Flexible Planning

Press [Enter], and the screen shown in Figure 11.18 appears. Click the **Choose Chars** button, which brings up the option to select characteristics from the catalogs. For this example, select the following characteristics from three catalogs:

- **SD: Sales Organization (order)**
  - **Sales Organization**
  - **Distribution Channel**
  - **Division**
- **SD: Article (order)**
  - **Material**
  - **Plant**
- **SD: Units (delivery)**
  - **Document Currency**
  - **Statistics Currency**

If the selections are made in the correct order, the resulting screen will look as shown in Figure 11.18.

...

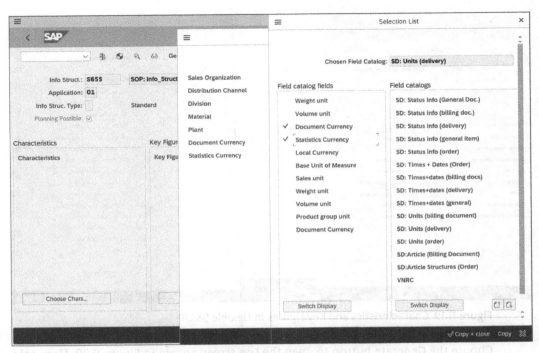

Figure 11.18 Characteristics and Key Figures in Flexible Planning

Next, to select the key figures, click **Choose Key Figures**, then select the key figures from the following catalog. For this example, select the following key figures from two different catalogs:

- **Key Figures: SOP**
  - **Sales**
  - **Production**
  - **Stock Level**
  - **Target Stock Level**
  - **Available Capacity**
- **SD: Values, Prices (Order)**
  - **Net Price**
  - **Net Value**

All the key figures that are selected in Figure 11.18 are copied to a temporary area, and a user confirms the selection by choosing **Copy + Close**. If the selections are made in the correct order, the resulting screen will look like the **Key Figures** area in Figure 11.19.

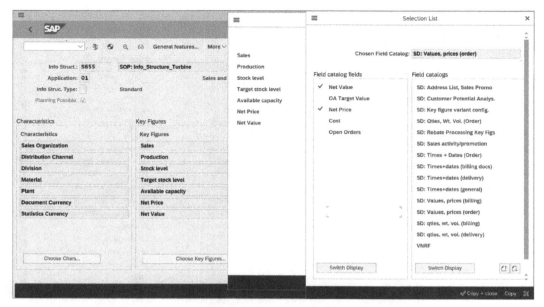

Figure 11.19 Characteristics and Key Figures in Flexible S&OP

Choose the **Generate** button to open the **Log** screen shown in Figure 11.20. Here, info structure S655 is successfully created in the form of an SAP table. If there are any errors, a warning or error message will appear, thus enabling the user to address the problem to avoid issues during the planning activity phase.

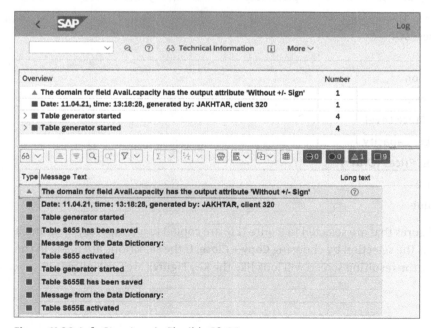

Figure 11.20 Info Structure in Flexible S&OP

The next step in the info structure for flexible planning is to define the *planning method*. The SAP system offers two types of planning methods, as we've already discussed:

- Consistent planning
- Level-by-level planning

The planning method determines the method of disaggregation of data and the storage of data at various levels of planning. Refer to Section 11.1.5 for details.

To set up a planning method for the self-defined info structure, follow menu path **SAP IMG • Production • Sales & Operations Planning (SOP) • Master Data • Set Parameters for Info Structures and Key Figures**, or use Transaction MC7F. In the overview screen of the various info structures available, double-click the info structure (**Table**) **S655**. The screen shown in Figure 11.21 appears, wherein you assign the **Planning Method** as "K" (for consistent planning) and the **Planning Plant** as "1105" so that the system will automatically use this plant during transfer of key figures to demand management.

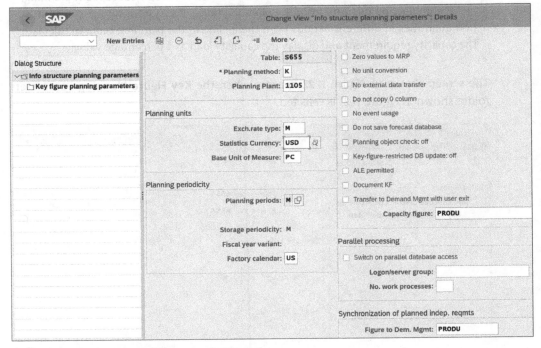

Figure 11.21 Planning Parameters in Info Structure

Two other important fields are **Statistics Currency** and **Base Unit of Measure**. For this example, assign "USD" and "PC", respectively, to these two fields. The **Statistics Currency** field enables the system to use it as a base currency, whereas the **Base Unit of Measure** is the smallest unit of measure in which the inventory figures are shown. If a material has a different base unit of measure than what is being used in planning, then the conversion factor must be defined.

By entering the **Capacity Figure** field value "PRODU", a planner can work with production line values from the planning table while carrying out rough-cut capacity planning. Similarly, by entering the **Figure to Dem. Mgmt** value "PRODU", a planner ensures that the system uses the production line values while transferring the planned values to demand management.

Finally, assign "US" in the **Factory Calendar** field, which will enable the system to refer to the working days and holidays during rough-cut capacity planning.

[»]

> **Note**
>
> A planner can perform rough-cut capacity planning in a planning table to see if the planned forecast values are within the constraints—for example, available capacity at a critical work center. If they aren't, then adjust the planned forecast values until the capacity load value is shown within permissible limits. For rough-cut capacity planning, use the production quantity from the planning table. The system selects the production quantities of different periods from the PP line in the planning table to calculate the capacity requirement and display the capacity load as a percentage value.

The screen shown in Figure 11.22 appears when the **Key Figure Planning Parameters** folder shown in Figure 11.21 is selected.

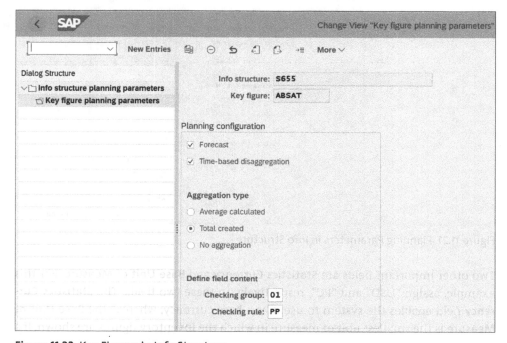

Figure 11.22 Key Figures in Info Structure

The lower half of Figure 11.22 lists all the key figures selected during the info structure creation. Double-click **ABSAT** and, on the screen that appears, choose between two options:

- **Forecast**
  Choose this checkbox to allow forecasting. If **Forecast** isn't selected for the key figures, then forecasting isn't possible for the key figure in the planning table.

- **Time-Based Disaggregation**
  This determines the type of aggregation with three possible options: the average value of the total key figures value of a lower level is aggregated to the higher level; the total of key figure values of the lower level is aggregated to the higher level; or no aggregation is to be carried out at all from the lower level to the higher level. It's always recommended to use the total aggregation method.

11.2.2 Planning Hierarchy

In standard S&OP, only level-by-level planning is possible. Although the characteristics of the info structure already fine-tune the planning levels, a planner must still assign characteristic values to them to carry out planning at those levels. For this example, the custom info structure S655 contains the sales organization, distribution channel, division, material, plant, document currency, and statistics currency characteristics.

A planning hierarchy also enables the planner to define the proportional factor of each of the characteristics and in the same sequence of the characteristics in which they are supposed to be planned. A planning hierarchy is created for the following important reasons:

- To let the SAP system know how the characteristic values are involved in S&OP.
- To let the SAP system know the percentage proportional weight of each of the characteristic values in the organizational hierarchy. This is known as the *disaggregation percentage*, which is used by the system to disaggregate or aggregate the data across various levels during planning and consolidation. We covered aggregation and disaggregation in Section 11.1.5.

In level-by-level planning, the disaggregation percentage is used directly for disaggregation/aggregation purposes. In consistent planning, the disaggregation percentages are used to calculate the proportional factors used in aggregation and disaggregation.

The following prerequisites must be fulfilled for successfully creating a planning hierarchy:

- Create an info structure with an active status.
- Configure the planning parameters for an info structure.
- Create the update rules and activate these rules (if applicable).

A planner can only create one planning hierarchy for a given info structure. In addition, note that a planner can only use one info structure in consistent planning, whereas in level-by-level planning, a planner can use one or multiple info structures.

To maintain the planning hierarchy for the self-defined info structure S655, use SAP menu path **Logistics** • **Logistics Controlling** • **Flexible Planning** • **Planning Hierarchy** • **Create**, or use Transaction MC61.

Enter **Info structure** "S655" as shown in Figure 11.23. In the ensuing **Characteristics** popup, enter all the details. Note that if the details aren't maintained at a specific level, the system triggers the planning hierarchy to maintain the proportional factor. For example, if a planner doesn't enter any details for **Division**, then the next three characteristics, **Material**, **Plant**, and **Document Currency**, will enable a planner to reflect the planning hierarchy in which, for example, a planner enters multiple material numbers with a proportional factor for each.

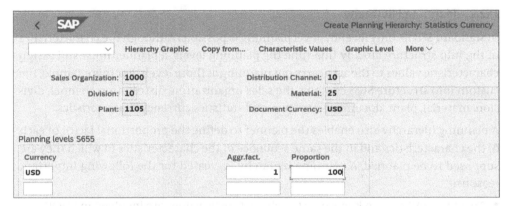

Figure 11.23 Creation of Planning Hierarchy

On the **Create Planning Hierarchy: Statistics Currency** screen, maintain **Currency** as "USD" with a **Proportion** of "100".

Next, navigate from the higher level to the next level by selecting the characteristic values and choosing the **Next Level** icon (not shown) or by just double-clicking a characteristic value. Also, check out the graphical representation by clicking the **Hierarchy Graphic** button in the **Maintain Planning Hierarchy** screen or directly with Transaction MC67.

[+]

> **Tips and Tricks**
>
> A planner can also have the system automatically create the planning hierarchy along with the disaggregation percentages based on the historical data available in the info structure and its version by using Transaction MC9A (Generate Master Data). It can simulate the creation of a planning hierarchy as well.

11.2.3 Planning Type

With the planning hierarchy already in place, the next step is to maintain the planning type, which then becomes an underlying template or layout in the planning table.

As mentioned previously, in maintaining a planning type for flexible planning, a planner can define their own macros, assign events, allocate rough-cut capacity planning, and deploy planning versions. The planning type then becomes a format, layout, or template of the planning table, containing key figures and arranged in the desired way. A planning type is similar to a Microsoft Excel program, in which a user can, for example, include the headings on the left-hand side of the worksheet and the data for the headings on the right-hand side of the sheet.

A planner can also create multiple planning types for a given info structure. Each planning type arranges the key figures of the info structure as desired on a planning table that has its own macros to convert or translate the available data of an info structure. Having multiple planning types enables the planner to plan the same data arranged in different templates and from different perspectives to arrive at a feasible operations plan. Alternatively, if a planner is going to use only one planning type, then save the data under different planning versions and then finalize one final planning version, activate it, and transfer the finalized planning data to demand management.

> **Note**
>
> In flexible planning, it's only possible to transfer the finalized planning to demand management if you have the plant characteristic and the material characteristic included in the different characteristics defined in the planning hierarchy.

A planner creates the planning types with reference to an info structure (in this example, it's S655). The name of the planning table must start with a Z or Y only. The name of the planning type can be up to 11 characters.

To create a planning type, use SAP menu path **Logistics** • **Logistics Controlling** • **Flexible Planning** • **Tools** • **Planning Type/Macro** • **Create**, or use Transaction MC8A. On the **Planning Type: Create** screen (see Figure 11.24), enter **Planning Type** "Z655", select the **Line Layout** and **Macros** checkboxes, and press Enter.

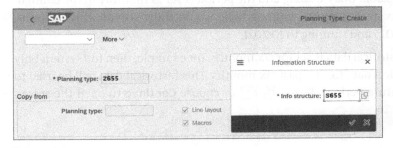

Figure 11.24 Planning Type

When the popup appears, enter **Info Structure** "S655", then press Enter again to open the **Define Planning Type** dialog box (see Figure 11.25).

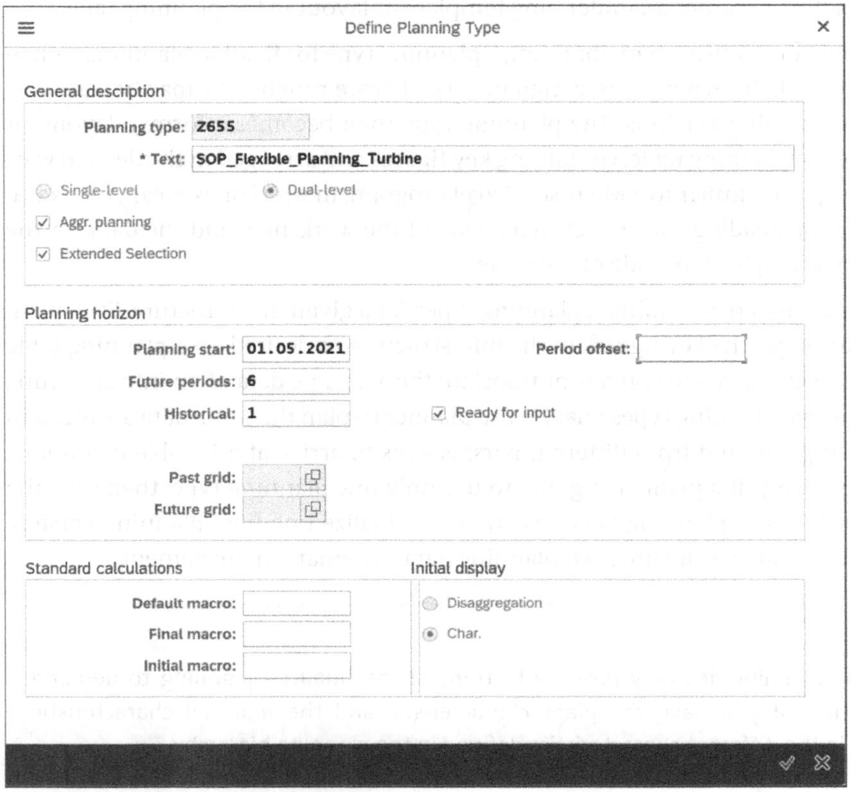

Figure 11.25 Creation of Planning Type

Define the planning horizon by entering the **Planning Start** date, the **Future Periods** involved in forecasting, and the **Historical** data that needs to be pulled in from the info structure.

The planning start date is the date or the period from which you want to begin planning. This is the start of the future periods; that is, if you've opted for six future periods starting from 01.05.2021 (May 1, 2021), and the period is set as monthly in the configuration for the info structure, the planning table would show six monthly columns, starting from 05.2025 and running to 10.2021.

Similarly, if the historical data is set for six months, for example, then the system only pulls in the historical data for the past six months. This historical data will be used to forecast for the future periods. Press Enter or choose **Continue** to open the screen shown in Figure 11.26.

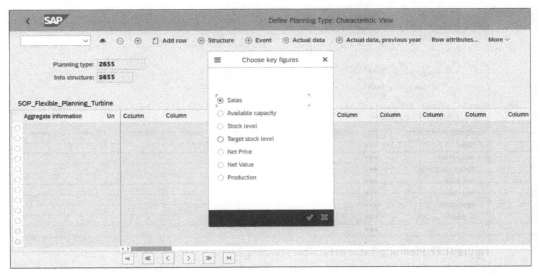

Figure 11.26 Structure Assignment in Planning Type

It's possible to add key figures to the planning type by clicking the **Structure** button to add the key figures, clicking the **Add Row** button to insert a blank row, and clicking the **Actual Data** button to add a row that will bring in the actual data in the planning table belonging to version 000 (which contains the actual data) of the info structure. To have the actual data brought in for a key figure, first keep the cursor on the key figure for which a planner wants to have the actual data brought in, and then choose the **Actual Data** button. For example, if the cursor is placed on the **Sales** key figure and then **Actual Data** chosen, then the system adds a row called **Actual Sales** below the **Sales** key figure.

The actual data row is a noneditable row, although it's possible to use it in formulas (macros) to arrive at the data of other rows. A planner can use the actual data row to compare the actual data to the planned data.

[+]

Tips and Tricks

A planner can also bring in external data for a key figure using the EXIT_SAPMMCP6_001 user exit. To create a row for the external data, keep the cursor on a key figure and then go to **More • Edit • User Exit Data**.

Figure 11.27 shows how the planning type will look after successfully incorporating all of the needed key figures in the planning table and in the desired sequence. A planner will need to repeatedly click **Structure** to bring each key figure into the planning table in the desired order or sequence. When finished, save the planning type.

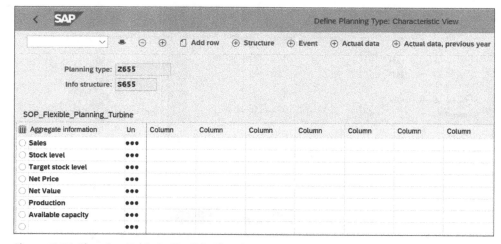

Figure 11.27 Planning Table in Flexible Planning

11.2.4   Working with Self-Defined Macros in Flexible Planning

Next, create self-defined macros in the planning type by using the menu options **More · Macro · Create**. Follow these steps:

1. In the **Define Macro** window, enter the **Macro** name and the **Description** of the macro, and then press Enter.

2. Select the **Display** and **Calc. Selected Area** checkboxes shown in Figure 11.28.

3. Place the cursor on the **Operand** field in Figure 11.28, and either use drilldown or press F4 to select a key figure in the ensuing window. For this example, select the key figure **Sales**, and choose **Continue**.

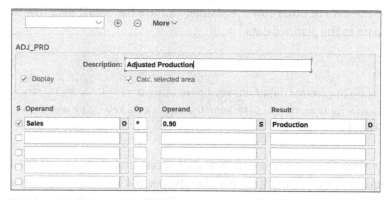

Figure 11.28 Self-Defined Macro

4. Use the drilldown for the **Op** field and, on the screen in Figure 11.29, all of the normal operands (addition, multiplication, etc.) are available to choose from to perform mathematical calculations.

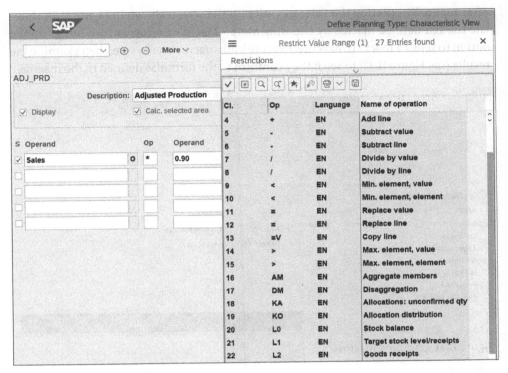

Figure 11.29 Available Operands

5. Enter the value "0.90" as the second **Operand**, and the calculated results (output) should appear as the **Production** key figure in the **Result** field on the previous screen.

   In other words, whenever a planner manually enters values or makes available the data in the **Sales** key figure of the planning table and executes the Adj_Prod macro, the **Sales** key figure will be multiplied by 0.9, and the results will be shown in the **Production** key figure.

6. Save the macro.

For the second example of using macros, define a second macro, TOTAL, which multiplies the key figure **Sales** by **Net Price** to result in a **Net Value** key figure, as shown in Figure 11.30.

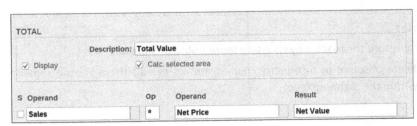

Figure 11.30 Second Self-Defined Macro

After manually entering the **Sales** quantity on the screen shown in Figure 11.31, simulate the self-defined macros by choosing **More • Macro • Execute**, which brings up the option to select a macro to execute. Execute both macros one by one, then examine the results (see Figure 11.32) to see if they conform to the formulas defined in the macros.

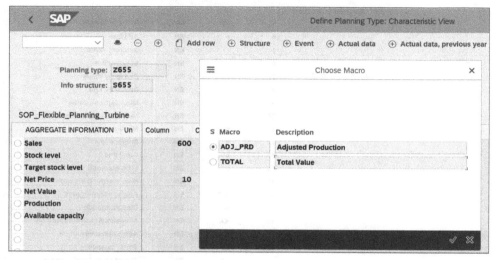

Figure 11.31 Executing Macros

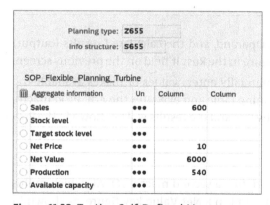

Figure 11.32 Testing Self-Defined Macros

[+] **Tips and Tricks**

It's possible to record the macros by choosing **More • Macro • Record**.

If needed, delete obsolete or incorrectly created macros or edit them via the same menu path within the planning type.

11.2.5   Row Attributes in a Planning Type

For any of the key figures, simply double-click the key figure or select it and choose the **Row Attribute** icon to set its properties or attributes, as shown in Figure 11.33. A key field can be marked as a **Planning Line** (input required), an **Output Line** (display only), a **Text Line** (information-only key figure), or an **Auxiliary Line**, which can be used as a variable in macros. An aggregation type of the key figure can also be determined by choosing the relevant radio button. In Figure 11.33, we changed the standard description of the **Production** key figure to **Adjusted Production**.

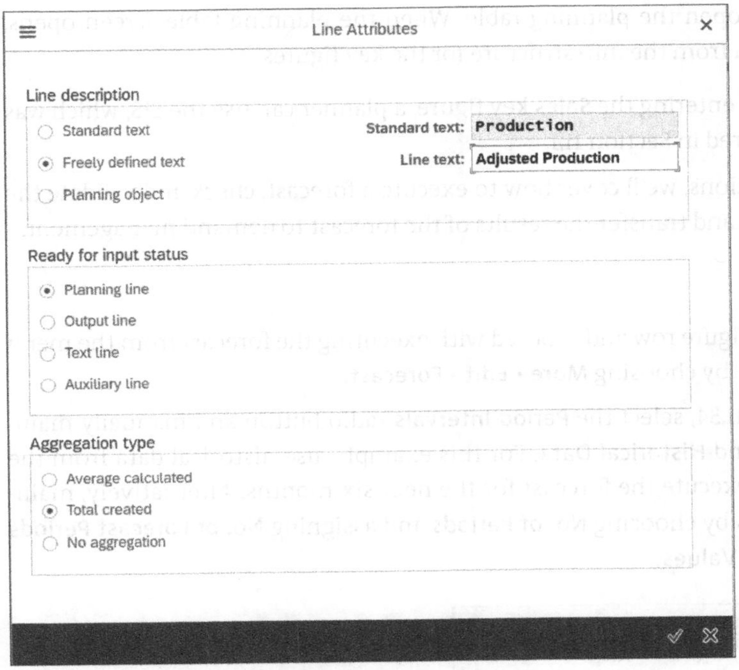

Figure 11.33 Line Attributes in Planning Type

11.2.6   Planning in the Planning Table

Apart from entering the sales, calculating the production quantities, or running macros, a planner can also perform the following functions (all covered in this chapter, with the exception of transfer to CO-PA):

- Forecasting historical data in the planning table (see the Execute Forecast section ahead, as well as Section 11.1.4)
- Transfer to demand management (Section 11.1.4)
- Capacity planning (rough-cut planning; Section 11.1.5)
- Events (Section 11.1.6)
- Transfer to CO-PA

To create a new plan in flexible planning for the self-defined info structure, use menu path **Logistics** · **Logistics Controlling** · **Flexible Planning** · **Planning** · **Create**, or use Transaction MC93. Follow these steps:

1. Enter the planning type as "S655" for this example. Alternatively use, for example, "Z655" for the planning type to clearly indicate a link with info structure Z655.

2. Enter the characteristics combinations for which to create the planning table.

3. Enter the **Version** number, "001", for the info structure data that is to be used in the planning table. Planning version 001 is an inactive version.

4. Press [Enter] to open the planning table. When the planning table screen opens, maintain the data from the info structure for the key figures.

Instead of manually entering the **Sales** key figure, a planner can use the SIS, which was also separately covered in Section 11.1.

In the following sections, we'll cover how to execute a forecast, check and validate the self-defined macros, and transfer the results of the forecast to demand management.

Execute Forecast

Select the **Sales** key figure row and proceed with executing the forecast from the menu in the planning table by choosing **More** · **Edit** · **Forecast**.

As shown in Figure 11.34, select the **Period Intervals** radio button and manually maintain both **Forecast** and **Historical Data**. For this example, use historical data from the past six months to execute the forecast for the next six months. Alternatively, maintain the same details by choosing **No. of Periods** and assigning **No. of Forecast Periods** and **No. of Historical Values.**

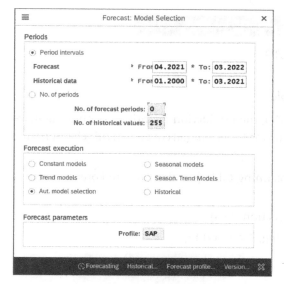

Figure 11.34 Executing Forecast in Flexible Planning

Next, in the **Forecast Execution** area, select the forecast model, such as **Seasonal Models**. The historical values can be changed or updated by choosing the **Historical** button. A planner also can manually enter or correct the historical values, as we've done in this example. When choosing the **Forecasting** button, depending on the forecast model selected, there may be a need to enter further details, such as **Alpha Factor** and **Gamma Factor** (see Figure 11.35).

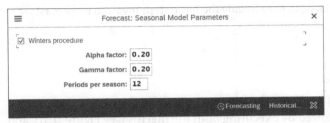

Figure 11.35 Additional Forecast Parameters

Tips and Tricks

To save from manually entering all of the preceding details, use the **Forecast Profile** button shown in Figure 11.34. Creating forecast profiles is discussed in Section 11.4.3.

Execute the forecast by clicking the **Forecasting** button shown in Figure 11.35. This brings up the **Forecast: Results** screen that shows the forecast values for the next few months (see Figure 11.36). Choose **Continue**, and all of the forecast figures are automatically copied to the **Sales** key figure of the planning table.

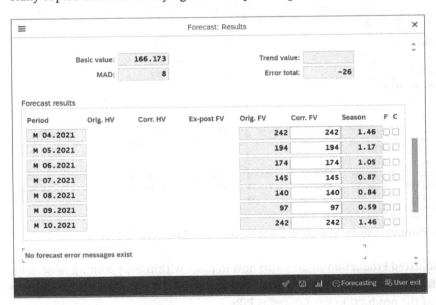

Figure 11.36 Results of Forecast

The result is a graphical comparison of the historical and forecast figures for the period under consideration—that is, the defined months of historical figures and of forecast figures.

Note

Because we've separately covered forecasting in sufficient detail in this chapter, we've intentionally limited the discussion here to only the basic steps involved in forecasting in the planning table.

Validate Self-Defined Macros

After the **Sales** figures are in place from the forecasting activity, the next step is to manually enter the **Net Price**, followed by executing both the macros (see Figure 11.37), and the system automatically fills in the **Net Value** and **Adjusted Production** key figures (Figure 11.38).

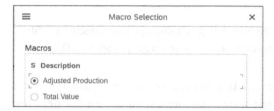

Figure 11.37 Executing Macros

Aggregate Information	Un	M 04.2021	M 05.2021	M 06.2021	M 07.2021	M 08.2021	M 09.2021	M 10.2021
Sales	PC	242	193	174	145	140	97	242
Stock level	PC							
Target stock level	PC							
Net Price	USD	150.00	200.00	130.00	140.00	160.00	110.00	100.00
Net Value	USD	36300.00	38600.00	22620.00	20300.00	22400.00	10670.00	24200.00
Adjusted Production	PC	217	173	156	130	126	87	217
Available capacity	PC							

Sales Organization: 1000, Division: 10, Plant: 1105, Version: 001 Version 001, Distribution Channel: 10, Material: 25, Document Currency: USD, Inactive. SOP_Flexible_Planning_Turbine

Figure 11.38 Planning Figures after Executing Forecast and Running Macros

With the **Adjusted Production** figures also now in place within the planning table, let's now transfer the same to demand management, in which the system will reflect the quantities of the production key figures as PIRs.

Transfer Key Figures to Demand Management

While remaining within the planning table, select the **Production** row, and choose **More · Extras · Transfer to Demand Management**.

Alternatively, you can use menu path **Logistics · Logistics Controlling · Flexible Planning · Environment · Transfer Material to Demand Management**, or use Transaction MC90 (Figure 11.39).

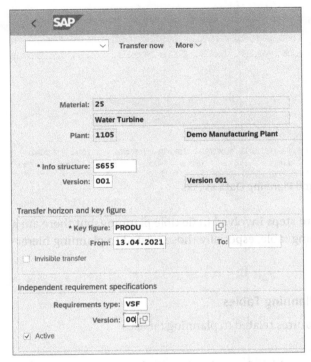

Figure 11.39 Transfer of Planning Data to Demand Management

Assign **Version** "001" of **Info Structure** "S655" for transfer to demand management. The **Key Figure** for this example is **PRODU** (production), and the transfer horizon begins from **13.04.2021** (April 13, 2021).

Further, specify the requirement type and the version of PIR within which the system transfers the values. For this example, assign **Requirement Type** "VSF" and **Version** "00", and then choose the **Transfer Now** button from the menu bar.

A message log appears after the transfer of key figures to demand management.

Transfer Results Validation in Demand Management

To check and confirm whether production figures were successfully transferred to demand management as PIRs, follow SAP menu path **Logistics · Production · Demand Management · Planned Independent Requirements · Display**, or use Transaction MD63.

On the initial screen that appears, enter the selection parameters, such as **Material** "25", **Plant** "1105", **Requirements Type** "VSF", and **Version** "00", which were all previously defined in Figure 11.39. Press ⌜Enter⌝, and on the screen shown in Figure 11.40, notice that the transferred quantities are complete and correct. The correctness of the transferred data can also be checked for a product group by entering the relevant product group, which in this example is TURBINE_SOP, in the initial parameters selection screen in Transaction MD63.

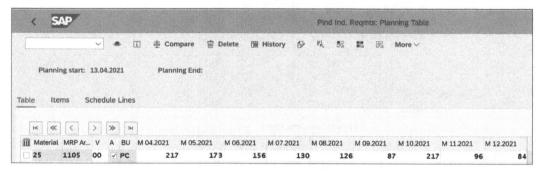

Figure 11.40 Validation of Transferred Planning Data as PIRs

This brings an end to the standard steps involved in flexible planning, but there are a few salient features of the planning table, especially those related to planning hierarchy, that are discussed next.

11.2.7   Additional Features of Planning Tables

Following are some additional features related to planning tables:

- **Checking header information**
  To check the header information, which shows the planning hierarchy levels, choose **More · Settings · Choose Header Info** in the planning table.

- **Firming/unfirming key figure data**
  During consistent planning and to ensure that aggregation and disaggregation won't change the key figures data, a planner can firm or unfirm the key figure data. Choose **More · Settings · Firming · Switch On**. It's recommended to follow this sequence in the firming process:
  - Activate fixing
  - Change the value
  - Deactivate fixing

  Fixing can also be deactivated by choosing **More · Settings · Firming · Unfirm Period**.

- **Determining decimal places and rounding**
  To determine the number of decimal places and also allow rounding of key figures, press ⌜F8⌝ or choose **More · Settings · Places after Decimal Point**.

- **Copying key figure data from another info structure**
  To copy data for a key figure from another info structure, choose **More · Extras · Copy Data**. The copy of key figure data goes from the source info structure for a given period to the target info structure.

- **Showing row totals**
  To show the row totals, choose **More · Settings · Show Row Totals**.

- **Transferring all planning table data**
  To transfer the entire data of the planning table to Excel, choose **More · Extra · Microsoft Excel**.

- **Moving up or down the planning hierarchy**
  Use the following options to move up or down the planning hierarchy within the planning table:
  - **Member**
  - **Owner**
  - **Next Member**
  - **Previous Member**
  - **All Members**

11.3   Version Management

In the info structure, the planning data is retained in versions. This enables the planner to carry out simulations. A planner can assign any number to a version, and these remain inactive with the exception of two specific versions with defined meanings and functions: version 000 always contains actual data, and version A01 is the active version.

Every version that is created and for which data is stored in the planning table, all of the values for each of the key figures, and characteristic combinations entered either manually or evaluated by macros, events, or forecasts are directly updated in the info structure against the respective version number.

It's possible to copy one version's data to another version and to delete obsolete or unwanted versions, as discussed in the following sections.

11.3.1   Copy a Version

Depending on whether a planner is using standard S&OP or flexible planning, use the following menu paths or transactions to copy one version to another:

- **Standard S&OP**
  Choose **Logistics · Production · SOP · Planning · Version Management · Copy**, or use Transaction MC78.

- **Flexible planning**
  Choose **Logistics · Logistics Controlling · Flexible Planning · Planning · Version Management · Copy**, or use Transaction MC8V.

To copy the PIR details of the source version to the target version of an info structure, enter values for **Version** in the **Source Version** (in this example, "001") and **Target Version** (in this example, "A00") areas, and choose **Copy** at the top of the screen (see Figure 11.41). Alternatively, maintain the date range (**Period**) to copy the PIR details of the source version to the target version.

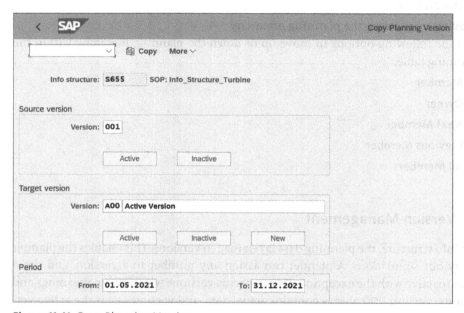

Figure 11.41 Copy Planning Version

11.3.2   Delete a Version

Depending on whether you're using standard S&OP or flexible planning, use the following menu paths or transactions to delete planning versions:

- **Standard S&OP**
  Choose **Standard SOP: Logistics · Production · SOP · Planning · Version Management · Delete**, or use Transaction MC78.

- **Flexible planning**
  Choose **Logistics · Logistics Controlling · Flexible Planning · Planning · Version Management · Delete**, or use Transaction MC8W.

To delete one or several versions of an info structure, select the relevant checkboxes next to the version numbers and choose **Delete** at the top of the screen.

11.3.3 Scheduling a Copy Version or Scheduling a Delete Version

To schedule a background job to delete or copy a planning version or to activate an existing planning version, use Transaction MC8K. To schedule a copy from one target version of one info structure to another info structure, use Transaction MC8Q.

11.4 Forecasting

A *forecast* is a prediction of future requirements and is based on the past consumption trend in a given period of time. These consumptions can be, for example, material withdrawals against the production order, process orders, or even cost centers. Whenever a new material is created in the system, the system automatically incorporates the info in the **Consumption** tab in the **Additional Data** area of the material master. The consumption for finished goods can be against the sales order. Hence, forecasting offers enormous benefits to plan any material type, whether it's a raw material, a consumable, a packing material, a semifinished good, or even a finished good, based on historical consumption figures. While each withdrawal or consumption updates the information in the system, a planner can also manually enter the past consumption figures of a material to help drive and facilitate the forecasting.

A detailed analysis of the consumption figures provides a pattern or other valuable information on the consumption pattern—that is, a constant consumption, a moving average, or a seasonal trend model. Therefore, the system offers several standard forecasting models to choose from. If a planner isn't sure which forecast model to select, then the system allows the planner to select **Automatic Model Selection** to facilitate forecasting. However, using this option has its disadvantages.

[!]

Warning

SAP doesn't recommend using **Automatic Model Selection** for forecasting because it eventually ends up incorporating one of the several forecast models (e.g., constant, moving average, or seasonal) available in the material master. The SAP-recommended forecasting model may not be in line with the actual business scenario.

[+]

Tips and Tricks

When using the forecasting tool, take a couple of materials as test cases and run the entire forecasting cycle. This forecasting cycle includes maintaining historical values, selecting the right forecasting model, and maintaining additional forecasting parameters. Finally, execute the forecast and see if the forecast results closely match with what the system is expected to do. If it doesn't, consider evaluating other available forecasting models or refining the forecasting parameters. After gaining the necessary experience with a limited number of materials, replicate the same steps for other similar materials. Be sure to periodically review and update the forecasting parameters to ensure reliable material planning results.

This section covers the forecasting options available in S&OP (which are standard and flexible planning), as well as the options available in the material master in case you want to run forecasting on a consumable material or a packing material, which isn't part of S&OP. We'll begin with covering the fields and options available in the forecasting view of the material master (e.g., forecast models and configuring and using the forecast profile). Finally, we'll cover the weighting group and splitting indicator that can be used in forecasting.

11.4.1   Forecasting View in the Material Master

The forecast parameters are maintained in the forecasting view of the material master with Transaction MM02. Figure 11.42 shows the **Forecasting** view of **Material 25** for **Plant 1105**. Details of all the important fields on the screen are given in the subsequent sections of this chapter.

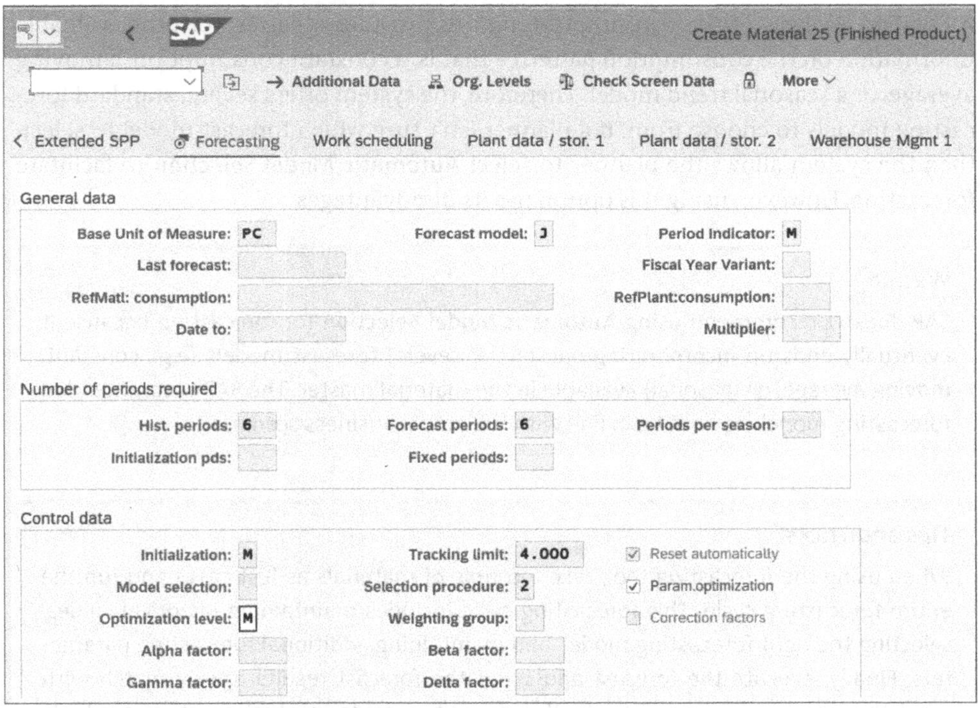

Figure 11.42 Forecasting View in Material Master

When a planner runs the forecast for a material-plant combination (Transaction MP30) or for the entire plant (Transaction MP38), the system uses information from the material master and offers no option to make changes to the forecast parameters.

[«]

> **Note**
>
> Navigate to the **Forecast** menu in SAP system via menu path **Logistics** • **Production** • **Production Planning** • **Materials Forecast**.

Forecasting can also be executed in the following planning areas:

- S&OP for materials or for product groups
- Flexible planning

When executing a forecast in either of these areas, the system provides the options to select the forecast profile and make changes to the default data defined in the forecast profile. A planner can also carry out forecasting for consumption-based materials; essentially, the concepts and the fundamentals remain the same.

Table 11.4 covers the fields shown in Figure 11.42.

Field	Description
Forecast Model	Indicates the chosen forecast model. For example, a forecast model **N** (no forecast/external model) enables the SAP system to create forecasts from external sources, such as an Excel file or even a legacy system (Section 11.4.2, in which we cover this topic in detail).
Period Indicator	The periods in which the consumption values and the forecast values are managed.
Fiscal Year Variant	The fiscal year in which the consumption values and the forecast values are managed.
RefMatl: Consumption	The consumption data a material that the system uses to forecast values of a new material. If two or more materials have a similar consumption history, then one material can form a reference material for other, and yet a multiplier can still apply to individual material to account for any increase or decrease in consumption values and forecast values (see the definition of **Multiplier** below).
Date To	Date up to which the system uses the consumption values of the reference material to calculate new material forecast values.
RefPlant: Consumption	The plant of the reference material.

Table 11.4 Parameter Details of Forecasting Screen in Material Master

Field	Description
Multiplier	The multiplication factor that the system uses for the reference material's historical values to calculate new material forecast values.
Hist. Periods	Indicates the number of historical values the system uses for a material forecast.
Forecast Periods	Indicates the number of period splits for which the forecast values should be created.
Periods per Season	Indicates the number of periods that belong to a season. Use this option only if the forecast model is a seasonal forecast model.
Initialization Pds.	Number of periods used for initialization. Initializing is resetting the system's settings, which can be automatically or manually enabled. Initialization takes place when the material is forecast for the first time or when there are structural changes to a material's time series, such as a change in a material's forecast model, a change in historical values, or a change in forecast values.
Fixed Periods	Number of periods for which the system won't recalculate the forecast values in the next forecast. This option is helpful to avoid fluctuation in a forecast's calculation or because the production can no longer react to changed planning figures within the planning horizon.
Model Selection	Specifies if the system should check for the values for trend *or* seasonal fluctuation, or for a trend *and* seasonal fluctuation. Set this indication if the system should help in automatic forecast model selection.
Optimization Level	Specifies the increment (rough, middle, finer) by which the system optimizes the forecast parameters.
Alpha Factor	Specifies the smoothing factor for updating the basic values. If left blank, the default value is **0.2**.
Gamma Factor	Specifies the smoothing factor for updating the seasonal index. If left blank, the default value is **0.3**.
Tracking Limit	Specifies the amount (or number of times) by which the forecast values may deviate from the actual values. Every time a forecast runs, the system compares the tracking limit with the tracking signal. The tracking signal, which is calculated internally, is the quotient and the mean average deviation (MAD). The system uses the tracking signal to control the accuracy of the forecasts. If the tracking signal is greater than the tracking limit, the system issues an exception message and asks the planner to (re)check the selected forecast model.

Table 11.4 Parameter Details of Forecasting Screen in Material Master (Cont.)

Field	Description
Selection Procedure	Defines the procedure by which the system selects the optimum forecast model. In the standard system, there are two methods that the system uses: ■ **1**: Uses a significant test to determine whether a trend or a seasonal pattern is present and then select the forecast model based on the basis of results. ■ **2**: Uses more precise and granular calculation than procedure 1 but consumes more system resources. This procedure carries out the forecast using all models, optimizes the parameters, and then selects the model with the smallest MAD.
Weighting Group	Indicates how many historical values are used to calculate the forecast and what weighting is given to each of the historical values.
Beta Factor	Specifies the smoothing factor for the trend value. If left blank, then a default value of **0.1** is used.
Delta Factor	Specifies the smoothing factor for the MAD. If left blank, then the default value is **0.3**.
Reset Automatically	If selected, the system automatically resets the forecast model if the tracking limit is exceeded. The system also selects a new model during the next forecast run.
Param.Optimization	If selected, the system optimizes the smoothing factors needed by the given forecast model. When this indicator is set, parameter optimization is carried out both for the first and for subsequent forecasts. The system calculates a number of different parameter combinations and selects the one that produces the lowest MAD.
Correction Factors	If selected, the system calculates the forecast values by taking into account the correction factors, as defined in the configuration.

Table 11.4 Parameter Details of Forecasting Screen in Material Master (Cont.)

Tips and Tricks

When SAP S/4HANA is implemented for the first time, there aren't any historical consumption values available in the system that can form the basis of forecasting. In such scenarios, it's possible to manually enter the unplanned or total consumption quantities of a material. When maintaining consumption values for a large number of materials, creating an upload program is a more practical approach. To manually enter the total consumption values in the material master (Transaction MM02), select the **Additional Data** button, followed by choosing the **Consumption** tab. Also, define the plant for which the consumption values are maintained and for which forecasting is being executed.

11.4.2   Forecast Models

Forecast modeling has been devised to aid in forecasting particular events. The forecast model is designed around factors that the client believes are important in influencing the future use of a material. The client also uses past consumption of a material to determine its future use. Both of these methods should produce a reliable forecast. A number of forecast models are available within SAP S/4HANA, as follows:

- **Constant model**

  The constant model assumes that the use of material is constant. This isn't to say that the use of material is the same each month but that the variation in material usage fluctuates little and a constant mean value is calculated. This forecast model applies to electricity consumption in an office, for example. Although summer months raise electricity consumption due to increased air conditioning use, the consumption doesn't vary a great deal from the mean value over a longer period of time, such as a year.

- **Trend model**

  The trend model is used when there is an identifiable increase or decrease of a material over a period of time. The trend may include areas of movement away from the trend, but the overall movement follows the trend. For example, a downward trend over time may represent the use of printer cartridges for top-selling printers that become obsolete over a short period of time, perhaps only 12 to 18 months. As the purchase and use of the printer decreases, the cartridges used in that printer will slow also.

- **Seasonal model**

  The seasonal model affects many businesses due to the weather, holidays, or vacations. The seasonal model is defined as a pattern that repeats for each period. For example, the annual seasonal pattern has a cycle that is 12 periods long, if the periods are months. A seasonal model may be applicable to a company that makes patio furniture, which experiences a greater demand in the months of May through September, and this pattern is repeated each year.

- **Seasonal trend model**

  The seasonal trend model is similar to the seasonal model, except that instead of the same pattern occurring each period, the pattern is moving further away from the mean value, either positive or negative. For example, California sparkling wine manufacturers can see a positive seasonal trend. They have a seasonal pattern in demand for their products, and for them the seasonal pattern has a positive trend, as sales have continued to rise. A negative seasonal trend can be shown for beer manufacturers, who have a seasonal market, but the overall trend continues to be negative as sales slow each year.

> **Tips and Tricks**
>
> If a client hasn't developed forecast models in the past or doesn't know which forecast model fits best, it may want to allow the SAP system to analyze the historical data and determine an appropriate forecast model to use. The forecast model J (automatic model selection) is available in SAP S/4HANA. After the model has been selected, the client can use this as a starting point and make modifications in the future. However, it's equally important to revisit the system-proposed and selected forecast model to ensure it closely matches the consumption trend.

11.4.3 Forecast Profile

A forecast profile consists of user-defined values (parameters), which then become available during the execution of forecasting. A planner can, however, still make changes to these values (parameters) in the forecast profile before executing the forecast. To create a forecast profile, follow menu path **SAP IMG • Production • Sales & Operations Planning (SOP) • Functions • Forecasting • Maintain Forecasting Profiles**, or use Transaction MC96.

Figure 11.43 and Figure 11.44 show a standard available forecast profile, SAP, which can be copied to create a new profile and make desired changes.

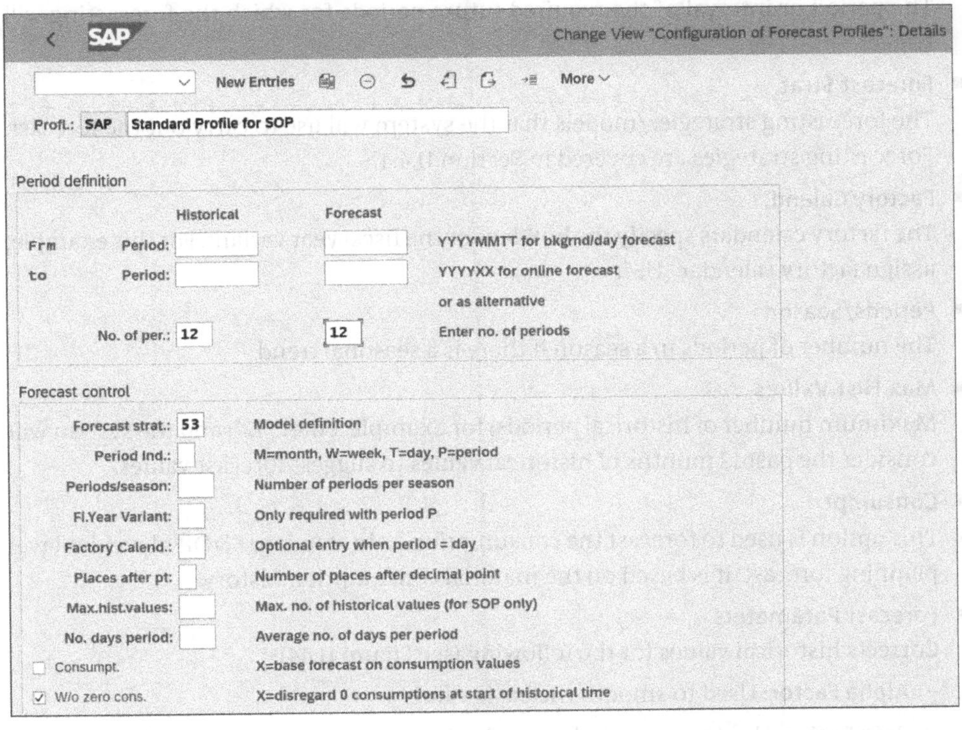

Figure 11.43 SAP Forecast Profile

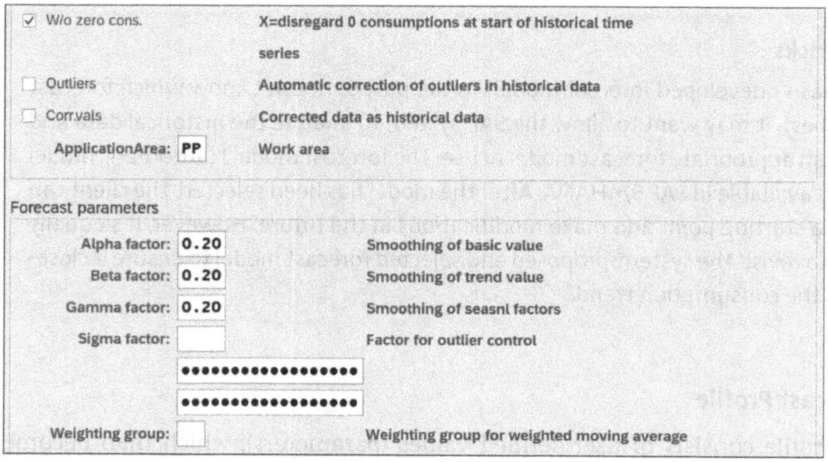

Figure 11.44 SAP Forecast Profile: More Options

Details of the important fields in the forecast profile are given in the following list:

- **Frm Period/To Period**

  The period or intervals for the historical data and for forecast data, which you'll use during forecasting.

- **Period Ind.**

  The period or interval of the required future periods for which the forecasting will trigger.

- **Forecast Strat.**

  The forecasting strategies/models that the system will use to carry out the forecast. Forecasting strategies are covered in Section 11.4.4.

- **Factory Calend.**

  The factory calendars specify the holidays or the fiscal year variant. For this example, assign factory calendar "US".

- **Periods/Season**

  The number of periods in a season if there is a seasonal trend.

- **Max.Hist.Values**

  Maximum number of historical periods; for example, enter "12", and the system will consider the past 12 months of historical values to suggest forecast values.

- **Consumpt.**

  This option is used to forecast the consumption as in standard S&OP's level-by-level planning forecast. It is based on the material consumption history.

- **Forecast Parameters**

  Corrects historical values for the following (see Figure 11.44):

  - **Alpha Factor**: Used to smooth the basic value.
  - **Beta Factor**: Used to smooth the trend value.

– **Gamma Factor:** Used to smooth the seasonal index.
– **Sigma Factor:** Used to correct the historical figures that lie outside the predefined upper and lower tolerances. The lower the sigma factor, the greater is the control on forecast figures. SAP recommends using a value between 0.6 and 2.0.

11.4.4   Forecast Strategy

Table 11.5 lists the relationships of various forecast models and corresponding forecast strategies. For each forecast strategy (or model) selection, maintain details of the parameters, such as the alpha factor, beta factor, or gamma factor, which are highlighted in the Additional Information column of the table. For example, if the demand of a product is generally constant throughout the year, then select the constant model. Similarly, to maintain an average quantity of material in the warehouse, use the moving average model. For the moving average, it adds up the total quantity of the material from historical figures and then divides this total quantity by the period under consideration to arrive at an average number. So, it's important to evaluate the consumption figures for a given historical period that the forecasting model fits best to meet your business requirements.

Time Series Development	Forecast Model	Forecast Strategy	Additional Information
Constant progression	Constant model	10	The end results are constant figures.
Constant progression	Constant model with first-order exponential smoothing	11	Maintain an alpha factor to smooth the basic values.
Constant progression	Constant model with automatic alpha smoothing factor adoption	12	First-order exponential smoothing is used.
Constant progression	Moving average model	13	Averages out the values based on the number of historical values.
Constant progression	Weighted moving average model	14	Maintain a weighting group.
Trend-like pattern	Linear regression	20	Evaluates the trend in values to come up with plausible trend values.

Table 11.5 Forecast Models and Forecast Strategies

Time Series Development	Forecast Model	Forecast Strategy	Additional Information
Trend-like pattern	First-order exponential smoothing	21	Maintain alpha and beta factors to smooth out the basic and trend values.
Trend-like pattern	Trend model of second-order exponential smoothing	22	Maintain alpha and beta factors to smooth out the basic and trend values.
Trend-like pattern	Automatic alpha smoothing factor adoption	23	Maintain second-order exponential smoothing with or without model parameter optimization.
Season-like pattern	Seasonal model (winters procedure)	31	Maintain alpha factors, gamma factors, and periods per season for basic and seasonal smoothing.
Season-like pattern	Seasonal model of first-order exponential smoothing	40	Maintain alpha, beta, and gamma factors and periods per season.
Automatic model selection		50	The system takes its own calculation and factors into account and determines/suggests the appropriate model.
Automatic model selection		52	This is more time- and resource-consuming, but it provides more reflective results.
Historical data way		60	The system will use the past or historical values as is, without automatically making any corrections or adjustments.

Table 11.5 Forecast Models and Forecast Strategies (Cont.)

Figure 11.45 shows the dropdown list of some of the forecast strategies available to choose from and assign the same in the forecast profile.

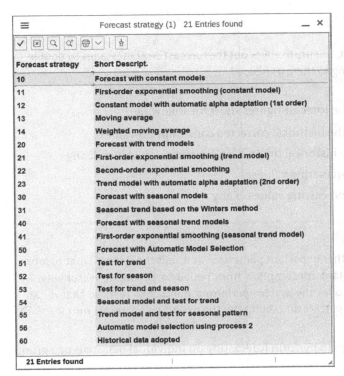

Figure 11.45 Forecast Strategy

11.4.5 Using the Forecast Profile

If you select **Forecast Profile** while executing the forecast, the **Forecast: Forecast Profile** popup appears, in which you can select the relevant forecast profile. The system considers all of the forecast parameters during forecasting. If there's still a need to make any last-minute changes to the values defined in the forecast profile, then choose the **Change** option to make the desired changes and execute the forecast. To configure a new forecast profile, use Transaction MP80.

We already covered how to execute a forecast in Section 11.2.6, so we'll just summarize some of the more important topics of forecasting here.

On forecast execution, the system calculates the MAD, the trend value, and the error total of the forecast values. The MAD option helps the planner identify the degree of variability and a subsequent decision on buffering strategies to avoid stock-outs. For example, an error total of 44 is divided by the MAD value of 13 (44 ÷ 13 = 3.385) and is compared with the tracking limit set at 4.000 (in the material master) to decide if the forecast model is still applicable or warrants selecting a new or a different forecast model. An error total is the sum of all errors in the past consumption series (refer to Figure 11.36).

Tips and Tricks

When executing a forecast, be sure to check out the forecast error messages by double-clicking them and attending to them as needed.

The graphical versions of the forecast figures show the following:

- In yellow, the details of the historical corrected consumption values
- In blue, the details of the historical originating consumption values, if any
- In red, the originating forecasting values
- In green, the corrected forecasting values, if any

Tips and Tricks

The forecast model is another important parameter as it tells the system what to look for: a trend pattern, constant consumption from period to period, or seasonality. A planner can also choose to let the system perform a number of tests so that it can automatically identify the pattern and set it after the executing a forecast run.

Here are three different ways to perform forecasting on individual materials or a group of materials:

- At a single material and plant level, use Transaction MP30.
- At the total materials and plant level, use Transaction MP38.
- At a single material and plant level, use Transaction MM02.

Tips and Tricks

To view or print the consumption values and the forecast values of individual materials or all materials in a plant, here are the transaction codes:

- Individual material: Transaction MP32
- Total forecast: Transaction MPDR

11.4.6   Weighting Group

The weighting group defines how many of the consumption values the system takes into account during the forecast run and what weight should be given to each value. Often, recent consumption values get higher weights than past values.

The weighting group works only for the weighted moving average forecast model or forecast model W. The delta factor can be set up to smooth out the forecast values using this forecast model. To set up a weighting group, follow menu path **SAP IMG · Materials Management · Forecast · Weighting Groups for Weighted Moving Average**.

11.4.7 Splitting Indicator

In forecast-based planning, it's mandatory to execute material forecasts first. Based on the results of the forecast, the system calculates and plans future consumption quantities. A planner can select the forecasting periods to be in days, weeks, months, or for the entire year. The system can consider safety stock in the net requirement calculations. The system takes receipts into account to ensure the demand from the forecast is met. If the demand isn't met, then the system creates procurement proposals.

It's possible to specify the number of historical periods that the system uses in forecasting and also the future forecast horizon (periods) for each material. After the planning run, the system makes material available in the beginning of the period. A planner has the option to further divide or split these material requirements into finer detail by using the **Splitting Indicator** option in the **MRP 3** view of the material master.

The period pattern for the forecast (day, week, month, or posting period) and the number of prediction periods can be defined separately for each material. However, the period pattern of the forecast may not be detailed enough for MRP because it may not provide the required granularity. For this reason, use **Splitting Indicator** to define for each material how the forecast requirement values may further be distributed to a more detailed period pattern for MRP purposes.

Maintain the **Splitting Indicator** option in configuration by following menu path **SAP IMG · Materials Management · Forecast · Define Splitting of Forecast Requirements for MRP**. The splitting indicator contains the number of periods to be considered and the number of days and/or weeks for which the splitting is to be carried out.

The following are the three possible forecast requirements:

- **No. of Days**
  How many periods are to be calculated to the day in MRP

- **No. of Weeks**
  How many periods are to be calculated to the week in MRP

- **No. of Periods**
  For how many periods—in addition to the periods to be split—the system is to carry out the net requirements calculation in the planning run

> **Note**
> As per SAP Note 2268100, SAP plans to replace the current material forecast solution in the future. The future solution will perform the forecasting algorithm in SAP HANA by utilizing SAP HANA's forecasting library, improving the material forecast performance. In the meantime, the material forecast transactions, such as Transaction MP30, can still be used as there is no functional equivalent yet in SAP S/4HANA.

11.5   Rough-Cut Planning Profile

To carry out capacity analysis in standard S&OP or in flexible planning, a planner needs to maintain master data for the capacity requirements for production of a base quantity of the material or product group. This master data is known as a *task list*, and it can be a routing, rate routing, master recipe, or rough-cut planning profile. Normally, a rough-cut planning profile is created for the material-plant combination because it provides a rough estimation of the capacity requirements.

[!]

> **Warning**
>
> An important point to consider is that not every info structure created or used in S&OP has a plant as a characteristic. This makes capacity planning very difficult. It's for this reason that a planning plant should be entered in the **Set Parameters for Info Structure and Key Figures** configuration screen (Transaction MC7F). Also, without reference to a plant and material, transfer of key figures to PIRs isn't possible.

Because the capacity evaluation is performed at the plant level, it's advisable to include it in the info structure and percentage splits given to them for disaggregation and aggregation purposes.

Also on the **Set Parameters for Info Structure and Key Figure** screen (Transaction MC7F), enter a key figure in the **Capacity Figure** field; the numbers for this key figure in the planning table will be considered in capacity planning. For this example, we used the PRODU value in the capacity figure (refer to Figure 11.21).

Based on the details given in the rough-cut planning profile, the resource leveling calculates the resource load for the operations plan and thus enables a planner to quickly estimate feasibility in terms of capacity.

Next, we'll cover the rough-cut planning profile and how the system reflects pegged requirements.

11.5.1   Create a Profile

To create a rough-cut planning profile, use SAP menu path **Logistics • Logistics Controlling • Flexible Planning • Tools • Rough Cut Planning Profile • Create**, or use Transaction MC35.

On the initial screen of a rough-cut planning profile, enter info structure "S655", and click **Execute**, which opens the popup shown on the right-hand side of Figure 11.46. Enter all of the characteristic details and press [Enter]. The **General Data** screen shown in Figure 11.47 appears.

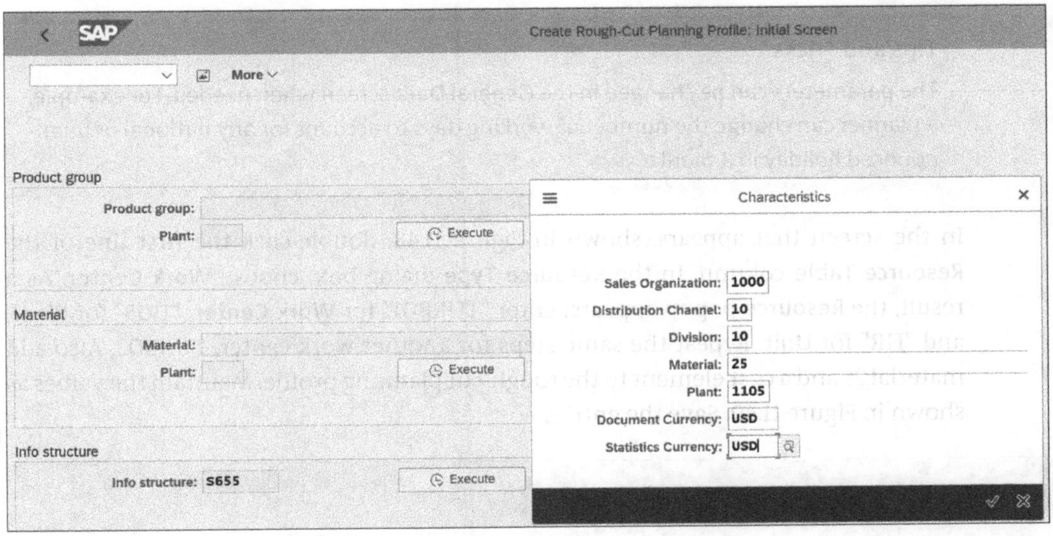

Figure 11.46 Initial Screen for Characteristic Assignments

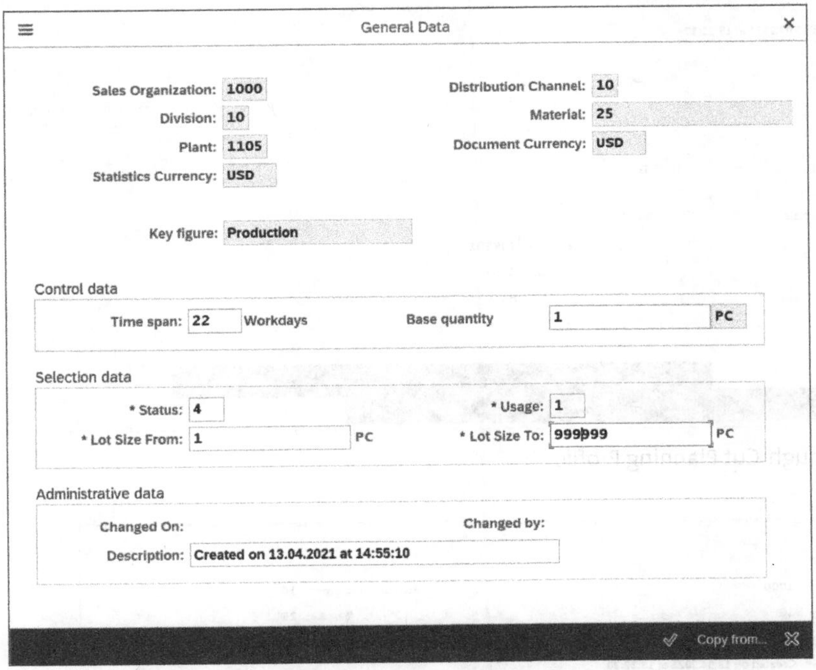

Figure 11.47 General Data in Rough-Cut Planning Profile

On this screen, enter "22" in the **Time Span** field, and enter "1" **PC** in the **Base Quantity** field. Set the **Status** to "4" (for **Released**) and set the **Usage** to "1" (for production), then press [Enter].

[+]
Tips and Tricks

The parameters can be changed in the **General Data** screen when needed. For example, a planner can change the number of working days to account for any national or unannounced holiday in a month.

In the screen that appears, shown in Figure 11.48, double-click the first line of the **Resource Table** column. In the **Resource Type** dialog box, choose **Work Center**. As a result, the **Resource** popup appears: enter "TURB01" for **Work Center**, "1105" for **Plant**, and "HR" for **Unit**. Repeat the same steps for another work center, TURB02. Also add material 25 and a cost element to the rough-cut planning profile. Maintain the values as shown in Figure 11.49. Save the entries.

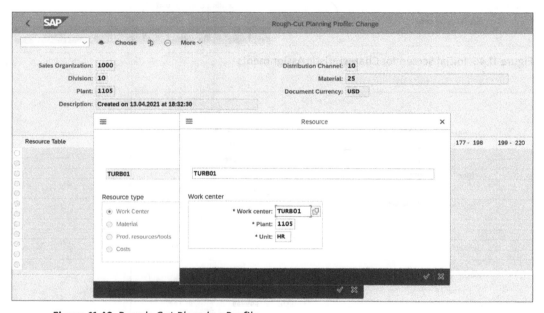

Figure 11.48 Rough-Cut Planning Profile

Resource Table	Un	0 - 22	23 - 44	45 - 66	67 - 88	89 - 110	111 - 132	133 - 154	155 - 176
TURB01	HR	10	120	140	50	20	180	60	
TURB02	HR	25	6	120	900	20	400	45	
Mat25	PC	450	460	60	450	90	25	350	
Costs_C_Eelement		289	269	250	6	35	45	80	

Figure 11.49 Rough-Cut Planning Profile with Relevant Data

In Transaction MC94, the planning table displays the available capacity and capacity requirements via menu path **More · Views · Capacity situation · Rough-cut planning · Show** (see Figure 11.50).

In the **Planning Table** area, the system shows the capacity requirements against the available capacity at the work center, based on the monthly production figures.

The capacity utilization is immediately calculated when the plan changes, which facilitates the interactive adjustment of the operations plan to the capacities. However, the resource-leveling process doesn't provide any standard function for adapting the production plan to the available capacity.

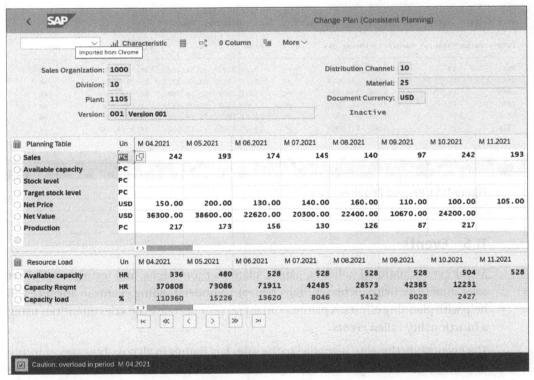

Figure 11.50 Rough-Cut Planning View in Planning

If a capacity is overloaded, a corresponding message is displayed in the footer. For this example, this is the case for April 2021. There's also a capacity overload for the next several months, as shown with the blue font in the monthly columns for the **Capacity Load** row. Scroll down in the same section and the capacity requirements details of the second work center, TURBO2, will also appear.

Use the same menu path to view the costs and the material values—that is, **More · Views · Capacity situation · Rough-cut planning · Show**—and choose the relevant option.

11.5.2   Pegged Requirements

Within the planning table, pegged requirements offer a quick way to gain a better understanding of a workload on a resource, whether it's a work center, a material, or a PRT, to evaluate pegging. The term *pegging* is synonymous with *association* or *attachment*, which means one planning element is attached to another. To view the pegged requirements within the planning table, choose **More • Views • Pegged Requirements** to open the **Source of Requirements** screen (see Figure 11.51). Alternatively, double-click the **Capacity Reqmt** field shown in Figure 11.50 so that the screen in Figure 11.51 appears.

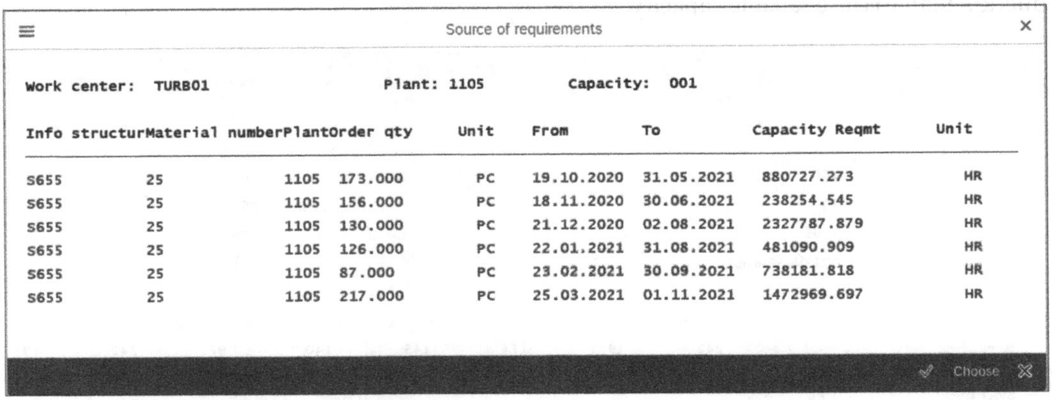

≡				Source of requirements					×

Work center:	TURB01		Plant: 1105		Capacity:	001		
Info structur	Material number	Plant	Order qty	Unit	From	To	Capacity Reqmt	Unit
S655	25	1105	173.000	PC	19.10.2020	31.05.2021	880727.273	HR
S655	25	1105	156.000	PC	18.11.2020	30.06.2021	238254.545	HR
S655	25	1105	130.000	PC	21.12.2020	02.08.2021	2327787.879	HR
S655	25	1105	126.000	PC	22.01.2021	31.08.2021	481090.909	HR
S655	25	1105	87.000	PC	23.02.2021	30.09.2021	738181.818	HR
S655	25	1105	217.000	PC	25.03.2021	01.11.2021	1472969.697	HR

Choose

Figure 11.51 Pegged Requirements

11.6   Events

Major events, national holidays, games, planned promotions, and festivals can affect sales quantities (with increases or decreases), so understanding events in advance will help with planning efforts. A planner can increase or decrease the sales quantities using a functionality called *events*.

The events functionality is applied to the sales key figures in all possible cases or to any other key figures that give the sales quantities or sales values. The system provides the option to assign events across all characteristic levels or for a specific characteristic level for which the event should be applied.

For example, let's say that initially a planner used the forecasting tool and seasonal model to come up with planned sales figures. Later, the company decides to participate in an important and relevant trade show that should have a positive impact on the company's sales. To attend to this anticipated surge in product sales (or demand), a planner can incorporate this event (the trade show) into the planned sales figures to enable the system to account for the increase. The events are assigned to the planning types and thus come into play in the planning table.

[«]

> **Note**
> Creating an event isn't a mandatory activity in the planning process, so a planner can opt out of the event option in the planning situation, if needed.

The SAP system provides two ways of modeling an event: *cumulative modeling* and *percentage modeling*. For cumulative events, the sales quantity affected by the event is maintained as a difference quantity in absolute figures. The overall sales quantity is represented as the total of normal sales and includes the event. For percentage events, the sales quantity affected by the event refers to the quantity planned in the **Sales** key figure.

In the following sections, we'll discuss how to create events and assign them to planning. We'll also show how an event's assignment impacts materials planning.

11

11.6.1 Create Events

To create events, use menu path **Logistics • Logistics Controlling • Flexible Planning • Tools • Events • Create**, or use Transaction MC64.

The initial screen to create an event is shown in Figure 11.52. For this example, enter the **Event Number** as "S655: SOP EVENT", then press ⌷Enter⌷. In the **General Information** popup, select the **Proportional** radio button, then press ⌷Enter⌷ again.

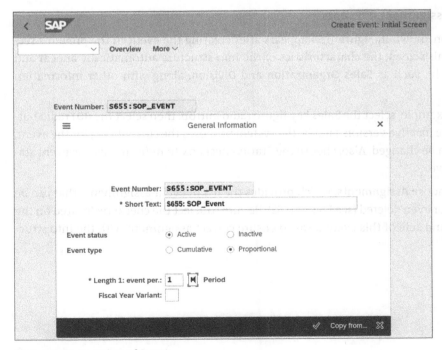

Figure 11.52 Creation of Event

In the **Proportional Event** screen shown in Figure 11.53, enter the monthly **Change** in percentage, and then choose **Assignment**, which opens the **Info Structure** popup. In this popup, assign the **Info Structure** as "S655".

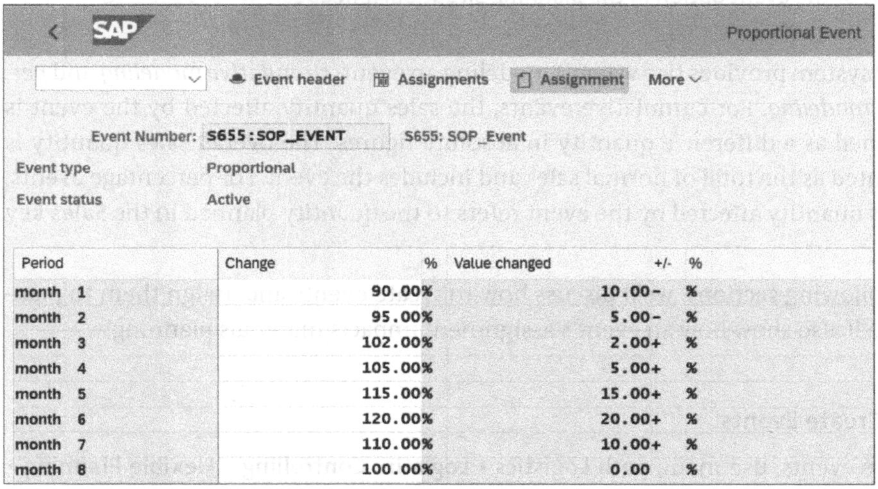

Period	Change	%	Value changed	+/-	%
month 1		90.00%		10.00-	%
month 2		95.00%		5.00-	%
month 3		102.00%		2.00+	%
month 4		105.00%		5.00+	%
month 5		115.00%		15.00+	%
month 6		120.00%		20.00+	%
month 7		110.00%		10.00+	%
month 8		100.00%		0.00	%

Figure 11.53 Assigning Event to Info Structure

Now that an event is created, the next step is to assign the event.

11.6.2   Assignment of Events

The screen shown in Figure 11.54 appears after creating the event in the previous section. In this screen, the characteristics of the info structure automatically appear and are filled in, such as **Sales Organization** and **Division**, along with other information shown.

For this example, select the **Sales** key figure radio button, then select the **001** radio button for the inactive version. Finally, the system proposes the current data for the event, which can be changed. Also, choose the **Status** checkbox to indicate that the event status is active.

Finally, choose **Assignments**, which provides the list of event assignments that can be changed or even deleted (see Figure 11.55). Be sure to select the checkbox located on the far left-hand side of this event so as to ensure correct assignment with the info structure.

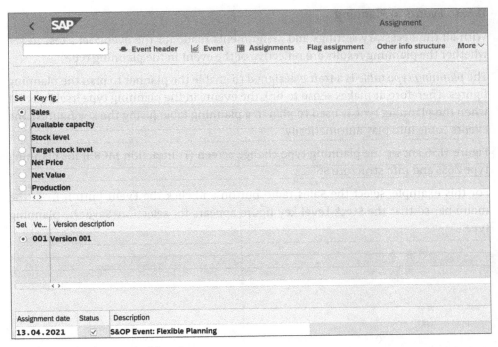

Figure 11.54 Assignment of Event

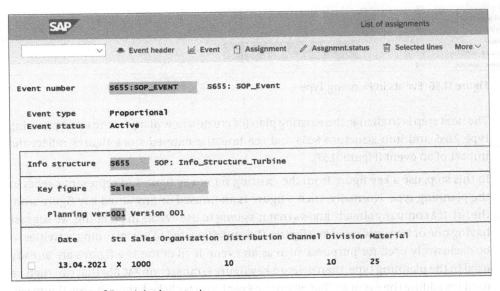

Figure 11.55 List of Event Assignments

11.6.3 Events in Planning

With all the necessary settings and assignments made for the event, let's test to see whether the planning results are reflective of the event in the planning type.

The *planning type table* is a frame designed to enable the planner to plan the planning figures. Therefore, it makes sense to link the events in the planning type itself, so that when the planning type is used to plan in a planning table (using the key figures), the events come into play automatically.

Figure 11.56 shows the planning type change screen (Transaction MC8B) for planning type Z655 and info structure S655.

For this example, select the **Sales** radio button and click the **Event** button from the menu bar so that the **Stock Level** key figure appears for selection. Save the planning type.

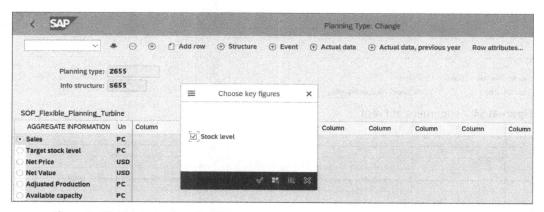

Figure 11.56 Events in Planning Type

The next step is to change the existing plan (or create a new plan) for the same planning type Z655 and info structure S655 and see how the entered stock figures reflect the impact of an event (Figure 11.57).

In this step, use a key figure from the existing set of key figures to represent events in the planning type. Normally, such a figure is an unused or unwanted key figure from the list. If a company already knows that it's going to use events in planning, we suggest having one or two unwanted key figures that aren't related to any planning activities to be exclusively used for purposes such as an event. If all of the key figures are already used in the planning type, then delete a key figure (Transaction MC8B) that can then be used for adding the event so that when the **Event** icon is clicked, then the key figure will be shown as available for addition.

In the planning type, place your cursor on a key figure (in a location where a planner wants the event-related key figures to appear—preferably below **Actual Sales** or **Sales Quantities**), and then choose **Event**. This action shows a list of unused key figures from which to choose. Select one and press ⌈Enter⌋; the system will draw in four other new event-related key figures in its place. In short, the system requires a key figure that can be overwritten with the four new key figures required for planning events.

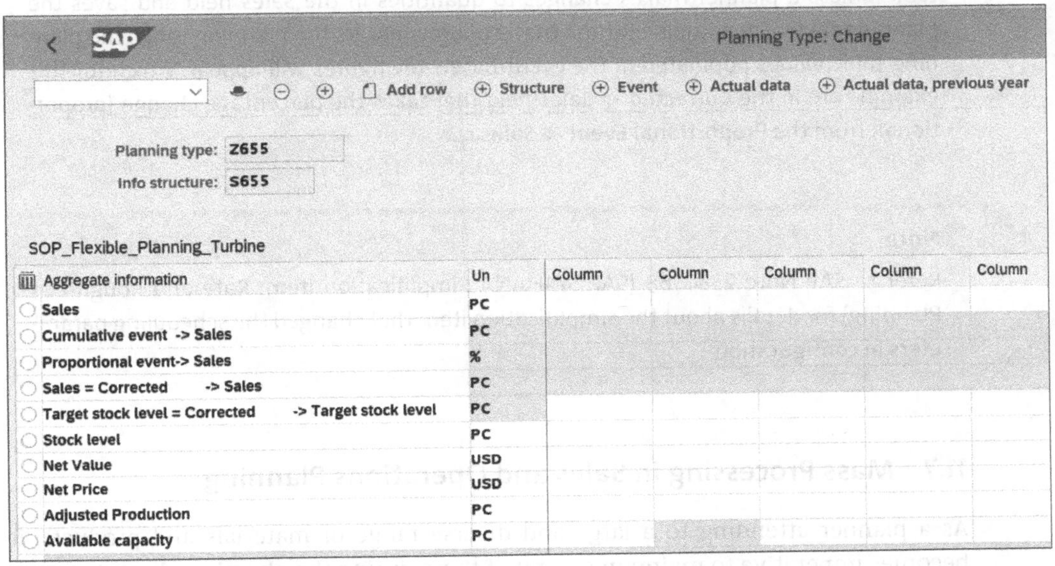

Figure 11.57 Events in Flexible Planning: Part 1

Figure 11.58 shows the change mode screen (Transaction MC94), in which you can manually enter quantities for each month in the **Sales** field. Notice that the **Proportional Event -> Sales** field reflects the details of the event (event number: S655:SOP Event; not shown).

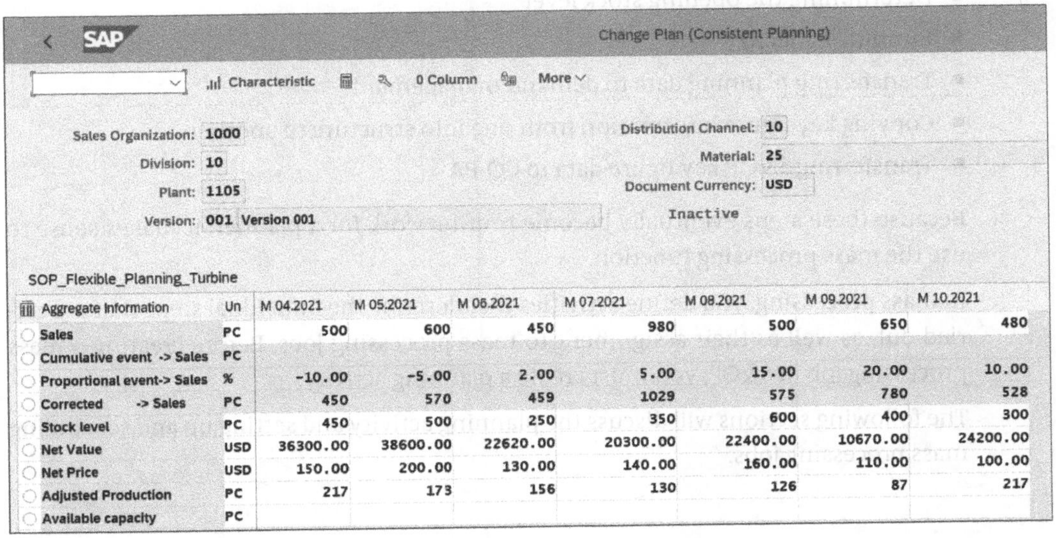

Figure 11.58 Events in Flexible Planning: Part 2

[»]

Note

It's very important to note that the impact of an event won't be visible in the planning table unless a planner makes changes to quantities in the **Sales** field and saves the planning table. Then, the next time that a planner enters the planning table, the planning table values populated in the event-based key figures will appear, which for this example are in the **Corrected -> Sales** field that takes the percentage change (proportional) from the **Proportional Event -> Sales** row.

[»]

Note

Refer to SAP Note 2380568 (SAP S/4HANA Simplification Item: Rate and Rough-Cut Planning) for details about the simplification item that changed the scheduling parameters in configuration.

11.7   Mass Processing in Sales and Operations Planning

As a planner attending to a large and diverse range of materials and products, it becomes imperative to maintain several of these during the planning phase. In many planning steps, it's crucial that the planner performs the requisite functions online and interactively; however, planners can automate a few planning steps in the mass processing functionality of S&OP. Some of the mass processing steps that a planner can perform are listed here:

- Forecasting
- Determining the opening stock level
- Running a macro
- Transferring planning data to demand management
- Copying key figure information from one info structure to another
- Transferring S&OP key figure data to CO-PA

Because these steps eventually become routine work for a planner, it makes sense to use the mass processing function.

In mass processing, you define activities that describe the individual steps that are carried out, as well as their assignment to mass processing jobs. Before creating a mass processing job in S&OP, you must create a planning activity.

The following sections will discuss the planning activity and setting up and scheduling mass processing jobs.

11.7.1 Planning Activity

A *planning activity* defines the function that a planner will execute through a given mass processing batch job. The planning activity consists of function profiles, which define the functions in detail. A planner will need to create each of the function profiles separately before the creation of the planning activity in SAP.

To create a planning activity, use menu path **SAP IMG • Production • Sales & Operations Planning (SOP) • Functions • Mass Processing • Define Activities**, or use Transaction MC8T.

Enter the name of the planning activity in the **Key F.plng.activity** field (for this example, "SOP"), the **Planning Type** ("Z655"), the planning activity type, and the corresponding activity profile that needs to be executed through this planning activity. For a given function that requires mass processing execution, choose the relevant activity type. After selecting the relevant activity, the corresponding activity profiles, such as **Macro**, **Transfer Profile**, or **Copy Profile**, become available to select among.

11.7.2 Setting Up a Mass Processing Job

To set up the mass processing job, you need to perform the following steps in the given sequence:

1. Assign a name to the mass processing job.
2. Assign the info structure and version.
3. Assign the planning type.
4. Assign a name to the variant.
5. Select the selection screens.
6. Define the characteristic values, activity, and aggregation level.
7. Save the variant.

To create the mass processing job, follow SAP menu path **Logistics • Logistics Controlling • Flexible Planning • Planning • Mass Processing • Create**, or use Transaction MC8D. (Use Transaction MC8E to change the job and Transaction MC8F to delete it.)

The following steps are involved:

1. Create a planning job. For this example, enter the **Job Number** as "SOP_SAP" and a short description of the **Job Name** as "SOP_SAP_Flex_Plan".
2. Choose **Execute**, and maintain **Info Structure** "S655" and **Version** "001" to apply the mass processing job to this info structure and version.
3. Choose **Execute**, and maintain **Plng.Type** "Z655", which is the specific planning type within the info structure with which the system will perform the mass processing function.

4. Select a planning type, and then maintain the **Variant Name** for the selection screen details.

5. Enter the variant name in the **Create Variant** field, which in this example is "SOP_ Flex_Plan", and choose **Create** to create the variant and enter the selection screen details.

6. Select the **Created** checkbox and choose **Continue** to proceed with maintaining the selection screen details.

After a planner has finished creating the planning job, perform the following functions:

1. Select the characteristic levels on which the system will run the mass processing job, the **Aggregation Level** and the **Planning Activity**. The planning activity was configured in Section 11.7.1. The planning activity consists of functions that the system performs through mass processing. It contains the profiles for the respective functions that are configured.

2. Click the **Attributes** button to go to the **Variant Attributes** popup.

3. Select whether to run the mass processing in the background only by selecting the relevant checkbox. Save the variant attributes.

11.7.3   Scheduling the Mass Processing Job

The mass processing job can be scheduled using Transaction MC8G. Here, specify the variant name and use the standard batch scheduling function.

Mass processing jobs can be monitored using Transaction SM37. Use Transaction MC8I to obtain an overview of a specific job. To delete a mass processing job, use Transaction MC8F.

11.8   Standard Analysis in Flexible Planning

Now that we've discussed most of the options and features available in flexible planning, we'll cover a lesser-known functionality of standard analysis in flexible planning. In Chapter 23, we'll discuss how to take advantage of the large number of standard analysis reports available using predefined and preconfigured info structures in all the logistics areas of the SAP system. However, this section covers a user-defined info structure (not a predefined info structure) that can still be used in standard analysis. User-defined standard analysis helps when a planner wants to evaluate all the desired key figures in one report (analysis report) by using one info structure. This eliminates the need to refer to two or more predefined info structures to obtain the desired information.

The following summarizes the steps involved in creating a standard analysis in flexible planning:

1. Maintain a self-defined info structure (Transaction MC21).
2. Set parameters for the info structure and key figures (Transaction MC7F).
3. Create update rules for the info structure (Transaction MC24). Maintain an update rule for each key figure, then click **Activate Updating**. You may use the **Check** icon to simulate update rules. Finally, click the **Generate** icon to generate the update rules for the info structure.

In flexible planning, update the rules for key figures within the info structure so that when running the standard analysis report, the system brings up the relevant information.

The step to define the update rule occurs right after creating and activating the info structure. Using Transaction MC24, create the update rules for the characteristics and key figures of the info structure.

Update rules enable the system to do the following:

- Know which characteristics and key figures the system must update when the user performs the business transactions.
- Know the SAP tables from which the system needs to fetch the data for given key figures and characteristics. They also include information for the dates the system should use for records or data that is populated in the structures.

The *update group* is equally important because it defines the business areas and the tables that will be used for updating the info structure. Multiple update rules can be maintained for a given key figure by copying an existing rule.

The SAP system offers functional areas such as Materials Management, Sales and Distribution, Production Planning, Quality Management, Project System, and Plant Maintenance, among others.

[!]

Warning

Only include the key figures for which there is a need to update the info structure from SAP system tables of the application area to ensure that the system isn't overburdened.

[«]

Note

To update groups in configuration, follow menu path **SAP IMG** · **Logistics Information System (LIS)** · **Logistics Data Warehouse** · **Updating** · **Updating Definition** · **Specific Definition Using Update Rules** · **Maintain Update Rules**.

Before the activation is done, check the consistency of the set update rules by choosing the **Generate** button to check for any errors or warning messages and eliminate them.

An info structure with errors won't be generated, and no data will be populated in the info structure.

After attending to the update rules, the next step is to configure the parameters to update data in the info structure. The period split must match with the period for planning—that is, **Set Planning Parameters for the Info Structure** (Section 11.2.2). To configure the parameters, follow these steps:

1. Perform the business transactions, such as creation of sales order or production order.

2. Create the necessary transaction data in the SAP system to test the update of the info structure in the SAP tables. For example, create a sales order with an order quantity and order value (if these two key figures are used in the self-defined info structure), and see if the data is automatically updated in the info structure (table) by using Transactions SE16N or SE11 and giving the details of the self-defined info structure.

3. Run standard analysis for the self-defined info structure (Transaction MC9C). On the initial screen, enter the self-defined info structure S655, and enter version 001 (actual data). Press ⌈Enter⌉; on the next screen, defined characteristics will be available to choose from (see Figure 11.59).

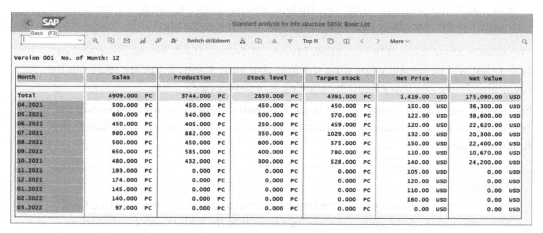

Version 001 No. of Month: 12

Month	Sales	Production	Stock level	Target stock	Net Price	Net Value
Total	4909.000 PC	3744.000 PC	2850.000 PC	4391.000 PC	1,419.00 USD	175,090.00 USD
04.2021	500.000 PC	450.000 PC	450.000 PC	450.000 PC	150.00 USD	36,300.00 USD
05.2021	600.000 PC	540.000 PC	500.000 PC	570.000 PC	122.00 USD	38,600.00 USD
06.2021	450.000 PC	405.000 PC	250.000 PC	459.000 PC	120.00 USD	22,620.00 USD
07.2021	980.000 PC	882.000 PC	350.000 PC	1029.000 PC	132.00 USD	20,300.00 USD
08.2021	500.000 PC	450.000 PC	600.000 PC	575.000 PC	150.00 USD	22,400.00 USD
09.2021	650.000 PC	585.000 PC	400.000 PC	780.000 PC	110.00 USD	10,670.00 USD
10.2021	480.000 PC	432.000 PC	300.000 PC	528.000 PC	140.00 USD	24,200.00 USD
11.2021	193.000 PC	0.000 PC	0.000 PC	0.000 PC	105.00 USD	0.00 USD
12.2021	174.000 PC	0.000 PC	0.000 PC	0.000 PC	120.00 USD	0.00 USD
01.2022	145.000 PC	0.000 PC	0.000 PC	0.000 PC	110.00 USD	0.00 USD
02.2022	140.000 PC	0.000 PC	0.000 PC	0.000 PC	160.00 USD	0.00 USD
03.2022	97.000 PC	0.000 PC	0.000 PC	0.000 PC	0.00 USD	0.00 USD

Figure 11.59 Standard Analysis for Self-Defined Info Structure S655

[+] **Tips and Tricks**

Check the update log by using Transaction MC30. Enter the user ID and choose **Execute**. Keep the cursor on the info structure number and choose the **Details** button to check the data updated in detail. Choose the **Analysis** button to check the programs used in updating the info structure.

> **Note**
>
> All of the master data and transactions for flexible planning are listed in one place, under the following SAP menu path: **Logistics • Logistics Controlling • Flexible Planning**.

11.9 Summary

S&OP offers significant optimization to the business processes by helping the planner use standard S&OP or flexible planning. For standard S&OP, the product group is used to define the percentage or the proportional factor of each material within the group or hierarchy, whereas in flexible planning, the planning hierarchies are used.

A planner can extensively use standard or self-defined macros and also create large numbers of planning versions. The final operations plan gets transferred to demand management via PIRs. The forecasting tool is also available in standard S&OP and in flexible planning to facilitate proposing realistic planning figures. Events help a planner take any specific spike or dip in planning figures into account. The rough-cut planning profile provides better visibility into capacities and materials commitments. A large amount of routine planning work can be performed by using the mass processing functionality. A planner can also use flexible planning to perform standard analyses for the self-defined info structure.

The next chapter covers demand management.

Chapter 12
Demand Management

It's important to establish a balance between anticipating demand for products and ensuring that the right production, procurement, and distribution processes are in place to fulfill that demand for eventual consumption. It's also vital to take advantage of several available planning tools to determine realistic planning figures in demand management.

Demand planners in companies are always striving to maintain a balance between the anticipated demands of a product from customers and ensuring its timely availability. Demand management today is much more than using the forecasting tool to predict what to produce and when. In fact, it has evolved into taking a much closer and more critical look at each step of the entire sales, production, procurement, and distribution process for ensuring an optimal balance. This balance is necessary so that the optimum inventory of raw material is maintained in the company's warehouses, and the machines' capacities aren't booked for those products that won't sell well or suddenly have several unexpected and unanticipated customer-specific orders, resulting in undue long lead time and delayed deliveries.

The overall goal of production planning (PP) in general and demand management in particular is to better serve customers by reducing the following:

- Replenishment lead times
- Storage costs

To achieve these goals, one of the effective materials planning approaches is to group materials according to their individual demand patterns. Depending on the business and reporting needs, as few groups as possible for better transparency on the shop floor and as many as necessary for flexibility should be created. To make this materials grouping logical and easier to understand, we've structured similar strategy groups in such a way that all make-to-stock (MTS) or make-to-order (MTO) groupings can be found in relevant sections of this chapter.

We begin this chapter by discussing important elements of demand that will form the foundation of PP in SAP S/4HANA. Next, we'll cover various planning strategies—from MTS to MTO to assemble-to-order (ATO)—so that a planner can make informed decisions on which strategy to use either for an individual material or for a group of materials. Although standard strategies available in the SAP system are sufficient for most business needs, we'll also cover how to create a customized requirement class for a strategy to meet any specific or unique business needs. Finally, and after all these demand management concepts and foundations are in place, we'll show some examples of demand management working in the SAP S/4HANA system.

Let's begin with discussing the core elements of demand management that are used throughout this chapter and then in the rest of book.

12.1   Elements of Demand Management

The main elements based on which demand management works can be broadly categorized into the following four areas:

- Consumption modes and logic
- Determining the requirement type
- Availability check
- Total replenishment lead time (TRLT)

We'll discuss each of these in the following sections.

12.1.1   Consumption Modes and Logic

A *consumption mode* determines whether consumption of planned production quantities is to be carried out as backward or forward consumption, or whether both consumption types are allowed. In *backward consumption*, the system looks for the planned independent requirement (PIR) quantity that exists directly before the sales order. In *forward consumption*, the system looks for the PIR quantity that exists directly after the sales order. There's also a need to maintain the consumption period in the **MRP 3** view of the material master or in the configuration for demand management. The consumption period (forward or backward) is specified in workdays and is valid from the current date. Sales orders, material reservations, and dependent requirements then consume the PIR quantities that lie within the consumption period and after (for forward consumption) or before (for backward consumption) the requirements date.

In the consumption process, the system compares PIR quantities and dates of materials with actual customer requirements or demand, such as sales orders. The consumption process is defined for every planning strategy by combining a requirements type from demand management and a requirements type from sales order management. This step means that the requirements type entered when maintaining PIRs is compared to the customer requirements type specified in configuration.

The following prerequisites must be met for consumption mode: Maintain the **Consumption Mode** field in the material master record (**MRP 3** view, as shown in Figure 12.1).

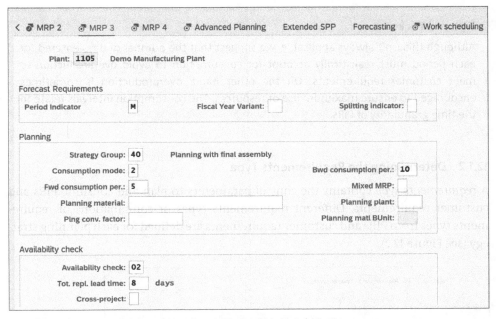

Figure 12.1 Consumption Mode in MRP 3 View of Material Master

The **Consumption Mode** field offers the following five options (available as dropdown options when you place your cursor on the field and press ⌞F4⌟):

- **1** – (backward consumption only)
- **2** – (backward/forward consumption)
- **3** – (forward consumption only)
- **4** – (forward/backward consumption)
- **5** – (period-specific consumption)

The customer requirement consumes the PIR quantity that either directly precedes or follows it. If the PIR quantity directly preceding the customer requirements doesn't cover the customer's requirement, then the system looks for the next closest PIR in the future or past. During this process, the system refers to the consumption periods maintained in the material master or in configuration for demand management. The consumption periods determine the intervals (for backward or forward consumption) within which customer requirements consume PIRs. Customer requirements that lie outside the consumption period aren't consumed. If no consumption periods have been maintained, you can only consume requirements that are planned on the same day. The allocation of customer requirements to PIRs is carried out dynamically. This step means that if sales orders or planning are rescheduled, the allocation is deleted and redefined. In period-based consumption, sales orders, dependent requirements, or material reservations consume planned independent requirements that lie within the consumption period of the planned independent requirement.

Tips and Tricks

Although this isn't always applicable, we suggest that the number of days entered for each period must realistically account for consumption to avoid overproduction to meet customer requirements. On the other hand, overproduction is sometimes encouraged to ensure maximum use of resources. The consumption intervals relate to the time granularity of PIRs.

12.1.2   Determining the Requirements Type

A *requirements type* contains the control parameters to plan and consume PIRs and customer requirements. Different requirements types or combinations of requirements types from PIRs and customer requirements are defined for each planning strategy (see Figure 12.2).

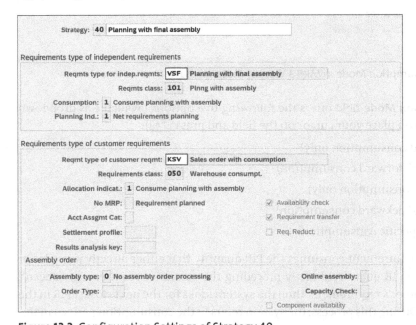

Figure 12.2 Configuration Settings of Strategy 40

Note

There may not be a need to define any new strategies because SAP's standard delivery provides all strategies to meet most business needs. There may only be a few cases that require defining customized planning strategies, as covered in Section 12.7.

If a planner wants the system to automatically determine the requirements type when creating the PIRs, enter strategy groups for the corresponding materials in the material master record. If the strategy group allows a number of planning strategies, the system proposes the requirements type from the main strategy.

Referring to Figure 12.1, notice that **Strategy Group 40** is assigned to the material. Figure 12.2 shows that for **Strategy 40**, the associated **Reqmts Type for Indep.Reqmts** is "VSF" (**Planning with Final Assembly**). The associated **Reqmt Type of Customer Reqmt** is "KSV" (**Sales Order with Consumption**).

The planning strategies represent the business procedures to plan and produce a material. In the system, the planning strategies are recorded in configuration by a combination of requirements types from demand management and sales order management (refer to Figure 12.2). This combination determines either the consumption of PIRs by customer requirements or how the availability check is to be carried out.

By assigning a planning strategy to a particular material, the system determines the correct requirements type (and all the control parameters of the requirements class) when creating PIRs or sales orders. The following assignments have to exist to assign the requirements classes to PIRs and sales orders:

- Planning strategy to a strategy group (from demand management) so that a material can be planned with various planning strategies
- One main strategy and up to six alternative strategies
- Strategy group to the material (in the material master record) so that the system can automatically determine the correct requirements type
- Planning strategy to the material requirements planning (MRP) group (assigned in the configuration for demand management) in which the MRP group is assigned to the material in the material master record

Figure 12.3 shows how various elements of requirement classes and planning strategy link up with each other in. In Section 12.7, we'll cover the step-by-step approach to configuring the elements shown in Figure 12.3.

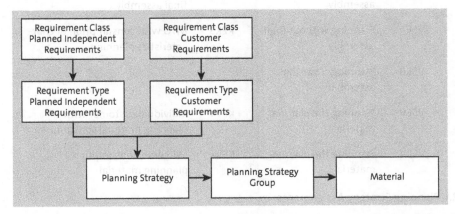

Figure 12.3 Relationships among Requirements Type, Requirements Class, and Planning Strategy

Table 12.1 shows how requirements types for independent requirements link up with requirement types for customer requirements. Refer to Figure 12.2 and the associated strategy 40; the same details of strategy 40 are covered in Table 12.1.

Strategy	Requirements Type for Independent Requirements		Requirements Type for Customer Requirements	
10	LSF	MTS production	KSL	Sale from stock without independent requirement reduction
11	BSF	Gross PIRs	KSL	Sale from stock without independent requirement reduction
20			KE	Individual sales order without consumption
25			KEK	MTO with configurable material
26			KEL	MTO for material variants
30	LSF	MTS production	KL	Sales order manufactured by lot size
40	VSF	Planning with final assembly	KSV	Sales order with consumption
50	VSE	Planning without final assembly	KEV	MTO with consumption
52	VSE	Planning without final assembly	KSVS	Sales order with consumption
54	VSE	Planning without final assembly	KEKT	MTO with consumption
55	VSE	Planning without final assembly	KELV	MTS with consumption without final assembly
56	VSE	Planning without final assembly	KEKS	MTO with consumption of characteristics planning
59	VSEB	Planning; phantom assemblies		
60	VSEV	Planning the planning material	KEVV	Individual customer with planning material consumption
63	VSEV	Planning the planning material	KSVV	MTS with consumption of planning material

Table 12.1 Planning Strategy Assignments

Strategy	Requirements Type for Independent Requirements		Requirements Type for Customer Requirements	
65	VSEV	Planning the planning material	ELVV	MTO variant with planning material
70	VSFB	Planning for assemblies		
81			KMSE	Assembly planned order
82			KMFA	Assembly with production order
89	VSE	Planning for assemblies	KMSE	Assembly planned order

Table 12.1 Planning Strategy Assignments (Cont.)

12.1.3   Availability Check and Total Replenishment Lead Time

A crucial element of effective production planning is the way a material's availability is checked in the sales order and how the demand is transferred from the delivery proposal to the production schedule. To set up this process, maintain an availability check and a TRLT in the **MRP 3** view of the material master that also includes the strategy group and the consumption rules. The availability check with its associated rule and scope of check will drive what happens when a sales order is entered using Transaction VA01. On sales order creation, an availability check is triggered; if the customer's requested delivery date can't be met, a view with a delivery proposal pops up. The delivery proposal attempts to address the following questions:

- Is a one-time delivery in full on the customer-requested delivery date possible?
- When is the complete delivery of all requested items possible?
- When can partial deliveries be made?

The availability check in a sales order shows two dates separated by a forward slash (/). The first date is the ship date, and the second is the material availability date that is relevant for MRP and will show in Transaction MD04 if some other conditions are met and the dates and quantities are fixed. Depending on what proposal is selected and agreed upon with the customer, the checkbox next to the delivery proposal can be selected to confirm the dates. Those dates will then be relevant for production and materials planning, and everything in planning works toward meeting these dates. How these dates were determined depends on the scope of the check.

A combination of the availability check (set in the **MRP 3** view of the material master) and the checking rule (set according to the option chosen to carry out the availability check) determine the delivery date to the customer. Other factors that can be defined are objects, parameters, and elements that the system considers (or doesn't consider) in the procedure to check for availability.

One of the most relevant settings in the scope of the check is the decision of whether a planner checks with or without TRLT. TRLT is a measure primarily used in MTO because it's the time it takes to replenish the product in question if there is nothing readily available in stock. If the system checks *with* TRLT (the field **Scope of Check** checkbox is unchecked), the availability check only looks out to the end of the lead time. If it doesn't find enough quantity to fulfill the demand in that period, it confirms *any* quantity just after the TRLT. Subsequently, the next MRP run will generate an additional order proposal to fulfill the demand.

In the next sections, we'll discuss various planning strategies for MTS, followed by MTO. We'll also cover strategies relevant to ATO, planning components, and, finally, planning strategies relevant to variant configuration.

12.2   Strategies for Make-to-Stock Production

The planning strategies explained in this section are designed for planning procurement (production or purchasing) of components by planning the final products. Choose an MTS strategy if the following is true:

- The materials aren't segregated; that is, they aren't assigned to specific sales orders.
- Costs need to be tracked at the material level and not at the sales order level. If the stock is produced independently of sales orders, always use MTS production because it's then possible to immediately provide goods to the customers from that stock. A planner may even want to produce goods without having sales orders in anticipation that there might be customer demand in future. This means that MTS strategies can support a close customer-supplier relationship because the objective is to quickly provide the customers with goods from the stock. Returns that have passed quality inspection and other unexpected goods receipts (GRs) can be used for other sales orders.

Avoid maintaining unreasonably high stock levels by doing the following:

- Create a production plan in advance (in demand management) to plan the stock. If this option is used, then also decide whether sales orders exceeding the production plan are to affect the actual production or not.
- Receive sales orders as early as possible (e.g., using scheduling agreements).

MTS strategies generally consist of up to five stages. Table 12.2 illustrates which stages are involved in which strategies; 1 denotes allocations and 2 denotes reduction of planned independent requirements (PIRs). A PIR of a finished goods material is a planning quantity that the company expects to sell in the future but want to pre-produce earlier on.

	Planning Strategies					
Stages in order	40	30	10	11	52	63
Demand management (creation of PIRs)	Yes	No	Yes	Yes	Yes	Yes
Procurement before sales	Yes	No	Yes	Yes 2	Yes	Yes
Sales order	Yes 1	Yes	Yes	Yes	Yes 1	Yes 1
Procurement after sales	No	Yes	No	No	Yes	Yes
Goods issue (GI) for delivery and reduction of PIRs	Yes	Yes	Yes	Yes 2	Yes	Yes

Table 12.2 Five Stages of MTS Strategies

Let's now discuss the MTS planning strategies in detail.

12.2.1   Strategy 40: Planning with Final Assembly

This strategy is probably the most widely used MTS strategy. If a planner can forecast production quantities for the final product, it makes sense to use this planning strategy. PIRs are consumed by incoming sales orders so that the master plan is always adjusted to suit the current requirements situation. Therefore, the important feature of this planning strategy is that a planner can react quickly to a customer's requirements. The smoothing of the master plan is less important here. Moreover, strategy 40 has the following qualities:

- PIRs are entered at the finished product level and trigger the procurement and production of the necessary assemblies and components before receipt of the sales orders.
- It's possible to use information from the sales forecast, information from the sales information system, or other planning tools to plan production quantities.
- As soon as the sales order is received, it consumes the PIRs. This step means that a planner can compare the PIRs situation with the actual customer requirements situation.
- An accurate availability check is performed according to available-to-promise (ATP) logic during sales order processing.
- The system checks whether sufficient PIRs have been planned to cover the sales order.
- Requirements from the sales orders are passed onto production and can lead to changes being made to procurement if the requirements from the sales orders exceed the PIR quantities.

- If there is insufficient coverage of components—that is, the sales order quantities exceed the PIR quantities—the sales orders can't be confirmed. The system therefore automatically adjusts the master plan.

- PIR quantities that are left unconsumed increase the warehouse stock of the finished product. However, the system doesn't create additional production orders if sufficient stock exists.

When using this strategy, maintain the following master data for the finished product in the material master:

- **Strategy Group** "40" in the **MRP 3** view

- Consumption parameters (**Consumption Mode, Bwd Consumption, Fwd Consumption**) to allow consumption of independent requirements

- Default values taken from the MRP group if no consumption parameters are maintained in the material master

- Item category group (e.g., "NORM") in the **Sales: Sales Org. Data 1** view

> **Note**
>
> Unlike other planning strategies, planning strategy **Planning with Final Assembly (40)** doesn't require the material master MRP availability check to contain a specific value. This field doesn't impact the strategy 40 planning process. A planner can also use the sales and distribution (SD) checking rule with (or without) replenishment lead times, which can be seen in the sales order under **Edit · Item Availability · Goto · Scope of Check.**

MTS strategy 40, illustrated in Figure 12.4, starts with the entry of the forecast ❶. This can be done manually via Transaction MD61, through upload from a spreadsheet, or via transfer out of sales and operations planning (S&OP) in the SAP system by use of info structures, product groups, or a flexible planning hierarchy. The long-term planning (LTP) or predictive material and resource planning (pMRP) components can be used in the system to simulate various versions and to set the **Active** checkbox for a specific version in demand management, which is basically the PIR. The MRP run then generates supply proposals ❷ that can be sequenced, leveled, and scheduled within available capacity ❸ and then collectively checked for missing parts.

The resulting production schedule will fill up the inventory before the sales orders drop in. Any customer request for product can now be directly fulfilled from freely available, neutral inventory ❹, and as the orders come in, they find the remaining quantities of the forecast (looking backward, forward, or both according to the rules set in **MRP 3**) and consume it with the respective quantities of the orders ❺. This allows for comparing and monitoring forecasted quantities against the actual order quantities.

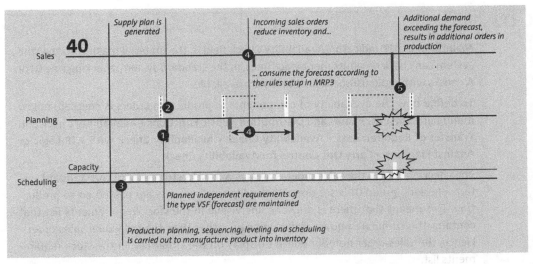

Figure 12.4 Strategy 40: MTS

12.2.2   Strategy 30: Production by Lot Size

In strategy 30, procurement is based only on sales orders, and no planning for the finished product is involved. Depending on the dates, several sales orders can be grouped together for production in one single lot. Moreover, strategy 30 has the following qualities:

- It's not possible to use information from other SAP planning tools, such as forecasting, sales information systems, or S&OP (except when combined with schedule line agreements).

- An accurate availability check is performed according to ATP logic during sales order processing.

- Lot size optimization and rounding mechanisms are possible. Depending on the dates, several sales orders can be grouped and collectively produced in a single lot. The lot size in this procedure can depend on various aspects of production, such as pallet size or production optimization.

- Leftover stock from previous procurements can be used. Using leftover stock for other sales orders is particularly useful for companies that mainly produce goods for major customers but also want the option to sell smaller requirements from stock.

- PIRs aren't consumed by sales and stock orders. However, the delivery "consumes" the schedule lines or sales order items because it updates goods as delivered. If an issue is made for a particular sales order, the system reduces the sales order quantity.

- Stock orders are reduced when the goods are sold from stock.

[»]

> **Note**
>
> Maintain the ATP indicator (**Availability Check** field in the material master) so that the system can check replenishment lead times. In the standard system, checking rule **01** or **A** checks with replenishment lead times are available.
>
> To define how the availability of components in production orders is checked, follow menu path **SAP IMG • Sales and Distribution • Basic Functions • Availability Check and Transfer of Requirements • Availability Check • Availability Check with ATP Logic or Against Planning • Carry Out Control for Availability Check**.
>
> The checking rule in the sales order is always **A** in MTS strategies. In the standard system, checking group 01 is set up so that daily requirements are passed on to production. This means that there is only one line visible in the stock/requirements list that contains the cumulated quantity for one day, rather than the individual sales orders. Hence, the sales order number doesn't display on the **Order** line in the stock requirements list.

As shown in Figure 12.5, nothing happens unless a sales order is entered ❶ and the availability check determines a feasible delivery date for confirmation. The MRP run will then create an order proposal with a larger lot size (rounding or minimum) ❷, and the lot size is produced into inventory. The sales order will then take the requested quantity from inventory ❸, and the rest remains in inventory for future orders to consume ❹ until the inventory runs out. As soon as a new sales order demands more product than what remains in inventory, the cycle will repeat itself.

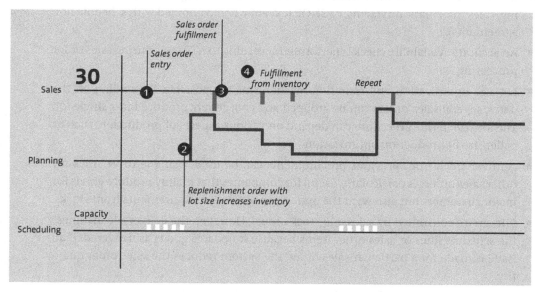

Figure 12.5 Strategy 30

Tips and Tricks

While using this strategy type, there's no need for a PIR. However, we suggest not removing the PIR from the configuration settings because it may be used if necessary.

The following master data prerequisites need to be maintained for the finished product:

- Maintain **Strategy Group** "30" in the **MRP 3** view of the material master.
- Use the **Availability Check** field (in the **MRP** view and the **Sales: General/Plant** view) so that the system will perform an availability check with replenishment lead times ("01" in the standard system).
- Set the item category group (e.g., "NORM") in the **Sales: Sales Org. 2** view of the material master.
- Because procurement is based only on sales orders, no planning for the finished product is involved here, which means knowing the sales order situation in advance. Therefore, with regard to the production time and replenishment lead times of the components, this strategy is sometimes combined with scheduling agreements.
- The necessary components can also be procured with the following:
  - Individual planning of the components—for example, using strategy 70 (Section 12.5.1)
  - Consumption-based components
  - Kanban components

Note
For setting up kanban in the SAP system, refer to Chapter 9.

12.2.3   Strategy 10: Net Requirements Planning

Strategy 10 is particularly useful in mass production environments. It's often combined with repetitive manufacturing (REM). Choose this strategy if a planner wants production to be determined by a production plan (demand management) and doesn't want sales orders to directly influence production. One of the most important features of this planning strategy is that it enables a planner to smooth the demand program.

This planning strategy is used in the customer packaged goods industry because it's possible to plan the demand for ice cream, for example, but a single order should not affect production. This strategy is also used for products with seasonal demand where production needs to be smoothed. Moreover, strategy 10 has the following qualities:

- Procurement is only determined by PIRs, which leads to smoothing of production that is unaffected by irregular sales orders.

- An accurate availability check is performed using ATP logic during sales order processing. Sales orders can be displayed for information purposes only. They don't affect production quantities. Goods are sold from stock.

- The PIRs are reduced at GI for the delivery. A planner can compare the PIRs situation with the actual customer requirements.

- PIRs left unreduced increase the warehouse stock of the finished product and cause procurement to be decreased or, due to netting, to not take place at all in the next period.

- If a planner wants the system to reduce future PIRs when it makes withdrawals for unplanned sales orders, maintain the appropriate consumption period.

[+]

Tips and Tricks

It's recommended to work with an availability check that checks without TRLT (e.g., 02 in the standard system). For this strategy, it usually makes sense to create a new checking rule that combines the **Check without TRLT** setting with passing on daily requirements.

First the forecast is generated, as shown in Figure 12.6 ❶. This can happen through manual input into Transaction MD61, an upload from an Excel or Access datasheet, or using the system's forecasting component in the logistics information system (LIS) with a subsequent transfer of demand. After the forecast has been generated, it becomes relevant to MRP.

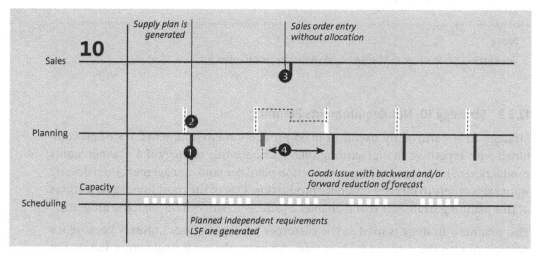

Figure 12.6 Strategy 10

The MRP run will generate order proposals to meet the forecast in the respective periods ❷. The order proposals are now turned into supply elements and inventory is built up accordingly. Incoming sales orders have absolutely no impact on that supply (or production) program and are fulfilled from available inventory ❸. This is where strategy 10 differs from other MTS strategies: it protects the production schedule and allows for the smooth flow of the replenishment process. To make sure the process works in its entirety, ensure that the sales availability checking rule doesn't use the TRLT. After a GI is posted (to a sales order or not), the PIR is reduced (unallocated) ❹.

While using this strategy type, maintain the following master data prerequisites for the finished product:

- **Strategy Group** "10" in the **MRP 3** view
- Item category group (e.g., "NORM") in the **Sales: Sales Org. 2** view
- **Availability Check** field in configuration so as to perform an availability check without replenishment lead times (in the standard system, enter "02")

12.2.4   Strategy 11: Gross Requirements Planning

The *gross requirements planning* MTS strategy is particularly useful in mass production environments and is often combined with REM. This strategy is particularly useful if a planner needs to produce, regardless of whether there's stock or not. This strategy is often useful for steel, fertilizer, or cement manufacturing, in which it's not possible to shut down production. A blast furnace or a cement factory must continue to produce, even if this means producing stock. For example, if a planned demand is 100 pieces, and there are 50 pieces in inventory, the MRP run will generate an order proposal for 100 pieces, ignoring the 50 that are already available.

This planning strategy is to some extent similar to net requirements planning (strategy 10). However, the following differences exist:

- There is no netting of stock with demand; only the planned quantities are produced.
- Production is only determined by PIRs, which leads to production smoothing.
- PIRs are reduced during GR for an order (planned order in REM, production order, process order, or purchase order).

Gross requirements planning (strategy 11) also has the following features in common with net requirements planning (strategy 10):

- Production quantities can be planned relatively effectively by means of PIRs.
- It uses information from the sales information system (SIS), flexible planning, or other planning tools to plan production quantities. Therefore, production and procurement of the required components are triggered before the sales order stage.
- Individual sales orders, which can be somewhat irregular, don't affect production.
- An accurate availability check is performed according to ATP logic during sales order processing.

- Using lot size or rounding keys, perform *lot size optimization* during planning so that a planner always plans convenient lot sizes in demand management or during the MRP run (lot sizes are covered in Chapter 13, Section 13.5).

[»]

> **Note**
>
> It's recommended to work with an availability check that functions without checking the replenishment lead time. These details are covered in production by lot size (strategy 30) and net requirements planning (strategy 10).

When using this strategy type, maintain the following master data for the finished product:

- Maintain **Strategy Group** "11" in the **MRP 3** view.
- Set the **Mixed MRP** indicator to "2" in the **MRP 3** view.
- Set the item category group (e.g., "NORM") on the **Sales: Sales Org. 2** view.
- Maintain the **Availability Check** field so that the system performs an availability check without the replenishment lead time (checking group "02" in the standard system).

12.2.5   Strategy 52: Planning with Final Assembly and without MTO

This strategy, along with planning with a planning material and without MTO (63), discussed in the next section, allows a planner to procure components based on PIRs. Production of the finished product, however, is based on actual sales orders, similar to MTO strategies. This planning strategy ensures that a planner can react quickly to customer requirements, even if the finished product has a long overall lead time. A planner can avoid the main value-added process until there's a customer. This strategy is very similar to strategy 50, which uses MTO production.

Production quantities can be planned relatively effectively with PIRs for the finished product. It's possible to use information from the sales forecast, SIS, or other planning tools to plan production quantities. Only the procurement of the component is triggered before the sales order stage. Final assembly takes place after a sales order has been entered.

Strategy 52 is very similar to MTO strategy 50, except that the actual sales orders aren't segregated in individual segments in Transaction MD04 (Stock/Requirements List) but rather are listed in the **Net Requirements** section. Moreover, strategy 52 has the following qualities:

- The PIRs are consumed during the sales order stage. Therefore, a planner can compare the PIRs situation with the actual customer requirements.
- An availability check is performed on the basis of the PIRs.

- Demand from sales orders is passed on to production and triggers production after the sales order stage, even if insufficient components are planned. However, the sales orders can't be confirmed if there is insufficient coverage of components.

- PIR quantities for the finished products that are left unconsumed increase the warehouse stock and cause procurement to decrease or not take place at all in the next period. This procedure is known as *netting*.

- From a costing perspective, this is an MTS strategy, in contrast to strategy 50, which is MTO. This means that stock of the finished material isn't linked to each customer order. As such, this strategy doesn't take stock that exceeds the PIRs (due to customer returns, overproduction, etc.) into account when creating a sales order. Stock for finished goods should be handled through an exception process.

Maintain the following master data for the finished product:

- Set **Strategy Group** "52" in the **MRP 3** view.

- Lot size key "EX" must be set in the **MRP 1** view because lot size optimization would be incompatible with the allocation logic, which could result in overplanning and incorrect results in the ATP check.

- Ensure that no rounding profile or rounding values are taken into account.

- Maintain consumption parameters (**Consumption Mode, Bwd Consumption, Fwd Consumption**) so that the independent requirements can be found.

- Set the item category group (e.g., "NORM") on the **Sales: Sales Organization 2** view.

[«]

Note

In this strategy, there is only an availability check against PIRs. A material is considered available if a PIR can be consumed. Therefore, unplanned stock (returns or unplanned production quantities, e.g., overdeliveries) isn't taken into account. The **Availability Check** indicator (**MRP** and **Sales: General/Plant Data** screens) isn't relevant in this case because an availability check according to ATP logic doesn't take place.

[+]

Tips and Tricks

A bill of materials (BOM) is required for the finished product, and there are no major implications for the BOM components. However, for the components, it's important to set the following:

- **MRP Type** to P* (or M*) on the **MRP 1** view to plan the components in MRP
- **Individual/Coll.** indicator to "2" in the **MRP 4** view as a starting point for the master data setup (see Figure 12.7)

12

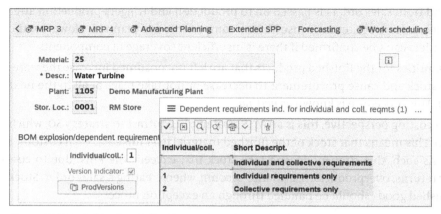

Figure 12.7 Individual or Collective Options in MRP 4 View

12.2.6   Strategy 63: Planning with a Planning Material and without MTO

This strategy enables planning of different sizes or packages for one product. For instance, a company may want to sell a product in packages, such as the following:

- Containing one liter, two liters, and one gallon
- Labeled in English, German, and Hindi

All variants are set up with different material numbers. In addition, a planning material that consists of only *nonvariant components*, which means that it excludes the packaging materials that form the variants, is usually set up. All variants are linked to the planning material with the correct conversion factors. The packaging materials (boxes or cartons for the different sizes or different labels) can be planned based on consumption because they aren't too expensive. Moreover, strategy 63 has the following qualities:

- The planning material could be sold in the same way as any *variant* product. However, it's generally used as an "artificial" material that only contains the nonvariant parts. The BOMs of the variant products contain additional components that diversify the product. These variant components can't be planned exactly using this strategy.
- It handles the variant components in the following way:
  - The variant components are consumption-based.
  - The variant components are planned independently using a planning strategy for components.
  - Overplanning or underplanning of the variant components is accepted.
  - If products have a high level of variance, then use characteristics planning to automate the planning of components.

- This strategy can also be used as a cross-plant version of strategy 52.

- It procures nonvariable components based on the PIRs of a planning material.

- Production of the finished product is based on actual sales orders. This procedure guarantees that a planner can quickly react to customer requirements, even if the finished product has a long overall lead time, and avoid the main value-added process until there is a customer.

- It has the same basic features as planning without final assembly and without MTO (strategy 52). In addition, more than one material can consume the PIRs of one planning material.

- It lends itself to the planning of variants of one product. (The term *variant* here indicates similar products, not variant configuration.) For example, imagine similar parts sharing a BOM group (which isn't necessary in this strategy) so that a planner can easily exchange a component in all similar BOMs. A planner usually has up to several dozen variants, whereas variance would be much higher in variant configuration.

Tips and Tricks

This strategy is often used to manage a simple but effective method of capacity planning. The PIRs for the planning material represent a given capacity situation. All variant materials require a similar capacity, and there is an allocation of given capacity with requested capacity at the order entry stage. Using the total requirements list, a planner can easily check the capacity situation.

In the next section, we'll discuss planning strategies associated with MTO production.

12.3   Strategies for Make-to-Order Production

The planning strategies covered in this section are designed to produce a material for an individual sales order. That is, production of finished products only begins on receiving a sales order. Therefore, MTO strategies always support a close customer-supplier relationship because sales orders are closely linked to production. MTO can also be used in production using variant configuration and ATO environments. The usage in these areas is due to the close link between the sales order and production that exists in a MTO environment and is required in ATO and variant configuration.

Choose a MTO strategy if both of the following are true:

- The materials are segregated and uniquely assigned to specific sales orders.

- Costs need to be tracked at the sales order level and not at the material level.

> **Note**
>
> For the sake of clarifying the master data settings, MTO strategies should always be combined with lot-size key EX (lot-for-lot), and rounding values should not be used. Even if other lot-size keys or rounding values are maintained, these values don't take effect in MTO strategies.

Several options exist that enable procurement of components for specific sales order items. It's also possible to use a different planning strategy to procure components without having a sales order yet. Using one of these planning strategies allows you to keep your replenishment lead time low, as follows:

- Plan on the basis of the finished product, such as planning without final assembly (strategy 50) or planning with a planning material (strategy 60).

- Plan at the component level (Section 12.5).

- Use consumption-based or Kanban-controlled components.

- Know that customer stock can exist on any BOM level.

- Note the close link of sales orders to stock results in the customer section of the stock/requirements list.

- In the basic MTO strategy, MTO production (strategy 20), no specific product structures are required. Therefore, it doesn't matter if the material has a BOM or not. The material can be produced in-house or procured externally. No planning is involved in this strategy.

- Planning without final assembly (strategy 50) and planning with a planning material (strategy 60) do require a specific product structure (i.e., a BOM, which means the BOM header material is always produced in-house). These planning strategies assume that a planner wants to plan the procurement (production or purchasing) of the components by planning the finished products. This strategy means a planner needs a fairly stable demand for the finished products. But if you can plan more easily at the component level than at the finished product level, refer to Section 12.5.

Let's cover each of the MTO strategies in more detail.

12.3.1   Strategy 20: Make-to-Order Production

As the name suggests, in MTO production, a product is produced specifically for an individual sales order. This planning strategy is used when planning of the (parent) product is neither required nor possible. Demand management isn't involved in this process, nor is there an allocation mechanism. Orders are taken as they come. This strategy represents a production procedure where, in theory, each product is only produced once, although over time the same or similar production processes are repeated.

Each product is specifically produced for an individual customer; therefore, the finished product is rarely placed in stock. Out of the three buffers—inventory, capacity, and time—only the latter two are available to the MTO process.

While considering this strategy, the following requirements have to be met for the components:

- Procure all necessary components within the TRLT.
- Plan at the component level, if required.
- Use consumption-based components or Kanban-based components.
- Alternatively, receive the sales orders at a very early stage to account for the replenishment lead time of the components.

Moreover, with strategy 20, note the following:

- The sales order quantities are planned for production using the sales order number.
- The quantities produced for the individual sales orders can't be changed. Each quantity is maintained specifically for the individual sales order. A separate segment is created in the MRP list (Transaction MD04) for MTO production.
- Starting from the sales order, apply this type of planning to as many levels of the BOM as needed.
- Assemblies and components are also produced or procured specifically for the pegged order, and stock is also managed separately for this sales order.
- The production and procurement costs are maintained for each sales order in either a settlement order or in a project at the sales order item level. A detailed analysis of the planned and actual costs is ensured.
- A special aspect to consider is the indicator "E" entry in the **Acct Assgt Cat.** field under **Requirements Type of Customer Requests**, which drives the posting of any value added during the replenishment process to the customer-specific account throughout all levels of the BOMs.
- This production technique can also be used to create ATOs. The assembly order triggers the creation of either a production order or a planned order and provides a precise delivery schedule. The delivery schedule is based on availability and the production requirements of the relevant assemblies and components (Section 12.4).

In Figure 12.8, a sales order is entered first ❶. If the customer requests the delivery within the TRLT, the availability check in the sales order allows confirmation only for the first date after the lead time counting from today ❷. That date, after being fixed in the delivery proposal of the sales order, then drives the MRP availability date, and the MRP run can generate the replenishment or order proposal ❸. Only then can the production scheduler find time in the schedule to fit production in ❹.

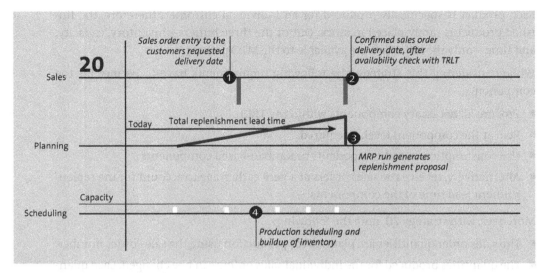

Figure 12.8 Strategy 20

While using strategy 20, maintain the following master data settings for the finished product:

- **Strategy Group** "20" in the **MRP 3** view
- Item category group (e.g., "NORM") in the **Sales: Sales Org. 2** view

12.3.2 Strategy 60: Planning with a Planning Material

This planning strategy is particularly useful for planning BOMs that contain variable and nonvariable parts. The important feature of this strategy is the flexibility to procure nonvariable components based on planning in demand management. Production of the finished product is based on actual sales orders. This procedure ensures that a materials planner is able to quickly react to customer requirements even if the finished product has a long overall lead time. The main value-added process can begin upon having a sales order from a customer.

This strategy has the same basic features as strategy 50. In addition, many materials can consume the PIRs of one planning material. For more information on the differences between these strategies, Section 12.3.3.

In strategy 60, the nonvariable parts are planned using the BOM of a *planning material*. In this instance, the planning material is used purely for planning purposes. It's not actually produced itself but rather used to pass on the dependent requirements of the nonvariable parts from the finished product. The variant parts can be planned using the strategy planning at assembly level (strategy 70) as discussed in Section 12.5.1. The advantage of planning with a planning material is that a planner can plan all the nonvariable parts included in several finished products together.

These variant components can't be planned exactly using this strategy. Instead, ensure the following are true regarding the variant components:

- They're consumption-based.
- They're independently planned using a planning strategy for components.

Alternatively, simply accept overplanning or underplanning of the variant components.

While using strategy 60, the following prerequisites need to be met:

- Create a separate material master record for the planning material and enter the planning material in the material master record (on the **MRP** screens) of all finished products that are to be planned using this planning strategy.
- There are no major implications for the BOM components. However, enter "P*" or "M*" for **MRP Type** (in the **MRP** view) to plan the component in MRP.
- Consider setting the **Individual/Coll.** indicator (on the **MRP 4** view) to **2** for an MTS procurement of components in an MTO environment.

12.3.3   Strategy 50: Planning Without Final Assembly

It makes sense to use this planning strategy when the main value-added process is final assembly. This strategy and planning with a planning material (strategy 60) are probably the most widely used strategies in an MTO environment. Like all MTO strategies, use strategy 50 if production is unique for every customer, where it's impossible or difficult to change the stock for different sales orders.

This strategy is preferred for MTO processes because the lead time to the customer is shortened due to only the top level of the BOM structure being procured to order instead of the entire BOM. An inventory/order interface is introduced just below the level of the finished product. The intermediates are procured into stock so that they are available after the sales order comes in, and the only time it takes to finish is the time for final assembly. This is achieved by way of statistical (planned) orders of the order type VP. Moreover, strategy 50 has the following qualities:

- Production quantities can be planned effectively. Use information from the sales information system, S&OP, or other planning tools to plan production quantities.
- Procurement of the components is organized by means of PIRs entered at the finished product level. The system creates special planned orders at the finished product level for these PIRs. These orders are only relevant for production after a sales order for the finished product exists.
- PIRs that are scheduled using this particular strategy are listed in a separate segment in the MRP list. The planned orders are created with the order type VP and are unconvertible. The sales orders for this strategy are entered as individual customer requirements and maintained in a separate segment in the planning run.

- The assemblies are produced or procured before the sales order is entered. Production is carried out up to one level before the finished product level, and the assemblies and components required for producing the finished product are placed in stock to await the incoming sales order.

- Final assembly is triggered after a sales order has been entered.

- An availability check is performed on the basis of PIRs. Therefore, unplanned stock (e.g., returns) isn't considered for sales.

- The incoming sales order consumes the PIRs, and this in turn reduces the unconvertible planned order quantity.

- The system creates a new convertible planned order for the sales order quantity. If the unconvertible planned order quantity isn't exhausted by the sales order quantity, it remains in the system. If the sales order quantity exceeds the PIR quantity, the unconvertible planned order quantity is increased.

- The PIR quantities that remain unconsumed increase the warehouse stock of the components and cause procurement to decrease or not take place at all in the next period.

- In this strategy, there is only an availability check against PIRs. A material is considered available if a PIR can be consumed. Therefore, unplanned stock (returns or unplanned production quantities, e.g., overdeliveries) isn't taken into account. The **Availability Check** indicator (**MRP** and **Sales: General/Plant Data** screens) isn't relevant in this case because an availability check according to ATP logic doesn't take place.

The following prerequisites need to be in place when using strategy 50:

- Maintain **Strategy Group** "50" in the **MRP 3** view of the finished product.

- Maintain consumption parameters (**Consumption Mode, Bwd Consumption, Fwd Consumption**) so that the independent requirements can be found. If no independent requirements can be found, default values are taken from the MRP group.

- Maintain the item category group (e.g., "NORM") in the **Sales: Sales Org. 2** view.

- A BOM is required for the finished product. There are no major implications for the BOM components. However, maintain the following settings for the BOM components:

  - Set the **MRP Type** to "P*" (or "M*") to plan the components in MRP (or use consumption-based components).

  - Set the **Individual/Coll.** indicator to "2" for an MTS procurement of components in an MTO environment.

While strategies 50 and 60 are very similar to strategies 52 and 63, differences do exist, as listed in Table 12.3.

Strategy	50, 60	52, 63
Costing, settlement, work-in-process (WIP), etc.	MTO	MTS
Finished product stock (and component stock (if required)	Segregated per sales order item	Not segregated
Lot-size indicator and rounding values	Lot-size indicator and rounding values ignored	User ensures that the appropriate values are set

Table 12.3 Differences between Strategies 50/60 and 52/63

The next section covers planning strategies for ATO or assembly orders.

12.4 Strategies for Assemble-to-Order

Strategies for ATO provide the functionality required to carry out an availability check at the component level when the sales order (or customer quotation or inquiry) is created, with the following results:

- The committed order quantity of the sales order is based on the component with the smallest available quantity.
- The confirmed delivery date of the sales order is based on the availability date of the component that is latest on the available time axis.
- Changes to quantities or dates in the sales order affect production and procurement. Changes to dates or quantities in production and procurement change the confirmation date and the committed quantity in the sales order.

When a sales order is created with the *assembly processing* planning strategy, the system automatically creates a procurement element—the assembly order. Choose among the following procurement elements for the assembly order:

- Planned order
- Production order
- Process order
- Network (project)

Scheduling is carried out for the assembly order. When creating the sales order, capacity planning is also possible. Further, the BOM is usually exploded for the assembly order to determine the corresponding components. The availability check is carried out automatically for the components. The check can be carried out either according to ATP logic or against PIRs (at the assembly level). This check determines the committed quantity for the desired delivery date. If no quantity can be committed for the desired delivery date, the system calculates and displays the missing parts. If necessary, it also determines a partial quantity and a total confirmation date (if ATP logic is used for checking).

If a material is configured in the sales order, the results of the configuration are copied to the assembly order, and the system checks the availability of the components selected on the basis of the configuration. Any changes to the date or the quantity in the sales order are immediately passed on to the assembly order.

When working with planned orders, the changes made to sales orders affect planned orders at all times. The following is valid for the production order:

- Changes made to the sales order are only valid for the production order until it's released.

- Changes to the assembly order automatically adjust the committed quantities and dates in the sales order. It's also possible to set the system so that any changes made to the assembly order don't affect the sales order.

The following procedures (assembly types) also are supported:

- A 1:1 procedure—that is, exactly one procurement element for each sales order item (static procedure)

- A loose link between sales order items and procurement elements, via which a planner can split quantities and dates in the sales orders and production (dynamic procedure)

Let's now discuss the associated planning strategies of ATO.

12.4.1   Strategy 81: Assembly Processing with Planned Orders

Assembly processing with planned orders (strategy 81) is particularly useful if production control is managed using the following:

- **Production orders**
  A planner doesn't want to create the production order along with the sales order. Instead, use the planned order for adjusting planning and then convert it into a production order at a later date.

- **REM**
  The planned order is then the run schedule quantity, which a planner can plan using the planning and control tools provided by REM. With this procedure, the GR for the material can be posted with reference to the sales order number. Thus, the costs can also be directly assigned to the sales order, even in REM.

Strategy group 81, assembly processing with planned orders, is predefined for planned orders. In this strategy, the dynamic procedure (i.e., the loose link between the planned order and sales order) is preset as the assembly type. Strategy group 81 refers to both the following requirements type and requirements class in the standard system:

- Requirements type KMSE
- Requirements class 200

Use assembly processing with REM if several of the following situations are applicable:

- Production of the finished product is carried out in clear and simple steps.
- The assembly is produced in a constant flow over the production lines.
- Simple routings are used, or assembly can be carried out without routings.
- The components can be staged anonymously at the production lines.
- The components are procured—for example, with Kanban—using consumption-based planning or with the subassembly planning strategy.
- The effort required for production control and backflushing needs to be reduced.
- The production process is kept as simple as possible. There are only a limited number of production levels involved in producing the product. The number of components is relatively low, however, and it's fully possible to produce a large number of finished products due to configuration options.
- The components required for final assembly are selected through the configuration in the sales order and are staged at the production line anonymously.
- The finished product is assembled without a routing, and the operations are similar. The planning table in REM provides the planner with an overview of the production rates. At this point, the planner can also check capacities for the production lines and distribute the ordered quantities to the production lines with available capacity.
- When production is complete, the GR for the finished product is posted with reference to the sales order number (a special function exists in REM for this step). After the GR posts, the goods are withdrawn for the specific sales order, and the assembly order is deleted.

For these scenarios, a planner can also work without using the planning functions of REM. In this case, capacity planning isn't carried out from the planning table in REM, but instead using the capacity leveling functions in capacity planning (see Chapter 18 on capacity requirements planning). However, it's possible to still use the backflushing functions in REM.

Whether or not to use the planning table for REM depends on the following:

- Use the planning table in REM to assign the production quantities to production lines or to carry out capacity planning, for example. If a planner wants to use the planning table, then maintain the following data in the material master record:
  - Allow REM for the material. To do so, maintain a REM profile. Various control parameters are contained in this profile—for example, for the movement types in backflushing and for posting costs (see Chapter 5 and Chapter 8).

- Use a profile for which a cost collector has to be created manually, as a cost collector isn't required for MTO production.

- The REM profile also determines whether the costs are posted with or without activities (machine costs, labor costs, etc.) when backflushing. If a planner decides to post with activities, they are automatically posted with the final backflush.

- Create a production version containing the data relevant for production (alternative BOM, group, group counter, production line, etc.). If a planner works without routings, then enter at least the BOM and the production line in the production version.

- If a planner doesn't want to use the planning table to plan the run schedule quantities, they may instead, for example, want to use the following:

  - The current stock/requirements list from MRP to gain an overview of the run schedule quantities

  - The capacity leveling functions from the stock/requirements list or from capacity planning to adjust the master plan

If a planner chooses not to work with the planning table, then include the appropriate settings in the material master record.

Maintain a REM profile in the material master. Various control parameters are contained in this profile (e.g., for the movement types in backflushing and for posting costs). As mentioned previously, we recommend using a profile for which a cost collector has to be created manually, as a cost collector isn't required for MTO production. The REM profile also determines whether the costs are posted with or without activities (machine costs, labor costs, etc.) during backflush. If a planner decides to post with activities, they are automatically posted with the final backflush. Note that the special GR posting with reference to the sales order is available whether working with or without the planning table.

12.4.2   Strategy 82: Assembly Processing with Production Orders

Assembly processing with production orders is particularly useful, when one or more of the following is true:

- **Status management functionality is required.**
  Status management, for example, can be used to do the following:

  - Document the current processing status of an object.

  - Allow or forbid certain business transactions.

  - Group or select objects by status (e.g., all orders with the status **Released**, or all components with the status **Missing Part**).

  - Trigger rework functions automatically (using trigger points).

- **A planner wants to carry out business functions at the operation level, such as the following:**
  - Releasing operations
  - Printing shop papers
  - Entering completion confirmations
- **A planner needs to keep track of costs during the production process.**
  Every confirmation or goods movement carried out for the production order causes an update of the actual order costs.
- **A planner wants to use the collective order functionality.**
  A collective order is a structure that links production orders over several manufacturing levels. It offers the following advantages:
  - Any changes to dates or quantities have an immediate effect on any dependent orders within the collective order.
  - No goods movements are required for subassemblies.
  - It allows you to carry out an availability check across all production levels.
  - Each production order is automatically settled to the superior production order. The top production order is then automatically settled to the sales order.

  Collective orders are especially suited to the following types of production:
  - Continuous flow production
  - Production using parallel production lines
  - MTO production
- **A planner wants to use the rework functionality.**
  Use the rework functionality to compensate for malfunctions or errors that occur during the production process. With *unplanned* malfunctions/errors, a planner can do the following:
  - Insert rework operations.
  - Insert reference operation sets.
  - Create rework orders.

  With *planned* malfunctions/errors, a planner can control rework by using trigger points.
- **A planner wants to produce coproducts.**
  Only if a planner set up assembly processing with production orders can they use coproducts.

The following options are available when creating a sales order:

- Create a production order directly and immediately use all the production order functionalities (e.g., the status maintenance).
- Create a planned order first, which is converted into a production order at a later date.

In this case, implement planning decisions (e.g., external procurement or in-house production) later on in the assembly process. Note that in assembly processing, a planner can only convert planned orders into production orders if a strategy group or requirements class with a *dynamic* assembly type is used.

All configuration settings required for assembly processing with production orders, such as strategy group, requirements class, and order type, are already predefined by SAP in the standard system.

Strategy group 82, assembly processing with production orders, is predefined for production orders. In this strategy, the static procedure (i.e., the 1:1 link between the production order and sales order) is preset as the assembly type.

Strategy group 82 refers to both the following requirements type and requirements class in the standard system:

- Requirements type KMFA
- Requirements class 201

Order type PP04, production order with assembly processing, is predefined in requirements class 201. If, for some reason, a planner wants to use an order type different from the one predefined by SAP, ensure that the following scheduling parameters are set for that order type:

- Enter **Backward Scheduling**.
- Select **Adjust Basic Dates**.

If all the available standard system settings are used, there's no need to make any additional settings in configuration.

12.5   Strategies for Planning Components

The purpose of planning at the component level is to procure components to stock (without sales orders) and quickly react to customer demand. The planning strategies explained in this section are designed to plan the procurement (production or purchasing) of components by planning the components. These strategies are particularly useful if one or more of the following is true:

- A variety of finished products exist, possibly with an irregular demand pattern where planning isn't possible.
- The finished products are consumption-based.
- The planning of components also lends itself to separate organizational departments. Component planning in one department isn't influenced by the planning of the finished product in another department.

Choose the relevant strategy (either 70 or 59) for planning components if the following hold true:

- The components aren't segregated; that is, they aren't uniquely linked at specific orders.
- Costs must be tracked at the component (material) level and not at the order level.

Strategies for planning components can be used for both MTS and MTO scenarios. To use a strategy for an MTS planning of components in an MTO environment, set the **Individual/Coll.** indicator (on the **MRP 4** view) to "2" as a starting point for your master data setup.

The planning of components has the following in common with MTS strategies:

- A planner can automate the planning stage by using information from the forecast and pass on the results from these applications directly to demand management.
- MTS costing applies.
- Smoothing of production against customer requirements may be an important aspect.
- Strategies for planning components are usually combined with a lot-size key different from EX or with rounding values.

In planning at assembly level (strategy 70), no specific product structure of the component is required. In other words, it doesn't matter whether the component has a BOM. The material can be produced in-house or procured externally (e.g., raw materials). Planning at the phantom assembly level (strategy 59) requires a special product structure.

In the following sections, we'll discuss planning strategies at the assembly levels.

12.5.1   Strategy 70: Planning at Assembly Level

If a more reliable forecast can be produced for certain assemblies than for the multitude of product variants, this planning strategy is particularly useful for manufacturers of products with variants.

This strategy is very similar to planning with final assembly (strategy 40) covered earlier. The difference is that PIRs are allocated to consumption of production orders (or schedule lines in REM) and not to consumption of sales orders. The material to be planned is a component in a larger structure, often referred to as an *assembly* or *subassembly*.

Take the following factors into consideration when using strategy 70:

- Stock for the assembly usually exists.
- PIRs are entered at the assembly level.

- Procurement (planned by means of the PIRs) is therefore triggered before the production order stage (or schedule line in REM).
- The planned orders for the assembly/components are convertible.
- A planner can smooth procurement according to order demand.
- An accurate availability check is performed according to ATP logic during order processing.
- Requirements from production orders (or planned orders) are passed on to production and can lead to changes being made to procurement after the sales order stage if the order quantities exceed the PIR quantities. However, order quantities can't be confirmed if there is insufficient coverage of components. Therefore, the system automatically adjusts the master plan.
- The PIRs are consumed during the production stage. Therefore, the PIR situation can be compared with the actual order requirements.
- The unconsumed PIR quantities increase the warehouse stock of the component and cause procurement to decrease or not take place at all in the next period (i.e., netting).

Here are the master data of the assembly perquisites for using strategy 70:

- Maintain strategy group "70" in the **MRP 3** view.
- In the **MRP** view, enter "1" for assembly planning (the **Mixed MRP** indicator).
- Set consumption parameters (**Consumption Mode, Bwd Consumption, Fwd Consumption**, on the **MRP** view) to allow for consumption of PIRs.
- If this strategy in an MTS environment is used, then maintain "2" for the **Individual/Coll.** indicator.

12.5.2   Strategy 59: Planning at Phantom Assembly Level

This strategy can be used for a set of components that meet all of the following criteria:

- Components are always assembled together in various finished products.
- Components are planned together.
- Components don't make up an assembly (they constitute a *phantom* assembly).

Moreover, take the following factors into consideration when using strategy 59 (this strategy is similar to planning at assembly level [strategy 70]):

- Component requirements can be planned relatively effectively. Procurement, planned by means of PIRs, is triggered before the production order stage.
- Procurement can be smoothed based on order demand.
- An accurate availability check is performed according to ATP logic during production order processing. An availability check at the component level is possible in the production order.

- If the order quantities exceed the PIR quantities, requirements from production orders (or schedule lines) are passed on to production and can lead to changes being made to procurement after the sales order stage.
- The PIRs are consumed during the production stage. The PIR situation can be compared with the actual order requirements.
- Due to its phantom nature, in contrast to strategy 70, stock doesn't exist for the assembly in strategy 59.

The following master data prerequisites for the phantom assembly need to be ensured while using strategy 59:

- Maintain strategy group "59" in the **MRP 3** view.
- For assembly planning and the **Mixed MRP** indicator, enter "1".
- Maintain consumption parameters (**Consumption Mode, Bwd Consumption, Fwd Consumption**, in the **MRP** view) to allow for consumption of PIRs.
- Maintain "50" in the **Special Procurement** field in the **MRP** view (phantom assembly).
- Enter "2" for the **Individual/Coll.** indicator in the **MRP 4** view.
- To maintain the master data of the components in the phantom assembly, enter "1" in the **Backflush** field ("2" may also be possible) in the **MRP** view. Backflushing is essential because the components are planned with only one PIR and not with individual PIRs. Subsequently, the strategy can only work correctly if all reservations are simultaneously reduced. This procedure is only possible when the GI for the components is posted at a later stage, as in backflushing.
- In addition, all components of the phantom structure have to be linked to the same operation. BOMs must be maintained for the finished products and for the phantom assembly.

12.6 Production with Variant Configuration

This section explains the issues involved in the planning of configurable materials. It's important to note that this section isn't about variant configuration as such. We expect that you're already familiar with variant configuration. All planning strategies are MTO.

The variance or variety of products is the key driver to choosing the right planning strategies. Planning with only a few variants differs fundamentally from planning thousands or millions of variants. Some examples of configurable products are bicycles, computers, or cars. This series of products shows an increasing variance:

- A bicycle might have only a few characteristics—for example, color and frame type.
- A computer might have more characteristics—for example, hard disk, case, CPU, country, or color.

- A car might have hundreds of characteristics, each with a number of characteristics values.

The number of characteristics and characteristic values leads to different approaches to how these materials could be planned. To make this point clear, consider the number of possible variants:

- A bicycle might have seven colors and two frame types, which results in $7 \times 2 = 14$ variants.
- A computer might have two hard disk types, three case types, two CPU types, two country versions, and three possible colors, resulting in $2 \times 3 \times 2 \times 2 \times 3 = 72$ variants.
- A car with some dozens of configurations can easily have a million or more variants.

After further examination, you could reduce the variants for planning purposes:

- The colors of the bicycle are typically cheap and based on planned consumption, so it may be more practical to plan only the two variants of the frame type.
- A similar reduction could be applied to the computer as well. For example, a planner could use consumption-based procurement for cheap components, and then would plan only the expensive components (e.g., a planner might want to plan only CPU types and casing types, resulting in six variants).
- Similar planning approaches can be used for more complex products, such as cars or elevators.

If a company lets its customers configure a product fully, then in that case it's possible to plan the components directly (e.g., using strategy planning at the assembly level [70]). This approach would result in one set of PIRs for all components (which aren't procured as consumption-based or Kanban-controlled). The generation of these PIRs could be performed manually, from a technical point of view. But to simplify this process, it's recommended to plan the characteristics directly and have the system generate the PIRs of the components.

A totally different approach, even for complex products such as cars, would be to define a set of variants that are produced in an MTS process. The advantage of this approach is that the customers can be served immediately from stock. The downside is that the customers can't fully configure the product; they need to willingly buy from stock.

This section describes potential ways to cope with products that have a practical limited number of possible permutations of characteristics and characteristic values (*low variance*). Essentially, it describes the use of variants to sell configurable materials. Variants can be used to facilitate work with configurable materials. Variants of a configurable material are, for example, defined to prefabricate frequently required configurations and place them in stock (for that reason, variants were formerly called *stockable types*). For some configurable materials, it may be difficult to determine the possible variants. To use strategies for variants effectively, a planner must have an estimate of the future consumption for each variant. If the configuration isn't changed during the sales order stage, then production can occur at the production before the sales order stage.

Variants can be planned on the finished product level using any MTO strategy, such as planning without final assembly (50) or planning with a planning material (60). These strategies were already covered previously in this chapter. The planning of variants with MTO strategies combines the advantages of MTO production (i.e., very short delivery time or cost tracking on the sales order level) with the advantages of variant configuration (i.e., one BOM and one routing for a whole product family).

Table 12.4 illustrates which stages are involved in which strategies.

Strategy/Stage	55	26	65
Similar MTO Strategy	50	20	60
1. Demand management	Yes	No	Yes
2. Procurement before sales	Yes	No	Yes
3. Sales order	Yes	Yes	Yes
4. Procurement after sales	Yes	Yes	Yes
5. GI for delivery and reduction of PIR	Yes	Yes	Yes

Table 12.4 Production with Variant Configuration

The MTO for material variants strategy (26) is similar to the MTO production strategy (20). The difference is that MTO for material variants (26) lets a planner change the configuration of the variant. See Table 12.5 for differences and commonalities between strategies 25 and 26.

Strategy/Stage	25	26
Configuration (of a variant)	Must	Can
Material used in sales order	Configurable material	Variant
Default configuration (frequently used configurations can be stored)	*One* configuration defaulted per configurable material using the defaults in characteristics	Several configurations can be stored (i.e., one configuration can be stored per variant)
Entry in SD order	Configurable material	Variant

Table 12.5 Difference between Strategies 25 and 26

As already discussed in the beginning of this chapter, the SAP standard planning strategies are generally sufficient to cater to most business processes and scenarios;

however, there are always exceptions, and therefore a need exists to create a custom requirement class and associated planning strategy. This is covered in the next section.

12.7 Create a Custom Requirement Class

It's possible to create your own planning strategies—for example, for assembly processing—because there's a need to do one of the following:

- Create assembly orders with your own order types.
- Use specific availability checking methods for the components (e.g., to display a missing parts list).
- Use specific methods for a capacity check.

In fact, the planning strategies delivered in the standard system for assembly processing provide examples of how to proceed. Planning strategies 81, 82, and 86 are similar to the planning strategy MTO production (strategy 20) in terms of production planning. That is, no real production planning is involved; the order is merely created without the leveraging procurement started by PIRs.

However, it's also possible to set up planning strategies for assembly processing that would work similar to planning without final assembly (strategy 50) or planning with a planning material (strategy 60). That is, planning strategies could be set up in which creating PIRs first to procure the components and then assemble the finished product by using assembly processing is possible.

[!]

Warning

SAP recommends the following when maintaining requirements classes:

- Never change existing requirements classes.
- If necessary, try to choose an existing requirements class with the desired properties. First, check to see if the requirements specification can be covered with existing strategies/requirements classes.
- If there is no requirements class with the desired properties, copy an existing one and change the copy.
- In this case, create a new requirements type and strategy as well. Don't change existing strategies and requirements types.

To construct your own planning strategy for assembly processing requires the following steps (for each step, use a number range starting with *Z* or *9*; see Figure 12.9):

1. Copy the relevant requirements classes into the custom requirements class.
2. Create a requirements type, and include the newly created requirements class.
3. Create a planning strategy, and include the newly created requirements type.

4. Create a strategy group, and include the newly created planning strategy.

5. Assign the strategy group to the MRP group.

6. Assign the MRP group to the **MRP Group** field in the **MRP 1** view of the material master via Transaction MM01 or Transaction MM02. Because assigning an already configured object into master data, such as a material master, is a frontend activity, this step isn't covered in detail.

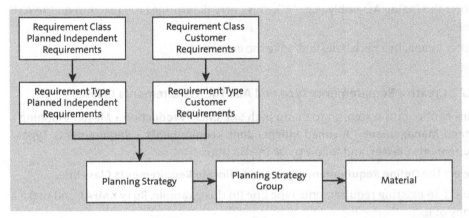

Figure 12.9 Relationships among Requirements Type, Requirements Class, and Planning Strategy

The following sections describe each of these steps in detail.

12.7.1   Copy Standard Requirements Class

In this step, go to menu path **SAP IMG · Sales and Distribution · Basic Functions · Availability Check and Transfer of Requirements · Transfer of Requirements · Define Requirements Classes**, and follow these instructions:

1. Select an existing requirements class line (e.g., **ReqC 201**), and click **Copy as**. Each requirement class contains a number of control functions.

Tips and Tricks

When choosing requirements class lines, select the requirements class:

- 200, 201, or 040 to get a planning strategy similar to MTO production (strategy 20)
- 045 to get a planning strategy similar to planning without final assembly (strategy 50)
- 060 to get a planning strategy similar to planning with a planning material (strategy 60)
- 200 to get a planning strategy similar to assembly processing with characteristics planning (strategy 89)

---

2. Change the **Reqmts Class** key, and add short text (to change the key, use a number range starting with *Z* or *9*).

3. Under **Assembly**, enter your **Assembly Type** (e.g., "2").

4. Enter the **Order Type** (e.g., "PP10"). Change this field for production and process orders; leave it blank for planned orders.

5. Select **Avail. Components** if desired.

6. Enter the **Dialog Assembly** (e.g., "3"). This entry determines the reaction on the ATP check.

7. Enter a capacity check if desired. Save the entries.

12.7.2   Create a Requirements Type and Add the Requirements Class

In this configuration step, go to menu path **SAP IMG • Production • Master Planning • Demand Management • Planned Independent Requirements • Requirements Types/ Requirements Classes**, and follow these instructions:

1. Select the **Define Requirements Types and Allocate Requirements Class** line.

2. Select an existing requirements type line (in this example, **RqTy KMFA**), and make a copy of it.

3. Change the **RqTy key**. Use a number range starting with "Z" or "9" (e.g., change "KMFA" to "ZMFA").

4. Enter short text for **Requirements Type**.

5. Under **ReqCl**, enter the new requirements class created in the previous section. This step links the requirements type to the requirements class. Save the entries.

12.7.3   Create a Planning Strategy

In the step, go to menu path **SAP IMG • Production • Master Planning • Demand Management • Planned Independent Requirements • Planning Strategy**, and follow these steps:

1. Select the line **Define Strategy**.

2. Select an existing line (e.g., **Strategy 82**), and create a copy by clicking **Copy As**.

3. Change the **Strategy** key (use a number range starting with *Z* or *9*), and add short text.

4. Link this strategy to the newly created requirements types from the previous step. Save the entries.

[+]   **Tips and Tricks**

To link newly created requirements types, one of the following is possible:

- Leave the **Reqmt Type for Indep Reqmts** section blank. In **Reqmt Type of Customer Reqmt**, enter the copy of the requirements type that links to requirements class 200, 201, or 040 to get a planning strategy similar to MTO production (strategy 20).

- In the **Reqmts type for indep. Reqmts** section, enter requirements type "VSE" (which links to requirements class 103). In the **Reqmt Type of Customer Reqmt** section, enter the copy of the requirements type that links to requirements class 045 to get a planning strategy similar to planning without final assembly (strategy 50).

- In the **Reqmts Type for Indep. Reqmts** section, enter requirements type "VSEV" (which links to requirements class 104). For the **Reqmt Type of Customer Reqmt** section, enter the copy of the requirements type that links to requirements class 060 to get a planning strategy similar to planning without planning material (strategy 60).

- In the **Reqmts Type for Indep. Reqmts** section, enter requirements type "VSE" (which links to requirements class 103). For **Reqmt Type of Customer Reqmt**, enter a copy of the requirements type that links to requirements class 200 to get a planning strategy similar to assembly processing with characteristics planning (strategy 89).

12.7.4 Create a Strategy Group and Include the Newly Created Planning Strategy

In this step, go to menu path **SAP IMG • Production • Master Planning • Demand Management • Planning Strategy**, and follow these steps:

1. Select the **Define Strategy Group** line.

2. Select an existing line (e.g., **Strtgy Grp 82**).

3. Make a copy, and change the **Strategy Group** key (use a number range starting with Z or 9).

4. Maintain short text in the **Description** field, and enter the new planning strategy in **Main Plg. Straty** to link to the newly created planning strategy. Save your settings.

12.7.5 Assign Strategy Group to a Material Requirements Planning Group

To assign the strategy group to an MRP group, follow menu path **SAP IMG • Production • Production Planning • Demand Management • Planned Independent Requirement • Planning Strategy • Assign MRP Group to Strategy Group** (see Figure 12.10).

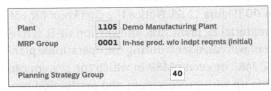

Plant	1105	Demo Manufacturing Plant
MRP Group	0001	In-hse prod. w/o indpt reqmts (initial)
Planning Strategy Group	40	

Figure 12.10 Assignment of Strategy Group to MRP Group and Plant

The planning strategy can now be used in the material masters. In the following sections, we'll cover how to create various requirements, such as PIRs and customer independent requirements, and we'll discuss these evaluations.

12.8   Business Processes in Demand Management

In the following sections, we'll show how to either manually maintain PIRs or copy the planning figures from one of the several planning tools available, such as forecasting or LTP. Customer independent requirements are covered next, followed by evaluating all requirements. Finally, we'll show how to reorganize or delete PIRs that are either too old or no longer needed for planning purposes.

12.8.1   Planned Independent Requirements

PIRs are the direct outcome of S&OP and form an integral part of demand management. During the MRP run, the system refers to PIRs with an active version to come up with procurement proposals.

> **Note**
>
> Refer to Chapter 11 for information about S&OP and how the data and information flows into demand management.

PIRs can be created independently. In fact, demand management offers a far greater number of options to create PIRs than S&OP does. To create PIRs, follow menu path **Logistics • Production • Production Planning • Demand Management • Planned Independent Requirements • Create**, or use Transaction MD61.

Figure 12.11 shows the initial view to create PIRs. For this example, enter **Material** "25" and **Plant** "1105", and also assign **Version** as "00" (**Requirements Plan**).

Define the planning period in months so that the system brings up the relevant field for data input. Notice that you can also enter default user parameters by choosing the **User Parameters** button and then entering the relevant details. These parameters then form the default settings for PIRs. However, if a requirements type is preset, this overrules the strategy settings and is therefore not recommended.

Press ⏎Enter, and the PIR view appears, in which a planner can manually enter monthly production figures for **Version 00** (Figure 12.12). Notice the checkbox for column **A**, which indicates that the PIR for material 25, plant 1105, and version GP is active. An *active* version indicates that the system will consider it during the operational planning run (MRP). This compares with LTP MRP or even pMRP in which the system can also consider an inactive version to come up with procurement and production proposals (simulated).

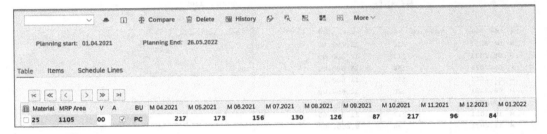

Figure 12.11 Initial Screen of Planned Independent Requirements

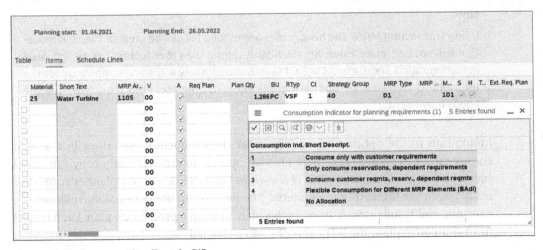

Figure 12.12 PIRs

Figure 12.13 shows the **Items** tab of the PIR for material 25, wherein the system assigns the requirement types of PIRs based on the strategy type defined in the material master.

Figure 12.13 Consumption Type in PIRs

For this example, the system assigns requirement type VSF, which is for planning strategy 40. Pressing F4 while keeping the cursor in the **CI** (consumption indicator) field reveals that **Consumption 1** to **Consume Only with Customer Requirements** applies.

Figure 12.14 shows the detailed **Schedule Lines** view of the PIRs. Because the planning period was chosen to be in months on the initial PIRs view, the same can be changed, if needed. The system also shows the planning (financial) values of the quantities. However, there are other options available to change the time granularity to daily or weekly.

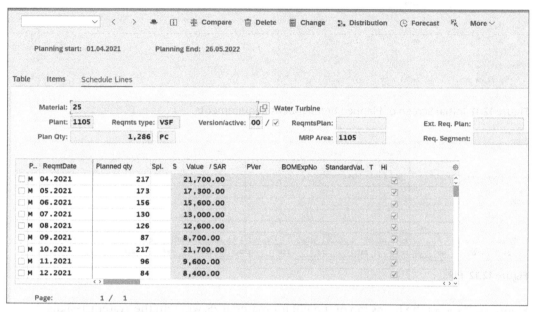

Figure 12.14 Schedule Lines in PIRs with Financial Values

> **Note**
>
> Using Transaction MD61, the history of changes for a PIR can be seen, but the PIR reduction will not be shown. However, the history during the PIR reduction can be activated in configuration Transaction OMP4. PIR reduction history will always appear under the user ABBAU-, which is an internal identification, not the user who actually posted the goods movement.

In addition to the option to manually enter the production quantities in the view shown earlier in Figure 12.12, there are also options to automatically copy PIRs from several other planning tools. This is shown in Figure 12.15, where a planner copies the results from the forecast of the material (the forecast on the material must already be executed and results saved), from a sales plan, or from a production plan. Even results from simulative planning (LTP) or pMRP can be copied.

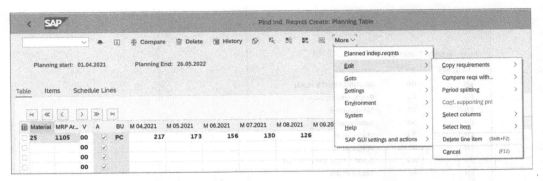

Figure 12.15 Options Available to Create PIRs

Note

LTP is covered in Chapter 16, and pMRP is discussed in Chapter 17.

Another highly intuitive feature of PIR creation is that a planner can also compare the PIR quantities with consumption, with the forecasting results, and with the sales or production plans. To do this, choose **More** • **Edit** • **Compare Reqs With**.

When the quantities are entered in the PIR or transferred for S&OP, it's important to assign a version number, which denotes different demand plans. There may be several inactive versions and even some simulation versions available in the system. The inactive or simulation versions are used in a simulation tool, such as LTP or pMRP, whereas an active version becomes part of operative planning (MRP). The recommendation for the SAP system is to have version 00 as the one and only active version, whereas all other versions must remain either inactive or used in simulations (LTP and pMRP).

Although the standard version numbers available are generally sufficient for the business processes in a company, it's possible to create new version numbers if needed or to amend the existing ones to make them more reflective of business needs. To create a new version, use menu path **SAP IMG** • **Production Planning** • **Demand Management** • **Planned Independent Requirements** • **Define Version Numbers** (see Figure 12.16), or use Transaction OMP2.

Apart from creating and changing PIRs in the SAP GUI transactions, SAP S/4HANA also offers the possibility to manage a demand plan in an SAP Fiori application, Maintain PIRs (see Figure 12.17).

When using this application, a list of materials with KPIs related to the PIRs will appear. Here, the key figures, the accuracy in the current period, the accuracy in the last week, and the accuracy in the last month, where the accuracy is the percentage of PIRs consumed/reduced by actual demand, can be seen.

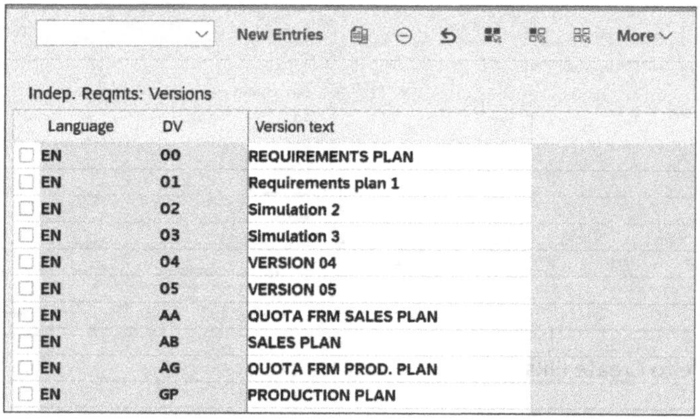

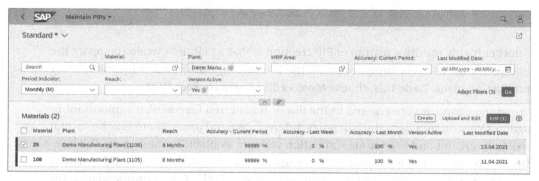

Figure 12.16 Versions for PIRs

Figure 12.17 Manage PIRs App

When selecting one or more materials, the **Edit** option allows you to change the PIRs, or the **Upload and Edit** option allows you to upload a CSV file with the PIR quantities and then change the uploaded values.

If the option to upload a file is chosen, a popup screen will appear, as shown in Figure 12.18 ❶, wherein the user can choose the file to be uploaded. This option to upload PIRs is a major innovation of this new SAP Fiori application. It wasn't present in the previous application, and there's no simple feature to upload PIRs in SAP GUI. After the file upload, or if you simply chose the **Edit** option, you'll see a new option to change the existing or the newly uploaded PIR quantities. As shown ❷, this screen will be very similar to Transaction MD62 in SAP GUI, in which there are different materials and PIR quantities in the period buckets. In the upper-right corner, there's a **Mass Maintenance** option, in which a value can be set for a given period for all the materials displayed. The **Download to Spreadsheet** option can be used to download a demand plan as a CSV file ❸. This CSV file can be used as a model for uploading PIRs, as shown earlier.

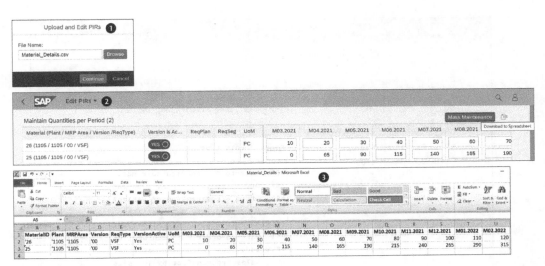

Figure 12.18 Uploading PIRs from Manage PIRs App

12.8.2 Customer Independent Requirements

When the user enters the sales order in the system, the system immediately adjusts it with the PIR as consumption. While sales orders and associated activities, such as outbound delivery and posting GI, form the basis of consumption and PIR adjustments, it's also possible to independently create customer independent requirements in demand management without reference to a sales order.

To create customer independent requirements, follow menu path **Logistics • Production • Production Planning • Demand Management • Customer Requirements • Create**, or use Transaction MD81. Figure 12.19 shows the initial view to create the independent requirement. When you drill down in the **Requirements Type** field (by pressing F4 while keeping the cursor on the field), a large number of standard requirement types specific to the customer will be available to choose from. If you've assigned a strategy group in the **MRP 3** view of the material master, the system automatically assigns a requirement class to the customer independent requirements.

> **Note**
> While the system automatically fills in the **Requirements Type** field whenever a strategy group is assigned to the material master, it can be overwritten if alternative strategies are defined n the strategy group.

Press Enter and the screen in Figure 12.20 appears. Here, enter **Material** number "25" and an **Order Quantity** of "250" for **Plnt** "1105". Save the customer independent requirements, and the system generates an internal number for the customer requirement, which in this example is 50000003.

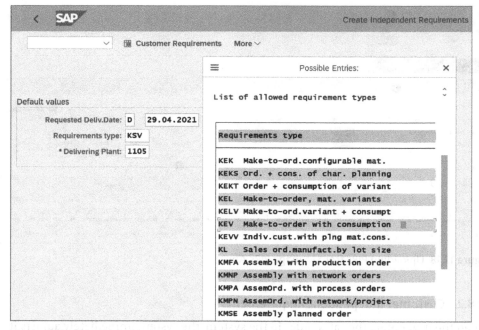

Figure 12.19 Creation of Independent Requirements

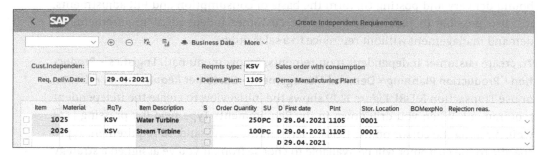

Figure 12.20 Independent Requirements with Requirement Type KSV

Next, run the MRP to see how the system accounts for the customer requirements in the planning run.

12.8.3   Planning and Stock/Requirements List for Independent Requirements

To plan for the independent requirement, run the MRP on material 25 and plant 1105 using Transaction MD01N.

To evaluate the stock/requirements list, including independent requirements after the MRP run, use the menu path **Logistics · Production · Production Planning · Demand**

Management • Environment • Stock/Requirements List, or use Transaction MD04. As shown in Figure 12.21, the customer requirement is shown as **CusReq** in the **MRP Element** column.

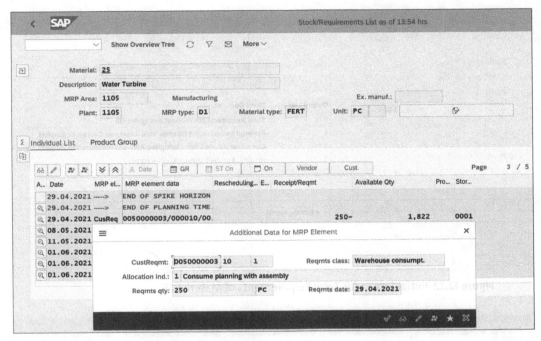

Figure 12.21 Results of MRP with Customer Requirements

12.8.4 Total Independent Requirements: Evaluation

At any given time, a planner can evaluate the total PIRs of a material and its consumption. The system displays the **Planned Qty.** as available in the system, whereas the **Total Assignment** column shows the consumption figures. Use menu path **Logistics • Production • Production Planning • Demand Management • Evaluations • Display Total Reqmts**, or use Transaction MD73. Figure 12.22 shown the initial view. Here, enter **Material** "25", enter **Plant** "1105", and select the **Output List 1** option from the dropdown list.

Press Enter, and the **Display Ind Requirements with Assigned Cust. Requirements** view shown in Figure 12.23 appears. Here, the monthly planned quantity previously entered is visible in the upper half of the view, along with the customer requirement.

When a planner has maintained only the dynamic consumption, then this is shown in the **Total Assgmnt** column. If the entire process is finished—that is, the sales order is delivered—the system shows the quantity in the **Withdrawal Qty** column.

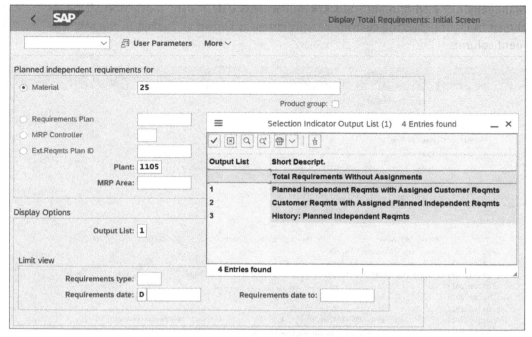

Figure 12.22 Initial Screen for Total Requirements of Material 25

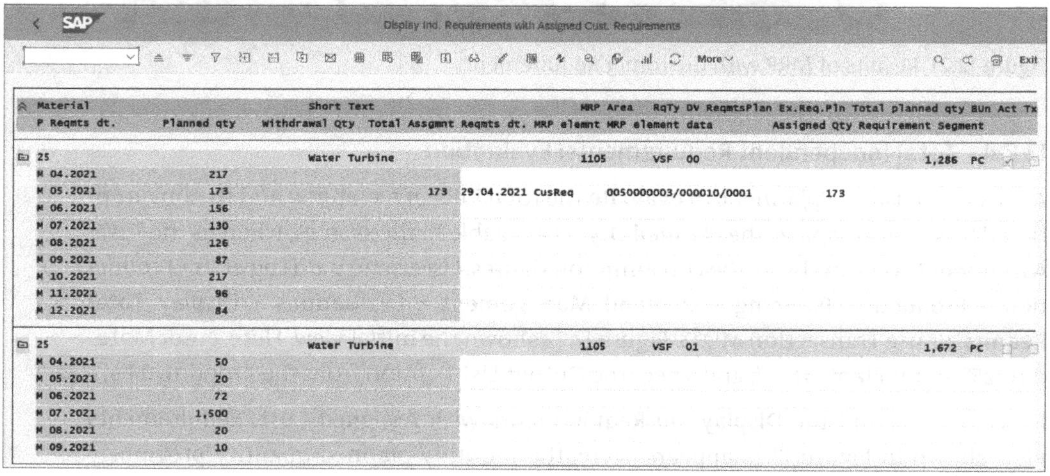

Figure 12.23 Total PIR and Requirements for Material 25

12.8.5   Total Independent Requirements: Reorganization

Although the PIRs are automatically reduced, a planner must regularly and periodically evaluate the PIRs in the system to see if the same needs to be eliminated (or adjusted).

This helps ensure that old and nonrelevant planning data no longer becomes part of the planning process during the MRP run.

To evaluate the PIR, use menu path **Logistics · Production · Production Planning · Demand Management · Environment · Independent Requirements: Reorganization · Adjust Requirements**, or use Transaction MD74. In the initial view, maintain the initial parameters so that when the system is executed, it only brings up the relevant results for consideration and action. Notice that there's flexibility to evaluate the results of the organization in **Test Mode (No Database Changes)** (see Figure 12.24). This lets you evaluate the results in simulative mode before actual reorganization.

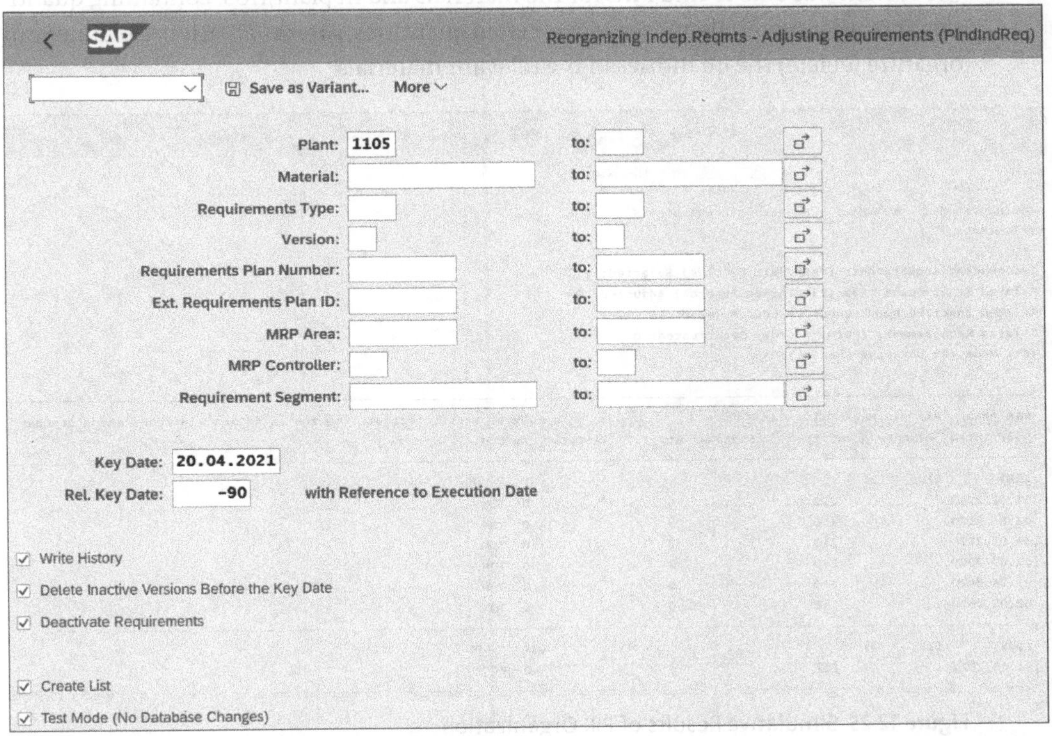

Figure 12.24 Initial Screen for Reorganizing PIRs

The **Key Date** field refers to the date *until which* the system should bring up the PIR data for reorganization. For this example, it's **20.04.2021** (April 20, 2021), so here the system should consider all of the PIRs *until* the month of April in 2021. It's important to highlight that such PIR reorganization is ensured for past/old PIRs only, ones the company no longer wants to plan or account for in demand management. The **Rel. Key Date** field specifies the relative key date, with reference to today, for which the demands will be processed. For example, if -60 days is entered, then the system selects and processes all demands that lie 60 days in the past and earlier.

Tips and Tricks

To define the plant-level PIR reorganization, use Transaction OMP8, wherein the number of days is defined. The system subtracts these days from today's date to come up with the reorganization date. The system reorganizes all PIR data older than the reorganization date.

After maintaining the initial parameters, choose **Execute** to open the view shown in Figure 12.25. This view brings up the data for the six months, until April 2021, in which the system was able to find PIRs for the materials and in plant 1105, containing quantities and other materials and their associated quantities. After evaluation, a planner can organize (delete) the quantities of the relevant materials.

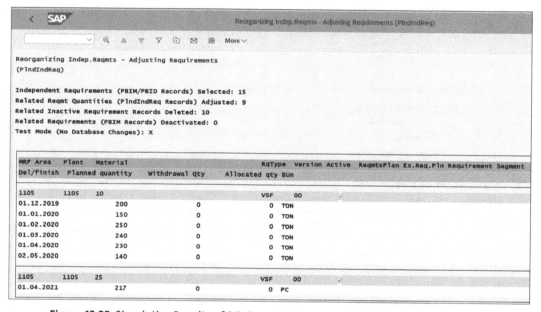

Figure 12.25 Simulative Results of PIR Organization

12.8.6   Planned Independent Requirements: Reduction

PIRs are reduced during GI. Unlike consumption, the PIRs are actually reduced and not just consumed. During MTS production using strategy 10, the oldest PIR is reduced first. However, the reduction can also affect PIRs in the future if relevant strategies are used with consumption, such as reduction in consumption strategies 40, 50, 60, and so on.

Here, reduction simply takes place according to the current consumption situation when posting the GI. For this strategy to work, the configuration data needs to be set accordingly. The configuration is performed using Transaction OMJJ. For nonconsumption strategy 10, this setting is available in the requirements class. This transaction is in the domain of materials management (MM), wherein relevant settings per movement type are made. For nonconsumption strategy 10, these settings are available in the requirements class.

After executing Transaction OMJJ, provide the movement type—for example, "601" (GI against delivery)—in the **Updating Control** area, as shown in Figure 12.26. Select the **Ind. Rqmts Reduction** checkbox to enable the system to reduce the PIRs at the time of GI (e.g., movement type 601) against a sales order.

During assembly planning, the PIR is reduced when goods are withdrawn for the production order.

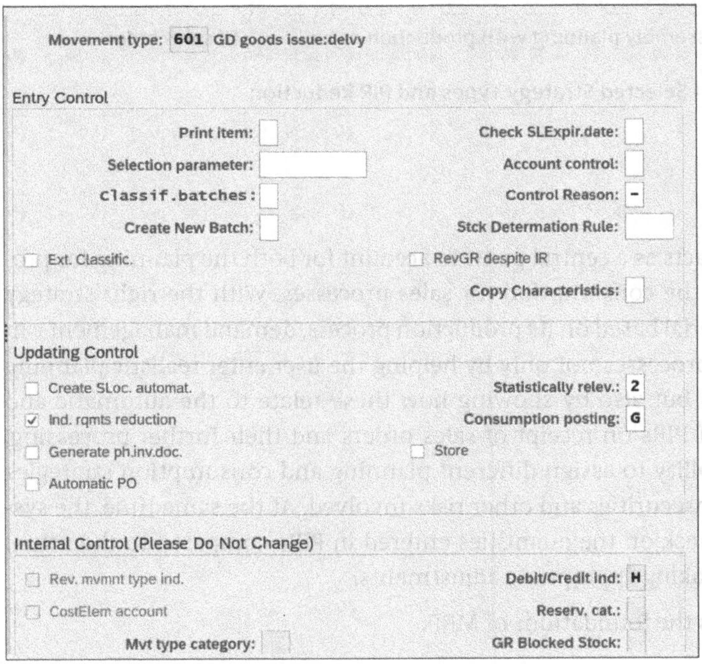

Figure 12.26 Configuration Settings of PIR Reduction

Table 12.6 provides an overview of common (selected) planning strategy types for which the system reduces the PIRs, based on specific transactions, such as GI against a sales order or production order.

Planning Strategy	Planning Strategy Description	PIR Reduction
10	MTS production	GI (sales order, MTS)
20	MTO production	GI sales order
30	Production by lot size	GI (sales order, MTS)
40	Planning with final assembly	GI sales order
50	Planning without final assembly (MTO)	GI sales order
52	Planning without final assembly (MTS)	GI production order
60	Planning with planning material (MTO)	GI sales order
63	Planning with planning material (MTS)	GI production order
70	Subassembly planning	GI production order
82	Assembly planning with production order	GI sales order

Table 12.6 Relationship of Selected Strategy Types and PIR Reduction

12.9   Summary

Demand management acts as a central point to account for both the planning for production processes and the consumption for sales processes. With the right strategy type used for each material based on its production process, demand management can optimize the business processes not only by helping the user enter realistic planning quantities such as PIRs but also by showing how these relate to the automatic and dynamic adjustment of PIRs on receipt of sales orders and their further processing, including GI. The flexibility to assign different planning and consumption strategies broadly mitigates the insecurities and other risks involved. At the same time, the system keeps a realistic check on the quantities entered in PIRs compared to the actual demand situation by making appropriate adjustments.

The next chapter covers the foundations of MRP.

Chapter 13
Foundations of Material Requirements Planning

Material requirements planning is an integral part of production planning and materials management. This chapter will build the foundations required to use this tool for optimizing a company's logistics and supply chain planning processes.

Material requirements planning (MRP) is a highly versatile and intuitive planning tool that generates procurement proposals to fulfill in-house production and external procurement demands in order to help production and procurement planners optimize their business processes. Furthermore, it generates these procurement proposals for all levels of production-based materials and also takes lead times, scrap quantities, external procurements, special procurements, planning cycles, planning calendars, and lot sizes into account. MRP isn't limited to quantity calculations; it includes scrap and stock considerations and also provides in-depth scheduling solutions and capacity requirements.

To use the results of MRP effectively, a planner needs to provide complete, correct, and comprehensive master data as often as possible. To facilitate this initiative, the system also offers several helpful tools: planned delivery time calculation for external procurement, statistical analyses for in-house production times or external procurement times, forecasting tools, calculation of safety stock, and reorder point planning. With the passage of time and with more experience and reliable data, a planner can continue to update the planning data (the MRP data in four different MRP views of a material) and continue the refining and optimization process.

This chapter begins with a process overview of MRP, including the important role of MRP in all of supply chain planning. It covers both types of MRP—that is, MRP for deterministic replenishment procedures and for stochastic replenishment procedures—and their variants.

We'll cover important influencing factors involved in ensuring calculation of reliable planning results, such as MRP types, lot sizes, scrap, and safety stocks. We'll also discuss scheduling, procurement proposals as well as rounding the lot sizes. Wherever applicable, we also cover the necessary configuration to get MRP up and running in your system.

[»]

> **Note**
>
> Although this chapter primarily helps to build the foundations, concepts, and understanding of MRP, see Chapter 16 on long-term planning (LTP) to see how to put MRP to actual use via a real-life example. Chapter 14 covers running MRP Live and its associated topics.

13.1 Process Overview

During an SAP system implementation project, or even later on when a company wants to start taking advantage of planning tools such as MRP, be sure to follow a step-by-step approach in identifying materials to plan with MRP. Just about any kind of material can be planned with MRP. Broadly, as a planner, you should consider the following factors and take the following steps:

1. To begin, prepare a comprehensive list of all materials (e.g., in a Microsoft Excel file). This Excel file may be a template that the SAP system consultant will make available. Materials can be finished goods, components, assemblies, raw materials, packing materials, consumables, or maintenance spares. It's also possible to plan materials with special procurement types, such as subcontracting materials, phantom assemblies, pipeline materials, procurement from another plant, production in another plant, stock transport orders (interplant transfer), and so on.

2. Segregate the materials to plan from those that aren't worth the time, effort, or cost involved in planning, and then eliminate the latter from the Excel file.

3. For materials to including in planning, segregate them further by classifying them as A, B, or C types). Type A materials are high-value ones and generally include finished goods, semifinished/assemblies, raw materials, packaging materials, and so on. Types B and C are medium- to low-value materials, such as consumables, routine maintenance spares, and so on.

Using deterministic replenishment procedures for all A-type materials, individually evaluate each and every important factor involved in MRP to see how these fit in planning to give the desired results. For example, as a planner, ask the following questions:

- What should the safety stock of this material be?
- How many days in the planning window are needed so that the system doesn't make any automatic changes to the production (or procurement) plan?

- When there is a requirement for a material, how much should the system plan (exact quantity, minimum quantity, maximum quantity, etc.)?
- How should the incoming sales orders consume the planning figures?
- Is this material make-to-stock (MTS) or make-to-order (MTO)?
- Is there a need to produce this material for a specific project or customer (MTO)?
- Is this assembly produced in-house or at another plant of the company?
- How much scrap (as a percentage) does the production of a material generate for a product or subassembly, so it can be incorporated in planning?
- Does it make sense to first forecast material requirements by using a forecasting tool and then adjust forecast values before proceeding with material planning?

A planner needs to ask these (and many more) questions for each material and correspondingly enter or update the information in the Excel file.

For raw materials or packaging materials, which are externally procured, get answers to questions such as the following:

- What is the planned delivery time of this material?
- What is the goods receipt (GR) processing time?
- How much underdelivery and overdelivery of a material is allowed?
- Is there a scheduling agreement or a contract (quantity or value) with a vendor for a material?
- Is there a quota arrangement in place, in case of multiple vendors for the same material?

We suggest involving procurement personnel (materials management [MM]) to help with answering these (and many more) questions because they have firsthand knowledge and experience regarding the procurement.

For B- and C-type materials, consider using consumption-based planning or stochastic replenishment procedures. For consumption-based planning, choose whether to use reorder-based planning, which can manually or automatically suggest the reorder point of each material based on historical consumption. For manual reorder point planning, enter the reorder point quantity, which may be based on past experience or on consumption figures available in another planning program (not the SAP system). Further, also take advantage of the forecasting tool to help with planning future consumption. Forecasting also uses historical consumption data available in the system.

Because planning is a continuously evolving and ongoing process, it's recommended to continue fine-tuning the planning parameters of materials to help the system come up with planning results that can be used in the production and procurement processes almost immediately (and without need for significant adjustments). For example, say that when a planner first entered the planned delivery time of a material, it was five days, but as the system built up a significant database of this information (planned delivery time) in the past year, the average delivery time turned out to be seven days. This information must be updated in the **MRP** view of the material master so that future planning results of MRP are more reflective of this reality. The system also makes available a tool (Transaction WPDTC) to provide a comparison between the information maintained in the material master and the actual planned delivery time that the system recorded for each delivery. Several such analysis reports and tools are available in the SAP system.

Whether it's MRP or consumption-based planning—that is, deterministic or stochastic replenishment procedures, respectively—a large number of factors are defined in the four different **MRP** views of the material master to influence the planning results of MRP. In fact, the system refers to this detailed information in the **MRP** views to come up with procurement proposals. Some of these factors may be how the system performs the net requirements calculations, what percentage of safety stock to consider in planning, the lot-sizing procedures to use, if forecasting is a necessary prerequisite to planning, and how to manage special procurement types. In the following sections, we cover the important factors and parameters needed to set up and achieve the desired planning results from MRP, which can be subsequently used in the production and procurement activities.

Figure 13.1 provides an overview of the role of MRP in the planning and production areas of the SAP system.

The planning process starts with requirements coming from sales and distribution (SD), from the next-generation cloud-based SAP HANA tool known as SAP Integrated Business Planning for Supply Chain (SAP IBP), and from the sales and operations planning (S&OP) planning process as a forecast, eventually becoming a part of demand management. Companies can also use master production scheduling (MPS) for planning finished products, important semifinished products, or products that will use bottleneck production lines. After the MPS planning run, the capacity leveling functionality in capacity requirements planning (CRP) can be used to ensure that the plan proposed by MPS will not exceed the critical resources capacity. An alternative to MPS is to use the production planning and detailed scheduling (PP-DS) tool, now embedded into the SAP S/4HANA digital core. PP-DS supports advanced planning features that are not available in MPS or MRP, such as planning with finite capacity (i.e., considering capacity restrictions on the work centers), planning considering the batch shelf life, planning with complex heuristics, or even using the PP-DS optimizer tool to make a feasible plan based on cost considerations.

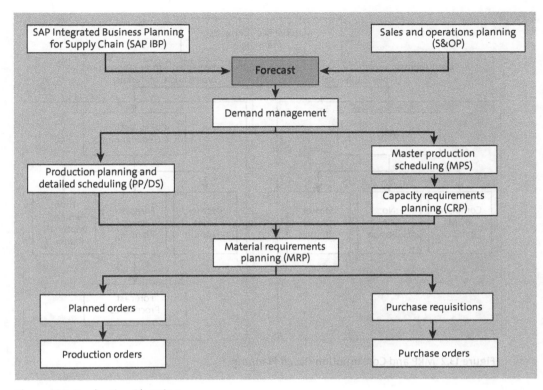

Figure 13.1 Production Planning

The system also takes customer requirements into account and reflects all the demand from the demand management as *planned independent requirements* (PIRs). The PIR with an active version consists of quantities of the material for which a planner wants to run MRP. The system runs MRP based on the details given in the demand program, and the outcome of the MRP run is the creation of procurement proposals. These procurement proposals can be planned orders (order proposals), purchase requisitions for external procurement, or delivery schedules for scheduling agreements with vendors. The procurement proposals distinctively divide up into two separate yet interlinked areas: procurement for externally procured materials and production for in-house produced materials.

Figure 13.2 shows how to categorize materials for planning purposes into two major subareas: deterministic and stochastic replenishment procedures.

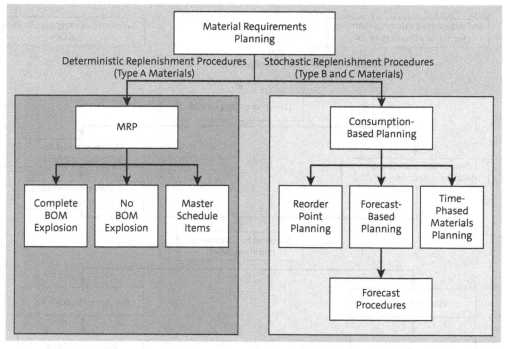

Figure 13.2 MRP and Consumption-Based Planning

[+] **Tips and Tricks**

Transactions MC40 and MC41 are quite helpful for letting a material planner segregate materials into A, B, or C types based on their usage or consumption values (past) or even requirement values (future). For example, use ABC analysis to classify those customers that generate 75% of sales volume as A customers, the next 15% as B customers, and the rest as C customers. Similarly, classify materials by aggregating their consumption values (or sales volume) of materials until they reach 80% (or whatever boundaries are defined) of the total value and then designate all these materials as A items.

These ABC analyses can then be incorporated into the **ABC Indicator** field in the **MRP1** view of the material master. Note the A, B, or C indicators that can be made part of their respective material masters in Figure 13.3.

Figure 13.3 accessed using Transaction MC41 ❶ shows the ABC analysis based on requirements values. The other screen ❷ shows an ABC analysis based on consumption values (Transaction MC40).

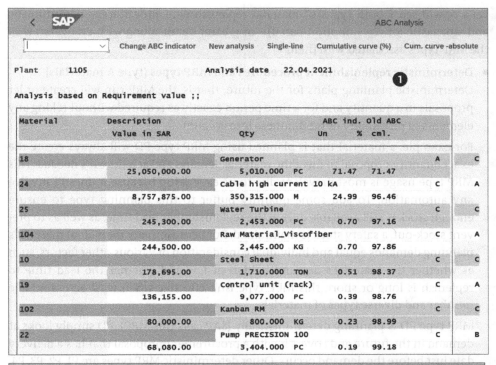

SAP — ABC Analysis

Change ABC indicator | New analysis | Single-line | Cumulative curve (%) | Cum. curve -absolute

Plant 1105   Analysis date 22.04.2021

Analysis based on Requirement value ;;

Material	Description / Value in SAR	Qty	Un	%	cml.	ABC ind.	Old ABC
18	Generator					A	C
	25,050,000.00	5,010.000	PC	71.47	71.47		
24	Cable high current 10 kA					C	A
	8,757,875.00	350,315.000	M	24.99	96.46		
25	Water Turbine					C	C
	245,300.00	2,453.000	PC	0.70	97.16		
104	Raw Material_Viscofiber					C	A
	244,500.00	2,445.000	KG	0.70	97.86		
10	Steel Sheet					C	C
	178,695.00	1,710.000	TON	0.51	98.37		
19	Control unit (rack)					C	A
	136,155.00	9,077.000	PC	0.39	98.76		
102	Kanban RM					C	C
	80,000.00	800.000	KG	0.23	98.99		
22	Pump PRECISION 100					C	B
	68,080.00	3,404.000	PC	0.19	99.18		

SAP — ABC Analysis

Change ABC indicator | New analysis | Single-line | Cumulative curve (%) | Cum. curve -absolute

Plant 1105   Analysis date 22.04.2021

Analysis based on Consumption/usage value ;;

Material	Description / Value in SAR	Qty	Un	%	cml.	ABC ind.	Old ABC
104	Raw Material_Viscofiber					A	
	5,000.00	50.000	KG	26.88	26.88		
24	Cable high current 10 kA					A	
	3,750.00	150.000	M	20.16	47.04		
19	Control unit (rack)					A	
	2,850.00	190.000	PC	15.32	62.37		
17	Running gear					B	
	2,100.00	175.000	PC	11.29	73.66		
22	Pump PRECISION 100					B	
	2,000.00	100.000	PC	10.75	84.41		
16	Turbine casing					C	
	1,600.00	160.000	PC	8.60	93.01		
20	Lubrication unit					C	
	800.00	100.000	PC	4.30	97.31		

Figure 13.3 ABC Analysis Using Transactions MC40 and MC41

Let's now discuss both types of material replenishment procedures—deterministic and stochastic (or consumption-based)—in greater detail, along with an overview of the MRP types associated with them.

- **Deterministic replenishment procedures and MRP types (type A materials)**
  Deterministic planning plans for the future; that is, the MRP run will create order proposals in a quantity and for a time period exactly as required without taking any elements of probability or randomness into account.

  For example, a material that is planned using MRP type PD will always create the exact quantity proposal to meet the material demand and at a time it's needed. This MRP type usage is most prevalent due to its easy setup because it doesn't involve any automation. To add some quantity buffer to this planning type to ensure enough stock is still available during the replenishment lead time, as well as to prevent stock-out, a safety stock is maintained. But because every individual material's planning demands equal and individual consideration of various other factors, such as whether the material's demand is high or low and whether the lead time to replenish is long or short, this MRP type isn't effective when used across a large number and diverse types of materials.

  MRP type PD is planning deterministically (SAP calls this MRP). PD simply looks at demand in the future and covers it with a procurement proposal that has a delivery date just before the demand occurs. Other deterministic MRP types are P1, P2, P3, P4, and D1. They require a planning time fence to be set, and they help a planner by keeping planned orders that are generated by the MRP run out of that period of time. These MRP types can also protect a short-term production program and are fixed automatically when they fall within the frozen zone. MRP type M0 is used to plan important finished (or unfinished) products separately from the rest. It has its own master production scheduling (MPS) planning run and is meant to cut down on processing time before the plan is released to the bill of materials (BOM) structure. As in the P series, the M1, M2, M3, and M4 types allow for the protection of a planning time fence and automatic fixing of procurement proposals. MRP type D1 (demand-driven replenishment [DDR]) works the same as MRP type M1 with the difference that stocks are replenished to the maximum level.

- **Consumption-based replenishment procedures and MRP types (type B and type C materials)**
  These procedures are also called *stochastic* and have some degree of randomness and an element of probability. The future planning of their demand and correspondingly the supply availability of these materials is based on past consumption patterns. Hence, there is a probability and randomness to this process that can be buffered with safety stocks, capacity, or time.

  In stochastic planning procedures, the system tries to cover future requirements by making stock levels available that fulfill these future requirements with the least amount of inventory investment. That is why consumption-based replenishment policies underlie an estimating process. Here, the safety stock settings for these procedures play an equally important role. Because future stockholdings are predicted to the best of the procedure's capabilities and because there is some level of randomness and variability in demand, a buffer in the form of safety stock in most cases is indispensable to avoid stock-outs.

The need for a buffer level depends on the length of the replenishment lead time, the variability of that lead time, the variability in demand, and a desired, stipulated service level that communicates the planner's percentage of acceptable stock-outs to the system. Using these parameters, the system—or for manual procedures, the planner—can calculate a safety buffer that should deliver the expected results in terms of availability and stockholding. The first groupings of consumption-based replenishment procedures are the reorder point types. Reorder level planning is a consumption-based method because it requires inventory to be available at all times and doesn't wait until there is demand before replenishment is triggered. The next grouping is forecast-based planning procedures, such as MRP type VV. Finally, the third grouping is time-phased planning procedures, such as MRP types R1 and R2.

Let's now discuss the deterministic replenishment procedures and the associated MRP types available in the SAP system in the following section. The section after that will then cover stochastic replenishment procedures and their associated MRP types.

13.2   Deterministic Replenishment Procedures

When a planner decides to plan a material using MRP, one of the first parameters to define in the material master is the MRP type. An MRP type is a control function used to control several subsequent steps. For example, if the MRP type ND, for no planning, is assigned to a material, then the system won't plan the material at all. If MRP types that start with P* (e.g., PD, P1, P2, etc.) are used, they control how the system takes the net requirements calculations into account and how it firms the procurement proposals for MRP during the MRP runs. The net requirements calculation takes the plant stock and all receipts into account and then subtracts the requirement quantities. If the net requirements calculation comes up with a shortage or deficit quantities, the system creates procurement proposals during the MRP run.

In the net requirements calculation, the system determines the available stock based on the following formula:

Plant stock – Safety stock + Open order quantity (purchase orders, production orders, fixed procurement proposals) – Requirement quantity (PIRs, customer requirements, material reservations, forecast requirements for unplanned additional requirements) = Available stock

If it evaluates that there is no shortage, then the system doesn't create procurement proposals.

> **Note**
>
> We'll cover only the standard materials replenishment procedures and their associated MRP types, to develop the necessary foundations and understanding required to use them first before opting for customization.

13.2.1   MRP Type PD

MRP type PD is planning deterministically. In its initial configuration, PD may also include a forecast of unplanned consumption (see the **Forecast Ind.** and **Cons. Ind. Forecast** fields). When a forecast model is maintained in the **Forecasting** screen, the PD will forecast unplanned consumption (the unplanned consumption can be seen in the consumption history) and display additional requirements (**Unpld. Cons.**) in the stock requirements list (Transaction MD04).

PD simply looks at demand in the future and covers it with a procurement proposal that has a delivery date just before the demand occurs, as shown in Figure 13.4.

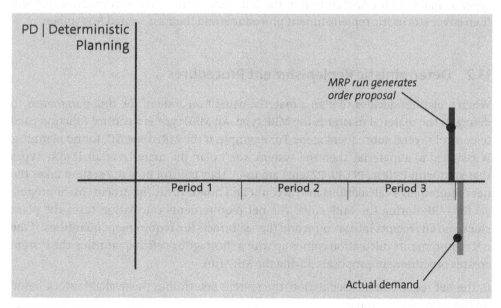

Figure 13.4 MRP Type: PD

Because PD is deterministic, it waits for demand to arrange supply. If there is demand, and the MRP run is executed, a supply proposal is generated to cover that demand. This MRP type is well suited for expensive purchased parts that are costly to store, for which consumption is highly variable and unpredictable, and for which the lead time to procure is short.

This type of planning is carried out for the quantities planned in PIRs or quantities planned in incoming sales orders (MTO or MTS), dependent requirements, and stock transfer requirements—that is, any requirement that is MRP-relevant. In this type of net requirements calculation and its planning, the following apply:

- The system doesn't consider nor ask for any forecast information or historical consumption values. Material planning is ensured only on the basis of absolute requirements or demands in hand.

- The system determines the available stock in the planning run, which is required to meet the demands, with the following logic:

  Plant stock + Scheduled receipts from production and purchase – All of the demands (e.g., from sales orders, material reservations, and PIRs)

If the available stock is unable to fulfill the demand, then depending on the settings of the planning run, it creates planned orders for in-house production, as well as purchase requisitions, delivery schedules/scheduling lines, or purchase requisitions for external procurement.

As mentioned earlier, other deterministic MRP types are P1, P2, P3, and P4, which require a planning time fence to be set and help a planner by keeping planned orders that are generated by the MRP run out of that period of time. The differences between these four MRP types lie in firming or not firming of the procurement proposals and what requirements in which period are considered.

Similarly, MRP type M0 is used to plan important finished (or unfinished) products separately from the rest. As in the P series, the M1, M2, M3, and M4 types allow for the protection of a planning time fence and automatic fixing of procurement proposals.

Let's consider an example of firming type P1 to explain how firming works. In firming type P1, the system automatically firms the existing procurement proposals so long as these are within the defined planning time fence. It also creates new order proposals when it evaluates that there is going to be a shortage of material within the planning time fence. However, the system pushes the new procurement proposals outside the planning time fence to ensure that the production plan isn't disturbed. When the newly created procurement proposals begin to fall within the planning time fence, the system automatically firms them and makes them a part of the production plan.

To ensure greater stability in the production and procurement plans, a planner can take advantage of firming logic and the planning time fence. The *firming logic* defines how the system should handle the existing or new procurement proposals by automatically firming the planned orders, allowing an option for manual firming, or allowing neither of those. The *planning time fence* allows for the definition of a range within which MRP doesn't create, change, move, or delete any procurement proposals. This can be a great reliability factor for the production department if a planning time fence such as the following is used: for the next five days starting from today, the production plan will not be changed, not even if there are new sales orders.

The planning time fence can be maintained in the **MRP 1** view of the material master or in configuration. The planning time fence is the number of workdays (not calendar days) within which a planner can protect the master plan. The system firms the procurement proposals to protect them from any changes. However, a planner still has the flexibility to make any last-minute manual changes, if needed. Firming of the procurement proposals (planned orders, purchase requisitions, delivery schedules) falling within the planning time fence prevents the proposals from being adapted in the next planning run. In other words, in the planning time fence, the system doesn't create or delete any procurement proposals, nor does it change the existing proposals.

The system calculates the planning time fence from the current date and adds up the number of working days incorporated as the planning time fence in the material master (**MRP 1** view). The planning time fence can also be defined in the configuration settings of the MRP group because it's easier to just assign the MRP group to the material master. When the system moves forward in the time scale, it's logical that any procurement proposal that was previously outside this planning time fence will start to move into the planning time fence. When that happens, the proposal is automatically firmed for protection from changes. That means the horizon keeps rolling with time.

There are two firming options for procurement proposals: automatic firming and manual firming.

There are 10 MRP types with firming available in the system (M0, M1, M2, M3, M4, P1, P2, P3, P4, and D1), and these differ with regard to the automatic firming of elements within the planning time fence and also with regard to the creation of new elements.

It's important to note that firming type M0 behaves just like MRP type PD; that is, the planning time fence is inactive for this MPS time.

Note

Firming type M refers to MPS, whereas firming type P refers to MRP.

Technically, MPS and MRP in SAP S/4HANA are almost the same thing, and the same transaction (MD01N) can be used. However, because neither MPS nor MRP takes capacity restrictions into account, it's recommended to split the planning run between MPS and MRP and to run capacity leveling for the products planned with MPS *before* running MRP.

Table 13.1 shows the similarities of firming types for both MRP (firming type P) and MPS (firming type M).

Firming Types	0	1	2	3	4
MRP Types	PD MO	P1 M1 D1	P2 M2	P3 M3	P4 M4
Firming methods of existing procurement proposals (within the planning time fence)					
No firming of procurement proposals within the planning time fence.	✓				
Automatic firming of procurement proposals within the planning time fence.		✓	✓		
Manual firming of procurement proposals within the planning time fence (no automatic firming of procurement proposals).				✓	
Firming methods of new order proposals (within the planning time fence)					
Automatic creation of new procurement proposals to cover the shortages within the planning time fence. However, the system pushes the dates of these new procurement proposals outside the planning time fence.		✓		✓	
No new procurement proposals created to cover the material shortages within the planning time fence.			✓		✓

Table 13.1 Firming Types in Planning

A planner can also set how the system should account for roll-forward. A *roll-forward* defines the number of workdays starting from today (both forward and backward) in which the system can proceed to delete the firmed planned orders if they aren't converted to either production orders or purchase requisitions. For example, a planner may want to delete all of the firmed planned orders older than five days during the next MRP run. To do this, select an MRP type with firming (e.g., **P1**) and select the **Delete Firm Planned Orders** option from the **Roll Forward** field. Next, define "–5" in the **Roll Forward** field in the MRP group parameters for a specific plant (Transaction OPPR). The negative value (number of days from today) is for deletion of the past and firmed planned order, and a positive value is to manage deletion of the firmed planned orders in the future. In the same MRP group settings (Transaction OPPR), assign the number of workdays (from today) that the system can use to firm the planned orders for the relevant firming type.

Figure 13.5 shows the **MRP 1** view of the material master and shows various **MRP Types** in the dropdown menu, as well as the **Planning Time Fence** field.

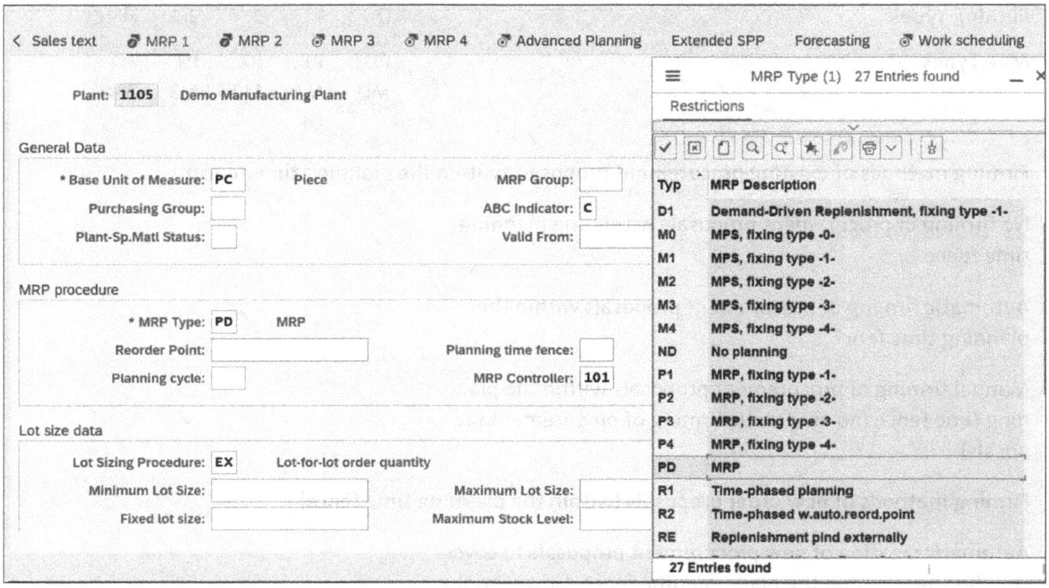

Figure 13.5 Planning Time Fence

13.2.2   MRP Type VB

VB is the simplest and most manual of the reorder point MRP types. When using MRP type VB, a planner has to calculate and set the reorder point manually and maintain it in the **Reorder Point** field in the material master. The reorder point may be based on historical consumption values or even a best guess. Although not required, it's recommended to maintain safety stock when using this MRP type.

Further, it's suggested to look at the past consumption of the material in question and derive an estimated, future daily consumption quantity from that amount. Then, simply multiply this quantity by the number of working days (days in which a company consumes the material) within the total replenishment lead time (TRLT). That lead time should be maintained in the **MRP 2** screen of the material master record (the **Planned Delivery Time** + **GR Proc.Time** + **Purchasing Time** fields). The product of future daily consumption with the lead time gives an inventory point that, if reached, will enable the system to reorder so that a company doesn't run out of stock before the next receipt comes in. Depending on the variability in the estimated consumption or lead time, it may be necessary to raise the reorder point by a safety stock when the record point shifts below the safety stock (see Figure 13.6).

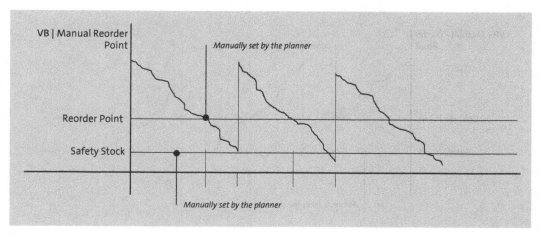

Figure 13.6 Reorder Point Planning

Tips and Tricks

There are many ways to calculate and guess future daily consumption. Transaction MC.9, for example, gives that history. However, when looking at the table with key figures and characteristics, only monthly totals are available, and even though it's possible to divide the monthly total by the number of working days in that month, there is some sense of doubt about consistent consumption day by day. But the consumption graphic is displayed in the logistics information system (LIS), where a number of helpful tools can be applied to get all the information you need. This way, it's possible to see if there's consistency in the consumption over time and figure out how much inventory is needed to get through the lead time without any stock-outs. Then add a safety stock and maintain it in the material master's **MRP 2** view. Subsequently, maintain **MRP Type VB** and also **Reorder Point** in the **MRP 1** view of the material master. The reorder point quantity is the estimated consumption within the TRLT plus the safety stock quantity.

We mentioned that though it's not required to maintain a safety stock at all in **MRP 2**, it's recommended to have that kind of information readily available (see Figure 13.7). The system creates an exception message 96 (see Chapter 14, Section 14.2.3, on exception messages) every time the stock falls into that range, which gives an indication over time of whether the reorder point is too low or there's an opportunity to lower it (and with it, the average stockholding of this material). The more often exception message 96 appears, the more likely the reorder point is too low. But if exception message 96 appears only rarely, it's time to look into lowering that reorder point.

We'll show an example of reorder point planning in Chapter 14, Section 14.4.

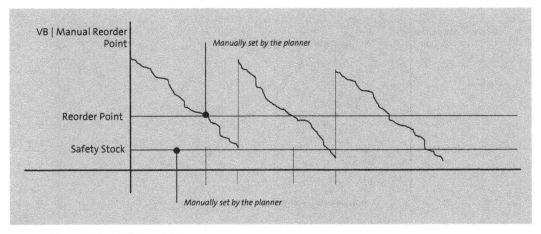

Figure 13.7 MRP Type VB

The MRP procedure (see Figure 13.8) that the system uses in the MRP type can be configured.

MRP Type:	VB	Manual reorder point planning

MRP Procedure: B Reorder Point Planning

Control Parameters

Firming type:

Roll forward: Do not delete firm planned orders

Plan regularly:

Include ext. reqmts: Ignored

Additional External Requirements in Reorder Point Planning

Subcontracting: Order reservation: PM/network reserv.:

ReleaseOrd.StkTrans.: Purch. req. release: Sched.armt.DelySch.:

Use of Forecast for Material Requirements Planning

Forecast ind.: * Optional forecast

Cons. Ind. Forecast: G Total Consumption

Material Doc.:

MRP Ind. Forecast: Not to be included in planning

Reduce forecast:

Figure 13.8 Reorder Point Planning

Place your cursor on the **MRP Procedure** field, then click on the dropdown option or press F4. Figure 13.8 shows the configuration screen of manual reorder point planning (**MRP Type VB**). Notice that a planner can take advantage of the system's functionality to automatically calculate safety stock and reorder points. For configuration of the MRP type, refer to Section 13.4.

> **Tips and Tricks**
>
> Use the fixed lot-sizing procedure for reorder point based planning so that the system procures the fixed lot size instead of only creating a proposal for the deficit quantity.

13.2.3 MRP Type VM

To achieve more automation and greater accuracy in the reorder point procedure, MRP type VM can be used. MRP type VM eliminates guesswork and lets the system do the figuring. But the system can only figure and calculate reliable and authentic values if the underlying basic data and specifically the historic consumption are accurate. This procedure requires timely and accurate GR/GI postings because it's using that data to figure mean absolute deviation (MAD) and therefore consistency in consumption, lead time deviation, and various settings (e.g., planned delivery time and service level) to come up with a reorder point. If any of this information isn't maintained correctly, VM will produce reorder points that either cause stock-outs or drive the inventory to potentially very high levels. In any case, VM uses the material master's **Forecasting** screen to automatically calculate the reorder point and a safety stock quantity via the following procedure:

1. On the **Forecasting** screen, use its settings and historical consumption to calculate a past MAD. The system does so by comparing an ex post forecast to the actual past consumption.

2. Use the service level being maintained in the **MRP 2** view of the material master and a standard formula to calculate a safety stock quantity.

3. Calculate the future anticipated daily consumption by running a forecast in the material master record.

4. Multiply the working days in the TRLT with the future anticipated daily consumption. This is the basic value that will appear in the forecasting results.

5. Add the safety stock quantity to the basic value. This is the calculated reorder point.

6. During this procedure, the **Forecasting** screen is used for simulation purposes only. The forecasted quantities won't become MRP-relevant. The forecast is simply used to perform an ex post forecast that allows for the determination of MAD, which is

then used to determine the degree of variability for the calculation of reorder point and safety stock (see Figure 13.9).

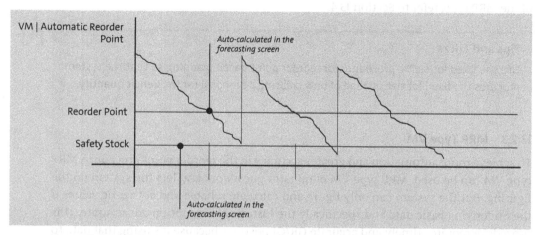

Figure 13.9 MRP Type VM

When deciding to use this planning procedure, take the following factors into consideration:

- The higher the degree of variation (MAD), the higher the safety stock requirement and the higher the reorder point will be.
- The longer the replenishment lead time, the higher the reorder point needs to be to get through the replenishment lead time.
- The longer the replenishment lead time, the greater the chance of an unforeseen consumption. This is increasing variability and, with it, safety stock requirements and the reorder point.
- The higher the service level percent maintained in **MRP 2**, the higher the safety stock requirement and, with it, the reorder point.
- The higher the daily consumption, the higher the reorder point. At the same time, the forecast is obligatory and uses total consumption.

Figure 13.10 shows the automatic reorder point calculation, safety stock calculation, and other calculations.

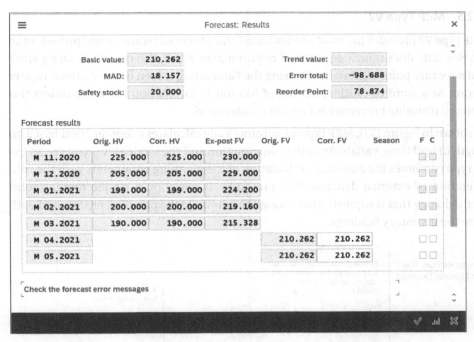

Figure 13.10 Safety Stock and Reorder Point Calculation Using MRP Type VM

13.2.4 MRP Type V1

MRP type V1 acts exactly like VB, except that it takes external requirements into consideration. The safety stock and reorder point have to be set and calculated manually for this procedure. It's possible to choose and configure what those external requirements are, such as order reservations, released stock transport orders, and released purchase requisitions. If there is a sales order reservation within the replenishment lead time (set **Ext. Reqmts** as "2"), then the order is triggered early because the amount of demand from the reservation is taken into account for the determination of when the reorder point is broken.

While using this MRP type, it's helpful to use a lot-size procedure that adds those external requirements within the lead time to the ordering quantity. Because these demands are already known, it makes sense to add them to the order size so that at the time of receipt, the consumption can be replenished in full. Therefore, the V1 type offers an advantage over both the VB and the VM types in that it's not purely driven by the past but is a little more proactive and includes future requirements in the planning process.

13.2.5   MRP Type V2

MRP type V2 provides the *most* sophisticated and advanced reorder point procedure so far. Not only does it include external requirements, but it also calculates safety stock and a reorder point automatically using the **Forecasting** screen in the material master record. As a word of caution, beware of too much automation too soon, unless this material planning procedure is first fully understood.

As shown in Figure 13.11, MRP type V2 automatically calculates a reorder point based on length of lead time, variability in the consumption and the service level you set. So the V2 type combines the automatic calculation of the planning parameters with the consideration of external demand. This procedure is based on a simple reorder point methodology that is sophisticated enough to automate the planning process and optimize the inventory holdings.

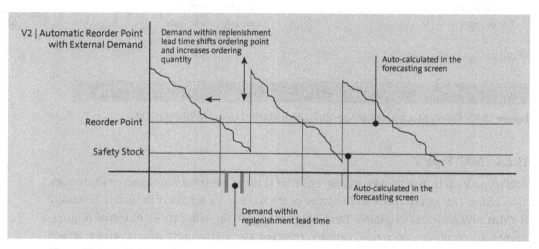

Figure 13.11 MRP Type V2

13.2.6   MRP Type D1

In DDR, the planning run creates a new supply element, such as a purchase requisition, a planned order, or a stock transfer requisition, when the net flow position of a material falls below the reorder point maintained in the material master. The aim of the planning run is to create supply elements to fulfill demand by using a better quality of demand signal. This means that it's possible to create supply elements that meet real customer demand more accurately. This in turn achieves improved service levels on the one hand while lowering inventory levels and bound capital on the other.

As this MRP type uses firming type 1 (like MRP type M1), the procurement proposals within the planning time fence are firmed automatically as soon as their date is at least one day before the end date of the planning time fence. The date of new procurement proposals created in the planning time fence is moved to the end date of the planning time fence. As a result, these new procurement proposals aren't firmed.

The equation for generating supply elements is the net flow equation:

On-hand stock + Open supply − Open past (including today's) demand − Qualified spike demand

In this equation, the quantity of stock on hand is added to the quantity of open supply. Then the total quantity of open demand (including today's demands) plus the qualified spike demand is subtracted. This results in the net flow position. If the day's net flow position is below the reorder point, a supply element is created for the amount that will bring the stock level back up to the maximum stock quantity.

> **Note**
>
> See Chapter 15 on DDR.

13.3   Stochastic Replenishment Procedures

Some of the stochastic replenishment or consumption-based MRP procedures require executing and saving the forecast before the system carries out MRP. In such cases, the **Forecasting** indicator in the relevant MRP type is marked as mandatory/obligatory, rather than optional. When a forecast on a material is executed, the system looks for the forecasting parameters that are maintained in the forecasting view of the material master, such as forecasting model and historical or forecast (future) periods. Further, depending on the model selected, it also considers smoothing factors, such as alpha, beta, gamma, or delta. In forecasting, the system considers the planned and unplanned consumption quantities of the material for the periods under evaluation and comes up with forecast (future) figures. When the forecast results are saved, the MRP for forecast-based consumption planning uses these forecast figures to create procurement proposals after the MRP run.

The following stochastic replenishment procedures require executing a forecast as a prerequisite to an MRP run:

- Forecast-based planning
- Time-phased materials planning

In the following sections, we cover forecast-based and time-phased materials planning.

13.3.1 MRP Type VV

The system updates the consumption data in the material master as total consumption (planned consumption and unplanned consumption) or unplanned consumption. To view the consumption details of the material, go to the **Basic Data** view of a material master (Transaction MM02), and click the **Additional Data** icon. Of the several tabs available, the **Consumption** tab holds consumption quantities. Per the MRP reservations, the system updates the consumption data of the planned consumption. If consumption isn't planned per MRP reservations, or if the material issuance quantity is greater than the reservation quantities, then the system updates the unplanned consumption.

In MRP type configuration, choose the type of historical consumption of a material to plan whether the system uses total consumption or unplanned consumption. Also, choose the reduction method for forecast requirements. The default system setting is reduction by consumption.

As we've already covered forecasting in detail in Chapter 11, we'll only briefly cover details relevant to forecast-based consumption planning here. The consumption forecast for components is based on material withdrawals. Maintain the forecast parameters in the **Forecasting** view of the material master, as shown in Figure 13.12.

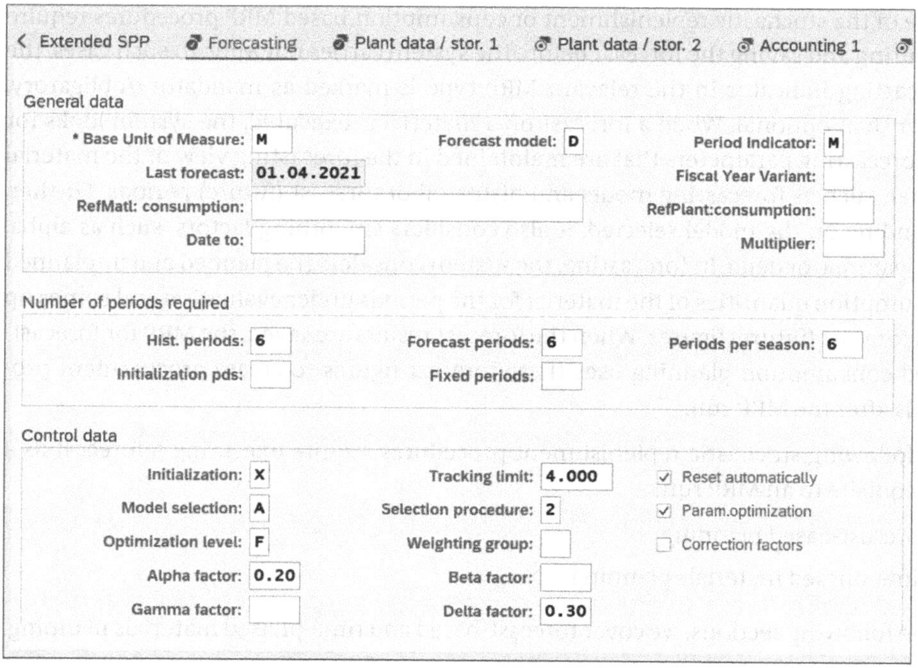

Figure 13.12 Forecasting View of the Material Master

The parameters include the *granularity* of the forecast—that is, whether it's carried out on the basis of monthly, weekly, or daily values. The granularity can be defined using the **Period Indicator** field. Other entries specify the number of historical periods based on which the forecast is carried out, as well as the number of forecast periods. Either specify the forecast model directly or have it determined automatically. Some of the possible forecast models include the following:

- Constant model (**D**)
- Trend model (**T**)
- Seasonal model (**S**)
- Seasonal trend model (**X**)
- Moving average (**G**)

The **Execute Forecast** button (not shown), located further down the screen shown in Figure 13.12, enables carrying out a forecast in the material master, while the other two buttons, **Consumption vals** and **Forecast values**, allow editing the historical values and the forecast values respectively.

An individual forecast for a material or an overall forecast for several materials can be run. For an individual material forecast, use Transaction MP30. After executing the forecast, a planner can change the forecast results and also correct forecast values interactively. The forecast values can be changed using Transaction MP31. To display the forecast, use Transaction MP32.

For the overall forecast, use Transaction MP38 to restrict the planning scope by plants, materials, and ABC indicators. The ABC indicator can be maintained in the **MRP 1** view of the material master.

In MRP type VV, the forecast is carried out at an individual material level. In fact, each material can have its own forecasting screen activated in the material master. MRP type VV can also be used for finished goods. There are many situations that call for setting up a finished product as VV. MRP type VV is a consumption-based replenishment strategy in that it maintains inventory in anticipation of actual demand. The inventory is replenished to a forecast, which is based on the material's own consumption history—hence the name *material forecast*. This is a good strategy when demand is predictable but the lead time to replenish is long. By putting "artificial" demand out there by using the forecasting functionality, MRP can generate all supply elements far ahead of time. All that is required is to convert the requisition into an order on the date that the system suggests a planner do so (see Figure 13.13).

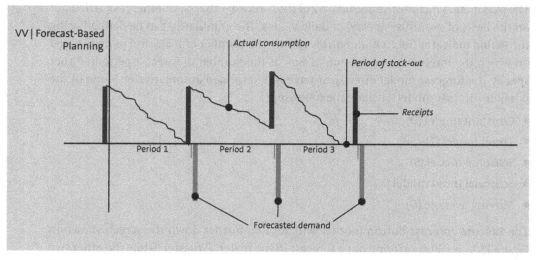

Figure 13.13 MRP Type VV

Warning

VV doesn't take demand spikes into consideration. Any changes in demand will flow into the consumption pattern and eventually be picked up by the forecast module. The system might increase or decrease the forecast or state that the current underlying model isn't applicable anymore. So, like all the other strategies, use MRP type VV if and when it meets your business needs.

For MRP type VV to function, maintain all the parameters in the **Forecasting** screen of the SAP system. Identify the periodicity by which to run the forecast to create demand with the **Period Indicator** in the **Forecasting** view of the material master. This setting will eventually determine with what frequency the forecast is run automatically for the material in question. The options are listed here:

- **Daily (D)**
  Results in daily demand records for every working day visible in Transaction MD04 and relevant to the MRP run. Be aware, however, that a daily forecast will also result in daily replenishment and may be an unnecessary consumption of the system's resources.

- **Weekly (W)**
  The most often used periodicity allows for relatively low average inventory holding because doing so brings in less inventory than in a monthly periodicity. It's also flexible and quick to detect spikes and periods of low consumption.

- **Monthly (M)**
  Used for less important or less expensive items because it brings in large quantities with few orders.

- **Posting period (P)**
  Freely definable according to a period to set up in financial accounting (FI). After the **Period Indicator** is set, decide how many periods from the past to include in the forecast calculation. It's also possible to set aside a number of periods for an ex post forecast, and the number of periods for which the forecast run generates demand can be identified.

To maintain the **SI** (splitting indicator) details, use menu path **SAP IMG · Production · Material Requirements Planning · Forecast · Define splitting of Forecast Requirements for MRP. Splitting Indicator** contains the number of periods to be considered, as well as the number of days and/or weeks for which splitting is to be carried out (see Figure 13.14).

Plnt	Name 1	SI	Per. Ind.	Period Ind. Descr.	No.Day	No. Wk	Per
☐ 1105	Demo Manufacturing Plant	A	M	Monthly	1	2	4
☐ 1105	Demo Manufacturing Plant	A	W	Weekly	4		16

Figure 13.14 Distributing the Forecast Values to Different Periods

In the **MRP 3** view of the material master, assign the previously-configured splitting indicator in the **Splitting Indicator** field (Figure 13.15).

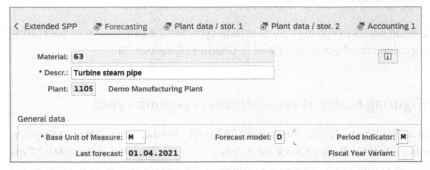

Figure 13.15 Splitting Indicator in Material Master (MRP 3 View)

13.3.2 MRP Types R1 and R2

Materials that are replenished using a time-phased planning method are scheduled so that the MRP run considers them for planning only on specific dates in the week. This is determined by the planning cycle in which the MRP run is only triggered on specific days of a week. Time-phased planning can be carried out with consumption-based—stochastic—procedures or with deterministic ones. MRP type R1 simply plans for an MRP run on the days scheduled by the planning cycle, which might lead to stock-outs when large consumption happens on a day not included in the planning cycle. This is where MRP type R2 is the better choice because it calculates a reorder point automatically and triggers the planning run whenever the reorder point is broken.

For example, if a vendor always delivers a material on a certain day of the week due to its own internal route and delivery planning, then it makes sense for a company's planning run to follow the same cycle and be displaced by the delivery time. Similarly, if the company procures or produces certain material during specific times of the year only, then time-phased planning is used. For example, chocolate manufacturers in a few hot and humid climatic countries cease production during the summer months. In such cases, all production and procurement planning is confined to the defined planning cycle only.

To plan a material based on time phases, use Transaction MM02 to enter the MRP type for time-phased planning and the planning cycle in the material master (see Figure 13.16). A forecast is also used in this planning concept, and the general procedure is very similar to forecast-based planning, with the difference that the procurement intervals are predefined.

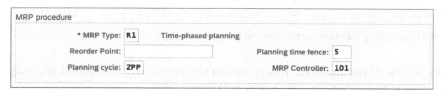

Figure 13.16 Time-Phased Materials Planning

The configuration basics of setting up a planning cycle are the same as those for setting up a planning calendar, which is described in Chapter 14, Section 14.3.

13.4   Configuring Material Requirements Planning Types

To configure an MRP type, follow menu path **SAP IMG · Production · Material Requirements Planning · Master Data · Check MRP Types**. Here the detailed view of **MRP Type PD** is shown (see Figure 13.17). Almost all options available on this screen, such as the firming type, forecast indicator, and consumption indicator, were previously discussed.

To control the MRP procedure that the system uses in the MRP type, place the cursor on the **MRP Procedure** field and click the dropdown option or press F4 . Figure 13.18 shows the resulting available list of MRP procedures.

> **Note**
>
> MRP procedure **X Without MRP, with BOM Explosion** is used in the production planning and detailed scheduling (PP-DS) area of SAP S/4HANA. The use of this MRP procedure and its associated MRP type X0 (see Table 13.2) is covered in Chapter 19, which discusses PP-DS.

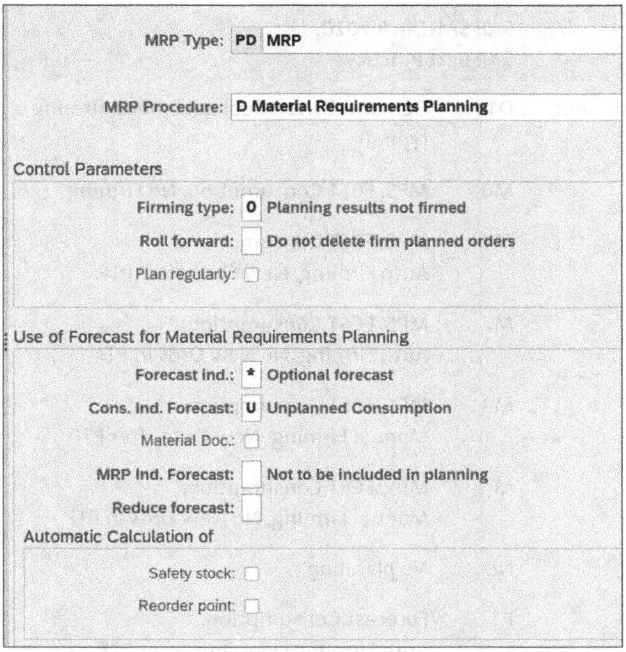

Figure 13.17 Configuration (Transaction SPRO) of MRP Type PD

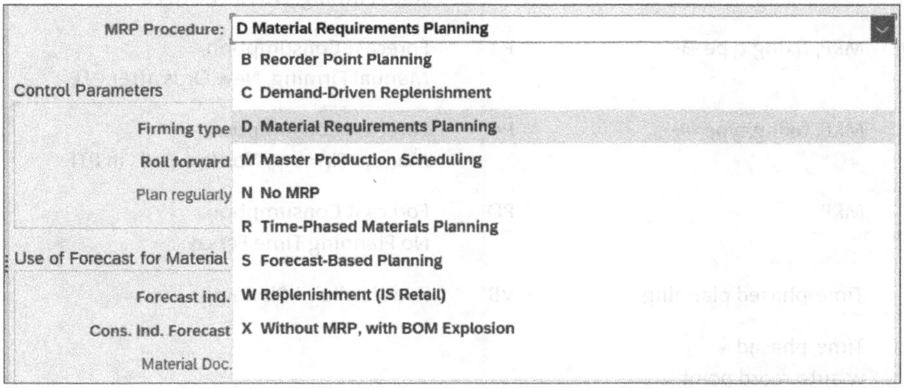

Figure 13.18 MRP Procedures

Table 13.2 is a side-by-side comparison of the available MRP types in a standard (blank) SAP client and SAP Best Practices client. For the sake of providing as much coverage of different MRP types as possible, we chose to cover the standard client in this chapter.

SAP S/4HANA 2020: Blank Client		SAP S/4HANA 2020: SAP Best Practices	
D1	Demand-Driven Replenishment, fixing type -1-	D1	Demand-Driven Replenishment, firming type -1-
M0	MPS, fixing type -0-	M0	MPS, FCST Consumption, No Firming
M1	MPS, fixing type -1-	M1	MPS, FCST Consumption, Auto Firming, New Ords after PTF
M2	MPS, fixing type -2-	M2	MPS, FCST Consumption, Auto Firming, No New Ords in PTF
M3	MPS, fixing type -3-	M3	MPS, FCST Consumption, Manual Firming, New Ords after PTF
M4	MPS, fixing type -4-	M4	MPS, FCST Consumption, Manual Firming, No New Ords in PTF
ND	No planning	ND	No planning
P1	MRP, fixing type -1-	P1	Forecast Consumption, Auto Firming, New Ords after PTF
P2	MRP, fixing type -2-	P2	Forecast Consumption, Auto Firming, No New Ords in PTF
P3	MRP, fixing type -3-	P3	Forecast Consumption, Manual Firming, New Ords after PTF
P4	MRP, fixing type -4-	P4	Forecast Consumption, Manual Firming, No New Ords in PTF
PD	MRP	PD	Forecast Consumption, No Planning Time Fence
R1	Time-phased planning	VB	Reorder-Point Planning
R2	Time-phased w.auto.reord.point		
RE	Replenishment plnd externally		
RF	Replenish with dyn.TargetStock		
RP	Replenishment		
V1	Manual reord.point w. ext.reqs		
V2	Autom. reord.point w. ext.reqs		

Table 13.2 Available MRP Types

SAP S/4HANA 2020: Blank Client		SAP S/4HANA 2020: SAP Best Practices
VB	Manual reorder point planning	
VI	Vendor Managed Inventory	
VM	Automatic reorder point plng	
VS	Seasonal MRP	
VV	Forecast-based planning	
X0	W/O MRP, with BOM Explosion	

Table 13.2 Available MRP Types (Cont.)

13.5   Lot Sizing Procedures

After performing a net requirements calculation, when the system determines a material shortage, it looks to information maintained in the **Lot Sizing Procedure** field in the **MRP 1** view of the material master. The lot sizing specifies the quantity that the system should propose when it comes across a quantity shortage of a material. For the system to create the correct lot size as a procurement proposal, it also looks for other information, such as safety stock, maximum or minimum lot size, static or dynamic safety stock, scrap percentage, and rounding value.

It's very important to determine lot sizes to ensure optimum inventories and good service levels. Suppliers occasionally demand minimum order quantities, which end up as excess inventory levels, especially for slow-moving items. It's possible to maintain inventory controls or gates that are then easier to manage. Between procurement or purchasing and materials planning there is a gate, which means that materials planning should generate the most economical lot size, generate an order proposal with that optimal lot size, and initiate the purchasing process.

The advantage of having these kinds of gates is that a company can build a basis for negotiations with suppliers. For example, if the materials planner applies the conditions in the **Minimum Lot Size** field in the material master, then the MRP run will always generate order proposals using the minimum quantity. Lot sizing procedures in the SAP system help the planner find the most optimal quantities to order. An MRP run not only automatically generates the order proposal but also suggests the perfect lot size to bring in so that availability is assured without holding too much inventory. There are several lot sizing procedures already preconfigured and available in the standard SAP system.

The lot sizing procedure is assigned in the **MRP 1** view of the material master (Transaction MM02). For the example in Figure 13.19, assign the **Lot Sizing Procedure** as "EX" (**Lot-for-Lot Order Quantity**).

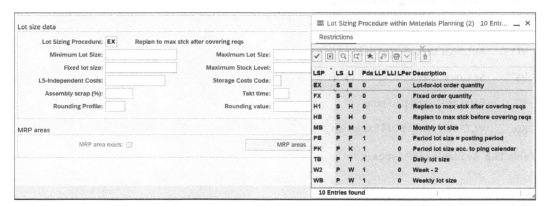

Figure 13.19 Lot Sizing Procedure in Material Master

There are three different lot sizing procedures in the SAP system:

- Static lot sizing procedures
- Periodic lot sizing procedures
- Optimum lot sizing procedures

We'll discuss these procedures in the following sections before moving on to configuring lot sizes.

13.5.1 Static Lot Sizing Procedures

Static lot sizing procedures can further be categorized as exact lot sizing, fixed lot sizing, fixed lot sizing with splitting, and replenish to maximum stock level, as described in the following sections.

Lot Size: EX (Exact Lot Sizing)

The system creates planned orders or procurement proposals to cover the exact shortage requirement only. For example, if a net requirement quantity of a material is 110 units, the system creates the procurement proposal for 110 units only (see Figure 13.20).

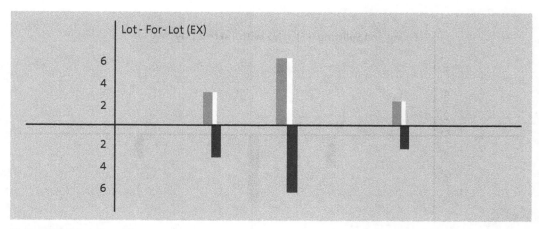

Figure 13.20 Lot Size: EX

Lot Size: FX (Fixed Lot Sizing)

The system proposes the total requirement in multiples of fixed lots. For example, if the lot size is fixed as 60 units, and the shortage quantity is 240, then the system creates four planned orders to cover the shortages.

Lot Size: FS (Fixed Lot Sizing with Splitting)

The system proposes the total requirement in multiples of fixed lots with overlap. This lot sizing is generally preferred if a company can't procure a large quantity at once and hence must split the quantity with an overlap. Using this lot sizing procedure entails assigning a fixed lot quantity together with a rounding value. The rounding value must be a multiple of the fixed lot quantity. For example, if the lot size is fixed as 100 units, and the rounding value is 20 units, then the system creates five planned orders to cover the shortages (see Figure 13.21).

It's also possible to shift the orders by a certain takt time, which means using a control parameter for scheduling based on *takts* (i.e., physical areas of a production line). This procedure avoids the simultaneous scheduling of numerous orders and thus ensures that the actually required lead time is observed. If splitting is used in combination with a fixed lot size, the rounding value must be a multiple integer of the fixed lot size. The takt time indicates the offset between order dates in terms of workdays. The different orders overlap in time and are shifted against each other by the takt time.

For example, assign **Lot Sizing Procedure** as "FS" (**Fixed Lot with Splitting**) and give a **Fixed Lot Size** of "100". Next, set the **Rounding Value** as "25" (it should be a multiple of the fixed lot quantity). Finally, maintain a **Takt Time** of "3" days (workdays). When the system runs the MRP, assuming there is no existing stock of the material in the plant, it will create four planned orders of 25 each for the total quantity of 100 and will also delay the start date of each planned order by three workdays (takt time).

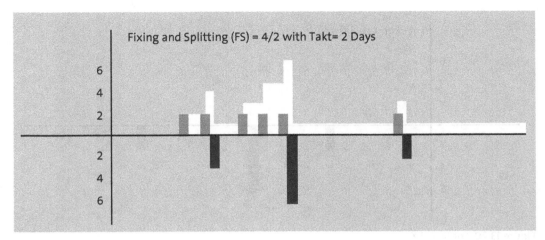

Figure 13.21 Lot Size: FS

Lot Size: HB (Replenish to Maximum Stock Level)

The system creates planned orders to fill to the maximum stock level. The maximum stock level has to be defined in the relevant field of the **MRP 1** view of the material master. For example, if the maximum stock level is 300 units, and the demand quantity is 50 units, the system creates a planned order of 350. It first ensures that the 300 units of stock fill up, and then the demand quantity is added to it.

When the reorder point is broken, the MRP run figures the difference between the current stock level and the maximum stock level desired and creates a replenishment quantity correspondingly.

When using this lot sizing procedure, some consumption occurs during the replenishment lead time, and when the replenishment quantity is received, the stock level might be considerably lower than at the time the replenishment quantity was calculated. One way to address this issue is the inclusion of demand within the replenishment lead time by making relevant configuring settings in a lot sizing procedure, as covered in Section 13.5.4.

13.5.2   Periodic Lot Sizing Procedures

Periodic lot sizing procedures can be further categorized into daily lot sizing, weekly lot sizing, monthly lot sizing, or lot sizing of any other periodicity. For example, if the lot sizing procedure is daily, then the system considers demand with all the receipts for that day and creates a daily shortage proposal in case a shortage exists. If it's a weekly lot size, then the system combines all the requirements for a week and comes up with one procurement proposal.

In other words, several demands can be covered with a single supply element. These procedures all collect demand in a specified period and create exactly one supply element to cover the total demand quantities in that period. However, it's important to mention that the longer the period, the more inventories need to be maintained. This is because the MRP run generates an order proposal that brings in the entire quantity needed in that period to the date of the first demand. For example, if a planner is using a three-month period, and there's a demand of one piece on the first date of the first month, the order proposal would bring in the entire quantity needed for three months' worth of demand on the first day. This will result in higher inventory, carrying a cost if the item in question is of high value. Periodic lot size procedures are effective when used with cheap items with low inventory carrying costs.

Tips and Tricks

Use Transaction OMI4 to set the availability date as either the start or the end of the period (Section 13.5.4).

13.5.3 Optimum Lot Sizing Procedures

In the optimum lot sizing procedure, the production or purchase of materials entails fixed lot size costs, such as setup costs for machines or PO costs, and variable costs, which are referred to as capital tie-up due to stockholding. To minimize the variable costs, ensure that you procure quantities that are as small as possible. To minimize the fixed costs, procure quantities as large as possible. Optimum lot sizing procedures consider variable and fixed costs and determine optimal lot sizes according to different procedures based on these costs.

Example

Phosphoric acid is the main component used in the production of specialized fertilizer, diammonium phosphate. The company wants to replenish to the maximum stock of phosphoric acid at the time of placing new orders. However, there are supplier requirements regarding minimum and maximum order limits for shipment. To cater to this business need, create a new MRP lot size (which may also be a copy of MRP lot size HB: replenish to maximum stock level) and also select the **Check Min. Lot Size** and **Check Max Lot Size** checkboxes. Assign this self-defined MRP lot size to the **MRP 1** view of the material master. The system now prompts you to enter the minimum and maximum lot sizes of the material. Not only will the system now make sure to replenish the material to the maximum stock level, but it will also take the minimum and maximum lot sizes into account while creating procurement proposals.

To illustrate this example further, the storage tank capacity for phosphoric acid is 40,000 MT (metric tons), the minimum lot size is 20,000 MT, and the maximum is

25,000 MT. Currently, the stock in the storage tank has dropped to 10,000 MT. The system creates one planned order for 25,000 MT, which ensures that this is the maximum lot size it can go up to and still remain within the maximum storage tank capacity of 40,000 MT. If the minimum or maximum lot sizes had not been maintained, then the system would have created a planned order of 30,000 MT to replenish the existing stock of 10,000 MT to the maximum of 40,000 MT.

Optimum lot sizing procedures strive to strike a balance between ordering cost and stockholding cost. They therefore optimize the total cost of inventory. For example, let's look at the EX lot sizing procedure, which brings in—in its simplest version— exactly as much as is needed at exactly the time that it's needed. In other words, there's no need to carry inventory forward to meet any other demand; whatever comes in is consumed immediately. However, there's certainly an ordering cost that needs to be paid every time there is a demand. So if there are five demands in one month, a company will end up paying for five orders. This is different with a monthly lot sizing procedure, in which there's only one order per month. But if the same situation with five demands is taken into account, the order will bring in the total quantity to meet all demands throughout the months to the first demand, and a planner will have to carry forward the stock that isn't consumed by the first demand. On the other hand, there's cost of only one order.

When using an optimum lot sizing procedure instead, the system (the MRP run) will figure out automatically—for any given demand situation—what the optimum order quantity and order frequency is to arrive at the minimum between the ordering cost and stockholding cost. It does so by using various formulas, such as the least unit cost formula, the Groff formula, or the part-period balancing formula. These all aim to strike the optimum balance between ordering and stockholding costs.

To determine the variable costs, maintain the storage costs percentage specified in the storage costs indicator (**Storage Costs Ind.**). Enter the storage costs indicator along with the ordering costs in the **MRP 1** view of the material master. The system calculates the variable costs according to the following formula:

Variable costs = Requirement × Price × Storage costs [%] × Storage duration ÷ 365

In the **MRP 1** view of the material master, maintain **Storage Costs Ind.**, as well as **Ordering Costs**.

13.5.4   Configuring Lot Size

Table 13.3 is a summary of a selection of standard MRP lot sizes with lot sizing procedures. When selecting a certain lot size, some of them require additional information and must be maintained in the material master, as noted in the final column.

MRP Lot Size	Lot Sizing Procedure	Lot Size Indicator	Fields
EX: Exact lot size calculation	Static lot size	E: Exact lot size	
FK: Fixed lot size for customer MTO production	Static lot size	F: Fixed lot size	
FS: Fixed/splitting	Static lot size	S: Fixed with splitting	**Fixed Lot Size, Rounding Value, Takt Time**
FX: Fixed order quantity	Static lot size	F: Fixed lot size	**Fixed Lot Size**
HB: Replenish to maximum stock level	Static lot size	H: Replenishment to maximum stock level	**Maximum Stock Level**
MB: Monthly lot size	Lot size according to flexible period length	M: Monthly lot size	
PK: Lot size according to flexible period length and planning calendar	Lot size according to flexible period	K: Period based on planning calendar	
TB: Daily lot size	Lot size according to flexible period length	T: Daily lot size	
WB: Weekly lot size	Lot size according to flexible period length	W: Weekly lot size	
WI: Least unit cost procedure	Optimization lot size	W: Least unit cost procedure	**Ordering Costs, Storage Costs Ind.**
DY: Dynamic lot size creation	Optimization lot size	D: Dynamic planning	**Ordering Costs, Storage Costs Ind.**
GR: Groff lot-sizing procedure	Optimization lot size	G: Procedure according to Groff	**Ordering Costs, Storage Costs Ind.**
SP: Part-period balancing	Optimization lot size	S: Part-period balancing	**Ordering Costs, Storage Costs Ind.**

Table 13.3 Selection of MRP Lot Sizes and Lot-Sizing Procedures

Although standard lot sizes available in the SAP system are generally sufficient to fulfill most business needs, the MRP lot size can be configured to attend to any specific business process.

To configure the MRP lot size, use menu path **SAP IMG · Logistics · Production · Material Requirements Planning · Planning · Lot Size Calculation · Check Lot Sizing Procedures**, or use Transaction OMI4. Figure 13.22 displays MRP lot sizing procedure EX for an exact lot size calculation.

A planner can also set different applicable lot sizing parameters for short-term and long-term horizons. Procurement/production always takes place with the lot size of the short-term horizon. The long-term horizon enables the forecast function (mostly aggregated, e.g., via monthly periodic lot sizing). This is often useful in reducing the number of requirement coverage elements, especially if fixed lot sizes are used that are smaller than the average requirement quantity. Typically, a period-based lot size is used for the long-term horizon.

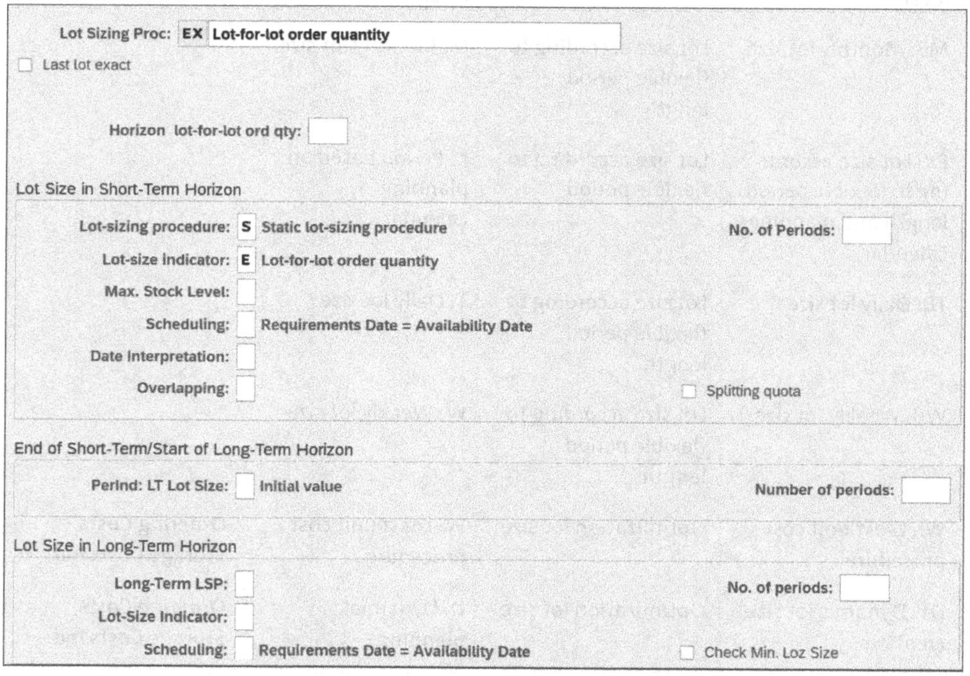

Figure 13.22 Lot Size Configuration

[+]

Tips and Tricks

If fixed lot sizes are used for financial or practical reasons, without any technical need, avoid surplus procurements by setting the **Last Lot Exact** checkbox in the configuration of the MRP lot size. This is particularly applicable for higher-value goods.

13.6 Rounding

In some cases, it's useful to round the quantities of the procurement proposals. In the simplest business scenario, a rounding value is used. In this case, the order quantity of the requirement coverage element always represents a multiple of the rounding value. In more complex scenarios, in which the rounding value depends on the requirement quantity, a rounding profile can be used. The rounding profile enables you to, for example, model different pack sizes.

The system offers static and dynamic rounding profiles. The *static* rounding profiles round up the value after a threshold value has been reached. If the rounding value exceeds the threshold, the system continuously rounds the value until it reaches the next threshold. Rounding profiles can be created by using Transaction OWD1.

> **Example**
>
> If the rounding value is 30 units, the procurement quantity is 75 units, and the minimum lot size is 15 units, then the system always rounds up the planned order to a multiple of 30 units, specifying the rounding to a quantity of 30 units. In this example, the system rounds off the procurement quantity of 75 units to 90. The **Rounding Value** option in the **MRP 1** view of the material master can be used in almost all lot sizing procedures.

The static rounding value method may not fulfill all business scenarios in which a given rounding value is used and the procurement proposals are rounding to that value. There may also be business processes in which the rounding value may change based on the size of the procurement proposal. In such instances, you can use a static rounding profile. For example, you can configure the system to have a rounded value of 10 units if the procurement quantity is at least one unit. For the procurement quantity of 31 units or more, the system should round this off to 50 units.

Using Transaction OWD1, the example in Figure 13.23 ❶ shows that a **Rounding Profile PP01** has been created for **Plant 1105**. Click the **Static** button, and the next screen ❷ pops up. Enter the threshold values and the rounding values. Click the **Simulation** button to bring up the **Simulation Selection** dialog box ❸. Enter the **Quantity Simulation** of "1" unit and **To Qty** of "150", and choose **Continue**. The system then displays the simulation results ❹.

If there's a business need to specify how the system acts when it reaches a certain threshold value by either adding up or reducing the quantity to the defined percentage, you can do that too. Go back to Figure 13.23 ❶. This time, choose the **Qty T/B Added/Subtracted** button, and the screen shown in Figure 13.24 appears. Here, define the threshold values and then enter the percentage that the system should add to or subtract from the procurement quantity. So, if the procurement quantity is less than or equal to 100 PC, the system will add up to 10% of it. When the procurement quantity is greater than 100 but less than or equal to 200, it will reduce the quantity by 15%.

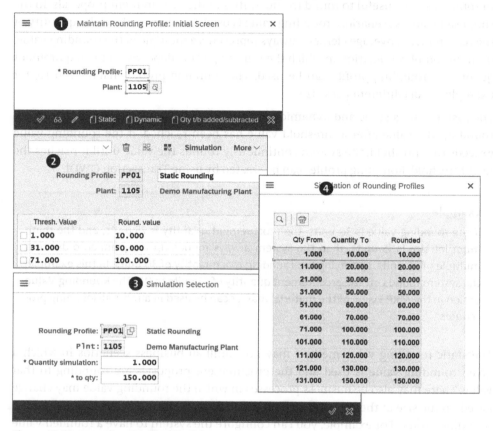

Figure 13.23 Rounding Profile (Static)

Figure 13.24 Quantity Addition/Subtraction Profiles

In a dynamic rounding profile, define the rounding off method, as well as the rounding rule. The rounding off method may be a multiple of the order unit or sales order. Also, consider using an available customer exit to define any unique rounding method. For a rounding rule, round the threshold value either up or down by the defined percentage.

13.7 Scrap

Companies are often faced with problems relating to materials they can't use, known as *scrap*, whether from defective finished goods produced, excess consumption of raw material due to wastage in the production process, or operational inefficiencies. The system offers several options to maintain scrap or waste details at every level—the assembly or the component (raw material) level—so that production and procurement planning are closely synchronized with actual and practical situations.

Based on historical data or practical experience, maintain assembly and component scrap as master data, which subsequently facilitates production and procurement processes. Scrap is treated differently in the SAP system. Scrap in real life can be available or even sold but isn't treated as inventory in the SAP system.

The two types of scrap described here are as follows:

- **Assembly scrap**
  This is completely unusable finished or semifinished product for which the raw material was issued in accordance with a BOM. Assembly scrap is different from coproducts or by-products, which are inventory-managed in the SAP system.

- **Component scrap**
  This allows the system to increase the issuance quantity of the component against a production order by the defined percentage to account for scrap or wastage during production.

Successfully assigning assembly and component scrap in master data enables the system to consider scrap not only during production planning—either by increasing production quantity to account for assembly scrap or increasing the issuance quantity to account for component scrap—but also during procurement planning. During the MRP run, the system takes the scrap percentage into account and reflects it in the planning proposals generated.

To maintain the details of assembly or component scrap in the MRP view of the material master, follow menu path **Logistics • Materials Management • Material Master • Material • Change • Immediately**, or use Transaction MM02.

In the following sections, we'll provide additional details about the different types of scrap and also explain how to maintain details of their different uses.

13.7.1 Assembly Scrap

Maintain assembly scrap in the **MRP 1** view of the material master. Here, enter the assembly scrap in the form of a percentage in the **Assembly Scrap (%)** field. If this material is then used as an assembly, the system considers it during scrap calculation by correspondingly increasing the production order quantity. For example, say an assembly scrap of 10% is defined for the material. When a production order is created, say for a quantity of 100 PC, the system automatically increases the production order quantity to 110 PC to account for 10% scrap. At the same time, it also issues an information message. Because the production order quantity increased to 110 PC, the system accordingly increases the components' quantities also, as it reads this information from the material's BOM (and multiplies the production order quantity, which in this case is now 110 PC with the components' quantities).

13.7.2 Component Scrap

Maintain component scrap in the **MRP 4** view of the material master in the form of a percentage. If this material is then used as a component in the BOM, the system considers it during scrap calculation. For example, entering 10% scrap for 100 M of a component material increases the component issuance quantity in the production order to 110 M (see Figure 13.25).

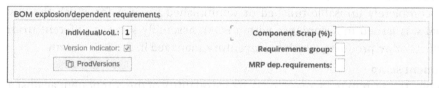

Figure 13.25 Component Scrap

13.7.3 Operations and Component Scraps in Bill of Materials

In Transaction CS02, to change a BOM for a material, click the **Item Overview** column. In the screen that appears (see Figure 13.26), maintain operation scrap and component scrap in percentages. When maintaining operation scrap in a percentage, also select the **Net ID** checkbox.

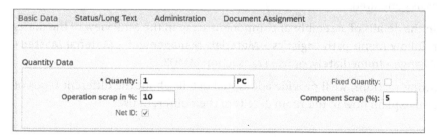

Figure 13.26 Operation and Component Scrap in BOM

If both operation scrap and component scrap in the BOM are maintained, then the system takes *both* of them into account. For example, for the component quantity of 1.00 M, the system calculates the final component issuance quantity as 1.21 M, after first taking operation scrap and then component scrap into account. That is, it used the calculations 1.00 M × 1.10 = 1.10 M and then again 1.10 M × 1.10 = 1.21 M.

[+]

Tips and Tricks

Maintaining a component scrap percentage in a material master (Figure 13.25) will enable the system to consider the *same* scrap percentage whenever and wherever this component is used in any material's BOM. However, if there's a business scenario to maintain different scrap percentages of the component used in different products, then it makes sense to maintain the component scrap details in each material's BOM (Figure 13.26).

For example, raw tomatoes are used as a component in producing different products. If the *same* quantity of raw tomatoes is wasted (as scrap) in producing different products, then maintain this scrap percentage in the material master for fresh or raw tomatoes. However, if raw tomatoes wastage percentages are *different* for different products, such as tomato ketchup, tomato paste, tomato puree, and tomato soup, then maintain these individual wastage (scrap) percentages in each of the four tomato-based products so that the SAP system correctly calculates the raw tomato quantities required to procure and/or produce each of the four products and their associated wastages.

13

13.7.4 Scrap in Routing

Use Transaction CA02 to change a routing for a material. In the **Item Overview** column, go to the **General Data** area (see Figure 13.27). Maintain operation scrap as a percentage. When a production order is created, the system increases the component issuance quantity by the defined percentage to account for operation scrap in the routing.

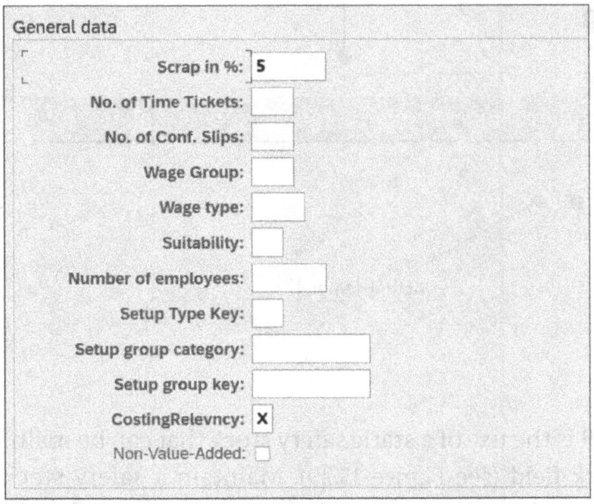

Figure 13.27 Scrap in Routing

13.8   Safety Stock

Safety stocks are quantity or time buffers to account for variability in supply and demand. The system offers two types of safety stock: static (i.e., absolute) safety stock and dynamic safety stock (i.e., safety days' supply).

In the following sections, we'll cover how the safety stock availability can be used in net requirements calculation and also the selection method that the system uses for receipts.

13.8.1   Static Safety Stock

The static or absolute safety stock enables the system to subtract it from material availability calculations (net requirements calculation). The safety stock must always be available to cover for unforeseen material shortages or unexpected high demand (see Figure 13.28).

The static safety stock certainly has its uses, especially when the objective is to guarantee 100% availability of a cheap part; however, for most situations, the system will drive up dead stock because the variability in demand may lead to a constant availability of stock that may never really be used.

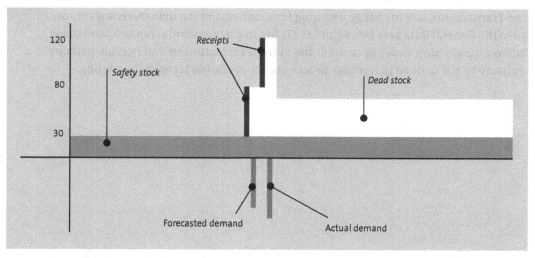

Figure 13.28 Static Safety Stock

The simplest buffering strategy of all is the use of a static safety stock that can be maintained manually in the **Safety Stock** field (see Figure 13.29). Maintain a safety stock quantity, and the MRP run will ignore that quantity for planning purposes and set it aside for bad times. In fact, the **Stock/Requirements List** area in Transaction MD04 subtracts that safety stock in the first line and then works without it for everything it does and looks at.

Figure 13.29 Safety Stock and Safety Days' Supply

Figure 13.30 (Transaction MD04) shows that the safety stock quantity is immediately subtracted from free available stock and simply ignored for all future planning.

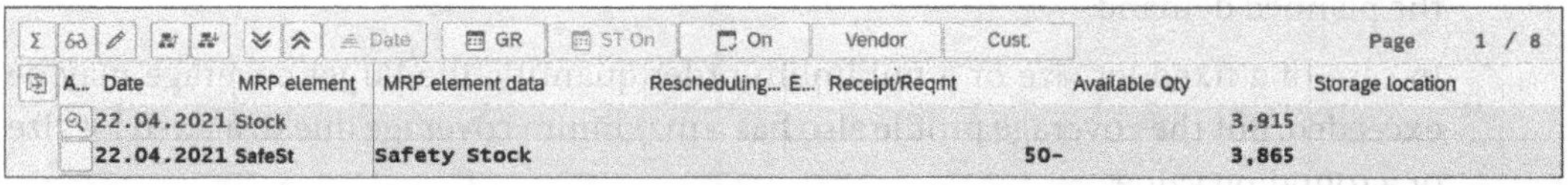

A..	Date	MRP element	MRP element data	Rescheduling... E...	Receipt/Reqmt	Available Qty	Storage location
	22.04.2021	Stock				3,915	
	22.04.2021	SafeSt	Safety Stock		50–	3,865	

Figure 13.30 Not Considering Safety Stock as Available Quantity

13.8.2 Safety Stock Availability

To avoid the unnecessary creation of planned orders for a smaller quantity, which can otherwise be covered by the safety stock, define the percentage (share) of safety stock that the system can use in such business scenarios. For example, during the MRP run, the system assesses a shortage of 2 PC of a material. However, a safety stock of 40 PC is maintained for this material, which the system doesn't consider in the MRP run. If a 10% safety stock has been defined to account for smaller shortages, which for this example means that 4 PC come from safety stock, then the system can cater to this small requirement or shortage of 2 PC from the 4 PC available from safety stock and no longer creates a procurement proposal.

To define the safety stock parameters, use menu path **SAP IMG • Logistics • Production • Material Requirements Planning • Planning • MRP Calculation • Stocks • Define Safety Stock Availability**. For this example, the system can consider 10% of the safety stock for **Plnt 1105** and **MRP Group 0000** for net requirements calculation (see Figure 13.31). Next, assign this MRP group in the **MRP 1** view of the material master.

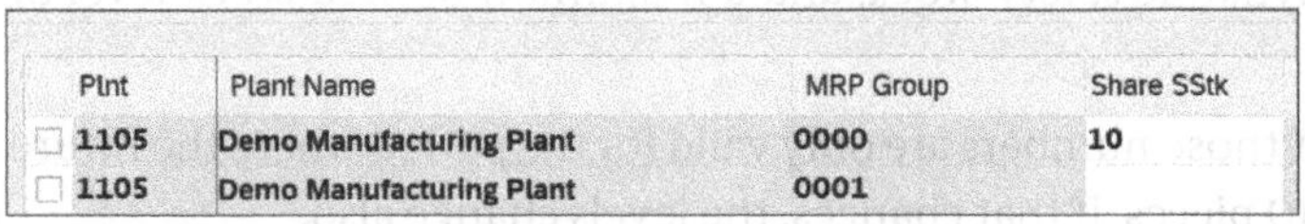

Plnt	Plant Name	MRP Group	Share SStk
☐ 1105	Demo Manufacturing Plant	0000	10
☐ 1105	Demo Manufacturing Plant	0001	

Figure 13.31 Share of Safety Stock

13.8.3   Dynamic Safety Stock with Range of Coverage Profile

A dynamic safety stock in the SAP system can be employed by use of the **Range of Coverage** profile. With the receipts-forecasted demand safety stock profile, a target dynamic safety stock, a minimum level, and a maximum level can be set. If effectively implemented, then the MRP run will always try to keep the target dynamic safety stock available for planning. But other than with the static safety stock, no additional quantities are brought in unless the safety stock falls below the minimum. Therefore, if the minimum low in planning is set, then all safety stock is used as a buffer. In addition, if the actual demand turns out to be less than what was planned, the maximum level in the coverage profile keeps the stock from blowing up in case of underconsumption of the planned demand.

In case of a fixed lot size or a minimum order quantity, the target coverage may be exceeded. But the coverage profile also has a maximum coverage due to a fixed lot size or a rounding value.

In a coverage profile, the levels (minimum, target, and maximum) aren't set in quantities but are managed in days of coverage. That fact provides the dynamic part of the safety stock because the objective is to hold three days of future demand in safety to buffer demand and supply variability. That means that if the demand goes up, there's more safety stock, and if the demand goes down, it'll be less.

To set up the range of coverage profile, follow menu path **SAP IMG • Production • Material Requirements Planning • Planning • MRP Calculation • Define Range of Coverage Profile (Dynamic Safety Stock)**, or use Transaction OMIA (see Figure 13.32).

The **Determine Range of Coverage** area is used to calculate the future daily demand. This is done by collecting demand over a horizon (you have to set the horizon here in the first section), and then the total is divided by the number of days within that horizon (working days or calendar days must be identified in this section) to arrive at a future average daily demand. This future average daily demand is then multiplied with the levels set in the **Determine Average Requirements** area. Therefore, when calculated, a planner will end up with a quantity for minimum target and maximum target. For example, if the levels are Min. = 1, Tgt = 5, and Max. = 20, and the future average daily demand was 10 pieces for the next three months, then the levels will be 10 pieces minimum, 50 pieces target dynamic safety stock, and a maximum desired stock level of 200 pieces.

It's important to note that those numbers are only valid for the period where the future average daily demand is 10 pieces. If that changes, the levels change also.

Figure 13.32 shows **Coverage Profile** set to "001" and **Plant** to "1105".

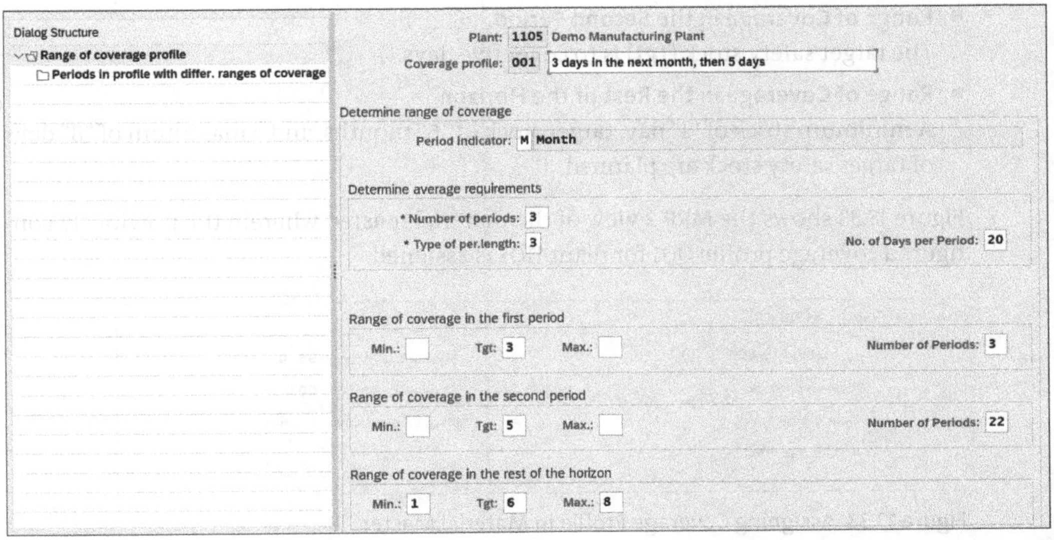

Figure 13.32 Range of Coverage Profile

The dynamic safety stock is calculated by this formula:

Dynamic safety stock = Average daily requirement × Range of coverage

In this equation, the average daily requirement is calculated by this formula:

Requirements in the specified periods ÷ Number of days in the total period length

For the calculation of the average daily requirements, the following parameters must be maintained:

- **Period Indicator**
  This indicator determines the calendar period for which average daily requirements need to be carried out. The following values can be maintained: weeks (**W**), months (**M**), and periods according to the planning calendar (**K**). For this example, maintain "M" for a monthly coverage of safety stock.

- **Type of Per.Length**
  This indicator is used to determine the length of the individual periods in detail. The following values can be maintained: workdays, calendar days, or standard days. If standard days is selected as a period length, the number of days determined per period must be maintained in the field.

- **Number of Periods**
  The number of periods is defined and used to calculate the average daily requirements.

- **Range of Coverage Profile in the First Period**
  The **Number of Periods** is three months. The **No. of Days per Period** is 20 days.

- **Range of Coverage in the Second Period**
  The target safety stock (**Tgt**) is to cover five days.

- **Range of Coverage in the Rest of the Horizon**
  A minimum stock of "1" day, target stock of "6" months, and a maximum of "8" days of target safety stock are planned.

Figure 13.33 shows the **MRP 2** view of the material master, wherein the previously configured coverage profile 001 for plant 1105 is assigned.

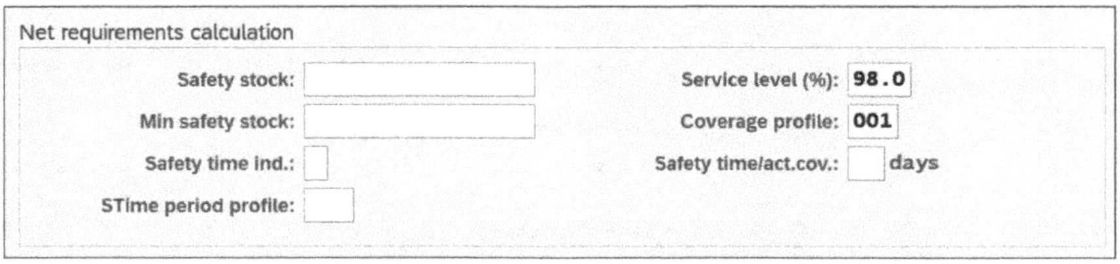

Net requirements calculation			
Safety stock:		Service level (%):	98.0
Min safety stock:		Coverage profile:	001
Safety time ind.:		Safety time/act.cov.:	days
STime period profile:			

Figure 13.33 Assigning Coverage Profile in Material Master

With these configuration and master data settings in place, let's now show the dynamic safety stock calculation with an example.

Figure 13.34 shows the monthly requirement (PIRs; Transaction MD61) shown in the **Planned Qty** column for the next five months for **Material 132** and **Plant 1105**.

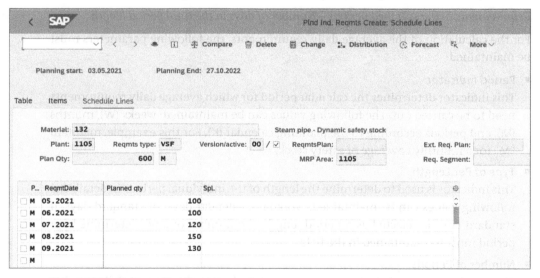

P...	ReqmtDate	Planned qty	Spl.
M	05.2021	100	
M	06.2021	100	
M	07.2021	120	
M	08.2021	150	
M	09.2021	130	
M			

Figure 13.34 Independent Requirements

After running MRP Live (Transaction MD01N), go to the stock/requirements list (Transaction MD04).

Let's evaluate the planning results in detail. Because it's already April, the system calculates safety stock requirements for the *next* month (May) by considering average daily requirement for the next three months (May, June, and July). Here the system considers three months because in the coverage profile, the period maintained was three months:

((100 + 120 + 150 M) PIRs) ÷ (3 (Period) × 20 (Standard days of each period)) = 370 ÷ 60 = 6.16 M of daily average requirement

> **Note**
> All requirements and calculations are in M (meters), and all calculations are rounded off to two decimal places.

Because the target days of first period in coverage profile is maintained as three days of daily average requirements (6.16 M), the amount to cover this requirement of three days of safety stock (dynamically calculated) is calculated as:

6.16 (Average daily requirement) × 3 (Three days of target safety stock) = 18.51 M of safety stock (period 1)

Figure 13.35 shows that in June 2021, the system created a planned order 7159 for quantity 118.51 M (100 M was the original requirement, while 18.51 M was to account for three days of safety stock).

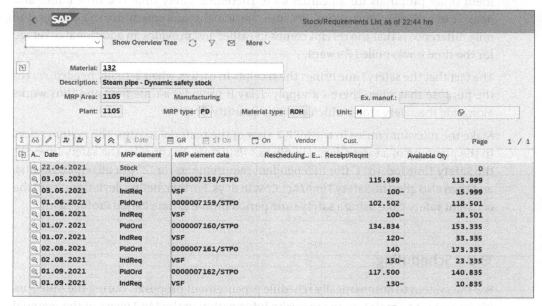

A... Date	MRP element	MRP element data	Rescheduling... E...	Receipt/Reqmt	Available Qty
22.04.2021	Stock				0
03.05.2021	PldOrd	0000007158/STPO		115.999	115.999
03.05.2021	IndReq	VSF		100-	15.999
01.06.2021	PldOrd	0000007159/STPO		102.502	118.501
01.06.2021	IndReq	VSF		100-	18.501
01.07.2021	PldOrd	0000007160/STPO		134.834	153.335
01.07.2021	IndReq	VSF		120-	33.335
02.08.2021	PldOrd	0000007161/STPO		140	173.335
02.08.2021	IndReq	VSF		150-	23.335
01.09.2021	PldOrd	0000007162/STPO		117.500	140.835
01.09.2021	IndReq	VSF		130-	10.835

Figure 13.35 Procurement Proposals Created after MRP Run

Figure 13.36 shows the summarized view, in which the **Targ.** (target) **Stock** column validates the safety stock calculations shown earlier.

A.. Period/Segm...	Plnd ind.reqmts	Requirem...	Receipts	Avail. Quantity	ATP quantity	Actual Coverage	Stat. coverage	T...	Daily Reqmt	Min. covera...	Targ. Stock	Minimum stock	Maximum ...	
Stock				0	0	6.0	0.0	00		0	0	0	0	
03.05.21	100-	0	115.999	15.999	115.999	19.2	3.0	35.333		3	15.999	15.999	0	
01.06.21	100-	0	102.502	18.501	102.502	21.2	3.0	36.167		3	18.501	18.501	0	
01.07.21	120-	0	134.834	33.335	134.834	21.2	5.0	56.667		5	33.335	33.335	0	
02.08.21	150-	0	140	23.335	140	21.2	5.0	54.667		5	23.335	23.335	0	
01.09.21	130-	0	117.500	10.835	117.500	999.9	5.0	52.167		5	10.835	10.835	0	

Figure 13.36 Actual Coverage and Days' Supply

13.8.4   Safety Stock and Safety Time

For days' supply/safety time, the system plans the GR in advance by the period specified as safety time. Thus, planned days' supply of the stock, in fact, corresponds to the number of days specified as safety time. The system shifts back the date of the receipts by the number of working days and also takes the factory calendar into account.

In the **MRP 2** view of the material master, the **Safety Time/Act.Cov.** field is available. The system uses the number of days maintained in this field to simulate the requirements to an earlier date, displaced exactly by that number of days. By using this field, a planner pulls the requirements in so that the MRP run creates the receipts for replenishment order proposals for an earlier date. Therefore, safety time is a time buffer and doesn't increase any quantities. Because the actual requirement doesn't change, the only difference is that the receipt comes in earlier and provides an additional coverage for the time it was pulled forward.

The fact that the safety time brings the receipts in earlier, when actually needed, serves the purpose that when there's a supply delay it provides a time float and thus works alongside the safety stock, which acts as a quantity float.

Make the relevant entries in the **MRP 2** view of the material master. The system refers to the planning of a safety days' supply as *safety time*. To consider the safety time, set the **Safety Time Ind.** to "1" (for independent requirements) or "2" (for all requirements), and then also give the **Safety Time/Act.Cov.** in days. Further, define deviations from the constant safety time using a safety time period profile (**STime Period Profile** field).

13.9   Scheduling

For the system to automatically schedule procurement proposals during the MRP run, it's important to maintain the requisite information in the MRP views of the material master. In the following sections, we'll discuss the options to maintain lead time details for in-house and external procurement that then enable the system to ensure effective planning and scheduling of both in-house and externally procured materials.

13.9.1   Scheduling In-House Production

A planner can schedule the in-house production in the planning run, and the system creates planned orders in two different ways:

- **Basic date determination**
  The system schedules the dates based on the production time defined in the material master.
- **Lead time scheduling**
  The system schedules the dates (and time) based on the information in the routing (or master recipe). Besides a more detailed scheduling result, the MRP run can also generate capacity requirements for the planned orders and perform capacity planning, sequencing, leveling, and scheduling with planned orders.

In an MRP run, select the option for the system to schedule based on basic date determination or lead time scheduling.

13.9.2   Basic Date Determination

Basic date determination is a type of scheduling that determines the basic dates within which production is to take place. For this reason, the in-house production time defined by the basic dates should be greater than or equal to the in-house production time defined by the routing explosion. In an MRP run, the system first calculates the basic order dates from the data in the material master. Then, in detailed planning, it uses the data in the routing. In the context of basic date scheduling, no operation dates are defined and no capacity requirements are generated. The determination of the in-house production time can be carried out as quantity-dependent or quantity-independent. In both cases, the system refers to the entries in the material master and also takes the factory calendar into account.

Tips and Tricks

Use Transactions CA96 and CA97 to update the **In-House Production** parameter in terms of **Days** in the **MRP 2** view of the material master (see Figure 13.37). At the same time, Transaction CA97 helps with updating the **Assembly Scrap** field in the material master, which is taken from the total operation scrap in the routing of material.

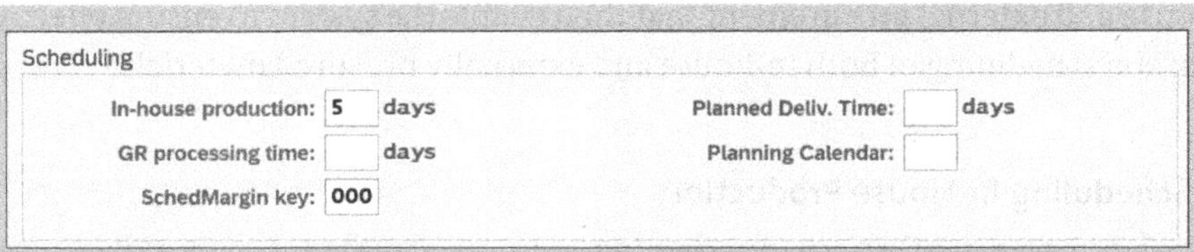

Figure 13.37 In-House Production Time and Scheduling Margin Key

Note

The scheduling margin key (SMK) is the float consisting of the number of days it takes to release a production order and the number of days before and after production when the material finally becomes available. SMKs are buffer times for scheduling.

The next two sections cover in-house production times that are either dependent or independent of the quantity produced.

Quantity-Independent In-House Production Time

In this case, the in-house production time doesn't depend on the order quantity; that is, small quantities require the same amount of time as large quantities. This assumption is valid for planning if the order quantity is limited by the lot sizing procedure, if experience has shown that order quantities usually don't differ very much, or if the daily granularity can cover the fluctuations of the order quantity.

Quantity-Dependent In-House Production Time

If it's no longer possible to ignore the influence of the order quantity on the in-house production time, then calculation of the in-house production time as quantity-dependent is possible. For this purpose, carry out a detailed evaluation of the in-house production times and maintain the **Setup Time**, **Interoperation**, and **Processing Time** fields as well as the **Base Quantity** in the **Work Scheduling** view of the material master (see Figure 13.38). The interoperation time represents a summary of move times, wait times, and safety times. Only the processing time is quantity-dependent because it depends on the base quantity. The setup and interoperation times are quantity-independent and are added to the processing time.

The following formula describes the quantity-dependent in-house production time:

In-house production time = Setup + (Order quantity ÷ Base quantity) × Processing time + Interoperation time

Maintain these parameters either for the quantity-independent or quantity-dependent in-house production time (see Figure 13.38).

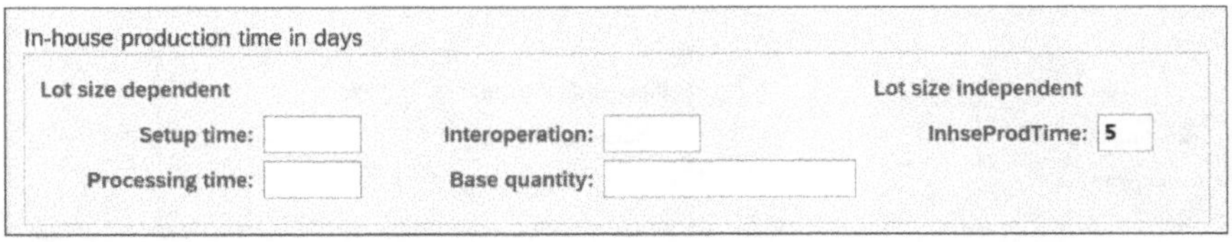

In-house production time in days

Lot size dependent | | Lot size independent
Setup time: [ ] | Interoperation: [ ] | InhseProdTime: [5]
Processing time: [ ] | Base quantity: [ ] |

Figure 13.38 In-House Production Time in Days

13.9.3 Planned Order Dates

In backward scheduling, a planner can derive the dates for the planned order from the requirement date. To do this, they must deduct the various periods, including opening period, in-house production time, and GR processing time, from the requirement date.

In forward scheduling, the system shifts the order start date to the current date, and the opening period is omitted. Forward scheduling occurs in the MRP run only if the requirement date is too close to the current date.

Figure 13.39 shows the **Dates** area for the planned order for the material, in which it takes the various dates into account to arrive at the start and finish dates of the order. Because this is backward scheduling, enter the **End** (order finish) date as "03.05.2021". The system uses SMK 001 to come up with the basic date calculations. All dates are in workdays (Monday through Friday) per the factory calendar.

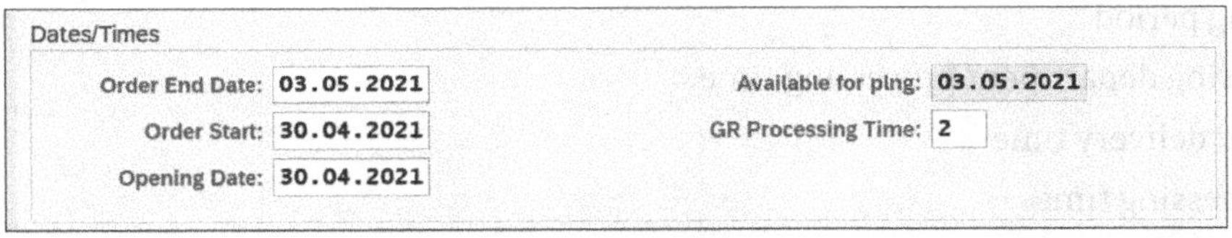

Dates/Times

Order End Date: [03.05.2021] | Available for plng: [03.05.2021]
Order Start: [30.04.2021] | GR Processing Time: [2]
Opening Date: [30.04.2021] |

Figure 13.39 Basic Dates Determination in Planned Order

While remaining on the **Change Planned Order** screen, also perform scheduling by clicking the relevant icon. In scheduling, the system accurately calculates the time it takes to perform each activity at every operation of the work center.

13.9.4 Scheduling External Procurement

When planned orders for externally procured materials or purchase requisitions are created, the system refers to the **Planned Deliv. Time** information in the material master to calculate how long (on average) it will take for the supplier to deliver the requisite material (see Figure 13.40).

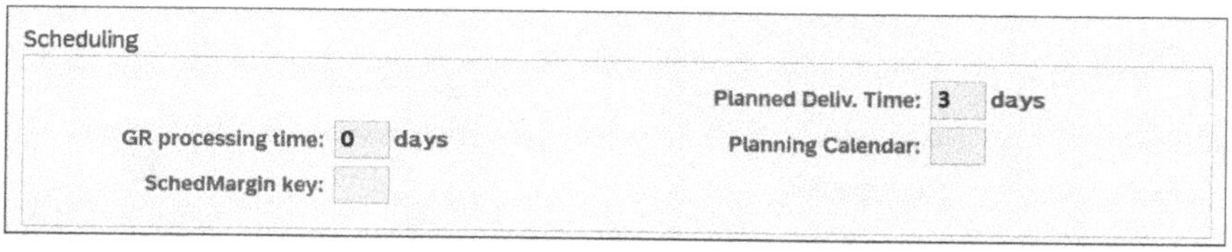

Scheduling

GR processing time: 0   days
SchedMargin key:

Planned Deliv. Time: 3   days
Planning Calendar:

Figure 13.40 Scheduling for Planned Delivery Time

The *planned delivery time* refers to workdays that appear in the factory calendar, provided a planning calendar hasn't been specified. As an alternative to determining the planned delivery time from the material master, a planner can determine the planned delivery time from the purchasing info record. To do this, the scheduling type must be allowed in the plant parameters. Moreover, the source list for the material must contain a relevant entry.

[+]

Tips and Tricks

Use Transaction WPDTC to calculate and compare the planned delivery time of a material (or group of materials) in the material master, purchasing info record, and vendor.

The scheduling process for external procurement is carried out similarly to that of in-house production, except that it uses four periods (for backward scheduling):

- Opening period
- Purchasing department processing time
- Planned delivery time
- GR processing time

These periods are deducted from the requirement date. The purchasing department processing time is maintained in the **Plant Parameters** area (see Figure 13.41). These options are described in Section 13.11.3.

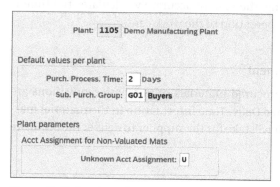

Plant: 1105 Demo Manufacturing Plant

Default values per plant

Purch. Process. Time: 2   Days
Sub. Purch. Group: G01 Buyers

Plant parameters

Acct Assignment for Non-Valuated Mats

Unknown Acct Assignment: U

Figure 13.41 Purchase Processing Time in Configuration

13.9.5   Forward and Backward Scheduling

A distinction between the scheduling types regarding whether to use backward scheduling or forward scheduling can be made, as well as choosing whether production takes place in-house or externally.

Similarly, the following interdependencies also exist for different MRP procedures:

- Materials planned in forecast-based planning
- MRP

For the two MRP procedures, the start dates are known, and the planning should ensure that materials are available on these dates. The determination of basic dates for in-house production and of the release date for purchasing therefore occurs as *backward scheduling* in these MRP procedures. Only if the basic date determined during scheduling is in the past does the system automatically switch to *forward scheduling* from today's date (when the MRP run took place).

In reorder point planning, the dates are defined by means of forward scheduling. After falling short of the reorder point during the MRP run, a planner needs to initiate the procurement activities. The availability date of the materials is determined based on the date of the material shortage.

For external procurement, the *order finish date* corresponds to the delivery date, while the *order start date* corresponds to the release date. Here, the processing time in purchasing, the GR processing time in terms of workdays, and the planned delivery time of the material in terms of calendar days are all taken into account. For external procurement, the system creates either a planned order or a purchase requisition. Purchase requisitions for external procurement plan the external procurement quantity. After the system completes the planning, a planner can convert the planned order into a purchase requisition, and then the purchase requisition is converted into a purchase order. In the initial screen of the planning run, use the **Creation** indicator for purchase requisitions to define whether the system should directly create purchase requisitions or whether it should first create planned orders.

If a delivery plan exists for a material, and the source list contains an MRP-relevant entry, then directly generating delivery schedules in MRP is possible. This applies if there's a scheduling agreement of materials with the vendor. This is achieved by specifying the **Creation** indicator for delivery schedules in the initial screen of the planning run.

13.10   Procurement Proposals

When the MRP is run in the system, the system looks for procurement type information to decide if the ensuing procurement proposals entail in-house production, external procurement, or both. The procurement type in the **MRP 2** view of the material master defines which of the alternatives applies to the material in the plant (see Figure 13.42). If both in-house production and external procurement are allowed, MRP assumes in-house production by default. For example, the raw material is generally not sold or produced in-house, so it makes sense to maintain the procurement type as external. Similarly, the finished product isn't procured but instead is produced in-house, so it makes sense to assign it an in-house procurement type. Finally, the semifinished good may be produced in-house as well as procured externally, so the procurement type as both can be assigned.

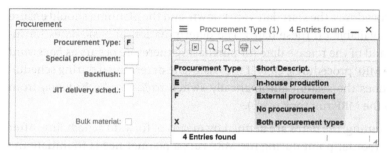

Figure 13.42 Procurement Type in Material Master

In the MRP run, the system creates planned orders. These planned orders are converted into a production order (or process order) for in-house production. For external procurement, the purchase requisitions can be converted into a PO or PO item.

In the following sections, we'll discuss how to interactively create planned orders from a stock/requirements list. We'll also show you how to independently create a purchase requisition for a material and the planned order profile it uses. Finally, you'll see how to check for component availability, including available-to-promise (ATP) logic.

13.10.1 Planned Orders

Planned orders contain an order quantity, a start date, and a finish date. The start and finish dates are the result of the scheduling process and are based on the factory calendar. The availability date can occur after the finish date if a GR processing time has been maintained.

In addition, the planned order contains the dependent requirements from the BOM explosion, as well as organizational data.

There are a couple of ways in which you can manually create planned orders:

- While remaining in the stock/requirements list (Transaction MD04)
- By using Transaction MD11, which is the planned order creation transaction

For this example, we'll show you how to create a planned order in the stock/requirements list. We'll also show how to manually create a planned order using Transaction MD11.

Planned Order Creation with Interactive Planning

To carry out interactive planning by specifically creating planned orders, use Transaction MD11, or use interactive MRP for material and plant via Transaction MD43. In the latter case, the system displays the current requirement and stock situation. The **Planning** button enables a planner to trigger automatic MRP (see Figure 13.43). The system displays the planning result, which is still only a simulation at this point.

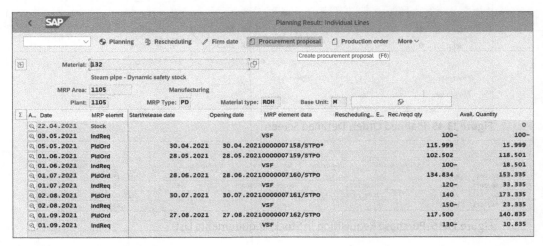

Figure 13.43 Planning Results

The system doesn't create the planned order until the planning results are saved. Moreover, Transaction MD43 also enables a planner to create and reschedule specific procurement proposals manually, when the **Procurement Proposal**, **Production Order**, or **Rescheduling** button is clicked.

Figure 13.43 shows the planning results for material 132 and plant 1105. While remaining in interactive planning, choose **Create Procurement Proposal** (see Figure 13.43). In the **Select Procurement Proposal** popup (see Figure 13.44), select the procurement proposal, which for this example is a purchase requisition with the purchase requisition key (or document type) **NB**. Chose **Continue** or press Enter to open the **Purchase Requisition** creation screen (see Figure 13.45). Enter the details, such as order quantity, start date, and so on, and choose **Continue**. The system incorporates a purchase requisition for the material (see Figure 13.46). For this example, it creates the purchase requisition number 100000237.

Select Procurement Proposal
Planned order
Purchase requisition
Delivery schedule
Plnned order profile: LA
Purch.reqisition key: NB

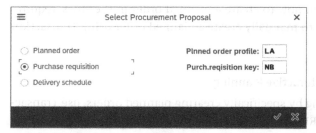

Figure 13.44 Interactively Creating Planned Order

Purchase requisition
Purchase Requisition:
NB
* Quantity: 50
Item cat.: 0
Deliv.date: 25.08.2021
Release Dt: 25.08.2021
Purch.org.: G001
AccAssgnTy:
GR pr.time:
Stor. Loc.:
BOMexpl.no:
Agreement:
Fixed
Fixed vend:

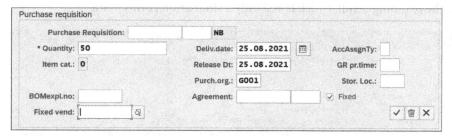

Figure 13.45 Planned Order: Detailed Screen

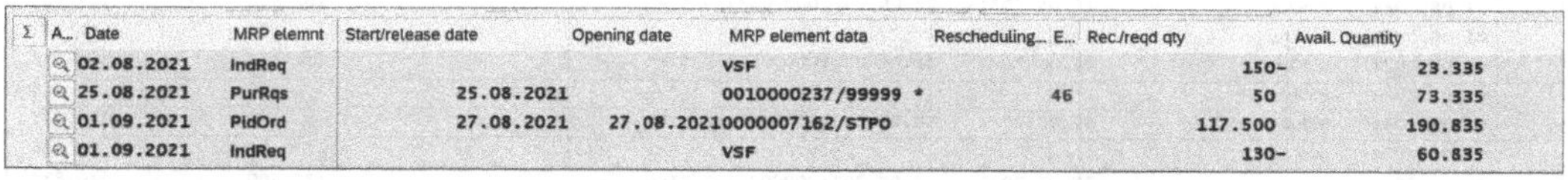

A... Date
MRP elemnt
Start/release date
Opening date
MRP element data
Rescheduling... E...
Rec./reqd qty
Avail. Quantity
02.08.2021 IndReq VSF 150- 23.335
25.08.2021 PurRqs 25.08.2021 0010000237/99999 * 46 50 73.335
01.09.2021 PldOrd 27.08.2021 27.08.20210000007162/STPO 117.500 190.835
01.09.2021 IndReq VSF 130- 60.835

Figure 13.46 Purchase Requisition in Stock/Requirements List

Manual Creation of Planned Order

Use Transaction MD11 to manually create a planned order. On the initial screen that appears, enter "LA" for **Plnned Order Profile**, which supports MTS production. Press [Enter], and provide the material number, the plant, the order quantity, and the basic dates, as shown in Figure 13.47. A manually created planned order is always firmed, and the system denotes it with an asterisk (*) in the stock/requirements list (Transaction MD04). The **Conversion Ind.** checkbox ensures that the planned order can eventually be converted either into a production order (or a process order) for in-house production or into a purchase requisition for external procurement.

Next we perform three functions: check the availability of the material's components to ensure smooth production, check the components' ATP, and also check for any capacity overload. Figure 13.48 shows the BOM (component) details of material 132. Make any desired changes, if needed.

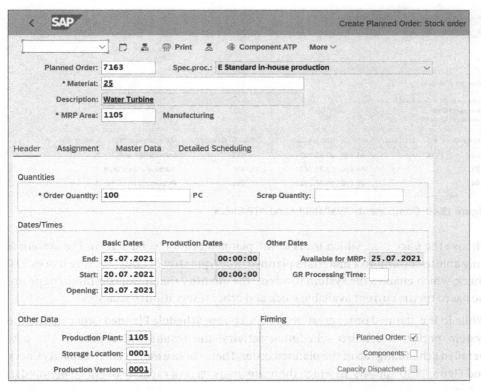

Figure 13.47 Planned Order Creation

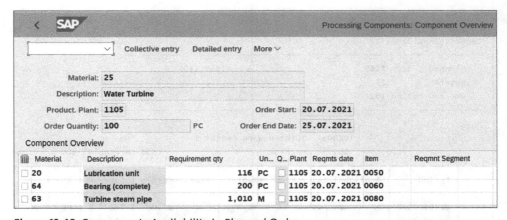

Figure 13.48 Components Availability in Planned Order

Increase the planned order quantity of material 132 to 10,000 units (or any large quantity), and then choose **Comp. ATP** (see Figure 13.47) to open the **Availability Check** screen (see Figure 13.49). Notice that the available component quantities are shown with green lines (if any), while the system reflects the shortages with yellow lines.

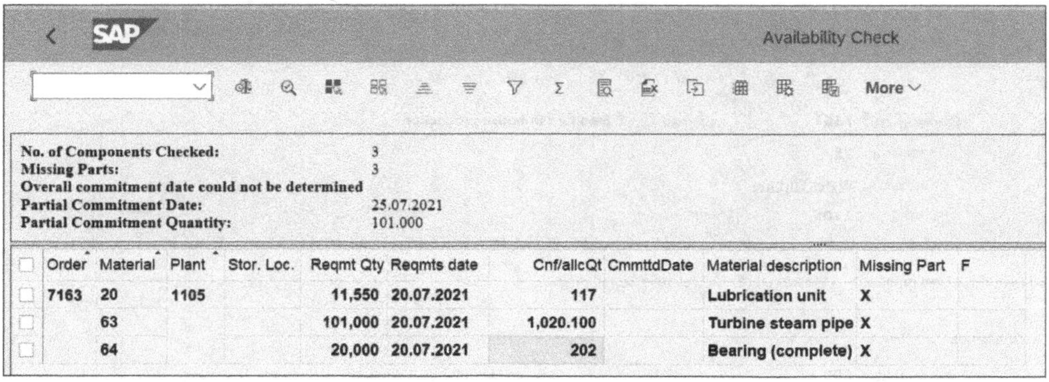

Figure 13.49 Components Availability and ATP Check

Choose the **Back** icon, which leads to the planned order header screen. The system is only able to commit to a material's planned order quantity of 1,000 because it uses ATP check, which enables the system to advise the quantity that it can commit to or promise based on the current available stock and other reservations/issuances.

While in the planned order creation screen, choose **Schedule Planned Order** so that the system performs detailed scheduling activity; the results will appear in the new **Detailed Scheduling** tab in the planned order. Then, choose **More • Edit • Capacity Check** and Figure 13.50 appears, in which there are many days of capacity overload denoted in red rows.

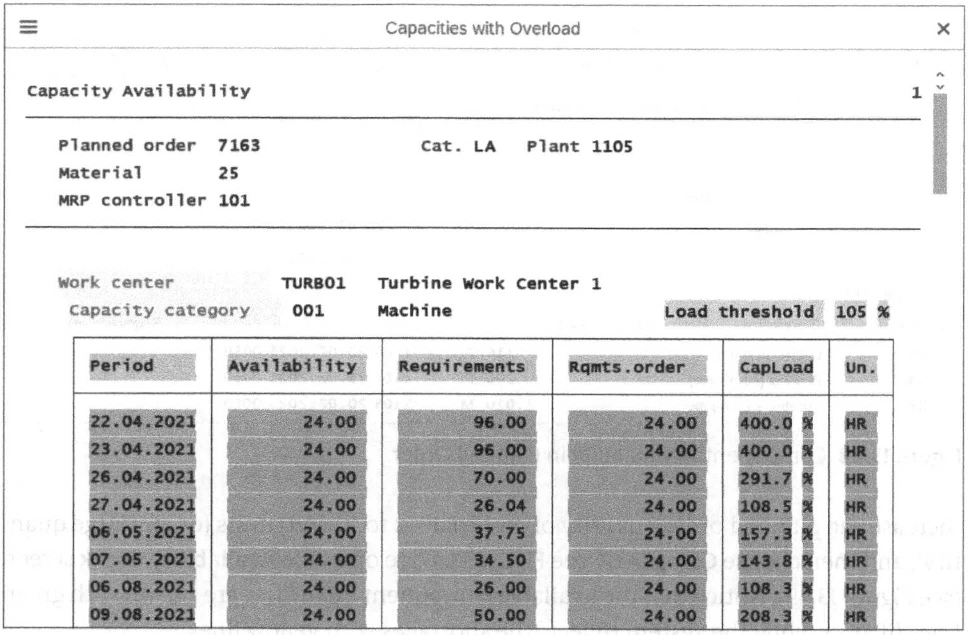

Figure 13.50 Capacity Check

13.10.2   Collective Availability Check of Planned Orders

Transaction MDVP can be used to perform collective availability check of a large number of planned orders (see Figure 13.51). When the selection is executed, a list of planned orders will be displayed with the results of the last availability check, including the **Confirmation Factor** (the percentage of the total order quantity that could be committed), **Committed Date**, and **Committed Quantity** values. A traffic light is shown in the first column to indicate the results of the availability check:

- A green light means the availability check was carried out and the total order quantity was committed.
- A yellow light means the availability check was not yet carried out.
- A red light means the availability check was carried out, but there were missing components.

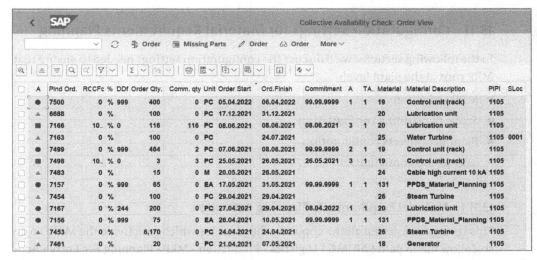

Figure 13.51 Collective Availability Check of Planned Orders

> **Note**
>
> To run the mass availability check as a background job, schedule a job with program RLD05000. In this case, the relevant parameters are in the **Check Mode (Background Processing)** box.
>
> Collective availability checks can also be carried out for planned orders using Transaction COHV.

13.10.3   Planned Order Profile

As already seen during the planned order creation, the user has to enter a planned order profile. To define the order profile, follow menu path **SAP IMG • Production •**

Material Requirements Planning · Procurement Proposals · Planned Orders · Define Order Profile. The order profile is used for both planned orders (**Object Type 1**) and purchase requisitions (**Object Type 2**), and it contains information on the permitted procurement types and special procurement types.

Other available object types include the following:

- Reservation
- Production order
- Simulation order

To create a new planned order profile, choose **New Entries**. Enter a name for the planned order profile and select the object type. Finally, in the detailed screen, enter the procurement type or even special procurement control parameters.

13.11   Configuration Settings for Material Requirements Planning

In the following sections, we'll discuss the configuration settings needed to ensure that MRP runs at the plant level:

- MRP activation
- Scope of planning configuration
- Plant parameters configuration
- MRP group configuration

13.11.1   Material Requirements Planning Activation

This configuration step allows choosing the plant for which to activate the MRP. To do so, follow menu path **SAP IMG · Logistics · Production · MRP · Planning File Entry · Activate MRP and Set Up Planning File**, or use Transaction OMDU.

13.11.2   Scope of Planning Configuration

When running plant-level MRP with Transaction MD01, the scope of MRP generally refers to a specific plant. However, it's possible to also refer to several plants if this is defined in the corresponding planning scope. To define the planning scope, use menu path **SAP IMG · Production · Material Requirements Planning · Planning · Define Scope of Planning for Total Planning**.

13.11.3   Plant Parameters Configuration

MRP can be configured up to the following three levels:

- Plant parameters
- MRP groups
- Material master (MRP views)

Material master settings have higher priority than MRP group parameters, which in turn have higher priority than plant parameters. No setting can be found on all three levels, but they can be on up to two of them. Therefore, plant parameters are usually used to set defaults, which can be overruled if necessary.

The plant parameters of MRP contain a view of numerous configuration settings that are relevant to MRP. The plant parameters screen shows whether certain configuration settings have been maintained or whether they are still in their initial status. Using this screen enables a user to navigate directly to the relevant configuration area.

In the plant parameter configuration step, the following buttons are some of the configurations:

■ **Reference Plant**	■ **Conversion of Planned Orders**
■ **Number ranges**	■ **Dependent Requirements Availability**
■ **Direct Procurement**	■ **Floats (Schedule Margin Keys)**
■ **Available Stock**	■ **BOM Explosion**
■ **Rescheduling**	■ **BOM/Routing Selection**
■ **External Procurement**	

To configure plant parameters, follow menu path **SAP IMG • Logistics • Production • Material Requirements Planning • Plant Parameters**, or use Transaction OPPQ. Click the **Maintain** button. A popup appears; enter the **Plant** as "1105", then click the **Maintain** icon. A detailed screen appears for maintaining individual plant parameters.

13.11.4   Material Requirements Planning Group Configuration

Materials can be grouped together by using MRP groups and then assigning the MRP groups in the **MRP 1** view of the material master. Each of the MRP groups can have its own set of MRP parameters. When working with an MRP group, the following options that are specific to a material or group of materials are available:

- Strategy group
- Settlement type and horizon
- Rescheduling horizon and planning horizon
- Production storage location selection
- Conversion order types of planned orders
- Planning horizon
- Planning time fence and roll-forward periods

- BOM and task list selection IDs
- Direct procurement parameters
- Planned order scheduling parameters
- Start number of days allowed in the past
- Availability checking groups
- Period split for distributing the independent requirement
- Maximum MRP intervals
- Availability of safety stock for MRP
- BOM explosion
- Direct procurement of nonstock items
- Creation indicators for purchase requisitions
- Scheduling of external procurement according to the information record
- Checking rule for dependent demand

To configure MRP groups, follow menu path **SAP IMG · Logistics · Production · Material Requirements Planning · MRP Groups · Carry out Overall Maintenance of MRP Groups**, or use Transaction OPPR.

On the initial screen, enter the **Plant** as "1105", and click the **Maintain** button. In the popup that appears, enter **MRP Group** "0001", and click the **Maintain** button. Figure 13.52 and Figure 13.53 show part of the **MRP Group** detailed screen for maintaining individual parameters of the MRP group.

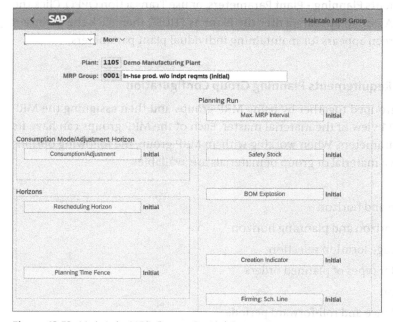

Figure 13.52 Maintain MRP Group: Partial Screen 1

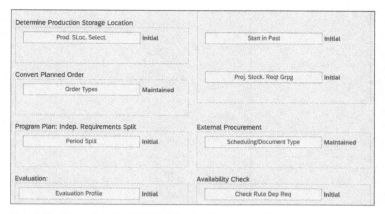

Figure 13.53 Maintain MRP Group: Partial Screen 2

When a MRP group is configured and saved, assign it in the **MRP 1** view of the material master (see Figure 13.54).

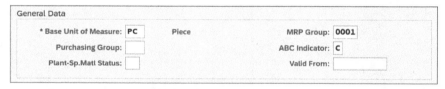

Figure 13.54 MRP Group in Material Master

> **Note**
>
> While this example covers the maintenance of an MRP group, it's also possible to create a new MRP group, delete an existing MRP group, or copy an MRP group from an existing one. You can also assign the MRP group to a material type by following menu path **SAP IMG • Logistics • Production • Material Requirements Planning • MRP Groups • Define MRP Group for Each Material Type**.

13.12 Summary

A company can take enormous advantage of the MRP functionality in the SAP system to help improve and optimize the business processes. A planner can plan all types of materials, including high-, medium-, and low-value materials. The various lot-sizing procedures and safety stocks ensure that there's neither an overstock nor a stock-out situation. The planning calendar helps a planner plan materials that are specific to particular calendars only.

The next chapter covers running MRP in the SAP system.

Figure 13.53 Maintain MRP Group, Partial Screen 2

When a MRP group is configured and saved, assign it in the MRP 1 view of the material master (see Figure 13.54).

Figure 13.54 MRP Group in Material Master

Note

While this example covers the maintenance of an MRP group, it is also possible to create a new MRP group, delete an existing MRP group, or copy an MRP group from an existing one. You can also assign the MRP group to a material type by following menu path SAP IMG • Logistics • Production • Material Requirements Planning • MRP Groups • Define MRP Group for Each Material Type.

13.12 Summary

A comprehensive set of tools are offered as part of the MRP functionality in the SAP system to help improve and optimize the business processes. A planner can plan all types of materials, including high-, medium-, and low-value materials. The method for setting procedures and safety stocks ensure that there's a buffer to reduce out-of-stock situations. The planning calendar helps a planner plan for material for a specific time frame to meet demand.

The next chapter covers running MRP in the SAP system.

Chapter 14
Running Material Requirements Planning

The material requirements planning foundations built in the previous chapter can now be put to use by running MRP Live and evaluating the planning results. Storage location planning can be tailored with MRP area functionality.

During the course of an SAP S/4HANA implementation project, a question is often raised regarding which of the many planning tools available in SAP to use to make planning and operations more efficient. Although there's no "right answer" that fits all situations, it's best to strive to use as many tools as possible to get a greater return on investment from the SAP S/4HANA system. The follow-on question is how often these planning tools should be used. Again, effort needs to be made to maintain a balance while using a planning tool.

For example, it doesn't make sense to run material requirements planning (MRP) very frequently as doing so disturbs procurement and production schedules. But not running MRP as often as required is also to be discouraged because without running MRP, the system won't be able to calculate the net requirement situation of each material, and thus the company risks stock-outs or even overstock situations. A logical approach to using these planning tools is to consider long-, medium-, and short-term planning horizons and then leverage these tools.

For example, based on historical consumptions of materials, forecasting can be used for a longer-term planning horizon. Then, either long-term planning (LTP) or predictive material and resource planning (pMRP) can be used to simulate the forecast figures to see if the company has the resources to produce or store the materials. When LTP results are found satisfactory, these can be used for rough-cut planning or even sales and operations planning (S&OP) for an eventual transfer to demand management, which may only be used for the medium-range planning horizon. Finally, master production scheduling (MPS) for critical materials followed by MRP for regular materials and then capacity requirements planning (CRP) can be used as short-term planning tools to ensure smoother operations management.

There's no constraint or limitation on using any planning tool at any time, so these can be used as standalone tools or together in a logical and structured manner.

MRP consists of the following steps, as shown in Figure 14.1:

❶ Check the planning file to avoid planning materials that aren't needed.

❷ Determine the material shortage quantity (or surplus quantity) by carrying out a net requirements calculation.

❸ Calculate the procurement quantity to include lot sizes for planned orders or purchase requisitions.

❹ Schedule basic dates or lead time (for in-house production only).

❺ Select the source of supply by determining the procurement proposal.

❻ Determine the requirement of subordinate parts on the basis of the bill of materials (BOM) explosion by carrying out a dependent requirements determination.

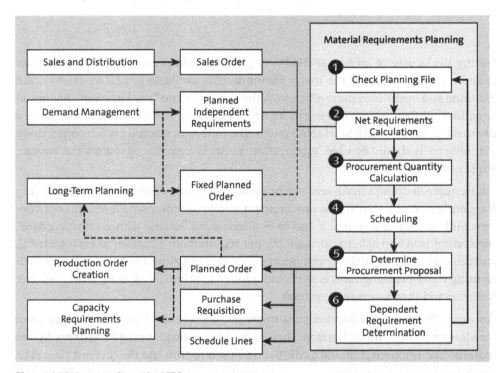

Figure 14.1 Process Steps in MRP

Now that we've covered the basics of MRP, we need to bring together all the concepts and understanding developed previously in Chapter 11, Chapter 12, and Chapter 13. We'll put all this know-how to actual and practical use in this chapter by showing how to run MRP Live, followed by evaluating the planning results. Next, we cover how to configure and use a planning calendar. This is then followed by covering configuration and business processes of using the MRP planning areas. We'll also briefly discuss classic MRP, as well as different types of planning runs.

Let's begin with MRP Live.

14.1 MRP Live

MRP Live is the new version of MRP, developed to achieve maximum performance when using an SAP HANA database. In MRP Live, the entire MRP logic is carried out directly in SAP HANA, including database selection. This means that all the MRP steps, from net requirements calculation to the creation of the replenishment proposal, are carried out in SAP HANA.

Let's first discuss how MRP Live differs from the classic MRP transactions, including the main functionalities, restrictions, and transactions available for MRP Live, compared with classic MRP.

The new Transaction MD01N was created specifically to run MRP Live. In classic MRP, there were different transactions available to execute a total MRP run (Transaction MD01); a single-item, multilevel MRP run (Transaction MD02); and a single-item, single-level MRP run (Transaction MD03). Transaction MD01N replaces all of those classic MRP transactions and provides more flexible selection criteria with more fields and options for selection, as shown in Figure 14.2.

However, it's not possible to replace multilevel, make-to-order (MTO) planning (Transaction MD50) and individual project planning (Transaction MD51) with MRP Live. For such business scenarios, the classic MRP transactions should be used, or the header material should be planned within MRP Live, with the **BOM Components** checkbox selected so that all the components are also checked.

Transaction MD01N was also designed via the simplification concept. Therefore, compared with the classic MRP transactions, some changes are as follows:

- The creation indicator for purchase requisitions and schedule lines doesn't exist in Transaction MD01N. This means that MRP Live directly creates purchase requisitions for materials procured externally or creates a schedule list.

- The creation indicator for MRP lists is also not available in MRP Live for performance reasons. This means that MRP lists aren't created by MRP Live. If it's necessary for a planner to create MRP lists, the material should be planned with the classic MRP transactions (e.g., Transaction MD01). Otherwise, use the stock/requirements list (Transaction MD04) to analyze the MRP results.

- The scope of planning is no longer necessary because it's now possible to select one or more plants in Transaction MD01N. MRP Live can also automatically determine the sequence of plants for planning, so the scope of planning becomes obsolete with MRP Live.

- Processing key NETPL (net change in the planning horizon) isn't available in Transaction MD01N. This processing key was created to restrict the MRP run on the planning horizon for a faster MRP run. Because the MRP performance is much better with MRP Live, this processing key and the planning horizon concept are obsolete.

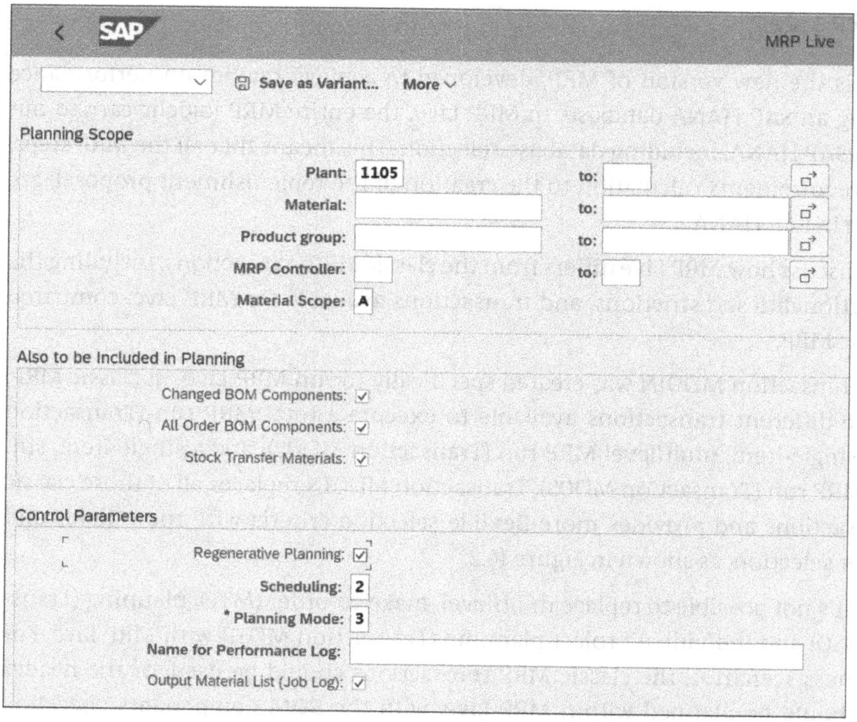

Figure 14.2 MRP Live

- The flag to determine if parallel processing should be used isn't available in MRP Live; parallel processing is automatically triggered by the system. In addition, it's no longer required to define the destinations for parallel processing in Transaction OMIQ because they will be determined automatically based on the server group.

- The user exit key and user exit parameter fields aren't available. In the classic MRP transactions, user exits SAPLM61C_001 and EXIT_SAPMM61X_ 001 allowed the user to select which materials would be planned by MRP, and their most common use was to plan all the materials of a specific MRP controller. In Transaction MD01N, the MRP controller is already available as a selection criterion. If a different selection criterion is necessary, it's possible to use the product group or the multiple material selection as a selection criterion.

Besides changes related to the transaction design, there are some changes to the MRP process that must be considered:

- **Total requirements aren't supported on MRP Live.**
  Just like the classic MRP transactions, total dependent and sales requirements aren't supported on MRP Live.

- **Subcontracting on MRP Live is only supported with MRP areas.**
  In classic MRP transactions, a separated planning segment is created for each vendor

in a subcontracting scenario. In MRP Live, however, this functionality is no longer available. This means that the subcontracting scenario must be mapped with MRP areas. Therefore, you need to create an MRP area for each vendor in configuration and assign this MRP area to the materials that will use the subcontracting scenario. See Section 14.4 for more on MRP planning areas.

- **Replenishment proposals aren't reusable.**
  In classic MRP transactions, unfirmed planned orders and purchase requisitions weren't necessarily changed during the MRP run in the case of a quantity or date change. Now, in MRP Live, if the date or quantity of a replenishment proposal must be changed by MRP, the replenishment proposal is deleted and a new one is created. Basically, this means that the number of existing planned orders and purchase requisitions may be changed more frequently in MRP Live than in the classic MRP.

> **Note**
>
> As MRP Live is a new material planning tool, some very specific settings aren't yet implemented; a complete overview of those restrictions can be found in SAP Note 1914010.

Under very specific scenarios, the number of replenishment proposals generated by MRP Live can differ from the number of replenishment proposals generated by classic MRP. This happens, for example, when using a reorder point MRP type with external requirements (e.g., MRP type V1) or a safety stock. This happens because, in classic MRP, the safety stock (or reorder point) quantity is added to the replenishment proposal created to cover the first requirement. In MRP Live, on the other hand, a separate replenishment proposal is created to cover the safety stock. Even though there may be more replenishment proposals in MRP Live, the total quantity of the replenishment proposals generated should be the same as the total quantity in classic MRP. This will be shown with an example in Section 14.4.

> **Note**
>
> A new set of MRP applications collectively called the *MRP simulation cockpit* was delivered in the latest versions of SAP S/4HANA. These applications are enhanced, and new applications were created as an alternate way to evaluate MRP results. For the SAP Fiori applications of the MRP simulation cockpit, a strong focus is placed on identifying and resolving shortages that may lead to supply chain disruptions. Refer to Chapter 24, where several of these apps are discussed in detail.

To access MRP Live, follow menu path **SAP Menu • Production • MRP • Planning • MRP Live**, or use Transaction MD01N (see Figure 14.2).

There are far more materials planning options available in MRP Live, such as selecting a specific group of materials and saving them as a variant. Planning can happen via product group and MRP controller, and you can even choose a material scope to decide whether MRP Live is to run on master production scheduling (MPS) materials only, MRP materials only, or both. BOM components can also be planned. Enter the parameters shown in Figure 14.2, and click **Execute**.

Whenever MRP Live finds a material planning setting that is still not supported, it automatically switches to the classic MRP logic to plan without further problems. However, this isn't the best approach to achieve optimal performance with MRP Live. A planner can identify for which materials a restriction was found and classic MRP was executed by analyzing the MRP Live results in Transaction MD01N. On the MRP Live results screen, the system displays how many materials were planned directly in SAP HANA and how many were planned using the classic MRP logic. By clicking the **Materials with Messages** button on the results screen (see Figure 14.3), a planner can see exactly which materials could not be planned with MRP Live and which restrictions caused them to be planned via classic MRP logic.

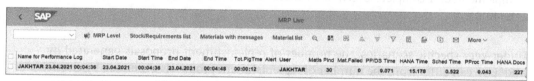

Name for Performance Log	Start Date	Start Time	End Date	End Time	Tot.PlgTme	Alert User	Matls Plnd	Mat.Failed	PP/DS Time	HANA Time	Sched Time	PProc Time	HANA Docs
JAKHTAR 23.04.2021 00:04:36	23.04.2021	00:04:36	23.04.2021	00:04:48	00:00:12	JAKHTAR	30	0	9.071	15.178	0.522	0.043	227

Figure 14.3 Planning Results from MRP Live

Figure 14.4 shows that eight materials were planned at the finished goods level (those materials with **000** in the **Cde** column) via MRP Live, while no materials were planned at code level **001**. One material was planned using classic MRP; the details are shown in Figure 14.5.

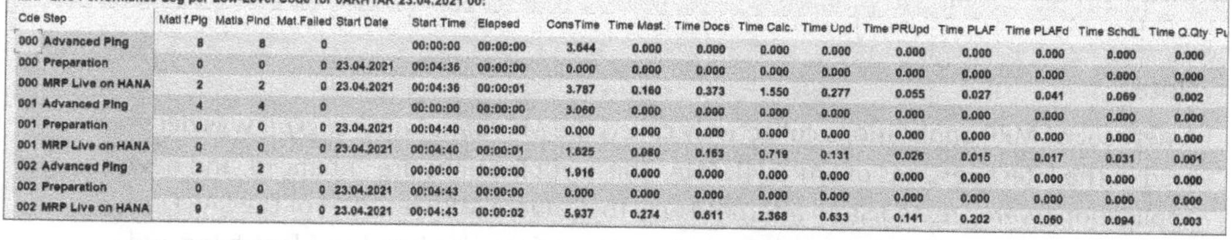

MRP Live Performance Log per Low-Level Code for JAKHTAR 23.04.2021 00:

Cde Step	Matl f.Plg	Matls Plnd	Mat.Failed	Start Date	Start Time	Elapsed	ConsTime	Time Mast.	Time Docs	Time Calc.	Time Upd.	Time PRUpd	Time PLAF	Time PLAFd	Time Schdl	Time Q.Qty	Pl
000 Advanced Plng	8	8	0		00:00:00	00:00:00	3.644	0.000	0.000	0.000	0.000	0.000	0.000	0.000	0.000	0.000	
000 Preparation	0	0	0	23.04.2021	00:04:36	00:00:00	0.000	0.000	0.000	0.000	0.000	0.000	0.000	0.000	0.000	0.000	
000 MRP Live on HANA	2	2	0	23.04.2021	00:04:36	00:00:01	3.787	0.160	0.373	1.550	0.277	0.055	0.027	0.041	0.069	0.002	
001 Advanced Plng	4	4	0		00:00:00	00:00:00	3.060	0.000	0.000	0.000	0.000	0.000	0.000	0.000	0.000	0.000	
001 Preparation	0	0	0	23.04.2021	00:04:40	00:00:00	0.000	0.000	0.000	0.000	0.000	0.000	0.000	0.000	0.000	0.000	
001 MRP Live on HANA	0	0	0	23.04.2021	00:04:40	00:00:01	1.825	0.080	0.163	0.719	0.131	0.026	0.015	0.017	0.031	0.001	
002 Advanced Plng	2	2	0		00:00:00	00:00:00	1.916	0.000	0.000	0.000	0.000	0.000	0.000	0.000	0.000	0.000	
002 Preparation	0	0	0	23.04.2021	00:04:43	00:00:00	0.000	0.000	0.000	0.000	0.000	0.000	0.000	0.000	0.000	0.000	
002 MRP Live on HANA	9	9	0	23.04.2021	00:04:43	00:00:02	5.937	0.274	0.611	2.368	0.533	0.141	0.202	0.060	0.094	0.003	

Figure 14.4 Materials Planned via MRP Live and Classic MRP

Figure 14.5 shows the materials with messages after the MRP Live execution. Clicking the **Solve Issue** button will redirect the planner to the master data configuration where this restriction is found (generally the material master) so that the settings can be changed to avoid this restriction and ensure that the material is planned with MRP Live.

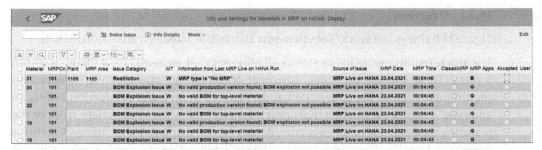

Figure 14.5 Materials with Message from MRP Live

After running MRP, the materials planner spends more time in the stock/requirements list evaluating the supply-demand situation of the material and taking actions where required.

14.2 Stock/Requirements List

We'll now briefly explain a few of the available analysis and evaluation functions of the stock/requirements list after an MRP Live run. The stock/requirements list is not only a materials evaluation tool but also an intuitive dashboard that a materials planner can use to create, change, or delete planning elements.

From accessing the planning, production, sales, or procurement details of either an individual material or collectively several materials, the stock/requirements list details the parameters, such as MRP type, lot size, or the replenishment lead time, used in material planning. The logical and structured grouping of exception messages enables a materials planner to immediately see which materials need urgent action, such as expediting procurement or production to meet customer orders or even canceling or delaying procurement or production orders that are no longer needed as early as originally planned. Evaluation tools, such as stock overview or day's supply, provide planners with complete visibility into demand and supply situations of materials.

> **Stock Overview**
>
> There is another important report—the stock overview report—that isn't discussed in this section. The stock overview report provides the current stock situation of the material and is quite helpful for material planners. Use Transaction MMBE to access the stock overview report. In the initial parameter screen, enter the **Material** number, together with the **Plant**, and select other parameters, such as **Storage Location** or **Special Stock Indicator**. With the stock overview report, a planner can only view the stock details of one material at a time. Choose **Execute** or press F8.
>
> If there's a need to view the warehouse stock of a large number of materials all at the same time, then use Transaction MB52.

14.2.1   Overview

Figure 14.6 shows the **Stock/Requirements List: Initial Screen** (Transaction MD04).

The stock/requirements list describes all MRP-relevant elements for a material within a plant. These include the stock, customer requirements and planned independent requirements (PIRs), dependent demands, planned orders, and production orders. In addition, it shows parameters that are relevant to MRP, such as the safety stock or the planning time fence. For all elements, details can be displayed and changed, if this is permitted. Usually, the system displays the availability date of a goods receipt (GR). But it's also possible to display the GR date instead—for example, to plan actions in case of delays. We'll also discuss the following options available in the stock/requirements list, along with several other options:

- Display of exception messages
- Jump into the detail view
- Jump into the order report
- Display GR date or availability date
- Show the replenishment lead time
- Change the MRP elements

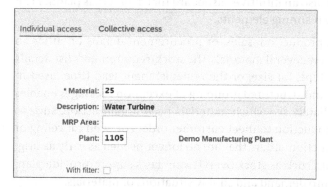

Figure 14.6 Initial Screen of Stock/Requirements List: Individual Access

Figure 14.7 shows the stock/requirements list, and clicking the **Expand Header Details** icon on the top-left of the screen will reveal all the parameters used by the system in planning the material. In other words, there's no longer a need to separately view the MRP parameters in the material master; you can do so while remaining in the stock/requirements list.

Let's evaluate some more details shown in Figure 14.7. On **23.04.2021** (April 23, 2021), the opening **Stock** of material **25** in the **Available Qty** column is **795**. There are quite a few customer orders, as well as a few production and planned orders.

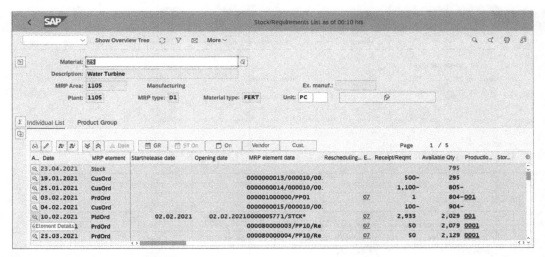

Figure 14.7 Stock/Requirements List

To interactively convert a planned order into a production order, click the **Element Details** icon (the magnifying glass) next to **MRP Element 5771** in Figure 14.7, and the popup shown in Figure 14.8 will appear.

Figure 14.8 offers more details about the system-generated (automatic) planned order **5771** for quantity **2,933**. The MRP controller can both display this planned order and make any manual changes if needed. Further, it's also possible to convert this planned order into a production order. To do so, click **-> Prod.Ord.** and Figure 14.9 appears.

Figure 14.8 Converting Planned Order into Production Order

Figure 14.9 shows a production order; clicking the **Assignment** tab here will show the automatically assigned planned order number **5771** in the lower half of the screen (not shown). Save the production order, and the system will create a production order number, which in this example is **80000106**.

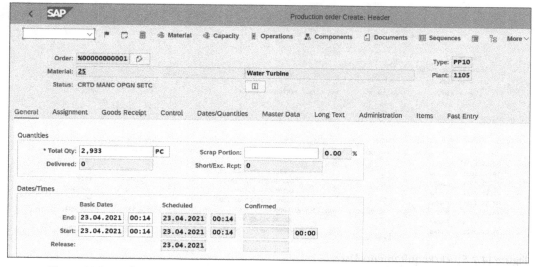

Figure 14.9 Production Order Created from Planned Order Conversion

Figure 14.10 is the stock/requirements list (Transaction MD04) after conversion of the planned order **5771** into a production order. Production order **80000106** is displayed for a quantity of **2,993**.

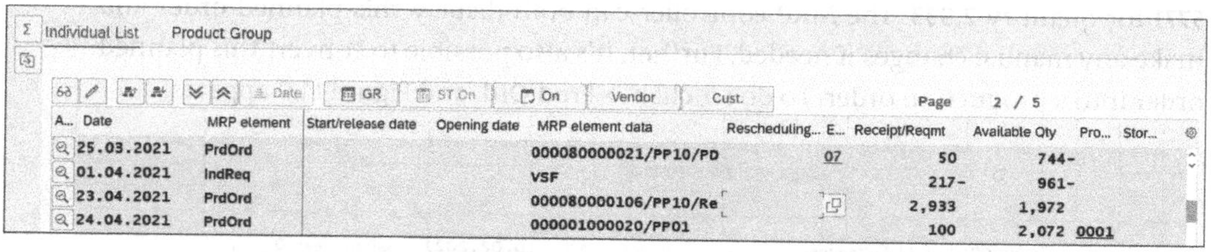

A... Date	MRP element	Start/release date	Opening date	MRP element data	Rescheduling...	E...	Receipt/Reqmt	Available Qty	Pro...	Stor...
25.03.2021	PrdOrd			000080000021/PP10/PD	07		50	744–		
01.04.2021	IndReq			VSF			217–	961–		
23.04.2021	PrdOrd			000080000106/PP10/Re			2,933	1,972		
24.04.2021	PrdOrd			000001000020/PP01			100	2,072	0001	

Figure 14.10 Converted Production Order in Stock/Requirements List

Refer to the initial screen of Transaction MD04, as shown in Figure 14.6, but this time choose **Collective Access**, and enter any of the several selection parameters, such as **MRP Controller 101**. Doing so will bring up a list of materials for which MRP controller 101 is responsible for planning. Transaction MD07 can also be used for collective access of stock/requirements list.

14.2.2   Traffic Lights for Days' Supply and Receipt Days' Supply

The red, yellow, and green traffic lights in both Transaction MD06 and Transaction MD07 in Figure 14.11 give a quick indication in the list view of potential overstocking or understocking:

- A red light will appear if a demand in the past is still unfulfilled. How far in the past this demand element lies is specified by the negative days of supply shown in a column in the list display.

- A green light doesn't mean everything is in order. It can also mean that there is more stock than needed to fulfill requirements in the future. Green lights, therefore, can alert a planner if there is too much inventory held.

- Yellow lights are assigned to materials for which demand and supply are in perfect balance.

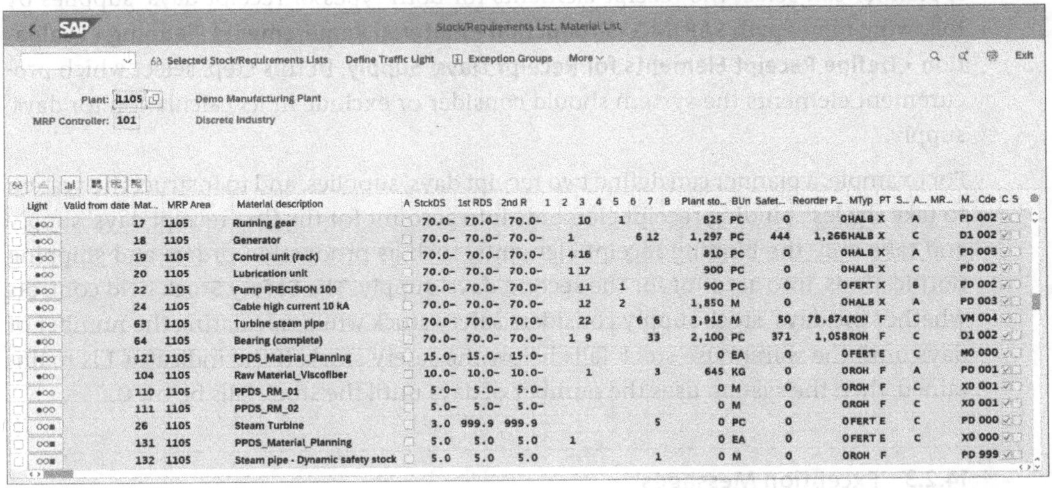

Figure 14.11 Stock/Requirements List: Collective Access

SAP allows changes to the traffic light settings to tell the system when a material's planning should be alerted with a red or green light and what range is acceptable for an item with balanced demand and supply.

A traffic light system can be developed to provide relevant and useful information. For example, consider setting up the list so that traffic lights are sorted from the most urgent material handling down to long-term opportunities. One such scenario can involve setting the monitor so that materials with stock days of supply below safety levels (and not only after they are overdue) have a red light. Anything that has receipts coming in to cover demand within an acceptable time frame gets a yellow light, and anything that has too many receipts coming too early—and which therefore needs to be expedited out—gets a green light.

The traffic lights can also be used for exception messages: the exception groups considered more important are sorted above the ones that aren't so urgent, combined with the ranges of coverage.

In the stock/requirements list or in the MRP list, the system calculates the number of days on the time axis for which the existing stock of material can fulfill the requirements.

Receipt days' supply indicates how long the current stock and the expected receipts can cover the requirements. The system offers two different types of receipt days' supply:

- Receipt days' supply 1
- Receipt days' supply 2

A planner can select the receipt elements for both types of receipt days' supplies by following menu path **SAP IMG • Production • Material Requirements Planning • Evaluation • Define Receipt Elements for Receipt Days' Supply**. In this step, select which procurement elements the system should consider or exclude in its calculation for days' supply.

For example, a planner can define two receipt days' supplies, and to instruct the system to take the less binding receipt elements into account for the first receipt days' supply and take only the binding receipt elements, such as production orders and shipping notifications, into account for the second days' supply. The **Safety Stock** field controls whether the days' stock supply considers safety stock while calculating the number of days until the warehouse stock falls below the safety stock. If the indicator 1 is maintained, then the system uses the number of days until the stock falls below 0.

14.2.3 Exception Messages

The system generates exception messages in MRP when it encounters alerts during the planning run. The system displays exception messages for each relevant procurement element in the stock/requirements list (refer to the **Exception** column in Figure 14.10). The exception elements can also be viewed by choosing **More • Edit • Find in the List**.

The main elements of exception messages are priority, assignment to group, suppress message, create MRP list, and text of exception message. Exception messages are displayed primarily in four transactions:

- Transaction MD04 to display the dynamically created stock requirements situations for an individual material
- Transaction MD05 to display the MRP list, a snapshot from the time when the MRP run last planned the material
- Transaction MD06 to display a collective list of materials with their respective MRP lists
- Transaction MD07 to display a collective list of materials with their respective stock/requirements situations

> **Tips and Tricks**
>
> The text of exception messages can be changed to denote the importance of an exception. For example, changing the text to "Warning: stock fallen below safety stock level" will help a planner quickly segregate exception messages with a warning from exception messages with information. To make limited changes to the existing exception messages, follow configuration menu path **SAP IMG** • **Production** • **Material Requirements Planning** • **Evaluation** • **Exception Messages** • **Define and Group Exception Messages**.

Let's now briefly discussion the eight different exception message groups.

Group 1 Exceptions

An MRP run generates exception messages in group 1 when the date that was determined using the opening period is in the past. For example, the start date of a planned order might be November 15. That is the date when the planned order must be converted to a process order so that the goods are produced on time to fulfill a demand. From this date, the system then subtracts the working days—for example, four days—from the opening period (the number of days maintained for the opening period in the scheduling margin key) and arrives at the opening date of the planned order, which in this example will be November 11. If the planned order isn't converted to production order after November 11, the system will display a message in this group. In other words, it's an extra time buffer to alert the planner to convert an order proposal into a fixed supply element.

Group 2 Exceptions

This group contains exception messages that inform you about missing the release date to convert a purchase requisition or planned order into a PO or production order, respectively. The release date can be seen in Transaction MD04. There are actually two hidden columns—one for the opening date and the other one for the release date. If the **Start/Release Date** and **Opening Date** columns aren't visible in Transaction MD04, then be sure to make them visible. Move the cursor so that the two lines can be seen, and then drag the columns open. These columns provide valuable information about opening and conversion dates for the order proposals.

The release date was calculated by subtracting the lead time from the requirements date (backward scheduling); therefore, it represents the latest date an order proposal has to start (fixed, converted, a PO sent out to supplier, a production order sentd to the shop floor) so that the material can be received on the required date. If this date is missed, on-time material availability might not happen, thereby causing service levels to degrade.

As in group 1, an exception informs the user of a new order proposal, 03, and an exception informs the user of an existing order proposal. This time, however, it's the start (or release) date that is relevant. To address why the **03 New, and start date in the past** message is issued, evaluate possible lead time errors in the master data, or look at the availability checking rule, which might have allowed a requirement to drop in within the replenishment lead time. It's also possible to maintain configuration settings so the system switches to forward scheduling from today's date onward in case the start date falls in the past. The **06 Start date in the past** message informs the user of an existing order proposal that has missed its conversion date. To address these errors, get all these elements up to date and release them on time with the correct lead time, which will determine the correct start/release date. If there's a need to reschedule an order proposal instead of release it, then check the basic data setup to see if it's faulty and doesn't generate the correct dates automatically. When exception **63 Production start before order start** appears, it's due to incorrect configuration settings. The system has suggested a production start that lies before the order start in lead time scheduling. This message can be fixed by selecting the option to adjust the basic dates in the scheduling parameters for the order proposals (Transaction OPU5).

Group 3 Exceptions

Group 3 messages reflect a more serious problem as they not only inform you about missing the start/release date of the order, but indicate that the finish date has passed as well. With the **04 New, and finish date in the past** message, the MRP run keeps trying to adjust the proposals to match supply with demand. Dates are adjusted with new order proposal creation, which creates a bullwhip effect in the planning process. The exception monitoring needs to be prioritized to ensure finish dates in the past don't happen at all or occur at an absolute minimum.

The **07 Finish date in the past** message is very critical because it alerts the user of an impending outage, unless there's enough safety stock to get through the demand that's waiting for that order to be received. Message 07 can come from a purchase requisition, a planned order, a PO, or a production/process order. In all cases, an immediate action is warranted. Under no circumstances should there be orders in the system for which the finish date has passed. This actually means that the finish date (or the GR date, in the case of a purchase order) lies in the past.

Also part of group 3 for late finishing is exception message **64 Production finish after order finish**, which informs the user of an inconsistency in scheduling. The production finish, which was calculated using the routing's lead time, lies after the basic date (calculated from the material master's lead time). Again, this is because the basic dates aren't adjusted—due to a setting in configuration Transaction OPU5.

Group 4 Exceptions

Exceptions from group 4 are general messages and are for information only to address master data or configuration inconsistencies. These exceptions can only be in Transaction MD06 (Collective MRP Lists), not in Transaction MD07 (Collective Stock/Requirements Situation), because the system can't tell when the last planning run was as the dynamically created stock/requirements situation (in Transaction MD07) has no time stamp and therefore the system doesn't know the new from the old.

The following are some of the exception messages in group 4:

- **01 Newly Created Order Proposal**
  An order proposal was newly created in the last planning run. This message is generated if there is new demand in the system or when MRP runs use planning mode 3 (delete planning dates).

- **42 Order Proposal Has Been Changed**
  The order proposal was changed in the planning run, either because of a change in demand situation or because of changes made in the master data settings after the last planning run.

- **44 Order Proposal Re-exploded**
  The order proposal's BOM was re-exploded in the planning run, and new dependent requirements were created.

- **46 Order Proposal Has Been Manually Changed**
  The order proposal was manually changed in the single-item planning run.

Group 5 Exceptions

Group 5 exception messages result from errors in the BOM explosion during the MRP run. Message **50 No BOM Exists** means there is most likely no BOM for the material, or, in sales order processing, a sales order BOM could be missing. If the MRP run generates a planned order to cover demand, but it can't find a BOM suitable for the order, message **52 No BOM Selected** appears. It could be that there are BOMs assigned to the material, but the selection criteria can't assign the appropriate one to the planned order.

If exception message **53 No BOM Explosion Due to Missing Config.** appears, it's due to missing configuration and customization because the line items in the BOM didn't receive dependent requirements.

Message **54 No Valid Run Schedule** is an exception when using repetitive manufacturing. A run schedule is like a planned order, and the correct quantities couldn't be determined by the MRP run.

Group 6 Exceptions

Group 6 exceptions result from an availability check that evaluates stock shortages or excess stock. All messages in this group are related to quantities and stock levels. For example, message **25 Excess Stock** points to the planned available stock's coverage to be greater than the maximum stock coverage specified in the range of coverage profile. Because the range of coverage profile is used to keep a check on minimum, target, or maximum stock levels, the MRP run checks to see inventory below the defined levels. However, if there is a rounding value, fixed lot size, or minimum order quantity maintained in the policy, this maximum will be exceeded.

For customer individual stock segments to manage individual customer stock, exception **26 Shortage in Individual Segment** will alert the user to higher stock levels than planned for in a range of coverage profile. When using a planning time fence with fixed types (P2 or P4 in deterministic planning), message **56 No Requirements Coverage** can alert the user of a shortage within the planning time fence.

Message **57 Disc. Matl (discontinued material)** describes a situation wherein a material is partly replaced by a follow-up or replacement material used in the discontinuation process. As a planner can replace a part with a follow-up material in the discontinuation process, there may be a business need to receive an alert if the discontinued part was only partially replaced by the substitute material. Another exception in discontinuation is message **58 Uncovered Reqmt after Effective-Out Date**, which is generated if a requirement exists after the effective-out date for a part that is to be discontinued and therefore can't be covered by planned stock. And if there is a receipt—maybe from a previously generated PO—that brings in stock after the effective-out date of a discontinued part, the exception message **59 Receipt after Effective-Out Date** will appear. These are very helpful alerts to manage discontinuation of parts without interruptions, stock-outs, or leftover unconsumed stock.

When using quota arrangements, a planner can source parts or materials from various vendors with an equal or unequal distribution of required quantities, called a *quota*. For example, a planner could order a quantity of 100 pieces for the same part from three different vendors with quotas of 40%, 35%, and 25% of the required total quantity. Should the MRP run, for whatever reason, exceed the maximum release quantity of the quota, then exception **70 Max. Release Qty—Quota Exceeded** appears.

An exception message that may then appear often is **96 Stock Fallen below Safety Stock Level**, which informs the user that the static safety stock set in the MRP 2 screen of the material master record is low. If a planner never or rarely receives this message, then the inventory level is probably too high, and all the safety stock turns into unused dead stock. So it's a good thing to receive the occasional message 96 because it means you're making good use of the buffer without binding too much cash in inventory holdings. In addition, when a material has exception message 96, its traffic light turns to red, and its **Days of Supply** turns to −999.9, which means that all materials whose safety stocks are breached can be seen at the top of the list in Transaction MD07. This might help in managing priorities and effectively addressing exception messages.

Group 7 Exceptions

Four exception messages are contained in this group. One is for nonfixed order proposals (30), and the other three are for fixed replenishment elements, such as POs and production orders. The latter three require manual rescheduling of the orders because they are fixed, and the MRP run doesn't change them anymore. The system does suggest the date to reschedule to. The four messages are explained in more detail here:

- **10 Bring Process Forward**
  When a demand date or quantity has changed and a certain quantity of goods is needed at an earlier time, instead of creating another order proposal, the MRP run suggests bringing the already ordered quantities in for an earlier delivery date so they can be used to fulfill the changed demand. The rescheduling has to happen manually, and the process is often called expediting because the planner will need to reach out to the supplier to see if expediting the delivery to an earlier date, faster than the originally agreed upon lead time, is possible.

- **15 Postpone Process**
  This message informs the user that the opposite has to happen: the ordered quantities aren't needed as early as was originally agreed to. It would be better if the supplier could deliver later because the demand has moved out to a later date. Not postponing as suggested by message 15 will lead to having too much inventory too early.

- **20 Cancel Process**
  This message occurs when a demand is reduced or disappears altogether. This message only appears for fixed supply elements such as a PO or a production/process order. At an earlier time, there must have been a demand causing the creation of an order proposal that must have been converted to a fixed supply order. Subsequently, the demand disappeared or was reduced, but because the supply was fixed, the MRP run can't delete the order.

- **30 Plan Process According to Schedule**
  The MRP run isn't able to fulfill the demand because, according to master data or routing settings, the lead time is too long to bring the materials in on time.

Group 8 Exceptions

As with group 4, messages out of group 8 can't be seen in Transaction MD07 but only in Transaction MD06. If the planning run was terminated for a material, users see message **98 Abnormal End of Requirements Planning**. This message may appear due to defective master data that prevents planning or even a prerequisite not being met, such as mandatory forecasting on the material not being performed prior to the MRP run.

When dealing with exception messages, the following are some of the ways to prioritize handling them:

1. Group 8 is the most important of all the groups, so look at the abnormal ends first where the planning run aborts. Address these materials first.

2. Next, look at group 5. These concern structural problems, and the planning run can't even come up with a date or quantity because the demand doesn't get exploded down to the lower level.

3. Then check out group 3. Not only was a date to firm a receipt missed, it's already too late when the receipt was supposed to come in to fulfill a demand.

4. After that, attend to the group 2 problems, wherein the date was missed when a proposal needed to be firmed, so that a planner can receive the quantity after the regular lead time. If a date is missed, rescheduling and manual expediting is the only option.

5. Group 1 exceptions are only relevant while using the opening horizon to have an additional check when external procurement is triggered first by a planned order and then by a purchase requisition.

6. Therefore, group 7 messages ought to be tackled next. These require expediting and may take much more time to get through, but at least a planner can create a list at this point. The list can be worked on later in the day (call vendors, check with purchasing, check the warehouse for inventory, etc.).

7. Next deal with group 6. Inventory excess or shortages usually require a change in strategy. Again, make a list and see how to reduce these exceptions over time, applying a different MRP type, changing the lot sizing procedure, looking at safety stock levels, and so on.

8. Finally, review the general messages in group 4 to see why there is a new proposal or why they have changed. These messages are information only and don't necessarily require action.

14.2.4   Order Report

Access the screen shown in Figure 14.12 via Transaction MD4C or CO46. The order report shows each element of the stock/requirements list. In this example, it shows that production order 80000005 of main material component 25 doesn't provide the requirements coverage, as denoted by the red traffic light. The green traffic light further down the report represents a satisfactory stock situation, whereas the red one represents a signal for the planner to take action.

[»]

Note

To create a custom profile that can then be used in an order report, follow menu path **SAP IMG • Production Planning • Material Requirements Planning • Evaluation • Define Profiles for Order Report.**

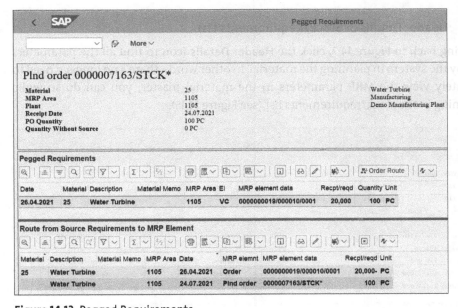

Figure 14.12 Order Report

14.2.5 Pegged Requirements

The order report finds all the receipts assigned to the requirements in a multilevel, top-down pegging overview, but it's also possible to run a bottom-up pegging analysis to find which requirements are assigned to a given receipt element. Use Transaction MD09 to determine the pegged requirements (see Figure 14.13). Choose the **Order Route** and it will show the pegged requirements level by level in the lower half of the screen.

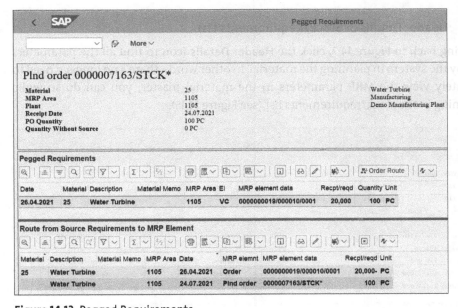

Figure 14.13 Pegged Requirements

14.2.6 Material Requirements Planning Elements

Because the system denotes each planning element separately, use the dropdown or filter function so that the system only displays the desired information (see Figure 14.14).

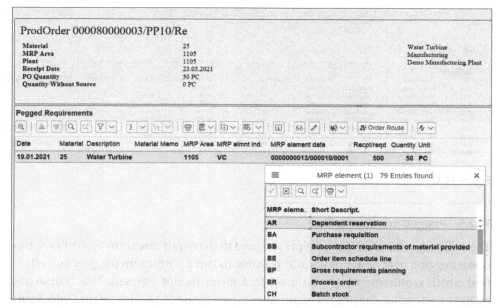

Figure 14.14 MRP Elements in Procurement without Requirements

14.2.7   Header Details of Stock/Requirements List

Referring back to Figure 14.7, click the **Header Details** icon to find all the parameters used by the system in planning the material. In other words, there's no longer a need to separately view the MRP parameters in the material master; you can do so while remaining in the stock/requirements list (see Figure 14.15).

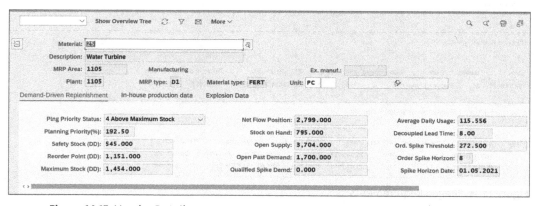

Figure 14.15 Header Details

14.2.8   Interactive Conversion of Procurement Elements

When the **Additional Data for MRP Element** icon (the magnifying glass icon on the left-hand side of the stock/requirements list) is clicked for any procurement element (e.g., a planned order), a popup appears for a planner to perform the interactive conversion of a planned order either into a purchase requisition for external procurement or a production/process order for in-house production.

14.2.9 Summation View

Figure 14.16 shows that a planner can toggle between the summation and detailed view of all planning elements (receipts, issuances/requirements, etc.). This icon is shown on the left-hand side of Figure 14.16 (next to **Individual List**).

A.. Period/Segment	Plnd ind.reqmts	Requirement	Receipts	Avail. Quantity	ATP quantity	Actual Coverage
M 05/2021	0	0	210	2,032	210	999.9
03.05.21 End of Planni						
M 06/2021	156–	0	200	2,076	200	999.9
M 07/2021	130–	0	100	2,046	100	999.9

Figure 14.16 Summation View of Stock Requirement List

14.2.10 Stock Statistics

The screen shown in Figure 14.17 appears when **More · Goto · Stock Statistics** in the stock/requirements list is chosen. The stock statistics provide comprehensive details of the stock situation of the material.

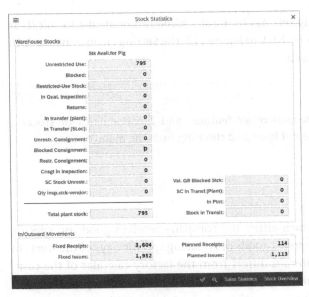

Figure 14.17 Stock Statistics

The stock/requirements list also provides a complete overview of the capacity situation of the in-house produced materials so that a planner can act or react to any unusual capacity overload on specific work centers. To view the capacity situation, navigate to **More · Goto · Capacity Situation** in the stock/requirements list (see Figure 14.18).

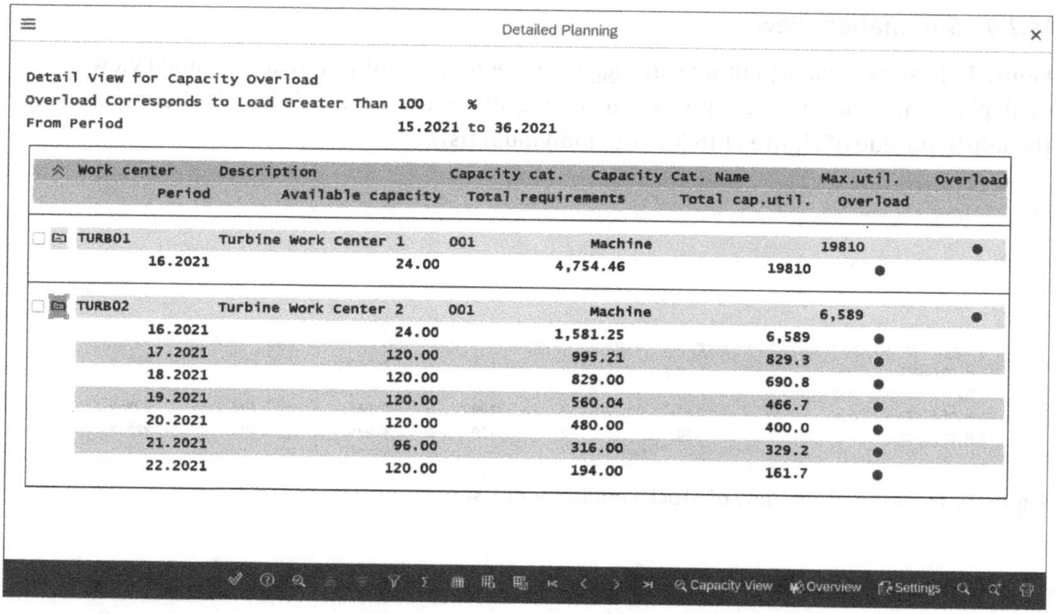

Detail View for Capacity Overload
Overload Corresponds to Load Greater Than 100   %
From Period   15.2021 to 36.2021

| ∧ Work center | Description | Capacity cat. | Capacity Cat. Name | Max.util. | Overload |
Period	Available capacity	Total requirements	Total cap.util.	Overload	
▣ TURB01	Turbine Work Center 1 001		Machine	19810	●
16.2021	24.00	4,754.46	19810	●	
▣ TURB02	Turbine Work Center 2 001		Machine	6,589	●
16.2021	24.00	1,581.25	6,589	●	
17.2021	120.00	995.21	829.3	●	
18.2021	120.00	829.00	690.8	●	
19.2021	120.00	560.04	466.7	●	
20.2021	120.00	480.00	400.0	●	
21.2021	96.00	316.00	329.2	●	
22.2021	120.00	194.00	161.7	●	

Figure 14.18 Capacity Situation

14.2.11   User Settings

A user can save individual display settings in the stock/requirements list to suit their preferences or business needs. Refer back to Figure 14.7: the **Settings** icon is available in the top-right hand side of the screen.

> **Note**
> We encourage exploring the several other features and functionalities of stock/requirements list by clicking different icons and choosing from the menu options.

14.3   Planning Calendar

There are several instances in which either the company receives goods on specific days of the week or the vendor supplies goods only during specific days of the week. In other words, the planning of materials differs from the factory calendar of the company. For example, several agricultural products used in the production process of edible products are produced only during specific periods of the year. The company must procure them and also store them to ensure they are available for consumption during the production process. For example, red chilies, an agricultural product, are only produced from January to April. The company uses a planning calendar to ensure the system creates procurement proposals for this raw material (red chilies) within that four-month time period.

It's also possible to specify a planning date in the planning run. This option is useful because it enables a planner to bring the planning run forward to an earlier date. If the planning run is set for Monday, for example, this planning run can be performed on a Friday.

The planning calendar is assigned in the **MRP 2** view of the material master (Transaction MM02). Figure 14.19 shows the **Planning calendar** field for maintaining the planning calendar.

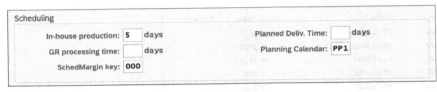

Figure 14.19 Planning Calendar in Material Master

To create a new planning calendar, follow menu path **SAP IMG · Production · Material Requirements Planning · Master Data · Maintain Planning Calendar**, or use Transaction MD25.

On the screen shown in Figure 14.20, define the **Planning Calendar** as "PP1" for **Plant** "1105" and select the **Following Working Day** radio button if the period start date isn't on a working day.

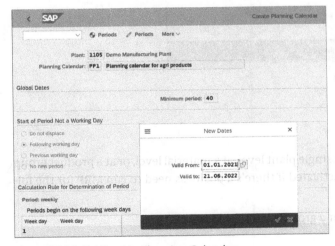

Figure 14.20 Setting Up Planning Calendar

Define a minimum number of periods that the system must generate in the planning calendar in the **Minimum Period** field. On pressing Enter, a popup appears to select weekdays, work week, workdays, work months, and so on. Next, choose the **Periods** button, and the **New Dates** popup appears to define the start and end date of the planning calendar. Choose **Continue**.

In Figure 14.21, notice that all period planning starts on a Monday, and this is the same as is defined in the lower half of the first screen shown in Figure 14.20.

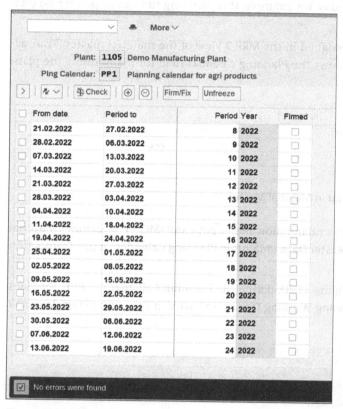

Figure 14.21 Planning Calendar

14.4   Planning Areas

Apart from running MRP at a single plant level, at a material level, or at a product group level, the MRP areas can be activated if there's a business need to run MRP for the following:

- A single storage location or a group of storage locations
- A subcontractor

The advantage of setting up MRP areas is that materials can be planned at the storage location level, which allows planning of materials differently at the storage location level than MRP planning of the material at the plant level. For example, if there are consumable materials that are stored at several storage locations in a plant, then set the MRP type of this material as "ND" (no planning) at the plant level. However, for two specific storage locations with high consumption of this consumable material, set the MRP type as "VB" (reorder point planning) to ensure that the system helps in replenishment of this material as soon as it drops below the reorder point level in those two storage locations. MRP areas make this material planning possible.

In this section, we show the configuration of MRP areas; activating the MRP areas in the material master, including defining important planning parameters; running the MRP for MRP areas; and finally evaluating the planning run's results.

[!]

> **Warning**
>
> It isn't possible to deactivate the MRP areas after activating them in the SAP system. Therefore, it's important to consider the use of MRP areas extensively before proceeding to implement them.

14

14.4.1   Configuration

The two main configuration steps involved in setting up MRP areas are setting the **MRP Area Active** checkbox and defining the MRP areas, as described here for a storage location:

1. To activate MRP areas, use menu path **SAP IMG • Production • Material Requirements Planning • Master Data • MRP Areas • Activate MRP for MRP Areas**. Here, select the **MRP Area Active** checkbox and save.

2. To define MRP areas, use menu path **SAP IMG • Production • Material Requirements Planning • Master Data • MRP Areas • Define MRP Areas**.

3. Choose **New Entries**, set **MRP Area** as "1105–0001", and provide a description.

4. For **MRP Area Type**, select **02** from the dropdown menu, which is for storage location MRP. Assign the **Plant** as "1105", and press ⌜Enter⌟.

5. On the left-hand side of the screen, double-click **Assign Storage Locations**, which leads to the screen shown in Figure 14.22.

[«]

> **Note**
>
> MRP area type 02 is the standard type to define additional MRP areas on the storage location level. MRP area type 01 is for the plant MRP areas and is created automatically by converting the planning file for MRP areas. MRP area type 03 is for subcontracting, in which a company's stock is maintained at a vendor's premises, and it ensures materials planning.

6. Assign **Recg. Stor. Loc.** (receiving storage location) as "0001" for **Plant** "1105", and save the entry.

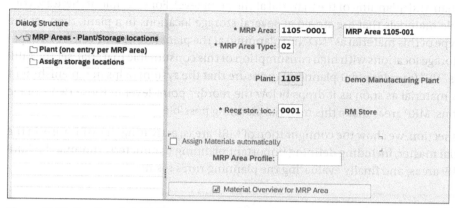

Figure 14.22 Configuring MRP Areas for Storage Location

For this example, we used a single storage location for the plant, but more than one storage location can be grouped under one MRP area. This storage location (or locations) will be planned separately and independently from planning at the plant level. In addition, in a subcontracting scenario involving MRP areas, define subcontracting MRP areas within a plant to enable planning and material availability at the subcontractor (vendor) level.

14.4.2   Set Up the Material Master

With the necessary configuration settings for MRP areas in place, you can activate the storage location MRP for the material 132 for plant 1105 and for storage location 0001.

Using Transaction MM02 for the change in the material master, enter **Material** "132" for **Plant** "1105", and for **Stor. Loc. 0001**, select the **MRP 1** view. On the screen shown in Figure 14.23, click the **MRP areas** button so that the **Change MRP Area** screen shown in Figure 14.24 appears. Select the configured **MRP Area 1105–0001**.

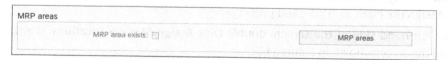

Figure 14.23 MRP Areas in Material Master

[»]

> **Note**
>
> If an error message reading **MRP area 1105–0001 does not exist as SCM location** appears, then execute report /SAPAPO/CREATE_LOCATION for MRP area 1105-0001 using Transaction SE38.

Assign the MRP type as VB for manual reorder point planning at the MRP area level and set **Reorder Point** as "200". Assign other parameters, such as **MRP Controller** "101" and **Fixed Lot Size** "100.00", as shown in Figure 14.24. Choose the **MRP 2** tab.

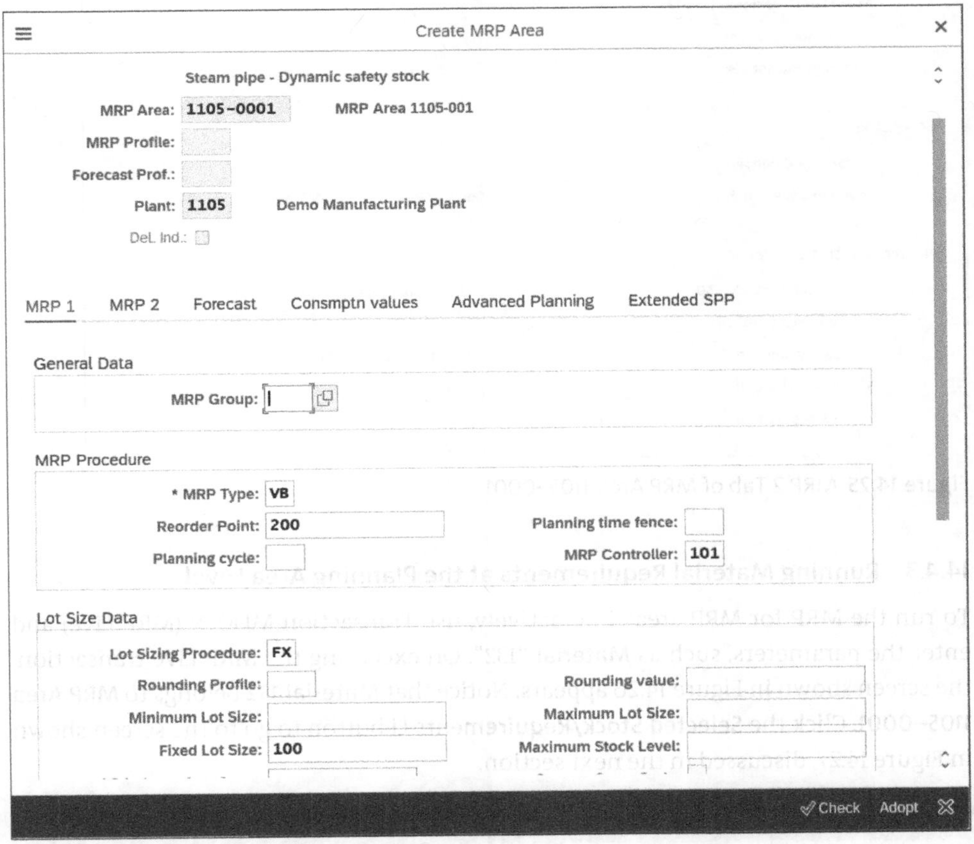

Figure 14.24 MRP Area Settings for Storage Location in Material Master

In the **MRP 2** tab, more planning options are available at the material level, such as defining a **Safety Stock** of "70.000" at the MRP areas level (Figure 14.25). Enter a **Planned Deliv. Time** in days, and choose the **Forecast** tab.

The **Forecast** tab page enables a planner to enter forecast parameters and also interactively execute a forecast of the material. Finally, choose the **Consmptn Values** tab, and maintain the planned and unplanned consumption values. Choose **Adopt** in MRP areas, then save the material master settings.

| MRP 1 | MRP 2 | Forecast | Consmptn values | Advanced Planning | Extended SPP |

Procurement

Special procurement: |
Prod. stor. location:
Storage loc. for EP:

Scheduling

Planning Calendar:
Planned Deliv. Time: ☐ Consider Planned Delivery Time

Net requirements calculation

Safety stock: **70**   Service level (%):
Coverage profile:
Safety time ind.:   Safety time/act.cov.:   Days
STime period profile:
MRP dep. reqmts:

Figure 14.25 MRP 2 Tab of MRP Area 1105–0001

14.4.3   Running Material Requirements at the Planning Area Level

To run the MRP for MRP areas interactively, use Transaction MD01N (MRP Live) and enter the parameters, such as **Material** "132". On executing the MRP Live transaction, the screen shown in Figure 14.26 appears. Notice that **Material 132** belongs to **MRP Area 1105–0001**. Click the **Selected Stock/Requirements Li** button to go to the screen shown in Figure 14.27, discussed in the next section.

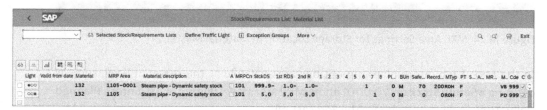

Figure 14.26 Planning Results from MRP Live Using MRP Area

14.4.4   Planning Results

Figure 14.27 shows the planning results of material 132 in MRP area 1105–0001. Because there was no opening stock, and the stock has fallen below the safety stock in the warehouse (storage location of the MRP areas), the system creates new purchase requisitions 100000238 and 100000239 with a fixed quantity of 100 each (this is because we defined a fixed lot size in Figure 14.24). Notice **Exception 96**, which denotes: **Stock Fallen below Safety Stock Level** (message details in the lower half of the screen).

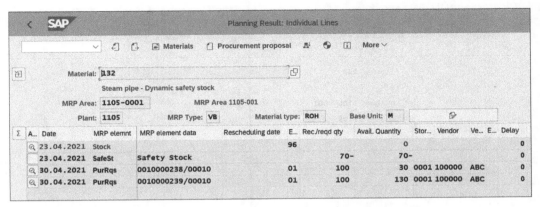

Figure 14.27 Planning Results of Material 132 for MRP Area 1105–0001

Note

SAP S/4HANA also offers report RMMDDIBE (via Transaction SE38) for the mass maintenance of the MRP area settings in the material master. With this report, the MRP area
settings can be copied with a reference, created or changed with an MRP or forecast
profile, created or changed with data, and have the deletion indicator set or reset (see
Figure 14.28).

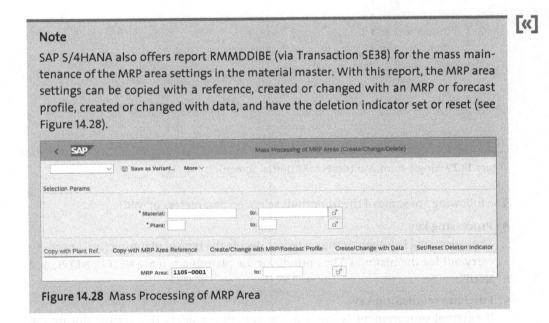

Figure 14.28 Mass Processing of MRP Area

14.5 Classic Material Requirements Planning

Now that we've already covered MRP Live and associated business processes, let's also
briefly cover the basics of classic MRP and some of the important functionality it offers.
Access the screen shown in Figure 14.29 using Transaction MD02 to run MRP for a single material at MRP area level 1105–0001.

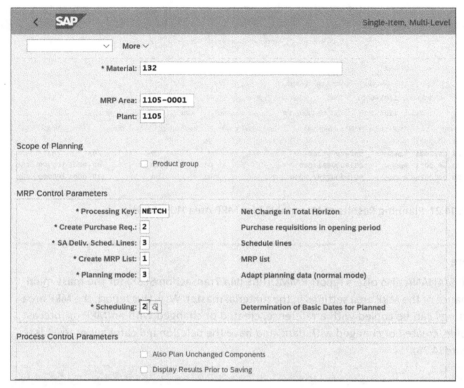

Figure 14.29 Single-Item, Multilevel MRP (Initial Screen)

The following are some of the important selection parameters of MRP:

- **Processing key**
  The processing key enables the system to decide the type of planning run it needs to carry out for the material. The options for the planning run are **NETCH**, **NETPL**, and **NEUPL**.

- **Purchase requisition key**
  If external procurement is implied, the system considers this setting during the planning run. If necessary settings are in place, then the system can directly create purchase requisitions for all externally procured materials. Alternatively, the system can create planned orders that you can convert into purchase requisitions.

- **Delivery schedules**
  If a source list for the material is maintained and the same has been incorporated in scheduling agreements with vendors, the system can create schedule lines.

- **Creation of MRP list**
  The system includes the results of the planning run in the MRP list after the planning run. An MRP list is a static or frozen list of stock/requirements situations with the date and time immediately after the planning run. This indicator controls how

the system should create the MRP list. The available options are for the system to create an MRP list for all planned orders, to create an MRP list for planned orders with exceptions, or not to create any MRP list at all. Exceptions are alerts in the system that the planner needs to keep an eye on.

- **Planning mode**

  During the planning run, the system plans various procurement elements, such as the unfirmed planned orders, purchase requisitions, and scheduling agreements, once again in the next planning run. It's possible to control how the system should proceed with the planning data that are already there (from the latest planning run or due to interactive activities of the MRP planner). Three options are available:

  - **Adopt Planning Data**

    If there is any change in requirement quantities, dates, or lot sizing procedures for the unfirmed planned orders (or other procurement elements), the system re-explodes the BOM for the new quantities in the MRP run.

  - **Re-explode BOM and Routing**

    The system re-explodes the BOM and routing if there is a change in the BOM master data, routing, production versions, or BOM explosion numbers. This helps to ensure that the system re-explodes the BOM for the existing unfirmed planned orders. The procurement proposals created in the previous planning aren't deleted but are adjusted to take the changes into account.

  - **Delete and Recreate Planning data**

    The system deletes the existing procurement proposals (i.e., the entire planning data of the previous planning run), unless they are firmed, and re-explodes the BOM and routing, thereby creating altogether new procurement proposals.

- **Scheduling types**

  For in-house-produced materials, the system offers two types of scheduling options:

  - Basic date scheduling
  - Lead time scheduling

  After entering the parameters on the initial screen of Transaction MD02, press [Enter] twice (first to confirm the MRP parameters, causing the entered parameters to turn red, and then to execute the MRP run), and the system brings up the planning result screen for a large number of materials. In this result screen, not only the finished or semifinished goods (132) are planned but also all the components of the BOM. The planning result of a material can be viewed by double-clicking it.

14.6   Types of Planning Runs

Depending on the business process, a planner can use one of several types of planning run available in the SAP system. A *planning run* denotes the level and mode at which a planner wants to run MRP. For example, a planner may want to run MRP on an individual plant or group of plants, individual material or group of materials (product group), in online mode, or in background mode.

Some of the planning runs include the following:

- Total planning online
- Total planning background
- Single-item planning, sales order
- Single-item planning, project

We discuss each of the planning runs in the following sections.

14.6.1   Total Planning Online

In this type of planning run, the system carries out a multilevel planning run—that is, for all the materials in a plant, for all the materials in multiple plants, or for MRP, as defined through **Scope of Planning**, which is available in the selection screen. Total planning online is carried out using Transaction MD01.

If the business process requires considering and using other parameters in the MRP run, either define them or use a user exit. For example, if a company wants to carry out the MRP run for a set of MRP controllers only or for a specific procurement type (E: In-house managed, F: Externally procured, X: Both), then use a user exit. The user exit enhancement is M61X00001, and it's recommended to engage an ABAP consultant for this.

14.6.2   Total Planning Background

With the total planning background method, a planner can carry out the planning in the background, as opposed to the foreground or online. Using Transaction MDBT, create a variant of the Transaction MD01N screen and schedule it in the background on a periodic basis. The program name for Transaction MDBT is RMMRP000. Use Transaction SE38, give the program name, and define the variant to execute the MRP in the background.

14.6.3   Single-Item Planning, Sales Order

For MTO production, use single-item planning for a sales order. Enter the sales order number together with the line item of the sales order and use Transaction MD50 to execute the planning. The system not only creates a procurement element or receipt with the sales order reference for the finished good but also plans all the components defined in the BOM of the finished good.

14.6.4 Single-Item Planning, Project

It's also possible to execute separate planning for engineer-to-order (ETO) materials. If the material—a finished good or a spare part for a raw material—is assigned to a work breakdown structure (WBS) element, then use Transaction MD51 to execute planning.

> **Note**
>
> Materials planning is a very complex topic and requires a much deeper understanding of how to formulate material planning rules and policies in a company that can then be mapped in the SAP system. Here, we recommend *Material Requirements Planning with SAP S/4HANA* (*www.sap-press.com/4966*, SAP PRESS, 2020), which does complete justice to this topic.

14.7 Summary

This chapter focused on some of the latest planning innovations available in SAP S/4HANA. MRP Live provides far more options for improved planning and scheduling of materials and capacity. MRP areas can be implemented to plan materials at the storage location or subcontracting vendor level.

The next chapter covers demand-driven replenishment (DDR) in SAP S/4HANA.

Chapter 15
Demand-Driven Replenishment

From system configuration to the SAP Fiori apps used for planning and execution, this chapter covers each stage of a demand-driven replenishment project. Learn how SAP S/4HANA takes the classic material requirements planning elements—classifications, stock positioning, lead time, and buffers—and recalculates them using demand-driven replenishment for lower variability and to improve materials planning accuracy.

Logistics and supply chain management today is far more volatile, uncertain, complex, and ambiguous (VUCA) than it has ever been, making it a no-win battle for a company to manage the chaos that exists between customer demand and the company's capability for timely supply. The traditional approach to materials procurement and production planning using enterprise resource planning (ERP) tools isn't helping with the ever-widening gaps between demand and supply.

Let's take a close look at both of these situations—the VUCA world of supply chain and even the most sophisticated ERP tools' inability to bring sanity to supply chain challenges.

An almost infinite variety of products for a customer to choose from, diverse and globalized sources of supply, and the complexity involved in manufacturing a product in which outsourcing is now playing an increasingly important role are some of the latest challenges of the supply chain world. Adding to these challenges are shortened product lifecycles, demand from companies finance departments to reduce working capital, and less tolerance on the part of customers to wait for a product before they begin seeking alternatives. All these factors are responsible for the intense competition a company faces within and outside, all while working to increase market share, capture new opportunities, and reduce working capital.

The plethora of ERP tools for materials, scheduling, and capacity planning currently available aren't able to calm the nervousness of today's VUCA world. Despite using these planning tools, poor inventory performance is common, with companies having an overstock of products that don't sell, stock-outs of in-demand products, low inventory turnover, and high obsolescence. Meeting inventory and service key performance indicators (KPIs)—such as high fill rate, high service level, and on-time, in-full requests from customers for shorter delivery times for products—forces companies to spend significant resources on expediting expenses.

Let's take a look at the limitations of the available materials and resource planning tools, the importance of material and relevant information flows and keeping them smooth and uninterrupted, and how demand-driven replenishment (DDR) plays an important role in bringing stability to the logistics and supply chain processes.

15.1   Limitations of Current Materials Planning and Replenishment Tools

Let's first evaluate why traditional materials planning tools are falling short of addressing the challenges of the VUCA world. Equally important to understand is that while many of these planning tools effectively work in isolation, they aren't able to work cohesively enough to reduce or eliminate the bullwhip effect. As each material planning tool is evaluated to explain why they are falling short, it's equally important to understand that implementing a DDR solution doesn't entail discarding all these planning tools, such as forecasting, material requirements planning (MRP), safety stock, or reorder point planning. Rather, it requires using selected and effective features of several of these planning tools to improve the flow of materials and relevant information. For example, DDR still uses MRP for quantity calculation and scheduling of components, but it stops at stocked or buffered positions. In contrast, MRP starts at the lowest level of a bill of materials (BOM), which is often the highest level of the product (e.g., a finished product), and continues quantity calculation and scheduling of all components of the BOM until it reaches the highest level of a BOM (often the raw materials and packing materials). Similarly, the forecasting tool is still a required planning tool in the overall context of using DDR, as is using the capacity requirements planning (CRP) tools in the context of overall supply chain planning.

> **Bullwhip Effect**
>
> The *bullwhip effect* is a cascading and incremental increase in the logistics and supply chain's variability as a result of a small change in customers' demand.

The most important material planning tools and their current limitations are as follows:

- **Forecasting**
  Forecasting uses historical data to predict or forecast future requirements and uses forecasting models, such as constant, moving average, seasonal, and trend. All forecasts also have a degree of error to account for deviations (mean average deviations) between forecast figures and the confidence on these figures. However, forecasts start out wrong, and they are riddled with errors that only increase with time. Forecasts are also more inaccurate when they are made at the individual stock-keeping unit (SKU) level. Imagine trying to accurately forecast or predict the number of air

conditioners of a specific model (individual SKU) to produce a year from now (long time horizon) when there just isn't enough information available now, and predicting how hot the weather is going to be a year from now is unreliable.

- **Sales and operations planning (S&OP)**
  Forecasting often forms the basis for S&OP. A sales and operations plan ensures that the annual sales plan matches up with the production (operations) plan. The mutually agreed-upon sales and operations plan then enables a company to evaluate the warehouse space, the machines' capacities, and the procurement commitment (value) it will need for the entire year. However, when inaccurate forecasting forms the basis of S&OP, the sales and production plans are most certainly bound to change in the near-term horizon when the actual sales and demand are better known.

- **Demand management**
  Demand management is the last step for a materials planner to check and validate a sales or a production plan (the plan is driven from the S&OP of the previous step) to use for production and procurement planning by using the master production scheduling and MRP tools. The basis of demand management is an unreliable forecast, leading to precisely wrong procurement and proposals generation.

- **Master production scheduling (MPS)**
  An MPS program plans and schedules production of critical materials and ensures that there are no changes to the production plan within the defined time horizon, such as within a week. No changes are made to the master production scheduling after an MRP run. MPS runs before MRP so that critical products and components are planned first in the planning process. As the demand management plan is fed into MPS, it's clear to see why MPS only adds to the supply chain chaos.

- **Material requirements planning**
  MRP explodes the BOMs of finished products to calculate the quantities of semifinished, packing, and raw materials required to produce the finished products.

- **Materials planning using safety stock**
  Safety stock refers to the buffer stock of materials that planners turn to in case of a sudden and unforeseen demand spike or a supply disruption. Although it's possible to automatically calculate safety stock, safety stock is unable to account for the dynamic nature of supply and demand variabilities. Further, the safety stock calculation method isn't the primary materials planning tool and therefore is unable to truly act as a buffer between demand and supply deviations.

- **Reorder point planning**
  When stock falls below a reorder point, replenishment is triggered. The replenishment's proposal quantity is often a fixed or minimum lot to prevent the ERP system from creating an unnecessarily large number of procurement proposals of small quantities each time there's a material shortage (or when a material's stock falls below the reorder point). Like safety stock, it's possible to calculate the reorder point

15

of a material automatically; however, reorder point planning can't reflect the replenishment priorities of different materials.

15.2   Material and Information Flows

According to George W. Plossl, author of *Production and Inventory Control: Principles and Techniques*, "All benefits will be directly related to the speed of *flow* of information and materials." Now and more than ever, this concept is enhanced by adding that the flow of materials and information must be *relevant* to the required out-of-market information because in today's hyperconnected world, companies are drowning in data but starving for relevant information to help them navigate the VUCA challenges of the modern supply chain. Further, the words *all benefits* can be further broken down into the following benefits or KPIs that companies closely monitor:

- Exceptional customer service ensures timely and quality products.
- Revenue increases or at least remains stable.
- The quality of products and services keeps getting better.
- Inventories of purchased, work-in-process (WIP), and produced products stay at optimal levels.
- Expenses remain minimal by eliminating expedited freight costs, rework, or unplanned partial deliveries.
- Cash flow is greatly improved.

With these points in mind, it's critically important to ensure that distortions leading to relevant information or material flows are addressed as often and as soon as possible for a smoother supply chain.

First, let's look at why distortions to relevant material and information occur, as illustrated in Figure 15.1. Starting at the bottom of Figure 15.1, materials planners use MRP ❶ to calculate future demand for the products to ensure timely production and procurement. However, due to the inherent logic of MRP, it treats everything as dependent and acts as one big calculator to suggest production and procurement quantities of materials on specific dates. In today's complex and globalized supply chain, the time it takes to procure and produce a product is much longer than it has ever been before. At the same time, customers today have far more options to choose from, thereby leading to shrinking customer tolerance time for a company to deliver or ensure availability of a product ❷.

To better predict customers' demand and feed that into the MRP program, companies use a forecasting tool ❸. Unfortunately, using even the best forecasting model or program always has a degree of error. The longer the forecast horizon is, such as yearly, quarterly, or even monthly, the greater is the degree of error ❹. The more detailed level at which the forecasting is done, such as at the individual product or SKU level, the more amplified is the forecasting error, leading to the distortion of relevant information ❽.

Refer again to the bottom of Figure 15.1. While MRP uses forecasting to predict demand ❸, when the actual customers' demand is known, adjustment between forecasted demand versus actual demand must happen ❺, leading to nervousness ❻ in the logistics and supply chain. These conflicting and often-changing demand signals ❼ lead to the distortion of relevant information ❽. This distorted or unreliable information used for materials planning is one of the two major reasons for the *bullwhip effect*, the amplification of supply variability as the result of demand variability, which has cascading and negative ripple effects on the supply chain.

The second effect of nervousness ❻ is that companies often use materials planning, such as production or procurement planning in time horizons of one-week or even two-week buckets ❾, to bring some sanity to production or procurement plans and to prevent frequent changes to these plans. In doing so, planners use latent signals ❿ that again result in distortion to relevant information ❽.

The third factor that adds nervousness to the supply chain is when materials planners attempt to flatten BOMs ⓫ to reduce material quantities or scheduling variabilities. In doing so, materials planners end up using oversimplified signals ⓬ for procurement or production planning, further adding to the distortion of relevant information ❽. When distorted information ❽ is used, it's no surprise that the products or materials required aren't ready or available when needed ⓭, eventually culminating in the distortion of relevant materials ⓮. When relevant materials are distorted, companies either end up with products that don't sell (overstock scenario) or with no products to deliver on time to meet demand (out-of-stock scenario); both scenarios lead to missed business opportunities and lost customers.

Let's now go back again to the bottom of Figure 15.1 to understand how the MRP program that treats all materials as dependent ❶ leads to the same distortions to relevant materials created by nervousness in the supply chain previously. The MRP program performs a level-by-level explosion of BOMs of finished goods to calculate quantities of semifinished, packing, and raw materials (just like a big calculator) required at specific times; the resultant MRP plans of quantities and schedules are based on all these dependencies ⓯. Because the MRP program is designed to ensure that quantities of all materials in a BOM eventually net to zero after taking any safety stock into account, any change in plans, variability, or disruption on the supply side has multiplying effects on all dependent requirements, leading to the accumulation of delays ⓱. The delays accumulate, but the gains do not, and thus material planners have MRP-generated production and procurement plans that are never properly synchronized ⓲ between demand and supply. The end results are the same as before: companies end up with overstock of slow-moving products or products that don't sell, while stock-outs occur for high-demand products.

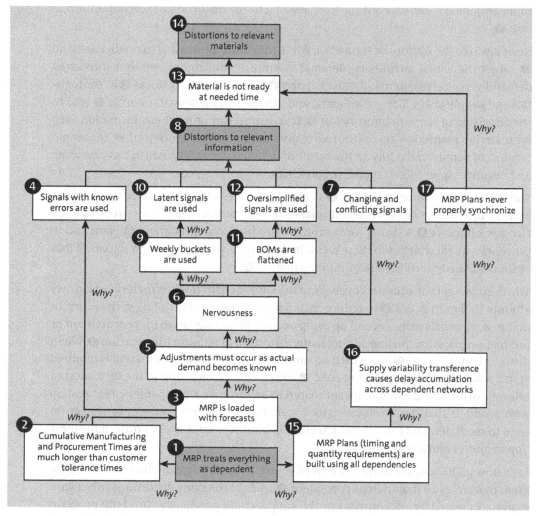

Figure 15.1 Factors Leading to Information and Material Distortions (©Demand Driven Institute, used with permission)

In the following sections, we'll look at how decoupling can serve as a solution to this problem, along with covering demand-driven material requirements planning (DDMRP) basics and its components.

15.3   DDMRP Basics and Components

The solution to the distortion of relevant information and the quagmire of material flows lies in decoupling the logistics and supply chain to reduce the bullwhip effect.

Decoupling entails disconnecting the ever-present and constantly increasing variability between demand and supply by placing buffers at strategic points, known as *decoupling points*. Materials planners then regularly monitor the buffers in the material value chain—from procurement to interplant transfer to production to distribution—to ensure timely action and interventions where necessary. There are three types of buffers:

1. **Stock buffer**
   The stock situation at each buffer is closely monitored to ensure that there's no shortage of the required materials. The ▼ icon denotes a decoupled position and maintains a stock buffer in DDR.

2. **Time buffer**
   This buffer manages demand and supply variability that may impact production or procurement scheduling. The time buffer icons are these: ⊽ .

3. **Capacity buffer**
   This buffer at production lines or work centers provides the cushions required for smoother flow to in-house-produced materials. The capacity buffer icons are these: ⊟ ⊞ .

The three color codes represent different buffer statuses: red points the materials planners to areas that need immediate attention or urgent action, yellow requires closely monitoring the buffer situation, and green reflects a comfortable buffer situation. Each color of buffer is also accompanied by a percentage to denote the buffer remaining or unconsumed in relation to the overall buffer size. For example, a work center, such as a tablet-packing line, might show a red color in the tricolor buffer status to indicate 12% remaining (unconsumed) capacity. All reports and metrics used to represent buffers show red at the top (or highest) level to reflect the criticality or severity of the buffer situation, while green gets the lowest position. Exceptional situations such as stock-outs, overstocks, or overcapacities are denoted by different colors, such as deep red for stock-outs or overcapacities, and deep blue for overstocks or excess available capacities. As this chapter will discuss later, these deep red and dark blue zones are often the best candidates for bringing improvements to material and information flows.

> **Note**
> SAP introduced DDR in SAP S/4HANA Cloud 1708 and SAP S/4HANA 1709. DDR is based on the DDMRP methodology from the Demand Driven Institute (DDI). Carol Ptak and Chad Smith, partners at DDI, have committed themselves to promoting and proliferating DDMRP and associated concepts and working throughout the world. In the *DDMRP: Demand Driven Materials Requirement Planning* book (3rd edition, Industrial Press, 2019), Ptak and Smith provide a deep-dive into and authoritative resource on DDMRP and associated concepts.

Figure 15.2 shows an example planning screen of DDR for several parts, with varying priorities denoted by corresponding tricolor buffer status.

Today's Date: July 15											
Part#	Planning Priority	On Hand	On-Order	Qualified Demand	Net Flow Position	Order Recommendation	Request Date	Top RED	Top YELLOW	Top GREEN	Lead Time
406P	RED 19.8%	401	506	263	644	2606	4-Aug	750	2750	3250	20
403P	YELLOW 43.4%	1412	981	412	1981	2579	23-Jul	1200	3600	4560	8
402P	YELLOW 69.0%	601	753	112	1242	558	24-Jul	540	1440	1800	9
405P	YELLOW 74.0%	3400	4251	581	7070	2486	24-Jul	1756	7606	9556	9
401P	YELLOW 75.1%	2652	6233	712	8173	2715	25-Jul	2438	8938	10888	10
404P	GREEN 97.6%	1951	1560	291	3220	0		1050	2550	3300	6

Easily demonstrable RELATIVE PRIORITY is a crucial aspect of DDMRP

Figure 15.2 Example of DDR Planning Screen (©Demand Driven Institute, used with permission)

Figure 15.3 represents the supply chain. Starting from the left, a buffer is placed at the decoupling point ❶, which is between the component manufacturing and subassembly steps. Notice the reduction in the variability wave ❷ to dampen the bullwhip effect and the associated lead time reduction ❸.

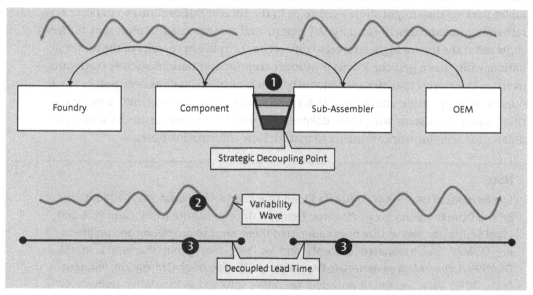

Figure 15.3 Decoupling to Reduce Bullwhip Effect (©Demand Driven Institute, used with permission)

In the following sections, we'll discuss not only where to implement DDR in the logistics and supply chain but also the five main components of DDMRP.

15.3.1   Where to Implement Demand-Driven Replenishment

The following are the four areas in the logistics and supply chain in which implementing DDR can be beneficial:

1. **Purchasing**
   Purchased parts often experience supply variability.

2. **Operations**
   Production operations that produce several common parts or work centers with bottleneck capacities are the prime candidates for DDR. For semifinished goods sold by a company directly to its customers, implementing DDR can mitigate the risks of demand variability due to customers' changing requirements for a company's products.

3. **Distribution**
   Finished goods or even services' spare parts are distributed to different distribution centers and experience significant demand variability.

4. **Interplant**
   Companies with several manufacturing units or even warehouses spread across various locations of a country, different countries, or even continents have materials with short, medium, or long lead times. Due to the special procurement types of such materials, some of them are prime candidates for DDR.

15.3.2   DDMRP Components

The five components of DDMRP (see Figure 15.4) show a materials planner how to effectively *position* buffers at strategic inventory locations, *protect* the flow of materials and relevant information by evaluating buffer profiles, and then dynamically adjust these buffers. Finally, an efficient *pull* system is put in place to reduce variabilities between demand and supply through demand-driven planning.

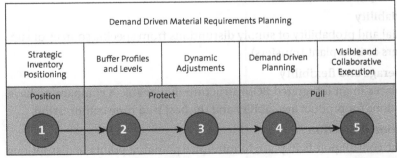

Figure 15.4 Five Components of DDMRP (©Demand Driven Institute, used with permission)

This is followed by execution while ensuring that the changing supply and demand dynamics adapt to the logistics and supply chain.

Strategic Inventory Positioning

In this component (see Figure 15.4), a materials planner decides *which* items to stock and *where*. Materials with long lead times, with significant supply or demand variability, with a component used in manufacturing several products, or facing a production capacity bottleneck are prime candidates for consideration. The planner chooses materials from the stock buffers, as well as the decoupling points in the logistics and supply chain. As already covered previously, the buffers at decoupling points are denoted by the ▽ icon.

Two immediate questions arise when choosing a decoupling point, as follows:

- What important factors should a materials planner consider while selecting a decoupling point in the logistics and supply chain?
- Where should a materials planner position a decoupling point in the logistics and supply chain?

The six factors to consider when choosing a decoupling point are as follows:

- **Customer tolerance time**
  The maximum amount of time customers are willing to wait for delivery or availability of a product before seeking alternatives.

- **Market potential lead time**
  Lead time that will allow an increase in price or an opportunity to capture additional business through existing or new customer channels.

- **Demand or sales order visibility horizon**
  The time period during which the demand for dependent requirements is known or when there's visibility into actual sale of products as recorded in a sales order.

- **External variabilities**
  - **Demand variability**
    The probability of spikes and swings in demand that may overwhelm resources such as capacity, stock, and cash flow.
  - **Supply variability**
    The potential and probability of supply disruptions from specific sources of supply (suppliers or interplant transfers).

- **Inventory leverage and flexibility**
  The specific places in an integrated BOM structure that enable a company to have maximum options for product availability and the best lead time compression.

- **Critical operation protection**
  Putting specific control points in place to minimize potential points of disruptions in the supply chain, such as placing control points at work centers or production

resources with bottleneck capacities or where demand/supply variabilities can quickly accumulate or amplify.

Based on these six factors for choosing decoupling points, Figure 15.5 shows an example of strategically placed buffers. These buffers are based on the following considerations:

- The FPG and 201 buffers enable satisfaction of quickly taking advantage of additional business opportunities.
- The FPG stock position is minimized due to the 101 buffer.
- The 101 and 102P buffers allow for a make-to-order (MTO) strategy on FPH.
- The 201 and 204P buffers protect the Z resource as best as possible at the product structure (BOM) level.
- The 301P buffer minimizes the inventory liability at 201.
- The 201 and 101 buffers can direct the shared components to actual requirements.

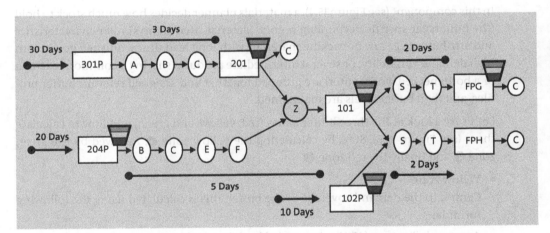

Figure 15.5 Strategically Placed Buffers (©Demand Driven Institute, used with permission)

The following are the six tests to consider when evaluating a decoupling point:

- **Decoupling test**
  The lead time on the supply side should decrease when compared with the lead time chain of the nonbuffered components.
- **Bidirectional benefit test**
  The demand side should show a compressed or reduced lead time and higher availability of a product or a component. The supply side should get cumulative demand requirements to provide a materials planner with better and more efficient order management of the recommended order quantity.
- **Order independence test**
  The stock in the buffers isn't specific to any production order, sales order, or stock

transport order (interplant transfer). This test therefore ensures that there's as little WIP as possible while making stock available for any demand.

- **Primary planning mechanism test**
  The buffered part at a decoupling point should be able to manage all demand and supply requirements independently by taking the net flow position into account.

- **Relative priority test**
  The buffered position needs to account for both planning and execution of not just the buffered part but also its priority in relation to other buffered parts and positions.

- **Dynamic adjustment test**
  The buffered part needs to adjust dynamically to account for supply and demand variations within the defined time horizon.

Buffer Profiles and Levels

In this component (see Figure 15.4), a materials planner decides how much stock to hold (the buffers) at specific decoupling points. Materials that share similar characteristics and attributes (e.g., raw or packing materials with long lead times, finished goods with high demand variability, or several intermediate products sharing a common machine or a bottlenecked work center) are grouped together and assigned relevant buffer profiles, and then buffer levels are maintained.

Let's take a look at the three buffer zones (red, yellow, and green) and how to calculate them (see Figure 15.6). Start by calculating the yellow zone ❶, followed by the green zone ❷, and finally the red zone ❸.

- **Yellow zone**
  Central to the demand coverage in the buffer, this is calculated using the following formula:

  Average daily usage (ADU) × Decoupled lead time (DLT)

- **Green zone**
  This determines the order frequency and the size of each order. There are three ways to calculate the green zone, and the *largest* value of the three calculations forms the green buffer zone:

  - *Minimum order quantity (MOQ)*
  - *Desired order cycle (DOC) × DLT*
  - *ADU × DLT × Lead time factor (LT factor)*

- **Red zone**
  This is the embedded safety in the buffer. The red zone is the sum of the red zone base and red zone safety, as follows:

  - *Red zone base: ADU × DLT × LT factor*

– *Red zone safety: Red zone base × Variability factor (VF)*
– *Red zone = Red zone base + Red zone safety*

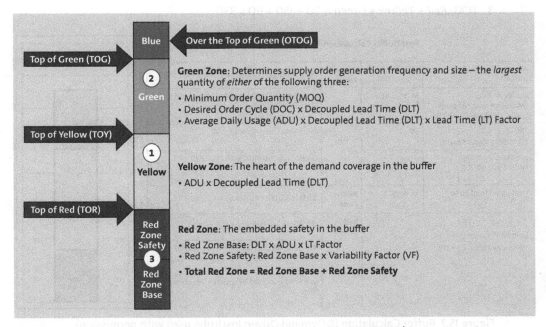

Figure 15.6 Buffer Zones (©Demand Driven Institute, used with permission)

To get a better sense of buffer positions, consider the following four abbreviations and their meanings:

- **Top of red (TOR)**
  The highest point of the red zone. When the stock, schedule, or capacity breaches the red zone, it signals an urgent action or immediate attention.

- **Top of yellow (TOY)**
  The highest point of the yellow zone. Breaching TOY means a warning of a buffer situation. *TOY = Red zone + Yellow zone.*

- **Top of green (TOG)**
  The highest point of the green zone that reflects a comfortable buffer position until it crosses into the TOY zone. *TOG = Red + Yellow + Green.*

- **Over the top of green (OTOG)**
  A situation in which the on-hand or available stock is over the top of the defined green zone (TOG) and signals excess inventory position.

Figure 15.7 shows an example of calculating the buffer zones. Start out with calculating the yellow zone, followed by the green zone, and finally the red zone. Data required for calculating all three zones is also shown in Figure 15.7. The three zones are calculated as follows:

1. TOR: 90
2. TOY: *Red + Yellow* = 90 + 150 = 240
3. TOG: *Red + Yellow + Green* = 90 + 150 + 90 = 330

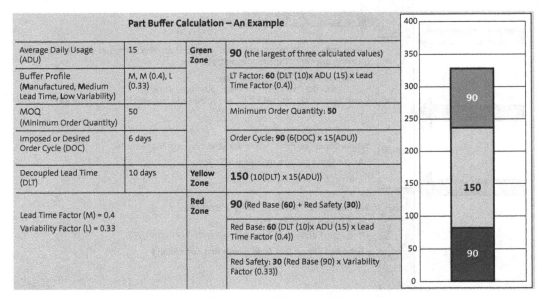

Part Buffer Calculation – An Example				
Average Daily Usage (ADU)	15	Green Zone	**90** (the largest of three calculated values)	
Buffer Profile (**Manufactured, Medium Lead Time, Low Variability**)	M, M (0.4), L (0.33)		LT Factor: **60** (DLT (10)x ADU (15) x Lead Time Factor (0.4))	
MOQ (Minimum Order Quantity)	50		Minimum Order Quantity: **50**	
Imposed or Desired Order Cycle (DOC)	6 days		Order Cycle: **90** (6(DOC) x 15(ADU))	
Decoupled Lead Time (DLT)	10 days	Yellow Zone	**150** (10(DLT) x 15(ADU))	
Lead Time Factor (M) = 0.4 Variability Factor (L) = 0.33		Red Zone	**90** (Red Base (**60**) + Red Safety (**30**))	
			Red Base: **60** (DLT (10)x ADU (15) x Lead Time Factor (0.4))	
			Red Safety: **30** (Red Base (90) x Variability Factor (0.33))	

Figure 15.7 Buffer Calculation (©Demand Driven Institute, used with permission)

Dynamic Adjustments

In this component (see Figure 15.4), a materials planner oversees dynamic adjustments to buffers to account for product seasonality, stage of a product maturity such as a soon-to-be-discontinued product or a new product introduction, and capacity adjustments, and then prebuilds the requirements in anticipation of future demand or slowdown. Buffers, such as stock buffers, also adjust dynamically to account for supply variability, a procurement or production schedule mismatch, or a machine reaching an overload capacity situation. As already covered, the stock, schedule, and capacity buffers adjust dynamically to ensure elimination of distortions to relevant information and materials flows.

Demand-Driven Planning

In this component (see Figure 15.4), a materials planner uses the visual planning tools to create replenishment orders where necessary. Replenishment orders are created based on the *net flow equation*:

Net flow equation: On-hand + On-order – Qualified sales order (or demand)

In this equation, *on-hand* is the available stock in the warehouse, *on-order* refers to the quantities of materials ordered and awaiting receipt, and *qualified sales order (or demand)* refers to the sales orders due today, those past due, and qualified future spikes. The qualified future spike considers the quantity threshold within a defined time horizon in a *daily* time bucket to decide if the spike qualifies to be included in net flow equation calculation. For example, a qualified future spike is included in the net flow equation calculation when the demand quantity of the material is 50 units or more (the quantity threshold) on a single day (daily time bucket) and within the time horizon of one week.

Visible and Collaborative Execution

In this component (see Figure 15.8), materials planners take action to convert suggested replenishment orders into procurement orders, production orders, or stock transport orders. Further, material planners use material lead times or scheduling synchronization alerts to quickly attend to any material or scheduling disruptions that threaten to destabilize the supply chain. DDR is a priority-based pull system that alerts planners visually whenever a situation warrants action or attention.

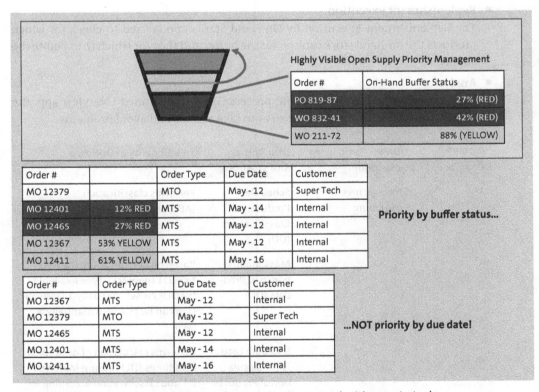

Figure 15.8 DDMRP Execution (©Demand Driven Institute, used with permission)

Table 15.1 shows the DDMRP components mapped to the available DDR apps in SAP S/4HANA. The following is a brief introduction to each component, and we'll dive into them further in later sections:

- **Buffer positioning**
  DDMRP starts with the product classification using the Schedule Product Classification app. After the classification, the Buffer Positioning app can be used to select where the decoupling point buffers should be positioned. Finally, the products are classified according to the lead time using the Schedule Lead Time Classification of Products app. Alternatively, manually classifying the products using the Mass Maintenance of Products (DD) app is also possible.

- **Buffer sizing**
  In this step, the actual buffer calculation will be executed with the Schedule Buffer Proposal Calculation app. The calculated buffers can be reviewed using the Manage Buffer Levels app.

- **Replenishment planning**
  The Replenishment Planning by Planning Priority app will be used to evaluate which products are below the reorder point.

- **Replenishment execution**
  The Replenishment Execution by On-Hand Status app is used to check for which products the on-hand stock can't cover the buffer and thus for which to expedite the supply.

- **Analytics**
  This is the last step of the DDMRP process. With the Planned Overview app, the DDMRP-related KPIs can be found so as to take actions and avoid problems.

DDMRP Component	DDMRP Component Description	DDR App in SAP S/4HANA	Functionality of DDR App
1	Strategic Inventory Positioning	Schedule Product Classification (DD)	Performs classification (ABC, EFG, PQR)
		Mass Maintenance of Products (DD)	Based on classification, the MRP type D1 (new MRP type available for DDR) is set manually. Classification can be changed manually as well.
		Schedule Lead Time Calculation of Products (DD)	Performs calculation of decoupled lead times (DLTs) using MRP type D1 and classification according to EFG.

Table 15.1 DDMRP Components Mapping with DDR Apps in SAP S/4HANA

DDMRP Component	DDMRP Component Description	DDR App in SAP S/4HANA	Functionality of DDR App
2	Buffer Profiles and Levels	Schedule Buffer Proposal Calculation	Calculates buffers based on DLTs using MRP type D1.
		Manage Buffer Levels	Enables users to adjust calculated values of buffers.
3	Dynamic Adjustments	Replenish Planning by Planning Priority	The Replenish Planning by Planning Priority app is used to evaluate which products are below the reorder point.
4	Demand-Driven Planning	MRP Run	Creates receipt elements.
		Replenishment Execution by On-Hand Status	With the Replenishment Execution by On-Hand Status app, a materials planner can check for which products the on-hand stock can't cover the buffer and expedite the supply.
5	Visible and Collaborative Execution	Planner Overview	The Planner Overview app helps with finding DDMRP-related KPIs to take actions and avoid supply chain problems.

Table 15.1 DDMRP Components Mapping with DDR Apps in SAP S/4HANA (Cont.)

The first three sections of this chapter discussed the DDR concepts in detail and laid the foundations that will form the basis of mapping these DDR concepts with actual setup in the SAP S/4HANA system, which is discussed in detail in the following sections.

15.4 DDMRP Setup

To begin, this section will focus on the configuration settings to explain how they impact the DDR master data and even the business processes. Then we'll discuss setting up the minimal DDR-specific master data to get the DDR process up and running in the system. Next we cover some transactions or real-time business processes that DDR takes into consideration in order to calculate its own set of parameters. These parameters calculate the three difference zones (green, yellow, red) and set up the right classifications (ABC, EFG, PQR, XYZ, etc.).

As the entire DDR process is embedded in various stages of the logistics and supply chain, such as procurement, production, distribution, and sales, it's best that all relevant stakeholders gain a better understanding of an end-to-end DDR process flow.

Let's discuss configuration settings first.

15.4.1   Configuration Settings

The configuration settings related to DDR are buffer profile, key terms, MRP type, and lot sizing, and these are discussed in the following sections.

Buffer Profile

According to the DDMRP principles, products must first be classified according to various classifications, such as the usage value (ABC classification), lead time (EFG classification), BOM usage (PQR classification), and variability (XYZ classification).

Depending on the settings of the variability and the lead time classification made in a buffer profile, SAP S/4HANA will determine a variability factor (VF) and a lead time factor (LT factor). Both of these factors are predetermined in a buffer profile and are used to calculate the buffer. Figure 15.9 shows the standard buffer profile delivered by SAP, which can be found in the Buffer Profile Maintenance app. Alternatively, the buffer profile can also be accessed using Transaction PPH_DD_BUF_PROF in the SAP S/4HANA system.

Let's consider an example of how the system determines the VF and the LT factor from the buffer profile. For a material purchased externally (referred to as **Buy**) with a medium variability indicator and a short lead time, as shown in Figure 15.9, the VF is 0.50 and the LT factor is 0.80. This is noted in the first row of the buffer profile in Figure 15.9.

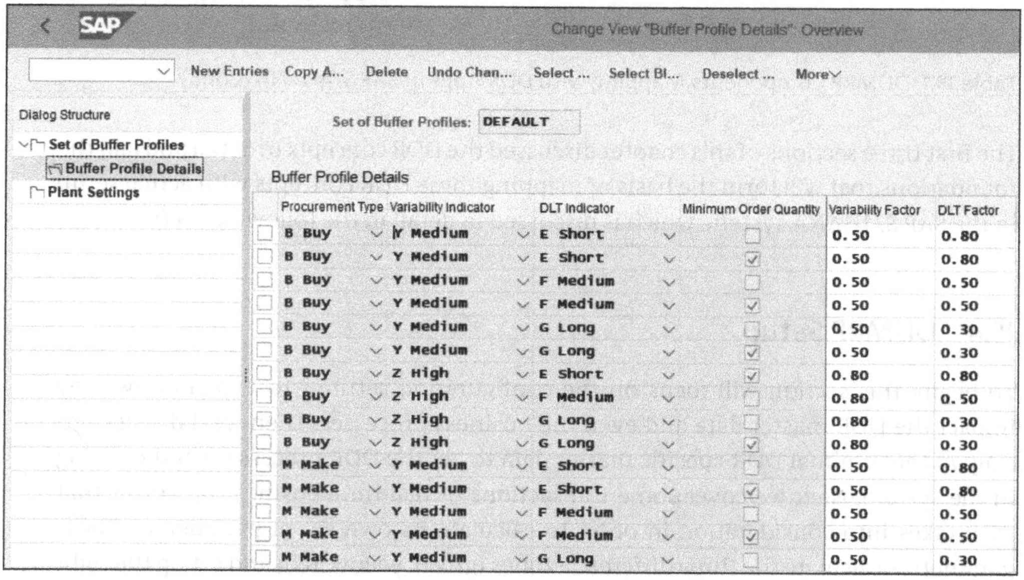

Figure 15.9 Standard Buffer Profile

If necessary, a new buffer profile can be created with adjusted factors or a different buffer profile can be assigned to each plant (in this case, plant 1105, as shown in Figure 15.10). Plant 1105 will be used as an example throughout this chapter.

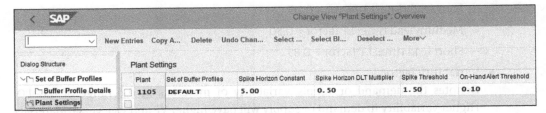

Figure 15.10 Plant-Specific Settings of Buffer Profile

The next section discusses some of the key DDR terms, which are helpful to refer to when considering Figure 15.9 and Figure 15.10.

Key Terms

The following lists some important DDR terms and their meanings. These terms are either defined in supply chain associations, such as APICS, or by the DDI:

- **Item type**
  Categorizes various material types, such as procured (P), intermediate (I), semifinished (SF), manufactured (M), and distributed (D). In the SAP S/4HANA buffer profile, procured materials are referred to as **Buy**, the produced components are referred to as **Make**, and the interplant transfer (stock transport orders) of materials are referred to as **Transfer**.

- **Average daily usage (ADU)**
  The average consumption of a material in a given time period.

- **Minimum order quantity (MOQ)**
  The minimum procurement quantity imposed by the supplier, or the minimum production quantity or economic order quantity of a material. In SAP S/4HANA, this information is maintained in the **Minimum Lot Size** field in the **MRP1** view of a material master.

- **Imposed or desired order cycle (DOC)**
  The frequency of procuring a material, either imposed from the supplier side or a company's own ordering cycle.

- **Decoupled lead time (DLT)**
  The longest but reduced unprotected or unbuffered lead time in the BOM to procure or produce a material. In SAP S/4HANA, this information is maintained or updated in the **Total Replenishment Lead Time** field of a material master (in the **MRP 3** view of a material master).

- **Lead time factor (LT factor)**
  Denotes a factor in the lead time to procure or produce a material in the *range* of 0.0–1.0. Longer lead times will have smaller LT factors and vice versa. Materials planners mutually agree to define the lead time categories (long, medium, and short) and then assign an LT factor to each lead time category. Here's an example:

- Long lead time: LT factor = 0.20
- Medium lead time: LT factor = 0.50
- Short lead time: LT factor = 0.85

- **Variability factor**

Denotes the demand or supply variability of materials in the range of 0.0–1.0. Higher variability in demand or supply will have higher VF and vice versa. Materials planners mutually agree to define the VF categories (stable, intermittent, and unstable/unpredictable demand/supply) and then assign VF to each category. Here's an example:

- Erratic supply/demand (high variability): VF = 0.85
- Semi-stable supply/demand (significantly high variability): VF = 0.70
- Mostly stable supply/demand (medium variability): VF = 0.30

- **Buffer profile**

A logical grouping of materials sharing similar characteristics, such as materials being procured, manufactured, or distributed across warehouses. The buffer profile also mentions the LT factor and VF of each material. A buffer profile consists of an item part, lead time category (and LT factor), and variability category (and VF). For example, a buffer profile M, M (0.4), L (0.33) means the following:

- Part is manufactured (M)
- Has medium lead time (M) with a LT factor (0.4)
- Has low (L) demand/supply variability with a VF (0.33)

- **On-hand alert threshold**

It's defined as a percentage of the safety stock and is maintained in the Buffer Profile Maintenance app (refer to the last column of Figure 15.10). For example, if the safety stock of a material is 1,000 PC, and an on-hand alert threshold is maintained as 0.10 in the buffer profile, then the system will issue a red alert in the Replenishment Execution by On-Hand Alert app as soon as the stock falls to 100 or below (1,000 × 0.10 = 100 PC).

- **Spike horizon**

The spike horizon is a time window that starts the day after today and comprises the DLT multiplied by a factor called the spike horizon DLT multiplier (SHT), with the addition of an offset called the spike horizon constant. The idea is that DDR will also react to a demand within this time window to ensure product availability. Referring to Figure 15.10 again, and as an example, the **Spike Horizon Constant** is maintained as **5** (days), while the **Spike Horizon DLT Multiplier** is maintained as **0.5**. Now, if the DLT calculated by the DDR process is eight days, then the calculation for **Spike Horizon** is *Spike horizon = 5 (spike horizon constant) + (8 (DLT) × 0.5) = 9 days.*

- **Spike threshold**
  DDR won't react to all the demand within the spike horizon but only to qualified demands. To be considered a qualified demand, a requirement quantity must be greater than the spike threshold, which is calculated by multiplying the safety stock by the *spike threshold factor*. Only those highlighted demands will be considered qualified demands because they are within the spike horizon and above the spike threshold. Let's discuss this with an example: A safety stock (red zone) of 1,000 is calculated by the DDR process. A qualified spike demand of 1,500 is taken into account by DDR because it's greater than the order spike threshold of 1,500. An order spike threshold is a multiplication between the safety stock (in this example, 1,000) and the **Spike Threshold** (1.50) as defined in the buffer profile (refer to Figure 15.10). Therefore, 1,000 × 1.5 = 1,500, which is the order spike threshold. So, any sales order with quantity of 1,500 or more and within the spike horizon (nine days; see previous bullet point) is considered a qualified demand.

Material Requirements Planning Type

DDR uses the MRP type D1 that has **Firming Type 1—Automatic Firming and Order Proposals Rescheduled Out**. This setting entails that any existing planned order that lies within the time fence will be automatically considered firm and won't be changed by MRP. If there is a shortage within the time fence, a new planned order will be created, but it will be rescheduled out (i.e., it will be created outside the time fence). As soon as this newly created planned order falls within the planning time fence, the system will automatically firm it.

If the planning time fence is 15 days, then in a stock/requirements list (Transaction MD04), the MRP results when using MRP type P1 will uniquely identify the **End of Planning Time Fence** when this 15-day period ends. A DDMRP type can be any MRP type with **MRP procedure C**, such as the standard MRP type D1, and will be used throughout this chapter. A DDMRP type acts like a reorder point MRP type, wherein the yellow buffer zone is the reorder point, the green zone represents the maximum stock level, and the safety stock is the red zone.

Lot Sizing

A lot sizing procedure defines the rules for the quantity of the replenishment proposal created by MRP. The lot sizing procedures available in SAP S/4HANA can be grouped into the following categories:

- Static lot sizing procedures
- Period lot sizing procedures
- Optimum lot sizing procedures

DDR belongs to the static lot sizing procedures. In the static lot sizing procedures, the quantity will be calculated according to the quantity specifications defined in the material master. To achieve the correct MRP results for DDR, it's also important to choose a lot sizing procedure that will replenish up to the maximum stock level after covering the requirements. For this, standard lot sizing procedure H1 is available in the system.

Positioning a buffer for a product in DDR entails selecting a DDMRP type, such as the standard MRP type D1, as well as using the standard lot sizing procedure H1 so that MRP can correctly replenish up to the maximum stock level. Technically, these settings can be made directly in the material master, but SAP also offers the Buffer Positioning app (Section 15.5.5 will discuss this app), which was specially developed for this purpose. When using this application, filters are available so that a planner can select the products to process. Those products will be listed with their respective classifications and further details, such as the lead time and the DLT. This information can be used to help determine whether a buffer should be positioned or not.

15.4.2   Master Data Settings

The following sections list the critical master data setup required for the DDR process.

Material Master

For material master 25 in plant 1105, the **MRP Type** field is assigned "D1", while the **Lot Sizing Procedure** field is assigned "H1". This material-plant combination will be used as a DDR example throughout this chapter. Meanwhile, for the sake of this example only, maintain the numeric values for different fields in the material master as noted in Table 15.2, which also includes the purpose they serve.

Field in Material Master	Field Value in Material Master	Purpose in DDR
Maximum Stock Level	"500"	TOG
Reorder Point	"100"	TOY
Safety Stock	"50"	TOR
Procurement Type	"E"	For materials produced in-house: value "E" For procured materials: value "F"
Special Procurement Type	"40"	To be maintained only for inter-plant transfer materials

Table 15.2 Material Master Fields Maintenance for Buffers in DDR

[«]

> **Note**
>
> As this is just an example, simply maintain any reasonable values in all stock-related fields. The DDR process will automatically calculate and update these fields based on actual material usage or consumption data, which is discussed in Section 15.4.3.
>
> Second, for all the materials that are part of the DDR process, such as raw materials, packing materials, and semifinished materials, maintain the relevant data in the respective material masters.

Figure 15.11 shows the **Demand-Driven Replenishment** tab available in the **Stock/Requirements List** (Transaction MD04), in which the **Net Flow Position** is shown along with other details. The **Demand-Driven Replenishment** tab will only appear in the **Stock/Requirements List** for only those materials that are DDR-managed. Further, scroll to the far-right side (slide the gray bar located at the center of the screen to the right side) of Figure 15.11 to see some more DDR classifications, such as the variability indicator or the DLT indicator, among other information.

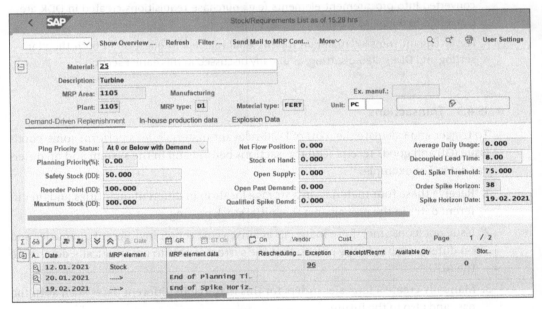

Figure 15.11 Stock/Requirements List for DDR Material

Bill of Materials

A material's BOM consists of components grouped together with the relevant quantities that are needed to produce the material in the production process. For example, if vanilla ice cream is the main product, then its BOM will consist of all the ingredients (referred to as *components*) needed to produce it. Similarly, to produce an automobile requires an engine, a chassis, a body, and a large number of other components.

15

To create the BOM of a material, use Transaction CS01. On the initial screen, enter **Material** "25" and **Plant** "1105". Maintain material numbers for the individual components, together with the quantity for each. Although it contains quite a number of materials, only materials 18, 63, and 64 are relevant to DDR (in addition to the main material 25).

> **Note**
>
> Although only BOM details are covered here, it's also important to maintain the other manufacturing data, such as routing data for discrete manufacturing (master recipe for process manufacturing) and production version. This master data setup will ensure that the planning elements created by DDR can be successfully converted into production elements (e.g., planned orders created in DDR are converted to production or manufacturing orders).
>
> Similarly, for procured materials, at least maintain a purchasing info record, which is a one-to-one procurement relationship between a material and a supplier. This master data setup will ensure that the planning elements created in DDR can be successfully converted into procurement elements (e.g., purchase requisitions created in DDR are converted to purchase orders).
>
> For interplant transfer, maintain the material masters in question in both the plant setting and DDR-related setting, as already discussed in this earlier section.

15.4.3   Transactions

To trigger and calculate the ADU of DDR-relevant materials, let's perform some goods issue (GI) and goods receipt (GR) transactions beforehand in the system and on different dates. For example:

1. Receive these four materials in a storage location in different quantities and on different dates in the past against the initial stock posting.

2. Issue out (consume) these materials against a cost center in different quantities and on different dates in the past so that the system is able to automatically determine the ADU.

3. Manually create a few sales orders for this material in different dates such as in the past and also in the future.

4. As DDR now also enables planning for the future to account for any forecast/predicted requirements, maintain some values in the planned independent requirements (PIRs). This step will then enable the system to calculate the ADU for future consumption too.

All the steps just mentioned are briefly covered in the following sections.

Goods Receipts/Goods Issue

In this example, when these DDR and non-DDR materials are created in the SAP S/4HANA system, there are no initial stocks nor any history of past receipts or consumptions. To maintain some stocks of different materials and on different dates in the past, the GR process is performed.

Use Transaction MIGO, and choose **Goods Receipt** from the first dropdown list followed by choosing **Other** from the second dropdown list. Ensure that movement type **561** is used for initial entry of stock balances (**Init.entry of stBal.**), as shown on the right-hand side of the screen.

In this example, four DDR-based materials are received in a quantity of 100 each on January 1, 2021 (**Posting Date**). A few more similar GR transactions are undertaken but in varying quantities and on different dates. These receipts of materials on different dates and of different quantities will enable the system to calculate the LT factor and supply VF.

In a real-time, actual supply chain scenario, such GRs are undertaken with reference to purchase orders for procured materials, via production or process orders for in-house-produced materials, and via stock transport orders for interplant transfer materials.

To begin GI— that is, to record consumption of materials with reference to a cost center—make selections from both the dropdowns: choose **Goods Issue** from the first dropdown on the left-hand side, and then select **Other** in the relevant options dropdown that appears. Ensure that movement type **201** is used in the **GI for Cost Center** field for consumption of materials against the cost center, as shown on the right-hand side of the screen. A few more similar GIs are undertaken, but in different quantities and on different dates. These issuances or consumption of materials on different dates and quantities will enable the system to calculate ADU.

In the real-time supply chain scenario, goods are issued either with reference to production or process orders (movement type 261), cost centers (movement type 201), sale orders (movement type 601), or stock transport orders (movement type 541).

Planned Independent Requirements

As of SAP S/4HANA 1909, PIRs can be used to project ADU in the future and allow the system to calculate a projected buffer for the future. This is especially relevant, for example, if it's known in advance that there will be an event that might affect the product consumption, such as a marketing campaign or a seasonal increase in demand. The horizon in the future for which the system will look for PIRs can be defined in the Mass Maintenance of Products (DD) app.

To create the PIRs of a material, use either Transaction MD61 or MD64. For this example, enter **Material** "25" and **Plant** "1105", and assign the **Version** as "00" (**Requirements Plan**). Define the **Planning Horizon** and the **Planning period** in days so that the system brings up the relevant fields for data input. Press ⏎ Enter ⏎ to arrive at the screen shown in Figure 15.12.

Figure 15.12 shows the day-wise future demand of material 25 in plant 1105. It's important to select the checkbox in column **A** (active) so that the system will consider these PIRs during the MRP run.

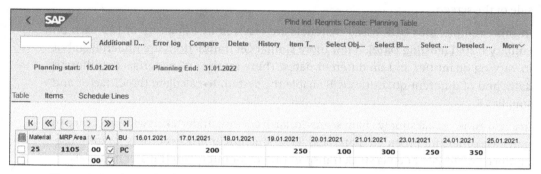

Figure 15.12 Planned Independent Requirements

Open Past Demand

Open past demand refers to sales orders for which the delivery dates have already passed, but they aren't delivered yet. To create open past demand—that is, to create a sales order—use Transaction VA01. Enter the standard sales **Order Type** "OR", as well as the organizational data details, such as **Sales Organization** "1000", **Distribution Channel** "10", and **Division** "00", and then press ⏎ Enter ⏎.

As shown in Figure 15.13, enter the customer, which in this case is **Sold-To Party** "300010". At the item level, enter **Material** "25" and the **Order Quantity** "600" **PC**.

Notice that the **Req. Deliv.Date** (required delivery date) in this case is **14.01.2021** (January 14, 2021). This is the date that DDR will consider when evaluating both the open past demand (sales orders that aren't partially or fully delivered to the customers yet) and any future demand that lies within the spike horizon in order to make them a part of the net flow equation. Save the sales order, and, for this example, the system creates sales order number 14.

If there are several line items in a sales order, then the system considers the **First Date** field for scheduling and DDR calculation purposes. It's important to note that DDR only consider sales orders for demand and not customer requirements (Transactions MD81).

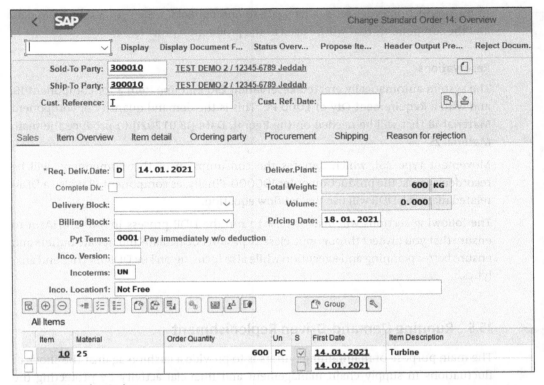

Figure 15.13 Sales Order

Open Orders

Open orders are basically the production orders or process orders for in-house-produced materials, purchase orders for procurement-related materials, and stock transport orders for interplant transfer-related materials whose goods are partially delivered or not delivered yet but are expected to be (i.e., open orders).

To create a production order, use Transaction CO01 (use Transaction COR1 for creating a process order). On the initial production order screen that appears, enter **Material** "25", production **Plant** "1105", and standard order **Type** "PP01". Choose **Continue**.

The header data screen of the production order consists of information that is applicable to the entire order, such as production order number, material number, plant, and order type. The **Total Qty** field is relevant, and the quantity 100 is the open order quantity of material 25 in plant 1105 that hasn't been delivered yet and hence is considered in the net flow equation of DDR. The **Dates/Times** section is equally important as these dates form the basis for when the system expects the goods to be delivered to the warehouse.

In the production order screen, navigate to **Components**, which shows the BOM data and the components that will be used in the production process.

Reservations

The system automatically created **Reservation 250** and line item **3** for component 18, and with a **Requirement Qty** of **1,000 PC**. This is the demand quantity of component **Material 18** that will be needed on the **Reqmt. Date (18.01.2021)** to produce the main **Material 25**.

Movement type 261, which denotes the consumption of this component, will be recorded against the production order 100000. Finally, as component 18 is also a DDR-related material, DDR will use the net flow equation.

The following sections will discuss how to run the DDR process in SAP S/4HANA to ensure that you protect throughput, classify products, calculate and update buffers and ensure better planning and execution while also focusing on key DDR metrics and analytics.

15.5 Running Demand-Driven Replenishment

The main purpose of maintaining buffers is to provide a cushion against the shock of fluctuations in supply chain management and financial activity by protecting the throughput. *Throughput* is defined as the rate at which material is exiting in the manufacturing process. *Lead time* is the time it takes to move through the manufacturing process, and WIP, as mentioned previously, is the amount of inventory contained between entry and exit points of the manufacturing process. Therefore, throughput = (WIP ÷ lead time).

The following sections will discuss how to protect throughput, classify materials based on ABC, PQR, and XYZ, position buffers, and classify materials based on lead time.

15.5.1 Protecting Throughput

DDR builds on the same buffer concept to achieve the following two primary objectives:

- Provides shock absorption by providing inventory, thereby ensuring to protect the downstream uses from fluctuations in demand and supply
- Reduces the lead time required to deliver a product by removing anything upstream from the buffer from the cumulative lead time

To achieve these objectives, a series of DDR-specific steps are undertaken in SAP S/4HANA, such as classifying products for variability or usage value, positioning buffers, and finally classifying products based on the lead time.

Classification is a central step in determining the decoupling points in a multilevel BOM structure as part of the DDR approach. The planning objects' product/plant or product/plant/MRP areas are valuated according to their essential characteristics and are then assigned to classes on this basis. This classification helps in identifying the appropriate settings for each planning object, which should be selected based on these characteristics.

In the context of DDR, these settings are defined in a certain way. The results of classification lead to the assignment of buffer profiles in a subsequent step: buffer positioning. As a result, classification is a central building block in the planning process of the DDR approach in SAP S/4HANA. In SAP S/4HANA, classification is carried out exclusively based on SAP Fiori apps.

15.5.2   Classification

The Schedule Product Classification (DD) app, along with other DDR-related apps, is available after activating DDR in SAP S/4HANA. These apps are available via the SAP Fiori launchpad.

Some SAP Fiori apps for DDR need to be executed at the start of using DDR as a solution, whereas operational SAP Fiori apps for DDR are used on a daily basis. This section will walk through the DDR implementation steps, beginning with classifying the products. Technically speaking, buffer positioning may take place before the classification, but the product classification is an important factor to be considered when deciding where a buffer should be positioned, so a materials planner should always start with the product classification.

> **Note**
>
> Because the product classification will help identify where a buffer should be positioned, it's recommended to classify all the products that may potentially be planned with the DDR logic.

After opening the app, an overview screen appears that displays the job runs of the past. Choose **Create** to start an application job for making the necessary settings for the classification run. The **Job Template** in Figure 15.14 ❶ is preselected, while a user-defined **Job Name** can be maintained to clearly distinguish the individual application jobs. Scroll down, and then choose the **Start Immediately** ❷ checkbox to begin the application job right away. To schedule an application job, choose **Define Recurrence Pattern** ❸, which opens the popup shown in Figure 15.15. When scheduling a new job, it's important to first define the scheduling options that will set the job start date and the recurrence pattern.

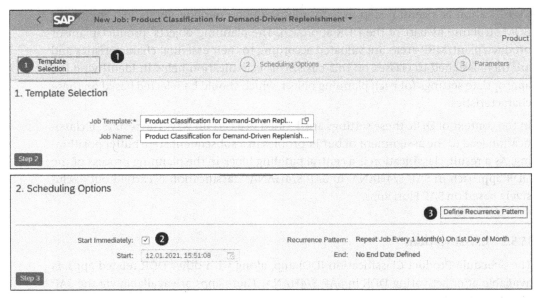

Figure 15.14 Product Classification

When choosing the relevant option from the **Recurrence Pattern** dropdown scheduling options shown in Figure 15.15, the next few fields will prompt the user to maintain the application job recurrence's details. For this example, choose **Single Run**, and then choose **OK**; the screen in Figure 15.16 will appear.

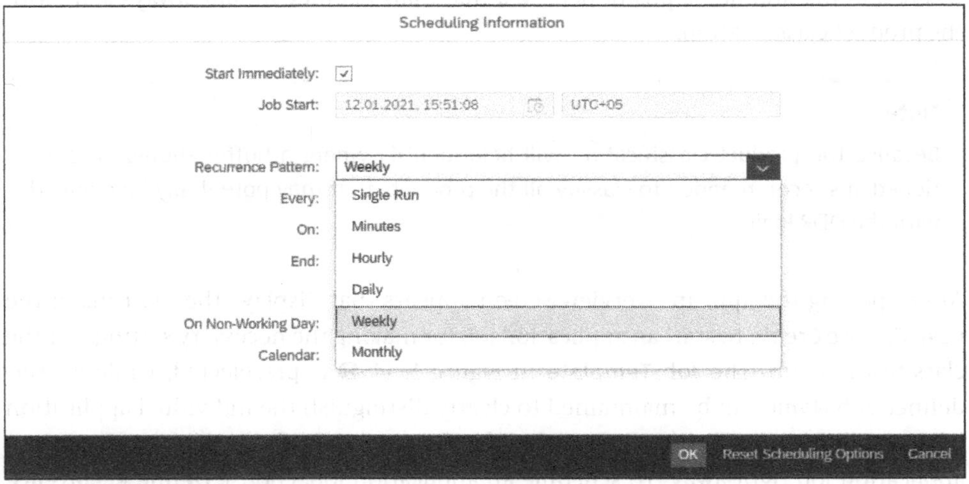

Figure 15.15 Scheduling Options

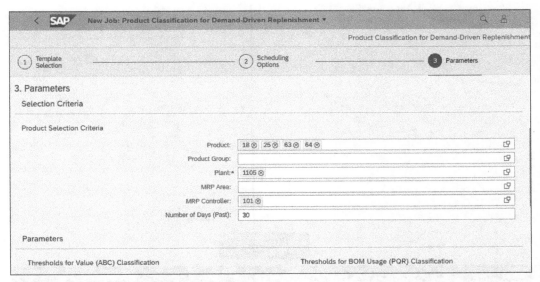

Figure 15.16 Selection Criteria for Products

Following the scheduling step, the next step is to define the **Selection Criteria** settings that will be used to select which products will be classified in the job. Figure 15.16 shows four entries in the **Product** field, the relevant **Plant**, and the **MRP Controller** value as selection criteria, so the application job will classify all the products that meet these criteria.

An important parameter included in the selection criteria is the **Number of Days (Past)** value. This will represent the number of days in the past for which the system will look for goods movements (goods issuances/consumptions) to calculate the ADU. In this example, the **Number of Days (Past)** value is maintained as "30", so the system will look for goods issued in the past 30 days to determine the ADU. Scrolling down the **Selection Criteria** section in Figure 15.16 will bring up the screen area shown in Figure 15.17, where the thresholds for the value, BOM usage, and variability classifications can be defined.

While this app analyzes material movements to determine past consumption in the specified period, it isn't possible to influence the selection of material documents that form the basis of consumption. Only the threshold values that are used to delimit the previously mentioned classes can be influenced and can be maintained as percentage values in the app, as shown in Figure 15.17.

Maintain the relevant classification parameters for ABC, XYZ, and PQR in Figure 15.17. Then choose **Check** to validate all settings made, and the message noted at the bottom of the screen will appear. Finally, choose **Schedule** to schedule the application job.

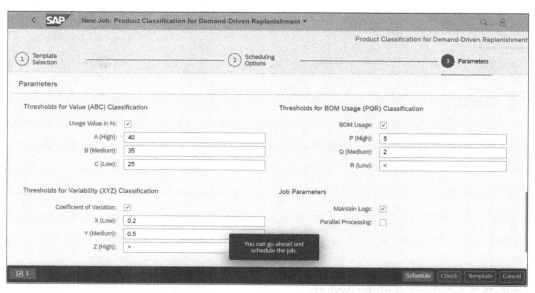

Figure 15.17 Thresholds Settings

The settings for three different classification procedures can be made:

- ABC analysis
- XYZ analysis
- PQR analysis

The ABC classification evaluates the relative importance of a material/plant or material/plant/MRP area combination in relation to the other planning objects analyzed on the basis of historical consumption. The objects are divided into three groups:

- **A materials**
  Relative to all objects analyzed in a run, these have had the highest consumption value in the past.
- **B materials**
  These materials have a lower proportion of total consumption compared to A materials.
- **C materials**
  These materials have the lowest proportion.

For classification, the consumption value is determined on the basis of the material documents. The materials involved in the classification run are then sorted in descending order according to their consumption value. An A is assigned to a planning object until the threshold value of, for example, 70% is reached cumulatively across all materials of the class. The subsequent materials are then assigned a B classification until, say, the next 20% of the consumption value is reached; the remaining materials are classified as C materials. The Schedule Product Classification (DD) app can perform this analysis at the level of material/plant combinations, as well as at the level of material/plant MRP area; other levels aren't possible.

The **Value (ABC) Classification** setting will be used to define if a product belongs to the group of products with the largest GI value (classification A), to the intermediate group with a medium GI value (classification B), or to the group of products with the lowest GI value (classification C). SAP S/4HANA will calculate the total GI value of these products within the interval defined in the selection criteria, sort materials according to this value, and then define to which group each product belongs, according to the percentages defined in these thresholds. This means that the input for these thresholds will be a percentage, and the sum of the three values should be 100%.

SAP S/4HANA will calculate the total GI value within the period; that is, both the material price and the number of issues will be considered. This means that a material with a high price but without too many GIs may have the same classification as a material with a low price and a high number of GIs.

ABC analysis is therefore a way of dividing the planning objects into classes according to their value-based significance. This analysis method is now being combined with two other methods that bring in further important aspects for the identification of key characteristics, thus facilitating the goal of being able to assign optimal settings to a planning object, for example, with regard to buffer configuration. One of the two additional classification methods provided by the app is XYZ analysis, which is used to assess the predictability of future demand on the basis of past consumption. Analogous to the ABC analysis, there are three classes:

- **X materials**
  These materials have the most constant consumption, so it's assumed that future consumption can be predicted with high accuracy, and therefore buffers for the coverage of uncertainties can be reduced.

- **Y materials**
  The materials in this class have greater variations in consumption than X materials.

- **Z materials**
  These materials show the greatest variations in consumption, so it's assumed that predictability accuracy is low.

The criterion for assessing predictability is a statistical fluctuation factor called the *coefficient of variation*, which determines, squares, and sums up the deviation of each individual observed historical values from the mean value. This sum is then divided by the number of observed values and normalized to the mean value to obtain a relative fluctuation measure.

Similar to ABC analysis, the app enables the maintenance of threshold limits for the XYZ analysis. Unlike ABC analysis, however, these are absolute values, not percentage values.

The **Variability (XYZ) Classification** setting will classify products according to the demand variability. Products with the classification X will have a low variability, products with classification Y will have medium variability, and products with classification Z will have high variability. The total sum of sales orders overdue, sales orders due on the current date, and order spikes are considered as the actual demand.

With the mean and standard deviation of the actual demand, a coefficient of variation is calculated. This coefficient is used as the threshold for variability: the higher the coefficient, the higher the variability.

The last possible classification methodology within the framework of the app is the PQR analysis, which can be used to analyze the planning objects to determine how many BOMs they are used in. The reason for this type of analysis is to find out whether there is a single use or multiple use and thus how many recipients are relevant for the object.

The **BOM Usage (PQR) Classification** setting is used to determine if a material is used in a high number of BOMs (classification P), a medium number of BOMs (classification Q), or a low number of BOMs (classification R). The value defined for each threshold is basically the total number of material BOMs in which a product is used, and it will be classified accordingly.

The three classification methods mentioned can be used to classify material/plant combinations or material/plant/MRP area combinations according to the following essential characteristics:

- How important they are in relative terms in the material spectrum
- How predictable the future demand is
- How many objects are used

These three characteristics are then used to determine the central settings of the DDR process, mainly to define how these objects are controlled and whether inventory needs to be maintained. Therefore, the results of the classification will play an important role in the next step: buffer positioning.

[»]

EFG Analysis According to Replenishment Lead Times

In SAP S/4HANA, another possibility to classify objects is referred to as *EFG classification* and is based on the replenishment lead time. However, before deciding how to classify an object on the basis of the replenishment lead time, it's important to first calculate the decoupled replenishment lead time that doesn't exist at this early stage. Therefore, this type of classification can only be executed with a different app in a later process step. This topic in the context of the lead time determination will be discussed in Section 15.5.4.

A summary of the results of the classification run can be viewed in the application log of the Schedule Product Classification (DD) app. The log can be assessed directly in the initial screen of the app or by clicking the **Back** button in the job settings overview. From the overview screen, two more detailed views are available:

1. **Job Log**
   Shows messages that have been identified by the system during runtime. In this context, it's also possible to filter by message types.

2. **Job Details**
   Provides settings selected for the job, such as threshold values or selections.

The results of the classification are often used together with other information to make the previously mentioned decisions, which will play a role at a later stage. If, in addition to the mathematically deductible criteria of the classifications, additional criteria that can't be mathematically derived are used to make appropriate decisions, this is referred to as a *grouping*. For example, it can make sense to treat a simple standard part different from a more complex electronic part with a similar consumption behavior—that is, with comparable classification results. When classes and groups are combined, the term *clusters* is often used.

After the first step of product classification, the information needed to position the decoupling buffers of the DDR products is available. To position those buffers, the results of the previous classification to determine if a product is a good candidate for a buffer can be considered. The product classification, however, isn't the only factor to be considered: there are external factors, and the planner can also use their own experience to determine when a buffer is necessary. There are some situations in which a buffer may be a good option:

- A semifinished product is classified as P because it's used in too many BOMs.

- Because it's a key component and it's used to produce many products, it might be a good idea to position a buffer for this product, avoiding stock-outs that might have far-reaching effects.

- The source of supply of a given component purchased externally isn't reliable, and there are too many delayed deliveries. In this case, adding a buffer would mean that the demand for this product would be absorbed by the safety stock if there is a delay.

- An important product has a long lead time to be produced, so any late demand arriving would mean a long delay.

- In an MTO scenario, a customer can't wait for the whole total replenishment lead time to have the product delivered. In this case, adding a buffer to strategically selected components will reduce the lead time, as the demand for this customer will be absorbed by the buffer.

15

15.5.3   Buffer Positioning

When entering this application, use the filters to select which products will be processed. Those products will be listed with their respective classifications and further details, such as the lead time and the DLT. This information can be used to help determine whether a buffer should be positioned or not (see Figure 15.18).

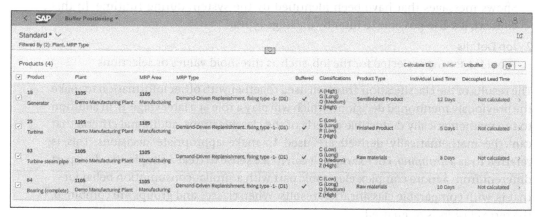

Figure 15.18 Unbuffered Products without Decoupled Lead Time

A product can be directly buffered or unbuffered from the initial screen of the Buffer Positioning app by clicking the **Buffer** or **Unbuffer** button (see Figure 15.18). On selecting one of these options, a popup appears to select a new MRP type, the new lot sizing procedure, and additional DDR-related material master settings. Any changes made here will be saved directly in the material master. It's also possible from the initial screen to trigger the DLT calculation for one or more products as done in this example and shown in Figure 15.19.

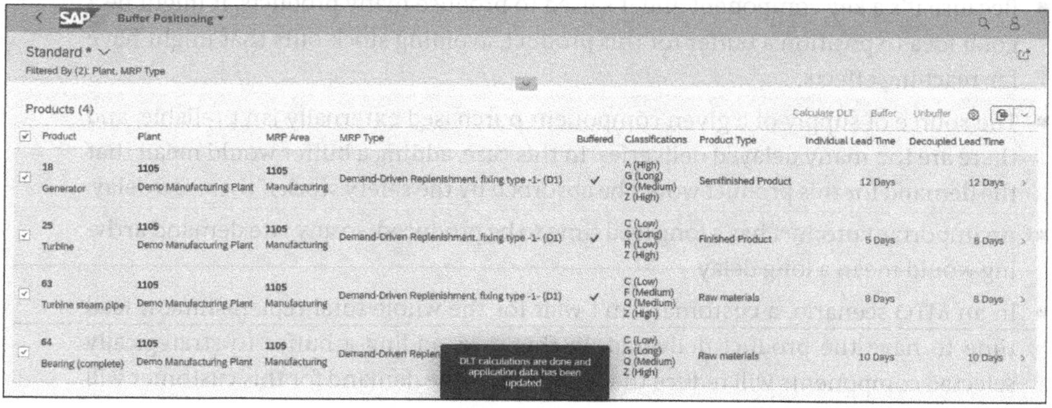

Figure 15.19 Unbuffered Products with Decoupled Lead Time

The **Decoupled Lead Time** column in Figure 15.19 shows that the DLT isn't calculated for these four selected products. On selecting these four products and then choosing **Calculate DLT**, the calculated DLT (in days) will appear as shown in Figure 15.19.

Before deciding whether a buffer should be positioned for a specific product or not, select a specific product, and navigate to the Buffer Analysis app, where extensive details are available to support the decision (see Figure 15.20).

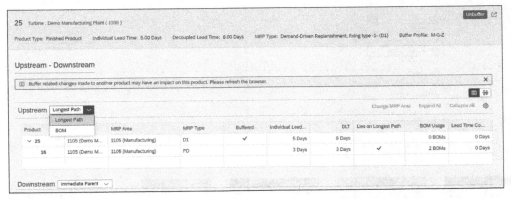

Figure 15.20 Buffer Analysis

To navigate from the Buffer Positioning app (refer to Figure 15.19) to the Buffer Analysis app, select the relevant material, which in this example is material 25, and click the forward arrow icon located on the far-right side of an individual material. The screen shown in Figure 15.20 appears.

Figure 15.20 shows all the information related to the **Upstream** and **Downstream** values. In this situation, *upstream* refers to product components, for which there is the longest path or the whole BOM. *Downstream* refers to product parents, for which information is displayed that is related to all the BOMs in which a product is used (see Figure 15.21).

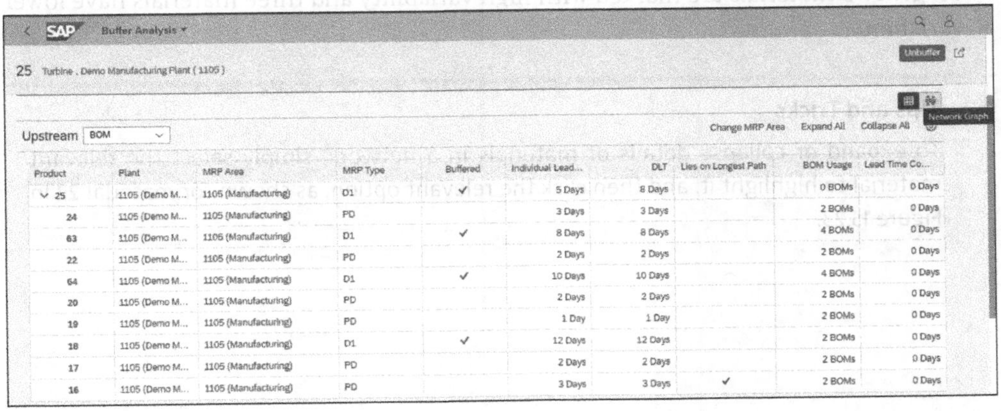

Figure 15.21 Upstream

To analyze a product with too many levels of components, it's recommended to switch to the **Network Graph** view (see Figure 15.21), where there is a graphical representation of the upstream and downstream values and multiple display options, as shown in Figure 15.22.

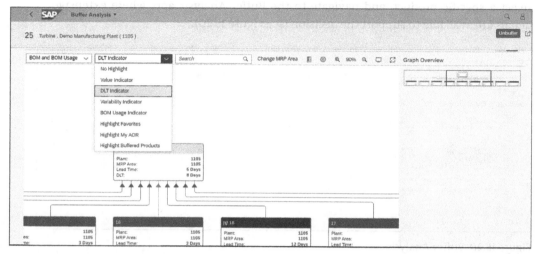

Figure 15.22 Network Graph

In Figure 15.22, it's possible to show, for example, the longest path, the product flow, or the entire BOM and BOM usage from the first dropdown located on the top-left side of the screen. There are different options to highlight specific products in the network, such as buffered products, products under an area of responsibility (AOR), products selected as favorites, or products in one of the product classifications.

The example in Figure 15.23 shows a partial view of the whole BOM of a product (**25**) with the characteristic (**DLT Indicator**) chosen from the dropdown in Figure 15.22. The BOM components are highlighted in red, yellow, or green, depending on the BOM usage. Two materials are marked with high variability and three materials have lower variability.

> **[+] Tips and Tricks**
>
> To expand or collapse details of materials in a network, simply select the relevant material to highlight it, and then click the relevant option, as shown for material **22** in Figure 15.23.

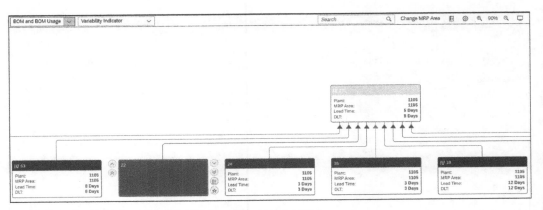

Figure 15.23 Partial View of BOM with Lead Time Variability

15.5.4   Lead Time Classification

The Schedule Lead Time Classification of Products (DD) app uses the DDR planning characteristics maintained in the previous step of buffer positioning to determine the DLTs. These DLTs are the basis for buffer level determination.

The second main task of the Schedule Lead Time Classification of Products (DD) app is to carry out a fourth classification method: the EFG classification by replenishment lead time. Unlike the three classification methods explained earlier, this classification can only be carried out after the DDR-dispatching characteristics have been maintained because the decoupling points aren't available in the system at the beginning of the process.

After calling up the Schedule Lead Time Classification of Products (DD) app, a selection screen appears to create a new analysis run. In addition to the job name and start time, it's important to define the objects—for example, **Product**, **Product Group**, **Plant**, and **MRP Controller**—for which the system should perform the analysis. Another central setting is the horizon for historical replenishment (see **Number of Days (Past)** in Figure 15.24).

Figure 15.24 shows an overview of the possible settings regarding the classification thresholds of the EFG analysis.

This app classifies the products according to the lead time (EFG) classification. Just like the Schedule Product Classification app, the initial screen of this app will show an overview of the jobs already completed, in process, or scheduled. On this screen, the option to create a new job, copy an existing job, or check the results of the finished jobs are available.

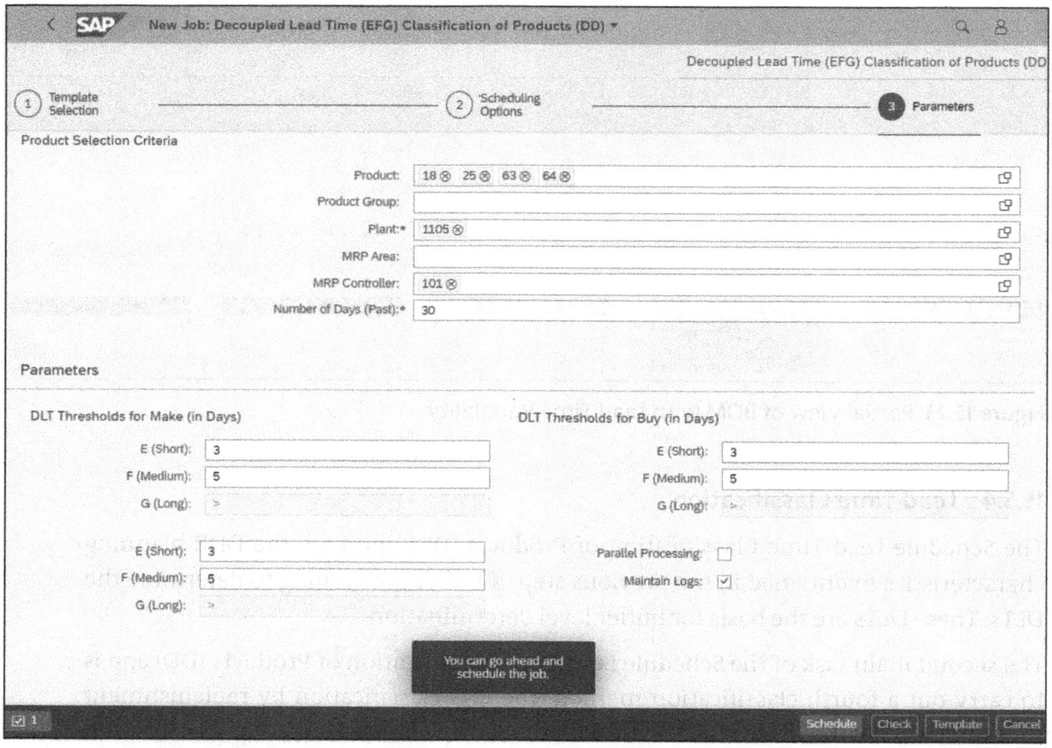

Figure 15.24 Job Settings for EFG Analysis

The thresholds defined here are only for the EFG classification, but a materials planner can define different thresholds depending on the procurement type. The following options are available:

- **DLT Threshold for Buy**
  This is used for products procured externally—that is, with procurement type F.

- **DLT Threshold for Make**
  This will be considered for products manufactured internally—that is, products with procurement type E.

- **DLT Threshold for Transfer**
  This is used for products with a stock transfer special procurement type, which are supplied by means of a stock transfer from another plant.

In these thresholds, a materials planner can define how many days is considered a short, medium, or long lead time for products manufactured, purchased, or transferred. This differentiation of thresholds depending on the procurement type happens because the lead time to manufacture a product may be very different from the lead time to buy the components.

In addition, appropriate thresholds must be specified for the EFG classification. This classification methodology is executed for material/plant combinations with a DDMRP type based on their DLTs, which are also determined in this run together with the single-level replenishment lead times. Different threshold values in calendar days for in-house production, external procurement, and stock transfers can be used. In all three cases, the materials are divided into three groups:

- **E materials**
  Short replenishment lead times according to the respective value definition.
- **F materials**
  Average replenishment lead times according to the threshold value definition.
- **G materials**
  Long replenishment lead times according to the threshold value definition.

While the EFG classification and, by its very nature, the determination of the DLTs are only carried out for decoupled materials with a DDMRP type, the single-level replenishment lead times are determined for all selected objects, including those for which no buffering is planned.

For in-house production, the system determines the production or process orders in the selected analysis horizon. For all identified objects, the time period between order creation and final confirmation is determined as a single-level replenishment lead time and then aggregated as an average value on the material/plant combination. If no element is found in the selected horizon, the system uses the in-house production time of the material master, which is independent of lot size.

The procedure for external procurement is the same, which means the purchase orders within the horizon are selected accordingly, and the period between purchase order creation and the date on which the final delivery indicator is set is determined. As is true for in-house production, there is a fallback scenario for external procurement in case no element is found within the selected horizon. In this instance, the system first uses the planned delivery time of the info record or contract that the MRP run selects as the preferred source of supply according to the settings. The system uses an explosion with lot size 1 and the explosion date of the run. If no replenishment lead time can be determined, the planned delivery time of the material master is used.

For interplant transfer materials, the system evaluates the time when the goods/materials were issued from a supplying plant against a stock transport order until these goods were received at the receiving plant.

The determination of the DLTs is based on the single-level replenishment lead times determined as described earlier, by using the multilevel sum of the longest critical path in each case.

An active Business Add-In (BAdI) implementation is delivered that enables the automated maintenance of the values into the material master. Maintenance takes place in the master data fields that were specified previously as a fallback option for determining replenishment lead times—that is, into the lot-size-independent in-house-production time for in-house production and into the planned delivery time of the preferred source of supply or the material master in the case of external procurement. The DLT is updated in the **Tot. Repl. Lead Time** (total replenishment lead time) field (**MRP 3** view) of the material master.

15.5.5   Buffer Level Determination

These areas are now used to derive buffer levels. The following areas are distinguished:

- **Top of red**
  This area marks the upper end of the red buffer zone.

- **Top of yellow**
  This buffer level is the sum of the buffer zones red and yellow.

- **Top of green**
  This buffer level is the sum of the buffer zones red, yellow, and green.

If the inventory position is lower than TOY, a replenishment to TOG will be triggered in the planning run. If the stock is above TOG, this is called the blue zone. This depiction of the buffer zones and their levels is shown in Figure 15.25.

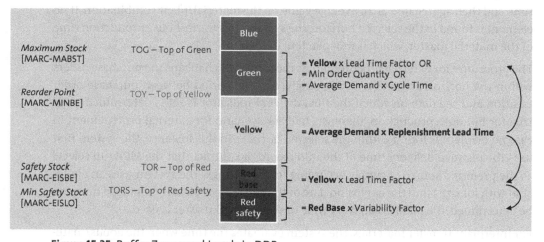

Figure 15.25 Buffer Zones and Levels in DDR

The following sections will discuss how to schedule buffer level calculation, position buffers, evaluate buffer levels and average daily usage, and how to adjust buffers.

Schedule Buffer Level Calculation

The last step in DDR implementation is the actual buffer calculation, which can also be scheduled as a background job using the Schedule Buffer Proposal Calculation app. On the initial screen, there are options to manage the already scheduled and finished jobs and to schedule a new background job execution. The selection screen provides the scheduling parameters and allows you to select which products should be included in the buffer calculation, as shown in Figure 15.26.

The Schedule Buffer Level Calculation app performs the calculation of the buffer zones according to the DDR logic, which means the central buffer zones and levels are calculated. After calling up the Schedule Buffer Level Calculation app, a planner can configure an analysis run, including selecting whether the ADU is to be calculated—that is, the average demand per day. It's based on the previous step of classification, in which the material movements (GIs and GRs) were used. Figure 15.26 shows the possible settings in the Schedule Buffer Proposal Calculation app. It's also important to specify here whether the results should be saved or just adopted within the defined tolerances. Further, the option to adopt DLT from the material master can be used or recalculated by selecting the relevant radio button located on the bottom-right side of the screen.

There's an option to choose if the buffer will be adopted only if the new value is within a tolerance interval (**Adopt with Tolerance**), if it will be always adopted (**Always Adopt Proposals**), or if it will never be adopted (**Do Not Adopt Proposals**). If the planner chooses either **Adopt with Tolerance** or **Do Not Adopt Proposals**, the planner then needs to review the calculated buffer later in the Manage Buffer Levels app. Further, a materials planner can also choose whether the ADU will be calculated based on a fixed interval or on a rolling interval and whether the DLT will come from the material master values or will be recalculated.

For this example, choose **Do Not Adopt Proposals**. After clicking **Check** and then finally **Schedule**, the system will create a log for the scheduled job.

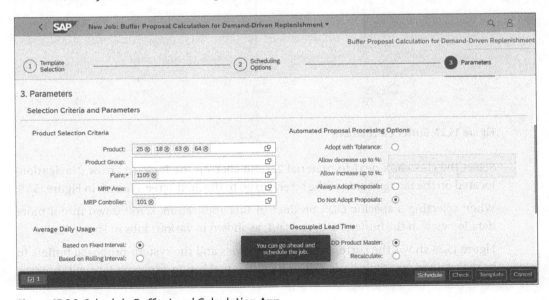

Figure 15.26 Schedule Buffer Level Calculation App

[»]

> **Note**
>
> The PIRs can also be used to project an ADU in the future and allow the system to also calculate a projected buffer for the future. This is especially relevant, for example, if it's known in advance that an event might affect product consumption, such as a marketing campaign or a seasonal increase in demand. The future horizon for which the system will look for planned independent requirements can be defined in the Mass Maintenance of Products (DD) app, discussed later in Section 15.5.5.

For jobs already completed, a flag on the initial screen will appear under the **Log** column, which will show the status of the background job execution. On double-clicking this flag, the log details will appear, including any warning or error messages that may prevent the buffer calculation.

Position Buffers

Next, use the Manage Buffer Levels app to evaluate the results. Figure 15.27 shows an example of buffer level management by manual intervention. The system proposes to decrease the **Current** stock of **2,218 PC** to **Proposed 1,454 PC**. The **Buffer Levels** field first shows the current buffer levels followed by showing the proposed buffer levels right below (in a tricolor horizontal bar). The **Average Daily Usage (Historical and Future)** column provides insight on the ADU of material **25**, or the yellow zone (75.733 PC). The last three columns are the zone-wise suggestions for the proposed buffers, and we'll discuss them in detail soon.

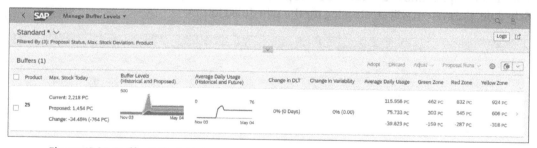

Figure 15.27 Buffer Calculation

Select the checkbox next to material **25**, and click on the forward arrow (**Navigation**) located on the far-right side of the screen to go to the next screen shown in Figure 15.28.

When selecting a specific DDR product in this application, scroll down into a more detailed view of the buffer, ADU, and DLT, as shown in various tabs in Figure 15.28.

Figure 15.28 shows the current lower buffer levels and the system-proposed buffers to be maintained on a daily basis. Clicking a horizontal bar on a specific date will show the date and details of the respective zones, which, in this example, shows that as of February 3, 2021, the **Yellow Zone** is **606** PC, **Green Zone** is **303** PC, and **Red Zone** is **545** PC.

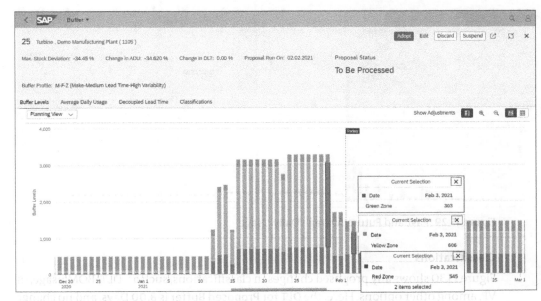

Figure 15.28 Planning View of Redefined Buffer Levels

Select another view from the **Planning View** dropdown, such as the **Comparison View**, and the system will show comparisons of various stock levels. The **Settings** icon lets you switch between viewing the details as zones or as stocks, while using the **Legends** icon provides details of this visual representation. These icons are located on the top-right side of the screen.

Buffer Levels

The calculated buffer levels can be reviewed in the Manage Buffer Levels app. When entering this application, there'll be a list of products and the respective buffer levels calculated by the system, including a graphical representation of the historic and projected buffer levels and the ADU. Scroll down the screen shown in Figure 15.28 so that Figure 15.29 appears (or choose the **Average Daily Usage** tab in Figure 15.28).

Average Daily Usage

The blue bars in Figure 15.29 represent the ADU during the past 30 days based on actual GIs. The orange bar represents future ADU based on the planned independent requirements maintained for material 25 in plant 1105 as well as the settings maintained in the screen for mass adjustments (shown later in Figure 15.34). The past and future horizons are also shown as **Horizon for Past** and **Horizon for Future**, respectively, on the top-left side of Figure 15.29.

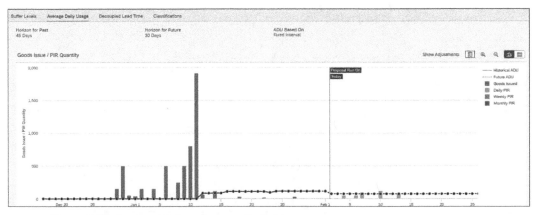

Figure 15.29 Past and Future Average Daily Usage

Classifications

Figure 15.30 shows any proposed changes in classifications, such as, DLT, BOM usage, or VF, among other options. Here, the **DLT for Proposed Buffer** is **8.00 Days**, and no change in the DLT is proposed.

Figure 15.30 Decoupled Lead Time

Figure 15.31 is the summary of all the current versus proposed changes (if any) to the classification of a DDR-based material. Here the **Variability Factor** is **0.80**, and the **DLT Factor** is **0.50**.

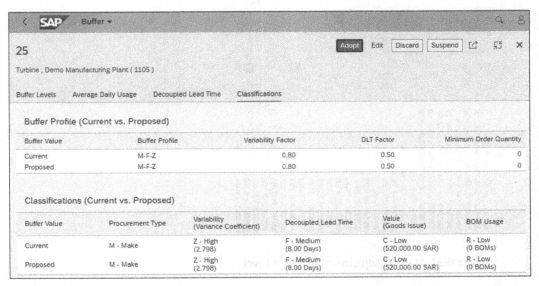

Figure 15.31 Classifications

Buffer Adjustments

You also can switch to edit mode and make manual adjustments in the calculated buffer level by adding an adjustment factor for each zone. The value originally calculated for each zone will be multiplied by this factor within the period defined for this buffer adjustment. After entering edit mode, select the **Show Adjustments** option to see all the existing zone adjustments per period. There's an option to add a new adjustment or to delete an existing one. Figure 15.32 shows an example in which an adjustment was created from February 8 to February 12, 2021, with a factor of 1.50, 2.50, and 0.80 for red, yellow, and green zones respectively. On adding a new zone adjustment, choose **Simulate Changes** to see the changes reflected in the chart.

Based on information and data available let's first summarize the classification of material 25 undertaken through the DDR process and then understand how the three buffer zones were calculated. All data and calculations are based on the date the DDR process was run—that is, on February 3, 2021.

- ADU = 75.733 PC
- DLT = 8 Days
- VF = 0.8
- DLT Factor = 0.5

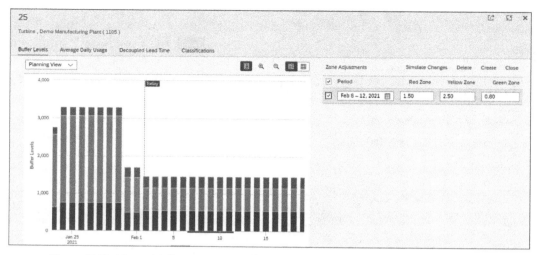

Figure 15.32 Manual Adjustment in Buffer Levels

Therefore, on February 3, 2021, the *yellow zone = ADU × DLT = 75.733 × 8 = 606 PC* (rounded off; can be validated in Figure 15.28).

The green zone is calculated as the *yellow zone × DLT factor = 606 × 0.5 = 303 PC* (can be validated in Figure 15.28).

Because the red zone consists of red base and red safety, let's calculate them first:

- *Red base = Yellow zone × DLT factor = 606 × 0.5 = 303 PC*
- *Red safety = Red base × VF = 303 × 0.8 = 242 PC*
- *Red zone = Red base + red safety = 303 + 242 = 545 PC* (can be validated in Figure 15.28)

Next let's discuss how these three calculated zones update the various fields in the material master (or product):

- *TOR = Safety stock or the red zone = 545 PC* (see the **Safety stock (DD)** field in Figure 15.33 ❶)
- *TOY = TOR + yellow zone = 545 + 606 = 1,151 PC* (see the **Reorder Point (DD)** field in Figure 15.33 ❶)
- *TOG = TOY + green zone = 1,151 + 303 = 1,454 PC* (see the **Maximum Stock (DD)** field in Figure 15.33 ❶)

Note that data in Figure 15.33 ❶ is only updated after the buffer proposal is adopted by clicking **Save and Adopt** in the screen shown in Figure 15.30. Adopting a buffer proposal automatically updates the relevant fields of the material master with updated values. These fields are **Safety Stock**, **Reorder Point**, **Maximum Stock**, and **Total Replenishment Lead Time**.

> **Note**
>
> Because product characteristics, such as lead time or usage, may change over time, it's best practice to periodically review the product classifications. In addition, the buffer also should be periodically reviewed and recalculated because the ADU varies over time. For this, use the scheduling options available in the relevant DDR apps.

As soon as the buffer proposal is accepted, the next step is to run MRP Live (Transaction MD01N) so that the system creates replenishment proposals. After MRP Live runs, the stock/requirements list (Transaction MD04) is updated accordingly, as shown in Figure 15.33 (see the upper half of the stock requirements list ❶ ❷). All stock fields, such as **Maximum Stock**, **Reorder Point**, and **Safety Stock**, are updated along with other demand-driven fields. Recall that all these fields were blank when the DDR process wasn't initiated on material 25 and for plant 1105 in Section 3 of this chapter.

More fields and associated calculations shown in Figure 15.33 ❶ ❷ are discussed in the next section.

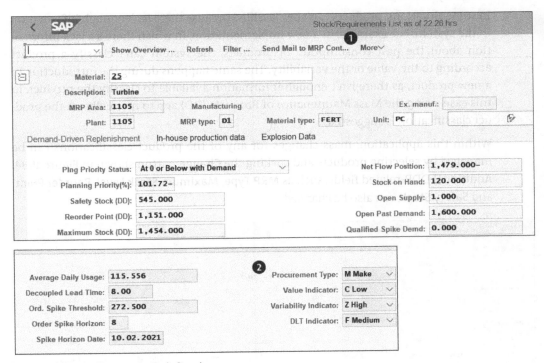

Figure 15.33 Buffer Levels Redefined

Finally, when a buffer proposal is created and adopted, the system sets the following values as defaults for a product:

- *Individual lead time = (Planned delivery duration or in-house production duration, based on the procurement type) + GR processing time*
- *DLT = Individual lead time or total replenishment lead time*
- *ADU = (Reorder point – safety stock) ÷ DLT*
- *LT factor = (Maximum stock – reorder point) ÷ (reorder point – safety stock)*
- *VF = (Safety stock ÷ (maximum stock – reorder point)) – 1*

As a self-learning DDR exercise, use the safety stock (545), reorder point (1,151), maximum stock (1,453), and decoupled lead time (eight days) data to calculate and validate the ADU, LT factor, and VF of 75.7, 0.5, and 0.8, respectively, from the preceding three equations.

It's also important to note that running MRP Live is one way of replenishing the stock. The next section shows how to interactively manage all DDR planning with SAP Fiori apps and without needing to run MRP Live.

Mass Adjust Buffers

In some situations, products can't be classified because there isn't enough information in the system. For example, in a new implementation, in which there's a lack information about the past consumption of products, the system can't classify a product according to the value or the variability. The same happens during the introduction of a new product, as there isn't enough information available to classify the product. In this case, using the Mass Maintenance of Products (DD) app to manually set the product classification is suggested.

Within this application, mass changes for any of the product classifications can be managed by selecting products and clicking the **Change** button shown in Figure 15.34. Additional DDR-related fields, such as **MRP Type**, **Maximum Stock Level**, **Reorder Point**, and **Safety Stock**, can also be changed.

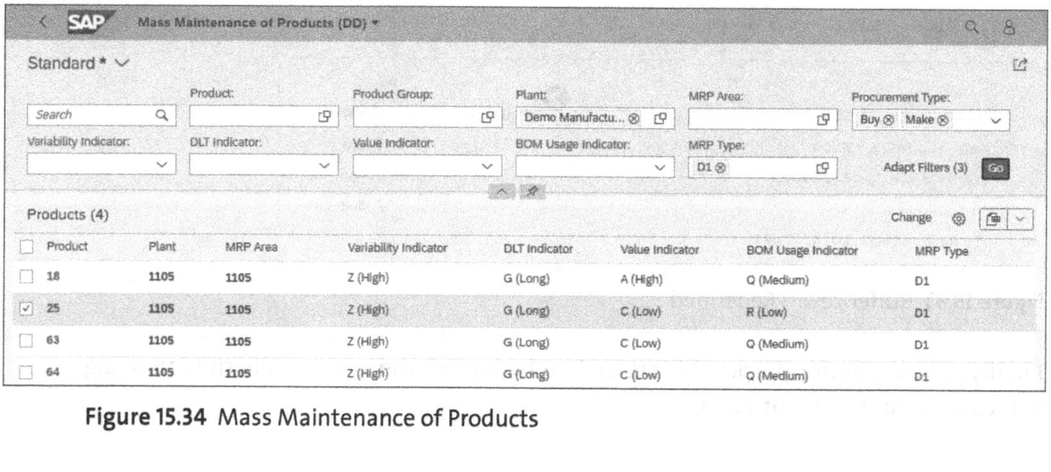

Figure 15.34 Mass Maintenance of Products

Figure 15.35 ❶ and ❷ show the popup screen to implement the mass changes after clicking the **Change** button. Here, select which fields should be changed and for which fields to keep the existing values. For example, you can manually define values for the **Variability Indicator** and the **Value Indicator** dropdowns because these can't be calculated automatically without enough GIs posted in the past.

In this application, you can also define the **Lead Time Calculation Method**, **Horizon for Past (in Days)** and **Horizon for Future (in Days)** settings. By default, the system will calculate the lead time based on the values defined in the material master, but different methods are available in which the lead time will be calculated based on confirmed production orders. These fields will define the method and the number of days used by the system to find confirmed production orders and calculate the lead time. For this example, maintain a value of "30" in the **Horizon for Future (in Days)** field ❷ so that the system considers the future planning horizon of 30 days with demand, which is basically PIRs, during the buffer level determination.

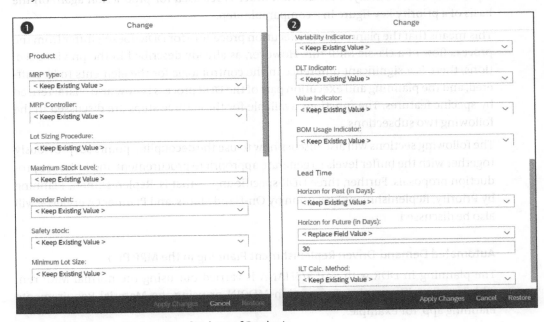

Figure 15.35 Mass Adjustments of Values of Products

> **Note**
>
> The **ILT Calc. Method** field shown in Figure 15.35 ❷ is used to calculate the lead time. Lead time can be calculated based on its historic average, which is the default method. Lead time, when predicted, is calculated using machine learning and will grow more accurate over time. Note that in the initial stages, there might be a mismatch in the predictions when compared to the actual lead times.

> To maintain relevant configuration settings so that they appear in the **ILT Calc. Method** field in Figure 15.35 **❷**, use the following configuration menu path in the SAP S/4HANA system: **SAP IMG · Production · Demand-Driven Replenishment · Define Lead Time Calculation Method**.

15.5.6   Planning and Execution

Now we'll discuss the procedures that have been defined in SAP's automated planning to generate procurement proposals such as purchase requisitions and planned orders. This is followed by interactive planning executed by the user to postprocess the results of the planning run. Here, there are two substeps involved. Priority key figures support the decision to convert a procurement proposal (e.g., a planned order) into a fixed element (a production order or a process order) or to convert a purchase requisition into a purchase order. Finally, a production order is released for production again on the basis of a priority key figure in a comparable step.

This means that the planning and execution procedure for DDR doesn't differ from the process flow of a classic MRP run. However, as already described in the previous sections, there is a significant difference in the control logic for the elements to be buffered, and the planning and execution part of the DDR process is now also characterized by specific features. The functions available for these three steps are discussed in the following two subsections.

The following sections will also discuss how to use the decoupling points set previously together with the buffer levels to generate appropriate procurement and in-house production proposals. Further, three DDR-specific apps—that is, Replenishment Planning by Priority, Replenishment Execution by On-Hand Status, and Planner Overview—will also be discussed.

Automated Demand-Driven Replenishment Planning in the MRP Run

The planning in DDR with SAP S/4HANA is carried out using the normal MRP run, which starts with running Transaction MD01N or using the Material Requirements Planning app, for example.

Using the MRP type previously maintained, the planning run identifies the materials for which the DDR logic is to be used. These must have planning procedure C indirectly via the MRP type. The net flow equation is used for generating receipt elements:

On-hand stock + Open supply – Open past (including today's) demand – Qualified spike demand

In the planning run, the net flow position calculated as described is compared with the buffer level TOY. If the net flow position is lower than TOY, a receipt element is created that raises the stock quantity to TOG. Figure 15.36 shows the results of a DDR planning run as an example.

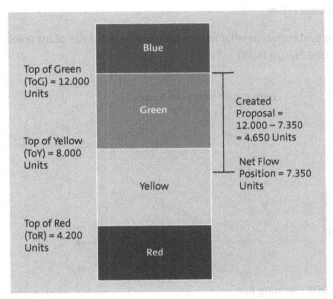

Figure 15.36 Results of DDR Planning Run (Example)

The following input factors are used for the calculation:

- **On-hand stock**
  Quantity available for the planning run that would also be used in other planning procedures in the MRP run.
- **Open supply**
  All receipts that have already been ordered but aren't yet available.
- **Open demand (past, including current day):**
  - Dependent requirements
  - Sales and distribution requirements (schedule lines, outbound deliveries, open sales order quantities)
  - Stock transfer order requirements
  - Stock transfer reservations (movement type 541)

  This explicitly excludes dependent requirements, PIRs, and stock transport requisitions.
- **Qualified spike demand**
  In particular, high demand is to be taken into account when determining the qualified spike demand. This is a future daily requirement that lies above the spike threshold within the spike horizon (see Figure 15.37). The spike threshold is defined

by a factor of the TOR, which is maintained at the plant level. The spike horizon is calculated as follows:

Today + factor × DLT + constant offset

The input values for the factor and constant offset are also maintained at the plant level and in the Buffer Profile app (see Figure 15.38).

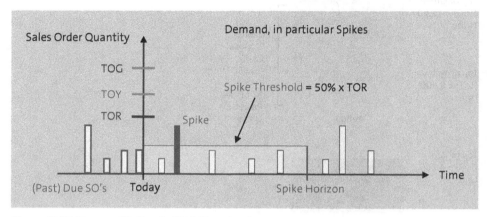

Figure 15.37 Usage of Spikes in DDR Planning Run

Plant	Set of Buffer Profiles	Spike Horizon Constant	Spike Horizon DLT Multiplier	Spike Threshold	On-Hand Alert Threshold
1105	DEFAULT	5.00	0.50	1.50	0.25

Figure 15.38 Buffer Profile Settings at Plant Level (Plant 1105)

Forward scheduling is applied by using the DLT, whereby the GR processing times and the safety times of the horizon key are also included in the same way as for normal MRP. It's recommended to eliminate these times to avoid multiple consideration.

To calm the planning results, use a planning time fence with firming type 1 (MRP Type D1 for DDR) so that a new element that has been moved by one day can't be created in the subsequent planning run.

Evaluating the DDR Results after MRP Run

Figure 15.39 and Figure 15.40 are part of the same screen and show an example of the MRP results for **Material 25** in the **Stock/Requirements List** screen (Transaction MD04). On expanding the **Header Details** screen, notice the **Demand-Driven Replenishment** tab and associated DDR information.

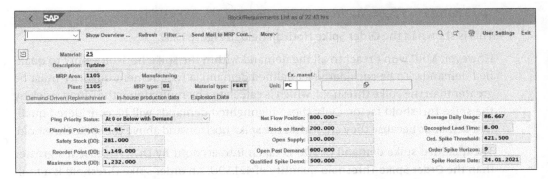

Figure 15.39 Stock/Requirements List

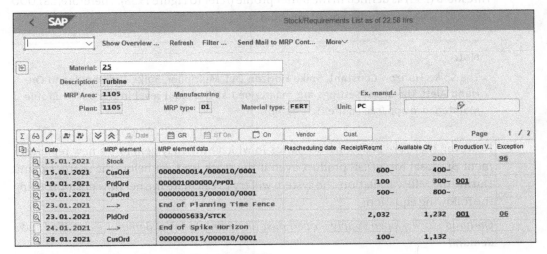

Figure 15.40 Stock/Requirements List: Detailed View

Let's discuss and evaluate the DDR results for material 25 in plant 1105. The material's **Stock on Hand** is **200**, which is below the reorder point. The **Open Supply** quantity is **100** and is basically a production order for which the goods aren't delivered to the warehouse yet. The **Open Past Demand** quantity (from sales order) is **600**, whereas the **Qualified Spike Dmd** is **500** (customer order for which the delivery date is within the **Spike Horizon Date** of **24.01.2021**).

The *spike horizon* is a time window that starts the day after today and comprises the DLT multiplied by a factor called the *spike horizon DLT multiplier*, with the addition of an offset called the *spike horizon constant*. The purpose here is that DDR will only react to a demand within this time window to ensure product availability.

So, in this example, the **Spike Horizon Constant** is 5 (days), and the **Spike Horizon DLT Multiplier** is 0.5. Referring to Figure 15.39 again, the DLT is 8 days. So, the calculation for the spike horizon is as follows:

Spike horizon = 5 (Spike horizon constant) + (8 (DLT) × 0.5) = 9 days

This is shown in the **Order Spike Horizon** field in Figure 15.39.

However, MRP won't react to all the demand within the spike horizon—only to qualified demands. To be considered a qualified demand, a requirement quantity must be greater than the spike threshold, which is calculated by multiplying the safety stock by the spike threshold factor. Only those highlighted demands will be considered qualified demands because they are within the spike horizon and above the spike threshold.

The qualified spike demand of 500 is taken into account by DDR because it's greater than the **Order Spike Threshold** quantity of 421.500. An order spike threshold is a multiplication between the safety stock (in this example, 281.000) and the **Ord. Spike Threshold** (1.50) as defined in the buffer profile (refer to Figure 15.38). Therefore, 281.000 × 1.5 = 421.500 is the order spike threshold.

> **Note**
>
> The **Spike Horizon Constant**, **Spike Horizon DLT Multiplier**, **Spike Threshold**, and **On-Hand Alert Threshold** settings are maintained at the plant level in the Buffer Profile Maintenance app (see Figure 15.38 again).

However, there are additional scenarios in which MRP may generate a new replenishment proposal for a DDR product even if the stock isn't yet below the reorder point. During the MRP calculation, the system will try to calculate the net flow position, using the following equation:

On-hand stock + open supply – open past (including today's) demand – qualified spike demand

Referring to Figure 15.39 and this equation, the net flow position of -800 is calculated as follows:

Net flow position: 200 + 100 – 600 – 500 = -800

So, the MRP run not only creates a replenishment proposal that addresses this shortage of 800 but also ensures that replenishment extends up to the maximum stock (which is 1,232; see the **Max Stock (DD)** field in Figure 15.39) *after* addressing this shortage. Therefore, the expected replenishment proposal after the MRP run will be for 2,032 (800 + 1,232 = 2,032), as shown in Figure 15.40, wherein a planned order 5633 for quantity 2,032 (in the **Receipt/Reqmt** column) reflects the same logic.

Figure 15.39 shows another example, in which there's an open past demand of 600. The reorder point is 1,149, and the on-hand stock is currently 200 while the open order is 100, so it's technically below the reorder point. Because the open past demand and any qualified spike demand are also considered in the equation, the available quantity would be below the reorder point. Therefore, MRP will create a new replenishment proposal to replenish up to the maximum stock level.

In the equation, the qualified spike demand, as well as Figure 15.40, shows that we have a line with the **End of Spike Horizon**, so it's important to define those terms for better understanding of the MRP results for a demand-driven product.

Replenishment proposals created for a DDR product will always be forward-scheduled, considering today as the start date and using the DLT to calculate the finish date for both externally and internally procured products. As shown in Figure 15.39 and Figure 15.40 earlier, in which the stock/requirements list for a demand-driven product is shown, there's also a planning time fence when using a demand-driven MRP type. This time fence is always equal to the DLT and uses fixing type 1 by default. This time fence exists to prevent the dates of a planned order created by MRP for a demand-driven product from being changed in the following MRP run.

Figure 15.40 shows the stock/requirements list (Transaction MD04) for **Material 25** in **Plant 1105** as of **15.01.2021** (January 15, 2021). The opening **Stock** or the available quantity is **200**, while an open order **PrdOrd** (production order) is **100**. **CusOrder** (customer order or sale order) **14** is the demand past due (or today's demand), whereas **CusOrder 13** is considered by DDR because it lies *within* the **End of Spike Horizon (24.01.2021)**, calculated by the system as 9 days (previously discussed in this section). Notice, however, that **CusOrder 15** lies *outside* the spike horizon (**28.01.2021**) and therefore isn't considered by DDR as a qualified spike demand. **PldOrd** (planned order) **5633** of quantity **2,032** is created as the result of the MRP run that takes the net requirements calculation into account. Details of how the MRP arrived at this calculation of 2,032 has also been previously covered.

The MRP run is usually executed daily as a background job, and it should ensure that there are enough replenishment proposals to cover the DDR buffer. In addition to the MRP run, a materials planner can also use the Replenishment Planning by Planning Priority app and Replenishment Execution by On-Hand Status app to monitor the buffer coverage and take actions to avoid shortages, such as manually creating a new replenishment proposal or expediting an existing order. These two apps are discussed in the following sections.

Replenishment Planning by Planning Priority

The planning run is postprocessed using the Replenishment Planning by Planning Priority app. After calling up the app, a buffer level overview is displayed. The planning priority is used for sorting, which results in a percentage comparison of TOG with the following value:

On-hand stock + Receipts – Relevant requirement elements

The results displayed are used to convert planned orders into production orders and process orders, or to convert purchase requisitions into purchase orders. Within the Replenishment Planning by Planning Priority app, a list of products within the user's AOR for which the net flow position is below the reorder point are displayed. However, this can be changed by using the filter option to add more planning priority statuses if there's a need to see additional products. All those products will be sorted according to the planning priority, which is the percentage of the buffer covered by the net flow position. The lines are highlighted in color according to the respective planning priority status. Figure 15.41 shows an example in which the first three lines are highlighted in red because the net flow position is below the safety stock, and the fourth line is highlighted in blue because the net flow position is above the maximum stock level.

There are five different planning priority statuses:

- Above maximum stock
- At 0 or below with demand
- Below reorder point
- Below safety stock
- Below or at maximum stock

Figure 15.41 shows an example of a planning run result sorted according to planning priority.

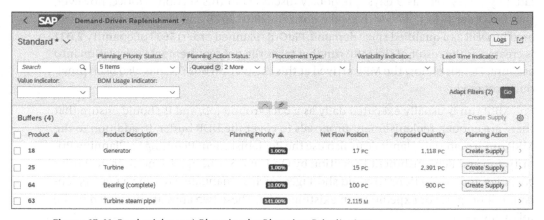

Figure 15.41 Replenishment Planning by Planning Priority App

As shown in Figure 15.41, a **Create Supply** button is displayed for those lines for which the net flow position is below the reorder point or the safety stock. On choosing this option, DDR will create a new planned order to replenish this product up to the maximum stock level. The scheduling logic for this planned order will be similar to the logic used by MRP: with forward scheduling, considering today as the start date, and using the DLT to calculate the finish date.

Select a specific line in Figure 15.41, and then click the forward arrow located on the far-right side of the screen. This brings up the **Supply/Demand List** tab and additional information about the product, as shown in Figure 15.42.

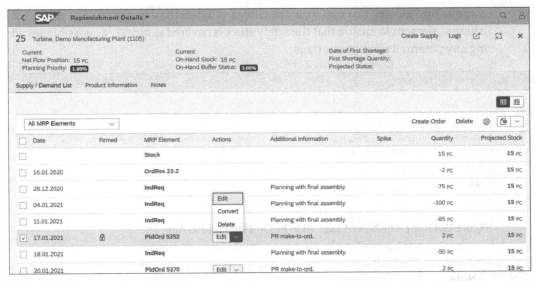

Figure 15.42 Supply/Demand List

The **Supply/Demand List** tab consists of information about the existing demand and replenishment elements. You can edit or deleting an existing replenishment element or manually create a new planned order by defining the quantity, date, and source of supply.

The Replenishment Planning by Planning Priority app shown in Figure 15.42 focuses on the planning side because it's based on the comparison of the net flow position with the reorder point. Meanwhile, the Replenishment Execution by On-Hand Status app (see Figure 15.43), discussed next, is used to manage short-term execution. It focuses on the comparison of the on-hand stock with the safety stock.

Replenishment Execution by On-Hand Status

Replenishment execution according to the DDR logic is performed with the Replenishment Execution by On-Hand Status app. In this app, the current warehouse stock situation is displayed, and the on-hand status is used for prioritization, which is calculated as follows:

On-hand stock (without receipt and requirement elements) compared to TOR (in %)

This app will show, by default, a list of products for which on-hand stock is below the safety stock (the red zone), but additional products can be included by changing the default filters. Figure 15.43 shows this list of products, where the icons in the **On-Hand Buffer Status** column highlight products with the stock below the safety stock.

Whenever there is an open replenishment proposal for a product for which the stock is below the safety stock, the **Expedite Supply** button will appear in the **Execute Action** column. By choosing this option, it's possible to change the dates of an existing replenishment element to ensure that the safety stock is covered as quickly as possible, avoiding any potential product shortage.

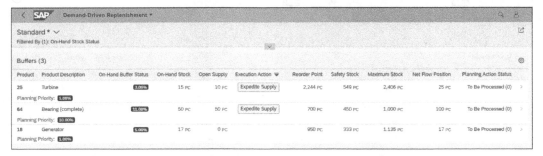

Figure 15.43 Replenishment Execution by On-Hand Status App

Note

By default, the Replenishment Planning by Planning Priority app will only show the option to create a new supply, and the Replenishment Execution by On-Hand Status app will only show the option to expedite an existing supply. However, you can change the column settings (via the filter option) in both applications to include a column for the missing action. Additional columns with important information, such as the reorder point or the safety stock, can also be included.

When choosing the option to **Expedite Supply** in Figure 15.43, a popup appears (see Figure 15.44) in which a list of the existing replenishment proposals and additional information, such as the source, status, and order progress (in case of production orders) are displayed. The date in the **Planned Availability Date** column is changeable, thereby allowing you to expedite the replenishment proposal.

Expedite Supply

Product: 25 (Turbine)
Plant: 1105 (Demo Manufacturing Plant)

On-Hand Buffer Status: 3.00%
On-Hand Stock: 15 PC

Below On-Hand Alert Threshold by: 424 PC
Below Safety Stock by: 534 PC

Orders

ID	Quantity	Planned Availability Date	Source	Status	Order Progress
PldOrd 5385	10 PC	12.01.2021	Production Version (001)	Firmed	
PldOrd 5485	2,381 PC	20.01.2021	Production Version (001)	Created	
PldOrd 5352	2 PC	17.01.2021		Firmed	
PldOrd 5486	2 PC	20.01.2021	Production Version (001)	Created	

Save and Expedite   Cancel

Figure 15.44 Expedite Supply

Alternatively, instead of choosing the option to expedite a replenishment proposal as shown in this example, simply click one of the lines to see the **Supply/Demand List** and additional information about the demand-driven product, exactly as in the Replenishment Planning by Planning Priority app shown earlier in Figure 15.41.

Planner Overview

The Planner Overview app displays an overview for all materials that need to be treated manually. Therefore, one or both of the following considerations are taken into account:

- Buffer level calculation results need attention or action.
- Planning status/on-hand status need attention or action.

There are three different tiles in this application, as shown in Figure 15.45:

- **Buffer Level Management**
  This tile shows the products with deviating buffers that a planner should approve.

- **Replenishment Planning**
  Similar to the Replenishment Planning by Planning Priority app, this tile shows products with a net flow position below the reorder point.

- **Replenishment Execution**
  Similar to the Replenishment Execution by Planning Priority app, this tile shows products with a stock level below the safety stock level.

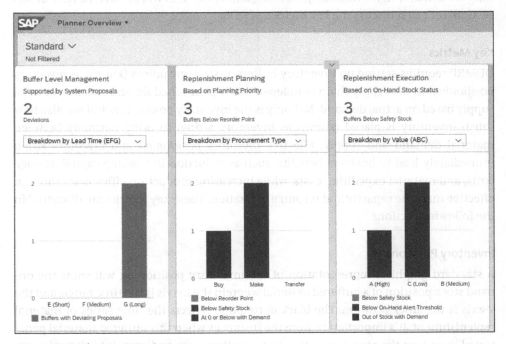

Figure 15.45 Planner Overview

The Planner Overview app enables you to choose the breakdown by procurement type or by each DDR product classification (ABC, EFG, PQR, or XYZ) by choosing the relevant option from the dropdown available in all three tiles. Within this app, it's also possible to click any of the bars in the charts to drill down into the application and see the respective list of products. For example, in Figure 15.45 there is one product with the **Buy** procurement type in the chart for the **Replenishment Planning** tile. Clicking this bar will branch into the Replenishment Planning app, and this specific product will be displayed. Therefore, this application can used as a central place of entry to monitor the main DDR KPIs and to take actions to correct problems and deviations.

The next section will discuss important KPIs and metrics relevant to DDR, including inventory position and inventory sizing. Further, it will discuss the factors that affect DDR process.

15.5.7   Metrics and Analytics

As discussed in Section 15.2, the key to ensuring success in materials planning and a smoother supply chain using the DDR approach requires focusing on protecting and promoting relevant material and information flows. Doing so is only possible by setting up metrics (KPIs) and leveraging the power of analytics to bring constant improvements.

The three factors responsible for smoother and more efficient demand-driven planning are demand signal reliability, stability, and velocity, as will be covered later in this section. Let's first discuss the key metrics of DDR.

Key Metrics

DDMRP requires setting up inventory buffers at strategic points (known as *inventory positioning*) in the supply chain to independently plan, schedule, and execute material supply based on actual demand. Not only is the inventory position critical but also how much inventory is placed (known as inventory sizing) to bring harmony between material demand and supply. Effective *inventory positioning* and *inventory sizing* immediately lead to business benefits, such as reduction in working capital, storage costs, and material expediting costs, while increasing production efficiencies through effective machine capacity and resource utilization. These key metrics are discussed in the following sections.

Inventory Positioning

A standard graphical representation of the inventory positioning will show the on-hand stock position of a buffered material wherein the x-axis is the time range, and the y-axis is the stock position. The black dotted line reflects the time series of material replenishment. It's important to note the instances when this buffered material penetrated deep into the alert zones, that is, the yellow zone and even into the red zone.

Evaluating such instances by addressing the root causes that led to these zone penetrations often reveals the prime areas for improvement. Some of the root causes for such situations can be the fact that the materials planner didn't place a timely replenishment order (i.e., waited too long) or a supplier's inordinate delay or a production breakdown led to these zone penetrations. Similarly, companies often evaluate a supplier's performance based on the number of times there were stock-outs due to that particular supplier's delayed material delivery, how long such delays lasted, and how many parent materials were affected. Using analytics, these key supplier metrics (KPIs) help the company make informed decisions on whether to continue with the same supplier, work on an improvement plan, or simply look for alternative sources of supply.

Figure 15.46 is another view of key metrics for stock (left side of the figure) and capacity (right side) buffers. Again, the dashed lines in both figures are situations worth evaluating for improvement for understock, overstock, and capacity. To provide a more holistic view of such alert zones, such as dark red, red, or yellow, it often makes sense to evaluate them over a longer period horizon than over a shorter one. Doing so will ensure that the analytics are able to depict a broader trend over a relatively longer period of time instead of showing a sudden erosion of zones due to a one-time supplier's delay or an unforeseen machine breakdown.

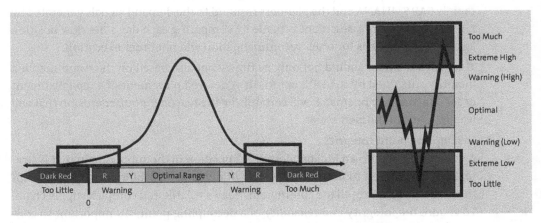

Figure 15.46 Focusing on Outliers (©Demand Driven Institute, used with permission)

Inventory Sizing

Similarly, evaluating a group of materials with similar characteristics (e.g., materials with long lead times, several materials ordered from the same supplier or a group of suppliers, and production materials facing delays due to bottleneck capacities at specific work centers) provides greater insights for improvement initiatives than evaluating individual materials' replenishment situations at the decoupling points.

Here's an example of typical stages or phases wherein analytics are used to monitor the replenishment's critical metrics and then to undertake improvement initiatives to monitor the progress of these critical metrics. Stage 1 shows a bimodal distribution of material stock wherein there were many deep penetrations into the yellow, red, and dark red zones for both stock-outs and overstock situations. This alarming situation is reflected with the dashed lines at both ends of the two curves. At stage 2, the DDR's implementation takes place, and the situation improves significantly. However, notice that there are still outliers on both sides of the curve, as shown by the dashed lines. There's still some room for improvement at both ends, that is, eliminating the stock-out and the overstock situations. Additional buffer improvement initiatives, such as procuring materials from alternative sources that may be slightly more expensive but greatly reduce the replenishment lead time, finally result in stage 3.

Factors Affecting Demand-Driven Replenishment

Finally, let's discuss the three factors that play a critical role in measuring demand-driven metrics and providing reliable analytics, as follows:

- **Signal integrity**
  Signal integrity in the supply chain monitors whether there's complete, correct, and timely communication of the required data and relevant information to ensure timely replenishment. In other words, signal integrity status is a measure of how rapidly SAP S/4HANA and the planners respond to the demand signals generated by SAP S/4HANA. This assessment is made by comparing each day's net flow position against TOG, which is for order recommendation and not order execution.

  This replenishment should not only be timely but also based on the recommended quantity suggested by the DDR approach. A delayed placement of a replenishment order or a quantity mismatch will certainly be the reason for buffer erosion that will lead into one of the alert zones.

- **Decoupling point integrity**
  A decoupling point is an independent stock position in the supply chain that is strategically positioned to absorb the effects of demand variability or supply disruptions—factors that are all too common in today's volatile and complex supply chain. To ensure the integrity and reliability of a decoupling point, it's important to constantly evaluate the reasons, factors, and causes responsible for deviations in relevant material and information flows. Using analytics, materials that exhibit a large variability between planned and actual supply order management are immediate candidates for attention and corrective actions. With analytics, the on-hand inventory value is compared with TOY (the execution zone) to generate a status expressed as a percentage.

- **Decoupling point velocity**
  The velocity at a decoupling point measures the frequency between planned and actual placement of supply orders, and this measurement is known as order frequency variance. For example, after implementing DDR planning, 10 purchase

orders for a material are planned to be placed to a vendor on a monthly basis. However, in actuality, 14 purchase orders were placed within the same time period. This deviation between planned and actual purchase orders points to an area where order frequency needs to increase. Similarly, a group of materials belonging to the same classifications or attributes are measured for flow index, that is, how their ordering frequencies compare with their ADU. In addition, although the focus is often on the materials that move too slowly or are ordered too infrequently, an equally important factor to look into are those materials that are ordered very frequently. They mask the actual velocity of materials' movements and therefore are candidates for improvement in materials flow. With analytics, such critical material flow metrics are monitored and action taken to improve the flow index.

15.6 Summary

DDR shifts the entire paradigm from the "supply" side of planning to the "demand" side, wherein only the materials in demand are procured and produced to reduce stockouts and overstock situations. This chapter covered the necessary DDR configuration and master data setup, then performed a few relevant transactions to accurately and correctly reflect them in the DDR business processes. The DDR business processes consist of classifying products, buffer positioning, and buffer calculation. We also discussed the planning and execution steps of DDR.

The next chapter covers long-term planning (LTP), a materials and capacity planning simulation tool to help improve logistics and supply chain management.

15

Chapter 16
Long-Term Planning

Long-term planning allows a company to test various business models to make the best choices without affecting the standard planning database. The beneficiaries of long-term planning are various stakeholders in the company—the production planner, the procurement in charge, the inventory controller, and the capacity planner.

Long-term planning (LTP) is used to simulate various business scenarios to help in production and procurement planning by using existing master data and other information. Companies can use this tool to test various hypothetical assumptions affecting business decisions. When compared with material requirements planning (MRP), LTP doesn't affect the database of results that was created while running normal (operative) MRP. However, the simulation mode can be used in operational MRP to get similar results as in LTP.

LTP is a separate planning area in which you can undertake all simulation-related planning. However, if the results from simulative planning in LTP are satisfactory, you can also transfer them to operative planning in standard MRP. While it's easy to set up LTP, it's equally easy to delete the planning scenarios when you no longer need them. For example, you quickly set up a planning scenario to test procurement quantities of materials that you need for the next six months, including the associated financial values (capital tie-up). When you no longer need this information, you can delete the planning scenario from the system.

LTP results in the following benefits for specific business roles:

- Capacity planners are better able to plan their machine resources and manpower resources.
- The purchasing department uses the information about future requirements quantities to estimate and plan future procurement orders.
- The inventory controller gains greater comprehension of warehousing requirements.
- Vendors are able to get a preview of a company's future procurement needs, which enables them to foresee and take action to meet impending demands of the company.
- The product costing team can get a preview of the associated costs of producing products.

16

807

Note

SAP doesn't consider LTP to be a target architecture for SAP S/4HANA in the future, but it's still a relevant tool that can still be used for planning simulations. The alternate simulative planning tool is called *predictive material and resource planning* (pMRP), which should replace LTP. The capabilities of pMRP are discussed in Chapter 17.

This chapter will cover the steps needed to prepare the master data and planning data for LTP using a real-life business case from the keyboard manufacturing industry. We also cover the logistics information system (LIS) with particular reference to LTP, focusing on the purchasing and inventory controlling subsets of the LIS. Finally, we also discuss further planning options offered by LTP to cater to various business scenarios.

Note

LTP isn't confined to just the long-term planning needs of the company but can be equally beneficial for short-term to medium-term planning.

For short-term simulation, a materials planner has the option to include sales orders, firm receipts from production, or purchase orders, whereas for long-term simulation, scrap calculations and other checks can be switched off to gain a broader view of the planning.

16.1 Long-Term Planning Master Data and Planning Data

LTP derives its details from existing information in the SAP system, including the planning data in the four different MRP views of the material master. Similarly, multilevel planning of the material is planned in LTP, and the system uses bills of materials (BOMs) and routings. To run an LTP simulation, ensure that the planning data is set up in the SAP system on which to run the simulation. For example, enter month-wise planning quantities of a finished or a semifinished good as planned independent requirements (PIRs). Then, define all of these quantities in a specific planning version number. The same material can have different month-wise planning quantities separately defined in different version numbers. Using inactive versions in LTP, execute various simulative LTP scenarios and evaluate the results separately. The following data is needed in the SAP system before running LTP:

- **Master data**
  The material for LTP (i.e., the material to be planned using LTP) and the BOM and routing of the material. The planning scenarios are also part of master data that you need to set up.

- **Planning data**
  The planning quantities of the material that will be entered as PIRs.

- **Planning scenario**
  The planning scenario that forms an integral part of master data setup for LTP.

We'll now cover master and planning data in detail.

16.1.1   Master Data

This example will show on how to perform LTP for manufacturing a keyboard, which is the main material, and its associated components in the BOM, as shown in Table 16.1. All of these materials and their planning data in the MRP views must already be maintained in the system, including the material BOM and routing. Table 16.1 also lists the details of some of the hypothetical BOM components for the keyboard. As previously explained, LTP uses the same planning data that had been defined in the MRP views of materials, so there's no need to define any additional data.

Number	Material Number	Material Description	BOM Components
1	72	Desktop Keyboard	1
2	19	Control unit (rack)	1
3	64	Bearing (complete)	5
4	24	Cable	5

Table 16.1 Unpacked Urea Bulk and Its Components in BOM

Example

For BOM components that aren't planned, the **MRP Type** defined in the **MRP 1** view of the material master is **ND**, which means **No Planning**. Therefore, the system will eliminate them from all planning activities in LTP. They won't be part of the operational MRP run either. Only in exceptional circumstances are such materials not planned in MRP or LTP; otherwise, we suggest on ensuring the data modeling for MRP or LTP to include all components of a material. For example, in the production of caustic soda, one of the raw materials is raw salt. Raw salt is not only very cheap but also readily available in countries with huge salt mines. Further, there's no specific warehousing requirement for raw salt so it can be placed in open space. With no significant capital tie-up and no inventory controlling requirement, it makes sense not to plan this material (raw salt).

Other planning parameters that were defined in the MRP views are applicable in LTP. For example, if a fixed lot size or minimum lot size for a material was defined in the material master, then the system will consider the lot sizing procedures during LTP. This also applies if, for example, a planning calendar was defined for external procurement.

The BOM for the keyboard was also previously defined, and once again LTP uses this information. For the rest of this example, we'll focus on the main material (material 72) for LTP.

Figure 16.1 shows the initial screen for BOM display. It includes a **BOM Usage** field, which indicates the application of the BOM, whether it's a production BOM, a costing BOM, an engineering/design BOM, or another usage. For this example, enter **BOM Usage** "1", which indicates **Production** use. To display the BOM, follow menu path **Logistics · Production · Master Data · Bill of Material · Bill of Material · Display**, or use Transaction CS03.

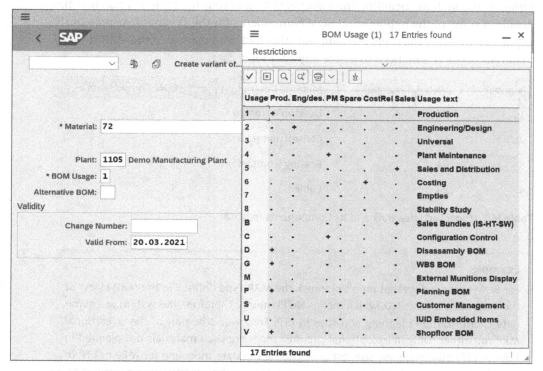

Figure 16.1 Production BOM with Usage 1

<table>
<thead>
<tr><th>Usage</th><th>Prod.</th><th>Eng/des.</th><th>PM</th><th>Spare</th><th>CostRel</th><th>Sales</th><th>Usage text</th></tr>
</thead>
<tbody>
<tr><td>1</td><td>+</td><td>.</td><td>.</td><td>.</td><td>.</td><td>.</td><td>Production</td></tr>
<tr><td>2</td><td>.</td><td>+</td><td>.</td><td>.</td><td>.</td><td>.</td><td>Engineering/Design</td></tr>
<tr><td>3</td><td>.</td><td>.</td><td>.</td><td>.</td><td>.</td><td>.</td><td>Universal</td></tr>
<tr><td>4</td><td>.</td><td>.</td><td>+</td><td>.</td><td>.</td><td>.</td><td>Plant Maintenance</td></tr>
<tr><td>5</td><td>.</td><td>.</td><td>.</td><td>.</td><td>.</td><td>+</td><td>Sales and Distribution</td></tr>
<tr><td>6</td><td>.</td><td>.</td><td>.</td><td>.</td><td>+</td><td>.</td><td>Costing</td></tr>
<tr><td>7</td><td>.</td><td>.</td><td>.</td><td>.</td><td>.</td><td>.</td><td>Empties</td></tr>
<tr><td>8</td><td>.</td><td>.</td><td>.</td><td>.</td><td>.</td><td>.</td><td>Stability Study</td></tr>
<tr><td>B</td><td>.</td><td>.</td><td>.</td><td>.</td><td>.</td><td>+</td><td>Sales Bundles (IS-HT-SW)</td></tr>
<tr><td>C</td><td>.</td><td>.</td><td>+</td><td>.</td><td>.</td><td>.</td><td>Configuration Control</td></tr>
<tr><td>D</td><td>+</td><td>.</td><td>.</td><td>.</td><td>.</td><td>.</td><td>Disassembly BOM</td></tr>
<tr><td>G</td><td>+</td><td>.</td><td>.</td><td>.</td><td>.</td><td>.</td><td>WBS BOM</td></tr>
<tr><td>M</td><td>.</td><td>.</td><td>.</td><td>.</td><td>.</td><td>.</td><td>External Munitions Display</td></tr>
<tr><td>P</td><td>+</td><td>.</td><td>.</td><td>.</td><td>.</td><td>.</td><td>Planning BOM</td></tr>
<tr><td>S</td><td>.</td><td>.</td><td>.</td><td>.</td><td>.</td><td>.</td><td>Customer Management</td></tr>
<tr><td>U</td><td>.</td><td>.</td><td>.</td><td>.</td><td>.</td><td>.</td><td>IUID Embedded Items</td></tr>
<tr><td>V</td><td>+</td><td>.</td><td>.</td><td>.</td><td>.</td><td>.</td><td>Shopfloor BOM</td></tr>
</tbody>
</table>

Tips and Tricks

We recommend creating a new BOM exclusively for LTP simulation. This provides greater visibility from a planning perspective. A dedicated BOM for LTP not only eliminates the chances of error while creating a normal production BOM of a material but also ensures that it's used for LTP purposes only. It then becomes easier for the person managing the production planning master data to segregate the normal production BOM from the LTP BOM. BOM usage is maintained in configuration. The selection ID enables a materials planner to use separate BOMs for LTP purposes. To do this, create a separate BOM usage and assign it to a selection ID by using the order of priority for BOM usages (Transaction OS31).

In Section 16.1.4, we address the significance of defining a separate BOM usage for LTP. Refer to Chapter 3, in which we explain how to define and set up BOMs (Section 3.2) and routing selection (Section 3.4).

16.1.2   Planning Data: Planning Quantity

Table 16.2 presents the monthly planning quantities for the main material (keyboard). These quantities are entered as PIRs for this example. LTP will simulate the production and procurement requirements based on this information (PIRs).

Number	Month/Year	Quantity (Metric Tons)
1	04.2021	1,000
2	05.2021	1,200
3	06.2021	1,500
4	07.2021	1,800
5	08.2021	1,500
6	09.2021	1,200

Table 16.2 Planning Quantities

16.1.3   Planning Data: Planned Independent Requirements

The purpose of having multiple versions of PIRs in the SAP system is to account for various planning situations and scenarios, each of which is identified by its version number. A simulation version is the identified demand plan. One demand plan can be a sales plan while another can be a production plan, each having its own planning quantities of the same material. There can be several inactive versions available for simulation and comparison, but we recommend only having one active (operational) version.

> **Note**
> Although the standard SAP system provides several PIR versions, more versions can be created if there's a need to attend to specific business processes in configuration Transaction OMP2.

For this example, use **Version 02** (simulation 2) for LTP (see Figure 16.2). To enter planning quantities in the PIR, follow menu path **Logistics · Production · Production Planning · Demand Management · Planned Independent Requirements · Create**, or use Transaction MD61.

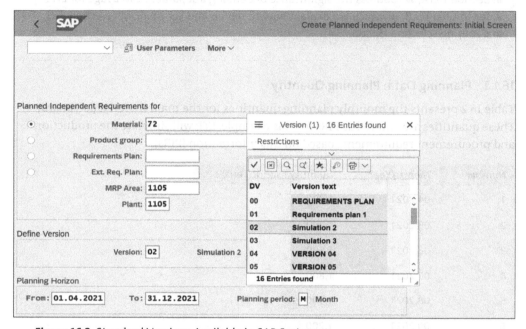

Figure 16.2 Standard Versions Available in SAP System

Figure 16.3 shows the monthly PIR figures as maintained in Table 16.2. Notice the **A** (active) checkbox isn't selected, which means LTP can consider planning materials without the checkbox selected. In contract, MRP only considers those materials that have this checkbox selected.

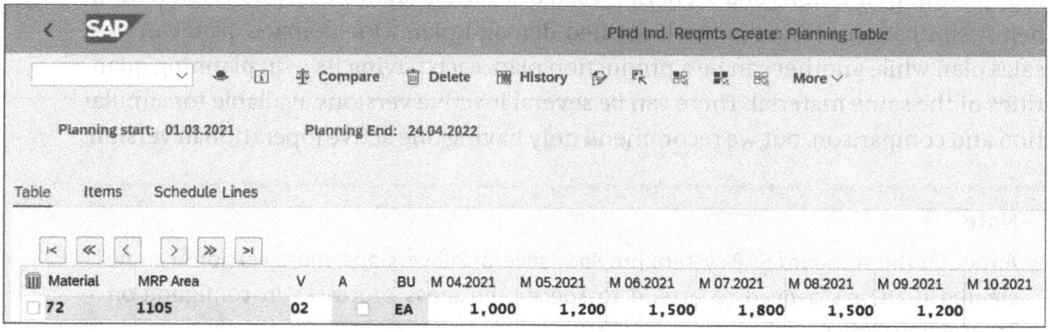

Material	MRP Area	V	A	BU	M 04.2021	M 05.2021	M 06.2021	M 07.2021	M 08.2021	M 09.2021	M 10.2021
72	1105	02	☐	EA	1,000	1,200	1,500	1,800	1,500	1,200	

Figure 16.3 Planned Independent Requirements

16.1.4   Create a Planning Scenario

To create a planning scenario, follow menu path **Logistics • Production • Production Planning • Long-Term Planning • Planning Scenario • Create**, or use Transaction MS31. These are the important steps in creating a planning scenario:

1. On the first screen that appears, define the planning scenario. For this example, define the **Planning Scenario** as "110" and also provide a short description.

2. Choose the **Long-Term Planning** radio button to denote that it's LTP in which the safety stock is used as the opening stock, and dependent requirements are created for reorder point materials. There are two other radio buttons on the first screen. **Gross Long-Term Planning** is similar to the long-term planning scenario, but the scrap calculation is deactivated, and a gross lot-sizing procedure can be selected. The **Short-Term Simulation** radio button enables the system to consider plant stock as the opening stock, and existing sales orders and firmed planning elements will be considered in the simulation.

3. Press ⏎ Enter so that the screen shown in Figure 16.4 appears.

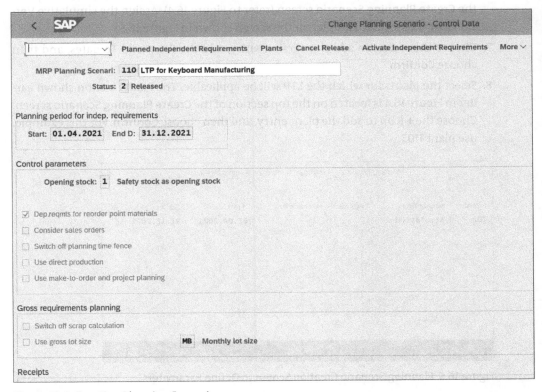

Figure 16.4 Creating Planning Scenario

We'll now explain the step-by-step procedure for running the LTP process, which we'll discuss in more detail in upcoming sections:

1. On the screen shown in Figure 16.4, enter "01.04.2021" and "31.12.2021" in the **Planning Period for Indep. Requirements** area of the screen. The system will carry out LTP for the specified period only.

2. Enter "1" (**Safety Stock as Opening Stock**) in the **Opening** stock field.

3. Select other parameters as deemed appropriate.

4. Scroll down and select the **BOM Selection ID 01** (not shown), which is the production BOM for this example. If an LTP-specific BOM usage was specifically created, then assign it here.

5. If there's a business need to consider a different shift schedule or perhaps a different capacity utilization, then choose a different active version for the available capacity under the **Available Capacity** section (not shown but located further down the same screen).

6. Click on the **Planned Independent Requirements** button located on the top section of the **Create Planning Scenario** screen (refer to Figure 16.4). Assign the simulative **Version** (use **02** for this example) on the screen shown in Figure 16.5.

7. Choose the **+** icon to add the version entry, add the **From** and **To** dates, and then choose **Confirm**.

8. Select the plants for which the LTP will be applicable. The **Plants** button shown earlier in Figure 16.4 is located on the top section of the **Create Planning Scenario** screen. Choose the **+** icon to add the plant entry, and then choose **Confirm**. For this example, use plant **1105**.

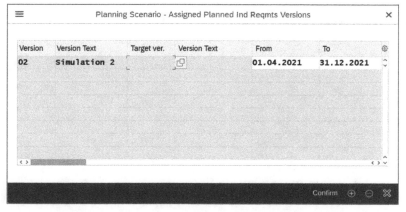

Figure 16.5 Planning Scenario Creation Screen to Define Parameters

9. Choose the **Release + Save** button shown earlier in Figure 16.4 to save the planning scenario. After a planning scenario has been released, parameters maintained in a scenario can no longer be changed. However, it is possible to undo the release within the planning scenario, make the desired changes and then re-release the planning scenario again.

10. The system automatically creates planning file entries in due course. When the planning scenario is released, the system creates entries in the planning files and this is confirmed via a popup message to confirm if the planning entries be created online or in the background. However, when release of the planning scenario is cancelled, the system correspondingly deletes the entries from the planning file. The new report PPH_SETUP_MRPRECORDS_SIMU is used to set up and check for consistencies in the LTP planning file entries; this is the report executed in a background job when a scenario is released.

16.2   Long-Term Planning: Business Process

Now that we've covered the master data and the planning data that needs to be set up for LTP, let's cover the business processes involved in LTP. After creating the planning scenario, perform the following series of activities in sequential order:

1. Enter the PIR in a simulative version (already covered in Section 16.1.3).
2. Run LTP (simulative MRP) and save the results.
3. Evaluate the LTP stock/requirements list.

> **Note**
>
> When working with LTP in the SAP system, it may take several rounds to achieve a satisfactory production plan. It's helpful, then, to know that the basics and the underlying principles involved in LTP are very similar to MRP—adjusting, planning, evaluating, and comparing until the results are satisfactory.
>
> The LTP example that we present in this chapter is a straightforward one, and the objective is to help a materials planner understand the sequence of steps involved in running LTP. For example, the planning quantities in the PIR can be set up much earlier than setting up LTP. We present it here to show that creating a PIR is one of the several steps that need to be undertaken in the initial stages of master data setup for LTP.

16.2.1   Run Long-Term Planning (Simulative MRP)

To run the LTP interactively (simulative MRP), follow menu path **Logistics · Production · Production Planning · Long-Term Planning · Long-Term Planning · Single Item, Multi-Level**, or use Transaction MS02. Here, define the initial parameters to run the LTP. Enter the **MRP Planning Scenario** as "110", as well as the **Material** code (72) and the **Plant** (see Figure 16.6).

Just like the MRP, define the parameters that will eventually influence the results of LTP. For this example, define that during LTP, the system should re-explode the BOM and routing to read the latest data and perform lead time scheduling to account for capacity planning (see Figure 16.6).

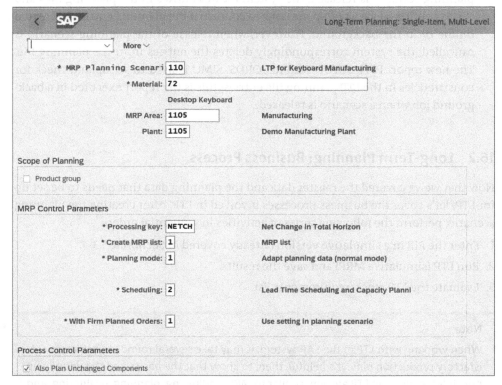

Figure 16.6 Initial Screen to Run LTP

Press [Enter], and the system issues a warning message to check all of the planning parameters. Press [Enter] again to confirm, and the system runs the LTP.

Figure 16.7 shows the planning results of **Material 72**, which is the first of the BOM materials selected for LTP planning. Click **Save and continue** so that the screen shown in Figure 16.8 appears.

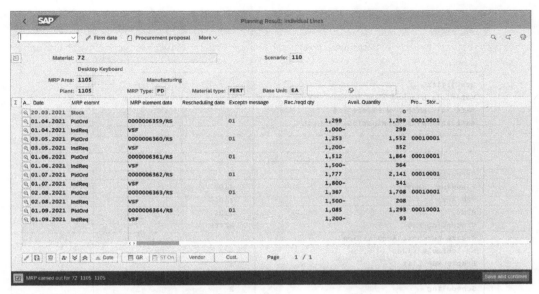

Figure 16.7 LTP List (Simulative MRP List) Generated

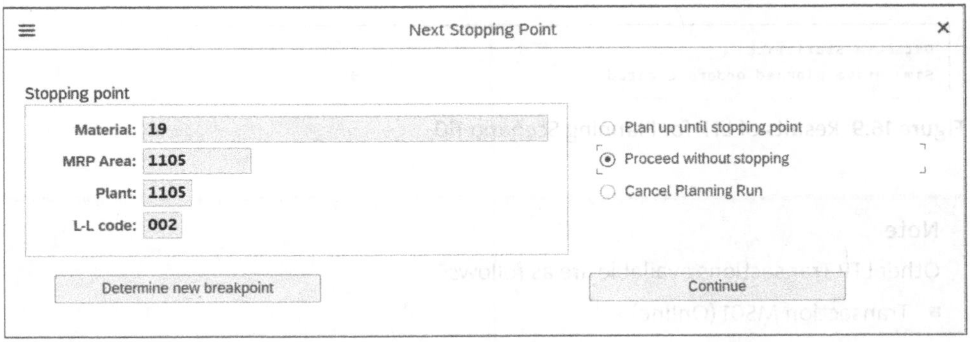

Figure 16.8 LTP of BOM Component

After the LTP planning of the keyboard, Figure 16.8 shows that the next BOM component, **Material 19**, is ready to be planned. Choose the **Proceed without Stopping** radio button and then choose **Continue** so that the system plans all BOM components without stopping at each breakpoint.

Figure 16.9 shows the LTP report of single material, multilevel LTP in which a total of four materials were planned via LTP.

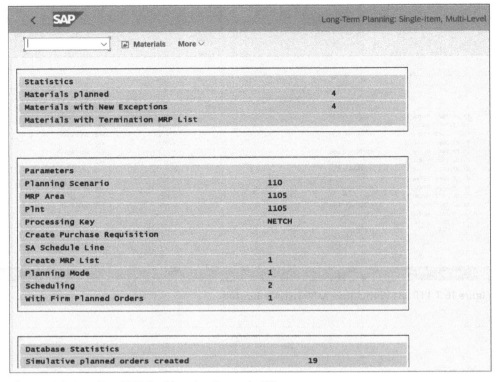

Figure 16.9 Results of LTP for Planning Scenario 110

> [»] **Note**
>
> Other LTP Transactions available are as follows:
>
> - Transaction MS01 (Online)
> - Transaction MS03 (Single Level Single Item Planning)
> - Transaction MSBT (As Background Job)
> - Transaction MS50 (Single Item Planning, Sales Order)
> - Transaction MS51 (Single Item Planning, Project)

16.2.2   Evaluate the Long-Term Planning Stock/Requirements List

It's now time to evaluate the results and outcome of the LTP in the form of an LTP stock/requirements list. Follow menu path **Logistics • Production • Production Planning • Long-Term Planning • Evaluations • Stock/Requirements List**, or use Transaction MS04. The screen shown in Figure 16.10 appears after entering parameters for planning scenario 110, material number, and plant.

Note

In the standard display layout of a stock/requirements list, the system shows individual planning elements, including independent requirements, planned orders, and so on. However, we've changed the layout to show how the monthly quantities entered in the PIR are shown in the stock/requirements list. Notice that the first column is the monthly **Period/Segment**, whereas the second column is the **Plnd Ind.Reqmts**.

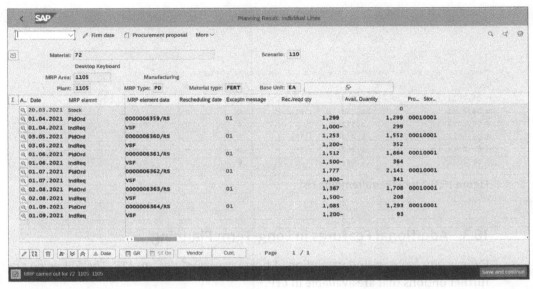

Figure 16.10 Stock/Requirements List

Tips and Tricks

The layout can be aggregated to period total in the stock/requirements list by choosing the **Aggregate** icon. Click the **Days**, **Weeks**, or **Months** tabs to view the aggregate details. Refer to Chapter 13 and Chapter 14 on MRP for more information.

Figure 16.10 doesn't have any opening stock. This is because we selected the safety stock as the opening stock balance while creating planning scenario 110. All figures are available as shown in Table 16.2, which shows the planning quantities for the keyboard.

Figure 16.11 shows the results of component control unit (rack) of the finished product. The dependent requirements of control unit (rack) calculated by LTP are based on the PIRs and the BOM explosion details given in Table 16.2. The calculated quantities are shown in the **Receipt/Reqmt** column.

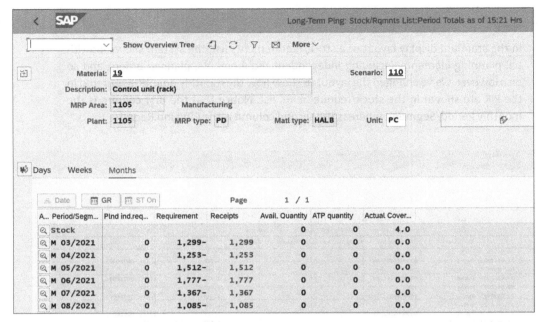

Figure 16.11 Stock/Requirements List

16.3   Additional Features in Long-Term Planning

By now you have an understanding of how to successfully run LTP. The following are further options that are available in LTP:

- Manually creating a simulative planned order
- Firming the simulative planned order using a firming date
- Copying PIRs or firmed planned orders from LTP to operative planning
- Cleaning up the LTP data

Some of these options aren't commonly known; we'll explain them in the following sections.

16.3.1   Manually Create a Simulative Planned Order

While LTP provides complete automation in planning and proposal generation, including the creation of planned orders, it's often necessary to manually create a simulative planned order to meet any additional requirements during the simulation phase. For example, say that while evaluating results from LTP, a materials planner realizes that there's a need to account for additional demand for a specific component. Instead of making changes to the PIR of a finished product and then re-exploding the BOM to come up with the component's quantity, simply create a simulative planned order for that specific component. This simulative planned order then becomes available in all evaluations (e.g., the stock/requirements list) and information systems (e.g., purchasing and inventory controlling) and is also firmed. The system won't make changes during the next LTP run to this manually created simulative planned order.

To create a simulative planned order, follow menu path **Logistics · Production · Production Planning · Long-Term Planning · Simulative Planned Order · Create**, or use Transaction MS11. Figure 16.12 shows the screen for the creation of a simulative planned order. For this example, create a simulative planned order for a quantity of 100 EA and also associate it with planning scenario 110. In addition, set the **Firming** indicator (not shown) so that during the next LTP run, the details of this simulative planned order aren't changed.

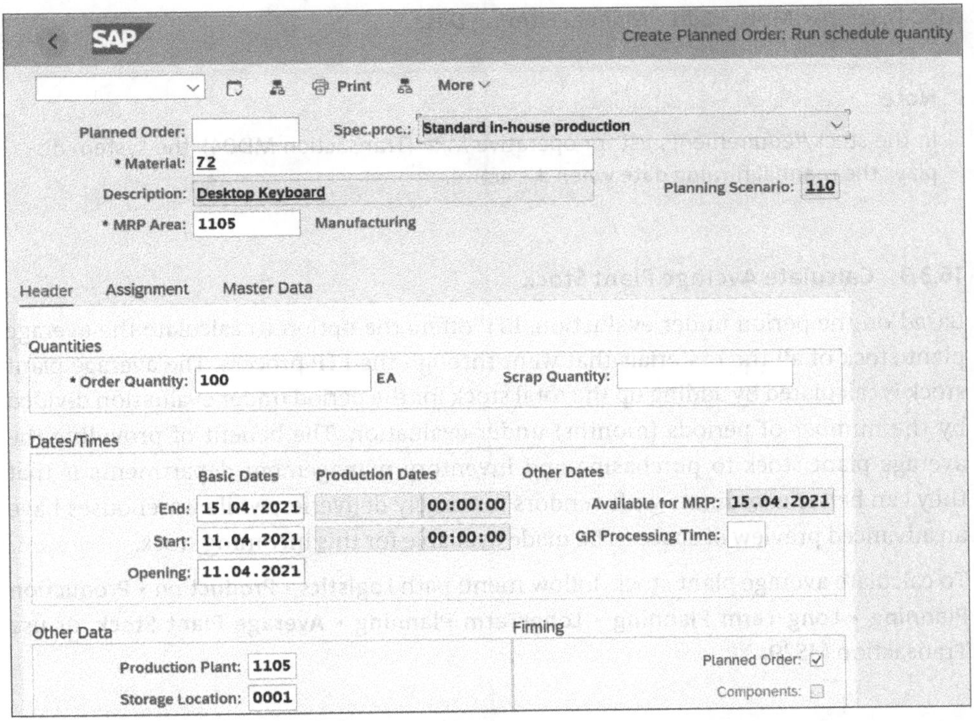

Create Planned Order: Run schedule quantity

Planned Order:		Spec.proc.:	Standard in-house production
* Material:	72		
Description:	Desktop Keyboard	Planning Scenario:	110
* MRP Area:	1105	Manufacturing	

Header   Assignment   Master Data

Quantities

| * Order Quantity: | 100 | EA | Scrap Quantity: | |

Dates/Times

	Basic Dates	Production Dates	Other Dates	
End:	15.04.2021	00:00:00	Available for MRP:	15.04.2021
Start:	11.04.2021	00:00:00	GR Processing Time:	
Opening:	11.04.2021			

Other Data

| Production Plant: | 1105 |
| Storage Location: | 0001 |

Firming

| Planned Order: | ☑ |
| Components: | ☐ |

Figure 16.12 Manual Creation of Simulative Planned Order

When processing a simulative planned order, you can take actions such as firming, scheduling, or using it for capacity analysis, for example. It isn't possible to run an availability check for this kind of order, though, and the available-to-promise (ATP)-related menu button will not be displayed. Further, to copy the LTP planned orders to operational MRP, you need to trigger the interactive MRP in Transaction MD43 and then choose the **More · Edit · Copy Simulative LT Planned Orders** menu option. From the subsequent popup, choose from which planning scenario you're copying the firm planned orders and a date interval from which the planned orders should be copied.

After copying the planned orders, it's highly recommended to trigger the MRP planning within Transaction MD43 to ensure that all the requirements are covered and that there are no shortages for the material because the previously existing planned orders were deleted.

16.3.2   Firm the Simulative Planned Order Using a Firming Date

The process of manually firming planned orders ensures that all future LTP runs don't impact or overwrite the existing simulative planning data. In firming, a date is specified, and all of the simulative planned orders generated from LTP are then firmed until that date. During the next LTP run, these manually firmed simulative planned orders aren't changed or deleted. While remaining in the stock/requirements list (Transaction MS04), choose **More** · **Edit** · **Manual Firming Date**.

> **Note**
>
> In the stock/requirements list for operative MRP (Transaction MD04), the system displays the manual firming date when it's active.

16.3.3   Calculate Average Plant Stock

Based on the period under evaluation, LTP offers the option to calculate the average plant stock of all the materials that went through the LTP process. The average plant stock is calculated by adding up the total stock for the period under evaluation divided by the number of periods (months) under evaluation. The benefit of providing the average plant stock to purchasing and inventory management departments is that they can better coordinate with vendors for timely deliveries, while warehouses have an advanced preview of space to be made available for this incoming stock.

To calculate average plant stock, follow menu path **Logistics** · **Production** · **Production Planning** · **Long-Term Planning** · **Long-Term Planning** · **Average Plant Stock**, or use Transaction MS29.

16.3.4   Copy Long-Term Planning Results to Operative Planning

After all of the necessary simulations (LTP) have been completed, the business often needs to move the results of one of the simulations of LTP to operative planning, based on which the actual MRP run can be executed. For this example, proceed with the understanding or assumption that the entire supply chain team is satisfied with the results of LTP and wants to copy the PIR to operative planning. In an actual business scenario, there may be several rounds of PIR updating and planning simulations within LTP before copying the agreed-upon PIR into operative planning. The agreed-upon PIR for transfer to operative planning will be the one in which the supply chain is satisfied with the LTP simulation results. While this example focuses on copying PIRs, the firmed (simulative) planned orders can also be copied to operative planning.

The option to copy a PIR of simulative planning to operative planning saves an enormous amount of work already done during the LTP process and eliminates redundancy in data entry. Further, during the copy function, there's a flexibility to make changes in operative planning with respect to LTP. After the PIR is in operative planning, assign the **Active** status to it and run the MRP.

To copy the LTP's PIR to operative planning, follow menu path **Logistics • Production • Production Planning • Long-Term Planning • Planned Independent Requirements • Copy Version**, or use Transaction MS64. Figure 16.13 shows the initial screen to define parameters to transfer the results of the simulative planning of version 02 to the operative planning in version 03.

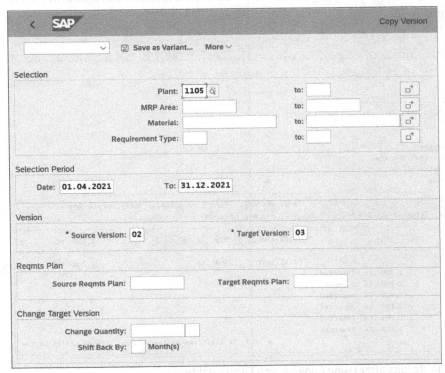

Figure 16.13 Copying Source Version 02 to Target Version 03 of PIR

Tips and Tricks

Although we're deliberately taking the longer route in this example to show the steps involved in the copy function, use Transaction MS32 (Change Planning Scenario) and the **Active Independent Requirements** icon to copy PIRs to the target version.

Here, source version 02 is specified as the version to be copied to target version 03. Other parameters to define include dates of transfer from version 02 to 03. Changes in quantities between the source and target versions can also be made, as well as the number of months by which a materials planner wants to displace the planning data to operative data during transfer. *Displacement* refers to moving quantities forward or backward in time from version 02 to version 03 during copying of simulative data to operative data. Also select the **No Database Changes (Simulation)** checkbox to enable the copy function in the simulation mode and to check for any errors or other deviations before performing the actual transfer.

After execution (by pressing F8), the screen shown in Figure 16.14 shows the simulated results copied to target version 03 with all the quantities successfully transferred to version 03. Go back to the previous screen and deselect the **No Database Changes (Simulation)**, then press F8 again; this time, the copied results are available in the PIR under version 03.

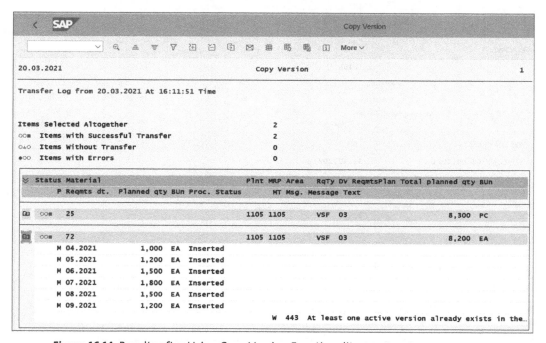

Figure 16.14 Results after Using Copy Version Functionality

[»]

Note

While this example shows the transfer of a PIR from version 02 to version 03, we suggest using version 00, which is the active version in the system, to transfer LTP PIRs to operative planning (MRP).

After copying the LTP planning results of source version 02 to operative planning in version 03, check to see if the outcome of the copy function is that the LTP PIR data of version 02 is now available in version 03. To check the PIR, follow menu path **Logistic · Production · Production Planning · Long-Term Planning · Planned Independent Requirements · Change**, or use Transaction MD62. Confirm that the system successfully executed the copy function and that the simulative figures of version 02 are now transferred to 03. Refer to the third column (with the heading **V**) to note that it's version 03, and consider the activated **Active** field (the checkbox) right next to it.

[+]

> **Tips and Tricks**
>
> Use Transaction MD74 to delete or reorganize old or inactive PIRs on a regular basis. Transaction MS08 can be used to reorganize (delete) MRP lists created for LTP.

16.3.5   Cleaning Up Long-Term Planning Data

After running all the desired LTP simulations, there might be a need to restart the simulation from scratch or simply reuse the same planning scenario for a different simulation. In the standard SAP S/4HANA system, there is no LTP archiving object as it's simply a simulation tool, but SAP offers options for deleting the LTP scenario-dependent data and the whole planning scenario. The deletion of dependent data can be carried out independently of the planning scenario deletion. There are different alternatives to delete the planning scenario-dependent data, and each one can be used for a different purpose.

If you're firming simulative planned orders and an MRP type with roll-forward isn't used, then it might occasionally be necessary to delete the old firmed planned orders because they will not be converted or backflushed like the operational MRP planned orders. If there's a need to delete firm planned orders, the simplest option is to run report RMPLAF00 (using Transaction SE38); just select for which specific planning scenario planned orders need to be deleted, and decide if you want to activate the **Set Planning File Entries** flag so that all the materials with deleted planned orders are planned again in the next LTP run. The report also offers an option to run in test mode, which will tell you how many planned orders will be deleted before the actual deletion. If you're setting manual firming dates for the materials in Transaction MS04, it will cause simulative planned orders to be automatically firmed during the LTP run. When the manual firming date is no longer required, use report RMMDFD00 to delete those entries so that they will no longer be relevant to LTP.

Another way to delete the planning scenario-dependent data is to run report RMPLSC00. This report will not only delete the planned orders but also provides options to select specific elements to be deleted by checking the **Planning File Entries**,

MRP Lists, Manual Firming Data, Data in Purchasing Info System, Data in Inventory Controlling, and **Average Plant Stocks** flags in the selection screen (see Figure 16.15).

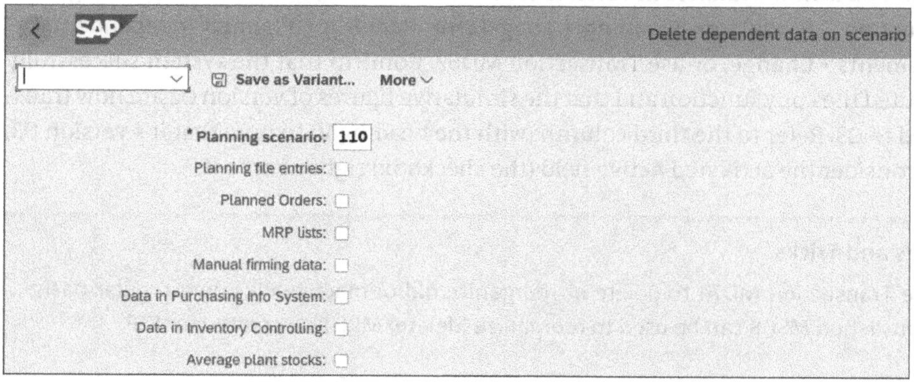

Figure 16.15 Deleting LTP Data

Finally, the data and the planning scenario itself can be deleted when changing the planning scenario in Transaction MS32. Both options can be selected through the **More** • **Planning Scenario** • **Delete** menu option when changing the planning scenario. If you choose the option to delete dependent data in Transaction MS32, then a popup appears. Here, choose which planning elements will be deleted and whether the deletion will be executed immediately or in the background; the system will only allow marking those planning elements that actually exist for the planning scenario.

The actual deletion of the planning scenario will be possible only after all the dependent data is deleted, and it can be carried out directly in Transaction MS32. After the deletion, reusing the same number for the creation of a new planning scenario is possible.

16.4   Evaluate Information Systems

The LIS is available for all core logistics areas in the SAP system. The LIS for each area provides a multitude of standard analysis reports. It derives the data and information from all of the transactions performed in the system, thus ensuring the availability of comprehensive information for evaluation and decision-making purposes. An information system is a reporting option available in the system to display the desired information based on the user-defined criteria. Therefore, there is also a comprehensive information system for LTP, catering to both purchasing and inventory controlling functions.

In the following sections, we'll explain how to set up and evaluate the results of the information systems for purchasing and inventory controlling in LTP. There'll be a need to first set up the data for these two information systems before the system displays the planning results of a planning scenario. There's no need to set up any data for capacity requirements for work centers for a given planning scenario.

16.4.1   Setting Up a Purchasing Information System for LTP

Let's set up data before the purchasing information system for LTP is ready for use and evaluation. To get to the initial screen for the data setup (Figure 16.16), follow menu path **Logistics · Production · Production Planning · Long-Term Planning · Evaluations · Purchasing Information System · Set Up Data**, or use Transaction MS70.

To set up the data, select the relevant parameters (e.g., **MRP Planning Scenario**). For this example, select **MRP Planning Scenario 110**. For order value calculation, choose **Standard/Moving Avg.Price**, which the system will read from the material master. If the planned prices of the material are to be used to form the basis for purchasing value calculation, then choose **Plnd Price** (planned price) and enter one of the three planned prices available. Press F8 to execute.

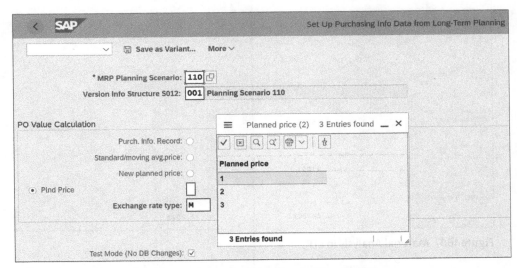

Figure 16.16 Set Up Screen for Purchasing Information System for LTP

[!]

Warning

Make sure you deselect the **Test Mode (No DB Changes)** checkbox shown in Figure 16.16 to execute in the system.

16.4.2   Evaluating with the Purchasing Information System for LTP

The purchasing information system for LTP is now ready for use for evaluation purposes. Follow menu path **Logistics · Production · Production Planning · Long-Term**

Planning • Evaluation • Purchasing Information System • Material, or use Transaction MCEC. Enter the relevant parameters, as shown in Figure 16.17. These parameters are **MRP Planning Scenario**, **Standard/Moving Avg.Price** (or other value calculation), **Material** number, **Plant**, and the **Period to Analyze**.

Planning scenario 110 and the results for the materials are shown in Figure 16.18. Monthly order quantities along with values are reflected. The monthly purchase order quantity and the monthly total value in local currency is shown as well.

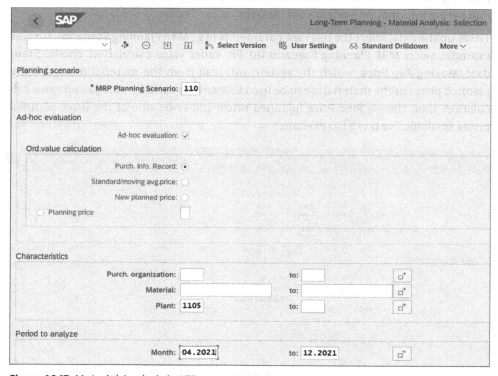

Figure 16.17 Material Analysis in LTP

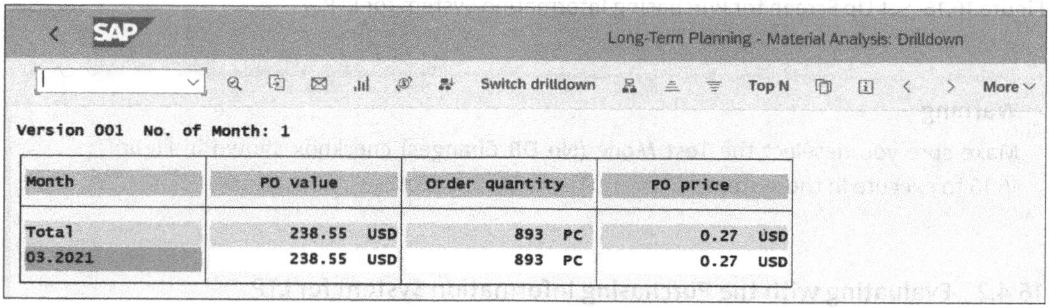

Month	PO value		Order quantity		PO price	
Total	238.55	USD	893	PC	0.27	USD
03.2021	238.55	USD	893	PC	0.27	USD

Figure 16.18 Evaluation in Purchasing Information System for Materials

The planning results of simulative planning data of the planning scenario can be compared with operative planning. Use Transaction MS44 to bring up the material-specific or plant-specific comparison. Then choose whether to run a comparison with the current operative planning situation (corresponding to the stock/requirements list) with the last operative planning run (corresponding to the MRP list) or with another planning scenario. The presentation of the comparison can be defined by means of a layout; in this case, we chose the standard layout, SAPSOP. This layout displays the issues, receipts, and available quantity for LTP and operative planning (indicated by comparative data in this case).

16.4.3   Setting Up an Inventory Controlling Information System for LTP

Similar to setting up a purchasing information system for LTP, you have to set up data before the inventory controlling information system for LTP is ready for use. To set up the data, follow menu path **Logistics • Production • Production Planning • Long-Term Planning • Evaluations • Inventory Controlling • Setup Data**, or use Transaction MCB&.

In Figure 16.19, the selection parameters are **Plant**, **Material**, **Period to analyze**, and **MRP Planning Scenario** (which is **110** for this example). After the parameters are defined as shown, choose the **Execute** icon or press F8 . This is all that is needed to set up data for the inventory controlling information system for LTP.

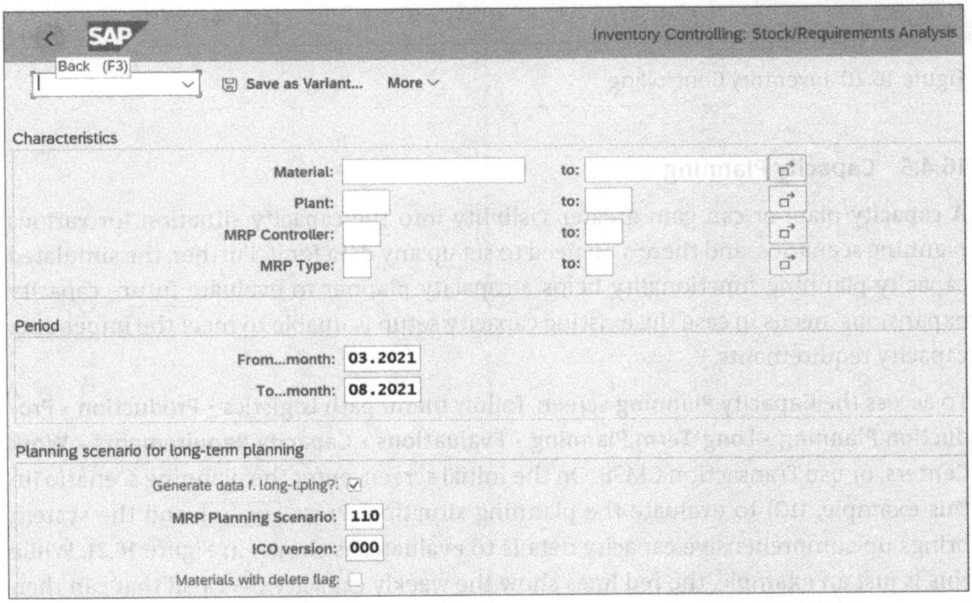

Figure 16.19 Setup of Inventory Controlling Information System for LTP

16.4.4 Evaluating the Inventory Controlling Information System for LTP

The inventory controlling information system for LTP is now ready for use for evaluation purposes. To get to the **Inventory Controlling** screen, follow menu path **Logistics · Production · Production Planning · Long-Term Planning · Evaluations · Inventory Controlling · Evaluation**, or use Transaction MCB). Figure 16.20 reflects the inventory situation of some components for individual months. The total monthly requirements are shown first, followed by the stock situation, and finally by how much quantity must be received per month against procurement proposals generated by MRP/LTP (as shown in the **GdsReceipt (MRP)** column).

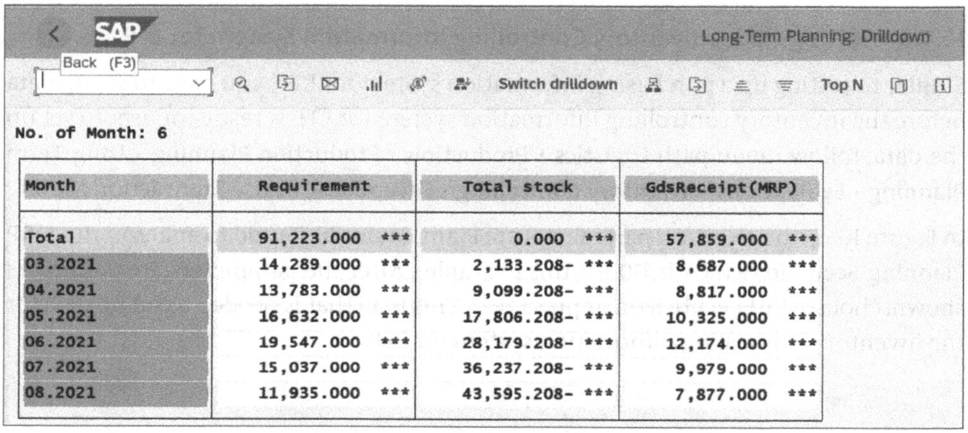

Month	Requirement	Total stock	GdsReceipt(MRP)
Total	91,223.000 ***	0.000 ***	57,859.000 ***
03.2021	14,289.000 ***	2,133.208- ***	8,687.000 ***
04.2021	13,783.000 ***	9,099.208- ***	8,817.000 ***
05.2021	16,632.000 ***	17,806.208- ***	10,325.000 ***
06.2021	19,547.000 ***	28,179.208- ***	12,174.000 ***
07.2021	15,037.000 ***	36,237.208- ***	9,979.000 ***
08.2021	11,935.000 ***	43,595.208- ***	7,877.000 ***

No. of Month: 6

Figure 16.20 Inventory Controlling

16.4.5 Capacity Planning

A capacity planner can gain greater visibility into the capacity situation for various planning scenarios, and there's no need to set up any data for it. Further, the simulated capacity planning functionality helps a capacity planner to evaluate future capacity expansions' needs in case the existing capacity setup is unable to meet the impending capacity requirements.

To access the **Capacity Planning** screen, follow menu path **Logistics · Production · Production Planning · Long-Term Planning · Evaluations · Capacity Requirements · Work Centers**, or use Transaction CM38. On the initial screen, enter the planning scenario (in this example, 110) to evaluate the planning situation. Press ⌈Enter⌋, and the system brings up comprehensive capacity details to evaluate, as shown in Figure 16.21. While this is just an example, the red lines show the weekly capacity overload that can then help the capacity planner to consider shifting some production to other time periods (the capacity leveling process).

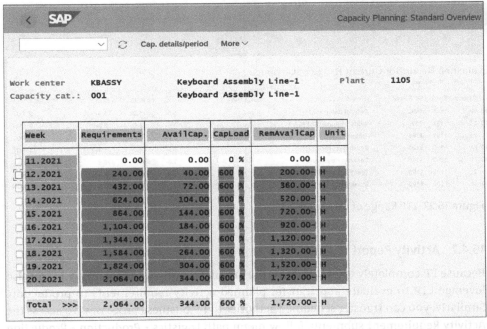

Figure 16.21 Capacity Evaluation with LTP

> **Note**
> Refer to Chapter 18 on capacity requirements planning (CRP) for more information.

16.4.6 Long-Term Planning Evaluation for Range of Coverage

The *range of coverage* reflects the number of days during which the current stock will cover future stock issues, and it's based on past stock and issue values. In other words, the range of coverage indicates how long existing inventory will last, assuming that the average future stock issues will be the same as those in the past. The usage-based range of coverage is calculated as follows:

Current stock ÷ Average usage per day

The requirements-based range of coverage is calculated as follows:

Current stock ÷ Average requirement per day

Using the range of coverage in LTP, a company can identify materials with excess coverage and take action to reduce unnecessary inventory. The opposite is also true when it comes to identifying a potential shortage situation early on to take corrective measures. Using Transaction MSDO, access the screen shown in Figure 16.22 for LTP evaluation of several materials for which there isn't adequate coverage, including our example material 72.

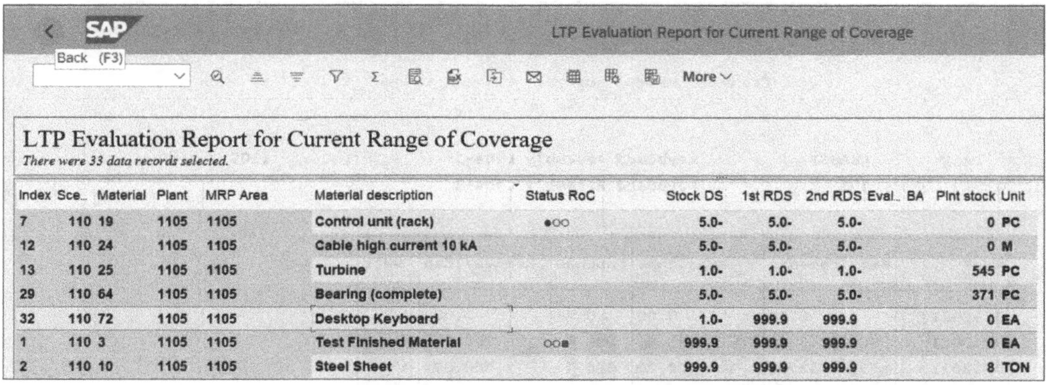

Figure 16.22 LTP Range of Coverage

16.4.7   Activity Report

Because PP completely integrates with the product costing functionality, you can also leverage LTP to evaluate and transfer planned activity requirements to production. Similarly, you can transfer scheduled activities to PP business processes. To access the **Activity Requirement** submenu, follow menu path **Logistics · Production · Production Planning · Long-Term Planning · Environment · Activity Requirement**.

16.5   Summary

LTP is able to attend to several business scenarios in simulation mode, as well as to matters such as average plant stock, production quantities, procurement quantities and values, and capacities over a given period of time. LTP uses the same concepts and fundamentals as MRP. Even the system navigation and functions of LTP and MRP offer great similarities.

The next chapter is on pMRP, the next-generation materials and capacity simulation tool.

Chapter 17

Predictive Material and Resource Planning

Predictive material and resource planning is a new feature introduced in SAP S/4HANA that allows capacity, production, and procurement planners to simulate demand changes and check if there are capacity overloads. It's built on several of the same concepts as its predecessor, long-term planning.

A new functionality called *predictive material and resource planning* (pMRP), designed to provide simulation capabilities and to validate a forecast based on the work center capacity, was introduced in SAP S/4HANA 1909. The overall concept behind pMRP is similar to LTP and can be considered a successor of LTP, but with more functionalities and an intuitive user interface. pMRP is designed with an intuitive, SAP Fiori-based user interface and uses a simplified planning logic.

As in LTP, the main input for the pMRP simulation will be also a demand plan, reflected in the system as planned independent requirements (PIRs). The system will consider this input to run a simulated planning run so as analyze the capacity of the work centers. It can also be used to simulate the required quantity for a specific raw material during the time period under evaluation (see Figure 17.1).

Within the pMRP simulation, users can interactively analyze the results of the simulation, taking actions to resolve a work center capacity issue, such as the following:

- Change the forecasted demand to reduce the capacity requirements in the work center.
- Increase the work center available capacity to accommodate the capacity requirements for the forecasted quantities.
- Change the source of supply to use a different work center.
- Preproduce a component to distribute the requirements for this component across multiple months.

Once the necessary changes and adjustments to a simulation is undertaken, it can be released to operational planning so that the quantities adjusted in the simulation can be saved into the PIRs. pMRP is also designed to consider the new demand-driven material requirements planning (DDMRP) concept (see Chapter 15): the forecast requirements are released as PIRs for components planned with a DDMRP type once the simulation is released.

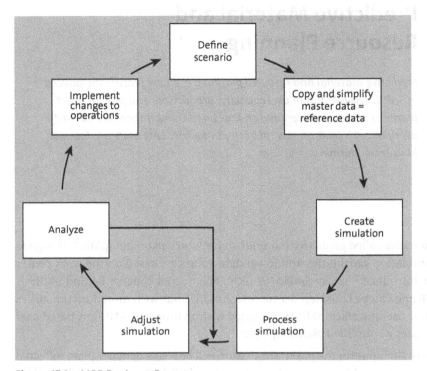

Figure 17.1 pMRP Business Processes

pMRP is mainly accessed through two SAP Fiori applications: the Schedule pMRP Simulation Creation app (in which the simulation is created) and the Process pMRP Simulations app (in which the simulation can be processed and copied). Both are accessed through the SAP Fiori launchpad.

The following sections will discuss the end-to-end pMRP process in a step-by-step way, starting with the basic setup required to run pMRP followed by creating a new simulation before moving on to how to process this simulation. Finally, we conclude with releasing the simulation results of pMRP to operational planning.

17.1   pMRP Basics

pMRP doesn't requires any configuration settings at all. This means that pMRP can be used right away as long as the proper operational MRP configuration is in place, such as a valid plant, MRP controllers, and so on. pMRP does, however, need basic master data and transactional data already in place. That data is also used by MRP for planning a material, such as the following:

- **Material master**
  Any MRP-relevant material can be used for a pMRP simulation.

- **BOM**
  A valid BOM with the BOM usage set to **1—Production** should exist for a material that will be used in a simulation.

- **Work center**
  The work center used in a simulation should have at least one capacity relevant for finite scheduling.

- **Routing**
  A valid routing should exist, and the operation in the bottleneck resource operation should be relevant for capacity planning.

- **Production version**
  At least one valid production version referring to the BOM and routing should exist. If there is more than one valid production version, then it's possible to change the source of supply during the simulation.

- **Planned independent requirements**
  PIRs for the relevant materials are maintained.

Before starting to use pMRP, all the relevant master data should be available in advance. As one of the main objectives behind pMRP is to allow the user to check if there is enough capacity to produce the forecasted quantities, it's very important to correctly set up the routing and the work center with the standard values and the proper formulas.

From a transactional data perspective, the main input for pMRP is a forecast plan, represented by PIRs (Transaction MD61). The planning strategy used isn't relevant because it supports any requirement type and it's also possible to use an active or an inactive PIR version. When choosing an inactive version, the capacity planner will need to select the version number during the simulation creation.

17.2   pMRP Setup

The first step in the pMRP process is to create a pMRP simulation. This step in pMRP is similar to the creating an LTP scenario; the difference is that the long-term planning scenario is created for a whole plant, whereas in pMRP a planner can choose to restrict a set of master data for simulation purposes. When a simulation is created, it's possible to select which top-level materials or work centers will be considered for pMRP. Another difference between pMRP and LTP is that all the planning will happen during the simulation creation itself, whereas in LTP the planning scenario must first be released and then a planning run execution takes place (as many times as needed). In pMRP, a planner will be able to process the simulation immediately after the creation is finished and will not have to wait for a planning run. A third difference is that whereas LTP generally runs with the same MRP type and lot sizing procedure used by operational MRP, pMRP uses a simplified planning logic, in which all materials will use a deterministic MRP and a lot-for-lot procedure.

Before the simulation creation, ensure that the relevant master data has been created. It's also important to have PIRs created: they will be the main input for the pMRP simulation. The system will plan the selected materials and determine the work center capacity requirements based on those PIRs.

A word of caution here: when a simulation is created, master data will be copied into it, so subsequent changes to master data may not be considered.

The pMRP simulation creation is basically a background job that can be scheduled through the Schedule pMRP Simulation Creation app. This application can also be used to manage background jobs that are already finished, scheduled, or in process.

As shown in Figure 17.2, an icon in the **Log** column will show the status of the finished background executions, and another icon is shown in the **Results** column. Clicking the icon in the **Log** column will show the details of success, warning, or error messages that may have been triggered during each step of the simulation creation.

You can create, copy, and delete a simulation creation (although deletion is only possible for scheduled jobs). To create a new application job, choose **Create** in the screen shown in Figure 17.2, which brings up the screen shown in Figure 17.3.

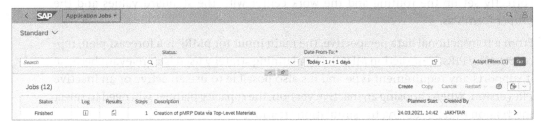

Figure 17.2 Application Jobs

Figure 17.3 shows that a planner can choose between the following two different job templates and, depending on the selection in the **Job Template** field, different selection criteria will appear:

- **Creation of pMRP Data via Top-Level Materials**
  Object selection is based on the material master, so selection criteria will be focused on the material master information, such as material number, MRP controller, or low-level code. The system will look for PIRs for the relevant materials and run simplified MRP to determine the required quantity for each level and the capacity allocated in the work center.

- **Creation of pMRP Data via Work Center**
  Object selection is based on the work center, so the selection criteria will be focused on the work center. The system will look for capacity requirements in the selected work centers and then identify the top-level materials and the respective PIRs.

For this example, choose the first option from the dropdown in Figure 17.3 ❶, then Choose **Step 2**.

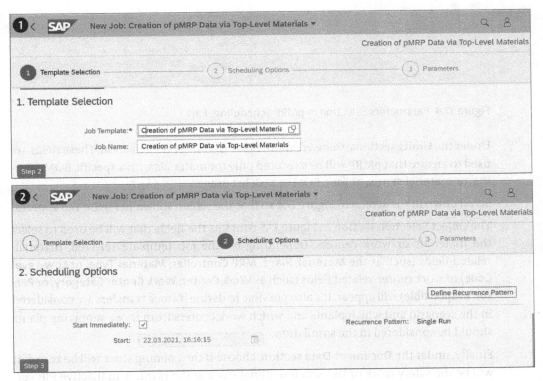

Figure 17.3 Scheduling pMRP

In the **Scheduling Options** section ❷, define whether the job will be executed immediately or scheduled to run on a future date. The creation of the pMRP simulation will be executed only once; therefore, it should not be executed as a periodic job, and the **Recurrence Pattern** value is set to **Single-Run** by default. Choose **Step 3** in the screen in Figure 17.3 so that the screen shown in Figure 17.4 appears.

In the **Parameter** section in Figure 17.4, fill in the **ID for Reference Plan** and **Simulation ID** fields, which are used to identify the simulation. These should be unique values; the reference ID and simulation ID cannot be the same. The ID for the reference plan will represent the set of master data selected according to the selection criteria, and new simulations can be added later under the same reference ID. Under the **Parameter** section, select the bucket category (daily, weekly, or monthly buckets) and the start and end date for the simulation.

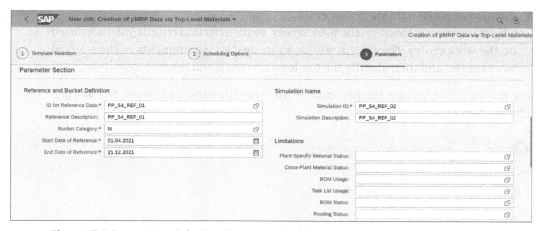

Figure 17.4 Parameters Selection in pMRP Scheduling: Part 1

Under the **Limits** sections, there are more fields to restrict the selection. These fields are used to ensure that pMRP will be executed only for materials with a specific BOM, routing, or material status, or for a BOM or task list usage.

Scroll down in the screen in Figure 17.4 so that the screen shown in Figure 17.5 appears.

The **Object Selection** section in Figure 17.5 contains the fields that will be used to select the materials or work centers. Depending on the job template selected, material-related fields (such as the **Material, Plant, MRP Controller, Material Type,** or **Low-Level Code**) or work center-related fields (such as **Work Center, Work Center Category,** or **Person Responsible**) will appear. It's also possible to define if stock transfers are considered in the scenario and which plants and which work centers from those supplying plants should be considered in the simulation.

Finally, under the **Document Data** section, choose if the opening stock will be zero, if it will be the safety stock or the actual material stock at the plant, if an inactive PIR version will be considered instead of the active version, and if the simple discontinuation will be considered.

All those settings are defined in the reference plan during the simulation creation. They cannot be changed later when you're adding new simulations into the same reference plan. Once the **Schedule** button is clicked, the background job to create the new simulation will be scheduled. Depending on the number of materials selected for the simulation, it may take some time because an actual planning run is executed. It's highly recommended to first check the completeness and correctness of the data maintained by choosing **Check**; the message shown at the bottom of screen will confirm if the application job can be scheduled.

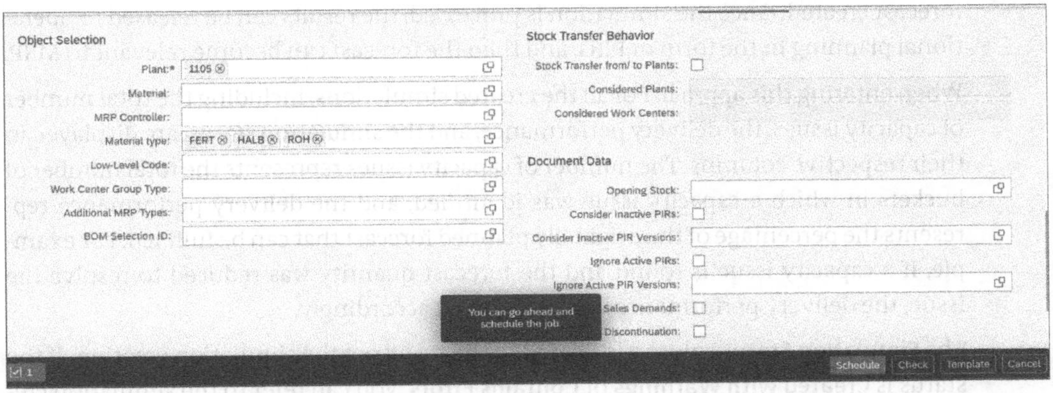

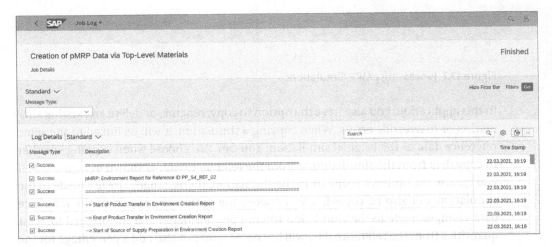

Figure 17.5 Parameters Selection in pMRP Scheduling: Part 2

Figure 17.6 shows the details of the simulation creation logs, including the success and error messages being triggered. When clicking the icon under the **Results** column (not shown here, but shown previously in Figure 17.2), the screen will jump into the spool, where a list of the materials and work centers selected for the simulation are listed.

Figure 17.6 Application Log

After the pMRP simulation creation, a planner will be able to process the simulation in the Process pMRP Simulations app, as discussed in the next section.

17.3 Managing pMRP

In the Process pMRP Simulations app, the planner will actually work with the simulation, analyze the planning results, identify and resolve capacity issues, and validate the forecast created. Once the simulation is processed, the results can be released to operational planning in the form of PIRs, and then the forecast can become relevant to MRP.

When entering this app, a list of all the created simulations, including the total number of capacity issues, the delivery performance, and the simulation status, are displayed in their respective columns. The number of capacity issues represents the total number of buckets in which a capacity issue was identified, and the delivery performance represents the percentage of the originally planned forecast that can be fulfilled. For example, if a capacity issue is found and the forecast quantity was reduced to resolve the issue, the delivery performance will be adjusted accordingly.

The **Simulation Status** column is related to the results of the simulation creation; if the status is **Created with Warnings** or **Contains Errors**, you can refer to the simulation creation logs shown in Figure 17.7.

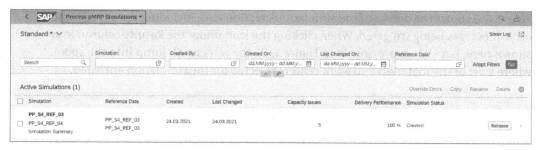

Figure 17.7 Processing pMRP Simulations

In this application, you also have the option to copy, rename, or delete an existing simulation or to override errors. When copying a simulation, it will be linked to the same reference data as the original simulation. You can also choose when copying whether to copy data from the simulation or from the reference data, as shown in Figure 17.8. If you choose the option to copy from the simulation, then changes already made to the simulation will also be copied; if you choose the option to copy from the reference data, changes made to the simulation will not be considered and the original forecast quantities from the reference data will be copied. You can also add a percentage for the **Overload Tolerance** value so that pMRP will not consider a work center overload until reaching the tolerance.

When clicking one of the simulations, the **Demand Plan Simulation** screen will appear (see Figure 17.9) . This screen shows the lines with the materials selected for this simulation, where each column will represent the forecast quantity for a specific bucket. Some cells are highlighted in red because there is an issue with a capacity overload in the work center: the forecasted quantities will require more time to be produced than is available with the current shift schedules in the work centers. The capacity issue may be related either to the top-level materials or to a semifinished product in the BOM's lower levels.

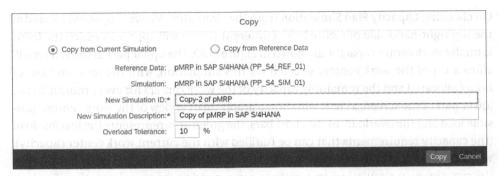

Figure 17.8 Copying pMRP Simulation

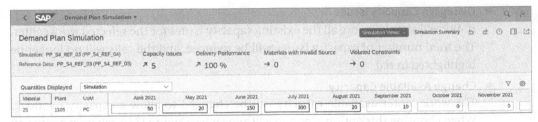

Figure 17.9 Demand Plan Simulation

The **Demand Plan Simulation** screen shows the number of capacity issues and the delivery performance. The number of capacity issues will not necessarily match the number of highlighted cells; two or more cells may be highlighted due to the same capacity issue in a specific work center. In this example, the delivery performance is still **100%** because the originally forecasted quantities were not yet changed, but this number may change when a supply chain planner try to resolve the capacity issues caused by the forecasted quantities.

Here, choose from the following options for the **Quantities Displayed** dropdown:

- **Simulation Only**
  The forecast quantities related to the simulation are shown.

- **Reference/Simulation**
  Two columns will appear: the original quantity from the reference and the simulation quantities. With this option, you can compare the changes made to the simulation with the original quantities for a better estimation of the impact of the changes over the originally forecasted quantity.

- **Delta of the Reference and Simulation**
  This column will only show the difference between the reference and the simulation. This view is also useful to estimate the impacts of the changes made in the simulation.

On choosing **Capacity Plan Simulation** from the **Simulation Views** dropdown located at the top right-hand side of Figure 17.9, a different screen will appear in which the focus is on the work center capacity, as shown in Figure 17.10. The upper part of the screen will show a list of the work centers selected for this simulation, with the total number of hours allocated and the remaining capacity of the work centers for every month. In the lower part of the screen, a chart will show a graphical overview of the work centers' possible load and the overload. In the chart bars, the green area represents the feasible load (the capacity requirements that can be fulfilled with the current work center capacity), whereas the red area represents the capacity overload that is causing the issue. From the capacity plan simulation, two buttons correspond to the two alternatives for dealing with the capacity issues:

- **Disregard Capacity Issues**
  pMRP will simply ignore all the existing capacity issues for the selected work center. The total number of capacity issues will be reduced, and the cells will no longer be highlighted in red.

- **Change Available Capacity**
  The work center available capacity can be changed to allow a capacity overload. When choosing this option, a popup will appear (see Figure 17.11), wherein a capacity planner can choose months and the percentage of overload allowed. Months with a capacity issue will be highlighted in red; the system will also propose a capacity utilization that can resolve the capacity issue for each month.

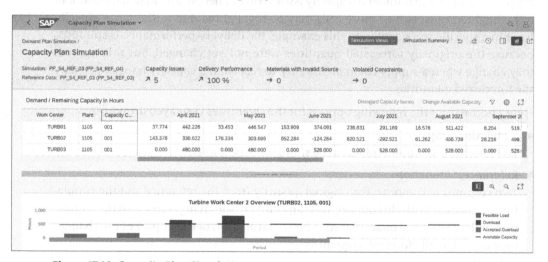

Figure 17.10 Capacity Plan Simulation

From both the **Capacity Plan Simulation** and the **Demand Plan Simulation** screens, choosing the **Object Inspector** view will display a side panel with additional information about the selected object (see Figure 17.12). When using the Object Inspector from the capacity plan simulation, the inspected objects will be the work center and the capacity allocated for the selected month, and the Object Inspector will also show the top-level materials related to the capacity allocated in the work center.

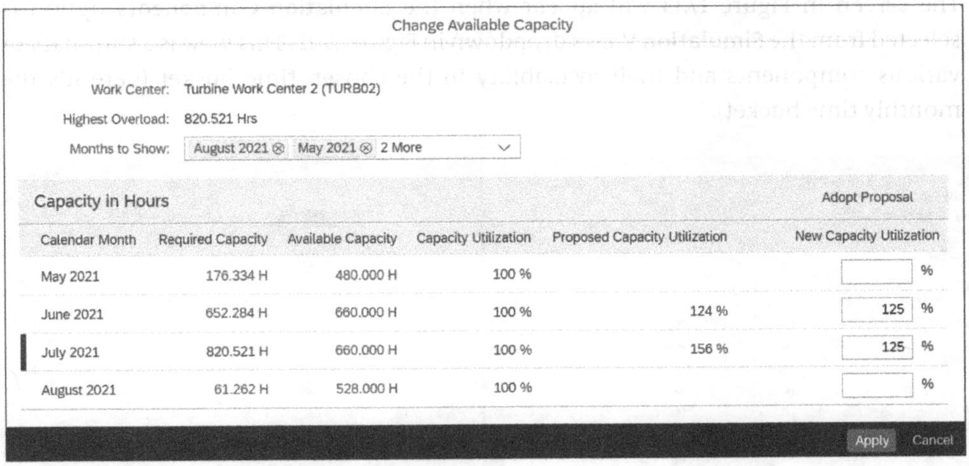

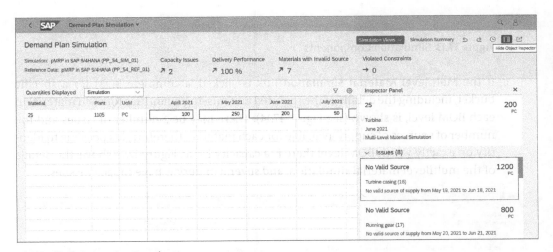

Figure 17.11 Changing Available Capacity

Figure 17.12 Inspector Panel

If the Object Inspector tool is used from the demand plan simulation, then the inspected objects will be the material and the quantity forecasted for the selected month. It will also display the capacity issues related to the forecast created for this specific top-level material, even if it's caused by a material in the lower BOM levels. When using the Object Inspector for the demand plan simulation, a link will appear that, when clicked, will bring up the multilevel material simulation for the selected demand.

Figure 17.12 shows the **Object Inspector** view for a demand plan simulation. The link to **Multi-Level Material Simulation** and the link to the capacity plan simulation for the work centers with capacity issues (not shown, but scrolling down will reveal it) are available

The screen in Figure 17.13 will appear when the **Simulation Components** option is selected from the **Simulation Views** dropdown in Figure 17.12. This view is a summary of various components and their availability in the chosen time bucket (here it's the monthly time bucket).

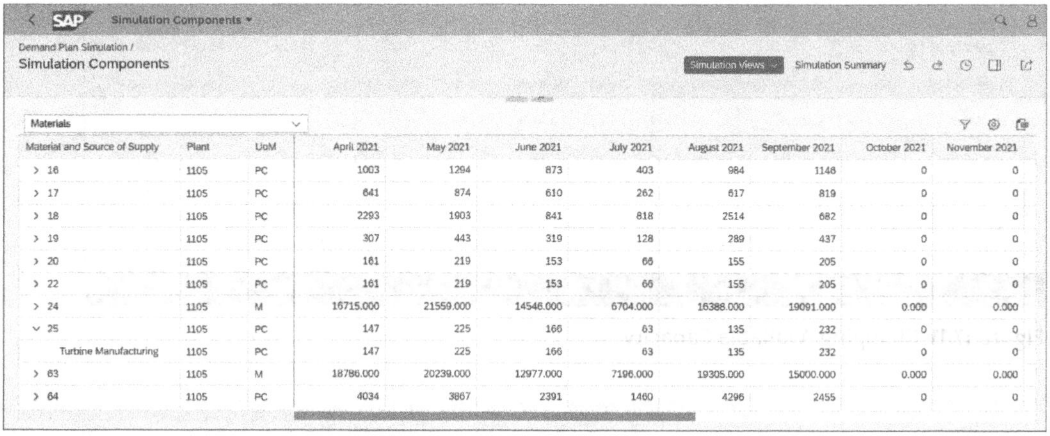

Material and Source of Supply	Plant	UoM	April 2021	May 2021	June 2021	July 2021	August 2021	September 2021	October 2021	November 2021
> 16	1105	PC	1003	1294	873	403	984	1146	0	0
> 17	1105	PC	641	874	610	262	617	819	0	0
> 18	1105	PC	2293	1903	841	818	2514	682	0	0
> 19	1105	PC	307	443	319	128	289	437	0	0
> 20	1105	PC	161	219	153	66	155	205	0	0
> 22	1105	PC	161	219	153	66	155	205	0	0
> 24	1105	M	16715.000	21559.000	14548.000	6704.000	16388.000	19091.000	0.000	0.000
⌄ 25	1105	PC	147	225	166	63	135	232	0	0
Turbine Manufacturing	1105	PC	147	225	166	63	135	232	0	0
> 63	1105	M	18786.000	20239.000	12977.000	7196.000	19305.000	15000.000	0.000	0.000
> 64	1105	PC	4034	3867	2391	1460	4296	2455	0	0

Figure 17.13 Simulation Components

If the **Multilevel Material Simulation** link is clicked, a complete BOM for a specific bucket, including the details of the required and missing quantities for each material in each BOM level, is shown (see Figure 17.14). There may be a number of issues and the number of sources of supply available for each material; therefore, it's possible to identify on exactly which BOM level there is a capacity issue. Figure 17.14 shows the details of the multilevel material simulation, and several materials have capacity issues.

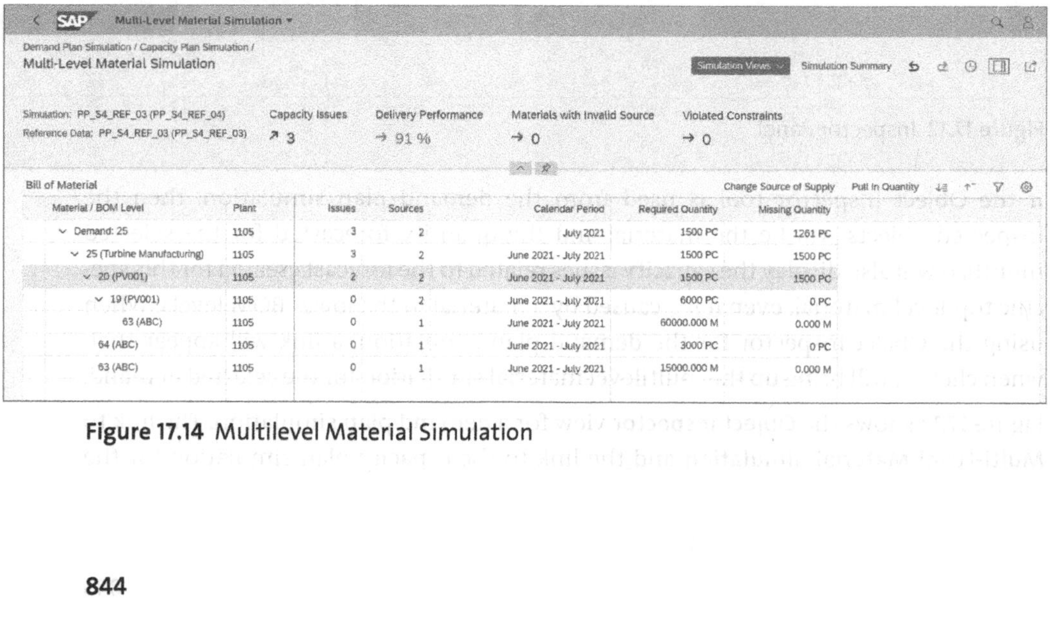

Material / BOM Level	Plant	Issues	Sources	Calendar Period	Required Quantity	Missing Quantity
⌄ Demand: 25	1105	3	2	July 2021	1500 PC	1261 PC
⌄ 25 (Turbine Manufacturing)	1105	3	2	June 2021 - July 2021	1500 PC	1500 PC
⌄ 20 (PV001)	1105	2	2	June 2021 - July 2021	1500 PC	1500 PC
⌄ 19 (PV001)	1105	0	2	June 2021 - July 2021	6000 PC	0 PC
63 (ABC)	1105	0	1	June 2021 - July 2021	60000.000 M	0.000 M
64 (ABC)	1105	0	1	June 2021 - July 2021	3000 PC	0 PC
63 (ABC)	1105	0	1	June 2021 - July 2021	15000.000 M	0.000 M

Figure 17.14 Multilevel Material Simulation

In the multilevel material simulation, it's also possible to resolve the capacity issues for the top-level and lower-level materials. For materials with several sources of supply (and thus with several valid production versions), select the **Change Source of Supply** option, and a different production version can be selected. When choosing this option, a popup appears (see Figure 17.16) in which the forecasted quantity can be distributed among the different production versions available for the selected material. Here, an overview of the available capacity for each source of supply and a proposed distribution of the forecast quantity among the different production versions are available. Also, you can manually define the quantity distribution or select the **Adopt Proposal** option (see Figure 17.15) to automatically adopt the proposed distribution. Figure 17.15 shows that the demand for the month of July 2021 is being shifted to June 2021 (preproduction) so to balance the capacity overload at the given work center.

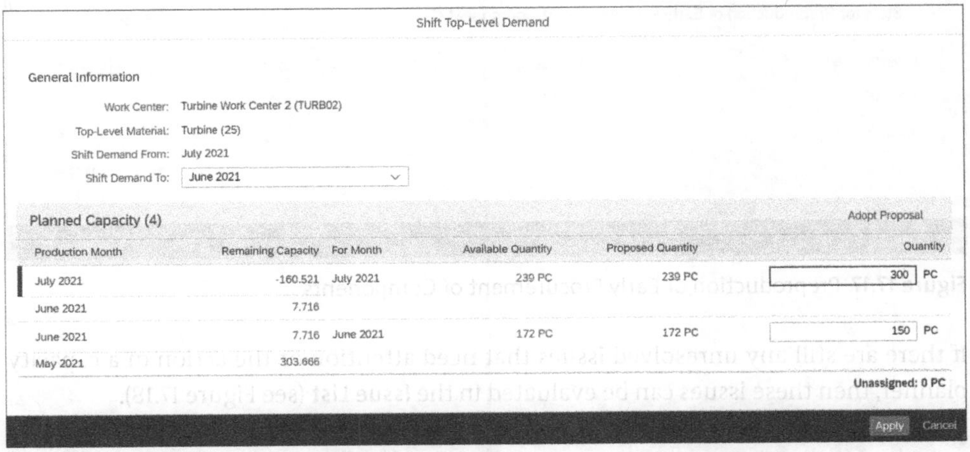

Figure 17.15 Shifting Top-Level Demand

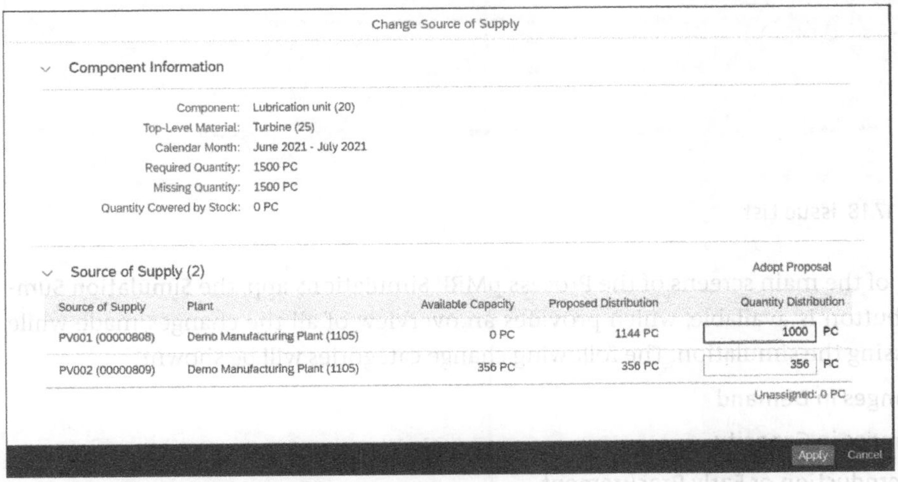

Figure 17.16 Changing Source of Supply

The **Pull-In** option shown in Figure 17.14 will enable the capacity and materials planner to either preproduce an in-house-produced material or request an early procurement of an externally procured material (see Figure 17.17).

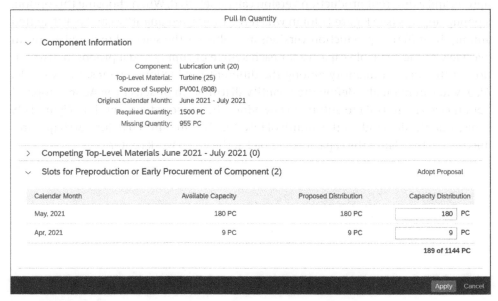

Figure 17.17 Preproduction or Early Procurement of Components

If there are still any unresolved issues that need attention or the action of a capacity planner, then these issues can be evaluated in the **Issue List** (see Figure 17.18).

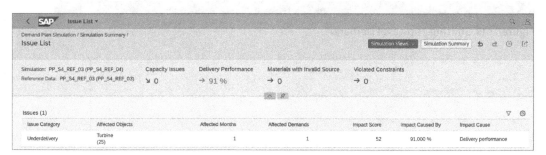

Figure 17.18 Issue List

In any of the main screens of the Process pMRP Simulations app, the **Simulation Summary** button is available, which provides an overview of all the changes made while processing the simulation. The following change categories will be shown:

- **Changes in Demand**
- **Changes in Capacity**
- **Preproduction or Early Procurement**

- **Changes in Source of Supply**
- **Unresolved Issues**
- **Disregarded Capacity Issues**

Figure 17.19 shows the **Simulation Summary** screen, with tabs for the different change categories and the total number in each category. This table can be also exported to a spreadsheet so that the forecast changes can be further discussed and validated.

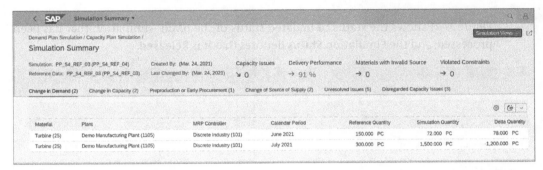

Figure 17.19 Simulation Summary

17.4   Releasing pMRP Results to Operative MRP

Once the simulation process is complete and all the capacity issues are identified and resolved, or if the capacity planner decides to disregard them, the pMRP simulation can be released. This release is made by choosing the **Release** button on the initial screen of the Process pMRP Simulations app. This brings up a popup (see Figure 17.20) to confirm whether the simulation can be released, and the forecast will be transferred to the top-level materials in an inactive version **01**, even if the simulation was created with active PIRs as reference. The option to transfer PIR in an active version also exists in the same popup (see **Version Active—Yes**). Also, and as mentioned in the beginning of this chapter, in the latest version of SAP S/4HANA, DDMRP can also consider PIRs for the buffer calculation. This means that the pMRP simulation results will be an input for DDMRP. When the simulation is released, if there are DDMRP materials in the BOM's lower levels, then PIRs will be created for DDMRP materials even if there was no PIR for those materials before the simulation creation. Therefore, the buffer calculation will take into consideration any demand variability that can be anticipated by the forecast.

Further, inactive PIRs created by DDMRP can be copied to the active version in Transaction MD70. Alternatively, simply check the **Active** flag in Transaction MD62 to activate PIRs. On releasing a simulation, the **Show Log** option (not shown) will provide a complete log of PIRs transferred. If needed, checking the **Subassembly Components** checkbox in will bring up the option to transfer the subcomponents of the main assembly in the chosen version (**Requirements Version*** in Figure 17.20).

17

Figure 17.20 Releasing pMRP Simulation

Figure 17.21 shows the status of updated status of the pMRP simulation that has been processed, and the **Simulation Status** denotes that it is **Released.**

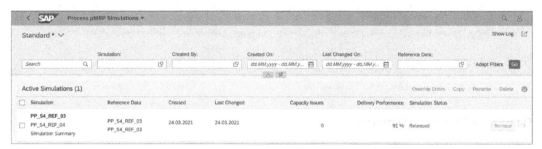

Figure 17.21 Processed Simulation and Released to Operative MRP

Figure 17.22 is accessed via Transaction MD62 and shows that material 25 in plant 1105 now has updated PIRs transferred through pMRP simulation. Because this PIR is now already in the operative planning, it's ready for the MRP run.

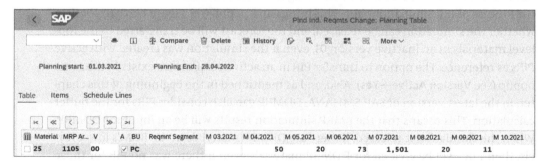

Figure 17.22 Updated Planned Independent Requirements

17.5   Summary

pMRP is the latest innovation in SAP S/4HANA, and it offers simulation capabilities that can be used by production and capacity planners to make a forecast from a work center capacity point of view both practical and achievable. With pMRP, a supply chain planner can change the forecasted quantities and evaluate the results, test different sources of supply for different products, and consider the preproduction of certain critical products in order to avoid a capacity overload in a specific month.

Compared to LTP, which is a mature solution, pMRP is still in the development phase, and more innovations are expected to be delivered in future releases of SAP S/4HANA.

The next chapter is on capacity requirements planning, which includes capacity evaluation and capacity leveling.

17

Chapter 18
Capacity Requirements Planning

Apart from materials availability, capacity availability plays a central role in the entire production process. Capacity requirements planning helps companies ensure that the relevant resources become available at the required time for optimum and uninterrupted production.

Building on the concepts and understanding that you developed in Chapter 3 and Chapter 6 for capacity requirements planning (CRP) , this chapter focuses on the *short-term* capacity planning after a production planner creates or releases production orders. The medium- to long-term capacity planning were covered by sales and operations planning (S&OP; Chapter 11) and long-term planning (LTP; Chapter 16). The CRP details for discrete manufacturing that we cover in this chapter are equally relevant and applicable to the process manufacturing and, to a certain extent, repetitive manufacturing (REM) types. For example, when deciding to assign relevant profiles for a capacity evaluation or capacity leveling, the system offers profiles with "REM" in the naming convention for REM and with "PI" in the naming convention for process manufacturing. For discrete manufacturing, the profiles have a naming convention that includes "SFC" (for shop floor control). Because the system uses the same principles that we cover in this chapter in Plant Maintenance and Project System, the available profiles have naming conventions that include "PM" or "PS," respectively.

This chapter will start with an overview of the processes involved in capacity planning and will then cover the capacity requirements and capacity evaluations. We cover both standard and variable capacity evaluations. Next, we cover how capacity requirements at different work centers can be combined and hot to perform real-time checks on capacity availability, either during order creation or order release.

The chapter then moves on to cover dispatching and the associated profiles, the dispatching sequence, sequence-dependent setup, and finally the midpoint scheduling. We also cover how to use the mass processing function to expedite the business processes, such as dispatching or deallocation. Finally, we cover some of the more important features available in both the graphical and tabular versions of capacity planning tables.

18.1   Process Overview

The objective of CRP is to schedule operations within the availability capacity and to check their feasibility when creating logical sequences of operations.

CRP can be implemented for production orders and for planned orders from material requirements planning (MRP) and LTP. The relevant configuration settings can be made to enable the system to also consider planned orders in capacity planning. This option works best if a company's business processes are mature enough and there's a significantly high confidence in the planning results that MRP creates. Because there are often frequent and at times high numbers of last-minute changes between the planning and actual production and execution, it may not be wise to book capacities based only on planning results. In doing so, a company may be compromising the capacity availability, which in turn may have an impact on the actual production schedule. At the same time, there may be a genuine business need that entails converting planned orders earlier on into production orders to book the capacities based on production orders. Still others prepare a comprehensive and feasible production plan based only on planned orders.

Apart from scheduling operations, CRP involves two important processes:

- **Capacity evaluation**
  The *capacity evaluation* provides a comparison between available capacities with capacity requirements, with reference to the work center or specific production order.

- **Capacity availability check**
  The *capacity availability check* uses the same information to check whether the available capacity at the requisite work center is sufficient to manage the operation of the production order. Depending on the configuration settings, the system can perform the capacity availability check during production order creation or during its release. If there is insufficient capacity, three options are available:
  - The system won't create or release the production order.
  - The system will create or release the production order.
  - The system prompts the production planner to decide on creating or releasing the production order, despite the capacity shortage.

[»]

> **Note**
> Refer to Chapter 6, in which we covered available capacity.

If there is insufficient capacity, or to account for capacity restrictions, the system performs *finite scheduling* to look for periods when sufficient capacity is available. Insufficient capacity at the work center leads to rescheduling the operation, but a production planner still has to perform the *dispatch* function to give a formal go-ahead to proceed with production on the given work center. The dispatch function can take place either from the capacity planning table or from the tabular capacity planning table. If there is an incorrect or inadvertent dispatch, it's possible to interactively *deallocate* the operation.

On dispatch, the system performs the following four functions:

- Determines the dispatch dates
- Creates the dispatching sequence
- Performs finite scheduling of the operation to be dispatched
- Performs midpoint scheduling of nondispatched operations of the production order

On dispatch of an operation, the system assigns it the status DISP (dispatched) and no longer schedules the operation automatically.

> **Note**
>
> Implementing CRP makes greater sense in companies that have a diverse range of products and also want to ensure that all of their products are produced in sufficient quantities for availability in the market. If a company produces products that use up all of its available capacities or produces single products such as fertilizer, cement, caustic soda, or iron bars, then implementing CRP doesn't add much value to business processes.
>
> During SAP system implementation, it's best to discuss and evaluate how implementing CRP will improve business processes and then decide on whether to implement CRP.

Capacity management describes a sequenced system of repeatable tasks. Each of these tasks serves to balance resource availability with the capacity load it has to cope with. To do so, capacity management can be broken down into the following phases (see Figure 18.1, in which the broad arrows denote the capacity management process):

- Planning
- Sequencing
- Leveling
- Scheduling
- Evaluation

A production scheduler is tasked with scheduling a pool of orders within a certain time frame. To do so, the orders first have to be put into a sequence according to some sort of criteria (maybe heijunka or setup optimization) and then leveled on the work centers or production line as available hours permit. For sequencing, many options are preconfigured and available in the SAP system. It can be sorted according to setup optimization, first in, first out (FIFO), or heijunka, and there are many more that can be customized. For any given period, a sequence record is saved, which is used in the next step for the distribution within available capacity. Leveling uses the order's load and the work center's availability to figure out at what specific point in time the order will be placed.

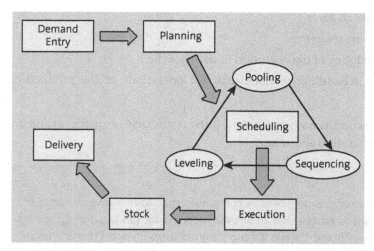

Figure 18.1 Capacity Management

Two Invaluable Rules of Planning

For a production and a capacity planner, following two specific rules in capacity planning will bring tremendous sanity to the production process:

- There is a point in time at which planning activities must end.
- Plan resources in the medium and long term and manage demand. Plan the resources and sequence in the short term. Then, schedule and manage the supply of materials required for production.

Now that a basic understanding of how CRP works is developed, let's delve into the details needed to know to understand how it works in the system, alongside the relevant business requirements.

18.2   Capacity Requirements and Capacity Evaluation

The system reflects the day-to-day business processes in place, including creation and release of production orders, their confirmations, the delays in production, and the extra time it takes to set up or process the product in capacity requirements. The capacity evaluation enables a capacity planner to view the capacity load or overload at various work centers in a large number of standard and variable evaluation options. These two business processes—that is, capacity requirements and capacity evaluation—are essential before getting started with the actual CRP process, and we'll discuss them in more detail in the following sections.

In the following sections, we'll cover how to understand the capacity requirements that the system creates, their evaluations, and the steps that can be taken for capacity leveling.

18.2.1   Capacity Requirements

As already mentioned, the system uses the settings that were already configured in Chapter 3 for CRP and also the information that was entered in the production planning (PP) master data, such as work center and routing from Chapter 6. Here, we briefly cover these details.

The system determines the capacity requirements during lead time scheduling if the **Det. Cap. Reqmnts** option in the control key was set. Furthermore, the system takes into consideration the formulas that were entered in the work center, the default values in the routing, and the order quantity. It's important to emphasize that the formulas for scheduling aren't used in CRP. For each component of an operation, such as setup, processing, and wait times, there is an earliest and latest date. The schedule formula is set to one of the operation dates. In the standard settings, this is the latest setup start date or processing start date, if the operation doesn't provide for any setup time. An operation can span several periods, and because the system bases the capacity evaluation on this information, the distribution key determines how the system distributes capacity to different periods.

The *distribution key* itself consists of the distribution strategy and the distribution function. The distribution key defines the operation dates and on what basis it carries out the distribution—for example, on the factory calendar, Gregorian calendar, or operation time. The distribution key, distribution strategy, and distribution function can be maintained through menu path **SAP IMG · Production · Capacity Requirements Planning · Operations · Capacity Requirement · Distribution**.

The system determines the capacity requirement during lead time scheduling and has to go through the capacity availability check and finally the dispatching process. If the system confirms the operation during the capacity availability check, it assigns the capacity requirement with the system status **BSTKZ**. It does the same when an operation is dispatched. In this way, the system converts the capacity requirement into a component called a *basic load*.

The basic load has an important role to play in the capacity availability check because available capacity represents the difference between the available capacity and the basic load. The system reduces the capacity requirements when any of the following tasks is performed:

- Confirm an operation.
- Set the status of a production order as technically complete.
- Lock the production order.
- Set the deletion flag in the production order.

The system also updates the capacity requirements when you partially confirm an operation, and it correspondingly reduces part of the capacity requirements for the operation.

18.2.2   Standard Evaluation of Capacity Utilization

The system offers several methods of *capacity evaluation*. Each standard evaluation has its own transaction code, whereas for variable evaluation, a user selects the relevant profile to enable the system to display the requisite information.

In standard evaluations, the system displays the capacity requirements in direct comparison to the available capacities. The following are some of the standard capacity evaluations:

- **Standard overview (Transaction CM01)**
  The system aggregates the load on a weekly basis.
- **Detailed capacity list (Transaction CM02)**
  The system shows the load per order and week.
- **Pool of orders/operations (Transaction CM03)**
  The system presents only the load of released operations.
- **Overload (Transaction CM05)**
  The system only shows work centers with overload.
- **Extended selection, work center view (Transaction CM50)**
  The system displays an aggregated view of the daily load.
- **Extended selection, order view (Transaction CM52)**
  The system displays an aggregated view of the weekly load for all work centers that the selected orders occupy.

To access the capacity planning evaluation, follow SAP menu path **Logistics • Production • Capacity Planning • Evaluation • Work Center View • Load**, or use Transaction CM01. Figure 18.2 shows the standard overview (load) of the **Work center TURBO1** and **Plant 1105** combination. It shows the capacity requirements for each calendar week that result from the creation or release of production orders. The screen also shows the available capacity (**AvailCap.**) of the work center and the resulting percentage of load (**CapLoad**), as well as the remaining available capacity (**RemAvailCap**).

For example, in calendar week 11.2021, a capacity requirement of **140.18** hours (**H**) leads to a utilization (or an overload) of **116.8%** based on an available capacity of **120.00 H**. The system displays the periods with an overload in red.

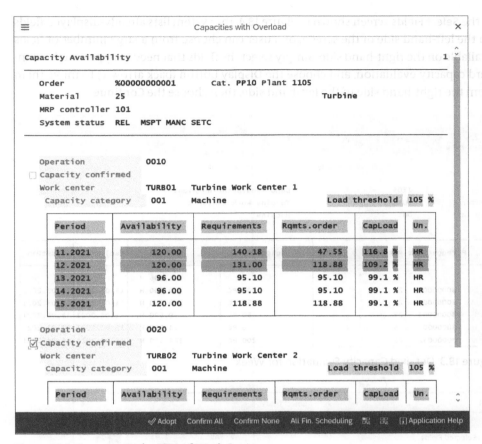

Figure 18.2 Capacity Evaluation of Work Center

Warning [!]

The utilization rate on the production lines should never exceed 100% for an extended period of time. It shouldn't even get close because the closer it gets to a full utilization (100%), the less a capacity planner can cope with variability in the process. It's a fact that when capacity utilization approaches 100%, variability multiplies. The urge to do this, however, comes from the standard model of finance or costing departments that asks for maximum utilization of resources because the business should make as many products or units as possible, with the available capacity used to spread the overhead costs thinner over more units and make the individual product cheaper.

Use Transaction CM02 and the screen shown in Figure 18.3 appears, showing the evaluation list of the capacity requirement of each operation, including the production order number, the header material, and the order quantity. The **Choose Fields** button enables a user to display additional fields of the operation, such as its start time. A user can also directly jump into the production order from here.

In the **Select Fields** screen shown in Figure 18.4, the system lists already-displayed fields on the left-hand side of the screen, or a user can choose from a large number of fields available on the right-hand side. Simply select the fields that need to appear in the standard capacity evaluation, and choose the **Display** button (back arrow **<**) to move them from the right-hand side to the left-hand side, then choose the **Continue**.

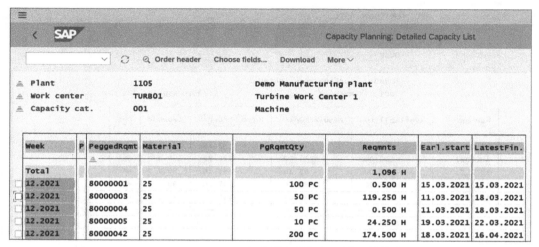

Figure 18.3 Detailed Capacity Evaluation for Week

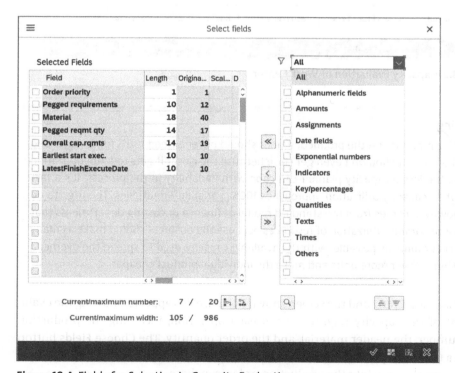

Figure 18.4 Fields for Selection in Capacity Evaluation

Because a user can select many fields, it's recommended to use the filter options to narrow down the available choices. For example, if you use the **Quantities** filter available in the dropdown on the right-hand side of the screen, the system brings up the quantities fields to choose from and eventually displays them in the standard capacity evaluation.

18.2.3   Variable Evaluation of Capacity Utilization

In *variable evaluations*, a capacity planner can base the capacity evaluation on individual requirements. In this process, the system requires an overall profile that defines the evaluation. Standard profiles are available for this purpose, or profiles can be configured to meet specific business needs.

For a variable evaluation of capacity utilization, follow SAP menu path **Logistics • Production • Capacity Planning • Evaluation • Variable**, or use Transaction CM07. The **Planning** screen in Figure 18.5 shows the variable evaluation using overall profile **SAPSFC010**. In contrast to the standard overview (Transaction CM01 or overall profile SAPX912), this profile displays only the requirements of the basic load.

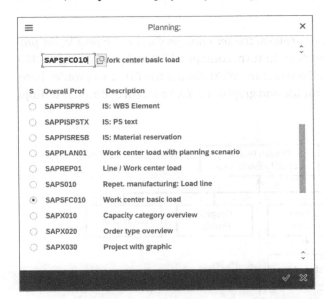

Figure 18.5 Selection of Variable Evaluation: Overall Profile SAPSFC010

Here, select **Overall Prof SAPSFC010**. On the ensuing screen, enter the **Work Center** "TURBO1" and **Plant** "1105", and then press $\boxed{\text{Enter}}$ or choose **Variable Overview**.

The **Variable Overview** screen that appears (see Figure 18.6) is similar to the standard evaluation, but it displays only those requirements that affect the basic load. The system shows the capacity requirements that have been dispatched.

Variable evaluation can be defined using profiles, which we'll discuss next.

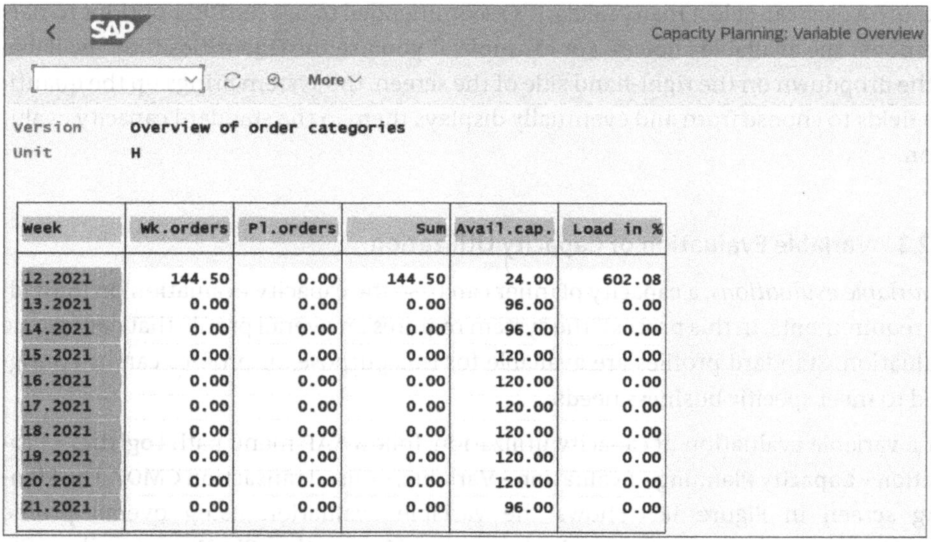

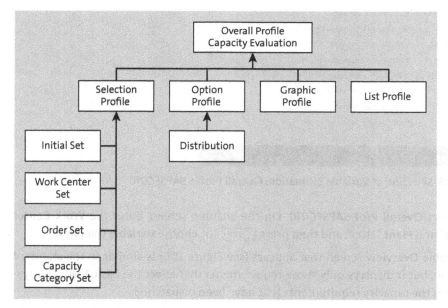

Figure 18.6 Variable Evaluation Using Overall Profile SAPSFC010

Overall Profile

The *overall profile* consists of four profiles: the *selection profile*, *option profile*, *list profile*, and *graphic profile*. These profiles, in turn, contain additional profiles. Figure 18.7 provides an overview of the profile structure. We'll discuss the first two profiles here; the remaining two profiles (list profile and graphic profile) contain additional settings to display a standard evaluation.

Figure 18.7 Profiles for Variable Evaluation

To create or make changes to an overall profile, follow menu path **SAP IMG · Production · Capacity Requirements Planning · Evaluation · Profiles · Define Overall Profiles**, or use Transaction OPA6. Figure 18.8 shows the assignment for **Overall Prof. SAPSFC010**.

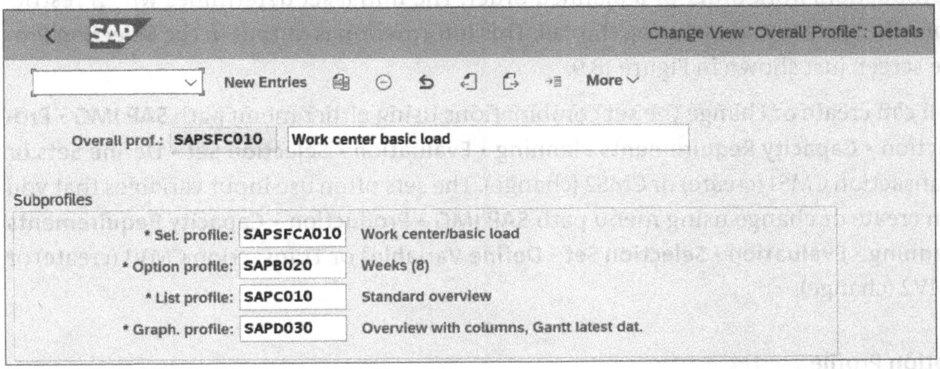

Figure 18.8 Overall Profile for Variable Evaluation

Selection Profile

The *selection profile* determines which capacity requirements the system should read. To create or make changes to a selection profile, follow menu path **SAP IMG · Production · Production · Capacity Requirements Planning · Evaluation · Profiles · Define Selection Profiles**, or use Transaction OPA2. Figure 18.9 shows **Sel. Profile SAPSFCA010**, which it assigns to overall profile SAPSFC010.

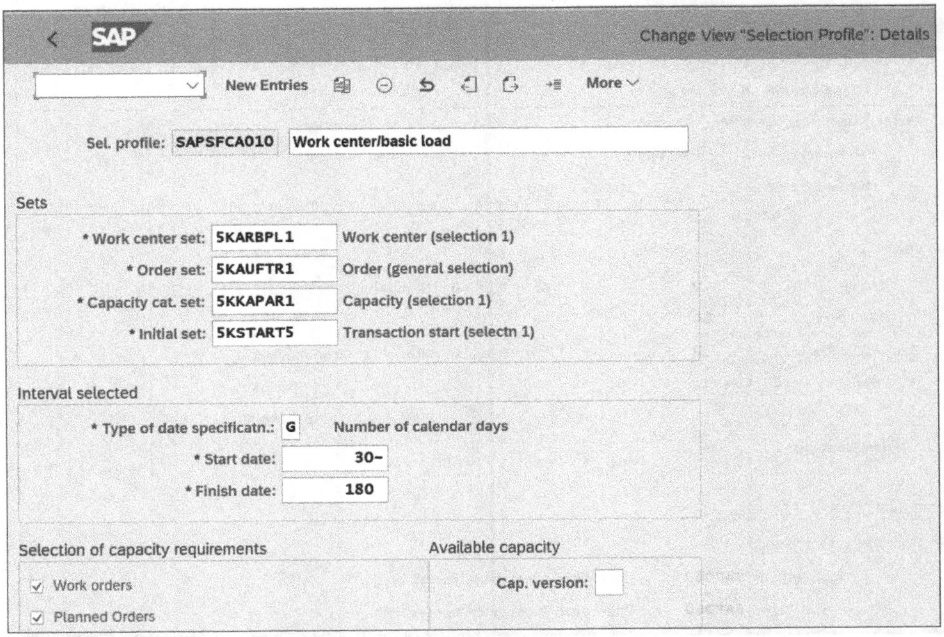

Figure 18.9 Selection Profile for Variable Evaluation

The objects for which the system reads the capacity requirements are determined on the basis of the set combinations for the work center, capacity category, and the order. These can also be determined on the basis of the *order categories*—that is, whether it's a production/work order or a planned order. The initial set determines which restrictions the system makes during the call. This information is output in the **Selection Profile** screen just shown in Figure 18.9.

You can create or change the set combinations using either menu path **SAP IMG · Production · Capacity Requirements Planning · Evaluation · Selection Set · Define Sets** or Transaction CMS1 (create) or CMS2 (change). The sets often use input variables that you can create or change using menu path **SAP IMG · Production · Capacity Requirements Planning · Evaluation · Selection Set · Define Variables** or Transaction CMV1 (create) or CMV2 (change).

Option Profile

The *option profile* contains items to include in backlogs, to cumulate the capacity requirements and the available capacity (Section 18.2.4), and to distribute the capacity requirements. Figure 18.10 shows **Option profile SAPB020**, which is also used for standard evaluation.

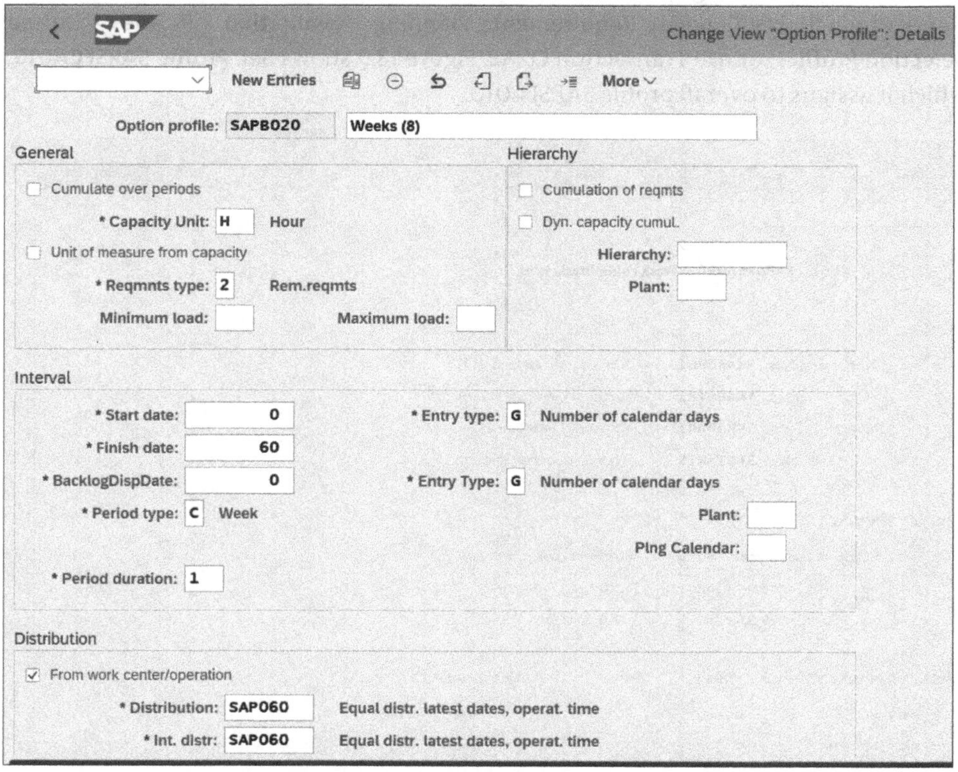

Figure 18.10 Option Profile for Variable Evaluation

To create or make changes to an option profile, follow menu path **SAP IMG · Production · Capacity Requirements Planning · Evaluation · Profiles · Define Options Profiles**, or use Transaction OPA3.

The *list profile* can be set up by using Transaction OPA4, and the *graphic profile* can be set up using Transaction OPA5. Both profiles contain additional settings to display the standard evaluation.

18.2.4   Cumulating the Capacity Requirements

For evaluation purposes, especially when large numbers of orders at various work centers are taken into consideration, it's often helpful to cumulate the capacity requirements. This provides a broader overview of the capacity situation at each work center. Capacities can be cumulated either statically or dynamically from work center hierarchies. When statically cumulating the capacity, the system only refers to the work center and its available capacity. To carry out capacity evaluation in cumulated form—that is, to cumulate both available capacity and capacity requirements—CRP must be cumulated dynamically.

In the **Hierarchy** area shown previously in Figure 18.10, the options to cumulate capacities dynamically and the **Hierarchy** work center for the plant are available.

18.2.5   Checking Capacity Availability

When a production order is created, capacity availability can be checked in the order before dispatching it. This step helps a production planner to decide whether it's possible to dispatch the order or not. The system considers period-based information by checking it to find out whether the available capacity in the period of operation is bigger than or equal to the capacity requirement of the operation. The length of the period is set in the period profile, which we'll cover later in this chapter. The shortest possible period is one day. When the system performs a period-based check, it only indicates that the capacity is available (or unavailable) within the given period, not on the planned operation date.

The available capacity represents the difference between the permitted capacity overload defined in the work center and the basic load. The basic load doesn't contain all of the capacity requirements. By default, only dispatched operations and those for which the capacity has been confirmed affect the basic load. The basic load can be displayed using the variable evaluation (Transaction CM07) and profile SAPSFC010.

Tips and Tricks

If no capacity availability check has been carried out over a long period of time, or if it's being used for the first time, it's recommended to create the basic load on the basis of the existing (unchecked) capacity requirements using Transaction CM99. In this case, all capacity requirements will be confirmed.

Often, due to delays in actual production, the system creates a backlog (e.g., noncon-firmed operations from the past). Use the **Overall Capacity Load** checkbox in the strat-egy profile and the backlog dispatching date (**BacklogDispDate 0**; refer to Figure 18.10) to define whether to include them in the determination of the available capacity. We cover strategy profiles in Section 18.4.2. If these are included, the capacity requirements of the past are temporarily scheduled forward into the current period and, if necessary, into subsequent periods and added to the basic load.

An operation can last for several periods. In this case, the distribution key determines the way in which the system distributes the capacity requirement to different periods. The capacity check uses the distribution key that is assigned to the *evaluation profile* (Section 18.4.2). The capacity availability check is carried out for each individual order, and all operations are checked one after the other, according to their numerical order. A restriction on this capability is that only those operations are checked that exist in work centers relevant to finite scheduling. Therefore, it makes sense to define critical work centers (work centers with bottleneck capacities) as finite to ensure there are enough degrees of freedom in the capacity planning.

The capacity availability can be checked interactively during production order creation or its release. Alternatively, an interactive capacity availability check from the produc-tion order is also possible, as shown in Figure 18.11. The **Check Capacity Availability** popup appears when a user chooses the **Capacity** button in the production order header. The system checks for capacity during production order creation of the turbine manufacturing process.

In the example in Figure 18.11, there is at least one operation where the work center doesn't have sufficient capacity. More detailed information is available, as well as the option to use finite scheduling to shift the operations into periods with sufficient capacity. Choose the **Detailed Info** button to see the detailed information for this capac-ity availability check, provided in the **Capacities with Overload** screen that appears (see Figure 18.12).

Here, the capacity problem exists in the first **Operation** at **Work center TURBO2**, and in the **Period 17.2021** because the requirement of **205.36** hours far exceeds the available capacity of **120.00** hours. Because this situation leads to a load of 171.1%, the system can't confirm the operation. Notice that there are weeks when the availability capacity meets the capacity required.

The system determines the load threshold on the basis of the permitted overload specified in the capacity master data, and it can exceed 100%.

However, it's possible to confirm the capacity requirement interactively by setting the **Capacity Confirmed** checkbox (left-hand side of the screen), if the planner wants to do that, and then choosing **Adopt**.

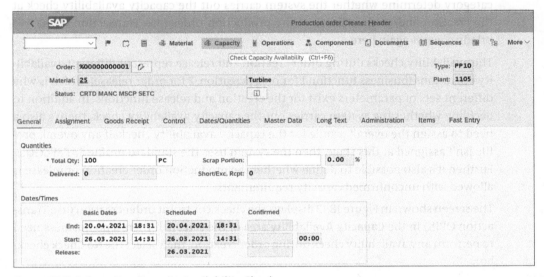

Figure 18.11 Interactive Capacity Availability Check

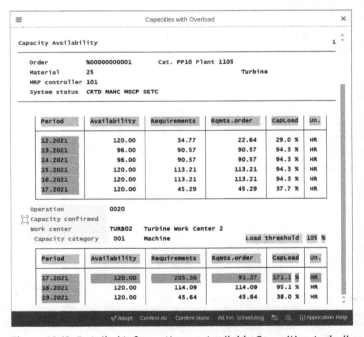

Figure 18.12 Detailed Information on Available Capacities, Including Overload

Let's now discuss category-specific check control and various capacity profiles available in the system.

Category-Specific Check Control

In Chapter 3, we covered that the check control settings specific to the plant and order category determine whether the system carries out the capacity availability check at the creation and/or the release of the production order (use Transaction OPJK). We briefly cover it again here.

The availability checks during order creation and release represent different availability operations (business function 1 for order creation, 2 for order release), which is why different sets of parameters exist for the creation and release functions. In addition to deciding whether the system carries out the capacity availability check, there's also a need to assign the overall profile for the capacity availability check. If any overall profile isn't assigned at this stage, then the system uses the standard profile SAPSFCG013. Further, it's also possible to define whether the production order creation or release is allowed with unconfirmed capacity requirements.

The screen shown in Figure 18.13 displays the check control at order creation (use Transaction OPJK) in the **Capacity Availability** area of the screen. If there's no business need to perform any availability check during order creation, then select the **No Check** checkbox.

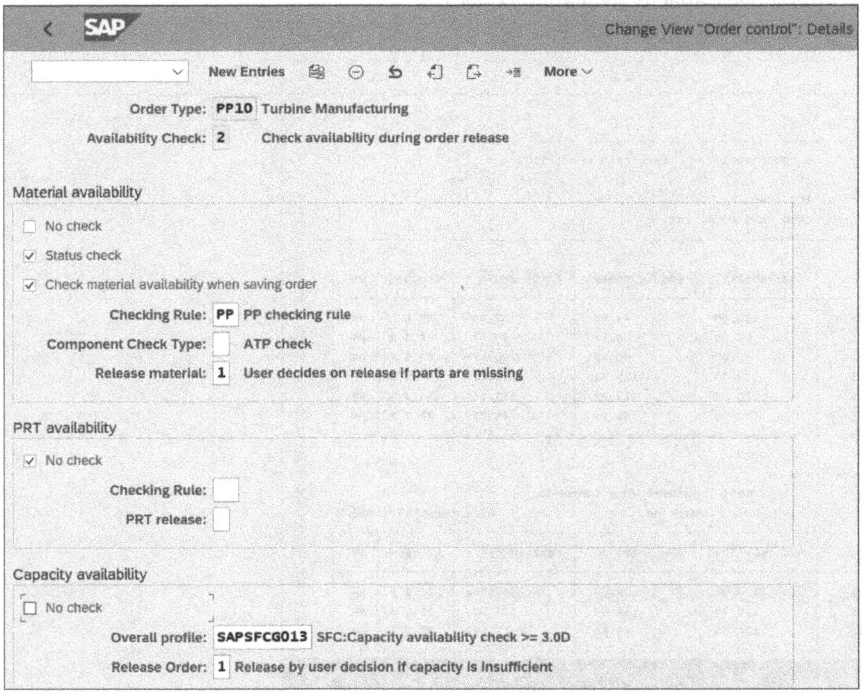

Figure 18.13 Check Control for Capacity Availability Check

If the system is unable to confirm the capacity requirement of an operation, then make the following settings in the production scheduling profile (Transaction OPKP) and assign it in the **Work Scheduling** view to the material master:

- Define whether the confirmed capacity requirements are transferred to the basic load or whether all capacity requirements are discarded.

- Define whether finite scheduling should be carried out. Figure 18.14 displays the corresponding fields in the production scheduling profile (**Prod. Sched. Profile**) 101 for **Plant 1105**. These settings are only relevant to collective processing. Here, set the **Overall Profile** for capacity leveling and define the parameters for **Availability Check**.

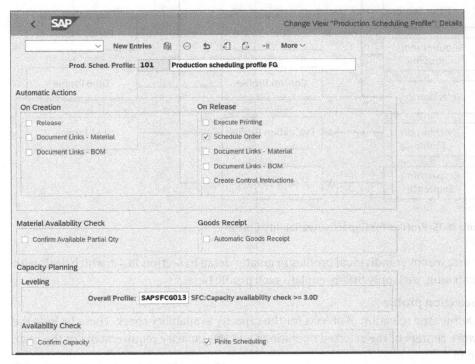

Figure 18.14 Production Scheduling Profile

Profiles

Note that the system doesn't use the overall profile for capacity leveling for the capacity availability check but instead uses it for dispatching. The overall profile for the capacity availability check has the same structure as the overall profile for dispatching. In contrast to dispatching, however, the capacity availability check doesn't use the overall profile from the production scheduler. Instead, it uses the overall profile from the capacity check control; if there is no profile available there, it uses overall profile SAPSFCG013.

Figure 18.15 provides an overview of the profiles involved in the capacity availability check.

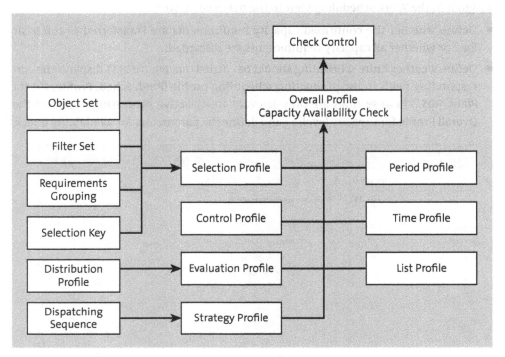

Figure 18.15 Profiles for Capacity Availability Check

Because we cover individual profiles in greater detail in Section 18.4.2, which deals with dispatching, we'll only briefly explain each profile here:

- **Selection profile**
  Defines the selection of objects for the capacity availability check. These include the work centers of the selected operations and the capacity requirements of the basic load.

- **Control profile**
  Defines the preparation of the data.

- **Evaluation profile**
  Assigns the distribution key for distributing the capacity requirements, among other parameters.

- **Strategy profile**
  Contains the sequence and search direction for finite scheduling, among other parameters.

- **Period profile**
  Defines the length of the period for the check.

- **Time profile**
  Defines the time fences for the capacity requirements in question.
- **List profile**
  Contains settings for the results output.

The result of the capacity availability check is the confirmation of the capacity requirements, if the available capacity is sufficient. If the available capacity within the period is insufficient, the finite scheduling process can be triggered to find a period with a sufficient capacity and to confirm the capacity requirement in that new available period. The system doesn't automatically dispatch the operation by either the capacity availability check or by finite scheduling. A capacity planner will have to manually dispatch the operation, either individually or in the mass processing step. We'll cover these options later in Section 18.4.1 and Section 18.4.6, respectively.

18.3   Finite Scheduling

If the available capacity is insufficient to meet the capacity requirement of an operation on the requested date, the *finite scheduling* option can be used to find the next possible date on which the available capacity is sufficient for the operation. Finite scheduling can either be performed during the capacity availability check or during dispatching.

While performing finite scheduling, the system refers to the strategy profile to search for the direction in which to perform the scheduling (backward or forward scheduling). A search in the direction of today's date is based on backward scheduling and represents the standard case, whereas a search into the future is based on forward scheduling. However, much of this also depends on the company's business processes and needs, where only forward scheduling is considered to look for free or available capacity in the future. If insufficient capacity is found in one direction, then the search direction can also be reversed.

The screen shown in Figure 18.16 appears during the capacity availability check In the next capacity overload popup, choose the **Finite scheduling** icon (not shown). The system proposes the new latest date (**NewLtStart**) and time (**NewStTim**) after it performs finite scheduling. At this stage, a capacity or production planner can confirm the capacity by selecting the **Cap. Confirm.** checkbox and then choosing **Adopt**.

When an operation (lower half of Figure 18.17) is dispatched at the work center (upper half), the system automatically performs finite scheduling and assigns the operation immediately next to the already assigned operation.

18

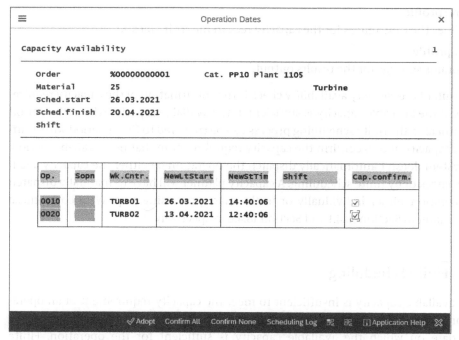

Figure 18.16 Finite Scheduling Results (after Capacity Availability Check)

Figure 18.17 Dispatching Orders in Capacity Planning Table

18.4   Dispatching

In the *dispatching* process, the system creates a workable or feasible production plan in which the capacity is available. To achieve this objective, there should be a sequence of dates set up for the individual operations in the work centers. The nondispatched operations form the pool of orders/operations for the capacity planner/production scheduler to work on. To dispatch an operation, the capacity planner selects the operation, which is ready for dispatch from the capacity planning table or from the tabular capacity planning table, and initiates the dispatching function.

In this section, we'll go over the process steps of dispatching and then get into the details of the different profiles, sequencing, and setup.

18.4.1 Process Steps

When dispatching takes place, the system carries out the following steps:

- **Determine dispatching dates**
  The standard setting uses the operation dates as dispatching dates. However, a planner can also enter dates interactively or define the dispatching date using drag and drop in the capacity planning table.

- **Create dispatching sequence**
  If a planner wants to dispatch several operations in one step, then create a dispatching sequence based on specific sorting criteria (Section 18.4.3) or on optimal setup times. The default settings stipulate dispatch at the latest date.

- **Finite scheduling if no capacity is available**
  If no capacity exists on the dispatching date, the system needs to run finite scheduling to come up with a feasible dispatching date.

- **Dispatch operation**
  The system dispatches the operation and assigns it the status **DISP** (if successful).

- **Midpoint scheduling**
  A planner needs to adjust the dates of the nondispatched operations in such a way that the system carries out the midpoint scheduling process for them. In midpoint scheduling, the system schedules the nondispatched operations so that earlier ones are scheduled backward and later ones forward. Midpoint scheduling is covered later in Section 18.4.5.

> **Note**
>
> It may be impractical from a particular practice or business point of view, but a planner can also base the dispatching processing on an infinite capacity assumption. To do this, deselect the finite scheduling option in the strategy profile. However, with bottleneck capacities at critical levels, work centers hardly ever permit this option.

During dispatching, a planner may realize that it's not possible to meet the basic dates of the order. Because the system carries out dispatching for each operation, it's also possible to compromise on the sequence of operations for the dispatch. For this, use the strategy profile to define the extent to which the system allows inconsistencies within the operations of an order. However, the capacity planner needs to monitor the external dependencies, such as the date-based dependency between orders and customer requirements, to ensure timely production.

Whenever a planner performs the dispatch or the deallocate function, the system updates the planning and the scheduling logs. In fact, it issues a message to inform the capacity planner to check the planning and/or scheduling logs. The planning log can be called from the respective application—for instance, from the capacity planning table or from finite scheduling in the interactive capacity availability check. Figure 18.18 displays a sample planning log that contains two information messages.

Planning Table: SAPSFCG001 Finite scheduling forw./all functs.activ
More
Message log created on: 26.03.2021
Number of Messages Collected
Information Messages: 2
Warning Messages: 0
Error Messages: 0
Termination Messages: 0
Total: 2

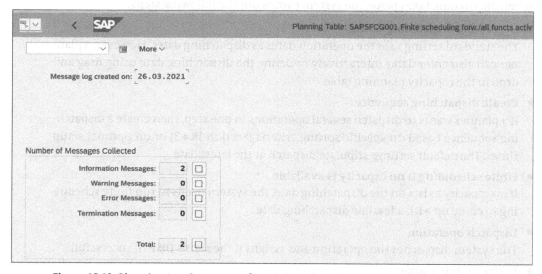

Figure 18.18 Planning Log Summary after Finite Scheduling

Double-click the information or warning messages, and a log that displays information messages appears—for instance, that the system successfully dispatched operation 0010. It provides the dispatching date and time as well (in the second information message), as shown in Figure 18.19.

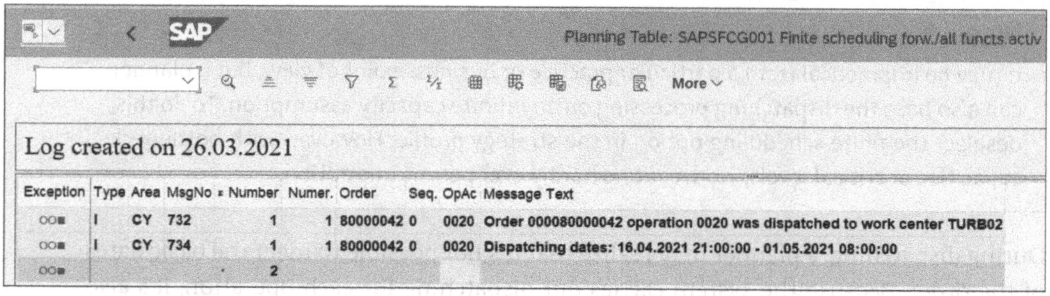

Planning Table: SAPSFCG001 Finite scheduling forw./all functs.activ
More
Log created on 26.03.2021
Exception Type Area MsgNo Number Numer. Order Seq. OpAc Message Text
I CY 732 1 1 80000042 0 0020 Order 000080000042 operation 0020 was dispatched to work center TURB02
I CY 734 1 1 80000042 0 0020 Dispatching dates: 16.04.2021 21:00:00 - 01.05.2021 08:00:00
2

Figure 18.19 Detailed Scheduling Message Log after Finite Scheduling

18.4.2 Profiles for Dispatching

Capacity leveling uses a large number of profiles, which are primarily interconnected, to perform capacity leveling and differentiate between different tasks. In this section, we briefly cover some of the most-used profiles and the associated settings in each. Later in this chapter, when we cover the business processes of capacity leveling, we'll cover greater details of the associated profiles and explain their roles where necessary.

Building on the same principles as for profiles in capacity evaluation, the system cumulates profiles for capacity leveling in an overall profile. Figure 18.20 illustrates the relationships of various profiles with each other. We explain some of the more important profiles in the following sections.

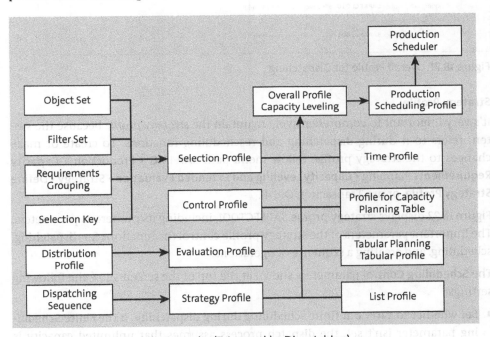

Figure 18.20 Finite Scheduling Results (Triggered by Dispatching)

Overall Profile

To create or make changes to an overall profile in capacity leveling, follow menu path **SAP IMG · Production · Capacity Requirements Planning · Capacity Leveling and Extended Evaluation · Define Overall Profile**, or use Transaction OPDO.

The screen shown in Figure 18.21 displays the standard overall profile SAPSFCG011 and different subprofiles.

There's no need to maintain the **Period Profile** field for the overall profile because it's relevant for a capacity availability check only. The following sections describe some of the individual profiles shown on this screen.

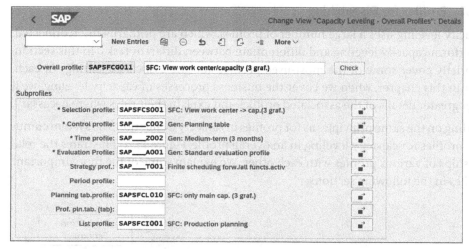

Figure 18.21 Overall Profile for Dispatching

Strategy Profile

It's very important to comprehensively maintain the *strategy profile* because the system refers to it during dispatching and rescheduling functions. To create or make changes to the strategy profile, follow menu path **SAP IMG • Production • Capacity Requirements Planning • Capacity Leveling and Extended Evaluation • Strategy • Define Strategy Profile**, or use Transaction OPDB.

Figure 18.22 displays strategy profile SAPSFCT001, including its numerous parameters. The important parameters of the strategy profile control the functions for dispatching, scheduling, and creating a sequence of operations.

The **Scheduling Control** parameters shown at the top of the screen allow the following settings:

- Set whether to carry out finite scheduling during dispatching. If the **Finite Scheduling** parameter isn't set, the dispatch process assumes that unlimited capacity is available. If there is insufficient available capacity, the dispatching attempt becomes unsuccessful.

- When the **Dispatch at Earliest Point in Time** parameter is used, the system doesn't consider interdependencies with other operations and dispatches the operation as early as possible.

- The **Dispatch at Best Time for Setup** parameter chooses the dispatch date on the basis of the existing setup sequence in such a way that the increase in the overall setup time is kept as small as possible. This entails the system having the provision to shift the already dispatched operations. To attend to this need, also set the **Insert Operation** parameter. The system supports this function in the capacity planning table, and it makes sense only if setup matrices for sequence-based setup are in place. We explain the setup matrices later in Section 18.4.4.

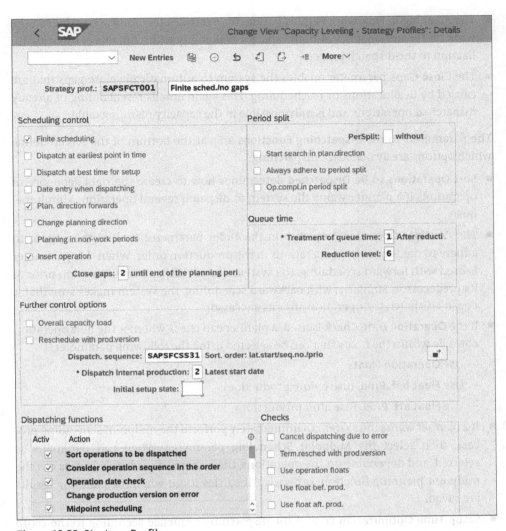

Figure 18.22 Strategy Profile

- The **Date Entry when Dispatching** parameter ensures that instead of using the operation date during dispatching, a popup window appears and prompts the user for an interactive date entry.
- The default setting for the planning direction is backward from the dispatch date. However, this setting can be changed when the **Plan. Direction Forwards** parameter is activated. When the system is unable to find available capacity within the planning horizon, and the **Change Planning Direction** parameter has also been set, the system continues to search for available capacity in the opposite direction.

- The **Planning in Non-work Periods** parameter overrides the nonwork periods in the work center and suggests 24-hour capacity availability with a full rate of capacity utilization to the dispatch process.

- The **Close Gaps** parameter enables the system to automatically close gaps that are caused by deallocations or rescheduling. This again entails rescheduling of already dispatched operations and is only possible in the capacity planning table.

The parameters in the **Dispatching Functions** area at the bottom of the screen define which options are available for dispatching:

- **Sort Operations to Be Dispatched** determines how to create the right sequence of operations if a planner wants the system to dispatch several operations simultaneously.

- The **Consider Operation Sequence in the Order** parameter enables the system to adhere to the sequence of operations in the production order. When this parameter is used with forward scheduling, the system doesn't dispatch the operation prior to its predecessor. Similarly, with backward scheduling, the system makes sure that it doesn't dispatch the operation after its successor.

- If the **Operation Date Check** is used, a planner can check whether the new operation dates lie within the floats that can be selected using the following parameters:
  - **Use Operation Floats**
  - **Use Float bef. Prod.** (use before production)
  - **Use Float aft. Prod.** (use after production)

- If a planner wants the system to immediately perform the midpoint scheduling process, then select the **Midpoint Scheduling** parameter. When this parameter is selected, and depending on the operations, the system immediately carries out the midpoint planning function; otherwise, it carries it out when the planning results are saved.

- **Setup Time Optimization** creates the dispatching sequence according to the setup time minimization criterion.

- If the **Cancel Dispatching Due to Error** parameter is set, the system doesn't allow dispatch of operations outside the floats.

Selection Profile

The *selection profile* enables a planner to define which capacity requirements the system should consider for dispatch. To create or make changes to the selection profile, follow the configuration menu path **SAP IMG · Production · Capacity Requirements Planning · Capacity Leveling and Extended Evaluation · Define Selection Profile**, or use Transaction OPD1 (see Figure 18.23).

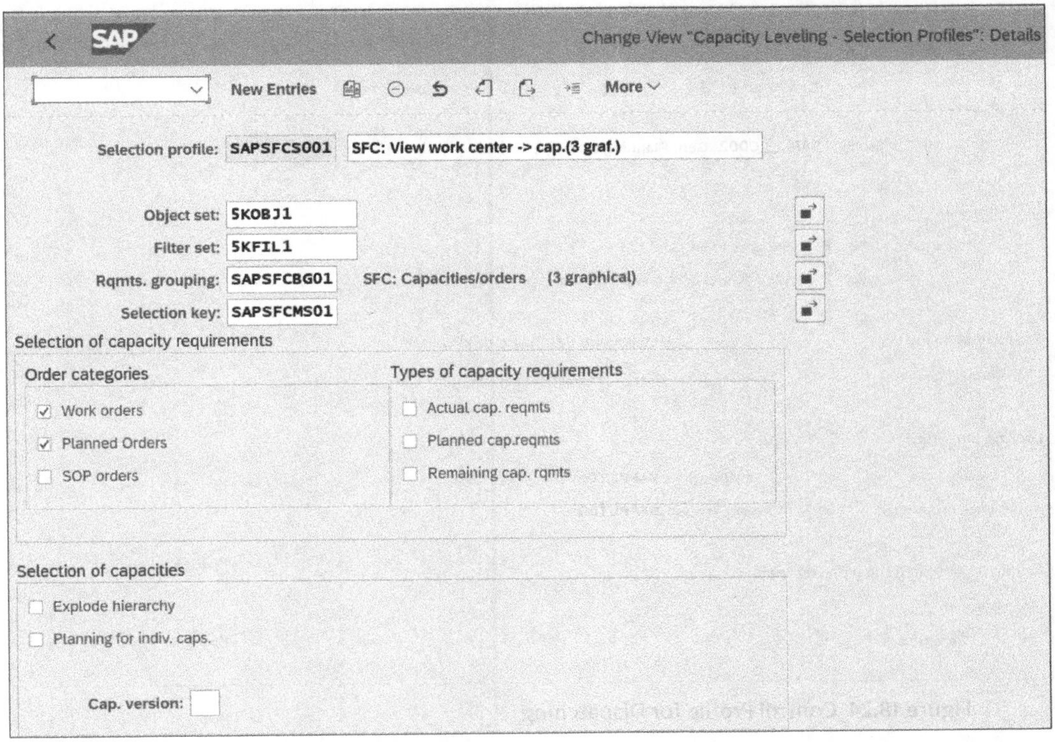

Figure 18.23 Selection Profile for Dispatching

Control Profile

The *control profile* defines how the system presents the data. It can be presented continuously over time for the capacity planning table, or it can be based on periods for the tabular capacity planning table. An important parameter of the control profile defines whether a planner can modify the operations and at which stage the system should set the locks to avoid any further changes to the operations.

To create or make changes to the control profile, follow the configuration menu path **SAP IMG · Production · Capacity Requirements Planning · Capacity Leveling and Extended Evaluation · Define Control Profile**, or use Transaction OPDE (see Figure 18.24).

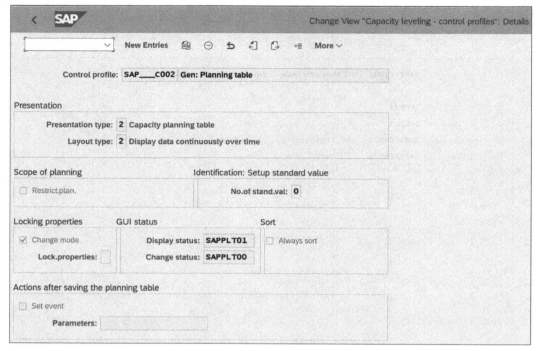

Figure 18.24 Control Profile for Dispatching

Evaluation Profile

The *evaluation profile* enables a planner to maintain the distribution keys for the capacity requirements, the units of measure, and the details to cumulate the capacity requirements. To create or make changes to the evaluation profile, follow menu path, **SAP IMG · Production · Capacity Requirements Planning · Capacity Leveling and Extended Evaluation · Strategy · Define Evaluation Profile**, or use Transaction OPD3.

Time Profile

The *time profile* contains the time horizons for importing the data records, as well as for evaluation and planning. The planning horizon must be smaller than or equal to the evaluation period, which in turn must be smaller than or equal to the database read period. Another entry concerns the date for dispatching the backlog to which the system dispatches all backlog capacity requirements—provided it considers the backlog.

To create or make changes to the time profile, follow menu path, **SAP IMG · Production · Capacity Requirements Planning · Capacity Leveling and Extended Evaluation · Define Time Profile**, or use Transaction OPD2. Figure 18.25 displays the details of time profile SAPSFCZ002.

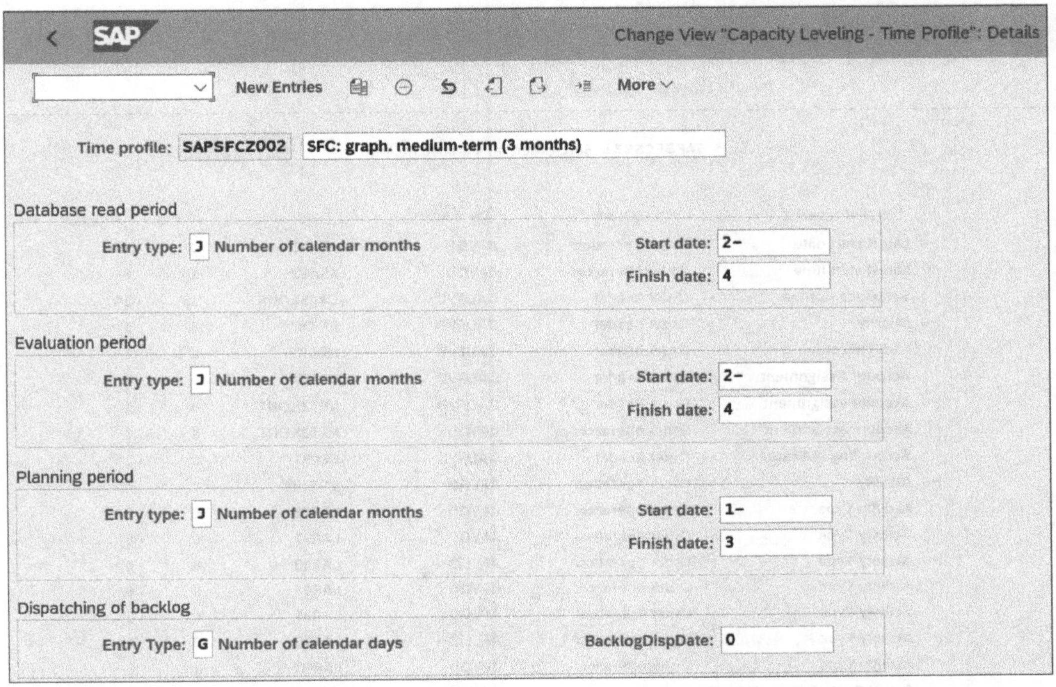

Figure 18.25 Time Profile for Dispatching

18.4.3 Dispatching Sequence

In general, a planner will carry out the dispatching function manually, individually, and interactively. But when there's a large and drastic change in the production plan, which also greatly impacts the operations involved, it makes sense to dispatch several operations according to specific rules. The easiest and most straightforward rule that most companies follow in dispatching is according to the start dates and times of operations. Similar rules can be implemented by using the sorting function, whereas the layout key enables a planner to implement sorting from a large number of available fields.

The layout key can be set using Transaction CY39 in Customizing (see Figure 18.26). On this screen, select the fields that a planner wants to sort and then eventually make available in dispatching. After selecting the fields, choose the **Sequence/Heading** button.

The field details allow managing the sorting in ascending or descending order. Then, the layout key is assigned to the strategy profile.

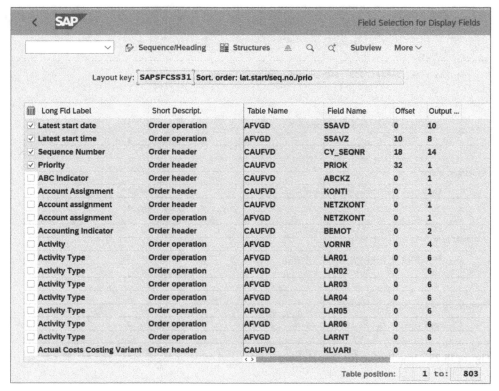

Figure 18.26 Layout Key for Sequence Creation during Dispatching

---

[+]   Tips and Tricks

In addition to the layout key, user exit CYPP0001 is also available to sort the capacity requirements. Engage an ABAP resource to define the parameters in the user exit.

The sequence in which the operations are dispatched may not necessarily match the sequence in the work center, as certain conditions of the dispatching process can trigger the system to dispatch some operations differently. For example, if a long-duration operation doesn't fit into any gap that has been created on the basis of operations already dispatched, the system dispatches that long-duration operation further in the planning horizon.

18.4.4   Sequence-Dependent Setup

In some production processes, the setup time depends on the sequence in which the product is produced or the physical state of the machine left behind after an operation.

For example, if an automotive company has a paint shop and it paints doors and hoods in light color such as gray or white first and then a dark color such as dark blue or black afterwards, this might not be that critical because the setup time for dark might be of standard length. But if the dark color is painted first and gray afterward, the setup time for gray might be much higher because the paint shop machines need to be cleaned very thoroughly from the dark color.

The dependency of setup work on a processing sequence can be configured by assigning the setup groups in respective operations of the routing. The assignment takes place at two levels: the setup group category and the setup group key. A setup group category can contain several setup group keys; for example, a setup group category can be color, and the setup group keys can be black, white, and yellow. The fact that the assignment occurs at two different levels has the advantage of enabling both detailed maintenance between setup group keys and less detailed maintenance between setup group categories.

Setup Group Categories

Group categories and setup group keys can be configured using Transaction OP43. Figure 18.27 shows the list of setup groups available for plant 1105.

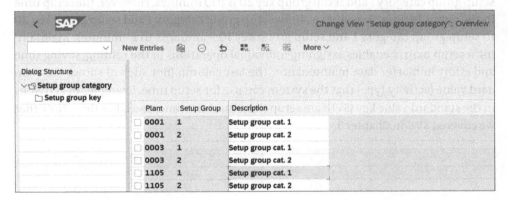

Figure 18.27 Setup Group Category

Select the **Setup group category** folder, then double-click the **Setup group key** folder on the left-hand side of the figure. Finally, in the operations details of the routing (Transaction CA02), assign the setup group categories and keys (see Figure 18.28).

The setup time between the setup group categories and the setup group key in a setup matrix can be maintained via menu path **SAP IMG · Production · Capacity Requirements Planning · Master Data · Routing Data · Define Setup Matrix**, or by using Transaction OPDA. The setup matrix is unique for each plant.

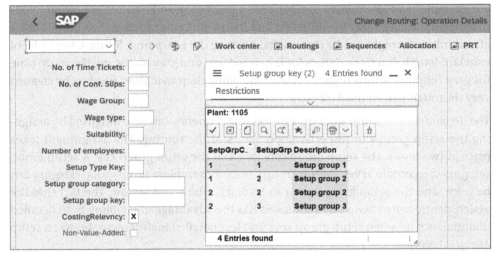

Figure 18.28 Assignment of Setup Group Category and Setup Group Key in Routing

Figure 18.29 illustrates an example in which the setup time from a previous operation with setup group category 1 and setup group key 10 to a subsequent operation with setup group category 1 and setup group key 20 is 100 minutes. However, the setup time in the opposite direction—that is, from setup group category 1 and setup group key 20 to setup group category 1 and setup group key 10—amounts to 25 minutes. Maintaining a setup matrix enables assigning individual operations in the routing, saving time and effort in master data maintenance. The last column (not shown) shows the standard value (activity type) that the system can use for setup time. Examples of activities in the standard value key (SVK) are setup time, machine time, and labor time. Note that we covered SVK in Chapter 3.

Figure 18.29 Setup Matrix

Setup Time

When a planner is using the capacity planning table, the system offers the following planning functions for planning with sequence-dependent setup times:

- Interactive change of default values
- Automatic adjustment of default values
- Dispatch at best time for setup
- Setup time optimization

In the capacity planning table, a planner can also make automatic or manual changes to the setup time by following menu path **Functions · Adjust Setup Time · Manually**. In the screen that appears, make changes to the setup time in the **Setup** field.

The setup time can be increased or decreased. When making this setup time adjustment, the system carries out a new scheduling process. If an operation was already dispatched, the system deallocates it when the setup adjustment takes place. With automatic setup time adjustment, the system calculates the setup times of operations on the basis of their sequence and reschedules them accordingly. To carry out the automatic setup function, first set the **Plan. Direction Forward** and **Insert Operation** parameters in the strategy profile. To close gaps that occur when the system reduces the setup times, also set the **Close Gaps** parameter in the strategy profile.

When using the **Dispatch at Best Time for Setup** function, the system doesn't try to dispatch the operation at the predefined dispatch date. It will do this at a point when the overall setup time is minimal for all operations increases. To use this function, set the **Dispatch at Best Time for Setup** and **Insert Operation** parameters in the strategy profile and make sure that the parameter for the **Setup Time Optimization** dispatch function is *not* set.

To enable the system to propose an optimum time for setup, it compares the dispatch times of operations with each other. If several optimal setup times exist, the system uses the latest of the optimal setup times. During dispatch, the system doesn't adjust the setup time of operations according to the sequence of operations. Instead, it requires an automatic setup time adjustment in the next step. To dispatch several operations at the same time, the system uses the dispatch sequence defined in the strategy profile.

The setup time optimization establishes an optimal setup sequence for a group of operations. The system dispatches the sequence in the work center without gaps and also automatically adjusts the setup times. The setup time optimization function is useful to redesign the planning because it ensures that the sequence of operations is optimal even after the dispatch. But if the dispatch period contains operations that have already been dispatched, the system deviates the new sequences from the previously determined optimal sequence.

18

For setup time optimization, select the **Setup Time Optimization** and the **Plan. Direction Forward** parameters in the strategy profile.

18.4.5   Midpoint Scheduling

Midpoint scheduling behaves in the same way as lead time scheduling, except that the basis of scheduling isn't the order start or finish date. Instead, it starts with the date of the dispatched operation of the order and carries out a backward or forward scheduling process from the operation, according to the planning direction that you've defined in the strategy profile. The system considers the other dispatched operations of the order as fixed. The dispatch occurs for each individual operation. During the dispatch of an operation, the dates of the operation can change. In such cases, you can use midpoint scheduling to adjust the dates of nondispatched operations to the changed dates of a dispatched operation.

For example, out of three operations, if the dispatch of the second operation took place, then midpoint scheduling can adjust the date of the nondispatched operations, which are the first and third ones. See Figure 18.30 for midpoint scheduling of three operations of an order.

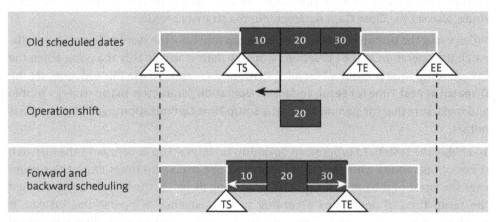

Figure 18.30 Midpoint Scheduling

18.4.6   Mass Processing

Often, if there are several operations or orders for which you want to perform a mass function, such as dispatch or deallocation, it's best to use the mass processing functionality available in capacity planning. To maintain the mass processing settings, follow SAP menu path **Logistics • Production • Capacity Planning • Leveling • Variable • Background • Execute**, or use Transaction CM40.

In the initial screen that appears, assign, for example, **Overall profile SAPSFCG011** for capacity leveling. Enter the **Job name** as "PP10", and choose **Save Parameters** in the **Call**

Up Function area of the screen. Next, click on **Save**, or press Ctrl + S . On saving parameters for the first time, the system prompts a user to enter work center parameters, in which text related to the **Work Center**, **Plant**, **Capacity Category**, or **Capacity Planner Grp** fields can be maintained.

Next time, when Transaction CM40 is used, a planner can use one of the three available actions, such as **Dispatch**, **Deallocate**, or **User Exit** (i.e., user exit CY190001) in the **Action** area of the screen. In the **Call Up Function** area of the screen, define whether to dispatch the job at a later stage (**Save Parameters**), dispatch it directly, or execute it directly.

Use Transaction CM41 to display the logs of the dispatch jobs.

18.5 Capacity Planning Table

Two types of capacity planning tables are available in the system: graphical and tabular. Our focus will primarily remain on the graphical capacity planning table, but all of the concepts and functions available in the graphical capacity planning table are also available in the tabular capacity planning table.

The highly interactive and intuitive nature of the graphical capacity planning table enables a capacity planner to perform several activities and functions:

- Make changes to an order.
- Make changes to an operation.
- Make changes to capacity.
- Dispatch operations.
- Deallocate operations.

While we'll discuss the final two functions in the preceding list in individual sections, there are relevant options available in the graphical capacity planning table for all the remaining change functions. Some of these change functions that we'll discuss in the following sections are making real-time changes to production or process orders, making changes to operations, or making changes to available capacities.

18.5.1 Changing Orders, Operations, or Capacity

To provide an example of the change functions, let's say a planner wants to make changes to a specific order. First, choose **Change Order**, and the system navigates to the production order change screen (Transaction CO02), in which the desired changes are made. The options to change operations and capacity details are also available.

A planner can also make changes in the strategy profile in the capacity planning table to perform the desired functions and achieve the requisite planning results.

To access the capacity planning table, follow SAP menu path **Logistics • Production • Capacity Planning • Leveling • Work Center View • Planning Table (Graphical)**, or use Transaction CM21. Figure 18.31 shows the capacity planning table that appears after entering the initial parameters, such as the **Work Center** and **Plant**. Here, choose **Execute**.

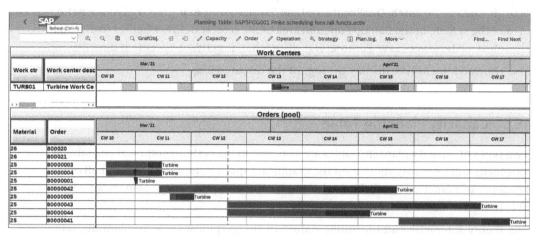

Figure 18.31 Capacity Planning Table

[+]   Tips and Tricks

Transaction CM25 can also be used, and it offers even greater options for capacity leveling.

If the system is able to find capacity requirements in the given period for work centers or orders, it displays the capacity information. The upper-left pane displays the work centers, whereas the upper-right pane displays the dispatched operations. The lower-left pane displays the pool of operations and the corresponding production orders. The lower-right pane displays nondispatched operations.

The sort profile of the pane can be defined to enable the system to sort from the pool of orders/operations. The system uses the order start date in the standard setting for sorting. However, the sort sequence gets disturbed when a planner deallocates the operations because the system adds new objects to the end of the list. Choose **More • Edit • Sort New** to reestablish the previous sort sequence.

The *time-based scaling* of the planning table can be modified by choosing **More • Settings • Scale** or by pressing the ⌈Ctrl⌋ key and simultaneously dragging a section of the screen.

The search function is helpful in navigating through the planning table, especially in finding relevant information where there is a large amount of data or information available. The search window can be called via **More • Edit • Search** or by pressing the key combination Ctrl + F.

The system facilitates navigation in the capacity planning table by highlighting objects that belong together. Let's say a planner wants the system to highlight the orders that belong to the same material (in this example, 25). To do this, choose **More • Edit • Highlight • Objects That Belong Together** (see Figure 18.32). The lower-right pane now shows all the objects belonging together in dark green.

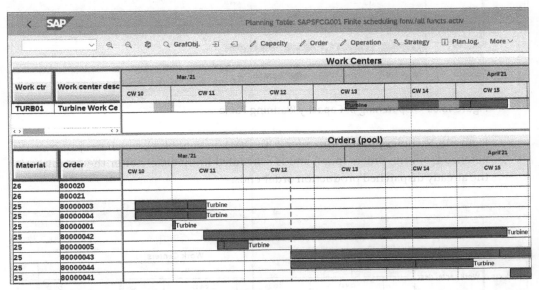

Figure 18.32 Highlighting All Objects Belonging Together

You can also highlight the objects that belong together with other criteria, such as order start date, target quantity, or planner group. To do this, choose **More • Edit • Highlight • Selection**. In the resulting screen, check the selection field to group and enter the field value that matches the purpose. Choose **Continue**, and the groupings will again appear in dark green.

18.5.2 Dispatch Operations

In the capacity planning table, there are two ways to dispatch operations. A planner can call the dispatch function by clicking **Dispatch** from the menu bar or can drag and drop the operation using the mouse. In both cases, first select the operations that need to be dispatched from the pool of orders/operations. The screen shown in Figure 18.33 displays the dispatch using the dispatch function in the menu bar. From the lower-right pane, select the operation to dispatch; on selection, the horizon bar turns to light blue. Then, choose **Dispatch** from the top menu bar and the system moves it to the upper-right pane (see Figure 18.34).

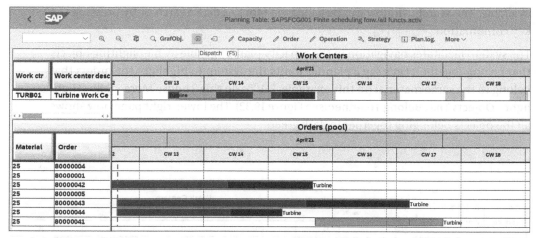

Figure 18.33 Dispatching in Capacity Planning Table

Figure 18.34 shows production order 80000041 (in light blue), which has just been dispatched from the orders (pool) and is scheduled immediately after the operation for the already dispatched production order ends.

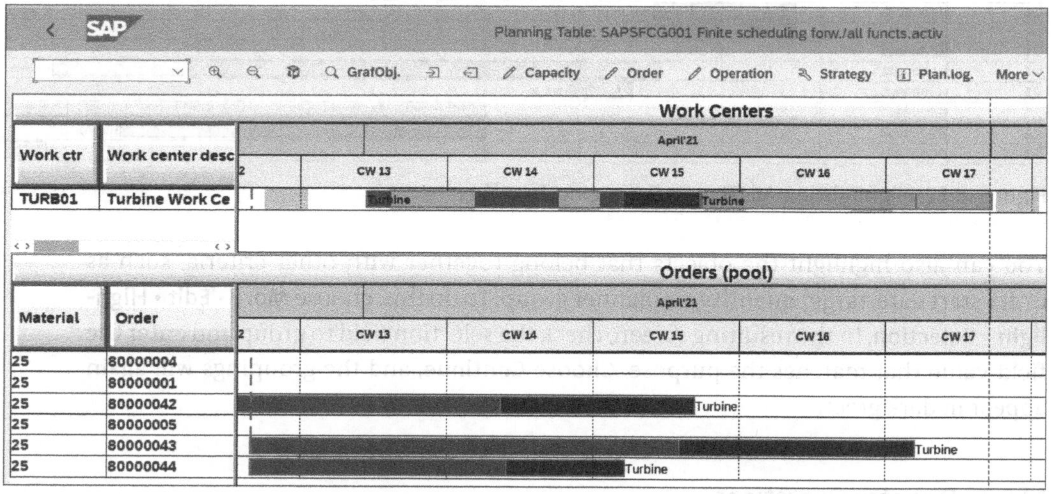

Figure 18.34 Dispatched Operation

The dispatch date is the scheduled operation date, which by default is the latest start date. If capacity is available on that date, the system dispatches the operation on the dispatch date. If capacity is unavailable on the dispatch date, finite scheduling determines the next possible date on which capacity is available, and the system then accordingly dispatches the operation on that date. If using the drag-and-drop method for dispatching the operation, the "drop" date represents the dispatch date.

18.5.3   Deallocate

The *deallocation* process is similar to the dispatching process. An operation can be deallocated either through **Deallocate** in the menu bar (located right next to the **Dispatch** option in Figure 18.33, or denoted by the back arrow) or by using drag and drop in the pool of orders/operations pane.

18.5.4   Options in the Graphical Planning Table

We've already covered in the sequence-dependent setup that the system requires specific settings in the strategy profile to enable it to plan effectively in the capacity planning table. The capacity planning board allows a planner to change the strategy profile by navigating to **More • Settings • Strategy**. Temporary changes can also be made to the selected strategy profile. These changes then apply to the dispatches that are carried out immediately after that, but the system won't store these settings when a planner leaves the capacity planning table.

If the available capacity is insufficient, it can be increased from within the capacity planning table—for example, by adding another shift or an interval. The available capacity can be adjusted from the capacity planning table by choosing **More • Goto • Capacity • Change**. Similarly, changes to the production order or to the operations can be made from within the capacity planning table by clicking the relevant options available in the menu bar.

The planned increase in material stock can be displayed in the capacity planning table. To display the **Material Stock** pane for selected materials (Figure 18.35), choose **More • Extras • Material Stock • Show**. This pane appears toward the bottom of the capacity planning table.

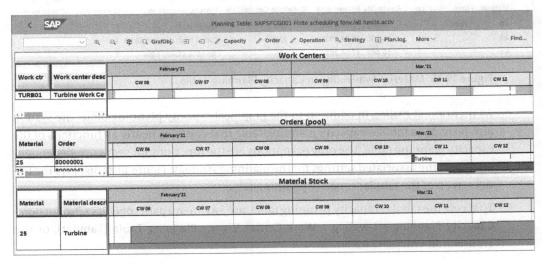

Figure 18.35 Material Stock Pane

Depending on how the capacity master data is set up, several operations can occupy a work center at the same time. In such cases, a green line below the operations indicates a multiple commitment. Choose **More • Edit • Multiple Commitment • Show** to display the multiple commitments of the selected work centers.

> **Note**
>
> The system enables a planner to leverage objects and layouts for display in the capacity planning table. We encourage exploring these options, especially from the **More** menu. Here options for **Scale, Increment, Shift Calendar,** and **Time Line,** among others, can be found.

18.5.5   Material Availability before Dispatching

To ensure smoother production, also check to see if the components required to produce a product are available prior to dispatching an operation to a work center. Figure 18.36 shows that a production order has three missing parts (components) out of the nine components required.

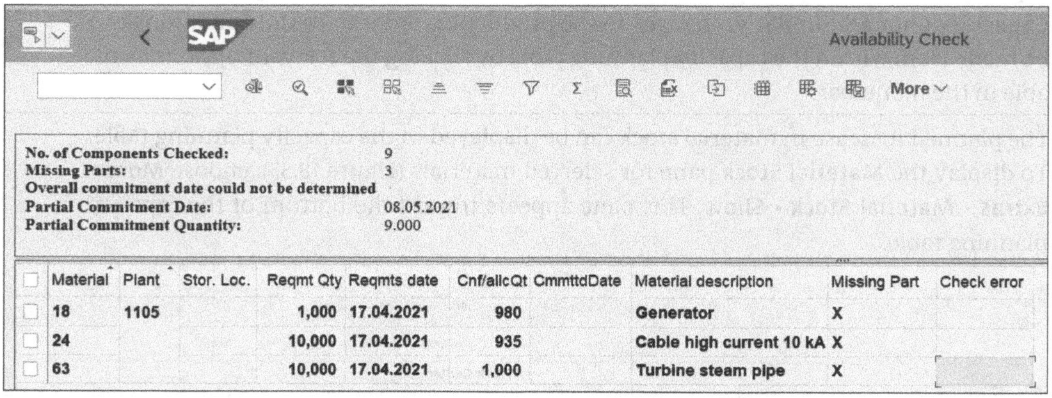

	SAP															Availability Check
																More ∨

No. of Components Checked: 9
Missing Parts: 3
Overall commitment date could not be determined
Partial Commitment Date: 08.05.2021
Partial Commitment Quantity: 9.000

	Material	Plant	Stor. Loc.	Reqmt Qty	Reqmts date	Cnf/allcQt	CmmttdDate	Material description	Missing Part	Check error
☐	18	1105		1,000	17.04.2021	980		Generator	X	
☐	24			10,000	17.04.2021	935		Cable high current 10 kA	X	
☐	63			10,000	17.04.2021	1,000		Turbine steam pipe	X	

Figure 18.36 Material Availability in Capacity Planning Table

As mentioned earlier, in addition to the graphical capacity planning table, the system also provides a tabular capacity planning table that contains nearly all functions of the capacity planning table. The only exceptions are the functions for sequence-dependent setup and the associated settings for the planning strategy. Figure 18.37 displays the initial screen of the tabular capacity planning table.

To access the tabular capacity planning table, use SAP menu path **Logistics • Production • Capacity Planning • Leveling • Work Center View • Planning Table (Tabular),** or use Transaction CM22.

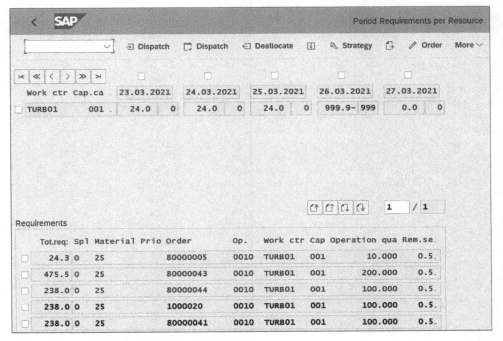

Figure 18.37 Tabular Capacity Planning Table

Due to the extensive similarities between the capacity planning tables in graphical form and tabular form, and with almost all of the properties and functions covered in this chapter, a planner can easily conduct the planning process in the tabular capacity planning table if necessary.

18.6   Summary

CRP helps a planner ensure that the system plays its part in making important business decisions, from dispatching the right operation in the right work center to evaluating the possibilities of increasing a shift or an interval. It can also be ensured that the system performs finite scheduling if there is a capacity shortage, or midpoint scheduling can be performed to account for on-ground production and capacity realities.

The next chapter discusses the production planning and detailed scheduling functionality.

Chapter 19
Production Planning and Detailed Scheduling

The primary objective of the production planning part of PP-DS production planning and detailed scheduling is to ensure that the right product is available at the right time and the right place to be delivered to customers and ensure the raw materials are available for production. The detailed scheduling part PP-DS supports the sequencing and scheduling of production operations by taking into consideration the available resource capacity (machines and human resources) and the availability of materials. In addition, detailed scheduling ensures optimal usage of resources.

SAP S/4HANA offers a new embedded production planning and detailed scheduling (PP-DS) area, which means that the PP-DS functionality is now part of the SAP S/4HANA core and there's no longer a need to have an SAP Advanced Planning and Optimization (SAP APO) system to use PP-DS. The embedded PP-DS functionality offers most of the features present in PP-DS in SAP APO. All PP-DS transactions can be accessed directly in SAP S/4HANA. In addition, new SAP Fiori apps for capacity monitoring and capacity planning are available, and most existing PP-DS transactions can also be accessed through the SAP Fiori launchpad. Embedded PP-DS also ensures master data harmonization. In addition, creating sources of supply has also been simplified.

In embedded PP-DS, the core interface (CIF) has also been simplified. The CIF is responsible for integration between PP-DS and SAP S/4HANA. The CIF integration occurred through remote function calls (RFCs) and inbound and outbound queues in which data was processed when received or sent. Because PP-DS runs on an SAP S/4HANA core, there's no longer a need to use RFCs to integrate data between systems, which means simplified integration, synchronous commits, and consistent data between both systems. Immediate error handling in most situations is possible. The new MRP Live, introduced in SAP S/4HANA and already covered in Chapter 14, is now also capable of planning with PP-DS heuristics. Due to the embedded nature of PP-DS in SAP S/4HANA, the material master and work center creation is also synchronous. In other words, a material or a work center that has just been created in SAP S/4HANA can be immediately available for planning in PP-DS.

In the following sections on PP-DS, it will instantly become clear that many of the concepts, foundations, and pieces of knowledge developed in this book will equally be applicable to PP-DS processes. For example, by now, you're familiar with concepts related to work centers, bills of materials (BOMs), routings, and production versions. Similarly, familiarity with pegging, planned independent requirements (PIRs), demand management, stock/requirements lists, and MRP Live, among other concepts, and their workings have already been discussed in various chapters of this book. So, in the interest of giving maximum coverage to the topic under discussion—that is, PP-DS—these already covered topics or topics covered in more detail later in this book aren't repeated or previewed here. Only topics or definitions relevant to PP-DS that need more detailed coverage for understanding PP-DS itself are discussed.

Further, while it's true that now PP-DS is "embedded" in SAP S/4HANA, the CIF still needs to be configured and set up even when the source and the target SAP systems are both the same—that is, SAP S/4HANA. Similarly, to use the PP-DS optimizer tool to optimize the production flow, it still needs to be set up in SAP S/4HANA. Finally, due to the same or similar terminologies, such as planned orders and PIRs, used in both SAP S/4HANA and PP-DS, the following sections will specifically mention when an element belongs either to SAP S/4HANA or to PP-DS.

Following are some of the key features in PP-DS that we'll cover in this chapter:

- Production planning heuristics
- Interactive planning tools
- Detailed scheduling heuristics
- PP-DS optimizer
- Interactive detailed scheduling tools
- Background planning and scheduling tools
- Planning procedures
- Pegging relationships
- Alert monitor
- Plan monitor

The following sections will adopt the same approach to cover PP-DS in SAP S/4HANA that has been followed throughout. We'll cover the basic configuration needed to set up PP-DS, which will then be followed by covering master data specific to PP-DS. Next, the PP-DS master data is put to use by covering the associated PP-DS business processes. We'll also be discussing heuristics, the production planning run, and the optimizer. The last section covers the alert monitor and the plan monitor. The chapter will conclude with a discussion on reporting, including SAP Fiori apps relevant to PP-DS.

Let's begin with the necessary PP-DS configuration.

19.1 Configuration

A number of steps are necessary to start using embedded PP-DS in SAP S/4HANA, such as checking the relevant business functions and other configuration settings.

Embedded PP-DS was introduced as business function SCM_PPDS_ON_ERP, and it should be active by default on an SAP S/4HANA system. Still, it's recommended to confirm if the business function is active by executing Transaction SFW5 and checking if the traffic light is green on the screen the system displays. To activate embedded PP-DS, the **Advanced Planning** checkbox must be activated by following menu path **SAP IMG · Advanced Planning · Basic Settings · Activate Advanced Planning and Scheduling**.

> **Note**
>
> All PP-DS configuration options are available via menu path **SAP IMG · Advanced Planning**.

With embedded PP-DS, there's no need to create integration models to transfer transaction data between SAP S/4HANA and PP-DS or vice versa. The transfer of the transaction data can be activated by following configuration path **Advanced Planning · Basic Settings · Activate Advanced Planning and Scheduling · Settings For Data Transfer**. The order types relevant for advanced planning can be set as relevant for transfers between PP-DS and SAP S/4HANA (see Figure 19.1).

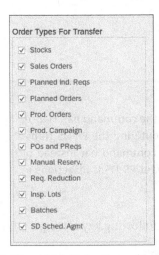

Figure 19.1 Order Types for Transfer

Embedded PP-DS needs the model and version set up. Model 000 and version 000 are the locations in which the active planning data products and resources relevant to advanced planning are stored. Additional simulated planning versions can be created for assessing the planning situation. The model and version are created via Transaction

/SAPAPO/MVM (see Figure 19.2). Here, maintain the **PP-DS Planning Horizon** in calendar days as a time frame during which the system will automatically be able to create, change, or delete receipts. Outside of the PP-DS horizon, receipts can only be planned manually.

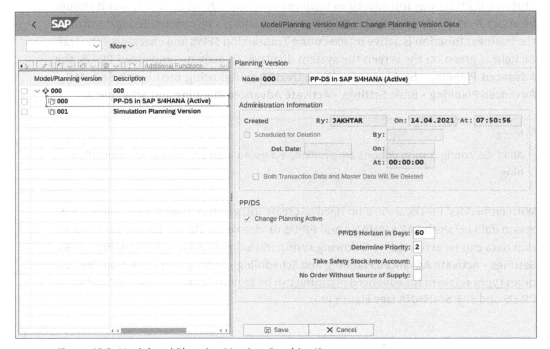

Figure 19.2 Model and Planning Version Combination

[+]   Tips and Tricks

The system doesn't recognize a PP-DS transaction entered in the command bar. Hence, all PP-DS transactions are preceded with "/N", followed by entering the PP-DS transaction code. For example, enter "/N/SAPAPO/MVM" in the command bar instead of "/SAPAPO/MVM". To avoid repetition, we'll denote the relevant PP-DS transactions in this chapter without repeating "/N".

Select the **Change Planning Active** checkbox, then make the following key settings:

- **Standard Planning Horizon (Days)**
  The PP-DS horizon in days defines the number of calendar days within which the PP-DS system is allowed to create, change, and delete procurement proposals during a planning run execution. Beyond the PP-DS horizon, it's possible to create procurement proposals manually using the PP-DS transactions. There is no option to set any

material-specific planning horizon in embedded PP-DS, and all the advanced planning products will use the PP-DS horizon defined in the planning version settings.

- **Determine Priority**
  In PP-DS, it's possible to assign priorities to the procurement proposals (e.g., planned orders). These order priorities are used in PP-DS functions such as scheduling heuristics to reduce the delays in manufacturing an order that has higher priority.

- **Take Safety Stock into Account**
  Safety stock is the requirement element used in the plan to cover any unplanned demand that may result in a stock-out situation. PP-DS supports safety stocks in planning.

- **No Order Without Source of Supply**
  In PP-DS, when orders are created, the source of supply, such as a production data structure (PDS) or an external procurement relationship (e.g., info record), is assigned to the orders. If there are no suitable sources of supply found, the orders can still be created, but the order dates can't be correct as the source of supply determines the duration it takes to procure or produce a material. In the planning version, define whether to create orders when no suitable source of supply is available or how the system should react when no source of supply is determined.

Activate the business transfer event (BTE) application indicator. This indicator is required to trigger the transfer of the relevant data into the embedded PP-DS. In Transaction BF11, select the **ND-APO** checkbox to set the flag (see Figure 19.3).

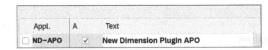

Appl.	A	Text
☐ ND–APO	☑	New Dimension Plugin APO

Figure 19.3 Activating ND-APO Checkbox

Although creating integration models for the transaction data transfer isn't required, basic settings for the CIF still need to be maintained. In addition, certain master data objects such as purchasing contracts, info records, and scheduling agreements still need to be created in an integration model to send these objects to the PP-DS side. Therefore, maintaining the basic CIF settings is an important step of using embedded PP-DS. It's possible to change basic settings for creating the system landscape and for including SAP S/4HANA with system type SAP_APO and the corresponding release so that an integration model can point to itself (act as its own system and client) and logical system and queue types can be maintained. Maintain basic CIF settings by following the Customizing path **SAP IMG • Advanced Planning • Integration via Core Interface**.

Global settings and defaults for PP-DS must be maintained via Transaction /SAPAPO/ RRPCUST1 or by following configuration path **SAP IMG • Advanced Planning • Global Settings • Maintain Global Parameters and Defaults** (see Figure 19.4).

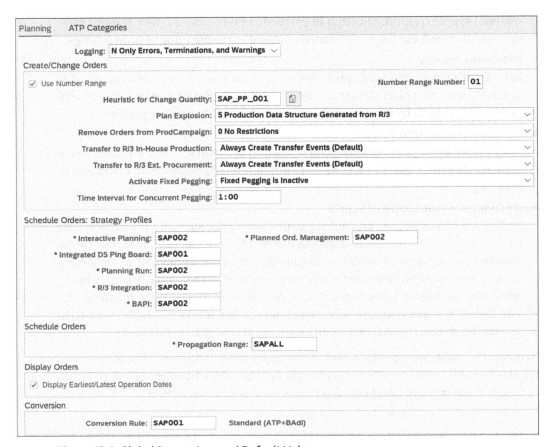

Figure 19.4 Global Parameters and Default Values

Let's discuss some of the important fields or data transfer options shown in Figure 19.4:

- **Number Range Number**
  This optional setting determines whether orders created in PP-DS contain a number that corresponds to the PP-DS number range. As soon as an order is transmitted to SAP S/4HANA via CIF, it receives an order number in SAP S/4HANA that is based on the SAP S/4HANA number range. The order number is then transferred to PP-DS. A number range for PP-DS orders needs to be defined in advance and can then be assigned here.

- **Transfer to In-House Production**
  Define whether planned orders or purchase requisitions are transferred to SAP S/4HANA or whether the transfer occurs only after conversion in production orders or purchase orders (POs).

- **Planning Run**
  The settings made here are relevant if no other explicit settings are made within specific applications.

Note

Notice the *available-to-promise* (ATP) *categories* for PP-DS. These are used to define the receipt and requirement elements of production and detailed planning. They are already present in the delivery system, so specify a category only if the executing system isn't an SAP S/4HANA system (see the **ATP Categories** tab in Figure 19.4).

The *MRP-based DS scenario* is the special form of process modeling that uses PP-DS in the context of production order processing in a targeted manner. Before the advent of embedded PP-DS in SAP S/4HANA, the basic material requirements planning (MRP) was supposed to be done in SAP S/4HANA, while PP-DS was supposed to be used only for detailed scheduling. Against this background, the MRP-based DS in master data modeling doesn't require a transfer and mapping of routings and BOMs in production data structures (PDSs) or production process models (PPMs) and can omit the associated implementation effort (production versions and associated integration with change transfers).

It's possible to consider manufacturing order networks from SAP S/4HANA (direct procurement/in-house production special procurement key) in the PP-DS capacity planning with this scenario. Within the scope, implement a scheduling and a retransfer of the new time schedule to SAP S/4HANA when converting planned orders into production orders. A special feature is that this conversion is done locally in SAP S/4HANA by way of exception; but when the production orders are posted, the earlier PP-DS scheduling takes effect nevertheless. Additional changes and transfers can follow iteratively. To make the relevant configuration settings, access the screen shown in Figure 19.5 via Transaction CFDS and select the relevant options to automatically transfer or not transfer some or all planning and scheduling data from PP-DS to SAP S/4HANA.

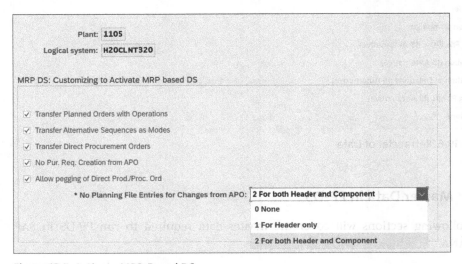

Figure 19.5 Activate MRP-Based DS

Another *retransfer of the planning result* can be set between PP-DS and SAP S/4HANA. These settings are relevant if the quantity of a production order (or any other data element) that originates from PP-DS is changed in SAP S/4HANA, for example. The changed quantity is transferred to PP-DS, where the order is rescheduled. The new dates are retransferred to SAP S/4HANA only if this is configured in Transaction /SAPAPO/CP3 (see Figure 19.6). Here, choose elements such as in-house production, external procurement, PIRs, or reservation data to retransfer between PP-DS and SAP S/4HANA in a bidirectional manner.

This brings an end to the minimal configuration required to set up and run PP-DS in SAP S/4HANA. The next section is on maintaining the necessary PP-DS master data to be able to run the associated business processes.

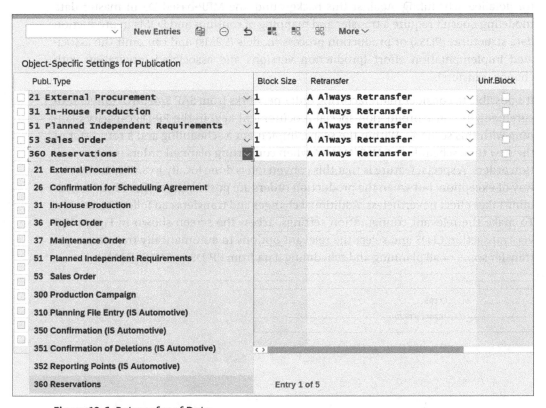

Figure 19.6 Retransfer of Data

19.2   Master Data in PP-DS

The following sections will cover the master data required to run PP-DS in SAP S/4HANA.

19.2.1   Location

A location can represent a plant, a business partner, a shipping or receiving point, or an MRP area. To create locations in PP-DS, use Transaction SE38 followed by executing report /SAPAPO/CREATE_LOCATION. With this report, a location is immediately created, with no integration queues, and an error message will be displayed immediately if an error occurs (see Figure 19.7). ABAP program /SAPAPO/UPD_ LOC_SP_PL can be used to update the location data in embedded PP-DS when changes are performed for the corresponding data in SAP S/4HANA.

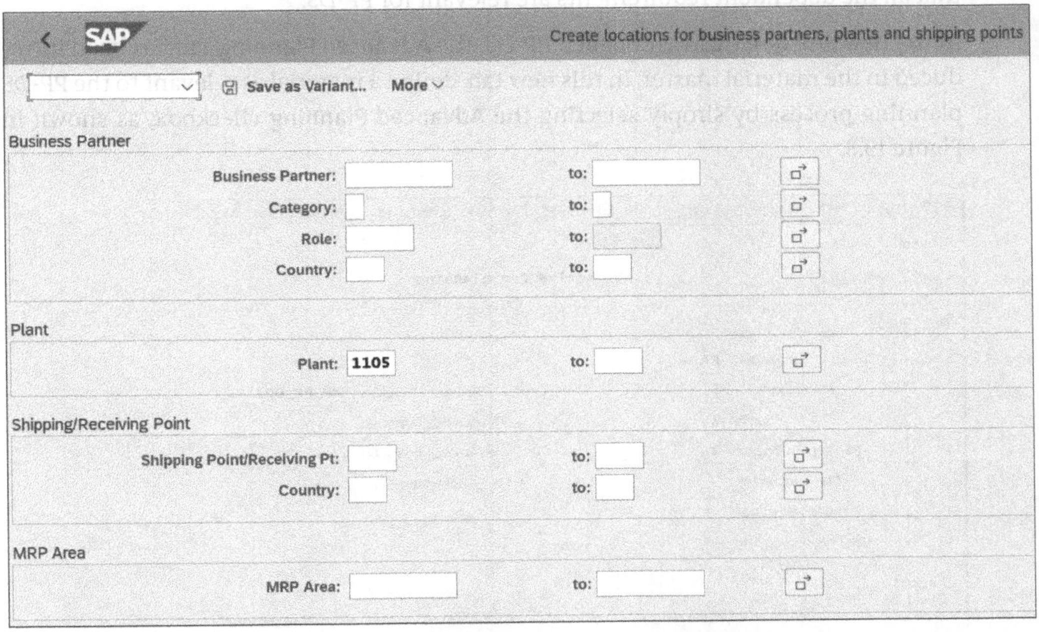

Figure 19.7 Create Locations, Business Partners, Plants, and Shipping Points

Note
Transactions pertaining to the master data, business processes, and reporting of PP-DS can be accessed via **SAP Menu · Logistics · Advanced Planning**.

After transferring the plant location, the plant location of location type **1001** (production plant) is created in embedded PP-DS. The location master can be accessed from Transaction /SAPAPO/LOC3 or via menu path **Logistics · Advanced Planning · Master Data · Location · Location**. After entering the **Location** and **Location Type**, choose **Change** to change the info and add additional PP-DS information to the location master.

19.2.2   Material Master

When an advanced planning material is planned in MRP Live, the system uses the default heuristic and further settings defined in the **Advanced Planning** tab of the material master. For materials to be planned with PP-DS heuristics, define MRP type "X0" in the **MRP1** tab. Whenever a semifinished material is to be planned with PP-DS heuristics, the parent material should also be planned with PP-DS. Therefore, when designing a BOM, ensure that the parent material is an advanced planning material if at least one of its components is an advanced planning material. This design is necessary to ensure that all the dependent requirements are relevant for PP-DS.

In the new SAP S/4HANA embedded PP-DS, the **Advanced Planning** tab has been introduced in the material master. In this new tab, define a material as relevant to the PP-DS planning process by simply selecting the **Advanced Planning** checkbox, as shown in Figure 19.8.

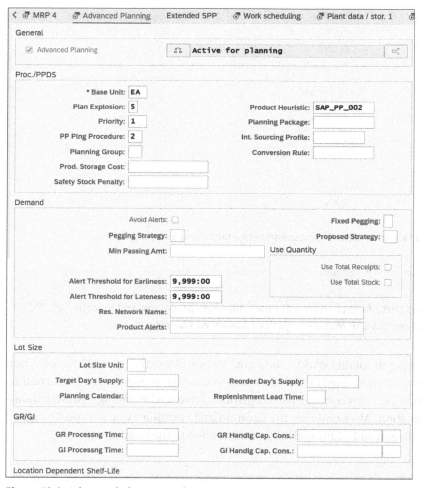

Figure 19.8 Advanced Planning Tab in Material Master

Let's discuss some of the important fields of PP-DS. Figure 19.8 shows the **Advanced Planning** view of the material master. Some of the important fields are as follows:

- **PP Plng Procedure**
  For each planning-relevant material in PP-DS, and any event occurring at a location product level (that is a material), an action is triggered by PP-DS. For customer requirements, the PP planning procedure also determines whether the desired quantity or the confirmed quantity of a schedule line is relevant for pegging. For example, a planning-relevant event such as a goods movement for a product or a change in the product master takes place. Possible actions by PP-DS can include immediately calling up a product heuristic for the product or creating a planning file entry. A *heuristic* is a planning function in PP-DS that executes planning for selected objects, such as products, resources, operations, or line networks.

- **Plan Explosion**
  This field specifies the task list type, such as a BOM and routing, that the system uses to create receipts in PP-DS.

- **Product Heuristic**
  Just as there are MRP types in SAP S/4HANA that control the type of planning a material will have, product heuristics are the planning methods for PP-DS.

- **Avoid Alerts**
  On setting this checkbox, the system will attempt to create the pegging relationships between requirements and receipts, if possible, without quantity or date alerts. The system first links receipts and requirements that are compatible on a time and quantity basis, then the remaining receipts and requirements in a second step.

- **Alert Threshold for Earliness**

  The system creates a date/time alert for a fixed or a dynamic pegging relationship if the earliness exceeds the alert threshold—that is, if the availability date/time is earlier than the specified time frame before the requirements date. To specify the time frame, use format HHHHHH:MM (hours:minutes). For example, 1000:10 means 1,000 hours and 10 minutes and 20:20 means 20 hours and 20 minutes. If no value is specified, then the system uses the value 100000:00. Therefore, the system only creates an alert if an availability date/time is more than 100,000 hours before the requirements date.

- **Alert Threshold for Lateness**

  Similar to the alert threshold for early receipt, the system creates a date/time alert for a fixed or a dynamic pegging relationship if the delay exceeds the alert threshold—that is, if the availability date/time is later than the specified time frame after the requirements date.

- **Pegging Strategy**

  Using the pegging strategy, you can determine in which time sequence the system should cover requirements for the product with dynamic pegging and in which time sequence the system should use the product receipts in the *pegging interval* to cover a requirement. Thus, the pegging strategy controls the following:

  - Which requirement the system should cover first

  - Which receipts the system should use first

  In general, for dynamic pegging, the system begins by covering the earliest requirement, and then processes the next requirement, and so on. Because there may be several receipts for the availability dates/times within the pegging interval, it's important to specify which receipt the system should use first. The following options exist:

  - **Use current receipts**

    Here the system uses the current receipt where possible to cover a requirement. Starting from the requirement date, the system first searches to the beginning of the pegging interval. If there are no receipts in this direction, the system will search to the end of the pegging interval.

  - **Use the earliest receipt (first in, first out [FIFO])**

    Here the system uses the earliest receipts in the pegging interval to cover a requirement—that is, first the first receipt in the pegging interval, then the second, and so on. With this strategy, excess receipts only become available later.

- **Res. Network Name**
  This indicates the name of the resource network. A resource network describes the physical links between resources in a plant, such as processing units, reactors, vessels, and so on. It explains the flow of materials through a plant.

- **Product Alerts**
  In this field, specify whether
  - the system determines direct alerts for a requirement or a receipt of a product or
  - the product is relevant to network alerts.

  If a product is relevant to network alerts, the system evaluates the direct alerts that it determines for this product for receipts or requirements at the superordinate levels of the pegging structure as well.

  It's possible to hide alerts for less critical components and thus
  - increase the clarity and transparency of the network alerts and
  - improve performance.

  If the **Avoid Alerts** option is selected, the system won't determine any direct alerts for the product. Thus, the product also isn't relevant in regard to the network.

> **Note**
>
> A planner needs to specify whether and which alerts are actually displayed by the system in the planning interface or in the alert monitor in the PP-DS alert profile to be used for planning. The alert monitor is discussed in detail in Section 19.7.

- **Lot Size Unit**
  This indicates the valid unit of measure (UoM). The following options are available:
  - No lot size units maintained: The base UoM maintained for the product applies.
  - A unit of measure (alternative or base UoM) can be maintained which can be converted to the base UoM. If an alternative UoM is entered, the conversion to the base UoM must be maintained on the **Units of Measure** tab. The alternative units of measure must be able to be converted to the base UoM for the product; otherwise, the unit won't be accepted. For example, the alternative UoM is kilogram (kg). The base UoM is piece (pc). In this case, 5 kg corresponds to three pieces.

- **Target Days' Supply**
  The PP-DS standard heuristic SAP_PP_002 (Planning of Standard Lots) and the Supply Network Planning (SNP) heuristic takes into account the target days' supply if one of the following target stock level methods are selected:
  - **No entry**: Target days' supply from the product master.
  - **111**: Target stock level equals maximum stock level + safety stock.
  - **5**: Maximum from maximum stock level/target days' supply (product master).

- **6**: Total from maximum stock level/target days' supply (product master).
- **7**: No target stock level.

To plan location products using target stock level methods, use the standard heuristic SAP_PP_002 (planning of standard lot sizes).

The heuristic-based planning uses the SNP heuristic. The SNP heuristic plans the demand over the entire supply chain network (cross-location planning) and creates a medium-term production and distribution plan. It doesn't take into account any constraints or costs, so the plan created won't necessarily be feasible. In a second step, after the heuristic run, the planner can then adjust the plan using capacity leveling in interactive SNP planning to create a plan that is feasible.

- **Reorder Days' Supply**
  Specify the reorder days' supply if **Reorder Point Method 2** for the location product has been defined.

- **GR Processing Time**
  This is the time in between the delivery or the production of a product and its availability as stock. This time is used, for example, as handling time or time for quality checks and is added to the transportation duration or the production time of a product.

- **GR Handling Cap. Cons.**
  This is used by the heuristic and PP-DS optimizer to calculate how much handling resource capacity is consumed by the product for a particular plan. For example, if the handling resource can handle 1,000 liters per day, and the handling capacity consumption of 10 liters per piece is defined, the maximum rate is 100 pieces per day.

- **Loc. Shelf Life**
  In this area, a planner can control if the system should consider the resource location-dependent shelf life of a product and, if so, then the standard, minimum, and maximum shelf lives a product needs to have. A location in PP-DS can be a plant, distribution center, storage location, MRP area, customer, transportation lane, or business partner (vendor).

- **Proposed Strategy**
  The strategy group maintained in the **MRP 3** view of the material master is directly linked to the PP-DS strategy, as shown in Table 19.1. If other strategies or keys are entered in SAP S/4HANA, the relevant field in the PP-DS product master remains blank or is unchanged.

Strategy Description	SAP S/4HANA Strategy Group	PP-DS Strategy
Anonymous make-to-stock (MTS)	10	10
Planning with final assembly	40	20

Table 19.1 Different Strategy Keys in SAP S/4HANA and PP-DS

Strategy Description	SAP S/4HANA Strategy Group	PP-DS Strategy
Subassembly planning	70	20
Planning without final assembly	50	30
Planning with planning product	60	40
Make-to-order (MTO) production	20	Blank

Table 19.1 Different Strategy Keys in SAP S/4HANA and PP-DS (Cont.)

After selecting the **Advanced Planning** checkbox for an existing material, use Transaction SE38 to execute report /SAPAPO/PPDS_DELTA_ORD_TRANS for this material. This report allows the integration of existing planning elements for this material into PP-DS without the creation of an integration model. The only input parameters to add are the material and the plant. Enter these parameters in the **Material** and **Plant** fields shown in Figure 19.9.

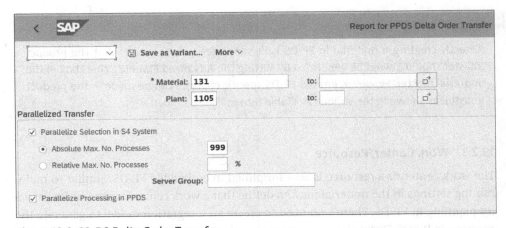

Figure 19.9 PP-DS Delta Order Transfer

Tips and Tricks

Use the mass maintenance transactions available for the material master, such as Transaction MASSD or MM17, to maintain the PP-DS fields in the material master.

After saving a material master for which the **Advanced Planning** option has been selected, the changes will be immediately reflected in the product master. Review the product master with Transaction /SAPAPO/MAT1; Figure 19.10 shows product master 131, created for this material. Recall that these same details were maintained in the material master and are now visible in the product master.

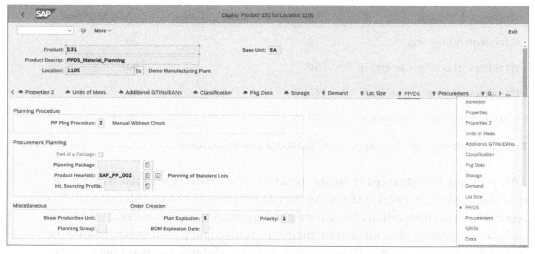

Figure 19.10 Product Master in PP-DS

> **Note**
>
> Directly creating a material in PP-DS isn't supported, which means that the product master should always be generated by setting the **Advanced Planning** checkbox in the material master. However, limited PP-DS specific changes can be made in the product master, as shown in the various available tabs in Figure 19.10.

19.2.3   Work Center/Resource

The work center or a resource is also simplified in embedded PP-DS. Similar to maintaining settings in the material master, define that a work center is relevant for capacity planning in PP-DS. There's no need to create an integration model to generate the resource in PP-DS. During the work center creation or maintenance (Transaction CR01), simply select the **Advanced Planning** flag as shown in Figure 19.11, and a corresponding PP_DS resource is then automatically created. Figure 19.11 shows work center PPDSWC2 for plant 1105 with the **Advanced Planning** option selected in the **Basic Data** tab.

> **Note**
>
> We'll be using the same work center PPDSWC2 and plant 1105 combination throughout this chapter while discussing PP-DS.

Next, choose the **Capacities** tab shown in Figure 19.11 and then choose the **Capacity Header**, which brings up the screen shown in Figure 19.12.

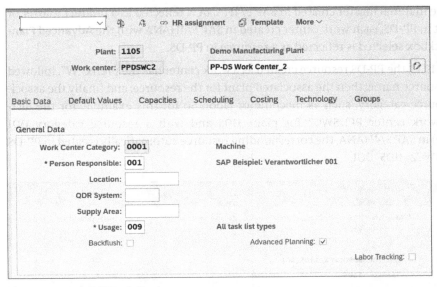

Figure 19.11 PP-DS Work Center

In Figure 19.12, choose the **APO Resource** button located on the top-right-hand side, and maintain the PP-DS specific details in the popup screen. The time stream validity is determined by the fields **Days -** (days in past) and **Days +** (days in future), and the same is used to create the SAP liveCache time stream in PP-DS.

Figure 19.12 APO Resource in Work Center

Just as the material master created in SAP S/4HANA is reflected as a product master or a product in PP-DS, each work center created in SAP S/4HANA with the **Advanced Planning** checkbox selected is reflected as a resource in PP-DS.

In Figure 19.13, the PP-DS resource created as a work center has the prefix "W", followed by the resource name, then the associated plant for the resource, and finally the associated resource category, such as machine or labor. So for this example, for the just-created work center PPDSWC2 for plant 1105 and with a resource category 001 (machine) in SAP S/4HANA, the corresponding resource automatically created in PP-DS is WPPDSWC2_1105_001.

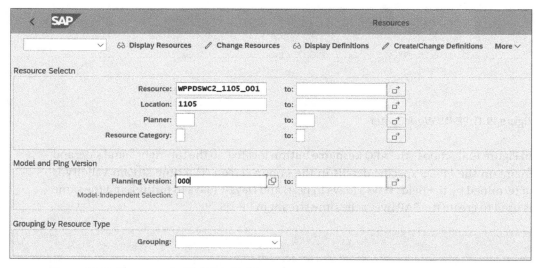

Figure 19.13 Resources in PP-DS: Initial Screen

Access the newly created PP-DS resource shown in Figure 19.13 via Transaction /SAPAPO/RES01, and enter the details as shown, followed by clicking **Display Resources** so that the screen shown in Figure 19.14 appears.

As already mentioned, embedded PP-DS provides synchronous commit; that is, the PP-DS resource information will be always consistent with the SAP S/4HANA work center information. As shown in Figure 19.14, the PP-DS resource is created immediately after the creation of the work center. In the resource, the **Planner Gr (group)** field is important. The PP-DS planner is location independent and is created in the **Specify Person Responsible (Planner)** configuration activity. The planner is also used to select the area of responsibility for PP-DS reporting, including in SAP Fiori apps.

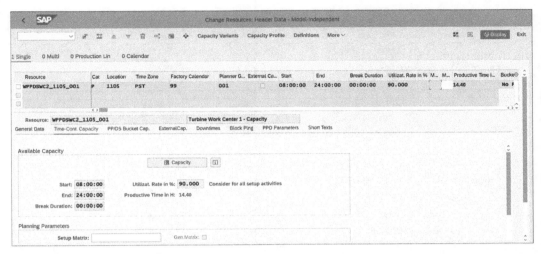

Figure 19.14 Resource in PP-DS

[«]

Note

Just like the material master-product combination, manually creating PP-DS resources also isn't allowed, and a PP-DS resource can only be created together with a work center. However, deleting a PP-DS resource should be handled manually when the respective work center is deleted. Creating a work center won't be allowed if the respective resource already exists in the PP-DS side.

It's important to enable target system-independent settings in the CIF for the resource transfer in Transaction CFC9. Values defined for the **Days in Past** and **Days in the Future** fields and resource type will be used when a PP-DS resource is created. In addition, the *no change transfer* change transfer mode isn't supported in embedded PP-DS (see Figure 19.15).

[«]

Note

Remember to also create the remaining PP master data, such as the BOM of material 131 and its routing that uses work center PPDSWC2. Finally, also create a production version that combines the routing and BOM details of material 131.

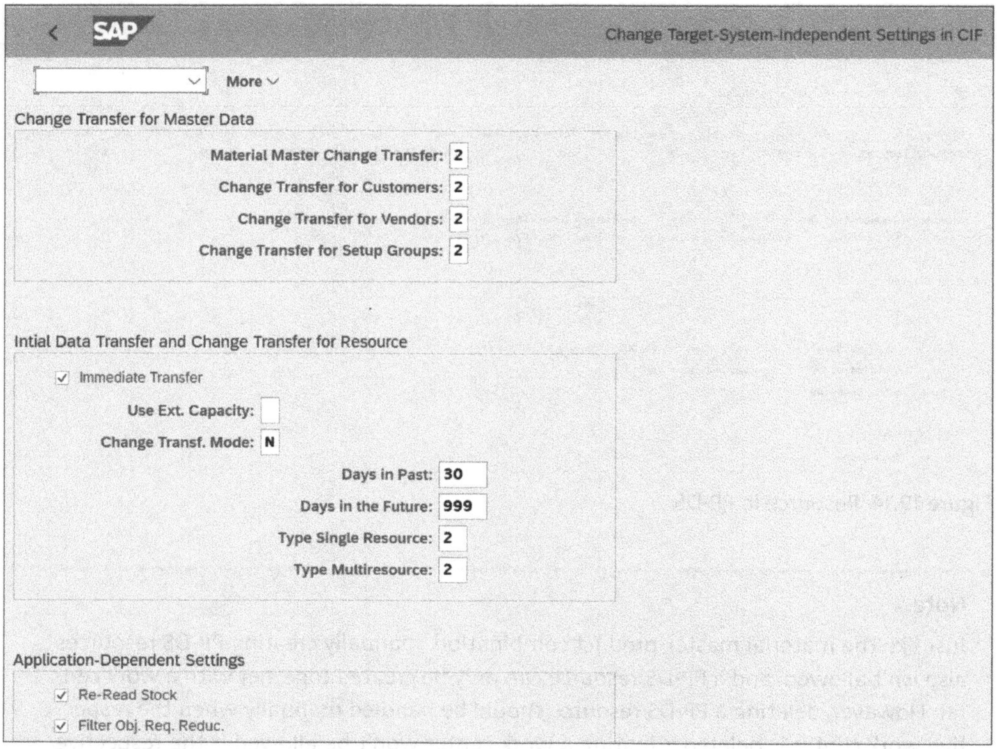

Figure 19.15 Configuration Settings for Data Transfer

19.2.4   Sources of Supply

Sources of supply define how the materials are procured. The sources of supply for materials produced in-house (internal procurement) and sources of supply for the materials sourced from a vendor or another plant (external procurement) are examined in the following sections.

Internal Procurement

For a material produced internally, the PP-DS source of supply is the PDS, which represents a combination of BOM, routing, and production version.

Although creating the PDS in PP-DS isn't as simple as the creation of the product (i.e., material in SAP S/4HANA) and the resource (i.e., work center in SAP S/4HANA), there's still no need create an integration model to do it. By using Transaction SE38 and executing report PPDS_ERP_CUSLNTRTO_CIF_REPORT, you can generate the PDS based on the production versions. Figure 19.16 shows the selection screen of report PPDS_ERP_CUSLNTRTO_CIF_REPORT ❶, and the results of the report execution are visible ❷, showing a successful transfer of the PDS.

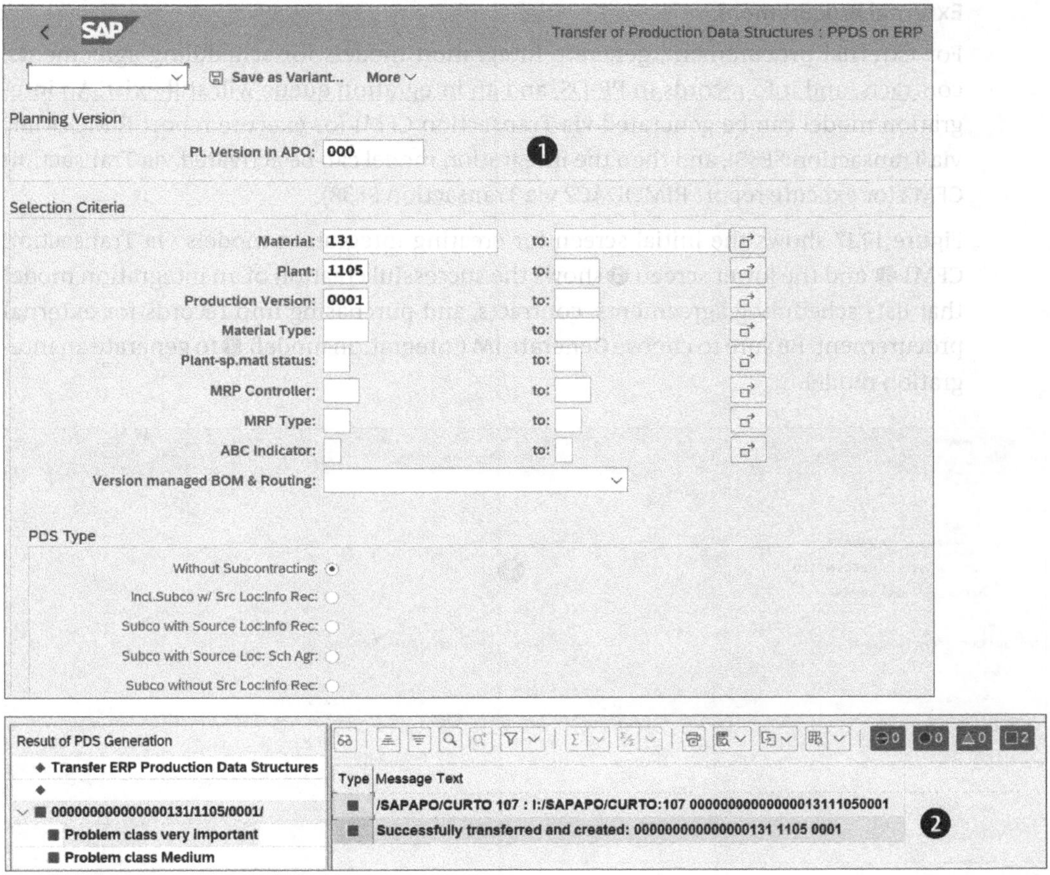

Figure 19.16 Product Data Structure

As shown, this transaction offers flexible selection criteria, allowing you to choose, for example, which materials or plants for the PDS will be generated. You can also choose between an **Absolute Transfer**, in which everything will be transferred, or **Change Transfer**, in which only the PDS for which the master data was changed since the last transfer will be transferred. Because PDS transfers are synchronous, the results are visible immediately after running the transaction. Any errors that may have occurred during the transfer are also revealed. Figure 19.16 ❷ shows the results screen of PDS generation for **Material** "131", **Plant** "1105", and **Production Version** "0001".

> **Note**
> Transaction CURTOADV_CREATE can also be used to generate the PDS. Use Transaction /SAPAPO/CURTO_SIMU to view PDS.

External Procurement

For external procurement, generate integration models for scheduling agreements, contracts, and info records in PP-DS, and an integration queue will still exist. An integration model can be generated via Transaction CFM1 (or execute report RIMODGEN via Transaction SE38), and then the integration model can be activated via Transaction CFM2 (or execute report RIMODAC2 via Transaction SE38).

Figure 19.17 shows the initial screen for creating integration models via Transaction CFM1 ❶, and the lower screen ❷ shows the successful creation of an integration model that lists scheduling agreements, contracts, and purchasing info records for external procurement. Be sure to choose **Generate IM** (integration model) ❷ to generate an integration model.

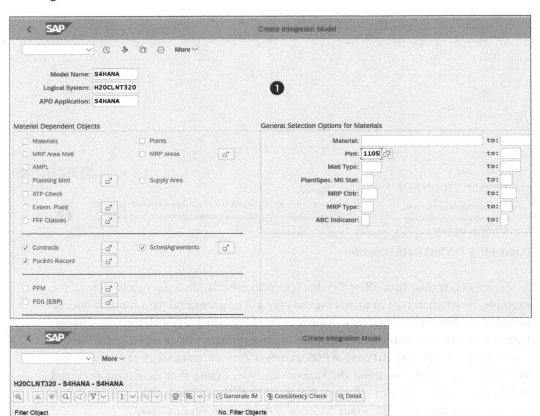

Figure 19.17 Creating Integration Model

After creating the integration model in Transaction CFM1, use Transaction CFM2 (see Figure 19.18) to activate the model.

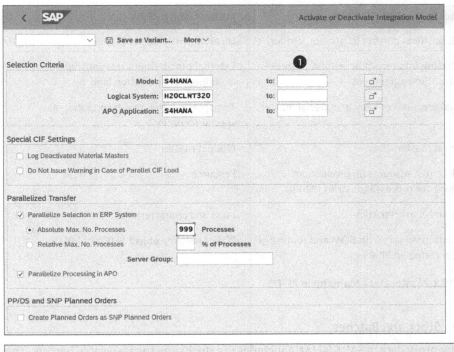

Figure 19.18 Activating or Deactivating Integration Model

> **Note**
>
> In addition to creating and activating the integration model, Transaction CFM4 can be used to display it. Transaction CFM5 can be used to search for the integration model that a particular master data object is part of. Transaction CFM7 is used to delete integration models.

[«]

> **Note**
>
> Due to the highly integrated nature of working between production and procurement, we recommend engaging an MM consultant to ensure that the necessary master data is correctly created for a correct and smooth planning and scheduling of procured materials that are planned through PP-DS.

[«]

Table 19.2 summarizes the master data mapping between SAP S/4HANA and PP-DS.

Master Data in SAP S/4HANA	Master Data in PP-DS
Plant, business partner (customer, vendor)	Location (with location type)
Purchasing info record, scheduling agreement, outline agreement	External procurement relationship, including transportation lane
Special procurement key in material master	Transport relation or interpretation as a special scenario
Material master	Product master
Work center, resource (in production planning for process industries [PP-PI])	Resource
Class and characteristics	Class and characteristics
Production version with BOM and routing or master recipe (in PP-PI)	PDS or runtime object (RTO), or PPM

Table 19.2 Master Data Mapping in PP-DS

19.2.5 Stock and Batches

The inventory data in SAP S/4HANA includes the stocks and the associated batches. The stock information is transferred to embedded PP-DS along with the batch information if the material is batch-managed. The stocks are maintained at the plant level, and for planning purposes the stock is considered at the MRP area level in SAP S/4HANA if an MRP area is assigned to the plant. The plant-level stock will be transferred as stock to the PP-DS plant location, and the stocks at the MRP area in SAP S/4HANA are transferred to the MRP area location in embedded PP-DS. The batches associated with the stock are transferred to embedded PP-DS; they are referred to as versions in the PP-DS planning tools. In embedded PP-DS, the stock update counters are activated by default and can't be turned off. The stock data transferred to embedded PP-DS uses the relative stocks, which refers to the delta between the current stock and the stock to be received or issued. The initial transfer of stock can be triggered by the CIF reconciliation tool (Transaction /SAPAPO/CCR) or the initial transfer report (Transaction /SAPAPO/PPDS_DELTA_ORD_TRANS). Whenever a stock posting happens in SAP S/4HANA, it's immediately transferred to embedded PP-DS, along with its batch and storage location information.

This brings an end to the discussion of PP-DS master data. In the following sections, we'll discuss the important business processes of PP-DS.

19.3 Business Processes

The PP-DS product view is the equivalent of an MRP transaction, the stock/requirements list (Transaction MD04), which we covered in Chapter 14, Section 14.2. The demand/supply situation for one specific product can be monitored in the product view. It's also possible to create different planning versions for simulation purposes.

To access the product view, use Transaction /SAPAPO/RRP3. In the popup that appears, asking you to enter a variant, simply enter a dummy number such as "1" and press [Enter]. The initial screen in Figure 19.19 shows the product view featuring the planning version (Plng Version), Product, and Location fields as the main selection fields. Enter the details as shown and click Continue.

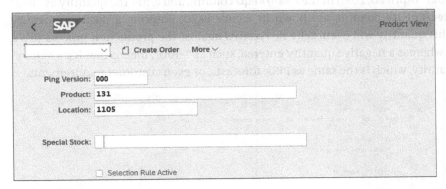

Figure 19.19 Product View

19

> **Note**
>
> Although this example is mostly focused on using the product view (Transaction /SAPAPO/RRP3), there are the following other available views:
>
> - Transaction /SAPAPO/RRP4: Receipts View
> - Transaction /SAPAPO/RRP1: Requirements View
> - Transaction /SAPAPO/RRP2: Order Processing
> - Transaction /SAPAPO/PCMT: Production Campaign
> - Transaction /SAPAPO/PPT1: Product Planning Table
> - Transaction /SAPAPO/POV1: Product Overview
> - Transaction /SAPAPO/PEG1: Pegging Overview
>
> As always, we encourage exploring these PP-DS views after reading the chapter.

Because the product view is an interactive planning transaction, options for making changes in the product planning version are available, such as the following:

- Generating a new forecast requirement
- Creating a new PP-DS planned order
- Executing the product heuristic
- Executing a variable heuristic
- Checking logs and alerts
- Changing the planning strategy

Choose the **Change** button in the top menu bar to enable data entry. When this button is clicked, the button will change to **Update**.

To start the planning activity in the product view, for example, enter the date as "20.04.2021" (April 20, 2021) in the **Avail/ReqD** column, and enter the quantity as "100" in the **Rec/RqtQty** column, as shown in Figure 19.20. Entering a positive quantity means this quantity will eventually be *received* against the production process (it's a receipt), whereas a negative quantity entered, such as "–100", means that it's a *requirement* quantity, which is the same as PIRs, forecasts, or even customer requirements.

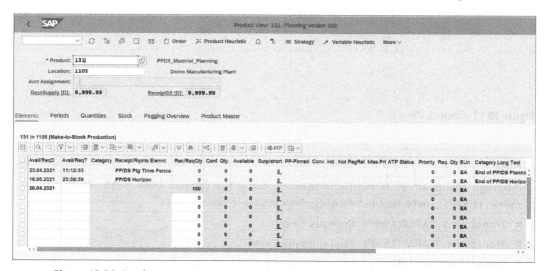

Figure 19.20 Product Master in PP-DS

As soon as a user selects the row with a quantity of 100 and performs another planning function, such as **ATP Check** or even selecting the **Conv. Ind.** (conversion indicator) checkbox, the system will create a relevant planning element—which in this case is a planned order number (**PlOrd. (F)**), **341**, as shown in Figure 19.21.

In Figure 19.21, either double-click the PP-DS planned order **341** or select the relevant line item, then click the **Context of an Order** icon located in the top menu bar so that the screen shown in Figure 19.22 appears.

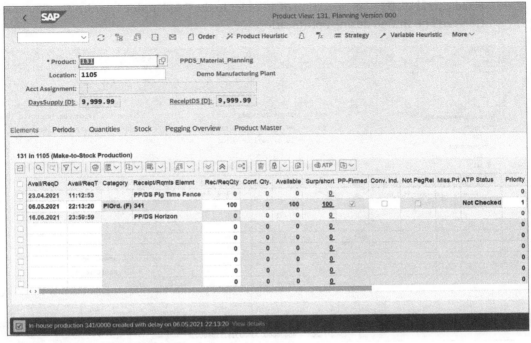

Figure 19.21 Planning Elements

[+]

Tips and Tricks

A user can always double-click any element in not just the product view but any view of PP-DS to navigate to the detailed view of the element. In other words, a user doesn't have to always select an element and click the **Context of an Order** icon; simply double-clicking will lead to a detailed screen.

Figure 19.22 shows order 341. the left-hand side of the screen shows the entire product structure, that is, the components 2 and 111 (which is the BOM for product 131) in the form of requirements, and the various operations, such as setup and produce. These operations are basically the routing of material 131, including the previously created PP-DS resource WPPDSWC_1105_001.

A user can firm individual orders manually. When a user changes orders manually, the associated firming flags are set automatically, and firming can be cancelled at any time. The **Output Firmed** checkbox prevents the quantities of an order from being changed during automatic planning. The status corresponds to freezing the order header of an SAP S/4HANA planned order. The **Input Firmed** checkbox freezes the dependent requirements of an order. The PDS can no longer be changed for this order. This status corresponds to the **Components** flag in the SAP S/4HANA planned order. The **Date**

Fixed checkbox fixes an operation of an order in the DS planning board. A fixed operation can't be shifted during optimization.

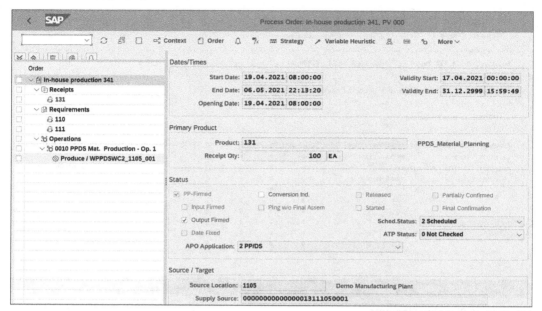

Figure 19.22 Detailed View of PP-DS Planned Order

Choose **Back** to return to the screen shown earlier in Figure 19.21. Other tabs in the product view, such as **Periods**, **Quantities**, **Forecast**, or **Pegging Overview**, will provide more detailed insight into the planning situation. Let's review these tabs one by one in detail.

Figure 19.23 shows the pegging structure of order 341 and how these elements are all interlinked through procurement and production processes. The PP-DS planned order 341 is automatically converted to SAP S/4HANA planned order 7154 (as shown at the top of the screen) because the planning results were saved, and that lead to an automatic creation of the planned order in SAP S/4HANA. As we'll show later, choosing **Conversion Ind.** will automatically convert this planned order into a production order.

Two purchase requisitions (**PurRqs**) are automatically created for external procurement of two corresponding components (materials 2 and 111). The details of these automatically created purchase requisitions can also be checked via Transaction ME53N.

Pegging involves a link that creates a logical relationship between the receipt elements and requirements elements of a product within a location. The system uses these pegging relationships to assign requirements to receipt elements. The links always result from availability and requirements dates within a pegging area, in which product, location, and account assignment (MTS or MTO, etc.) correspond to each other. Pegging involves an analysis that refers to existing orders and requirements. It occurs independently of requirements planning. The primary applications of pegging include the analysis of production planning, capacity planning, and optimization.

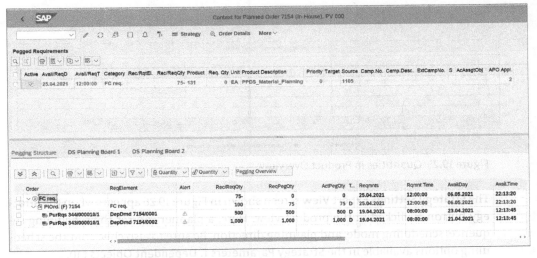

Figure 19.23 Pegging Structure in Product Overview

There are two types of pegging relationships: fixed and dynamic. Fixed pegging enables a planner to fix a pegging relationship that will not be changed automatically by the system. In dynamic pegging, the system attempts to adjust the dates and quantities to closely meet the production and the procurement plan.

For pegging relationships to be created, the product, location, account assignment (MTS and MTO production), and planning version must be the same.

Click **DS (Detailed Scheduling) Planning Board 2** on the screen shown in Figure 19.23 to open the screen showing the PP-DSWPPDSWC2_1105_001 PP-DS resource and the operations details of PP-DS planned order 7154 (Figure 19.24).

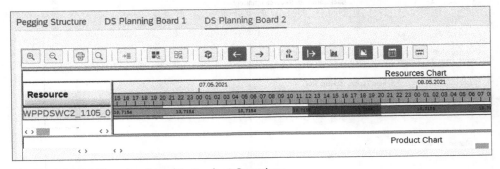

Figure 19.24 DS Planning Board in Product Overview

Figure 19.25 shows the **Quantities** tab of the product view of product 131 and plant 1105. Cumulated requirements and receipts along with available quantities are shown in a graphical representation.

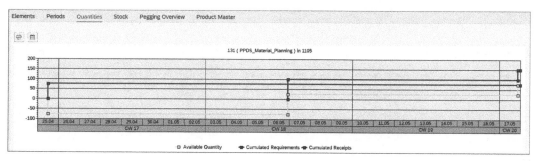

Figure 19.25 Quantities in Product Overview

The **Strategy Settings Expert View** screen shown in Figure 19.26 appears when the **Strategy** button is clicked in the product view. Here, a planner can set the scheduling sequence, scheduling mode, and planning direction. Be sure to also check out the scheduling options available in the **Strategy Parameters f. Dependent Objects** tab.

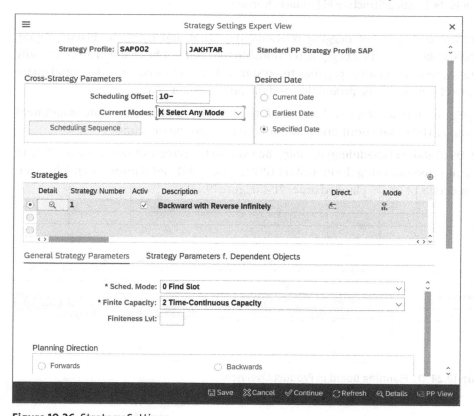

Figure 19.26 Strategy Settings

Figure 19.27 shows the **User Settings** details of a product view. Here, assign relevant profiles so that the system is able to perform necessary planning functions. Be sure to check out the tabs available in the user settings and maintain necessary information as required.

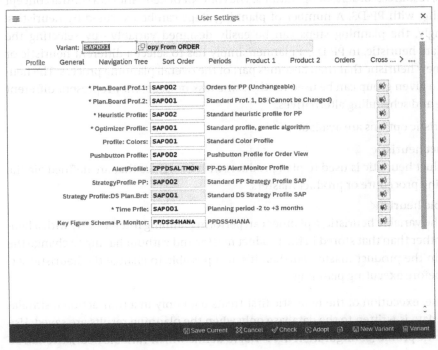

Figure 19.27 User Settings

Figure 19.28 appears when a planner clicks the **Display Logs** button in the product view. The maintained log keeps a record of all the planning activities performed and any information, warning, or error messages generated during the planning process. Refer to the **Logging** field shown in Figure 19.4 and choose the relevant option for how the system maintains logs of all the steps and activities performed.

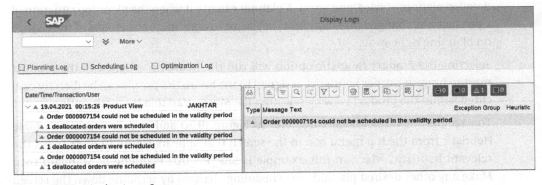

Figure 19.28 Display Logs Screen

19.4   Heuristics

A *heuristic* is a planning function that can be parameterized and used to execute planning or a planning step for selected objects. The planning objects of heuristics can be products, resources, orders, or operations. The concept of heuristics is a central concept in planning with PP-DS. A number of planning steps can be executed by heuristics. Accordingly, the planning steps can be easily designed variably—by selecting the appropriate heuristic. In PP-DS, a planner simply has to select a different heuristic or create a new heuristic that then becomes part of the overall planning process. The heuristics of a given group can be used for the same task or issue; they represent different planning and scheduling alternatives.

Two heuristic options are available:

- **Product heuristic**
  A product heuristic is used to plan products with heuristics that are defined via the planning procedure or product masters.

- **Variable heuristic**
  With the variable heuristic, a planner can perform planning interactively with a heuristic other than that stored in the product master and without having to change the entry in the product master. Further, it's also possible to change the heuristic settings before executing planning.

In any case, execution of the heuristic first treats data only in a transactional simulation. The data is written to the database only when the planning results are saved. Use the heuristic profile (configuration in PP-DS) to define which variable heuristics can be selected. Three standard heuristic profiles are available:

- Profile SAP001 for the detailed planning board
- Profile SAP002 for the product view
- Profile SAPREM for the product planning table

With interactive heuristic planning, a planner executes planning for a product. This function can also be performed from the product view, the product planning board, the detailed planning board, and so on. A planner can use it when the planning situation of a product was changed manually and they want to determine the effects of the change on planning right away.

Selecting the **Product Heuristic** option will run the heuristic assigned to the product master; however, other heuristics assigned to the heuristics profile can be directly executed within the product view by selecting the **More · Variable Heuristic** option.

To execute the variable heuristic, refer to Figure 19.20 and choose **Execute Variable Heuristic** from the top menu bar. In the screen that appears Figure 19.29 ❶, select the relevant heuristic, which in this example is **SAP_PP_002 Planning of Standard Lots**. Make any other desired planning or scheduling changes by scrolling down the screen and choosing relevant options. In addition, to cross-check which materials are being planned via a heuristic, click the **Products** tab. Next, click the **Heuristics** button from the top menu bar to see the heuristic results ❷.

As already mentioned, product heuristics define the planning of a product. They can be entered explicitly in the PP-DS tab in the product master. If no entry is present in the product master, the standard heuristic of the planning procedure is used.

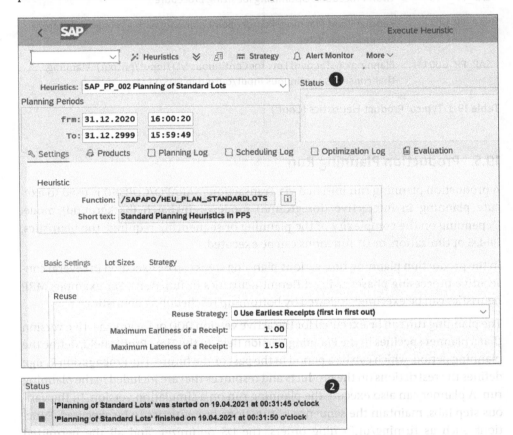

Figure 19.29 Executing Variable Heuristic in PP-DS

Table 19.3 lists some typical product heuristics.

Heuristic	Short Description
SAP_PP_002	Planning of Standard Lots: "Normal" planning of the product based on the lot size stored in the product master
SAP_PP_003	Planning of shortage quantities: Planning only of shortage quantities; existing orders remain as is; relevant for capable to promise (CTP)

Table 19.3 Typical Product Heuristics

Heuristic	Short Description
SAP_PP_004	Planning of standard lots in three horizons: Planning with various lot sizes in three time horizons
SAP_PP_005	Part-Period Balancing: Optimizing lot sizing procedure
SAP_PP_013	Groff Procedure: Optimizing lot sizing procedure
SAP_PP_007	Reorder Point Planning: Reorder point planning with a reorder point from the product master
SAP_PP_C001	Planning of Standard Lots for Continuous I/O (input/output): Planning that considers continuous input/output in PDS/PPM

Table 19.3 Typical Product Heuristics (Cont.)

19.5   Production Planning Run

A production planning run initiated via Transaction /SAPAPO/CDPSB0 is used to execute planning in interactive (foreground) mode or in batch (background) mode. Depending on the complexity of the planning or sequencing required, the heuristics, PP-DS optimization, or DS functions can be executed.

In the production planning run, various planning steps can be executed in several consecutive processing phases using different heuristics or functions. For example, MRP heuristics can be executed, followed by bottom-up rescheduling heuristics.

The planning run can be executed for the active version 000 or for any inactive version that a planner specifies in the **Planning Version** field. In the **Time Profile** field, define the planning period, which can be a period in the past or the future. The **Propagation Range** defines the restrictions on the products and resources that are included in the planning run. A planner can also execute the planning run on a simulation version. In the various step tabs, maintain the sequence of functions or heuristics to be executed. Functions such as firming/unfirming orders, the DS optimizer, and all the permitted heuristics can be selected. Based on the functions or heuristics you select, the relevant products and resources are controlled. For example, if you select the schedule sequence heuristic, then the system is forced to use resources or order selections instead of products when applying the heuristic (see Figure 19.30).

The results of the planning run can be analyzed immediately and examined interactively by selecting the **Display Logs** checkbox in the selection screen.

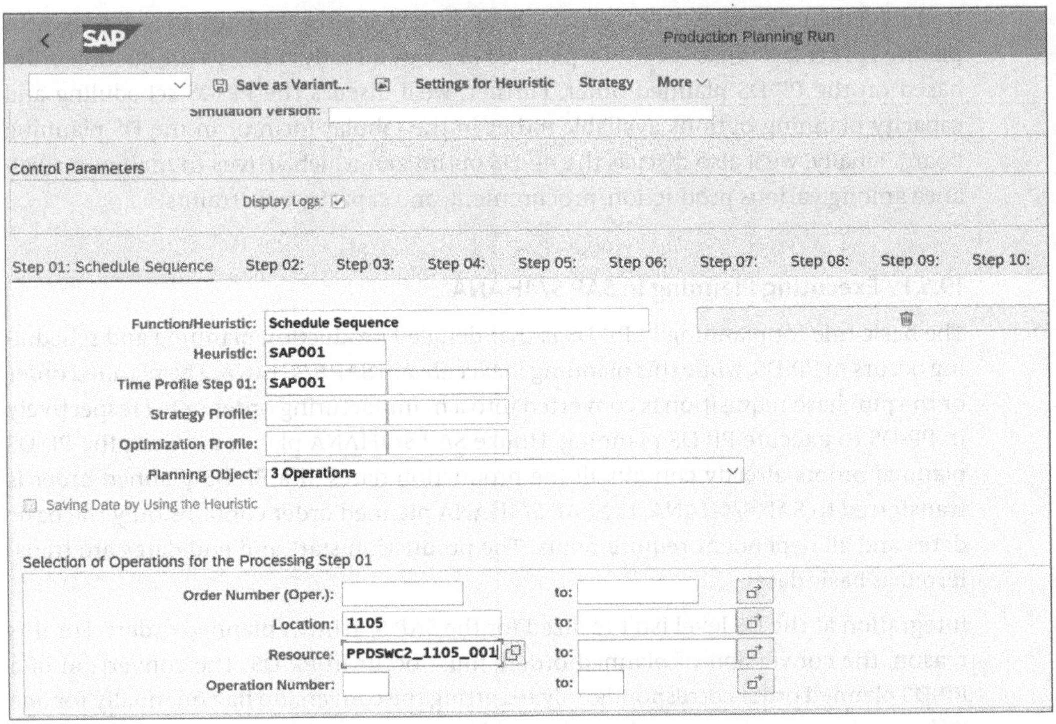

Figure 19.30 Planning Several Heuristics

[+] **Tips and Tricks**

After the planning run has been executed in interactive mode or in background processing, the logs are stored and can be analyzed in evaluation transactions, such as Transaction /SAPAPO/RRPLOG1. The selection variants saved in the PP-DS production planning run can be used in a background planning run executed via Transaction /SAPAPO/CDPSB1.

[«] **Note**

Heuristic SAP_PP_002 (Planning of Standard Lots) is particularly important and corresponds to the normal planning of a product with the use of the lot size defined in the product master. It's the standard heuristic in planning procedure 111 (Planning in the Planning Run) and therefore represents the normal case for product planning. In heuristic SAP_PP_002, you can set a reuse mode (e.g., for new planning or change planning). If nothing is specified, the reuse mode from the planning file is used. Normal planning of a product with the lot sizes defined in the product master occurs with heuristic SAP_PP_002.

In the following sections, we'll discuss how MRP Live either creates an SAP S/4HANA planned order that links the PP-DS planned order or directly creates a production order based on the PP-DS planned order. Further, we'll discuss the PP-DS scheduling and capacity planning options available either in the tabular form or in the DS planning board. Finally, we'll also discuss the PP-DS optimizer, which strives to maintain a balance among various production, procurement, and capacity constraints.

19.5.1   Executing Planning in SAP S/4HANA

The basic rule for planning in PP-DS is that detailed production planning and scheduling occurs in PP-DS, while this planning is *executed* in SAP S/4HANA. The planned order or the purchase requisition is converted into a manufacturing order or PO respectively in PP-DS to execute PP-DS planning. Unlike SAP S/4HANA planned orders, the PP-DS planned orders already contain all the production dates. If a PP-DS planned order is transferred to SAP S/4HANA, the SAP S/4HANA planned order contains only the basic dates and all dependent requirements. The production start and end dates are transferred as basic dates.

Integration at the DS level isn't realized for the SAP S/4HANA planned orders. For this reason, the conversion of planned orders must occur in PP-DS. The conversion of a PP-DS planned order corresponds only to setting the conversion flag (manually for one order or via mass conversion for orders and purchase requisitions). If a PP-DS planned order with the conversion flag is transferred to SAP S/4HANA, a corresponding manufacturing order is created in SAP S/4HANA. The SAP S/4HANA planned order assumes the production dates determined in the PP-DS planned order. The integration of the orders is maintained.

Status information or production confirmations that are created in SAP S/4HANA and are relevant to planning are transferred from SAP S/4HANA to the PP-DS order. All data relevant to planning must remain consistent. In addition, the SAP S/4HANA production order also contains a variety of functions to execute production—functions that don't require integration with the PP-DS order, such as printing of order papers and consumption.

We've now covered the PP-DS side of the product view of product 131 and the receipt quantity of 100. The next step is to run MRP Live (Transaction MD01N) and see how the planning results for product 131 from PP-DS transfer to creating a planned order in SAP S/4HANA so that it can be converted into a production order.

Figure 19.31 shows the MRP results from MRP Live (Transaction MD01N). After the planning run, the performance log is displayed, showing information about the number of materials planned, the number of materials with errors, and the time spent in each step.

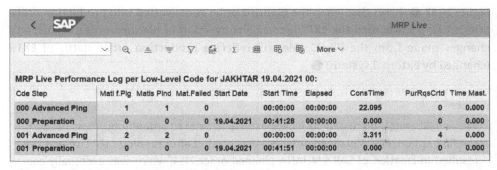

Figure 19.31 Results of MRP Live for PP-DS Material

Tips and Tricks

The standard system lacks the option to plan only PP-DS materials or to exclude PP-DS materials from the planning run. However, an ABAP programmer can be engaged to create an implementation of the MRP_DISPATCHER_BADI Business Add-In (BAdI) to bring additional selection fields into the MRP Live selection screen. We can add, for example, the MRP type as a selection criterion and filter for materials with MRP type X0.

Access the **Stock/Requirements List** screen shown in Figure 19.32 ❶ via Transaction MD04, and you'll see that the system created planned order 7154 for a quantity of 100.

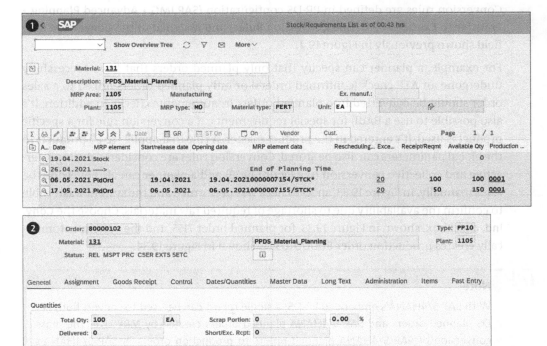

Figure 19.32 PP-DS Production Order after Running MRP Live

Figure 19.32 ❶ shows that when the planned order is converted into production order 80000102, it's accorded the **EXPL** (external conversion of planned order) status; any changes made from the PP-DS side will reflect a production order status of **EXTS** (changed by external system) ❷.

[»]

Note

We've deliberately discussed both options here to cater to different business needs. In the first option, PP-DS planned order 341 was created after running MRP Live and this resulted in creation of SAP S/4HANA planned order 7154, which was eventually converted into production order 80000102. The second option entails automatic and direct creation of an SAP S/4HANA production order as soon as a PP-DS planned order is assigned a conversion indicator (the settings are controlled via PP-DS configuration). Refer to the control functions available for the **Transfer to R/3 In-House Production** field in Figure 19.4.

19.5.2   Conversion of PP-DS Planned Orders

It's also possible to use a conversion rule to define which planned orders should be converted into manufacturing orders. During a collective conversion of planned orders using Transaction /SAPAPO/RRP7 (Conversion of Orders and Purchase Requisitions), the conversion rule lets a planner convert only specific orders into production orders. Conversion rules are defined in PP-DS configuration (**SAP IMG • Advanced Planning • Transfer to Execution • Define Conversion Rules**) and assigned in the **Conversion Rule** field shown previously in Figure 19.4.

For example, a planner can specify that only planned orders that have successfully undergone an ATP check (confirmed orders) or only planned orders linked to a sales order should be converted into planned orders (requirements check). In addition, it's also possible to use a BAdI) for special requirements. If a conversion rule for a specific product is used, it's entered in the product master. A rule that applies to all products in the global parameters can also be stored. Conversion rules are considered during interactive and collective conversion (see Figure 19.33) and a planner can also override the rules manually. In Figure 19.33, an ATP check was performed and the system wasn't able to confirm the availability due to shortage of required raw materials. Choose the **Conv. Ind.** checkbox, shown in Figure 19.33, for planned order 7155, and the system automatically creates production order 80000103, as shown in Figure 19.34.

[»]

Note

With SAP S/4HANA's embedded PP-DS, a single report can be used to convert both PP-DS planned orders and SAP S/4HANA planned orders created by MRP Live. The mass conversion of SAP S/4HANA planned orders to production orders in SAP S/4HANA's embedded PP-DS can be executed using report /SAPAPO/PROD_ORDER_CONVERT, while mass processing of converted orders is executed by report /SAPAPO/PROC_ ORDER_CONVERT via Transaction SE38.

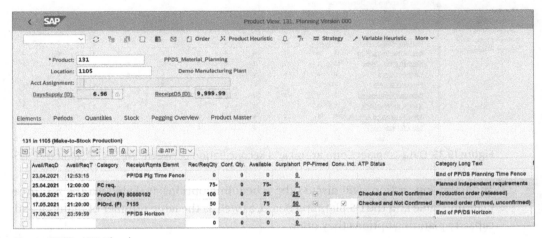

Figure 19.33 ATP Check

Avail/ReqD	Avail/ReqT	Category	Receipt/Rqmts Elemnt	Rec/ReqQty	Conf. Qty.	Available	Surp/short	PP-Firmed	Conv. Ind.	Not PegRel	Miss.Prt
23.04.2021	12:56:47		PP/DS Plg Time Fence	0	0	0	0				
25.04.2021	12:00:00	FC req.		75-	0	75-	0				☐
06.05.2021	22:13:20	PrdOrd (R)	80000102	100	0	25	25	✓			☐
17.05.2021	21:20:00	PrdOrd (C)	80000103	50	0	75	50	✓			☐
17.06.2021	23:59:59		PP/DS Horizon	0	0	0	0				
				0	0	0	0				

131 in 1105 (Make-to-Stock Production)

Elements | Periods | Quantities | Stock | Pegging Overview | Product Master

Figure 19.34 Interactive Conversion of Planned Order into Manufacturing Order

Tips and Tricks

To resolve such a transactional data inconsistency between SAP S/4HANA and PP-DS, use Transaction /SAPAPO/CCR (CIF Comparison/Reconciliation Function).

Figure 19.35 shows the differences between the numbers of various elements, such as manufacturing orders or purchase requisitions, that exist between SAP S/4HANA and PP-DS. For example, four **Purchase Requisitions** don't exist in SAP S/4HANA (**Not in R/3**). To transfer the data between SAP S/4HANA and PP-DS, select the **Purchase Requisitions** folder from the left-hand side of the screen so that a complete list of purchase requisitions appears. Then, select all the purchase requisitions, and click the relevant icon (→**APO** or ←**R/3**) to transfer elements to the relevant systems (either SAP S/4HANA or PP-DS).

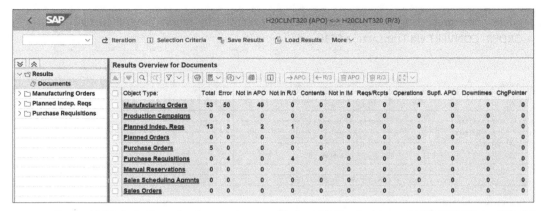

Figure 19.35 Data Transfer Comparison and Reconciliation between SAP S/4HANA and PP-DS

The following sections will discuss the scheduling options available via the resource planning table and the DS planning board, as well as the large number of material and capacity planning options they offer.

Scheduling in Production Planning-Detailed Scheduling

DS in PP-DS helps a planner schedule order operations while considering constraints such as material and resource availability. The basic functions of the scheduling tools are to schedule, reschedule, and deallocate operations. Other parameters, such as scheduling direction (forward/backward) and order relationships, also can be used to influence DS behavior. DS can be performed interactively from the scheduling tools or can be executed in the planning run as a step.

Scheduling via the Resource Planning Table

A resource planning table is an alternative to the DS planning board that displays scheduling data in tabular format. A resource planning table can be used to handle sequencing or scheduling problems on resources. The selection screen for data to be included in the resource planning table is similar to the selection screen for the DS planning board. Additional tools, such as the alert monitor, plan monitor, and the PP-DS optimizer, are integrated into resource planning tables, as shown in Figure 19.36. A clipboard function is available in the resource planning table so a planner can copy a list of operations and sequence and schedule them on the resource. Operations and activities can be interactively sequenced using drag-and-drop or pick-and-drop options. The scheduling heuristic assigned to the heuristics profile used in the resource planning table enables a planner to execute the scheduling heuristic. Planning multiple resources or bucket resources isn't supported by the resource planning table. However, **Alert Monitor** and **Plan Monitor** functions are available in the resource planning table.

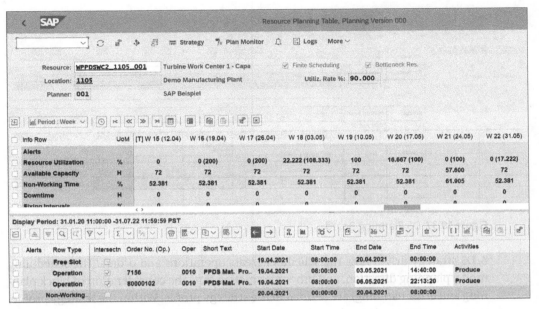

Figure 19.36 Resource Planning Table

Detailed Scheduling Planning Board

The DS planning board is a widely used scheduling tool in PP-DS. From the DS planning board, all scheduling options, including executing various DS heuristics, the PP-DS optimizer, and manual scheduling, are possible. DS is launched with a time profile that determines the time period during which data is displayed (**Display Start** and **End of Display** fields) and the data is available for DS (**Planning Start** and **Planning End** fields).

A planner can manually select resources, products, and orders via Transaction /SAPAPO/CDPS0 (see Figure 19.37). In the DS planning board, graphical objects represent the different statuses of the scheduling of the planning objects, such as orders and operations. A work area can also be used to determine the resources and products and is defined in Transaction /SAPAPO/CDPSC3.

The user settings and the DS planning board profile settings determine the charts displayed in the DS planning board and also the availability and behavior of the scheduling and monitoring tools loaded into the DS planning board. Apart from the charts within the DS planning board, such as the **Resources Chart**, the **Product Chart**, and the **Product Stock**, there is a graphical representation of the network view of the orders, as well as the pegging relationships among activities, operations, and orders (see Figure 19.37). On this screen, notice that a planner can **Reschedule** and **Deallocate** operations in similar ways as in capacity requirements planning (CRP) in SAP S/4HANA (Transactions CM21 and CM25), as we covered in Chapter 18.

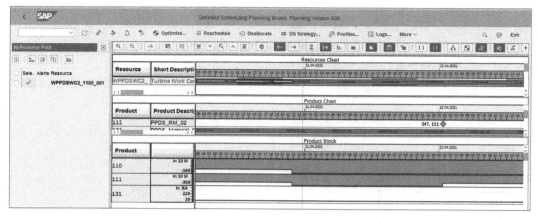

Figure 19.37 DS Planning Board

A DS strategy drives how the scheduler treats operations and orders. The scheduling mode, planning direction, and other parameters (e.g., the consideration of block planning and error handling) are defined in the strategy profile. Within the strategy profile, the parameters for dependent objects (the orders and operations that depend on other objects scheduled within the DS planning board) are also defined, as shown in Figure 19.38.

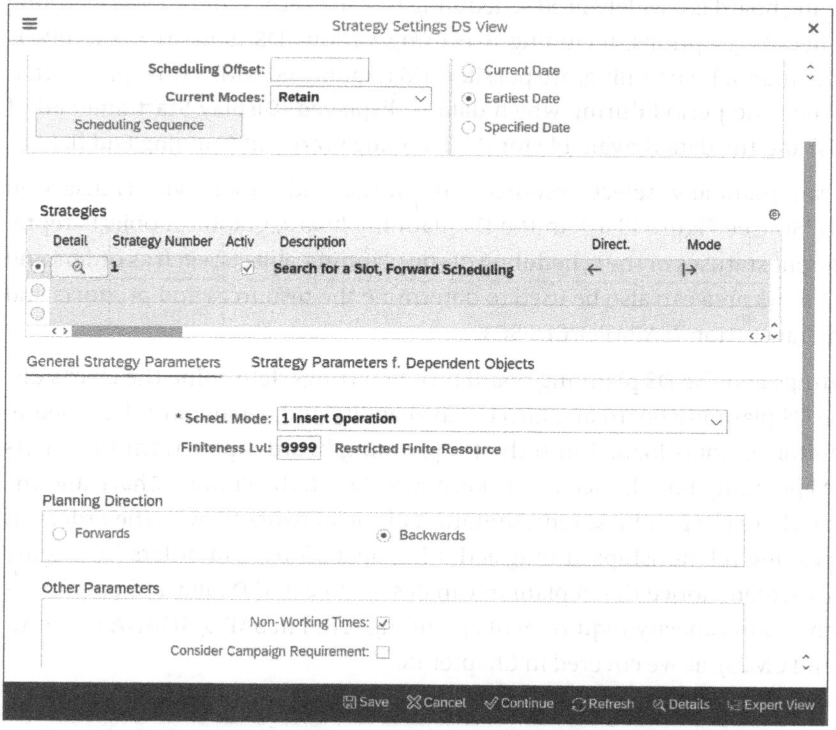

Figure 19.38 Strategy Settings

Tips and Tricks

When launching the DS planning board, the system generates a simulation version by copying the planning data from the current version. As a result, a planner can simulate multiple scheduling options; after a desirable scheduling situation is achieved, can then save the data to the current planning version. Simulation versions can be accessed via Transaction /SAPAPO/CDPSS0. These simulation versions can be processed further in both graphical and tabular options and can also be adopted into the active version.

19.5.3 Production Planning-Detailed Scheduling Optimizer

The PP-DS optimizer has specific properties that distinguish it significantly from the calculation procedure of heuristics. Solving complex scheduling problems requires consideration of several constraints that the PP-DS optimizer is able to address. The effort needed to find an exact solution to the problem increases with the number of possible permutations. To put it more exactly, the effort needed increases by the factorial of the orders to be planned. In this case, even a small, two-digit number of orders to be planned would require hundreds of years of computer time to find an exact analytical solution. Therefore, the PP-DS optimizer uses selective procedures that lead to realistic computing times (in minutes)—but without a guarantee that the absolute optimum solution for the problem has been found. From the set of possible solutions, it's very likely that some solutions are found by the PP-DS optimizer, but not all of them. In comparison, a heuristic leads to exactly one solution. Using the same constraints, several optimization runs can produce different results. Based on these properties, it's clear that the computing time entered by the user as a termination criterion for the optimization run is extremely important. In general, the higher the amount of computing time, the higher the quality of the solution. However, the reverse isn't always true: more computing time doesn't guarantee the improvement of a solution that has already been found.

The PP-DS optimizer isn't called as an independent transaction; instead, it's called from within corresponding applications. It can be called interactively in the DS planning board or product planning table (Transaction /SAPAPO/PPT1). The PP-DS optimizer can also be run with specification of an optimization profile in the production planning run. The PP-DS optimizer in embedded PP-DS can't create orders, but other functionalities are supported. The PP-DS optimizer can be executed in the background in a production planning run (Transaction /SAPAPO/CDPSB1) or via interactive scheduling tools such as the DS planning board (refer to Figure 19.37).

To use the PP-DS optimizer, click **Optimize** on the screen shown in Figure 19.37. In the ensuing popup, enter the start and end dates of optimization horizon, and choose **Optimize** again to open the **PP-DS Optimizer** screen shown in Figure 19.39.

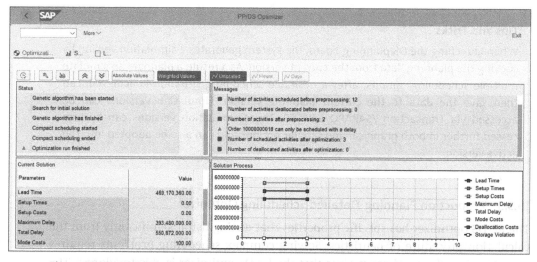

Figure 19.39 PP-DS Optimization Log

Before we discuss Figure 19.39 in detail, choose the **Optimization profile** icon (wrench) at the top of the screen to bring up the **Settings** box shown in Figure 19.40. Here, different information, such as the total setup costs, the maximum delay costs, or the total mode costs, can be maintained in relative terms. Various optimization settings can also be made in different tabs.

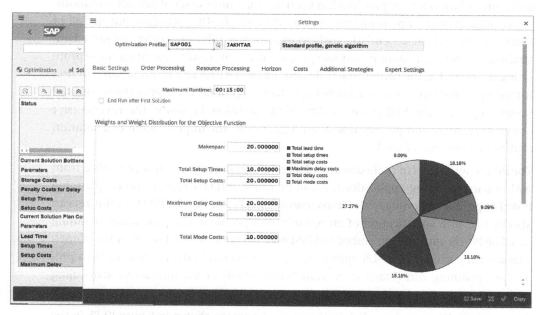

Figure 19.40 PP-DS Optimization Profile

Select basic settings for the PP-DS optimizer through the optimization profile, by customizing the DS planning board or the product planning table, or using Transaction /SAPAPO/CDPSC5. When a planner starts the PP-DS optimizer, it's possible can adjust or change some of these basic settings based on the current planning situation (see Figure 19.40).

The PP-DS optimizer works based on costs, and therefore the objective of optimization is to minimize the overall production costs. This cost reduction is achieved with an *objective function* made up of individually weighted key figures. Use the following weighting factors (Wi, where i = 1...6) to influence the orientation of optimization:

Production costs = (W_1 × Makespan) + (W2 × Total of the setup times) + (W3 × Total of the setup costs) + (W4 × Maximum delay costs) + (W5 × Total of the delay costs) + (W6 × Total of the mode costs)

Now let's discuss the fields shown in Figure 19.40.

- **Makespan**
  Minimizing the *makespan*, or the overall lead time, aims at a maximum load on the optimized bottleneck resources in the short term. The system attempts to minimize the overall time needed to process orders and operations with consideration of the existing constraints.

- **Total Setup Times**
  Minimizing the total of the setup times is possible if the time needed to set up from one setup status to the next is dependent on exactly that sequence (setup-status-dependent setup time with *dynamic setup*). In a paint shop, for example, the time required to set up from a dark color to a light one is likely longer than in the opposite direction. In such cases and in similar cases, an optimization objective can be to create an optimal sequence from the standpoint of the total of the required setup times. The result is that the system summarizes the operations of similar setup statuses into blocks. Long setup times would then appear only when changing between two different setup statuses.

- **Total Setup Costs**
  Minimizing the total of the *setup costs* is necessary only when the system needs to have the costs and setup times described independently of each other. This can be the case when identical setup times differ for various resources in terms of cost-related evaluation and must therefore be decoupled from the setup time. Otherwise, the setup time criterion is sufficient.

- **Maximum Delay Costs**
  The PP-DS optimizer can penalize *delays* that occur in terms of the defined requirements date/time that lie within the optimization horizon with delay costs. Two approaches are available:

- Permit short delays in similar forms, which will help you avoid individual, significant delays, resulting in a minimization of the maximum delay costs.
- Formulate the total of the delays as a target value and calculate a minimum value across the overall delay for all orders. This approach doesn't exclude individual, obvious delays. In general, you can define delay costs as dependent on the order priority; you would use higher costs for sales orders with a higher priority. This approach should help to avoid delays for high-priority orders.

■ **Total Delay Costs**
This is the cost of delayed production and enables planners to decide which materials need to be produced first so as to minimize the associated costs.

■ **Total Mode Costs**
Mode costs penalize the frequent (via fixed costs) and long-lasting (as defined with variable costs) use of alternative work centers. The alternative work centers must already be available in the system in master data and contained in the propagation range. You can link them to optimization via *alternative modes*.

■ **Trade-offs**
It should be obvious that optimization usually works within somewhat contradictory constraints and different interests, such as sales interests and production interests. This is referred to as a *trade-off*.

It's also clear that the influencing factors have somewhat different natures (costs and times) and therefore possess different physical units. To enable a comparison of the individual totals within the formula for calculating the production costs, costs are converted into times. The following rule applies here: a standardized cost of 30 corresponds to 30 seconds.

Referring to Figure 19.39 again, note the information about the quality of the solution that has been found both during and after successful optimization. The three charts shown here display information on the status of the optimization messages, the values of the related optimization parameters (including deallocation costs), and the solution process over time in a graphic. From this evaluation view, use a button to view the parameters of the optimization and to change the parameters set by the optimization profile to some extent, as well as to start optimization (or restart it) interactively.

To start the PP-DS optimizer, click the **Start Optimization Run** icon (the clock or the execute icon) at the top left-hand side of Figure 19.39, and the system will start generating messages as shown at the top-right-hand side of the screen. Notice that the optimization run shows that order 10000000018 can only be scheduled with a delay. The two bottom-half sections show the numerical and the weighted values of the optimized solution. Click the **Disp. Solution** tab located at the top-left-hand side of Figure 19.39 to open the results screen shown in Figure 19.41.

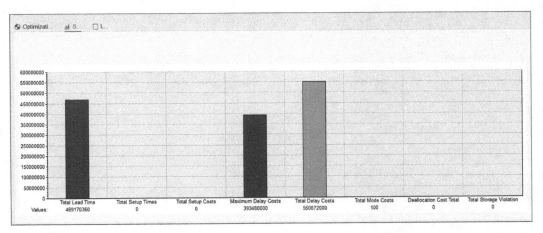

Figure 19.41 PP-DS Optimizer Results

Figure 19.41 shows the graphical representation of the results of the PP-DS optimization run and the associated total delay costs (the tallest bar) due to a delayed start of the order. It's possible to carry out more optimization runs if needed. Alternatively, make changes to the settings shown in Figure 19.40 and then rerun the PP-DS optimizer.

Next, in the following sections, we'll cover some of the PP-DS reporting tools, including SAP Fiori apps.

19.6   Reporting and Monitoring Apps

Scheduling reports for PP-DS orders, operations, and resources can be accessed from Transaction /SAPAPO/CDPS_REPT. In these reports, the selection criteria are globally restricted by the planning version, time profile, or evaluation start and end dates. Based on the type of evaluation selected, a planner may be prompted to define more filters—for example, if choosing **Resource Utilization** in the **Evaluation List** area (see Figure 19.42) will prompt the planner to make further selections for resources, periods, and views in the **Resource and Period Selection** dialog box, shown on the right-hand side of the screen.

Figure 19.43 shows the month-wise capacity availability and its utilization of resource WPPDSWC2_1105_001.

Figure 19.44 shows the web UI of the resourcing planning table that a planner can user to interactively plan resources. The relevant transaction is /SAPAPO/RPT.

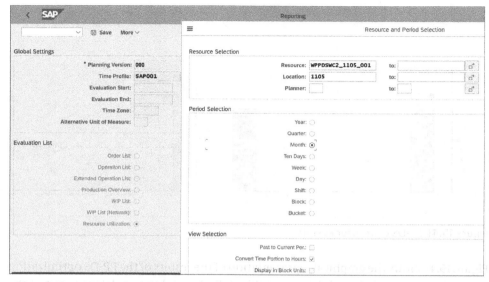

Figure 19.42 Parameters Selection Screens of Reporting

Figure 19.43 PP-DS Reporting

Figure 19.44 Resource Planning Table

In the following sections, we'll discuss three SAP Fiori apps of PP-DS—two of which are relevant to the production and capacity planning, while the third helps with an efficient procurement process.

19.6.1 Production Scheduling Board

The Production Scheduling Board app is not only a report but also an interactive planning app that lists capacity requirements for each resource and where changes to the operations schedule can be performed interactively. Figure 19.45 shows all the operations assigned to resource WPPDSWC2_1105_001 within the time frame defined by the time profile. The time profile defines the start and end dates for the planning and display periods. The two dropdowns, **Scheduling** and **Order**, enable interactive production planning, scheduling, and operations management.

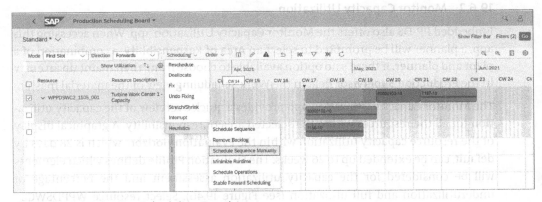

Figure 19.45 Production Scheduling Board App

Within the Production Scheduling Board app, a planner can drag and drop operations to achieve the desired scheduling, or simply run a PP-DS heuristic and let the system automatically optimize the operation scheduling. The following heuristics are supported within the SAP Fiori app:

- SAP001—Schedule Sequence
- SAP002—Remove Backlog
- SAP003—Schedule Sequence Manually

- SAP004—Minimize Runtime
- SAP005—Schedule Operations
- SAP_DS_01—Stable Forward Scheduling
- SAP_DS_02—Enhanced Backward Scheduling
- SAP_DS_03—Change Fixing/Planning Intervals
- SAP_DS_04—Activate Seq.-Dependent Setup Activities

Within the SAP Fiori app, a planner can also create (using a template), change, or delete orders; check logs/alerts; and adopt, save, or reset results. However, campaign planning, block planning, creating downtimes, and fixing intervals aren't supported within the Production Scheduling Board app.

19.6.2 Monitor Capacity Utilization

Embedded PP-DS also offers the Monitor Capacity Utilization app. When accessing this app, a planner will be prompted to select an **Area of Responsibility**, a combination of a plant and planner. If there's no option available to choose from, then maintain an entry in the **Production Supervisor** field in the **Work Scheduling** view of the material master.

The Monitor Capacity Utilization app provides a quick overview of the capacity utilization for all the resources within the selected area of responsibility. A graphical display of the resource capacity utilization within the **Evaluation Horizon**, which is 28 days by default, can be extended up to 26 weeks. The **Evaluation Profile** defines which elements will be considered for the capacity utilization assessment and the percentage of underutilization and full utilization (see Figure 19.46). Select resource WPPDSWC2_1105_001 in Figure 19.46, and click the **Navigation** icon located on the far right-hand side of the screen.

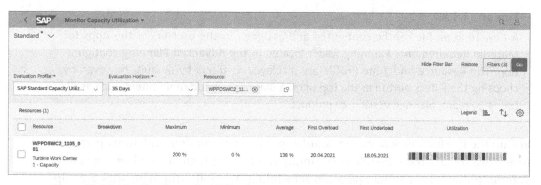

Figure 19.46 Monitor Capacity Utilization App - 1

> **Note**
>
> This area of responsibility isn't the same as the one defined for MRP SAP Fiori apps, and the planner here isn't the same as the MRP controller. This planner is assigned to a PP-DS resource.

The detailed screen appears for resource WPPDS2_WC_1105_001 in a graphical form (Figure 19.47). Notice the **Operation Issues** column, showing scheduling or material availability (missing parts) alerts (see Figure 19.48). Further, clicking **Edit** at the top right-hand side of the **Capacity Utilization** screen will enable a planner to manually adjust the operation dates and other details of an individual order.

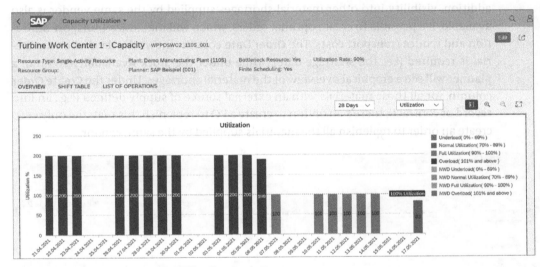

Figure 19.47 Monitor Capacity Utilization App - 2

OVERVIEW | SHIFT TABLE | LIST OF OPERATIONS

List of Operations (5) | Find Slot | Forwards | Search

Order	Operation Number	Product	Start Date	End Date	Planning Status	Pegged Requirement	Operation Quantity	Operation Issues
80000102	10	131 PPDS_Material_Planning	Today 08:00 AM	06.05.2021 10:13 PM	Deallocated, Released		100.00 EA	
7156	10	131 PPDS_Material_Planning	Today 08:00 AM	03.05.2021 02:40 PM	Deallocated	Orders	75.00 EA	
80000104	10	131 PPDS_Material_Planning	In 1 day 09:46 AM	07.05.2021 11:59 PM	Deallocated, Released		100.00 EA	
80000105	10	131 PPDS_Material_Planning	In 1 day 09:46 AM	07.05.2021 11:59 PM	Deallocated, Released		100.00 EA	

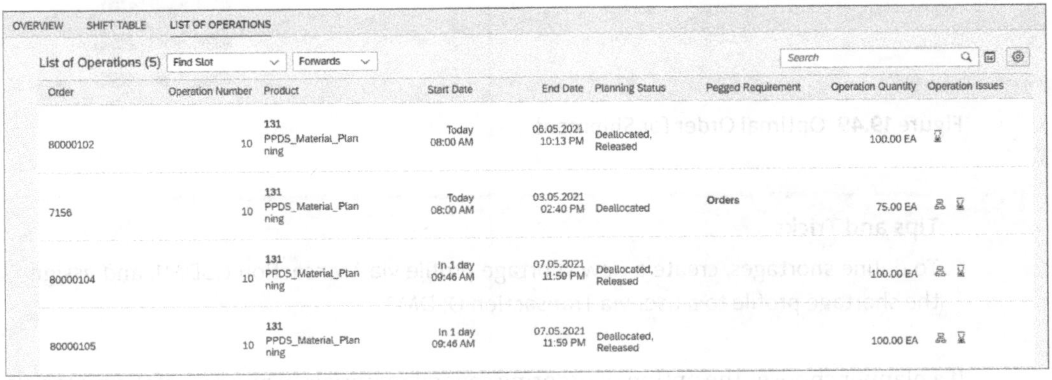

Figure 19.48 Operations in Monitor Capacity Planning App

Tips and Tricks

It's possible to configure a new evaluation profile and assign the profile to a user under the **Apps for Material Requirements Planning** folder in the **Advanced Planning** configuration.

19.6.3   Create Optimal Orders for Shipment

Recall that in the beginning of this chapter, material/product 131 included a few externally procured components. The Create Optimal Orders for Shipment app can be used to identify shortages and to generate POs to cover these shortages (see Figure 19.49). In addition, visibility into other material shortages supplied by the same vendor is also available. It's possible to create optimal orders, which will maximize transport utilization and reduce transport costs. The **Order Date** column shows the date when a material is required (i.e., the shortage date), while under the **Stock Availability** column, a planner will see a graphical overview of the material shortages. Under the **Create Order** column, for all those materials with an external source of supply defined (e.g., an info record or contract), there's an option to create a PO to replenish this material only or to create an order to replenish all the materials supplied by the same vendor.

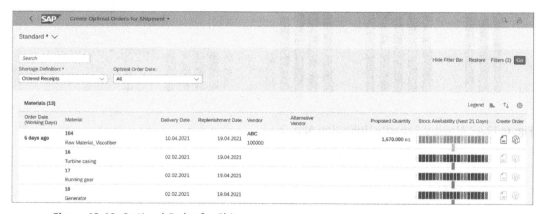

Figure 19.49 Optimal Order for Shipment

Tips and Tricks

To define shortages, create a new shortage profile via Transaction OSDM1, and assign the shortage profile to a user via Transaction OSDM2.

If a planner chooses the option of ordering several materials in any one of the materials with shortage, a screen will appear showing all the materials with shortages that are supplied by the same vendor. On this screen, define a capacity limit for the shipment.

Then, after you click the **Propose Quantities** button in the lower-right corner, the system will propose replenishment quantities, trying to clear the shortages while respecting the capacity limits.

The next section discusses the alert monitor in PP-DS.

19.7 Alert Monitor

The alert monitor in PP-DS is a tool that a planner can use during planning to manage and evaluate exception messages centrally. Messages about problems are transferred automatically from the application to the alert monitor. Each exception message relates to a specific problem situation. The primary task of the alert monitor is to list exception messages in a structured manner. The messages correspond to the defined selection criteria. The alert monitor provides information on situations that require adjustments in planning. Note the distinction between the reason for the exception and its properties. Using exception messages, the alert monitor can provide general information on the problem situation itself but not necessarily on why the exception occurred.

Let's first discuss how to set up the alert monitor before showing how it works in planning and scheduling.

To create a new alert monitor profile, use Transaction /SAPAPO/AMON1, and click **Alert Profile** on the initial screen. Figure 19.50 shows alert profile ZPPDSALTMON, for which checking the relevant checkboxes in the **Selection** column will trigger relevant alerts. A planner can also define ranges or specific values so that the system brings up information, warning, or error alerts on meeting the specified values. In this example, the **Product Too Early (Fixed Pegging)** alert type shows alert thresholds for information, warning, and error alerts.

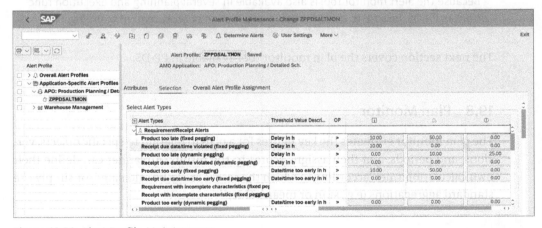

Figure 19.50 Alert Profile Maintenance

[»] **Note**

After creating an alert profile, assign it to an overall profile so that the system is able to display alerts within an application (refer to Figure 19.27 to see how the defined alert profile ZPPDSALTMON in Figure 19.50 is assigned to **User Settings**).

Figure 19.51 is accessed via Transaction /SAPAPO/RRP3 (Product View), followed by clicking the **Alert Monitor** icon. Note the large number of error, warning, and information alerts in the top half of the screen. On clicking the relevant checkbox in the **Selection** column, details of each alert are displayed in the lower half of the screen. For this example, resource WPPDSWC2_1105_001 has four error alerts.

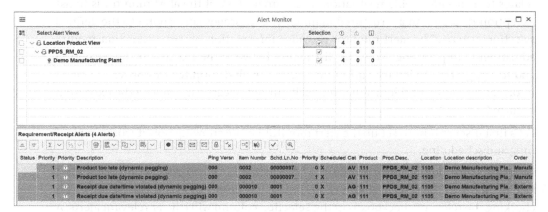

Figure 19.51 Alerts in Transaction /SAPAPO/RRP3

[»] **Note**

Because the alert monitor tool is also available in several planning and execution functions in PP-DS, be sure to use it for better production or procurement planning.

The next section covers the plan monitor tool available in PP-DS.

19.8   Plan Monitor

The plan monitor evaluates the key figures for a plan in relation to specific objects, versions, and periods, and then assigns scores to the results. A planner can define their own calculation rules, according to which the scores are to be calculated, or simply use standard aggregations (e.g., sum or mean value).

The plan monitor can be used to do the following:

- Determine the quality of the current planning situation.
- Compare various planning and simulation versions with each other.
- Compare planning over different periods.

The plan monitor considers the key figures for which a planner has created key figure variants in the key figure schema. These key figures can be displayed in a tabular or graphical version, or both.

For example, a production planner plans in a three- to four-week horizon but is faced with new expectations every day that impact many areas of the plan over the upcoming weeks. Here, the plan monitor can help.

Key figures in the following areas of the plan monitor are available:

- Key figures for order quantities
- Key figures for order times
- Key figures for pegging relationships
- Key figures for stocks
- Key figures for resources

Let's see how to put the plan monitor to use in a step-by-step way:

1. In the initial screen of Transaction /SAPAPO/PMON, choose **Definition: Key Figures Schema** to open the screen shown in Figure 19.52.

2. In the **General** tab, maintain initial details such as **Key Figure Schema**, which, in this example, is, "PPDSS4HANA", and add a short description.

3. In the **Display** area, choose relevant display options, such as to only display the grid, the graphic, or both. Choose whether individual values in the graphic can be displayed by checking the relevant checkbox.

4. Choose the **Key Figures** tab.

5. On the screen shown in Figure 19.53, first select **Key Figure Cat.** (category) from the dropdown (in this example, **9032 Orders: Quantities**), followed by choosing the relevant key figure (**Open Order Quantity**). The lower left-hand side offers available calculations, such as using minimum, maximum, or average values of key figures.

   Key figures can be displayed individually or collectively by choosing relevant options in the **Display Area**. Further, it's possible to check the correctness of a defined key figure by clicking the **Check** button before choosing **Adopt**.

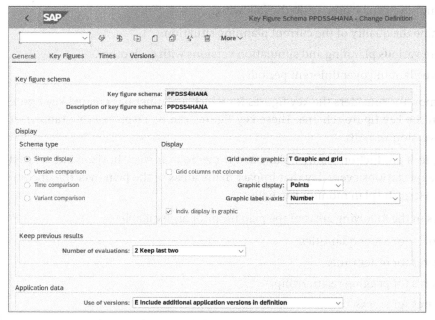

Figure 19.52 Key Figure Schema in Plan Monitor

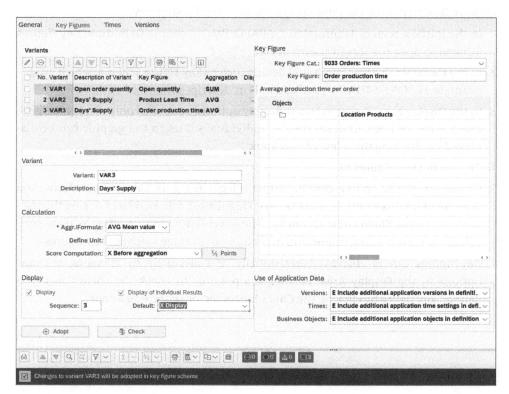

Figure 19.53 Key Figures in Plan Monitor

6. Each key figure can be saved as an individual variant; in this example, variants VAR2 and VAR3 are created for two different key figures. Be sure to select the **Location Products** checkbox on the right-hand side of the screen.

7. Choose the **Times** tab.

8. On the screen shown in Figure 19.54, maintain the start and end of the evaluation horizons in the lower half so that the system displays key figures within the defined horizon.

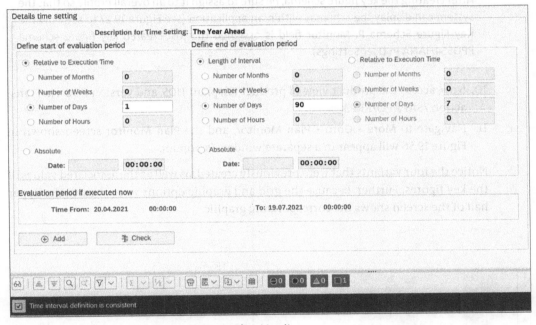

Figure 19.54 Times and Versions Setting in Plan Monitor

9. Choose the **Versions** tab shown in Figure 19.54, and maintain the planning and the simulation versions as shown (see Figure 19.55). Save the settings.

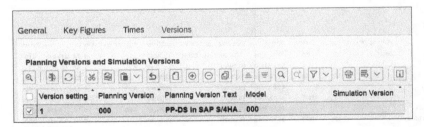

Figure 19.55 Version in Plan Monitor

[+] **Tips and Tricks**

Be sure to check the completeness and correctness of the defined key figure schema by choosing **Check Key Figure Schema** in the top menu bar, as shown in Figure 19.53.

[»] **Note**

After creating the key figure schema, be sure to assign it to an overall profile so that the system can display the schemas within an application (see Figure 19.27 to see how the **Key Figure Schema P. Monitor** field is assigned the just-created key figure schema PPDSS4HANA in **User Settings**).

10. Now, access the product view of product 131, plant 1105, and version 000 via Transaction /SAPAPO/RRP3.

11. Navigate to **More · Goto · Plan Monitor**, and the **Plan Monitor** screen shown in Figure 19.56 will appear in a separate window (a popup).

Notice the four variants that were previously created, as well as the associated values of the key figures. Further, because the grid and graphic options were chosen, the upper half of the screen shows the corresponding graphic.

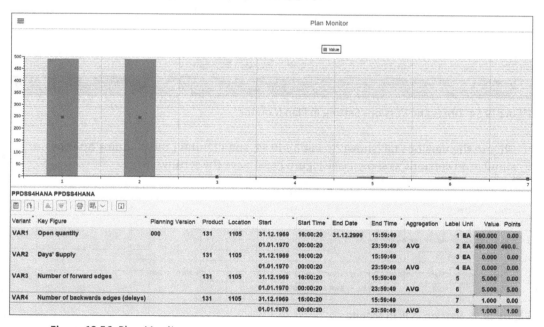

Figure 19.56 Plan Monitor

19.9 Summary

In this chapter, we covered important configuration, master data, business processes, and reporting of PP-DS in SAP S/4HANA. The PP-DS optimizer attempts to maintain a balance between costs and benefits for producing or not producing products and to determine where trade-offs are necessary. The user-defined alerts in the alert monitor and monitoring key figures in the plan monitor keep various checks and balances in place for smoother production and procurement planning. SAP Fiori apps for PP-DS not only report via dashboards but also enable intuitive planning.

The next chapter discusses SAP Manufacturing for production engineering and operations.

Chapter 20
Production Engineering and Operations

SAP S/4HANA Manufacturing for production engineering and operations is one of the latest introductions in the manufacturing space in SAP S/4HANA as an embedded solution. It caters to large, complex, turnkey projects, such as those in the aerospace, aircraft, ship building, defense, and space industries, and it's an extension of discrete manufacturing production types.

SAP S/4HANA Manufacturing for production engineering and operations is now also embedded in SAP S/4HANA. It's gaining significant traction in complex, low-volume, and extended manufacturing processes and is an extension of discrete manufacturing processes. Due to the extensive design and development stages involved in a complex, large-scale, turnkey manufacturing process, production engineering and operations attempts to bring a greater balance between design changes (engineering bills of materials [EBOMs]) and their impact on operations/manufacturing (manufacturing bills of materials [MBOMs]).

Here are some of the traits to consider when deciding to implement production engineering and operations:

- Highly engineered products
- Engineer-to-order (ETO)
- Make-to-order (MTO)/configure-to-order
- Complex assembly production
- Low volume of orders
- High number of engineering change requests
- Labor-intensive processes
- Long cycle times (days, weeks, months)
- High number of components and operations

Materials with some or all of the above traits are prime candidates to be considered for production via the production engineering and operations.

Figure 20.1 shows the key building blocks of production engineering and operations, and Figure 20.2 focuses on the key business processes of production engineering and operations that we'll discuss in this chapter.

20

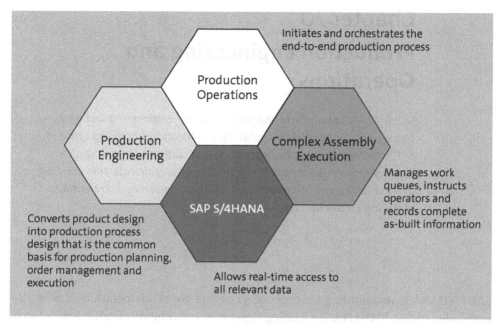

Figure 20.1 Building Blocks of Production Engineering and Operations

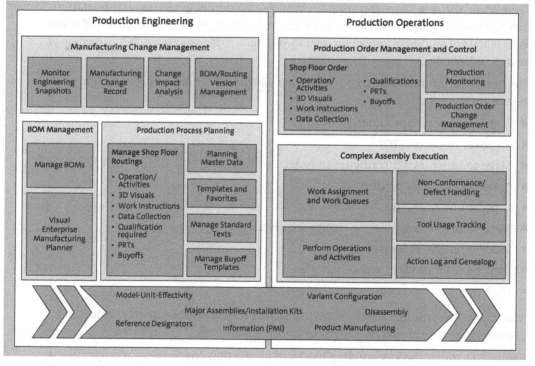

Figure 20.2 Business Processes Overview

This chapter begins with an overview of production engineering and operations and implementation concepts to develop an understanding of production engineering and operations, including production engineering and production operations. The system configuration, roles, and authorizations required for using production engineering and operations are discussed. Then we explain the core business processes of production engineering and the master data setup requirements and version management to support the production engineering and operations processes. Comparisons are provided to show key differences between the master data setup required for production engineering and operations and that of standard discrete manufacturing. An example is used to walk through the process of transitioning from engineering to manufacturing execution operations and the tools to handover the processes from product lifecycle management (PLM) systems to SAP systems. Then, the business processes of production operations are discussed in a step-by-step manner. Further, integration of production engineering and operations with other SAP S/4HANA areas, such as Materials Management, Quality Management, SAP Document Management service, and SAP Human Capital Management for SAP S/4HANA, are also briefly touched upon. Lastly, as production engineering and operations processes entail significant engineering changes to the products being manufactured, change management and impact analysis are discussed too.

> **Note**
>
> Because production engineering and operations processes significantly resemble discrete manufacturing processes, we recommend reading Chapter 3 and Chapter 6 first. We'll only be discussing the processes briefly herein so as to stay focused on production engineering and operations.

20.1 Key Terminologies

In Figure 20.2 you'll see some of the key terminologies used in production engineering and operations:

- **Production engineering**
  Bridges the gap between product engineering and production operations by converting the product design into production process design, which is the basis for production order management and shop floor execution.

- **Manufacturing change management**
  Orchestrates the end-to-end production engineering process:
  - The Monitor Engineering Snapshots app informs you of new sets of EBOM versions and triggers the production engineering process.
  - The Manufacturing Change Record app is used to orchestrate the whole production engineering process and keeps track of all changes made to manufacturing objects when incorporating a new EBOM version.

- – The Change Impact Analysis app identifies all objects that are impacted by a product engineering change.
- – BOM and routing version management control the lifecycle and usage of different revision levels.

- **Visual enterprise manufacturing planner (VEMP)**
  Used for the handover from the EBOM to the MBOM by converting the design-driven EBOM structure into a manufacturing, built-sequence-driven MBOM structure.

- **Production process planning**
  Used to create shop floor routings that include all information needed for production planning, production costing, and shop floor execution:

  - – Operations are used for planning and costing purposes as in classic PP-SFC (shop floor control/discrete manufacturing).
  - – Operation activities are used for shop floor execution and describe in detail how an operation has to be performed: work instructions, data collection required, qualifications needed, production resources/tools (PRT), buyoff procedures.

  Production process planning includes a set of "supporting" features:

  - – Distinguishing BOMs and routings used for planning (MRP, PP-DS) from those used for shop floor execution. The usage of BOMs and routings for different purposes is defined in the Manage Production Version app.
  - – Using templates and favorites significantly increases user efficiency when maintaining routings.
  - – In the Manage Standard Texts app, a manufacturing engineer can maintain a library of reusable text elements for efficient work instruction authoring.
  - – Buyoff templates can be defined and used during routing maintenance as an approval process.
  - – Qualification requirements can be predefined for work centers and materials and are inherited by related operations and activities.

The next section describes the basic configuration and setup activities needed to use production engineering and operations.

20.2   Configuration Settings and Production Engineering and Operations Setup

In the following sections, we'll discuss the configuration settings and the basic production engineering and operations setup that need to be in place in the SAP S/4HANA system.

20.2.1   Activating Extended Manufacturing Features

In this configuration step, the production engineering and operations features are activated as these are not a part of the standard SAP S/4HANA Enterprise Management license.

For each plant, activate the following manufacturing features. As in the rest of the book, we'll be using plant 1105 as an example. To activate the required features in production engineering and operations, navigate to the configuration menu path **Production • Manufacturing for Production Engineering and Operations • General Settings • Activate Features and Acknowledge License Obligations** (see Figure 20.3). For this example, the following production engineering and operations features are activated:

- **Buyoffs**
- **Change Alerts**
- **Extended Manufacturing Engineering**
- **Extended Production Operations**
- **Qualifications**

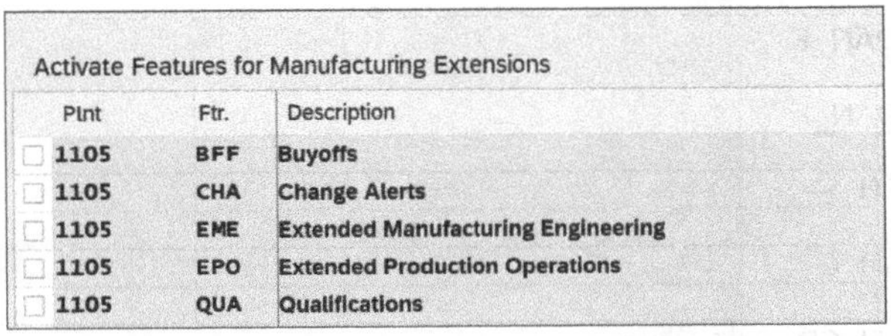

	Activate Features for Manufacturing Extensions	
Plnt	Ftr.	Description
☐ 1105	BFF	Buyoffs
☐ 1105	CHA	Change Alerts
☐ 1105	EME	Extended Manufacturing Engineering
☐ 1105	EPO	Extended Production Operations
☐ 1105	QUA	Qualifications

Figure 20.3 Activating Features for Manufacturing Extensions

20.2.2   Roles and Authorizations Assignment

Engage an SAP NetWeaver expert to assign the business roles listed in Table 20.1.

Business Role	Role Description
SAP_BR_PRODN_ENG_DISC_CAM	Production engineer—discrete manufacturing (CAM)
SAP_BR_PRODN_ENG_DISC_EME	Production engineer—discrete manufacturing (EME)
SAP_BR_PRODN_OPTR_DISC_EPO	Production operator—discrete manufacturing (EPO)
SAP_BR_PRODN_PROC_SPCLST_CAM	Production process specialist (CAM)
SAP_BR_PRODN_PROC_SPCLST_EPO	Production process specialist (EPO)
SAP_BR_PRODN_SUPRVSR_DIS _CAM	Production supervisor—discrete manufacturing (CAM)
SAP_BR_PRODN_SUPRVSR_DIS _EPO	Production supervisor—discrete manufacturing (EPO)

Table 20.1 Business Roles

Business Role	Role Description
SAP_BR_PRODN_SUPERVISOR_DISC	Production supervisor—discrete manufacturing
SAP_BR_QUALITY_ENGINEER_EPO	Quality engineering (EPO)
SAP_BR_BOM_ENGINEER	BOM engineer

Table 20.1 Business Roles (Cont.)

20.2.3 Number Ranges

Use Transaction SNUM to assign the number ranges to the various objects listed in Table 20.2. Enter the number range object and choose **Interval Editing**. For each object, create the number range number 01 for the full range and ensure that the **External** checkbox is deselected.

Number Range Object	Number Range Object
MPE_AHF_K	MPE_OAN
MPE_BUYOFF	MPE_OAN_E
MPE_COMP_A	MPE_OAN_I
MPE_EVENT	MEP_SFI
MPE_GROUP	MPE_SFI_C
MPE_HOLD	MPE_SFI_CD
MPE_LOG_ID	MPE_USR_TR
MPE_OA	MPE_WI
MPE_OA_C	QCHARGRP

Table 20.2 Number Ranges in Production Engineering and Operations

20.2.4 Create Business Partners and Manufacturing Users

In production engineering and operations, all SAP users need to be manufacturing users too, regardless of their roles.

With SAP S/4HANA, a *business user* is defined as a natural person who is represented by a business partner and is linked to a user in the SAP S/4HANA system. Business users interact with the SAP system in the context of a business process—for example, in the role of a production engineer, a production supervisor, or a production operator. For more information, see SAP Note 2570961.

Using the Maintain Employees app, create a business partner; while doing so, assign the user ID of the user from the SAP S/4HANA system. Figure 20.4 shows the **User** is assigned **Business Partner 131**, which can be confirmed by using Transaction SU3. This business partner (131) will be used throughout this chapter. Because production engineering and operations entails working across various teams and business functions, create a few additional business partners and assign their SAP user IDs accordingly.

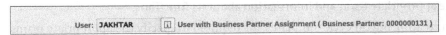

User: **JAKHTAR**   ⓘ User with Business Partner Assignment (Business Partner: 0000000131)

Figure 20.4 SAP User ID Mapping with Business Partner IDs

For creating manufacturing users, create business partners as just discussed, then use them as manufacturing users. Figure 20.5 ❶ shows that a manufacturing user is created using the Manage User Settings app, in which not only the previously created business partner 131 is assigned but also the relevant work center and plant.

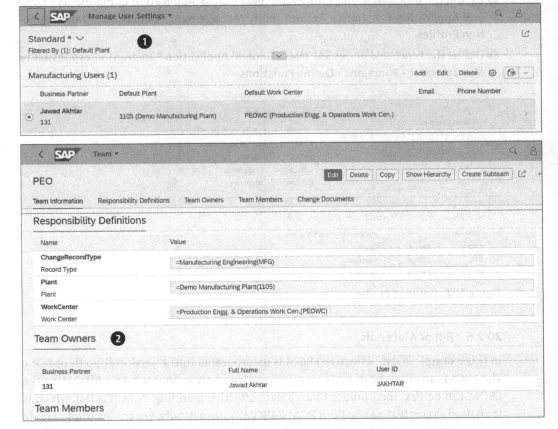

Figure 20.5 Manufacturing Users and Setting Up Teams

Also use the Manage Teams and Responsibilities app to create teams that will be managing the production engineering and operations business processes and assign team members accordingly ❷. For several functions in production engineering and operations, it's important to create appropriate teams and responsibilities. This is required for the following functions, for example:

- When adding a buyoff to operation activities in the routing, it's best practice to specify the appropriate team and information about its functions.

- When creating buyoff cycle templates, it's required to specify the appropriate teams and information about their functions.

20.2.5   Profiles

Maintain the buyoffs by defining business functions and function profiles as per the following configuration menu paths (see Figure 20.6):

❶ Define the function profiles under **SAP IMG · Cross-Application Components · General Application Functions · Responsibility Management · Functions · Define Function Profiles**.

❷ Define the functions under **SAP IMG · General Application Functions · Responsibility Management · Functions · Define Functions**.

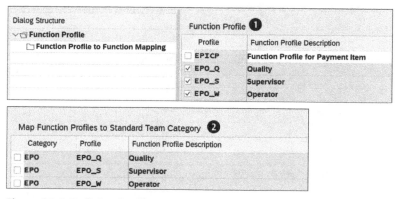

Figure 20.6 Defining Profiles

20.2.6   Bill of Materials

In this example, a date-effective EBOM is incorporated into a version shop floor BOM. The EBOM can either be directly incorporated into a shop floor BOM (or MBOM) or the EBOM can be first incorporated into a date-effective planning BOM (EBOM), which is then used to create the shop floor BOM (MBOM) automatically. For this example, create two new BOM usages, P and V, to represent the EBOM and MBOM for the shop floor

BOM by using Transaction OS20 (see Figure 20.7). For BOM usage P, ensure that **Eng/ Des.** is enabled; for BOM usage V, **Prod.** must be enabled by choosing the **+** sign.

	BOM Usg	Prod.	Eng/des.	Spare	PM	Sales	CostRel	Usage text
☐	P	.	+	–	–	–	.	Planning BOM
☐	S	–	–	–	.	–	–	Customer Management
☐	U	.	–	–	.	–	–	IUID Embedded Items
☐	V	+	–	–	–	–	.	Shopfloor BOM

Figure 20.7 BOM Usages

Because production engineering and operations extensively uses version management functionality in the BOM and routing, maintain the control data for the BOM usages to enable the creation of version BOMs. The two BOM usages (P and V) are the same that were configured in the last step and are now assigned in production engineering and operations. To do this, follow the configuration menu path **SAP IMG · Production · Manufacturing for Production Engineering and Operations · Production Engineering · Define Control Data for BOM Usage** (see Figure 20.8).

BOM Usage Control Data

	BOM Usg	Versn Ctrl	Prod Relevance Usage
☐	2	E Date Validity Controlled	
☐	D	V Version Controlled	D Disassembly Template
☐	P	E Date Validity Controlled	P Production Planning
☐	V	V Version Controlled	E Production Execution

Figure 20.8 BOM Control Usage

20.2.7 Routing

To differentiate the shop floor routing in production engineering and operations from standard routing in discrete manufacturing, configure the work center usages for routing types V (shop floor routing) and P (planning routing) by following the configuration menu path **SAP IMG · Production · Basic Data · Work Center · General Data · Define Task List Usage.** Figure 20.9 shows the work center u 009 with two new task list types, P and V. This newly configured work center usage will be assigned to the work center responsible for managing production engineering and operations processes.

Further, it's important to define material type assignments to task lists for all material types that are going to be used in shop floor routings and have to be assigned to task list type V. To do so, follow the configuration menu path **SAP IMG · Production · Basic Data · Routing · General Data · Define Material Type Assignments** (see Figure 20.10).

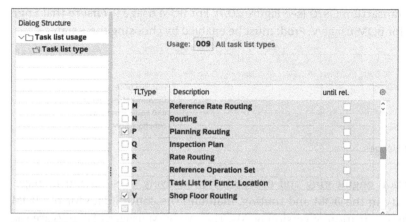

Figure 20.9 Task List Usage

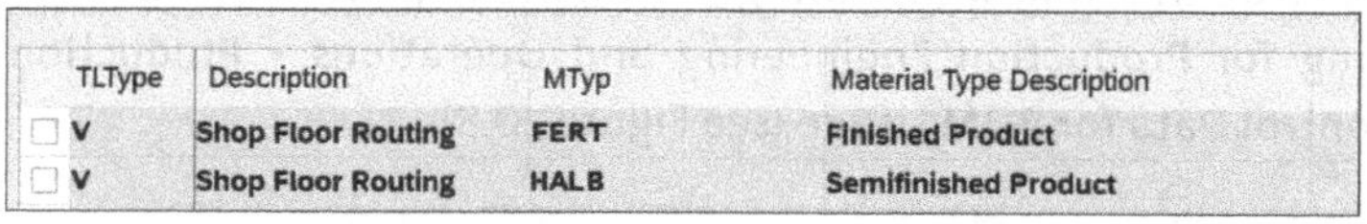

TLType	Description	MTyp	Material Type Description
☐ V	**Shop Floor Routing**	FERT	**Finished Product**
☐ V	**Shop Floor Routing**	HALB	**Semifinished Product**

Figure 20.10 Task List to Material Type Mapping

Similarly, maintain the following configuration settings for task lists via menu path **SAP IMG · Production · Basic Data · Routing · Routing Selection · Select Automatically**:

- **Select Automatically: Selection ID 01, priority 05, TL type P, Usage 1, Status 2**
- **Select Automatically: Selection ID 01, priority 06, TL type V, Usage 1, Status 4**

20.2.8   Control Key

Because production engineering and operations business processes also entail rework scenarios, create a control key that allows rework by selecting the **Rework** checkbox for the control key in the configuration menu path **SAP IMG · Production · Shop Floor Control · Master Data · Routing Data · Define Control Key**.

20.2.9   Order Type-Dependent Plant Parameters

It's recommended to configure a separate order type for production engineering and operations scenarios so as to differentiate it from normal or regular production processes in discrete manufacturing. For this example, ensure that for production order type PEO1 in plant 1105, the previously configured routing type V shop floor routing is assigned via the configuration menu path **SAP IMG · Production · Shop Floor Control · Master Data · Order · Define Order-Type-Dependent Parameters** (see Figure 20.11).

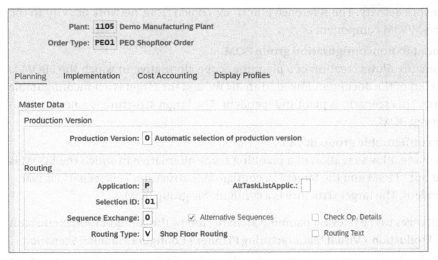

Plant: **1105** Demo Manufacturing Plant
Order Type: **PEO1** PEO Shopfloor Order

Planning   Implementation   Cost Accounting   Display Profiles

Master Data

Production Version

Production Version: **0** Automatic selection of production version

Routing

Application: **P**   AltTaskListApplic.: ☐
Selection ID: **01**
Sequence Exchange: **0**   ☑ Alternative Sequences   ☐ Check Op. Details
Routing Type: **V** **Shop Floor Routing**   ☐ Routing Text

Figure 20.11 Order Type-Dependent Parameters

20.2.10   Planning Scenarios

The next configuration step lets you activate or deactivate the planning scenarios for creating a planning scope alternative. A *planning scenario* defines the parameters and the associated scope based on which the system undertakes the planning in production engineering and operations. Here are some of the important planning scenarios that can only be activated or deactivated (a new planning scenario cannot be created):

- **Document-based nonconfigurable**
  This scenario allows a planner to create a planning scope alternative in which the EBOM is derived out of the document linked to an RH file and the target is a nonconfigurable structure. We'll use this planning scenario as an example to demonstrate end-to-end business process in this chapter.

- **Document-based purchased part**
  This scenario allows creation of a planning scope alternative for a purchased part. The planning scope alternative of a purchased part is not available for planning.

- **PSM-based configurable**
  This scenario allows creation of a planning scope alternative in which the EBOM is derived out of the product structure manager (PSM) and the target is a configurable structure.

- **Document to nonconfiguration with network**
  This scenario allows creation of a planning scope alternative in which the EBOM is derived out of the document linked to an RH file and the target is a nonconfigurable structure. It also allows loading a Project System network and assign components to

20

the network activity. The reference points are copied from network activity to the assigned MBOM components.

- **Document to nonconfiguration group BOM**
  This scenario allows creation of a planning scope alternative in which the EBOM is derived out of the document linked to an RH file and the target is a nonconfigurable structure. This scenario is plant-independent. The target structure is a nonconfigurable group BOM.

- **PSM to configurable group BOM**
  This scenario allows creation of a planning scope alternative in which the EBOM is derived out of PSM and the target is a configurable structure. This scenario is plant-independent. The target structure is a configurable group BOM.

To make changes to the relevant planning scenario, follow the configuration menu path **SAP IMG • Production • Visual Manufacturing Planner • Configure Planning Scenario**.

On the screen shown in Figure 20.12, assign the previously configured planning BOM usage P to planning scenario 01, and also assign V, which is the shop floor BOM usage, to planning scenario 05.

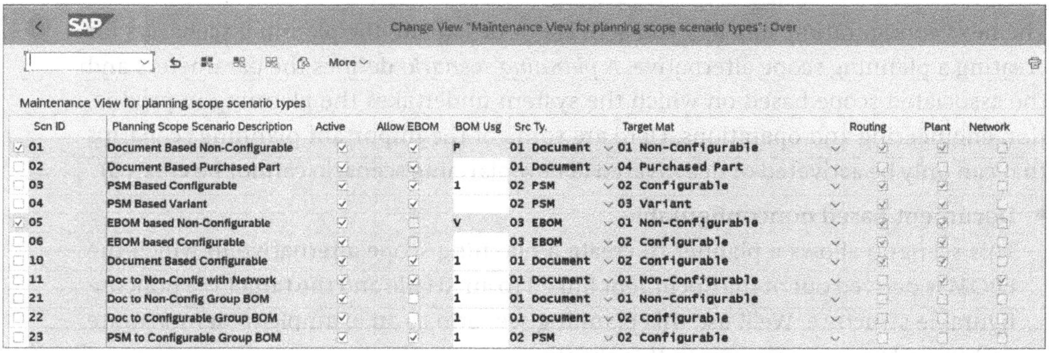

Scn ID	Planning Scope Scenario Description	Active	Allow EBOM	BOM Usg	Src Ty.		Target Mat		Routing	Plant	Network
01	Document Based Non-Configurable	✓	✓	P	01 Document		01 Non-Configurable		✓	✓	
02	Document Based Purchased Part	✓	✓		01 Document		04 Purchased Part				
03	PSM Based Configurable	✓	✓	1	02 PSM		02 Configurable		✓	✓	
04	PSM Based Variant	✓	✓		02 PSM		03 Variant		✓	✓	
05	EBOM based Non-Configurable	✓		V	03 EBOM		01 Non-Configurable		✓	✓	
06	EBOM based Configurable	✓			03 EBOM		02 Configurable		✓	✓	
10	Document Based Configurable	✓	✓	1	01 Document		02 Configurable		✓	✓	
11	Doc to Non-Config with Network	✓	✓	1	01 Document		01 Non-Configurable			✓	✓
21	Doc to Non-Config Group BOM	✓		1	01 Document		01 Non-Configurable				
22	Doc to Configurable Group BOM	✓		1	01 Document		02 Configurable				
23	PSM to Configurable Group BOM	✓	✓	1	02 PSM		02 Configurable				

Figure 20.12 Planning Scenarios

In the next section, we'll discuss the master data setup required for production engineering.

20.3   Production Engineering Master Data Setup

In this following section, we'll discuss the master data setup required for the production engineering part of production engineering and operations. Figure 20.13 shows the end-to-end business processes in production engineering, including the associated master data.

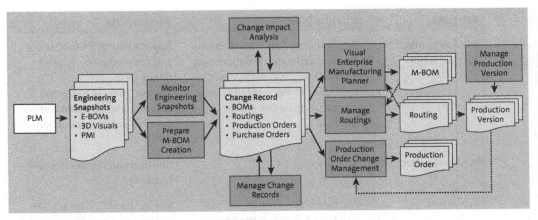

Figure 20.13 Business Processes in Production Engineering

20.3.1 BOM Management

To create a BOM version in production engineering and operations, you must use the Maintain Bill of Materials app; the standard Transaction CS01 for creating a BOM will not offer the required options to create BOM versions.

Table 20.3 lists the attributes to differentiate the classical BOM in discrete manufacturing with the version-controlled BOM used in production engineering and operations.

Attributes	Classical BOM	Version BOM
Identification	Identified by material, plant, usage, alternative.	Identified by material, plant, usage, alternative and version.
Change states	For a BOM with history, the change states are identified using engineering change numbers (ECNs).	No change states of BOM header or BOM item. Each version is a distinct instance of the BOM. Any change in one BOM version will not affect another version.
Edit control	The BOM alternative is always open for editing. ECNs are used to ensure the date effectivity of the change states.	Once released, a BOM version is frozen and does not allow any further changes. If changes are necessary, a planner will have to create a new version of the BOM alternative by copying the previous version.

Table 20.3 Classical BOM versus Version BOM

20

Attributes	Classical BOM	Version BOM
BOM determination for production	Applicability of an MBOM alternative for production is determined by the production version, but applicable components are determined based on the production date.	Applicability of an MBOM version for production is determined by the production version. There is no further determination of BOM components as per the production date.
Parameter effectivity	Supported.	Unitized parameter effectivity supported.
App access	Accessible using the legacy SAP GUI transaction and the new Manage Bill of Materials app.	Not accessible via legacy SAP GUI transactions; must use the Maintain Bill of Materials app.

Table 20.3 Classical BOM versus Version BOM (Cont.)

With the Maintain Bill of Materials app, a planner can display and manage all BOMs. Using the available filters, a user can find and view existing BOMs, drill down to the level of detail needed, and perform any necessary actions (such as copying or deleting BOMs or assigning change records to BOMs). A new BOM, whether classical, version-based, or alternative, can be created, and the relevant components—along with the required data, including any attachments—can be assigned.

Figure 20.14 shows the Maintain Bill of Materials app. Here, choose **Create Version BOM**.

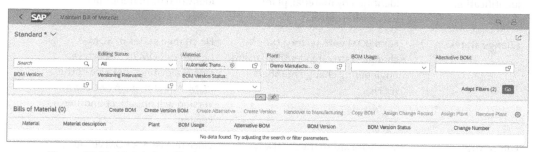

Figure 20.14 Maintain Bill of Materials App

On the screen shown in Figure 20.15, maintain the material number, plant, and the previously configured BOM usage V, and choose **OK**. We'll be using material 143 throughout this chapter.

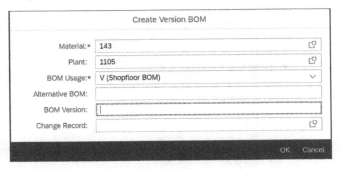

Figure 20.15 Creating Version BOM

On the screen shown in Figure 20.16, maintain the components and the component quantities. Then click the forward arrow located on the far right-hand side of the screen to navigate to additional screens or the detailed screen of a component. Be sure to choose **Release** to release the MBOM, and assign a change record number if it's already created. Assigning a change record number will ensure that the system will be able to evaluate the impact of any changes made to the BOM and be able to reflect them in the Change Impact Analysis app that we'll discuss in Section 20.5.5.

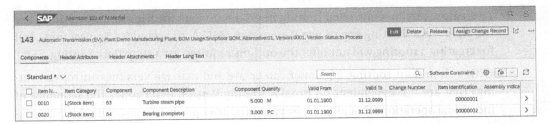

Figure 20.16 Version BOM

20.3.2 Maintain Work Center

Production engineering and operations can ensure labor tracking. To activate this option, follow menu path **Logistics • Production • Master Data • Work Centers • Work Center • CR02**. Enter the relevant plant and work center. In the **Basic Data** tab, choose the **Labor Tracking** checkbox to activate this feature (see Figure 20.17), and incorporate usage 0009 that was previously configured. In the **Default Values** tab, select a control key that allows the rework process in production engineering and operations, as discussed in Section 20.2.8.

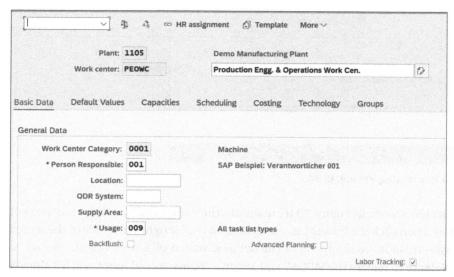

Figure 20.17 Work Center

20.3.3   Manage Shop Floor Routing

To create a version-controlled routing in production engineering and operations, use the Shop Floor Routing app or use Transaction MSFR4; the standard Transaction CR01 for creating a routing will not offer the options required for a shop floor routing.

With a shop floor routing, a planner can create and manage version-controlled routings that are not dependent on time. A routing version determines the sequence of individual operations that are necessary to produce a product. It also contains information on where the work is performed and the work center's resources that will be consumed with all the necessary technical specifications, such as the standard times, capacity requirements, and work instructions. The operation activities can be used to describe the production process in more detail. Once released, a production version for the routing version and BOM version can be used in production execution. A released routing version can no longer be changed.

Table 20.4 lists the attributes to differentiate the classical routing of discrete manufacturing from the version-controlled shop floor routing used in production engineering and operations.

Attributes	Classical Routing	Shop Floor Routing
Identification	Identified by group and group counter for task list type N.	Identified by group and group counter version.
Change states	In case of routings with history, the change states are identified using ECNs.	No status change of shop floor routing is allowed once it is released. Each version is a distinct instance of the routing. Any change in one routing version will not affect another version.
Edit control	Routing is always open for editing. ECNs are used to ensure date effectivity of change states.	Once released, a routing version is frozen and cannot be changed. If changes are required, a new version of the routing is created by copying the previous version.
Routing determination for production	Applicability of routing for production is determined by production version but applicable operations are determined based on production date.	Which routing version and BOM version are to be used for production is determined by the production version. There is no further determination of BOM components and routing operations according to the production date.
Parameter effectivity	Supported.	Unitized parameter effectivity supported.
App access	Accessible using SAP GUI transaction.	Can be accessed using the new Manage Shop Floor Routings app and using SAP GUI Transaction MSFR4.

Table 20.4 Classical Routing versus Shop Floor Routing

Access the screen in Figure 20.18 using the Manage Shop Floor Routings app, and choose **Create** from the dropdown, followed by choosing **New Routing**.

On the screen in Figure 20.19, maintain the details as shown, including the material number and the version BOM created in the previous step with the correct BOM usage, V. Because this example is for a nonserialized product, be sure to choose the **Non-serialized Product** option from the dropdown.

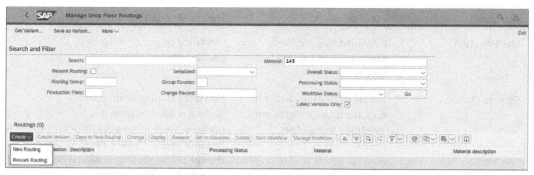

Figure 20.18 Manage Shop Floor Routing

Figure 20.19 Header Details

Figure 20.20 shows the structure workplace of the shop floor routing. Choose **Add Operation** from the dropdown ❶ and maintain the operations details ❷.

Select **Structure Workspace** in Figure 20.20 ❶, then choose **Component Assignment Workspace** (see Figure 20.21).

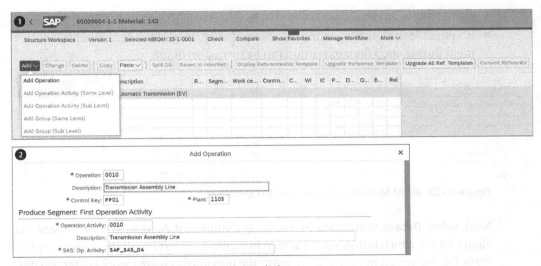

Figure 20.20 Adding Operation in Structure Workplace

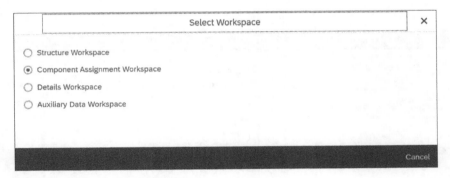

Figure 20.21 Workspace Selection

On the screen in Figure 20.22, select the BOM components and assign them to the operation activity. The BOM components are automatically available as the details were already maintained on the initial screen of the shop floor routing creation. Some additional functions available are as follows:

- One or more BOMs can be assigned to a routing (depending on routing profile).
- MBOMs that are not yet released can be assigned.
- Upgrading to a newer MBOM version is possible without losing the corresponding component assignments.
- An MBOM can be released in the routing application.
- The BOM items are displayed in the left pane, which shows the current status of component allocation.

20

- Components can be partially allocated to different activities in an operation.
- It's possible to explicitly define the assembly sequence of the components. Enforcement during shop floor execution can be turned on or off.

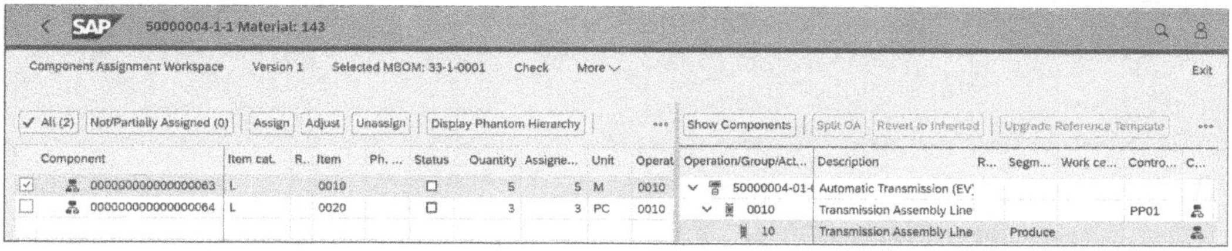

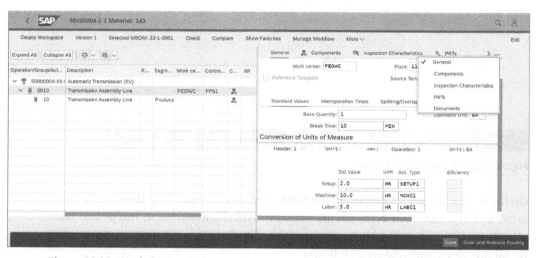

Figure 20.22 Bill of Materials Assignment to Operation

Next, select **Details Workspace** by choosing **Component Assignment Workspace** (see Figure 20.22), which brings up the screen in Figure 20.21 to choose the relevant option from. On the screen in Figure 20.23, enter the previously created work center, **PEOWC**, in the **General Data** tab, and then maintain activity times, such as setup, machine, and labor.

Figure 20.23 Work Center Assignment

Figure 20.24 shows an example where a change record 20000021 of record type MFG ❶ is created and assigned to the shop floor routing. Later on, we'll show how this change record 20000021 ❷ can be used to assign additional objects, such as a production order, an MBOM, an EBOM, or a planning scope, to analyze the impacts on various objects due to any changes made to them.

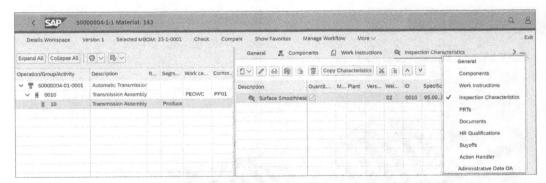

Figure 20.24 Creating and Assigning Change Record

It's possible to define and assign inspection characteristics to the operation activities. These readings can be utilized for quality management or for analytical purposes, such as root cause analysis. Predefined master inspection characteristics can be used, or inspection characteristics specifically for the routing can also be created interactively. Characteristics can also be grouped together to capture the readings in a table format. Appropriate characteristics from other routings can also be copied, and the data for the inspection is collected by operators and can be maintained using the Perform Work app, which is discussed Section 20.5.3 (see Figure 20.25).

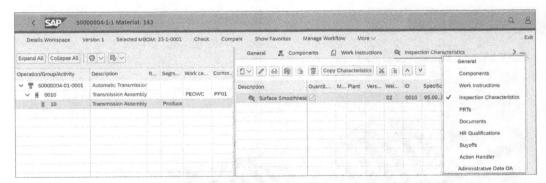

Figure 20.25 Integration Quality Management with Shop Floor Routing

Select the **Work Instruction** tab. If available, a 3D visual can be shown next to the MBOM item list. A selected item in the MBOM list is highlighted in the 3D image and vice versa. Other available options for work instructions are as follows:

- Rich text work instructions can be defined for each operation activity.
- The work instructions editor enables creating content using rich text, which can be authored directly in the editor. The editor supports features such as background

color, foreground color, font selection, font size selection, highlighting, and bulleting.

- The instruction can also contain images based on an external source or using the attachment feature from SAP Document Management service.
- Standard texts can also be used to enrich the work instruction content. The standard texts are rich text snippets that can be reused across several work instructions.
- Work instructions and standard texts can be authored in different languages. During execution, they will be shown in the logon language of the operator.
- Interactive work instructions allow the production operators to record the data collection required for component serial numbers and batches, as well as the readings for inspection characteristics.
- Clickable hyperlinks can be added in the work instruction which, when selected, highlight the corresponding part in the component list and the 3D model in the Perform Work app.
- Serial number and batch collection for components can be configured.
- The inspection characteristics can also be collected multiple times in an easy-to-use table format.

Figure 20.26 shows a partial view of a work instruction; the lower half shows a partial image.

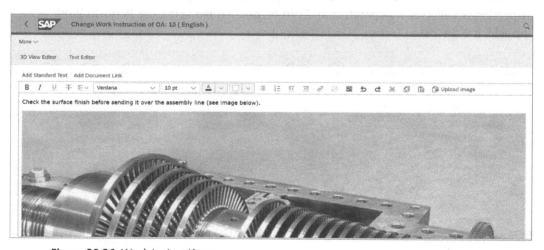

Figure 20.26 Work Instructions

Note

Frequently used work instructions can be created as templates or standard text via the Manage Standard Texts app (see Figure 20.27). Such templates can then be selected by choosing **Add Standard Text**, shown in Figure 20.26.

Figure 20.27 Manage Standard Texts

Figure 20.28 **❶** shows the required HR qualifications and the proficiencies of the persons who'll be involved in the production engineering and operations processes. One or more qualifications can be assigned to operation activities. Only an operator with the required or a higher qualification is allowed to perform the operation activity. Use Transaction PPPM to create and assign qualifications to relevant users (or engage the human capital management [HCM] expert on this integration point) **❷**.

In the Manage Object Qualification Assignments app, in the **Qualification** field, maintain relevant data, such as the work center and plant and the materials that will be managed with the production engineering and operations business processes.

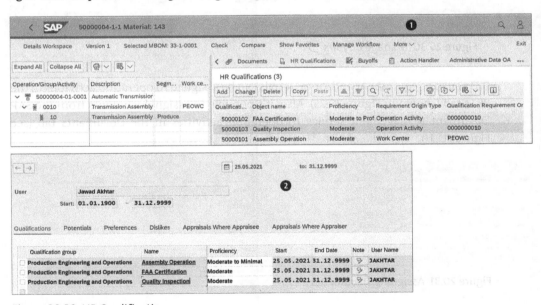

Figure 20.28 HR Qualifications

The *buyoff* is a process to sign off on a complex task by getting it reviewed by experts. A sequence of buyoffs can be defined for an operation activity. A buyoff step consists of the description and the team and/or function that can perform the step. Some buyoff steps may require qualification checks too. These buyoff steps can only be performed by personnel with required qualifications (see Figure 20.29).

Figure 20.29 Buyoffs in Shop Floor Routing

> **Note**
>
> Buyoffs can also be copied using the buyoff template via the Manage Buyoffs app (see Figure 20.30). Such templates can then be selected by choosing **Add from Template**, shown in Figure 20.29.

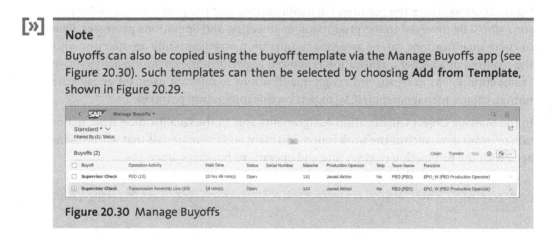

Figure 20.30 Manage Buyoffs

PRTs such as equipment and/or materials can be assigned to operation activities in the **PRTs** tab (shown in Figure 20.25). Also, it's possible to assign documents from the SAP Document Management service to operation activities in the **Documents** tab (see Figure 20.31).

Figure 20.31 Assigning Documents

Referring to Figure 20.31 again, the action handlers contain business logic—for example, checks or determinations. Different action events can be assigned to operation activities. If a production operator triggers the action during production order execution, the system executes the checks or events associated with the action handlers.

Figure 20.32 again shows the structure workspace of the shop floor routing; this time, it provides a summary of the information maintained so far in the routing. The following are some of the additional features available:

- Different versions of a routing can be compared by turning the compare mode on.
- For each operation, operation activity, and operation activity object (inspections, characteristics, PRTs, etc.), a planner can see whether they are the same in both versions.
- The system also shows the attributes of both versions for a given element (such as standard values).
- Work instructions are compared for all available languages, and differences are highlighted.
- A planner can easily copy operations, operation activities, or operation activity details from one version to another.
- The shop floor routing can be checked via the **Check** function to check for completeness and correctness of the information maintained.
- Customer-specific data can be maintained for the routing header, operation, and operation activity.
- Production version creation and updates during shop floor routing release is possible. This streamlines the process for engineers as there's no need to navigate to another app.

Choose **Save and Release Routing**.

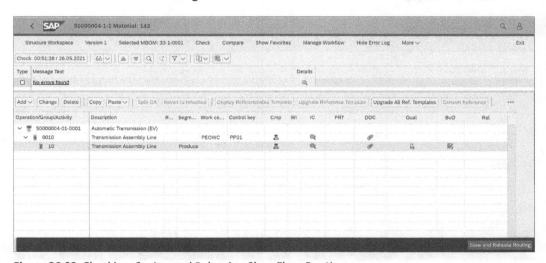

Figure 20.32 Checking, Saving and Releasing Shop Floor Routing

Figure 20.33 shows the popup in which the option to maintain a production version is offered.

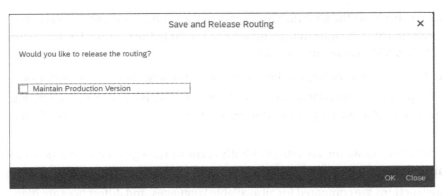

Figure 20.33 Production Version Creation Popup

20.3.4   Manage Production Versions

A production version is used to combine a BOM alternative with a shop floor routing alternative (group counter) and therefore describes a method that can be used to manufacture a material. The valid from and valid to dates and the lot size determine when a certain production version is to be used. The screen shown in Figure 20.34 is accessed using the Manage Production Versions app, in which the previously created master data, such as the BOM and its specific usage, the shop floor routing, and the task list type details, are maintained for material 143 in plant 1105. Make sure that you use the **Check** option to check for the completeness and correctness of the production version before saving it.

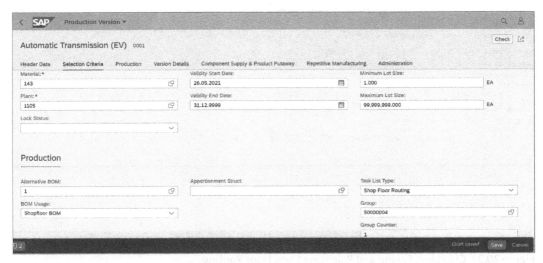

Figure 20.34 Manage Production Version

20.4   Planning in Production Engineering

As discussed earlier, we'll focus on planning scenario 01 (using a document of the SAP Document Management service as a source and converting it into a nonconfigurable material as a target). Because we've been using material 143 all along, we'll use it again as an example. Using Transaction CVO2N, access the screen in Figure 20.35 ❶, wherein document 10000000011 and document type VED will be used as an example for the rest of this section. Here, material 143 is linked via the object link functionality that links a document with the relevant object, which in this example is the document 10000000011. Further, in the **Originals** tab ❷, a sample drawing (in the Transmission.rh file) is attached and checked into the content server. The file type extension used here is .rh (right hemisphere), but other file types can also be configured and used. The file is checked in and stored in the content server so that it can be accessed by other applications later on.

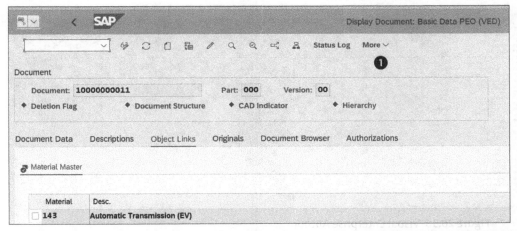

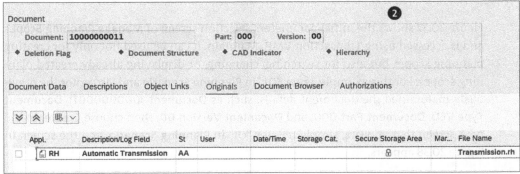

Figure 20.35 Document in SAP Document Management Service

> **Note**
>
> It's recommended to engage an SAP Document Management service expert to ensure the necessary configuration is in place. Further, engage an SAP NetWeaver expert to install related applications of manufacturing execution, such as visual enterprise author (VEA), visual enterprise viewer (VEV), and visual structure manager (VSM).

Although the relatively simple example used here is using the native SAP Document Management service in SAP S/4HANA, there are other PLM/computer-aided drawing (CAD) engineering drawing and authoring tools that can be used, such as AutoCAD, CATIA V5, Team Center, Windchill, or even SAP's own authoring tool, SAP 3D Visual Enterprise Author (see Figure 20.36). These can be used to convert complex EBOMs into MBOMs.

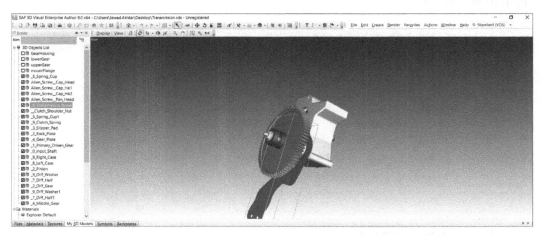

Figure 20.36 Visual Enterprise Author

Figure 20.37 shows the initial parameters selection screen of **Manage Planning Scopes** and is accessed using Transaction VMP_Maintain. It can be used not only for creating planning scopes but also for searching, changing, or displaying already created planning scopes. For this example, enter "01" in **Planning Scenario** and also enter the previously maintained the document details, such as **Document 10000000011, Document Type VED, Document Part 000**, and **Document Version 00**, then choose **Create**. In the next screen that appears, simply reenter "01" in **Planning Scenario**, and the screen in Figure 20.38 appears.

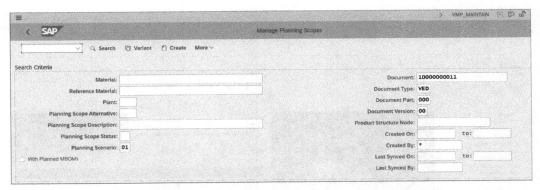

Figure 20.37 Manage Planning Scopes

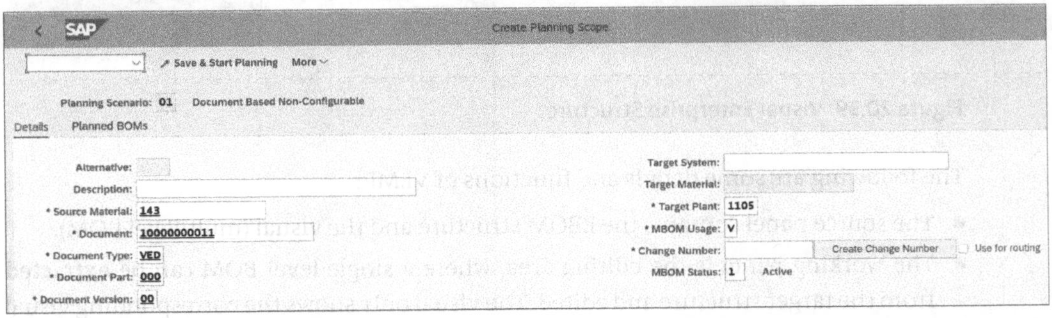

Figure 20.38 Create Planning Scope

Figure 20.38 is divided between the source details (left-hand side) and the target details (right-hand side) of the planning scope creation. Maintain or confirm all the previous details, such as **Source Material 143**, and the document details, such as **Document 10000000011, Document Type VED, Document Part 000** and **Document Version 00**. In the target section, maintain **Target Plant** "1105", as well as **MBOM Usage** "V", and choose **Save & Start Planning**.

Figure 20.39 shows the visual enterprise manufacturing planner (VEMP) and consists of three panels. The left-hand side shows the **Source Panel**; the upper-right-hand side shows the **Working Panel**; and the lower right-hand side shows the **Target Panel**. The header shows the same material 143, and the drawing is fetched from the SAP Document Management service, where it was previously checked in or stored in the content server. VEMP enables the handover of the engineering structure (EBOM) to the manufacturing structure (MBOM), assisted by an interactive 3D model.

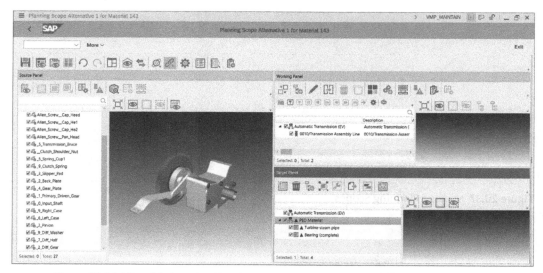

Figure 20.39 Visual Enterprise Structure

The following are some details and functions of VEMP:

- The source panel contains the EBOM structure and the visual (multilevel BOM).

- The working panel is the editing area, where a single-level BOM can be extracted from the target structure and edited. The visual only shows the corresponding visual of the single-level BOM.

- The target panel contains the MBOM structure and corresponding visual (multilevel BOM).

- The components in the source panel are disabled once they are fully planned/converted in the MBOM.

- VEMP reconciles the EBOM (source) with the MBOM (target) to check whether any component is over- or underassigned. If any discrepancy is found, it's highlighted in the corresponding nodes.

- VEMP allows restructuring the EBOMs in a different MBOM structure using a quantity or parameter effectivity-based split or merge of EBOM components into MBOMs.

- Synthetic MBOMs, which are only relevant for manufacturing, can be created using VEMP while ensuring the design intent in the EBOM and the EBOM component coverage.

- A routing can be loaded in the working panel to allocate the components to the relevant operations.

- Planning BOMs are created by VEMP) based on EBOMs that may be version-controlled or date-effective.

- Shop floor BOMs can be created from the planning BOMs. Phantoms will be flattened out and data-effectivity will be turned into versions.

- VEMP can be used to derive shop floor BOMs from the EBOM structure.

- For various reasons, such as material availability or production process reasons, you might need to use a different part in production than the one that has been specified by the product design.

- During the handover from an EBOM to MBOM in VEMP, the production engineer can decide to replace an EBOM material with a manufacturing substitute. If required, the quantity can also be adjusted (e.g., when substituting a big plate with two small ones).

- The system will automatically remember and consider the substitution when handing over future EBOM changes and during EBOM/MBOM reconciliation.

After the necessary changes are made and finalized between the EBOM and MBOM, choose **Save and Exit Planning** from the dropdown located on the top left-side hand side.

> **Note**
>
> VEMP is a user-friendly and intuitive planning tool, and we recommend exploring it in detail. Choose a component in any of the three panels (working, source, and target) and right-click it to see more options to choose from.

The next section is on production operations.

20.5 Production Operations

Production operations is about initiating, preparing, executing, and documenting the actual end-to-end production process. The *shop floor production order* is an extended version of the PP production order of discrete manufacturing. We'll cover many additional details of the shop floor production order in production engineering and operations here.

Figure 20.40 shows the end-to-end process flow that we'll discuss in these sections, and the following additional details:

- Operations are used for planning and costing as in classic PP-SFC.

- Activities are used for shop floor execution and describe in detail how an operation has to be performed—that is, work instructions, data collection required, qualifications needed, PRTs, buyoff procedures, and so on.

- Production monitoring provides a comprehensive overview of the expected and actual status and progress of production orders and operations by automatically detecting exceptions, providing decision support, and allowing for immediate actions.

- Engineering change incorporates and updates production orders with the latest engineering changes.

- Complex assembly execution is primarily designed for complex, low-volume production processes with high change frequency and a focus on manual work—typical for complex assembly and engineer-to-order businesses.

- Work assignment and work queues orchestrate the actual execution of production order operations and activities. Operators can access their tasks in a work center's work queues, or supervisors can explicitly distribute work to their team members by moving tasks to personal work queues.

- The Perform Work app supports production operators in executing their tasks by guiding them through the production process with the help of interactive work instructions, 3D visual support, data collection with real-time valuations, and so on.

- Defect handling manages nonconformance issues by placing holds on orders or parts, creating defects to be followed up on by quality engineers, and executing final usage decisions.

- Tool usage tracking documents which tool instances were used when executing an operation activity.

- Serialized parts are tracked and traced during the entire production process. The genealogy and action log collect all data and create a complete and detailed record of how a serialized part has been produced and how an order has been executed.

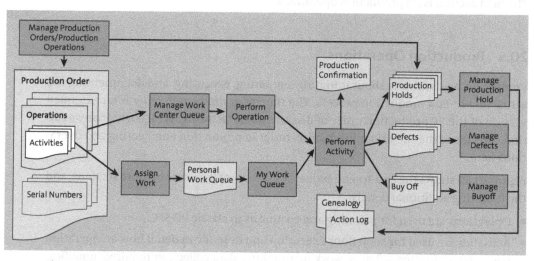

Figure 20.40 Process Flow in Production Operations

In the following sections, we'll create a production order for material 143 in plant 1105 and will maintain the requisite details. This will be followed by assigning work to specific operators who then perform and record the assigned work by using the Perform Work—Order/Operation app.

20.5.1 Production Order

The screen in Figure 20.41 is accessed using Transaction CO03 for the previously configured production order type PEO1. The production order number is 800060 for material 143 in Plant 1105. The **Master Data** tab shows the task list (TL) type V that was also previously configured and then subsequently assigned to production order type PEO1. We'll use the same production order number 800060 for material 143 and plant 1105 in the remaining sections.

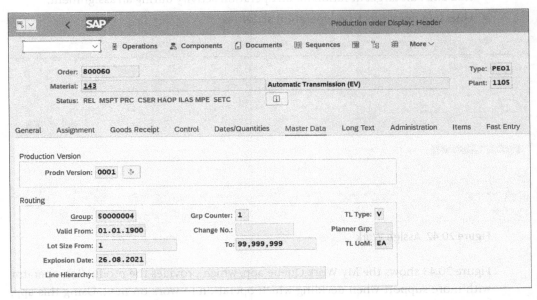

Figure 20.41 Production Order

20.5.2 Assign Work

The Assign Work app lists all operations to be performed at a given work center. It supports the operator in picking the next operation to be worked on based on order and operation status, priority, scheduled start/end, start feasibility and issues such as holds, missing components, and delays (see Figure 20.42). Production supervisors can see all their operators with their currently assigned workloads and labor statuses.

Supervisors can assign additional operation activities to operators while considering their qualifications and work center assignments. Supervisors can also remove operation activities from the operator's worklist and maintain target times for each operation activity assigned to an operator.

Some additional available functions are as follows:

- Select all unassigned operation activities or check existing assignments.
- Assign one or more production operators to individual operation activities to distribute the workload.
- Filter operators' names by matching work centers and qualifications during an assignment.
- View a number of current operators' assignments.
- Add and edit target duration for an operation activity during an assignment.
- Unassign operators from operation activities.

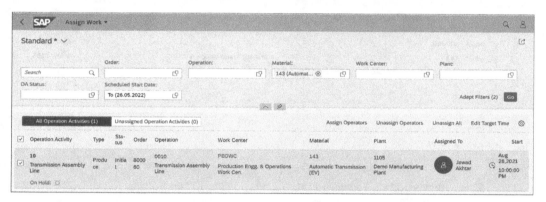

Figure 20.42 Assign Work

Figure 20.43 shows the My Work Queue app, which provides the production operator with more support when deciding which operation to work on next. Using this app, operators can access the operation activities directly assigned to them. Operators can also do the following:

- View the work (operation activities) that has been assigned to an individual operator.
- Sort, filter, and group the displayed operation activities.
- Start working on an operation activity by choosing **Execute**, after which the system navigates to the Perform Operation Activity app, which is discussed next.

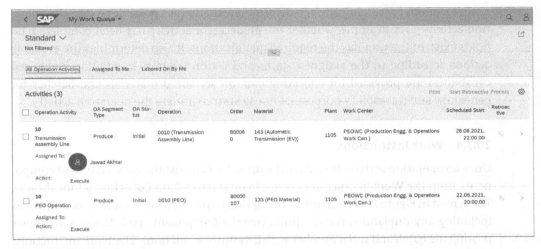

Figure 20.43 Work Queue

20.5.3   Perform Operation Activity

Figure 20.44 shows the Perform Work—Order/Operation app for production order 800060 and operation 0010, wherein a production operator can perform and record work on the operation activities assigned by the production supervisor.

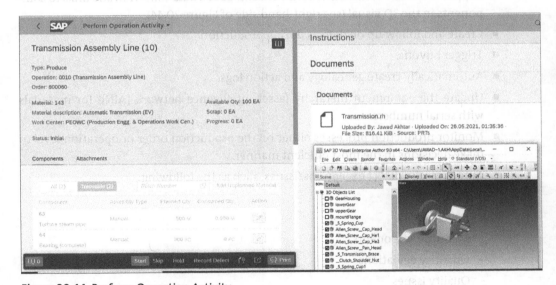

Figure 20.44 Perform Operation Activity

The app contains everything needed to carry out the work, giving full visibility into the tasks to be performed on the shop floor at the operation activity level. Besides displaying the key data that's needed, the app has integrated functions that allow an operator quickly deal with any issues encountered in production and thus react accordingly. To ensure smooth processing, the app determines whether it's possible to start the operation activity—for example, whether the predecessor activity has been completed, no holds exist, or the user has the required qualifications. It also determines the available actions according to the assigned status and action schema. In addition, enhanced capabilities are provided for collecting data on serialized materials and batches for genealogy and traceability purposes. Choose **Start** to initiate the operation activity.

20.5.4   Work Instructions

Once an operation activity is started, the operator can post the goods issues of components from the **Work Instructions** screen in **Interactive Data Collection** 9 (not shown). The screen in Figure 20.44 also offers the option to record components' consumptions, including any unplanned consumption (see the **Components** tab). The system allows posting the batch and serial number with inventory validations. The Work Instructions app can also do the following:

- Perform and confirm activities on orders or on individual parts (serial numbers).
- Enforce execution and provide actions for reporting activity progress and status.
- Display a dynamic 3D visualization showing the parts already assembled and parts to be added next.
- Support rich text work instructions with embedded data collection and links to components in the 3D visual (see right-hand side of Figure 20.44).
- Create and follow-up on defects during production.
- Trigger buyoffs.
- Automatically create genealogy and action logs.
- Update the equipment hierarchy (asset intelligence network [AIN]) for materials with serial numbers.
- Monitor production processes either on the production order or operation level to make decisions in the most efficient manner.
- Automatically detect exceptions/issues, such as the following:
  - Holds
  - Delays
  - Missing components
  - Quantity deviations
  - Quality issues
- Provide contextual information for root cause analysis and decision support:
  - Order schedule and history
  - Work center schedule and history
  - Material availability in plant and supply area

- Operation activity details, providing a complete overview of the activity layer
- Information on the inspection characteristics collected and the results in the operation activity details

- Provide immediate actions:
  - Placing holds (for one or multiple production orders simultaneously) and releasing holds
  - Manual order adjustments including order dates and quantities
  - Order update with latest master data
- Support the operator in performing and confirming activities for orders or individual parts (serial numbers).
- Validate proper execution.
- Provide actions for reporting activity progress and status:
  - Start/undo start, skip/undo skip, pause/undo pause, complete/undo complete
  - Partial confirmations
  - Support the operator in understanding the task
  - Support interactive data collection
  - Serial/lot numbers consumed
  - Inspection characteristics results recording

Further, the Perform Work app ensures that the defined sequence of operation activities is considered during execution, considering any order or parallel execution of operation activities. If multiple activities are available to start, an operator can choose which one to start with. It can also do the following:

- Provide a buyoff timeline, increasing visibility of buyoff history and upcoming steps.
- Provide an option to record defects during execution against production order or individual serial numbers.
- Provide the option of scrapping serialized parts.
- The labor tracking functionality can now be enabled for a work center that is later associated with an operation in the shop floor routing to track the time a production operator is logged on to work on the operation activity at that work center.
- Provide a possibility for multiple operators to collaborate on a task that has been already started by another operator.
- The system starts tracking the time spent on the serialized product or an operation activity when a production operator starts the labor tracking functionality on.
- At the end of a shift, for example, one production operator labors off an operation activity, while another operator can still continue working on the operation activity.

- The system automatically stops labor tracking for all production operators currently labored on to an operation activity on completion of the operation activity.

- Buyoffs verify the proper execution of an operation activity. Experts of different domains have to check the work defined for an operation activity and approve a buyoff.

- Operation activities can have a buyoff procedure with multiple steps. Every step has to be approved by a different domain expert. The Manage Buyoff app shows who has already approved buyoffs for the same operation activity.

- Ad hoc buyoff lines can be added during buyoff execution. That is, the buyoff cycle of an activity can be enhanced, if necessary.

- The Manage Buyoff app shows all open buyoffs that a domain expert can approve (or reject).

Figure 20.45 shows a partial view of the Perform Work app after some of the business functions, such as consumption of two components and the defect details, are recorded. All business functions can be performed by choosing the relevant options from the menu bar located on the bottom-left-hand side of Figure 20.45.

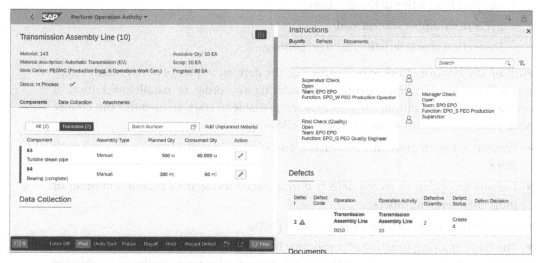

Figure 20.45 Recording Operation Activities

Let's now discuss defect handling, production hold, yield and scrap recording, and the action log, as well as the Change Impact Analysis app.

Defects Handling

The defects handling functionality shown in Figure 20.45 provides an option for production operators to record defects during the execution of production activities. Further, it also can do the following:

- Support the recording of a defect with and without hold.
- Provide an option for the production supervisor to process defects.
- Support follow-up decisions, such as use as-is or scrap
- After a decision has been made, it becomes available for the production operator in the defects list.
- Prevent the usual completion of a serialized product if a scrap decision has been made. The production operator is then forced to scrap the product.
- Display the list of all recorded defects in the Perform Operation Activity app (see Figure 20.46).

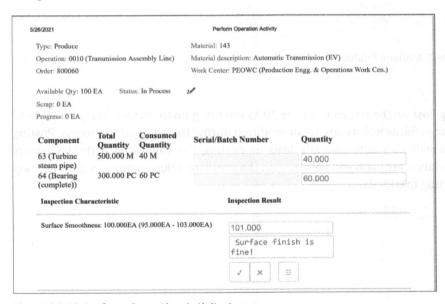

Figure 20.46 Perform Operation Activity App

Hold

The hold functionality shown in Figure 20.45 provides an option to temporarily block production by placing a hold on orders, materials, operations, work centers, or serial numbers. Here are some of the business functions that the hold functionality:

- When placing an object on hold, a reason code and note can be maintained.
- If something is put on hold, production operators cannot continue with their activities until the hold has been released.
- Holds are shown as an important exception on all supervisor and operator user interfaces. Once the issue has been solved, the hold can be released.
- You can monitor all production holds in the Manage Production Holds app, with drill-down capability to view the hold details (see Figure 20.47).

Figure 20.47 Manage Production Hold

Yield

Choosing **Post** on the screen in Figure 20.45 will bring up the screen in Figure 20.48 to record the yield, as well as any scrap produced during the production process. Posting the yield will also automatically lead to posting the calculated activities (setup, machine, labor, etc.) and will be based on the standard values maintained in the shop floor routing master data.

Figure 20.48 Posting Yield

Action Log

Choosing **Action Log** on the screen in Figure 20.45 will bring up the action log, as shown in Figure 20.49.

An *action log* is a complete as-built and where-used report for individual parts and displays serial/batch numbers for consumed components. It maintains a detailed log of activities and actions performed for an individual part, such as the following:

- Date/time
- User

- Activities started, completed, paused, skipped
- Buyoffs approved, rejected, canceled
- Holds applied and released
- Nonconformances raised
- Inspection characteristics

Action	Action Message	Reason Code	Note	Performed On	Performed By
				Action Log for Operation Activity 10	
	Items (9)				
Confirm Scrap	Scrap quantity 10 EA for operation activity Transmission Assembly Line has been posted			May 26, 2021 2:25 AM	Jawad Akhtar
Confirm Yield	Yield quantity 80 EA for operation activity Transmission Assembly Line has been posted			May 26, 2021 2:25 AM	Jawad Akhtar
Defect Created	Defect (2) has been created			May 26, 2021 2:20 AM	Jawad Akhtar
Labor On	User JAKHTAR started work on OA Transmission Assembly Line			May 26, 2021 2:20 AM	Jawad Akhtar
Labor Off	User JAKHTAR stopped work on OA Transmission Assembly Line			May 26, 2021 2:20 AM	Jawad Akhtar
Component Assembly	60 ST of component 000000000000000064 assembled in OA Transmission Assembly Line			May 26, 2021 2:19 AM	Jawad Akhtar
Component Assembly	40 M of component 000000000000000063 assembled in OA Transmission Assembly Line			May 26, 2021 2:19 AM	Jawad Akhtar
	Action Start for operation activity Transmission			May 26, 2021	

Close

Figure 20.49 Action Log

Figure 20.50 and Figure 20.51 show the Manage Work Center Queue and Manage Production Operations apps, which show here the current status of production order 800060, including issues in the **Issues** area, such as quality issues, scheduling issues, component shortage issues, and others.

With these apps, an operator can have a complete overview of the operation activities in a specific operation of a shop floor order. From here, it's possible to start executing the production tasks, view key information at a glance, or drill down into detailed information for each operation activity. The features available in these apps enable smooth and efficient processing of production tasks by increasing transparency into the progress in production and allowing a faster response to issues in production apps available for production planning.

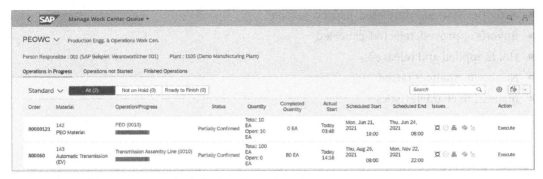

Figure 20.50 Manage Work Center Queue App

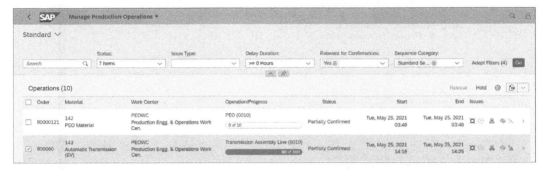

Figure 20.51 Manage Production Operations App

20.5.5   Change Impact Analysis

Before we delve into discussing the Change Impact Analysis app, let's first briefly discuss another SAP Fiori app: Manage Engineering Changes. A change record can be created at any stage of the production engineering and operations business process by using the Create Change Record app. However, it's highly recommended to create a change record as early as possible so that all objects affected by the changes are part of the change record. The primary purpose of a change record is to contain references to all the objects that are relevant for the change cycle. The following objects are supported:

- *Master data*: EBOM, MBOM, shop floor routing, planning scope
- *Transactional data*: production order, purchase order

Change items can be configured depending on the change record type. The context of the object in the change record is indicated using the change relevance setting—for example, **Create**, **Change**, **New Version**, **Reference**, and so on. The status network of the change record is also configurable.

A manufacturing engineer can use the change record as a single entry point to access all the relevant objects for the change cycle. The change record enables an engineer to navigate to the corresponding apps to view or manipulate the objects.

Access the screen in Figure 20.52 by opening the Manage Engineering Changes app, followed by selecting change record 200000021. This is the same change record that was created while creating the shop floor routing. More objects, such as planning scopes, manufacturing material BOMs, and even production order 800060 were added to this change record later on to analyze the impact of changes made to any or all of these objects. Choose **Analyze Impact** on the screen shown in Figure 20.52.

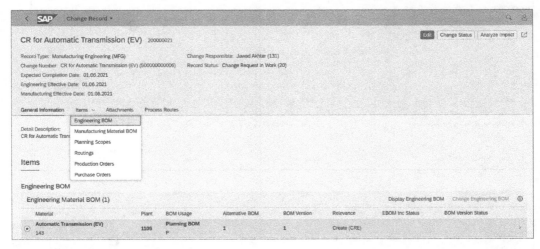

Figure 20.52 Change Record

The change impact analysis can be triggered from different master data objects: EBOMs, MBOMs, and shop floor routings. It determines the net change of the trigger objects and identifies all manufacturing objects that are impacted by those changes: MBOMs, shop floor routings, production orders, project networks, and directly related purchase orders (direct procurement, purchase-to-order, purchase-to-project). The change impact analysis also determines which parts (BOM items, operations, operation activities) of an object are impacted by the change (see Figure 20.53). Some additional functionalities available in the Change Impact Analysis app are as follows:

- Select one or more objects from the context of the change record as the trigger object for the analysis (Figure 20.53 ❶).

  The analysis result can be displayed in a list or in a network view mode. While the list is useful to display all the impacted objects in a consolidated manner, the network (Figure 20.53 ❷) provides insights into the relationships between the objects.

- Details of the impacted objects can be visualized in the details area.
- Items, operations, and operation activities affected by the change are highlighted to visualize where the impact is.
- For model/unit effectivity, the change impact analysis also identifies the units impacted by the change.
- Some quick actions can be performed for the impacted objects—for example, add to a change record, hold an order, and so on.

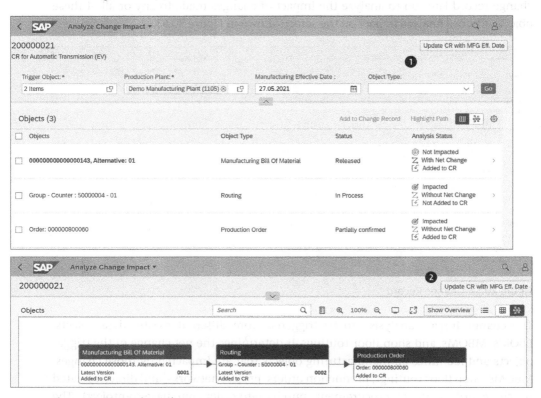

Figure 20.53 Analyze Change Impact

Figure 20.54 ❶ and ❷ show the Manage Unassigned EBOMs and Manage Unassigned MBOMs apps. Here, an engineer can not only create a change record but also assign the unassigned EBOMs or MBOMs to respective change records.

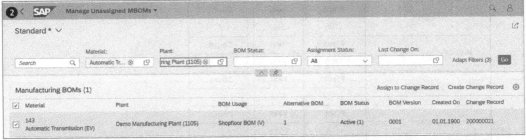

Figure 20.54 Manage Unassigned EBOMs and Manage Unassigned MBOMs Apps

20.6 Reporting

The Data Subject Information report is a comprehensive report that shows the activity-level details of an individual user.

Individual texts for each of the object types can be written and used—for example, routings, production orders, or buyoffs. Each text is assigned to a specific plant so as to allow creating different texts for different object types in different jurisdictions if required.

These texts are then inserted into the report above the tables containing the objects that the user created. For some objects, if there is no data included in the table, the report doesn't contain the texts that were created. Instead, only the table and a standard text are shown. Most data is stored under the user name. However, if a user has a business partner name, then data can also be recorded for this.

For each plant, enter the technical names of the text modules that contain the legal texts. To print or view a preview of the report for a data subject, enter the user name or business partner name of the data subject.

Figure 20.55 shows a partial view of the report.

Use Transaction SE38, followed by entering "RMPE_DATA_SUBJECT_INFO", to access this report.

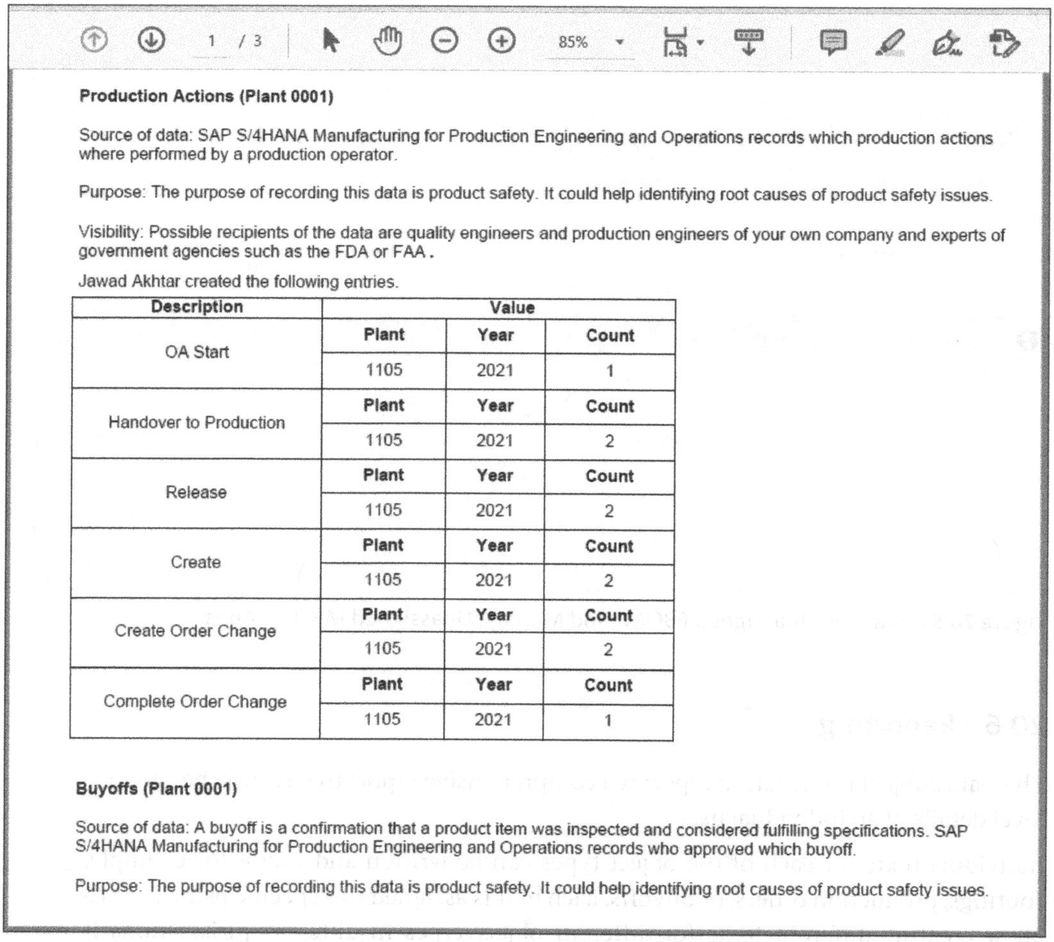

Production Actions (Plant 0001)

Source of data: SAP S/4HANA Manufacturing for Production Engineering and Operations records which production actions where performed by a production operator.

Purpose: The purpose of recording this data is product safety. It could help identifying root causes of product safety issues.

Visibility: Possible recipients of the data are quality engineers and production engineers of your own company and experts of government agencies such as the FDA or FAA.

Jawad Akhtar created the following entries.

Description	Value		
OA Start	Plant	Year	Count
	1105	2021	1
Handover to Production	Plant	Year	Count
	1105	2021	2
Release	Plant	Year	Count
	1105	2021	2
Create	Plant	Year	Count
	1105	2021	2
Create Order Change	Plant	Year	Count
	1105	2021	2
Complete Order Change	Plant	Year	Count
	1105	2021	1

Buyoffs (Plant 0001)

Source of data: A buyoff is a confirmation that a product item was inspected and considered fulfilling specifications. SAP S/4HANA Manufacturing for Production Engineering and Operations records who approved which buyoff.

Purpose: The purpose of recording this data is product safety. It could help identifying root causes of product safety issues.

Figure 20.55 Data Subject Information of Individual Users

To activate the required functions for each plant, navigate to the configuration menu path **SAP IMG · Production · Manufacturing for Production Engineering and Operations · General Settings · Get Data About Data Subjects.**

Note

To learn more about production engineering and operations, refer to the SAP Help article at this link: *http://s-prs.co/v216702*.

20.7 Summary

In this chapter, we covered some of the important configuration, master data, business processes, and reporting for SAP S/4HANA Manufacturing for production engineering and operations. We also discussed a business example in which an engineering drawing stored in the SAP Document Management service was used for production engineering to create a MBOM, and then the same was used in production operations.

The next chapter discusses the Early Warning System (EWS).

20

PART V

Monitoring and Evaluating Production Planning

Chapter 21
Early Warning System

The Early Warning System informs a supply chain manager whenever any deviation or exception to an important business process occurs, allowing for timely action to optimize and monitor your business processes.

The Early Warning System (EWS) is built on the same SAP S/4HANA logistics information structures as other standard analysis tools and reports, with added flexibility that allows a supply chain manager to monitor and receive alerts for only the specific exceptions on important business processes. It provides real-time updates and can be tailored to individual needs without the involvement of any custom ABAP development.

EWS is delivered as part of the logistics functionality and can provide alerts to individual business process owners in all of the logistics functions, such as the logistics information system (LIS), shop floor information system, purchasing information system, and plant maintenance information system. The alerts help business process owners quickly make important decisions or take actions as deemed necessary.

This chapter will explain the benefits of EWS, and then provide a step-by-step approach to set it up and run it in the SAP system.

21.1 Overview

There are many instances in production planning (PP) in which EWS can come in handy, depending on what is important to the business. This chapter will explain how easy and intuitive it is to set up EWS by following the steps in logical and sequential order. If the business requirements change at any time, then a supply chain manager can make changes or even delete the EWS alerts that had previously been set up.

Some examples of when EWS can be used are listed here:

- When the production scrap is recorded at greater than 5% of total production
- When sales figures show a decreasing trend for a high-running, high-profit item for the past three months
- When quality specifications of an important raw material are out by more than 3%

21

1003

- When a vendor continues to make late deliveries of critical components
- When inventory of precious metal exceeds a certain value

In any of these situations, EWS can be configured to the individual exception so as to receive timely alerts and have the necessary actions taken immediately. Although EWS can be set up in any logistics area, we use an example in PP. The relevant information structures available for PP are listed in Table 21.1.

Information Structure	Description
S021	Production order
S022	Operation
S023	Material
S024	Work center
S025	Run schedule header
S026	Material usage
S027	Product costs
S028	Reporting point statistics
S029	Kanban
S225	Goods receipts (GR): Repetitive manufacturing
S226	Material usage: Repetitive manufacturing
S227	Product costs: Repetitive manufacturing

Table 21.1 Standard Information Structures Available for Production Planning

[»]

Note

When EWS is set up in logistics, the relevant information structures are automatically made available by SAP S/4HANA. For example, if EWS is set up for use with the materials management (MM) functionality, all MM-related information structures become available.

Setting up EWS entails the creation of an exception by selecting the desired information structure from Table 21.1, followed by the characteristics and key figures. The requirements of each key figure need to be defined next, then, you configure the follow-up function. The third and final step is periodic analysis, in which you define the frequency with which the system monitors the exceptions and issues alerts. In summary, the required steps are as follows:

1. Create an exception.
2. Group the exceptions.
3. Create a periodic analysis.

> **Note**
>
> If there are several exceptions from the same information structure, they can be combined to create a *group exception*, which is a list of individual exceptions. Like the first step, the follow-up function for this step involves determining whether an email alert to an individual suffices or if it should be communicated to the entire distribution list.

Let's move on to discuss the first step in the following section: creating an exception.

21.2 Exceptions

An *exception* is an important data element that a production planner wants to monitor from a business point of view. The sequence of steps in creating an exception is as follows:

1. Choose the characteristics.
2. Define the key figures.
3. Define the characteristics values.
4. Choose the requirements.
5. Define the requirements.
6. Define the follow-up processing.

For this example, we've created an exception in PP (shop floor), ZPP10, using information structure SO21 (production order). In exception ZPP10, we specified that the system should issue an alert whenever material 25 has the following characteristics:

- Shows a negative trend of planned versus actual quantity deviation
- Exceeds actual scrap quantity of the material by 10 EA
- Quantity of goods received against a production order less than 80 EA

If the system records an exception in the SAP system, you want a popup message to appear, highlight the exception in red in EWS reporting, and send an email message to the SAP inbox. In the following sections, we'll cover the steps you need to perform to set up EWS in SAP S/4HANA.

21.2.1 Set Up Exceptions

Use menu path **Logistics** • **Logistics Controlling** • **Shop Floor Information System** • **Early Warning System** • **Exception** • **Create** or use Transaction MC=1 to set up the exception (see Figure 21.1). Follow this step-by-step process to create exception ZPP10:

1. Enter **Exception** "ZPP10", a short description, and **Info Structure** "S021" (info structure S021 corresponds to the production order).

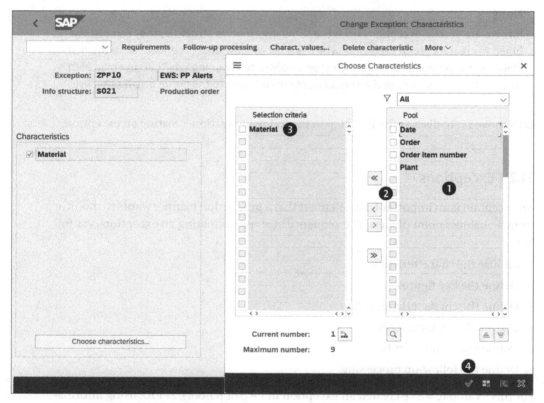

Figure 21.1 Characteristics Setup in EWS

2. In the selection screen, click **Choose Characteristics** to select the characteristics for which EWS needs to be activated.

3. In the popup screen that appears in Figure 21.1 ❶, move **Material** ❸ to the left column by choosing it from the available characteristics in the right-hand column and clicking **Choose** ❷. Choose **Execute** ❹ and the screen in Figure 21.2 appears. More than one characteristic can be selected from the right-hand column.

4. For each characteristic in Figure 21.2, provide the corresponding value or a range from which to choose. Click the **Material** characteristic ❶, then click the **Charact. Values** ❷ button at the top.

5. In the popup window that appears, enter the desired value or range of values for which the system should monitor EWS (Figure 21.2). For this example, enter "25" ❸ for the material. Choose **Copy** ❹.

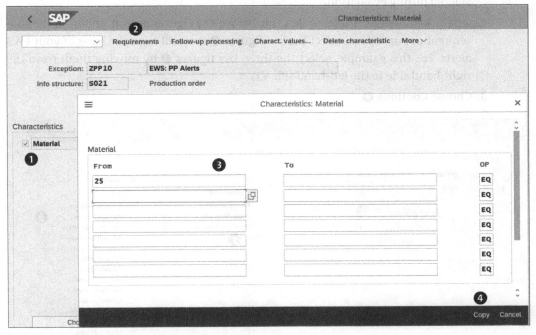

Figure 21.2 Characteristics Value for Material 25

> **Note**
>
> A range of materials can be given for EWS to monitor by filling out both the **From** and **To** fields shown in Figure 21.2. Alternatively, leaving these fields blank means EWS considers all materials in the alert.

21.2.2 Define Requirements

Now that the value for the characteristic material is defined, the next step is to define the requirements—that is, the information that a supply chain planner needs EWS to monitor in day-to-day business processes. Select the **Requirements** button shown previously in Figure 21.2 to define requirements for the material.

For this example, choose three key figures for the material (Figure 21.3) by following these steps:

1. Define the **Period to Analyze** fields ❶, which stipulate the past and future periods for which EWS must evaluate deviations. By defining **Previous Periods** as "12", you indicate that all key figures for the past 12 months that meet the conditions must be considered during evaluation.

2. On the **Requirements** screen, click the **Choose Key Figures** button, and from the subsequent popup screen, select the key figures ❸ that will form the basis of your EWS alerts. For this example, select the three key figures ❸ by moving them from the right-hand side to the left-hand side ❷.

3. Choose **Continue** ❹.

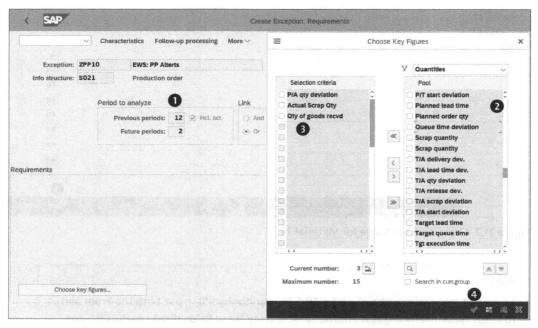

Figure 21.3 Key Figures for EWS

4. After selecting the key figures, choose **Define Requirement** to specify the limits or other details that form the basis for EWS alerts (Figure 21.4). The requirement has to be defined for each key figure. The options available are **Threshold Val. Anal.**, which requires a value to be specified, or **Trend Analysis**, which is used to monitor positive or negative trends and requires specifying the percentage of deviation in the trend.

5. For the first key figure shown in Figure 21.4, **P/A Qty Deviation** ❶, place the cursor on the key figure and double-click it. Alternatively, click the **Define Requirement** button, and a popup will appear ❷.

6. In the popup window, select the **Trend Analysis** radio button, and choose the **Continue** button. In the next popup window that appears, click the **Negative Trend** radio button ❸, then choose the **Continue** ❹ button.

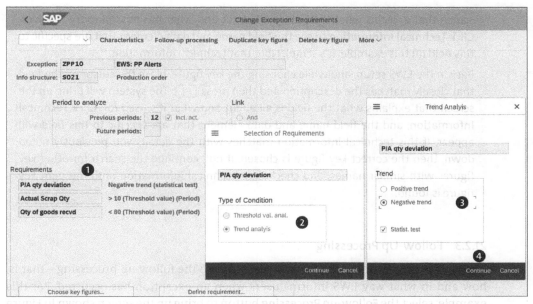

Figure 21.4 Define Requirements for Key P/A Quantity Deviation

7. For the second key figure, follow the same steps as for the first key figure. When the popup window appears, enter ">10" for **Actual Scrap Qty**, and then choose the **Continue** button.

8. Repeat the preceding step for the third key figure, **Qty of Goods Recvd**, with a threshold value of "<80".

Note

All other standard operands, such as less than, greater than, equal to, and not equal to, are available for use when setting threshold values.

Tips and Tricks

Given that there are so many key figures available with similar names or descriptions when setting up EWS, it often gets confusing to choose the right key figure to ensure that an alert will be issued for deviation through EWS. For this example, the **Actual Scrap Qty.** key figure differs from its description in the confirmation screen, where it's mentioned only as **Scrap**. In such cases, correct key figure selection in EWS can be ensured through technical names. In this example, the field name (technical) for scrap is XMNGA, and the field element is MC_XMNGA.

For example, say a production planner wants to monitor scrap quantity during confirmation of an operation via EWS. To do so, and while in the confirmation (Transaction CO11N), place the cursor on the **Scrap** field and press [F1]. The system will bring up the

21

screen that explains what the field is all about and what business purpose it serves. Click **Technical Information** to see the field name and data element that are specific to this field (in this example, it's scrap). Note that technical information.

Back in the EWS setup, and while choosing the key figure, place the cursor on the field that closely matches the description and then press F1. The system will bring up the screen that explains what the field is all about and what it's used for. Click **Technical Information**, and the field name and data element that are specific to this field will appear. If this technical information matches with the details you previously noted down, then the correct key figure is chosen. If not, continue the search for other key figures with similar names, and check their technical information until the right key figure is found.

21.2.3   Follow-Up Processing

The next step in defining an exception is to define the follow-up processing—that is, how and in what way EWS informs users when an exception has occurred. For this example, select the **Follow-up Processing** button to bring up the screen shown in Figure 21.5. Here, it's specified that whenever exception ZPP10 occurs, the details are to be marked in red and sent as a table to the entered mail recipient. This info also needs to be communicated by email to the corresponding SAP Inbox.

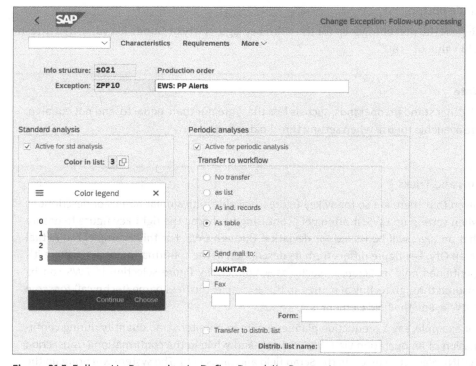

Figure 21.5 Follow-Up Processing to Define Requisite Parameters

Tips and Tricks

Select both the **Active for Std** (standard) **Analysis** and **Active for Periodic Analysis** checkboxes shown in Figure 21.5, as these will be subsequently checked whenever running analysis reports in EWS.

21.2.4   Group Exceptions

If more than one exception from the *same* information structure needs to be monitored in EWS, it's convenient and practical to group them together in exception groups for ease of reporting. For example, if the same material's scrap is monitored for its upper tolerance limit with the color red and its lower tolerance limit with the color yellow, then grouping these two different exceptions provides details in one list or report in EWS. Let's clarify this further. A production planner defines that whenever the material scrap is exceeded by greater than 10% (upper tolerance limit), the system highlights it in red in EWS. When the material scrap is less than 10% (lower tolerance limit), the system highlights it in yellow in EWS.

If no such requirement exists, then there's no need to define the exception grouping.

Note

For this example, exception grouping isn't used. However, the concepts and other details covered in this chapter are sufficient for a user to quickly set up exception grouping. Exception grouping is found in the same menu path as EWS.

21.3   Set Up Periodic Analysis

Now that the exceptions have been defined, the last step in setting up EWS is to define the frequency with which the system should alert the person who set up EWS (e.g., every eight hours, daily, once a week, or once a month). For this example, we need to set up periodic analysis for exception ZPP10 by setting up the variant and defining the frequency of the analysis.

To get to the **Periodic Analysis** screen, follow menu path **Logistics • Logistics Controlling • Shop Floor Information System • Early Warning System • Periodic Analysis • Area to Analyze • Create**, or use Transaction MC=7. Then follow these steps:

1. Enter "ZPP10" for **Exception** to indicate the exception for periodic analysis, and choose **Create** (Figure 21.6 ❶). A popup window appears asking for the name of the variant to create ❷.

2. Define ZPP10 as the variant. Click the **Create** button in the popup window to open the **Variants: Change Screen Assignment** screen ❸.

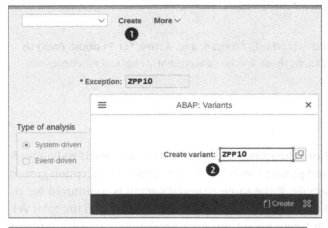

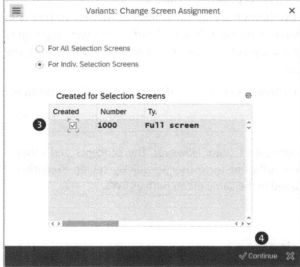

Figure 21.6 Setting Up Periodic Analysis

3. Define this variant as applicable for the individual screens (**For Indiv. Selection Screens**), which means that the parameters of variant ZPP10 and material 25 are automatically available for selection on the EWS screen for info structure S021, number 1000. If the **For All Selection Screens** radio button is chosen, then these parameters are available for all the different screens of EWS by default. Click the **Continue** button ❹.

4. On the screen shown in Figure 21.7 ❶, define the initial screen parameters for the variant. For this example, define that the system should automatically select material 25 ❷ and make it available as the default.

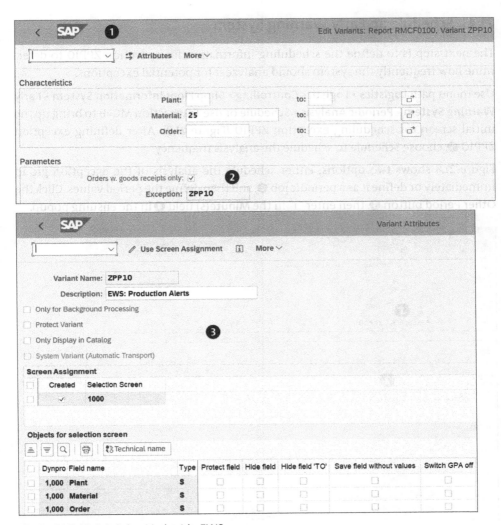

Figure 21.7 Maintaining Variant in EWS

5. After defining the parameters, choose **Attributes** ❶, and provide a meaningful description of the variant ❸. This description is communicated whenever EWS needs to alert an exception, in both the form of a popup window and also when it's delivered to an SAP Inbox as a list or table. An example of a meaningful description is "Production material is out of specification," which immediately alerts the concerned person to respond, instead of a more generic and vague description, such as "PP Specs. are out." This approach also helps if the same alert is sent to many people in the form of a distribution list. For this example, enter "EWS: Production Alerts" in **Description** ❸. Finally, click **Save** or press ⌃Ctrl⌃+⌃S⌃ to save the periodic analysis.

A message appears to confirm that variant ZPP10 is saved with all the values on the selection screen.

21.4   Schedule an Early Warning System

The next step is to define the scheduling information for exception ZPP10 to determine how frequently the system should analyze it for potential exceptions.

Use menu path **Logistics • Logistics Controlling • Shop Floor Information System • Early Warning System • Periodic Analysis • Schedule** or use Transaction MC=B to bring up the initial screen for scheduling exception ZPP10 (Figure 21.8). After defining exception ZPP10 ❶, choose **Schedule** to schedule the analysis frequency.

Figure 21.8 shows two options: either schedule the analysis of the exception group immediately or define it as a periodic job ❷, and then define the period values. Click the **Other Period** button ❸, then enter "1" in the **Minute(s)** field ❹ in the ensuing popup.

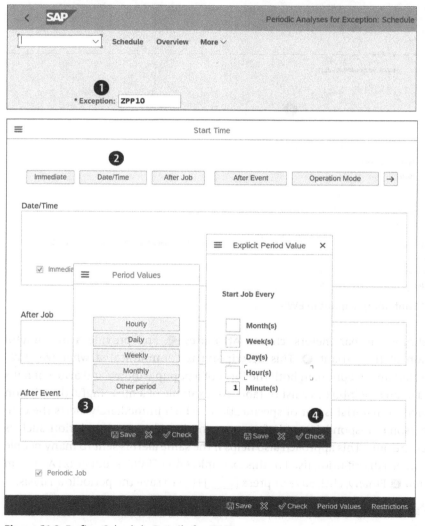

Figure 21.8 Define Schedule Details for EWS

The option to schedule the job immediately ensures that any new exception is immediately reported. However, if the **Date/Time** button is used, for example, then exception monitoring and reporting start on that specified date and time only, as a scheduled job.

The second option for scheduling a periodic job helps ensure that system resources aren't unduly overburdened.

[+]

> **Tips and Tricks**
>
> The scheduling frequency should be practical and within a reasonable gap—for example, daily. Under the **Daily** scheduling option, all exceptions for the entire day are consolidated into one issued alert. This allows the person who set up the alert to attend to all exceptions in one sitting.

Choose **Save** to save the scheduling details. After saving, a message appears to confirm that the background job for exception ZPP10 has been successfully planned.

This ends the discussion of how to set up EWS. The next section shows how EWS works in the system when the user performs day-to-day business functions, and how the system alerts the user who sets up EWS when an exception occurs. The business users can continue to perform and report their daily activities in SAP, such as performing GRs against purchase orders, reporting daily production with scrap percentages, and recording the quality results of inspection lots. Actual monitoring occurs and alerts are triggered in EWS based on this day-to-day information.

21.5 Triggering an Early Warning System

21

For this example, the business process owner (the production supervisor) creates a production order for material 25. The production supervisor records the actual production and the scrap via the production confirmation transaction in SAP. The details recorded in confirmation form the basis of the EWS. Any negative trend in the production of material—that is, any scrap greater than 10 EA or quantity of the produced material below 80 EA—causes EWS to alert the person who set it up. For this example, the alert is sent as a popup, and an email is sent to the person's SAP Inbox.

To create a new production order, follow menu path **Logistics • Production • Shop Floor Control • Order • Create • With Material**, or use Transaction CO01. If EWS is set up for a process order, then use Transaction COR1 to create a new process order.

Enter **Material** as "25", **Production Plant** as "1100", and **Order Type** as "PP10" and press `Enter`. On the **Production Order** screen (see Figure 21.9), enter **Total Qty** (planned) as "200 EA", and release the production order by clicking **Release Order**. Release and save the production order, and, for this example, the system then generates production order number 80000021.

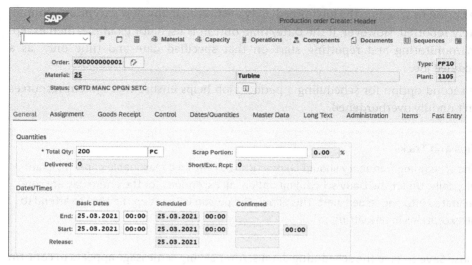

Figure 21.9 Production Order Creation

The next step is to record the production quantities and the scrap in the confirmation of the production order. To record confirmation of the production order, follow menu path **Logistics · Production · Shop Floor Control · Confirmation · Enter · For Order**, or use Transaction CO15 (Figure 21.10).

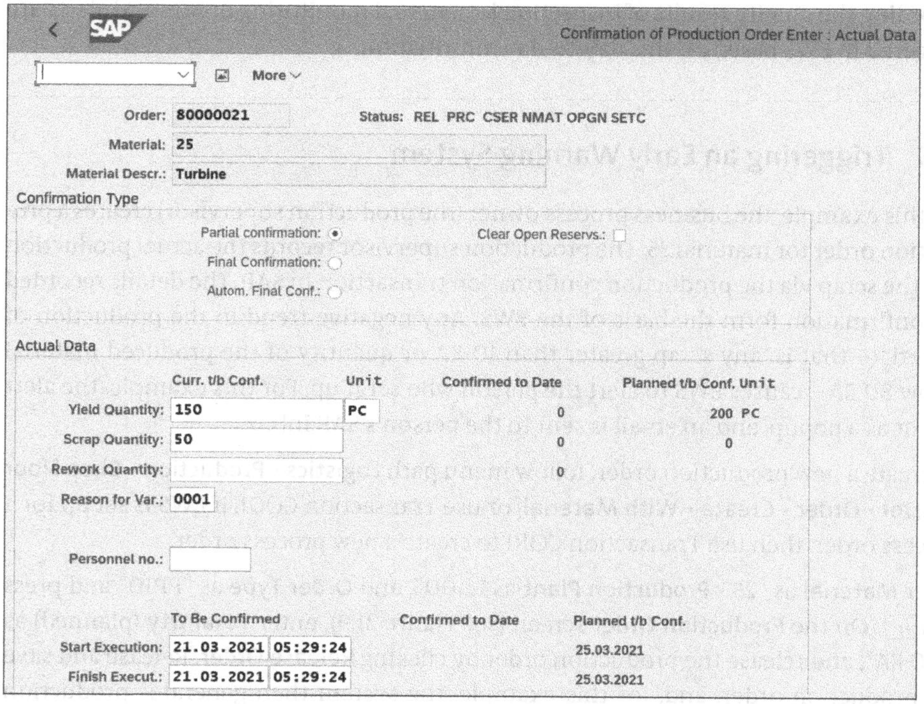

Figure 21.10 Production Order Confirmation with Scrap Quantity

Enter "80000021" in **Order** for the production order number, then press ⌜Enter⌟. In the **Confirmation of Production Order Enter: Actual Data** screen, enter the production quantity (**Yield Quantity**) as "150 EA" and **Scrap Quantity** of "50". Save the confirmation.

As soon as the confirmation is saved, the system issues a popup (see Figure 21.11) message about the deviation (exception).

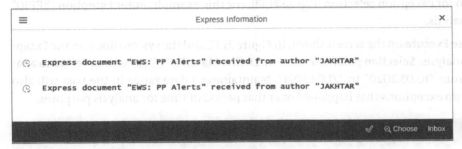

Figure 21.11 Popup Alert Issued by EWS as Soon as Exception Takes Place

Figure 21.11 shows that two of the three exceptions (deviations) have occurred:

- The planned versus actual production shows a negative trend. That is, the planned production quantity was 200 EA but actual production was 150 EA, hence the negative trend.
- The production scrap recorded in the confirmation was 50 EA, which is greater than the 10 EA or more limit set to issue an EWS alert.

The third exception hasn't occurred, which is if the production quantity during confirmation was less than 80 EA. For this example, the produced quantity (yield) was 150 EA for production order 80000021.

The system also delivers the same exception message in the SAP inbox.

> **Tips and Tricks**
>
> While maintaining scheduling to analyze for individual exceptions or exception groupings, make sure you eliminate duplication of information so that the system doesn't present the same information repeatedly—first in an individual exception and then in an exception grouping. This is achieved by adopting a well-thought-out approach prior to setting up EWS—for example, by making a list of all important materials for which there's a need to monitor parameters for deviations.

21.6 Exception Analysis

Finally, we'll show how to analyze exceptions with EWS in the shop floor information system. While alert monitoring is certainly a valuable EWS tool to promptly alert a supply chain planner of any deviations and exceptions, it's often required to have detailed information about the exceptions. Fortunately, EWS is supported by PP, which ensures that comprehensive details related to all exceptions are instantly available.

Follow menu path **Logistics • Logistics Controlling • Shop Floor Information System • Early Warning System • Exception Analysis**, or use Transaction MCYJ to get to the initial screen for exception selection (Figure 21.12). For this example, enter **Exception** "ZPP10" for analysis.

Choose **Execute** on the screen shown in Figure 21.12, and the system displays the **Exception Analysis: Selection** parameter screen. Define **Material** "25", as well as **Period to analyze** from "10.03.2020" to "21.03.2021". Maintaining a date range in the past will also bring up exceptions that happened over that period of time for analysis purposes.

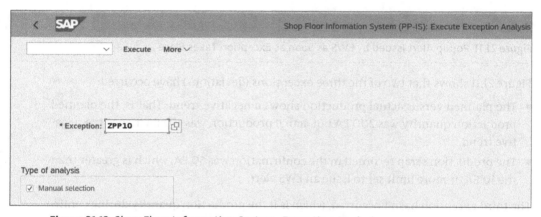

Figure 21.12 Shop Floor Information System: Exception Analysis

Select the **Order w. Goods Receipts Only** checkbox to denote that the system should only take those production orders into account for which the GRs in the warehouse have been undertaken.

Execute the exception analysis report (by pressing `F8` or clicking **Execute**) on the screen in Figure 21.12, and the system displays the results, as shown in Figure 21.13.

This exception analysis shows the three defined key figures ❶ with data in separate columns. Further, the color is red for the entire row of the **Material** column, as we originally defined in Figure 21.5. Keep the cursor on a key figure and click **Choose**. In the ensuing popup, not only will all key figures appear but also the key figures with exceptions will be highlighted in red.

As with all standard analyses reports, use the **Switch Drilldown** button ❷ to view details on a production order basis or on a day (date) basis. The lower half of the figure provides production order details. For this example, production order 80000021 ❸ contains all the correct details that were previously entered in various business transactions, such as production order, confirmation, and GR for production order.

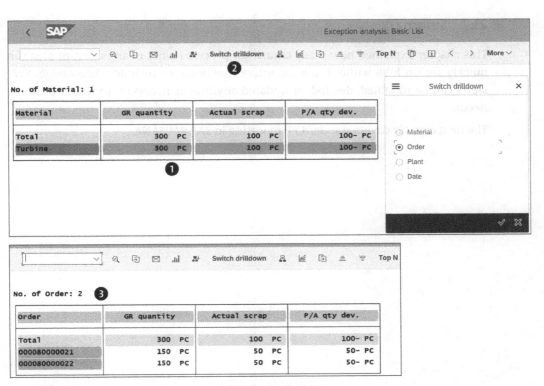

Figure 21.13 Exception Analysis Report of EWS for Material 25

Access the screen shown in Figure 21.14 via Transaction SBWP, which is the SAP inbox. You'll see the two EWS alerts, as well as the relevant details based on which the SAP system created those alerts.

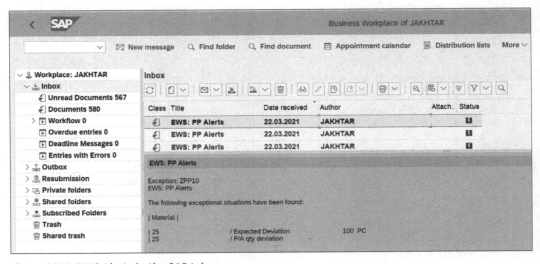

Figure 21.14 EWS Alerts in the SAP Inbox

21

21.7   Summary

This chapter explained how easily a business process owner in any relevant area can quickly set up EWS without any extensive functional or technical knowledge. EWS alerts can be modified, deleted, or updated anytime as necessary to reflect business needs.

The next chapter covers standard PP reporting in SAP S/4HANA.

Chapter 22
Production Planning Reporting

Timely, accurate, and comprehensive information helps a company make better business decisions. A planner can immediately start to use a large number of information systems and standard reports available in SAP S/4HANA for production planning, as well as for logistics.

This chapter provides detailed guidance on how to leverage a large number of standard reports that are available in all the logistics areas of SAP S/4HANA. Once you're familiar with the features and functions for reporting, including tools and icons, it becomes easier to navigate to unexplored areas of reporting.

22.1 The Basics of Reporting

To fully take advantage of SAP S/4HANA, it's essential to become familiar with the icons and other features frequently available for use in reports. Because these icons and functions are the same in all the information systems and analyses, a user can navigate faster and be able to get to desired information more quickly, or even find tips and tricks to manage the display and availability of data as needed.

> **Note**
>
> It's important to note that you may find similar icons in master data and transactions such as the repetitive manufacturing (REM) planning table (Transaction MF50) or the stock/requirements list (Transaction MD04), but these icons may have different meanings and functions. For example, in a standard business process, clicking the **Details** icon brings up the **Item** details screen for the object. In the reporting function, however, this icon brings up a comprehensive list titled **All Key Figures**.

Information systems present a large amount of data and information in logically structured lists and sections. The following menu paths and transaction codes for both discrete manufacturing and process manufacturing are provided to make the information systems easier to use:

- **Discrete manufacturing**
  Choose **Logistics • Production • Shop Floor Control • Information System • Order Information System**, or use Transaction COOIS.

- **Process manufacturing**
  Choose **Logistics • Production – Process • Process Order • Reporting • Order Information System**, or use Transaction COOISPI.

22.2   Report Parameters

When we talk about the *order information system*, it can be either the production order information system or the process order information system. The former is specific to discrete manufacturing reporting, while the latter is for process manufacturing reporting.

An *information system* consists of the most up-to-date information about a specific object and is based on the transactions that the user has performed as part of the business process. For example, when a planner executes the operations list in a production order information system, the system displays the current status of various operations, including those that are completely or partially confirmed. If the same report is run or executed again after six hours—for example, when the user has recorded more confirmations for production orders—at that time the system shows up-to-date (and different) information. Another example is that when the user first uses the sales information system (SIS), the system shows the creation of 10 sales order for a specific material. After six hours, when the user again runs the report (in SIS), the number of sales orders has increased to 18. This information helps to reflect the accurate and up-to-date status of various activities and business processes.

In the order information system, we've divided the large number of available options for parameters selection into several figures in the following sections for ease of understanding and comprehension.

22.2.1   Selection Screen at the Header Level

Figure 22.1 shows the **Process Order Information System** screen (Transaction COOISPI). Here you need to first select the list from the **List** dropdown menu; further parameter selection directly relates to the list.

Based on the list option that you select, you can then define further selection parameters. If **Components** is selected from the dropdown list in Figure 22.2, then the user will need to give selection parameters in the screen shown in Figure 22.3 (in the next section) under **Selection at Component Level**. If **Operations/Phases** is selected from the dropdown list, then the user will provide greater details in the **Select. at Operation Level** area in Figure 22.1.

This all-in-one report caters to the reporting requirements of all major business processes of production. Notice that a user can also provide the sales order number with a sales order item number, if a company has make-to-order (MTO) process order (or production order) scenarios. Similarly, if a process order references any work breakdown structure (WBS) element, enter that information in the selection criteria at the header level.

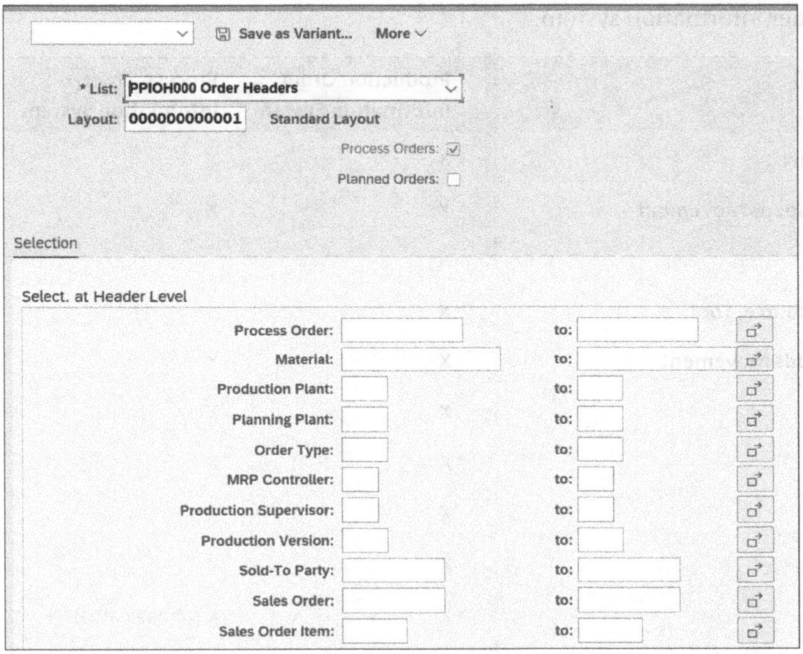

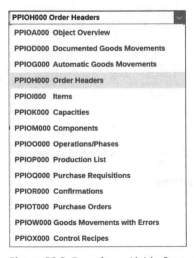

Figure 22.1 Selection Screen for Process Order Information System

Figure 22.2 Dropdown List in Process Order Information System

For the example shown previously in Figure 22.1, select **Order Headers** from the drop-down list, and then on the header level, define **Production Plant** as "1105".

A user can select an option from 18 available lists in discrete manufacturing and 14 available lists for process manufacturing. In fact, selection of the list is the first step that a user will need to complete before running the order information system.

Table 22.1 shows the available lists in the production order information system and in the process order information system.

List	Production Order Information System	Process Order Information System
Object Overview	X	X
Documented Goods Movement	X	X
Trigger Points	X	
Production Resource/Tool	X	
Automatic Goods Movement	X	X
Order Headers	X	X
Items	X	X
Capacities	X	X
Components	X	X
Operations	X	X (phases also)
Production List	X	X
Purchase Requisitions	X	X
Confirmations	X	X
Sequences	X	
Purchase Orders	X	X
Documents Links	X	
Goods Movements with Errors	X	X
Control Recipes	X	X (control recipe)

Table 22.1 Comparison of Available Lists in Information Systems

22.2.2 Selection at the Operations and Components Levels with Options

Scrolling down in the screen shown previously in Figure 22.1 leads to several different views in which a user can enter selection details at the operation and component levels in the **Select. at Operation Level** view shown in Figure 22.3. A user can also select a specific system status (**System Status**) with the **Excl.** checkbox selected to exclude information having the specified status. For example, if a user doesn't want to see partially confirmed operations/phases in the report, then enter "PCNF" in the **System Status** field and select the **Excl.** checkbox.

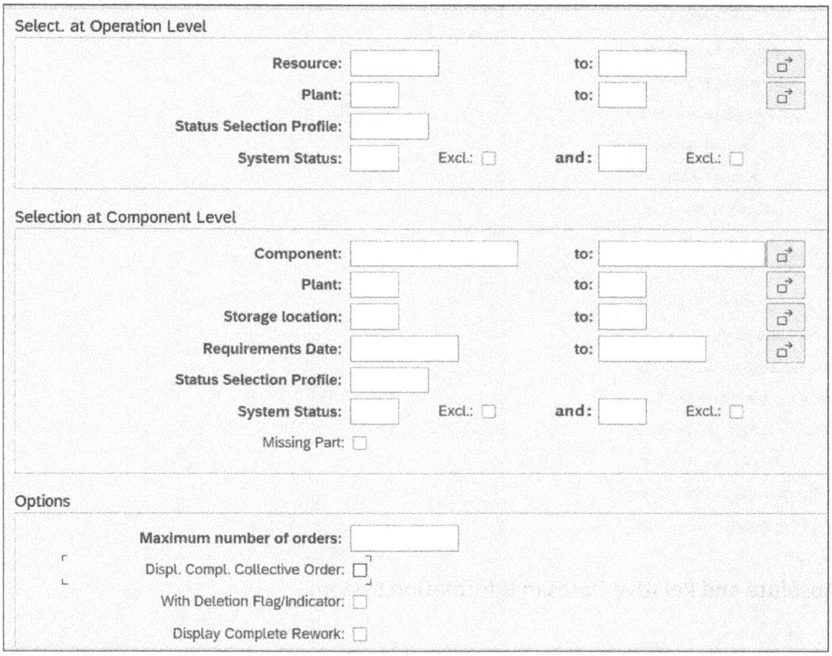

Figure 22.3 Selection Options at Operation and Component Levels

Select the **Missing Part** checkbox so that the system displays the components with the missing parts status in the process orders. The missing parts status is denoted by **MSPT**.

A user can also limit the number of process orders that the system displays so that it's displaying only collective process orders or process orders with deletion flags by selecting the relevant checkboxes.

22.2.3 Selection Screen for Dates

Scrolling further down, there is a large number of choices of dates. If a user wants a report to show from a certain start date to end date in the process order, then define this in basic start dates, actual start dates, or even according to the release dates of the process orders.

1025

The **Relative Dates at Header Level** area (see Figure 22.4) corresponds to the time interval between today's date and any other date, either in the past or future. For example, if you want to see all the process orders for the past 100 days and for the next 50 days, then you enter "100–" in the **Relative Basic Start Date** field and "50" in the **To** field. Dates in the past are denoted by adding the negative sign after entering the number (e.g., 100–).

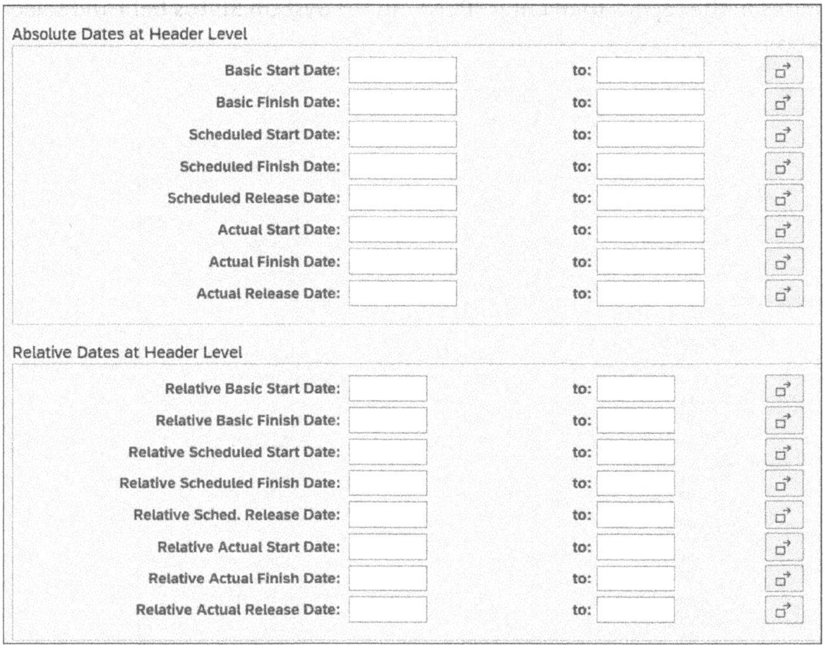

Figure 22.4 Absolute and Relative Dates in Information System

22.2.4   Multiple Selection

So far, on the selection screen of a report, the option has been available to enter any parameter in a range or an interval. For example, for the **Relative Basic Start Date** field shown in Figure 22.4, a user can only enter a selection interval. But what if a user wants to exclude a certain period within the date range on the selection screen or include two specific dates, apart from the dates given in the interval? This and several other options are available via the **Multiple Selection** settings in all information systems and reports of all components.

Click the **Multiple Selection** icon shown in Figure 22.5 for the **Process Order** fields. In the resulting screen, four tabs allow a user to include or exclude single values or even an entire range. Enter information in each of the four tabs, and the ensuing output (report) will show the desired results. Further, there are additional available icons to facilitate the user, such as copying data from a clipboard, adding or deleting a line within the values, or using the **Multiple Selection** option. The **Multiple Selection** icon enables a user to select multiple values by clicking the requisite checkboxes.

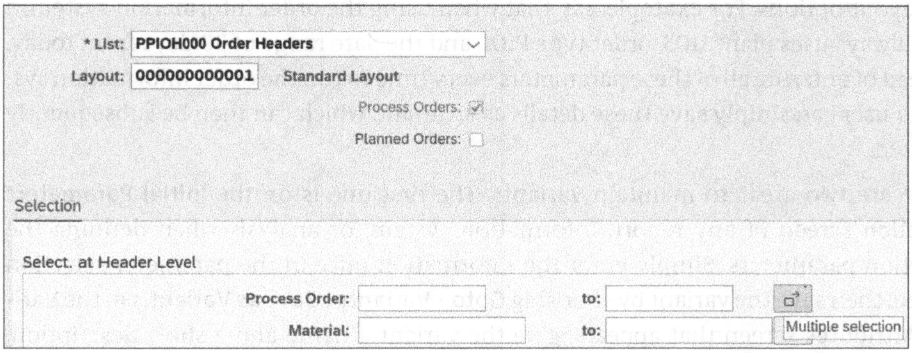

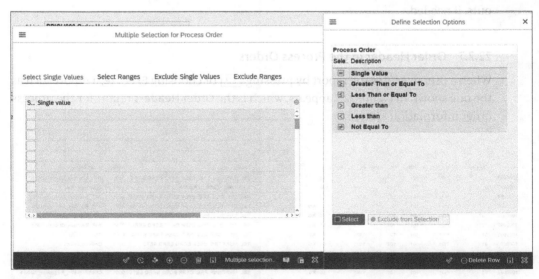

Figure 22.5 Multiple Selection Option in Order Information System

22.2.5   Maintain Selection

A frequently used and available option is the **Maintain Selection** option. When **Maintain Selection** is clicked, the **Maintain Selection Options** screen appears, as shown earlier in Figure 22.6. Use any of the available options in this screen. Alternatively, a shortcut to reach the **Maintain Selection Options** screen is to double-click the relevant field of the selection screen of any report.

Figure 22.6 Maintain Selection Option in Order Information System

22.2.6 Maintain Variant

Maintaining a variant in SAP S/4HANA is similar to saving a layout, which is then available for repeated use when needed. A user can also set a variant as default by managing the layout options. For example, say that when using the order information system, a user always uses plant 1105, order type PI01, and the date range of 30 days from today. Instead of entering all of these parameters every time to run the order information system, a user can simply save these details as a variant, which can then be subsequently selected.

There are two areas to maintain variants. The first one is on the **Initial Parameters Selection** screen of any report, information system, or analysis when defining the selection parameters. Simply enter the information once in the parameter selection screen, then save the variant by choosing **Goto • Variants • Save as Variant**. On the **Variant Attributes** screen that appears, give the variant a name and a short description, then choose whether to make each field required, hidden, or protected from data entry. With the variant saved, next time simply choose **Goto • Variants • Get** to get the variant. Incorrect or unwanted variants can also be deleted.

The second option to save a variant is used when an analysis report is already executed in the order information system. The system displays all list fields, and a user has made the required changes—or example, any filter set, any sorting of columns in ascending or descending order performed, or aggregation. Choose **Select Layout** and select the **Save Layout** option from the dropdown. In the ensuing popup, enter the name of the layout and a short description. Here again, a user can change or delete the saved layouts, if needed.

22.2.7 Order Header in the Process Orders

When a user executes the report by pressing [F8] or choosing **Execute**, a report such as the one shown in Figure 22.7 appears, which is the **Order Headers** report for the process order information system.

Order	Material	Icon	Order Type	MRP ct.	Pr.Superv.	Plant	Target Qt		System Status	Version	Material description
1000098	107		PI01	101	101	1105	10	Choose Layout...	REL CNF DLV PRC CSER BASC BCRQ BRRQ*	0001	WIP_Batches_Chemical Mix
1000085	81		PI01	101	101	1105	100	Change Layout...	CRTD PRC CSER BCRQ MANC SETC	0001	Chemical Mix
1000094	107		PI01	101	101	1105	10	Save Layout...	REL CNF DLV PRC CSER BCRQ BRRQ GMPS*	0001	WIP_Batches_Chemical Mix
1000095	107		PI01	101	101	1105	10 KG	Manage Layouts	REL CNF DLV PRC CSER BCRQ BRRQ GMPS*	0001	WIP_Batches_Chemical Mix
1000096	107		PI01	101	101	1105	10 KG		REL CNF DLV PRC CSER BASC BCRQ BRRQ*	0001	WIP_Batches_Chemical Mix
1000097	107		PI01	101	101	1105	10 KG		REL CNF DLV PRC CSER BASC BCRQ BRRQ*	0001	WIP_Batches_Chemical Mix
1000091	81		PI01	101	101	1105	10 KG		REL MSPT CNF DLV PRC CSER BASC BCRQ*	0001	Chemical Mix
1000092	81		PI01	101	101	1105	10 KG		REL MSPT PRC CSER BCRQ BRRQ SETC	0001	Chemical Mix
1000093	81		PI01	101	101	1105	10 KG		REL MSPT PRC CSER BASC BCRQ BRRQ SET.	0001	Chemical Mix
1000061	91		PI01	101	101	1105	10 KG		REL MSPT CRCR CNF PRC CSER BCRQ BRR.	0001	Chemical Mix_Resource_Netwo.
1000062	91		PI01	101	101	1105	10 KG		REL MSPT CNF PRC CSER BCRQ BRRQ SETC	0001	Chemical Mix_Resource_Netwo.
1000063	91		PI01	101	101	1105	10 KG		REL MSPT CNF DLV PRC CSER BCRQ BRRQ*	0001	Chemical Mix_Resource_Netwo.
1000064	91		PI01	101	101	1105	10 KG		REL MSPT CNF DLV PRC CSER BCRQ BRRQ*	0001	Chemical Mix_Resource_Netwo.

Figure 22.7 Order Headers in Order Information System

In the following sections, we'll explore a few important options that are available in this report, such as aggregation, setting a filter, or viewing the information in a graphical presentation. Some of the common and obvious options, such as sorting by ascending or descending order of information and changing or displaying objects, aren't covered.

Fields Selection

Figure 22.7, shown previously, displays only a limited number of columns and information, whereas a user can display and manipulate an enormous amount of information and even save the display layout, if it's routinely used.

When a user chooses **Change Layout**, the **Change Layout** screen appears, as shown in Figure 22.8. The columns or fields already displayed in the report are shown on the left-hand side, whereas the fields or columns that can be displayed in a report are shown on the right-hand side. To further facilitate the user in selecting fields, use several filters to group together relevant fields so that it's easier for a user to choose and display the desired fields in the report. For this example, use the **Quantities** filter, and then only quantity-relevant fields are available for users to choose from. Click the relevant field shown in Figure 22.8 and move it with the left-arrow icon so the system displays the content in the report (see Figure 22.9).

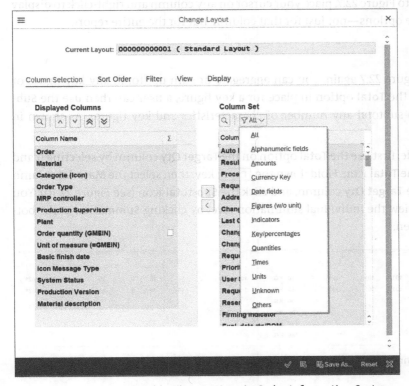

Figure 22.8 Layout and Fields Filter Options in Order Information System

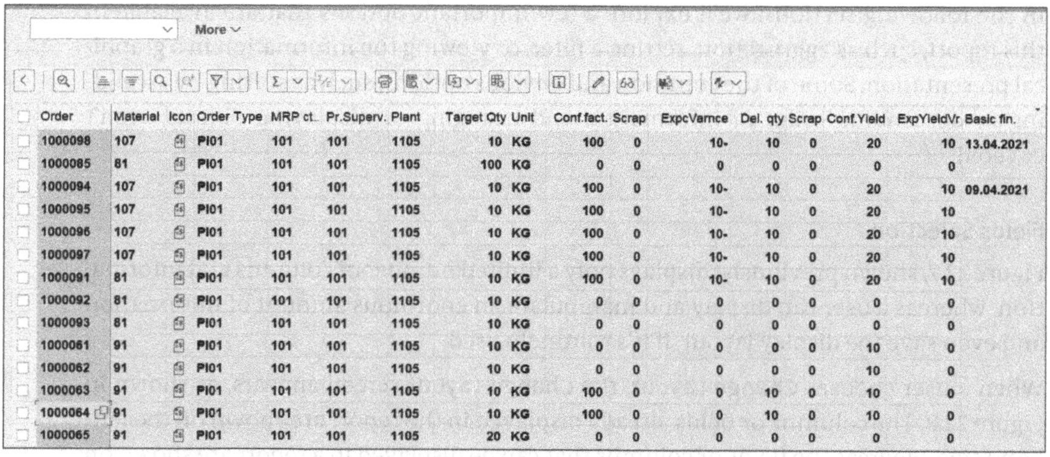

Order	Material	Icon	Order Type	MRP ct..	Pr.Superv.	Plant	Target Qty	Unit	Conf.fact.	Scrap	ExpcVarnce	Del. qty	Scrap	Conf.Yield	ExpYieldVr	Basic fin.
1000098	107		PI01	101	101	1105	10	KG	100	0	10-	10	0	20	10	13.04.2021
1000085	81		PI01	101	101	1105	100	KG	0	0	0	0	0	0	0	
1000094	107		PI01	101	101	1105	10	KG	100	0	10-	10	0	20	10	09.04.2021
1000095	107		PI01	101	101	1105	10	KG	100	0	10-	10	0	20	10	
1000096	107		PI01	101	101	1105	10	KG	100	0	10-	10	0	20	10	
1000097	107		PI01	101	101	1105	10	KG	100	0	10-	10	0	20	10	
1000091	81		PI01	101	101	1105	10	KG	100	0	10-	10	0	20	10	
1000092	81		PI01	101	101	1105	10	KG	0	0	0	0	0	0	0	
1000093	81		PI01	101	101	1105	10	KG	0	0	0	0	0	0	0	
1000061	91		PI01	101	101	1105	10	KG	0	0	0	0	0	10	0	
1000062	91		PI01	101	101	1105	10	KG	0	0	0	0	0	10	0	
1000063	91		PI01	101	101	1105	10	KG	100	0	0	10	0	10	0	
1000064	91		PI01	101	101	1105	10	KG	100	0	0	10	0	10	0	
1000065	91		PI01	101	101	1105	20	KG	0	0	0	0	0	0	0	

Figure 22.9 Quantity-Related Fields in Information System

The following sections will show some more reporting features, such as the quick menu, aggregation, filter settings, and downloading data.

Quick Menu in Report

Referring back to Figure 22.7, place your cursor on any column and right-click to display all the available options—not just for that column, but for the entire report.

Aggregation

Referring to Figure 22.7 again, you can aggregate or sum up (total) any key figure or quantity. With the **Total** option in place for a key figure, a user can then use the **Sub-total** option to subtotal any number of characteristics and key figures, as shown in Figure 22.10.

For this example, first use the **Total** option on the **Target Qty** column by selecting it and then clicking the **Total** icon. Hold down the Ctrl key, then select the **Material** column followed by the **Target Qty** column, and click the **Sub-total** icon (see Figure 22.10). You can then also view the individual summation level by clicking **Summation** at the bottom of the screen.

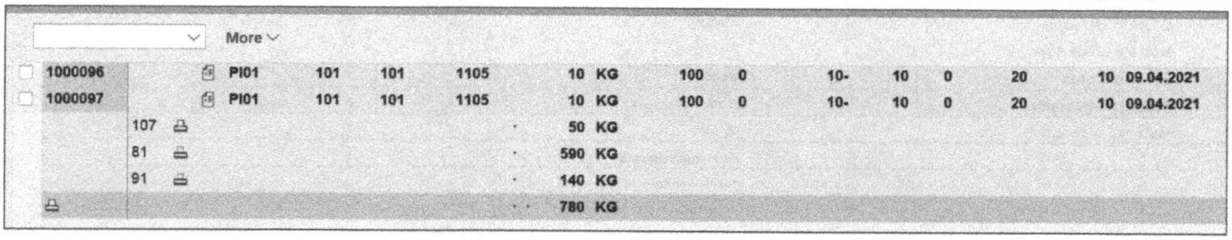

1000096			PI01	101	101	1105	10	KG	100	0	10-	10	0	20	10	09.04.2021
1000097			PI01	101	101	1105	10	KG	100	0	10-	10	0	20	10	09.04.2021
	107						50	KG								
	81						590	KG								
	91						140	KG								
							780	KG								

Figure 22.10 Summation (Total and Subtotal) in Order Information System

22.2.8   Filter Settings

While evaluating a report, sometimes it becomes important to filter out some information so that the system displays only the desired information.

Refer to Figure 22.7 once again. As shown in Figure 22.11, select the **Target Qty** column, click the **Filter** icon, and choose **Set Filter** to set the filter. In the popup that appears, either double-click the **Target quantity** field or use the **Maintain Selection** icon, which opens the popup window. Select **Greater Than or Equal To**, and choose **Continue**. Enter "50" in the **Order quantity** field so that the report should now only show target quantities equal to or greater than 50. This screen shows that the filter is in place with a little black arrow pointing downward on the **Target qty** column. The red arrows denote the list is sorted in descending (upward red arrow) or ascending (downward red arrow) order.

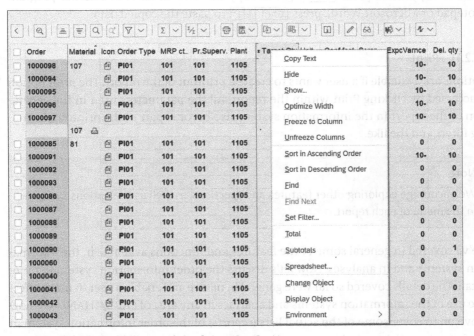

Figure 22.11 Setting Filter in Order Information System

Note

The system will interchangeably show the **Target Qty** or **Order Quantity** fields in this report. Either is basically the production order quantity (the GMEIN field).

22.2.9   Download

When executing a report or conducting a standard analysis, a user can also download the information in one of the several formats available by choosing the **Download** option. A user can also send the information as an email attachment or even perform an ABC analysis in the information system, although this is also available in the standard analysis reports.

22.2.10   Copy Selective Data to Microsoft Excel

A user can copy selected data if they don't want to download all the entire data from SAP S/4HANA into Excel or a different format. Press $\boxed{\text{Ctrl}}$+$\boxed{\text{Y}}$ to select the fields or content within the report. This enables block selection, in which you select the block of fields to copy. Then press $\boxed{\text{Ctrl}}$+$\boxed{\text{C}}$ to copy the data. In Excel or another program (Notepad or Microsoft Word), press $\boxed{\text{Ctrl}}$+$\boxed{\text{P}}$ to paste the copied data.

22.2.11   Print

Options are available if a user wants to create a printout of the report. The print option is accessed by clicking **Print** within the report. All the parameters used in the generation of the report in the information system also become part of the printout, including filters and the like.

[»]
> **Note**
> We encourage exploring other features and functions, as well as the options available in the menu of each report.

We've covered in general some of the features and functions available in the information systems and in analyses. Now let's discuss the order information system in more detail. The details covered so far were general in nature and enable a user to make effective use of the information systems and analyses in any area of SAP S/4HANA. We now move on to cover some of the actual lists (reports) of the order information system in the following sections and encourage exploring the others available. All of the following reports can be accessed via Transaction COOIS.

22.3   Order Information System Reports

Now that the basic understanding of icons and features of standard reports is covered, the following sections will cover some of the actual order reports, such as automatic goods movement, capacities, document links, and execution steps.

22.3.1   Automatic Goods Movement

In automatic goods movement, the system performs one or both of the following functions:

- If the **Backflush** functionality is activated, the component's consumption or goods issue (GI) is automatically recorded at the time of confirmation against the process order. This is denoted by movement type 261.

- If the **Auto-GR** functionality is activated, the system automatically performs the goods receipt (GR) for the process order of the confirmed production quantity when the user performs the confirmation for the process order. This is denoted by movement type 101.

From the **List** dropdown option shown earlier in Figure 22.1 (we'll be referring to this **List** dropdown for each of the report options discussed next), select **Automatic Goods Movements**. Figure 22.12 shows the **Mvmt type** (movement type) column for backflush and auto-GR.

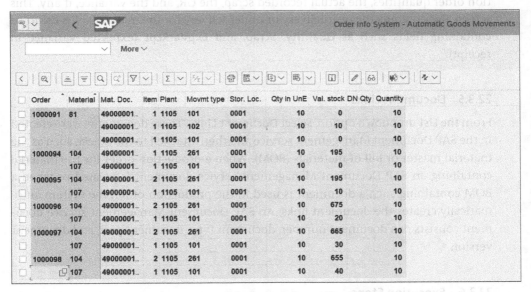

Order	Material	Mat. Doc.	Item	Plant	Movmt type	Stor. Loc.	Qty in UnE	Val. stock	DN Qty	Quantity
1000091	81	49000001...	1	1105	101	0001	10	0		10
		49000001...	1	1105	102	0001	10	10		10
		49000001...	1	1105	101	0001	10	0		10
1000094	104	49000001...	1	1105	261	0001	10	195		10
	107	49000001...	1	1105	101	0001	10	0		10
1000095	104	49000001...	2	1105	261	0001	10	195		10
	107	49000001...	1	1105	101	0001	10	10		10
1000096	104	49000001...	2	1105	261	0001	10	675		10
	107	49000001...	1	1105	101	0001	10	20		10
1000097	104	49000001...	2	1105	261	0001	10	665		10
	107	49000001...	1	1105	101	0001	10	30		10
1000098	104	49000001...	2	1105	261	0001	10	655		10
	107	49000001...	1	1105	101	0001	10	40		10

Figure 22.12 Automatic Goods Movements in Order Information System

22.3.2   Capacities

From the **List** dropdown option, select **Capacities**. Based on the information from the routing of the material, the system automatically calculates the required capacities when the user creates a production order. When the user confirms an operation of the production order, the system correspondingly reduces the capacity requirements of the work center.

This will display the work centers, the operation quantities, and the remaining processing time (in hours) for each of the production orders.

22.3.3 Production Resources/Tools

From the **List** dropdown option, select **Production Resource/Tool** (PRT). Although not directly involved in the production process, PRT plays a pivotal role in the manufacturing process.

The available PRT categories are material (**M**), equipment (**E**), document (**D**), or miscellaneous (**O**). The details in **Usage Value** denote the duration for which a PRT is needed during the production process for a production order.

22.3.4 Items

From the **List** dropdown option, select **Items**. This will display the items of the production order quantities, the actual recorded scrap, the GR, and the variance, if any. This screen also contains the overdelivery or underdelivery for the material, plus columns containing fields such as **Quantity**, **Scrap**, and **ExpVarRcpt** (expected variance in receipt).

22.3.5 Document Links

From the **List** dropdown option, select **Document Links**. These documents were created in the SAP Document Management service and then attached to the object, such as the material master or bill of materials (BOM). When a production order for the material containing an SAP Document Management service document is created or when a BOM containing such a document is used in the production order, the system automatically creates the document links. An SAP Document Management service document consists of a document number, document type, document part, and document version.

22.3.6 Execution Steps

In the production order information system, a user will see the same information in the **Control Recipe** list as is shown in the process order information system. Execution Steps (XSteps) or control recipes are used in process manufacturing, depending on the option the company chooses for control instructions in process management. For discrete manufacturing, the company can only implement the XSteps option in process management.

From the **List** dropdown option, select **Control Recipe**. This screen shows the status of the control recipe for the specific process order (**Created**, **Sent**, **Executed**, or **Terminated**), the **Batch** details, the destination details (**Dest. Type**, **Destinatn**, **Destination**

Address columns) of the control recipe, and the in-process (during production) **Inspection Lot** details (see Figure 22.13).

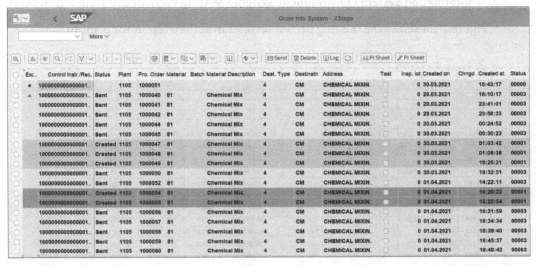

Figure 22.13 Execution Steps

We've now covered a few reports from the process order information system and the production order information system, and the remaining reports follow the same pattern, while containing information pertaining to a specific area or application.

22.4   Missing Parts Information System

Having access to a standard SAP S/4HANA report that contains information about missing parts of components in the production or process order is highly valuable for a company's production planner. Production or process orders with missing components are shown with the system status **MSPT**. When a user executes the report, the system not only shows the requirements quantity but also the committed or available quantity, as well as the shortage quantity.

The missing parts information system can be accessed for all of the different production types—that is, discrete manufacturing, process manufacturing, or REM. The menu path/transaction for each is listed here:

- **Discrete manufacturing**
  Choose **Logistics • Production • Shop Floor Control • Missing Parts Info System**, or use Transaction CO24.

- **Process manufacturing**
  Choose **Logistics • Production—Process • Process Order • Reporting • Missing Parts Info System**, or use Transaction CO24.

- **Repetitive manufacturing**
  Choose **Logistics · Production · Repetitive Manufacturing · Environment · Shop Floor Information System · Environment System · Missing Parts**, or use Transaction CO24.

Figure 22.14 shows the missing parts information system report for plant 1105.

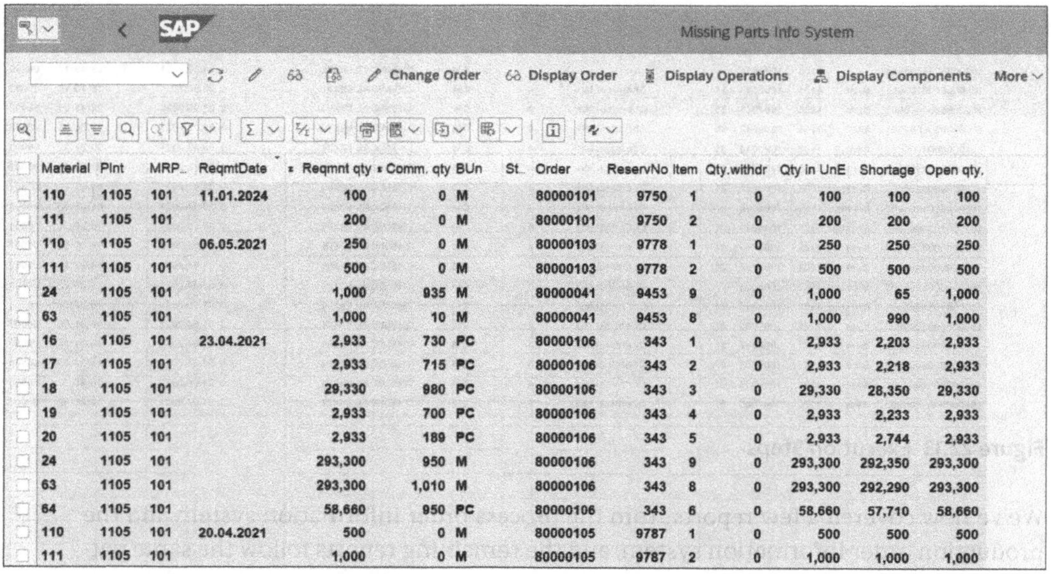

Material	Plnt	MRP_	ReqmtDate	± Reqmnt qty	± Comm. qty	BUn	St_	Order	ReservNo	Item	Qty.withdr	Qty in UnE	Shortage	Open qty.
110	1105	101	11.01.2024	100	0	M		80000101	9750	1	0	100	100	100
111	1105	101		200	0	M		80000101	9750	2	0	200	200	200
110	1105	101	06.05.2021	250	0	M		80000103	9778	1	0	250	250	250
111	1105	101		500	0	M		80000103	9778	2	0	500	500	500
24	1105	101		1,000	935	M		80000041	9453	9	0	1,000	65	1,000
63	1105	101		1,000	10	M		80000041	9453	8	0	1,000	990	1,000
16	1105	101	23.04.2021	2,933	730	PC		80000106	343	1	0	2,933	2,203	2,933
17	1105	101		2,933	715	PC		80000106	343	2	0	2,933	2,218	2,933
18	1105	101		29,330	980	PC		80000106	343	3	0	29,330	28,350	29,330
19	1105	101		2,933	700	PC		80000106	343	4	0	2,933	2,233	2,933
20	1105	101		2,933	189	PC		80000106	343	5	0	2,933	2,744	2,933
24	1105	101		293,300	950	M		80000106	343	9	0	293,300	292,350	293,300
63	1105	101		293,300	1,010	M		80000106	343	8	0	293,300	292,290	293,300
64	1105	101		58,660	950	PC		80000106	343	6	0	58,660	57,710	58,660
110	1105	101	20.04.2021	500	0	M		80000105	9787	1	0	500	500	500
111	1105	101		1,000	0	M		80000105	9787	2	0	1,000	1,000	1,000

Figure 22.14 Missing Parts Information System

22.5 Summary

In this chapter, we covered a large number of features and functions of standard reports, as well as the standard analysis available. We also covered the actual order reports, such as automatic goods movement, capacities, document links, and XSteps. Finally, we discussed the missing parts information system, a helpful tool for the production planner.

The next chapter covers standard planning analysis.

Chapter 23
Standard Planning Analysis

Standard analyses in SAP S/4HANA provide great insight into many of the important logistics and supply chain management key performance indicators to help companies make informed decisions. Standard analyses aren't just available in production planning but also in all logistics and supply chain management areas of SAP S/4HANA.

Standard analyses enable users to draw information from the available standard info structures in SAP S/4HANA. The difference between the shop floor information system (reports) and standard analyses is that in the information systems, the information is dynamic and changes when the user performs the relevant business functions. In standard analyses, the system instead draws from historical information to enable the user to make better business decisions. In other words, the data and information from the information systems flow into the analyses.

This chapter will cover some of the standard analyses for discrete manufacturing. We also show a few features and functionalities available only in analyses and not in information systems, such as time series analysis and ABC analysis. The concepts underlying standard analyses for discrete manufacturing that are discussed in this chapter will enable a user to explore standard analysis of process manufacturing and repetitive manufacturing (REM), for which we've provided the necessary menu paths, as well as the associated transaction codes.

> **Note**
>
> Refer to Table 23.1 through Table 23.3 for the transaction codes of the various available standard analyses in discrete manufacturing, process manufacturing, and REM, respectively. We'll also provide the relevant SAP S/4HANA menu paths to access the standard analyses of each production type.

23.1 Discrete Manufacturing/Production Order

To access the standard analyses of discrete manufacturing, follow menu path **Logistics • Production • Shop Floor Control • Information System • Shop Floor Information System • Standard Analyses**. Table 23.1 lists the transaction codes of various standard analyses available for discrete manufacturing, all of which we'll discuss in the following sections. Standard analysis for material consumption (Transaction MCRE) provides day-wise consumption figures (quantity and value) of components consumed in producing a product. After gaining an understanding of the various standard analyses we cover in this chapter, as an exercise and to reinforce the learning, we recommend running the material consumption analysis and exploring the various options it offers.

Standard Analysis	Transaction Code
Work center	MCP7
Operation	MCP1
Material	MCP5
Production order	MCP3
Product costs	MCRI
Material consumption	MCRE

Table 23.1 Standard Analyses for Discrete Manufacturing

23.1.1 Work Center

The screen shown in Figure 23.1 is accessed via Transaction MCP7. No information has been provided on the selection criteria screen for the standard analysis for the work center; we simply executed the report. Choose **Switch Drilldown** to open the **Drilldown** screen. Select the **Work Center** radio button to change from the plant-level to work center-level display of data. In the **Drilldown** screen, there are **6** work centers listed, along with target lead time (**TgtLeadTm.**) and actual lead time (**ActLeadTm.**) details. The smallest/minimum time unit (using shorter intervals can be derived via decimal format) is in days.

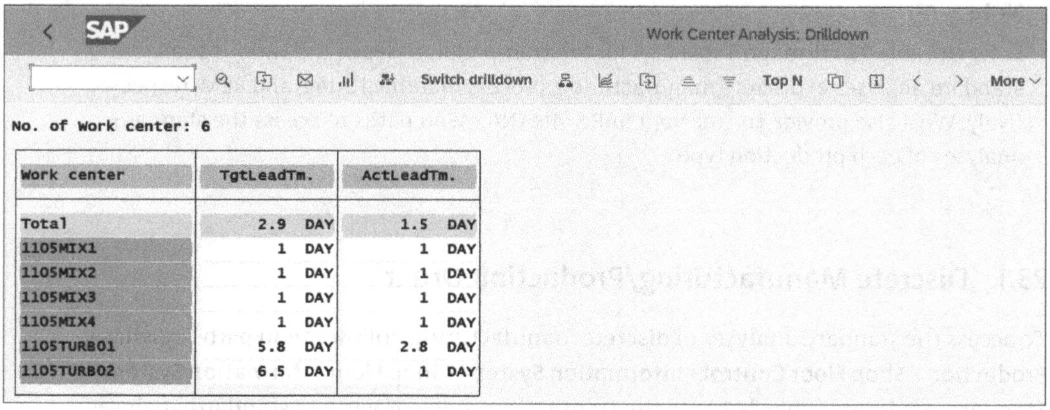

Work center	TgtLeadTm.	ActLeadTm.
Total	2.9 DAY	1.5 DAY
1105MIX1	1 DAY	1 DAY
1105MIX2	1 DAY	1 DAY
1105MIX3	1 DAY	1 DAY
1105MIX4	1 DAY	1 DAY
1105TURB01	5.8 DAY	2.8 DAY
1105TURB02	6.5 DAY	1 DAY

Figure 23.1 Switch Drilldown in Work Center Analysis

Tips and Tricks

If you want to know more details about any field of a standard analysis or the purpose or function of a field, simply place the cursor on the field in question and press F1. Use this tip while choosing the fields to display in standard analyses, as shown in Figure 23.2.

A large number of fields can be displayed on the screen in Figure 23.1, just as was possible in the order information systems. To display hidden fields, choose **More • Edit • Choose Key Figures** from the menu bar, and the popup screen shown in Figure 23.2 appears. The left-hand side of this screen shows the fields already displayed in Figure 23.1, whereas the right-hand side shows a large number of fields to choose from. Also notice that there are filters for key figures—**All**, **Figures (w/o Unit)**, and **Quantities**—which help you quickly identify and select the desired fields for the report.

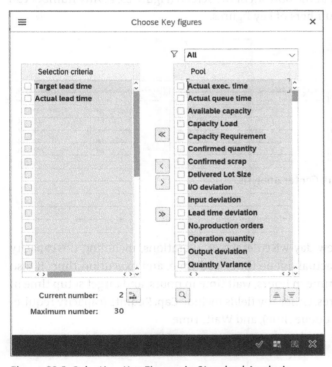

Figure 23.2 Selecting Key Figures in Standard Analysis

For this example, select a few key figures from the list shown in Figure 23.2 for display. Here, notice the input deviation of planned start date of operation and actual start dates. The values are averaged out. The same concept applies for the output deviation, which is the deviation between the planned end date of operation at the work center and the actual end date entered in the confirmation of the operation (Figure 23.3). It also shows details about the available capacity versus the capacity requirements of different work centers.

No. of Work center: 6							
Work center	e	Avail. capacity	Capacity reqmts	Confirmed qty	Confirmed scrap	Delvrd Lot Size	I/O deviation
Total	DAY	3,504.0 HR	1,209.8 HR	1,068.000 ***	135.000 ***	1,145.000 ***	1.1 DAY
1105MIX1	DAY	480.0 HR	0.0 HR	120 KG	0 KG	60 KG	0.2 DAY
1105MIX2	DAY	480.0 HR	0.0 HR	20 KG	0 KG	20 KG	4 DAY
1105MIX3	DAY	0.0 HR	0.0 HR	18 KG	0 KG	20 KG	3 DAY
1105MIX4	DAY	480.0 HR	0.0 HR	20 KG	0 KG	20 KG	4 DAY
1105TURBO1	DAY	1,032.0 HR	832.8 HR	625 PC	125 PC	750 PC	0.4 DAY
1105TURBO2	DAY	1,032.0 HR	377.0 HR	265 PC	10 PC	275 PC	2 DAY

Figure 23.3 More Key Figures of Work Centers

Place your cursor on the **Capacity Reqmts** key figure, and navigate to **More · Top N**. Enter **Number** as "3" to then see the top three capacity requirements; the remaining deviations are shown as **Rest** at the bottom of the screen (Figure 23.4). Any number can be entered to view the top numbers of key figures.

Work center	tLeadTm.	Actual exec.tm.	Act. queue time	Avail. capacity	Capacity reqmts Capacity Requirement	Confirmed qty
Total	1.5 DAY	0.5 DAY	1 DAY	3,504.0 HR	1,209.8 HR	1,068.000 ***
1105TURBO2	1 DAY	0 DAY	1 DAY	1,032.0 HR	377.0 HR	265 PC
1105TURBO1	2.8 DAY	1.9 DAY	0.9 DAY	1,032.0 HR	832.8 HR	625 PC
1105MIX4	1 DAY	0 DAY	1 DAY	480.0 HR	0.0 HR	20 KG
Rest	0.3 DAY	0 DAY	0.3 DAY	960.0 HR	0.0 HR	158 KG

Figure 23.4 Ranking List in Work Center Analysis

23.1.2   Operations

Use Transaction MCP1 to view day-wise details of operations, including the capacity requirements in hours, the actual queue time, lead time, and execution time. It also shows the target processing time in hours, wait time in hours, and target setup time in hours, among other key figures. Other key fields include **Cap. Reqmts** (capacity requirements), **ActQueueTm** (actual queue time), and **Wait. Time**.

23.1.3   Material

Use Transaction MCP5 to view the material analysis, which covers the quantity and duration details of various materials. This includes the order quantity, the goods receipt (GR) quantity, the scrap, and also the deviations. The duration details consist of delivery time deviation, lead time deviation, and durations, such as target queue time and target execution time.

23.1.4   Production Order

Figure 23.5 shows the standard analysis production orders (Transaction MCP3). Select the first key figure, **GR Quantity**, by placing your cursor on it and navigating to **More · Edit · ABC Analysis** from the menu bar. In the popup that appears, set **Strategy** for ABC analysis as **Total GR Quantity (%)**, then choose **Continue**.

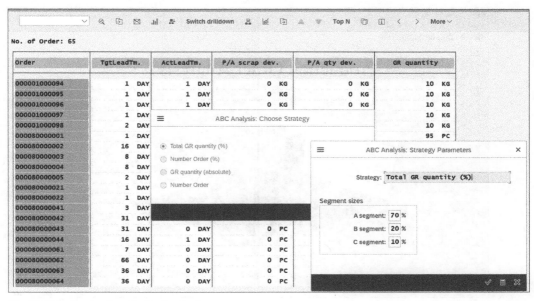

Figure 23.5 Production Order Analysis

The options in ABC analysis are as follows:

- **Total GR Quantity (%)**
  The GR quantity is divided by the defined percentage.

- **Number Material (%)**
  The number of materials is divided by the defined percentage.

- **GR Quantity (Absolute)**
  The actual GR quantity is divided into A, B, or C segments.

- **Number Material**
  The number of materials is divided into A, B, or C segments.

ABC analysis enables a user to select the right strategy and then divide the key figures into the top three groupings. Further, there's flexibility to define what percentage of a key figure should be listed in the A, B, or C segments.

The system-suggested segment sizes for A, B, and C can be overwritten. For this example, enter **A Segment** as "70", **B Segment** as "20", and **C Segment** as "10". These three entries cause the system to divide and display the **Total GR Quantity** (%) in such a way that the top 70% will be categorized in segment A, 20% in segment B, and the bottom 10% in segment C in a sequential order.

Click **Calculate** to open **SAP Business Graphics** as a graphical representation of the ABC analysis. Click **Graphics** in the menu bar so that the screen shown in Figure 23.6 appears.

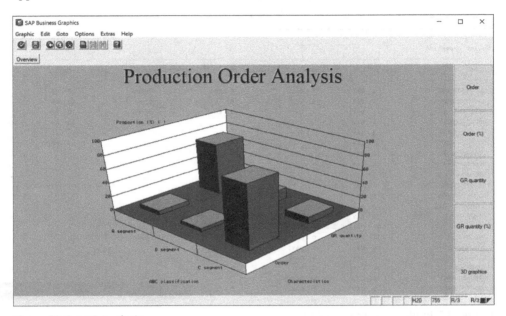

Figure 23.6 ABC Analysis

23.1.5 Product Costs

In Transaction MCRI, the screen shown in Figure 23.7 shows the standard analysis of the product cost. Choose the **Value COCurr** field and then choose **Time Series** to open the **Time Series** dialog box. A *time series* denotes the breakdown of a key figure of a characteristic, which in this case is **Material**.

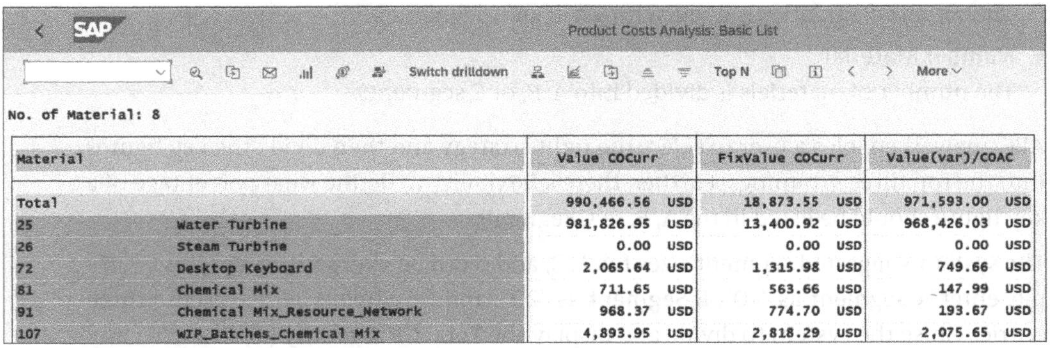

No. of Material: 8

Material		Value COCurr	FixValue COCurr	Value(var)/COAC
Total		990,466.56 USD	18,873.55 USD	971,593.00 USD
25	Water Turbine	981,826.95 USD	13,400.92 USD	968,426.03 USD
26	Steam Turbine	0.00 USD	0.00 USD	0.00 USD
72	Desktop Keyboard	2,065.64 USD	1,315.98 USD	749.66 USD
81	Chemical Mix	711.65 USD	563.66 USD	147.99 USD
91	Chemical Mix_Resource_Network	968.37 USD	774.70 USD	193.67 USD
107	WIP_Batches_Chemical Mix	4,893.95 USD	2,818.29 USD	2,075.65 USD

Figure 23.7 Product Costs Analysis

23.2   Process Manufacturing/Process Order

To access the standard analyses of process manufacturing, follow menu path, **Logistics • Production—Process • Process Order • Reporting • Shop Floor Information System**. Table 23.2 lists the transactions for the various standard analyses available for process manufacturing.

Standard Analysis	Transaction
Resource	MCRW
Operation	MCRU
Material	MCP5
Process Order	MCRV
Material Consumption	MCRX
Product Costs	MCRY

Table 23.2 Standard Analyses for Process Manufacturing

23.3   Repetitive Manufacturing

To access the standard analyses of REM, follow menu path **Logistics • Production • Shop Floor Control • Information System • Shop Floor Information System • Standard Analyses • Repetitive Manufacturing**. Table 23.3 lists the transactions for the various standard analyses available for REM.

Standard Analysis	Transaction Code
GR statistics	MCP6
Reporting point statistics	MCRM
Material consumption	MCRP
Product costs	MCRK

Table 23.3 Standard Analyses for REM

23.4   Additional Analysis Functions

In the following sections, we'll cover some additional analysis functions, such as key figures, icon texts replacing the icons in SAP S/4HANA, and how to quickly navigate to other info structures in standard analysis.

Let's now discuss some of the standard analyses of PP.

23

23.4.1   Key Figures

Sometimes, a user may want to see all the key figures of one characteristic. Double-click any entry of the characteristic, and the system displays all the key figures of that characteristic, as shown in Figure 23.8.

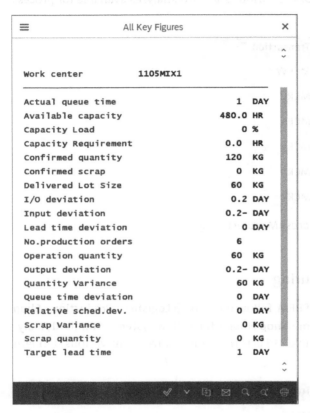

Figure 23.8 All Key Figures

23.4.2   Icons

In the new SAP Fiori-themed user interface (UI) of SAP S/4HANA standard analyses, SAP has mostly done away with icons in both the parameters selection screen (see Figure 23.9) and in the standard analyses themselves (see Figure 23.10).

Icons are now mostly replaced with icon texts to enable users to quickly find the relevant icons required to perform specific functions. With icon texts in place, users no longer have to hover over an icon to see an icon's text and then decide if it accesses the function they want to use.

Because icon texts take more screen space than the icons themselves, always look for **More** in the menu bar (usually located on the far right-hand side of the screen) to search for functions that aren't visible in the main menu bar or at the bottom of the screen.

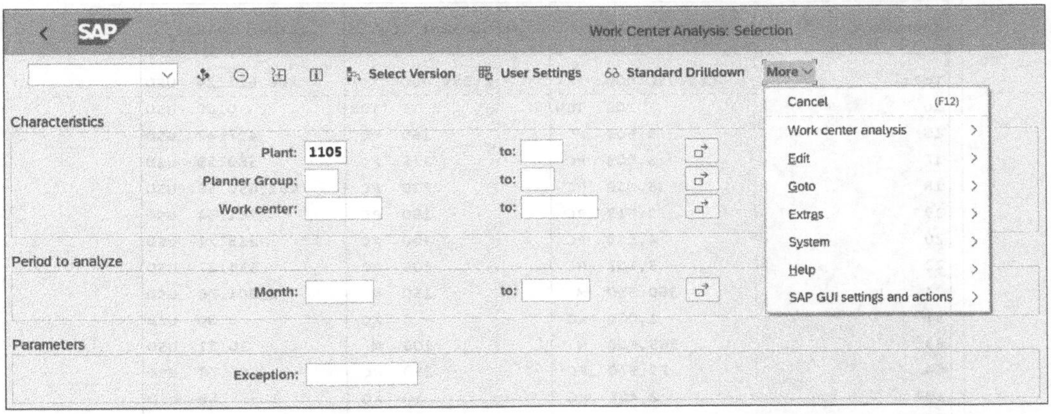

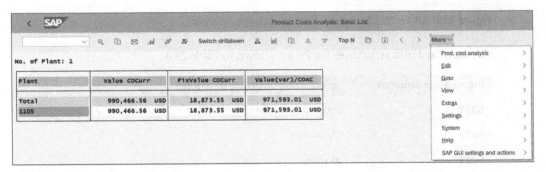

Figure 23.9 Parameters Selection Screen

Figure 23.10 Standard Analysis

23.4.3   Other Info Structures

It's also possible to navigate to the **Other Info Structure** screen within the standard analysis. To do so, choose **More • Goto • Other Info Structure**, and in the ensuing popup, enter the name of the new info structure, or use the dropdown menu to select one. In this example, info structure SO26 (not shown) for material usage analysis is selected (see Figure 23.11).

23

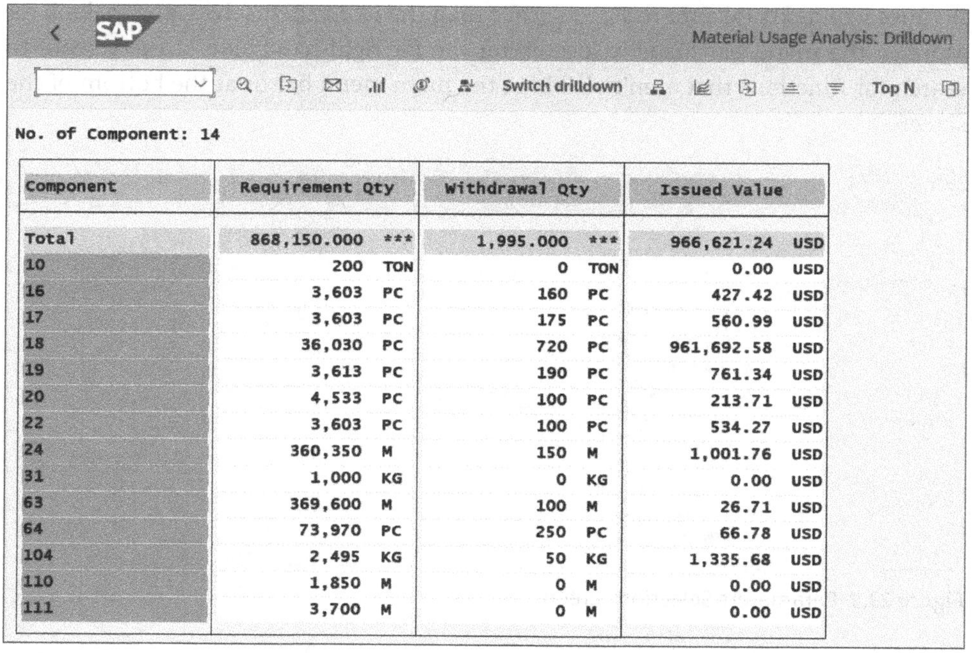

Component	Requirement Qty		Withdrawal Qty		Issued Value	
Total	868,150.000	***	1,995.000	***	966,621.24	USD
10	200	TON	0	TON	0.00	USD
16	3,603	PC	160	PC	427.42	USD
17	3,603	PC	175	PC	560.99	USD
18	36,030	PC	720	PC	961,692.58	USD
19	3,613	PC	190	PC	761.34	USD
20	4,533	PC	100	PC	213.71	USD
22	3,603	PC	100	PC	534.27	USD
24	360,350	M	150	M	1,001.76	USD
31	1,000	KG	0	KG	0.00	USD
63	369,600	M	100	M	26.71	USD
64	73,970	PC	250	PC	66.78	USD
104	2,495	KG	50	KG	1,335.68	USD
110	1,850	M	0	M	0.00	USD
111	3,700	M	0	M	0.00	USD

Figure 23.11 Other Info Structure (Material Usage Analysis)

The standard info structures for PP are shown in Table 23.4.

Information Structure	Information Structure Description
S021	Production order
S022	Operation
S023	Material
S024	Work center
S025	Run schedule header
S026	Material usage
S027	Product costs
S028	Reporting point statistics
S029	Kanban
S225	GR: REM
S226	Material usage: REM
S227	Product costs: REM

Table 23.4 Standard Information Structures Available for PP

> **Note**
>
> Now that you have a decent understanding of standard analyses in PP, we recommend exploring the many hidden and latent features available. These can bring ongoing improvements in business processes—not just in logistics, but in the entire supply chain.

[«]

23.5 Summary

This chapter covered some of the more frequently used standard analyses of PP. All analyses of logistics and the supply chain are available in one spot to facilitate quick and comprehensive access to the needed information.

The next chapter discusses SAP Fiori apps for PP in SAP S/4HANA.

23

Chapter 24
SAP Fiori Apps for Production Planning

Timely, accurate, and comprehensive information helps companies make better and faster business decisions. A large number of SAP Fiori apps are available not just for production planning but also for logistics and supply chain management and can be used immediately.

SAP Fiori is the next-generation web-based user experience for working with the SAP S/4HANA system, and each app is accessed via a tile in the SAP Fiori launchpad. A large number of SAP Fiori apps are available in SAP S/4HANA, and the apps library is constantly expanding. Apps for master data, transactional data, reporting, and analytics in all SAP areas are available in the SAP Fiori library. We'll cover some of them in this chapter, after taking a quick look at the SAP Fiori launchpad and the library for all SAP Fiori apps.

24.1   SAP Fiori Launchpad and Apps Library

Figure 24.1 shows the initial screen of the SAP Fiori launchpad, wherein individual apps are represented as tiles. The apps can be grouped together based on different roles, such as materials planner, production planner, or inventory controller. They can also be grouped together based on functional areas such as production planning (PP), materials management (MM), or quality management (QM), as shown in the different tabs in Figure 24.1. Due to the highly intuitive nature of apps, they make it easier to quickly get up to speed. Further, most master data and transactional data apps and even several reporting apps in SAP Fiori still give the look and feel of the SAP GUI by showing the same menu options, menu bars, buttons, and icons. The top-right-hand corner of the SAP Fiori launchpad provides an option to search for an app by its name or by transaction code, such as COR2 (change process order).

The library of SAP Fiori apps is constantly expanding at a rapid pace for both SAP S/4HANA and SAP S/4HANA Cloud. To search for and explore the latest or most relevant SAP Fiori apps, go to *http://s-prs.co/v216700* and click the **Home** icon. On the initial screen of the SAP Fiori apps library, you can search for a relevant app on the left-hand side, and app details can be viewed on the right-hand side of the screen. To make relevant apps available for use, reach out to your SAP Fiori consultant with an app's details and the specific role or group to which it needs to be assigned.

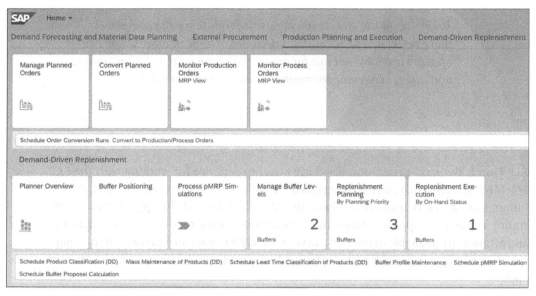

Figure 24.1 SAP Fiori Launchpad Homepage

24.2   SAP Fiori Applications

In the following sections, we'll cover some of the SAP Fiori apps of PP, such as Monitor Material Coverage, Monitor External and Internal Requirements, and Manage Work Center Capacity, among others.

24.2.1   Monitor Material Coverage

This app enables a production planner to monitor all the materials in a selected area of responsibility. This includes make-to-stock (MTS) and collective requirements materials, make-to-order (MTO) and engineer-to-order (ETO) materials, and materials for direct production and direct procurement. The app also provides a list of all materials with a net requirement segment or individual segments. These materials might have coverage issues according to a specified shortage definition. The shortage definition a planner chooses contains a set of rules that the system uses for calculating the material shortages. These rules define the scope of the shortage calculation—that is, the supply and demand elements to be considered and the conditions that have to be met to be a relevant shortage.

Figure 24.2 shows the Monitor Material Coverage app, showing a few materials for which the green bars represent a comfortable stock availability situation. The red bars represent a situation that the inventory or materials planner needs to pay greater attention to in order to avoid stock-outs or unavailability of required material on the desired date. The displayed columns show the shortage quantity and when the first shortage is likely to happen. More columns can be displayed too. Multiple dropdowns on the left-hand side provide options so that the materials or production planner can filter materials based on different criteria. After applying a new filter, click **Go**. A planner can also use the default **Time till Shortage**, **Material**, and **Individual Segment** filters to narrow down the scope of the list.

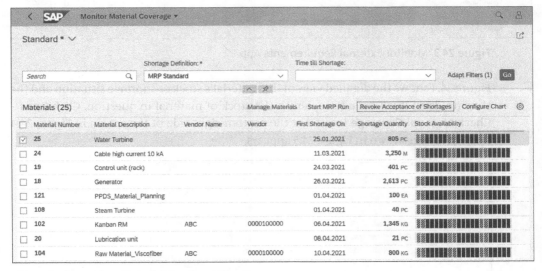

Figure 24.2 Monitor Material Coverage App

24.2.2   Monitor External Requirements

The Monitor External Requirements app offers monitoring of the uncovered requirements originating from sales orders and stock transport orders in a selected area of responsibility. The default **Time till Requirement Date** filter can be used to determine the period in which a planner wants to check for uncovered external requirements. Only one shortage definition is available for calculating uncovered requirements and is displayed for information purposes. This app is helpful for a materials planner, providing necessary information to be able to react to the shortage situation and fulfill customers' demands on time. Click a material code on the screen shown in Figure 24.2—for example, **25**—and the screen shown in Figure 24.3 appears.

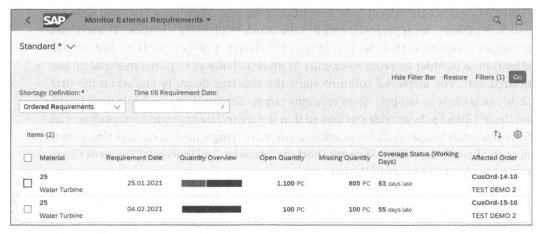

Figure 24.3 Monitor External Requirements App

Figure 24.4 shows the detailed view of the material's stock or shortage situation and the time (in days) it will take to replenish the stock of material in question. Click **Open •
Check Material Coverage** located at the bottom-right side of the screen in Figure 24.4 and the screen shown in Figure 24.5 appears.

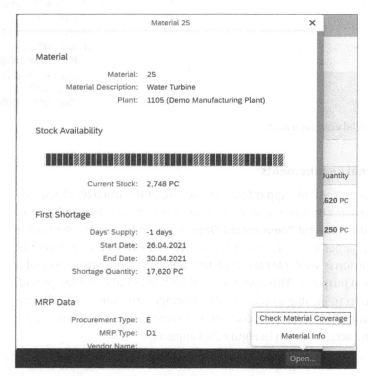

Figure 24.4 Details of Individual Material Coverage

Tips and Tricks

You can also directly navigate to the Manage External Requirements app (Figure 24.5) to view details of the selected delayed items. You can check different solutions by selecting an item on the screen in Figure 24.3 and clicking **Manage Item** at the bottom-right side of the screen (not shown).

The screen shown in Figure 24.5 is similar to the stock/requirements list (Transaction MD04), but it offers more features, including the ability to run material requirements planning (MRP) interactively (see **Start MRP Run** at the bottom-right side of the screen). The **Material Information** tab shows the detailed material planning settings for a material.

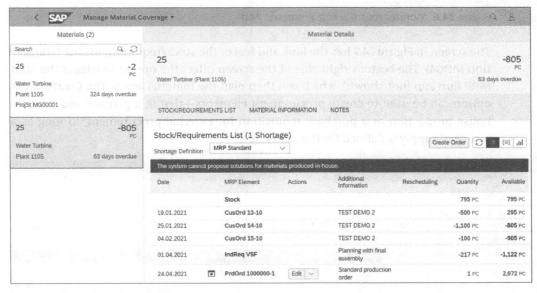

Figure 24.5 Manage External Requirements

24.2.3 Monitor Internal Requirements

With the Monitor Internal Requirements app, it's possible to ensure that components are available in the right quantity and in time so that internal requirements originating from production orders, process orders, maintenance orders, and network orders can be fulfilled. To determine which receipts and requirements are included in the coverage calculation, a shortage definition is available and displayed in the app. The app provides all the necessary information to react quickly to critical situations. From this app, a user can directly navigate to the Manage Internal Requirements app to view details of the selected materials and check different solutions for the shortages. Click any material on the screen shown in Figure 24.6 to see the screen shown in Figure 24.7.

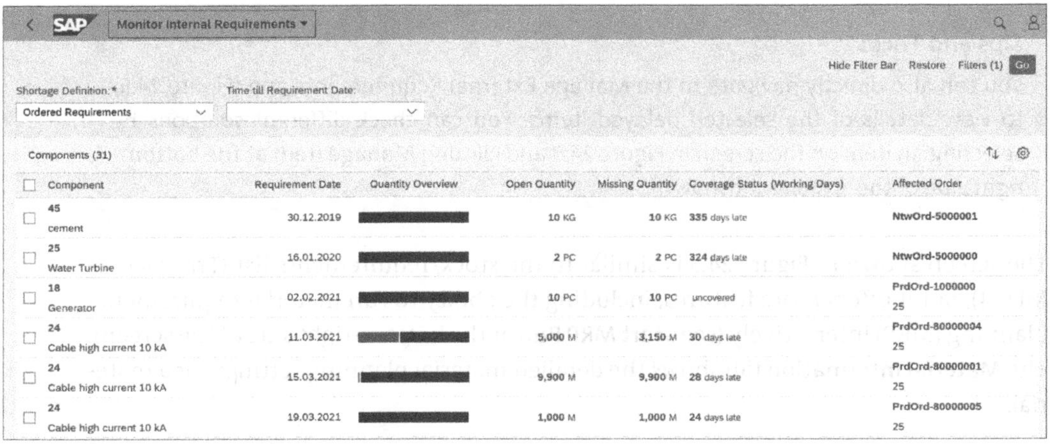

Figure 24.6 Monitor Internal Requirements App

The screen in Figure 24.7 has the look and feel of the stock/requirements list (Transaction MD04). The bottom-right side of the screen offers the option to trigger the Start MRP Run app (not shown), which will then plan the material again. The **Create Order** option can be used to create procurement elements—that is, a planned order for in-house production or a purchase requisition for external procurement, as long as a source of supply is defined for the material.

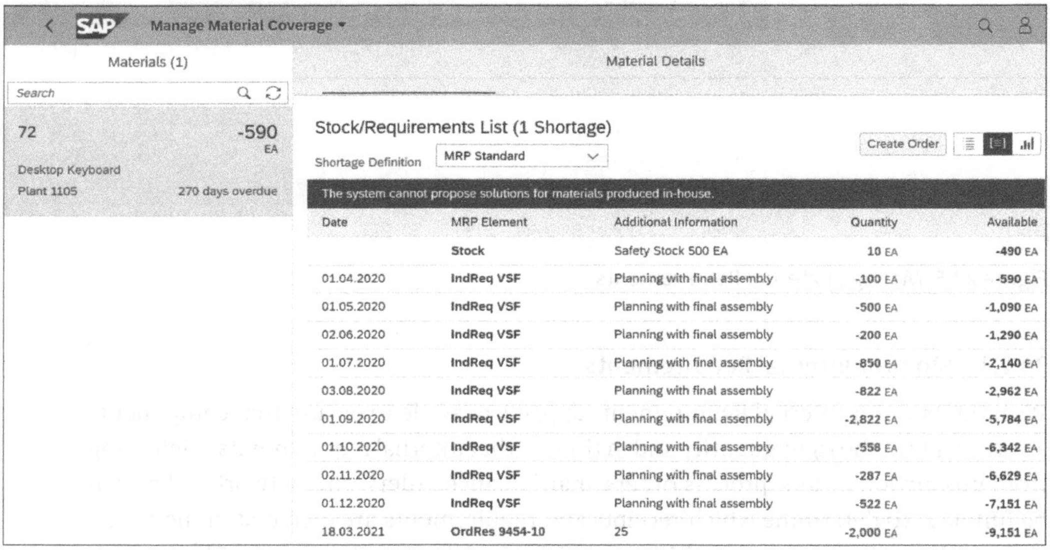

Figure 24.7 Manage Material Coverage App: Detailed Screen

24.2.4   Manage Production or Process Orders

With the Manage Production Orders and Manage Process Orders apps, it's possible to manage those production orders or process orders that have issues based on the settings made in the Monitor Production Orders and Monitor Process Orders apps. A planner can view details regarding delayed materials and missing components, as well as the status of operations and milestones. This app provides all the necessary information to react quickly to critical situations and avoid delays in production. The **Issues** column shown in Figure 24.8 includes icons in each row for four important categories: material shortage, scheduling delay, quality issues, and material delay. For each category, if there's an issue, the related icon turns blue. Select an item, and then choose **Check Components**—for example, the number of missing components required to produce a product. Choosing a process order and then clicking the **Details** button (forward arrow > located on the far right hand side of the screen) will bring up a detailed screen that can be used not only for evaluating the current status of an order but also for performing several important business functions. Some of the functions are changing an order, confirming an order, confirming an operation, and setting an order to the technically complete status. The mini charts at the top of the screen provide a summary of the status of various process orders and can be clicked to get greater insight into the issues.

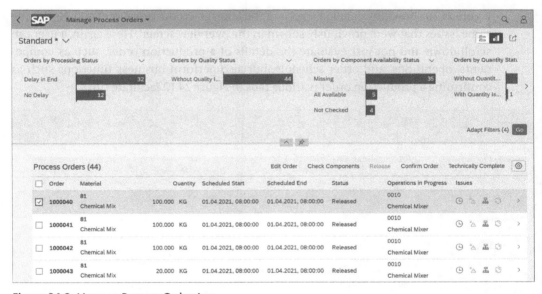

Figure 24.8 Manage Process Order App

Figure 24.9 shows the Manage Production Order app, showing similar information as in the Manage Process Order app. Here, the issues are denoted with red icons. Choosing a production order will enable the user to perform additional processes such as changing the dates and quantities in the production order, releasing a production order, or even rereading the master data. Choose a production order, followed by clicking the forward arrow (>) located on the far right-hand side of the screen, and the screen shown in Figure 24.10 appears.

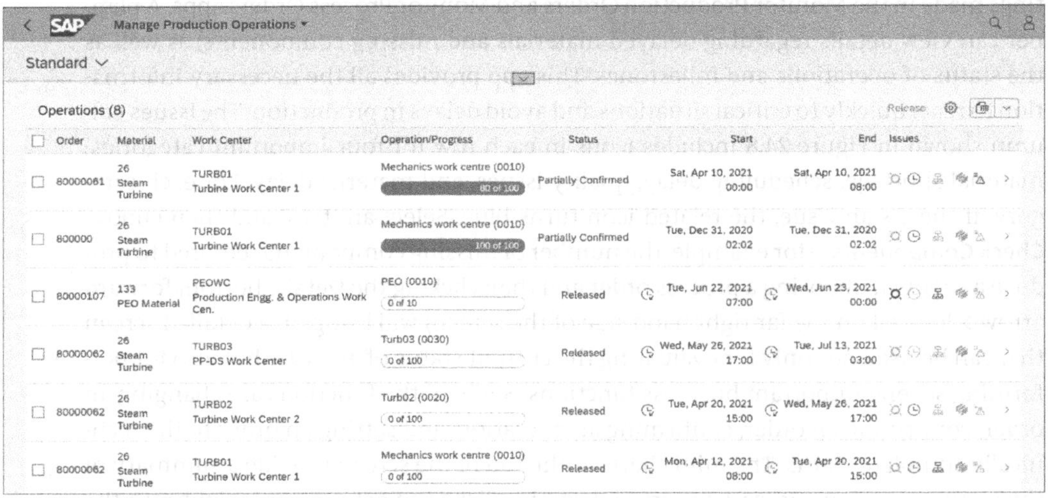

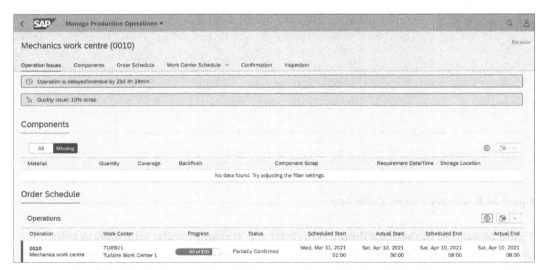

Figure 24.9 Manage Production Order App

Figure 24.10 shows the detailed screen of the Manage Production Order app. Notice the same issues that were previously shown in the overview screen. Here again, a user can scroll down and not just evaluate the details of a production order, such as components, operations, and order schedule, but also perform business functions such as confirming a production order (various tabs in Figure 24.10 facilitate this).

Figure 24.10 Detailed Screen of Individual Production Order

Figure 24.11 shows the Manage Order app, with comprehensive details of an individual production order, including any component shortages, quality issues, scheduling conflicts, or capacity overloads. Be sure to explore the various tabs to get end-to-end visibility into an individual production order.

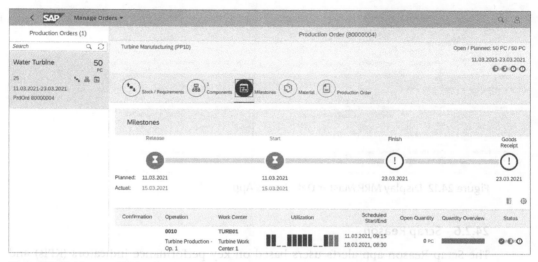

Figure 24.11 Manage Order App

24.2.5 MRP Master Data Issues

The Display MRP Master Data Issues app provides details of the materials in a specific plant for which an issue occurred in the last MRP run. Both types of information display are possible—that is, materials for which messages were created in the MRP run or those that may not have been planned at all. Information about the responsible MRP controller and the date and time that the last planning run was carried out is also displayed. After addressing the issues faced during materials planning, materials can be planned correctly in future planning runs. Figure 24.12 shows the overview of the issues faced in planning for several materials. For material 24, the message **No valid production version found; BOM explosion not possible** needs to be addressed before the system can plan this material.

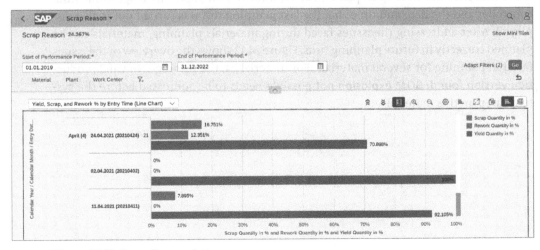

Figure 24.12 Display MRP Master Data Issues App

24.2.6   Scrap Reason

The Scrap Reason app alerts users based on key performance indicators (KPIs) and enables a step-by-step data analysis from different perspectives to identify the root causes for scrap in the production process. The app shows information on the distribution of actual scrap recorded in production confirmations in the dimensions of time, work center, material, plant, and reason for variance. As a production planner, analyzing the confirmed scrap and rework makes it possible to work on the reasons or root causes of the greatest loss of production, which will help prevent problems in the future (see Figure 24.13).

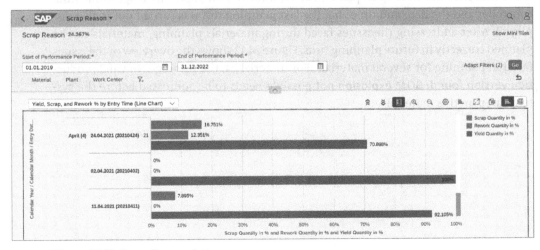

Figure 24.13 Scrap Reason App

Be sure to check out more display options from the **Yield, Scrap, and Rework % by Entry Time (Line Chart)** dropdown. The chart types can also be changed—for example, from the horizontal bars shown to a pie chart, selected from the chart options available on the right-hand side of the screen. The data can also be displayed in tables.

24.2.7 Operation Scrap

Figure 24.14 shows the Operation Scrap app, which enables a planner to compare actual scrap figures recorded in the production confirmations with the expected scrap that was defined in the order operation. It allows implementing a feedback loop for updating the expected scrap percentage in the order operation. The app shows the work centers where the expected scrap percentage most differs from the actual scrap percentage.

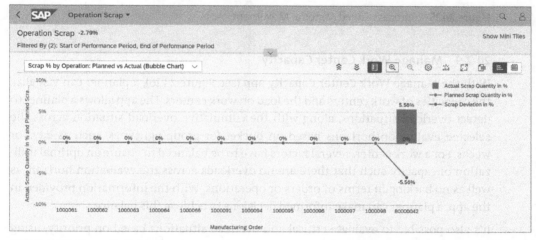

Figure 24.14 Operations Scrap

24.2.8 Reprocess Failed Material Movements

The Reprocess Failed Material Movements app enables the viewing of and also processing of unsuccessful materials movements and also provides the reason these goods movements failed. From this app, it's possible to navigate to the root cause of the problem, such as missing storage location or incorrect posting period, and then correct the problem. To correct a failed material movement issue, select a material and choose **Reprocess**.

Figure 24.15 shows the SAP Fiori version of Transaction COGI (Reprocess Failed Material Movements), which was covered in Chapter 6, Section 6.9.1. Here it shows that all five goods movements failed due to missing storage locations.

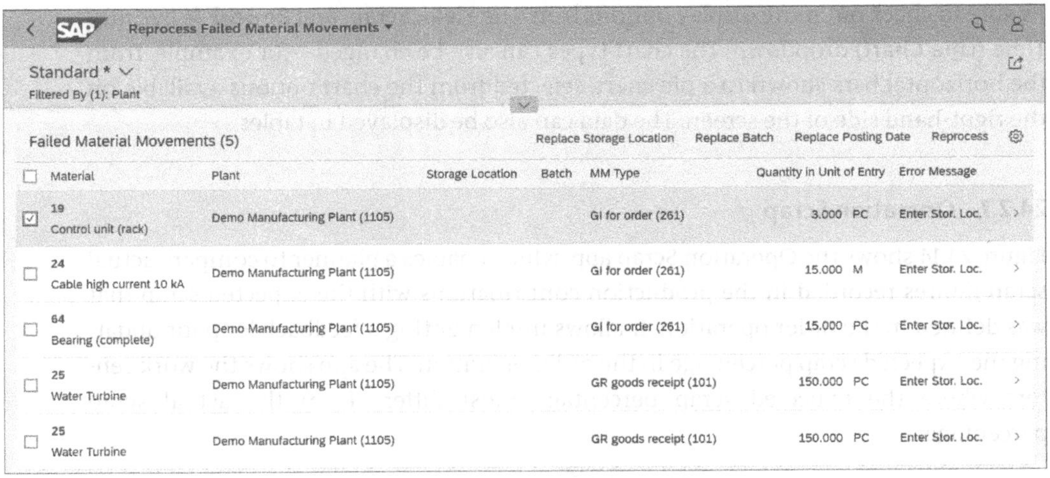

Figure 24.15 Reprocess Failed Material Movements App

24.2.9   Manage Work Center Capacity

With the Manage Work Center Capacity app (see Figure 24.16), a planner can visualize the capacities of work centers and the load on work centers. The app allows a planner to detect overload situations, along with the cumulative overload situation across the selected evaluation horizons based on bucket (or grouping) types, such as days or weeks. For a work center, several factors have to be balanced to ensure an optimal utilization of capacity such that there are no overloads across the evaluation horizon, as well as no backlog in terms of orders or operations. With the information provided in the app, a planner can make informed decisions to achieve this balance.

It's also possible to evaluate critical and overload situations based on priority, using KPIs such as first critical load, first overload, and maximum load. These critical and normal load levels can be personalized as per the requirement that anything above critical will be considered an overload.

With the app, a planner can view the capacity required to fulfill all the open orders, such as planned, production, and process orders, in a set evaluation horizon. Choose a work center and click the forward arrow (>) located on far right-hand side of the screen, and the screen shown in Figure 24.17 appears.

With the Work Center Capacity app, it's possible to get details of the capacity situation a of work center and the loads on the work center. The app offers an ability to detect overload situations across select evaluation horizons based on bucket (or grouping) types, such as days or weeks. For a work center, a planner attempts to balance several factors to ensure an optimal utilization of capacity so that there are no overloads across the evaluation horizon, as well as no backlog in terms of orders or operations. With the information provided in the app, a planner can make informed decisions to achieve this balance (see Figure 24.17).

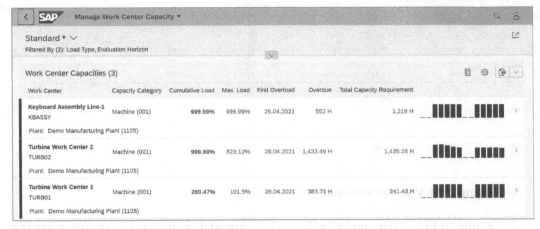

Figure 24.16 Manage Work Center Capacity App

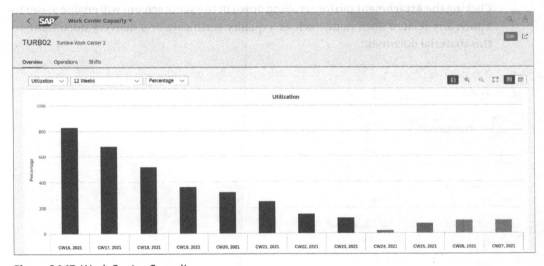

Figure 24.17 Work Center Capacity

24.2.10   Material Documents Overview

Figure 24.18 shows the Material Documents Overview app, which has a similar look and feel to SAP GUI Transaction MB51. The top half of the figure offers several filters that can be used to display only the required information, as shown in the lower half of the screen. Choose a material document and click the forward arrow (>) located on far right-hand side of the screen, and the screen shown in Figure 24.19 appears.

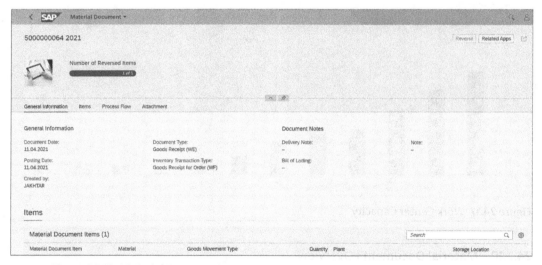

Figure 24.18 Material Documents Overview App

Figure 24.19 not only provides details of a material document but also provides the option for user to reverse it, via the **Reverse** option located at the top-right-hand side. Clicking the **Attachment** tab (or scrolling down in the same screen) will enable a user to attach any related document, such as a quality certificate or a delivery document, to this material document.

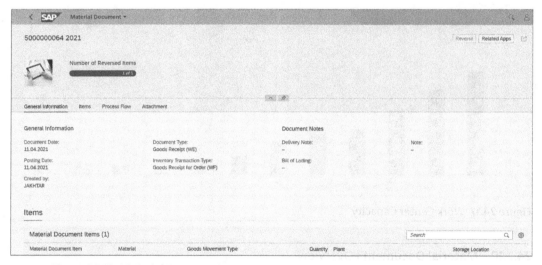

Figure 24.19 Material Document

24.2.11   Manage Production Version

A *production version* is the link between the BOM of a product and its routing, master recipe, or rate routing. It determines which BOM relates to the relevant routing or master recipe to produce a material or plan a material. There may be different production versions based on the lot sizes and validity dates. With the Manage Production Version app, a user can create, edit, copy, and delete various production versions. Figure 24.20 shows the SAP Fiori version of the Transaction C223 (Manage Production Version) screen covered in Chapter 6, Section 6.2.5.

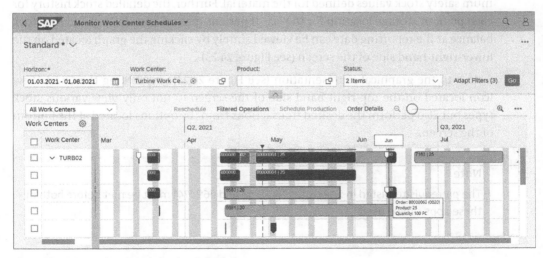

Figure 24.20 Manage Production Version App

24.2.12 Monitor Work Center Schedules

The Monitor Work Center Schedules app is a new app in which a production planner can preschedule the orders to be dispatched from a work center based on their priority. A planner can select the source of supply (production version) and the work centers to dispatch the orders on the chosen dates. A work center with the capacity duration that meets the capacity required to complete the operation gets highlighted for ease of selection. The app uses midpoint scheduling to adjust the operational time (of dispatch, reschedule, etc.) according to the strategy that has been set. The production versions can be switched when the work center capacity is insufficient or orders can be rescheduled that overlap in a time slot (see Figure 24.21).

Figure 24.21 Monitor Work Center Schedules

24.2.13   Kanban Board

The Kanban Board app that was discussed in detail in Chapter 9 is a tool that a planner uses for monitoring circulating kanban containers and evaluations, providing an overview of work progress and material consumption. The kanban board presents a clear picture of missing part situations and bottlenecks, for example, for every supply area. For this purpose, the statuses of the kanban containers and the error situations are represented by different colors. The kanban board can also be used to trigger the kanban signal (see Figure 24.22).

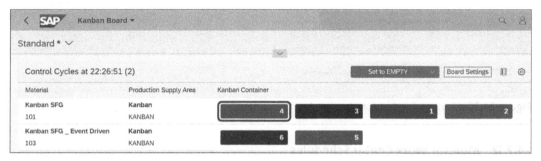

Figure 24.22 Kanban Board App

24.2.14   Stock—Single and Multiple Materials

With the Stock—Single Material app, a planner and an inventory controller can get an overview of the material stock. Stock can be reviewed by the plants and storage locations for which a planner is responsible. The app can display the stock information as a table or a diagram.

It also features a comparison of the stock information with the safety stock and minimum safety stock values defined for the material. Further, the detailed stock history for each plant or storage location for the last 11 periods (period-end closing) and the stock balance at the reporting date can be viewed simply by clicking the graph located on the lower-right-hand side of the screen (see Figure 24.23).

Switch to the graphical representation (see Figure 24.24) by clicking the **Chart View** icon located on the top-right-hand side of the screen to not only view various stock types but also perform the desired transactions from the options located at the bottom of the screen.

Note

The prerequisites listed in SAP Notes 2404856 and 2694741 must be met before both of these apps can be used.

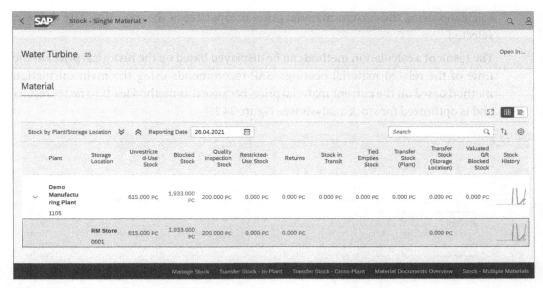

Figure 24.23 Stock—Single Material App

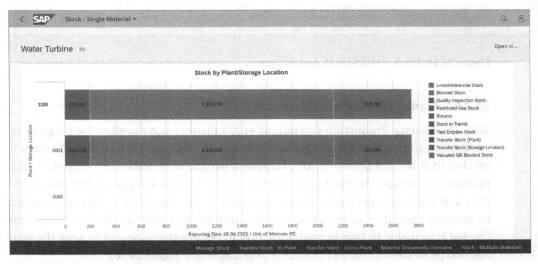

Figure 24.24 Graphical View of Stock—Single Material App

The Stock—Multiple Materials app can be used to get an overview of material stocks. Stock can be reviewed for the plants and storage locations for which a planner or an inventory controller may be responsible. The app can also display the stock information as a table.

The app calculates the stock values based on the stock quantity of the selected reporting date multiplied by the current material price. This means that the app always calculates using the current material price, irrespective of the reporting date that was selected.

The result of a calculation method can be displayed based on the historical prices at the time of the related material postings. SAP recommends using the main calculation method based on the current material price, because this method leads to faster results and is optimized for stock analysis (see Figure 24.25).

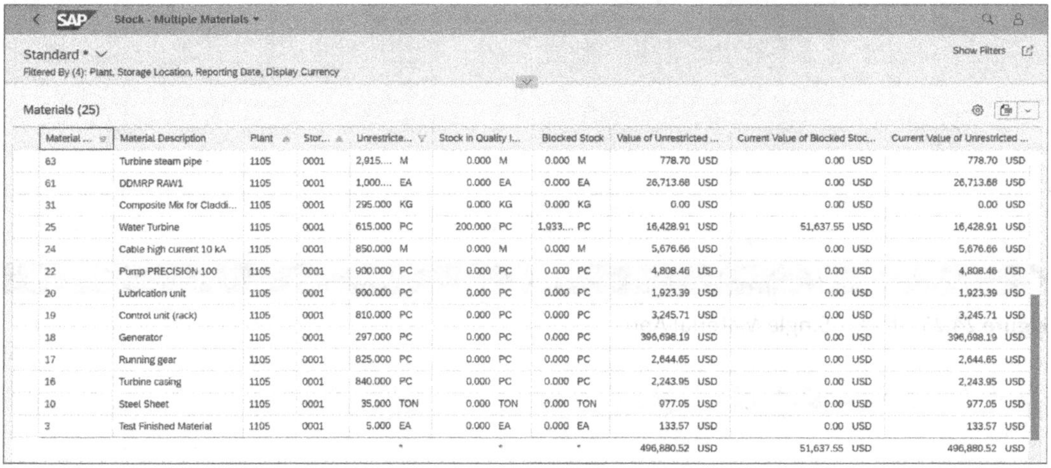

Material ...	Material Description	Plant	Stor...	Unrestricte...	Stock in Quality I...	Blocked Stock	Value of Unrestricted ...	Current Value of Blocked Stoc...	Current Value of Unrestricted ...
63	Turbine steam pipe	1105	0001	2,915.... M	0.000 M	0.000 M	778.70 USD	0.00 USD	778.70 USD
61	DDMRP RAW1	1105	0001	1,000.... EA	0.000 EA	0.000 EA	26,713.68 USD	0.00 USD	26,713.68 USD
31	Composite Mix for Claddi...	1105	0001	295.000 KG	0.000 KG	0.000 KG	0.00 USD	0.00 USD	0.00 USD
25	Water Turbine	1105	0001	615.000 PC	200.000 PC	1,933.... PC	16,428.91 USD	51,637.55 USD	16,428.91 USD
24	Cable high current 10 kA	1105	0001	850.000 M	0.000 M	0.000 M	5,676.66 USD	0.00 USD	5,676.66 USD
22	Pump PRECISION 100	1105	0001	900.000 PC	0.000 PC	0.000 PC	4,808.46 USD	0.00 USD	4,808.46 USD
20	Lubrication unit	1105	0001	900.000 PC	0.000 PC	0.000 PC	1,923.39 USD	0.00 USD	1,923.39 USD
19	Control unit (rack)	1105	0001	810.000 PC	0.000 PC	0.000 PC	3,245.71 USD	0.00 USD	3,245.71 USD
18	Generator	1105	0001	297.000 PC	0.000 PC	0.000 PC	396,698.19 USD	0.00 USD	396,698.19 USD
17	Running gear	1105	0001	825.000 PC	0.000 PC	0.000 PC	2,644.65 USD	0.00 USD	2,644.65 USD
16	Turbine casing	1105	0001	840.000 PC	0.000 PC	0.000 PC	2,243.95 USD	0.00 USD	2,243.95 USD
10	Steel Sheet	1105	0001	35.000 TON	0.000 TON	0.000 TON	977.05 USD	0.00 USD	977.05 USD
3	Test Finished Material	1105	0001	5.000 EA	0.000 EA	0.000 EA	133.57 USD	0.00 USD	133.57 USD
				*	*	*	496,880.52 USD	51,637.55 USD	496,880.52 USD

Figure 24.25 Stock—Multiple Materials App

24.2.15 Manage Production Operations

With the Manage Production Operations app, a planner can monitor the progress of production and also have an overview of the current situation, with all the information needed to solve any issues. If, for example, a particular operation is delayed, then a planner can navigate to the details (see Figure 24.27) to see at a glance why the operation is delayed: perhaps there are missing components, the resource may be occupied by another operation, or the previous operation hasn't finished. All the information needed is available to take immediate action to resolve the issue and to keep the production processes running as smoothly as possible (see Figure 24.26).

Figure 24.27 not only shows the issues at hand but also enables a planner to perform various business functions, such as any date changes or confirming an operation (refer to the various tabs in Figure 24.27, which also can be accessed simply by scrolling down in the same screen).

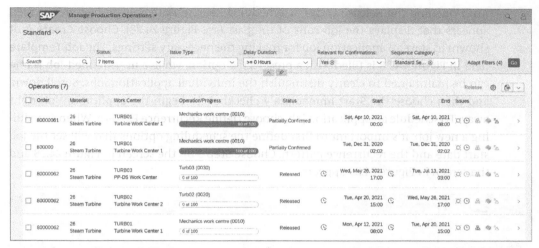

Figure 24.26 Manage Production Operations App

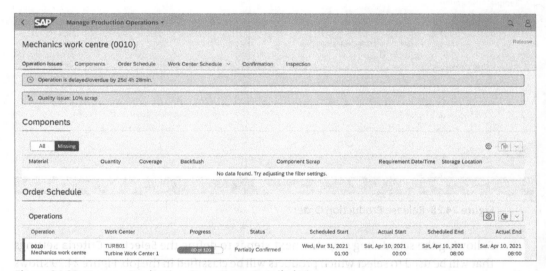

Figure 24.27 Manage Production Operations: Detailed View

24.2.16 Release Production Order

Apart from individually or collectively releasing production orders, it's also possible to schedule their release based on the defined frequency, as well as to specify the parameters that the system will look for while releasing production orders.

After opening the Release Order at Scheduled Release Date app, an overview screen appears that displays the job runs of the past (see Figure 24.28). Choose **Create** (not shown) to start an application job for making the necessary settings. The **Job Template** field in Figure 24.28 is filled with a preselected option, while a user-defined **Job Name** can be maintained to clearly distinguish the individual application jobs. Scroll down, and then choose the **Start Immediately** checkbox to begin the application job right away. To schedule an application job, choose **Define Recurrence Pattern**. When scheduling a new job, it's important to first define the scheduling options that will set the job start date and the recurrence pattern. Choose **Step 3** on the screen in Figure 24.28 and the screen in Figure 24.29 appears.

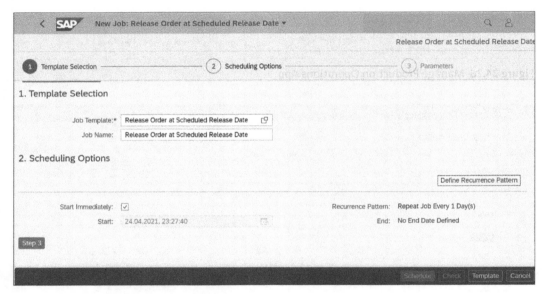

Figure 24.28 Release Production Order

Following the scheduling step, the next step is to define the **Selection Criteria** settings that will be used to select which products will be classified in the job. Figure 24.29 shows some entries for the relevant plant as selection criteria, so the application job that meets these criteria will be scheduled for releasing production orders based on the defined frequency. On this screen, the option to create a new job, copy an existing job, or check the results of the finished jobs are available.

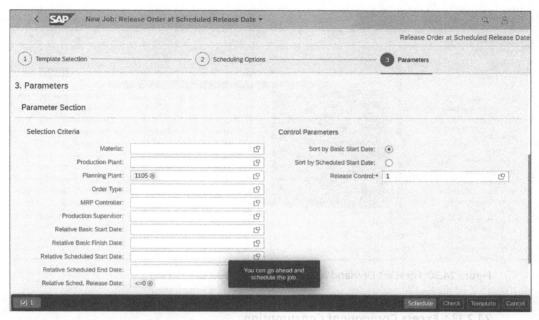

Figure 24.29 Release Production Order: Scheduled Job

24.2.17 Analyze PIR Quality

With the new Analyze PIR Quality app, a planner can analyze how accurately the forecast matches the planned independent requirements (PIRs) for materials. It's also possible to determine how well the forecasted demands for sales orders matched the quantities that were actually delivered to customers. This data can be analyzed for monthly periods in the past.

The fields in the **Available Fields** area shown in Figure 24.30 can be simply dragged and dropped as rows or columns to create the necessary hierarchy to view the results. Not only can the data can be filtered or sorted but a large number of business functions can be performed, as shown in the **Tools** dropdown. If the displayed data has a single unit of measure, then the same also can be visually presented by choosing the **Graphical Display** option.

24

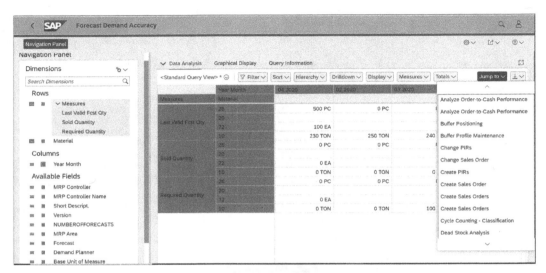

Figure 24.30 Forecast Demand Accuracy

24.2.18   Excess Component Consumption

The Excess Component Consumption app provides a comparison of the expected component scrap percentage defined in the BOM item with the actual excess consumption recorded in the production confirmation. The problems that created the largest excess component consumption in the past can be analyzed, and means to prevent these problems in the future can be suggested (see Figure 24.31).

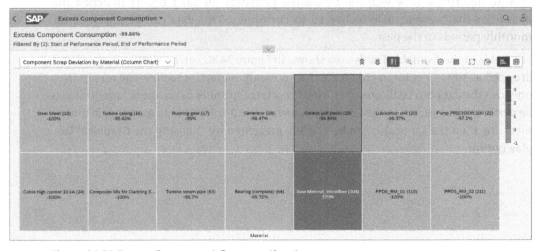

Figure 24.31 Excess Component Consumption App

24.2.19 Analyze Costs by Work Center/Operation

The Analyze Costs by Work Center/Operation app provides reports on the cost information at the work center or operation level to help a planner analyze overall production costs. Figure 24.32 shows the graphical version of various costs at the work center, cost center, and activity levels in the local or company code currencies. Clicking any of the mini graphs will bring up additional relevant cost-related details of the selection made.

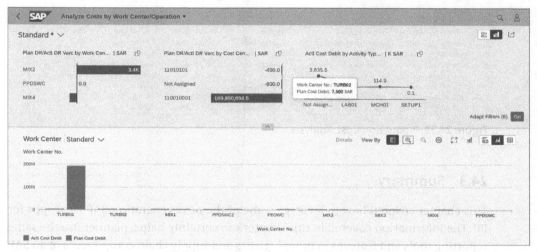

Figure 24.32 Analyze Costs by Work Center/Operation App

24.2.20 Production Cost Analysis

The Production Cost Analysis app provides reports on the cost information at the individual production order level to help a planner analyze overall production costs. Figure 24.33 shows the tabular version of various costs of individual production orders in the local or company code currencies. Choose **Settings** to display or hide the desired fields. Choosing the forward arrow located on the far right-hand side of the screen will bring up more cost- and quantity-related details of individual production order.

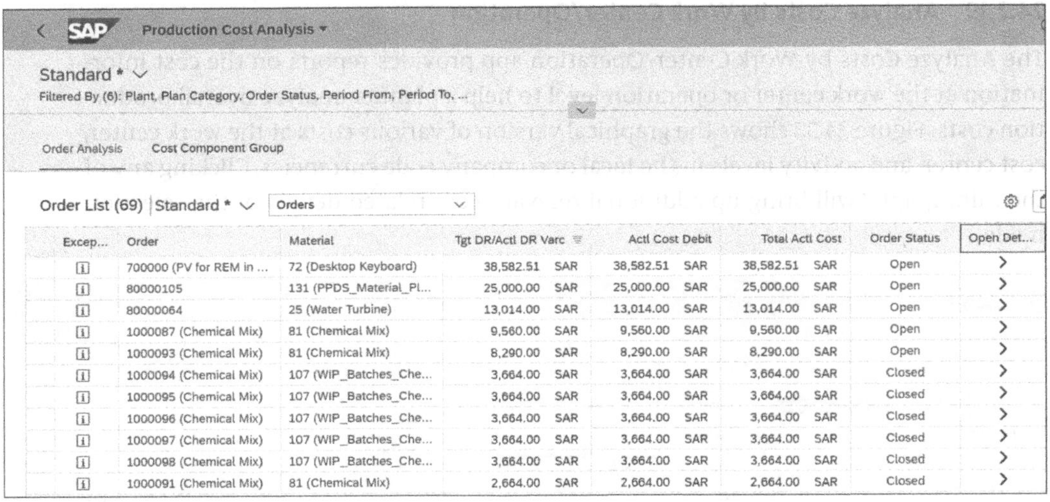

Figure 24.33 Production Cost Analysis

24.3   Summary

This chapter covered how to leverage some of the next-generation SAP Fiori apps for PP. The information covered in this chapter can certainly help a planner use the same reporting tools and features in other logistics and supply chain components of an SAP system.

To conclude, PP in the SAP S/4HANA system is quite comprehensive and offers in-depth and practical solutions for a large number of business processes and scenarios in a diverse range of industries. It also offers options to implement and integrate PP in all the important business processes. However, the actual return on investment for the SAP system implementation can be ensured only when a company strives to understand the integration of various SAP system components with each other. Achieving flawless integration during an SAP system implementation is possible by maintaining extensive collaboration and intense coordination among the various stakeholders of the company. In addition, those who are working in supply chain management roles have seen how the PP function is vital to many processes in the logistics and supply chain.

The Author

 **Jawad Akhtar** is an SAP logistics and supply chain management expert with a focus on business sales and delivery. He earned his chemical engineering degree from Missouri University of Science and Technology in the United States. He has more than 20 years of professional experience, 16 of which have been spent working with SAP systems. He has experience working on several large-scale, end-to-end SAP project implementation lifecycles, including rollouts. He works with SAP clients to help them identify root causes of business issues and address those with the appropriate SAP products and change management strategies. He now focuses on next-generation SAP products such as SAP S/4HANA, SAP Integrated Business Planning for Supply Chain, SAP Ariba, and SAP Customer Experience.

Akhtar is also a technical advisor to SAPexperts, an ASUG speaker, and a contributor to SearchSAP, where his "Ask the Expert" column shares real-life lessons and best practices gleaned from SAP implementations, ways to avoid common project pitfalls, and features of various SAP products that solve key business issues.

Index

- Configure embedded PP-DS in SAP S/4HANA for advanced manufacturing

- Run production planning and detailed scheduling step by step

- Master planning, service, and scheduling heuristics

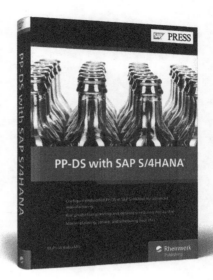

Mahesh Babu MG

PP-DS with SAP S/4HANA

Are you ready for embedded PP-DS? Advance your production planning and detailed scheduling with this comprehensive guide! Discover how the PP-DS integration model has been simplified with SAP S/4HANA. Then follow step-by-step instructions for configuring and running PP-DS in your system, from determining your requirements to monitoring your results. With details on advanced features, troubleshooting, and migration, this is your all-in-one PP-DS resource.

476 pages, pub. 02/2020
E-Book: $79.99 | **Print:** $89.95 | **Bundle:** $99.99
www.sap-press.com/4951

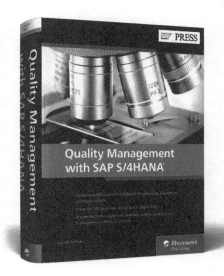

- Configure and run MRP Live and classic MRP with SAP S/4HANA

- Evaluate your MRP results with classic transactions and SAP Fiori apps

- Explore planning with demand-driven and predictive MRP

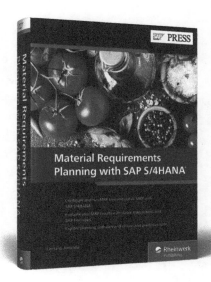

Caetano Almeida

Material Requirements Planning with SAP S/4HANA

With this comprehensive guide, master MRP in SAP S/4HANA from end to end. Set up master data and configure SAP S/4HANA with step-by-step instructions. Run classic MRP, MRP Live, or both; then evaluate your results with SAP GUI transactions or SAP Fiori apps.

541 pages, pub. 07/2020

E-Book: $79.99 | **Print:** $89.95 | **Bundle:** $99.99

www.sap-press.com/4966

- Configure and run MRP Live and classic MRP with SAP S/4HANA

- Evaluate your MRP results with classic transactions and SAP Fiori apps

- Explore planning with demand-driven and predictive MRP

Caetano Almeida

Material Requirements Planning with SAP S/4HANA

With this comprehensive guide, master MRP in SAP S/4HANA from end to end. Set up master data and configure SAP S/4HANA with step-by-step instructions. Run classic MRP, MRP Live, or both; then evaluate your results with SAP GUI transactions or SAP Fiori apps.

541 pages, pub. 07/2020
E-Book: $79.99 | **Print:** $89.95 | **Bundle:** $99.99
www.sap-press.com/4966

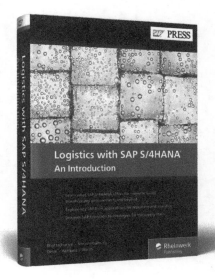

- Learn what SAP S/4HANA offers for manufacturing, warehousing, procurement, and beyond
- Explore key SAP Fiori applications for reporting and analytics
- Discover SAP Leonardo technologies for the supply chain

Deb Bhattacharjee, Vadhi Narasimhamurti, Chaitanaya Desai, Guillermo B. Vazquez, Tom Walsh

Logistics with SAP S/4HANA

An Introduction

Transform your logistics operations with SAP S/4HANA! With this introduction, see what SAP has in store for each supply chain line of business: sales order management, manufacturing, inventory management, warehousing, and more. Discover how SAP Fiori apps and embedded analytics improve reporting, and explore the intersection between your supply chain processes and new SAP Leonardo technologies. Take your first look at SAP S/4HANA logistics, and see where it will take your business!

589 pages, 2nd edition, pub. 01/2019
E-Book: $69.99 | **Print:** $79.95 | **Bundle:** $89.99

www.sap-press.com/4785

Interested in reading more?

Please visit our website for all new book
and e-book releases from SAP PRESS.

www.sap-press.com